Private Security and the Law
Fifth Edition

Private Security and the Law
Fifth Edition

Charles P. Nemeth

CRC Press
Taylor & Francis Group
Boca Raton London New York

CRC Press is an imprint of the
Taylor & Francis Group, an **informa** business

CRC Press
Taylor & Francis Group
6000 Broken Sound Parkway NW, Suite 300
Boca Raton, FL 33487-2742

First issued in paperback 2021

ISBN 13: 978-1-03-209631-5 (pbk)
ISBN 13: 978-1-138-73875-1 (hbk)

Library of Congress Cataloging-in-Publication Data

Names: Nemeth, Charles P., 1951- author.
Title: Private security and the law / by Charles P. Nemeth.
Description: Fifth edition. | Boca Raton, FL : CRC Press, [2018] | Includes bibliographical references and index.
Identifiers: LCCN 2017015342| ISBN 9781138738751 (hardback : alk. paper) | ISBN 9781315184449 (ebook)
Subjects: LCSH: Private security services--Law and legislation--United States. | Police, Private--Legal status, laws, etc.--United States.
Classification: LCC KF5399.5.P7 N46 2018 | DDC 344.7305/289--dc23
LC record available at https://lccn.loc.gov/2017015342

Visit the Taylor & Francis Web site at
http://www.taylorandfrancis.com

and the CRC Press Web site at
http://www.crcpress.com

To Smiling John and Mighty Joe, twin sons who continue to be not only gifts, but also young men I am deeply proud of.

Thirty years later, these twin sons continue down a remarkable path—both of them men of honor and decency—both of them the sons fathers always hope for.

To Saint Thomas Aquinas

It is lawful for any private individual to do anything for the common good, provided it harm nobody: but if it be harmful to some other, it cannot be done, except by virtue of the judgment of the person to whom it pertains to decide what is to be taken from the parts for the welfare of the whole.

Summa Theologica, II–II, Question 64, Article 3

Contents

Acknowledgments

The fifth edition of *Private Security and the Law* traces a most remarkable geneaology in the life and times of the private security industry. As done in previous editions, I continue to marvel at the industry's staying power and ability to adapt to an evolving law enforcement marketplace. Onward and upward, the industry goes with the reality of "privatization" now a full-fledged reality. From street and community protection, to the perpetual protection of assets and people, the private sector shows no signs of being stuck in the status quo. In fact the complete opposite is true. Private sector justice will just keep gobbling up once sacrosanct public policing functions. Whole neighborhoods and communities are now part of the delivery system. Dramatic growth everywhere—prisons, courts, policing, energy, art and cultural, educational and medical, community services—to name a few are now part and parcel of private security delivery.

As these obligations rise, so too the concerns for legal liability, legal oversight, and compliance. Despite the evolution of many legal principles, the state of legal application in the world of private security remains remarkably consistent. While there are always efforts to impute new and novel legal protections to those claiming an entitlement or procedural protection, private security finds itself in remarkably similar shape over the last 60 years. This is not to say that courts and legislators, regulators and policymakers, do not tinker or intervene—to be sure, there is a hard court press used at making the private into the public domain. And that is the thrust of this fifth edition—to show recent case law and statutory constructions relevant to private security as well as the maze of regulatory initiatives that seek to deliver oversight to this industry.

Whether constitutional or civil, criminal, or adminsitrative, security management now need a fixed eye on all things legal.

As in the other editions, the project relies on a wide range of people. First, the willingness of CRC Press to continue this legacy is most appreciated. Editor Mark Listewnik continues his unbridled support for the private security industry and displays a strong knack for knowing what is essential in this academic sector. The historical overview provided early in the text remains as fresh and accurate as the day my brother, James E. Nemeth, an historian in his own right, penned. At John Jay College I am forever blessed by a strong crop of undergraduate and graduate students who provide research assistance, particularly Manny Zevallos, Jose Rodriguez, John Carleton, and Alexis Tabak.

Editorial assistance, as has been the custom in so many of my works, was provided brilliantly by Hope Haywood. I never take for granted the details, the organizational and administrative aspects of book production and without Hope, these ideas would still be on the drawing board. Remarkably, Hope has been there since the first edition printed in 1988.

Finally, John Jay College provides a supportive and nurturing environment for research and scholarship—a legacy promoted by our President, Jeremy Travis, and the Provost of the College, Dr. Jane Bowers. Both are leaving the institution for either retirement or a return to teaching. In matters of research and scholarship, each left an indelible mark.

As in all my productions, family drives the enterprise. I know I owe the deepest of gratitudes to my beloved family, Jean Marie, wife and friend for 46 years, and the children we have been blessed with—Eleanor, Stephen, Anne Marie, John, Joseph, Mary Claire, and Michael Augustine. It is impossible to imagine life without these incredible blessings.

About the Author

Charles P. Nemeth is a recognized expert in homeland security and a leader in homeland security education. An educator for more than 30 years, Dr. Nemeth's distinctive career is a blend of both theory and practice. He has authored more than 40 books on law, security, law enforcement, and homeland security and is currently chair of the Department of Security, Fire, and Emergency Management at John Jay College in New York City. Dr. Nemeth is formerly the editor for the peer-reviewed journal *Homeland Security Review* and also currently serves as the director of the newly established Center for Private Security and Safety at John Jay College in New York City. He is a much sought-after legal consultant for security companies and a recognized scholar on issues involving law, morality, and ethics.

Chapter 1

Historical Foundations of Private Security

1.1 Introduction: The Concepts of Self-Help and Self-Protection

Historically, the concepts of self-help and self-protection were considered foundational to the enforcement of law and the assurance of social order. The private citizen was, by most measures, the chief party responsible for the safety and security of a community. Public law enforcement is a much more novel concept. Whether private or public in design, ideas about policing and protection arise from a variety of influences. Like any other type of institution, its practices and procedures are not fixed in a day but emerge in an evolutionary sense.[1] For any clear and accurate assessment of private security or public sector justice, first the historical underpinnings need to be examined.

These principles, derived from English law and the Anglo-Saxon tradition, and subsequently adapted to American jurisprudence, provide a panorama for how public and private protection systems not only emerged but legally operate. For example, what were the early parameters for protection of property? Within the common law and even early codifications of English law was the right of self-help first recognized. A man's home was indeed his castle, if he was fortunate enough to possess one. To protect his property and life, a person was entitled to use even deadly force. And have there been historical preferences regarding public protection or private oversight—a tendency to protect oneself instead of waiting for others to protect? Early emanations of self-defense and self-protection can be traced to the earliest civilizations. For example, the maintenance of law and order in the Greek and Roman empires were primarily the function of the military and its command structure. Order was maintained in the empire not because of some formal entity, but because the power base was rooted in military authority. Weaving its way through this very mentality was the natural, almost universal view that citizens had a right to self-defense and had the obligation to defend self and others and to do so without much state interference. The Greek philosopher Demosthenes correlated the power of self-defense with a vision of natural law and natural rights common to every human person. "Is it not monstrous, is it not manifestly contrary to law—I do not mean merely the statute of law but to the unwritten law of our common humanity—that I should not be permitted to defend myself against one who violently seizes my goods as though I were an enemy?"[2]

> Although the word "police" has a classical origin—the Greek *politeuein* "to act as a citizen of a polis"—the metropolitan police forces we are accustomed to did not exist in the ancient world. A few cities had some form of institutionalized keepers of the peace—"magistrates of the peace"—but municipal police forces are a nineteenth century phenomenon: the British "bobbies" named for the Prime Minister Robert Peel appear in the 1830s.[3]

Upholding the law and the protection of private and communal person and property was, and is still considered, the responsibility of the individual and the community.[4] It is as the great jurist Blackstone indicated in the eighteenth century—a most "natural right to security from the corporal insults of menaces, assaults, beating, and wounding"[5] of others. Inherent in our own autonomy is this view that self-defense and self-preservation could not be more natural.

The law is most effectively served by those who serve themselves. "An unwritten tenet of democracy places enforcement of the law within the domain of ordinary citizens … under the principles of common law any man still possesses wide authority to protect himself, his family, and to some degree the general peace of the land."[6] Coupled with this reality, in a free and capitalist society, some would argue, are the market forces that dictate what things have value and what needs protection based on that value. To be sure, self-help directly ties its undergirding to a philosophy of ownership and personal protection. In other words, the society's decision on how to parse up its enforcement model, whether it be public or private in design is inexorably tied to demand.[7]

Although self-help in the protection of one's life and property was socially acceptable, other factors often dictated the practice as the only viable form of law enforcement. For much of European and American history, sparsely populated areas, rugged geography, and a strong distrust of any proposed national police organization forced individual citizens and communities to enact and enforce the law through the best available means. Oftentimes, private individuals acting on their own, or at the behest of communal interests, would be forced to take the law into their hands. This was best demonstrated in the tribal "blood feuds" of the Dark Ages. Order and protection was threatened by nomadic bands of rogues and barbarians, territorial fiefdoms, and blood feuds. Anguished communities were held captive by hordes of intruders.[8] Primitive justice centered on the retribution of wrongs:

> An injury done was primarily the affair of the party injured and of his kindred. It was for him and them to avenge the wrong on the wrongdoer and his kin, and to prosecute a "blood feud" against them until the wrong originally done was wiped out by retaliation.[9]

Although the self-help protection philosophy gave no clear-cut parameters as to what was fair and equitable justice, the origins of common law did develop from a notion of reasonable, nonlethal force in the protection of one's property. When criminal action threatened only property, the law did not condone the use of deadly, retaliatory force. The law rightfully considered human life more precious than mere property.[10]

The issue of self-protection did not, however, exclude the use of deadly force in the protection of life. To be a legitimate use of deadly force, the use of force had to be justifiable, and not disproportionate to the force threatened.[11] A person, with justifiable cause, could use force in defense of family and self, and also in the defense of others.[12] Under the feudal system, the relationship between lord and vassal resembled the present-day system of contract security.

1.1.1 Historical Foundations

1.1.1.1 The Middle Ages

Although modern law enforcement, security organizations, and policing/security functions were not initiated during the Middle Ages, an idea of the need and design for law enforcement and security did originate during this era. While most of the Middle Ages maintains its preference for private justice over centralized public systems, there was a growing recognition that centralized authority may assure a more even result in terms of justice. Yet at the same time, the period fully held fast to the necessity of self-defense, self-protection and self-help as an essential feature of a civil society. Katherine Fisher Drew's masterful work on this public–private comparison during this same captures the full essence of the dilemma:

> For the purposes of justice, all these kingdoms recognized the need for self-help and the usefulness of belonging to either a strong family or kin group or enjoying the protection of a more powerful individual, whether he was your lord and you his humble servant or tenant, or whether he was the lord who accepted your free service and provided protection in return.[13]

It is important to understand the chaos and circumstances of Medieval England and Europe that led to the establishment of private, self-policing forces. The vassal–lord relationship had developed a reciprocal self-help approach to the security of one's life and property. Life in feudal times centered on the manors and villages, each responsible for their own protection. Small villages provided their own citizen-police, centering on the ancient "hue and cry" by which the able-bodied men could be summoned to lend assistance when criminal acts occurred or a felon needed to be apprehended.[14] This method proved effective, but only within the limited range of the feudal territory or lord's domain. With each lord having his own system of security and no codified system of English law, the issue of national or regional security was a muddled mess of self-interests and conflicting jurisdictions. As the small manors of feudalism evolved into towns, villages, and eventually cities, the old system of self-help could not keep up with the rising crime rate.

From 1000 to 1300 AD, the developmental seeds of an ordered system of law enforcement began in England.[15] The king appointed shire-reeves, who had law enforcement responsibilities in English counties or precincts. "The shire-reeve seems to have developed from the king's reeve, the local official who looked after the king's business."[16] He was a royal representative, and it was intended that he would protect the royal interests if they conflicted with the local claims of anyone, including the lord of the county. Above all, the shire-reeve was still the chief officer of the county.[17] Within a manor, an appointed officer known as a "constable" was responsible for dealing with legal matters. Both the shire-reeve, later shortened to sheriff, and the constable were the forerunners of modern sworn police officers.

The system of English legal protection continued to expand and define itself more clearly. Under the Statute of Winchester of 1285 a system of "watch and ward" was established to aid constables.[18] The watch and ward system was comprised of a justice of the peace, constable, constable's assistants, and night watchmen whose primary function was the care and tending of a designated area of a town or city known as a "ward."[19] Even today political subdivisions are often broken down into the ward structure. Regular patrols of citizens were established to stand watch nightly and to arrest criminals and strangers found wandering at night. When an offender was caught in a criminal act, the "hue and cry" was raised.[20]

It was then the duty of all men in the community, fifteen years and older, to rally at the scene and uphold justice. In addition, they were required by law to carry arms and form a *posse comitatus* to pursue criminals.[21] Maintaining the king's peace and enforcing the law remained a public responsibility.[22]

Although all men had the general duty and the right to make arrests, the constables and sheriffs had additional specific peacekeeping duties and powers. Unfortunately, the officers were ill-equipped to handle the urban growth that created cities with huge populations. Because constables were unpaid, ill-trained, and ill-equipped, English law enforcement was in dire straits. Lord Chancellor Bacon, in 1618, complained that constables were "of inferior stock, men of base conditions."[23] The towns and cities of England, especially London, fell into virtual anarchy because of the lack and inadequacy of publicly appointed and underpaid professional peacekeepers. Unfortunately, the bulk of the watchmen and constables lacked the essential qualities for success.[24] In his book, *Hue and Cry*, Patrick Pringle states:

> Such is our respect for institutions that when an established system breaks down we are quick to blame people and defend the system; but the lesson of history seems to be that systems must be made for people, because people cannot be made for systems. To be effective, any system—whether political, religious, economic, or judicial—must expect people to be base and selfish and venal.[25]

Due to the rising crime rate, and the inability of the poorly organized English system of law enforcement to effectively combat it, private persons and businesses developed their own means of protection. As towns and cities expanded, merchants and artisans banded together for mutual protection. In his book *On Guard*, Milton Lipson relates how:

> Guild members united to perform the duty of watching their contiguous property in the heart of these medieval towns, serving as watchmen themselves, later assigning their apprentices and thereafter hiring special guards. In these practices are the visible roots of both modern insurance and private security.[26]

What is clear is that the American fore into law enforcement has not been as clean or transitionally predicable as one might hope and, in fact, can be properly described as a "tangled web of what are typically referred to as public and private police forces."[27]

Other forces played into the impetus for a more formal law enforcement system. The expanding trade and transportation of vital goods and services were temptations for criminals. It also demanded the need for protection of private interests, property, and self. From this arose the concepts of proprietary and contract security. Throughout the sixteenth century, different kinds of police agencies were privately formed. Individual merchants hired men to guard their property and merchant associations created merchant police to guard shops and warehouses.[28] The status of these private guards "was by no means uniform; some were sworn in as constables, while others continued in employment as private watchmen or guards. There were also no general scales of payment, rules of conduct, or assigned duties for these newly created private security forces."[29] These areas were solely under the discretion of the employer. The essence of private security was born in the chaos of the Middle Ages, especially that of the "contract" variety, but the standardization of its organizational hierarchy, duties, and pay was yet to come.[30]

1.1.1.2 *Colonial America*

The influence of the English culture and tradition in America is quite evident in our legal system, and especially evident in early colonial law enforcement. Colonial America incorporated the systems of sheriff, constable, and watch as its earliest forms of law enforcement. With subsequent empire building came further pressure to regularize and formalize the protection system. However, the concept of a uniform police force was still far in the future. George O'Toole contends in his book, *The Private Sector*, that

> ...police, public or private, are not one of America's oldest traditions: the Republic was nearly 70 years old before the first public force was organized, the infant nation had few laws to enforce, and the protection of life and property was largely a do-it-yourself matter in the tiny wilderness communities that made up the frontier.[31]

As in Medieval England and Europe, population and geographic factors in Colonial America favored a loosely structured communal law enforcement system. Generally, the sheriff served in unincorporated areas, the constables in towns and villages.[32] In Colonial America, the sheriff was charged with the execution of all warrants directed to him, both civil and criminal. He shared with other peace officers special powers of arrest without warrant, but did not serve as an important agent in the detection and prevention of crime.[33]

In 1607, the first constable was appointed in Jamestown, Virginia, becoming the first duly appointed law officer in the New World.[34] As in England, the constable's position was difficult to fill. His duties were many and varied, the pay was minimal, the hours long, and the prestige associated with the job was low.[35] The constable was, however, the main law enforcement officer for the local American government in the 1800s.[36]

The watch system in America was derived as colonists coming to the New World banded together for mutual safety and business protection.[37] The first night watch formed in Boston in 1634.[38] Serving as a watchman was the duty of every male citizen over the age of 18. The tour of duty usually began at 9 or 10 p.m. and ended at sunrise.[39] As in the selection of constables, finding men of high caliber to serve watch was difficult. The powers of the night watch were more limited than those of constables, and they had no policing power and limited arrest authority.[40]

Primarily, the early colonial need for security did not center on proprietary or commercial interests, but on the fear of fire, vagrants, and Indian attacks. As urban populations grew, the system of sheriffs, constables, and the watch proved inadequate in meeting law enforcement needs. The diversity of the original colonies did not promote any concept of uniform law enforcement practices or national police. Even with increasing urban congestion and a rising crime rate, little would change in American law enforcement. "Watchmen remained familiar figures and constituted the primary security measures until the establishment of full-time police forces in the mid-1800s."[41] The seemingly unchanging organization of colonial American law enforcement was not so much a sign of social stability, but more likely a wariness of any public or national force controlled by a federal government. "The principle of states' rights had a profound and continuing impact upon law enforcement."[42] Americans, especially right after the American Revolution, were leery of any federal entity that sought to control and administrate over state and local matters. Law enforcement and security, like other facets of life, were to be controlled by state and local government, which reflected the "states' rights" mentality of the age and the supremacy of a decentralized federalism. Although local and state jurisdictions might have felt politically comfortable with the watch system of security, other factors necessitated a change in American security practices. As in

England, the old systems of law enforcement became outdated and inadequate in facing the security problems of the growing nation. "The basic deficiencies of the watch and constable systems rendered them ill-prepared to deal with the unrest that occurred in many American cities during the first half of the nineteenth century."[43] New methods of organizing and defining public and private law enforcement were needed to combat urban problems.

1.1.1.3 Law Enforcement in the Industrial Revolution

The first half of the nineteenth century saw a rise in urbanization, crime, and the need for better law enforcement.[44] Private security existed, but only on a small scale for business and merchant protection. Although private police greatly contributed to keeping the peace, it became obvious, particularly in the cities, that a centralized public police department was a necessity. Even so, the clamor did not always match the support for a governmental system that controlled the day-to-day activities of the people.[45] In many ways the move to a public perception regarding law and order came tediously. Charles Reith's observations on the ambiguity could not be clearer when he notes, "The new Police found, as soon as they appeared in the streets, that their creation had united against them, in a demand for their immediate disbandment, all parties, classes, and factions in the state."[46]

In England, an early version of public policing was affectionately labeled the "Bow Street Runners," since their activities emanated from London's Bow Street in Covent Garden. A magistrate's court would instruct these early "police" types to run after and pursue criminals. The first legitimate police force would arise in England. The Metropolitan Police Act, passed in 1829 under the sponsorship of Sir Robert Peel, created a carefully selected corps of policemen trained and organized in a military fashion.[47] Sir Robert Peel, the oldest son of a wealthy cotton manufacturer, was educated at Harrow and Oxford University.[48] Peel's system, although it "spread slowly and sporadically,"[49] became the primary model for efficient urban public policing. Peel, widely known as the "father of policing," recognized the need for a more effective police force to replace the old watch and ward system as well as the limited capabilities of the Bow Street Runners. Peel believed that by organizing a group of professionally trained full-time police officers, he would be able to reduce the level of crime through proactive prevention techniques instead of relying solely on prevention through punishment. To accomplish this evolutionary process, Peel promulgated new rules for police operations, including the following:

- To prevent crime and disorder.
- To recognize that the power of the police is dependent on public approval and respect.
- To secure the respect of the public means also securing the cooperation of the public.
- To seek and to preserve public favor by constantly demonstrating impartial service to law, without regard to the justice or injustices of individual laws, without regard to wealth or social standing; by exercise of courtesy and friendly good humor; and by offering of individual sacrifice in protecting and preserving life.
- To use physical force only when necessary on any particular occasion for achieving a police objective.
- To recognize always the need for strict adherence to police-executive functions.
- To recognize always that the test of police efficiency is the absence of crime and disorder.[50]

Peel's *Principles of Law Enforcement*, authored in 1829, still remain highly instructive for both the public and the private police models. His major tenets are outlined in Figure 1.1.[51]

Sir Robert Peel's Principles of Law Enforcement 1829

1. The basic mission for which police exist is to prevent crime and disorder as an alternative to the repression of crime and disorder by military force and severity of legal punishment.

2. The ability of the police to perform their duties is dependent upon *public approval* of police existence, actions, behavior and the ability of the police to secure and maintain *public respect.*

3. The police must secure the willing cooperation of the public in voluntary observance of the law to be able to secure and maintain public respect.

4. The degree of cooperation of the public that can be secured diminishes, proportionately, to the necessity for the use of physical force and compulsion in achieving police objectives.

5. The police seek and preserve public favor, not by catering to public opinion, but by constantly demonstrating absolutely impartial service to the law, in complete independence of policy, and without regard to the justice or injustice of the substance of individual laws; by ready offering of individual service and friendship to all members of society without regard to their race or social standing, by ready exercise of courtesy and friendly good humor; and by ready offering of individual sacrifice in protecting and preserving life.

6. The police should use physical force to the extent necessary to secure observance of the law or to restore order only when the exercise of *persuasion, advice and warning* is found to be insufficient to achieve police objectives; and police should use only the minimum degree of physical force which is necessary on any particular occasion for achieving a police objective.

7. The police at all times should maintain a relationship with the public that gives reality to the historic tradition that *the police are the public* and *the public are the police;* the police are the only members of the public who are paid to give full-time attention to duties which are incumbent on every citizen in the intent of the community welfare.

8. The police should always direct their actions toward their functions and never appear to usurp the powers of the judiciary by avenging individuals or the state, or authoritatively judging guilt or punishing the guilty.

9. The test of police efficiency is the *absence* of crime and disorder, not the *visible evidence* of police action in dealing with them.

Figure 1.1 Sir Robert Peel's Principles of Law Enforcement.

The Peelian model was extremely influential in nineteenth-century American law enforcement. "The riots of the 1840s provided an impetus for finding a more effective means of dealing with urban unrest."[52] The need for a unified public force would begin to override the self-interest protection provided by private security. However, both fields would continue to grow together, defining themselves as separate, yet cooperating, law enforcement sectors.

The early 1800s witnessed the birth of American policing as a viable peacekeeping force. New York City had started the rudiments of a police department in 1783, and by 1800 had established the first paid daytime police force. Daytime police forces were also started in Philadelphia (1833) and Boston (1838).[53] These early departments did not supplant the system of the watch but worked as the daytime counterpart. Since the day and night watches would prove inadequate in fighting crime, New York City became the first city to combine its day and night watches into a unified police force in 1844.[54] "Other large cities began to follow the lead—Chicago in 1851, New Orleans and Cincinnati in 1852, and Providence in 1864. The snowballing effect stimulated the modernization of American policing."[55]

Find out about the full and comprehensive history of the New York City Police Department by visiting https://www.nycpm.org/

The rapid development of the modern police force in no way sounded the death knell of private security. On the contrary, private security forces would continue to grow, expand, and complement other law enforcement agencies in fighting crime. Now, two arms of law enforcement were becoming more closely defined along public and private lines.[56]

By 1830 in England, and within a decade or so thereafter in the United States, the beginnings of a separation of the security function into two spheres of responsibility were taking place. Public police departments, with their sworn duties, were charged with maintaining law and order. The burden of security for private property and personal safety thereon had to be redefined. The world of private security was to be limited.[57] With public police forces centering their efforts on the enforcing of law and order, private security would expand and grow as guardians of the corporate sector.

1.1.2 Coming of Age: Private Security

Despite the growth and formalization of public policing, the private sector police model continued down an unabated and parallel path.[58] Major factors that served as the impetus for the growth of the private security industry included the growth of the commercial sector, the strained administrations of public law enforcement agencies, and the great westward expansion of America in the 1840s and 1850s. All of these dynamics combined to entrench the private police model.

1.1.2.1 Lack of an Effective Public Force

It became apparent that with the growth of the private business and commercial sector in the United States during the 1800s, the newly created public police agencies were unable or unwilling to provide for their security needs. Public police organizations had little experience or capabilities in handling wide-scale security protection services. With the newly created sworn police serving mainly in metropolitan areas, their jurisdictions were strictly limited to their own territory. Local sheriff and watch were also restricted to local, county, or state lines.[59] Big business and industries found criminal problems surpassing the jurisdictional and functional capabilities of the public police. With interests that often covered vast areas and multiple jurisdictions, businesses and commercial associations began to hire their own protective sources.

1.1.2.2 Movement of Goods and Services

The transportation industry was instrumental in developing the private security industry. Henry Wells and William G. Fargo had established the American Express Company and Wells Fargo in the 1850s as protective services for commercial shipments both in the East and the Far West. Wells Fargo's security measures included the use of armed guards, ironclad stagecoaches, and an expert investigative service.

The railroad industry also had substantial security needs. As the greatest source of commercial transportation of the nineteenth century, railroads were also susceptible to criminal activity. Prior to the Civil War, the railroads contracted with private detective companies, namely the Pinkertons. After the war, the trend was toward developing company-owned internal police forces. The railroad police became instrumental in pursuing train robbers, watching out for petty theft and embezzlement, and securing the trains from unwanted vagrants.[60] On industry-wide problems, the security forces of different railroad companies often cooperated, increasing the security and efficiency of the industry as a whole. Railroad police, with their far-reaching jurisdictions and official powers, would represent the closest America would ever come to a national police force. During the latter half of the nineteenth century, only the railroad police agencies were with full police powers. In many areas, especially the West, the railway police provided the only security services until effective local government units were established.[61]

1.1.2.3 The Pinkerton Factor: Industrialization and Unionization

As the industrial revolution matured, economic interests for both company and worker solidified. To be sure, workers—whether in coal mines or steel works—no longer saw themselves as mere rabble to enrich the elites. Grumblings and rumblings of worker dissatisfaction were commonly heard, particularly in the industrial cities and centers for major industries.[62] Security firms were crucial players in this company–worker dynamic. Allan Pinkerton started the first contract private security agency in America.[63] Scottish immigrant and barrel maker by trade, Pinkerton developed an interest in detective work and had been named the city detective of Chicago in 1849. In 1850, he formed his own North-Western Police Agency, the first private detective agency in America. Capitalizing on the rapid growth of the country's railroad industry, Pinkerton began to contract his security forces to protect the railroads of the Midwest. The Illinois Central, Michigan Central, Michigan Southern and Northern Indiana, Chicago and Galena Union, Chicago and Rock Island, Chicago, Burlington, and Quincy Railroads all utilized Pinkerton's protective services.[64] It was through his association with the railroad industry that Pinkerton met George B. McClellan, vice-president and chief engineer of the Illinois Central Railroad, and later commander in chief of the Union Army during the Civil War. With the outbreak of the Civil War, McClellan would take Pinkerton and his detectives along as the United States' first military intelligence unit.

Pinkerton's early success helped define the role and abilities of the private security industry.[65] For more than 50 years, the "Pinks" were the only officers involved in interstate activities such as the provision of security for transcontinental railroads and multilocation industrial concerns.[66] Pinkerton had definitely developed into the biggest protective service in the United States, but it would be in post-Civil War America where the greatest test for the fledgling industry would take place.

Postwar industrial expansion, fed by an increasing flow of immigrants, also helped Pinkerton's business. With growth came labor unrest and movements to organize workers. In the strife that ensued, the use of private security guards to combat efforts to unionize became commonplace. Pinkerton and his company were used by industry, especially railroads and mining groups.[67]

While Pinkerton officers were serving as the protectors of American railroads and as, basically, the only uniform system of law in the West, labor–management conflicts developed in the latter decades of the nineteenth century in the East. As America was immersed in its Industrial

Revolution, a growing consensus of American laborers, usually immigrants who toiled in the mines and mills, worked for the development of labor representation. In many instances, management refused to bargain with labor organizations and would send in strike-breakers to dismiss the mobs. On the other hand, labor unions and secret societies often used unethical tactics in their determination to change unfair labor practices. Pinkertons, Baldwin-Felts, and others were often hired by business management to disrupt and disband labor activities. In all, Pinkerton's agency would involve itself in over 72 labor–management disputes in the second half of the nineteenth century.[68]

One of the first labor disputes the Pinkerton Company contracted out for involved the Molly Maguires. The Molly Maguires was a secret society that originated out of nineteenth-century Ireland, a country then racked by poverty and hunger. Their life in America had improved little as they toiled in the coal mines of northeastern Pennsylvania.

Find out about how the Molly Maguires played a crucial role in the life of the security industry at http://ehistory.osu.edu/exhibitions/gildedage/content/mollymaguires

---

Pinkerton used undercover agents such as James McParland, who lived and worked with the Molly Maguires under the assumed name Jim McKennon, from 1873 to 1886. It was McParland's subsequent testimony in a murder trial, changing certain important players in the organization that effectively ended the Molly Maguires as an effective labor organization. At the same time in southern West Virginia the Baldwin-Felts Detective Service was assigned by management to uphold justice and disband union experts in the coal mining towns.[69]

Another landmark labor–management dispute that involved the Pinkerton Agency was the Homestead Steel Strike of 1892.[70] In July of 1892, workers at the Carnegie Steel Company in Homestead, Pennsylvania went on strike, protesting a proposed pay cut set forth by Carnegie Steel's new manager, Henry Clay Frick. Frick cited poor business as the reason for the designed wage cuts. Instead of acquiescence to management's demands, the striking steel workers blockaded and fortified the steel plant. In response, Frick secretly ordered his hired Pinkerton men to regain control of the plant.[71]

As 300 armed Pinkerton guards attempted to sneak up the river side of the plant, an estimated 10,000 angry steelworkers confronted the Pinkerton force. In the intense battle that ensued, eight were killed (three Pinkerton officers and five steelworkers). The Pinkerton officers were surrounded, forced to surrender, and were physically escorted to the railroad station. The Homestead Massacre was a debacle that ultimately hurt the image of private security agencies, and for a time the Pinkerton Company. The name Pinkerton became synonymous with labor spying and strike-breaking during the late nineteenth and early twentieth centuries. Its image was so badly tarnished that a House Judiciary Subcommittee began a formal investigation of Pinkerton and the private security industry in 1892. In 1893, the House passed the Pinkerton Law, which stated:

> … an individual employed by the Pinkerton Detective Agency, or similar organization, may not be employed by the government of the United States or the government of the District of Columbia.[72]

In the aftermath of the Pinkerton Law, Pinkerton announced it would no longer take sides in any labor disputes. Again, the roles and parameters of the private security industry were being redefined. Strike-breaking was out and labor surveillance within legitimate bounds was in.

For a full survey of Pinkerton History, see: https://www.pinkerton.com/about-us/history/

1.1.2.4 Western U.S. Expansionism

While the labor disputes of the nineteenth century were an important watershed in the development of private security, they certainly did not signal a decline in the uses and demand for private security forces. Pinkerton and other private security forces were attaining a booming business in the as yet unsettled frontiers of the American West. With Pinkerton controlling the security and investigative services of the railroads, and Wells Fargo controlling the stages, law enforcement in the towns and territories of the West was largely in the hands of sheriffs or private individuals. The ancient legal tenet of self-help saw its last vestiges of practice in the American West.

See the history of the Wells Fargo Company at: https://www.wellsfargohistory.com/history/

As the guilds and businesses had done in a previous age, western businessmen, traders, bankers, and ranchers banded together for mutual benefit. "Business sponsorship of law enforcement started with the earliest days of the frontier … railroads, ranchers, mining concerns, oil field operators—all established their own investigating and law enforcement agencies."[73]

In some cases, private security was provided by an association of businesses in the same area of commerce. A system of Merchant Police was formed in the towns and cities to safeguard mercantile interests. Cattle ranchers in the West joined forces to create associations that frequently employed agents to prevent and investigate cattle rustling.[74] These detectives, although paid by private groups, were often given official state or territorial recognition, and sometimes were given powers as official public law enforcement officers. Detective forces, each specializing in various forms of business and trade, appeared on the western scene in increasing numbers. F. Prassel's work, *The Western Peace Officer*, described their purpose:

> At their worst, such security organizations constituted a combination of the protection racket and violence for hire… At its best, a private detective force could provide real services with integrity and discretion.[75]

By contemporary standards, western justice and law enforcement had less regard for procedural due process. Vigilantes, private individuals with no formal authority acting in self-interest or in the interests of a specific group, served as enforcers. The first American vigilantes, the South Carolina Regulators, appeared in 1767, but only really flourished after 1850.[76] Both the Los Angeles and San Francisco police departments originated as volunteer vigilante forces.[77] "The true vigilante movement was in social conformance with established procedures and patterns of structural leadership."[78] This was not often the case, as abuses of legal power became commonplace. Wyoming had such a distrust of private security forces as to adopt a statute in 1889, which stated:

> No armed police force, or detective agency, or armed body, or unarmed body of men, shall ever be brought into this state, for the suppression of domestic violence, except upon the application of the legislature, or executive, when the legislature cannot be convened.[79]

Other western states passed similar laws in attempts to curb abuses by private individuals or security forces. For many years, only private security forces served as the quasi-law enforcement agencies in the West. All major transportation systems and various commercial interests were protected by private security forces in one way or another.

1.1.3 Contemporary Private Security

World War II and the years that followed would have a profound effect on the type, organization, and need for American private security. The secrecy and vulnerability of war usually brings a demand for more internal security. With the dual need for fighting soldiers and security protection, the government could not solely rely on the depleted ranks of the local and state police. "Wartime requirements compelled local police establishments, already strapped because their young men had gone to war, to take on tasks beyond those it normally assumed. Industrial plants, drinking water and its sources, utilities and their transmission lines, and other vital services had to be guarded."[80]

With these massive security problems facing the United States, thousands of men and women served their country in the ranks of private security forces. By war's end, over 200,000 individual private security personnel had worked for the government.[81] With the end of World War II, the importance and usefulness of private security personnel would be a given, and the need for various forms of security increased dramatically. The Private Security Task Force of 1976 claims that, "after the war, the use of private security services and products expanded from an area of defense contractors to encompass all segments of the private-public sectors."[82]

The United States, assuming the status of a world power, heightened security problems and increased political and governmental suspicion and secrecy. Cold War reality and rumor led to an increased use of private security forces to protect government installations and secrets. Protection against information theft also became a growing security field. The fears of the 1950s allowed former Federal Bureau of Investigation (FBI) agent George R. Wachenhut and three other former agents to found the Wachenhut Corporation.[83] With a long list of experienced personnel, the Wachenhut Corporation grew to be one of the largest private security contractors in the United States. Remarkably, Wachenhut was also able to skirt the previous legislative intention of the Pinkerton Law of 1893 by gaining security contracts for government installations, including National Aeronautics and Space Administration (NASA) and the Department of Defense.

Since then, the private security industry has faced steady growth. "Private security personnel also significantly outnumber sworn law enforcement personnel and nonmilitary government guards by nearly 2 to 1."[84] Today, the public interacts with and depends upon a private-sector model whose tentacles reach into every aspect of communal living. ASIS International sees the opportunities present in the field now and in the future, and states that the demand for heightened security is being increased by theft of information, workplace violence, terrorism, and white collar crime. The security industry in the United States is a $100 billion a year business and growing. Opportunities exist at all levels with the security industry. All businesses, no matter how small, have security concerns such as fraud, theft, computer hacking, economic espionage or workplace violence.[85]

The developing complexity of the world marketplace, the technological evolution of goods, services, and the transference of money and other negotiable instruments, served as a catalyst to private security growth. By way of example, ponder the cyclonic revolution in the banking industry, from automated teller machines (ATMs) to paperless checks, from wire transactions to credit card issuances. These practices are essentially novel, and at the same time, the subject of some inventive criminality. Look at the range of security concerns one division of Citibank of New York has: "traveler's checks, money orders, official checks, and other instruments issued by the Citicorp financial organization."[86] Its security response is quite sophisticated:

The 33-member staff, located in eight countries around the world, is a blend of individuals from various law enforcement backgrounds—including the Royal Hong Kong Police, the Belgium Police, Scotland Yard, the New York City Police Department, and the Drug Enforcement Agency.[87]

Private security engages citizens even more than its public counterpart. And it has done so without the fanfare to match its astonishing rise. David Sklansky's *The Private Police* targets the central implications.

> For most lawyers and scholars, private security is terra incognita—wild, unmapped, and largely unexplored… Increasingly, though, government agencies are hiring private security personnel to guard and patrol government buildings, housing projects, and public parks and facilities, and a small but growing number of local governments have begun to experiment with broader use of private police.[88]

The quiet revolution[89] of private security could not have greater impact. More than ever, the enormous public demands piled upon the private security industry call for professional planning and policy making, and a renewed dedication to the advancement of this dynamic industry. Combine technology with a rampant wave of economic crime and the climate of accommodation to the private security industry could not be better.

There is no question that much "ordinary crime"—burglary, larceny, robbery, for example—substantially affects business. In retailing, the U.S. Department of Commerce estimates that the combination of shoplifting by customers and internal pilferage by employees add as much as 15% to customer retail prices (see Figure 1.2).[90]

Crime in the workplace includes such white-collar crimes as fraud and embezzlement. Computer-related crime is perhaps the most devastating of these crimes, because losses are often in the hundreds of thousands of dollars. In 2006, total credit and debit card fraud losses are estimated at $3.718 billion.[91]

The rise of these sorts of criminal behaviors gives impetus to privatized services.

Problems of Retail Theft are now global challenges. See the Barometer of data at: http://www.retailresearch.org/grtb_currentsurvey.php

---

Sources of inventory shrinkage

- 35% Shoplifting
- 43% Employee theft
- 15% Administrative error
- 4% Vendor fraud
- 3% Unknown

Figure 1.2 Sources of Shrink in the United States.

On top of this, there is an emerging preference for private sector involvement in American foreign policy. Throughout the Middle East, Iraq, and Afghanistan, the fingerprint, or better said, the footprint, of the private security industry, could not be more apparent.[92] Labeled either as private military specialists or the "dogs of war" mercenaries will say much about the tension this new dimension causes. For those in favor, the private sector soldier provides "great flexibility, with an ability to create unique solution for each case, knowledge about the problem area and operational expertise, business integrity, secure confidentiality, and a generally apolitical nature."[93] Critics charge that the privatized military operations "exploit violence for personal gain, serve as agents for unsavory power, or happily promote repression, turmoil, and human rights violations..."[94] Neither of these cases is fully accurate and the caricature that the Blackwater firm has turned into provides a poor illustration of this new and emerging dynamic.[95] The role of private security firms play in armed conflicts is a natural progression of mission and privatization.[96]

Whole-scale security systems in the war on terror have come to depend on the private sector system. The fit of private sector justice in the world of military action, seems, at first glance rather odd, yet the deeper the correlation is considered, the more sense it makes. Private security companies now "possess great flexibility, with an ability to create unique solutions for each case, knowledge about the problem area and operational expertise, business integrity, secure confidentiality and a general apolitical nature."[97] Put another way, the private security industry can provide a mercenary force that sees the problem dispassionately and thus, is an agency more reasonable and rational in outlook.

This turning over of the guard, whether it be executive protection, private prison processing, community and neighborhood intelligence, diplomatic protection, to name just a few functions, manifest a change in the overall paradigm.[98] In both war and peace one witnesses the staggering interlocking of a private justice model in public functions. Whether in military action or block security, the trend to privatization is undeniable and unstoppable. What was normative in the early annals of the American experience, namely self-help and self-reliance, appears again on the front burner.[99]

> Privatization is now predictable nomenclature in the world of public policy and the delivery of governmental services. Coming full circle, legislators and policymakers now evaluate programs and their delivery considering outsourcing, private contracts, delegable services and partnerships with the private sector. No longer is this sort of thinking on the fringe. Although the shift has now become self-evident, the transition troubles many. Scott Sullivan's excellent discourse, "Private Force/Public Goods" keenly lays out the dilemma: The privatization of governmental services has repeatedly arisen as a controversial topic of legal scholarship. The controversy inherent to privatization largely flows from a difficulty in identifying a definitive line separating core public responsibilities. This ambiguity, along with a renewed enthusiasm for cost-efficiency and belief in the virtues of the market, has spurred increased privatization of a variety of public goods and services over the course of the past forty years. As privatization has spread, the universe of government activities viewed as unmistakably public, and thus unmistakably inappropriate for privatization, has diminished.[100]

The National Institute of Justice has insightfully discerned the shift back to privatized justice in the form of nonpublic law enforcement:

Such expanded use of private security and increased citizen involvement signals an increasing return to the private sector for protection against crime. The growth and expansion of modern police reflected a shift from private policing and security initiatives of the early nineteenth century. Now the pendulum appears to be swinging back. Despite the expanded role of the police in crime prevention in recent years, it appears that the private sector will bear an increased prevention role while law enforcement concentrates more heavily on violent crimes and crime response. Economic realities are forcing law enforcement to seek ways to reduce workloads.[101]

In the final analysis, there is something empowering about this reality, and as some have described a "participatory democratic self-government."[102] In what greater sense does the citizen bear responsibility for the world around them than when that citizen assumes the responsibility of self-help and self-protection?

It appears private security's role in the administration of American justice is both multifaceted and entrenched. Its areas of service not only entail private, individual, or property security, but loss prevention, insurance, military intelligence and related functions, as well as computer security. Security as a practice, process, and system is embedded in the nation's tradition and is an essential contributor to justice in modern America.

DISCUSSION QUESTIONS

1. Historically, policing efforts were private by design. Could the converse have been true? Can you envision a context in which the public police model would have been first and private sector justice second?
2. What other areas in the private sector economy has the private security industry fit and served well?
3. Does a right to self-help or the calling of a posse still exist?
4. How does modern western law enforcement reflect its historical heritage, particularly in states like California, Texas, and Arizona?
5. By the nature of its mission, would it have been possible for the private security industry to have been supportive of the union movement rather than antagonistic to it?
6. Is private security's tradition the protection of assets and business and commercial property rather than persons?
7. Can you name the oldest contract security company in your geographic region?
8. Did early law enforcement processes in the American Colonies imitate the British system?
9. Is it fair to conclude that the bulk of policing history has essentially been more private than public in design and delivery?
10. If you had to project, where and what ways will privatization continues without much resistance? Could one conclude that the golden age of public policing is now over?

NOTES

1 For an interesting look at one side of the evolution, namely bounty hunting, see Rebecca B. Fisher, *The History of American Bounty Hunting as a Study in Stunted Legal Growth*, 33 N.Y. U. Rev. L & Soc. Change 199 (2009); see also Joshua Horwotz and Casey Anderson, *A Symposium on Firearms: The Militia and Safe Cities: Merging History, Constitutional Law and Public Policy*, 1 Alb. Gov't. Rev. 496 (2008).

2 Demosthenes, *Oratio 23 against Aristocrates*, in: James Herbert Vince (trans.), *Demosthenes against Meidias, Androtion, Aristocrates, Timocrates, Aristogeiton*, Cambridge, MA: Harvard University Press (1935), 212–367, at pp. 253–255 [sec. 61 of the Oratio]; see also Jan Amo Hessbruegge, *Human Rights and Personal Self-Defense in International Law*, New York: Oxford University Press (2017).

3 Fred Mench, *Policing Rome: Maintaining Order in Fact and Fiction*, at https://intraweb.stockton.edu/eyos/page.cfm?siteID=78&pageID=35, last accessed 01/08/2017; see also: Trevor Jones and Tim Newburn, *Private Security and Public Policing* (1998); James F. Pastor, *Privatization of Police in America: An Analysis and Case* (2003).

4 See *Blackstone's Commentaries* concerning these foundational components of a free society at: William Blackstone, *Commentaries* 1:120–41, (1765), http://press-pubs.uchicago.edu/founders/documents/amendIXs1.html.

5 William Blackstone, Commentaries 1:120–41, 1765 part 3 http://press-pubs.uchicago.edu/founders/documents/amendIXs1.html.

6 Frank R. Prassel, *The Western Peace Officer* 126 (1972).

7 M. Rhead Enlon, *Constitutional Limits on Private Policing and the State's Allocation of Force*, 59 Duke L. J. 519. 527 (2009).

8 See Geoffrey R. Radcliffe, E. L. Cross, *The English Legal System* (1970); Max Radin, *Handbook of Anglo-American Legal History* (1936); and William Holdsworth, *A History of English Laws* (1927).

9 Radcliffe and Cross, at 6.

10 Rollin M. Perkins, *Perkins on Criminal Law* 1926–1927 (1969).

11 Franklin F. Russell, *Outline of Legal History* 93–94 (1929).

12 Holdsworth, at 313.

13 Katherine Fischer Drew, *Public vs. Private Enforcement of the Law in the Early Middle Ages: Fifth to Twelfth Centuries*, 79 Chi-Kent L. Rev. 1583, 1585 (1995), available at http://scholarship.kentlaw.iit.edu/cgi/viewcontent.cgi?article=3001&context=cklawreview.

14 See generally 4 Leon Radzinowicz, *A History of English Criminal Law* 105 (1968).

15 See Drew, at 1585–1591.

16 Radcliffe and Cross, at 4.

17 Radin, at 170–171.

18 Holdsworth, at 6–7.

19 Patrick Pringle, *Hue and Cry: The Story of Henry and John Fielding and Their Bow Street Runners* 43 (1955).

20 Elaine Reynolds, *Before the Bobbies: The Night Watch and Police Reform in Metropolitan London*, 1720–1830 (1998).

21 Thomas A. Critchley, *A History of Police in England and Wales* 3 (1966).

22 See Reynolds; Peter John Stephens, *The Thief-takers*, New York: W. W. Norton, 1970; James F. Richardson, *The New York Police* 38 (1970); Roger Lane, *Policing the City: Boston: 1822–1885* 7 (1975); Seldon Bacon, *The Early Development of American Municipal Police* 44 (1939).

23 Critchley, at 1.

24 Reynolds, at 40–41.

25 See Pringle.

26 Milton Lipson, *On Guard* 13 (1975).

27 See Enlon.

28 Gion Green, *Introduction to Security* 5 (1981).

29 2 Leon Radzinowicz, *A History of English Criminal Law* 205 (1956).

30 Pringle describes the situation in eighteenth-century London at pp. 29–30 of *Hue and Cry*. See also Patrick Colquhoun, *A Treatise on The Commerce and Police of the River Thames* (1800); Patrick Colquhoun, *A Treatise on The Police of the Metropolis* (1796).

31 George J. A. O'Toole, *The Private Sector* 21 (1975).

32 Gloria G. Dralla et al., *Who's Watching the Watchmen? The Regulation, or Non-Regulation, of America's Largest Law Enforcement Institution, The Private Police*, 5 Golden Gate L. Rev. 442 (1975); see also Pat Rogers, *Henry Fielding* 232–233 (Scribner's); Henry Goddard, *Memoirs of a Bow Street Runner* xi (Morrow); See Colquhoun.

33 Lane, at 7; Visit the City of Boston Web location to experience the rich history of the Boston Police Department at: http://bpdnews.com/history/.

34 Green, at 8.

35 Richardson, at 38.

36 Lane, at 9.

37 Charles F. Hemphill, *Modern Security Methods* 5 (1979).

38 Bacon, at 44.

39 Hemphill, at 5.

40 Dralla et al., at 443.

41 National Advisory Commission on Criminal Justice Standards and Goals, *Private Security Task Force Report* 30 (1976).

42 Green, at 9.

43 Dralla, et al., at 443.

44 For a fascinating look at entirely western law enforcement see John Boessenecker, *Lawman*, Norman, OK: University of Oklahoma Press (1998).

45 See Charles Reith, *Preventive Principle of Police*, 34 J Crim. Law & Criminology 206 (1943), available at http://scholarlycommons.law.northwestern.edu/cgi/viewcontent.cgi?article=3224&context=jclc.

46 Charles Reith, *Preventive Principle of Police*, 34. *J Crim. Law Criminology* 307 (1943), available at http://scholarlycommons.law.northwestern.edu/cgi/viewcontent.cgi?article=3224&context=jclc.

47 Prassel, at 71–72.

48 Reynolds, at 211–213.

49 David A. Sklansky, *The Private Police*, 46 UCLA L. Rev. 1165, 1204 (1999).

50 See Reynolds, at 211–213.

51 Sir Robert Peel's Principles of Law Enforcement at https://www.durham.police.uk/About-Us/Documents/Peels_Principles_Of_Law_Enforcement.pdf, last visited 2/20/17.

52 Dralla et al., at 445. Even today the influence of Robert Peel can be felt in matters of community policing. See Sandra Mazemi, *Sir Robert Peel's Nine Principals of Policing*, Los Angeles Community Policing Website at http://www.lacp.org/2009-Articles-Main/062609-Peels9Principals-SandyNazemi.htm, last visited February 20, 2017.

53 Erik Beckman, *Law Enforcement in a Democratic Society* 34.

54 Lipson, at 21.

55 Beckman, at 34.

56 Id. at 19.

57 Id.

58 Elizabeth E. Joh provides a good historical overview at *The Paradox of Private Policing*, 95 *J. Crim. Law Criminology* 49 (2004); See also Sklansky.

59 Beckman, at 23.

60 O'Toole, at 21–22.

61 Charles Chamberlain, *A Short History of Private Security Assets Protection* 38 (1979).

62 Sklansky, at 1212.

63 Chamberlain, at 21.

64 Lipson, at 35.

65 James D. Horan, *The Pinkertons* 516 (Bonanza Books, 1968).

66 Chamberlain, at 37.

67 Lipson, at 27.

68 Id. at 28.

69 Hadsell & Coffey, *From Law and Order to Chaos Warfare: Baldwin-Felts Detectives in the S.W. Virginia Coal Mines*, 40 W. Va. Hist. 268–286 (1979).

70 Lipson, at 28.

71 For some general background on the Pinkerton and his company, see *Old West Legends: Pinkerton Detective Agency – for 150 Years*, Legends of America Website at http://www.legendsofamerica.com/we-pinkertons.html, last visited 2/20/17.

72 O'Toole, at 21–22.

73 Prassel, at 132.

74 Id. at 126–149.

75 Id. at 133.

76 Lawrence M. Friedman, *The Development of American Criminal Law* 17 (1979).

77 Id. at 18–19.

78 Prassel, at 131.

79 See Id. for an interesting discussion.

80 Lipson, at 42.

81 Green, at 12.

82 National Advisory Commission, at 35.

83 O'Toole, at 30; see also Wesley, *Thirty Years of Security: An Overview*, 4 J. of Sec. Admin. 26 (1981); William C. Cunningham, John J. Strauchs, and Clifford W. Van Meter, *Private Security: Patterns and Trends* (1991); See also Ronald van Stedena and Rick Sarre, *The Growth of Private Security: Trends in the European Union*, 20 Security J. 222–235 (2007).

84 Total private security employment in 1982 is conservatively estimated at 1.1 million persons (excluding federal, civil, and military security workers), 449,000 in propriety security and 641,000 in contract security. These rises continue unabated throughout the Western World. Our neighbors to the north have seen a shrinking to stagnant public police model replaced by a vibrant private policing system. See Statistics Canada, *Table 1: Police Officers, Private Investigators and Security Guards Canada 1991, 1996, 2001 and 2006* (December 3, 2009) at http://www.statcan.gc.ca/pub/85-002-x/2008010/article/10730/tbl/tbl1-eng.htm, last visited February 20, 2017.

85 For a current picture of theft losses at the retail level alone, see Ernie Deyle, *Global Retail Theft Barometer: 2013-2014*, LPM Insider (1/19/15), at http://losspreventionmedia.com/insider/inventory-shrinkage/the-global-retail-theft-barometer, last visited 2/20/17.

86 Karen K. Addis, *The Business of Security*, 10 Sec. Mgmt. 76 (Oct. 1991).

87 Id.

88 Sklansky, at 1177.

89 Id.

90 Ernie Deyle, *Global Retail Theft Barometer: 2013-2014*, LPM Insider (January 19, 2015), at http://losspreventionmedia.com/insider/inventory-shrinkage/the-global-retail-theft-barometer, last visited February 20, 2017.

91 Richard J. Sullivan, Federal Reserve Bank of Kansas City, *The Changing Nature of U.S. Card Payment Fraud: Issues For Industry And Public Policy* 11, presented at the 2010 Workshop on the Economics of Information Security, Harvard University (May 21, 2010) available at http://weis2010.econinfosec.org/papers/panel/weis2010_sullivan.pdf; see William C. Cunningham and Todd H. Taylor, *The Growing Role of Private Security*, National Institute of Justice Research in Brief, Oct. 1984, at 4; William Cunningham et al, *Private Security Trends 1970–2000, The Hallcrest Report II* 237 (1990); US Private Security Services, *Market Report* (Freedonia, 2008) available at http://www.reportlinker.com/p091920/US-Private-Security-Services-Market.html.

92 E. L. Gaston, *Mercenarism 2.0? The Rise of the Modern Private Security Industry and its Implications for International Humanitarian Law Enforcement*, 49 Harvard Internat'l L. J. 221 (2008), available at http://www.harvardilj.org/2008/01/issue_49-1_gatson.

93 Robert Mandel, *The Privatization of Security*, 28 Armed Forces & Society 129, 132 (2001); see also Joshua S. Press, *Crying Havoc Over the Outsourcing of Soldier and Democracy's Slipping Grip on the Dogs of War*, 103 NW U. L. Rev. Colloquy 109 (2008).

94 Mandel, at 129.

95 Mark Calaguas, *Military Privatization: Efficiency or Anarch?* 6 Chi-Kent J. Int'l & Comp. L 58 (2006).

96 Jon Cadieux, *Regulating the United States Private Army: Militarizing Security Contractors*, 39 Cal. W. Int'l L. J 197 (2008).

97 Mandel, at 132.

98 Christopher Kinsey, *Corporate Soldiers and International Security, The Rise of Private Military Companies* (2006); Thomas Jäger and Gerhard Kümmel, *Private Military and Security: Companies Chances, Problems, Pitfalls and Prospects* (2007).

99 For a full analysis of the reasons and rationales for increased privatization, see Charles P. Nemeth, *Introduction to Private Security* (2017) and *Private Security and the Investigative Process 3rd* 1–9 (2010).

100 Scott M. Sullivan, *Private Force/Public Goods*, 42 Conn. L. Rev. 853, 857–858 (2010); See also Ellen Dannin, *Red Tape or Accountability: Privatization, Publicization, and Public Values*, 15 Cornell J. L. and Pub. Pol'y 111, 113 (2005); Jody Freeman, *The Contracting State*, 28 Fla. St. U. L. Rev. 155, 170 (2000); Clayton P. Gillette and Paul B. Stephan III, *Constitutional Limitations on Privatization*, 46 Am. J. Comp. L. 481, 490 (Supp. 1998); David A. Super, *Privatization, Policy Paralysis, and the Poor*, 96 Cal. L. Rev. 393, 409–10 (2008).

101 Cunningham and Taylor, at 3.

102 David A. Sklansky, *Private Police and Democracy*, 43 Am. Crim. L. Rev. 89 (2006).

Chapter 2

Regulation, Licensing, Education, and Training: The Path to Professionalism in the Security Industry

2.1 Introduction: The Impetus for Increased Regulation

Much needs to be said about the security industry's call for increased professionalism and standards. Is it merely shallow puffery—calling for respect, skilled personnel, occupational status, and direction—without taking the requisite steps to insure that reality? Or is private security following the path to professionalism, insisting on well-regulated personnel, highly proficient in the field's varied tasks, properly educated and motivated to continuous training and professional improvement? "Professionalism carries with it certain responsibilities as well as certain privileges," according to Sackman.[1]

Any quest for professionalism mandates serious licensing requirements and quantifiable standards or levels of personal achievement, education, and experience. Security personnel must be both aware and strictly attentive to the dramatic surge of law and legislation outlining required levels of training and standards. "The private security field is entering a new era—an era of governmental regulation...and training of the guard force is a major focus of this regulatory thrust."[2]

The National Private Security Officer Survey, whose respondents included security directors, facilities and plant managers, security executives, and professional organizations, manifests an appreciation for regulation, either of a public or private variety, to insure a quality workforce.[3] Some findings were

- 75% check personal references
- 24% use psychological evaluation
- 40% use drug screening
- 53% believe there will be increased federal regulation of security officers
- 40% favor increased regulation[4]

Governments have not been shy about jumping into the oversight role of the private security industry, and this tendency has heightened since 9/11. A bipartisan bill, the Private Security Officer Employment Standards Act of 2002, sponsored by Senators Levin, Thompson, Lieberman, and McConnell, sought a review of past criminal histories of private security personnel. The legislative intent concerning the Act is plain on its face:

Congress finds that

1. Employment of private security officers in the United States is growing rapidly;
2. Private security officers function as an adjunct to, but not a replacement for, public law enforcement by helping to reduce and prevent crime;
3. Such private security officers protect individuals, property, and proprietary information, and provide protection to such diverse operations as banks, hospitals, research and development centers, manufacturing facilities, defense and aerospace contractors, high-technology businesses, nuclear power plants, chemical companies, oil and gas refineries, airports, communication facilities and operations, office complexes, schools, residential properties, apartment complexes, gated communities, and others;
4. Sworn law enforcement officers provide significant services to the citizens of the United States in its public areas and are supplemented by private security officers;
5. The threat of additional terrorist attacks requires cooperation between public and private sectors and demands professional security officers for the protection of people, facilities, and institutions;
6. The trend in the nation toward growth in such security services has accelerated rapidly;
7. Such growth makes available more public sector law enforcement officers to combat serious and violent crimes;
8. The American public deserves the employment of qualified, well-trained private security personnel as an adjunct to sworn law enforcement officers;
9. Private security officers and applicants for private security officer positions should be thoroughly screened and trained; and
10. Standards are essential for the selection, training, and supervision of qualified security personnel providing security services.[5]

Terrorism alone has justified a new vision of professionalism and corresponding oversight.[6] The U.S. State Department paints a grim picture of terrorism's impact on asset and facility integrity. Terrorism has changed the landscape. Data on numbers of international attacks from 1998 to 2003, shown in Figure 2.1, unfortunately charts an inclined plane with no end in sight.[7]

The security industry itself wishes some level of standardization in matters of licensure, regulation, and professional standards. Because private security personnel are increasingly involved in the detection and prevention of criminal activity, use of ill-trained, ill-equipped, and unsophisticated individuals is not only unwarranted but foolhardy (see Table 2.1).[8]

Consider the potential liabilities, both civil and criminal, that can potentially arise from a security employee who has little or no training, or has not been diligently screened. J. Shane Creamer, former attorney general for the Commonwealth of Pennsylvania, argues decisively:

There is a variety of problems involving abuse of authority which impact society itself. These range from very serious instances in which a private security officer shoots someone to a minor instance of using offensive language. These actions occur in the context

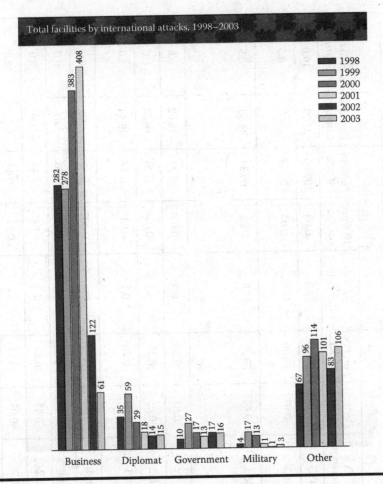

Total facilities by international attacks, 1998–2003

Legend:
- 1998
- 1999
- 2000
- 2001
- 2002
- 2003

Business: 282, 278, 383, 408, 122, 61
Diplomat: 35, 59, 29, 18, 14, 15
Government: 10, 27, 17, 13, 17, 16
Military: 4, 17, 13, 1, 1, 3
Other: 67, 96, 114, 101, 83, 106

Figure 2.1   Facilities struck by international terrorist attacks.

of an attempted arrest, detention, interrogation or search by a guard or a retail security officer. There is a striking consistency among private security executives' views, personal-injury claims statistics, responses of security personnel, complaints recorded by regulatory agencies, court cases, and press accounts. One is led to the inescapable conclusion that serious abuses occur—even if their frequency is unknown.[9]

Lack of proper standards, training, and educational preparedness results in a predictable shortage of skilled and dutiful security practitioners. Promotion of these traits and professional characteristics could and does curtail a plethora of common private enforcement problems, including

- Unnecessary use of force
- False imprisonment claims
- False arrest assertions
- Improper or illegal search and seizure techniques
- The proliferation of lawsuits
- Misuse of weaponry
- Abuse of authority

Table 2.1   Employment by Industry, Occupation, and Percent Distribution, 2008 and Projected 2018

33-9021   *Private detectives and investigators*
(Employment in thousands)
Industries with fewer than 50 jobs, confidential data, or poor quality data are not displayed

Industry		Employment	2008 Percent of ind	Percent of occ	Employment	2018 Percent of ind	Percent of occ	Percent Change	Employment Change
TOT001	Total employment, all workers	45.5	0.03	100.00	55.5	0.03	100.00	21.98	10.0
WSE100	Total wage and salary employment	36.1	0.03	79.30	44.6	0.03	80.34	23.58	8.5
WSE110	Wage and salary employment, except agriculture, forestry, fishing, hunting, and private households	36.1	0.03	79.30	44.6	0.03	80.34	23.58	8.5
220000	Utilities	0.2	0.03	0.35	0.1	0.03	0.24	−16.62	0.0
221000	Utilities	0.2	0.03	0.35	0.1	0.03	0.24	−16.62	0.0
221100	Electric power generation, transmission, and distribution	0.1	0.03	0.26	0.1	0.03	0.17	−19.44	0.0
310000-330000	Manufacturing	0.1	0.00	0.13	0.1	0.00	0.11	−3.10	0.0
440000-450000	Retail trade	1.6	0.01	3.53	1.7	0.01	2.98	2.81	0.0
445000	Food and beverage stores	0.2	0.01	0.54	0.2	0.01	0.44	−0.86	0.0
445100	Grocery stores	0.2	0.01	0.54	0.2	0.01	0.44	−0.86	0.0
448000	Clothing and clothing accessories stores	0.2	0.01	0.35	0.2	0.01	0.29	−0.50	0.0

(Continued)

Table 2.1 (Continued) Employment by Industry, Occupation, and Percent Distribution, 2008 and Projected 2018

33-9021 *Private detectives and investigators*
(Employment in thousands)
Industries with fewer than 50 jobs, confidential data, or poor quality data are not displayed

Industry		2008			2018					Employment Change
		Employment	Percent of ind	Percent of occ	Employment	Percent of ind	Percent of occ	Percent Change		
448100	Clothing stores	0.1	0.01	0.31	0.1	0.01	0.26	1.13		0.0
452000	General merchandise stores	1.1	0.04	2.43	1.1	0.03	2.05	2.96		0.0
452100	Department stores	0.7	0.05	1.57	0.6	0.04	1.06	−17.27		−0.1
452900	Other general merchandise stores	0.4	0.03	0.86	0.5	0.03	0.99	39.83		0.2
480000–490000	Transportation and warehousing	0.4	0.01	0.95	0.4	0.01	0.81	3.66		0.0
482000	Rail transportation	0.2	0.07	0.37	0.2	0.07	0.30	−1.47		0.0
482100	Rail transportation	0.2	0.07	0.37	0.2	0.07	0.30	−1.47		0.0
510000	Information	0.5	0.02	1.08	0.5	0.02	0.89	0.59		0.0
517000	Telecommunications	0.4	0.03	0.77	0.3	0.03	0.56	−11.53		0.0
517100	Wired telecommunications carriers	0.2	0.03	0.51	0.2	0.03	0.37	−12.91		0.0
517200	Wireless telecommunications carriers (except satellite)	0.1	0.03	0.12	0.1	0.03	0.09	−6.69		0.0

(Continued)

Table 2.1 (*Continued*) Employment by Industry, Occupation, and Percent Distribution, 2008 and Projected 2018

33-9021 Private detectives and investigators
(*Employment in thousands*)
Industries with fewer than 50 jobs, confidential data, or poor quality data are not displayed

Industry		2008			2018				
		Employment	Percent of ind	Percent of occ	Employment	Percent of ind	Percent of occ	Percent Change	Employment Change
18000-9000	Data processing, hosting, related services, and other information services	0.1	0.02	0.16	0.1	0.02	0.18	37.45	0.0
520000	Finance and insurance	3.9	0.06	8.53	4.3	0.07	7.71	10.27	0.4
521000-2000	Monetary authorities, credit intermediation, and related activities	2.4	0.09	5.22	2.7	0.09	4.82	12.75	0.3
522000	Credit intermediation and related activities	2.4	0.09	5.22	2.7	0.09	4.82	12.75	0.3
522200	Nondepository credit intermediation	0.6	0.09	1.28	0.5	0.09	0.95	−8.83	−0.1
522290	Other nondepository credit intermediation, including real estate credit and consumer lending	0.3	0.08	0.73	0.3	0.08	0.56	−6.14	0.0
522300	Activities related to credit intermediation	0.1	0.05	0.28	0.1	0.05	0.26	12.50	0.0

(*Continued*)

Table 2.1 (Continued) Employment by Industry, Occupation, and Percent Distribution, 2008 and Projected 2018

33-9021   Private detectives and investigators
(Employment in thousands)
Industries with fewer than 50 jobs, confidential data, or poor quality data are not displayed

Industry	2008			2018				Employment Change
	Employment	Percent of ind	Percent of occ	Employment	Percent of ind	Percent of occ	Percent Change	
523000 Securities, commodity contracts, and other financial investments and related activities	0.1	0.02	0.32	0.2	0.02	0.28	7.14	0.0
524000 Insurance carriers and related activities	1.3	0.06	2.93	1.4	0.06	2.55	6.07	0.1
524100 Insurance carriers	0.5	0.04	1.20	0.5	0.04	0.91	−8.01	0.0
524120 Direct insurance (except life, health, and medical) carriers	0.3	0.06	0.69	0.3	0.06	0.52	−9.10	0.0
524200 Agencies, brokerages, and other insurance-related activities	0.8	0.09	1.72	0.9	0.09	1.64	15.89	0.1
524210 Insurance agencies and brokerages	0.1	0.02	0.30	0.2	0.02	0.27	8.53	0.0
524290 Other insurance-related activities	0.6	0.27	1.42	0.8	0.27	1.37	17.46	0.1
540000 Professional, scientific, and technical services	2.3	0.03	5.02	3.2	0.03	5.85	42.15	1.0
541000 Professional, scientific, and technical services	2.3	0.03	5.02	3.2	0.03	5.85	42.15	1.0

(Continued)

Table 2.1 (Continued) Employment by Industry, Occupation, and Percent Distribution, 2008 and Projected 2018

33-9021 Private detectives and investigators
(Employment in thousands)
Industries with fewer than 50 jobs, confidential data, or poor quality data are not displayed

Industry	2008			2018			Percent Change	Employment Change
	Employment	Percent of ind	Percent of occ	Employment	Percent of ind	Percent of occ		
541100	Legal services	1.3	0.12	2.95	1.9	0.13	3.37	39.38	0.5
541300	Architectural, engineering, and related services	0.1	0.01	0.24	0.1	0.01	0.25	25.62	0.0
541500	Computer systems design and related services	0.4	0.03	0.94	0.6	0.03	1.07	38.80	0.2
541600	Management, scientific, and technical consulting services	0.2	0.02	0.54	0.5	0.02	0.81	83.62	0.2
541700	Scientific research and development services	0.1	0.02	0.29	0.2	0.02	0.29	23.43	0.0
541710	Research and development in the physical, engineering, and life sciences	0.1	0.02	0.28	0.2	0.02	0.28	24.12	0.0
550000	Management of companies and enterprises	1.2	0.06	2.69	1.4	0.07	2.54	14.90	0.2
551000	Management of companies and enterprises	1.2	0.06	2.69	1.4	0.07	2.54	14.90	0.2
551100	Management of companies and enterprises	1.2	0.06	2.69	1.4	0.07	2.54	14.90	0.2

(Continued)

Table 2.1 (Continued) Employment by Industry, Occupation, and Percent Distribution, 2008 and Projected 2018

33-9021 *Private detectives and investigators*
(Employment in thousands)
Industries with fewer than 50 jobs, confidential data, or poor quality data are not displayed

Industry		2008				2018				
		Employment	Percent of ind	Percent of occ	Employment	Percent of ind	Percent of occ	Percent Change	Employment Change
560000	Administrative and support and waste management and remediation services	19.6	0.24	43.16	25.4	0.27	45.84	29.55	5.8
561000	Administrative and support services	19.6	0.26	43.16	25.4	0.28	45.84	29.55	5.8
561100	Office administrative services	0.1	0.03	0.26	0.1	0.03	0.26	19.30	0.0
561200	Facilities support services	0.1	0.08	0.23	0.1	0.08	0.25	31.98	0.0
561300	Employment services	0.3	0.01	0.75	0.4	0.01	0.75	22.31	0.1
561400	Business support services	0.3	0.04	0.75	0.4	0.05	0.77	25.48	0.1
561600	Investigation and security services	18.5	2.30	40.78	24.1	2.51	43.47	30.05	5.6
561610	Investigation, guard, and armored car services	18.5	2.68	40.73	24.1	2.95	43.42	30.06	5.6
561900	Other support services	0.2	0.06	0.39	0.2	0.06	0.34	4.67	0.0
610000	Educational services, public and private	0.2	0.00	0.36	0.2	0.00	0.32	8.85	0.0

(Continued)

Table 2.1 (Continued) Employment by Industry, Occupation, and Percent Distribution, 2008 and Projected 2018

33-9021 *Private detectives and investigators*
(Employment in thousands)
Industries with fewer than 50 jobs, confidential data, or poor quality data are not displayed

Industry		2008			2018				
		Employment	Percent of ind	Percent of occ	Employment	Percent of ind	Percent of occ	Percent Change	Employment Change
611000	Educational services, public and private	0.2	0.00	0.36	0.2	0.00	0.32	8.85	0.0
620000	Health care and social assistance	0.1	0.00	0.31	0.2	0.00	0.29	16.05	0.0
621000-3000	Health care	0.1	0.00	0.21	0.1	0.00	0.19	11.09	0.0
622000	Hospitals, public and private	0.1	0.00	0.17	0.1	0.00	0.16	10.72	0.0
710000	Arts, entertainment, and recreation	0.1	0.01	0.27	0.1	0.01	0.24	7.11	0.0
713000	Amusement, gambling, and recreation industries	0.1	0.01	0.26	0.1	0.01	0.22	6.50	0.0
713100	Amusement parks and arcades	0.1	0.05	0.18	0.1	0.05	0.15	3.50	0.0
720000	Accommodation and food services	0.1	0.00	0.27	0.1	0.00	0.24	6.49	0.0
721000	Accommodation, including hotels and motels	0.1	0.01	0.27	0.1	0.01	0.23	6.55	0.0
721120	Casino hotels	0.1	0.02	0.12	0.1	0.02	0.11	12.06	0.0

(Continued)

Regulation, Licensing, Education, and Training ■ 31

Table 2.1 (Continued) Employment by Industry, Occupation, and Percent Distribution, 2008 and Projected 2018

33-9021 Private detectives and investigators
(Employment in thousands)
Industries with fewer than 50 jobs, confidential data, or poor quality data are not displayed

Industry		2008			2018				
		Employment	Percent of ind	Percent of occ	Employment	Percent of ind	Percent of occ	Percent Change	Employment Change
721110,90,300	Hotels (except casino), motels, and all other traveler accommodation	0.1	0.00	0.14	0.1	0.00	0.12	1.83	0.0
810000	Other services (except government and private households)	0.3	0.01	0.64	0.3	0.01	0.61	16.92	0.0
813000	Religious, grantmaking, civic, professional, and similar organizations	0.2	0.01	0.41	0.2	0.01	0.38	14.58	0.0
813400-900	Civic, social, professional, and similar organizations	0.2	0.02	0.38	0.2	0.02	0.36	14.94	0.0
813900	Business, professional, labor, political, and similar organizations	0.2	0.3	0.38	0.2	0.03	0.36	14.94	0.0
930000	Government	5.3	0.05	11.65	6.3	0.05	11.39	19.28	1.0

(Continued)

Table 2.1 (*Continued*)   Employment by Industry, Occupation, and Percent Distribution, 2008 and Projected 2018

33-9021   *Private detectives and investigators*
(Employment in thousands)
Industries with fewer than 50 jobs, confidential data, or poor quality data are not displayed

Industry		2008			2018				
		Employment	Percent of ind	Percent of occ	Employment	Percent of ind	Percent of occ	Percent Change	Employment Change
932000	State and local government, excluding education and hospitals	5.3	0.06	11.65	6.3	0.07	11.39	19.28	1.0
933300	State government, excluding education and hospitals	3.47	0.15	8.09	4.4	0.16	7.92	19.42	0.7
934300	Local government, excluding education and hospitals	1.6	0.03	3.56	1.9	0.03	3.47	18.96	0.3
SE1000	Self-employed and unpaid family workers, all jobs	9.4	0.08	20.70	10.9	0.09	19.66	15.86	1.5
SE1300	Self-employed workers, all jobs	9.4	0.08	20.70	10.9	0.09	19.66	15.86	1.5

Certainly, state legislatures, federal authorities, and even local governing bodies are mindful. "On the local level, governmental regulation dealing with training is proliferating. Cities, counties, and states are contemplating, or have already enacted, legislation or ordinances mandating standards for private security guards within their jurisdiction—standards that rarely fail to include training requirements."[10] Oversight is fairly expected and sensibly demanded of our governmental bodies.

> The states have the authority to regulate and license the private security industry, whether private detectives, watchmen, guard services, security agencies or any other activity related to personal and property security. The state may set reasonable standards and requirements for licensing. The courts stand ready to examine the regulations but only when these enactments appear unreasonable, capricious in purpose or arbitrary in design. Furthermore, they stand ready to examine either the uniformity or disparateness of impacts when implementing the regulations.[11]

The ramifications of inadequate regulation and licensing are far reaching. The 1985 study, *Crime and Protection in America: A Study of Private Security and Law Enforcement Resources and Relationships*,[12] by the National Institute of Justice, categorized how abuses and unprofessional behavior usually manifests itself in conduct such as

- Deceptive advertising
- Improper equipment
- Conflicting uniform designs
- Aggressive, unprofessional techniques
- Deceptive sales techniques
- Fictitious bidding processes
- High turnover rates (personnel)
- Lack of business longevity
- Internal fraud and criminal corruption
- Avoidance of confrontation
- Lack of liability insurance
- Low-grade personnel[13]

Even from an industry self-interest point of view, increased standards and regulatory requirements seem to correlate to eventual salary and position. The ASIS International database and study, *Compensation in the Security Loss Prevention Field*, corroborates the correlation:

> The survey serves as a benchmark, confirming what many industry professionals have known: For instance, unarmed security officers rank at the low end of the salary spectrum, with an average income of less than $16,000 a year. The compensation study also highlights some more novel findings, pointing to the Certified Protection Professional (CPP) designation as a distinct factor in higher income.[14]

Salaries also vary by geographic region and by armed or unarmed status. In 1993, unarmed salaries ranged between $12,000 and $21,000, and salaries for armed security officers ranged between $13,000 and $35,000.[15] Salaries will also vary by position and assigned responsibility. In 2015, the American Society of Industrial Security confirmed the continuous rise of salary and compensation for the managerial class in private security.[16] With increased compensation levels comes increased expectations of professional performance.

As the public justice system privatizes further, increased regulation and licensing will occur. Without it, abuse of authority will only escalate. At present, there is no national regulatory consensus to ensure a uniform design though most states fall into one of these categories:

1. Some jurisdictions have absolutely no regulatory oversight in the private security industry.[17]
2. Some jurisdictions heavily regulate armed security professionals, but disregard other private security activities.[18]
3. Some jurisdictions use existing state and municipal police forces to regulate the industry, while others promote self-regulation and education.[19]
4. Some jurisdictions cover the activities of alarm companies, while others exempt them.
5. Some jurisdictions devise separate regulatory processes for private detectives, but not for security guards or officers, while others make no distinction.[20]
6. Most jurisdictions have little education or training requirements, though the trend is toward increased education.[21]
7. Jurisdictions that require examinations for licensing are in the minority.
8. Those that regulate have an experience requirement.
9. Criminal record checks for prospective private employees for those states that regulate are increasing.

At present, the regulatory climate is a hodgepodge of philosophies exhibiting increasing uniformity. Moreover, regulation at the state and local levels has often been hastily developed and quickly enacted following media accounts alleging abuses of power by security guards and the commission of criminal actions by guards.[22] Usually, one hears about the regulatory crisis when scandal erupts or some criminality occurs within the security community. It is indisputable that there is a linkage between the behavior, good or bad, and the level of regulatory requirements and oversight in the security industry. More effective licensing and regulation for the private security industry can be attained by statewide preemptive legislation and interstate licensing agency reciprocity. With the number of national private security companies, the legislatures must address these two critical components of the licensing and regulation process. In states with a proliferation of local licensing ordinances, legislatures must take a leadership role in establishing uniform and fair legislation.

In addition, states must participate in interstate licensing reciprocity similar to that used by public law enforcement agencies in such matters as auto licenses, driver's licenses, and similar regulation. Currently, the national security companies are required to be licensed in many states. This is not cost-effective either for the security companies or ultimately the users of security services. The same burden is experienced by many smaller security companies that operate in several jurisdictions in adjacent states.[23]

Given these dynamics, a call for professionalism both from industry sources as well as governmental entities has been continuous and steadfast and there are signs of significant progress. At both the federal and state level, the push is on for increased controls, but our examination will weigh these questions:

Federal and State Regulation—What is the present level of governmental regulation of the security industry? Has there been increased attention given to qualifications? To education and training? Is a movement afoot to professionalize legislatively?

Education and Training—How much education and training has been legislated for security personnel? Is security education a viable academic exercise? What forms of specialized education should be legislatively or administratively required?

Model Statutory Designs that Promote Security Professionalism—How are statutes that involve the security industry composed? What types of statutory designs exists? What types of statutory authority promote professionalism in the security industry?

As the security industry takes on higher levels of responsibility in the elimination of crime, the enforcement of law, and the maintenance of the community, legislation and regulatory policy can only accelerate.

2.1.1 Federal Regulation

Aside from the states' efforts to professionally regulate the security industry, the federal government, through both direct and indirect means, has had some input into this industry's current standing. Historically, private security's union/business activities, from the Molly Maguires to the Homestead Steel Strike, have forced national scrutiny of the industry.[24] Recent events of paramilitary security contractors engaged in covert activities in the Middle East, especially in Iraq and Afghanistan, only heighten this penchant for oversight. Through the opinions of the U.S. attorney general and congressional passage of the Anti-Pinkerton Acts, private security has been the subject of continuous governmental oversight.[25]

The administrative agencies of the federal government, who extensively contract out for private security services, also influence private sector qualifications through their numerous requirements. These regulatory agencies have set standards on age, experience, education, and character:

- Department of Homeland Security
- Federal Aviation Administration
- Department of Defense
- Interstate Commerce Commission
- Nuclear Regulatory Commission
- Securities and Exchange Commission
- Food and Drug Administration
- Office of the Inspector General
- General Accounting Office[26]

Federal legislation that impacts private security practice is another means of regulatory control. Throughout the Clinton and Bush years, and certainly since the debacle of 9/11, various bills have been proposed to nationalize and standardize the security industry and its practice. In reaction to terrorism, Congress has enacted a host of measures which deliver security services in many contexts.[27] The Homeland Security Act of 2002[28] signifies a major reorientation in the legislative landscape. In 2003, the mission of the Homeland Security Agency noted, "In technology and safety, rules and facilities practices, the security world has been turned on its head."[29] In addition, there is an expectation that private security companies and corporations will continue to be active, cooperative players in the defense of a nation as to terror. The Department of Homeland Security (DHS) promotes the integration of private sector security firms working in conjunction with public law enforcement. More specifically, DHS erected a Private Sector Office and Outreach Group dedicated to these ends.[30]

The federal system entangles itself in all sorts of activities prompted by laws and legislation. Data collection, information gathering, and its maintenance are often the subject of federal legislation such as

- *The Fair Credit Reporting Act*[31]
- *The Freedom of Information Act*

Polygraphs have also been the subject of congressional oversight with the passage of the Polygraph Protection Act of 1980[32] and the Employee Polygraph Protection Act.[33] With extensive limitations on pre-employment screening and further encumbrances on internal investigations, employees and polygraph vendors see little promise in the future role of the polygraph,[34] yet the statutes manifest a federal nervousness about the industry.

There is momentum for increased regulation, particularly since the terrorist attacks of 2001. At the federal level, The Law Enforcement and Industrial Security Cooperation Act of 1996 (H.R. 2996)[35] was introduced, though not passed. H.R. 2996 encouraged cooperation between the private and public sectors. If passed, this bill would have been a solid step for the security industry to take toward an active role in opening the lines of communication with law enforcement and in turn, sharing ideas, training, and working in conjunction with each other, all indirectly influencing standards. The content of the proposed bill is instructive and certainly foretells an active future for the security industry. The rationale for bill adoption is fourfold:

1. Seventy percent of all money invested in crime prevention and law enforcement each year in the United States is spent by the private sector.
2. There are nearly three employees in private sector security for everyone in public law enforcement.
3. More than half of the responses to crime come from private security.
4. A bipartisan study commission specially constituted for the purposes of examining appropriate cooperative roles between public sector law enforcement and private sector security will be able to offer comprehensive proposals for statutory and procedural initiatives.[36]

The Private Security Officer Employment Standards Act of 2002[37] represents formidable federal involvement.

The impetus for federal legislation is real and forceful. So much of what the industry does has grave consequences. Technical and electronic intrusions into the general citizenry, especially in the technological age, raise many concerns. The private security industry must be attuned to legal and human issues that involve privacy. The industry must adopt policies and practices that achieve "a delicate balance between the forces of liberty and authority—between freedom and responsibility."[38]

2.1.2 State Regulation

Few would argue the enhanced trend toward regulation. Even police organizations such as the International Association of Police Chiefs (IACP) have promulgated minimum standards. All private security officers must meet the applicable statutory requirements and the established criteria of the employer, which may exceed minimum mandated requirements. Federal law mandates that candidates for employment must be citizens or possess legal alien status prior to employment. All applicants who are hired or certified as a private security officer should meet the minimum criteria listed below.

1. Be at least 18 years of age—"unarmed" private security officer.
2. Be at least 21 years of age—"armed" private security officer and comply with U.S. Public Law 104-208 Section 658 (The Omnibus Consolidated Appropriations Act of 1997).
3. Possess a valid state driver's license (if applicable).
4. Not have been:
   a. Convicted or pled guilty or nolo contendere to a felony in any jurisdiction.
   b. Convicted or pled guilty or nolo contendere to a misdemeanor involving moral turpitude, acts of dishonesty or acts against governmental authority, including the use and/or possession of a controlled substance within a seven-year period.
   c. Convicted or pled guilty or nolo contendere to any crime in any jurisdiction involving the sale, delivery, or manufacture of a controlled substance.
   d. Declared by any court to be incompetent by reason of mental disease or defect that has not been removed or expunged.
5. Submit two sets of classifiable fingerprints and two passport-sized photographs, along with applicant's name, address, date of birth, social security number, citizenship status, and a statement of conviction of crimes in order to conduct a state criminal record check, and a FBI criminal history check, prior to permanent employment as a private security officer. In all instances, these actions must be taken prior to the private security officer's being armed.
6. Furnish information about all prior employment through the employer making a reasonable effort to verify the last seven years of employment history, and checking three personal references.
7. Successfully pass a recognized pre-employment drug screen.

Suggested nonregulated pre-employment applicant criteria include the following:

1. High school education or equivalent
2. Military discharge records (DD 214)
3. Mental and physical capacity to perform duties for which being employed
4. Armed applicants shall successfully complete a relevant psychological evaluation to verify that the applicant is suited for duties for which being employed[39]

An overwhelming majority of American states have passed legislation governing the security industry. This legislation promulgates standards on education and training, experiential qualifications, and personal character requirements.

That the power to regulate is quite extraordinary is indisputable. The grant or denial of a license has economic and professional implications and regulatory authority must be attentive to due process and constitutional challenges. Most case law reviews not the constitutionality of the regulatory power, but the procedural rules and due process that accompany the industry's oversight. Appellate cases that challenge the process of oversight are fairly common. In Moates v. Strength,[40] an appeals court granted summary judgment to the licensing authority because appellant was incapable of showing a disregard for procedural regularity. The court noted, "The court cannot recognize a party's subjective belief that wrongdoing will occur as a viable claim for deprivation of that party's civil rights."[41]

While it is not the function of this section to review every piece of legislation promulgated by the states, the reader will be provided with a broad-based overview of legislative trends and standards. To commence, review the complete Florida Act given in Appendix 1. In Florida, as in most jurisdictions, state legislation tends to emphasize these regulatory categories:

- Age
- Experience requirements
- Gradations of licensure
- Personal character
- Education and training

2.1.2.1 Age

Age and its relation to eligibility are evident in most regulatory frameworks. Does age provide any assurance of better performance, ethical adherence, and professional demeanor? When one considers the seriousness of many security tasks, it seems logical that age is a crucial factor in licensing and regulation. Connecticut's statutory provision is a case in point:

> The applicant for a private detective or private detective agency license shall be not less than twenty-five years of age and of good moral character and shall have had at least five years' experience as a full-time investigator, as determined in regulations adopted by the commissioner pursuant to section 29-161, or shall have had at least ten years' experience as a police officer with a state or organized municipal police department.[42]

Most states are less rigorous than Connecticut, though age is usually a factor correlating with the type of license applied for. In many jurisdictions, age limitations are outlined when applying for a private investigator's license. Examples include the following states:

Hawaii	Be not less than 18 years of age;[43]
Indiana	is at least 21 years of age;[44]
Delaware	Be at least 25 years of age;[45]
Arkansas	Be at least 18 years of age.[46]

More typically, state legislatures propose minimal age requirements. Iowa makes a qualification for a license conditional on being at least 18 years of age.[47] Other jurisdictions following the 18-year-old rule for numerous licensed positions in security include Maine[48] and Georgia.[49] All in all, most jurisdictions allow applicants to be admitted at the legal age of majority.

2.1.2.2 Experience Requirements

A majority of states have an experience requirement, a fact somewhat inconsistent with the age qualifications. North Carolina experience provisions are more stringent than most states:

Experience Requirements/Security Guard and Patrol License

1. In addition to the requirements of 12 NCAC 07D.0200, applicants for a security guard and patrol license shall:

    a. *provide security guard and patrol services on an individual employer–employee basis to any person, firm, association or corporation which is not engaged in a contract security guard and patrol business.*

    b. *Law enforcement officers, while off-duty, may be employed by a licensed security guard and patrol business provided such officer is registered with the Board.*

    c. *A law enforcement officer employed by a proprietary security organization at times when the officer is not scheduled for work with the employing law enforcement agency shall not be considered as being employed regularly and exclusively as an employee in connection with the business affairs of such employer.*[50]

Requiring experience in justice-related occupations seems the norm. Georgia's experience requirements represent this tendency:

(7) The applicant for a private detective company license has had at least two years' experience as an agent registered with a licensed detective agency, or has had at least two years' experience in law enforcement, or has a four-year degree in criminal justice or a related field from an accredited university or college; and the applicant for a security company license has had at least two years' experience as a supervisor or administrator in in-house security operations or with a licensed security agency, or has had at least two years' experience in law enforcement, or has a four-year degree in criminal justice or a related field from an accredited university or college;[51]

The Georgia legislature allows police and law enforcement training as a substitute for the experience requirement. Other substitute activities for the experience requirements are as follows:

Have a minimum of two years of experience, education or training in any one of the following areas, or some combination thereof:

Course work that is relevant to the private investigation business at an accredited college or university;[52]

Employment as a member of any United States government investigative agency, employment as a member of a state or local law-enforcement agency or service as a sheriff;

Employment by a licensed private investigative or detective agency for the purpose of conducting the private investigation business;

Service as a magistrate in this state; or

Any other substantially equivalent training or experience;[53]

an insurance adjuster;[54]

an internal investigator or auditor while making an investigation incidental to the business of the agency or company by which the investigator or auditor is singularly and regularly employed.[55]

The emphasis placed on experience is a positive sign in the industry's quest for professionalism. Inept and inexperienced persons should not be entrusted with the obligations of private security. This trend toward security professionalism is further evidenced by the statutory reciprocity that exists between public and private justice, namely credit granted for law enforcement experience, or a waiver of the experience qualifications for those who have served in public law enforcement. Hawaii's statute is typical of this reciprocity:

Experience requirements. The board may accept the following:...
(3) Have had experience reasonably equivalent to at least four years of full-time investigational work;[56]

While great strides are evident in the jurisdictional experience rule, many states blatantly disregard the experience issue. Kansas lacks experience requirements.

75-7b05. License, initial or renewal; fee set by attorney general.
  a. Every application for an initial or a renewal license shall be accompanied by a fee in an amount fixed by the attorney general pursuant to K.S.A. 2008 Supp. 75-7b22, and amendments thereto.
  b. In addition to the application fee imposed pursuant to subsection (a), if the applicant is an organization and any of its officers, directors, partners or associates intends to engage in the business of such organization as a private detective, such officer, director, partner or associate shall make a separate application for a license and pay a fee in an amount fixed by the attorney general pursuant to K.S.A. 2008 Supp. 75-7b22, and amendments thereto.[57]

Equally silent on experience is New Jersey.[58]

2.1.2.3 Licensure

Regulation by license is the state's effort to regularize security practice and its particular positions. By overseeing occupations and professions, from lawyers to security officers, the state gives credence to the field's influence and importance and symbolizes a need to quality control those engaging in its activities. Review the Private Detective, Private Alarm, Private Security, and Locksmith Act of 2004.[59] Licensure classifications are as follows:

- *Classes of Individual Licenses*
  - Private detective[60]
  - Private security contractor[61]
  - Private alarm contractor[62]
- *Classes of Business Certification*
  - Private detective agency[63]
  - Private security contractor agency[64]
  - Private alarm contractor agency[65]

Varying degrees of experience, education and training, bond, and age are cited, depending upon the license desired. Not surprisingly, the licensure requirements impose the heaviest burdens on those who can exert force, handle weaponry, or those owning and operating a security agency.

These statutory gradations are testimony to the dynamic growth and maturation of the security industry. Legislators, as a rule, make laws when pressed or prodded by the ebb and flow of social and political pressure. At times, political action comes from enlightened activism, at other times the impetus is scandal or some reactionary setting. "This new era—an era of regulation for the private security industry offers a great challenge, and that challenge will be met if the interested parties recognize their common business interests as well as their collective responsibility to the community at large."[66]

The Florida legislature poses another set of licensure categories even more grandiose:

5N-1.116 Classification of Licenses; Insurance; Fees.
(1) Classifications. The following shall be the classifications of licenses:

PRIVATE INVESTIGATION

Agency	Class "A"
Private Investigator	Class "C"
Armed Private Investigator	Class "C" & Class "G"
Branch Office	Class "AA"
Manager	Class "C," Class "MA," or Class "M"
Intern	Class "CC"

PRIVATE SECURITY

Agency	Class "B"
Security Officer	Class "D"
Armed Security Officer	Class "D" & Class "G"
Branch Office	Class "BB"
Manager	Class "MB" or Class "M"

REPOSSESSION ACTIVITY

Agency	Class "R"
Recovery Agent	Class "E"
Branch Office	Class "RR"
Manager	Class "MR" or Class "E"
Intern	Class "EE"

COMBINED PRIVATE INVESTIGATION AND SECURITY

Agency	Class "A" & Class "B"
Branch Office	Class "AB"
Manager	Class "M"

SCHOOLS

Security Officer School/Training Facility	Class "DS"
Security Officer Instructor	Class "DI"
Recovery Agent School/Training Facility	Class "RS"
Recovery Agent Instructor	Class "RI"

FIREARMS

Instructor	Class "K"
Statewide Firearm License	Class "G"

MANAGERS

Private Investigative Agency or Branch	Class "C," "MA," or "M"
Private Security Agency or Branch	Class "MB" or "M"
Recovery Agency or Branch	Class "E" or "MR"
Armed Manager	Appropriate Manager's License & Class "G"[67]

Florida licensing law promotes an interplay and reciprocity between public and private law enforcement by granting credit for public law experience. Equally stressed is education, its level obtained and degree correlating to the security position. In sum, the more complicated the position, the higher the regulatory demand. For example, a private investigator applicant may substitute some of the experiential requirements by adhering to the following regulatory pattern:

1. Private investigative work or related fields of work that provided equivalent experience or training;
2. Work as a Class "CC" licensed intern;
3. Any combination of paragraphs (a) and (b);
4. Experience described in paragraph (a) for one year and experience described in paragraph (e) for one year;
5. No more than one year using:
   a. College coursework related to criminal justice, criminology, or law enforcement administration; or
   b. Successfully completed law enforcement-related training received from any federal, state, county, or municipal agency.[68]

Additionally, the Florida statute fully recognizes the serious burden that is placed upon the armed security officer. Both armed personnel and their instructors are placed under stringent guidelines:

In order to qualify for the Class "G" license, you must have successfully completed 28 hours of range and classroom training provided by a licensed Class "K" Firearms Instructor within the preceding 12 months. The Firearms Instructor will issue a

Certificate of Firearms Proficiency (Form DACS-16005) to you upon completion of this training. A copy of this certificate must be included with your application.

Acceptable Alternatives for the 28 Hours of Range and Classroom Training

1. If you are certified by FDLE's Criminal Justice Standards & Training Commission (CJSTC) as a law enforcement officer or correctional officer AND you are currently employed in either of these capacities, a copy of your valid ID card issued to you by your employing law enforcement agency will satisfy the training requirement.
2. If within the preceding 12 months you have successfully completed a training program approved by the CJSTC for certification of graduates as law enforcement officers or correctional officers, a copy of your certificate of completion from that program will satisfy the training requirement.
3. If you qualify for a Class "K" Firearms Instructor License in accordance with the requirements set forth in s. 493.6105(7(a), FS, a copy of one of the law enforcement or security firearms instructor certificates listed in this section will satisfy the training requirement.[69]

Licensure grades and requirements vary according to the level of responsibility exerted. Some states need the security agency itself to perform internal oversight of its own employees. Thus, the security firm or proprietor needs a license that includes a right to supervise or evaluate those under its command. Given the growth of security personnel, it makes good sense to transfer the task of policing one's own to those in occupational proximity—the agency itself. New Mexico sets up such a policy in its list of qualifications for operation of business. The statute holds

A licensee shall at all times be legally responsible for the good business conduct of each of his employees, including his managers.[70]

Those holding themselves out Armed Security Officers need adhere to licensing and regulatory requirements. In *U.S. v. Kelly*[71] police officers checked on security officers at local nightclubs and found them lacking proper licensure and certification. Law enforcement confiscated those weapons. In sum, these legislative classifications are further evidence of the technical, business, and professional sophistication evolving in the security industry. As the field matures and develops, legislative activity and regulation mirrors the development.

2.1.2.4 Personal Character

Traditionally, "good" character was the chief criteria for license issuance. Stating such criteria is easy. Definition and interpretation of these criteria is highly subjective. The diversity of good character definitions is testimony to the creative draftsmanship of legislators. The desire is plain—to license only those individuals who are not thieves, liars, untrustworthy scoundrels, or other reprehensible characters. Character bespeaks loudly the man or woman's suitability for the job.

In North Carolina, a license will be issued to a person who "is of good moral character and temperate habits."[72] Who is the judge of temperance? Can this trait be objectively measured? Indiana tries to make it plain by denying a license to applicants who have not:

(c) The board may deny a license unless the applicant makes a showing satisfactory to the board that the applicant or, if the applicant is a business entity, the officer or partner referred to in subsection (b):

1. has not committed an act which, if committed by a licensee, would be grounds for the suspension or revocation of a license under this chapter;
2. has not been convicted of a:
   A. felony; or
   B. misdemeanor that has a direct bearing upon the applicant's ability to practice competently;[73]

While this legislative guidance is commendable, the lawmaker and regulator must be keen on the clarity of the act in question. Imprecision of language leads to abuse of discretion. Character is a difficult thing to measure precisely. Ohio provides more objective criteria.

(a) Has a good reputation for integrity, has not been convicted of a felony within the last twenty years or any offense involving moral turpitude, and has not been adjudicated incompetent for the purpose of holding the license, as provided in section 5122.301 [5122.30.1] of the Revised Code, without having been restored to legal capacity for that purpose.[74]

With this statutory definition, the evaluator measures the applicant by a past criminal history. Arizona does an even better job of delineating the notion of good character.

The applicants shall:

Within the five years immediately preceding the application for an agency license, not have been convicted of any misdemeanor act involving:

1. Personal violence or force against another person or threatening to commit any act of personal violence or force against another person.
2. Misconduct involving a deadly weapon as provided in section 13-3102.
3. Dishonesty or fraud.
4. Arson.
5. Theft.
6. Domestic violence.
7. A violation of title 13, Chapter 34 or 34.1 or an offense that has the same elements as an offense listed in title 13, Chapter 34 or 34.1.
8. Sexual misconduct.[75]

Arkansas adds further criteria in its search for acceptable conduct and character—alcohol and drug abuse. The statute holds that before issuance of a license prospective security professionals should not be suffering from habitual drunkenness or from narcotic addiction or dependence.

No license shall be granted to any person who has within five (5) years been convicted of a willful violation of any law of the United States, or of any state, relating to opium, coca leaves, or other narcotic drugs, or to any person who is a narcotic drug addict.[76]

Other states, such as New Jersey[77] and New York,[78] attempt to prove character by relying on the judgment of others. New York specifically requests:

(5) Such application shall be approved, as to each person or individual so signing the same, by not less than five reputable citizens of the community in which such applicant resides or transacts business.[79]

Statutory constructions sometimes measure character acceptability by reliance on one's moral order or disorder. The historic term for a deficit in character is "moral turpitude." "Moral turpitude" is defined as an act of baseness, vileness, or depravity in the private and social duties a person owes to another person, or to society in general, contrary to the accepted and customary rule of right and duty between persons, and conduct which is contrary to justice, honesty, or good morals. The following is a nonexclusive list involving moral turpitude:

1. Any act involving dishonesty or fraud
2. Any criminal act involving deception
3. Any act involving sexual misconduct and
4. Any offense with an element of specific criminal intent

Iowa illustrates the difficulty of dealing with the definition of good character though it delineates the unacceptable.

1. Applications for a license or license renewal shall be submitted to the commissioner in the form the commissioner prescribes. A license or license renewal shall not be issued unless the applicant:
   a. Is eighteen years of age or older.
   b. Is not a peace officer.
   c. Has never been convicted of a felony or aggravated misdemeanor.
   d. Is not addicted to the use of alcohol or a controlled substance.
   e. Does not have a history of repeated acts of violence.
   f. Is of good moral character and has not been judged guilty of a crime involving moral turpitude.
   g. Has not been convicted of a crime described in section 708.3, 708.4, 708.5, 708.6, 708.8, or 708.9.
   h. Has not been convicted of illegally using, carrying or possessing a dangerous weapon.
   i. Has not been convicted of fraud.
   j. Provides fingerprints to the department.
   k. Complies with other qualifications and requirements the commissioner adopts by rule.[80]

Efforts to define and measure character are never easy due to the subjective nature of character and moral determinations. While there is much that can be agreed upon as to the nature of what constitutes good character, there are distinct outlooks that are either more tolerant or judgmental in design and scope. Finding a balance is the best approach for the regulator.

Visit the National Association of Security Companies (NASCO) and find a rich database of information on the regulatory process at: http://www.nasco.org/member-area/state-agencies-associations/

Also, so dedicated is NASCO to this standardization of qualification that it has supported the creation of an electronic database for all American jurisdictions.

2.1.2.5 Education and Training

Professionalism for the security industry remains an empty promise without a commitment to education, scholarly research and development, and academic rigor. Regulatory bodies throughout the United States have been placing heightened emphasis on education and training as part of the minimum qualifications of an applicant.[81] The Private Security Advisory Council,[82] a federally funded consortium of public law enforcement specialists and private security experts, has made numerous recommendations concerning the upgrading of educational standards. The Council notes eloquently:

> [W]hile private security is a vast crime prevention and reduction resource, it will for the most part remain only a potential resource until steps are taken to eliminate incompetence and unscrupulous conduct. Many private security personnel are only temporary or part-time employees who are often underpaid and untrained for their work. The protection of lives and property is an awesome societal responsibility, and the public interest demands that persons entrusted with such responsibilities be competent, well-trained, and of good moral character.[83]

In the early 1990s the National Private Security Officer Survey portrayed an industry pool in need of higher educational achievement, reporting that most positions require a high-school diploma.[84] The requirements seem to be elevating on some levels. The 2002 Virginia Security Officer Study reported that over 55 percent of the survey respondents possessed at least some college level education[85] (see Figure 2.2).

From the lowest echelon employee in a security organization to the highest supervisory personnel, education and training is inexorably tied to occupational development.[86] A 1973 study, Private Police in the United States: Findings and Recommendations, heralds education as a remedy to deficiencies in the security industry. Insisting on minimums, the study relays the following:

- All types of private security personnel should receive a minimum initial training program of at least 120 hours.

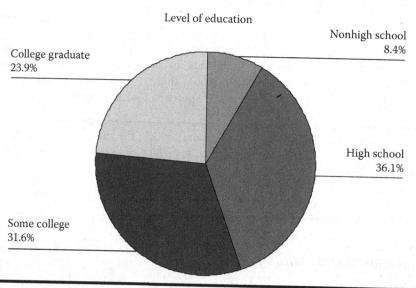

Figure 2.2 Security Officer education levels.

- Federal funds should be made available to develop appropriate training programs, including curricula, materials, and methodology.
- State regulatory agencies should require minimum training programs—in terms of quality, curriculum, and hours of instruction for all types of private security personnel.
- Appropriate higher education, such as a bachelor's degree in police science and administration, should also be a substitute for part of the minimum experience requirements.[87]

The Private Advisory Council, as well as a RAND Study on private security,[88] critique the paucity of the education and training provided to security personnel. The RAND Study concludes:

> 65% of private security personnel had no training at all prior to commencing job assignments. Approximately one-half of private security personnel carried firearms, but less than 20% had ever received any firearms training in their present job.[89]

The National Association of Private Security Industries, Inc. of Dallas, Texas, confirms the urgent need for training and education for the contract guard firm. A recent report by the National Association of Private Security Industries stated that contract guard firms want their officers to be trained in liability avoidance, documentation and reports, patrol techniques, mid-level security supervision, laws of arrest, and first aid.[90]

The call for increased education and training has been broad-based.[91] "In security, as in other functions of an organization, the higher an executive climbs the broader is his need for education."[92] Education of public and private law enforcement can "dismiss prior notions or opinions, that is, to motivate them to think on a factual basis. The appalling lack of knowledge of the law can be corrected by immersing the officer in a study of the legal problems. Topics such as powers and restrictions on private police, law of arrest, search and seizure procedures, electronic eavesdropping, civil liabilities, and licensing statutes can be studied. Perhaps through an educational experience, an officer may not allow enthusiasm to overcome judgment in his daily rounds.[93]

The National Association of Security Companies corroborates the urgent need for educational preparation for the industry and concludes the causal connection between professionalism and education.

> The National Association of Security Companies (NASCO) is the nation's largest contract security trade association, representing private security companies that employ more than 250,000 of the nation's most highly trained security officers servicing every business sector. NASCO is leading efforts to set meaningful standards for the private security industry and security officers by monitoring state and federal legislation and regulations affecting the quality and effectiveness of private security services.[94]

At the collegiate and university level, the development and legitimization of the academic discipline of security studies has been both steady and impressive. Currently there are 1476 institutions in the United States that offer some coverage of security and protective studies, though most do not offer full-fledged degrees.[95] Some of the institutions offering degrees and courses in the field are

- Alabama State University
- American University

- Auburn University—Montgomery
- Baylor University
- California State University—various locations
- California University of Pennsylvania
- Eastern Kentucky University
- Fairmont State College
- Farleigh Dickinson
- George Washington University
- Jackson State University
- Jersey City State University
- John Jay College of Criminal Justice
- Marquette University
- Sam Houston State University
- Seton Hall University
- Texas A & M University
- Xavier University

For a complete listing of universities and colleges offering security-related education, see the ASIS International listing of participating institutions at: https://www.asisonline.org/Membership/Library/Academic-Student-Center/Documents/Academic-Programs-in-Security.pdf

How security studies grows and evolves is likely a parallel story to how the academic discipline of criminal justice came to be. Criminal justice education illustrates the long and sometimes vicious battle for legitimacy within traditional academic circles. Now an academic discipline firmly entrenched in more than 1100 colleges and universities, criminal justice's search for legitimacy in stodgy academic environs may soon be over.[96] Security training has been an integral course within criminal justice studies but is in its seminal stage at the undergraduate and graduate levels. "Growth in security academic programs has been significant. Nationwide, there were 33 certificate and degree programs 15 years ago. By 1990, the total had increased to 164. According to the Criminal Justice Degree school database, there are currently approximately 1400 schools in the US which offer criminal justice degrees."[97]

In a degree-granting framework there has been steady growth particularly at the graduate level.[98] ASIS International, through its foundation, established a master's degree in security management at Webster University. "The Webster curriculum features a Master of Arts (MA) and a Master of Business Administration (MBA) option and reflects current security theory and practice. The program, guided by the Foundation, will be frequently revised to better meet the needs of students and will reflect input from university studies, corporate surveys and other assessments."[99] Its core curriculum contains seven required business courses, including statistical analysis, business accounting systems, business information systems, financial planning, operations and production management, economics for the firm, and business policy. The program also requires eight security courses, which are the same courses required for the M.A. degree covering legal and ethical issues in security management, management and administration courses, asset protection, information systems security, emergency planning, and an integrated studies course.[100] At John Jay College of Criminal Justice, graduate degrees in the interdisciplinary field of protection management are offered as well as a national, online Master's in Security Management. Both curricula are cutting edge in that the programs integrate traditional security conceptions with emergency and fire content. In addition, both programs value managerial skills to train future supervisors and directors. The programs are housed under the department of Security, Fire and Emergency Management.[101]

Jim Calder of the University of Texas argues that as long as protective security studies is so heavily tethered and entangled with criminal justice, its growth will be slower than expected:

> Security Studies must move from separate-but-equal status to total interaction with other aspects of criminal justice education. My premise is that the criminal justice system cannot reduce property crime profoundly (because of social structural limitations) and thus must rely more heavily on security forces.[102]

There has been discussion about whether security studies need to exist independently or as an aligned subject matter with criminal justice. Christopher Hertig, CPP, remarks:

> Security curricula exist on many campuses today, and an increasing number of criminal justice programs include courses in security, loss prevention, or safety. While many people dispute the wisdom of having security courses attached to criminal justice programs, the reality is that the majority of courses are within criminal justice curricula. This is not likely to change anytime soon. I believe that working with an existing program is generally more productive than idly wishing for something that may never be.[103]

Since 9/11, certificates and degrees are continually evolving in the young academic discipline of "homeland security."[104] If anything, security education is a major complement to traditional criminal justice and police science programs. "Security studies can offer criminal justice education an end to the past overbearing concern for the quantity of crime as the primary indication of social and political controls. Security is less concerned with quantity than it is about location, specifically, whether crimes of all types are committed within a social location under its control."[105]

The argument for security education and training is compelling, particularly when coupled with the drive toward professionalism. One certainly cannot exist without the other as Richard Post lucidly poses:

> Is security a profession? No, probably not to the extent that law enforcement or many of the other areas of criminal justice are professions ... But, we have made a start. Things are beginning to move forward, and it is entirely possible that security may be considered the profession of the future.[106]

Considering these arguments, have the states enhanced educational requirements for licensure? Does the legislative process recognize the role education and training play in the future of security as an industry and the privatization movement? Legislative analysis manifests some sound redirection in favor of education and training. While some states like Colorado[107] are constitutionally unable, at least at this juncture, to mandate licensure requirements, and others simply do not require it, more and more states require some level of training for personnel.

Education and training can take many forms, such as that mandated in Arizona. Figure 2.3[108] outlines the training topics that security companies are required by law to provide to their personnel.

Other states require applicants to pass an examination covering a broad range of topics. State administrative agencies even provide bibliographic lists to help applicants prepare.[109] Recent

Arizona Department of Public Safety

Unarmed Security Guard
8 Hour Training Syllabus
February 2, 2007

This syllabus was developed by the DPS Security Guard Licensing Unit and meets the **mandatory 8-hour pre-assignment training requirement** that must be completed prior to submitting a security guard license application. All training must be conducted by an authorized instructor – Training may not be performed using videos alone, however, they may be used to supplement the instructor's training.

- **Trainers:** Training shall be **at least 8-hours** in duration and **does not** include a lunch break. Ten minute breaks each hour are permissible and will not count against the 8-hours. Establish and maintain (5 years) a sign-in roster for each class.
- The agency shall ensure the application and training verification has been signed by the instructor or designee.
- Guards **may not** work a security post until they are in possession of a valid security guard card and are wearing the DPS **approved** uniform (as applicable).

1.   **Orientation - Introduction to Security**

2.   **Criminal Law / Laws of Arrest** (Legal Authority) *The law and legal portion of this course is a vital block of instruction for security guard applicants. Instructors must cover all topics listed below. References include ARS Title 13 and the AZ DPS website: Arizona Department of Public Safety-Licensing Unit. Much of the text "Legal Issues Relating to the Use of Deadly Force" by Michael Anthony (found on the AZ DPS CCW website) is also applicable, however, this text was primarily designed for the CCW course, not security guards. Edit out specific references to CCW issues. References to specific section numbers* **(bold - within parenthesis)** *are for use with the "Legal Issues Relating to the Use of Deadly Force" text, which security guard instructors may find useful.*

   A.   Authority and Responsibility of a Security Guard

   1) Definitions

   2) ARS Title 32, Chapter 26, Security Guard Regulation. *Sections 2632.D, 2633, 2634, 2635, 2636, 2637, 2638, 2639.D, and 2642. Additionally, specifically state that security guards may not work a post unless they are physically in possession of a valid guard card and in the proper uniform – guards working under a "pending" application are in violation of State law.*

   3) ARS Title 13, Chapter 4, Justification: *All relevant subsections to include 401, 402.B.2, 403.3, 403.4, 403.6, 404, 405, 406, 407, 408, 409, 410, 411, 412, 413, 416, 417, 418 & 419* **(Section V)**. *Subsections that do*

1

Figure 2.3   Arizona Unarmed Security Guard training syllabus.   *(Continued)* *not pertain to security guards carrying weapons may be omitted. This chapter is the most crucial section of the law and legal training requirement and all instructors must be thoroughly knowledgeable of this section.*

B.   Laws of Arrest

1) Interface with Law Enforcement/Assisting Law Enforcement (Be a good witness but do not physically assist law enforcement unless asked).

2) A.R.S. 13-3801, Preventing offenses; aiding officers (Briefly Discuss)

3) A.R.S. 13-3802, Right to command aid for execution of process; punishment for resisting process (Briefly Discuss)

4) A.R.S. 13-3881, Arrest

5) A.R.S. 13-3882, Time of Making Arrest

6) A.R.S. 13-3884, Arrest by Private Person

7) A.R.S. 13-3889, Method of Arrest by Private Person

8) A.R.S. 13-3892, Right of Private Person to Break into Building

9) A.R.S. 13-3893, Right to Break a Door or Window to Effect Release

10) A.R.S. 13-3894, Right to Break into Building in Order to Effect Release of Person Making Arrest Detained Therein

11) A.R.S. 13-3895, Weapons to be Taken from Person Arrested

12) A.R.S. 13-3896, Arrest After Escape or Rescue; Method of Recapture

13) A.R.S. 13-3900, Duty of Private Person After Making Arrest (Call the Police)

C.   Search and Seizure

1) 4th Amendment Rights (Briefly Discuss)

2) Unlawful Search and Seizure, A.R.S. 13-3925 (Briefly Discuss)

D.   Criminal Law and Recognizing Crimes *(Security guards should be able to identify these crimes):*

1. Briefly discuss ARS Title 13, Chapter 11, Homicide *(Section III.A)* 13-1102, 1103 *(Use of force aspects relating to security guards)*

2

Figure 2.3 (Continued)   Arizona Unarmed Security Guard training syllabus.   *(Continued)*

2. Briefly discuss ARS Title 13, Chapter 12, Assault and Related Offenses *(Section III.B)* *13-1201, 1202, 1203, 1204.*

3. Briefly discuss ARS Title 13, Chapter 15, Criminal Trespass and Burglary *(Section III.C)* *Cover aspects that pertain to security guards.*

4. Briefly discuss ARS Title 13, Chapter 16, Criminal Damage to Property *Cover aspects that pertain to security guards.*

5. Briefly discuss ARS Title 13, Chapter 17, Arson *Cover aspects that pertain to security guards.*

6. Briefly discuss ARS Title 13, Chapter 18, Theft *1802, 1803, 1804, 1805, 1816, and 1817- Cover aspects that pertain to security guards.*

7. Briefly discuss ARS Title 13, Chapter 19, Robbery *Cover aspects that pertain to security guards.*

8. Briefly discuss ARS Title 13, Chapter 24, Obstructing Government Operations *Chapters 2402, 2403, 2404, 2406, 2409, and 2411 Cover aspects that pertain to security guards.*

9. Briefly discuss ARS Title 13, Chapter 29, Offenses Against Public Order – Disorderly Conduct *(Section III.D)* *2904, 2905, 2907, 2907.01, 2908, & 2911).*

10. Briefly discuss ARS Title 13, Chapter 31 Weapons and Explosives *(Section III.E)* *13-3101, 3102, 3107. Cover aspects that pertain to security guards.*

11. Briefly discuss ARS Title 4, 4-244.29 *Patrons may not bring firearms into commercial establishments that serve alcohol for consumption on the premises (except peace officers).*

12. Request students visit the AZ DPS Licensing website at: http://www.azdps.gov/license/default.asp.

3. **Uniform and Grooming**

 A. Arizona Law Pertaining to Uniforms

  1) Authorized Uniform by Law and Agency

  2) Responsibility to Wear the Authorized Uniform

 B. Basic Hygiene Policy

3

Figure 2.3 (Continued)   Arizona Unarmed Security Guard training syllabus.   *(Continued)*

4. **Communications**

   A.   Written

   1) Report Writing

   2) Note Taking

   3) Steps in Writing a Report

   4) Grammar and Spelling

   5) Report Forms

   B.   Human Relations / Communications

   1) Verbal Control

   2) Physiological Responses to Stress

   3) How to Bring Down Stress

   4) Bridging Barriers of Communication

   C.   Use of Force / Levels of Force

   1) Define Use of Force and When Can it be Used

   2) Elements of Resistance

   3) Escalation and De-Escalation of Force

   4) Handcuffs/Restraints

   5) Physical Force

   6) Non-Lethal Weapon Use and Company Policies (Tasers, Mace, Capstun, Batons, etc.)

   7) Deadly Physical Force (Choke Holds, Lethal Strikes, Unauthorized Weapons)

5. **Crime Scene Preservation/First Response**

4

Figure 2.3 (Continued)   Arizona Unarmed Security Guard training syllabus.   *(Continued)*

A.   Responsibilities

B.   Reasons for denial of entry to a crime scene

C.   Procedures for protecting a crime scene

D.   Emergency Response Procedures

E.   Practical Exercise

6.   **Ethics**

Include a basic ethics policy in regard to good moral character.

1) Guards on Duty

2) Guards off Duty (Incidents Leading to Loss of Guard Card)

3) Driving Courtesy (On Duty in Security Vehicles)

7.   **Sexual Harassment**

1) Verbal

2) Non-Verbal

3) Innuendos

8.   **General Security Guard Procedures (Post or Job Procedures)** Specific post responsibilities should be explained at the work location

9.   **Close of Training** – Sign Training Forms and Submit Applications – **Guards may not work a security post until they are physically in possession of a valid guard card and wearing the DPS approved uniform (as applicable).**

5

Figure 2.3 (Continued)   Arizona Unarmed Security Guard training syllabus.

statutory amendments in Illinois highlight the trend toward education and training. For the applicant in Illinois, a security training program of at least twenty hours must be documented. Topics include

1. The law regarding arrest and search and seizure as it applies to private security.
2. Civil and criminal liability for acts related to private security.
3. The use of force, including but not limited to the use of nonlethal force (i.e., disabling spray, baton, stun gun or similar weapon).
4. Arrest and control techniques.
5. The offenses under the Criminal Code of 1961 [720 ILCS 5/1-1 et seq.] that are directly related to the protection of persons and property.
6. The law on private security forces and on reporting to law enforcement agencies.
7. Fire prevention, fire equipment, and fire safety.
8. The procedures for service of process and for report writing.
9. Civil rights and public relations.
10. The identification of terrorists, acts of terrorism, and terrorist organizations, as defined by federal and state statutes.[110]

Education is the centerpiece of the Illinois legislation. When combined with undergraduate training and experience, the proviso rewards those seeking licensure with such backgrounds. Applicants can substitute certain experience requirements with postsecondary education. Specifically, for private security contractors, the educational provision states that in lieu of experience, the applicants may demonstrate that they have a degree:

> An applicant who has a baccalaureate degree or higher in police science or a related field or a business degree from an accredited college or university shall be given credit for two of the three years of the required experience. An applicant who has an associate degree in police science or in a related field or in business from an accredited college or university shall be given credit for one of the three years of the required experience.[111]

Additionally, Georgia insists on certification for all security personnel utilizing weaponry.

> The board shall have the authority to establish limits on type and caliber of such weapons by rule.
> The board shall have the authority to require periodic recertification of proficiency in the use of firearms and to refuse to renew a permit upon failure to comply with such requirement.[112]

Louisiana education and training for an armed security guard includes

1. Legal limitations on use of weapons.
2. Handling of a weapon.
3. Safety and maintenance.
4. Dim light firing.
5. A shoot, don't shoot program.
6. Stress factors.[113]

Just because the complexity increases in the license sought, one cannot be sure the content will reflect the added roles and responsibilities. To be sure, there is great variety in the private security industry. Tennessee, for example, requires training for the armed guard consisting of the following topics:

Training Requirements
Training includes an examination covering subjects in which the individual must have training. All candidates must complete a four hour basic course including one (1) hour each of:

- Orientation.
- Legal powers and limitations of a security guard/officer.
- Emergency procedures.
- General duties.
- Any additional training for weapons or other devices that are less than lethal he or she will use.
- An armed guard must complete eight additional hours in the classroom covering:
- Legal limitations on the use of a firearm:
    - Handling of a firearm
    - Safety and maintenance of firearms

In addition, an armed guard applicant must complete an additional four hours of marksmanship training and achieve a minimum of 70% on any silhouette target course approved by the commissioner.[114]

This curriculum seems hours short to a fault and leaves a poor impression of preparation and industry seriousness about the quality of the officers. In Washington state, an unarmed guard has far more preparation than the armed personnel in Tennessee. Washington's curricular content covers a broad range of topics and relevant knowledge essential to the security professionals.

1. *Basic principles*
    a. Basic role of the security guard.
    b. Washington State licensing laws.
    c. Observation.
    d. Proper actions, reactions, ethics and diversity.
    e. Homeland Security—Terrorism and Surveillance.
2. *Legal powers and limitations*
    a. Citizen arrest.
    b. Authority to detain, question, or search a private citizen.
    c. Authority to search or seize private property.
    d. Use of force.
    e. Building relationships with law enforcement.
    f. Avoiding liability.
3. *Emergency Response*
    a. How to define what is or is not an emergency situation.
    b. Response to fires.
    c. Response to medical emergencies.
    d. Response to criminal acts.
    e. Bomb threats.

4. *Safety and accident prevention*
   a. Hazardous materials including MSDS.
   b. Accident reporting.
5. *Report writing. It's a legal document*
   a. Elements and characteristics of a report.[115]

New York, by way of comparison, adopts a legislative design that combines classroom and actual training by mandating entry-level educational programs of eight hours and then within 90 days, a 16-hour on-the-job training course. If armed, a 47-hour firearms program must be successfully completed.

> § 89-n. Training requirements. 1. Security guards shall be required to satisfactorily complete training programs given and administered by security guard training schools, schools which provide security guard training programs or security guard companies prescribed, certified and approved by the commissioner pursuant to section eight hundred forty-one-c of the executive law to include
>
> 1. An eight-hour preassignment training course;
> 2. An on-the-job training course to be completed within ninety working days following employment, consisting of a minimum of sixteen hours and a maximum of forty hours, as determined by the council, generally relating to the security guard's specific duties, the nature of the work place and the requirements of the security guard company;
> 3. A forty-seven hour firearms training course for issuance of a special armed guard registration card;
> 4. An eight-hour annual in-service training course; and
> 5. An additional eight-hour annual in-service training course for holders of special armed guard registration cards.[116]

California authors a similar model to New York but with the additional sixteen-hour training requirement during the first year of service.

40 Hour Security Guard Training Requirement[117]

Prior to Being Assigned on Post	8 Hours
Training Required within the First 30 Days	16 Hours
Training Required within the First Six Months	16 Hours
TOTAL HOURS	40 HOURS

Naturally, as the complexity of security work increases, so too the educational and training requirements. Florida sets up a variable system of educational requirements, depending on job classifications. For example:

> Class "G" shall include, but is not limited to 24 statewide hours of range and classroom training, no more gun permit than 8 hours of such training shall consist of range training.[118]

Virginia lays out two distinct training curricula for these categories.

Unarmed Security Officer Training Requirements
18 Hours, Consisting of:

- 01E—Security Officer Core Subjects Entry-Level (18 hours)[119]

Armed Security Officer Training Requirements
50–53 Hours, Consisting of:

- 01E—Security Officer Core Subjects Entry-Level (18 hours)
- 05E—Armed Security Officer Arrest Authority (8 hours)
- 75E—Security Officer Handgun (24 hours)
- 08E—Shotgun Training Entry-Level (3 hours) - If Applicable[120]

The requirements are not staggering by any stretch of the imagination, but a start; a posture emphasizing the role education plays in attaining professionalism.

Delaware has mandatory firearms training for all private detectives and investigators. Delaware's Board of Examiners is the watchdog agency for the security industry and decided effective July 30, 1979, that

> No person duly licensed by the Board shall be permitted to carry a pistol, revolver, or any firearm, prior to the completion of a course of instruction as designed by the Division of State Police. Instruction shall include, but not be limited to, safety, use of deadly force and marksmanship training. Each person shall thereafter be recertified annually.[121]

Legislative coverage, at least in the education and training area, is becoming more specialized. With strong advocacy for specialized training and instruction in computer-based fields,[122] airport and aircraft,[123] and animal handling, both the industry itself and governmental authorities are focusing on training requirements.

2.1.2.6 Professional and Continuing Education

Certification programs play a critical role in the development of a professional class within the security industry. Certifications take many forms although nearly all of them highlight a specific subject matter that requires unique preparation of a body of specialized knowledge. In addition, certifications are usually the invention of the professional bodies and associations that are inexorably tied that body of knowledge needed for skilled implementation. ASIS International has been on the forefront of certifications for many generations. Its Certified Protection Professional (CPP) programs make a real contribution to substantive professionalism. The CPP program's chief objectives are

1. To raise the professional standing of the field and to improve the practice of security management by giving special recognition to those security practitioners who, by passing examinations and fulfilling prescribed standards of performance, conduct, and education, have demonstrated a high level of competence and ethical fitness.

2. To identify sources of professional knowledge of the principles and practices of security and loss prevention, related disciplines, and laws governing and affecting the practice of security.
3. To encourage security professionals to carry out a continuing program of professional development.[124]

The industry's professional associations and groups have played a distinct role in the delivery of education services. The Certified Protection Professional (CPP) program tests rigorously those wishing the designation. Topics covered are

- Emergency planning
- Legal aspects
- Personnel security
- Protection of sensitive information
- Security management
- Substance abuse
- Loss prevention
- Liaison
- Banking
- Computer security
- Credit card security
- Department of Defense
- Educational institutions
- Manufacturing
- Utilities
- Restaurants and lodging
- Retail security
- Transportation and cargo security
- Telecommunications[125]

Jon C. Paul, director of security services for a major hospital, applauds the CPP designation. "The CPP designation is the hallmark of excellence in our profession—a fact that is recognized in our industry and is becoming more widely recognized by the organizations we serve."[126] To be eligible for the exam, the individual must meet the following requirements.

- Nine years of security work experience, with at least three of those years in responsible charge of a security function
-or-
- A bachelor's degree or higher and seven years of security work experience, with at least three of those years in responsible charge of a security function[127]

ASIS International awards other certifications as well. "The Physical Security Professional (PSP)® credential provides demonstrable knowledge and experience in threat assessment and risk analysis; integrated physical security systems; and the appropriate identification, implementation, and ongoing evaluation of security measures. Those who earn the PSP are ASIS board certified in physical security."[128] Eligibility requirements include

- High school diploma, GED equivalent, or associate degree and six years of progressive physical security experience
  -or-
- Bachelor's degree or higher and four years of progressive physical security experience[129]

The emphasis here is obviously dedicated the mechanics, policy, and technology of physical security. The domain area for testing break down into these categories:

- Physical security assessment (33%)
- Application, design, and integration of physical security systems (38%)
- Implementation of physical security measures (29%)[130]

ASIS also awards a certification of Professional Certified Investigator (PCI) where the chief emphasis is on the protocols and practices of investigation, evidence collection, case management and evaluations as well as best practices in surveillance, interrogation, and evidence gathering. The PCI domains of knowledge include

- Case management (29%)
- Investigative techniques and procedures (50%)
- Case presentation (21%)[131]

Finally, ASIS International delivers a wide array of short term certificates in a host of topics relevant to the security professional. A few examples offered in 2016 include

- Soft Targets, Active Shooters, Workplace Violence: CPTED Solutions
- Security Leadership & Tools—Prepare Now for Tomorrow
- Successful Security Consulting
- Like Oil & Water, Physical and Cybersecurity Don't Mix. But Can They?
- Principles of Investigation and Interrogation
- Workplace Violence Prevention and Intervention
- Wharton/ASIS Program for Security Executives
- Security Documents and Project Management Process
- Physical Security Master Planning Workshop
- Risk, Threat, and Vulnerability Assessment
- ASIS Assets Protection Course™: Principles of Security (APC I)
- Executive Protection
- Crisis Management: Program Planning and Crisis Plan Development[132]

The American Bankers' Association awards the Certified Financial Services Security Professional (CFSSP) to those passing an exam covering banking practices. The Certified Financial Services Security Professional certification is designed to

- Establish a recognized standard of knowledge and competence for security professionals working in the financial services industry

■ Formally recognize those who meet these standards
■ Provide employers with a tool to identify skilled, knowledgeable professionals
■ Support the benefits of professional continuing education and development[133]

The International Association of Professional Security Consultants (IAPSC) administers the Certified Security Consultant test for eventual certification.[134] The organization promotes professionalism in the security industry and calls upon its members to adhere to the highest standards of ethics in the industry. To become a CSC requires both extensive experience and education but also verification of unimpeachable character as well as having made significant contributions to the industry.

Find out more about the CSC Exam at: https://iapsc.org/about-us/certification/qualifications

Other organizations and group devise membership requirements based upon education and experiential backgrounds. While not technically a certification, the membership designation represents proof of high-level preparation. A good illustration of this is the eligibility requirements at posed by the International Security Management Association whose requirements are as follows:

■ The applicant must be actively employed and operate autonomously as the senior security executive of the enterprise.
■ The enterprise must have gross revenues exceeding one billion ($1,000,000,000) or equivalent sum in local currency per annum.

The fundamental issue of "one company-one member" shall be determined by the following criteria:

■ Does the candidate control the security budget?
■ Is the candidate's compensation determined within that company?
■ Are security policies and procedures established within that company?
■ Is the direct report for the candidate within that company?
■ If the identified parent company is an ISMA member, does the CSO for that company sponsor the candidate's membership and confirm his/her autonomy?
■ The applicant must be a recipient of a baccalaureate degree or its international equivalent or have as a minimum six years of experience in a policy making role in the security profession in private industry.[135]

Other continuing education programs, training seminars, and advanced studies are provided by a wide array of professional associations and groups whose addresses and phone numbers are listed in Appendix 2.

CPP Chris Hertig advises busy security operatives that even Web-based education is now readily available. These newer programs take "correspondence courses" one step further. "There's the Certified Protection Officer (CPO) and Security Supervisor programs from the International Foundation for Protection Officers (IFPO) Bellingham, Wash., and Calgary, Canada," says Hertig. In addition, the Carrollton, Texas-based Professional Security Television Network offers a videocassette series. The U.S. Department of Defense offers distance learning for its facility security managers. And firms such as Defensive Tactics Institute in Albuquerque, New Mexico, offer video training and critiques in areas such as personal protection. Universities offering criminal justice and security degree programs may also have independent distance studies.[136]

From all perspectives—academically, legislatively, and industrially—there is a major push for increased education and training. The industry and its participants recognize the need to upgrade their image as a professional occupation and the parallel necessity of increased educational requirements. CPP Lonnie Buckels understands the interrelationship between education and professionalism:

> The designation of professional has to be earned. For example, look at the medical profession. For decades, practicing medicine was thought to be part of the black arts. In some regions of the world it still is. However, after years of hard work, coupled with agonizingly slow technical advancements, medical practitioners are honored professionals. We have made steady progress in our quest for professional designation in the security industry. But we must continue this progress and be patient—professionalism takes time.[137]

2.1.2.7 Model Educational Programs: Curricula

Previously we discussed the influence of the Private Security Advisory Council, whose many impacts include the development of model curricula for security professionals. Their recommended training program for armed security officers is reproduced below.

Minimum Training Standards for Armed Security Officers
Preassignment Training
Prior to assuming any actual duty assignment, each new security officer should receive at least 8 hours of formal classroom training and successfully pass a written examination on the subjects.

> Orientation and overview in security—2 hours
> Criminal justice and the security officer, including legal powers and limitations—
>   2 hours
> Emergencies—2 hours
> General duties—2 hours ·

Weapons Training
Prior to being issued a firearm or taking an assignment requiring the carrying of or having access to a weapon, the security officer should receive at least 6 hours formal classroom training, successfully pass a written examination on the subjects and successfully complete an approved 18-hour firearms target shooting course.

Classroom:

> Legal and policy restraints on the use of firearms—3 hours
> Firearms safety, care, and cleaning—3 hours

Range:

> Principles of marksmanship—6 hours

Single action course—6 hours
Double action course—6 hours

Basic Training Course

Within three months of assuming duties, a security officer should complete a 32-hour basic training course. At least 4 hours should be classroom instruction and up to a maximum of 16 hours may be supervised, on-the-job training.
Classroom:

Prevention in security systems—1 hour
Legal aspects and enforcement of rules—1 hour
Routine procedures—1 hour
Emergency and special procedures—1 hour

The IACP also promulgates minimum coverage in training. The following are recommended:

■ Minimum basic training requirements and relevant, continuous in-service training for private security officers should be required. A formal mechanism to establish curriculum requirements and hours of training should be established.
■ All private security officer training should be reviewed and approved for certification by a state regulatory agency. Instructors will also be certified by the state regulatory agency. All training will be validated by approved testing criteria.
■ Private security officer basic or in-service training should include the following elements based upon needs analysis related to job function:
  – Security officers fall into one or more of these categories based upon their job function:
    • Unarmed security officers
    • Armed security officers
    • Unarmed nonsworn alarm responder
    • Armed nonsworn alarm responder
    • Armored car guard
  – Security officers' training needs will be addressed in large part under these topic areas as appropriate:
    • Legal
    • Operational
    • Firearms
    • Administrative
    • Electronic
    • Armored transport
    • Use of force
■ Due to the varied nature of security tasks and duties along with the proper training for each, the demands for each specific setting should be assessed for the level of training certification to build public trust and confidence.[138]

Annual Firearms Proficiency Requalification

Each armed security officer must requalify at least once every twelve months in an 8-hour firearms proficiency course.

Legal and policy restraints on the use of firearms	3 hours
Range requalification in target shooting	5 hours[139]

States have utilized the PSAC advisory recommendations in designing their own curricula. Assess the similarities as well as differences in the educational components of the North Dakota plan.

Apprentice Security Officer Training Curriculum Outline (16 Hours)

SECTION I. SECURITY ORIENTATION/OVERVIEW:

1. Introduction and overview.
   a. To the course.
   b. To the employing organization.
2. Role of private security.
   a. Brief history of private security.
   b. Overview of organization's security operations.
   c. Role of security in crime prevention and assets.
   d. Protection.
   e. Components of private security services.
   f. Primary functions/activities of security personnel.
3. Ethical standards for security personnel.
   a. Code of ethics for private security personnel.
4. Qualities essential to security personnel.
   a. Attitude/public relations.
   b. Appearance.
   c. Personal hygiene.
   d. Physical fitness.
   e. Personal conduct/deportment.
   f. Discipline.
   g. Knowledge of responsibilities.

SECTION II. CRIMINAL JUSTICE AND SECURITY PERSONNEL:

1. The nature and extent of crime.
   a. Overview.
   b. The criminal law.
2. The criminal justice system.
   a. Overview.
   b. The security person's relationship.
3. Legal powers and limitations.
   a. Rights of a property owner.
   b. Detention/arrest powers (citizen's or statutory).
   c. Search and seizure.
   d. Use of force.

SECTION III. GENERAL DUTIES:

1. Patrol techniques.
   a. Functions of patrol.

    b. Types of patrol.
    c. Preparing for patrol.
    d. Dealing with juveniles.
    e. Personal safety on the job.
    f. Traffic control.
  2. Access control.
    a. Why access control.
    b. Types of access control systems.
    c. Controlling an entrance or exit.
  3. Note taking/report writing.
    a. Importance of note taking/report preparation.
    b. Daily/shirt reports.
    c. Incident/special reports.

SECTION IV. EMERGENCIES:

  1. Fire prevention and control.
    a. What is fire.
    b. Causes of fire.
    c. Classes of fire.
    d. Recognition and identification of fire hazards.
    e. Firefighting, control and detection equipment.
    f. Role in fire prevention.
    g. What to do in case of fire.
  2. Handling emergencies.
    a. Bomb threats and explosions.
    b. Natural disasters.
    c. Mentally disturbed persons.
    d. Medical emergencies.
    e. First aid.

Security Officer Training Curriculum Outline (32 Hours)

SECTION I. SECURITY SYSTEMS:

  1. Physical security.
    1. Definition.
    2. Purpose.
    3. Locks and key control.
    4. Barriers.
    5. Access control systems.
    6. Alarm systems.
  7. Information security.
    a. Definition.
    b. Information classifications.
    c. Information and document control procedures.
  8. Personnel security.
    a. Threats to employees.
    b. Employee theft.

SECTION II. EMERGENCY PROCEDURES:

1. Medical emergencies of other emergency procedures.
2. Defensive tactics.
3. Unusual occurrences.
   a. Strikes, demonstrations, etc.

SECTION III. ROUTINE PROCEDURES:

1. Patrol.
   a. Prevention.
   b. Response to calls for service.
   c. Response to crime-in-progress.
   d. Crime scene protection.
2. Reporting.
   a. Information collection.
   b. Report preparation.
3. Dealing with problems unique to the individual's assignment.

SECTION IV. LEGAL ASPECTS AND ENFORCEMENT OF RULES:

1. Legal authority.
   a. Authority of security personnel.
   b. Regulation of security personnel.
2. Observing and reporting infractions of rules and regulations.
   a. Organizational rules and regulations.
   b. Security rules and regulations.[140]

Arkansas also provides a formidable program of instruction for prospective security professionals.

17-40-208. Training of personnel.

1. The Director of the Department of Arkansas State Police shall establish minimum training requirements under this chapter for a private security officer, a commissioned security officer, and a commissioned school security officer.
2. For a private security officer, the minimum training requirements under this chapter include without limitation the following topics:
   a. Legal limitations on the use of firearms and on the powers and authority of the private security officer;
   b. Familiarity with this chapter;
   c. Field note taking and report writing; and
   d. Other topics that the director deems necessary.
3. For a commissioned security officer, the minimum training requirements under this chapter include without limitation the following topics:
   a. Legal limitations on the use of firearms and on the powers and authority of the commissioned security officer;
   b. Familiarity with this chapter;
   c. Field note taking and report writing;
   d. Range firing and procedure and handgun safety and maintenance; and

e. Other topics the director deems necessary.
4. For a commissioned school security officer, the minimum training requirements under this chapter include without limitation the following topics:
   a. Legal limitations on the use of firearms and on the powers and authority of the commissioned school security officer;
   b. Familiarity with this chapter;
   c. Field note taking and report writing;
   d. Fundamental use of firearms, including firearm safety drills, tactics, and required qualification on an approved course of fire;
   e. Active shooter training;
   f. Active shooter simulation scenarios;
   g. Trauma care;
   h. Defensive tactics;
   i. Weapon retention;
   j. Handgun safety and maintenance; and
   k. Other topics the director deems necessary.
5. When an individual meets the training requirements approved by the director, that individual shall not be required to be retrained until two (2) years after the private security officer, commissioned security officer, or commissioned school security officer is commissioned.[141]

2.1.3 *Ethical Considerations*

The true test of professionalism should be its unwavering dedication to ethical conduct, professional values, and occupational integrity. It is common knowledge that the industry has grappled with standards for a long time and has yet to announce or promulgate nationalized standards that are uniformly agreed to. While there are associations and governmental entities that issue general guidance, the diversity of approaches is quite dizzying for those hoping for uniform stands. Many states describe and outline conduct that is unlawful and thus unethical.

Most companies publish ethical standards and expectations for their personnel.[142] Securitas International, formerly Pinkerton's Security Inc., a massive security service provider, also publishes ethical standards for its employees (see Figure 2.4).[143]

At the association, made up of professional member bodies and other groups, appear the greatest opportunity for an ethical consensus. The industry's chief professional association, ASIS, has done an admirable though incomplete job in the matter of professional ethics. The ASIS International Code of Ethics is reproduced to demonstrate the continuing correlation between the professional duties and the framing of ethical standards (see Figure 2.5).[144]

The National Council of Investigators and Security Services publishes a well-rounded and reasoned code of ethics for security professionals. Its language and purpose gets right to the heart of the matter, forcing employees to think about how services are delivered both professionally and ethically.

NCISS Code of Ethics

■ A member shall provide professional services in accordance with local, state, and federal laws.
■ A member shall observe, and adhere to the precepts of honesty, integrity, and truthfulness.

STANDARDS OF CONDUCT

It is Pinkerton's policy that every action taken by the Company and by each employee satisfies the highest ethical, moral and legal standards. All employees should be alert and sensitive to situations that could result in the violation of Pinkerton policy or procedure. We must exemplify the virtues of honesty, integrity and hard work in our roles as Pinkerton representatives as well as citizens. Pinkerton will be better for it as will each and every employee. The basic virtues of kindness, courtesy and integrity are the elements that provide the framework for a pleasant and equitable working environment and should be practiced by all employees.

BUSINESS ETHICS

The success of any business is largely dependent upon the honesty and integrity of its employees. Compliance with ethical business standards is expected. Failure to observe such standards exposes Pinkerton and, possibly, its employees, to severe legal sanctions and may damage the reputation of the Company and its employees. It is the responsibility of each Pinkerton manager to ensure that all employees understand and adhere to every Company policy.

To maintain an efficient and safe environment, employees are expected to act in accordance with generally accepted standards of behavior. No "Standard of Behavior" can hope to spell out the appropriate moral conduct and ethical behavior for every situation with which we will be confronted. Where an employee has any doubt about the appropriateness of morality of any act, it should not be done. The employee should seek guidance from his/her departmental manager. We believe that our team works well together in conducting business and in resolving the problems that invariably arise. It is our conviction that this working relationship and the values we hold provide the most productive, rewarding and satisfying work environment.

Honest competition based on integrity, price, product quality, service quality and customer service serves the public interest. Ethical conduct is good business. The trust and respect of fellow employees, customers, suppliers, competitors, neighbors, friends, and the general public depend upon adherence to the

Pinkerton Proprietary 06/10

31

Figure 2.4   Securitas International's values.

(Continued)

highest ethical standards. It is Pinkerton's policy that our business be conducted according to such standards.

If an employee is asked to depart from an established policy or practice, whether by a manager, another Pinkerton employee, or by a Client, he/she has a responsibility to clarify any ethical questions. This includes addressing the matter with the appropriate departmental manager until a clear statement of policy or practice in question is obtained and understood.

COMPLIANCE GUIDELINES

Pinkerton has made a commitment to prevent and detect criminal and/or unethical conduct within our organization, to further our continuing effort to assure compliance with all applicable laws and to promote and maintain our reputation for integrity and honesty. We ask all Pinkerton employees to be diligent in accomplishing our goal to prevent and detect criminal and/or unethical conduct and promptly report all such offenses to their departmental manager, human resources representative, or the Pinkerton C&I Hotline. Questions regarding the legality of any transaction or conduct should be directed to Pinkerton's Administration Department.

ACCOUNTING RECORDS AND CONTROLS

Certain legal requirements in the United States require that the Company maintain accurate records and accounts that fairly reflect the Company's transactions. The Company is required to maintain a system of internal accounting controls to assure that:

- Transactions are executed and access to Company assets is permitted only in accordance with the appropriate management authorization, consistent with policy; and

- Transactions are recorded so that the Company may maintain accountability for its assets and prepare financial statements in accordance with generally accepted accounting principles.

Figure 2.4 (Continued)   **Securitas International's values.**   *(Continued)*

Each employee must fulfill his/her responsibilities to ensure that the Company's records and accounts are accurate and that they are supported by the appropriate documents. All vouchers, bills, invoices and other business records must be prepared with care and complete candor. False or misleading documents, accounting entries, bank accounts, funds or other assets which are not properly recorded in the Company's books will not be permitted. No payment shall be made with the intent or understanding that such payment, or any part thereof, is to be used for purposes other than those described in the documents supporting the payment.

Pinkerton expects that if an employee is in a position that requires the use of Company funds, or personal expenses that are reimbursed by the Company, the employee will use good judgment on the Company's behalf. Employees should spend Company monies responsibly for business purposes and never for personal benefit. Expenses must always be driven by business necessity, be consistent with Company policy, and be properly documented.

If an employee becomes aware of the misuse of Company funds, he/she must report such misuse to The Pinkerton C&I Hotline, Human Resources, or a departmental manager.

GOVERNMENT SECURITY INFORMATION

Pinkerton is committed to safeguarding the security of government-classified information to which it has access. The countries in which we operate have established security procedures with which Pinkerton will comply.

IN THE MARKETPLACE

Accurate Invoicing and Payments – Invoices submitted for payment must accurately reflect the true prices of products sold or services rendered as well as the terms of sale. Payments due must be made to Pinkerton customers, representatives, consultants and suppliers in accordance with contract stipulations unless otherwise approved by the Controller. Practices and procedures that might facilitate wrongdoing, bribery and kickbacks, as well as any illegal or improper payments or receipts, are strictly forbidden.

Pinkerton Proprietary 06/10

33

Figure 2.4 (Continued)   Securitas International's values.

(*Continued*)

Statements in Sales, Advertising, and Publicity – The truth must be the objective of all of our promotional efforts. A momentary advantage gained through the slightest misrepresentation or exaggeration can jeopardize Pinkerton's future success. This applies equally to our discussions with others.

Competition – It is unlawful in the United States and elsewhere to collaborate with competitors or their representatives for the purpose of establishing or maintaining prices at a particular level.

It is Pinkerton's policy not to discuss Client service rates with competitors at any time. Employees must never reveal information that might affect Client service rates to any individual outside Pinkerton's employ. Within Pinkerton, such information must be limited to those with a "need to know."

It is also unethical and unlawful to collaborate with competitors or their representatives to restrain competition in any form or fashion.

Estimates Must Be Reasonable – Those individuals who supply estimates to government procurement personnel, taxing authorities, audit agencies, customers and suppliers must have a reasonable basis for such estimates. For the purpose of this policy, "reasonable" means based upon known facts in instances where facts exist or, in the absence of facts, upon the estimator's plausible and honest judgment.

Reciprocal Dealing – It is Pinkerton's policy to sell its services by virtue of superior Client service. Coercion, expressed or implied, is unacceptable and inconsistent with Pinkerton's philosophy.

POLITICAL ACTIVITY / CONTRIBUTIONS

No contributions of Company funds, property or services for political purposes shall be made directly or indirectly by or on behalf of the Company, unless previously authorized by Pinkerton Consulting & Investigations' President. A "contribution" includes the rendering of services on behalf of the Company and the sale or use of Company assets for less than normal charges. Company facilities should not be made available to candidates or campaigns unless

Pinkerton Proprietary 06/10

34

Figure 2.4 (Continued)   Securitas International's values.   *(Continued)*

previously authorized, in writing, by the President of Pinkerton Consulting & Investigations.

This policy statement relates only to contributions made by or on behalf of the Company and is not intended to discourage employees from making contributions of their own resources or time to the candidates or political parties of their choice. The Company will not reimburse employees directly or indirectly for such contributions.

No employee will solicit political contributions while on Company premises. Freedom of choice in political posture and party affiliation is indigenous to the democratic process. It is Pinkerton's policy not to interfere with this basic and fundamental freedom.

APPEARANCE OF EMPLOYEES

The first impression of a company's professionalism is often made by the staff and their appearance. Each employee is expected to be neat, well groomed and dressed appropriately for the job. Employees should present a professional, businesslike image at all times. Supervisors are responsible for setting appropriate standards and determining compliance with dress code.

Generally, Pinkerton recognizes business dress. Appropriate business dress includes:

- Slacks
- Skirts, mid-length split skirts, dresses
- Sweaters, blouses, shirts with collars
- Collared shirts with the Pinkerton logo
- Loafers, boots, flats, with appropriate hosiery
- Ties, sport coats, and suits

The following items are inappropriate:

- Blue jeans
- Ripped, suggestive or disheveled clothing
- Gym and beachwear

Pinkerton Proprietary 06/10

35

Figure 2.4 (Continued)   Securitas International's values.

(Continued)

- Shorts, jean bib overalls, sweatpants, spandex
- T-shirts with promotional advertising
- Tank tops, tube tops or halter tops
- Mini-skirts, spaghetti strap or backless dresses
- Clogs, flip flops, slippers, sport or beach sandals, motorcycle or combat boots, tennis or other athletic shoes
- Hats and caps
- Attire which is worn out, stained or torn
- Excessive jewelry or inappropriately placed jewelry or accessories

Employees should wear appropriate professional business attire whenever so notified by Pinkerton management, or whenever necessary to present the appropriate image for client and/or vendor visits.

Hair should be clean, combed and neatly trimmed or arranged. Shaggy unkempt hair is not permissible regardless of length. Sideburns, mustaches and beards are to be neatly trimmed. Extreme hairstyles or multi-colored hair is not appropriate.

Reasonable accommodation will be made if religious beliefs require deviations from this policy.

COMMUNICATIONS

It is Pinkerton's practice that every effort be made to disseminate information in a timely manner to all employees, the general public, government authorities, claimants, applicants and all others who may have a need or interest. All information disseminated must be accurate and complete to the best of the Company's knowledge.

Pinkerton recognizes that employees may need to use Company telephones for personal reasons, however we strongly request that phone usage be reasonable and held to a minimum.

Voice mail and electronic mail (e-mail) systems are maintained by Pinkerton in order to facilitate Company business. Therefore, all messages sent, received, composed and/or stored on these systems are the property of Pinkerton. If a

Figure 2.4 (Continued) Securitas International's values.   *(Continued)*

message does not relate to Company business, and/or is not one the employee would want shared with his/her manager, it should not be sent utilizing Pinkerton equipment. Abuse of the voice mail and/or e-mail system could result in disciplinary action up to and including termination of employment.

INFORMATION TECHNOLOGY

Company documents and associated e-mail messages are the property of the Company and are strictly confidential. Similarly, information contained within the Company's information systems and databases is also the property of the Company and is considered confidential. The Company's highly distributed computing environment (PC's, servers, networks) provides users with access to proprietary Company information contained on screens, reports, diskettes, etc. Pinkerton employees will not disclose or provide access to any Company information to non-Company individuals, except in the legitimate course of conducting business in support of the Company.

The Company may gain access to, and disclose to authorized parties, the contents of employee electronic mail message or other computer system files. Such action will be taken for business or legal purpose, including but not limited to, investigations of theft, discloser of confidential business or proprietary information, or other business purposes which may be identified.

The sole purpose for which the Company provides computer hardware and software is to carry out legitimate business for the company. Computer equipment should not be used for any other purpose. No hardware or software should be loaned to non-company personnel. Employees are responsible for the computer equipment issued to them.

All computer hardware and software that is used for internal company business must be ordered through the Information Technology group. This group is responsible for setting standards for both hardware and software for the overall benefit of the Company.

Any person using a PC purchased for Company use must restrict the software used on the system to applications approved by the Information Technology

Pinkerton Proprietary 06/10

Figure 2.4 (Continued)   **Securitas International's values.**   *(Continued)*

group. This applies to applications downloaded from the Internet, personal software, shareware, games, screen savers, and other related software programs.

Most licensed software products are restricted to usage of only one copy of the software per licensed user. Software is typically owned by the manufacturer or its suppliers and is protected under United States copyright law or international treaty provisions. All employees should assume that copyright protection exists, and must therefore treat software like any other copyrighted material. Extra copies may not be made of licensed software except as specified by the original owner/manufacturer of the software. Employees must not loan, transfer, or permit the use of the software by or to any other person in any way.

Internet and related services are available to designated employees for the sole purpose of assisting in performing tasks within the scope of their employment. Such access is a business privilege conditional upon adherence to approval procedures set by the departmental manager. The Company is not responsible for any damages, costs, claims or expenses, direct or indirect, arising out of any employee's use or misuses of the Company's Internet or e-mail resources. Personal use of the Internet and e-mail system is prohibited. Forgery of e-mail messages is prohibited. Attempts to read, copy, modify, or delete e-mail messages of other users are prohibited. Sending, receiving, displaying, printing or otherwise disseminating material that is fraudulent, harassing, illegal, embarrassing, sexually explicit, obscene, intimidating, or defamatory is prohibited. Distribution of non-business related material, such as junk mail, jokes, or chain letters is prohibited. Employees are prohibited from using Internet or e-mail resources for commercial or personal advertisements, solicitations, promotions, destructive programs (i.e. viruses) religious material, political materials, or any other unauthorized use.

Company management has the right, but not the duty, to monitor any and all aspects of its computer systems, including, but not limited to, monitoring sites employees visit on the Internet, monitoring chat groups and news groups, reviewing materials downloaded or uploaded by employees, and reviewing e-mail sent and received by employees. Employees who are found misusing Internet resources may have privileges revoked. Gross violations may also result in disciplinary action up to and including termination of employment.

38

Figure 2.4 (Continued)   Securitas International's values.   *(Continued)*

EMPLOYEE ARRESTS & CONVICTIONS

Employees are required to notify Pinkerton management within three (3) days of any arrest, regardless of whether the employee was incarcerated. Failure to do so will result in immediate termination of employment. Upon notification to Pinkerton, the employee may be placed on an unpaid leave of absence for the duration of the legal proceedings.

CONFIDENTIAL INFORMATION

Pinkerton's and our clients' trade secretes, proprietary information and other internal information represent valuable assets. Protection of this information plays a vial role in Pinkerton's ability to remain a viable business competitor. As a matter of law, in most countries, a trade secret is treated as property, usually in the form of information, knowledge or "know-how." The possession of such information gives the owner an advantage over competitors who do not possess the "secret."

Employee's obligations with respect to the proprietary and trade secret information of Pinkerton and it's clients, are as follows:

- The information may not be disclosed to persons outside of Pinkerton.

- This information is not to be sued for one's own benefit or for the benefit of persons outside of Pinkerton.

- This information may be disclosed to other Pinkerton employees only on a "need to know" basis, and then only with a positive statement that the information is a Pinkerton trade secret.

Special safeguards should be observed for Pinkerton information classified "Pinkerton Private" or "Pinkerton Proprietary." These classifications impose restrictions of a "need to know" within Pinkerton. Trade secret and proprietary information includes, but is not limited to: Business and Strategic plans, divisional and regional revenues, hours of service, costs and profits, unpublished financial/pricing information, employee rosters, customer lists, vendor lists,

Pinkerton Proprietary 06/10

Figure 2.4 (Continued) Securitas International's values.

(Continued)

detailed information regarding customer requirements, preferences, business habits and plans, computer log-on codes, and passwords.

Employees who leave Pinkerton have an obligation to protect Pinkerton's and it's clients trade secret and proprietary information, unless the information becomes publicly available, or Pinkerton on longer considers it a trade secret. Correspondence, printed matter, documents of any kind, procedures, and special Pinkerton methodologies, whether classified or not, are all the property of Pinkerton.

CONFLICT OF INTEREST

Pinkerton needs all employees to devote their full effort, energy, and loyalty to the Company. Pinkerton strictly prohibits any outside employment or other activities or relationships that create any actual or potential conflict of interest. Employees should never use their positions in the Company for a purpose that is, or appears to be, motivated by the desire for private gain for the employee or for another. A conflict of interest may arise in many situations; some of the most common follow:

1. No employee, directly or indirectly, unless the employee has first made full discloser to, and received written approval from Pinkerton Consulting & Investigations' President, will:

    a. Have a financial interest in or a familial relationships with any vendor, contractor, supplier, customer, or competitor of the Company or in any other party doing or seeking to do business with the Company, or

    b. Have a financial interest in any transaction between the Company and any such party. (Ownership of less than one percent of any class of publicly traded securities of a company will not be considered a conflict of interest.)

Figure 2.4 (Continued) Securitas International's values.

(Continued)

2. Unless the employee has first made full discloser to, and received written approval from Pinkerton Consulting & Investigations' President, no employee will make or will attempt to influence any decision relating to any business transaction, if such transaction is between the Company and:

    a. A relative or domestic partner of such an employee, or

    b. Any firm of which such relative is a principal, director, officer or employee.

Any violation of this policy may result in disciplinary action, and possibly termination of employment. It is important for all employees to avoid any potential violations of this policy. Employees are encouraged to raise any questions regarding specific activities or questions involving this policy with the VP of Human Resources before becoming engaged in outside activities or relationships that could violate the policy.

OUTSIDE EMPLOYMENT

Pinkerton is committed to maintaining an employment environment based on loyalty and trust. To ensure this, we expect all employees to carefully review all outside employment arrangements with respect to conflict of interest.

The Company recognizes that occasionally an employee may need to seek outside employment while at Pinkerton. For the purposes of this policy, employment shall mean both self-employment and employment by others.

So long as the following conditions are met, outside employment is acceptable:

- The outside employment does not interfere with ability to successfully perform the job.

Pinkerton Proprietary 06/10

41

Figure 2.4 (Continued) Securitas International's values.

(Continued)

- The outside employment is not of such a nature to reflect unfavorably on Pinkerton.
- There is no conflict of interest (e.g., employees may not work with a competitor, supplier or Client of Pinkerton, as applicable).
- The outside employment is not conducted or solicited in any manner while on duty.
- The outside employment is not conducted or solicited from Company facilities or while using Company-owned equipment or supplies.

GIFTS AND ENTERTAINMENT

Employees are not to give or accept gifts, if such gifts would influence, or appear to influence, our relationship with our competitors, suppliers, or customers.

Moderation and common sense should be used when entertaining on behalf of Pinkerton or on behalf of any representatives of a company with which Pinkerton does business or is a competitor. Entertainment accepted from others must be on the same level of propriety and integrity as that required of Pinkerton employees in the course of business.

SMOKING AND TOBACCO PRODUCTS

Pinkerton has determined that the creation of a tobacco-free work environment is in the best interests of its employees. Smoking and use of all tobacco products is prohibited in all location facilities. Employees who violate this policy will be subject to disciplinary action, and possibly termination of employment.

POSSESSION OF FIREARMS AND WEAPONS

Employees may not possess firearms or weapons at work without written approval of their Vice President as outlined in the Firearms policy. This includes the carrying of personal weapons in a personal vehicle parked on Company

Figure 2.4 (Continued) Securitas International's values. *(Continued)*

property or at a Client site. Compliance with this policy is a condition of employment.

OTHER RULES OF CONDUCT AND DISCIPLINE

To maintain an efficient and safe environment, employees are expected to act in accordance with generally accepted standards of behavior. Violations of these standards can result in disciplinary action, including termination of employment. Examples of unacceptable behavior include but are not limited to:

- Insubordination, derogatory behavior or refusal of job assignment / walking off job.
- Breach of ethics.
- Falsification of any Company record.
- Failure to report to work.
- Breach of confidence, including misappropriation or unauthorized divulgence of confidential information.
- Theft, unauthorized taking or removal of Company property or the property of another person, or dishonesty.
- Serious misconduct of any kind.
- Misuse of company facilities and services.
- Deliberate damage to company property.
- Threatening or committing physical violence against another person, or any other act of violence.
- Disorderly conduct including profane or abusive language.
- Carrying a concealed weapon on Company or Client premises without authorization or in violation of Pinkerton's weapons policy.

Pinkerton Proprietary 06/10

43

Figure 2.4 (Continued) Securitas International's values.

(*Continued*)

- Conviction for or pleading guilty to any violation of any criminal statue or code, whether or not such a crime is committed against the Company or any of its employees when, in the Company's opinion, such conviction or guilty plea is reasonably related to the nature of the employee's work or relation with others and continued employment could jeopardize the Company's interests.

- Intoxication, use, possession or transmission of drugs.

- Intoxication, use, possession or transmission of alcohol on company or client property.

- Acts deemed unsafe to the employee, fellow employees or clients.

- Violation of Pinkerton's Code of Business Ethics, its sexual harassment policy or other forms of unlawful discrimination.

- Other offenses that in the supervisor's judgment threaten the well being of the Company, client, or any employee.

- Actions considered to be a violation of federal or state laws.

Figure 2.4 (Continued) Securitas International's values.

Code of Ethics

Aware that the quality of professional security activity ultimately depends upon the willingness of practitioners to observe special standards of conduct and to manifest good faith in professional relationships, ASIS adopts the following Code of Ethics and mandates its conscientious observance as a binding condition of membership in or affiliation with ASIS:

ARTICLE I

A member shall perform professional duties in accordance with the law and the highest moral principles.

Ethical Considerations

1-1 A member shall abide by the law of the land in which the services are rendered and perform all duties in an honorable manner.

1-2 A member shall not knowingly become associated in responsibility for work with colleagues who do not conform to the law and these ethical standards.

1-3 A member shall be just and respect the rights of others in performing professional responsibilities.

ARTICLE II

A member shall observe the precepts of truthfulness, honesty, and integrity.

Ethical Considerations

2-1 A member shall disclose all relevant information to those having a right to know.

2-2 A "right to know" is a legally enforceable claim or demand by a person for disclosure of information by a member. This right does not depend upon prior knowledge by the person of the existence of the information to be disclosed.

2-3 A member shall not knowingly release misleading information, nor encourage or otherwise participate in the release of such information.

ARTICLE III

A member shall be faithful and diligent in discharging professional responsibilities.

Ethical Considerations

3-1 A member is faithful when fair and steadfast in adherence to promises and commitments.

3-2 A member is diligent when employing best efforts in an assignment.

3-3 A member shall not act in matters involving conflicts of interest without appropriate disclosure and approval.

3-4 A member shall represent services or products fairly and truthfully.

ARTICLE IV

A member shall be competent in discharging professional responsibilities.

Ethical Considerations

4-1 A member is competent who possesses and applies the skills and knowledge required for the task.

4-2 A member shall not accept a task beyond the member's competence nor shall competence be claimed when not possessed.

ARTICLE V

A member shall safeguard confidential information and exercise due care to prevent its improper disclosure.

Ethical Considerations

5-1 Confidential information is nonpublic information, the disclosure of which is restricted.

5-2 Due care requires that the professional must not knowingly reveal confidential information or use a confidence to the disadvantage of the principal or to the advantage of the member or a third person unless the principal consents after full disclosure of all the facts. This confidentiality continues after the business relationship between the member and his principal has terminated.

5-3 A member who receives information and has not agreed to be bound by confidentiality is not bound from disclosing it. A member is not bound by confidential disclosures of acts or omissions that constitute a violation of the law.

5-4 Confidential disclosures made by a principal to a member are not recognized by law as privileged in a legal proceeding. In a legal proceeding, the member may be required to testify to information received in confidence from his principal over the objection of his principal's counsel.

5-5 A member shall not disclose confidential information for personal gain without appropriate authorization.

ARTICLE VI

A member shall not maliciously injure the professional reputation or practice of colleagues, clients, or employers.

Ethical Considerations

6-1 A member shall not comment falsely and with malice concerning a colleague's competence, performance, or professional capabilities.

6-2 A member who knows, or has reasonable grounds to believe, that another member has failed to conform to Code of Ethics of ASIS should inform the Ethical Standards Council in accordance with Article VIII of the Bylaws.

Figure 2.5 ASIS International Code of Ethics. (© 2017 ASIS International. Reprinted by permission.)

Maine Statutory Authority in Unlawful Conduct. Title 32, Section 9412.

1. *Acting without license; false representations*—It is a Class D crime for any person knowingly to commit any of the following acts:
   a. Subject to section 9404, to act as a security guard without a valid license;
   b. To publish any advertisement, letterhead, circular, statement or phrase of any kind which suggests that a licensee is an official police agency or any other agency, instrumentality or division of this State, any political subdivision thereof, or of the Federal Government;
   c. To falsely represent that a person is or was in his employ as a licensee;
   d. To make any false statement or material omission in any application, any documents made a part of the application, any notice or any statement filed with the commissioner; or
   e. To make any false statement or material omission relative to the requirements of section 9410-A, subsection 1, in applying for a position as a security guard with a contract security company.

2. *Failure to return equipment; representation as peace officer*—It is a Class D crime for any security guard knowingly to commit any of the following acts:
   a. To fail to return immediately on demand, or within 7 days of termination of employment, any uniform, badge, or other item of equipment issued to him by an employer;
   b. To make any representation which suggests, or which would reasonably cause another person to believe, that he is a sworn peace officer of this State, any political subdivision thereof, or of any other state or of the Federal Government;
   c. To wear or display any badge, insignia, device, shield, patch or pattern which indicates or suggests that he is a sworn peace officer, or which contains or includes the word "police" or the equivalent thereof, or is similar in wording to any law enforcement agency; or
   d. To possess or utilize any vehicle or equipment displaying the words "police," "law enforcement officer," or the equivalent thereof, or have any sign, shield, marking, accessory or insignia that may indicate that the vehicle is a vehicle of a public law enforcement agency.
   Paragraph A does not apply to any proprietary security organization or any employee thereof.

3. *Representations as to employees; failure to surrender license; posting of license*—It is a Class D crime for any person licensed under this chapter knowingly to commit any of the following acts:
   a. To falsely represent that a person was or is in his employ as a security guard;
   b. To fail or refuse to surrender his license to the commissioner within 72 hours following revocation or suspension of the license; or after the licensee ceases to do business subject to section 9410;
   c. To post the license or permit the license to be posted upon premises other than those described in the license; or
   d. To fail to cause the license to be posted and displayed at all times, within 72 hours of receipt of the license, in a conspicuous place in the principal office of the licensee within the State.

4. *Other unlawful acts*—It is a Class D crime for any person licensed under this chapter, or for any employee thereof, knowingly to commit any of the following acts:
   a. To incite, encourage or aid any person who has become a party to any strike to commit any unlawful act against any person or property;
   b To incite, stir up, create or aid in the inciting of discontent or dissatisfaction among the employees of any person with the intention of having them strike;
   c. To interfere with or prevent lawful and peaceful picketing during strikes;
   d. To interfere with, restrain or coerce employees in the exercise of their right to form, join or assist any labor organization of their own choosing;
   e. To interfere with or hinder lawful or peaceful collective bargaining between employers and employees;
   f. To pay, offer to give any money, gratuity, consideration or other thing of value, directly or indirectly, to any person for any verbal or written report of the lawful activities of employees in the exercise of their right to organize, form or assist any labor organization and to bargain collectively through representatives of their own choosing;
   g. To advertise for, recruit, furnish or replace or offer to furnish or replace for hire or reward, within or outside the State, any skilled or unskilled help or labor, armed guards, other than armed guards employed for the protection of payrolls, property or premises, for service upon property which is being operated in anticipation of or during the course or existence of a strike;
   h. To furnish armed guards upon the highways for persons involved in labor disputes;
   i. To furnish or offer to furnish to employers or their agents any arms, munitions, tear gas implements or any other weapons;
   j. To send letters or literature to employers offering to eliminate labor unions; or K. To advise any person of the membership of an individual in a labor organization for the purpose of preventing the individual from obtaining or retaining employment.

Figure 2.6   Maine Statutory Authority in Unlawful Conduct.   *(Continued)*

5. *Dangerous weapons at labor disputes and strikes*—It is a Class D crime for any person, including, but not limited to, security guards and persons involved in a labor dispute or strike, to be armed with a dangerous weapon, as defined in Title 17-A, section 2, subsection 9, at the site of a labor dispute or strike. A person holding a valid permit to carry a concealed handgun is not exempt from this subsection. A security guard is exempt from this subsection to the extent that federal laws, rules or regulations require the security guard to be armed with a dangerous weapon at the site of a labor dispute or strike.

6. *Class E crimes*—It is a Class E crime for any person licensed under this chapter or for any employee of such a person, to knowingly commit any of the following acts:

   a. To perform or attempt to perform security guard functions at the site of a labor dispute or strike while not physically located on property leased, owned, possessed or rented by the person for whom the licensee is providing security guards.

Figure 2.6 (Continued)   Maine Statutory Authority in Unlawful Conduct.

§ 3181. Unprofessional conduct

1. It shall be unprofessional conduct for a licensee, registrant, or applicant to engage in conduct prohibited by this section, or by 3 V.S.A. § 129a.

2. Unprofessional conduct means any of the following:

   a. Conviction of any felony or a crime involving fraud or dishonesty.

   b. Failing to make available, upon request of a person using the licensee's services, copies of documents in the possession or under the control of the licensee, when those documents have been prepared for and purchased by the user of services.

   c. Violating a confidential relationship with a client, or disclosing any confidential client information except:

      (A) with the client's permission;

      (B) in response to a court order;

      (C) when necessary to establish or collect a fee from the client; or

      (D) when the information is necessary to prevent a crime that the client intends to commit.

   d. Accepting any assignment which would be a conflict of interest because of confidential information obtained during employment for another client.

   e. Accepting an assignment that would require the violation of any municipal, state, or federal law or client confidence.

   f. Using any badge, seal, card, or other device to misrepresent oneself as a police officer, sheriff, or other law enforcement officer.

   g. Knowingly submitting a false or misleading report or failing to disclose a material fact to a client.

   h. Falsifying or failing to provide required compulsory minimum training in firearms or guard dog handling as required by this chapter.

   i. Failing to complete in a timely manner the registration of an employee.

   j. Allowing an employee to carry firearms or handle guard dogs prior to being issued a permanent registration card.

   k. Allowing an employee to work without carrying the required evidence of temporary or permanent registration.

   l. Allowing an employee to use or be accompanied by an untrained guard dog while rendering professional services.

   m. Failing to provide information requested by the board.

   n. Failing to return the temporary or permanent registration of an employee.

   o. Failing to notify the board of a change in ownership, partners, officers, or qualifying agent.

   p. Providing incomplete, false, or misleading information on an application.

   q. Any of the following except when reasonably undertaken in an emergency situation in order to protect life, health, or property:

      i. practicing or offering to practice beyond the scope permitted by law;

      ii. accepting and performing occupational responsibilities which the licensee knows or has reason to know that he or she is not competent to perform; or

      iii. performing occupational services which have not been authorized by the consumer or his or her legal representative.

   r. For armed and guard dog certified licensees, brandishing, exhibiting, displaying, or otherwise misusing a firearm or guard dog in a careless, angry, or threatening manner unnecessary for the course of the licensee's duties.

3. After conducting a hearing and upon a finding that a licensee, registrant, or applicant engaged in unprofessional conduct, the board may take disciplinary action. Discipline for unprofessional conduct may include denial of an application, revocation or suspension of a license or registration, supervision, reprimand, warning, or the required completion of a course of action.

Figure 2.7   Virginia Unprofessional Conduct Statute.

- A member shall be truthful, diligent, and honorable in the discharge of their professional responsibilities.
- A member shall honor each client contract, adhering to all responsibilities by providing ethical services within the limits of the law.
- A member shall safeguard confidential information and exercise the utmost care to prevent any unauthorized disclosure of such information.
- A member shall refrain from improper and unethical solicitation of business; including false or misleading claims or advertising.
- A member shall use due diligence to ensure that all employees and coworkers adhere to this same code of ethical conduct; respecting all persons, performing the job diligently and working within the limits of the law.
- A member shall never knowingly cause harm or defame the professional reputation or practice of colleagues, clients, employers, or any member of the NCISS.
- A member shall never undertake an assignment that is contrary to the Constitution of the United States of America or the security interests of this country.[145]

State legislatures give codified instruction on acceptable behavior. At the other edge of the regulatory continuum will reside federal, state, and local regulatory authority, which promulgates instruction on acceptable professional behavior. Some governmental entities do this by regulatory boards, or by and through state police or other agency. For example, the state of Maryland oversees the licensing requirements through the office of the Maryland State Police.[146] Other governmental entities, such as New York, designate an actual agency that assures compliance.[147]

In the majority of American jurisdictions, the licensure process of the private security industry has been codified by actual legislation. Review Figures 2.6 and 2.7 as examples of this effort. Will these guidelines promote professionalism?

2.2 Summary

Security's road to professionalism is filled with hidden dangers—rhetoric without substance, intentions without purpose, and commitment without resources. The security industry must take this professional sojourn seriously, if only because inaction will cause a legislative substitute. No doubt, many states are lagging behind in this impetus, but more states are set to raise age requirements, experience level, and educational qualifications as well as personal standards of conduct. The future appears inclined toward heightened regulation and standards.

DISCUSSION QUESTIONS

1. What level of qualifications is necessary for entry as an unarmed or armed security officer in your jurisdiction?
2. Determine how many private and public institutions of higher education provide academic studies in private security, security management, or other aligned degree?
3. What is the proper definition of good character? Should minor drug usage be and exclusionary basis for denial of a license?
4. Should a written examination be required before licensure as a security officer? What subjects should be included?

5. Devise a security training program totaling 100 hours of instruction.
6. Name at least two ethical considerations or concerns that constantly arise in the private security industry.
7. Should there be differing levels of qualification depending on the private security position?

NOTES

1 David W. Sackman, At the crossroads of professionalism, Sec. Mgmt., 30, 1986; 73. Alan Cribb and Sharon Gerowitz, *Professionalism,* Malden, MA: Polity Press, 2015.

2 Barak Richemond-Barak, Can self-regulation work? Lessons from the private security and military industry, *MI J. Int'l L.* 34, 2014, at http://repository.law.umich.edu/cgi/viewcontent. cgi?article=1069&context=mjil; see also Todd Savage, *Security Officers: New Demands Require New Training, Safety & Health,* 150, 1994; 64. Jeff Maahs and Craig Hemmens, Train in vain: A statutory analysis of security guard training requirements, *Int'l J. Comp. & Applied Crim. Justice,* 22, 1998; 91–101. Jay Akasie, Thwarting terrorists, *Forbes,* Sept. 21, 1998, at 162; Courtney Leatherman and Denise K. Magner, Notes on the curriculum, *Chronicle of Higher Education,* Mar. 9, 1994, at A19.

3 Note, survey yields new results on officer turnover, *Training,* 29, 1992; Sec. 71. See Savage, Leatherman and Magner; Reed A. Castle, *A Study of the Security Officer* 10, 2002.

4 Note, *Survey,* at 72; Castle, at 10.

5 107th Congress, 2d session, Senate Bill 2238, April 24, 2002; see generally Maahs and Hemmens.

6 United Nations Office on Drugs and Crime, *State Regulation concerning Civilian Private Security Services and their contribution to crime prevention and Community Safety,* Vienna: United Nations, 2014; available from https://www.unodc.org/documents/congress/background-information/Crime_Prevention/Civilian_Private_Security_Services.E.pdf.

7 U.S. Department of State, Patterns of Global Terrorism 2003, Appendix G: Total Facilities Struck by International Attacks, 1998–2003, 2004, available at https://www.state.gov/j/ct/rls/crt/2003/.

8 Bureau of Labor Statistics, 2008-18 National Employment Matrix: Private Detectives and Investigators (2009), available at https://www.bls.gov/ooh/protective-service/private-detectives-and-investigators. htm.

9 J. Shane Creamer, Private police in the United States: Findings and recommendations, *Sec. World* 66, 1973; 10. See also Castle, at 10.

10 Lukins; Maahs and Hemmens, at 91–101.

11 Richter H. Moore, Jr., Licensing and regulation of the private security industry: A historical view of the courts role, J. *Sec. Admin.,* 13, 1990; 37, 58–59. see also Maahs and Hemmens, at 91–101.

12 National Institute of Justice, Crime and Protection in America: A Study of Private Security and Law Enforcement Resources and Relationships, 1985; see also Operation Cooperation, Guidelines for Partnerships between Law Enforcement and Private Security Organizations, 2000; Clifford Shearing and Philip C. Stenning, The Interweaving of Public and Private Police Undercover Work in Private Policing, 1987; S. Ronald Hauri, Public–private security liaison: The synergy of cooperation, *Crime & Justice Internat'l,* Oct. 1997, at 16.

13 Crime and Protection in America, at 26–29; see also Operation Cooperation; Shearing & Stenning; Hauri.

14 Note, certification, firearms boost salaries, Sec. 69, 1993; 30. See also Michael Stack, Security professionals' salaries up 2% in 2012, *ASIS International,* August 2012, at https://www.asisonline.org/News/Press-Room/Press-Releases/2012/Pages/SecurityProfessionalsSalariesUp.aspx

15 Id.

16 See ASIS International, 2015 ASIS Compensation Survey Results, available at https://www. asisonline.org/Education-Events/Education-Programs/Webinars/Pages/2015-ASIS-International-Compensation-Survey.aspx

17 For example, Colorado, whose efforts to license were declared unconstitutional, given the language of the regulation.

18 For example, Pennsylvania, which requires significant firearms training.
19 For example, Delaware's State Police oversee the licensing aspects.
20 For example, New York.
21 For example, Pennsylvania, Arkansas, and Ohio.
22 Private police force is accused of abusing power, *The New York Times,* July 1993; see also Mark Button, *Security Officers and Policing, Powers, Culture, and Control in the Governance of Private Space.* New York: Ashgate Publishing, 2007.
23 William C. Cunningham, John J. Strauchs, and Clifford W. VanMeter, Private security trends 1970 to 2000: The Hallcrest Report II 1990, 322–23.
24 *See* Chapter 1. See also Rhead Enion, Constitutional limits on private policing and the states allocation of force, Duke L. J., Dec. 2009, 59.
25 James D. Horan, *The Pinkertons: The Detective Dynasty that Made History,* 1967; Jeremy Scahill, A very private war, *The Guardian,* July 2007, at https://www.theguardian.com/uk/2007/aug/01/military.usa; Milton Lipson, *The Business of Private Security,* 1975.
26 Bilek et al., 1980, at 34.
27 Note, The Security Officer Employment Standards Act of 1991, *Sec. Admin. Educ.* 1, 1992; 15 J. Note, Guardsmark Endorses Proposed Standards for Security Officers, 28, 1991; Sec. 48. Bill Zalud, Federal Security Officer Standards Proposed in Controversial Senate Bill, 28 Sec., 1991; 60, 62. Stephen C. George, New Officer Bill Sets Standards for Both Armed and Unarmed, 29, 1992; Sec. 53. Note, Zalud Report: Reports and Incidents that Impact Asset Protection, 30, 1993; Sec. 108. Note, Experts Rate New Officer Bill, 30, 1993; Sec. 66. Security Officers Quality Assurance Act of 1992, H.R. 5931, 102nd Cong., 1992; Security Officer Employment Standards Act of 1991, S. 1258, 102nd Cong., 1991. President's Remarks at Homeland Security Bill Signing. Department of Homeland Security Official Home Page. November 25, 2002, available at: http://www.presidency.ucsb.edu/you-tubeclip.php?clipid=63129&admin=43; Congressional Research Service, Critical Infrastructures: Background, Policy and Implementation, July 2011; See Katherine L. Hermann, Reviewing bush-era counter-terrorism policy after 9/11: Reconciling ethical and practical considerations, *Homeland Security Review,* 4, 2010; 139; See also Christie L. Richardson, The creation of judicial compromise: prosecuting detainees in a national security court system in Guantanamo Bay, Cuba, *Homeland Security Review* 4, 2010; 119.
28 6 C.F.R. pt. 25, 2003.
29 U.S. Department of Homeland Security, 68 Fed. Reg. 59,684, Oct. 16, 2003, 6 C.F.R. pt. 25, 2003.
30 Charles P. Nemeth, *Homeland Security: An Introduction to Principles and Practice* 2010; 168–169.
31 15 U.S.C. § 1681, 1970.
32 See 131 Cong. Rec., S. 1815, 1988.
33 29 U.S.C. § 2001; *Graham v. Beasley,* 180 F. Supp. 2d 760 (E. NC., 2001).
34 *Arkansas Gazette,* June 29, 1988; *see also* Charles P. Nemeth, Erosion of the privacy right and polygraphs, *Forensic Sci. Int'l.,* 103, 1984; 21.
35 The Law Enforcement and Industrial Security Cooperation Act of 1996, H.R. 2996, 104th Cong., 1996.
36 Id.
37 Private Security Officer Employment Standards Act of 2002, S. 2238, 107th Cong., 2002.
38 Darren W. Davis and Brian D. Silver, Civil liberties vs. security in the context of the terrorist attacks on America, *Am. J. Pol. Sci.* 28–46, 2004; 48.
39 Private-Sector Liaison Committee, International Association of Chiefs of Police, *Private Security Officer Selection, Training and Licensing Guidelines* 5.
40 57 F.Supp.2d. 1305, 1999.
41 Moates v. Strength, 57 F.Supp.2d. 1305, 1310, 1999.
42 Conn. Gen. Stat. § 29-154a, 2008.
43 Haw. Rev. Stat. § 463-6, 2009.
44 Ind. Code Ann. § 25-30-1-8, 2009.
45 Del. Code Ann. tit. 24, § 1319, 2010.
46 Ark. Code Ann. § 17-40-306, 2016. Be at least eighteen (18) years of age at the time of application.

47 Iowa Code §80A.4, 2008.

48 Me. Rev. Stat. Ann. tit. 32, §9405, 2009.

49 Ga. Code Ann. §43-38-6, 2009.

50 12 N.C. Admin. Code 07D.0301, 2015.

51 Ga. Code Ann. §43-38-6, 2009.

52 W. Va. Code §30-18-2, 2009.

53 Numerous jurisdictions waive many requirements for attorneys. See Iowa Code, §80A.2, 2009; Mont. Code Ann. §37-60-105(4)(a), 2009.

54 Mont. Code Ann. §37-60-105, 2009.

55 Mont. Code Ann. §37-60-105, 2009.

56 Haw. Rev. Stat. §463-6, 2009.

57 Kan. Stat. Ann. §75-7b05, 2008.

58 N.J. Stat. Ann. §45:19-8, 2010.

59 Ill. Admin. Code tit. 68, 1240.10 et seq., 2009.

60 Ill. Admin. Code tit. 68, 1240.10, 2009.

61 Ill. Admin. Code tit. 68, 1240.200, 2009.

62 Ill. Admin. Code tit. 68, 1240.100, 2009.

63 Ill. Admin. Code tit. 68, 1240.400, 2009.

64 Ill. Admin. Code tit. 68, 1240.400, 2009.

65 Ill. Admin. Code tit. 68, 1240.400, 2009.

66 Lukins at 35.

67 Fla. Admin. Code Ann. r. 5N-1.116, 2009.

68 Fla. Stat. §493.6203, 2010.

69 Florida Department of Agriculture and Consumer Services, Application for The Class "G" Statewide Firearm License, 3, 2010, available at http://www.doacs.state.fl.us/onestop/forms/16008.pdf.

70 N.M. Stat. Ann. §61-27A-10, 2016.

71 *US v. Kelly*, 917 F. Supp. 2d 553, 2013.

72 N.C. Gen. Stat. §74C-8, 2009.

73 Ind. Code Ann. §25-30-1-8, 2010.

74 Ohio Rev. Code Ann. §4749.03, 2010.

75 Ariz. Rev. Stat. §32-2612, 2010.

76 Ark. Code Ann. §20-64-204, 2010.

77 N.J. Stat. Ann. §45:19-8 et seq., 2010.

78 N.Y. Ins. Law §2108, Consol. 2010.

79 N.Y. Ins. Law §2108, Consol. 2010.

80 Iowa Code §80A.4, 2010.

81 Charles P. Nemeth, and K.C. Poulin, *Private Security and Public Safety: A Community Based Approach*, 2005; Ch. 9; Charles P. Nemeth, *A Status Report on Criminal Justice Education*, 1988; Savage; Maahs and Hemmens; Akasie; Leatherman and Magner; see also James F. Pastor, *Terrorism and Public Safety Policing: Implications for the Obama Presidency*, 2009; James F. Pastor, *Security Law & Methods*, 2006; James F. Pastor, *The Privatization of Police in America: An Analysis and Case Study*, 2003.

82 Private Security Advisory Council, Guidelines for the Establishment of State and Local Private Advisory Councils, 1976.

83 Id. at 7.

84 Note, *Survey* at 72.

85 Castle, at 10.

86 Agnes L. Baro, *Law Enforcement and Higher Education: Is There an Impasse? J. Crim. Just. Ed.* 57, 1999; 10.

87 Creamer, at 68.

88 National Advisory Commission on Standards and Goals, Private Security, Report of the Task Force Report on Private Security, 1976.

89 Private Security Advisory Council, at 8.

90 Note, Security Endorses Campus Incident Reporting; Divided on Same for Business, 28 (1991); Sec. 8, 9; See FBI Report: Frequency of Active Shooter Events has Increased, *Campus Safety*, January 27, 2014, http://www.campussafetymagazine.com/article/fbi-report-frequency-of-active-shooter-events-has-increased#, last visited August 31, 2016; Campus Safety and Security, Trend Data, US Department of Education, http://ope.ed.gov/campussafety/Trend/public/#/answer/4/401/trend/-1/-1/-1/-1, last visited August 31, 2016.

91 For example, The Law Enforcement and Industrial Security Cooperation Act of 1996, H.R. 2996 calls for increasing training and cooperation between public and private entities.

92 J. Fletcher and H. Borokawa, Non-security education, *J. Sec. & Pri. Police* 14, 1978; 1. See also Savage; Maahs and Hemmens; Akasie; Leatherman, and Magner.

93 J. Kostanoski, The private police and higher education, *J. Sec. Admin. & Pri. Police* 26, 1978; 1. see also Savage; Maahs and Hemmens; Leatherman and Magner; Claire Meyer, Addressing the human side of school security, *Sec. Mag.*, January 2014, at 28; See also: Private security turns big business, *Deccan Chronicle*, September 1, 2016, http://www.deccanchronicle.com/150505/nation-current-affairs/article/private-security-turns-big-business, last visited August 31, 2016.

94 National Association of Security Companies (NASCO), About NASCO, 2010, at http://www.nasco.org/about-nasco.

95 Data from a search conducted using the National Center for Education Statistics College Degree search tool at http://nces.ed.gov/ipeds/cool/Search.asp.

96 Charles P. Nemeth, *Directory of Criminal Justice Education, Including Criminology, Law and Justice Related Education*, 1991; Nemeth and Poulin; Nemeth, *Status Report*; Pastor, *Terrorism*; Pastor, *Security Law*; Pastor, *Privatization of Police*.

97 Cunningham et al., at 322; Criminal Justice Degree Schools at http://www.criminaljusticedegree-schools.com, last visited February 20, 2017.

98 Richard Post notes in his article (Toward rational curriculum development for private protective services, First National Conference on Private Security, 1978) that there are around 119 degree granting programs; see also Dr. Norman Bottom's annual compilation of security education programs in his *Journal of Security Administration*, showing around 165 programs. See also Pastor, *Terrorism*; Pastor, *Security Law*; Pastor, *Privatization of Police*.

99 Note, ASIS in action, *Sec. Mgmt.* 116, 1991; 35.

100 Peter Ohlhausen, Invest in security's future, *Sec. Mgmt.* 49, 50, 1991; 35.

101 John Jay College of Criminal Justice, Dept. of Security, Fire and Emergency Management, at http://www.jjay.cuny.edu/department-security-fire-and-emergency-management, last visited February 20, 2017.

102 James Calder, The security-criminal justice connection: toward the elimination of separate-but-equal status, J. *Sec. Admin.* 25, 1980; 3.

103 Joseph Straw, Q: What's your major? A: Homeland Security, *Sec. Mgmt.*, 2007; 51. Christopher A. Hertig, What course should we take? *Sec. Mgmt.*, 218, 1991; 35.

104 Scott Gold, 9/11 spawned big changes on campus, *LA Times*, January 20, 2004, August 31, 2011, at http://articles.latimes.com/2011/aug/31/nation/la-na-911-homeland-security-colleges-20110901; Kimberly Chase, Homeland security technology: A hot new academic specialty? *Christian Science Monitor*, January 20, 2004, at http://www.csmonitor.com/2004/0120/p18s02-legn.html. See also Certificate in Homeland Security/Emergency Management, Ohio Dominican eLearning Program, 1216 Sunbury Road, Columbus OH 43219, at http://elearning.ohiodominican.edu/programs/certificates/homeland_security.shtml.

105 Calder, at 33.

106 Richard Post notes in his article, Toward rational curriculum development for private protective services, First National Conference on Private Security, 1978; 6. *see also* Savage; Maahs and Hemmens; Akasie; Leatherman and Magner.

107 See *Colorado v. Romar*, 559 P. 2d 710, 1977.

108 Ariz. Rev. Stat. §32-2613, §32-2632, 2010; see also S.C. Code Ann. §40-17-40, 2010.

109 Some states requiring exams include North Dakota, Montana, Delaware, New York, Ohio, New Mexico, Vermont, Arkansas, and Iowa.

110 Ill. Admin. Code tit. 68, 1240.10 et seq., 2009.

111 Ill. Admin. Code tit. 68, 1240.10 et seq., 2009.

112 Ga. Code Ann. §43-38-10, 2009.

113 La. Rev. Stat. Ann. §37:3284, 2010.

114 Tennessee Department of Commerce and Insurance, Let a License Webpage, at https://www.tn.gov/commerce/article/prot-get-a-license, last visited February 20, 2017.

115 Washington State Department of Licensing, Preassignment Training Study Guide: Security Guards, at http://www.dol.wa.gov/business/securityguards/sgpreassigntrain.html, last visited February 20, 2017.

116 NY Gen Bus L § 89-N, 2012.

117 Security Guard Training HQ, Security Guard Requirement in California, at http://www.securityguardtraininghq.com/security-guard-training-california, last visited February 20, 2017.

118 Fla. Stat. Ann. §493.6106(6), West 2010.

119 Virginia Dept. of Criminal Justice Services, Unarmed security officer/courier, at https://www.dcjs.virginia.gov/licensure-and-regulatory-affairs/unarmed-security-officercourier, last visited February 20, 2017.

120 Virginia Dept. of Criminal Justice Services, Armed security officer, at https://www.dcjs.virginia.gov/licensure-and-regulatory-affairs/armed-security-officer, last visited February 20, 2017.

121 State of Delaware, Rules for the Board of Examiners for Private Detectives, Mandatory Firearms Training Program, 1979.

122 Jerome Lobel, Training: The missing line in computer security, *Sec. World* 28, 1980; 17. International Association of Chiefs of Police, Fifth Annual Law Enforcement Data Processing Symposium, 1981.

123 A. Potter, Security training: The airport operator's responsibility, *FBI L.E. Bul.*, 131, 1974; 43.

124 Note, Certified protection security and law enforcement, *Security Mgmt.*, 1980, at 75.

125 John T. Smith, Develop yourself professionally, *Sec. Mgmt.* 92, 92–93, 1991; 35.

126 Ian C. Paul, Certified Protection Professional Progress Report, *Sec. Mgmt.* 86, 1991; 35.

127 ASIS International, Certified Protection Professional, at https://www.asisonline.org/Certification/Board-Certifications/CPP/Pages/default.aspx, last visited February 20, 2017.

128 ASIS International, Physical security professional, https://www.asisonline.org/Certification/Board-Certifications/PSP/Pages/default.aspx, last visited February 20, 2017.

129 Id.

130 Id.

131 ASIS International, Professional Certified Investigator, https://www.asisonline.org/Certification/Board-Certifications/PCI/Pages/default.aspx, last visited February 20, 2017.

132 ASIS International, Classroom programs, https://www.asisonline.org/Education-Events/Education-Programs/Classroom/Pages/default.aspx, last visited February 20, 2017.

133 American Bankers Association, Certified Financial Services Security Professional (CFSSP), http://www.aba.com/Training/ICB/Pages/CFSSP_Maintain.aspx, last visited February 20, 20117.

134 International Association of Professional Security Consultants, Becoming a Certified Security Consultant, https://iapsc.org/about-us/certification, last visited February 20, 2017.

135 International Security Management Association, Membership Letter, at https://isma.com/cms/wp-content/uploads/2012/04/application-formREVISED_FILLABLE.pdf, last visited at February 20, 2017.

136 Note, Distance education: Learn from home, Sec. 8, 1993; 30. for a current listing of programs offered, visit the NCES' IPEDsCool search engine at http://nces.ed.gov/ipeds/cool/Search.asp.

137 Lonnie R. Buckels, Professionalism—An impossible task? *Sec. Mgmt.* 108, 1991; 35.

138 Private-Sector Liaison Committee, at 7.

139 Private Security Advisory Council; *see also* Case Western Reserve Law School, *Private Police Training Manual*, 1985.

140 N. D. Cent. Code §43-30-05-06, 2010.

141 Ark. Code Ann. §17-40-208, 2009.

142 US Security Associates, an industry leader in the private sector, has devised a comprehensive code of ethics for both national and international operations. See Ligue Internationale des Societes de Surveillance, Code of Conduct and Ethics, at http://www.ussecurityassociates.com/media-center/usa-social-responsibility/documents/international-code-of-conduct-and-ethics.pdf, last visited February 20, 2017.

143 Pinkerton/Securitas, Standards of conduct, at https://secure.ethicspoint.com/domain/media/en/gui/27743/code.pdf, last accessed February 20, 2017.

144 American Society for Industrial Security, Code of ethics, at https://www.asisonline.org/About-ASIS/Pages/Code-of-Ethics.aspx; see also R. Gallati, Introduction to private security, 1983; 181–182.

145 National Council of Investigation and Security Services website at http://www.nciss.org/about-us/nciss-code-of-ethics.php, last accessed August 26, 2016.

146 Maryland State Police, Licensing division website, available at http://mdsp.maryland.gov/Organization/Pages/CriminalInvestigationBureau/LicensingDivision.aspx, last accessed August 26, 2016.

147 New York State, Division of Licensing Services website, FAQ—Security Guard, available at http://www.dos.ny.gov/licensing/securityguard/sguard_faq.html, last accessed August 26, 2016.

Chapter 3

The Law of Arrest, Search, and Seizure: Applications in the Private Sector

3.1 Introduction

Private policing, as noted in *The Hallcrest* Report II, plays an integral role in the detection, protection, and apprehension of criminals in modern society. It is deemed by many interested sources as the more responsive, efficient, and productive player in the administration of justice.[1] While it may display an extraordinary capacity for efficiencies, some argue that the constitutional inapplicability of the Fourth, Fifth, Sixth, and Fourteenth Amendments may not be worth the price. Indeed, the industry has long held this advantage since its earliest days and this status has been further buttressed by the long-standing U.S. Supreme Court case, *Burdeau v. McDowell*.[2]

Although there are sporadic case decisions that seek to undermine this legal preference, the reality is that *Burdeau* and its many progeny still stand tall above the lower court outliers. That is the essence of this chapter—to lay out norm for public police and compare and contrast the private sector oversight from a constitutional perspective. The advantages of private sector justice are many and diverse.

Search WorldCat and find out where The Hallcrest Report II is in your area. http://www.worldcat.org/title/private-security-trends-1970-to-2000-the-hallcrest-report-ii/oclc/22892639

Aside from its efficiencies, private policing retains a strong procedural advantage in matters of constitutional scrutiny. Naturally, business and industry prefer to deal with private sector justice since their own private police forces are not constrained by constitutional dimensions. As Professor William J. O'Donnell eloquently notes:

The growth of the private security industry is having an increasingly controversial impact on individual privacy rights. Unlike public policing, which is uniformly and comprehensively controlled by applied constitutional principles, private policing is not. Across the various jurisdictions, both statutes and case law have been used to curb some intrusion into privacy rights but this protective coverage is neither standardized nationally nor anywhere near complete. The net result is that some rather debatable private police practices are left to the discretion of security personnel.[3]

Constitutionally, the private sector has the upper hand since the extension of traditional police protections have never materialized. However, that upper hand has largely related to matters involving the Fourth, Fifth, and Fourteenth Amendments, which include arrest, search and seizure, interrogation and rights, as well as due process and equal protection. The limited applicability of these principles does not preclude security officers from the exercise of individual constitutional rights. For example, privacy rights, religious express, and free speech rights may rightfully be exercised and defended.[4]

As the role of private security and private police develops in the marketplace and more citizens encounter the private version of police, criminal defendants and litigants will clamor for increased constitutional protection. Already, defense advocates argue that Fourth, Fifth, Sixth, and Fourteenth Amendment standards regarding arrest, search and seizure, and general criminal due process should be equally applied in both the public police and private police settings, though most appeals court reject these claims.[5]

The primary aim of this chapter is to provide a broad overview of the legal principles of arrest, search, and seizure in the private sector, analyzing the theoretical nexus between the private and public sector in the analysis of constitutional claims, and reviewing specific case law decisions, particularly at the appellate level. In addition, a review of the theory of citizens' arrest, both in common and statutory terms, is fully outlined. Finally, this chapter will highlight and focus upon novel and even radical theories that seek to make applicable constitutional protections in the private sector including the following:

- The significant involvement test
- The private police nexus test
- State action theory
- Platinum platter doctrine
- Common law and statutory review of private security rights and liabilities
- The parameters of private search rights

The precise limits of the authority of private security personnel are not clearly spelled out in any one set of legal materials. Rather, one must look at a number of sources in order to define, even in a rough way, the dividing line between proper and improper private security behavior in arrest, search, and seizure. Even traditional constitutional inquiry in the public sector can be complicated. So, when these same obtuse principles are applied to private security, confusion can result. The Private Security Advisory Council recognizes this complexity:

> In order to perform effectively, private security personnel must, in many instances, walk a tightrope between permissible protective activities and unlawful interferences with the rights of private citizens.[6]

Given the fact that the criminal justice system is already administratively and legally beleaguered, it is natural for both the general public and criminal justice professionals to seek alternative ways for stemming the tide of criminality and carrying out the tasks of arrest, search, and seizure. And couple this expectation and the driving reality of "privatization," the advocacy for extending constitutional protections for private security agents is a phenomenon that surely will not dissipate.[7] Few would disagree that privatized police services are here to stay and the role of private security industry will continue to play a critical role in the resolution of crime in modern society.[8]

Given all these forces at work, profound questions arise in the brave new world of private policing—none more compelling than the constitutional ones. Should private sector justice adhere to constitutional demands imposed on the public sector when detecting criminality or apprehending criminals? Should the Fourth Amendment apply in private sector cases? Are citizens who are arrested and have their persons and property searched and seized by private security personnel entitled to the same protections as an individual apprehended by the public police? Have public and private police essentially merged, or become so entangled as to prompt or advance similar constitutional protections? Does public policy and constitutional equity call for an expansive interpretation of the Fourth, Fifth, Sixth, and Fourteenth Amendments regarding private security actions? Or does the constitutional advantage presently owned by private security actually advance a more just system or protect those victimized by criminal behavior by making it less likely that a procedural argument frees a defendant while the facts confirm criminal culpability. In sum, the answers here are not the stuff of pithy demand and argument but issues grounded in the very structural framework of the American experience.

The ACLU has longed for an application of constitutional principles to private sector justice. See: http://acluva.org/4178/aclu-legal-filing-says-private-security-guards-bound-by-constitution-when-detaining-suspects/

3.2 Constitutional Framework of American Criminal Justice

Constitutional protections were originally implemented to protect the citizenry against governmental, state action that violates particular rights involving search, seizure, and interrogations. Most applicable is the Fourth Amendment, which provides:

> The right of the people to be secure in their persons, houses, papers, and effects, against unreasonable searches and seizures, shall not be violated and no warrants shall issue upon their probable cause supported by oath, affirmation and particularly describing the place to be searched and the persons or things to be seized.[9]

Responding to the clamor for individual rights, calls for a reduction in arbitrary police behavior and a general recognition that the rights of the individual are sometimes more important than the rights of the whole, judicial reasoning, public opinion, and academic theory for the last 50 years have suggested and formulated an expansive interpretation of the Fourth Amendment.[10] When and where police can be constrained and criminal defendants liberated appears to be the fixed legal trend.

On its face, and in its express text, the Fourth Amendment is geared toward public functions.[11] The concepts of a "warrant," an "oath," or "affirmation" are definitions that expressly relate to public officialdom and governmental action. When the Fourth Amendment employs language like "No state shall," it does not include the modern critic's claim that language be ready to include private action. As a result of these express terms, the courts have historically been reticent to extend those protections to private sector activities. In *Burdeau v. McDowell*,[12] the U.S. Supreme Court held unequivocally that Fourth Amendment protection was not available to litigants and claimants arrested, searched, or seized by private parties. The Court unequivocally remarked,

> The Fourth Amendment gives protection against unlawful searches and seizures.... Its protection applies to governmental actions. Its origin and history clearly shows that it was intended as a restraint upon the activity of sovereign authority and was not intended to be a limitation upon other than governmental agencies.[13]

The Court's ruling is certainly not surprising, given the historical tug-of-war between federal and states' rights in the application of constitutional law. Over the long history of constitutional interpretation, courts cannot discern any reasonable rationale to expand constitutional protections to cover the actions of private individuals rather than governmental actions. *Burdeau* has been continuously upheld in a long sequence of cases and is considered an extremely formidable precedent.[14] The *Burdeau* decision and its progeny enforce the general principle that the Fourth Amendment is applicable only to arrests, searches, and seizures conducted by governmental authorities. The private police and private security system have historically been able to avoid the constrictions placed upon the public police in the detection and apprehension of criminals.[15]

If constitutional protections do not inure to defendants and litigants processed by private sector justice, then what protections do exist for them? Could it be argued that the line between private and public justice has become indistinguishable, in terms of function or duty, or at least so muddled that the roles blur? Are private citizens, subjected to arrest, search, and seizure actions by private police, entitled to some level of criminal due process that is fundamentally fair and not overly intrusive? Does the Fourth Amendment's strict adherence to the protection of rights solely in the public and governmental realm blindly disregard the reality of public policing and how dependent the public system is upon privatized services? Is there evidence that the general citizenry suffers harm and abuse at levels worthy of a constitutional protection? Should the constitution be more generously applied to encompass the actions of private police and security operatives to minimize abuse and misconduct emanating from the private security industry? Or is the constitutional advantage something worth its maintenance for a just society? Is it an alternative mechanism to deal with crime, civil harms, and other communal challenges that need be left in place given the clarity of the Constitution on state action? To be sure, a host of advocates urge the expansion of these rights to private action. However, the implications of said extension cannot be done lightly or without deep concern with the eventual policy implications. If private security officers are judged under the same constitutional tests, then every citizen will be subject to the same systematic constitutional scrutiny. That sort of conclusion should cause great pause.

3.2.1 Arrest and Private Sector Justice

As a general proposition, private security officers, private police, and other private enforcement officials may exercise arrest rights at the same level of authority as any private citizen. "While many private security personnel perform functions similar to public law enforcement officers, they generally have no more formal authority than an average citizen. Basically, because the security officer acts on behalf of the person, business, corporation, or other entity that hires him, that entity's basic right to protect persons and property is transferred to the security officer."[16] When one considers the amazing similarity of service and operation between public and private police functions, the general assertion that security officers and other responsible personnel are guided only by the rights of the general citizenry seems something challengeable. Private police serve a multiplicity of purposes, including the protection of property and persons from criminal activity, calamity, and destructive events; the surveillance and investigation of internal and external criminal activity in business and industry; and the general maintenance of public order.[17] Therefore, it would seem prudent that private police be guided by some level of constitutional and statutory scrutiny. However, "unless deputized, commissioned, or provided for by ordinance or state statute, private security personnel possess no greater legal powers than any private citizen."[18]

As appealing as these arguments may be, these claims are less legal and far more equitable and sentimental. For the most part, the lack of express language in guiding constitutional documents that exclusively tend to matters of "state action," or governmental action, the private agent is left out of the mix. This is the stark reality when reading and interpreting constitutional texts.

Since private police do not derive their authority from a constitutional framework, the foundation for the arrest action rests in the common and statutory law—those codifications of legal traditions that simultaneously give the power of arrest to a private person. "The security officer has the same rights both as a citizen and as an extension of an employee's right to protect his employer's property. Similarly, this common law recognition of the right of defense of self and property is the legal underpinning for the right of every citizen to employ the services of others to protect his property against any kind of incursion by others."[19] The entire private arrest formula is labeled "citizen's arrest."

3.2.1.1 The Law of Citizen's Arrest—The Private Security Standard

The scope of permissible citizen's arrest has remained fairly constant in American jurisprudence over the last century. At common law, the private citizenry could make a permissible arrest for the commission of any felony in order to protect the safety of the public.[20] An arrest could also be effected for misdemeanors that constituted a breach of the peace or public order, but only when immediate apprehension and the presence of an arresting individual was demonstrated. Much of our contemporary analysis of reasonable suspicion and probable cause also relates to the citizen's right to subject another individual to the arrest process. "A citizen could perform a valid and lawful arrest on his own authority, if the person arrested committed a misdemeanor in his presence or if there were reasonable grounds to believe that a felony was being or had been committed by the arrestee although not in the presence of the arresting citizen."[21] Private citizens are also permitted to search individuals that they have arrested or detained for safety reasons, and this right is comparable to the incident to arrest or stop and frisk standard applicable in the public jurisdiction. "When an articulable suspicion of danger exists, granting a private policeman or citizen the authority to search for the purpose of finding or seizing weapons of an arrestee is at least equivalent to a pat down approved by Terry, and seems to be a necessary concomitant of the power to arrest."[22]

Review the opinion of the Wisconsin attorney general on the power of private security guards to make arrests at: https://www.doj.state.wi.us/news-releases/attorney-general-van-hollen-issues-informal-opinion-arrest-powers-private-security

When compared to public officialdom arrest rights, the private citizen has a heavier burden of demonstrating actual knowledge, the presence at the events, or other firsthand experience that justifies the apprehension. These added requirements of citizen's arrest should prompt an additional caution before executing arrest. In some states, a private citizen can arrest under any of the following scenarios:

1. For the public offense (misdemeanor) committed or attempted in his presence.
2. When the person arrested has committed a felony and the private citizen has probable cause to believe so, although not in his presence.
3. When the felony has been, in fact, committed and the private citizen has reasonable cause for believing the person arrested has committed that offense.

Statutorily, the scope of citizen's arrest varies according to jurisdiction. A list of statutory enactments, from Alaska to Florida, can be found in Appendix 1. Two legislative examples are given.

Alaska:

1. A private person or a peace officer without a warrant may arrest a person
   a. For a crime committed or attempted in the presence of the person making the arrest;
   b. When the person has committed a felony, although not in the presence of the person making the arrest; and
   c. When a felony has in fact been committed, and the person making the arrest has reasonable cause for believing the person to have committed it.[23]

New York:

§ 140.30. Arrest without a warrant; by any person; when and where authorized

1. Subject to the provisions of subdivision two, any person may arrest another person (a) for a felony when the latter has in fact committed such felony and (b) for any offense when the latter has in fact committed such offense in his presence.
2. Such an arrest, if for a felony, may be made anywhere in the state. If the arrest is for an offense other than a felony, it may be made only in the county in which such offense was committed.[24]

In Illinois, a police officer "can make an extraterritorial warrantless arrest in the same situation that any citizen can make an arrest."[25]

To thwart and effectively defend against citizen-based challenges to the regularity of the citizen arrest, the security officer conducting any arrest should complete documentation that justifies the decision making. First, an incident report, which details the events comprising the criminal conduct, should be completed (see Figure 3.1).[26] Second, an arrest report (Figure 3.2)[27] records the officer's actions. An arrest warrant is shown in Figure 3.3.

Generally, legislation, concerning citizen's arrest, lacks uniformity—although the major pieces seem similar such as knowledge, presence, and the type of offenses which trigger the right. Types and category of crimes, standards of action, time of day, and alternative retreat potential, to name a few, all guide the process. Critics have charged that attempts to codify a nationalized standard of "citizen's arrest" appear to be "more a product of legislation in discrimination than a logical adaptation of a common law principle to the conditions of modern society."[28] While legislators hope and wish for skilled, trained, and educated individuals to effect as many arrests as possible, the

Building Security Inspection Report

A security Inspection was made at _____ on date and at the time shown below. Conditions, if any, having a bearing on the protection of Company property are also noted below.

Security Representative _____

District _____

Complete Address of Property Inspected _____

Date _____ 20 ____

Time: From _____ AM

Central Office ( ) District ( ) Garage ( ) Locker ( ) Work Center ( ) _____ PM

Carrier Hut ( ) Vehicle ( ) Acctg. Bldg. ( ) Commerical Bldg. ( ) To _____ AM

_____ PM

Regular Means of Admittance Guard ( ) Locked Door or Gate ( ) Door Tele. ( )

Code Key Set ( ) Cable Box Lock ( ) Sesame Lock ( )

No.	Item		Satisfactory	Unsatisfactory	Remarks – Briefly describe Conditions That Prompted "Unsatisfactory" Classification and Corrective Action Taken
1.	Appropriate Ilumination				
2.	Condition of Locks				
3.	Condition of Fences				
4.	Condition of Gates				
5.	Basement Entrances				
6.	Outside Doors				
7.	Windows				
8.	Guard Services				
9.	Storage – Cable				
10.	Material Storage, Cages				
11.	Tool Storage				
12.	Talking Set Storage, Cages				
13.	Car or Bin Doors Unlocked				
14.	Fire Hazards				
15.	Identification & Accountability of Others Found on Premises	Employees			
		Non-employees			
16.	Responsible Department Advised:	Date:	Title:		Name:
17.	Repeated Condition:	Number ( ) above			
					Use other side if necessary

Figure 3.1 Incident report.

statutes have essentially sought a middle ground permitting arrests only when clearly essential. At the same time, these same laws tend to emphasize referral to public authority when at all possible. However, the process of citizen's arrest is "filled with legal pitfalls," which "may depend on a number of legal distinctions, such as the nature of the crime being committed, proof of actual presence at the time and place of the incident."[29] Throughout the United States, the array of variables that need be considered in formalizing a private arrest system can be a bit daunting—especially when one considers that this whole issue is about nonprofessionals conducting the arrest. The more common criteria that guide the private citizen power of arrest are critiqued below.

3.2.1.1.1 Time of the Arrest

Both common law and statutory rationales for the privilege or right of citizen's arrest impose time restrictions on the arresting party. In the case of felonies, the felon's continuous evasion of

ARREST REPORT		14 REP AREA	1 SUSPECT'S NAME (LAST, FIRST, MIDDLE)			1A M.O. NO.			2 COMPLAINT NO.	
15 LOCATION OF ARREST			3 SUSPECT'S ADDRESS		CITY				4 ARREST NO./GRADE	
16 DESCRIBE TYPE OF PREMISES			5 SEX RACE	D.O.B.	HT	WT	HAIR	EYES	6 I.D. NO	
17 DAY, DATE/TIME ARRESTED			7 N.C.I.C. CHECK	TIME		8 SOCIAL SECURITY NO.				
18 BREATHALYZER/OPERATOR/TIME READING	19 PARENT/GUARDIAN/TIME NOTIFIED ☐YES ☐ NO		9 PLACE OF BIRTH	10 WEAPON (DESCRIBE)					SERIAL NO.	
20 RESIST ☐YES ☐ NO	21 NARCOTIC? ☐YES ☐ NO	22 ARMED? ☐YES ☐ NO	11 OCCUPATION		12 RES. PHONE			13 BUS. PHONE		
23 WHERE SUSPECT EMPLOYED OR SCHOOL			24 DAY, DATE/TIME OCCURRED		125 DATE/TIME REPORTED					
26 SUSPECT OPERATOR'S LIC. NO.		STATE	27 FORMAL CHARGES					28 U.C.R.		
29 HOLD PLACED ON VEHICLE ☐YES ☐ NO		TOWED TO	30 CHARES CHANGED TO					DATE/TIME		
31 VEHICLE INVOLVED	YEAR-MAKE-MODEL	COLOR(S)	REG. NO. STATE YEAR		31A VEHICLE REGISTERED OWNER			ADDRESS		

CODE: C – COMPLAINANT   V – VICTIM   W – WITNESS   P – PARENT/GUARDIAN   CO - SUSPECT

32 NAME	CODE	RESIDENCE	CITY	RES. PHONE	BUS. PHONE
(1)					
(2)					
(3)					
(4)					
(5)					

33 ARREST PROCEDURE

(A) ARRESTED ____ HRS. (B) RIGHTS ____ (C) TRANSPORTED ____ HRS. (D) ARRIVED ____ HRS. (E) PROCESSED & RIGHTS ____ HRS. (F) INTERVIEWED ____ HRS. (G) ARRAINGNED ____ HRS. (H) RELEASED COMMITTED ____ HRS. (I) IMPLIED CONSENT LAW ____ HRS.

ITEM NO. | 34 NARRATIVE (1) CONTINUATION OF ABOVE ITEMS (INDICATE "ITEM NUMBER" AT LEFT) (2) DESCIRBE DETAILS OF INCIDENT NOT LISTED ABOVE (3) IDENTIFY ADDITIONAL WITNESSES, VICTIMS, ETC. FROM BLOCK NO. 32.

35 TRANSPORTING OFFICER	NO.	36 ARRESTING OFFICER	NO.	37 BOOKING OFFICER	NO.
38 TRANSPORTING OFFICER	NO.	39 ARRESTING OFFICER	NO.	40 SEARCHED BY	NO.
41 SUSPECT'S MONEY		42 SUPERVISOR APPROVING		43 DAILY BULLETIN ☐YES ☐ NO	PAGE OF

Figure 3.2   Arrest report.

(Continued)

44 OFFICER'S OBSERVATIONS

ODOR OF
ALCOHOL: STRONG ☐ MODERATE ☐ FAINT ☐ OTHER _____
COMPLEXION: FLUSHED ☐ MOTTLED ☐ PALE ☐ NORMAL ☐ OTHER_____
EYES: BLOODSHOT ☐ WATERY ☐ GLASSY ☐ CONTRACTED ☐ DILATED ☐ OTHER _____
      WEARING GLASSES ☐ CONTACT LENSES ☐
SPEECH: INCOHERENT ☐ CONFUSED ☐ JERKY ☐ PROFANE ☐ STUTTERING ☐ GOOD ☐ OTHER _____
BALANCE: STAGGERING ☐ SWAYING ☐ UNABLE TO STAND ☐ NEEDED ASSISTANCE TO WALK ☐ OTHER _____
MENTAL
ATTITUDE: POLITE ☐ EXCITED ☐ TALKATIVE ☐ HILARIOUS ☐ COMBATIVE ☐ STUPEFIED ☐ OTHER _____
CLOTHING
CONDITION: DISORDERLY ☐ ORDERLY ☐ SOILED BY VOMIT ☐ SOILED BY URINE ☐ PARTLY DRESSED ☐ OTHER _____
CLOTHING *(Describe Clothing and Color of Garments)* _____

DEFENDANT INJURED? Yes ☐ No ☐ Retained In Hospital? Yes ☐ No ☐ Doctor _____
NATURE OF INJURIES _____

45 REASON FOR STOP:

DRIVING TOO FAST/SLOW ☐ ACCIDENT ☐ DRIVING IN INAPPROPRIATE AREA ☐ WEAVING/DRIFTING ☐
NEARLY STIKING CAR OR OBJECT ☐ WIDE RADIUS TURN ☐ STOPS WITHOUT CAUSE ☐ LOOKS INTOXICATED ☐
NOT IN MARKED LANE ☐ EQUIPMENT VIOLATION ☐ RAN STOP SIGN/LIGHT ☐ FOLLOWING TOO CLOSELY ☐
BRIGHT/NO LIGHTS ☐
OTHER _____

46 FIELD TEST

1	**2**	**3**	**MARK**
WALK AND TURN	**ONE LEG STAND**	**ALCOTEST**	**LEVEL**
☐ CAN'T KEEP BALANCE WHILE LISTENING TO	☐ SWAYING WHILE BALANCING		**OF**
INSTRUCTIONS	☐ USES ARMS TO BALANCE		**DISCOLORATION**
☐ STARTS BEFORE INSTRUCTIONS FINISHED	☐ QUITE UNSTEADY		
☐ STOPS WHILE WALKING TO STEADY	☐ PUTS FOOT DOWN		
☐ DOES NOT TOUCH HEEL TO TOE	☐ CANNOT/REFUSES TEST (5)		
☐ LOSES BALANCE WHILE WALKING			
☐ INCORRECT NUMBER OF STEPS			
☐ CANNOT/REFUSES TO DO TEST (9)			

INSTRUCTIONS READ PER MTL. FORM _____ ☐

47 CHEMICAL TESTING

TIME OF TEST _____ SERIAL # _____
CHEMICAL BREATH TEST: ADMINISTERED BY _____ SERIAL # _____
DEVICE _____
RESULTS _____

URINE TEST SAMPLE: OBTAINED BY _____
SAMPLE STORED IN _____

BLOOD SAMPLE: TAKEN BY _____ AT _____ HOSPITAL
SAMPLE STORED IN _____ AT MTLP FOR TRANSPORTATION
TO _____ LAB _____

Figure 3.2 (Continued)   Arrest report.

authorities was considered a substantial and continuing threat against the public order and police. Therefore, an arresting party could complete the process regarding a felon at any time. Persons committing misdemeanors, however, were afforded greater protection from private citizen arrest actions. Some states require that the person committing a misdemeanor be arrested by a private citizen only when actually engaging in conduct that undermines the public order. However, other states have dramatically expanded the misdemeanor defense category beyond the breach of the public peace typology. More specifically, states have expanded the arrest power to include petty larceny and shoplifting,[30] and have provided a rational barometer of when citizens' arrests are appropriate.

Also relevant to time limitation analysis is "freshness" of the pursuit. A delay or deferral of the arrest process will result in a loss of the arrest privilege. Predictably, freshness in the pursuit may be

---

AO 442 (Rev. 01/09) Arrest Warrant

UNITED STATES DISTRICT COURT

for the

United States of America
v.

)
)
)   Case No.
)
)

_____
Defendant

ARREST WARRANT

To: Any authorized law enforcement officer

YOU ARE COMMANDED to arrest and bring before a United States magistrate judge without unnecessary delay
(name of person to be arrested) _____

who is accused of an offense or violation based on the following document filed with the court:

❒ Indictment   ❒ Superseding Indictment   ❒ Information   ❒ Superseding Information   ❒ Complaint
❒ Probation Violation Petition   ❒ Supervised Release Violation Petition   ❒ Violation Notice   ❒ Order of the Court

This offense is briefly described as follows:

Date: _____

                                                        _____
                                                        Issuing officer's signature

City and state: _____

                                                        _____
                                                        Printed name and title

Return
This warrant was received on *(date)* _____ , and the person was arrested on *(date)* _____   at *(city and state)* _____ .   Date: _____   _____   *Arresting officer's signature*   _____   *Printed name and title*

Figure 3.3   Arrest warrant.

(Continued)

AO 442 (Rev. 01/09) Arrest Warrant (Page 2)

**This second page contains personal identifiers provided for law-enforcement use only
and therefore should not be filed in court with the executed warrant unless under seal.**

(Not for Public Disclosure)

Name of defendant/offender: _____

Known aliases: _____

Last known residence: _____

Prior addresses to which defendant/offender may still have ties: _____

Last known employment: _____

Last known telephone numbers: _____

Place of birth: _____

Date of birth: _____

Social Security number: _____

Height: _____ Weight: _____

Sex: _____ Race: _____

Hair: _____ Eyes: _____

Scars, tattoos, other distinguishing marks: _____

History of violence, weapons, drug use: _____

Known family, friends, and other associates *(name, relation, address, phone number)*: _____

FBI number: _____

Complete description of auto: _____

Investigative agency and address: _____

Name and telephone numbers (office and cell) of pretrial services or probation officer *(if applicable)*: _____

Date of last contact with pretrial services or probation officer *(if applicable)*: _____

Figure 3.3 (Continued) Arrest warrant.

difficult to measure in precise terms. Timing restrictions "serve to compel reliance on police once the danger of immediate public harm from criminal activity has ceased."[31]

3.2.1.1.2 Presence and Commission

The presence during commission of the offence is a clear requirement in a case involving misdemeanors where firsthand, actual knowledge corroborates the arresting party's decision making.

"The purpose of the requirement is presumably to prevent the danger and imposition involved in mistaken arrests based upon uncorroborated or second hand information. Its principal impact is in cases where the citizen learns the commission of a crime and assumes the responsibility of preventing the escape of an offender."[32] If firsthand observation is called for, the arrest is properly based on an eyewitness view. In other cases, especially the full range of felonies, a citizen can arrest another person based on the standard of reasonable grounds, a close companion to the probable cause test. To find probable cause, one must demonstrate that someone has committed, is likely committing, or is about to commit a crime. Being present during an offense plainly meets this standard. But numerous other cases are just as probative despite a lack of immediate presence. Critics have charged that requiring presence as a basis for the privilege to arrest is nonsensical. A note in the *Columbia Law Review* gives an example by analogy:

> It is here that the requirement produces incongruous results. If a citizen hears a scream and turns around to see a bleeding victim on the ground and a fleeing figure, he can arrest the assailant with impunity. Yet if he comes upon the scene but a moment later under identical circumstances, his apprehension of the fugitive would be illegal.[33]

A few jurisdictions have attempted to reconcile this dilemma by allowing felony arrests to occur without the presence requirement. The presence is simply replaced with a reasonable grounds or reasonable cause criteria. The *Report of the Task Force on Private Security from the National Advisory Committee on Criminal Justice Standards and Goals* addresses this qualification.

> Under the statutes that authorize an arrest based on "reasonable cause" or "reasonable grounds" it has been held in most jurisdictions that these terms generally mean sufficient cause to warrant suspicion in the arrester's mind at the time of the arrest. Some jurisdictions have expanded the rule of suspicion to require a higher standard; yet, there are no uniform criteria emerging from the numerous decisions on the questions.[34]

A review of citizen's arrest standards on a state-by-state basis is provided in Table 3.1.

Note that Table 3.1 makes a distinction between minor and major offenses, namely between felonies and misdemeanors. It also outlines the general grounds leading to a finding of probable or reasonable grounds required to affect an arrest. Some general statutory conclusions can be made:

1. Probable cause, the standard utilized for arrest, search, and seizure by public officials is not commonly employed in the citizen's arrest realm.
2. Reasonable grounds is the standard generally employed by statutes outlining a citizen's right to arrest.
3. The presence is generally required in all minor offenses commonly known as misdemeanors.
4. The presence is required in a minority of jurisdictions in felony cases.
5. Before an arrest can be effected in a felony case, the private citizen must have some definitive knowledge that a felony has been committed.

In sum, hunches, guesses, or general surmises are not a satisfactory framework in which to conduct citizens' arrests. Just as the public police system must adhere to some fundamental standards of fairness regarding the arrest, search, and seizure process, so too must private sector justice. Arrest based on reasonable grounds is the benchmark.

Table 3.1 State by State Citizen's Arrest Standards

Column legend (top-level groupings → criteria):

Minor Offense — Type of Minor Offense:
1. Crime
2. Misdemeanor Amounting to a Breach of the peace
3. Breach of the peace
4. Public Offense
5. Offense
6. Offense other than an ordinance
7. Indictable offense

Minor Offense — Type of Knowledge Required:
8. Presence
9. Immediate Knowledge
10. View
11. Upon reasonable grounds that is being committed

Major offense — Type of Major offense:
12. Felony
13. Larceny
14. Petit larceny
15. Crime involving physical injury to another
16. Crime
17. Crime involving theft or destruction of property

Major offense:
18. Committed in presence
19. Information a felony has been committed
20. View
21. Reasonable grounds to believe being committed
22. That felony has been committed in fact
23. Is escaping or attempting

Certainty of Correct Arrest:
24. Summoned by peace officer to assist in arrest
25. Is in the act of committing
26. Reasonable grounds to believe person arrested committed
27. Probably cause

State	1	2	3	4	5	6	7	8	9	10	11	12	13	14	15	16	17	18	19	20	21	22	23	24	25	26	27
Alabama				X				X				X										X				X	
Alaska	X							X				X										X				X	
Arizona	X	X						X				X									X					X	
Arkansas								X				X										X				X	
California				X				X				X										X				X	
Colorado	X				X							X				X		X					X			X	X
Georgia									X							X		X							X		
Hawaii	X			X												X		X								X	X
Idaho				X				X				X									X					X	
Illinois						X					X	X									X						

(Continued)

Table 3.1 (Continued)   State by State Citizen's Arrest Standards

	Minor Offense											Major offense												Certainty of Correct Arrest			
	Type of Minor Offense							Type of Knowledge Required				Type of Major offense															
	Crime	Misdemeanor Amounting to a Breach of the peace	Breach of the peace	Public Offense	Offense	Offense other than an ordinance	Indictable offense	Presence	Immediate Knowledge	View	Upon reasonable grounds that is being committed	Felony	Larceny	Petit larceny	Crime involving physical injury to another	Crime	Crime involving theft or destruction of property	Committed in presence	Information a felony has been committed	View	Reasonable grounds to believe being committed	That felony has been committed in fact	Is escaping or attempting	Summoned by peace officer to assist in arrest	Is in the act of committing	Reasonable grounds to believe person arrested committed	Probably cause
Iowa				■				■				■										■				■	
Kentucky												■										■				■	
Louisiana												■										■					
Michigan												■										■		■			
Minnesota				■				■				■										■			■	■	
Mississippi							■	■				■						■				■			■	■	
Montana			■					■				■										■			■	■	
Nebraska					■							■		■								■			■	■	
Nevada				■				■				■										■			■	■	
New York					■			■				■										■					

(Continued)

Table 3.1 (Continued) State by State Citizen's Arrest Standards

	N. Carolina	N. Dakota	Ohio	Oklahoma	Oregon	S. Carolina	S. Dakota	Tennessee	Texas	Utah	Wyoming
Minor Offense — Type of Minor Offense											
Crime					■						
Misdemeanor Amounting to a Breach of the peace											
Breach of the peace	■								■		
Public Offense		■		■			■		■	■	
Offense											
Offense other than an ordinance											
Indictable offense											
Type of Knowledge Required											
Presence		■		■			■	■			
Immediate Knowledge											
View									■		
Upon reasonable grounds that is being committed											
Major offense — Type of Major offense											
Felony		■	■			■	■	■		■	■
Larceny											
Petit larceny											■
Crime involving physical injury to another	■										
Crime					■						
Crime involving theft or destruction of property	■										
Major offense											
Committed in presence					■		■				
Information a felony has been committed											
View				■			■				
Reasonable grounds to believe being committed		■									
That felony has been committed in fact		■	■			■		■			
Is escaping or attempting											
Certainty of Correct Arrest											
Summoned by peace officer to assist in arrest	■										
Is in the act of committing											
Reasonable grounds to believe arrested committed person		■	■	■			■	■		■	
Probably cause	■				■		■		■		

The *Restatement of the Law of Torts* cogently justifies a citizen's arrest in these circumstances:

1. If the other person has committed a felony for which he is arrested;
2. If a felony has been committed and the arrestor reasonably suspects the arrestee has committed it;
3. If the arrestee in the arrestor's presence is committing a breach of the peace or is about to renew it; and
4. If the arrestee has attempted to commit a felony in the arrestor's presence and the arrest is made at once or in fresh pursuit.[35]

Depending upon jurisdiction, another factor to be considered by security personnel in the arrest process is notice, an announcement advising a suspect of one's intention to arrest. The level of force utilized and the detention techniques for a person awaiting formal processing may also be significant factors in any resolution of the propriety of a citizen's arrest.

For a comprehensive look at the state laws on Citizens Arrest, visit the Solutions Institute at: http://solutions-institute.org/tools/citizens-arrest-laws-by-state/

3.2.2 *The Law of Search and Seizure: Public Police*

There are two fundamental ways in which a public peace officer can conduct a search and seizure—with or without a warrant. Warrants are expressly referenced in the Fourth Amendment and their probable cause determination is explicitly mentioned. Searches with warrants are mandated unless one of the various exceptional circumstances exists to justify a warrantless action. There are numerous exceptions to the warrant requirement from consent of the arrested party to exigency and safety. The exceptions have been shaped and crafted, not as an affront to the fundamental protection, but in full recognition of the practical reality and criminal activity and law enforcement policy. When public police search without justification or legal right, the evidence so taken is excluded due to the constitutional infringement. This restrictive policy is labeled the exclusionary rule.[36] In *Mapp v. Ohio*[37] the U.S. Supreme Court rendered evidence inadmissible, as it was obtained by public law enforcement officials in violation of the Fourth, Fifth, and Sixth Amendments of the U.S. Constitution. The Fourteenth Amendment has selectively incorporated these three amendments as they apply to state police action. For an example of a federal search warrant see Figure 3.4.

As part of routine procedure, a police officer who makes a lawful and valid arrest, with or without an arrest warrant, or at arm's length, is entitled to search the suspect and the area within his immediate control. At other times, the search and eventual seizure may arise from a "plain view" observation. Plain view permits any law enforcement official who sees contraband, weaponry, or other evidence of criminality within direct sight or observation to seize the evidence without warrants or other legal requirements. Police may search and seize contraband in any open space environment, such as agricultural centers for narcotics. This warrantless exception is often referred to as the "open field" rule.[38] Police can search and seize evidence in any abandoned property or place. Warrant requirements for police are waived in cases of extreme emergency known as *exigent* situations, as when there is a high likelihood of lost evidence. Naturally, police have also been given leeway to conduct warrantless searches when their personal safety is at risk. Auto searches and consent searches generally bypass the more restrictive warrant requirements due to the mobility of

AO 93 (Rev. 12/09) Search and Seizure Warrant

UNITED STATES DISTRICT COURT
for the

In the Matter of the Search of	)	
(Briefly describe the property to be searched	)	
or identify the person by name and address)	)	Case No.
	)	
	)	
	)	

SEARCH AND SEIZURE WARRANT

To: Any authorized law enforcement officer

An application by a federal law enforcement officer or an attorney for the government requests the search of the following person or property located in the _____ District of _____ *(identify the person or describe the property to be searched and give its location)*:

The person or property to be searched, described above, is believed to conceal *(identify the person or describe the property to be seized)*:

I find that the affidavit(s), or any recorded testimony, establish probable cause to search and seize the person or property.

YOU ARE COMMANDED to execute this warrant on or before _____
(not to exceed 14 days)

❏ in the daytime 6:00 a.m. to 10 p.m.   ❏ at any time in the day or night as I find reasonable cause has been established.

Unless delayed notice is authorized below, you must give a copy of the warrant and a receipt for the property taken to the person from whom, or from whose premises, the property was taken, or leave the copy and receipt at the place where the property was taken.

The officer executing this warrant, or an officer present during the execution of the warrant, must prepare an inventory as required by law and promptly return this warrant and inventory to United States Magistrate Judge

_____ .
(name)

❏ I find that immediate notification may have an adverse result listed in 18 U.S.C. § 2705 (except for delay of trial), and authorize the officer executing this warrant to delay notice to the person who, or whose property, will be searched or seized *(check the appropriate box)* ❏ for _____ days *(not to exceed 30)*.
❏ until, the facts justifying, the later specific date of _____ .

Date and time issued: _____   _____
                                                                        Judge's signature

City and state: _____   _____
                                                                Printed name and title

Figure 3.4   Federal search warrant.

(Continued)

AO 93 (Rev. 12/09) Search and Seizure Warrant (Page 2)

Return		
Case No.:	Date and time warrant executed:	Copy of warrant and inventory left with:
Inventory made in the presence of :		
Inventory of the property taken and name of any person(s) seized:		

Certification

    I declare under penalty of perjury that this inventory is correct and was returned along with the original warrant to the designated judge.

Date: _____

_____
Executing officer's signature

_____
Printed name and title

Figure 3.4 (Continued) Federal search warrant.

a vehicle. *Stop and frisk*, as outlined in *Terry v. Ohio*,[39] allows police to "pat down" a suspect if it's reasonable to suspect weaponry or other potential harm.[40]

Review the Handout summary prepared by Stanford University on the Terry doctrine and its inapplicability to Private Security Guards at: http://web.stanford.edu/group/streetlaw/cgi-bin/wordpress/wp-content/uploads/2011/10/Search-Seizure-Miranda_Updated.pdf

---

One other factor is worth mentioning as well, namely immunity. Historically, public officers operated under some level of "immunity" whether whole or qualified in design. That immunity-insulated government agents from liability as long as his or her "actions [are] taken in good faith pursuant to their discretionary authority."[41] Determining whether a public official is entitled to qualified immunity, then, "requires a two-part inquiry: (1) Was the law governing the state official's conduct clearly established? and (2) Under that law could a reasonable state official have believed his conduct was lawful?"[42] This standard "gives ample room for mistaken judgments by protecting 'all but the plainly incompetent or those who knowingly violate the law."[43,44] But that immunity does not preclude a judgment in a constitutional sense, although as this text has regularly witnessed, there is little proof that these constitutional remedies do little to change the behavior of errant officers in the public realm. Immunity is not a luxury given to the private sector.

3.2.3 *The Law of Search and Seizure: Private Police*

The rationale behind the exclusionary rule is to deter police misconduct and to halt illegal and unjustified investigative processes. As noted previously, in *Burdeau v. McDowell*,[45] the U.S. Supreme Court was unwilling to extend the exclusionary rule to private sector searches. *Burdeau* held exclusionary rule inapplicable since it was clear that there was "no invasion of the security afforded by the Fourth Amendment against unreasonable search and seizure as whatever wrong was done by the act of individuals in taking the property of another."[46] Trial attorney John Wesley Hall, Jr. writes in *Inapplicability of the Fourth Amendment*:

> One of the oldest principles in the law of search and seizure holds that searches by private or non-law enforcement personnel are not protected by the Fourth Amendment regardless of the unlawful manner in which the search may have been conducted. The Fourth Amendment historically only applies to direct governmental action and not the passive act of using relevant evidence obtained by a private party's conduct.[47]

Others disagree with these lines of legal explanation especially when one considers how extensive role private security plays in crime, critical infrastructure, privatized replacement services for public police activity, and other assumption of functions once left to the public sector exclusively. The regularity of arrest, search, and seizure processes in private security settings are now amply documented.[48] In retail establishments, security personnel regularly search individuals suspected of shoplifting. Security firms have now taken over entire neighborhood, housing projects and planned communities, and even cities and towns.

Searches are also seen in business and industrial applications. "These could include search of a car or dwelling for pilfered goods or the use of electronic surveillance devices to obtain information for use in making legal, business or personal decisions."[49] Additionally, surveillance by private security companies utilizing various forms of electronic eavesdropping, emerging technologies, and other interception devices, while still regulated to some extent in the public sector, are more readily utilized and commonly employed in the private sector.

The Private Security Advisory Council[50] ponders a noticeable lack of either common law or statutory authority governing private search parameters. Yet even with the industry's practices, this lack of restrictions in the private sector is inexcusable. However, the council does list these instances as legitimate private search actions:

1. Actual consent by a person
2. Implied consent as a condition of employment or part of an employment contract
3. Incidental to valid arrest
4. Incidental to valid conditions[51]

In some respects, these four categories parallel to the very conditions under which public law enforcement may permissibly conduct warrantless searches. "As a general consideration since the public police are intended to be society's primary law enforcers, the limitations on public police search should set the upper boundaries of allowable search by private police."[52] Of course, it is also critical to note that while constitutional restrictions may not yet apply in the private security realm without a more demonstrable showing, other remedies are available to those who have been illegally arrested, searched, or had personal effects or property unjustly seized. These tort actions and corresponding civil and criminal remedies include, but are not limited to

- Battery
- Theft
- Trespass
- False imprisonment
- Invasion of privacy or being placed in a false or humiliating light
- An action for false imprisonment or malicious prosecution as well as potential civil rights violations

To track a private sector search of the person, review the checklist at Figure 3.5.[53]

In summary, the constitutional guidelines and case law interpreting standards of public police practice have yet to make a remarkable dent in private security activity. Relying upon strong precedent, statutory noninvolvement, and a general hesitancy on the part of the courts and the legislatures to expand constitutional doctrines like the exclusionary rule, private security practitioners are still provided a safe haven in the law of arrest, search, and seizure.

3.3 Challenges to the Safe Harbor of Private Security

Despite this general resistance to expanding the constitutional dynamic to private sector police, legal advocates push hard for such reforms and a variety and steady stream of case law reaches appellate courts across the country each and every year. Some case law is more significant than others. Few cases have had much success in altering this legal landscape. An appeals decision from California carved out a noticeable precedent for those arguing for the expansion of these constitutional rights. In *People v. Zelinski*,[54] the California Supreme Court ruled that security officers were thoroughly empowered to institute a search to recover goods that were in plain view, but that any intrusion into the defendant's person or effects was not authorized as incident to a citizen's

1. What were the arresting security officers doing when you first saw them?
2. What were you doing when you first saw the security officers?
3. What were you wearing?
4. What did the arresting security officers say and do before they touched you?
5. Did you make any sudden move to conceal or dispose of anything in your possession in view of the security officers? Give details.
6. Were the security officers able to observe any incriminating objects on your person before they touched you? What?
7. Were there any bulges discernible to suggest incriminating objects concealed beneath your clothing?
8. Did you make any sudden movements that might appear to be threatening to the arresting security officers or other persons?
9. Did you attempt to escape or flee?
10. Describe the visibility in the area of the arrest.
11. Did the security officers ever tell you that you were under arrest, or utter words to that effect? What exactly did they say?
12. Did the security officers use force or threats to restrain you in any way?
13. Did the security officers tell you the reason you were being arrested?
14. Did they search your person? Describe in detail the manner and thoroughness of the search.
15. Did you resist the arrest or search in any way? Describe.
16. Did the security officers use force or threats of force to search your clothing or your person?
17. Did the arresting security officers search you at the place of the arrest?
18. If not, how long after the arrest were you searched?
19. How far from the site of the arrest was the search conducted?
20. Were you taken to your home or car before being searched?
21. Was anything else searched besides your person?
22. What was seized by the arresting security officers? Describe in detail.
23. How long had you been carrying it before the arrest and search?
24. From whom had you obtained it?
25. Did the security officers say or do anything to suggest that they knew in advance what they would find or where they would find it? Describe the acts and behavior of the security officers in detail.
26. Did anyone know you were carrying the objects seized? Who?
    a. Was he under investigation for any crime?
    b. Has he been in police custody recently?
    c. Has he a criminal record?

Figure 3.5   Search checklist.

arrest or protected under the *Merchant's Privilege Statute*. The court concluded that the evidence seized was "obtained by unlawful search and that the constitutional prohibition against unreasonable search and seizure affords protection against the unlawful intrusive conduct of these private security personnel."[55] The decision temporarily shook the status quo. The court fully recognized its own disregard of previous U.S. Supreme Court rulings, stating:

> Although past cases have not applied the constitutional restriction to purely private searches, we have recognized that some minimal official participation or encouragement may bring private action within the constitutional restraints on state action.[56]

Aside from the defective reasoning here, the Court simply mixes apples and oranges—for the excessive entanglement between public and private sector officers has long been a pathway for proper legal challenge. Using what is commonly excepted cannot justify a bold rejection of black-letter law offered up in *Burdeau*. Mindful of the facts of this case, the Supreme Court of California could not recite any cases including a connection or legal nexus between private and public police activity. Instead, the court simply dismissed previous decisions based upon a variety of rationales, including the security industry's new and dynamic involvement in the administration of justice.[57]

The court cited that the "increasing reliance placed upon private security personnel by local enforcement of criminal law"[58] particularly as it relates to privacy rights and procedural rights of defendants. In the end, the California Supreme Court relied upon its own Constitution, Article 2, Section 13, which ironically is a mirror image of the federal provision. Upon closer reading, the decision is a startling departure, at least at the state level. Stephen Euller, in his article *"Private Security in the Courtroom: The Exclusionary Rule Applies,"*[59] made a bold prediction:

> Like it or not the *Zelinski* rule is coming. There are good reasons why professionals should welcome it. The *Zelinski* court recognized that private security personnel play an important role in law enforcement and often act on the public's behalf. Part of the reason some people are concerned about abuse is simply because security professionals have at times demonstrated rather impressive investigative skills and sophistication. The new rules will encourage the private security industry to upgrade itself, its level of professionalism, to discipline itself, to erase the image of the lawless private eye.[60]

Just when the private act transforms into a public one is difficult to tell although it is certain that Euller's prophecy has not come around the bend. The level of public inducement, solicitation, oversight, and joint effect manifest a transformation. In *State of Minnesota v. Buswell*,[61] the court claims to have witnessed the transformation of private security personnel, at a racetrack who conducted searches on patrons, into a public persona. When cocaine was discovered, defendants assert that the private security agents had sufficient public connections to trigger a series of constitutional protections. The court qualified its public finding by corroborating the private–public interplay. It stated:

> In the instant case, a meeting occurred where public officials and private personnel reached an understanding regarding arrest procedures to be utilized upon the discovery of contraband by the private guards. Although this meeting dealt with the aftermath of searches, and not the manner of searching, the meeting produced a standing arrangement for contacts by the supervising security agent with police during the hours of operation, and a police officer was designated on call to assist with arrests.[62]

Adding to this reasoning was the adoption of the "public function" test—that imputes constitutional remedies when the nature and scope of private police conduct exhibits all the qualities and characteristics of a "public" act.[63] Regardless of direct police involvement, systematic use of random contraband searches serves the general public interest and may reflect pursuit of criminal convictions as well as protection of private interests. *Marsh v. Alabama*[64] supplies the basis for concluding that private investigators and police may be subject to the Fourth Amendment where they are with some regularity engaged in the "public function" of law enforcement.[65] Courts in the mold of *Buswell* look to corroborate the advocate's assertions. In short, does the private security officer act like a public police officer?[66]

Wearing police uniforms, and using police restraint processes "(handcuffing appellants to fences, conducting body searches), indicates the similarity of function and role."[67] Function infers a similarity of approaches and thereby awards an identical series of protections—at least in a theoretical sense. Finally, the court weighed the security agency hiring a full-time public police officer as further evidence of the transformation. Such officers are formally affiliated with the government and usually given authority beyond that of an ordinary citizen. Thus, they may be treated as state agents and subject to the constraints of the Fourth Amendment.[68]

Zelinski and *Buswell* manifest a voice of discontent and a resulting intellectual demand for change in traditional constitutional applications for the private security industry.[69] In this sense, *Zelinski* and *Buswell* signify a slow and very ineffective evolution. A quick glance at the precedential power of these cases attests to the firmness of the present legal foundation.

3.3.1 The Platinum Platter Doctrine

Challenges to the applicability of the exclusionary rule, whereby evidence is excluded for errant search, seizure, or arrest processes, are continuously witnessed in higher courts when the facts involve public officers. It is not a popular legal principle in more conservative quarters. Initially, the exclusionary rule was held applicable to federal action alone and was not applicable in state cases.[70] Federal agents realized this early on and clandestinely employed the services of state agents who delivered up evidence or other treasure while avoiding the constitutional challenges.[71] For state police officers, the delivery of the evidence, despite its procedural impropriety, was figuratively handed over on a "silver platter."[72]

These types of abuses, while inevitable, have long been minimized by the selective incorporation of the Bill of Rights by and through the Fourteenth Amendment. By this interpretation, state action becomes the type of governmental action that triggers constitutional demands. Consequently, state law enforcement and federal law enforcement play under identical rules. But private security is still exempt from these constitutional mandates and the silver platter is irrelevant. Even so, there are some advocates who claim that public law enforcement uses private sector justice operatives as conduits or feeders. As a result, private security gives life to another version of the platter—the platinum variety. Hence, the use by state and federal officials of private security operatives to arrest, search, or seize, without the usual constitutional oversight, has been labeled the *platinum platter doctrine*. In arguing that the entanglement of private sector/state involvement creates a relationship substantial enough to justify expansion of the Fourth Amendment, B. C. Petroziello, calls for a reexamination of the *Burdeau* doctrine. Referring to special police officers in Ohio as quasi-public figures, he argues that special police should no longer be permitted to hand over elicit evidence on a "platinum platter."[73] His comments provide food for thought:

> The confusion caused by the current state of the law could be obviated by the use of a much simpler and more preferable standard. The substance of this standard encompasses a different view of what is meant by private individual: no one should be considered private under *Burdeau* if he is employed or paid to detect evidence of crime or has delegated any more power possessed by the average citizen. Whenever a person meeting either of these qualifications tramples a defendant's rights the evidence so gathered is to be excluded at trial.[74]

For critics of unbridled private sector power, the more the private sector cooperates with public authority, the more its occupational role metamorphoses from private to public function. In essence, the entanglement and entwining is so complex and complicated that distinct roles have evaporated. As attractive as the theory is, it suffers conceptually. The principles of Burdeau should not be inapplicable simply because a person is employed or paid to detect criminality or because that person is chartered by the state or other governmental authority. If such reasoning were followed, then any attorney or licensed individual, including truck drivers, polygraph examiners, forest rangers, or park attendants, who are subject to governmental review, would fall within this scheme.

In *United States v. Brooks*[75] the nuances of the platinum platter doctrine were on full display. Here an apartment complex hired a security—the Tennessee Protection Agency—to check and screen visitors and tenants at a front gate complex. During the usual business of screening, the security officers discovered illegal drugs in a car and in subsequent seizure with public police nearby, confiscated the drugs. In response to the defendant's motion to suppress, the court lays out in clear and unambiguous terms why the platinum theory has no applicability to the private sector. The Fourth Amendment, however, does not provide protection against searches by private individuals acting in a private capacity.[76,77]

Despite the difficulties of merging public and private functions to the extent they are one and the same, it is equally undeniable that the private security industry is increasingly engaged in public activity, public protection and safety, and public function. The question of whether this "public" dimension is substantial enough to apply the constitutional regimen is still debatable. What is certain is that in the age of escalating privatization, adoption of a public function theory may be plausible in a host of contexts.

3.3.1.1 Private Action as State Action

A second strategy that attempts to apply the Fourth Amendment in private sector arrests, searches, and seizures is to characterize the action as being inherently "public" even though conducted by a private person. Put another way, the advocate argues that due to the multiple public points of contact or intermesh and that the private search really transforms into a public action. Some have alleged the line between the public and private law enforcement community is far more "tenuous" than most realize.[78]

If the government's role in the private search and seizure is significant enough, the argument concludes that private action is really state or public action and hence the Fourth Amendment applies.[79] State action constitutes not only cooperative partnerships between public and private officers, the latter acting at the behest of the public, governmental authority but also other forms of integration and oversight, such as licensing and regulatory control by state officialdom; levels of authority or classification for the security officers and respective powers and rights granted under some code or statute. Essentially, the private action metamorphizes into public action because the security officers are used by public officers to carry out specific tasks or functions upon request and the once clear line of demarcation becomes very muddled. Other commentators claim the debate about the blurring of the public and private lines has really become too difficult to decipher. In a recent law review commentary calling for clarity in "state action" reasoning, it was asserted that the "state action doctrine has been inconsistent and choppy at best, with the Supreme Court handing down a variety of state action determinative 'tests.'" This situation has prompted commentators to call this doctrine, among other things, "dysfunctional"[80] and "a conceptual disaster area," with Justice Black referring to the U.S. Supreme Court's jurisprudence on the issue as "a torchless search for a way out of a damp echoing cave."[81,82]

For the reformist, the ambition, despite the *Burdeau* doctrine, private conduct or actions should be subject to some level of constitutional scrutiny "if they are sufficiently impregnated with state actions."[83] Expansive judicial reasoning like this was used to justify a plethora of civil rights decisions during the mid-1960s and early 1970s.[84]

The principles of private action/state action have largely been argued in discrimination cases. Assess the historical underpinnings of this theory at: http://www.law.umkc.edu/faculty/ projects/ftrials/conlaw/stateaction.htm

Few functions, systems, enterprises, endeavors, or institutions are completely free from some level of governmental involvement or oversight. The tentacles of governmental influence weave their way into literally every facet of modern life. Whether it be business operation or licensing, environment or workplace safety, unions, and work rules, the heavy hand of government is discoverable just about everywhere. The security industry, like any other commercial concern, is subject to an endless series of oversights including:

1. State licensing requirements.
2. State and federal taxes.
3. State inspections.
4. Reporting requirements.
5. Statutory grant of authority to merchants, business, or industries to protect its property and interests.
6. Immunities and privileges granted by legislatures for certain conducts and behaviors.
7. Subcontractor and delegation rules.
8. Bonding requirements.
9. Regulatory compliance.

Some legal advocates and their plaintiffs think any interaction is sufficient to meet the public function theory. In *Copeland v. City of Topeka*,[85] the court threw out the allegation of private action as state action, commenting:

> Nothing in plaintiff's complaint sufficiently alleges that defendants, or either of them, engaged in acts under color of state law. Instead, the seizure and subsequent treatment of plaintiff at Dillons cannot be fairly attributed to the City of Topeka under any of the tests for state action. For a merchant or its security officers to call the police when they suspect shoplifting or destruction of property is insufficient to constitute state action. No acts allegedly taken by officers of the City of Topeka at the scene reveal prior collusion with defendants, or compliance with any requests by the defendants, or either of them, let alone the requisite joint action. Plaintiff's assertion that defendants "directed and controlled" the City police department is conclusory and unsupported by the facts alleged in the complaint.[86]

A recent North Carolina ruling[87] makes plain the power of *Burdeau* when the decision critically assessed the conduct of private officers appearing to be quasi-public. Even so, the Court construed that more than licensing and uniforms would win the day. The Court concluded:

> In determining whether a private citizen is a state actor for the purposes of the fourth amendment, we use a totality of the circumstances approach that requires special consideration of (1) "the citizen's motivation for the search or seizure," (2) "the degree of governmental involvement, such as advice, encouragement, knowledge about the

nature of the citizen's activities," and (3) "the legality of the conduct encouraged by the police." Importantly, "[o]nce a private search [or seizure] has been completed, subsequent involvement of government agents does not transform the original intrusion into a governmental search."[88]

A review of the trial court's applicable findings of fact reveals an absence of all three special considerations.

> The trial court did not address any of these exclusionary rule-related issues in its initial order. Although a determination that Lieutenant Shatley acted unconstitutionally would necessarily require the suppression of any evidence obtained at the time that he stopped Defendant's vehicle, the same is not necessarily true of evidence obtained after officers of the Chapel Hill Police Department arrived on the scene. Thus, in the event that the trial court concludes that a constitutional violation occurred at the time that Lieutenant Shatley stopped Defendant's vehicle, the trial court should, on remand, make findings of fact and conclusions of law addressing the issue of the extent, if any, to which evidence stemming from Defendant's arrest by officers of the Chapel Hill Police Department must be suppressed as the result of Lieutenant Shatley's conduct as well.[89]

Licensure and the state's grant to incorporate or operate as business form is a favorite of those hoping to prove the interplay and eventual integration of the public and the private. The theory concludes that the mere erection of the business form, which in turn seeks the approval of a governmental entity, is sufficient to change the private into the public. In turn, this "public" quality of the oversight, in whatever form or manner, justifies the imposition of new constitutional requirements.

Consider *United States v. Francoeur.*[90] Defendants sought to reverse a conviction by asserting a constitutional violation by private employees. While in a Disneyland amusement park, security personnel detained and emptied the pockets of multiple suspects. Subsequently, counterfeit bills were retrieved and these suspects were eventually found guilty of various offenses. To challenge the admission of the evidence, defendants claimed that since Disneyland was a public place, freely accessible, and open to the world, the security officials working within its borders were government officials. To uphold this appellate argument would have had far-reaching ramifications, and the Court reminded the defendants that any possible remedy was civil in nature rather than constitutional. It stated:

> The exclusionary rule itself was adopted by the courts because it was recognized that it was only by preventing the use of evidence illegally obtained by public officials that a curb should be put on overzealous activities of such officials. The Supreme Court has in no instance indicated that it would apply the exclusionary rule to cases in which evidence was obtained by private individuals in a matter not countenanced if they were acting for state or federal government.[91]

While most, if not all, security entities have some level of state involvement due to approval mechanisms, this is not the stuff of "institutional character, derived at least in part from grants of state authority and reflect[ing] governmental functions from which one may infer state action."[92] While this argument may be partially meritorious, it lacks the substantiality, the depth and breadth to be equated with state action. While modern constitutional jurisprudence has been comfortable elasticizing principles of state action in a variety of settings, especially in race and sex discrimination cases, these principles are a harder sell in the occupational marketplace. Even so, arguments regarding state action in the security environment do have a following. Arguably, a case of state action exists if there is direct participation and assistance by public police officers in the seizure of evidence by private security officers. John Wesley Hall comments:

> In view of the long-standing rule permitting private searches it will be incumbent on defense counsel to demonstrate some form of law enforcement participation in the search. Mere acceptance of the benefits of a private search by the prosecution authorities is not participation in the private search and seizure.[93]

Direct involvement or participation is not proven by inference, but instead, by a defendant's demonstration of direct involvement. In *United States v. Lima*,[94] the D.C. Appellate Court articulately espoused that private individuals can become agents or instruments of the state if the government is sufficiently involved in the development of actual plans or actions carried out by private persons. The *Lima* decision mandates "a significant relationship ... between the state and private security employees to find state action; something whereby the state intrudes itself into private entity."[95] The *Lima* case contends that mere licensing is not a sufficient basis for state action, and that the D.C. licensing statute vested no particular state authority to license security personnel.[96]

A second rationale for finding state action, outside of direct oversight or governmental scrutiny of some sort, is when private security personnel are found not to have acted alone but under the direct suggestion, supervision, or employment of the public police system.[97] In short, the private security officers act as fronts for the public police. This form of supervision, control, or direction would include instigation, encouragement, direct suggestions as to an operation, or any other strategy illustrating law enforcement involvement.[98] "Whether there has been enough police contact for an agency, the relationship to have existed is a question of fact to be answered by the court."[99]

In *Snyder v. State of Alaska*,[100] a defendant appealed his conviction, asserting that his Fourth Amendment rights were violated. An airline baggage employee had called police on at least 12 previous occasions to report the discovery of drugs and illegal goods. Police informed airline employees that they themselves were not permitted to open packages without a warrant, but that under Civil Aeronautics Board rules, airline employees had a right to open packages if they believed there was something wrong or that the items listed on the bill of lading did not accurately reflect what was in the parcels. The airline employee opened the package, on direction of the Alaskan Police authorities, and the defendant contended that this level of active involvement, encouragement, and investigation transformed private conduct into state action. The court denied that there was a sufficient level of conduct to find state action, holding that the airline employee was

> Performing his duties as private employee of a private company in opening the package received under circumstances reasonably arousing.... The prior contact, of a general nature, between the State police and airline employees did not cause the employees to become agents of the police. A zealous citizen does not subject his activities to the requirements of the Fourth Amendment in Article 1, Section 14 of the Alaskan Constitution.[101]

A similar result was reached in a Georgia case, *Lester v. State*.[102] Appellant moved to suppress as evidence pieces of copper tubing, which a fire investigator had taken from the ruins of the appellant's house. Claiming that the investigator engaged in governmental activity, the defendant sought to have his conviction overturned on Fourth Amendment principles. The Court ruled with little trepidation that:

> Even assuming arguendo that the appellant had standing to object to his search of these premises it was not error to overrule the motion. The investigator was dispatched by a private firm at the behest of the fire insurance company. He was not connected with any law enforcement agency nor did he communicate with one prior to conducting his investigation. Therefore the search could not have violated his Fourth Amendment rights.[103]

Governmental action, arising in a private policing context, requires a substantial correlation between public and private behavior. The case of *Gilette v. The State of Texas*,[104] in which the defendant asserted that security officers, spying on prospective customers in a fitting room, violated constitutional protection, is a failed but instructive case decision. The court cited *Burdeau v. McDowell* as doctrine, maintaining not only its precedential power, but resisting attempts to expand into novel constitutional territory. Similar denials of the state action theory regarding private conduct were also found in New York[105] and New Hampshire.[106] What is striking about these judicial decisions is their simplicity and firm renunciation of legal novelty. The tone could be described as abrupt and impatient over the attempts to unseat well-settled law. The majority of appellate-based decisions treat the argument of state action similarly.

The third and final situation where state action is arguable in the private security industry is when security personnel act in a quasi-police status as when commissioned as special police officers.[107] Professor Stephen Euller, in his article, *"Private Security and the Exclusionary Rule,"* notes:

> In such cases state action has been recognized when private officers have been formally designated "special police officers." States often commission "special police officers" to patrol retail stores or to perform occasional public law enforcement services such as traffic or crowd control at parties or sports events.[108]

These lines can be quite blurry. Consider the hiring of uniformed private security guards at a Job Corps Program—a federally funded retraining facility and program for disadvantaged youth. Job Corps is a public, tax-funded entity, which protects the physical facilities of the Job Corps where training for new employment opportunities occurs. In *State of Tennessee v. Hudson*,[109] the trial court held that the conduct of the security guard was sufficiently tied to government to make it a state action. Since the security guard wore a badge, was in uniform, was referred to as "officer," and worked on a program set up and funded by federal government money being funneled through from the Department of Labor, the trial judge concluded that the security guard's conduct was sufficient to constitute state action.[110]

The appellate court reversed the decision, finding that the private security company, contracted at this Job Corps facility was no more a government agency "than any other company or individual with whom the government contracts to supply a product or service of whatever nature." The court further remarked:

> It is common knowledge that both federal and state governments engage in thousands of contracts daily with many organizations of many types whose employees

have absolutely no connection with the government whatsoever other than being an employee of a government contractor.[111]

Another case, which manifests the delicate line between public and private function, is *State of Ohio v. McDaniel*.[112] The defendants/appellants sought to demonstrate that the security staff, consisting of about 45 full-time employees at a department store in Franklin County, Ohio, were governmental agents by their commission as special deputy sheriffs. Searches made by security employees resulted in the seizure of various incriminating goods. Defendants sought to overturn the seizures based upon Fourth Amendment protections and argued emphatically the state action theory. The court, recognizing that privacy was important to the defendant appellants, attempted to balance the interest of both parties. It found:

> The right to privacy is not absolute and the Constitution prohibits only unreasonable searches. Shoplifting is a serious problem for merchants. Merchants may utilize reasonable means to detect and prevent shoplifting. Where the merchant or his employee has probable or reasonable cause to believe that an apparent customer is in reality a thief planning to shoplift merchandise, the merchant or his employee may utilize reasonable means of surveillance and observation in order to detect and prevent the crime.[113]

The court further rejected the argument that simply being commissioned as special deputies is a sufficient basis for a finding of state action. It concluded:

> From the evidence herein it could only be concluded that Lazarus Security employees at the times in question were engaged in activity within the scope of their employment with Lazarus solely for the benefit of their employer, Lazarus, to detect and prevent thievery of Lazarus merchandise. They were acting outside of any public duty they might be authorized to perform as a commissioned special deputy sheriff and only one of the employees could have acted in that respect in any event. To hold in this case that the actions of the Lazarus Security employees constituted state action on their part would not only be contrary to the realities of the situation but would constitute an unwarranted extension of constitutional provisions to apply to the activities of corporations conducted through its employees.[114]

Deputization, a special commission, or other status, in and of itself, appears an insufficient basis for finding state action. State action requires meaningful participation, significant involvement, and intentional instigation, a series of conducts whereby the public police orchestrate the private activity.[115] "The exclusionary rule should apply then in cases where government officials directly instigate or supervise searches and seizures committed by private parties for the purpose of acquiring evidence for a criminal prosecution. If courts do not apply the rule of exclusion in these cases, government officials will be permitted to conduct improper searches by employing a private party to commit the physical search."[116] A more provocative argument emerges in *Austin v. Paramount Parks*,[117] where plaintiffs alleged that Kings Dominion Park Police where answerable, in a supervisory sense, to the public office of the local county sheriff. The case is further complicated by an employee manual that designates the necessary interaction of the private force with public authority. The manual listed a chain of command that undeniably integrates public policing into this private security context.

The Chain of Command and authority for all Kings Dominion Park Police shall be as follows involving official law enforcement:

1. Sheriff of Hanover County
2. Lieutenant of Kings Dominion Park Police
3. Kings Dominion Park Police Sergeant
4. Kings Dominion Park Police Corporal
5. Kings Dominion Park Police Officer[118]

Despite this clear entanglement of private/public law enforcement, the Austin majority rejected the plaintiff's allegation of sufficient public assumption to trigger constitutional protections. The court further held that the Park's Manager of Loss Prevention lacked all authority over the operations of the public force and dismissed the argument without hesitation.

> Put simply, there was no evidence that Hester, despite his title of Manager of Loss Prevention, in practice exercised any control over the decisions of the special police officer regarding detention and/or arrests of park guests suspected of criminal offenses in this case.... [T]he uncontradicted testimony was to the contrary. In fact, we find no support in the record for any specific policy-making authority given to or exercised by Hester regarding matters of law enforcement.... [W]e have no basis upon which to conclude that Hester exercised final policy-making authority concerning arrests effected by the special police officers of the Park Police Department. Because Austin's position on Paramount's liability ... rests entirely upon her theory that Hester was a "policymaker," we are satisfied that she failed to establish that any deprivation of her federal right was caused by ... Paramount.[119]

In *State v. Weaver*, a lower court found a significant enough interplay between the private and public system to apply constitutional protections when it declared:

1. The armed security guard ... [a]cted as an agent for the State[.]
2. The armed security guard is a state actor.
3. There was lack of reasonable suspicion to stop.
4. The search and seizure were unconstitutional.
5. The evidence acquired beyond the stop and detention should be excluded.[120]

However, on appeal, the Court rejected all of these conclusions and reaffirmed the traditional antagonism to forcing private entities under the constitutional umbrella, claiming that does not "extend to evidence secured by private searches, even if conducted illegally."[121]

As a practical matter, security operatives should not conduct any search without gaining the searched party's consent. See the examples of consent documents in Figures 3.6 and 3.7.

Assess how fixed and dependable the conclusion that the exclusionary rule does not apply to the private sector is in a recent New Mexico Supreme Court case at: http://www.nmcomp-comm.us/nmcases/NMSC/2009/09sc-045.pdf

Consent to Search

I, _____, having been informed of my Constitutional Right not to have a search made of the premises or vehicle hereafter described without a Search Warrant and of my right to refuse to consent to such a search, hereby authorize _____ and _____, who are Police Officers for the Borough of _____, to conduct a complete search of the premises of vehicle under my control described as _____.

This written permission is given by me voluntarily threats or promises of any kind being made to me.

Signed _____

Date _____

Location _____

WITNESSES:

_____

Name, Title, Date & Location

_____

Name, Title, Date & Location

Figure 3.6   Consent to search.

Consent to Search

I further acknowledge that nothing other than the items listed herein were removed by the investigating _____ Police Officers, and _____.

This written permission is given by me voluntarily threats or promises of any kind being made to me.

Signed _____

Date _____

Location _____

WITNESSES:

_____

Name, Title, Date & Location

_____

Name, Title, Date & Location

Figure 3.7   Consent to search.

3.3.1.2 The Public Function of Private Security

Proponents of the public function theory would expand and extend the protections of the Fourth Amendment and other aligned constitutional provisions by alleging the public nature of occupational tasks performed by private security. Under the public function test, a private entity is said to be performing a public function if it is exercising powers traditionally reserved to the state. The possibilities for confusion of role and function increase each day in diverse communities. For example, in gated communities, religious communities, and private lands, the use of private officers and private police forces is now common practice.[122] In other words, it is not the private officer that measures applicability but instead, the nature of what the private security is undertaking.[123]

In essence, "courts have limited the public function approach to those functions that are traditionally exclusive to the state. The Court has found few functions that satisfy this exclusivity requirement."[124] See Figure 3.8[125] for a portrayal of the many public functions performed by

FUNCTIONS OF PRIVATE SECURITY PERSONNEL
Guard and Patrol Services and Personnel

Guard and patrol services include the provision of personnel who perform the following functions, either contractually or internally, at such places and facilities as industrial plants, financial institution, educational institutions, office buildings, retail establishments, commercial complexes (including hotels and motels), health care facilities, recreation facilities, libraries and museums, residential and housing developments, charitable institutions, transportation vehicles and facilities (public and common carriers) and warehouse and goods distribution depots:

- Prevention and/or detection of intrusion, unauthorized entry or activity, vandalism, or trespass on private property;
- Prevention and/or detection of theft, loss, embezzlement, misappropriation or concealment of merchandise, money, bonds, stocks, notes, or other valuable documents or papers;
- Control, regulation, or direction of the flow or movement of the public, whether by vehicle or otherwise, to assure the protection of property;
- Protection of individuals from bodily harm; and
- Enforcement of rules, regulations, and policies related to crime reduction.

Investigative Services and Personnel

The major services provided by the investigative component of private security may be provided contractually or internally at places and facilities, such as industrial plants, financial institutions, educational institutions, retail establishments, commercial complexes, hotels and motels, and health care facilities. The services are provided for a variety of clients, including insurance companies, law firms, retailers, and individuals. Investigative personnel are primarily concerned with obtaining information with reference to any of the following matters:

- Crime or wrongs committed or threatened;
- The identity, habits, conduct, movements, whereabouts, affiliations, associations, transactions, reputation, or character or any person, group of persons, association or organization, society, other group of persons or partnership or corporation;
- Preemployment background checks of personnel applicants;
- The conduct, honesty, efficiency, loyalty, or activities of employees, agents, contractors, and subcontractors;
- Incidents and illicit or illegal activities by persons against the employer or employer's property;
- Retail shoplifting;
- Internal theft by employees or other employee crime;
- The trust or falsity of any statement or representation;
- The whereabouts of missing persons;
- The location or recovery of lost or stolen property;
- The causes and origin of or responsibility for fires, libels or slanders, losses, accidents, damage, or injuries to property;
- The credibility of informants, witnesses, or other persons; and
- The securing of evidence to be used before investigating committees, boards of award or arbitration, or in the trial of civil or criminal cases and the preparation thereof.

Figure 3.8 Functions of private security personnel.

private security. Not only is the occupation alleged to be "public," its multiple tasks and competencies are "public" in design and scope.

The theory of public function was first advocated in *Marsh v. Alabama*.[126] The case involved a company town, which was privately owned, though its services and functions mirrored a typical municipality or city. Services undertaken primarily for the benefit of the general public, and exercising functions traditionally associated with a form of sovereignty, can lead to a public function charge. Advocates of the public function doctrine assertively point out that all police functions are inherently public in nature and design. "Policing is one of the most basic functions of the sovereign when security personnel are hired to protect business premises, arrest, question and search for evidence against criminal suspects. They perform public police functions."[127] In the eyes of Professor William J. O'Donnell, in his article, *"Private Security, Privacy in the Fourth Amendment,"*[128] courts give far too much credence to the legal status of the party performing the public function rather than the function itself. He notes persuasively:

> On the other hand where status does not correspond with function courts have been too quick to rule out state action. Security guards who have not been deputized, specially commissioned, or otherwise formally charged to protect public interest are routinely equated with private persons by courts despite the fact they are hired to survey, apprehend, detain, and interrogate criminal suspects.[129]

Professor O'Donnell proposes a reorientation to function in place of occupational status. State action, therefore, is evaluated in light of what is done rather than who is doing it.

> This kind of problem exists, of course, largely because legal authorities continue to define state action principally on the basis of status rather than function—a *de jure* as opposed to a *de facto* orientation. As long as this remains the approach, however, the threats to individual privacy rights will increase in proportion to the privatization of policing. A functional approach ... subject[s] the greater portion of private security industry to Fourth Amendment coverage.[130]

That security performs an enormous array of public functions, which include, but are not limited to, arresting shoplifters, controlling crowds, keeping peace in educational institutions, correctional institutions, providing secure environments in banks, hospitals, and other institutions open to the general public, is not a debatable contention. If this be so, does participation in public functions automatically lead to public status? Did the framers of the Constitution intend constitutional coverage to be tied to questions of occupational function? Arguing that police work is "public" cannot rationally lead to the demand that private security officers conducting similar roles and functions are no longer private operatives. And if this legal argument be accepted would not toll collectors and maintenance workers be next in line for this constitutional scrutiny because they do public things? If this reasoning is adopted, the public function theory could be applied in numerous other environments, including all governmental agencies, social service centers, and welfare offices. While the comparison is not strictly valid, it does shed some light on the complexity of the public function doctrine. The intellectual and legal obstacles to the public function doctrine compel the "apparent hostility of the Supreme Court to expansion of any state action doctrines."[131] Despite this, some commentators are optimistic regarding the public function theory. The public function analysis is particularly persuasive when applied to cases involving private security protection because the roles and function of either group meld together so readily.

The demands of modern commerce have created a need for large numbers of private security forces to assist in the protection of persons and property. Private security companies and their personnel engage in activities that are normally and naturally reserved to the police. They often have authority to detain suspects, conduct investigations, and make arrests. Their actions can be as intrusive to individual privacy rights as those carried out by the police. Whether these activities can be construed or defined strictly as governmental functions and thereby as state action subject to the Fourth Amendment may be a breach too difficult to fill.[132]

On top of these considerations, the argument disregards the rights of citizens, businesses, and industries who purposely employ a chosen method or technique of private law enforcement to protect their property interests. Certainly, state action doctrines provide a vehicle for extending the Fourth Amendment to some private search cases, but to propose that the function controls legal application constitutes questionable legal logic. If function becomes the dominating factor, then status becomes irrelevant. In *People v. Holloway*,[133] a Michigan court emphatically stressed the Fourth Amendment's limits. The facts of the case involve a private security guard surveying a consumer acting in a suspicious manner, and according to the guard, about to shoplift. The guard noticed the bulge in the defendant's pocket and subsequent pat down revealed a .32 caliber pistol and knife. The defendant argued a violation of the Fourth Amendment which the court denied.

> Thus an individual has the right to address any wrongs which may have been committed by private citizens be they security guards or not. They can bring civil actions or file defenders. It is because the cloak of sovereign immunity is wrapped around law enforcement officials that the Fourth Amendment is applied to their actions. There is a growing feeling among the courts of the country that the exclusionary rule has been stretched far beyond its original and very useful purpose.[134]

A dissenting opinion in the *Holloway* case, by Judge Falkman, provides a thoughtful counter:

> Surely it will be argued that the mere fact of licensing alone does not a public official make. It is true that recitation of a familiar "talismanic formula" … has soothing effect on those who invoke it. Even fervent incantation cannot dispel the reality of what function is being licensed here, that of protection of person or property by an organized peacekeeping force.[135]

As eloquent as the reasoning may be, to uphold the public function argument may lead to greater difficulties than maintaining the status quo. Public function theorists posit that a private citizen's privacy rights are undermined when the unreasonableness of a search is "made to depend on the identity of the searcher rather than the activity itself and its infringement on his privacy."[136] This argument was unconvincingly made in *New Hampshire v. Keyser*.[137] The setting included a department store shopper who switched the contents of a $6.99 cooler with two tape decks worth a total of $150. The defendant claimed he had no knowledge of how the tape decks got into the box. Upon conviction, the defendant appealed, asserting that his Fourth Amendment rights were violated, not by the members of the local police department, but instead by the security guards. The court noted the issues:

> The question in this case is whether the Fourth Amendment protections extend to the action of the security guards because of their authority, official appearance and police-type function.[138]

Providing security in a retail store environment is an insufficient basis to invoke the exclusionary rule.[139] Hence, the future of the public function argument appears less likely to expand into the private security domain as other competitive theories.

3.3.1.2.1 Color of State Law: A Legislative Remedy

When constitutionalism cannot directly apply due to the private action defense, the appellate strategist considers legal actions based on a statutory schema that touches the constitutional theory although in a tangential way. The Civil Rights Acts, going back to the Civil War, sought to enforce the intent and purpose of the Bill of Rights and to ensure a fair and equitable application of the Bill of Rights when states and individuals sought to bypass it. Most of the early Civil Rights Act dealt with voting rights and equal opportunity that various Southern states sought to avoid after the end of the Civil War. Instead of a plea rooted in the Bill of Rights, the advocate urges remedial action based on a particular code or section of a particular act. For example, claims based on civil rights infractions and violations are commonly witnessed in the actions against private security personnel. Borrowing from the civil rights theater, plaintiffs assert civil rights violations, infractions, and other wrongs by utilizing the "color of state law" standard discoverable at 42 U.S.C. § 1983.[140] To act under the "Color of State Law" is to act under its approval—that government approves the particular action giving rise to harm.[141]

"To state a § 1983 claim, a plaintiff must show two things: that he or she has been deprived of a right, and that the party who caused the deprivation acted under color of state law…"[142] Put another way, the advocate does not claim a harm arising under a particular amendment but rather an injury to self or property caused by a specific action which eventually connects to some state action. That action is under the "color" of state authority. Hence, the public police officer is always acting under the "color of state law" by his or her very authority. The question of whether this remedy applies to the private security officer is obviously not as clear or applicable. For example, when a campus police officer, employed and overseen under a contract security relationship, works in a state-owned university of college, are the actions "public" enough to justify the application of 42 USC 1983? Some emphatically declare that this the proper conclusion.

Regardless of the source of authority, campus police forces often act with the broad power of law enforcement, such as the ability to make arrests, carry firearms, and make traffic stops. When considering whether campus police forces are state actors, courts have struggled to reconcile the near-uniform exercise of power with the varying methods of granting such power. Explicit, uniform statutes will help courts clarify and understand campus police forces' role in law enforcement and make their status as state actors explicit. Encouraging states to adopt similar standards when granting authority to campus police will consequently solve a procedural difficulty courts face, as well as the substantive problem of ensuring that no citizen is deprived of his or her rights without a remedy.[143]

In addition, the Act may call for some sort of relational proof as to matters of race, creed, or ethnicity—a sort of discriminatory motivation as impetus for the action. So matters of equal protection arise in a retail theft policy, which targets specific groups of people. Proof or demonstration that a state action caused a personal loss, affront, or indignity under the auspices of color of state law, are part and parcel of the *Civil Rights Acts*—and in select portions of said Acts, these allegations must be grounded in matters that are racially, religiously, or ethnically motivated. Examples might be arbitrary state licensing boards or bodies that reject applications on racial grounds, or denial or rejection of applicants based on religion or creed. Another claim might be a contrived or intentional plan to single out targeted minority groups in a shoplifting deterrence program.[144]

To discover how private casino employees can act under color of state law, see: http://www. martindale.com/business-law/article_Lewis-Roca-LLP_813180.htm

To claim that security officers or other personnel, in a retail theft plan, are acting under color of state law requires objective proof of a racial, religious, or gender motivation, or at least a demonstration that the acts alleged and the injury inflicted were done in contravention to approved laws relating to equal opportunity.[145] The *Civil Rights Acts* have leaned toward a more liberal application in recent years with its emphasis on personal harm arising because of government action by government personnel. *United States v. McGreevy*[146] provides instruction on the color of state law standard in regards to whether or not the government actor is acting under color of state law. McGreevy's facts consist of a security officer who held two jobs, one at a Federal Express company, and the other as an agent with the Drug Enforcement Administration (DEA). In his capacity as a security officer, he had the right to inspect and open packages that were not properly identified or appeared to be mislabeled or mismarked. During a routine investigation, he found a package that rattled, and upon inspection, illegal drugs were discovered. The defendant proposed that the employee with dual jobs was acting under color of state as a DEA agent. The court, much to the dismay of the defendant, disregarded his DEA affiliation and reminded the defendant that the opening of a package occurred under auspices of his Federal Express position. It held categorically:

> Here Petre was not acting under a color of state law when he opened a package. Petre did not hold his Federal Express position because he was a police officer. He carefully separated the two jobs. He knew of no understanding between Federal Express and the DEA for the disposal of contraband.[147]

A well-respected Pennsylvania Superior Court decision, *Commonwealth v. Lacey*,[148] assessed an appellant's claim that a statute governing security guard conduct provided a basis for a color of state law declaration. The Court, in interpreting a retail theft statute, dealt precisely with the color of state question:

> A peace officer, merchant, or merchant's employee, or an agent under contract with a merchant who has probable cause to believe that retail theft has occurred or is occurring on or about a store or other retail mercantile establishment and has probable cause to believe that a specific person has committed or is committing the retail theft may detain the suspect in a reasonable manner for a reasonable time on or off the premises for all or any of the following purposes: to require the suspect to identify himself, to verify such identification, to determine whether such suspect has in his possession un-purchased merchandise taken from the mercantile establishment, and, if so, to recover such merchandise, to inform a peace officer or to institute criminal proceedings against the suspect, such detention shall not impose civil or criminal liability on the peace officer, merchant, employee or agent so detaining.[149]

The appellant's reasoning concludes that the retail theft statute, in its terms and applicability, inherently bestows police powers on private persons which the Court completely rejected.

To prove color of state law requires proof of a direct relationship between a public official and private security agent. The evidence must demonstrate significant involvement of the private agent acting under a state law and as a result, causing injury. In *Bouye v. Marshall*,[150] a U.S. District

Court held, in the rarest of cases, that an off-duty county police officer crossed the line from private to public since he "wore a police sweatshirt and bullet-proof vest, displayed badge, was performing police function, and used police authority to detain and search visitor."[151]

To prove color of state law cases, the courts have devised a series of tests that seek to quantify the level of state involvement, such as the *significant involvement test*. The test mandates a look at how much state action and state oversight played a role in the harm inflicted while simultaneously looking for participatory schemes between state and federal officials. In *Byars v. United States*,[152] the Supreme Court held that evidence was inadmissible when the unreasonable search and seizure was performed by state officials concluding that state law enforcement was significant enough to satisfy the term "significant." In *Gambino v. United States*,[153] the Supreme Court also employed the *significant involvement test*, ruling inadmissible evidence that was seized and acquired by New York State Police in an unjustifiable search, met the color of state law standard. The Court was satisfied that the wrongful arrest, search, and seizure was performed for the benefit and exclusive purpose of federal prosecution, and therefore, "the state officers acting to enforce the federal law were subject to the Fourth Amendment just as if they acted under federal direction."[154] Finding significant involvement or participation between state and federal agents, however, is very different from deducing that the actions of the private security industry and police are equally in concert.

Another argument bolstering color of state law theory is the *police security nexus test*. "Under the nexus approach to state action analysis, a court considers the facts of the situation, looks for a contact between the private actor and the government, and makes a qualitative judgment as to whether there is enough involvement in a challenged action to say that it was an action of the state."[155] As in previous attempts to corral in the protection of the Fourth Amendment, liberal constructionists must show either a significant involvement; a private action fostered, authorized, or colored by state authority; or a public–private relationship conspiratorial in design. The natural procedural ties that develop between private security and public policing give further ammunition to those who propose an expansion of the color of state law theory. Since both public and private law enforcement seek similar ends, are hankering for increased cooperation, and are increasing their overall interaction, some critics call for an end to the immune status accorded private practice.[156] Not unexpectedly, public law enforcement has long been considered the private security industry feeder system for informants and assistance. There is a pipeline of trained investigators and security administrators moving from public law enforcement agencies into the private sector. These agencies train the personnel in patrol techniques, investigation, interrogation, arrest, search and seizure, and police administration. Years of experience working with these agencies give security officers a common language, a common method of operation, and common outlook with those who stayed beyond.[157]

Professor Euller, in his article in the *Harvard Civil Rights and Civil Liberties Law Review*, contends that police officers have no sense of changeover or "crossing over to the other side" when they join private security systems.[158]

Consequently, scholarly commentary has emphasized a reexamination of the state action in private security activities. Since a close and symbiotic relationship is emerging with public law enforcement, and since the procedural ramifications of private justice are starting to have a more marked impact on the public justice system, further study is necessary.

3.4 Constitutional Prognosis for Private Security

One of the chief reasons claimed for the phenomenal growth of the security industry is its ability to avoid the often complex and convoluted legalities that hamper public police operations. Equally crucial is the security industry's ability to avoid the political machinations that so encumber local, municipal, and federal police departments. Police departments, not security departments, are concerned with statistics, clearance sheets, and the general political issues that emerge in major municipal police departments. "Private agency police appear to be even less conviction-oriented than the public police. They seem to be concerned primarily with the protection of property and personnel."[159]

The hostility toward the expansion of rights into the private security realm has been fairly obvious in appellate case law review despite the academic clamor for that expansion. Even the United Nations is now parlaying an opinion on the need to regulate since it sees the industry as a global component in every security plan.[160]

A case in point includes *Sackler v. Sackler*,[161] from the New York Court of Appeals. A wife, appealing a grant of divorce on the basis of adultery, sought to exclude from evidence information acquired by private investigators employed by her husband. Surprisingly, defense counsel relied upon *Mapp v. Ohio*[162] as a basis for its decision, stating cynically:

> The theory seems to run like this: before *Mapp* the law of evidence in this state was the same as to all illegal searches whether governmental or not, that is, all evidence so produced was receivable. Now we are told that ... evidence which is the fruit of illegal government incursions is banned ... except when under non-governmental auspices. The argument goes too far and proves too much.[163]

The court, citing *Burdeau v. McDowell*[164] and other representative precedents, stated that neither "history, logic, nor law give any support for the idea that uniform treatment should be given to governmental and private searches to the evidence disclosed by such searches."[165] When research divulges such spirited appellate ponderings, the expansionists' reasoning pulls at straws. Creative, innovative approaches that afford protection to the general citizenry are always commendable, but to develop various theories of argumentation that fail to withstand legal rigor assures futility for Fourth Amendment applicability in private sector justice. The expansionist camp has to formulate rock-hard, substantive ideas based on the occupational nexus between private and public and criminal procedure. It would be foolhardy to argue a lack of parallels between the private and public police systems, but the similarities are not compelling enough to afford this extraordinary transformation. "Courts and commentators alike should be sensitive to the possibility that the existing powers and controls of private police may require alteration,"[166] but alteration does not require or lead jurors, practitioners, or academics to the conclusion that what is good for public justice is equally necessary in the private world of professional security. As Eugene Finneran, in his excellent text, *Security Supervision: A Handbook for Supervisors and Managers*, imparts:

> The other side of the controversy believes, as does the author, that it is impossible to separate security from a degree of law enforcement or to separate loss prevention from crime prevention. Even if it were possible to eradicate the joint history of public and private safety and security operations, it would be a mistake to do so. All previous expertise in the protection of assets through crime prevention must be maintained and built upon using this experience as solid base for developing all the skills necessary to become viable risk managers. All professional fields are constantly changing and searching for better methods and procedures for improving performance. Security is no exception.[167]

Clearly, private sector justice cannot infallibly mimic or imitate public sector justice. Its obligation rests principally in distinct though complimentary mission when compared to the public sector.[168] By any reasonable measure, it should draw from public sector justice the best it has to offer—namely the public police system's dedication to fundamental fairness and due process. Other public sector traits to emulate include the system's adherence to procedural guidelines, substantive rules and regulations that ensure equity, and an academic and political community of both practitioners and theorists who call to the forefront deficiencies in the American administration of justice. Probably the greatest catalyst in ensuring additional adherence to the public justice model will be the security industry's own desire and motivation as it treks down the long path of professionalism.

3.5 Summary

A review of case law, statutory materials, and common law principles concludes that the expansionists' theory of constitutional protection, as to the arrest, search, and seizure principles in private security, garners little intellectual or judicial support. Scholarly and academic materials urge increased constitutional oversight in private sector justice, but jurists and legislators alike have turned a deaf ear. The arguments posed throughout this section have included attempts, disguised in different forms, to show that the task of private sector justice is, at best, mimicry of public law enforcement. While there may be cooperation between public and private law enforcement in the fight against crime, and while there is frequent interaction between the two camps, only the public system, as the Constitution intends, is subject to the severest form of judicial scrutiny. The Constitution was designed and devised for the protection of the general citizenry from overzealous government regulation, taxation, and oversight. Arguably, the chief basis for the American Revolution was to remove the onerous restrictions and heavy-handed bureaucracy that government had thrust upon the colonists. From this it is fair to conclude that expansion of this ideology into the private realm, into private security itself, would be contrary to American legal tradition.

CASE EXAMPLES

State of Tennessee v. Gregory D. Hutson, 649 S.W. 2d 6 (1982)

Facts

On April 16, 1981, a security guard for the Knoxville Job Corps responded to an alarm indicating that someone was on the third floor of the Job Corps Center. He pushed the elevator button to go to that floor and found it to be already stopped there. Proceeding up the stairwell, he observed a person entering the elevator, and he watched as it descended to the first floor. When the elevator returned to the third floor, it was necessary for him to open the door with a key. In doing this, he found the defendant, Mr. Hutson, inside the elevator. Hutson was taken to the security office, where he was detained by other personnel. During the interrogation of Mr. Hutson, the security guard and other personnel felt that they had detained the right thief. As a result of this determination, Job Corps officials entered into the room of Mr. Hutson and ordered him to break the lock on his locker in his residential quarters. Once inside the locker, stolen goods related to the third floor thefts were found.

Issue

On a motion to suppress the admission of evidence based upon a constitutional violation of a search performed without a warrant, how should this court rule?

Private Search and Seizure—United States of America v. Lacey Lee Koenig and Lee Graf, 856 F.2d 843 (7th Cir. 1988)

Facts

On July 17, 1986, Federal Express Senior Security Specialist Jerry Zito was at the West Palm Federal Express station on what he described as a "routine station visit." While there, he conducted a visual inspection of packages received over the counter and detected an odor of laundry soap or fabric softener emanating from one of the boxes. The shipper of record was fictitious. The officer opened the package. Inside were two transparent plastic bags containing white powder that the DEA office identified as cocaine.

After replacing all but a small sample of the cocaine with cornstarch, the package was resealed. After consulting a DEA agent, the officer returned the package to the West Palm Beach Federal Express office with instructions to perform a controlled delivery. The package was routed through the Federal Express hub in Memphis, Tennessee. While in Memphis, the package was kept in a Federal Express safe and was opened on two occasions by Federal Express employees to check its contents. The box was once again opened upon its arrival in Peoria, Illinois, on July 19, this time by Illinois State Police and a Federal Express employee. Again the contents tested positive for cocaine. The package was again sealed and then delivered to its intended recipient, one Koenig. A federal search warrant was then obtained and executed on Koenig's apartment, resulting in the seizure of several items including the Federal Express package containing the packets of cornstarch and cocaine samples.

Issue

Have defendants been constitutionally violated by this warrantless search?

Answer

No, Federal Express security personnel opened the package for their own reasons and no evidence was introduced suggesting governmental control of Federal Express employees. The opening of the package and the placement of its contents in plain view of DEA destroyed any privacy interest the package might have initially supported.

DISCUSSION QUESTIONS

1. Constitutional remedies in cases involving private security investigators and detectives will be rare. Why?
2. Relay a fact pattern whereby a private security operative may trigger the exclusionary rule.
3. Private security industry's right to arrest is governed by what standard?
4. Which Supreme Court case indicated a reticence or hesitancy to extend constitutional protections to private sector justice?
5. Name five exceptions to the actual warrant requirement.
6. Under some merchant privilege statutes, even if the merchant is completely incorrect in carrying out an arrest, the merchant remains immune from a false imprisonment or arrest cause of action. Explain.
7. How does private conduct transform into state action?
8. Can it be argued that private security is continuously involved in public duties and functions?
9. What is the prognosis for constitutional protections, as to arrest, search and seizure, being applied in the private security industry?

NOTES

1 Charles P. Nemeth and K.C. Poulin, *Private Security and Public Safety: A Community-Based Approach*, 2005.
2 256 U.S. 465, 1921.

3 William J. O'Donnell, *Private security, privacy and the fourth amendment, J. Sec. Admin.* 9, 1984; 7.

4 For an interesting case on the mix of security guard services and the removal of Middle Eastern head dress, see: Fareed v. G4S Secure Solutions, 942 F.Supp.2d 738, 2013.

5 See Paul A. Campo, Note: The need for reform of Missouri's peace officer training requirements: A historical, economic and legal perspective, *UMKC L. Rev.* 681, 1998; 66; David A. Sklansky, The private police, *UCLA L. Rev.* 1165 (1999); 46; Lynn M. Gagel, Stealthy encroachments upon the Fourth Amendment: Constitutional constraints and their applicability to the long arm of Ohio's private security forces, *U. Cin. L. Rev.* 1807, 1995; 63; Malcolm K. Sparrow, Managing the boundary between public and private policing, *New Perspectives in Policing*, September 2014, https://www.ncjrs.gov/pdffiles1/nij/247182.pdf.

6 Private Security Advisory Council, Scope of Legal Authority of Private Security Personnel, Law Enforcement Assistance Administration, 3 (U.S. Department of Justice, 1979); See generally John D. Peel, *Fundamentals of Training for Security Officers*, 1970; Guy R. Rankin, *The Professional Handbook for Patrol and Security Guards*, 1977; Sullivan, *Legal Problems of Private Security Forces*, paper delivered at International Security Conference, October 3, 1972.

7 Andrew P. Morriss, *Returning justice to its private roots, U. Chi. L. Rev.* 551, 2001 68.

8 Leigh J. Jahnig, Under school colors: Private university police as state actors under Sec. 1983, *NW Univ. L. Rev.* 249 (2015); 110, http://scholarlycommons.law.northwestern.edu/cgi/viewcontent.cgi?article=1228&context=nulr.

9 U.S. Const. amend. IV.

10 Ernest W. Machen, Jr., *The Law of Search and Seizure*, 1950; Joseph A. Varon, *Searches, Seizures and Immunities*, 1974; Note, The concept of privacy and the Fourth Amendment, *U. Mich. J. L. Rev.* 154, 1972; 6; Note, From private places to personal privacy: A post-Katz study of Fourth Amendment protections, *N.Y.U. L. Rev.* 96, 1968; 43; Blancard, Clark, and Everett, *Uniform Security Guard Power To Arrest, Part II*, 1977; Fred E. Inbau, *Protective Security Law*, 1983.

11 Note, Seizures by private parties: Exclusion in criminal cases, *Stan. L. Rev.* 608, 608-609, 1967; 19.

12 256 U.S. 465, 1921.

13 *Burdeau v. McDowell*, 256 U.S. 465, 475, 1921.

14 See generally *Smith v. Maryland*, 59 U.S. (18 How.) 71, 76, 1855; *Barron v. Baltimore*, 32 U.S. (7 Pet.) 243, 250, 1833.

15 See *U.S. v. Janis*, 428 U.S. 433, 456 n. 31, 1976; *Coolidge v. New Hampshire*, 403 U.S. 443, 487, 1971; *Walter v. U.S.* 48 U.S. L.W. 4807, 1980; see contra *People v. Eastway*, 241 N.W. 2nd 249, 1976.

16 Note, The legal basis of authority, *Sec. Mgmt.* 50, 1982; 26; See also Rick Sarre, The legal basis for the authority of private police and an examination of their relationship with the "public" police (1992), available at http://www.aic.gov.au/publications/previous%20series/proceedings/1-27/~/media/publications/proceedings/23/sarre.ashx.

17 Nemeth and Poulin, *Public Safety*; see also Charles P. Nemeth and K.C. Poulin, *The Prevention Agency: A Public Safety Model for High Crime Communities in the 21st Century*, 2004.

18 National Advisory Committee on Criminal Justice Standards and Goals, Report on the Task Force on Private Security 391, 1976. Some prognosticators on the constitutionality of private security arrests argue that this question is still in flux. See James F. Pastor, *Security Law & Methods*, 2006; James F. Pastor, *The Privatization of Police in America: An Analysis and Case Study*, 2003.

19 *The Security Function* 67, 1980.

20 Note, The law of citizen's arrest, *Colum. L. Rev.* 502 (1965); 65. See also Lael Harrison, Citizen's arrest or police arrest? Defining the scope of Alaska's delegated citizen's arrest doctrine, *Wash. L. Rev.*, 2007; 82.

21 National Advisory Committee, at 393.

22 Note, Private police forces: Legal powers and limitations, *U. Chic. L. Rev.* 565, 1971; 38. See also Pastor, *Security Law*; Pastor, *Privatization of Police*.

23 Alaska Stat. § 12.25.030, 2010.

24 N.Y. C.P.L. § 140.30, 2010.

25 *People v. Niedzwiedz*, 268 Ill. App. 3d 119, 644 N.E.2d 53, 55, (Ill. App. Ct. 1994) cited in *Churney v. Downer's Grove*, 83 F.SUPP. 2d 925, 927 (N.C. Ill, 2000) (citing 725 ILCS5/107-3, stating that "any person may arrest another when he has reasonable grounds to believe that an offense other than an ordinance violation is being committed").

26 Edward T. Guy, John J. Merrigan, and John A. Wanat, *Forms for Safety and Security Management* 390, 1981.

27 Charles P. Nemeth, *Private Security and Investigative Process*, 3rd ed., 2010; 226–227.

28 *Note, Citizen's Arrest*, at 504.

29 National Advisory Committee, at 391.

30 Private Security Advisory Council, at 10.

31 *Note, Citizen's Arrest*, at 505.

32 Id. at 506.

33 Id. at 506–507.

34 National Advisory Committee, at 394.

35 *Restatement of the Law of Torts*, § 119 (1934; 2d ed. 1966).

36 *Weeks v. United States*, 232 U.S. 383, 1914.

37 367 U.S. 643, 1961; See also *Massiah v. U.S.*, 377 U.S. 201, 1964; *Miranda v. Arizona*, 384 U.S. 436, 1966; *Escobedo v. Illinois*, 378 U.S. 478, 1964; See generally Note, "Plain View"—Anything but Plain: Coolidge Divides the Lower Courts, 7 Loy. *L.A. L. Rev.* 489 (1974); Edward G. Mascolo, The role of abandonment in the law of search and seizure: An application of misdirected emphasis, *Buff. L. Rev.* 399, 1971; 20. *Annot. Admissibility, in Criminal Case, of Evidence Obtained by Search by Private Individual*, 36 ALR 3d 553.

38 For an interesting case on aerial search see *California v. Ciraolo*, 476 U.S. 207, 106 S. CT. 1009, 1986.

39 392 U.S. 1, 1968.

40 See *Aguilar v. Texas*, 378 U.S. 108; *Spinelli v. U.S.*, 393 U.S. 410, 89 S. CT. 584, 1969; *U.S. v. Haris*, 403 U.S. 573, 91 S.CT. 2075, 1971.

41 See *Harlow v. Fitzgerald*, 457 U.S. 800, 807, 102 S.CT. 2727, 73 L.ED.2d 396, 1982.

42 *Browning v. Vernon*, 44 F.3d 818, 822 (9th Cir. 1995) (citing Act Up/Portland v. Bagley, 988 F.2d 868, 871–872 (9th Cir. 1993).

43 *Hunter v. Bryant*, 502 U.S. 224, 229, 112 S.CT. 534, 116 L.ED.2d 589 (1991) quoting *Malley v. Brigges*, 475 U.S. 335, 343, 106 S.CT. 1092, 89 L.ED. 2d. 271, 1986.

44 *Corcoran v. Fletcher*, 160 F.SUPP.2d 1085, 1089 (C.D. Ca. 2001).

45 256 U.S. 465, 1921.

46 Id.

47 John W. Hall, Jr., *Search and Seizure Inapplicability of the Fourth Amendment*, 1982; 53.

48 Scope of Legal Authority of Private Security Personnel, https://www.ncjrs.gov/pdffiles1/Digitization/146908NCJRS.pdf.

49 Note, Private police forces: Legal powers and limitations, *U. Chic. L. Rev.*, 38, 1971; 565–566.

50 *Private Security Advisory Council*, at 3.

51 Id. at 15.

52 Id.

53 5 *Am. Jur. Trials* 389–391. Reprinted from *Am Jur Trials* with permission of Thomson Reuters.

54 594 P. 2d 1000 (1979).

55 Id.

56 Id. at 1002.

57 Id. at 1006.

58 Id. at 1005.

59 Stephen Euller, Private security in the courtroom: The exclusionary rule applies, *Sec. Mgmt.* 41, 1980; 24.

60 Id.

61 449 N.W.2d 471 (Minn. App. 1989).

62 *State of Minnesota v. Buswell*, 449 N.W.2d 471, 474 (Minn. App. 1989).

63 Private Security, *Public Order: The Outsourcing of Public Services and its Limits* (Simon Chesterman & Angelina Fisher, eds. 2009).

64 326 U.S. 501, 66 S.CT. 276, 90 L.ED. 265 (1946).

65 Id. at 506. See 1 W. LaFave, § 1.8(d) at 200. See also Feffer, 831 F.2d at 739; See also *State of Minnesota v. Buswell*, 449 N.W.2d 471, 474 (Minn. App. 1989).

66 For an interesting analysis of this transformation from the former Eastern bloc nation of Estonia, see Nele Parrest, Constitutional boundaries of transfer of public functions to private sector in Estonia, *Juridica International*, 44, 2009; 16, available at http://www.juridicainternational.eu/public/pdf/ji_2009_1_44.pdf.

67 *State of Minnesota v. Buswell*, 449 N.W.2d 471, 474 (Minn. App. 1989).

68 Id.

69 Note, The legal basis of authority, *Sec. Mgmt.* 54, 1982; 26.

70 See *Weeks v. U.S.*, 232 U.S. 383 (1914); *Wolf v. People of The State of Colo.* 338 U.S. 25, 1949.

71 Lacey Perkins, Note: A circumstantial defense: Determining the applicability of the good faith defense for campus security in Sec. 1983 Cases, 19 Suffolk *J. Trial & App. Advocacy* 176 (2013–2014).

72 See *Lustig v. U.S.*, 338 U.S. 74, 79, 1949; *Elkins v. U.S.*, 364 U.S. 200, 1960. See also Martin McGuinness, The "silver platter" In the context of state constitutional adjudication, *Albany Law Review*, 2008; available at http://www.albanylawreview.org/articles/McGuinness.pdf.

73 Note, The platinum platter in Ohio: Are private police really private? *U. Dayton L. Rev.* 290, 1977; 2.

74 Id. at 287–288.

75 Case No. 3:13-CR-00017, 2014 U.S. Dist. LEXIS (M.D.TN 2014).

76 *United States v. Lambert*, 771 F.2d 83, 89 (6th Cir. 1985) ("[T]he Fourth Amendment proscribes only governmental action and does not apply to a search or seizure, even an unreasonable one, conducted by a private individual not acting as an agent of the government or with the participation or knowledge of any government official."); *United States v. Coleman*, 628 F.2d 961, 965 (6th Cir. 1980) ("[T]he Fourth Amendment proscribes only governmental action, and does not apply to a search or seizure, even an unreasonable one, effected by a private individual not acting as an agent of the government or with the participation or knowledge of any governmental official"); see also *United States v. Smythe*, 84 F.3d 1240, 1243 (10th Cir. 1996) ("Fourth Amendment protection against unreasonable searches and seizures 'is wholly inapplicable to a search or seizure, even an unreasonable one, effected by a private individual.'") (citing *United States v. Jacobsen*, 466 U.S. 109, 113 (1984)); *United States v. Day*, 591 F.3d 679, 683 (4th Cir. 2010).

77 *U.S. v. Brooks*, Case No. 3:13-CR-00017, 2014 U.S. Dist. LEXIS 13732 (M.D. TN 2014) *7.

78 See: Julie K. Brown, Less is more; Decluttering the state action doctrine, *Mo. L. Rev.* 561, 2008; 73, http://scholarship.law.missouri.edu/cgi/viewcontent.cgi?article=3775&context=mlr.

79 Note, Private searches and seizures: An application of the public function theory, *Geo. Wash. L. Rev.* 185, 1980; 48.

80 Kevin L. Cole, Federal and state "state action": The undercritical embrace of a hypercriticized doctrine, *Ga. L. Rev.* 327, 343, 1990; 24.

81 Charles L. Black, Jr., Foreword: "State action," equal protection, and California's proposition 14, *Harv. L. Rev.* 69, 95, 1967; 81.

82 See Julie K. Brown, Less is more; Decluttering the state action doctrine, *Mo. L. Rev.* 561, 561, 2008; 73, http://scholarship.law.missouri.edu/cgi/viewcontent.cgi?article=3775&context=mlr.

83 See *Coolidge v. New Hampshire*, 403 U.S. 443, 487, 1971; *U.S. v. Guest*, 383 U.S. 745, 771–772, 1966.

84 See particularly *Burton v. Wilmington Parking Authority*, 365 U.S. 715, 1961.

85 Case No. 01-4016-SAC, 2003 U.S. Dist. LEXIS 9367 (Kansas May 23, 2003).

86 Copeland v. City of Topeka, Case No. 01-4016-SAC, 2003 U.S. Dist. LEXIS 9367 (Kansas May 23, 2003).

87 *State v. Verkerk*, 747 S.E.2d 658 (NC Ct. App. 2013).

88 *State v. Kornegay*, 313 N.C. 1, 10, 326 S.E.2d 881, 890, 1985.

89 *State v. Verkerk*, 747 S.E.2d 658,672 (NC Ct. App. 2013).

90 547 F. 2d 891, 1977.

91 *U.S. v. Francoeur*, 547 F. 2d 891, 1977.

92 Note, Sticky fingers, deep pockets, and the long arm of the law: Illegal searches of shoplifters by private merchant security personnel, *Or. L. Rev.* 279, 283, 1976; 55.

93 John W. Hall, Jr., Search and seizure inapplicability of the Fourth Amendment, 61, 1982.

94 *U.S. v. Lima*, 424 A. 2d 13, 1980.

95 Id. at 121.

96 Id. at 119–120.

97 Note, Developments in the law: State action and the public/private distinction, *Harv L. Rev.* 1248, 2010; 123 at http://www.harvardlawreview.org/media/pdf/DEVO_10.pdf.

98 G. Sidney Buchanan, A conceptual history of the state action doctrine: The search for governmental responsibility (pt. 1), *Hous. L. Rev.* 333, 336, 1997; 34.

99 Euller, at 655; see also *Tarnef v. State*, 512 P. 2d 923, 934, 1973; *People v. Agnosepoulous*, Misc. 2d 668, 354 N.Y.S. 2d 575, 576, 1974; 77. *U.S. v. Clegg*, 509 F. 2d 605, 609–611, 1975; *People v. Moreno*, 64 Cal. App. 3D Supp. 23, 135 Cal. Rptr. 340, 1976.

100 *Synder v. State of Alaska*, 585 P. 2d 229, 1978.

101 Id. at 232.

102 *Lester v. State*, 244 S.E. 2d 880, 1978.

103 Id. at 881.

104 *Gillett v. State of Texas*, 588 S.W. 2d 361, 1979.

105 *People v. Horman*, 22 N.Y. 2d 378, 1968.

106 *State v. Keyser*, 369 A 2d 224, 1977.

107 See generally *Griffin v. Maryland* 378 U.S. 130, 1964; *People v. Diaz*, 85 Misc. 2d 41, 376 N.Y.S. 2d 849 (1975); *People v. Frank*, 52 MISC. 2d 266, 275 N.Y.S. 2d 570, 1966; *State v. Bolan*, 27 Ohio St. 2d 15, 271 N.W. 2d 839, 1971.

108 Euller, at 606.

109 *State v. Hutson*, 649 S.W. 2d 9, 1982.

110 See an excellent commentary on how a private actor may become a state actor without much fanfare at: Michael Leotta, Julia Spiegel, and Haryle Kaldis, You may already be a government agent: *United States v. Carson* and what will turn a corporate internal investigation into "state action," *Bloomberg BNA White Collar Crime Report*, 8 WCR 127, 02/22/2013, http://www.wilmerhale.com/uploaded-Files/WilmerHale_Shared_Content/Files/PDFs/BNAinsights.WilmerHale.pdf.

111 *State v. Hutson*, 649 S.W. 2d 9, 1982; see also *People v. Tolivar*, 377 N.E. 2d 207, 1978.

112 *State v. McDaniel*, 44 Ohio App. 2d 163, 377 N.W. 2d 173, 1975; see also *U.S. v. Miller*, 668 F.2d 652, 1982.

113 Id. at 180.

114 Id.

115 See *State v. Scrotsky*, 39 N.J. 410, 189 A. 2d 23, 1963; *Moody v. U.S.*, 163 A.2d 337, 1960; *People v. Tarantino*, 45 CAL. 2d 590, 290 P.2d 505, 1955; *People v. Fierro*, 238 Cal. App. 2d 344, 46 Cal. Rptr. 132, 1965.

116 Note, Seizures, at 613.

117 195 F.3d 715 (4th Cir. 1999).

118 Id. at 730.

119 Id.

120 *State v. Weaver*, 752 S.E.2d 240, 242 (N.C. Ct. App. 2013).

121 *State v. Sanders*, 327 N.C. 319, 331, 395 S.E.2d 412, 420 (1990), cert. denied,498 U.S. 1051, 111 S.Ct. 763, 112 L.Ed.2d 782, 1991.

122 For an interesting contrast on public police and traditional Hasidic community police, see: Sarah M. Sternlieb, Comment: When the eyes and ears become an arm of the state: The danger of privatization through government funding of insular religious groups, *Emory L.J.* 1411, 2013; 62.

123 See also: Alison Wakefield, *The Public Surveillance Functions of Private Security*, 2 Surveillance & Society 529, 2004, http://ojs.library.queensu.ca/index.php/surveillance-and-society/article/view/3362.

124 Leigh J. Jahnig, Under school colors: Private university police as state actors under § 1983, *NW Univ. L. Rev.* 249, 258, 2015; 110, http://scholarlycommons.law.northwestern.edu/cgi/viewcontent.cgi?article=1228&context=nulr.

125 William C. Cunningham and Todd H. Taylor, The Hallcrest Report: Private Security and Police in America, 26, 1985.

126 *Marsh v. Alabama*, 326 U.S. 501, 1946.

127 Euller, at 658.

128 O'Donnell, at 11.

129 Id. at 12.

130 W. Clinton Terry, *Policing Society*, 1985.

131 Note, Private Searches and Seizures, at 185.

132 *People v. Holloway*, 82 Mich. App. 629, 267 N.W. 2d 454, 1978.

133 Id. at 456.

134 Id. at 460.

135 Note, Private searches and seizures, at 185.

136 *State v. Keyser*, 369 A 2d 224, 1977.

137 Id. at 225.

138 Id. at 226.

139 See *Smith v. Brookshire, Inc.*, 519 F.2d 93 (5th Cir. 1975); cert denied, 424 U.S. 915, 96 S. Ct. 1115, 47 L. Ed. 2d 320, 1976; *Duriso v. K-Mart* No. 4195, Division of Kresge Co., 559 F.2d 1274 (5th Cir. 1977); *El Fundi v. Deroche*, 625 F.2d 195 (8th Cir. 1980); *White v. Scraner Corp.*, 594 F.2d 140 (5th Cir. 1979).

140 See Civil liability for acts of off-duty officers—Part I, *AELE Mo. L. J.*, 101, 2007; 9 at http://www.aele.org/law/2007LRSEP/2007-09MLJ101.pdf.

141 See: Christopher Cross, Private security officers with state police powers March 9, 2016, at https://www.linkedin.com/pulse/private-security-officers-state-police-powers-christopher; See also: Michael Leotta, Julia Spiegel, and Haryle Kaldis, You may already be a government agent: *United States v. Carson* and what will turn a corporate internal investigation into "state action," *Bloomberg BNA White Collar Crime Report*, 8 WCR 127, 02/22/2013, http://www.wilmerhale.com/uploadedFiles/WilmerHale_Shared_Content/Files/PDFs/BNAinsights.WilmerHale.pdf.

142 Leigh J. Jahnig, Under school colors: Private university police as state actors under § 1983, *NW Univ. L. Rev.* 249, 251, 2015; 110, http://scholarlycommons.law.northwestern.edu/cgi/viewcontent.cgi?article=1228&context=nulr.

143 Id. at 252.

144 *Davis v. Carson Pirie Scott and Co.*, 530 F. Supp. 799, 1982.

145 See: Shaun L. Gabbidon, Racial profiling by store clerks and security personnel in retail establishments, *J. Contemp. Crim. Justice*, 2003; 19, http://consumerequality.com/pubs/03_Racial_profiling.pdf.

146 652 F.2d 849 (9th Cir. 1981).

147 *U.S. v. McGreevy*, 652 F.2d 849, 851 (9th Cir. 1981).

148 471 A. 2d 888 (Pa. Super. 1984).

149 *Commonwealth v. Lacy*, 471 A. 2d 888 (Pa. Super. 1984).

150 102 F.Supp.2d 1357 (N.D.Ga. 2000).

151 Id. at 1358.

152 273 U.S. 28 (1927).

153 275 U.S. 310 (1927); see also *Stonehill v. U.S.*, 405 F.2d 738 (9th Cir. 1968); *U.S. v. Mekjian*, 505 F.2d 1320 (5th Cir. 1975). See also Note, Private searches and seizures, at 185.

154 Euller, at 665.

155 Id.

156 See generally National Institute of Justice, *Crime and Protection in America: A Study of Private Security and Law Enforcement Resources and Relationships*, 1985.

157 Euller, at 668.

158 Id.

159 Note, Private police forces, at 572.

160 See: United Nations Office on Drugs and Crime, State Regulation Concerning Civilian Private Security Services and Their Contribution to Crime Prevention and Community Safety, 2014, at https://www.unodc.org/documents/justice-and-prison-reform/crimeprevention/Ebook0.pdf.

161 *Sackler v. Sackler*, 15 N.Y. 2d 40.

162 367 U.S. 643, 81 S.Ct. 1684, 6 L. Ed. 1081, 1961.

163 *Sackler v. Sackler*, 15 N.Y. 2d 42.

164 256 U.S. 465, 1921.

165 *Sackler v. Sackler*, 15 N.Y. 2d 42.

166 Note, Private police forces: Legal powers and limitations, *U. Chic. L. Rev.* 583, 1971; 38.

167 Eugene D. Finneran, *Security Supervision: A Handbook for Supervisors and Managers*, 1982.

168 Sven Bislev, *Privatization of Security as Governance Problem: Gated Communities in the San Diego Region*, 29 Alternatives: Global, Local, Political, 2004.

Chapter 4

Civil Liability of Security Personnel

4.1 Introduction

By all accounts, the past four decades have evidenced phenomenal growth of the private security sector.[1] In 1972, a benchmark study was performed by James S. Kakalik and Sorrel Wildhorn for the RAND Corporation,[2] which prophetically indicated the influential role security would play in the protection of people and assets. At the same time, the RAND Report harshly criticized the security industry, observing:

> [T]he vast resources and programs of private security were overshadowed by characterizations of the average security guard—under-screened, under-trained, under-supervised and underpaid and in need of licensing and regulation to upgrade the quality of personnel and services.[3]

The Bureau of Labor Statistics portrays a bright future for the security industry through 2018 (see Figure 4.1).[4]

With new and emerging opportunities come the natural liabilities for industry personnel and its employing agencies. In this chapter, the civil realm and its corresponding liabilities, as applied to private sector justice, receives intense analysis. The industry knows how liability impacts the bottom line better than any other constituency.[5]

Visit the risk and insurance management society and discover its many resources at: http://www.rims.org/Pages/Default.aspx

---

		Employment							Output				
		Thousands of jobs			Change		Average annual rate of change		Billions of chained 2000 dollars			Average annual rate of change	
Industry	2007 NAICS	1998	2008	2018	1998–2008	2008–2018	1998–2008	2008–2018	1998	2008	2018	1998–2008	2008–2018
Investigation and security services	5616	659.0	806.8	960.0	147.8	153.2	2.0	1.8	27.8	39.8	53.6	3.6	3.0

Figure 4.1 Projected security industry job growth, 1998–2018.

The *Hallcrest Report II* corroborates this picture escalating liability.

> Perhaps the largest indirect cost of economic crime has been the increase in civil litigation and damage awards over the past 20 years. This litigation usually claims inadequate or improperly used security to protect customers, employees, tenants, and the public from crimes and injuries. Most often these cases involve inadequate security at apartments and condominiums; shopping malls, convenience and other retail stores; hotel, motels and restaurants; health care and educational institutional; office buildings; and the premises of other business or governmental facilities. Frequently, private security companies are named as defendants in such cases because they incur 2 basic types of liability: (1) negligence on the part of the security company or its employees and (2) criminal acts committed by the security company or its employees.[6]

Private sector justice is deep in the mix of things, places, and circumstances where liability problems are most likely to occur. In retail and parking complexes, in government buildings and nuclear facilities, the industry will be exposed to liability just because of how and where it carries out its responsibilities. Other locales where liability is part of the territory include

- Shopping malls, convenience stores, and other retailers
- Apartments and condominiums
- Hotels, motels, casinos, bars, and restaurants
- Health care and educational institutions
- Security service and equipment companies
- Transportation operators such as common carriers, airports, and rail and bus stations
- Governmental and privately owned office buildings and parking lots
- Sports and special event centers[7]

As the industry continues taking on increased responsibility in novel and innovative frameworks, like the cybersecurity, cyber and economic crime within the financial sector, as well as assuming community policing roles in once public policing locales, liability issues will stay on the fixed horizon of potential problems.[8] Add to this striking growth in employment the trend toward privatization itself[9] and it is only logical that accentuated levels of responsibility and legal liability are part of the security industry landscape. With increased functionaries laboring in the private sector, there will be a corresponding increase in legal liability. The *Hallcrest Report II* sees nothing but continuous employment growth for private sector justice.

Total private security employment is expected to increase to 1.9 million by the decade's end. The present rate of change in employment from 1980 to 2000 is approximately 193%. The annual rate of growth in employment is anticipated to be about 2.3%, roughly double the rate of employment growth for the national workforce. By 2000 there will be 7 private security workers for each group of 1000 Americans, an increase of 1 from 1990. Further, by 2000 there will be about 13 private security employees for each group of 1000 workers in the nation—also an increase of 1 employee from the 1990 figure.[10]

The National Center for Policy Analysis (NCPA) foretells a further expansion of private justice function. Since the mid-1960s, the economic impact of private sector justice has been significant by any measure, as the NCPA notes:

■ There are nearly three times as many private security guards as public law enforcement officers, 1.5 million in 1990, and the private sector spends almost twice as much on private security as we pay in taxes to support the public police.
■ Private bounty hunters, or bail enforcements agents, make the private bail bonding system work for persons accused of crimes by tracking down and apprehending those who try to flee.
■ And the private sector on occasion has been used innovatively in other ways to prepare cases for district attorneys, to prosecute criminal cases, and to employ prisoners behind bars.[11]

At every level of the private security industry, including contract services, the growth continues its undeniable upward trend. The think tank Fredonia Group graphically charts this upward path for the next decade (see Figure 4.5).[12]

Increased functional responsibility begets enhanced civil liability. "Because the effects of liability cases are far reaching, potentially affecting all levels ... the more security personnel know about their responsibilities and exposure to liability, the less chance the company will be crippled with lawsuits."[13] Given the range and diversity of services of the private security industry, including "a whole spectrum of concerns, such as emergency evacuation plans, security procedures, bomb threats, liaisons with law enforcement agencies, electronic security systems, and the selection, training and deployment of personnel within institutions,"[14] liability is an ongoing policy issue. Dennis Walters, in his article, *"Training—The Key to Avoiding Liability,"* notes:

In the United States, where lawyers occupy a significant portion of the professional class, it is important to keep track of emerging legal trends when you are developing a comprehensive security training program. It is very helpful to know what forms of legal action are appearing that will affect the security industry.[15]

In fact, liability concerns are by nature part of the security managerial vision—a constant variable in the successful business and operation plan.[16] For examples, Stephen C. George highlights how legal liability become a planning dimension in the area of crowd control at events and entertainment venues.

Many professional security firms refuse to handle events that draw large crowds. They are often the best people equipped to deal with such situations, but they reject these jobs because of the concern over—and the potential for—liability. But if private security won't work these events, and police are reluctant to act, who's left to do the job?[17]

However, the fear of liability should not prevent a well-disciplined company from tackling this side of security and given the growth of event and venue security over the last three decades, there are clearly players in the business that anticipate the liability reality. The International Association of Chiefs of Police lays out some guiding principles for security services in large scale events:

■ Plan for worst-case scenarios extraordinary crimes, violence by protestors, a possible terrorist attack, natural disasters—but also be thoroughly prepared to deal with ordinary crimes and incidents (pickpockets, thefts from autos, disorderly conduct, etc.).

■ Weigh the security measures that conceivably could be taken (for example, street closures, searches, highly visible tactical units) against the jurisdiction's desire to produce events that are enjoyable, well attended, and profitable.

■ Establish new and effective—but temporary—organizational arrangements, management structures, and methods of communication.

■ Ensure that the event continues safely while respecting constitutional rights, including freedom of speech and assembly.

■ Anticipate unplanned activities and spur-of-the-moment gatherings—for example, on the eve of a major event.

■ Ensure that the rest of the jurisdiction receives essential law enforcement services, regardless of the size or importance of the event.

■ Ensure that appropriate federal officials, such as the Department of Homeland Security (DHS) state homeland security advisers, are informed in advance about events with national or international significance to guarantee federal awareness and possible support.

■ Develop an effective interoperable communications capability if multiple agencies are involved in the field.

■ Involve citizens and the business community in planning efforts.

■ Consider building event security training into basic and in-service training, if the jurisdiction routinely handles special events.[18]

Like all other security venues, the sports stadium or large-scale entertainment complex need full analysis and inspection before any security plan should be developed or implemented. First, know and identify the infrastructure to be secured. Second, identify its critical/key assets and components, which need the highest and even lowest levels of protection. Third, collect asset data that fully delineates the size and scope of the facility in need of protection. What is the capacity and how will certain events stress or strain that capacity, to name a few factors. Fourth, do all assessments necessary to prepare, plan, mitigate, and assume continuity in the facility. Hence threat and vulnerability analysis is central to any serious security plan as well as full-fledged risk assessment document that sets out priorities and involves all the major players of that facility, from management, to the security team, and local, state, and federal partners. Partnerships will be central to any meaningful event security operational plan because the size and scope of the crowd as well as the infrastructure make other players integral to the mission. Some examples of those in need of alliance and cooperation are

■ Event promoters/sponsors

■ Emergency services agencies (e.g., law enforcement, fire/rescue, emergency medical services, public health, and safety) and neighboring emergency managers and agency representatives (to coordinate mutual aid needs)

- Local planning agencies and individuals (e.g., community development agencies, city planners, and hazard-mitigation planner)
- Local emergency planning committees for hazardous materials information
- Public works agencies and utility companies
- State supporting entities, including the State Emergency Management Agency or National Guard
- Social service agencies and volunteer organizations (e.g., the American Red Cross and Salvation Army), including animal care and control organizations
- Medical community representatives (e.g., area hospitals, EMS agencies, medical examiner, coroner, mortician)
- Communications representatives (e.g., public information officer, local media, radio)
- Aviation and coastal authorities (e.g., state aviation authority, other air support representatives, port authorities, U.S. Coast Guard station)
- Chief financial officer, auditor, and heads of any centralized procurement and resource support agencies
- Business and retail communities that are directly impacted by the event
- The jurisdiction's legal counsel and leaders from labor and professional organizations
- Leaders of area facilities, including industrial and military installations, schools, and universities[19]

Finally, after amassing all of this information, issue and make recommendations concerning countermeasures to any potential or actual threats or risks. As in all stages of security, planning and preparing for the potential harm is more than half the battle to defend.[20]

Whether crowd supervision and control or security at defense installations, the industry's growth cannot escape the potential downside of an emerging economic force—that of legal liability. With the industry's tentacles around every place imaginable, private sector justice will have to mitigate and prevent liability.

This chapter's discussion involves the civil liability of security personnel and business entities from various angles. First, exactly what is the definition of civil liability and what types of civil liability are there? Second, how does negligence impact the security firm, especially as to its elements and requirements of due diligence? And how does negligence differ from the world of intentional torts and strict liability causes of action? How do these forms of civil liability impact the security officer, the security firm and related entities that provide supervision? Put another way, how can the security organization deliver its services without making mistakes or causing personal harm to others? Next, what types of intentional torts are most relevant to the private security industry assault, infliction of mental distress, false imprisonment, to name a few? How can the industry be held strictly accountable for harms that occur and what are those narrow examples where liability is imposed regardless of intent or motivation? Finally, what preventive steps can be taken to minimize these diverse forms of civil liability and how can the private security officer or firm avoid the many legal pitfalls that are often side by side with the delivery of private security services?

4.2 The Nature of Civil Liability

Civil wrongs or causes of action can be grounded in various remedies including negligence, intentional torts, and even strict liability findings. Private sector justice is exposed each and every day to both its protections and its corresponding liability. Consider this factual situation:

Mr. X and his fiancée Ms. Z were shopping in a large department store in the State of Missouri. The evidence indicated that Mr. X left the department store without purchasing a tool. Soon after, Mr. X was confronted by a security officer in a hostile fashion. Mr. X was handcuffed after engaging in a physical altercation with the security guard. Mr. X's face was bleeding, his ribs were bruised, and he suffered other injuries. Mr. X was eventually acquitted at trial on all charges brought forth by the department store.[21]

Who bears legal responsibility for these physical injuries? Is the liability civil and/or criminal in scope? Has there been an assault or battery? Was the restraint and confinement of the suspected shoplifter reasonable? Has there been a violation of Mr. X's constitutional or civil rights? How are civil actions distinguishable from criminal actions when reflecting on this situation?[22] At its core, a civil liability arises from an action that causes a particular and demonstrable harm on a personal level rather than a communal one. Civil wrongs, like criminal actions, have individual consequences and harms that include personal and very measurable damages.

A civil harm is a cause of action that is uniquely personal to one person. For example, an individual who is victimized by an unsafe driver is personally victimized. In contrast, the world of crime and criminality are gauged at a collective or communal level rather than an individual one since criminal acts are defined as a public harm, an action against the society as a whole that injures the public peace or public good. Crimes, despite their undeniable personal harm, do more to influence the common psyche of a neighborhood or family than any civil harm. A criminal act injures the world at large. While criminal law is chiefly concerned with protection of society and a restoration of the public good, the basic policy behind tort law is: "to compensate the victim for his loss, to deter future conduct of a similar nature, and to express society's disapproval of the conduct in question."[23] Civil remedies are more concerned with making injured parties economically and physically whole, while criminal remedies are more preoccupied with just desserts—namely punishment of the perpetrator either by fines or incarceration. Tort remedies involve damages, while criminal penalties result in incarceration or fines.[24]

Civil harms are further defined by their respective categories, namely negligence, intentional torts, and strict liability actions. Intentional conduct that causes civil harm is generally defined as a "tort." Some of the more common torts are

- Assault
- Battery
- Abuse of process
- Malicious prosecution
- Conversion
- Deceit
- Defamation
- False imprisonment
- Intentional infliction of emotional distress
- Invasion of privacy
- Trespass

Each cause of action requires a proof of its particular elements. And there is not an interchangeability to these categories for negligence action is not a strict liability claim nor an intentional tort the same as negligence. The elements are distinct. "When a party has alleged facts that cover every element of the cause of action, the party has stated a *prima facie* case."[25]

In *Cordoves v. Miami Dade*, the court grappled with literally every sort of civil harm definition. Here a patron at a local mall allegedly suffered posttraumatic stress disorder (PTSD) and needed the close attentiveness of a service dog—a puppy to assist her if suffering from a bout of stress. When told by security officers that dogs were not permitted in the mall, an altercation eventually ensued. Plaintiff argued all a host of civil liability theories including intentional torts—false imprisonment, false arrest, and infliction of mental distress, negligence, and civil rights violation based on the Americans with Disabilities Act. The court cautioned that one strata of remedy does not automatically support another. In rejecting the interchangeability, the court noted:

> Cordoves's second theory is Dadeland and Valor are negligent for allowing Cordoves to be falsely imprisoned and assaulted. Dadeland and Valor argue this theory fails as a matter of law. "A claim for negligence cannot be premised solely on a defendant's alleged commission of an intentional tort."[26] Assault and battery are intentional torts and therefore cannot form the sole basis of a claim for negligence. False imprisonment is also an intentional tort,[27] and therefore cannot form the sole basis of a claim for negligence.[28]

While there is much that distinguishes civil and criminal actions, "the same conduct by a defendant may give rise to both criminal and tort liability."[29] Selection of either remedy does not exclude the other, and in fact, success in the civil arena is generally more plausible since the burden of proof is less rigorous. Remember the evidentiary burden for the proof of a crime requires proof beyond a reasonable doubt. A successful civil action merely mandates proof by a preponderance of the evidence or by clear and convincing evidence.

The fact pattern portrayed above gives rise to a series of civil actions, including:

1. Assault:
   a. An act
   b. Intent to cause harm or apprehension of said harm
   c. Apprehension that is imminent
   d. Causation
2. Battery:
   a. A specific act
   b. Intent to cause harmful or offensive conduct
   c. Actual harmful or offensive conduct
   d. Causation
3. False Imprisonment:
   a. An act which confines a plaintiff completely within fixed boundaries
   b. Intent to confine plaintiff
   c. Plaintiff was conscious of his own confinement or was harmed by it
   d. Causation
4. Intentional infliction of emotional distress:
   a. An act that is extremely outrageous
   b. Intention to cause severe emotional distress
   c. Actual emotional distress is suffered
   d. Causation

Table 4.1   Civil versus Criminal Wrongs

Torts or Civil Wrongs	Crimes
Personal harm	Harm against society
Does not require intentional behavior	Generally requires intentional behavior
Requires proof by a preponderance of evidence	Proof beyond a reasonable doubt
Selection of civil remedy does not exclude a criminal prosecution	Selection of criminal prosecution does not exclude a civil remedy
Results in damage awards generally compensatory and sometimes punitive in nature	Results in fines, imprisonments and orders of restitution

5. Malicious prosecution:
   a. Initiation of legal proceedings
   b. Without probable cause
   c. With malice
   d. Favorable termination of legal proceedings regarding defendant[30]

Tortious conduct can be economically costly since the remedy is measured in damages—that judgment by jurist or jury that awards a dollar figure that reflects the harm. Of course, not all damage claims are accurate nor indicative of depth or breadth of the harm but to be sure, the imposition of damages can be economically devastating. It is difficult to get an exact figure on how many corporate dollars are lost through jury judgments against security personnel and their employers, but the fact that those losses are substantial is indicated by the circumstances of the legal climate as it affects security today. For example, jury awards in the past often amounted to only a few thousand dollars in many cases. Today, awards of $100,000 or more are becoming increasingly common.[31]

To get some insight into the size and scope of jury awards, search the well-regarded Verdict Search at: http://www.verdictsearch.com/index.jsp

Various industry authorities estimate that at least one suit involving security is filed in the United States every day.[32] A review of the literature indicates that cumulative damage awards are consistently increasing.[33] In sum, there are both similarities and differences between civil law and criminal law. Table 4.1 provides a concise overview.

4.3 Classification of Civil Wrongs/Torts

Security agencies and personnel need to become accustomed to the common civil actions that firms and their officers will likely encounter. Internal and external policies of security firms and the defensibility of its practices and procedures need constant evaluation to prevent litigation.

Civil harms are further divided into three main classifications:

1. Intentional torts
2. Negligence
3. Strict liability torts[34]

A review of common civil wrongs that regularly influence and affect security practice with illustrative case examples follows.

4.3.1 Intentional Torts

Intentional torts imply an understanding or willingness to act or cause a specific end. Intentional acts are not driven by carelessness, accident, or mistake, but a clear intentionality. In civil law, the specificity and clarity of mind and intent is less rigid than the criminal counterpart, although proof of intent remains a fundamental element. Criminal law insists on more intentionality with terms like premeditation, willfully, and purposely. In assessing criminal behavior, the law requires that the person choose consciously to perform a certain act, and not be under duress, coercion, or suffering from any other impediment that influences volition.

Civil intent partially mirrors criminal intent. "Evil motive or the desire to cause injury need not be the end goal; intent to cause the actual result is sufficient."[35] In the law of torts, intention can be strictly "without malice or desire to harm but with full knowledge to a substantial certainty that harm would follow."[36] Specific examples of intentional torts commonly applicable in security settings are highlighted below.

4.3.1.1 Assault

Since security personnel commonly deal with situations requiring detention and restraint, the potential for assault is not unexpected. An analysis of assault requires proof of the following elements:

■ An act
■ Intent to cause harmful or offensive contact or to cause the apprehension of harmful or offensive contact
■ The apprehension must be imminent
■ The defendant must cause the apprehension

Noticeably absent from this element list is an absolute requirement of offensive contact or actual touching. In most jurisdictions, an assault is considered to be an incomplete battery. Instead, the act of touching is in its threatened stage, symbolized by its tentativeness and lack of execution. Movement or an act of the defendant toward a prospective victim may consist only of eye movement or a slight jerk of the body. The plaintiff must reasonably anticipate, believe, or have knowledge that this potential action against the body is harmful. The proposed injury is imminent, immediate, or without any significant delay. Consider this factual scenario:

One evening in February 1976, George I. Kelley entered a Safeway store in southeast Washington, D.C. to shop for groceries. He noticed that an automatic exit door was not working properly and that it was necessary to exert pressure on the door to push it open. According to Kelley's testimony, he completed his shopping and later advised the cashier that he wanted to make a complaint about the broken door. The cashier suggested that Kelley talk to the assistant manager, Mr. Wheeler. When Kelley did so, the assistant manager responded that the door would be fixed in two to three months and that Kelley was always making trouble for him. Kelley testified that he had never made a complaint to Mr. Wheeler before that night and also stated that the assistant manager said to him, "boy, if you don't get out of this store I'm going to have you arrested." Kelley responded, "Well call the police, I want to file a complaint." Holding his bag of groceries, Kelley stood in front of the store to await the police. The Assistant Manager beckoned to a security guard, Larry Moore, who was assigned to the store by Seaboard Security Systems, Ltd. At the same time, the assistant manager asked someone in the back of the store to call the police. Within a few minutes, Officer Knowles of the Metropolitan Police Department arrived. According to Kelley, Knowles first spoke to the assistant manager, who called him over and then approached Kelley and said, "the Manager wants you to leave the store." Kelley testified that he was about to respond to the officer when the security guard approached from the rear, and grabbed him around the throat. Simultaneously, the police officer stuck his knee into Kelley's chest. The two pushed him to the ground and handcuffed him. Without any resistance from Kelley, the officer and the security guard took Kelley to the back of the store where he stood in handcuffs in view of store customers. After ten or fifteen minutes, a police car arrived and transported him to the precinct where the police charged him with unlawful entry.[37]

Using the elements of an assault or a battery action, does the plaintiff have a reasonable basis for filing a claim against Safeway and its employees? Clearly, a harmful or offensive contact took place but was there a reasonable apprehension of harm? In upholding the assault and battery determination the court held:

> Kelley alleges that although he offered no resistance, the Seaboard Guard grabbed him from behind, around the throat and pushed him to the ground before handcuffing him. Although witnesses were present each told different versions of the events. We find there was sufficient evidence upon which a jury could properly have found Safeway liable for assault and battery. Accordingly we affirm the jury finding liability on that account.[38]

The plaintiff's claim of assault was correctly struck down when the sole basis for the tort was a forty-five minute detention, in a state with merchant privilege, says *Josey v. Filene's*.[39] Even the assaults of third parties, bystanders, onlookers, and intermediaries are a security liability according to Charles Sennewald, founder and former president of the International Association of Professional Security Consultants. Sennewald highlights the pressing realty:

> Before stores were sued primarily for what they did. Now they are held accountable for acts of third parties against customers, such as muggings or purse snatchings in a store's parking lot.

This trend requires consultants to assess whether a store provides a reasonable level of security for invitees.

No matter the trends, the more enlightened retail security executives see the need for periodic outside objective advice. Firms that have failed to stay current, by not tapping into available consulting resources, have the most to lose. And some do![40]

4.3.1.2 Battery

Closely aligned to assault is the battery action. A battery requires an actual touching or offensive contact to another person without right, privilege, or justification. Proof of a battery requires a demonstration of

- A specific act or movement
- The intention to cause the contact or to possess knowledge of the consequences
- Actual physical impairment, pain, or illness to the body
- The conduct must be personally offensive based upon reasonable standards
- Causation between the defendant's act and the actual injury to the plaintiff

The primary concern in battery analysis is whether the touching or contact is offensive. While the term "offensive" possesses a certain amount of relativity, most courts have held that offensive does not mean "that the contact must be violent or painful."[41] Offensive contact can be touching, tapping, poking, spitting, and even indecent gestures. Given the constant interaction with customers in retail settings, battery is a predictable reality for security firms.[42] Security professionals should weigh and evaluate restraint techniques, detention policies, and use of force regimens as they carry out their many responsibilities always acting in a preventative way and anticipating potential liability problems. Clients and suspects will shape those policies. For example, the suspected shoplifter should be treated with far more restraint than the suspected rapist. Reflect further on the delicate balance that must be maintained between a proprietor's right to protect his or her property interest, and the right of a consumer not to be accused, confronted, or accosted without substantial cause. Creative legal minds easily conjure up a battery case under diverse factual scenarios, "since it is not necessary that the defendant intend to cause specific harmful injury, only that the contact itself was intended."[43] In the area of retail security, such as detention of a shoplifter, any security action has a battery prospect. Security specialists often walk the fine line of professional restraint and excessive force. Courts look to the totality of circumstances when assessing the difference.[44]

4.3.1.3 False Imprisonment

In order to prove a prima facie case of false imprisonment the following elements need demonstration:

- An act that completely confines a plaintiff within fixed boundaries.
- An intention to confine.
- Defendant is responsible for or the cause of the confinement.
- Plaintiff or victim was conscious, aware, and knowledgeable of the confinement or was harmed by it.

Industrial and retail settings provide fertile grounds for cases of false imprisonment. Evaluate the following facts:

> A United security guard detained the plaintiff as she was leaving the store and accused her of taking a gold necklace, which she was wearing around her neck. The plaintiff responded that the necklace had been given to her by her parents. The guard escorted her to the assistant manager's office and told the assistant manager that she had witnessed the plaintiff taking the necklace. The plaintiff again stated that the necklace was a gift from her parents and expressed a desire to leave so that she could contact her mother who was waiting in the parking lot outside. After the guard procured the necklace, the assistant manager accompanied the plaintiff outside the store to meet her mother. The latter confirmed the plaintiff's story as to where the necklace had come from, and all three proceeded back to the store office. There, the security guard produced a release form which she said would have to be signed. The mother refused, and the assistant manager informed her that the store's policy was not to prosecute minors. The mother replied that she intended to prosecute the store whereupon the necklace was returned to her and both the plaintiff and her mother were allowed to leave. The plaintiff also introduced evidence showing that the store did not stock necklaces of the same quality as the one the plaintiff was wearing when she was detained.[45]

Due to the tort's intentionality, it cannot be mere incompetence that will suffice in the proof of false imprisonment. For airline travelers, the waits on the tarmac and take points can border on a form of long-term imprisonment and confinement. A recent Jet Blue Airlines case, where passengers were stranded for hours and hours, pushed some passengers to sue for false imprisonment. While there was sympathy for the distress caused, the *Bisone v. JetBlue Airways Corp* decision from the New York Court of Appeals held that federal law preempted the remedies since it was guided by FAA requirements[46] as well the ADA standards. However, Biscone concludes there are cases when the preemption argument will falter because the conduct is too egregious. The Court held:

> Where the activity represents "outrageous conduct that goes beyond the scope of normal aircraft operations," the claims should not be preempted (id.). For example, if a flight attendant deals with a boisterous passenger by shooting the passenger, the state-law tort claim would not be preempted; if, however, the flight attendant acted in a rude or unprofessional manner in telling the passenger to be quiet, the state-law tort claim would be preempted.[47]

While there may be room for disagreement about the intentions of the security personnel, a close review of the facts reveals fulfillment of this tort's fundamental elements. First, the plaintiff was confined to a specifically fixed boundary. Second, it was the intention of the defendant to confine that party. Third, the defendant was clearly responsible for causing the confinement. Lastly, the plaintiff was conscious of it and, in her view, was harmed by it.

It is only natural that false imprisonment cases arise in the retail environment. Even good faith efforts to restrain suspected shoplifters are subject to mistakes. As a result, proprietors have been granted, in select jurisdictions, immunity in the erroneous detention of suspected shoplifters under merchant privilege laws. Merchant privilege laws usually provide that "[w]henever the owner or operator of a mercantile establishment ... detains, arrests, or causes to be detained or arrested any person reasonably thought to be engaged in shoplifting and, as a result ... the person so detained or arrested brings an action for false arrest or false imprisonment ... no recovery shall be had by the plaintiff in such action where it is established by competent evidence: (1) That the plaintiff had so conducted himself or behaved in such manner as to cause a man of reasonable prudence to believe that the plaintiff, at or immediately prior to the time of the detention or arrest, was committing the offense of shoplifting ... or (2) That the manner of the detention or arrest and the length of time during which such plaintiff was detained was under all the circumstances reasonable."[48]

Read the federal case at http://www.freelawreporter.org/flr3d/f3d/413/413.F3d.175.04-2251. html Explain why the court concluded that the Merchant Privilege Defense, while relevant, was not essential to a jury finding.

Though there is some variance in merchant privilege laws, most state laws adhere to a formula that blends the presumption of detention with a right of the merchant to protect his or her goods and services.[49] A typical construction might be

(c) *Presumptions*—Any person intentionally concealing unpurchased property of any store or other mercantile establishment, either on the premises or outside the premises of such store, shall be prima facie presumed to have so concealed such property with the intention of depriving the merchant of the possession, use or benefit of such merchandise without paying the full retail value thereof within the meaning of subsection (a), and the finding of such unpurchased property concealed, upon the person or among the belongings of such person, shall be prima facie evidence of intentional concealment, and, if such person conceals, or causes to be concealed, such unpurchased property, upon the person or among the belongings of another, such fact shall also be prima facie evidence of intentional concealment on the part of the person so concealing such property.

(d) *Detention*—A peace officer, merchant or merchant's employee or an agent under contract with a merchant, who has probable cause to believe that retail theft has occurred or is occurring on or about a store or other retail mercantile establishment and who has probable cause to believe that a specific person has committed or is committing the retail theft may detain the suspect in a reasonable manner for a reasonable time on or off the premises for all or any of the following purposes: to require the suspect to identify himself, to verify such identification, to determine whether such suspect has in his possession unpurchased merchandise taken from the mercantile establishment and, if so, to recover such merchandise, to inform a peace officer, or to institute criminal proceedings against the suspect. Such detention shall not impose civil or criminal liability upon the peace officer, merchant, employee or agent so detaining.[50]

Use of language like "reasonableness," "prudence," and "honest belief" manifests the legislative desire to assure protection from illegitimate claims of false imprisonment. Judgments for false imprisonment are not granted unless the plaintiff shows evidence of willful conduct, maliciousness, or wanton disregard.[51] The standard of "reasonableness" is commonly employed by appellate courts in determining civil liability. A Wisconsin case, *Johnson v. K-Mart Enterprises, Inc.*,[52] dismissed an action for false imprisonment after evaluating the total duration of imprisonment consisting of twenty minutes. The gentlemanly demeanor and behavior exhibited by the retail store's security personnel, coupled with a polite and formal apology given upon verification of the facts, favorably impressed the court.

The Appellate Court concurred in the dismissal noting that Wisconsin has a statute protecting merchants from liability where they have probable cause for believing that a person has shoplifted. Under the statute a merchant may detain such a suspect in a reasonable manner and for a reasonable length of time. The Court held that the K-Mart security guard did have probable cause to detain Johnson.[53]

While the facts enunciated above arguably prove the elements, security professionals should be aware that professionalism and courtesy during detention influence judicial reaction. A case in point is *Robinson v. Wieboldt Store, Inc.*,[54] whose facts are summarized:

On November 21, 1977, at about 6:30 p.m., the 66-year-old plaintiff was shopping at the Evanston Wieboldt Store. She purchased a scarf … with her credit card. Plaintiff chose to wear the scarf, removed the price tag, and handed it to the sales clerk. The sales clerk did not object when plaintiff put the scarf around her neck. The clerk handed plaintiff a copy of the sales receipt, which plaintiff put in her pocket. The plaintiff then took the escalator to the third floor of the store. As plaintiff stepped off the escalator a security guard grabbed her by the left arm near her shoulder. The guard gave his name and showed his badge. He asked her where she got the scarf and requested her to accompany him to a certain room. She told him she purchased the scarf on the first floor and had the receipt in her pocket. During the entire confrontation, the guard was holding tightly onto plaintiff's upper arm. Plaintiff, who was black, described the guard as white, weighing about 200 pounds, having dark hair and wearing a dark brown suit. The guard grabbed the receipt from the plaintiff's hand, continued to hold her upper arm, and plaintiff struggled to get the receipt back from the guard. Plaintiff testified that she felt very sick, as if her head was blown off and her chest was sinking in. She said she was frightened and that it seemed that the incident lasted forever. The guard took plaintiff down to the scarf department on the first floor. Plaintiff removed the scarf from her neck and noticed a small tag on the corner. This tag gave instructions on the care of the scarf. This was apparently what the security guard had seen before grabbing the plaintiff. The sales clerk told the guard the plaintiff had purchased the scarf a short time earlier. The guard told the sales clerk that she had caused plaintiff a lot of trouble and had embarrassed her. He then walked away without apologizing to the plaintiff.[55]

By the guard's actions, the plaintiff, for a period of time, was confined to a fixed boundary. Developing a restriction of this sort was the security agent's intention. The cause of the confinement can only be attributed to the security guard. Since the plaintiff was conscious of the confinement and certainly felt harmed by it, a prima facie case has legal support. Not surprisingly, the defendant security officer and the employing firm relied upon the statutory defense of a merchant privilege.[56] Given the facts of *Robinson v. Wieboldt*,[57] can a trier of fact conclude that the security official acted reasonably in this case? Were the actions of the security guard, especially in terms of the force exerted, reasonable in light of the age and stature of the plaintiff? The court held:

A review of the record reveals Plaintiff's assertions do in fact present a case of false imprisonment. She testified that the security guard grabbed her tightly on her upper arm while they were on the 3rd floor of Defendant's store, restricting her freedom of motion. Even after presenting the guard with a sales receipt she was forced to travel to the 1st floor of the store further restricting her liberty and freedom of locomotion. To claim that Plaintiff could have refused to go to the 1st floor and unilaterally ended the confrontation ignores the realities of the situation.[58]

False imprisonment cases can arise from distinct and differing contexts. For example, in a claim based on civil rights violations, the test is "objective reasonableness" of the security officer's conduct during that detention. The "reasonableness of an officer's conduct comes into play both 'as an element of the officer's defense' and 'as an element of the plaintiff's case.'"[59] For this reason, many courts have struggled with the application of qualified immunity.

Review the facts of *Lynch v. Hunter Safeguard*.[60]

> Defendant Donald Hunter, a ShopRite security guard, followed Plaintiff out of the store to her car, stopped her, took her keys and refund authorizations, and then escorted her back into the supermarket. Hunter then took Plaintiff to a storage room, restrained her wrists in handcuffs ... and fastened the handcuffs to a metal stairway. The handcuffs were so tight that they cut Plaintiff's skin, numbed her hands and fingers, and caused them to swell and darken. Plaintiff begged Hunter to allow her to use a bathroom. ... She finally lost control and urinated on herself. Hunter laughed and then photographed Plaintiff in her wet clothing. Plaintiff repeatedly asked Hunter to allow her to telephone her 69-year-old mother. ... Hunter ignored Plaintiff's requests. Plaintiff remained shackled to the stairway for three to four hours. ... Hunter directed other ShopRite employees to search Plaintiff's pocketbook. ... [and] Plaintiff's car ... two ShopRite managers, supported and encouraged Hunter's actions. "For a considerable length of time, neither Defendants ... telephoned the police or told anyone else to telephone the police about Plaintiff's detention, handcuffing or the shoplifting accusation against her."
>
> "Someone from the store" eventually telephoned the Philadelphia Police Department, and Officers. ... responded to the call ... Officer John Doe III immediately ordered Hunter to remove the handcuffs. Hunter ... told the two police officers that Plaintiff had shoplifted items from the supermarket, and asked them to arrest her. ... Officers John Doe III and Jones-Mahoney placed Plaintiff under arrest. ...
>
> At the police station, Plaintiff was placed in a "small, filthy, insect-infested cell with five other women, four of whom would not allow Plaintiff to sit down on a bench for several hours. Repeatedly, Plaintiff was inappropriately touched by one of these women." Plaintiff was incarcerated for twelve hours. ... She was not allowed to telephone her mother and "was not able to drink from the water fountain. ..." After seven hours, she was given food. Plaintiff was charged with Retail Theft ... but the charge was later dropped.[61]

In this case, the debate on false imprisonment is easily resolved after a cursory review of the security methods employed. It is likely that the conditions of the detention itself would elicit juror sympathy.

The security industry is paying dearly in false imprisonment cases. A few illustrations include

■ Retail customer awarded $20,850 in damages in false imprisonment case. Security manager refused to listen to customer's explanation.[62]

■ Award of $30,000 in punitive damages as well as $20,000 in compensatory damages for false imprisonment case upheld after trier believed security personnel were loud, rude, and unpleasant.[63]

■ Customer detained for over two hours in security office, searched, and questioned, even though he had a receipt that accounted for each and every item in his possession. Judgment for $85,867.85 plus costs upheld. *Daley v. Wanamaker, Inc.*, 464 A.2d 355 (Pa. Super. 1983).[64]

A recent ruling from New York, *Pelligrini v. Cervone*, highlights the diverse complexities of false imprisonment and false arrest cases—something easy to assert—although much more difficult to prove. The court rejects claims for both intentional torts by noting:

> In the present case, as an initial matter, Duane Reade's motion for summary judgment dismissing plaintiffs' third cause of action for false arrest and imprisonment is granted as Duane Reade has established that there is no issue of fact as to its liability under this claim. To establish a claim for false arrest or false imprisonment, plaintiff must establish that: "(1) the defendant intended to confine him, (2) the plaintiff was conscious of the confinement, (3) the plaintiff did not consent to the confinement, and (4) the confinement was not otherwise privileged."[65] "It is well settled in this State's jurisprudence that a civilian complainant, by merely seeking police assistance or furnishing information to law enforcement authorities who are then free to exercise their own judgment as to whether an arrest should be made and criminal charges filed, will not be held liable for false arrest or malicious prosecution."[66] "Nor does identifying plaintiff as the perpetrator of a crime, signing the summons or testifying at trial give rise to tort liability."[67] Rather, there must be evidence that defendant "encouraged the police to arrest plaintiff or intended to confine him."[68]
>
> Here, the court finds that no issues of fact exist as to Duane Reade's involvement in plaintiffs' arrest as the undisputed evidence demonstrates that Duane Reade did not encourage the police to arrest plaintiffs or intend to confine them. As an initial matter, the record indicates that Duane Reade employees neither confined plaintiffs in the store against their will, nor took part in the physical arrest of plaintiffs by the NYPD. Further, according to the criminal complaint, it is clear that plaintiffs' arrest was based upon NYPD's conversations with Chakraborty and the customer who was also involved in the altercation. Although the criminal complaint does not identify Chakraborty by name, it is clear from the record as a whole that the Duane Reade employee identified in the complaint must be Chakraborty as it is undisputed that he was the only individual who stopped plaintiff Cervone from exiting the store. As Chakraborty is not actually a Duane Reade employee but employed by Sottile, his actions cannot be attributed to Duane Reade to hold it liable. Thus, there is no evidence that Duane Reade encouraged the police to arrest plaintiffs and plaintiffs cannot maintain a claim for false arrest and imprisonment against Duane Reade.[69]

The method of detention weighs heavily on the court when reaching legal conclusions about false imprisonment. Detention is scrutinized and adjudged in light of many factors including

1. If physical force itself is used to cause the restraint
2. If a threat of force was used to effect the restraining and
3. If the conduct of the retail employee reasonably implied that force would be used to prevent the suspect from leaving the store[70]

All of these liabilities could have been avoided with sound security policies. As Leo F. Hannon suggests in his article, "Whose Rights Prevail?," "The bottom line seems to be that you can't beat common sense."[71]

Security professionals should design a system of detention and restraint that does not trigger, by its shortcomings, a false imprisonment action. For example, to confine does not require walls, locks, or other barriers. Since confinement can be the result of an emotional coercion or threat, establish a polite, cordial environment when detaining. Confinement is defensible if performed by an official that is legally empowered to act. While some protection is afforded in jurisdictions that have merchant privilege statutes, any action taken by private security personnel without that limited privilege will be subject to a false imprisonment claim. Other security professionals urge regularity and professionalism as the preventive steps to thwart off liability suits based on false imprisonment. John Francis' *The Complete Security Officer's Manual* corroborates this suggestion.

> A security officer is expected to be businesslike, alert, and helpful. He should treat people as he would like to be treated. He will more than likely be asked the same questions numerous times. He should remember the person standing in front of him is asking the question for the first time. He will be bombarded with questions all during his shift, and he must realize the people asking these questions have their own personal pride and they are certainly not going to ask for information that is otherwise easily obtainable to them. An officer should be sure when a person approaches him that he attempts to help them. If he cannot help them, because it is against facility rules/regulations, that should be explained. At least leave them with the knowledge that an attempt was made to help them. A simple word or a phrase: "Let me see if I can help you. Here are the rules and they cannot be changed. You will have to check with the person in charge, or call this number to get the assistance you need." Rather than saying, "This can't be done, it's against the rules, and you're not going to do it." Rudeness is no help to a person who needs help. An officer must be courteous. There is a saying that if, "courtesy is contagious, rudeness is epidemic." Security officers are expected to be courteous to people every day. By being rude to one employee in a facility, the word is spread throughout the facility that all the security officers are rude and inconsiderate.[72]

Even job announcements for positions in the private sector stress professionalism and appropriate demeanor. Examine the Guardian Security Announcement at: http://www.guardiansecurityinc.com/employment/job.asp

In contract guard settings, particularly when the company employing the security service defends itself as an independent contractor, the falsely imprisoned will argue liability on behalf of both the agent and the principal if the latter ratifies the former's conduct. "The liability of a principal for a wrongful restraint or detention by an agent or employee depends on whether the act was authorized or subsequently ratified, or whether the act was within the scope of the agent's or employee's employment or authority."[73]

4.3.1.4 Infliction of Emotional or Mental Distress

Often coupled with claims of assault, battery, and false imprisonment is the claim of intentional or negligent infliction of emotional or mental distress. Mental distress is the psychic portion of an injury—the pain and suffering portion of a calculable physical claim. Since only the minority of jurisdictions recognizes the negligent aspects of this tort, no further consideration will be given.[74] The majority of American jurisdictions do recognize the tort of intentional infliction of mental distress.[75] Many require that the tort be strictly parasitic in nature, that is, a cause of action resting upon another tort that causes actual physical injury or harm like assault and battery. Critics of the cause of action have long felt that without an actual physical injury that can be objectively measured, mental and emotional damages are too speculative to quantify. That position has now become a minority view since most jurisdictions recognize, or at least give some credence to, the soft sciences of psychiatry and psychology in matters of damage. Others have argued that the noncalculable quality of the damages, the noneconomic nature of the damage, make the claim suspect due to its immeasurability. The proof side of the damages have been called "fallacious" and subject to "distortions."[76]

For the security industry, the individual consumer, employee, or other party who is accosted, humiliated, or embarrassed by false imprisonment, battery, or assault will often attempt to collect damages tied to the emotional strain of the event. However, in an effort to provide quality control to mental damages, the elements of this tort are rather rigorous. Its basic elements are

- An act that is deemed extreme or outrageous
- The intention to cause another severe emotional distress
- The plaintiff actually suffers severe emotional distress
- The defendant is the actual cause of that distress

The general consensus regarding extreme and outrageous conduct is that it is behavior that the ordinary person deems outrageous. The borders of extreme and outrageous behavior encompass harsh insults, threats, handcuffing, physical abuse, and humiliation.[77]

At best, the term emotional distress is a series of "disagreeable states of mind that fall under the labels of fright, horror, grief, shame, humiliation, embarrassment, worry, etc."[78] The behavior complained of must be so extreme and outrageous as "to be regarded as atrocious, and utterly intolerable in a civilized community."[79] Furthermore, the emotional distress allegedly suffered must be serious.[80] A mere insult or petty bickering does not qualify.

The private security employee's very position may make seemingly innocent conduct outrageous or extreme.[81] The issue of emotional damages came to the forefront in *Montgomery Ward v. Garza*.[82] In assessing the damages of a plaintiff in a false imprisonment case, the court considered testimony by the plaintiff that he was embarrassed and humiliated.

> His son testified that Garza seemed confused, embarrassed, and frightened. He withdrew from his friends and he changed his eating habits after the incident. A psychiatrist testified that Garza was incapable of overcoming the emotional impact resulting from the false arrest, that Garza's epileptic condition could be aggravated by the event and that psychiatric treatment would be desirable. Garza's personal physician testified that Garza suffered from acute anxiety and depression and stated that he suffered an increased number of epileptic convulsions since his detention. The doctor has had to increase his medication and to add another tranquilizer in an effort to control Garza's attacks. Based on this evidence the Court found that the award of $50,000 was "not so excessive that it shocks our sense of justice and the verdict was therefore affirmed."[83]

In an age when psychiatric objectification is readily accepted and the judicial process welcomes the expert testimony of psychologists, it is not surprising that the bulk of tort actions seek emotional damages. The best preventive medicine that security professionals can ingest is to be certain, regardless of the innocence or guilt of the suspect, not to create conditions that could be characterized or described as extreme or outrageous. Just as public police must maintain an aura of decorum and professionalism, it is imperative that private justice personnel minimize the influence of emotion in daily activities. They must treat suspects with the utmost courtesy, and handle cases and investigate facts with dispassionate insight and objectivity.[84]

For a brief summary of case law, see LSU's web link at: http://biotech.law.lsu.edu/courses/tortsf01/iiem.htm

4.3.1.5 Malicious Prosecution

An unjustified claim or charge of criminal conduct or the affirmative use of the justice system to unlawfully prosecute may give rise to a claim of malicious prosecution. Accusations of criminality should never be made lightly, since the ramifications can be costly in both a legal and economic sense. The elements of this tort include

- The initiation of legal proceedings
- Without any probable cause
- With actual malice
- Legal proceedings terminate or result in favor of the accused

Proof that a charge lacked a reasonable basis in fact or in law was lacking in probable cause, or was prompted by actual malice, are the central issues in malicious prosecution. Probable cause, in a sense, is a defense to a claim of malicious prosecution for its finding imputes good faith in the action or a basis that justifies the action. To say that something has probable cause means minimally that it is arguable. And while its finding does not imply certainty, it is sure enough to justify the action. Probable cause deals with probabilities, not rigorous, scientific certitude. Probable cause conclusions verify the merit of any underlying cause of action.[85]

More challenging in proving a malicious prosecution is the showing of malice. Malice is the willful and intentional design to harm another.[86] Malice implies an improper motive—namely, that the initiation of legal action has little to do with a plaintiff's desire to bring the accused or the defendant to justice. Instead, the accused is unduly harassed by the improper filing of civil and criminal actions and victimized by the very processes that have been established to ensure justice. Instead of justice, spite, ill-will, politics, hatred, or other malevolent motive govern the decision to sue. In *Owens v. Kroeger Co.*,[87] a jury awarded $18,500 in damages in a malicious prosecution action when Mr. Owens was prosecuted for shoplifting 99¢ worth of potatoes. The exoneration, coupled with aggressive prosecution of Mr. Owens, convinced the trial jury that malice was the retailer's sole motive. The trial judge disagreed and overturned the jury's finding. Some jurisdictions, such as Georgia, bar an action for malicious prosecution even when the defendant is subsequently declared innocent if a probable cause basis triggered the arrest. In *Arnold v. Eckerd Drugs of Georgia, Inc.*,[88] a store customer was detained and prosecuted for shoplifting based upon probable cause. The court's decision noted:

With regard to appellant's claim for malicious prosecution, "[t]he overriding question ... is not whether [she] was guilty, but whether [appellee] had reasonable cause to so believe—whether the circumstances were such as to create in the mind a reasonable belief that there was probable cause for the prosecution." We have held that, under the undisputed evidence, appellee's agent had reasonable grounds to believe appellant to be guilty of shoplifting at the time of her arrest. Appellant produced no evidence that, subsequent to her arrest, appellee acquired further information tending to show that its earlier assessment of the existence of probable cause was erroneous.[89]

In *Butler v. Rio Rancho Public School*,[90] the U.S. District Court reiterated the need to prove the defendant's motivations, especially when the defendant misuses legal processes to accomplish illegal and unlawful ends.

4.3.1.6 Defamation

The cumulative effect of false imprisonment, intentional infliction of mental distress, assault and battery, and other related torts in security detention and restraint situations often lead to the tort of defamation. Defamation requires proof of the following elements:

- Defamatory statement by a defendant
- Statement concerns the plaintiff
- Publication
- Demonstration of actual damages
- Causation

When private security personnel make the accusation that "you have stolen an article" or "you are under suspicion for shoplifting" the potential for a defamation case exists.[91] An accusation of any criminal behavior may suffice. However, the defamatory remark must be "a statement of fact which in the eyes of at least a substantial and respectable minority of people would tend to harm the reputation of another by lowering him or her in the estimation of those people or by deterring them from associating with him or her."[92] If a security professional makes no accusation, at least in terms of verbal comment, or couches his interchange with the client in neutral, investigative jargon, few problems will arise. Again, common sense demands that security personnel be courteous and noncommittal and that they investigate all the facts necessary to come to an intelligent conclusion concerning the events in question.

In *Dauzat v. Dolgencorp*,[93] a defamation and false arrest civil action were simultaneously upheld—a conclusion demonstrating how multiples civil actions are likely more predictable than a sole theory of recovery. Of course, a false arrest and accusation, which is baseless and without merit, naturally gives rises to these civil actions. Since defamation is an intentional tort, the crux of intentionality is more than mere error or mistake as would be so in negligence but a knowing understanding of the potential for mischarging and false arresting another. The Court construed both actions as perfectly defensible when it remarked:

Included in Plaintiffs' evidence was surveillance video of Ms. Poarch observing Plaintiffs before she called the police. Plaintiffs argued against the application of a privilege on the basis that Ms. Poarch alerted the police knowing her statements were false. The trial court agreed declaring: "There is no evidence whatsoever on the surveillance video to implicate [P]laintiffs with the illegal activity of theft of goods." The trial court decided that Ms. Poarch's statements were defamatory per se and that it was her intent to cause Plaintiffs' damage. The burden then shifted to Defendants to rebut this presumption, and Defendants clearly failed in that effort. Ms. Poarch did not even appear at trial, and Defendants presented no evidence whatsoever.[94]

Defamation is not mere insult or "casual insults or epithets ... because such actions are not regarded as being sufficiently harmful to warrant invocation of the law's processes."[95] Another issue in the proof of a defamation action relates to the statement's verity. No action in defamation can be upheld if the statement, in fact, is true, and the defendant cannot demonstrate falsehood. The fact that a statement has been made is, of course, important. To whom the statement has been made is also a legal consideration, for the statement must be published or announced to others to be actionable. This is called the requirement of publication.[96] "Thus a derogatory statement made by a Defendant solely to the Plaintiff is not actionable unless someone else reads or overhears it."[97] Since many retail and industrial situations involving security personnel are in the public eye, it behooves security practitioners, when they make a claim, to do so discretely. Making accusations at the cash register or in other public settings is not intelligent discretion. Security personnel must be sensitive to the public nature of defamatory remarks. Beyond public comment, the tort arises from published comments or the dissemination of written material. "Preparation of and distribution of a letter to a personnel file and to other officers may constitute publication sufficient to support cause of action [for defamation]."[98]

An affirmative defense regarding defamation involves the proof of truth or falsity of the assertion. Truth defends the defamation as announced in *Nevin v. Citibank*[99] when a security guard alleged "a black female was making large purchases with a Citibank Visa card' and that, 'she makes purchases, she puts the merchandise in her vehicle and returns to the store."[100] Since these facts were true, the cause of action was dismissed.

4.3.1.7 Invasion of Privacy

Since much of the activity of private security is clandestine and investigatory in nature, the tortious conduct involving invasion of privacy can sometimes occur. Corporate spying—the practice of using security firms to monitor employee conduct manifests the fine line between invading privacy and conducting a legitimate investigative tactic. Alleged spying on prospective union organizers illustrates this tension. A Chicago firm enlisted to surveil union organizers "violated Illinois' privacy law by gathering information on employees' opinion about unions as well as such seemingly unrelated details as where a worker shopped, an employee's off-duty fishing plans, and a female worker's living arrangement."[101] The case elucidates the fine line between a privacy violation and legitimate corporate oversight. The use of such spies is widespread in American business and especially common among retailers with razor-thin profit margins. "Employee theft accounted for an estimated $11 billion of the $27 billion in shortages reported by U.S. retailers in 1992. ... Drug abuse is the other major reason for covert investigations."[102] These sorts of economic pressures on the profit margin prompt extraordinary measures.

The legal concept of invasion of privacy as an actionable civil remedy is a recent legal phenomenon spurred on by modern concerns for civil and constitutional rights.[103] Also supporting this legal remedy are recent efforts "expressed in federal and state statutes, in proposed legislation, and in judicial decisions."[104] The private justice sector's use of investigative technology and intrusive methodologies and practices further supports this legal remedy. When reviewing information gathering and investigative practices, security professionals should keep a few points in mind:

> Do not permit security personnel to use force or verbal intimidation or abuse in investigations of employees and customers; collect and disclose personal information only to the extent necessary; inform the subjects of disclosures to the greatest extent possible; avoid the use of pretext interviews; avoid the use of advanced technology surveillance devices whenever possible; know the standards adhered to by the consumer reporting agencies and other parties with whom you exchange personal information; train your employees in privacy safeguards; periodically review your information practices with appropriate personnel and counsel.[105]

There are four distinct types of the invasion of privacy namely:

- *Invasion of privacy*—Intrusion
  - An act which intrudes into someone's private affairs
  - The action is highly offensive to a reasonably prudent person
- *Invasion of privacy*—Appropriation
  - The unauthorized utilization of a plaintiff's name, trademark, or personality for the defendant's own benefit
- *Invasion of privacy*—public disclosure of private facts
  - Actual publicity
  - Concerning the private life of a plaintiff
  - Which is highly offensive to a reasonably prudent person
- *Invasion of privacy*—false light
  - Publicity, which places plaintiff in a false light and which is highly offensive to a reasonable person

Each of these types targets conduct that is an affront to public sensibility and personal integrity. In other words, to what extent or extremes can a party go to gain access to information or divulge the same? For example, how far can a media critic or newspaper reporter go when divulging the secret lives of the rich and famous? Are there not some activities that are uniquely personal and beyond the rabid publicity of a media without checks and balances? When, at least in this crazed age, does a public disclosure of a private fact in a private life offend individual and collective sensibilities? Politicians often complain about the intrusive stories concerning their sexual dalliances. Proponents of the disclosure hold that any public figure and his personal, moral, and sexual habits is fair game. Critics say that these disclosures are offensive to the average person.

For an excellent summation of Invasion of Privacy and corresponding case law, visit: http://www.cas.okstate.edu/jb/faculty/senat/jb3163/privacytorts.html

---

A recent American Law Reports annotation, "*Investigations and Surveillance, Shadowing and Trailing, as a Violation to the Right to Privacy,*"[106] addresses this very topic. Recognizing the increased use of private detective agencies and other investigatory boards, the annotation states:

> Those instances in which the surveillance, shadowing or trailing is conducted in an unreasonable and obtrusive manner, intent on disturbing the sensibility of the ordinary person, without hypersensitive reactions, is usually been held ... an actual invasion of the right to privacy.[107]

In the business of security, there are many private actions that become publicly disclosed. In divorce proceedings, private sector investigators delve into highly charged conduct that touches privacy. "Where the surveillance, shadowing and trailing is conducted in a reasonable manner, it has been held that owing to the social utility of exposing fraudulent claims, because of the fact that some sort of investigation is necessary to uncover fictitious injuries, an unobtrusive investigation, even though inadvertently made apparent to the person being investigated, does not constitute an actual invasion of his privacy."[108]

Drug screening, testing, and related monitoring programs have been challenged on privacy grounds. For the most part, private sector business and other entities are largely free to conduct such tests. The American Management Association recently reported that 63% of companies surveyed do test for drugs. Some 96% will not hire individuals who test positive. SmithKline Beecham Clinical Laboratories reports that 11% of 1.9 million people tested produced a positive test. This figure reflects a four-year decline in applicant test-positives.

Reid Psychological Systems continues to see increasing applicant drug use. In a study of more than 17,000 applicants in four major industries, 12% admitted to drug use on a written questionnaire.[109] Pinkerton Security and Investigation Services, Inc. and ENDS (Environmental Narcotics Detection Service) have instituted a partnership, whose singular purpose is to screen accurately and efficiently report drug testing results. ENDS helps employers detect traces of illegal drugs in the workplace. Pinkerton Security and Investigation Services collects test samples and the Woburn, Massachusetts-based Thermedics analyzes them. Clients receive results within 48 hours.[110]

Both alcohol and drug abuse in the workplace remain a substantial problem. The Bureau of Justice Statistics paints a distressing picture of workforce drug usage. A study, which focused on findings from the 1994 and 1997 *National Household Survey of Drug Abuse*, reported that:

- 70% of illicit drug users, aged 18–49, were employed full-time.
- 1.6 million of full-time workers were illicit drug users.
- 1.6 million of these full-time workers were both illicit drug and heavy alcohol users in the past.[111]

The picture is further edified by simply looking at data on arrests for drug crimes, which shows at Figure 4.2, a most unfortunate upward incline that shows no sign of abating.[112] Even emergency room data reflect this grim reality (see Figure 4.3).[113]

While most courts uphold the right to conduct such tests, any condemnation that does occur usually relates to the reliability of the methodology employed and the fairness relating to the test itself. Privacy questions need be balanced with the negative impact, the social and human costs that drugs cause in the workplace. Most American businesses allow a first offense, and upon individual rehabilitation, will reinstate the employee. See the agreement at Figure 4.4.

If employees complain about activities that invade their privacy, formally document their statement (see Figure 4.5).

DEA Domestic Arrests	
Calendar Year	*Number of Arrests*
2015	31,027
2014	30,035
2013	31,022
2012	31,085
2011	32,530
2010	31,417
2009	31,858
2008	28,607
2007	29,934
2006	30,691
2005	30,464
2004	30,552
2003	28,749
2002	30,259
2001	34,361
2000	39,772
1999	41,296
1998	38,470
1997	34,065
1996	29,273
1995	25,279
1994	23,135
1993	21,639
1992	24,540
1991	23,659
1990	22,770
1989	25,179
1988	24,853
1987	22,753
1986	19,884
Total	879,158

Source: DEA (SMARTS)
Defendant Statistical System (DSS)

Figure 4.2   DEA domestic arrest, 1986–2015.

Evaluate the fact patterns below to discern whether or not an arguable invasion of privacy has taken place.

■ Assume a merchant publicly posts lists of persons whose checks aren't acceptable due to past bounce experience. Could a damage action for $7,500 in actual damages as well as $50,000 in punitive damages be sustained under an invasion of privacy act?[114]

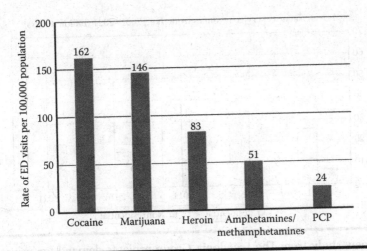

Figure 4.3 **Rates of ED visits per 10,000 population involving illicit drugs, 2011. Source: Center for Behavioral Health Statistics and Quality. SAMHSA, Drug Abuse Warming Network, 2011.**

EMPLOYEE REINSTATEMENT AGREEMENT

It is hereby agreed as follows:

1. Employee's name recognizes that the Company will conditionally reinstate him/her after he/she successfully completes a rehabilitation program at Name and location of rehabilitation program); provided the following conditions are met: List conditions:
2. If within the next Describe time , (employee's name) is unable to perform job duties due to alcohol or drug abuse, fails to continue an alcohol or drug rehabilitation program, or fails to meet the conditions set forth in "1" above, discipline up to and including termination may result.
3. I agree to cooperate in any additional alcohol and drug testing that the Company in its discretion deems appropriate during the (Time period) immediately following my reinstatement, or discipline up to and including termination may result.

(Date)

                                                                                                      (Employee)

                                                                                                      (Union Representative)

                                                                                                      (Employer)

Figure 4.4 Employee reinstatement agreement.

Answer: Maybe, but probably not.

■ If a merchant posts a sign informing customers of surveillance of fitting rooms, is this action an invasion of privacy?[115]

Answer: No

■ Can a retail department store search lockers as well as an employee's private personal property for purposes of reducing shoplifting problems? Does such an act constitute an invasion of privacy?[116]

Answer: No, for legitimate theft reduction, employers may conduct such searches as a condition of employment.

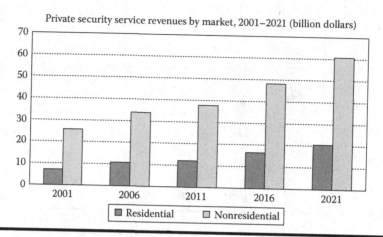

Figure 4.5 shows: Private security service revenues by market, 2001–2021 (billion dollars)

Figure 4.5   A new study from The Freedonia Group projects demand for private contracted security services in the United States to increase 5.4% annually to $64.5 billion in 2016. Source: The Freedonia Group, Inc.

Most companies and nonprofits have implemented various policies and work conduct expectations. Find out about a recommended toolkit which works for employers and employees at: http://www.nonprofitrisk.org/tools/workplace-safety/public-sector/topics/dfw/policy-ps.htm.

4.3.1.8 Negligence

In contrast to intentional conduct, civil law encompasses remedies based on negligent conduct—harms caused by errant conduct, carelessness and mistake. Instead of the intended harm, such as witnessed in assault and battery, defamation or false imprisonment, the negligent actor causes his or her harm without intentionality and does not intend the end or result. The negligent actor acts without the due care owed another, but lacks the malevolence and willfulness that intentional torts require.

Negligence theory examines harm that arises from accident or careless behavior and measures the damages. Negligence is the stuff of everyday life that people fail to do with due care. Forgetting to engage auto turn signals, failing to file documents such as a tax return, misreading a right of way, or missing an important court date, all illustrate the nature of negligence. Negligence evaluates acceptable levels of human conduct and expectation searching for what most people do in similar circumstances. The whole theory of negligence depends upon how the average man or woman would conduct themselves in traditional circumstances. Put another way, what would the "reasonable person" do? What should we expect from the average person in his or her dealings with others? Perfection? Infallibility? The reasonable person is an amalgam of human behavior, a predictable player on the world's stage. While mistakes are part of the human equation, the law of negligence, despite the predictability of human error, holds the negligent actor accountable. The law is even less tolerant of behavior that is either gross or reckless in design. And these expectations will additionally depend on the actor's level of preparation, education, and expertise. We surely expect more from doctors and lawyers than we do from janitors or construction workers. So, in this sense, the average, reasonable person acts reasonably under the circumstances they live and labor under.

How the legal system holds the reasonable person accountable will also depend on the particular industry the actor is employed in. What is certain is that the security industry will be held to its own standard of professional conduct and that injuries that result will be scrutinized in accordance with these expectations of professional performance and due care owed. Security's reasonable person will have to carry out the industry's diverse responsibilities without harm to others.[117]

In order to prove a case of negligence, the claimant must demonstrate the following elements:

1. A duty
2. A breach of duty
3. Proximate causation

Hence, negligence analysis initially considers human conduct in a global sense and then moves to the particular reality of a specific party whose level of obligation will trigger a corresponding expectation of due care and conduct. Here the ideas of duty and due care coalesce. To prove the principle elements of negligence, a duty must be demonstrated and a standard expectation of due care delineated; a harm, connected to the breach itself, then must occur due to a breach of said due care. The harm caused can then result in a finding of proximate causation.

4.3.1.8.1 Nature of Duty

What is duty, and to whom is it owed? When does the duty arise, and what is the standard in which there must be some level of uniformity and conformity? Duty depends not only on station and occupation, level of expertise, and sophistication of field, but also whether that particular duty is relevant in the events and conditions that surround the harm and injury. That duty must be more than a remote association as was evident in *Armor Elevator v. Hinton*,[118] where a security officer, who had just ridden an elevator, and experienced some malfunction, failed to warn other passengers of the defect. Here the court did not reach a conclusion of negligence since the scope and extent of the duty owed was unlikely to include warnings about elevators. While a "legal duty can arise not only by operation of law but by a contract between the parties,"[119] in the matter of elevator warnings, the security firm had no significant duty. That same analysis must be tailored to what the average person does or does not do in an occupation. In short, what does the average pediatrician do in these circumstances? Negligence never measures duty by the best and most sophisticated expert, but instead, employs the average practitioner as a guide. For an attorney, the same rule applies, that he or she owes a duty of competent, intelligent, and ethical representation to his client, as other attorneys in his or her same situation would offer. It does not require the highest level of advocacy, only a reasonable level of advocacy. Other examples of duty abound, including a parent to a child, teacher to student, and an engineer to a construction company. What standards of duty should apply in the assessment of security companies and security personnel in regard to clients or the general public? Is it not reasonable to expect that security personnel be competent in basic legal applications, or that they generally understand what techniques ensure the protection of people and property? And what is a reasonable expectation of duty owed to the consumer when entering a commercial premise? The duty of the premises owner is to provide a safe, secure environment. Even criminal conduct suffered by customers opens the doors to negligence actions.

The results have staggering personal and economic costs for companies and clients. An eight-year study by Liability Consultants, Inc. found the average jury verdict for a rape on a business premises to be $1.8 million. For a death, jurors awarded $2.2 million. The Framingham, Massachusetts, security consulting company compiled the survey results from verdicts voluntarily reported by attorneys to a national group of plaintiffs' lawyers.[120]

4.3.1.8.2 Duty and Foreseeability

Another essential factor in the analysis of duty is whether or not the harm suffered was reasonably foreseeable. By foreseeable, one means could the actor have predicted the result; was it possible for the actor to have predicted harm and injury would have resulted from the breach of that duty? In negligence law, the question is not only the defined duty, as well as its corresponding conduct expectation, but also the predictability and foreseeability of the injuries inflicted. In the case of security practice, the issue of duty is bound to its foreseeability. A recent case in a McDonald's restaurant confronts the duty question in light of foreseeability.[121] Restaurant management used security forces to prevent loitering and other problems in the parking lot and surrounding area. Sweeps of the area were dutifully performed every half hour. Despite this attention, trouble festered in the parking lot and a person was shot. The decedent's family called an expert criminologist who testified as to the paucity of protection and the failure of the McDonald's to provide a safe environment. In order to find negligence, the proof will evaluate the scope and extent of duty owed to the patrons of the McDonald's restaurant to its consumer base, and whether the restaurant chain breached that duty. How much safety and security does the proprietor owe the patron? How foreseeable were the events that led up to the wrongful death? What additional steps could the proprietor have taken to prevent harm? The appellate court analysis could find little evidence of foreseeably in these facts and exonerated McDonald's.

> We are of the opinion that McDonald's was not negligent in either failing to assist Kelly at the time of the encounter by not providing an armed security guard or by the Assistant Manager's failing to interject himself into the fray rather than call the police.[122]

In *Kroger v. Knox*,[123] the Mississippi Supreme Court affirmed the black letter law of forseeability based on reasonable knowledge and understanding the facts and reality of location. At a local Kroger, it was the correlation between the millions of visitors to a particular store and the paucity of criminal activity reported in that area, which led the court to conclude that one cannot foresee what is not reasonably forseeable. The majority opinion held to historic standards on the measure of knowledge needed to be liable.

> We find as a matter of law that—in the context of Kroger's more than three million customer visits over the course of three years—four incidences of criminal activity are wholly insufficient to establish an atmosphere of violence on Kroger's parking lot. And imposing liability without notice of an atmosphere of violence would be nothing short of strict liability for injuries caused by the criminal activity of third parties. It is well settled that a property owner is "not an insurer of an invitee's safety," but owes only "a duty to exercise reasonable care to protect the invitee from reasonably foreseeable injuries at the hands of another."[124,125]

Foreseeability, the ability to project and predict, relates to the duty of the security specialist. Here the security firm is unable to know, to see and predict, and thus, could not be held to a standard of duty and obligation it could not discern or foretell. If the criminal conduct was regular and continuous, or if the proprietor had advance notice, the story would be different. Due diligence, due care, and reasonable precaution cannot take place without some level of knowledge. The interplay between duty and foreseeability is somewhat more obvious in a decision from the Oregon Court of Appeals.[126] The facts include a 76-year-old shopper who exited the J.C. Penney's store at 7 p.m. and simply walked to her car in the parking lot. She was accosted, assaulted, and a victim of theft. A jury awarded her a verdict of over $20,000. The Oregon Court of Appeals held that the retail establishment is under no affirmative duty to provide security and protection in its parking lot unless it has reason to know of problems or conditions that make visitation troubling or potentially dangerous. In other words, if the retail establishment is put on notice of conditions that may cause harm to others, as was true in these facts, the duty standard is clear. The court held:

> Since the possessor is not an insurer of the visitor's safety, he is ordinarily under no duty to exercise any care until he knows or has reason to know that the acts of the third person are occurring or about to occur. He may, however, know or have reason to know, from past experience, that there is a likelihood of conduct on the part of third persons in general which is likely to endanger the safety of the visitor, even though he has no reason to expect it on the part of any particular individual. If the place or character of his business or his past experiences is such that he should reasonably anticipate careless or criminal conduct on the part of third persons, either generally or at some particular time, he may be under a duty to take precautions against it and to provide a reasonably sufficient number of servants to afford reasonable protection.[127]

If the facts lead a reasonable trier to conclude that harm could occur unless precautions were taken, negligence will be found. Again, an act of negligence is a breach of duty owed to others and a failure to exercise due care. In the retail or invitee environment, where customers are entreated to visit a location, that duty ratchets up a good bit more than for the uninvited trespasser. And commercial establishments are obliged to provide a safe and secure environment, especially when there is advance knowledge of unsafe and insecure conditions. Hence when a hotel or parking lot know of the criminal element taking over portions of a facility, the duty to provide security will be heightened. One who controls the premises does have a duty to use ordinary care to protect invitees from criminal acts of third parties if he knows or has reason to know of an unreasonable and foreseeable risk of harm to the invitee. But that duty is not unlimited but must be evaluated in light of what is known an understood. In sum, a duty exists only when the risk of criminal conduct is so great that it is both unreasonable and foreseeable.[128] "Judges face the questions of lawsuits where the customer already has been injured by the supposedly unforeseeable danger. The approach tends to exclude accurate predictions about what dangers are foreseeable."[129] Crafting a benchmark for duty and foreseeability is difficult. Some commentators merely suggest that merchants, business, and industrial leaders, and other parties take extra preventive precaution to protect against liability.[130] Companies cannot be held to a duty threshold when events are utterly unpredictable.[131] "The Courts have placed a public trust upon store owners, retailers must treat their security measures as public property or risk paying a financial penalty in the event of injury to a member of the public."[132]

The task of the security specialist is avoidance of these and every type of claim based on the theory of negligence. The costs are simply too high.[133] Foresee and foretell, predict and evaluate are professional expectations that security firms and their clients have rightfully come to expect and demand.

Consider third-party criminal conduct carried out in a hotel or motel on an innocent customer. How does the hotel proprietor predict or foresee this event?[134] Certainly, past regular criminal conduct at the facility puts the owner on notice of this criminal propensity. In an action by a motel patron against a motel to recover for a sexual assault, rape, and robbery that occurred after she opened her motel room door, a judgment in the patron's favor was upheld. A court may rightfully conclude that motel owners' negligence was the proximate cause of the guest's injuries. The court relied upon a series of evidentiary deductions including the hotel's highway intersection being a high-crime area, coupled with five armed robberies having occurred in the motel next door.[135]

On the other hand, reasonable minds could differ on this and lack the type of knowledge that leads to foreseeability. In *Satchwell v. LaQuinta Motor Inns, Inc.*[136] the court retorted the foreseeability claim since there was "no evidence of any significant criminal activity against motel guests within five miles of location of motel. ... Appellant called no expert witness, and did not present evidence of reasonable precautions that motel operator ... should have taken ... nor did appellant establish how the facts and circumstances of this case gave rise to the appellee's actual or constructive knowledge of any danger to motel guest from third party criminal assaults."[137] Other settings, like apartment complexes and other facilities with public traffic, manifest the complexities of forseeability for security firms. In *Abraham v. Raso*[138] the Court grants protection based on status. Invitees, that is consumer/customers that a business willfully seeks, get more security than the unwelcome trespasser though this principle is not without limitation. "Generally, 'the proprietor of premises to which the public is invited for business purposes of the proprietor owes a duty of reasonable care to those who enter the premises upon that invitation to provide a reasonably safe place to do so that which is within the scope of the invitation.'[139]... 'Whether a duty exists is ultimately a question of fairness. The inquiry involves a weighing of the relationship of the parties, the nature of the risk, and the public interest in the proposed solution.'"[140] Gate attendants at an apartment complex were held not accountable for criminal conduct by third parties since the security service was strictly defined in the contract between the provider and owner. In *Whitehead v. USA-One, Inc.*[141] the court held:

> [I]t is clear both from the contract here as well as from the deposition testimony ... that the employees of USA-One were at Sharpsburg Manor for the benefit of [the owner]. We are unpersuaded by the plaintiffs' ... that USA-One voluntarily assumed a duty to protect them. Here, the fact that the gate attendants patrolled the grounds of Sharpsburg Manor "more frequently" after the second assault is insufficient to establish that USA-One undertook to protect the residents of the apartment complex.[142]

Another locale of heightened interest to the security industry, at least in matters of duty and foreseeability, is the commercial parking lot—a locale where both civil harm and crime find a regular home. A landowner or commercial property owner has a duty to "take affirmative action to control the wrongful acts of third persons which threaten invitees where the [owner] has reasonable cause to anticipate such acts and the probability of injury resulting therefrom."[143] Such affirmative action would seem to mean that the owner or possessor of a parking facility should take reasonable security measures, such as adequate lighting and the presence of security guards, and, if practical, additional measures, such as strategically placed television cameras or alarm systems, warnings, and the availability of escort services.[144]

Discerning past and present criminal incidence rates is crucial to the owner's knowledge of what might occur. An important matter that should be investigated is the availability of any statistics concerning crime in the neighborhood where the crime occurred and, more specifically, in the parking lot facility itself. Some local police departments have computerized crime records that are kept in accordance with guidelines issued by the U.S. Department of Justice. It may be possible to have the department run a computer check of the parking facility address for up to three years preceding the crime in question.[145]

Factors that bear on the safety of the parking facility and the foreseeability of criminality are as follows:

- Occurrence of the crime
- Prior episodes of theft, vandalism, or attack
- Attraction of facility to criminals
- Design that makes concealment possible
- Remoteness of facility as inviting attack
- Foreseeability of event
- Duty of landowner to use reasonable care to guard against attack
  - Breach of duty by landowner
  - Causation unbroken by third-party criminal attack
  - Inadequate security at ramp
  - No warning of danger
  - Subsequent remedial events[146]

While the trend has been pro-victim in many jurisdictions, holding most criminal conduct by third parties preventable and foreseeable, there are more cases now challenging this conventional wisdom. To be sure, everywhere and everyplace sees crime. In *Ann M. v. Pacific Plaza Shopping Center*,[147] California altered its previous stand of assuming negligence when crimes occurred. Citing random, endemic, universal crime, the opinion takes a pro-defendant approach.

> Under the more pro-victim standard used in California prior to the recent ruling, evidence of all previous crimes, whether similar or dissimilar, could be considered by a jury as it decided whether a property owner should have known of the danger. Additional factors, such as lighting and other safety features, also could be considered. Courts applying this standard reason that the first victim of a particular kind of crime shouldn't be denied recourse merely because no analogous crime occurred previously. But with the recent ruling, California's high court is suggesting such an approach is no longer practical. For one thing, the court said, these days almost every property has been the site of all sorts of crimes.[148]

Negligence exerts extraordinary economic costs on all facets of the security industry for damages negatively impact the financial bottom line. Clearly damages must be paid by someone. While damages make whole, provide compensation and consequence, and reimburse for loss, the bill for said damages trickles everywhere in the lives of ordinary consumers, from the price of goods to insurance costs. Operationally, the security industry grapples with these liabilities and the effects on the balance sheet are never positive.

Adding to the compensatory framework of damages, where the harmed party is merely made whole, the firm must also be concerned about punitive damages. Punitive damages do what they imply—"punish" the party causing the harm since the results were so avoidable and the injuries so egregious. Punitive damages are computed as additional to compensatory and consequential damages. But this is not a conclusion without fail. Whether or not a security company knows or could have known that crimes could be committed on location is a question subject to multiple interpretations. To be sure, at common law, without knowledge, there was no obligation to make safe the locale. When awareness and understanding occurs, the obligation is ratcheted up a bit. In *Bowler v. Kings Plaza Shopping Center*,[149] the Court provides a well-reasoned template for determining when liability inures to the security firm. While in a jewelry store, a customer was punched by an unruly customer. The injured customer sued the jeweler for a failure to provide security. The Court correctly concluded:

> Further, at common law, when a criminal act is unforeseeable, such as the assault on the plaintiff in the instant case, the owner of the premises has no duty to protect persons from attack. ... Plaintiff ... Fails to demonstrate that the defendants knew or had reason to know from past experience that there is a likelihood of conduct on the part of third persons ... which is likely to endanger the safety of the plaintiff.[150]

In *Easterling v. Burger King*,[151] the Court insightfully deals with a host of negligence matters and is particularly keen on the matter of duty. Even when the company is aware of crime in perimeter of the facility and even though the company had taken preventative steps to secure that perimeter and even when previous injuries had been cataloged, the court accepted the reasonable efforts made by Burger King in securing its environment. The Court's language manifests a business and economic reality that accepts that not all situations can be perfectly safe. The Court plainly stated:

> Although Burger King previously hired an off-duty police officer, this was in response to a string of armed robberies in the area—not on its premises—and was only a temporary solution. Given the evidence regarding the nature of prior incidents at this Burger King location, as well as a lack of testimony from Easterling's expert calling for such a measure, we find it would be unreasonable to require Burger King to hire security personnel. Thus, we find Easterling failed to present a mere scintilla of evidence that (1) Burger King's preventative actions were unreasonable or (2) it should have expended more resources to curtail the risk of criminal activity on its premises.[152]

4.3.1.8.3 Negligence and Security Management

The analysis of negligence and its impact on security practice from a managerial point of view is an exercise worth serious energy. Negligent behavior on the part of lower echelon security personnel can give rise to multiple causes of action, both individually and vicariously. And those entrusted with supervision over on location security forces are always subject to multiple levels of negligence analysis.[153] More telling is the negligent behavior of management and policymakers of security companies. Supervision, training, personnel, policy making, and performance standards are the primary responsibility of security managers and the failure to carry out these professional obligations competently is a fertile ground for negligence actions.

4.3.1.8.3.1 Personnel Practices The security industry's costs of poor human relations and personnel practices are significant, and in hiring, supervision, and discipline, the industry needs to take its responsibility seriously.[154] "Private security companies or businesses which hire their own security forces should exercise great care in choosing security employees."[155] Hiring an individual without investigation of their background or improper placement of an individual in a position that requires higher levels of expertise than the applicant possesses, is a possible negligence case. In *Easly v. Apollo Detective Agency*,[156] the court found a security guard company negligent in the hiring of a security guard entrusted with a pass key for an apartment building. "Such negligence usually consist of hiring, supervising, retaining, or assigning the employee with the knowledge of his unfitness, or failing to use reasonable care to discover the unfitness, and is based upon the negligence of the employer to a third person entirely independent of the liability of the employer under the doctrine of *respondeat superior*."[157] While on duty the security guard entered, without license or privilege, a tenant's quarters with criminal intent. "The evidence showed that the company did not check any of the prior addresses or personal references listed by the guard on his application, nor did it require the guard to take any intelligence or psychological tests."[158] A company that appoints or hires an individual should be assured not only of competence, but of personal character too.[159] In *Violence in the Medical Care Setting*, hospital administrators are urged to not only carefully select, but also adequately train all security personnel.

> Pre-employment testing and evaluation, post-employment training and evaluation and adequate supervision corresponding to carefully drafted guidelines and policies are the new protective shields. Failure to take these minimal precautions in the highly explosive medical care environment leaves the employee the negligent supervisor and the entity facing liability unnecessarily.[160]

The entire company, its employees, and responsible policymakers must deal with the quality of employees. Employees should be enlisted to assure a safe, secure workplace inhabited by safe and secure personnel. "From the mail room to the executive suite, successful security awareness programs leave their mark. Once a luxury, awareness programs are evolving as a necessity to help curb security's high costs. Changing workplace demographics call for awareness training at all employee ranks."[161]

4.3.1.8.3.2 Negligent Retention When security management knows that present employees are professionally inept but willingly chooses to retain despite the employee flaws, the argument of negligent retention has legitimate merit. Case law and common sense dictate that retention of any troubled employee inevitably leads to larger problems for the firm and the client served.

Like negligent hiring, the courts have found liability under a theory of negligent retention when employers know or should have known, in the exercise of ordinary care, that their employees had violent tendencies. Employees with a history of sexual offenses, such as rape and sodomy, prompt strict scrutiny of the negligent retention. In addition, employees with checkered histories that include convictions of theft, larceny, embezzlement, and extortion are all prime candidates for a claim of negligent retention when offenses occur at the work location. Any employee with a propensity for violence should not be candidates for employment without a risk.[162]

Any personnel program must comprehensively examine the background of any prospective employees by the analysis of these variables:

- Identification information
- Records of conviction
- Proof of civil actions and other litigation
- Credit and financial history
- Educational records
- Neighborhood information
- Personal and business references
- Previous and current employment
- Opinions of previous and current employers
- Their financial data[163]

When security employees engage in misconduct, the company should give notice to the employer, specifying the exact nature of the misdeed (see Figure 4.6).[164]

If wrongful behavior persists, a warning formalizing future consequences for said behavior is warranted (see Figure 4.7).

If all corrective steps are futile, a discipline and/or termination report assures a significant record in the event of a challenge based on wrongful termination. Any legal action asserted by a third party for negligence in the handling of personnel can be rebutted by the due diligence these documents memorialize (see Figure 4.8).

4.3.1.8.3.3 Negligent Assignment and Entrustment

As personnel histories unfold, security firms can err in judgment at various stages: first, at initial hiring; second, at continued retention even when aware of employee problems as severe as criminal backgrounds; and finally, at the assignment and reassignment stage knowing full well that the assignment may cause difficulties for others. Once put on notice of employee problems, the employer should take remedial steps to assure that the employee is not assigned to any position or delegated tasks likely to create conflicts. With this knowledge, the employer will be negligent since he or she foreseeably knows the nature of the employee and realizes the real injury is likely. In *Williams v. The Brooklyn District Telephone Company*,[165] the security company was held liable for assigning a guard to a sensitive position that allowed easy access to larcenable items. "Rejecting the company's contention that it was not liable for the guard's theft because his act was outside the course and scope of his employment, the court held that the company was bound to exercise reasonable care in the selection of its guards and therefore could not be permitted to say that it had no responsibility for the unlawful acts of its guards."[166]

Allegations of negligence have even greater credibility when the claimant can demonstrate actual knowledge on the part of security management or administration. Assigning security officers who suffer from a bona fide alcohol or drug problem constitutes a negligent assignment or entrustment case.[167] The U.S. Court of Appeals, Fifth Circuit, issued a strongly wording ruling in *Aetna v. Pendelton Detectives*[168] where a company's substandard performance severely impacted a package delivery company. Indeed, the unprofessional security services caused the firm to fail in its core operations. Security was to assure delivery although the lack of it assured failure. The court objectively listed a series of variables that proved the negligent assignment.

Merchants presented the following evidence of Pendleton's negligent security practices: (1) guards slept on the job; (2) guards watched TV on the job; (3) guards drank on the job; (4) guards entertained guests of the opposite sex on the job; (5) guards left the gate to the warehouse open; (6) Pendleton's admission of failing to perform sufficient background checks on its guards; (7) the private investigator's conclusion

EMPLOYEE MISCONDUCT NOTICE

DATE:
TO PERSONNEL DEPARTMENT:

Time:

Name of Employee _____ No. _____ Dept. _____

The above-named employee has displayed the following misconduct, and has been warned that this misconduct will be entered on his Personnel Record.

MISCONDUCT (Check where applicable and specify details in section indicated below)

Smoking in Restricted Areas _____
Leaving Work Without Permission _____
Violation of Safety Rules or Dept. Rules _____
Refusal to Carry Out Supervisor's Instructions _____
Irregular Attendance (Specify No. of absences to date) _____
Violation of Eating Regulations _____
Breakage _____
Poor Service _____
General Inefficiency
  a) Quality _____
  b) Quantity _____
  c) Accuracy _____
Discourtesy Toward Guest _____
Discourtesy Toward Fellow Employee _____

_____
(Employee)

_____
(Union Representative)

_____
(Employer)

(Mention other Employee)
Attitude _____
Carelessness _____
Other _____

Specify Misconduct in Detail _____
_____
_____

EMPLOYEE COMMENTS _____
_____
_____

DISCIPLINARY ACTION TAKEN _____

Signature of Supervisor
(Reprimand) (Layoff) (Other)

I acknowledge receipt of this notice

_____
Signature of Employee

Figure 4.6 Employee misconduct notice.

```
┌─────────────────────────────────────────────────────────────────────────┐
│                          WARNING NOTICE                                   │
│                       SECURITY DEPARTMENT                                 │
│                                                                           │
│  Employee:                   Department:                    Date:         │
│                                                                           │
│  Rule(s) Violated: _____   │
│  _____    │
│  _____    │
│                                                                           │
│  Details of Violation: On_____        │
│                                   Date(s)                                 │
│  _____    │
│  _____    │
│  _____    │
│                                                                           │
│  Immediate satisfactory improvement must be shown and maintained of       │
│  further disciplinary action will be taken.                               │
│                                                                           │
│  Action to be Taken:    ____Suspension      ____Days      ____Discharge    │
│                         ____Warning                       ____Final Warning│
│                                                                           │
│  Supervisor        Date              Employee           Date              │
│  Sign Here                           Sign Here                            │
└─────────────────────────────────────────────────────────────────────────┘
```

WARNING NOTICE

SECURITY DEPARTMENT

Employee: ___ Department: ___ Date: ___

Rule(s) Violated: ___

Details of Violation: On___ Date(s) ___

Immediate satisfactory improvement must be shown and maintained of further disciplinary action will be taken.

Action to be Taken: ____Suspension ____Days ____Discharge
____Warning ____Final Warning

Supervisor Sign Here ___ Date ___ Employee Sign Here ___ Date ___

If Employee Refuses to Sign:
"This is to certify that the employee named in this report was warned by his superior in my presence concerning the subject matter contained therein."
If Employee Refuses to Accept Copy of Form:
"Employee refuses to accept his copy of this warning notice."
Witness: ___ Date: ___ Supervisor: ___ Date: ___

Figure 4.7 Security Department warning notice.

that night shift employees were responsible for the losses; (8) several of Merchants' night shift employees' confessions to stealing large amounts of food; (9) Pendleton's contractual obligation to provide security from 4 p.m. to 8 a.m. and 24 hours a day on weekends; (10) Merchants' repeated reports of suspected employee theft to Pendleton; (11) the report of a person wearing a Pendleton baseball cap selling Merchants' products from the trunk of his car; and (12) Merchants' security expert's testimony that it was more probable than not that Pendleton's lax security practices caused the losses.[169]

Few cases as clearly edify the principle of negligent assignment as *Aetna*.

DISCIPLINE AND TERMINATION FORM

1. Are there written rules or guidelines of conduct? __ Yes__ No
2. When and how are employees informed of employer rules? _____
   _____
3. Who is responsible for enforcing these rules? _____
   _____
4. Do persons responsible for enforcing rules have any power when determining the disciplinary penalty imposed once offense has occurred? ____Yes__No
5. Is there progressive discipline procedures? ____Yes __ No
6. How are managers/supervisors informed of the disciplinary procedure of an employee? _____
   _____
7. How and when are employees made aware of the disciplinary procedure?_____
   _____
8. Are disciplinary decisions made by supervisors reviewed? __Yes__No
9. How and when are employees informed of a decision of a disciplinary action? _____
   _____
10. Prior to being disciplined, is an employee given an opportunity to present his/her explanation? __Yes __No
11. Are employees given the opportunity to discuss the reasons for disciplinary actions?
    __Yes __No
    If yes, please explain._____
    _____
12. Are employees allowed to appeal disciplinary actions? __Yes __No
    If yes, please explain the appeal procedure. _____
    _____
13. Is an employee who is being investigated, permitted to have a person of his/her choice present at the investigation or negotiation meeting? __Yes__No
    If yes, are there exceptions? _____
    _____
14. If an employee receives more than one warnings or negative evaluations, are any of the following measures taken to remedy the problem: __Yes __ No
    a. Vertical transfer to place the employee in a position more closely suited to his/her abilities?
       ___Yes __ No
    b. Lateral transfer to reduce personality conflicts between the employee and supervisor or between the employee and workers? __Yes __ No
    c. Additional employee job training? ___Yes __No
    d. Other? Yes __No
15. Who is responsible for the termination process?
    _____
16. What is the procedure for documenting disciplinary decisions?
    _____
17. Is age or race ever used as a factor in a termination decision? __Yes__ No
    If yes, explain its use._____
    _____
18. Is sex ever used as a factor in a termination decision? __Yes__No
    If yes, explain its use._____
    _____
19. Is a terminated employee allowed to appeal to a higher-level manager of panel of officials? __Yes __ No
    If yes, please explain the procedure._____
    _____
20. Are employees given a written notice of termination? __Yes __ No

Figure 4.8 Discipline and termination form.

(Continued)

---

21. When are terminated employees given a final paycheck? _____

_____

22. Are terminated employees eligible for severance pay?   __Yes__ No

23. Are exit interviews conducted?
    By whom? _____   __Yes__ No

24. Are records maintained of all disciplinary actions?   __Yes __No

25. If yes, what records maintained and where._____

_____

26. Are copies of warnings and terminations placed in the Employee's personnel file? ___Yes __ No

27. Do warnings contain the following:
    a. Offense __Yes__No
    b. Action necessary for improvement __Yes__No
    c. Consequences of failure to improve __Yes__No

Figure 4.8 (Continued)   Discipline and termination form.

4.3.1.8.3.4 Negligent Supervision

Once hired and assigned, security managers have a continuing obligation to exercise a duty of due care relative to employee development and performance. A security company is vicariously liable for the actions of its employees, and a lack of supervision creates a presumption of negligence. Wayne Saiat, editorial director for *Security World Magazine*,[170] highlights the severe problem caused by a lack of supervision.

> Although security personnel and their employers can be subjected to legal action for a wide variety of causes, the vast majority of cases involve the action or inaction of security guards. But the suits generally do not name only a guard as a defendant; they will often name the guard's supervisor, the guard company, if one is involved, and the ultimate employer of the guard and the guard's company.[171]

Supervision takes on added importance when complicated by the temptations of technology. In *National Labor Relations Board v. J. Weingarten*,[172] the court fluently assessed the need for heightened supervision when security machinery is in use.

> There has been a recent growth of sophisticated techniques—such as closed circuit television, undercover security agents and lie detectors—to monitor and investigate the employees' conduct at their place of work. These techniques increase, not only the employees feeling of apprehension but also their need for experienced assistance in dealing with them.[173]

In *Sanders v. ERP Operating Ltd. Partnership*,[174] the Florida Supreme Court rejected a lower court directed verdict when it concluded that a security firm and its managerial personnel had failed to assure an adequate upkeep of security equipment such as the access gate and the complex under its protection rampant with crime and criminality. Here the Court sent back to the lower court to determine whether or not there was negligence in this operation of the security force that led to multiple deaths. The question of the "cause of death" was more complex than a directed verdict permits. The Court was troubled by the failure of the trial court to determine the sufficiency of oversight, when it relayed:

Whether or not proximate causation exists is a question of fact, involving an inquiry into whether the respondent's breach of duty foreseeably and substantially contributed to the plaintiff's injuries. This Court has made clear that plaintiffs alleging negligence in Florida must meet "the more likely than not standard of causation" as Florida courts "require proof that the negligence probably caused the plaintiff's injury."[175]

A failure to supervise or manage can be management's failure to hire sufficient personnel, to insufficiently or improperly train secondary managerial employees, or a failure to allot sufficient time and energy to train employees for appropriate tasks.

4.3.1.8.3.5 Negligent Training

The final theory under the negligence umbrella is negligent training. Sophisticated training, hopefully, will upgrade the quality and efficacy of security personnel. Critics have long argued that training presently required is superficial rather than substantive and the industry needs greater dedication to training. In *Training, The Key to Avoiding Liability*, the essential nature of training is espoused:

> The bottom line then is this: Your security officers must be adequately trained. Moreover, the training they receive must be sufficiently practical to enable them to demonstrate technical and legal competency commensurate with the duties they perform. Classroom theory is fine, but it isn't enough. Academics should be combined with performance exercises so that officers can try out and become confident with the techniques they may be required to use.[176]

The implications for this training theory reached an appellate course whereby those harmed by security officers alleged that a failure to train private security operatives in the complexities of constitutional law and civil liberties. The court, in *Royster v. Nichols*,[177] considered the argument but could not find a case of negligence in training when it asserted:

> First, "respondeat superior is inapplicable to claims under 42 U.S.C. § 1983."[178] Second, we have already determined that Officer Nichols's did not violate Royster's constitutional rights; therefore, Royster's "failure to train and failure to supervise claims ... [can]not be sustained absent an underlying constitutional violation by the officer."[179,180]

The security industry's response to education and training has been less than enthusiastic and often more rhetoric than substance.[181] While some strides are being made, industry foot dragging and a lack of legislative uniformity or standards influence the rigor and intensity of training. Saiat argues that security malpractice is on the horizon.

> While negligence implies a duty, malpractice implies reliance on the duty. Negligence implies a failure to perform with reasonable care, malpractice implies a failure to perform to a higher standard of care.[182]

Certain professional groups, such as American Society for Industrial Security (ASIS) International, have called for certification programs, like the Certified Protection Program (CPP) and the Certified Protection Officer (CPO). Security liability has given impetus to a host of educational delivery systems in the private sector, which is referred to as "niche" training. Certifications take many forms although nearly all of them highlight a specific subject matter that requires unique preparation of a body of specialized knowledge. In addition, certifications are usually the invention of the professional bodies and associations that are inexorably tied that body of knowledge needed for skilled implementation.

Some examples are

- Orleans Regional Security Institute, New Orleans, LA
  - Semi-automatic pistol training
  - Basic revolver handgun training
  - Security training course
  - CCP course
  - Basic investigator
  - Advanced investigator
  - Psychological stress evaluation training
- Sandia National Laboratories, Albuquerque, NM
  - Physical protection systems training course
- Bob Bondurant Security Services Division, Phoenix, AZ
  - Drivers training programs in antiterrorist/executive protection
  - Advanced antiterrorist driving course
  - Motorcycle training course[183]

ASIS International has also posed standards and guidelines for educational programs, which in turn ensure uniform preparedness and skills acquisition, something crucially necessary when defining acceptable or normative standards of professional conduct.[184] Its Certified Protection Professional (CPP) programs make a real contribution to substantive professionalism. The CPP program's chief objectives are

1. To raise the professional standing of the field and to improve the practice of security management by giving special recognition to those security practitioners who, by passing examinations and fulfilling prescribed standards of performance, conduct, and education, have demonstrated a high level of competence and ethical fitness.
2. To identify sources of professional knowledge of the principles and practices of security and loss prevention, related disciplines, and laws governing and affecting the practice of security.
3. To encourage security professionals to carry out a continuing program of professional development.[185]

The Certified Protection Professional (CPP) program tests rigorously those wishing the designation. Topics are broken down into distinct domains, which include

- Emergency planning
- Legal aspects
- Personnel security
- Protection of sensitive information
- Security management
- Substance abuse
- Loss prevention
- Liaison
- Banking

- Computer security
- Credit card security
- Department of Defense
- Educational institutions
- Manufacturing
- Utilities
- Restaurants and lodging
- Retail security
- Transportation and cargo security
- Telecommunications[186]

Jon C. Paul, director of security services for a major hospital, applauds the CPP designation. "The CPP designation is the hallmark of excellence in our profession—a fact that is recognized in our industry and is becoming more widely recognized by the organizations we serve."[187] Lastly, as noted in Chapter 2, there is a growing cadre of security service companies that present in-house training.

4.3.2 Strict Liability Torts

While intentional torts require a mental decision to act, defendants in cases of strict liability are held accountable regardless of their intentions. The act, in and of itself, is deemed serious enough to cause absolute, unconditional liability without mental intent. The burden of proof in strict liability cases is less rigorous than its negligence or intentional tort counterparts since the act alone suffices for liability. Certain types of activities, for public policy reasons, qualify for strict liability coverage. If an action is inherently dangerous, like explosives or wild animals, a tort claim needs no proof of intentionality. In the case of products, there is a body of strict liability case law. The elements of a strict liability case include

1. That there be a seller of a product or service
2. That the product is unreasonably dangerous to person and property
3. A user or a consumer suffers physical harm
4. That there be causation

Strict liability law is plainly in its infancy stage when applied to the security industry and its practices. Any ultra-hazardous action like the use of ballistics, explosives, underwater gear, and/ or injuries caused by wild, undomesticated, and uncontrollable animals would qualify. Outside of the ballistics and explosives area, there has been little litigation in the security industry.[188] One exception to this general rule is that strict liability may be imposed on security interests that operate by a "certificate of authority" issued by the state or other governmental entity.[189] "This means that such a private security company will be held liable for the acts of its employees regardless of whether the employee's acts were negligent or intentional as long as the acts were committed while the employee was actually on the job."[190] Alarm companies and other electronically sophisticated enterprises do have to consider the defensive or hazardous propensities of their products.

For an overview of strict liability and a refresher on all other torts, visit: http://www.aug.edu/~sbadph/mgmt2106/2106dph08.PDF

4.3.2.1 Vicarious Liability

Depending on the nature of a relationship, certain persons will be responsible or legally accountable for another's specific act or form of behavior even if they have not acted, solicited, or conspired in the action. To be responsible through another is to be vicariously responsible. By vicarious liability, the principal—characteristically an employer, a security supervisor, or a management team—having the right to govern, supervise, manipulate, and control the action of employees or agents, can be held accountable for the agent's actions. This legal relationship has sometimes been characterized as a master–servant relationship governed by the doctrine of *respondeat superior* (let the master answer).[191] Under the doctrine of *respondeat superior*, an employer is liable for injuries to the person or property of third persons resulting from the acts of his employee, which, although not directly authorized or ratified by the employer, are incidental to the class of acts, which the employee is hired to perform and are within the scope of his employment. Under the doctrine, the law imputes to the employer that act of the employee. Although employers have been held liable under this doctrine for the intentional and criminal acts of their employees under some circumstances, the viability of the doctrine is somewhat limited because intentional and criminal actions generally are not within an employee's scope of employment and usually are not committed at the request of or with the approval of an employer.[192] "The importance of this determination results from the general rule that a master is liable for the torts of his servants committed within the scope of a servant's employment, whereas the hirer of an independent contractor is ordinarily not liable for the torts of a contractor committed in carrying out work under the contract."[193]

Much of the security industry can be divided into these two classifications: employer–employee and independently contracted services.[194] Contract firms are hired by private companies or corporations to provide security services. The economic and legal advantages in contract services are many, since the company is not responsible for hiring, firing, tax liability, or any other administrative or procedural matters governing the security force. What type of workplace climate that employer provides bears on the question of liability.[195] In other words, the employer is generally only subject to an employee's misconduct when foreseeable and within the scope of the employee's responsibilities. Couple tortious conduct with poor management and cases of civil liability are bound to unfold. Bruce Harman lays out the types of business climate that indubitably lead to individual and vicarious liability.

- Failure to support elementary security and audit procedures
- Lack of climate for security and control consciousness
- Inept or complacent management without feedback to measure losses
- Inadequate implementation of plans and/or personnel and training procedures
- Dishonest management[196]

The assumption that the independent contractor status will hold harmless the employer from potential liability under either civil or criminal liability is not a foolproof defense and may be premature. By hiring independent contractors, employers hope to "convey all potential liability to the contract security company and to protect the security manager against joinder in a civil action that could arise out of a negligent or wrongful act by the security contractor."[197] However, while generally true, there are numerous exceptions to the rule:

1. Independent contractor status will not be upheld if the employer ratifies specific conduct.

2. Independent contractor status will not shield the employer from intentional torts.
3. Independent contractor status will not relieve the employer from strict liability tortious conduct.
4. Independent contractor status will not provide a defense to the employer if the duty is nondelegable.[198]

The doctrine of *respondeat superior*, the basic principles of agency and the common-law standard on master–servant relationship make unlikely an employer's complete insulation and isolation from legal responsibility for the acts of employees or independent contractors. Whether the security operative's action, tortious or not, are within the scope of his or her employment, is a seminal question in the imposition of vicarious liability. In *Sunshine Security & Detective Agency v. Wells Fargo Armored Services Corp.*,[199] a bank security guard robbed his employer. "The employee's tortious actions in conspiring to rob the bank he was hired by the defendant agency to guard, the court said, represented a classic case of an employee acting outside the scope of his employment."[200] Whether the relationship exists "depends on the particular facts of each case."[201] And the ultimate liability may depend on the status of the defendant in question. A 2016 Alabama decision offers up a curious result of how these principles play out. In *Martinez v. Espey*,[202] the Court deduced that a security officer—off job and moonlighting from a day job of public police officer, once he witnessed a crime could no longer maintain his or her status as a security officer. In this transformation, the police officer maintains his or her immunity as well as constitutional obligations that private security do not have. The endgame of this change causes a harmed party to lose particular remedies that might be collectible under damages caused by private security and now nonaccessible because of the recast public officer status. More particularly, the claim against the employer, in this case a Marriott Courtyard, under a theory of vicarious liability dissipates once the public officer alters his or her once private employee status where Marriott would remain liable. The Court reached this curious result by stating:

> When the officer witnessed the ethnic slurs and threatening gestures, his status changed from security guard to police officer. ... Therefore, Courtyard is not vicariously liable for the officer's failure to intervene in the altercation. The Court dismisses with prejudice Mr. Martínez's claims under respondeat superior for assault and battery, equal protection, and selective enforcement.[203]

Case law conservatively construes the definition of an independent contractor. The American Law Institute sought to distinguish a servant from an independent contractor by considering the following factors:

1. The extent of control, which, by agreement, the master may exercise over the details of the work
2. Whether or not the one employed is engaged in a distinct occupation or business
3. The kind of occupation with reference to whether, in the locality, the work is usually done under the direction of the employer or by a specialist without supervision
4. The skill required in the particular occupation
5. Whether the employer or the workman supplies the instrumentalities, tools, and the place for the person doing the work

6. The length of time for which the person is employed
7. The method of payment, whether by the time or by the job
8. Whether or not work is a part of the regular business of the employer
9. Whether or not the parties believe they are creating the relation of master/servant
10. Whether the principal is or is not in business[204]

In *Safeway Stores v. Kelley*,[205] a supermarket chain denied all liability for an abusive arrest process claiming that its guard service contract could only be characterized as an independent contractor relationship. In determining that the independent contractor status could serve as an employer shield, the court determined the following factors to be of particular pertinence:

> The contract was performed at the store; the store could determine which people the guards should investigate; the agency had no specific job or piece of work to perform; the agency rendered continuous service for which the store paid it weekly; and the store could terminate the particular service whenever it chose.[206]

A previously discussed case, *U.S. Shoe v. Jones*,[207] reiterated a common principle regarding the law's willingness to circumvent independent contractor status. In this case, which involved the intentional tort of false imprisonment, the court cited the well-respected *Noble v. Sears Roebuck & Co.*[208] decision.

Even though hirers of an independent security or protective agency have generally been held not liable for negligent torts of agency personnel, where the hirer did not exercise control over them, hirers have been held liable for the intentional torts that the agency personnel committed, in the scope of the agency's employment against the hirer's invitees.[209]

When private sector firms work oversees in military zones and operations, under the direct supervision and control of military personnel, these officers are said to have "dual servant" status, which negates traditional principles of vicarious liability. In this situation the employer, back in the states, is shielded from liability for the acts of his employees since his employees are now supervised by military authority.[210]

Principles of immunity also operate to minimize vicarious liability when a governmental authority, such as the military, supervises the security firm in a war zone. The *Federal Tort Claims Act* and other common law legislation provide immunity in combatant situations. Courts have struggled "when defining the term 'combatant activities.'"[211] Considering the types of activities service contractors perform demonstrates how slippery the concept of combatant activities can be.[212] While troop transport qualifies[213] road construction may not.[214] In addition, the *Alien Tort Claims Act (ATCA)*[215] seeks to pull in "actors responsible for their actions even though those actions may have taken place on foreign soil."[216]

To summarize, some principle points bear reiteration:

That liability for the tortious or criminal conduct of a security employee will extend to the security employer if the following relationships exist:

■ Master/servant governed by the doctrine of respondeat superior
■ Principal/agent
■ Employer/employee
■ An independent contractor who commits intentional tortious deeds

Generally, negligent conduct by an independent contractor is not the responsibility of a company procuring security services.[217]

Some courts will go to substantial extremes to maintain that status and protect the company utilizing the services of an independent contractor. In *Brien v. 18925 Collins Avenue Corp.*[218] a guard "supplied to a motel for protective purposes by a security corporation, under agreement with the owner of the motel, shot and killed Plaintiff's decedent whom the officer had stopped for questioning while patrolling the motel property."[219] Curiously deciding that the utilization of firearms was not an inherently dangerous activity, the court affirmed judgment in favor of the motel owner and essentially argued that "an owner is not ordinarily liable for the negligence of an independent contractor employed by him, noting there was nothing pleaded that the owner of the motel was himself in any way negligent."[220] A reverse judgment was demonstrated in *Ellenburg v. Pinkerton's Inc.*[221] upholding a civil action for invasion of privacy. The security agency hired to conduct surveillance did so improperly.

Determining whether a security agency is independent largely depends upon who controls the operation. In *Cappo v. Vinson Guard Service Inc.*,[222] a Louisiana court denied independent contractor status in an intentional battery case. Actions by the employer were largely imputed to by the conduct of the restaurant manager who:

1. Periodically checked on parking lot as part of his duties
2. Told security agent who to admit and exclude from parking lot
3. Had authority to replace security guard with other personnel
4. Had exercised his authority over security agent on night of incident by sending security agent home; in addition, trial court noted that security agent's activities during performance of his duties benefited restaurant as well[223]

There are numerous contrary decisions. In *Liability of Private Citizen or His Employer for Injury or Damage to a Third Person Resulting from Firing of Shots at Fleeing Felon,*[224] Caroll Miller outlines cases that hold security guards, as well as their employers, liable for the negligent operation of firearms, specifically when aimed at fleeing criminals. In *Giant Food v. Scherry,*[225] a security guard created a substantial risk to innocent bystanders when shooting at a fleeing robber as the bullets shattered a woman's apartment window.

4.3.2.1.1 Miscellaneous Issues in Vicarious Liability

4.3.2.1.1.1 Nondelegable Duty
The trend of judicial decision making in the area of vicarious liability has been pro-plaintiff, allowing victims as many "deep pockets" as possible. Asserting that the security services contracted were delegated provide another avenue to hold others vicariously liable. Nondelegable duty or skill is best understood by analogy, such as the artist or musician hired under a personal service contract or performance contract, which recognizes special skills or acumen. A contract between a security company and an employer may also be viewed as a personal service or performance contract that requires special skills and talents and is not conducive to assignment or delegation.[226] A grocery store was liable to a customer for false arrest committed by security guards employed by an independent contractor of the store where the store had a "nondelegable" duty to furnish the customer with a safe place to shop, where the independent contractor was employed exclusively by the store, and where the store provided place in which guards were to work and thus intentionally exposed customers to possible tortious conduct of guards.[227]

4.3.2.1.1.2 Principal's Liability for Punitive Damages

As a general rule, punitive damages should not be assessed against principal or master for an agent or servant's tortious acts.[228] While the principal may be liable for compensatory or actual damages, it is unfair to transfer or infuse the malicious, intentional, arbitrary, or capricious mental state of the tortfeasor. Punitive damages are not regularly awarded and are possible only on a more pronounced showing of defendant's irresponsibility. While the master is responsible for the actions of his servant, historically, he has not been responsible for the punitive consequences of his servant's acts.

Punitive damages have been successfully assessed against the principal in the following types of circumstances:

- Punitive damages have been assessed when the principal ratifies the conduct.[229]
- Punitive damages have been assessed when the principal actually authorizes or participates.[230]
- Punitive damages have been assessed against corporations and other business entities.[231]
- Punitive damages have been assessed against governmental bodies.[232]
- Punitive damages have been assessed against common carriers.[233]
- Punitive damages have been assessed against managerial or executive employees of a corporation.[234]

4.3.2.1.1.3 Contractual Limitations

Efforts by companies and agencies to contractually insulate themselves from potential liability resulting from negligent and intentional conduct are not generally successful. Many security firms utilize contractual forms to absolve liability. Limiting liability by contractual provisions is generally on two fronts: first, as relates to the amount of recoverable damages and second, as to what the conditions, events, or circumstances will trigger in liability. Susan Fettner, in her article, *Security System Service*, urges counsel for security companies to draft meticulous clauses that will protect their clients. She notes:

> In summary, we have seen that judgments against providers of security services may be had where those services failed to prevent a burglary. Liability, whether in contract or tort, becomes a question of fact. Because the subject of the bargain is the prevention of criminal intrusion or a mitigation of its results, the triers of the facts will be likely to find either a breach of the party's agreement or a causal relationship in the fact patterns presented to them. However, if liability is limited by contract, courts will enforce the limitation.[235]

One must pay close attention to the jurisdictional requirements of the security firm's area of representation and be certain to include legal language and clauses that are not contrary to warranty, mitigation of damages, and general disclaimer laws. These widely accepted principles will persistently evolve as new facts, conditions, and practices warrant. Consider the case of *Gulf Oil v. Williams*,[236] from the Texas Court of Appeals. The pertinent facts include:

> When Thomas Williams stopped at a Houston, Texas, Gulf Station for gasoline, he never expected to be mistaken for a robber and be shot by a security guard. Nonetheless, he was, for no apparent reason. Gulf Oil Corporation and Empire Security Agency, Inc. were held liable for $94,719.77 in actual damages and $50,000 in punitive damages. It appeared from the evidence presented that Gulf had a written contract with Manpower, Inc. by which Manpower furnished guards for security at Gulf stations.

Under this agreement, Gulf paid Manpower certain fees. Empire then agreed with Manpower, under a separate contract, to furnish security guards for Manpower's clients such as Gulf. Empire hired and fired these guards and furnished them to Gulf stations in accordance with this contract with Manpower. Gulf had no contractual agreement whatever with Empire, only with Manpower.

Empire hired Robert Gury as a guard, furnished him with his uniform and weapon, provided him training and instruction and paid him for the work. Empire assigned him to provide security for Gulf.[237]

Evidence at trial, and posed on appeal, posits a contradictory stance on the control of a gun-toting assailant. Gulf Oil Corporation failed to convince the majority panel of the court that ruled that companies exercise "joint control" when the "evidence was sufficient to sustain the joint liability."[238] The court assessed damages against both companies. In this sense, the case is a hybrid. Neither side supposedly exercised total control, though Gulf would dispute those facts. Commentary provided by Judge Federal indicates that the case is perplexing and certainly not illustrative.

> Suffice it to say here that each fact situation must be evaluated on its own merits, and when it appears that both security company and the retailer exercised joint control over the guard, then the courts will rule that both are liable for the guard's misconduct.[239]

4.4 Civil Remedies under the Civil Rights Act: 42 U.S.C. § 1983

The provisions of 42 U.S.C. § 1983 outline civil remedies available to certain individuals for harms tied civil rights violations. Initially, a review of this statute is in order:

> Every person who, under color of any statute, ordinance, regulation, custom or usage of any state or territory, subjects, or causes to be subjected, any citizen of the United States or any other person within the jurisdiction thereof to the deprivation of any rights, privileges, or immunities secured by the Constitution and laws shall be liable to the party injured in an action in law, suit in equity or other proper proceeding for redress.[240]

The historical underpinnings of 42 U.S.C. § 1983 sought to halt racial discrimination and prevent and eliminate slavery. Originally titled *The Ku Klux Klan Act of 1871*, the legislation was enacted to increase the power of the federal government relative to state's rights. "The Act of 1871 was passed by Congress to provide civil rights protection against inaction and the toleration of private lawlessness. While the act was intended to remedy the deficiencies of the southern states, there is little indication that Congress sought any way to impair the states' political independence."[241]

Like all law, the original legislative intent is sometimes altered as the enactment seeks to find its niche in the legal culture. The Act has certainly had a curious legislative history since the time of the Civil War Reconstruction. The statute's chief complexity rests in its vague language, especially the term "under color of state law."[242] It was not until 1961 that the Supreme Court, in *Monroe v. Pape*,[243] held that public police officers abusing their discretion and authority, face possible liability under the provisions of the Act. After *Pape*, the floodgates of litigation opened. Wayne W.

Schmidt, director for The Americans for Effective Law Enforcement, writes in his article, "Recent Developments in Police Civil Liability,"[244]

> During the five-year period, the number of civil suits rose from a projected 1741 in 1967 to 3894 in 1971. Reliable estimates indicated that by 1975, the number of suits alleging police misconduct exceeded 6000 per year. Because an average of 111 hours is consumed in defending a typical suit along with 97 hours of investigation, such increases have had a dramatic affect on the ability of many law enforcement agencies to adequately defend themselves.[245]

By 1971, the U.S. Supreme Court, in *Bivens v. Six Unknown Federal Narcotics Agents*,[246] interpreted the provisions of 42 U.S.C. § 1983 to include a violation of constitutional rights as a basis for a civil remedy. Since much of police conduct is subject to constitutional oversight, defendants frequently claim their Fourth Amendment rights "as the result of an alleged unlawful arrest or search; the Fifth Amendment as the result of an alleged improperly obtained confession or deprivation of liberty or property without due process; the Sixth Amendment for violations of the right to counsel; or the Eighth Amendment as the result of the incarceration of a plaintiff claiming to have been subjected to cruel and unusual punishment."[247]

An actual claim under 42 U.S.C. § 1983, must demonstrate two seminal issues: (1) that a defendant (state or other governmental entity) deprives plaintiff of some right or privilege guaranteed by the Constitution or the laws of the United States and (2) that the deprivation asserted was caused or effected under color of that law.[248] Examples of state conduct under color of state law by public affiliates are false imprisonment, false arrest, abuse of process, assaults and batteries, malicious prosecutions, illegal searches and seizures, and other claims.[249] Tortious conduct including negligence has also been successfully argued. Noted earlier, supervisory responsibility in the areas of negligent hiring, assignment, retention and entrustment, supervision, and training may also prompt a cause of action under 42 U.S.C. § 1983.[250]

Specifically, a plaintiff must show three elements to succeed on a state-created danger claim. First, the plaintiff must demonstrate that the state actor took affirmative actions that "either create or increase the risk that an individual will be exposed to private acts of violence."[251] Second, the plaintiff must show that the state actor created a "special danger," which can be done through a showing that the state's actions placed the specific victim at risk, as opposed to placing the general public at risk.[252] Third, the state actor must have known, or clearly should have known, that his actions "specifically endangered an individual."[253]

Vicarious liability, with its companion principles of respondeat superior, is not as readily established.[254] Standing in a civil rights action is generally only granted when the person asserting the claim has been personally aggrieved. From this it has rightfully been decided, that the respondeat superior doctrine cannot impose liability on an employer or master in public employment. There is generally thought to be no master/servant relationship between supervisors and subordinates. They are seen as different grades of employees in the service of the public, thus negating any application of traditional vicarious liability.[255] The burden of proof in this type of case is quite substantial. In order to be successful, an affirmative link must be demonstrated between the supervisory activity and that of his or her employees.[256] Finding the affirmative link between the supervisory behavior and the act that results in discrimination is the crux of the burden. If public police were ordered by their superiors to strip search all shoplifters, in full view of the public, supervisory accountability would be found. "Beyond such clear acts of malfeasance or misdeeds, finding accountability becomes much more complex."[257] In *Grant v. John Hancock*,[258] the U.S. District Court indicated the difficulty since there must be:

> Assessment of totality of circumstances, in which courts must consider both nature and circumstances of guard's conduct and relationship of the conduct to performance of his official duties; key determinant is whether actor, at time in question, proposes to act in official capacity or to exercise official responsibilities pursuant to state law.[259]

The legal ramifications of affirmative action press the security industry as well. Any discriminatory practices in hiring and firing practices of security firms may lend itself to a civil rights remedy under the various federal provisions enacted over the last three decades. An interesting trend has been the civil action based upon the federal *Employee Polygraph Protection Act.*[260] Security specialists are often asked to conduct internal investigations in the corporate sector to discern intentional and willful discriminatory trends. See Figure 4.9.

4.4.1 "Private" Applications of § 1983

It is well settled that public police functions fall under the aegis and descriptive language of 42 U.S.C. § 1983. But can the statutory protection be extended to the private justice sector? In reviewing the statute, could it be argued that the economic influences and occupational roles of private security and the obligations of private policing fall under 42 U.S.C. § 1983? "As governments increasingly delegate traditional public functions to private, for-profit entities, ... 42 U.S.C. § 1983 has the potential to play an important role in encouraging private entities to respect constitutional rights when they take on public duties."[261] However, the historic exemption as limitation as to private application, some say, "undermines" the full protection of rights.[262]

Is a security guard who detains a suspected shoplifter, and who is exercising authority granted by regulatory bodies and licensure agencies, and is empowered and protected by legislation such as a merchant's privilege statute, acting under the color of state law? Although some claimants have persuaded courts in the affirmative that private police action may be under color of state law,[263] these decisions are rare.[264] "Moreover, some courts have dismissed § 1983 actions based on arguments and facts virtually indistinguishable from those previously asserted with success by other 1983 plaintiffs in the same court. Thus, neither plaintiffs nor defendants can predict the character and extent of state involvement necessary to establish the Section 1983 liability of private police officers."[265]

Of more recent legal interest has been the argument that racially motivated shoplifting detection programs are violations of the various civil rights acts. This assumes that the security officer's fundamental reason for targeting and restraint is rooted in a bias or racial motive and lacks proper discretion. Under the provision of 42 USC 1981, a sort of commerce clause that promotes equal benefits under the law as to contract, the act states in part:

> All persons within the jurisdiction of the United States shall have the same right in every State and Territory to make and enforce contracts, to sue, be parties, give evidence, and to the full and equal benefit of all laws and proceedings for the security of persons and property as is enjoyed by white citizens, and shall be subject to like punishment, pains, penalties, taxes, licenses, and exactions of every kind, and to no other.[266]

JOB DESCRIPTIONS, ASSIGNMENTS, PROMOTIONS,
AND TRANSFERS AUDIT FORM

1. Are written job descriptions maintained? ___Yes ___ No
   If yes, explain how employees are informed of their obligations and duties. _____

2. Are there any job categories which contain criteria relating to a person's physical attributes? ___Yes ___No

3. Are females excluded from any job classifications because of state protective legislation regarding hours worked, work type, or weight-lifting restrictions?   ___Yes___No

   If yes, list classifications:_____

4. Describe the employer's policy for accommodating employees who can not work specified days or hours.

5. Are there any jobs which employees over age 40 are unable to perform?   ___Yes___No
   If yes, list and explain. _____

6 . Is there a minimum age for employment?   ___Yes___No
   If yes, what age? _____

7. What benefits are given employees on basis seniority?_____

8. How is seniority determined?_____

   Is age or sex used in determining seniority?   ___Yes___No
   If yes, explain. _____

9. When determining job task and transfers, are the following factors considered?
   a. Age
   b. Sex
   c. Race/Ethnic origin
   d. Handicap
   e. Union membership
   If yes to any factor, explain._____

   Are records made of this?   ___Yes___No
   If yes, at what location are they kept?_____

10. Has employment in any job been based on:
    a. Race
    b. Sex
    c. Age
    d. Handicap

11. Is a seniority system presently maintained which is based on service during the period when certain jobs or departments were segregated? ___Yes___ No

12. Are employees permitted to transfer into jobs or departments from which they were formerly excluded?
    ___Yes___No

13. Are job vacancies advertised or announced to current employees? ___Yes___No
    If yes, are records kept of who applies? ___Yes___No

Figure 4.9   Job descriptions, assignments, promotions, and transfers audit form.   *(Continued)*

14. Are records kept reflecting the reasonings of denial or award of a job to a current employee? ___Yes___No
    If yes, describe: _____
    _____

15. How does the employer evaluate whether an employee is permitted to move into another position?
    _____

16. Are any of the following factors used in determining whether an employee can move to another job?
    a. Race
    b. Sex
    c. Age
    d. Handicap
    If yes, explain its use._____
    _____

17. Are any jobs or departments limited to persons of one sex? ___Yes___ No
18. Are supervisors required to submit written decisions and reasons when employees are passed over for
    promotions? ___Yes___ No
19. Are employees promoted or transferred between facilities? ___Yes___No
    If yes, how often? _____
    _____

20. For each job category, describe the training programs used, indicating any employee participation prerequisites.
    _____
    _____
    _____

21. Describe the employee evaluating process.
    _____
    _____
    _____

    If a form is used, attach.
22. How frequently are evaluations conducted?_____
    _____

23. Are evaluations reviewed by someone other than the preparer? ___Yes___No
24. Describe evaluating performance review with employees. _____
    _____

25. Describe the training that supervisors receive regarding employee evaluations. _____
    _____
    _____

Figure 4.9 (Continued) Job descriptions, assignments, promotions, and transfers audit form.

Then, the foundation for the act clearly requires a status as a racial minority and an offending party, in commerce or contract, that intends to offend that minority for reasons of bias or racial motivation. Hence, private security forces operating in retail markets and loss prevention have been on the receiving end of this civil rights argument. In *Martin v. J.C. Penney*,[267] that argument was partially successful. For the full text of the opinion, see Selected Case Readings.

4.4.2 State Regulations as Providing Color of State Law

State regulation in the security industry has been amply documented.[268] The National Advisory Committee's Report of the Task Force on Private Security recommends implementation of a state board system as shown in Figure 4.10.[269]

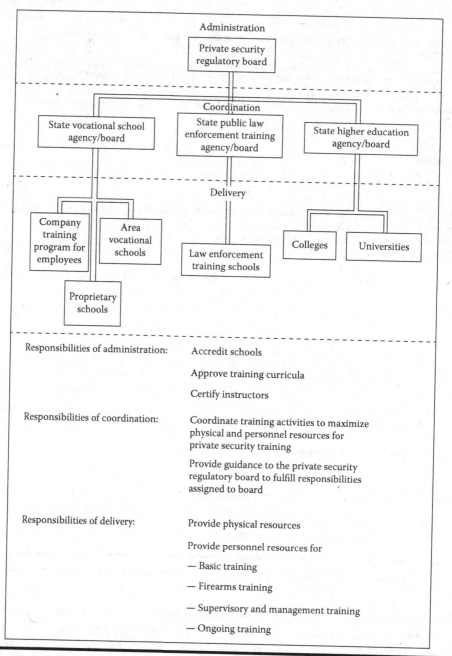

Figure 4.10 State board system sample hierarchy.

State involvement, such as licensure, which sets certain educational requirements, reviews past personal history and criminal records, and regulates by an administrative process is a definite governmental regimen. For a further demonstration of a clear state involvement, review Figure 4.11.[270]

This heightened call for quality control and the maximization of standards is largely the result of the security industry's own inability to regulate itself. Dr. Milton Cox, in his article, "*Guards*

STATE REGULATORY BOARDS

Standard 9.1: State Regulation
Regulation of the private security industry should be performed at the State level with consideration for uniformity and reciprocity among all States.

Standard 9.2: Regulatory Board for Private Security
State level of regulation should be through a regulatory board and staff responsible for the regulation of private security activities within that State. This board should have sufficient personnel to perform adequately and promptly their tasks of screening and investigating.

Standard 9.3: State Regulatory Board Membership
The State regulatory board should include, as a minimum, representatives of licensed security service businesses, businesses using proprietary security, local police departments, and consumers of security services; members of the general public; and individuals who are registered with the board and presently employed in the private security field.

Standard 9.4: Regulatory Board Hearing Procedure
The State regulatory board should establish a hearing procedure for consideration and resolution of the complaints of applicants, licensees, registrants, consumers, and the public. To assist in the implementation of this role, the board should be granted the means necessary to require appearance of witnesses and production of documents.

Standard 9.5: Regulatory Board Funding
The State regulatory board should be funded by nonconfiscatory license and registration fees and such general revenue funds as may be necessary for the effective operation of the board.

Standard 9.6: Regulatory Board Access to Criminal Record Information
The State regulatory board should be granted statutory authority for access to all criminal history record information so that it can conduct the necessary criminal history record check of all applicants for licenses and registration.

Figure 4.11 State regulatory board sample standards.

on *Guard Training*," calls for a "city or preferably a state regulatory agency to be appointed. This agency should have the authority and responsibility to formulate private security training standards, accredit training schools, approve training curricula, certify instructors for the private security industry, and enforce established standards for private security personnel."[271] If this is so, an act of regulation by public authorities may be a suitable private application to § 1983. In *Douglass Moore v. Detroit Entertainment, LLC*[272] the court was receptive to the color of state law rationale when finding for plaintiffs in a series of intentional tort and 1983 actions. The court found far too much by way of public authority in this case and concluded that the security officer "all possessed the power to arrest the plaintiff on casino premises for his alleged assault"[273]; detained the plaintiff" was a licensed entity and exercised powers traditionally reserved to the states.[274] The dissenting opinion displays an unusual foreboding and frustration about the majority holding.

> The fact that a private person has the power to arrest does not transform the person into a state actor. Rather, it would be the exercise of that power that would create the state action. That is why the presence of state action is fact specific ... determined on a case-by-case basis. It takes very little imagination to envision the havoc that would result from the application of the majority's holding. ... Thousands of everyday private actions would be distorted into state action for which plaintiffs will seek monetary remedies from taxpayer funds and overwhelm our already burdened courts.[275]

In *Tsao v. Desert Palace, Inc.*,[276] the court rejected in part and accepted in part efforts to recategorize a casino environment into a state-run or governmental entity. Again, state action varies in its interpretative approaches, but the mere alignment between casino operation with state licensing boards is not enough to transform a private action into a state action. However, if that security force was directed by state authority, policing supervision from public entities, and that there are sufficient proofs of points of contact between the private and the public, that picture can readily change to state action. The Court held:

> Thus, "the local police followed a policy that allowed [the security guard] to substitute his judgment for that of the police. "Such cooperative activity between the police department and a private party," the court concluded, "is sufficient to make [the guard] a party acting under color of state law."[277]

4.4.2.1 The Public Function Theory

As pointed out earlier, many of the occupational tasks of private security parallel or mimic public police functions. By analogy, the Supreme Court has held that certain seemingly private activities may be better characterized as quasi-public functions. Characteristic examples include the determination that a company town is really a municipality[278] or that the majority of services and operational qualities of a private park and shopping center serve the public sector more than the private interests.[279] Under the public function theory, the private entity has many public attributes, such as being open to the public and having public facilities or public restrooms despite its acclaimed private nature.[280] If segregated private clubs are subject to public control and thus characterized "public"; if parks and entertainment facilities are public because they are open to the general public; if publicly utilized shopping places are forced to grant free speech rights, it is hardly farfetched, by both analogy and implication, to apply constitutional rights to private sector justice. The argument has been posed relative to state universities.[281] This position is urged by proponents of federal expansionism. "The police function, then, with its special powers and privilege is a discretionary monopoly of government, the employment of which is particularly subject to the limitations imposed on government by the Constitution."[282] This is exactly the challenge made by *People v. Zelinski*,[283] a California decision imposing constitutional protections on private security operatives. Put another way, a public act prompts public scrutiny. On another front, the decision of *Maryland v. Collins*,[284] from Maryland's Court of Appeals exhibits sympathy for this argument in the matter of bail agents and private bondsman. But such a conclusion is a rarity even when public and private police work side by side. In *Crenshaw v. Rivera*,[285] and Illinois appeals court was unwilling to extend remedies under 42 U.S.C. § 1983 to private security officers while it was perfectly willing to allow that remedy to be applied against the public officers. The court held that while City of Chicago police were liable, the security office for Citizens Financial Bank lacked the public arrest powers to act under the color of state law. The court concluded that "{I}mposing liability on a defendant that has no control over the alleged wrong is an untenable position for the Court to endorse."[286]

4.4.2.2 The Nexus Theory

Admittedly a nebulous standard, the nexus theory was borne in the confusion of the public function analysis. In discerning the nexus theory, analysts and advocates look for evidence manifesting state interest, state support, or state solicitation in an improper activity. The court interprets the relationship as being "symbiotic."[287] The theory seeks to connect private action to a public model because that private action is so entangled with the public sector. The benchmark ruling under the nexus theory is *Burton v. The Wilmington Parking Authority*.[288] A parking authority owned by private interests serves a public function, namely providing parking facilities to individuals and businesses. In this case, the parking authority's policies and procedures discriminated against minorities. The burden of proof in the nexus argument rests upon the plaintiffs' ability to show sufficient "points of contact between the governmental entity and the action of the defendant."[289] The nexus theory of state action does not require a § 1983 claimant to convince the court that the defendant's conduct traditionally was performed by the state or other governmental authority, only that the state licensed or sponsored the action. In this case, the parking authority was made possible by governmental approvals and bonding mechanisms. The state needs not be involved at all in the improper activity. In the case of a parking authority, a sufficient nexus was shown. At no place is this argument as aggressively made as in the Blackwater setting—where private agents act in various military capacities.[290]

Security employees of private parcel carriers are frequently claimed de facto agents of the government. In *U.S. v. Koenig*,[291] a Federal Express carrier discovered a suspicious package, opened it, and discovered drugs later identified as cocaine. The DEA instructed Federal Express to deliver the package to its labeled location. The DEA then obtained a search warrant to seize the box at the delivery location. In rejecting a sufficient nexus between the public and private sector, the court remarked:

> We affirm the district court's finding that Koenig failed to prove the conditions she concedes are necessary to convert the actions of a private employee into an action of a governmental agent: Although the DEA may have known of Federal Express's security search policy, it is clear that Federal Express acted for its own private, business purposes. We note, however, that the factors Koenig identified are not independently sufficient to convert a private search into a governmental search. The effect such a transformation, a defendant must prove some exercise of governmental power over the private entity, such that the private entity may be said to have acted on behalf of the government rather than for its own, private purposes.[292]

Similarly, in *State v. Jensen*,[293] an Oregon Court of Appeals resolved this flawed contention. "On April 2, 1986, defendant was observed entering a fitting room in the store's ready to wear department by two security agents. The door to the fitting room had slats, through which one agent watched defendant remove her own pants, try on a pair of the store's pants, remove those, fold them and place them in the diaper bag. Both agents then followed defendant and her companion out of the store, where they detained defendant and took the merchandise from her companion. Defendant was thereupon released and arrested later at the store's request."[294]

Defense efforts to extend traditional constitutional protections were summarily dispensed:

> It is axiomatic that the provision is a limit on government authority of private persons acting on their behalf.[295] However, the provision does apply when private persons act at the behest of the state or under the mantel of its authority.[296] The determinative factor is "the extent of the official involvement in the total enterprise."[297,298]

Continuing this line of reasoning is *Tin Man Lee v. State of Texas*,[299] where a "patted down" defendant objected to the fruits of a negligent security guard. The Texas Court of Appeals, relying on *Burdeau*, maintains the precedent.

Appellant's argument refers only to provisions of the law that restrict searches and seizures by police officers or other governmental officials. In the instant case, Torres was not a police officer; he was employed as a private security guard for the Fantasia Club. Therefore, under the circumstances presented, the officers in this case were justified in conduction the search of appellant.[300]

A plaintiff employing the nexus theory, however, must reveal to the court evidence of state support of the wrongful conduct. Some specific examples of sufficient points of contact or other evidence manifesting a sufficient tie between the state and the illegal activity include these factors:

- A joint venture
- Cooperation in the activity
- An alliance in policy and planning
- Tacit encouragement
- Act in concert or conspiracy with the illegal activity
- The existence of a certificate of authority, state license, or other charter
- The encouragement argument
- The authorization and approval argument
- A grant of power

Advocates who urged the applicability of § 1983 to private policing pose as further argument recent studies that find a melding of private and public police concerns.[301] Both scholarly and practitioner argument is uniform on this score, urging less competition between public and private interests and, instead, a sharing of resources, skills, and capacities.

At the international level, there has been much criticism of private sector soldiers and mercenaries, who by their private status, avoid the implication and enforceability of human rights treaties and other binding oversight documents. The criticism, as noted at various places in this text, has been particularly acute when discussing Bosnia, Iraq, and Afghanistan. The perception, rightful or not, has been the member UN nations bypass human rights controls when using nongovernmental authority in police actions, such as private sector police instead of public representatives of a designated government.

To counter this ongoing criticism, various private security agencies and firms are being asked to be signatories to a Code of Conduct. Visit: http://www.news.admin.ch/NSBSubscriber/message/attachments/21143.pdf

4.4.2.3 The Police Moonlighter: A Merging of Public and Private Functions

Many occupational activities in private security and public law enforcement blur their once-distinct lines.[302] Examples include a private security officer who has been granted a special commission license or privilege by the state to perform clearly delineated activities. Certain jurisdictions designate individuals as "special policeman" or use other terminology to grant private security personnel public arrest privileges and rights.[303] This type of state involvement may meet the burden of 42 U.S.C. § 1983's color of state law standard. The fundamental premise behind the legislation is that the claimant must amply demonstrate an affirmative link between the private officer's conduct and the state or other governmental authority that involves itself directly or indirectly in the conduct.[304]

A classic merger of public and private interest occurs when public police officers moonlight within the security industry.[305] The Hallcrest Report II sees significant dual occupational roles in the private sector:

> These surveys revealed that 81% of the law enforcement administrators indicated that their department's regulations permit officers to moonlight in private security, while 19% prohibited or severely restricted private security moonlighting. Law enforcement administrators estimated that about 20% of their personnel have regular outside security employment to supplement their police salaries. Nationally, the Hallcrest researchers estimated that at least 150,000 local enforcement officers in the U.S. are regularly engaged in off-duty employment in private security. The three most common methods of obtaining off-duty officers for security work, in rank order, are (1) the officer is hired and paid directly by the business, (2) the department contracts with the business firm, invoices for the officer's off-duty work, and pays the officer, and (3) off-duty security work is coordinated through a police union or association.[306]

So common is moonlighting that the Fraternal Order of Police now offers liability coverage for public police officers engaged in this dual role. Visit: http://www.foplegal.com/files/Moonlighting_Fillable_Application2.pdf

The confusion of roles and functions often gives rise to ethical conundrums. What was once clear is a bit gray. Evaluate how moonlighting impacts ethical decision-making in the following questions:

1. Who is liable for a tortfeasor's behavior if the individual is off duty from public policing and working in a private security interest? How does the answer gel with a jurisdiction that requires police to be on call 24 hours per day?
2. What influence does moonlighting have upon the efficacy and productivity of police officers?
3. What potential conflict of interest exists?
4. Should an arrest, search, or seizure by a private security officer, working part-time while maintaining full-time public police employment, adhere to the rigorous standards of the Fourth, Fifth, and Fourteenth Amendments of the U.S. Constitution?
5. Which standard of constitutional protection should be accorded an appellant in a criminal case who has been victimized by a law enforcement person with both private and public connections?
6. How many hours per week should a publicly employed law enforcement officer be permitted to work in the private security industry?
7. Should a publicly employed police officer be permitted to operate as a private investigator, unrestrained by traditional constitutional protections granted in the public sector?

Others have argued that moonlighting suffers from inherent conflicts and is saddled with legal liability problems.[307]

Another factor courts weigh is the extent of the economic relationship. Is there a contract for private services? Does the proprietor want public officers to act privately or publicly? In *Otani v. City and County of Hawaii*,[308] the federal district court evaluated the question this way:

Plaintiff is correct in his assertion that "[a] private party may be liable under § 1983 if he was a willful participant in joint action with state agents."[309] However, "[a] claim of conspiracy or action in concert requires the allegation of 'facts showing particularly what a defendant or defendants did to carry the conspiracy into effect, whether such acts fit within the framework of the conspiracy alleged, and whether such acts, in the ordinary course of events, would proximately cause injury to the plaintiff.'"[310]

As the court explained, "it is possible that [the officer's] actions could have caused Plaintiff to be subjected to a deprivation of her civil rights while Safeway's actions did not; the Court merely holds that, whatever Safeway did, it did under color of state law."[311] To hold Safeway liable for the officer's actions, the plaintiff had to produce some evidence that Safeway "caused her to be subjected to a deprivation of her constitutional rights through its hiring and training policies, or the lack thereof."[312] A court is rightfully satisfied when the contract calls for the hiring of a public police officer to direct traffic at a construction site as a sufficient economic relationship.[313]

The inherent complexities moonlighting, both from an economic as well as legal point of view, make rock hard rules concerning entanglement difficult to come by. Some cases are easier than other. However, suspects of criminal behavior may be offered a menu of potential causes of action against an officer who is both publicly and privately employed. In *Faust v. Mendoza*,[314] a police officer was caught in an ethical dilemma representing two employers. The facts consisted of the following:

> At 10 PM on February 9, 1975 during Mardi Gras celebration in the French Quarter of New Orleans, Louisiana, a couple who had been enjoying the festivities and drinking all day stopped at the ice cream parlor in the Royal Sonesta Hotel. Apparently the man, John Faust, rested his head on the parlor's counter and ignored requests that he move. At this point, Officer John Mendoza entered to wait the 45 minutes until 11 PM when he was to begin work as a security guard for the parlor. He was to work until 3 AM in his police uniform at the parlor after completing 11 AM to 11 PM shift on police assignment controlling crowds around the Mardi Gras parades. After Mendoza approached Faust, testimony on what followed conflicts greatly. Although particular details are unclear, it appears that Mendoza struck both Faust and his female companion … Ingrid Pillar, with a billyclub, smashed the ice cream parlor window (either accidentally or by throwing him against it) and arrested Faust and Pillar for assault upon a police officer.[315]

The court held the police officer accountable. When these dual roles coalesce, some courts suspect a public law enforcement officer's intentional bypass of the more demanding public standards. In *Bauman v. State of Indiana*,[316] the court grappled with a suspect's right to Miranda warnings before a security officer could custodially interrogate. That security guard also happened to be an off-duty police officer. In affirming the convictions, the court did not accept the argument that Miranda rights were necessary because of the guard's public police officer status. The court was perfectly satisfied with the differentiation of occupational roles, holding that the security guard "was not acting in his capacity as a police officer at the time, but rather in his capacity as a private citizen security officer."[317] In *Leach v. Penn-Mar Merchants Assoc.*,[318] a county police officer, simultaneously employed as a security guard, made while on security duty an arrest at a traffic accident. The court construed his traffic altercation to be a public police function distinguishable from his security work. Other cases dealing with the differentiation of authority and the public/private status of law enforcement include the *City of Grand Rapids v. Frederick Impens*[319] and *Cinestate Inc. v. Robert T. Farrell, Administrator*.[320]

4.5 Summary

This chapter's main thrust involved the law of intentional torts, negligence, strict liability torts and civil rights, remedies, and damages. Specific causes of action were covered, including

- Assault
- Battery
- False imprisonment
- Infliction of emotional or mental distress
- Malicious prosecution
- Defamation
- Invasion of privacy
- Negligence
- Negligence and security management
- Strict liability torts

Other areas of interest dealt with vicarious inability, nondelegable duty, and the civil remedies provided by 42 U.S.C. § 1983. Also relevant to this discussion is the continual interplay between private and public security functions. In some respects, the distinctions presently drawn between private and public policing are academic. As increased funding and resources are placed in the private sector, there is a strong likelihood of increased regulatory oversight, causing heightened legal liabilities on the part of security personnel, agencies, and companies.

CASE EXAMPLES

False Imprisonment—Pamela Sue Peak, by her father and next friend,
Francis Wilber Peak v. W.T. Grant Company, 386 S.W. 685

Facts

A security officer saw a female customer acting suspiciously and holding tightly to a purse. The officer grabbed hold of her arm. The customer continued to scream and the officer reacted by covering her mouth. He dragged her by the arm across the store to a big safe located near the stairway to the basement offices. According to one witness, the officer was slapping her and knocking her into several counters as he dragged her along toward the basement steps. Until this time neither of the officers had identified themselves. They were not in any type of uniform. The officers had detained the wrong person.

Would the security company and its employees be liable for the false imprisonment?

Answer

When an employee of a corporation is authorized to arrest and detain shoplifters, and in endeavoring to do so mistakenly arrests and detains an innocent person, the security corporation is liable for false imprisonment.

Malicious Prosecution—*Arnold v. Eckerd Drugs of Georgia,*
Inc., 358 S.E.2d 632 (Ga. App. 1987)

Facts

After making purchases in a drug store, Mrs. Arnold attempted to leave the premises. The store had posted notice of its utilization of an anti-shoplifting device. As she approached the anti-shoplifting device, the alarm sounded. Mrs. Arnold claimed she had mistakenly put a pen in her pocket and had then forgotten to pay for it. The store manager had observed appellant's behavior after the anti-shoplifting alarm had sounded. Mrs. Arnold was arrested and charged with shoplifting, notwithstanding her after-the-fact explanation that she had simply forgotten about the pen. After a jury acquitted Mrs. Arnold of shoplifting, she brought a civil action for malicious prosecution.

Does probable cause negate a claim for malicious prosecution?

Answer

If there was probable cause to believe that Mrs. Arnold was shoplifting, the drug store cannot be held civilly liable for requiring that a jury in a criminal proceeding determine the credibility of her explanation.

Premises Security—*Opal Frederick, v. TPG Hospitality, Inc.*, et al., 56 F. Supp. 2d 76 (United States District Court for the District of Columbia 1999)

Facts

On October 21, 1994, Mr. John Frederick and his wife Opal were visiting Washington D.C., and they checked into the EconoLodge on New York Avenue for the night. In the very early morning hours of October 22, 1994, Mr. Frederick passed through the lobby on his way out to the garage. He spoke with the security guard on duty, Mr. Henry Gilmore, who was sitting in the lobby. Mr. Frederick then proceeded outside to the garage. When he got to his car, there was a light shining from underneath the car, and when he bent down to look under the car, he was struck in the face and robbed. Mr. Frederick suffered massive facial trauma from the attack and recently has passed away.

Plaintiffs have provided evidence that two elderly patrons of the EconoLodge were attacked in the EconoLodge garage approximately six months before Mr. Frederick was attacked. The plaintiffs contend that the EconoLodge is located in a high crime area and that a number of other attacks had taken place in the vicinity in the months prior to the attack on Mr. Frederick. Finally, it is established that the guards worked long shifts at the hotel; on the morning Mr. Frederick was attacked, Mr. Gilmore was nearing the end of a 14-hour shift.

Was the hotel negligent?

Answer

No, all Plaintiff's arguments were dismissed.

Vicarious Liability—*Shaffer v. Wells Fargo Guard Services*, etc. (1988 Fla App D3) 528 So. 2d 389, 13 FLW 562

Facts

A guard service company was hired to protect bank assets and assist in transportation. The security firm's contract lists explicitly this obligation. What if a bank employee was injured by third-party conduct? Under what theory would the case succeed or fail? Would the security firm be liable?

Answer

No, since it could not be fairly said that the guard service company contemplated protecting bank employees from hazards totally unconnected to activities or the business of the bank.

Negligence and Foreseeability—*Rosabel Brown v. J.C. Penney Company, Inc.*, 667 P. 2d. 1047 (1983)

Facts

Plaintiff and her husband, while shopping at a mall, were seriously accosted by assailants in the parking lot. The plaintiffs attempted to show that their injuries should have been foreseen in this particular public parking. They did so by producing a computer printout from the local police department that listed the criminal incidence rate. Plaintiff sued shopping center on a theory of negligence.

Issue

Should defendants reasonably have anticipated that careless or criminal conduct on the part of third persons would likely endanger the safety of business invitees?

Negligence and the Environment—*Ruth Nicoletti v. Westcor, Incorporated*, 639 P. 2d. 330 (1982)

Facts

Plaintiff was employed by a department store that required all employees to park at a temporary facility during the holiday season. As a result of this parking location, plaintiff and some other employees chose to take another direct route to the special parking lot. This shortcut took plaintiff through a highly shrubbed area, causing her to become tangled and to severely injure herself.

Issue

Could defendant company have foreseen these injuries?

State Action Theory—*Nicole Anderson v. Randall Park Mall Corporation*, 571 F. Supp. 1173 (1983)

Facts

A young woman attending a movie with friends at a mall was asked by security guards to quit speaking too loudly. As a result of a continuing disturbance, this young woman was among many others asked by security guards to leave the shopping mall. She was told that the mall was private property, that she was loitering, and that she would be arrested if she refused. Her refusal to leave the mall resulted in an arrest where she spent a short period of time in custody before being released. As a result of this 15-minute detention, she sued the Randall Park Mall Corporation on a claim that her civil rights were violated by its employees, the private security guards.

Issue

Are a private citizen's civil rights violated when deprived of a right to remain in a shopping mall? Does this fact pattern qualify for an action under 42 U.S.C. § 1983?

Third-Party Criminal Acts

Facts

Upon returning to her apartment unit at 11 p.m., a 21-year-old woman locked the sliding glass door, pulled the drapes, and immediately went to bed. Two hours later she was awakened by an individual who, with brutal force, caused her to perform sexual acts against her will. She brought suit against the owners and managers of the building complex, alleging that they had knowledge that other specific criminal acts had taken place within the complex and that they had negligently failed to take reasonable steps to protect their tenants. Plaintiff further alleged that the defendants failed to warn tenants of these prior crimes, thus denying tenants the opportunity to take increased self-protective measures.

Issue

Is this apartment complex negligent for the criminal acts of a third party?

DISCUSSION QUESTIONS

1. Compare and contrast the nature of a civil cause of action with a criminal act.
2. Which type of tort category would the private security industry most often come in contact with?
3. In a jurisdiction with a merchant privilege protection, how would this defense be effective in a case of false imprisonment or false arrest?
4. What causes of action must employers be concerned about in hiring, retaining, disciplining, and terminating personnel?

5. Businesses often feel that the hiring of security companies as independent contractors will shield them from potential liability. Is this belief generally dependable?
6. Name the types of civil remedies which exist under 42 U.S.C. § 1983.
7. Does moonlighting gives greater strength to a plaintiff's or claimant's argument that civil rights have been violated under 42 U.S.C. § 1983? Explain.

NOTES

1   Elizabeth E. Joh, The paradox of private policing, *J. Crim. L. & Criminology* 95 (2004) 49–50.
2   James S. Kakalik and Sorrel Wildhorn, The Private Police Industry: Its Nature and Extent (1972).
3   William C. Cunningham & Todd H. Taylor, The Hallcrest Report, *Private Security and Police in America* 4 (1985).
4   Industry Output and Employment Projections to 2018, Monthly Labor Rev., Nov. 2009, at Table 2.7, available at http://www.bls.gov/emp/ep_table_207.htm; see also William C. Cunningham, John J. Strauchs, & Clifford W. Vanmeter, Private Security Trends 1970–2000: The Hallcrest Report II 237 (1990).
5   Note, Security Indicators, 28 SEC. 10 (1991); see also *Elevating the Practice of Strategic Risk Management* (2010) available at http://marsh-africa.com/documents/MarshExcellenceinRiskManagementReport_April2010.pdf.
6   Cunningham et al., supra note 4, at 34–35.
7   Id. at 37–38.
8   For an interesting analysis of civil liability problems emerging from private sector contractors operating in theaters of war, see: http://jnslp.com/2012/04/16/dead-contractors-the-un-examined-effect-of-surrogates-on-the-publics-casualty-sensitivity/.
9   Charles P. Nemeth, *Private Security and the Investigative Process* 1 (3rd ed. 2010).
10 Cunningham et al., supra note 4, at 233.
11 Morgan O. Reynolds, Using the Private Sector to Deter Crime—NCPA Policy Report No. 181, at Executive Summary (National Center for Policy Analysis, 1994) at http://www.ncpa.org/pdfs/st181.pdf, visited Aug. 27, 2009; see also NEMETH, supra note 8, at Ch. 1.
12 Joel Griffin, Demand for private security services projected to rise in U.S., *SecurityInfoWatch* (Nov. 7, 2012) http://www.securityinfowatch.com/article/10826461/freedonia-group-study-projects-steady-increase-in-demand-for-private-security-services, last visited August 27, 2016.
13 Chamberlain, Understanding Your Exposure to Liability Increases Your Chance of Avoiding Litigation, *Sec. World* 20 (1983) 26; see also Victor E. Kappeler, Critical Issues in Police Civil Liability Ch. 1 (2001); Victor E. Kappeler, Police Civil Liability: Supreme Court Cases and Materials Ch. 1 (2002).
14 W.O. Dyer, D.S. Murrell, and D. Wright, Training for Hospital Security: An Alternative to Training Negligence Lawsuits, in Violence in the Medical Care Setting, A Survival Guide 1 (James T. Turner, ed., 1984); see also Kappeler, Critical Issues, supra note 11, at Ch. 1 (2001); Kappeler, Supreme Court Cases, supra note 11, at Ch. 1.
15 Dennis Walters, *Training—The Key to Avoiding Liability*, SEC. MGMT. 29 (1985) 79; see generally D. Carter and A. Sapp, *Higher Education as a Policy Alternative to Reduce Police Liability*, POLICE LIABILITY REVIEW 2 (1990) 1–3; H. E. Barrineau, *Civil Liability in Criminal Justice* (2nd ed. 1994).
16 For a pre-liability assessment tool, visit Triton Global Services Website at http://tritonglobalservices.com.
17 Stephen C. George, Playing the Liability Game SEC. 29 (1992) 56; see generally E. J. LittleJohn, Civil Liability and the Police Officer: The Need for New Deterrents to Police Misconduct Univ. Detroit Urban L. 58 (1976) 365–370; D. L. Ross, Emerging Trends in Police Failure to Train Liability *Policing: Internat'l J. Police Strategies & Mgmt.* 23 (2000) 169–193.
18 Ibid.; See also: ASIS International, Special Events Security Resources Webpage, https://www.asisonline.org/Education-Events/Pages/Special-Events-Security-Resources.aspx.
19 See: CNA, Managing Large-Scale Security Events: A Planning Primer for Local Law Enforcement Agencies (2013) https://www.bja.gov/Publications/LSSE-planning-Primer.pdf.

20 Ibid.

21 *Keenoy v. Sears Roebuck & Zeis*, 642 S.W.2d 665 (Mo. App. E.D. 1982).

22 In fact, this case resulted in a $75,000.00 damage award given to the accosted customer at a large department store.

23 Arthur J. Bilek, John C. Klotter, and R. Keegan Federal, Legal Aspects of Private Security 158 (1980); see also Barrineau, supra note 13.

24 For an overview of the distinctions between crimes and torts, see the Cornell University Legal Information Institute comparison at http://topics.law.cornell.edu/wex/tort.

25 William P. Statsky, *Torts: Personal Injury Litigation* 1 (1982).

26 *Brown v. J.C. Penney Corp., Inc.*, 521 F.App'x 922, 924 (11th Cir. 2013) (citing *City of Miami v. Sanders*, 672 So. 2d 46, 48 (Fla. 3d DCA 1996)).

27 see *Bartley v. Kim's Enter. of Orlando, Inc.*, 568 F. App'x 827, 831 (11th Cir. 2014); *Johnson v. Barnes & Noble Booksellers, Inc.*, 437 F.3d 1112, 1115 (11th Cir. 2006).

28 *Cordoves, v. Miami-Dade County*, Case No. 14-20114-CIV-ALTONAGA/O'Sullivan. March 12, 2015. United States District Court, S.D. Florida.

29 Bilek et al., supra note 18, at 158; see also Barrineau, supra note 13.

30 See generally Roger T. Weitkamp, Crimes and Offenses, *GA. St. U. L. Rev.* 16 (1999); 72, 73; Gloria F. Taft and Valeree R. Gordon, Criminal Law (Legislative Survey—North Carolina), *Campbell L. Rev.* 21 (1999) 353, 353.

31 Negligent Security Attorney, The Value of Inadequate Security Lawsuits, http://www.negligentsecurityattorney.com/verdicts-settlements, last accessed February 20, 2017.

32 Wayne Saiat, *The Need for Security and the Limits of Liability*, Sec. World 19 (1982); 23. See also Barrineau. See also: the volume of litigation in a structural or systematic sense should give pause to every security practitioner. United States Courts, *Judicial Business 2013*, at http://www.uscourts.gov/statistics-reports/judicial-business-2013, last accessed February 20, 2017.

33 See generally R. Keegan Federal and J. Jennifer L. Fogleman, *Avoiding Liability in Retail Security: A Casebook* (1986); Kappeler, *Supreme Court Cases*.

34 William L. Prosser, *Handbook of The Law of Torts* (1971); see generally Barrineau; Federal and Fogleman; Kappeler, *Supreme Court Cases*.

35 Bilek et al., at 158; Barrineau; John E. Douglas, *Crime Classification Manual* (1997).

36 Charles Friend, *Police Rights: Civil Remedies for Law Enforcement Officers* 93 (1979); Ross; Will Aitchison, *The Rights of Law Enforcement Officers* (4th ed. 2000).

37 *Safeway Stores v. Kelly*, 448 A.2d 856, 858 (D.C. 1982).

38 Id. at 864; see also *Note, Tort Liability for Threatening or Insulting Words*, 54 Canad. B.J. 563 (1976).

39 187 F. Supp. 2d 9 (D. Conn 2002).

40 Charles Sennewald, *Trends in Retail Security*, 30 Sec. 57 (1993); John E. Douglas, *Crime Classification Manual* (1997).

41 Friend, at 94 (1979); Barrineau; Aitchison.

42 See generally *Keane v. Main*, 76 A. 269 (Conn. 1910); J. Terry Griffith, *Respondent Superior and the Intentional Tort: A Short Discourse on How to Make Assault and Battery a Part of the Job*, 45 U. Cin. L. Rev. 235 (1976); see also *General Motors Corp. v. Piskor*, 340 A.2d 767 (Md. App. 1975).

43 Friend, at 94; see also Kappeler, *Supreme Court Cases*; Kappeler, *Critical Issues*.

44 *Threlkeld v. White Castle Systems*, 201 F. Supp. 2d 834 (N.D. Ill. 2002).

45 *U.S. Shoe v. Jones et al.*, 255 S.E.2d 73 (Ga. App. 1979).

46 See: *Biscone v. JetBlue Airways Corp.*, 103 AD3d 160 (2012).

47 Id at 174–175.

48 Ga. Code Ann. § 51-7-60 (2010). See also *Walker v. May Department Stores*, 83 F. Supp. 2d 525 (E.D. Pa. 2000).

49 Curtis Baillie, How litigation shapes retailers' security and loss prevention strategies, *Security Technology Executive*, March 19, 2010, at http://www.securityinfowatch.com/Features/how-litigation-shapes-retailers-security-and-loss-prevention-strategies.

50 18 Pa. Cons. Stat. § 3929 (2009).

51 See *Westview Cemetery v. Blanchard*, 216 S.E.2d 776 (Ga. 1975); *Standard Oil v. Mt. Bethel Church*, 196 S.E.2d 869 (Ga. 1973).

52 297 N.W.2d 74 (Wis. App. 1980); see also *Dawson v. Payless Shoes, Inc.*, 598 S.W.2d 83 (Ark. 1980).

53 *Americans for Effective Law Enforcement, Inc.* 102 Liability Reporter 9–10 (1981).

54 433 N.E.2d 1005 (Ill. App. 1982).

55 Id.

56 *Hampton v. Dillard Dept. Stores*, 247 F.3d 1091 (10th Cir. 2001).

57 Robinson, 433 N.E.2d at 1005.

58 Id. at 1009.

59 *Katz v. U.S.*, 194 F.3d 962, 967 (9th Cir. 1999); see also as to qualified immunity, *Corcoran v. Fletcher*, 160 F. Supp. 2d 1085, 1089 (C.D. Ca. 2001).

60 Civil Action No. 00-CV-1331, 2000 U.S.Dist. Lexis 13248 (E.D. Pa. 2000).

61 Id.

62 *Wal-Mart Stores, Inc. v. Yarborough*, 681 S.W.2d 359 (Ark. 1984).

63 *Daley v. Wanamaker, Inc.*, 464 A.2d 355 (Pa. Super. 1983).

64 *Landry v. Schwegmann*, 416 So. 2d 341 (La. App. 4 Cir. 1982); see also *Cobb v. Standard Drug Co. Inc.*, 453 A.2d 110 (D.C. 1982).

65 *Broughton v. State of New York*, 37 N.Y.2d 451, 456 (1975).

66 *Du Chateau v. Metro-North Commuter R. R. Co.*, 253 A.D.2d 128, 131 (1st Dept 1999).

67 Id.

68 *Berrios v. Our Lady of Mercy Med. Ctr.*, 20 A.D.3d 361, 362 (1st Dept 2005).

69 *Pellegrini v. Duane Reade Inc.*, NY Slip op 31352, NY Supreme Court 2015 Docket No. 156317/2012. Supreme Court, New York County July 22, 2015. At 2–3.

70 James Cleary, *Prosecuting the Shoplifter, A Loss Prevention Strategy* 215 (1986).

71 Leo F. Hannon, *Whose rights prevail?* Sec. Mgmt. 27 (1983) 27, 35.

72 John Francis, *The Complete Security Officer's Manual and Career Guide* 8 (1992).

73 *Peak v. W.T. Grant Co.*, 386 S.W.2d 685, 689 (Mo. App. 1965).

74 See Charles P. Nemeth, *Psychological Injuries: Civil Remedies for Police Officers*, Police J. (1983); Douglas; Kappeler, *Supreme Court Cases*.

75 See generally Prosser, at §12 at 52.

76 Herbert M. Kritzer, *An Exploration of "Noneconomic" Damages in Civil Jury Awards*, 55 Wm. and Mary L. Rev., (2014); 971, 974. http://scholarship.law.wm.edu/wmlr/vol55/iss3/9.

77 See generally *Restatement of Torts* § 46 (1965).

78 Statsky, at 510; Douglas; Kappeler, Supreme Court Cases.

79 *Yeager v. Local Union* 20, 453 N.E.2d 666, 671 (Oh. 1983) quoting *Res. 2D Of Torts* § 46, cmt. D (1965).

80 *Neuens v. City of Columbus*, 169 F. Supp. 2d 780, 790 (S.D. Oh. 2001).

81 Bilek et al., at 161.

82 660 S.W.2d 619 (Tex. App. 13 Dist. 1983).

83 Federal and Fogleman, at 98; Kappeler, Supreme Court Cases.

84 Robert L. Conason, Paul M. Deutsch, and Frederick A. Raffa, *Intentional Infliction of Emotional Distress, in Damages in Tort Actions* (2010).

85 See *Adams v. Williams*, 407 U.S. 143 (1972) (an excellent discussion of probable cause).

86 See *Van Hull v. Marriott Courtyard*, 87 F. Supp. 2d 771 (N.D. Oh. 2000).

87 430 So. 2d 843 (Miss. 1982); *Damages for injury to feelings in malicious prosecution and abuse of process*, Clev. L. Rev. 15 (1966); 15.

88 358 S.E.2d 632 (Ga. App. 1987).

89 Id. at 634.

90 245 F. Supp. 2d 1203 (D.N.M. 2002).

91 *Morris v. Dillard Dept. Stores*, 277 F.3d 743 (5th Cir. 2001).

92 Statsky, at 540.

93 La: Court of Appeals, 3rd Circuit 2016, No. 15-1096. April 6, 2016.

94 La: Court of Appeals, 3rd Circuit 2016, No. 15-1096. April 6, 2016. At 3 of 7.

95 Friend, at 149; Aitchinson.

96 For an interesting look at how defamation is now possible by online or internet publication, see E. Casey Lide, *ADR and Cyberspace: The Role of Alternative Dispute Resolution in Online Commerce, Intellectual Property and Defamation, Ohio St. J. Disp. Resol.* 12 (1996–1997); 193.

97 Friend; Aitchinson.

98 *Michaelson v. Minnesota Mining & Mfg. Co.*, 474 N.W.2d 174, 181 (Minn. App. 1991).

99 107 F. Supp. 2d 333 (S.D.N.Y. 2000).

100 Id. at 337.

101 David Dishneau, *Kmart Case Tests Limits of Corporate Spying*, Trib. Rev., Jan. 9, 1994 at H7.

102 Id.

103 Greg Trout, Invasion of privacy: New guidelines for the public disclosure tort, *Cap. U. L. Rev.* 6 (1976); 95. Aitchinson.

104 Robert R. Belair, Awareness of privacy rules is crucial for security pros, *Sec. Mgmt.* 23 (1979); 14.

105 Id. at 19.

106 13 A.L.R.3d 1025, Investigations and Surveillance, Shadowing and Trailing, as a Violation of Right and Privacy.

107 Id. at 1026; see also *Pinkerton v. Steven*, 132 S.E.2d 119 (Ga. App. 1963); *Schulz v. Frankfort*, 139 N.W. 386 (Wis. 1913); see contra *Tucker v. American Employers Ins. Co.*, 171 So. 2d 437 (Fla. App. 1965); *Forster v. Manchester*, 189 A.2d 147 (Pa. 1963).

108 13 A.L.R., at 1027.

109 Rebecca D. Russell, *Substance Abuse Police Takes Hold, Gains Acceptance*, Sec. 28 (1991); 49.

110 Note, Partnership offers site drug screening, Sec. 29 (1992) 51.

111 Substance Abuse and Mental Health Services Administration, Results from the 2013 National Survey on Drug Use and Health: Summary of National Findings, NSDUH Series H-48, HHS Publication No. (SMA) 14-4863. Rockville, MD: Substance Abuse and Mental Health Services Administration, 2014. http://www.samhsa.gov/data/sites/default/files/NSDUHresultsPDFWHTML2013/Web/NSDUHresults2013.pdf.

112 DEA, Domestic Drug Arrests, https://www.dea.gov/resource-center/statistics.shtml#arrests, last visited February 20, 2017.

113 Substance Abuse and Mental Health Services Administration, *Drug Abuse Warning Network, 2011: National Estimates of Drug-Related Emergency Department Visits. HHS Publication No. (SMA) 13-4760*, DAWN Series D-39. Rockville, MD: Substance Abuse and Mental Health Services Administration, 2013. https://www.samhsa.gov/data/sites/default/files/DAWN2k11ED/DAWN2k11ED/DAWN2k11ED.pdf; See also the American Council on Drug Education's foreboding analysis on the impact of drugs in the workplace at http://www.acde.org/employer/DAwork.htm.

114 *Mason v. Williams Discount Center*, 639 S.W.2d 836 (Mo. App. E.D. 1982).

115 *Lewis v. Dayton Hudson Corp.*, 339 N.W.2d 857 (Mich. App. 1983).

116 *K-Mart v. Trotti*, 677 S.W.2d 632 (Tex. App. 1 Dist. 1984); see also *Note, Uninvited Entry into Another's Living Quarters as Invasion of Privacy, Clev. Mar. L. Rev.* 16 (1967); 428.

117 For an excellent overview of reasonableness, see the Capsule provided by Lexis/Nexis at: http://www.lexisnexis.com/lawschool/study/outlines/html/torts/torts03.htm.

118 443 S.E.2d 670 (Ga. App. 1994).

119 Id. at 672–673.

120 Note, Premises—Liability suits become tougher for business to defend, *Wall St. J.*, Sept. 1, 1993 at B1.

121 *Kelly v. McDonald's Restaurant*, 417 So. 2d 556 (Miss. 1982).

122 Id. at 561.

123 *Kroger Co. v. Knox*, 98 So.3d 441 (2012).

124 *Double Quick, Inc. v. Lymas*, 50 So.3d 292, 298 (Miss.2010) (quoting *Simpson v. Boyd*, 880 So.2d 1047, 1051 (Miss.2004)).

125 *Kroger Co. v. Knox*, 98 So.3d 441, 444 (2012).

126 *Brown v. J.C. Penney*, 667 P.2d 1047 (Or. App. 1983).

127 Id. at 1049, quoting *Restatement (Second) of Torts* § 344, comment f (1965); see also *Tritch v. Burlington Northern, Inc.*, 458 N.W.2d 471 (Neb. 1981).

128 See: *Park v. Exxon Mobil Corp.*, 429 S.W.3d 142 (2014); Trammell Crow Cent. *Texas v. Gutierrez*, 267 SW 3d 9 - Tex: Supreme Court 2008.

129 Mark B. Rosen, Limiting liability, *Sec. World* 20 (1983); 47. See also Peters, *Determining Liability: There Are No Hard and Fast Rules*, *Sec. Mgmt.* 29 (1984); 44.

130 *Fontaine v. Ryan*, 849 F. Supp. 190 (S.D.N.Y. 1993).

131 *Hunley v. DuPont*, 174 F. Supp. 2d 602 (E.D. Mich. 2001).

132 Rosen, at 47.

133 Stephen R. Perry, Cost–benefit analysis and the negligence standard, *Vanderbilt L. Rev.* 54 (2001); 893.

134 Negligence and Foreseeability: Doctrine of Law or Public Policy (1999), at http://www.supremecourt.tas.gov.au/__data/assets/pdf_file/0003/53760/Negligence99.pdf.

135 *Murros v. Daniels*, 364 S.E.2d 392 (N.C. 1988).

136 532 So. 2d 1348 (Fla. App. 1988).

137 *Satchwell v. LaQuinta Motor Inn. Inc.*, 532 So. 2d 1348, 1350 (Fla. App. 1988).

138 997 F. Supp. 611 (N.J. 1998).

139 *Butler v. Acme Markets, Inc.*, 445 A.2d 1141, 1143 (N.J. 1982).

140 *Goldberg v. Housing Auth. of the City of Newark*, 186 A.2d 291, 293 (N.J. 1962) quoting *Butler v. Acme Markets, Inc.*, 445 A.2d 1141, 1148 (N.J. 1982); *Abraham v. Raso*, 997 F. Supp. 611, 613 (N.J. 1998).

141 595 So. 2d 867 (Ala. 1992).

142 Id. at 871–872.

143 *Taylor v. Centennial Bowl, Inc.*, 416 P.2d 793 (Cal. 1966).

144 Charles S. Parnell, Tort liability of owner or operator of public parking facility, *Am. Jur. Trials* 46 (1993); 17–18.

145 Id. at 29.

146 Id. at 51; Bill Zalud, Lots of parking bumps: IP, lighting and terrorism, *Sec. Mag.* (Jan. 2006) at 28; Bernard Scaglione, Determining and implementing successful access control solutions, *Sec. Mag.* (Jan. 2009) at 42; See also: Claire Meyer, Compounding technologies for more accurate intruder detection, *Sec. Mag.* (Feb. 2015) at 45.

147 863 P.2d 207 (Cal. 1993).

148 Junda Woo, Suing crime—Scene owner is made harder, *Wall St. J.*, Sept. 1, 1993 at B13.

149 2008 NY Slip Op 51202U, 2008 N.Y. Misc. Lexis 3517 (N.Y. Sup. Ct. 2008).

150 Id. at *6.

151 Opinion No. 5404. May 18, 2016. Court of Appeals of South Carolina.

152 *Easterling, v. Burger King*, Opinion No. 5404. May 18, 2016. Court of Appeals of South Carolina at 6.

153 See: *Jones v. Hiro Cocktail Lounge*, 2016 NY Slip Op 4110 - NY: Appellate Div., 1st Dept. 2016.

154 Mitsubishi paid $34 million in a sexual harassment case—the award partly was based on the negligent failure to have a published policy. Jennifer R. George, Put in a policy or pay the price, *Sec. Mgmt. Online* (July 2001) at http://www.securitymanagement.com/library/001075.html.

155 Bilek, et.al, at 164 (1980); Aitchison.

156 587 N.E.2d 1241 (Ill. App. 2 Dist. 1979); see also *Stein v. Burns International*, 430 N.E.2d 334 (Ill. App. 1981).

157 Phoebe Carter, Employer's liability for assault, theft, or similar intentional wrong committed by employee at home or business or customer, 13 A.L.R.5th 217, 230.

158 Security Guard Company's Liability for Negligent Hiring, Supervision, Retention or Assignment of Guard, 44 A.L.R.4th 620; see also Association news, *Sec. World* 19 (1982); 69.

159 Dyer, Murrell and Wright, *Training for Hospital Security: An Alternative to Training Negligence Lawsuits, Violence in The Medical Care Setting, A Survival Guide* 7 (James T. Turner, ed., 1984); see also Kirschenbaum, Security companies are liable for their employees, *Sec. Mgmt.* 24 (1984); 36.

160 Dyer, et al, at 9.

161 Brenda Moss, Security awareness at work, Sec. 28 (1991); 35.

162 Carter, at 231–232.

163 Nemeth, at 307.

164 Edward T. Guy, John J. Merrigan, Jr., and John A, Wanat, Forms for safety and security management 34 (1981).

165 33 N.Y.S. 849 (1895).

166 *Security Guard Company's Liability*, at 629; Aitchison; Barrineau; V. E. Kappeler, S. F. Kappeler, and R. V. Del Carmen, A content analysis of police civil liability cases: Decisions of the Federal District Courts, 1978–1990 (1993).

167 Walters, at 80; Carter and Sapp, at 1-3; Ross, at 169–193; Jeff Maahs and Craig Hemmens, Train in vain: A statutory analysis of security guard training requirements, *Internat'l J. Comp. & Applied Crim. J.* 22 (1998); 91–101.

168 182 F.3d 376 (5th Cir. 1999).

169 Id. at 378.

170 Saiat, at 23; Aitchison.

171 Saiat, at 24; Ross, at 169-93; Maahs and Hemmens, at 91–101.

172 420 U.S. 251 (1975).

173 *NLRB v. J. Weingarten, Inc.*, 420 U.S. 251, 265 at fn. 10 (1975).

174 157 So. 3d 273 - Fla: Supreme Court 2015.

175 *Gooding v. Univ. Hosp. Bldg., Inc.*, 445 So.2d 1015, 1018 (Fla.1984); See also 50 State Sec. *Service, Inc. v. Giangrandi*, 132 So. 3d 1128 - Fla: Dist. Court of Appeals, 3rd Dist. 2013.

176 Walters, at 82; Ross, at 169–193; Maahs and Hemmens, at 91–101.

177 698 F.3d 681 (2012).

178 *Bell v. Kan. City Police Dep't*, 635 F.3d 346, 347 (8th Cir.2011) (per curiam).

179 *Sitzes v. City of W. Memphis Ark.*, 606 F.3d 461, 470–471 (8th Cir.2010) (citing *City of Los Angeles v. Heller*, 475 U.S. 796, 799, 106 S.Ct. 1571, 89 L.Ed.2d 806 (1986) (per curiam); *Monell v. Dep't of Soc. Servs.*, 436 U.S. 658, 691, 98 S.Ct. 2018, 56 L.Ed.2d 611 (1978) ("Congress did not intend municipalities to be held liable unless action pursuant to official municipal policy of some nature caused a constitutional tort."); *Sanders v. City of Minneapolis, Minn.*, 474 F.3d 523, 527 (8th Cir.2007) ("Without a constitutional violation by the individual officers, there can be no § 1983 or Monell failure to train municipal liability.").

180 *Royster v. Nichols*, 698 F.3d 681, 692–693 (2012).

181 See Chapter 2.

182 Saiat, at 25; Ross, at 169–193; Jeff and Craig.

183 Note, Officer liability spurs niche training, Sec. 29 (1992); 69.

184 Wayne B. Hanewicz, New ASIS program guidelines—A preview, *J. Sec. Admin. & Pri. Police* 37–46 (1978).

185 Note, Certified protection security and law enforcement, *Sec. Mgmt.*, 1980, at 75.

186 John T. Smith, Develop yourself professionally, *Sec. Mgmt.* 35 (1991); 92, 92–93.

187 Ian C. Paul, Certified protection professional progress report, *Sec. Mgmt.* 35 (1991); 86.

188 See generally Annotation, liability of one contracting for private police of security service for acts of personnel supplied, 38 A.L.R.3d 1332; Annotation, Liability of hiring private investigator or detective for tortious acts committed in course of investigation, 75 A.L.R.3d 1175.

189 Ill. Rev. Stat. Ch. 11 § 2622 (10).

190 Products liability: Modern cases determining whether product is defectively designed, 96 A.L.R.3d 22.

191 See generally Principal's liability for false arrest or imprisonment caused by agent or servant, 92 A.L.R.2d 15; Brill, The liability of an employer for the willful torts of his servants, *Chic. - Kent. L. Rev.* 45 (1968); 1. Liability of one hiring private detective, 13 A.L.R.3d 1175.

192 Carter, at 229.

193 Hiring Private Detectives, at 1178.

194 Paul S. Bailin and Stanton G. Cort, Industry corner: Private contractual security services: The U.S. market and industry, *Business Economics* 31 (Ap. 1996) at 57; Joel Griffin, Demand for private security services projected to rise in U.S., SecurityInfoWatch (Nov 7, 2012), at http://www.securityinfowatch.com/article/10826461/freedonia-group-study-projects-steady-increase-in-demand-for-private-security-services, last visited August 27, 2016; Calvert Institute for Policy Research, Calvert Issue

Brief Vol. 3 (September 1999); See Bill Zalud, Enterprise-wide alignment drives contract or propri-etary decision, *Sec. Mag.* (Feb. 2007), available at http://www.securitymagazine.com/articles/78349-enterprise-wide-alignment-drives-contract-or-proprietary-decision-1, last accessed August 27, 2016.

195 *Howard v. J.H. Harvey Co., Inc.*, 521 S.E.2d 691 (Ga. App. 1999).

196 John Chuvala, Boss on Board: Get Your CEO Involved, 28 Sec. 19 (1991).

197 Walters, at 80; see generally Ross, at 169–193: Maahs and Hemmens.

198 Walters, at 80; see generally Liability for acts of security guards, 38 A.L.R.3d 1332; See also as to ratification: *Dillon v. Sears-Roebuck Co.*, 235 N.W. 331 (Neb. 1934).

199 496 So. 2d 246 (Fla. App. 1986).

200 Carter, at 272.

201 *Moorehead v. District of Columbia*, 747 A.2d 138 (D.C. 2000).

202 Case No. 2:14-cv-02318-MHH. United States District Court, N.D. Alabama, Southern Division. February 24, 2016.

203 *Martinez v. Espey*, Case No. 2:14-cv-02318-MHH. United States District Court, N.D. Alabama, Southern Division. February 24, 2016. At 3.

204 Restatement 2d of Agency § 220 (2) (1958).

205 448 A.2d 856 (D.C. 1982).

206 Id. at 861.

207 255 S.E.2d 73 (Ga. App. 1979).

208 33 Cal. App. 3d 654 (1973).

209 Id. at 661; see also *Greenbaum v. Brooks*, 139 S.E.2d 432 (Ga. App. 1964).

210 John P. Figura, The 2008 Randolph W. Thrower Symposium: Legal Science: An Interdisciplinary Examination of the Use and Misuse of Science in the Law, Comment: You're in the Army Now: Borrowed Servant, Dual Servants and Torts Committed by Contractors' Employees in the Theaters of U. S. Military Operations, *Emory L. J* 58 (2008); 513. See also Office of the Inspector Gen., U.S. Dep't of Def., Rep. No. D-2004-057, Acquisition: Contracts Awarded for the Coalition Provisional Authority by the Defense Contracting Command-Washington 15 (2004); U.S. Dep't of Def., Instruction No. 3020.41, Contractor Personnel Authorized to Accompany the U.S. Armed Forces ¶6.3.3 (2005), available at http:// www.dtic.mil/whs/directives/corres/pdf/302041p.pdf; Major Lisa L. Turner and Major Lynn G. Norton, *Civilians at the Tip of the Spear*, 51 A.F. L. REV. 1, 37 (2001) (summarizing issues confronting civilian contractors in contingency operations but not addressing the borrowed servant or dual servant doctrines); Major Karen L. Douglas, Contractors accompanying the force: Empowering commanders with emergency change authority, *A.F. L. Rev.* 55 (2004); 127, 135. Jeffrey S. Thurnher, Drowning in Blackwater: How Weak Accountability over Private Security Contractors Significantly Undermines Counterinsurgency Efforts, *Army Law.* 64 (2008); 2008. Craig S. Jordan, Who will guard the guards? The accountability of private military contractors in areas of armed conflict, *N.E. J. Crim. & Civ. Con.* 35 (2009); 309; Oliver R. Jones, *Implausible Deniability: State Responsibility for the Actions of Private Military Firms*, 24 Conn. J. Int'l. L. 239 (2009); Gable F. Hackman, *Lipping Through the Cracks: Can We Hold Private Security Contractors Accountable for Their Actions Abroad?*, Loy. J. Pub. Int. L. 9 (2008); 251.

211 See Donald L. Doernberg, *Sovereign Immunity or The Rule of Law* 74 (2005) (quoting William Blackstone, *Commentaries on the Laws of England* 235 (1765)); *United States v. Lee*, 106 U.S. 196, 205 (1882); Erwin Chemerinsky, *Federal Jurisdiction* 610-11 (4th ed. 2003); Federal Tort Claims Act, 28 U.S.C. §§ 1346(b), 2671–2680 (2008); 28 U.S.C. § 2680(j) (2008).

212 Andrew Finkelman, Suing the hired gun: An analysis of two federal defense to tort lawsuits against military contractors, *Brook. J. Int'l L.* 34 (2009); 395, 426.

213 *McMahon v. Presidential Airways, Inc.*, 502 F.3d 1331, 1336-38 (11th Cir. 2007).

214 See Hornstein, Protecting civilian logisticians on the battlefield, *Army Logistician* 38 (2006); 14. *Bentzlin v. Hughes Aircraft Co.*, 833 F. Supp. 1486, 1493 (C.D. Cal. 1993); *Johnson v. United States*, 170 F.2d 767, 770 (9th Cir. 1949); Chia Lehnardt, Private military companies and state responsibility, in from mercenaries to market: The rise and regulation of private military companies 139, 147–148 (Simon Chesterman and Chia Lehnardt eds., 2007).

215 See Charles Tiefer, The Iraq debacle: The rise and fall of procurement-aided unilateralism as a para-digm of foreign war, *U. Pa. J. Int'l L.* 29 (2007); 1, 13–19.

216 Matthew C. Dahl, Soldiers of fortune: Holding private security contractors accountable: The Alien Tort Claims Act and its potential application to *Abtan, et al. v. Blackwater and Training Center, Inc., et al..*, *Denv. J. Int'l L. & Pol'y* 37 (2008); 119, 120. E.L. Gaston, Note, Mercenarism 2.0? The rise of the modern private security industry and its implications for international humanitarian law enforcement, *Harv. Int'l L.J.* 49 (2008); 221, 221, 234–235 Jeremy Scahill, Blackwater: The Rise of The World's Most Powerful Mercenary Army xxi–xxii (2007).

217 See *Griffin v. Pinkerton's, Inc.,* 173 F.3d 661 (8th Cir. 1999); Philip Purpura, *Security and Loss Prevention: An Introduction* 79 (2008).

218 233 So. 2d 847 (Fla. App. 1970).

219 *Acts of Security Guards,* at 1342; see also *Principal's Liability for False Arrest or Imprisonment Caused by Agent or Servant,* 92 A.L.R.2d 15.

220 *Acts of Security Guards,* at 1342.

221 188 S.E.2d 911 (Ga. App. 1972).

222 400 So. 2d 1148 (La. App. 1981).

223 Id.

224 29 A.L.R.4th 144; see also *Peachtree v. Pandazides,* 327 S.E.2d 188 (Ga. 1988).

225 444 A.2d 483 (Md. App. 1982).

226 See *Nash v. Sears,* 163 N.W.2d 471 (Mich. App. 1968); *Adams v. F.W. Woolworth,* 257 N.Y.S. 776 (N.Y. Sup. 1932); *Hendricks v. Leslie Fay, Inc.,* 159 S.E.2d 363 (N.C. 1968); *Webbier v. Thoroughbred Racing,* 254 A.2d 285 (R.I. 1969).

227 *Dupree v. Piggly Wiggly Shop Rite Foods, Inc.* 542 S.W.2d 882 (Tex. Civ. App. 1976).

228 See generally 22 Am. Jur. 2d, *Damages* §§257, 260, 293.

229 See *Principal's Liability for Punitive Damages,* 93 A.L.R.3d 826 at 832.

230 Id. at 831.

231 See *Craven v. Bloomington,* 64 N.E. 169 (N.Y. 1902); *Thomas v. F. & R. Lazarus Co.,* 57 N.E.2d 103 (Oh. App. 1941).

232 For example, *Kieninger v. New York,* 384 N.Y.S.2d 11 (N.Y.A.D. 1976).

233 *Clairborne v. Chesapeake & O.R. Co.,* 33 S.E. 262 (W. Va. 1899).

234 *Standard Oil Co. v. Davis,* 94 So. 754 (Ala. 1922).

235 Susan Fettner, Security system service, Case & Comment 89 (1984); 12. see also Federal and Fogleman, at 209–216; Kappeler, *Supreme Court Cases.*

236 *Gulf Oil v. Williams,* 642 S.W.2d 270 (Tex. App. 6 Dist. 1982).

237 Federal & Fogleman, at 231.

238 Id. at 232.

239 Id. at 233.

240 42 U.S.C. § 1983 (1970). Civil Rights Act of 1871; Also pertinent 28 U.S.C. § 1343 (1970) conferring federal jurisdiction in the federal courts.

241 Barrineau.

242 See *Screws v. U.S.,* 325 U.S. 91 (1945).

243 365 U.S. 167 (1961).

244 Wayne W. Schmidt, Recent developments in police civil liability, *J. Pol. Sci. Admin.* 4 (1976); 197. See also Wayne W. Schmidt, *Survey of Police Misconduct Litigation* 1967–1971 (1971); Kappeler.

245 Schmidt, at 197; R. V. del Carmen, *Civil and Criminal Liabilities of Police Officers,* in *Police Deviance* (T. Barker & D. L. Carter, eds., 1994).

246 403 U.S. 388 (1971).

247 Jeffrey Higginbotham, Defending law enforcement officers against personal liability in constitutional tort litigation, *FBI L. Enf. Bull.* 54 (1985); 24.

248 *Allen v. Columbia Mall Inc.,* 47 F. Supp. 2d 605 (D. Md. 1998); *Orin v. Barclay,* 272 F.3d 1207 (9th Cir. 2001); see generally M. S. Vaughn and L. F. Coomers, Police civil liability under section 1983: When do police officers act under color of law, *J. Crim. Justice* 23 (1995); 395–415.

249 Barrineau, at 35–53.

250 Id. at 57–68; see also Comment, *City of Canton v. Harris.* Municipal liability under 42 U.S.C. Section 1983 for inadequate police training, *George Mason L. Rev.* 12 (1990); 757–774.

251 Kallstrom, 136 F.3d 1055, 1066 (6th Cir. 1998) (citing *Sargi v. Kent City Bd. of Educ.*, 70 F.3d 907, 913 (6th Cir. 1995).

252 Id.

253 *Neuens v. City of Columbus*, 169 F. Supp. 2d 780, 786 (S.D. Oh. 2001).

254 Steven D. Rittenmayer, Vicarious liability in suits pursuant to 42 USC 1983: legal myth and reality, *J. Pol. Sci. & Admin.* 12 (1984); 260. See also Comment, *City of Canton v. Harris.* Municipal liability under 42 U.S.C. Section 1983 for inadequate police training, *George Mason L. Rev.* 12 (1990); 757–774.

255 Rittenmayer, at 261.

256 See *Rizzo v. Goode*, 423 U.S. 362 (1975).

257 Rittenmayer, at 264; see also *Jordan v. Kelly*, 223 F. Supp. 731 (W.D. Mo. 1963); *Ritchard v. Downie*, 216 F. Supp. 621 (D. Ark. 1963); *Patrum v. Martin*, 292 F. Supp. 370 (W. Ky. 1968).

258 183 F. Supp. 2d 344 (D. Mass. 2002).

259 *Grant v. John Hancock*, 183 F.Supp. 2d 344, 345 (D. Mass. 2002).

260 29 U.S.C. § 2001 et seq. See *Graham v. Beasley Enterprises*, 180 F.Supp. 2d 760 (E.D. N.C. 2001).

261 Richard Frankel, Regulating privatized government through § 1983, *U. Chi. L. Rev.* 76 (2009); 1449.

262 Id.

263 See *Smith v. Brookshire Brothers, Inc.* 519 F.2d 93 (5th Cir. 1975); *DeCarlo v. Joseph Horne*, 251 F.Supp. (W.D. PA. 1966); see also M.S. Vaughn and L. F. Coomers, Police civil liability under section 1983: Who do police officers act under color of law? *J. Crim. Justice* 23 (1995); 395–415. Not all unlawful detentions are necessarily constitutional violations but sometimes error in processing or good faith mistake. See *Shoyoye v. County of Los Angeles*, 203 Cal. App. 4th 947 - Cal: Court of Appeal, 2nd Appellate Dist., 4th Div. 2012; See also the million-dollar damage claim case for improper detention in Cervantes v. County of Los Angeles, Dist. Court, CD California 2016.

264 An instructive case of the U.S. Supreme Court, *Wilson v. Layne* unanimously deduced "private action" of media working side-by-side with the police. *Wilson v. Layne*, 526 U.S. 603 (1999).

265 Vroman, The potential liability of private police under section 1983 of the Civil Rights Act, 4 L.F. 1185, 1186 (1976).

266 42 U.S.C.A. § 1981 (West).

267 28 F.Supp.3d 153 (2014).

268 See Chapter 2.

269 National Advisory Commission on Criminal Justice Standards and Goals, *Private Security Task Force Report* (1976).

270 Charles Buikema and Frank Horvath, Security regulation: A state-by-state update, *Sec. Mgmt.* 28:1 (1984); 39–43.

271 Milton Cox, Guards or guard training, *Sec. Mgmt.* 28 (1984); 73, 77.

272 755 N.W. 2d 686 (Mich. App. 2008).

273 Id. at 698.

274 Id.

275 Id. at 711.

276 698 F. 3d 1128—Court of Appeals, 9th Circuit 2012,

277 *Tsao v. Desert Palace, Inc.* 698 F. 3d 1128, 1141- Court of Appeals, 9th Circuit 2012.

278 *Marsh v. Alabama*, 326 U.S. 501 (1946).

279 *Evans v. Newton*, 382 U.S. 296 (1966); *Amalgamated Foods v. Logan Valley Plaza*, 391 U.S. 308 (1968).

280 Vroman, at 1192; see also Note, state action theories for applying constitutional restrictions to private activity, *Colum. L. Rev.* 74 (1974); 656.

281 Id; *Commonwealth v. Kneer*, 743 A.2d 942 (Pa. Super. 1999).

282 Note, private assumption of the police function under the Fourth Amendment, *Bost. U. L. Rev.* 51 (1971); 464–482.

283 24 Cal. 3d 357 (1979).

284 790 A.2d 660 (Md. 2002).

285 *Crenshaw v. Rivera*, No. 2:05-CV-440-PRC, slip op. (N.D. Ind. 2009).

286 Id. at 9.
287 Michael J. Dittener, Blackwater and beyond: Can potential plaintiffs sue private security companies for the due process violations via exceptions to the state action doctrine, including through 1983 actions, *Nova L. Rev.* 33 (2009); 627, 641
288 365 U.S. 715 (1961).
289 Vroman, at 1198.
290 Dittener, at 641; See Jonathan Finer, Recent development, holstering the hired guns: new accountability measures for private security contractors, *Yale J. Int'l L.* 33 (2008); 259, 259. E.L. Gaston, Note, mercenarism 2.0? The rise of the modern private security industry and its implications for international humanitarian law enforcement, *Harv. Int'l L.J.* 49 (2008); 221, 224. Jennifer K. Elsea et al., Private security contractors in Iraq: Background, legal status, and other issues 3 (Cong. Research Serv., CRS Report for Congress Order Code RL32419, Aug. 25, 2008), available at http://www.fas.org/sgp/crs/natsec/RL32419.pdf.
291 856 F.2d 843 (7th Cir. 1988).
292 Id. at 849; See also *Forbes v. City of New*, 2008 U. S. Dist. LEXIS 63021 (August 12, 2008).
293 *State v. Jensen*, 730 P.2d 1282 (Or. App. 1986).
294 Id. at 1283.
295 *State v. Olsen*, 317 P.2d 938 (Or. 1957); *State v. Okeke*, 728 P.2d 872 (Or. App. 1986).
296 Okeke, 728 P.2d at 872.
297 *State v. Lowry*, 588 P.2d 623, 630 (Or. App. 1978), rev. den. 285 Or. 195 (1979).
298 Jensen, 730 P.2d at 1283.
299 *Tin Man Lee v. State of Texas*, 773 S.W.2d 47 (Tex. App. 1989).
300 Id. at 49.
301 See James S. Kakalik and Sorrel Wildhorn, *The Private Police Industry: Its Nature and Extent* (1971).
302 See *Steven Cusack v. State* No. 49A05-1106-CR-274 (Ind. App., Jan. 10, 2012).
303 See *People v. Omeel*, 166 N.W.2d 279 (Mich. App. 1968); *Williams v. U.S.*, 341 U.S. 97 (1951); *Tarref v. State*, 512 P.2d 923 (Alaska 1973).
304 See Ohio Rev. Code Ann. §§4973.17.
305 *Payton v. Rush-Presbyterian-St. Luke's Medical Center*, 184 F.3d 623 (7th Cir. 1999).
306 Cunningham, et al., at 290.
307 Private delivery of public services, *The Lipman Report*, 1–4 (1989).
308 126 F.Supp. 2d 1299 (Haw. 1998).
309 *Ibarra v. Las Vegas Metropolitan Police Dept.*, 572 F. Supp. 562, 564 (D. Nev. 1983).
310 Id. at 565 (quoting *Hoffman v. Halden*, 268 F.2d 280, 298 (9th Cir. 1959)).
311 Id.
312 Id.
313 *Otani v. City and County of Hawaii*, 126 F. Supp. 2d 1299, 1306 (Haw. 1998).
314 415 So. 2d 371 (La. App. 1 Cir. 1982).
315 Federal & Fogleman, at 172.
316 468 N.E.2d 1064 (Ind. App. 4 Dist. 1985).
317 Federal and Fogleman, at 179.
318 *Leach v. Penn-Mar Merchants Assoc.*, 308 A.2d 446 (Md. App. 1973).
319 327 N.W.2d 278 (Mich. 1982).
320 290 S.E.2d 366 (N.C. 1982).

Chapter 5

Criminal Culpability and the Private Security Industry

5.1 Introduction: The Private Security Industry and Criminal Culpability

While civil liability problems are natural risks in the security industry, the panorama of liability extends beyond the civil realm and into the criminal context. While the term "liability" is acceptable in criminal settings, the more accurate term might be culpability. In short, how can and does the security operative become responsible for and culpable under criminal constructions? Can the security industry, as well as its individual personnel, suffer criminal liability? Can security personnel, in both a personal and professional capacity, commit crimes? Are security corporations, businesses, and industrial concerns capable of criminal infraction or can these entities be held criminally liable for the conduct of employees? Are there other criminal concerns, either substantive or procedural, that the security industry should be vigilant about?

As the privatization of once historic criminal justice functions continue, corresponding civil and criminal liability questions will remain and even accelerate. Security professionals engage the public in so many settings and circumstances that it is a sure bet that criminal conduct will be witnessed. While the content of this chapter will glance at procedural issues raised in Chapter 3, its main thrust shall be on criminal codification and analysis of criminal definition and how the security industry becomes entangled in these many offenses.

5.2 The Nature of Crime and Criminal Culpability

Before private security operatives can intelligently detect or enforce criminal behavior, they must master the essential elements of the alleged criminal behavior. More particularly, the industry must focus on the crimes more likely encountered by its field personnel.

Every crime consists of two basic elements:

1. The criminal act: *Actus Reus*
2. The mental intent: *Mens* Rea

In this way, guilt under nearly all criminal offenses calls for proof of both the act itself, and the mind that triggers, intends or prompts the act. In the mental faculty requirement, the actor must do more than merely act, but contemplate upon the act before its commission and present some sort of mental intentionality. One without the other is bound to lead to failure in the American conception of criminal culpability.

In some intellectual circles, there is a third element, namely causation, which demands proof that the act and the mind together, working in consort, lead to a particular consequence. While not necessary central to every criminal advocacy, it is wise to consider the question whether a criminal's mind, was prompted a particular act, which in turn caused a particular harm or injury. A more focused view of these primary components of a crime follows.

5.2.1 The Criminal Act (Actus Reus)

Not unexpectedly, criminal liability cannot attach without a deed, an act, an offense, or an omission of specifically enumerated conduct. Crimes are not inventions or fantasies but real human activity. Merely thinking about crimes, with rare exceptions, is not criminally punishable. Thoughts, no matter how bizarre or perverted, are not punishable unless put into action. Thus, to be found guilty of theft, an individual has to take overt steps toward the unlawful taking of another's property. He or she may think obsessively about the desire to be in possession of some object, but until some overt act or course of conduct is chosen, and put into effect, there is no *actus reus*.[1] Hence, every criminal construction insists on an act of some sort since acts alone are generally not sufficient except in narrow strict liability crimes.[2]

In addition, the criminal act must be a voluntary act. The law does not hold accountable those individuals who are mentally incapacitated or operating against their will, by either duress or coercion, or suffering from related or corollary disease or mental defect that substantially impacts the mental faculty.[3] The American Law Institute's *Model Penal Code*, in its proposed 1962 draft, defines the nature of a voluntary act for criminal liability purposes.

Requirement of Voluntary Act; Admission as Basis of Liability; Possession Is an Act.

1. A person is not guilty of an offense unless his liability is based on conduct which includes a voluntary act or the omission to perform an act of which he is physically capable.
2. The following are not voluntary acts within the meaning of this Section.
   a. A reflex or convulsion;
   b. A bodily movement during unconsciousness or sleep;
   c. Conduct during hypnosis or resulting from hypnotic suggestion;
   d. A bodily movement that otherwise is not a product of the effort or determination of the actor, either conscious or habitual.
3. Liability for the commission of an offense may not be based on an omission unaccompanied by action unless;
   a. The omission is expressly made sufficient by the law defining the offense; or
   b. The duty to perform the omitted act is otherwise imposed by law.[4]

Criminal liability does not attach unless the prosecution can demonstrate an act that is voluntary and not the result of unintentional, accidental, or nonvolitional circumstances. Acts by omission, that is, a failure to act when the law so dictates, such as the case of a parent who neglects his child, or fails to save the child when in peril, are also within the definition of *actus reus*.[5] In this sense, acts fall into two categories: commission and omission.

For a fascinating report on how federal codes are eroding the requirements of a mental state, read the Heritage Foundation's report at: http://www.heritage.org/research/reports/2010/05/the-criminal-intent-report-congress-is-eroding-the-mens-rea-requirement-in-federal-criminal-law

From the outset of any investigation concerning crime, the security investigator must look at the facts to determine whether an Act is proven. Use the Incident Report Form at Figure 5.1.[6]

5.2.2 The Criminal Mind (Mens Rea)

Determining the state of one's mind, the *mens rea* is a much more complicated exercise than the proof of a criminal act. It has long been a major tenet of American jurisprudence that persons not in control of their mind or fully functional in mental state are less likely to be criminally responsible. Subjectively or objectively appraising what is in a person's mind can be gleaned from the facts themselves, the *corpus delicti*; the statements and comments of the actor by oral or written form, as well as psychological and psychiatric evidence. These conclusions must all be linked to the crime in question. While most scholars and academics concede *mens rea* exists, it is, nevertheless, very subjective and difficult to prove.[7] That a defendant may intend the general consequences of a certain action is clear, but how intensely they actually desire to cause harm and at the actual injury level they intent is harder to quantify.[8] Consider the various descriptive adjectives and adverbs that are utilized to describe a person's state of mind:

- Felonious intent
- Criminal intent
- Malice aforethought
- Premeditated
- Guilty knowledge
- Fraudulent intent
- Willful with scienter
- With guilty knowledge
- Maliciously
- Viciously
- Intentionally
- With gross disregard
- With depraved heart
- With an evil purpose
- Wantonly
- Lawfully
- Without justification
- With a corrupted mind

SECURITY DEPARTMENT INCIDENT REPORT

OFFENSE CATEGORY		DATE-TIME RECEIVED	DAY OF WK.	DATE MO. DAY YR	TIME AM PM	INVESTIGATION NO.
	FORCED ENTRY	COMPLAINANT'S NAME				HOME PHONE
THEFT	PERS.PROP. COMPANY PROP COIN MACHINE	ADDRESS				BUSINESS PHONE
	AUTO	STATUS				

STATUS ☐ VISITOR ☐ EMPLOYEE ☐ OTHER (SPECIFY)

ROBBERY						

ASSAULT	DATE-TIME OF OFFENSE	DAY OF WK	DATE MO. DAY YR	TIME AM PM
RAPE				
MANSLAUGHTER	PLACE		WEAPON USED	
DISTURBANCE				
TRAFFIC	TRADEMARK			

OTHER (SPECIFY)

VICTIM'S NAME   ADDRESS

SEX ☐M ☐F	AGE	RACE	STATUS			

STATUS ☐ VISITOR ☐ EMPLOYEE ☐ OTHER (SPECIFY)

MECIAL TREATMENT ☐ YES (EXPLAIN) ☐ NO		DESCRIPTION OF LOST PROPERTY	VALUE

DESCRIPTION OF OFFENDERS

NO. 1	SEX ☐M ☐F	RACE	HEIGHT	BUILD	EYES	HAIR	GLASSES ☐ YES ☐ NO	COMPLEXION
	MARKS				AGE	HAT	COAT	SHIRT
NO. 2	SEX ☐M ☐F	RACE	HEIGHT	BUILD	EYES	HAIR	GLASSES ☐ YES ☐ NO	COMPLEXION
	MARKS				AGE	HAT	COAT	SHIRT

WITNESS NAME 1.	ADDRESS	TELEPHONE
WITNESS NAME 2.	ADDRESS	TELEPHONE

LAW ENFORCEMENT AGENCY NOTIFIED	TIME	PERSON
1.	AM PM	
2.	AM PM	

NAME OF PERSON ARRESTED 1.	ADDRESS
NAME OF PERSON ARRESTED 2.	ADDRESS

CHARGES

1.	2.

WAS PHYICAL FORCE USED? ☐ YES ☐ NO

SIGNATURE OF REPORTING OFFICER DATE	FOR SECURITY OFFICE USE ONLY APPROVED
	DATE NAME CARD COMPLETED

Figure 5.1 Incident report form.

(Continued)

NARRATIVE – BE SPECIFIC IN WRITING OF THIS REPORT. BE SURE TO USE THE GUIDELINES: WHO, WHAT, WHEN, WHY, WHERE AND HOW. DESCRIBE OFFENSE IN DETAIL. INCLUDE STATEMENTS UTTERED BY VICTIM, WITNESSES AND SUSPECTS. DESCRIBE SCENE OF OFFENSE AND CONTRIBUTORY CONDITIONS SUCH AS POOR LIGHTING, EXTREME ISOLATION, ETC. LIST EVIDENCE FOUND AT SCENE AND ALL OTHER RELEVANT INFORMATION SUCH AS SOBRIETY OF VICTIM, WITNESSES AND SUSPECTS, SAFEGUARD REPORT FOR REFERENCE.

FOR SECURITY DEPARTMENT USE ONLY

THIS OFFENSE IS DECLARED:

UNFOUNDED ☐

CLEARED BY ARREST ☐   SIGNED _____   DATE _____

EXCEPTIONALLY CLEARED ☐   SECURITY DIRECTOR

INACTIVE (NOT CLEARED) ☐

Figure 5.1 (Continued)   Incident report form.

- Criminally negligent
- With disregard for human life
- With depraved indifference
- Without moral turpitude
- Without justification
- Overtly
- With mischievous intent[9]

Admittedly, these terms can never fully describe the actor's mind—at best they infer the conduct's level of intentionality. Proving the mental state is often a deductive conclusion—looking to facts and conditions that comprise the criminality for defendants will rarely if ever proclaim the clarity of premeditation. Hence the usage of a deadly weapon leads the reasonable person to reach certain conclusions about what a person intends as do other facts.[10] Aligned to the normal difficulties of measuring the mental intent of any actor, the bulk of criminal actors suffer from some level of baggage or other mitigating or aggravating forces that make cool, collected rationality. Most criminal actors operate with external and internal forces that impact the clarity of the intellectual choice to commit the act.[11] Attempts to codify and categorize the nature of *mens rea*, while imperfect, are useful measures of the mental faculty in a criminal action.

Evaluate the PowerPoint presentation from the University of North Texas at: http://pacs.unt.edu/criminal-justice/Course_Pages/CJUS_2100/2100chapter2.ppt#329,10,Slide 10

Diverse descriptive states of culpability have been fully incorporated into the *Model Penal Code* and are fully discoverable throughout this chapter. State legislative chambers have utilized this basic guidance when fashioning crime codifications. "The Model Penal Code's (MPC) default provision desired to ensure a culpability element in all crimes…and its desire to codify particular mental states (purposely, knowingly, recklessly, and negligently)…"[12]

Foundationally, the MPC describes culpability in relation to each and every element of the crime. It promulgates some general requirements of culpability:

1. Minimum Requirements of Culpability. Except as provided in Section 2.05, a person is not guilty of an offense unless he acted purposely, knowingly, recklessly or negligently as the law may require, with respect to each material element of the offense.
2. Kinds of Culpability Defined.
   a. Purposely.
      A person acts purposely with respect to a material element of an offense:
      i. If the element involves the nature of his conduct or a result thereof, it is his conscious object to engage in conduct…
      ii. If the element involves the attendant circumstances, he is aware of the existence of such circumstances…
   b. Knowingly.
      A person acts knowingly with respect to a material element of an offense:
      i. If the element involved the nature of his conduct or the attendant circumstances, he is aware that his conduct is of that nature or he knows such circumstances exist and
      ii. If the element involves the result of his conduct he is aware that it is practically certain that his conduct will cause such a result.

c. Recklessly.
A person acts recklessly with respect to a material element of an offense when he consciously disregards a substantial and unjustifiable risk that the material element exists or will result from his conduct....

d. Negligently.
A person acts negligently with respect to a material element of an offense when he should be aware of a substantial and unjustifiable risk that the material element exists or will result from his conduct.[13]

Security professionals should be vigilant in their assessment of facts and conditions at a crime scene because conduct can be explained in more than one way. Instead of always assuming a crime occurred, look for secondary explanations, such as a mistake of fact or law regarding a right to property, inadvertent entry rather than an unlawful trespass, or an act of self-defense rather than an offensive touching. Security investigators and officers must not assume that the act is coupled with a criminal mind. Neither the act nor the mind alone will suffice since "criminal liability is predicated upon a union of act and intent or criminal negligence."[14]

Web Exercise: See Remarks of the Hon. Michael Mukasey, The Foreign Corrupt Practices Act panel, the Federalist Society's National Lawyers Convention, November 20, 2012, video available at http://www.fed-soc.org/publications/detail/the-foreign-corrupt-practices-act-event-audiovideo

---

5.3 Classification of Criminal Offenses and Related Penalties

Common law and statutory guidelines also characterize criminal behavior into various classifications or types. Those classifications generally include

- Felony[15]
- Misdemeanor[16]
- Summary offense[17]
- Treason[18] and other infamous crimes

The security industry's concern will be the detection and apprehension of misdemeanants and felons whose crimes comprise the basic menu of criminal charges including assault, battery, theft and related property offenses, sexual offenses, intimidation and harassment, and white collar crime including forgery, credit card fraud, and the like. Treason and other infamous crimes emerge in cases of international terrorism and homeland security, and given the rising influence of private sector justice in the global war on terror, they should give rise to more involvement. The entire aerospace industry is dependent upon personnel not only trained in security issues, but also the criminal law issues that surround breaches of security at airport facilities. Shoplifting and retail theft may be designated a "summary" offense. Summary offenses generally consist of public order violations, including failure to pay parking tickets, creating a temporary obstruction in a public place, public intoxication, or other offenses of a less serious nature that are rarely punishable by a term of imprisonment,[19] but are regularly witnessed by the security professional. At common law, the designation of an act as a felony constituted an extremely serious offense. Penal and correctional response to felony behavior included the death penalty and forfeiture of all lands, goods, and other personal property. Generally, a felony was any capital offense, namely murder, manslaughter, rape, sodomy, robbery, larceny, arson, burglary, mayhem, and other violent conduct.[20] An alternative way of defining a felony was the severity of its corresponding punishment. Felony was defined "to mean offenses for which the offender, on conviction, may be punished by death or imprisonment in the state prison or penitentiary; but in the absence of such statute the word is used to designate such serious offenses as were formally punishable by death, or by forfeiture of the lands or goods of the offender."[21] In other words, a crime could be a felony or a misdemeanor not because of its severity or subsequent impact but due to the term of incarceration. Modern criminal analysis shows a confused and perplexing legislative decision-making on the nature of a felony and a misdemeanor. The President's Commission on Law Enforcement and Administration of Justice, in its *Task Force Report on the Courts*, relates:

> A study of the Oregon Penal Code revealed that 1413 criminal statutes contained a total of 466 different types and lengths of sentences. The absence of legislative attention to the whole range of penalties may also be demonstrated by comparisons between certain offenses. A recent study of the Colorado Statutes disclosed that a person convicted of a first-degree murder must serve ten (10) years before becoming eligible for parole, while a person convicted of a lesser degree of the same offense must serve at least fifteen (15) years; destruction of a house with fire is punishable by a maximum twenty (20) years imprisonment, but destruction of a house with explosives carries a ten (10) years maximum. In California, an offender who breaks into an automobile to steal the contents of the glove compartment is subject to a fifteen (15) years maximum sentence but if he stole the car itself, he would face a maximum ten (10) years term.
>
> Although each offense must be defined in a separate statutory provision, the number and variety of sentencing distinctions which result when legislatures prescribe a separate penalty for each offense are among the main causes of the anarchy in sentencing that is so widely deplored.[22]

In defining the term misdemeanor, legislatures and jurists use a process of elimination holding that an offense not deemed a felony is, deductively, a misdemeanor. Usually misdemeanors are offenses punishable by less than a year's incarceration. The popular perception that misdemeanors are not serious offenses may be a faulty impression. Criminal codes surprise even the most seasoned justice practitioner, who frequently finds little logic in an offense's definition, resulting classification, and corresponding punishment. For examples of this confusion, review selected state code provisions on "sexual offenses."[23]

5.4 Types of Crimes and Offenses

Generally, the law of crimes divides into categories based on the victimized party, the subject matter of the criminality and the statutory or common law definition of the offense. To illustrate, property crimes are directed to special forms of property with value whether personal property, jewelry, stocks, bonds, and the like. Crimes that are sexual in motive, such as rape and aggravated sexual assault, focus on a sexually victimized human person or offenses against the person, run the gamut between the extreme of homicide and the nuisance of simple assault by profanity. The key for the security practitioner is to discern the elemental requirements in the proof of said offenses and then to determine how these offenses are often discovered in the world of private security.

5.4.1 Offenses against the Person

5.4.1.1 Felonious Homicide

The security industry cannot avoid the ravages of criminal homicide and, in fact, due to improper use of weaponry or mistaken identity, are sometimes the accused. Criminal acts of homicide are being recorded due to the installation, maintenance, and operational oversight of electronic surveillance systems and other technological equipment utilized to protect the internal and external premises of businesses. As the public sector continues to transfer and privatize many of its traditionally public police functions, such as courtroom and prison security, violent acts of homicide are unfortunately replayed. Airport terrorism, failed executive protection programs, and attempted or actual homicides on armored car money carriers, are other distressing examples of criminal homicide (see Figure 5.2).[24]

This subsection will deal only with felonious acts of homicide, and the security professional is reminded that nonculpable homicide occurs in cases of self-defense, necessity in time of war, or by legal right, authority, or privilege.[25] Criminal homicide is defined by the *Model Penal Code* as follows:

1. A person is guilty of criminal homicide if he purposely, knowingly, recklessly or negligently causes the death of another human being.
2. Criminal homicide is murder, manslaughter or negligent homicide.[26]

The *Model Penal Code*, after this general legislative introduction, precisely defines each type of homicide.

5.4.1.2 Murder

A charge of murder will be upheld when

1. It is committed purposely or knowingly or
2. It is committed recklessly under circumstances manifesting extreme indifference to the value of human life. Such recklessness and indifference are presumed if the actor is engaged or is an accomplice in the commission of, or an attempt to commit, or flight after committing or attempting to commit robbery, rape, deviate sexual intercourse by force or threat of force, arson, burglary, kidnapping or felonious escape.[27]

The *Code* as suggested requires a high level of mental faculty. While the law of criminal intent varies, most major capital offenses require what is known as specific intent.[28] Specific intent can be loosely described as premeditation or a mind possessive of malice aforethought. In other words, the criminal actor wants, desires, wishes, knows, and realizes the ramifications and repercussions of his or her activity. Although the law does not require an intelligent or an esoteric thinker, there is a clear, lucid mindset operating. The 2016 mass shooting at the Pulse Nightclub in Florida, by a licensed security officer with terrorist, radical Islamic intent, vivifies how intent motivates the actor.[29]

Read the transcript which captures the terrorist motivation at the mass shooting and killing at the PULSE nightclub in Orlando, Florida at https://www.fbi.gov/contact-us/field-offices/tampa/news/press-releases/investigative-update-regarding-pulse-nightclub-shooting

---

Department of Justice
Office of Public Affairs

FOR IMMEDIATE RELEASE
Wednesday, October 22, 2014

FOUR FORMER BLACKWATER EMPLOYEES FOUND GUILTY OF CHARGES IN FATAL NISUR SQUARE SHOOTING IN IRAQ

Jury Verdict Follows 2 ½-Month Trial

Four former security guards for Blackwater USA were found guilty today of charges stemming from the Sept. 16, 2007, shooting at Nisur Square in Baghdad, Iraq, that resulted in the killing of 14 unarmed civilians and the wounding of numerous others.

The jury verdicts, in the U.S. District Court for the District of Columbia, were announced by Ronald C. Machen Jr., U.S. Attorney for the District of Columbia, and Andrew G. McCabe, Assistant Director in Charge of the FBI's Washington Field Office.

The defendants include Nicholas Abram Slatten, 30, of Sparta, Tenn.; Paul Alvin Slough, 35, of Keller, Texas; Evan Shawn Liberty, 32, of Rochester, N.H.; and Dustin Laurent Heard, 33, of Maryville, Tenn. Slatten, who was accused of firing the first shots, was found guilty of one count of first-degree murder. Slough was found guilty of 13 counts of voluntary manslaughter, 17 counts of attempted manslaughter, and one firearms offense. Liberty was found guilty of eight counts of voluntary manslaughter, 12 counts of attempted manslaughter, and one firearms offense. Heard was found guilty of six counts of voluntary manslaughter, 11 counts of attempted manslaughter, and one firearms offense.

"This verdict is a resounding affirmation of the commitment of the American people to the rule of law, even in times of war," said U.S. Attorney Machen. "Seven years ago, these Blackwater contractors unleashed powerful sniper fire, machine guns, and grenade launchers on innocent men, women, and children. Today they were held accountable for that outrageous attack and its devastating consequences for so many Iraqi families. I pray that this verdict will bring some sense of comfort to the survivors of that massacre. I want to thank the prosecutors and law enforcement agents who have fought for the past seven years to bring justice to the memories of those who were gunned down in Nisur Square."

"Today's verdict demonstrates the FBI's dedication to investigating violations of U.S. law no matter where they occur," said Assistant Director in Charge McCabe. "International investigations such as this one are very complex and frequently dangerous. This case took a tremendous amount of coordination to bring over a large number of foreign witnesses in support of this prosecution. I commend the FBI Special Agents, Task Force Officers, Intelligence Analysts and Language Specialists and our partners at the U.S. Attorney's Office for working to bring those responsible to justice and conveying some measure of comfort to the victims' families in Iraq."

The verdicts came on the 28th day of jury deliberations and followed more than two months of trial. The Honorable Senior Judge Royce C. Lamberth ordered that the four defendants be detained pending sentencing. A sentencing date has not yet been set.

The murder charge against Slatten calls for a mandatory sentence of life in prison. Each of the voluntary manslaughter counts against the other defendants carries a statutory maximum of 15 years in prison. Each of the attempted manslaughter counts carries a statutory maximum of seven years of incarceration. The weapons offense carries a mandatory 30-year prison sentence.

Another Blackwater security guard, Jeremy P. Ridgeway, pled guilty in December 2008 to voluntary manslaughter and attempt to commit manslaughter. Ridgeway, who testified as a government witness in the trial, has not yet been sentenced.

The defendants worked for Blackwater USA, a private security contractor that was paid by the U.S. government to provide protective services to U.S. officials.

Figure 5.2 One of the most famous cases where private security officers were accused of homicide was the Blackwater killings in Iraq.

(Continued)

The trial began June 17, 2014. Over the next 10 weeks, the government presented testimony from 71 witnesses, including 30 from Iraq. This represented the largest group of foreign witnesses ever to travel to the United States for a criminal trial. The witnesses included 13 people who were wounded in the shootings, as well as relatives of many of those who died. The government's witnesses also included nine members of "Raven 23," the Blackwater team that was on the scene on the day of the shootings.

According to the government's evidence, at approximately noon on Sunday, Sept. 16, 2007, several Blackwater security contractors, including the four defendants, opened fire in and around Nisur Square, a busy traffic circle in the heart of Baghdad. When they stopped shooting, 14 Iraqi civilians were dead. Those killed included 10 men, two women, and two boys, ages 9 and 11. Another 18 victims were injured.

The four defendants and 15 other Blackwater security contractors were assigned to a convoy of four heavily-armed trucks known as a Tactical Support Team, using the call sign "Raven 23." Shortly before noon, Raven 23 learned that a car bomb had detonated in central Baghdad near a location where a U.S official was being escorted by a Blackwater personal security detail team. Raven 23 team members promptly reported to their convoy vehicles, and the convoy drove to a secured checkpoint between the Green Zone and Red Zone.

Once there, in disregard of an order from Blackwater's command, the team's shift leader directed Raven 23 to leave the Green Zone and establish a blockade in Nisur Square, a busy traffic circle that was immediately adjacent to the Green Zone. While occupying the southern part of the traffic circle, seven of the 19 members of Raven 23, including the four defendants and Ridgeway, fired their weapons, resulting in the deaths or injury of the unarmed Iraqi civilians there. While leaving the traffic circle, Slough continued to fire his weapon, resulting in additional deaths and injuries.

Finally, further away, north of the traffic circle, Slough and Ridgeway again fired their weapons, resulting in the injury of three more unarmed Iraqi civilians.

The first to be killed was Ahmed Haithem Ahmed Al Rubia'y, 21, an aspiring doctor, who was driving his mother to an appointment. His mother, Mahassin Mohssen Kadhum Al-Khazali, 44, a medical doctor, also was killed. Others who died included Ali Mohammed Hafedh Abdul Razzaq, 9, who was traveling with his family; Osama Fadhil Abbas, 52, a businessman who sold used cars and who was enroute to a business meeting; Mohamed Abbas Mahmoud, 47, a delivery truck driver, and his 11-year-old son, Qasim Mohamed Abbas Mahmoud; Sa'adi Ali Abbas Alkarkh, 52, a businessman; Mushtaq Karim Abd Al-Razzaq, 18, an Iraqi soldier who was standing at a military checkpoint; Ghaniyah Hassan Ali, 55, who was traveling with her daughter on a public bus, and who was in the area to get documentation for a trip to holy sites; Ibrahim Abid Ayash, 77, a gardener, who was traveling in another bus; Hamoud Sa'eed Abttan, 33, and his cousin, Usday Ismail Ibrahiem, 27, who were out looking for work with the Iraqi Army; Mahdi Sahib Nasir, 26, a taxi driver, and Ali Khalil Abdul Hussein, 54, a motorcyclist who was commuting to work.

The jury considered charges involving injuries to 14 men and three women. Because of travel issues, witnesses to support an 18th charge of attempted manslaughter did not appear at the trial, and the charge related to that victim's injuries was dismissed by the government.

This case was investigated by the FBI's Washington Field Office. The Iraqi Ministry of Interior and the Iraqi National Police provided cooperation and assistance in the investigation.

The case was prosecuted by Assistant U.S. Attorneys Anthony Asuncion, John Crabb, Jr., Christopher R. Kavanaugh, T. Patrick Martin, and David Mudd, of the National Security Section of the U.S. Attorney's Office for the District of Columbia. The case was originally indicted by Assistant U.S. Attorneys Jonathan M. Malis and Kenneth Kohl.

14-1162

Updated January 8, 2016

Figure 5.2 (Continued) One of the most famous cases where private security officers were accused of homicide was the Blackwater killings in Iraq.

The level of mind required for a charge of murder was clearly discerned in a Michigan case, *People v. Moran*.[30]

> Malice aforethought is the intention to kill, actual or implied, under circumstances which do not constitute excuse or justification or mitigate the degree of the offense of manslaughter. The intent to kill may be implied where the actor actually intends to inflict great bodily harm or the natural tendency of his behavior is to cause death or great bodily harm.[31]

Despite the legal attempts to objectify mental intentions, there will always be subjective underpinnings. The security practitioner must gauge conduct in light of all circumstances. He or she must ask him or herself whether the facts of a given case lead a reasonable person to the conclusion that the person not only knew what they were doing and wished both the method and the end result (see Figure 5.3).[32]

MOUNT VERNON MAN SENTENCED IN THE MURDER OF A SECURITY GUARD

🖨Print|+

111 Dr. Martin Luther King, Jr. Blvd.
White Plains, NY 10601
Tel: (914) 995-3586
Fax: (914) 995-2116

Oct. 01, 2015 -- Westchester County District Attorney Janet DiFiore announced that Dontan Jenkins (DOB 09/21/81) of 119 East 4th Street, Mount Vernon was sentenced today to seventeen years to life in prison on his July 2015 guilty plea to:

* one count of Murder in the Second Degree, a class "A" Felony,
* one count of Criminal Possession of a Weapon in the Second Degree, a class "C" Felony.

The defendant was a licensed, unarmed security guard supervisor at the Levister Towers Apartment complex in Mount Vernon. The victim, Richard Brown was also employed as a security guard at the building and had only been working in that position for 10 days at the time of the incident.

During those 10 days, Jenkins and Brown had 2 altercations including one on July 20, 2014 after another exchange of words during a change of shift.

At approximately 3:38 a.m. on the morning of July 21, 2014 the defendant returned to the apartment complex, approached the victim who was manning the security guard booth and fired 3 shots through the front plexi-glass window striking and killing the victim.

Mount Vernon Police responded to the scene commenced an investigation.

They developed information that led them to the defendant who was arrested a short time later.

Assistant District Attorney Perry Perrone, Chief of the Homicide Bureau, prosecuted the case.

Dontan Jenkins

a.net/

Figure 5.3   Security guard murders fellow coworker.

5.4.1.3 Manslaughter

Less crystalline as to intentionality, criminal codifications make room for a mindset that is impacted or effected by mitigation and other external forces. In homicide, the crime that fits this description is manslaughter. Most jurisdictions further grade felonious homicide into another central category: voluntary or involuntary manslaughter.[33] While specific intent is always required for a charge of murder, except in cases of strict liability such as cop killing and felonious homicide, actions and conduct that are not as intellectually precise, not as free from influential mitigating factors and provocation, sometimes qualify for a less rigorous mental state, that of general intent.[34] This is not to say that some jurisdictions do not have a specific intent requirement for a manslaughter charge for there are diverse ways of classifying the mind in the law of manslaughter. For the most part, a charge of manslaughter, whether voluntary or involuntary, has a significantly smaller burden of proof regarding the actor's objective state of mind. This distinct language is readily discoverable in the statute reproduced below.

2503. Voluntary Manslaughter

1. General rule—A person who kills an individual without lawful justification commits voluntary manslaughter if at the time of the killing he is acting under a sudden and intense passion resulting from serious provocation by
   a. the individual killed or
   b. another whom the actor endeavors to kill, but he negligently or accidentally causes the death of the individual killed.[35]

2504. Involuntary Manslaughter

1. General rule—A person is guilty of involuntary manslaughter when as a direct result of the doing of an unlawful act in a reckless or grossly negligent manner, or the doing of a lawful act in a reckless or grossly negligent manner, he causes the death of another person.[36]

Compared to the murder statute, the language of the voluntary manslaughter provision permits an evaluation of various mitigating circumstances including provocation, intense and emotional passion, and sudden and impetuous events.[37] In involuntary cases, the issue of gross negligence is appropriately weighed. In these cases, the court instructs the jury on the negligent nature of the act that causes harm. The defendant need not specifically intend the commission of any crime but could have or should have known the consequences. These are acts, mistaken and accidental in nature, unresponsive to others. Cases of automobile manslaughter or the mishandling of weapons while in a drunken stupor are good examples.[38]

In security settings, manslaughter is a more common event, particularly since practitioners are often called upon in hostile crowd control situations, in the maintenance of order at special events, and related activities.

Read and interpret a California Vehicular Manslaughter law at: http://codes.findlaw.com/ca/penal-code/pen-sect-191-5.html

---

5.4.1.4 Felony Murder Rule

Whether the jurisdiction has a felony murder rule (FMR) in operation is another security industry concern since the charge has far-reaching tentacles that pull in all operatives acting in consort with one another. Hence, if a team of four security officers are on a stake out, and one of them unlawfully shoots another, even one of the officers, and lacks privilege or right to do so, all will be held accountable. One of the officers would have to be engaged in felonious conduct. As outlined in the Code Section 210.1(a) above on Criminal Homicide, a charge of murder is appropriate when any individual dies during the commission of any major capital felony.[39] Coconspirators, accomplices, or other individuals, even though they did not pull the trigger, plan the murder, or personally wish or desire for the death of another can be felony murderers. Hence bank robbers or home invaders committing burglary, causing the death of any party, whether it be responding police, inhabitants, or even the partners in crime, will trigger the FMR.

The felony murder rule has been the subject of severe legal challenges in recent years. "There has been a discernible but not universal trend towards limiting the felony murder doctrine. The trend seems to be related to increasing skepticism as the extent to which the felony murder rule in fact serves a legitimate function or at least as to whether it serves its function or functions at an acceptable cost."[40] The most heated debate occurs when two or more persons are engaged in a theft, robbery, or burglary, obviously less serious offenses than murder or manslaughter, and someone dies by accident or negligence.[41] However, the strict liability nature of the felony murder rule forces criminals to think of the possible potential ramifications of their behavior, which surely includes the death of the participants and bystanders, during the commission of a felonious act.[42]

There are groups and associations solely dedicated to elimination of the Felony Murder Rule such as North Carolina. Visit: http://www.ncfelonymurder.org/Whats%20Wrong/whats-wrong.html

5.4.1.5 Assault

Aside from theft actions, no other crime is as regularly witnessed by security officers than assault and battery. In Chapter 4, readers were introduced to the concept of assault in a civil sense although there is a corresponding criminal definition as well. At common law, assault and battery were separate offenses, the former being a threat to touch or harm and the latter being the actual offensive touching. Most jurisdictions have merged the offenses, at least in a criminal context, though still distinguishing the offenses by severity and degree. The *Model Penal Code* poses the following construction:

1. *Simple Assault*. A person is guilty of assault if he:
   a. Attempts to cause or purposely, knowingly or recklessly causes bodily injury to another; or
   b. Negligently causes bodily injury to another with a deadly weapon; or
   c. Attempts by physical menace to put another in fear of imminent serious bodily harm.
2. *Aggravated Assault*. A person is guilty of aggravated assault if he:
   a. Attempts to cause serious bodily injury to another, or causes such injury purposely, knowingly or recklessly under circumstances manifesting extreme indifference to the value of human life or
   b. Attempts to cause or purposely or knowingly causes bodily injury to another with a deadly weapon.[43]

Most security specialists will encounter the crimes known as assault. Efforts to control crowds, secure buildings and installations, apprehend or detain a disgruntled employee, break up disputants in commercial establishments, and handle unruly and disgruntled shoppers in retail establishments are ripe settings to encounter assailants. Assault can be an extremely serious offense, particularly under the "aggravated" provision.[44] In fact, some jurisdictions have adopted reckless endangerment,[45] a new statutory design that describes even more severe conduct. See the example below:

> (3) A person acts recklessly with respect to a material element of an offense when he consciously disregards a substantial and unjustifiable risk that the material element exists or will result from his conduct.
>
> The risk must be of such a nature and degree that, considering the nature and intent of the actor's conduct and the circumstances known to him, its disregard involves a gross deviation from the standard of conduct that a reasonable person would observe in the actor's situation.[46]

Assaults are now a recurring concern for security officers working in domestic and international terrorism. It behooves security policymakers and planners to educate themselves as well as their staff on these criminal acts and corresponding statutes:

- Terrorist threats
- Use of tear gas or other noxious substances
- Harassment
- Ethnic intimidation[47]

Proof of an assault may or may not require proof of physical injuries. Any injuries alleged can be recorded in the Personal Injury Report shown in Figure 5.4.[48]

5.4.1.6 *Kidnapping and False Imprisonment*

Kidnapping and false imprisonment actions are relevant to the security industry because of its heavy involvement in executive protection and counterterrorism. Political figures, military commanders, and state guests, as well as traditional celebrities, provide instant targets for our enemies.

Kidnapping consists of the unlawful confinement or restraint of a victim, with an accompanying movement or transportation, for the purpose of ransom, political benefit, or other motivation, including the desire to inflict harm. The *Model Penal Code* sets out the essential elements:

> A person is guilty of kidnapping if he unlawfully removes another from his place of residence or business, or a substantial distance from the vicinity where he is found, or if he unlawfully confines another for a substantial period in a place of isolation, with any of the following purposes:
> 1. To hold for ransom or reward, or as a shield or hostage; or
> 2. To facilitate commission of any felony or flight thereafter; or
> 3. To inflict bodily injury on or to terrorize the victim or another; or
> 4. To interfere with the performance of any government or political function.[49]

While most of this codification is clear on its face, legal scholars and advocates frequently contest the transportation or "carrying away" requirement. Modern interpretation, which is generally rather liberal, rejects the view of geographic transfer that is from one locale to another, and adopts the "any movement" standard as being sufficient.[50]

Kidnapping is usually coupled with false imprisonment and rightfully so. Security professionals who detain or restrict the movements of a consumer in retail settings, unprotected by

PERSONAL INJURY REPORT FORM					
Director Security/Safety					
SECTION 1: (TO BE COMPLETED BY PERSON INJURED).					
A.	Name:		Age	Sex	S.S.#
	Address			Phone	
B.	Dept. In Which Employed				
	If Student Employee:	On Duty		Off Duty	
C.	Date And Time Of Accident				
D.	Place Of Accident				
	What Were You Doing?				
	How Accident Occurred:				
E.	Witnesses				
	Dept. Or Address			Tele. No	
F.	Injury Received				
	Treatment Received				
	By Whom: (Name)				
G.	Where (Address)			Tele. No	
	Person Injured Signature			Date	
SECTION 2: (TO BE COMPLETED BY IMMEDIATE SUPERVISOR)					
	Do You Agree With Above Information?			Yes	No
	If "No" -- Your Statement On Reverse Side				
	Did Employee Lose Time	Yes	No	How Much	
	Dates Absent Due To Accident			Days	Hrs
	Was There Any Unsafe Act?			Yes	No
If Yes Explain					
Any Unsafe Condition				Yes	No
If Yes Explain					
Recommendation					
Signature Of Supervisor				Date	

Figure 5.4 Personal injury report form.

merchants' privilege or other statutory immunity may be criminally liable for false imprisonment. False imprisonment is both a civil and criminal action. A typical construction might be:

A person commits a misdemeanor if he knowingly restrains another unlawfully so as to interfere substantially with his liberty.[51]

Any security-based investigation, whereby a suspect's freedom to move is abridged, rightly or wrongly, can give rise to the claim of false imprisonment. Kelley V. Rea, a principal in the security firm Legal and Security Services, Ltd., highlights this ongoing risk.

We also continue to read a surprising number of cases, arising out of investigations, with allegations of false imprisonment and infliction of emotional distress. Where a person is held against his or her will or where that person is subjected to "outrageous" conduct, such charges may arise. Conducting an "interview" that lasts more than an hour and giving the person interviewed the impression that he or she is not free to leave may trigger a charge of false imprisonment. Long, tough, threatening questioning, particularly if physical threats are made or physical force used, will often lead to infliction of emotional distress allegations.[52]

Aside from the physical harm, pain and suffering awards for psychic damages tend to be fairly generous when the confinement and detention is without justification.[53] The litigiousness of making an accusation or claim should at least prompt a cautious approach on the security claim operative. In cases of criminal conduct, it may be sound to completely turn over the case to public law enforcement.

For a series of damage awards in civil actions for false imprisonment, see: http://www.jvra.com/verdict_trak/professional.aspx?page=2&search=491

5.4.1.7 Sexual Offenses

Those entrusted with the task of ensuring safe business and industrial environments now must consider the ramifications of illegal sexual interaction between employers and employees and the increasing sexual victimization of guests, invitees, or licensees on the premises. The investigation and identification of sexual misconduct in the workplace is a major security responsibility. So too in the prison environment where private prisons operated by private personnel play a central role in providing a safe environment. Most states provide levels of protections and corresponding liability for failure to provide (see Figure 5.5,[54] which charts 50 jurisdictions).

Negligent hiring and supervision cases are frequently based upon the failure of supervision and oversight when hiring or disciplining employees who engage in sexual offenses.[55]

The American University Law School runs a clearinghouse that announces litigation relating to civil actions and awards in prison settings for sexual abuse. Visit: https://www.wcl.american.edu/endsilence/

The tragic violence of rape and aggravated sexual assault will, can, and does occur in any social, commercial, or business setting.[56]

The *Model Penal Code's* sample statute is outlined below.

1. Rape. A male who has sexual intercourse with a female not his wife is guilty of rape if
   a. He compels her to submit by force or by threat of imminent death, serious bodily injury, extreme pain or kidnapping, to be inflicted on anyone; or
   b. He has substantially impaired her power to appraise or control her conduct by administering or employing without her knowledge drugs, intoxicants, or other means for the purpose of preventing resistance; or
   c. The female is unconscious; or
   d. The female is less than ten (10) years old.[57]

CHECKLIST OF STATE CRIMINAL LAWS PROHIBITING THE SEXUAL ABUSE OF PERSONS IN CUSTODY OF LAW ENFORCEMENT, LOCK-UP AND JAIL AUTHORITIES

NOTE: *When the checklist indicates that a particular personnel or setting is covered under the law, either the words themselves (law enforcement, arrest, lock-up or jail) appear in the statute or a cross-referenced statute, or the law can reasonably be interpreted to cover those settings and/or personnel. Though staff sexual misconduct laws included in this chart may cover juveniles and private facilities, for the scope of this chart we have not analyzed the laws for their specific inclusion.*

STATE AND STATUTE	Covers Law Enforcement*	Covers Jails	Covers Lock-ups*	Covers Arrest^V	All Personnel Covered^+	Some Forms are Punishable as a Felony	Consent is Not a Defense
Alabama							
Custodial Sexual Misconduct ALA. CODE § 14-11-31 (2005).	✓	✓	✓[1]		Volunteers not covered	✓	✓
Alaska							
Sexual assault in the first degree. ALASKA STAT. § 11.41.410 (2006).	✓	✓	✓	✓	Volunteers not covered	✓[2]	Consent is not addressed
Sexual assault in the second degree. ALASKA STAT. § 11.41.420 (2006).							
Sexual assault in the third degree. ALASKA STAT. § 11.41.425 (2006).							
Sexual assault in the fourth degree. ALASKA STAT. § 11.41.427 (2006).							

[1] Alabama covers employees of government agencies that by court order have the responsibility for pretrial persons and thus the law appears to cover court holding facilities. ALA. CODE § 14-11-30(b)(2) (2006).

* Some state statutes use the word *police* or *sheriff*. For purposes of this checklist, if a statute uses the word *police* or *sheriff*, we assumed that all law enforcement is covered.

• If a state law contained the word jail and the word local correctional facility, local correctional institution, county or city facility etc., then we assumed that the state law intended to cover other local facilities such as lock-ups.

V If a state law contained the word "arrest" or covers law enforcement personnel and contains phrases such as "having custody over the victim", "in the offenders care under authority of law", or "under the supervision of a city or county" then we assumed that the law intended to cover arrest.

+ All personnel are covered if the statute includes paid employees, volunteers, other state agency employees, and private/contract employees.

Smith Consulting
February 2008

Do not use, publish or distribute without prior permission from authors. Please contact Prof. Brenda V. Smith at bvsmith@wcl.american.edu to obtain permission.

Page 1 of 23

Figure 5.5 State criminal laws prohibiting the sexual abuse of persons in custody.

(Continued)

CHECKLIST OF STATE CRIMINAL LAWS PROHIBITING THE SEXUAL ABUSE OF PERSONS IN CUSTODY OF LAW ENFORCEMENT, LOCK-UP AND JAIL AUTHORITIES

NOTE: When the checklist indicates that a particular personnel or setting is covered under the law, either the words themselves (law enforcement, arrest, lock-up or jail) appear in the statute or a cross-referenced statute, or the law can reasonably be interpreted to cover those settings and/or personnel. Though staff sexual misconduct laws included in this chart may cover juveniles and private facilities, for the scope of this chart we have not analyzed the laws for their specific inclusion.

STATE AND STATUTE	Covers Law Enforcement*	Covers Jails♦	Covers Lock-ups♦	Covers Arrest^V	All Personnel Covered+	Some Forms are Punishable as a Felony	Consent is Not a Defense
Arizona Unlawful sexual conduct; correctional employees; prisoners; classification ARIZ. REV. STAT. ANN. § 13-1419. (2006).	✓	✓	✓³	✓	Volunteers not covered	✓⁴	The defense of consent may be implied because the inmate is also penalized for the conduct
Arkansas Sexual assault in the first degree. ARK. CODE ANN. § 5-14-124 (2006). Sexual Assault in the second degree	✓	✓			Volunteers not covered	✓	✓

² Police are punished under First and Second Degree sexual assault and as felonies, where Department of Corrections Employees are punished under Third and Fourth Degree Sexual assault where third degree is a felony and fourth degree is a misdemeanor. ALASKA STAT. §§ 11.41.410(b), 11.41.420(b), 11.41.425(b) & 11.41.427(b) (2006).

³ In Arizona, custody is defined as actual or constructive restraint pursuant to a court order and thus would appear to cover court holding facilities. ARIZ. REV. STAT. ANN. § 13-2501 (2006).

⁴ In Arizona, the inmate is penalized for the misconduct. ARIZ. REV. STAT. ANN. § 13-1419B (2006).

* Some state statutes use the word *police* or *sheriff*. For purposes of this checklist, if a statute uses the word *police* or *sheriff*, we assumed that all law enforcement is covered.

♦ If a state law contained the word jail and the word local correctional facility, local correctional institution, county or city facility etc., then we assumed that the state law intended to cover other local facilities such as lock-ups.

V If a state law contained the word "arrest" or covers law enforcement personnel and contains phrases such as "having custody over the victim", "in the offenders care under authority of law", or "under the supervision of a city or county" then we assumed that the law intended to cover arrest.

+ All personnel are covered if the statute includes paid employees, volunteers, other state agency employees, and private/contract employees.

Smith Consulting
February 2008
Do not use, publish or distribute without prior permission from authors. Please contact Prof. Brenda V. Smith at bvsmith@wcl.american.edu to obtain permission.
Page 2 of 23

(Continued)

Figure 5.5 (Continued) State criminal laws prohibiting the sexual abuse of persons in custody.

CHECKLIST OF STATE CRIMINAL LAWS PROHIBITING THE SEXUAL ABUSE OF PERSONS IN CUSTODY OF LAW ENFORCEMENT, LOCK-UP AND JAIL AUTHORITIES

NOTE: When the checklist indicates that a particular personnel or setting is covered under the law, either the words themselves (law enforcement, arrest, lock-up or jail) appear in the statute or a cross-referenced statute, or the law can reasonably be interpreted to cover those settings and/or personnel. Though staff sexual misconduct laws included in this chart may cover juveniles and private facilities, for the scope of this chart we have not analyzed the laws for their specific inclusion.

STATE AND STATUTE	Covers Law Enforcement*	Covers Jails	Covers Lock-ups♦	Covers Arrest▽	All Personnel Covered+	Some Forms are Punishable as a Felony	Consent is Not a Defense
Arkansas Continued							
ARK. CODE ANN. § 5-14-125 (2006). Sexual assault in the third degree ARK. CODE ANN. § 5-14-126 (2006).							
California Employee or officer of detention facility; Engaging in sexual activity with consenting adult confined in detention facility. CAL. PENAL CODE § 289.6 (2006).	✓	✓	✓[5]		✓[6]	✓	✓

[5] California covers court holding facilities as well. CAL. PENAL CODE § 289.6(5) (2006).

[6] In California, the statute covers persons over the age of consent housed in juvenile facilities. Presumably, sexual offenses involving juveniles under the age of consent can be prosecuted under statutory rape or other sexual assault laws. The legislative history of the statute also suggests that the California Assembly knew that ANY sex between staff and juvenile inmates was already proscribed by law. "No mention was made of juvenile victims, presumably because legislators knew that the California Assembly knew that ANY sex between staff and juvenile inmates was already proscribed by law. Therefore, it was unnecessary to enact additional legislation criminalizing sexual activity between staff and juvenile inmates in their charge.

* Some state statutes use the word *police* or *sheriff*. For purposes of this checklist, if a statute uses the word *police or sheriff*, we assumed that all law enforcement is covered.

♦ If a state law contained the word jail and the word local correctional facility, local correctional institution, county or city facility etc., then we assumed that the state law intended to cover other local facilities such as lock-ups.

▽ If a state law contained the word "arrest" or covers law enforcement personnel and contains phrases such as "having custody over the victim", "in the supervision of a city or county" then we assumed that the law intended to cover arrest.

+ All personnel are covered if the statute includes paid employees, volunteers, other state agency employees, and private/contract employees.

Smith Consulting
February 2008

Do not use, publish or distribute without prior permission from authors. Please contact Prof. Brenda V. Smith at bvsmith@wcl.american.edu to obtain permission.

Page 3 of 23

Figure 5.5 (Continued) State criminal laws prohibiting the sexual abuse of persons in custody.

(Continued)

CHECKLIST OF STATE CRIMINAL LAWS PROHIBITING THE SEXUAL ABUSE OF PERSONS IN CUSTODY OF LAW ENFORCEMENT, LOCK-UP AND JAIL AUTHORITIES

NOTE: When the checklist indicates that a particular personnel or setting is covered under the law, either the words themselves (law enforcement, arrest, lock-up or jail) appear in the statute or a cross-referenced statute, or the law can reasonably be interpreted to cover those settings and/or personnel. Though staff sexual misconduct laws included in this chart may cover juveniles and private facilities, for the scope of this chart we have not analyzed the laws for their specific inclusion.

STATE AND STATUTE	Covers Law Enforcement*	Covers Jails	Covers Lock-ups*	Covers Arrest^v	All Personnel Covered[+]	Some Forms are Punishable as a Felony	Consent is Not a Defense
Colorado Unlawful Sexual Contact. COLO. REV. STAT. § 18-3-404 (2005).	✓	✓	✓	✓	✓	✓	Consent is not addressed
Sexual Conduct in Penal Institutions. COLO. REV. STAT. § 18-7-701 (2005).							
Connecticut Sexual assault in the second degree: Class C or B felony. CONN. GEN. STAT. § 53a-71 (2006).	✓	✓	✓	✓	Volunteers not covered	✓	Consent is not addressed
Sexual assault in the fourth degree:							
Class A misdemeanor or Class D felony. CONN. GEN. STAT. § 53a-73a (2006).							

* Some state statutes use the word *police* or *sheriff*. For purposes of this checklist, if a statute uses the word *police* or *sheriff*, we assumed that all law enforcement is covered.

♦ If a state law contained the word jail and the word local correctional facility, local correctional institution, county or city facility etc., then we assumed that the state law intended to cover other local facilities such as lock-ups.

^v If a state law contained the word "arrest" or covers law enforcement personnel and contains phrases such as "having custody over the victim", "in the offenders care under authority of law", or "under the supervision of a city or county" then we assumed that the law intended to cover arrest.

[+] All personnel are covered if the statute includes paid employees, volunteers, other state agency employees, and private/contract employees.

Smith Consulting
February 2008

Do not use, publish or distribute without prior permission from authors. Please contact Prof. Brenda V. Smith at bvsmith@wcl.american.edu to obtain permission.
Page 4 of 23

(Continued)

Figure 5.5 (Continued) State criminal laws prohibiting the sexual abuse of persons in custody.

CHECKLIST OF STATE CRIMINAL LAWS PROHIBITING THE SEXUAL ABUSE OF PERSONS IN CUSTODY OF LAW ENFORCEMENT, LOCK-UP AND JAIL AUTHORITIES

NOTE: When the checklist indicates that a particular personnel or setting is covered under the law, either the words themselves (law enforcement, arrest, lock-up or jail) appear in the statute or a cross-referenced statute, or the law can reasonably be interpreted to cover those settings and/or personnel. Though staff sexual misconduct laws included in this chart may cover juveniles and private facilities, for the scope of this chart we have not analyzed the laws for their specific inclusion.

STATE AND STATUTE	Covers Law Enforcement*	Covers Jails	Covers Lock-ups*	Covers Arrest▽	All Personnel Covered+	Some Forms are Punishable as a Felony	Consent is Not a Defense
Delaware Sexual relations in detention facility; Class G felony DEL. CODE ANN. tit. 11, § 1259 (2006).	✓[7]	✓[8]	✓[9]		Volunteers and contractors are not covered	✓[10]	✓[11]
District of Columbia First degree sexual abuse of a ward. D.C. CODE § 22-3013 (2006). Second degree sexual abuse of a ward. D.C. CODE § 22-3014 (2006).	✓	✓	✓[12]		Volunteers are not covered	✓	✓

[7] In Delaware, the activity must occur "on the premises of a detention facility" for it to be criminal. DEL. CODE ANN. tit. 11, § 1259 (2006).

[8] In Delaware, the activity must occur "on the premises of a detention facility" for it to be criminal. DEL. CODE ANN. tit. 11, § 1259 (2006).

[9] Delaware covers confinement pursuant to a court order and thus would appear to cover court holding facilities. DEL. CODE ANN. TIT. 11, § 1258(2) (2006). In Delaware, the activity must occur "on the premises of a detention facility" for it to be criminal. DEL. CODE ANN. tit. 11, § 1259 (2006).

[10] In Delaware, the inmate is penalized for the misconduct. DEL. CODE ANN. TIT. 11, § 1259 (2006).

[11] Although Delaware states that consent is not a defense to staff sexual misconduct, the law penalizes inmates for engaging in the conduct. DEL. CODE ANN. TIT. 11, § 1259 (2006).

* Some state statutes use the word *police* or *sheriff*. For purposes of this checklist, if a statute uses the word *police* or *sheriff*, we assumed that all law enforcement is covered.

* If a state law contained the word *jail* and the word *local correctional facility, local correctional institution, county or city facility etc.,* then we assumed that the state law intended to cover other local facilities such as lock-ups.

▽ If a state law contained the word "arrest" or covers law enforcement personnel and contains phrases such as "having custody over the victim", "in the offenders care under authority of law", or "under the supervision of a city or county" then we assumed that the law intended to cover arrest.

+ All personnel are covered if the statute includes paid employees, volunteers, other state agency employees, and private/contract employees.

Smith Consulting
February 2008

Do not use, publish or distribute without prior permission from authors. Please contact Prof. Brenda V. Smith at bvsmith@wcl.american.edu to obtain permission.

Page 5 of 23

(Continued)

Figure 5.5 (Continued) State criminal laws prohibiting the sexual abuse of persons in custody.

CHECKLIST OF STATE CRIMINAL LAWS PROHIBITING THE SEXUAL ABUSE OF PERSONS IN CUSTODY OF LAW ENFORCEMENT, LOCK-UP AND JAIL AUTHORITIES

NOTE: When the checklist indicates that a particular personnel or setting is covered under the law, either the words themselves (law enforcement, arrest, lock-up or jail) appear in the statute or a cross-referenced statute, or the law can reasonably be interpreted to cover those settings and/or personnel. Though staff sexual misconduct laws included in this chart may cover juveniles and private facilities, for the scope of this chart we have not analyzed the laws for their specific inclusion.

STATE AND STATUTE	Covers Law Enforcement*	Covers Jails	Covers Lock-ups*	Covers Arrest▽	All Personnel Covered+	Some Forms are Punishable as a Felony	Consent is Not a Defense
Florida Authorized use of Force; malicious battery & sexual misconduct prohibited; reporting required; penalties FLA. STAT. ANN. § 944.35 (2006). Sexual battery. FLA. STAT. ANN. § 794.011 (2006).	✓	✓	✓	✓	Volunteers not covered	✓	✓
Georgia Sexual assault against persons in custody; sexual assault against person detained or patient in hospital or other institution; sexual assault by practitioner of psychotherapy against	✓	✓		✓	Volunteers not covered	✓	✓

12 D.C. defines official custody as transportation for court appearances and thus would appear to cover court holding facilities. D.C. CODE § 22-3001(6)(b) (2006).

12 Hawaii defines custody as restraint pursuant to a court order and thus would appear to cover court holding facilities. HAW. REV. STAT. ANN. § 710-1000(3) (2006).

* Some state statutes use the word *police* or *sheriff*. For purposes of this checklist, if a statute uses the word *police* or *sheriff*, we assumed that all law enforcement is covered.

* If a state law contained the word *jail* and the word *local correctional institution, county or city facility* etc., then we assumed that the state law intended to cover other local facilities such as lock-ups.

▽ If a state law contained the word "arrest" or covers law enforcement personnel and contains phrases such as "having custody over the victim", "in the offenders care under authority of law", or "under the supervision of a city or county" then we assumed that the law intended to cover arrest.

+ All personnel are covered if the statute includes paid employees, volunteers, other state agency employees, and private/contract employees.

Smith Consulting
February 2008
Do not use, publish or distribute without prior permission from authors. Please contact Prof. Brenda V. Smith at bvsmith@wcl.american.edu to obtain permission.
Page 6 of 23

(Continued)

Figure 5.5 (Continued) State criminal laws prohibiting the sexual abuse of persons in custody.

CHECKLIST OF STATE CRIMINAL LAWS PROHIBITING THE SEXUAL ABUSE OF PERSONS IN CUSTODY OF LAW ENFORCEMENT, LOCK-UP AND JAIL AUTHORITIES

NOTE: When the checklist indicates that a particular personnel or setting is covered under the law, either the law itself, either the words themselves (law enforcement, arrest, lock-up or jail) appear in the statute or a cross-referenced statute, or the law can reasonably be interpreted to cover those settings and/or personnel. Though staff sexual misconduct laws included in this chart may cover juveniles and private facilities, for the scope of this chart we have not analyzed the laws for their specific inclusion.

STATE AND STATUTE	Covers Law Enforcement*	Covers Jails	Covers Lock-ups*	Covers Arrest▽	All Personnel Covered+	Some Forms are Punishable as a Felony	Consent is Not a Defense
patient. GA. CODE ANN. § 16-6-5.1 (2006).	✓						
Hawaii Sexual assault in the second degree. HAW. REV. STAT. ANN. § 707-731 (2006).	✓	✓	✓[12]	✓	Volunteers not covered	✓	Consent is not addressed
Sexual assault in the third degree. HAW. REV. STAT. ANN. § 707-732 (2006).							
Idaho Sexual contact with a prisoner. IDAHO CODE ANN. § 18-6110 (2006).	✓	✓	✓		Volunteers not covered	✓	Consent is not addressed

* Some state statutes use the word *police* or *sheriff*. For purposes of this checklist, if a statute uses the word *police* or *sheriff*, we assumed that all law enforcement is covered.

⁺ If a state law contained the word *jail* and the word local correctional facility, local correctional institution, county or city facility etc., then we assumed that the state law intended to cover other local facilities such as lock-ups.

▽ If a state law contained the word "arrest" or covers law enforcement personnel and contains phrases such as "having custody over the victim", "in the offenders care under authority of law", or "under the supervision of a city or county" then we assumed that the law intended to cover arrest.

⁺ All personnel are covered if the statute includes paid employees, volunteers, other state agency employees, and private/contract employees.

Smith Consulting
February 2008

Do not use, publish or distribute without prior permission from authors. Please contact Prof. Brenda V. Smith at bvsmith@wcl.american.edu to obtain permission.

Page 7 of 23

(Continued)

Figure 5.5 (Continued)   State criminal laws prohibiting the sexual abuse of persons in custody.

CHECKLIST OF STATE CRIMINAL LAWS PROHIBITING THE SEXUAL ABUSE OF PERSONS IN CUSTODY OF LAW ENFORCEMENT, LOCK-UP AND JAIL AUTHORITIES

NOTE: *When the checklist indicates that a particular personnel or setting is covered under the law, either the words themselves (law enforcement, arrest, lock-up or jail) appear in the statute or a cross-referenced statute, or the law can reasonably be interpreted to cover those settings and/or personnel. Though staff sexual misconduct laws included in this chart may cover juveniles and private facilities, for the scope of this chart we have not analyzed the laws for their specific inclusion.*

STATE AND STATUTE	Covers Law Enforcement*	Covers Jails	Covers Lock-ups*	Covers Arrest^V	All Personnel Covered+	Some Forms are Punishable as a Felony	Consent is Not a Defense
Illinois Custodial Sexual Misconduct 720 Ill. Comp. Stat. Ann. 5/11-9.2 (2005).		✓	✓[14]		Volunteers not covered	✓	✓
Indiana Sexual misconduct by service provider with detainee Ind. Code Ann. § 35-44-1-5 (2006).	✓	✓	✓[15]	✓	✓	✓	✓
Iowa Sexual misconduct with offenders and juveniles Iowa Code § 709.16 (2005).		✓			✓		Consent is not addressed

[14] Illinois includes employees of any governmental agency that by court order has the responsibility for pretrial persons and thus would appear to cover court holding facilities. 720 Ill. Comp. Stat. Ann. 5/11-9.2(g)(3) (2005).

[15] Indiana covers custody for purposes of court appearances and thus would appear to cover court holding facilities. Ind. Code Ann. § 35-41-1-18 (9) (2006).

* Some state statutes use the word *police* or *sheriff*. For purposes of this checklist, if a statute uses the word *police* or *sheriff*, we assumed that all law enforcement is covered.

♦ If a state law contained the word jail and the word local correctional facility, local correctional institution, county or city facility etc., then we assumed that the state law intended to cover other local facilities such as lock-ups.

^V If a state law contained the word "arrest" or covers law enforcement personnel and contains phrases such as "having custody over the victim", "in the offenders care under authority of law", or "under the supervision of a city or county" then we assumed that the law intended to cover arrest.

+ All personnel are covered if the statute includes paid employees, volunteers, other state agency employees, and private/contract employees.

Smith Consulting
February 2008
Do not use, publish or distribute without prior permission from authors. Please contact Prof. Brenda V. Smith at bvsmith@wcl.american.edu to obtain permission.
Page 8 of 23

(Continued)

Figure 5.5 (Continued) State criminal laws prohibiting the sexual abuse of persons in custody.

CHECKLIST OF STATE CRIMINAL LAWS PROHIBITING THE SEXUAL ABUSE OF PERSONS IN CUSTODY OF LAW ENFORCEMENT, LOCK-UP AND JAIL AUTHORITIES

NOTE: *When the checklist indicates that a particular personnel or setting is covered under the law, either the words themselves (law enforcement, arrest, lock-up or jail) appear in the statute or a cross-referenced statute, or the law can reasonably be interpreted to cover those settings and/or personnel. Though staff sexual misconduct laws included in this chart may cover juveniles and private facilities, for the scope of this chart we have not analyzed the laws for their specific inclusion.*

STATE AND STATUTE	Covers Law Enforcement*	Covers Jails	Covers Lock-ups+	Covers Arrest^V	All Personnel Covered+	Some Forms are Punishable as a Felony	Consent is Not a Defense
Kansas Unlawful sexual relations. KAN. STAT. ANN. § 21-3520 (2005).	✓	✓	✓		Volunteers not covered	✓	✓
Kentucky Sexual Abuse in the Second Degree. KY. REV. STAT. ANN. § 510.120 (2006).	✓	✓	✓16	✓	Community Corrections employees are not covered		Consent is not addressed
Louisiana Malfeasance in office; sexual conduct prohibited with persons confined in correctional institutions. LA. REV. STAT. ANN. § 14:134.1 (2006).	✓	✓	✓		Volunteers not covered Contract employees not covered Community Corrections	✓	Consent is not addressed

16 Kentucky defines custody as "restrain by a public servant pursuant to . . . an order of court for law enforcement purposes" and thus would appear to cover court holding facilities. KY. REV. STAT. ANN. § 510.010(2) (2006).

* Some state statutes use the word *police* or *sheriff*. For purposes of this checklist, if a statute uses the word *police* or *sheriff*, we assumed that all law enforcement is covered.

+ If a state law contained the word jail and the word local correctional facility, local correctional institution, county or city facility etc., then we assumed that the state law intended to cover other local facilities such as lock-ups.

^V If a state law contained the word "arrest" or covers law enforcement personnel and contains phrases such as "having custody over the victim", "in the offenders care under authority of law", or "under the supervision of a city or county" then we assumed that the law intended to cover arrest.

+ All personnel are covered if the statute includes paid employees, volunteers, other state agency employees, and private/contract employees.

Smith Consulting
February 2008
Do not use, publish or distribute without prior permission from authors. Please contact Prof. Brenda V. Smith at bvsmith@wcl.american.edu to obtain permission.
Page 9 of 23

Figure 5.5 (Continued) State criminal laws prohibiting the sexual abuse of persons in custody.

(Continued)

CHECKLIST OF STATE CRIMINAL LAWS PROHIBITING THE SEXUAL ABUSE OF PERSONS IN CUSTODY OF LAW ENFORCEMENT, LOCK-UP AND JAIL AUTHORITIES

NOTE: *When the checklist indicates that a particular personnel or setting is covered under the law, either the words themselves (law enforcement, arrest, lock-up or jail) appear in the statute or a cross-referenced statute, or the law can reasonably be interpreted to cover those settings and/or personnel. Though staff sexual misconduct laws included in this chart may cover juveniles and private facilities, for the scope of this chart we have not analyzed the laws for their specific inclusion.*

STATE AND STATUTE	Covers Law Enforcement*	Covers Jails	Covers Lock-ups♦	Covers Arrest^V	All Personnel Covered^+	Some Forms are Punishable as a Felony	Consent is Not a Defense
Maine	✓				employees not covered		
Gross sexual assault. ME. REV. STAT. ANN. tit. 17-A, § 253 (2005). Unlawful sexual contact ME. REV. STAT. ANN. tit. 17-A, § 255-A 1.E (2005). Unlawful sexual touching ME. REV. STAT. ANN. tit. 17-A, § 260.1-E (2005).		✓	✓[17]	✓	Volunteers not covered	✓	Consent is not addressed

[17] Maine defines official custody as custody pursuant to a court order and thus would appear to cover court holding facilities. ME. REV. STAT. ANN. tit. 17-A, § 755(3) (2005).

* Some state statutes use the word *police* or *sheriff*. For purposes of this checklist, if a statute uses the word *police* or *sheriff*, we assumed that all law enforcement is covered.

♦ If a state law contained the word jail and the word local correctional facility, local correctional institution, county or city facility etc., then we assumed that the state covered.

♦ If a state law contained the word jail and the word local correctional facility, local correctional institution, county or city facility etc., then we assumed that the state law intended to cover other local facilities such as lock-ups.

^V If a state law contained the word "arrest" or covers law enforcement personnel and contains phrases such as "having custody over the victim", "in the custody of a city or county" then we assumed that the law intended to cover arrest.

^+ All personnel are covered if the statute includes paid employees, volunteers, other state agency employees, and private/contract employees.

Smith Consulting
February 2008
Do not use, publish or distribute without prior permission from authors. Please contact Prof. Brenda V. Smith at bvsmith@wcl.american.edu to obtain permission.
Page 10 of 23

(Continued)

Figure 5.5 (Continued) State criminal laws prohibiting the sexual abuse of persons in custody.

CHECKLIST OF STATE CRIMINAL LAWS PROHIBITING THE SEXUAL ABUSE OF PERSONS IN CUSTODY OF LAW ENFORCEMENT, LOCK-UP AND JAIL AUTHORITIES

NOTE: When the checklist indicates that a particular personnel or setting is covered under the law, either the words themselves (law enforcement, arrest, lock-up or jail) appear in the statute or a cross-referenced statute, or the law can reasonably be interpreted to cover those settings and/or personnel. Though staff sexual misconduct laws included in this chart may cover juveniles and private facilities, for the scope of this chart we have not analyzed the laws for their specific inclusion.

STATE AND STATUTE	Covers Law Enforcement*	Covers Jails	Covers Lock-ups*	Covers Arrest[v]	All Personnel Covered[+]	Some Forms are Punishable as a Felony	Consent is Not a Defense
Maryland Sexual conduct between correctional or Department of Juvenile Services employee and inmate or confined child. MD. CODE ANN., CRIM. LAW § 3-314 (2006).	✓	✓	✓[18]	✓	Volunteers not covered Contractors not covered		Consent is not addressed
Massachusetts Punishments for sexual relations with inmate. MASS. ANN. LAWS ch. 268, § 21A (2006).		✓			Volunteers not covered	✓	✓
Michigan Criminal sexual conduct in the second degree; felony. MICH. COMP. LAWS SERV. §		✓	✓		✓	✓	Consent is not addressed

[18] Maryland defines correctional unit as a unit of government that is responsible under a court order for inmates and thus would appear to cover court holding facilities. MD. CODE ANN., CRIM. LAW § 8-201(g)(1) (2006).

* Some state statutes use the word *police* or *sheriff.* For purposes of this checklist, if a statute uses the word *police* or *sheriff,* we assumed that all law enforcement is covered.

⁺ If a state law contained the word jail and the word local correctional facility, local correctional institution, county or city facility etc., then we assumed that the state law intended to cover other local facilities such as lock-ups.

[v] If a state law contained the word "arrest" or covers law enforcement personnel and contains phrases such as "having custody over the victim", "in the offenders care under authority of law", or "under the supervision of a city or county" then we assumed that the law intended to cover arrest.

⁺ All personnel are covered if the statute includes paid employees, volunteers, other state agency employees, and private/contract employees.

Smith Consulting
February 2008
Page 11 of 23

Figure 5.5 (Continued) State criminal laws prohibiting the sexual abuse of persons in custody.

CHECKLIST OF STATE CRIMINAL LAWS PROHIBITING THE SEXUAL ABUSE OF PERSONS IN CUSTODY OF LAW ENFORCEMENT, LOCK-UP AND JAIL AUTHORITIES

NOTE: When the checklist indicates that a particular personnel or setting is covered under the law, either the words themselves (law enforcement, arrest, lock-up or jail) appear in the statute or a cross-referenced statute, or the law can reasonably be interpreted to cover those settings and/or personnel. Though staff sexual misconduct laws included in this chart may cover juveniles and private facilities, for the scope of this chart we have not analyzed the laws for their specific inclusion.

STATE AND STATUTE	Covers Law Enforcement*	Covers Jails	Covers Lock-ups◆	Covers Arrest∇	All Personnel Covered+	Some Forms are Punishable as a Felony	Consent is Not a Defense
750.520c (2006).							
Minnesota Criminal sexual conduct in the third degree. MINN. STAT. § 609.344 (2005). Criminal sexual conduct in the fourth degree. MINN. STAT. § 609.345 (2005).		✓	✓		✓	✓	✓
Mississippi Crime of sexual activity between law enforcement or correctional personnel and prisoners; sanctions. MISS. CODE ANN. § 97-3-104 (2006).	✓	✓	✓		✓	✓	✓
Missouri							

* Some state statutes use the word *police* or *sheriff*. For purposes of this checklist, if a statute uses the word *police* or *sheriff*, we assumed that all law enforcement is covered.

◆ If a state law contained the word *jail* and the word local correctional facility, local correctional institution, county or city facility etc., then we assumed that the state law intended to cover other local facilities such as lock-ups.

∇ If a state law contained the word "arrest" or covers law enforcement personnel and contains phrases such as "having custody over the victim", "in the offenders care under authority of law", or "under the supervision of a city or county" then we assumed that the law intended to cover arrest.

+ All personnel are covered if the statute includes paid employees, volunteers, other state agency employees, and private/contract employees.

(Continued)

Figure 5.5 (Continued) State criminal laws prohibiting the sexual abuse of persons in custody.

CHECKLIST OF STATE CRIMINAL LAWS PROHIBITING THE SEXUAL ABUSE OF PERSONS IN CUSTODY OF LAW ENFORCEMENT, LOCK-UP AND JAIL AUTHORITIES

NOTE: When the checklist indicates that a particular personnel or setting is covered under the law, either the words themselves (law enforcement, arrest, lock-up or jail) appear in the statute or a cross-referenced statute, or the law can reasonably be interpreted to cover those settings and/or personnel. Though staff sexual misconduct laws included in this chart may cover juveniles and private facilities, for the scope of this chart we have not analyzed the laws for their specific inclusion.

STATE AND STATUTE	Covers Law Enforcement*	Covers Jails	Covers Lock-ups*	Covers Arrest^V	All Personnel Covered+	Some Forms are Punishable as a Felony	Consent is Not a Defense
Missouri Continued							
Sexual contact with an inmate, penalty – consent not a defense Mo. Rev. Stat. § 566.145 (amended 2006) (current version at 2006 Mo. HB 1698 (2006)).	√[20]						
Montana Sexual assault Mont. Code Ann. § 45-5-502 (2005).		√	√[21]	√[22]	√	√	√

[20] Montana defines a peace officer as a person who by virtue of the person's office or public employment is vested by law with a duty to maintain public order or to make arrests for offenses while acting within the scope of the person's authority. Mont. Code Ann. §45-2-101 (55) (2007)

[21] Montana defines official detention as confinement of a person charged with an offense or detention by an officer pursuant to an arrest. Mont. Code Ann. §45-2-101 (50)(a) (2007).

[22] Montana defines official detention as confinement of a person charged with an offense or detention by an officer pursuant to an arrest. Mont. Code Ann. §45-2-101 (50)(a) (2007).

* Some state statutes use the word *police* or *sheriff*. For purposes of this checklist, if a statute uses the word *police* or *sheriff*, we assumed that all law enforcement is covered.

+ If a state law contained the word *jail* and the word local correctional facility, local correctional institution, county or city facility etc., then we assumed that the state law intended to cover other local facilities such as lock-ups.

V If a state law contained the word "arrest" or covers law enforcement personnel and contains phrases such as "having custody over the victim", "in the offenders care under authority of law", or "under the supervision of a city or county" then we assumed that the law intended to cover arrest.

+ All personnel are covered if the statute includes paid employees, volunteers, other state agency employees, and private/contract employees.

Smith Consulting
February 2008
Do not use, publish or distribute without prior permission from authors. Please contact Prof. Brenda V. Smith at bvsmith@wcl.american.edu to obtain permission.
Page 13 of 23

Figure 5.5 (Continued) State criminal laws prohibiting the sexual abuse of persons in custody.

(Continued)

CHECKLIST OF STATE CRIMINAL LAWS PROHIBITING THE SEXUAL ABUSE OF PERSONS IN CUSTODY OF LAW ENFORCEMENT, LOCK-UP AND JAIL AUTHORITIES

NOTE: *When the checklist indicates that a particular personnel or setting is covered under the law, either the words themselves (law enforcement, arrest, lock-up or jail) appear in the statute or a cross-referenced statute, or the law can reasonably be interpreted to cover those settings and/or personnel. Though staff sexual misconduct laws included in this chart may cover juveniles and private facilities, for the scope of this chart we have not analyzed the laws for their specific inclusion.*

STATE AND STATUTE	Covers Law Enforcement*	Covers Jails	Covers Lock-ups+	Covers Arrest^v	All Personnel+ Covered	Some Forms are Punishable as a Felony	Consent is Not a Defense
Sexual intercourse without consent MONT. CODE ANN. § 45-5-503 (2005).							
Nebraska							
Sexual abuse of an inmate or parolee. NEB. REV. STAT.ANN. § 28-322.01 (LexisNexis 2005).		✓	✓		Volunteers not covered	✓	✓
Sexual abuse of an inmate or parolee in the first degree; penalty NEB. REV. STAT. 28-322.02 (LexisNexis 2005).							
Sexual abuse of an inmate or parolee in the second degree; penalty NEB. REV. STAT. § 28-322.03 (2005).							
Nevada Voluntary sexual conduct between	✓	✓	✓	✓	Community corrections is	✓23	The defense of consent may be

23 In Nevada, the inmate is penalized for the misconduct. NEV. REV. STAT. ANN. § 212.187(2) (2006).

* Some state statutes use the word *police* or *sheriff*. For purposes of this checklist, if a statute uses the word *police* or *sheriff*, we assumed that all law enforcement is covered.

+ If a state law contained the word jail and the word local correctional facility, local correctional institution, county or city facility etc., then we assumed that the state law intended to cover other local facilities such as lock-ups.

^v If a state law contained the word "arrest" or covers law enforcement personnel and contains phrases such as "having custody over the victim", "in the offenders care under authority of law", or "under the supervision of a city or county" then we assumed that the law intended to cover arrest.

+ All personnel are covered if the statute includes paid employees, volunteers, other state agency employees, and private/contract employees.

(Continued)

Figure 5.5 (Continued) State criminal laws prohibiting the sexual abuse of persons in custody.

CHECKLIST OF STATE CRIMINAL LAWS PROHIBITING THE SEXUAL ABUSE OF PERSONS IN CUSTODY OF LAW ENFORCEMENT, LOCK-UP AND JAIL AUTHORITIES

NOTE: When the checklist indicates that a particular personnel or setting is covered under the law, either the law itself, or the words themselves (law enforcement, arrest, lock-up or jail) appear in the statute or a cross-referenced statute, or the law can reasonably be interpreted to cover those settings and/or personnel. Though staff sexual misconduct laws included in this chart may cover juveniles and private facilities, for the scope of this chart we have not analyzed the laws for their specific inclusion.

STATE AND STATUTE	Covers Law Enforcement*	Covers Jails	Covers Lock-ups+	Covers Arrest^v	All Personnel Covered+	Some Forms are Punishable as a Felony	Consent is Not a Defense
prisoner and another person; penalty. NEV. REV. STAT. ANN. § 212.187 (2006).					not covered		implied because the inmate is also penalized for the conduct
New Hampshire Aggravated Felonious Sexual Assault. N.H. REV. STAT. ANN. § 632-A2: (LexisNexis 2006). Felonious Sexual Assault. N.H. REV. STAT. ANN. § 632-A3: (2006).		✓			Volunteers not covered	✓	Consent is not addressed
New Jersey Sexual assault N.J. STAT. ANN. § 2C:14-2 (2006).		✓	✓		Volunteers not covered	✓	Consent is not addressed
New Mexico Criminal sexual penetration. N.M. STAT. ANN. § 30-9-11 (2006).		✓	✓		Volunteers not covered	✓	Consent is not addressed

* Some state statutes use the word *police* or *sheriff*. For purposes of this checklist, if a statute uses the word *police* or *sheriff*, we assumed that all law enforcement is covered.

+ If a state contained the word jail and the word local correctional facility, local correctional institution, county or city facility etc., then we assumed that the state law intended to cover other local facilities such as lock-ups.

^v If a state law contained the word "arrest" or covers law enforcement personnel and contains phrases such as "having custody over the victim", "in the offenders care under authority of law", or "under the supervision of a city or county" then we assumed that the law intended to cover arrest.

+ All personnel are covered if the statute includes paid employees, volunteers, other state agency employees, and private/contract employees.

Smith Consulting
February 2008
Do not use, publish or distribute without prior permission from authors. Please contact Prof. Brenda V. Smith at bvsmith@wcl.american.edu to obtain permission.
Page 15 of 23

(Continued)

Figure 5.5 (Continued) State criminal laws prohibiting the sexual abuse of persons in custody.

CHECKLIST OF STATE CRIMINAL LAWS PROHIBITING THE SEXUAL ABUSE OF PERSONS IN CUSTODY OF LAW ENFORCEMENT, LOCK-UP AND JAIL AUTHORITIES

NOTE: When the checklist indicates that a particular personnel or setting is covered under the law, either the words themselves (law enforcement, arrest, lock-up or jail) appear in the statute or a cross-referenced statute, or the law can reasonably be interpreted to cover those settings and/or personnel. Though staff sexual misconduct laws included in this chart may cover juveniles and private facilities, for the scope of this chart we have not analyzed the laws for their specific inclusion.

STATE AND STATUTE	Covers Law Enforcement*	Covers Jails	Covers Lock-ups*	Covers Arrest▽	All Personnel Covered⁺	Some Forms are Punishable as a Felony	Consent is Not a Defense
New York Sexual misconduct. NY PENAL LAW § 130.20 (Consol. 2006). Rape in the third degree. NY PENAL LAW § 130.25 (Consol. 2006).		✓	✓		Volunteers not covered Health care contractors are covered. Other contracted employees are not.²⁴	✓	✓
North Carolina Intercourse and sexual offenses with certain victims; consent no defense N.C. GEN. STAT. § 14-27.7 (2006).	✓	✓		✓	Volunteers not covered	✓	✓
North Dakota Sexual abuse of wards. N.D. CENT. CODE § 12.1-20-06 (2006).	✓	✓		✓	Volunteers not covered	✓	Consent is not addressed

²⁴ In New York, employees who perform professional duties including providing custody, medical or mental health services, counseling services, educational programs or vocational training are covered under the statute. NY PENAL LAW § 130.05(3)(e)(i) (2006).

* Some state statutes use the word *police* or *sheriff.* For purposes of this checklist, if a statute uses the word *police* or *sheriff,* we assumed that all law enforcement is covered.

* If a state law contained the word jail and the word local correctional facility, local correctional institution, county or city facility etc., then we assumed that the state law intended to cover other local facilities such as lock-ups.

▽ If a state law contained the word "arrest" or covers law enforcement personnel and contains phrases such as "having custody over the victim", "in the offenders care under authority of law", or "under the supervision of a city or county" then we assumed that the law intended to cover arrest.

⁺ All personnel are covered if the statute includes paid employees, volunteers, other state agency employees, and private/contract employees.

Smith Consulting
February 2008

Do not use, publish or distribute without prior permission from authors. Please contact Prof. Brenda V. Smith at bvsmith@wcl.american.edu to obtain permission.

Page 16 of 23

(Continued)

Figure 5.5 (Continued) State criminal laws prohibiting the sexual abuse of persons in custody.

CHECKLIST OF STATE CRIMINAL LAWS PROHIBITING THE SEXUAL ABUSE OF PERSONS IN CUSTODY OF LAW ENFORCEMENT, LOCK-UP AND JAIL AUTHORITIES

NOTE: When the checklist indicates that a particular personnel or setting is covered under the law, either the words themselves (law enforcement, arrest, lock-up or jail) appear in the statute or a cross-referenced statute, or the law can reasonably be interpreted to cover those settings and/or personnel. Though staff sexual misconduct laws included in this chart may cover juveniles and private facilities, for the scope of this chart we have not analyzed the laws for their specific inclusion.

STATE AND STATUTE	Covers Law Enforcement*	Covers Jails	Covers Lock-ups⁺	Covers Arrest▽	All Personnel Covered⁺	Some Forms are Punishable as a Felony	Consent is Not a Defense
North Dakota Continued							
Sexual assault. N.D. Cent. Code § 12.1-20-07 (2006).							
Ohio	✓	✓	✓	✓	Volunteers not covered	✓	Consent is not addressed
Sexual Battery, Ohio Rev. Code Ann. § 2907.03 (LexisNexis 2006).							
Oklahoma	✓	✓	✓	✓	Volunteers not covered	✓	Consent is not addressed
Rape Defined Okla. Stat. tit. 21, § 1111 (2005). Rape in the first degree - second degree Okla. Stat. tit.21, § 1114 (2005). Forcible sodomy Okla. Stat. tit. 21, § 888 (2005).							
Oregon	✓			✓	Volunteers not	✓	✓

* Some state statutes use the word *police* or *sheriff*. For purposes of this checklist, if a statute uses the word *police* or *sheriff*, we assumed that all law enforcement is covered.

⁺ If a state law contained the word jail and the word local correctional facility, local correctional institution, county or city facility etc., then we assumed that the state law intended to cover other local facilities such as lock-ups.

▽ If a state law contained the word "arrest" or covers law enforcement personnel and contains phrases such as "having custody over the victim", "in the offenders care under authority of law", or "under the supervision of a city or county" then we assumed that the law intended to cover arrest.

⁺ All personnel are covered if the statute includes paid employees, volunteers, other state agency employees, and private/contract employees.

Smith Consulting
February 2008

Do not use, publish or distribute without prior permission from authors. Please contact Prof. Brenda V. Smith at bvsmith@wcl.american.edu to obtain permission.

Page 17 of 23

(Continued)

Figure 5.5 (Continued) State criminal laws prohibiting the sexual abuse of persons in custody.

CHECKLIST OF STATE CRIMINAL LAWS PROHIBITING THE SEXUAL ABUSE OF PERSONS IN CUSTODY OF LAW ENFORCEMENT, LOCK-UP AND JAIL AUTHORITIES

NOTE: *When the checklist indicates that a particular personnel or setting is covered under the law, either the words themselves (law enforcement, arrest, lock-up or jail) appear in the statute or a cross-referenced statute, or the law can reasonably be interpreted to cover those settings and/or personnel. Though staff sexual misconduct laws included in this chart may cover juveniles and private facilities, for the scope of this chart we have not analyzed the laws for their specific inclusion.*

STATE AND STATUTE	Covers Law Enforcement*	Covers Jails	Covers Lock-ups*	Covers Arrest∇	All Personnel Covered+	Some Forms are Punishable as a Felony	Consent is Not a Defense
First Degree Custodial Sexual Misconduct Or. Rev. Stat. § 163.452 (2006).					covered		
Second Degree Custodial Sexual Misconduct Or. Rev. Stat. § 163.454 (2006).							
Pennsylvania Institutional sexual assault 18 Pa. Cons. Stat. § 3124.2 (2005).		✓			Volunteers not covered	✓	Consent is not addressed
Rhode Island Correctional employees — sexual relations with inmates — felony R.I. Gen. Laws § 11-25-24 (2006).		✓25	✓26		Volunteers not covered	✓	Consent is not addressed

[25] In Rhode Island, the law covers employees of the Department of Corrections. According to the structure of Rhode Island's Department of Corrections, all jails are governed under the state DOC. R.I. Gen. Laws § 11-25-24 (2006).

* Some state statutes use the word *police* or *sheriff.* For purposes of this checklist, if a statute uses the word *police* or *sheriff,* we assumed that all law enforcement is covered.

♦ If a state law contained the word jail and the word local correctional facility, local correctional institution, county or city facility etc., then we assumed that the state law intended to cover other local facilities such as lock-ups.

∇ If a state law contained the word "arrest" or covers law enforcement personnel and contains phrases such as "having custody over the victim", "in the offenders care under authority of law"", or "under the supervision of a city or county" then we assumed that the law intended to cover arrest.

+ All personnel are covered if the statute includes paid employees, volunteers, other state agency employees, and private/contract employees.

(Continued)

Figure 5.5 (Continued) State criminal laws prohibiting the sexual abuse of persons in custody.

CHECKLIST OF STATE CRIMINAL LAWS PROHIBITING THE SEXUAL ABUSE OF PERSONS IN CUSTODY OF LAW ENFORCEMENT, LOCK-UP AND JAIL AUTHORITIES

NOTE: When the checklist indicates that a particular personnel or setting is covered under the law, either the words themselves (law enforcement, arrest, lock-up or jail) appear in the statute or a cross-referenced statute, or the law can reasonably be interpreted to cover those settings and/or personnel. Though staff sexual misconduct laws included in this chart may cover juveniles and private facilities, for the scope of this chart we have not analyzed the laws for their specific inclusion.

STATE AND STATUTE	Covers Law Enforcement*	Covers Jails	Covers Lock-ups*	Covers Arrest^V	All Personnel Covered^+	Some Forms are Punishable as a Felony	Consent is Not a Defense
South Carolina Sexual misconduct with an inmate, patient or offender S.C. CODE ANN. § 44-23-1150 (2005).		✓			✓	✓	Consent is not addressed
South Dakota Sexual acts prohibited between prison employees and prisoners. S.D. CODIFIED LAWS § 24-1-26.1 (2006).		✓			Volunteers not covered	✓	Consent is not addressed
Tennessee Sexual contact with inmates	✓	✓	✓²⁷	✓	✓	✓	Consent is not

[26] In Rhode Island, the law covers employees of the Department of Corrections. According to the structure of Rhode Island's Department of Corrections, all intake centers (lock-ups) are governed under the state DOC. R.I. GEN. LAWS § 11-25-24 (2006).

[27] Tennessee defines custody as "restraint by a public servant pursuant to an order of a court" and thus would appear to cover court holding facilities. TENN. CODE ANN. § 39-16-601(2) (2006).

* Some state statutes use the word *police* or *sheriff*. For purposes of this checklist, if a statute uses the word *police* or *sheriff*, we assumed that all law enforcement is covered.

✦ If a state law contained the word jail and the word local correctional facility, local correctional institution, county or city facility etc., then we assumed that the state law intended to cover other local facilities such as lock-ups.

V If a state law contained the word "arrest" or covers law enforcement personnel and contains phrases such as "having custody over the victim", "in the offenders care under authority of law", or "under the supervision of a city or county" then we assumed that the law intended to cover arrest.

+ All personnel are covered if the statute includes paid employees, volunteers, other state agency employees, and private/contract employees.

Smith Consulting
February 2008

Do not use, publish or distribute without prior permission from authors. Please contact Prof. Brenda V. Smith at bvsmith@wcl.american.edu to obtain permission.
Page 19 of 23

Figure 5.5 (Continued) State criminal laws prohibiting the sexual abuse of persons in custody.

(Continued)

(Continued)

CHECKLIST OF STATE CRIMINAL LAWS PROHIBITING THE SEXUAL ABUSE OF PERSONS IN CUSTODY OF LAW ENFORCEMENT, LOCK-UP AND JAIL AUTHORITIES

NOTE: When the checklist indicates that a particular personnel or setting is covered under the law, either the words themselves (law enforcement, arrest, lock-up or jail) appear in the statute or a cross-referenced statute, or the law can reasonably be interpreted to cover those settings and/or personnel. Though staff sexual misconduct laws included in this chart may cover juveniles and private facilities, for the scope of this chart we have not analyzed the laws for their specific inclusion.

STATE AND STATUTE	Covers Law Enforcement*	Covers Jails	Covers Lock-ups*	Covers Arrest^V	All Personnel Covered+	Some Forms are Punishable as a Felony	Consent is Not a Defense
TENN. CODE ANN. § 39-16-408 (2006). Sexual battery by an authority figure TENN. CODE ANN. § 39-13-527 (2005).							addressed
Texas Violations of the Civil Rights of Person in Custody; Improper Sexual Activity with person in custody. TEX. PENAL CODE ANN. § 39.04 (Vernon 2005).	✓	✓	✓	✓	✓	✓	Consent is not addressed
Utah Custodial sexual relations – custodial sexual misconduct – definitions – penalties – defenses UTAH CODE	✓	✓		✓	✓	✓	✓

* Some state statutes use the word *police* or *sheriff*. For purposes of this checklist, if a statute uses the word *police* or *sheriff*, we assumed that all law enforcement is covered.

+ If a statute law contained the word jail and the word local correctional facility, local correctional institution, county or city facility etc., then we assumed that the state law intended to cover other local facilities such as lock-ups.

^V If a state law contained the word "arrest" or covers law enforcement personnel and contains phrases such as "having custody over the victim", "in the offenders care under authority of law", or "under the supervision of a city or county" then we assumed that the law intended to cover arrest.

+ All personnel are covered if the statute includes paid employees, volunteers, other state agency employees, and private/contract employees.

Smith Consulting
February 2008
Do not use, publish or distribute without prior permission from authors. Please contact Prof. Brenda V. Smith at bvsmith@wcl.american.edu to obtain permission.
Page 20 of 23

Figure 5.5 (Continued) State criminal laws prohibiting the sexual abuse of persons in custody.

CHECKLIST OF STATE CRIMINAL LAWS PROHIBITING THE SEXUAL ABUSE OF PERSONS IN CUSTODY OF LAW ENFORCEMENT, LOCK-UP AND JAIL AUTHORITIES

NOTE: When the checklist indicates that a particular personnel or setting is covered under the law, either the words themselves (law enforcement, arrest, lock-up or jail) appear in the statute or a cross-referenced statute, or the law can reasonably be interpreted to cover those settings and/or personnel. Though staff sexual misconduct laws included in this chart may cover juveniles and private facilities, for the scope of this chart we have not analyzed the laws for their specific inclusion.

STATE AND STATUTE	Covers Law Enforcement*	Covers Jails	Covers Lock-ups*	Covers Arrest^V	All Personnel Covered^+	Some Forms are Punishable as a Felony	Consent is Not a Defense
ANN. § 76-5-412 (2006).							
Vermont Sexual exploitation of an inmate VT. STAT. ANN. tit. 13, § 3257 (2006).		✓	✓		✓		Consent is not addressed
Virginia Carnal knowledge of an inmate, parolee, probationer, or pretrial or post-trial offender; penalty. VA. CODE ANN. § 18.2-64.2 (2006).		✓	✓		✓	✓	Consent is not addressed
Washington Custodial sexual misconduct in the first degree WASH. REV. CODE ANN. § 9A.44.160 (LexisNexis 2006). Custodial sexual misconduct in the second degree	✓	✓	✓	✓	Volunteers not covered	✓	✓

* Some state statutes use the word *police* or *sheriff*. For purposes of this checklist, if a statute uses the word *police* or *sheriff*, we assumed that all law enforcement is covered.

◆ If a state law contained the word *jail* and the word local local correctional facility, local correctional institution, county or city facility etc., then we assumed that the state law intended to cover other local facilities such as lock-ups.

^V If a state law contained the word "arrest" or covers law enforcement personnel and contains phrases such as "having custody over the victim", "in the offenders care under authority of law", or "under the supervision of a city or county" then we assumed that the law intended to cover arrest.

^+ All personnel are covered if the statute includes paid employees, volunteers, other state agency employees, and private/contract employees.

Smith Consulting
February 2008

Do not use, publish or distribute without prior permission from authors. Please contact Prof. Brenda V. Smith at bvsmith@wcl.american.edu to obtain permission.

Page 21 of 23

Figure 5.5 (Continued) State criminal laws prohibiting the sexual abuse of persons in custody.

(Continued)

CHECKLIST OF STATE CRIMINAL LAWS PROHIBITING THE SEXUAL ABUSE OF PERSONS IN CUSTODY OF LAW ENFORCEMENT, LOCK-UP AND JAIL AUTHORITIES

NOTE: When the checklist indicates that a particular personnel or setting is covered under the law, either the words themselves (law enforcement, arrest, lock-up or jail) appear in the statute or a cross-referenced statute, or the law can reasonably be interpreted to cover those settings and/or personnel. Though staff sexual misconduct laws included in this chart may cover juveniles and private facilities, for the scope of this chart we have not analyzed the laws for their specific inclusion.

STATE AND STATUTE	Covers Law Enforcement*	Covers Jails	Covers Lock-ups♦	Covers Arrest^V	All Personnel Covered+	Some Forms are Punishable as a Felony	Consent is Not a Defense
WASH. REV. CODE ANN. § 9A.44.170 (2006).							
West Virginia / Imposition of sexual intercourse or sexual intrusion on incarcerated persons; penalty W. VA. CODE ANN. § 61-8B-10 (2006).		✓	✓		Volunteers not covered	✓	✓
Wisconsin Second Degree Sexual Assault WIS. STAT. ANN. § 940.225 (West 2006).					✓	✓	Consent is not addressed
Abuse of residents of penal facilities WIS. STAT. ANN. § 940.29 (West 2006).		✓	✓	✓			
Wyoming	✓	✓		✓	Volunteers not covered	✓	Consent is not addressed

* Some state statutes use the word *police* or *sheriff*. For purposes of this checklist, if a statute uses the word *police* or *sheriff*, we assumed that all law enforcement is covered.

♦ If a state law contained the word jail and the word local correctional facility, local correctional institution, county or city facility etc., then we assumed that the state law intended to cover other local facilities such as lock-ups.

^V If a state law contained the word "arrest" or covers law enforcement personnel and contains phrases such as "having custody over the victim", "in the offenders care under authority of law", or "under the supervision of a city or county" then we assumed that the law intended to cover arrest.

+ All personnel are covered if the statute includes paid employees, volunteers, other state agency employees, and private/contract employees.

Smith Consulting
February 2008
Do not use, publish or distribute without prior permission from authors. Please contact Prof. Brenda V. Smith at bvsmith@wcl.american.edu to obtain permission.
Page 22 of 23

(Continued)

Figure 5.5 (Continued) State criminal laws prohibiting the sexual abuse of persons in custody.

CHECKLIST OF STATE CRIMINAL LAWS PROHIBITING THE SEXUAL ABUSE OF PERSONS IN CUSTODY OF LAW ENFORCEMENT, LOCK-UP AND JAIL AUTHORITIES

NOTE: When the checklist indicates that a particular personnel or setting is covered under the law, either the words themselves (law enforcement, arrest, lock-up or jail) appear in the statute or a cross-referenced statute, or the law can reasonably be interpreted to cover those settings and/or personnel. Though staff sexual misconduct laws included in this chart may cover juveniles and private facilities, for the scope of this chart we have not analyzed the laws for their specific inclusion.

STATE AND STATUTE	Covers Law Enforcement*	Covers Jails	Covers Lock-ups*	Covers Arrest^v	All Personnel Covered^+	Some Forms are Punishable as a Felony	Consent is Not a Defense
Sexual assault in the second degree WYO. STAT. ANN. § 6-2-303 (2006).							
United States (NOTE: This law also covers all federal United States territories including Guam, Northern Mariana Islands, Puerto Rico and the Virgin Islands) Aggravated sexual abuse 18 U.S.C.S. § 2241 (LexisNexis 2006). Sexual abuse 18 U.S.C.S. § 2242 (LexisNexis 2006). Sexual abuse of a minor or ward 18 U.S.C.S. § 2243 (LexisNexis 2006). Abusive sexual contact 18 U.S.C.S. § 2244 (LexisNexis 2006).	√[28]	√	√	√	√	√	Consent is not addressed

* Some state statutes use the word *police* or *sheriff*. For purposes of this checklist, if a statute uses the word *police* or *sheriff*, we assumed that all law enforcement is covered.

♦ If a statute contained the word jail and the word local correctional facility, local correctional institution, county or city facility etc., then we assumed that the state law intended to cover other local facilities such as lock-ups.

v If a state law contained the word "arrest" or covers law enforcement personnel and contains phrases such as "having custody over the victim", "in the offenders care under authority of law", or "under the supervision of a city or county" then we assumed that the law intended to cover arrest.

+ All personnel are covered if the statute includes paid employees, volunteers, other state agency employees, and private/contract employees.

Smith Consulting
February 2008

Do not use, publish or distribute without prior permission from authors. Please contact Prof. Brenda V. Smith at bvsmith@wcl.american.edu to obtain permission.

Page 23 of 23

Figure 5.5 (Continued) State criminal laws prohibiting the sexual abuse of persons in custody.

While the *Model Penal Code* lays out the generic elements of sexual offenses, the last four decades have witnessed extraordinary efforts to either reform or expand statutory coverage. Proponents of rape law reform have been successful in creating sexual offense legislation that is gender neutral, that does not require a traditional vaginal and penal contact, and does not weigh the substantiality of victim resistance.[58] Part of the reason why crime by security officers often occurs is the proximity to settings where bad behavior takes place, such as bars, taverns, entertainment facilities, and venues as well as large crowd events. Aberrant security officers take advantage of these settings and commit crimes that are hard to trace. Sexual offenses are not uncommon, especially when the crowd and client are inebriated.[59]

In business and commercial settings, cases of indecent assault or indecent exposure are not atypical. A representative statute from Pennsylvania covers the standard language:

> Indecent assault. A person who has indecent contact with another not his spouse, or causes such other to have indecent contact with him is guilty of indecent assault, a misdemeanor of the second degree, if:
>
> (1) the person does so without the complainant's consent; ...
>
> (4) the complainant is unconscious or the person knows that the complainant is unaware that the indecent contact is occurring; ...
>
> (6) the complainant suffers from a mental disability which renders the complainant incapable of consent;[60]
>
> Indecent exposure. (a) OFFENSE DEFINED.—A person commits indecent exposure if that person exposes his or her genitals in any public place or in any place where there are present other persons under circumstances in which he or she knows or should know that this conduct is likely to offend, affront or alarm.
>
> (b) GRADING.—If the person knows or should have known that any of the persons present are less than 16 years of age, indecent exposure under subsection (a) is a misdemeanor of the first degree. Otherwise, indecent exposure under subsection (a) is a misdemeanor of the second degree.[61]

Security companies charged with these types of investigations must memorialize complaints in document form (see Figure 5.6).[62]

Cases of sexual harassment are unfortunately recurring phenomena for security advisors and consultants. To ferret out the ruses from the legitimate cases of sexual harassment employ the evaluation checklist shown in Figure 5.7.[63]

5.4.2 Offenses against the Habitation and Other Buildings

The security industry is entrusted with protection of homes, business and commercial buildings, and residential settings. Whether by direct patrol or technological surveillance, the industry is increasingly controlling the safety of private residences and business settings.[64]

5.4.2.1 Arson

Industrial and business concerns have a grave interest in the protection of their assets and real property from arsonists.[65] Around-the-clock security systems, surveillance systems, and electronic technology have done much to aid private enterprise in the protection of its interests.[66]

SEXUAL HARASSMENT COMPLAINT FORM

Name

Position

Department

Shift

Immediate Supervisor

Describe the sexual harassment incident

Who was responsible for the sexual harassment?

List any witnesses to the sexual harassment incident

Where did the sexual harassment take place?

Identify the date(s) and time(s) that the sexual harassment occurred.

Employee   Date

Figure 5.6   Sexual harassment complaint form.

Arson, as defined in the *Model Penal Code*, includes the following provisions:

Arson. A person is guilty of arson, a felony of the second degree, if he starts a fire or causes an explosion with the purpose of:
1. Destroying a building or occupied structure of another; or
2. Destroying or damaging any property, whether his own or another's, to collect insurance for such loss.[67]

Client background, demeanor, and attitude

- Does the client appear to be telling the truth?
- Does the client relate her story with fervor and outrage?
- Does the client seem to be telling the truth when the story is approached from different angles?
- Will the client withstand a thorough background investigation?
- Has the client been responsive and truthful in disclosing personal facts?
- Has the client discussed any negative aspects of the case?
- Has the client fully discussed the nature of the sexual or other type of relationship with the person who committed the acts of sexual harassment?
- What kind of family support does the client have during litigation?
- Does the client's family or spouse encourage or discourage the pursuit of this litigation?
- Will the client pursue the litigation despite lack of support from her family or spouse?
- What impact, of any, would the litigation have on the relationship between the client and her family or spouse? Can that relationship withstand intense scrutiny?
- Has the client's accounting of the sexual harassment remained consistent throughout the initial interview and interviews?

Client motives

- What are the motives behind the clients desire to pursue the litigation?
- Is the client seeking revenge?
- Are the client's motives for bringing the matter to litigation sincere and believable?

Client's work record and job performance

- Obtain to the extent possible all relevant information as to the nature of the employment, duties, and functions of the client; attendance records; and work performance.
- Is there a legitimate nondiscriminatory reason that can be advanced by the employer?
- Are there any job evaluations that have been given to the client? If so, by whom?
- What was the relationship between the client and the person who gave the evaluations prior to any of the alleged incidents in question?
- What was the relationship between the client and the person who gave the evaluations after to any of the alleged incidents in question?
- Did the client complain to the employer about the alleged sexual harassment? If so, how many complaints were made, and to whom?
- How were these complaints or grievances handled and resolved?
- What observations or impressions can the client offer as to the resolution of prior grievances?
- Have there been any threats as to job security or the like been made to the client in respect to this litigation? If so, have the proper authorities been notified and has the matter been documented?
- What kind of additional documentation does the client have to support the claim of sexual harassment?
- Did the client make a diary while the incidents of sexual harassment were occurring?
- What are the employer's policies regarding the alleged incidents of sexual harassment?
- Is there a union agreement which may have a bearing on the facts of the case?
- Is there a personnel handbook or other company document which may be construed as a contract? If so, what did the employer promise to do when grievances as to sexual harassment were raised?

Number of potential witnesses

- To the extent possible, verify the experiences of each of the alleged witnesses to ensure the absence of a vindictive motive for agreeing to help the client.
- What kind of cooperation or support from either present of past employees does the client offer?
- Have there been other incidents experienced by other employees similar to that suffered by the client? If so, who were the participants, where are they presently employed, and what (if any) similarities exist?

Figure 5.7 Sexual harassment evaluation checklist. (*Continued*)

Other factors and considerations

- What are the statute of limitations or time restrictions involved in the case?
- Is there a requirement that state or federal administrative procedures be exhausted as a prerequisite to litigation?
- Were any unemployment insurance or compensation hearings held? If so, what was the disposition?
- Did the employer give any particular reasons for the cause of the employee's unemployment?
- Was the unemployment compensation hearing taped?
- Were the witnesses under oath?
- Were there any inconsistent statements made by witnesses at the unemployment insurance or compensation hearing?

Figure 5.7 (Continued) Sexual harassment evaluation checklist.

Judicial interpretation of arson statutes has been primarily concerned with either the definition of a "structure" or in the proof an actual burning or physical fire damage. Structure has been broadly defined as any physical plant, warehouse, or accommodation that permits the carrying on of business or the temporary residents of persons, a domicile, and even ships, trailers, sleeping cars, airplanes, and other movable vehicles or structures.[68] Any burning, substantial smoke discoloration and damage, charring, the existence of alligator burn patterns, destruction and damage caused as the results of explosives, detonation devices, and ruination by substantial heat meets the arson criteria. Total destruction or annihilation is not required.[69]

Most jurisdictions have also adopted related offenses:

- Reckless burning or exploding
- Causing or risking a catastrophe
- Failure to prevent a catastrophe
- Criminal mischief
- Injuring or tampering with fire apparatus, hydrants, etc.
- Unauthorized use or opening of a fire hydrant
- Institutional vandalism[70]

Find out about efforts of the DHS and other federal agencies to thwart arson attempts at churches and synagogues at: https://www.dhs.gov/xlibrary/assets/hsac/hsac-faith-based-security-and-communications-advisory-committee-final-report-may-2012.pdf

---

Proving a case of arson can be made easier with Figure 5.8.[71]

5.4.2.2 Burglary

Of major interest to the security industry is the crime of burglary, a crime whose felonious intent requires an illegal entry into a domicile or other structure for the purpose of committing any felony therein. Clark and Marshall's *Treatise on Crimes*[72] provides the common law definition of the crime of burglary:

1. The premises must be the dwelling house of another...
2. There must be a breaking of some part of the house itself. The breaking must be constructive, as well as actual.

INSPECTION AND TESTING FORM

DATE: _____

TIME: _____

SERVICE ORGANIZATION

Name: _____

Address: _____

Representative: _____

License No.: _____

Telephone: _____

PROPERTY NAME (USER)

Name: _____

Address: _____

Owner Contact: _____

Telephone: _____

MONITORING ENTITY

Contact: _____

Telephone: _____

Monitoring Account Ref. No.: _____

APPROVING AGENCY

Contact: _____

Telephone: _____

TYPE TRANSMISSION

❏ McCulloh
❏ Multiplex
❏ Digital
❏ Reverse Priority
❏ RF
❏ Other (Specify) _____

_____

SERVICE

❏ Weekly
❏ Monthly
❏ Quarterly
❏ Semiannually
❏ Annually
❏ Other (Specify) _____

_____

Control Unit Manufacturer: _____

Circuit Styles: _____

Number of Circuits: _____

Software Rev.: _____

Model No.: _____

Last Date System Had Any Service Performed: _____

Last Date that Any Software or Configuration Was Revised: _____

ALARM-INITIATING DEVICES AND CIRCUIT INFORMATION

Quantity	Circuit Style	
_____	_____	Manual Fire Alarm Boxes
_____	_____	Ion Detectors
_____	_____	Photo Detectors
_____	_____	Duct Detectors
_____	_____	Heat Detectors
_____	_____	Waterflow Switches
_____	_____	Supervisory Switches
_____	_____	Other (Specify): _____

(NFPA Inspection and Testing 1 of 4)

Figure 5.8 Arson inspection and test form. (Reproduced with permission from the National Fire Protection Association, Copyright © 2015.) *(Continued)*

ALARM NOTIFICATION APPLIANCES AND CIRCUIT INFORMATION

Quantity	Circuit Style	
_____	_____	Bells
_____	_____	Horns
_____	_____	Chimes
_____	_____	Strobes
_____	_____	Speakers
_____	_____	Other (Specify): _____

No. of alarm notification appliance circuits: _____

Are circuits monitored for integrity?   ❑ Yes   ❑ No

SUPERVISORY SIGNAL-INITIATING DEVICES AND CIRCUIT INFORMATION

Quantity	Circuit Style	
_____	_____	Building Temp.
_____	_____	Site Water Temp.
_____	_____	Site Water Level
_____	_____	Fire Pump Power
_____	_____	Fire Pump Running
_____	_____	Fire Pump Auto Position
_____	_____	Fire Pump or Pump Controller Trouble
_____	_____	Fire Pump Running
_____	_____	Generator In Auto Position
_____	_____	Generator or Controller Trouble
_____	_____	Switch Transfer
_____	_____	Generator Engine Running
_____	_____	Other: _____

SIGNALING LINE CIRCUITS

Quantity and style (See NFPA 72, Table 3-6) of signaling line circuits connected to system:

   Quantity _____   Style(s) _____

SYSTEM POWER SUPPLIES

a. Primary (Main):   Nominal Voltage _____ , Amps _____
   Overcurrent Protection: Type _____ , Amps _____
   Location (of Primary Supply Panelboard): _____
   Disconnecting Means Location: _____

b. Secondary (Standby):

   _____ Storage Battery: Amp-Hr. Rating _____
   Calculated capacity to operate system, in hours: _____ 24 _____ 60 _____
   _____ Engine-driven generator dedicated to fire alarm system:
   Location of fuel storage: _____

TYPE BATTERY

❑ Dry Cell
❑ Nickel-Cadmium
❑ Sealed Lead-Acid
❑ Lead-Acid
❑ Other (Specify): _____

c. Emergency or standby system used as a backup to primary power supply, instead of using a secondary power supply:

   _____ Emergency system described in NFPA 70, Article 700
   _____ Legally required standby described in NFPA 70, Article 701
   _____ Optional standby system described in NFPA 70, Article 702, which also meets the performance requirements of Article 700 or 701.

(NFPA Inspection and Testing 2 of 4)

Figure 5.8 (Continued)   Arson inspection and test form. (Reproduced with permission from the National Fire Protection Association, Copyright © 2015.)

(Continued)

PRIOR TO ANY TESTING

NOTIFICATIONS ARE MADE	Yes	No	Who	Time
Monitoring Entity	❑	❑	_____	_____
Building Occupants	❑	❑	_____	_____
Building Management	❑	❑	_____	_____
Other (Specify)	❑	❑	_____	_____
AHJ (Notified) of Any Impairments	❑	❑	_____	_____

SYSTEM TESTS AND INSPECTIONS

TYPE	Visible	Functional	Comments
Control Unit	❑	❑	_____
Interface Eq.	❑	❑	_____
Lamps/LEDS	❑	❑	_____
Fuses	❑	❑	_____
Primary Power Supply	❑	❑	_____
Trouble Signals	❑	❑	_____
Disconnect Switches	❑	❑	_____
Ground-Fault Monitoring	❑	❑	_____

SECONDARY POWER

TYPE	Visible	Functional	Comments
Battery Condition	❑		_____
Load Voltage		❑	_____
Discharge Test		❑	_____
Charger Test		❑	_____
Specific Gravity		❑	_____
TRANSIENT SUPPRESSORS	❑		_____
REMOTE ANNUNCIATORS	❑	❑	_____
NOTIFICATION APPLIANCES			
Audible	❑	❑	_____
Visual	❑	❑	_____
Speakers	❑	❑	_____
Voice Clarity		❑	_____

INITIATING AND SUPERVISORY DEVICE TESTS AND INSPECTIONS

Loc. & S/N	Device Type	Visual Check	Functional Test	Factory Setting	Meas. Setting	Pass	Fail
_____	_____	❑	❑	_____	_____	❑	❑
_____	_____	❑	❑	_____	_____	❑	❑
_____	_____	❑	❑	_____	_____	❑	❑
_____	_____	❑	❑	_____	_____	❑	❑
_____	_____	❑	❑	_____	_____	❑	❑
_____	_____	❑	❑	_____	_____		

Comments: _____
_____
_____

(NFPA Inspection and Testing 3 of 4)

Figure 5.8 (Continued) Arson inspection and test form. (Reproduced with permission from the National Fire Protection Association, Copyright © 2015.)
(Continued)

EMERGENCY COMMUNICATIONS EQUIPMENT	Visual	Functional	Comments
Phone Set	❑	❑	_____
Phone Jacks	❑	❑	_____
Off-Hook Indicator	❑	❑	_____
Amplifier(s)	❑	❑	_____
Tone Generator(s)	❑	❑	_____
Call-in Signal	❑	❑	_____
System Performance	❑	❑	_____

INTERFACE EQUIPMENT	Visual	Device Operation	Simulated Operation
(Specify) _____	❑	❑	❑
(Specify) _____	❑	❑	❑
(Specify) _____	❑	❑	❑
SPECIAL HAZARD SYSTEMS			
(Specify) _____	❑	❑	❑
(Specify) _____	❑	❑	❑
(Specify) _____	❑	❑	❑

Special Procedures: _____
_____
_____
_____

Comments: _____
_____
_____
_____
_____

SUPERVISING STATION MONITORING	Yes	No	Time	Comments
Alarm Signal	❑	❑	_____	_____
Alarm Restoration	❑	❑	_____	_____
Trouble Signal	❑	❑	_____	_____
Supervisory Signal	❑	❑	_____	_____
Supervisory Restoration	❑	❑	_____	_____

NOTIFICATIONS THAT TESTING IS COMPLETE	Yes	No	Who	Time
Building Management	❑	❑	_____	_____
Monitoring Agency	❑	❑	_____	_____
Building Occupants	❑	❑	_____	_____
Other (Specify)	❑	❑	_____	_____

The following did not operate correctly: _____
_____
_____

System restored to normal operation: Date: _____ Time: _____

THIS TESTING WAS PERFORMED IN ACCORDANCE WITH APPLICABLE NFPA STANDARDS.

Name of Inspector: _____ Date: _____ Time: _____
Signature: _____
Name of Owner or Representative: _____
Date: _____ Time: _____
Signature: _____

(NFPA Inspection and Testing 4 of 4)

Figure 5.8 (Continued) Arson inspection and test form. (Reproduced with permission from the National Fire Protection Association, Copyright © 2015.)

3. There must be an entry. The slightest entry of a hand or even an instrument suffices.
4. The breaking and entering must both be at night; but need not be on the same night.
5. There must be an intent to commit a felony in the house and such intent must accompany both the breaking and entry. The intended felony need not be committed.[73]

Statutory modification of these elements has been quite common. The definition of a dwelling house has been liberally construed and includes a chicken coop, a cow stable, a hog house, a barn, a smoke house, a mill house, and any other area or any other building or occupied structure.[74] The term "breaking" does not require an actual destruction of property, merely the breaking of a plane or point of entrance into the occupied structure.[75] Additionally, most jurisdictions have reassessed the nighttime determination and made the requirement nonmandatory, though make the time of the intrusion applicable to the gradation of the offense.[76]

Security operatives should, as in all other forms of criminality, take steps to prevent burglaries. See the checklist at Figure 5.9.[77]

Be aware that burglary is not necessarily motivated by a property offense. Appellate decisions continually instruct that burglary's requirement of entry be spurred on by an intent to commit any felony.[78] The benchmark question then becomes what was the intent of the accused at the precise time of his actual breaking and entry?[79]

A related act that has applicability to the security environment is criminal trespass.[80]

5.4.2.3 Trespass

1. Buildings and occupied structures. A person commits an offense if, knowing he is not licensed or privileged to do so, he enters or surreptitiously remains in any building or occupied structure or separately secured or occupied portion thereof. An offense under this Subsection is a misdemeanor if it is committed in a dwelling at night. Otherwise, it is a petty misdemeanor.[81]

To minimize burglary and trespass activity, adopt the policy considerations shown in Figure 5.10[82] when conducting a facility review.

5.4.2.4 Robbery

The unlawful acquisition or taking of property by forceful means constitutes a robbery.[83] In retail and commercial establishments, security officers and personnel are frequently endangered by the activities of felons. Robbery is more than a property crime since it is coupled with a violent thrust. The exact provisions of a general robbery statute include those outlined in the *Model Penal Code* provision.

1. Robbery Defined. A person is guilty of robbery if, in the course of committing a theft, he:
   a. Inflicts serious bodily injury upon another; or
   b. Threatens another with or purposely puts him in fear of immediate serious bodily injury; or
   c. Commits or threatens immediately to commit any felony of the first or second degree.

An act shall be deemed "in the course of committing a theft" if it occurs in an attempt to commit theft or in flight after the attempt or commission.[84]

BURGLARY PREVENTION CHECKLIST

PREVENTION TIPS	OK	NEEDED	RECOMMEND REPLACEMENT
Doors:			
Strong Pintumber locks:			
-Front Door			
-Back Door			
-Side Door			
-Basement Door			
Chain Latch:			
-Front Door			
-Back Door			
-Side Door			
-Basement Door			
Heavy-Duty Hinges:			
-Front Door			
-Back Door			
-Side Door			
-Basement Door			
Peephole:			
-Front Door			
-Back Door			
Doors with Windows:			
Need key to open inside and out			
Mailbox/Mail Slot in Door			
Garage Door Pintumbler Lock			
Windows:			
All windows with Pintumbers			
Bar or Strip of Wood (Patio Door)			
Bars or Grillworks:			
"Out-of-the-Way" windows			
Garage Windows			
Basement Windows			
Keys:			
Change tumblers when you move in or out if keys are lost			
Don't give out duplicate keys			
Keep home and automobile keys separate			
Don't put name and address on keys			
Keep house key hidden outside			

Figure 5.9 Burglary inspection checklist.

Distinguishing robbery from a larceny or a theft offense is not a difficult task since both judicial interpretation and statutory definitions insist upon a finding of force, violence, or a physical threat of imminent harm. Robbery can be accomplished by threats only if the threats are of death or of great bodily injury to the victim, a member of the victim's family or some other relative of the victim, or someone in the victim's presence. Threats to damage property will not suffice, with the

	Hazardous Conditions Requiring Special Attention
	Poorly lit areas
	Wet floors, holes or defects in floor covering
	Improper storage of flammable or sensitive materials; flammable liquids left uncovered; oily, flammable rags stored in open or improper containers.
	High voltage or electrical transformers not locked
	Fire fighting equipment out or order
	Broken windows
	Inadequate clearance between sprinkler heads and stored material (18"-24")
	Objects left on shelves or window sills that may fall off
	Use of boxes or chairs in place of ladders; damaged ladders, poor housekeeping, unsightly rubbish conditions, use of special equipment or machines without authorization, material piled in a dangerous manner, cigarettes not properly extinguished (extinguish those found/look for evidence of smoking in NO SMOKING AREAS;) other conditions peculiar to this location:
	Is the perimeter secure and in sound condition?
	Is the fire protection equipment in proper working order and accessible?
	Are the (Post Indicator Valves) P.I.V.'s in the OPEN position?
	Does the gauge on the RISER indicate the proper pressure?
	Are EXIT SIGNS, FIRE LIGHTS, and EMERGENCY LIGHTS working properly?
	Are flammable materials properly stored?
	Are aisles and pathways clear of obstructions and/or safety hazards?
	Are all doors and windows properly secured?
	Is there excess trash accumulation?
	Have all small appliances been turned off?
	Are there any leaks?
	Are there any strange noises?
	Are personnel loitering in the parking lot?
	Are all parking lot and roadway lights working properly?
	Are there any vehicles leaking fuel in the parking lot?
	Have the readings on all gauges required to check been recorded?
	Have alarms and sensitive areas been checked at the start of the shift?
	Are all the clients' vehicles secured?
	Have the names of employees that have entered the facility been recorded?
	Is all lawn sprinkler equipment working properly?
	Has the patrol vehicle been checked prior to the start of the shift?
	Does the Detex clock display the correct time?
	Have reports been made on all unusual or out of the ordinary incidents that occurred during the shift?
	Have all the clients' keys been accounted for?
	Be prepared to provide the relief officer with a complete briefing.
	Are general and special orders up-to-date?
	Is a copy of the emergency contact list available?
	Have all Sign-In Logs and Registrars been closed out at midnight?
	Have there been any accidents or employee complaints?
	Has all equipment that has been taken out of the facility been documented?
	Have any malfunctions or shortages or equipment been reported?
	Has the flag been raised and lowered in the proper manner?
	Are telephones working properly?

Figure 5.10 Burglary and inspection prevention checklist.

possible exception of a threat to destroy a dwelling house.[85] Considerations relevant to a finding of guilt in a robbery case include whether or not the victim was actually threatened with immediate harm; whether the force or violence exerted created substantial fear or simple apprehension in the robbery victim;[86] and whether the statutory guidelines demand that the victim be present when the unlawful taking occurs.[87]

5.4.2.5 Theft or Larceny

No other area of proscribed behavior affects the security practice as much as in the crime of theft or as it was once known at common law, larceny.[88] Shoplifting is a form of larceny and has become retail security's central concern as it seeks to devise loss prevention strategies.[89]

Visit and evaluate worldwide data on the scourge of property theft in the retail world at: http://www.globalretailtheftbarometer.com/

Stock pilferage, fraudulent accounting and record-keeping systems, embezzling of corporate funds, and theft of benefits and services are all criminal behaviors that significantly influence the profitable nature of business and industry. In the broadest definitional terms, larceny consists of

- A taking that is unlawful
- A carrying away or movement thereafter of personal property
- Property of which the taker is not in rightful ownership or possession
- With a mens rea that is felonious[90]

Outlined in Table 5.1[91] are the requisite elements needed for a successful charge of larceny.

Historical argument on what exactly could be the subject of a larceny is quite prolific, from disputes about whether rabbits and fish are larcenable, or whether vegetables, land, or the skins of deer could be the subject of theft.[92] In contemporary legal parlance, literally any type of property is potentially larcenable. Maryland delineates an extensive list of property classifications including

1. "Property" means anything of value.
2. "Property" includes:
   a. Real estate;
   b. Money;
   c. A commercial instrument;
   d. An admission or transportation ticket;
   e. A written instrument representing or embodying rights concerning anything of value, or services, or anything otherwise of value to the owner;
   f. A thing growing on, affixed to, or found on land, or that is part of or affixed to any building;
   g. Electricity, gas, and water;
   h. A bird, animal, or fish that ordinarily is kept in a state of confinement;
   i. Food or drink;
   j. A sample, culture, microorganism, or specimen;
   k. A record, recording, document, blueprint, drawing, map, or a whole or partial copy, description, photograph, prototype, or model of any of them;
   l. An article, material, device, substance, or a whole or partial copy, description, photograph, prototype, or model of any of them that represents evidence of, reflects, or records a secret:

Table 5.1 Elements of Larceny

I. Trespassory Taking § 12.06	II. Asportation § 12.05	III. Personal Goods § 12.01	IV. Of Another § 12.01	V. Felonious Intent § 12.04
A. Trespass de bonis asportatis is the type of taking required—at least under such circumstances as amount technically to a trespass	F. Some carrying away of the property.	H. Personal property only; real property excluded.	J. Special property in another is sufficient even against a general owner.	K. Animus furandi must exist both in the taking (I) and the carrying away (II).
B. From actual or constructive possession of owner.	G. There is sufficient asportation if the property (III) be entirely removed from the place it occupied so that it comes under the dominion and control of the trespasser though only for an instant.	I. Must be: 1. Thing which is recognized in law as being property and the subject of ownership. 2. Of some value, though slight value to owner will suffice.	1. Mere possession is enough as against others than the owner. See § 12.03.	1. Intent to deprive the owner permanently of his property in the good, or of their value or part of their value, viz., an intent to steal.
C. Without owner's consent.				2. There must be a fraudulent intent, and not a mistake or bona fide claim of right.
D. The taking may be by means of nonhuman agency, innocent human agent or by hands of the thief or thieves.				L. There is minority authority requiring that the taking shall be *lucri causa*—for the sake of gain.
E. Taking by violence from the person of another transforms this offense into robbery.				

      i. Scientific, technical, merchandising, production, or management information; or
     ii. Designed process, procedure, formula, invention, trade secret, or improvement;
  m. A financial instrument; and
  n. Information, electronically produced data, and a computer software or program in a form readable by machine or individual.[93]

Aside from the requisite form, the fact finder must then consider the claim or right of a possessor of property for larceny is an infringement on that right to possess. One need not own property to suffer a larceny but need be its rightful and privileged possessor. Finally, the taking of said property must not arise from violence or force for to take in the fashion would call for a robbery charge over that of larceny.

The *Model Penal Code's* provision on theft is fairly straightforward:

Theft by Unlawful Taking or Disposition.

1. Moveable Property. A person is guilty of theft if he takes, or exercises unlawful control over, moveable property of another with purpose to deprive him thereof.
2. Immovable Property. A person is guilty of theft if he unlawfully transfers immovable property of another or any interest therein with the purpose to benefit himself or another not entitled thereto.[94]

Security professionals should formally record any allegations of lost or stolen property in a report format (see Figure 5.11).[95]

REPORT OF LOST/STOLEN PROPERTY

1. Date and Time Loss Reported _____
2. By whom _____
                         Extension _____
3. Describe Property _____
_____
4. Estimated Value _____
5. Property is (check one) _____ Personal _____ Company
6. Loss occurred (note time last seen and time loss noticed)
_____

REMARKS
(List any known serial numbers, identifying marks, contents, special circumstances, etc.)

_____
_____
_____
_____
_____
_____
_____
_____
_____

Figure 5.11 Lost or stolen property report.

Given the diversity of property forms and the new and emerging means of taking things or items of value, traditional larceny definitions fail to encompass these many forms. Commentators at the American Law Institute have long advanced the need to consolidate these diverse thefts under one codified heading. The larceny should now be labeled theft and distinct provisions of theft will be divided up by other variables such as value of property, type, and form of property and tangible or intangible design. The call here is for consolidation of the myriad of theft offenses under one roof while allowing distinct elements to remain. As a result, "the general definition of theft consolidates into a single offense a number of heretofore distinct property crimes, including larceny, embezzlement, obtaining by false pretense, cheat, extortion and all other involuntary transfers of wealth except those explicitly excluded by provisions of this article."[96]

Therefore, security personnel must be concerned about the closely aligned theft provisions and correctly evaluate the facts to see the applicability of certain offenses. A summary review follows.

5.4.2.6 Theft by Deception[97]/False Pretenses

Be aware of individuals who are best described as "flim-flam" artists who create false impressions and deceive others into giving up their rightful possession of property.[98] In the case of false pretense, the criminal actor deceptively attains ownership in a deed, a stock certificate, auto title, or other form of property interest evidenced by a legal document.[99]

5.4.2.7 Theft by Extortion[100]

Theft's methods may employ threats that are futuristic in design. Future threats of bodily injury or even by words disclosing private matters or secrets, which will cause serious injury to a party are common artifices employed by those seeking funds illegally.[101] Public officials, refusing to cooperate in an official capacity, or by their offices cause harm or injury without justification, unless in receipt of sum kickback or other payback fall under the theft by extortion umbrella.

5.4.2.8 Theft of Property Lost, Mislaid, or Delivered by Mistake[102]

Security personnel must be particularly concerned about employees in retail establishments or other business concerns who have access to lost and found property departments, or who take advantage of incorrectly delivered warehouse shipments.

5.4.2.9 Receiving Stolen Property[103]

One often-discovered activity, especially in retail circles, is an internal network of illegal goods and services flowing either from employee to employee or to third-party outsiders.

5.4.2.10 Theft of Services[104]

Cable companies, electric utilities, hotel, motel, and other tourist facilities are subject to thieving scams as are rental car companies, entertainment venues, and telephone companies. At common law theft had to be of a tangible item. Services lacked that corporeal quality. Modern statutes incorporate services for these activities are things of value.

5.4.2.11 Retail Theft[105]

Considering the rampant onslaught of shoplifting cases in the judicial system and the need for specialized statutory designs that recognize the many demands that business labors under as its seeks to prevent the activity, retail theft is a major concern for private security policymakers. Modern retail theft statutes are distinctively less draconian in punishment. In addition, most provide some sort of immunity in the form of merchant's privilege or other protection. Some statutes permit and even promote alternative diversion or disposition of said cases. A typical construction might be.

1. OFFENSE DEFINED—A person is guilty of a retail theft if he:
    a. Takes possession of, carries away, transfers or causes to be carried away or transferred, any merchandise displayed, held, stored or offered for sale by any store or other retail mercantile establishment with the intention of depriving the merchant of the possession, use or benefit of such merchandise without paying the full retail value thereof;
    b. Alters, transfers or removes any label, price tag marking, indicia of value or any other markings which aid in determining value affixed to any merchandise displayed, held, stored or offered for sale in a store or other retail mercantile establishment and attempts to purchase such merchandise personally or in consort with another at less than the full retail value with the intention of depriving the merchant of the full retail value of such merchandise;
    c. Transfers any merchandise displayed, held, stored or offered for sale by any store or other retail mercantile establishment from the container in or on which the same shall be displayed to any other container with intent to deprive the merchant of all or some part of the full retail value thereof; or
    d. Under-rings with the intention of depriving the merchant of the full retail value of the merchandise.
    e. Destroys, removes, renders inoperative or deactivates any inventory control tag, security strip or any other mechanism designed or employed to prevent an offense under this section with the intention of depriving the merchant of the possession, use or benefit of such merchandise without paying the full retail value thereof.[106]

The economic impact of retail theft is incredibly high.[107] Economic crime impacts society in many direct and indirect ways, such as

■ *Business*
  − Increased costs of insurance and security protection
  − Costs of internal audit activities to detect crime
  − Cost of investigation and prosecution of suspects measured in terms of lost time of security and management personnel
  − Reduced profits
  − Increased selling prices and weakened competitive standing
  − Loss of productivity
  − Loss of business reputation
  − Deterioration in quality of service
  − Threats to the survival of small business.
■ *Local government*
  − Costs of investigation and prosecution of suspects
  − Increased costs of prosecuting sophisticated (e.g., embezzlement) and technology-related (e.g., computer) crime

- Costs of correctional programs to deal with economic crime offenders
- Cost of crime prevention programs
- Cost of crime reporting and mandated security programs
- Loss of tax revenue (e.g., loss of sales tax, untaxed income of perpetrator, and tax deductions allowed business for crime-related losses)
■ *The Public*
- Increased costs of consumer goods and services to offset crime losses
- Loss of investor equity
- Increased taxes
- Reduced employment due to business failures[108]

Employ the shoplifting checklist shown in Figure 5.12[109] when conducting an investigation.

The appearance of shoplifters has given way to some creative programs of civil recovery. The retailer, instead of formally prosecuting the shoplifter, bills him or her to recover the proceeds of the theft.

Thirty-eight states now permit civil recovery, according to R. Reed Hayes Jr., president, L P Specialists, Winter Park, Fla. Hayes, a pioneer in civil recovery who has watched the technique blossom after its 1973 Nevada start.

Typically, the business gives notice to a person by mail, asking for payment for money owed. If the person neglects a certain number of notices, civil action is initiated. More often, the person pays the money owed in one lump sum or in payments.[110]

An example of a firm that specializes in the tactics of civil recovery is at: http://www.lpinnovations.com/page/83-civil_recovery.

SHOPLIFTING INVESTIGATION CHECKLIST

1. How credible is my information?
2. Where did the information come from?
3. Is the information firsthand or hearsay?
4. What other evidence supports the allegation?
5. Who are the alleged culprits or suspects?
6. What method was adopted to commit the shoplifting?
7. When was the shoplifting perpetrated?
8. Where was the shoplifting committed?
9. What assets/specific personal property were taken?
10. What is the extent, dollar value, and amount of the loss?
11. What was the motivation of the perpetrator or perpetrators?
12. What was the motivation or the reason my source, informant or other aiding parties reported the event?
13. Are my sources credible and non-biased?
14. Will the source be capable of testifying if necessary?

Figure 5.12 Shoplifting investigation checklist.

5.4.2.12 Related Property Offenses: Fraudulent Behavior

The illegal acquisition of property may take place under fraudulent or deceptive circumstances. Criminals are inventive creatures who employ devious tactics and techniques to secure property not rightfully theirs to possess. If property cannot be taken outright, then the devious felon will invent a new technique, a new design to fraudulently acquire some property or interest.[111]

Problems with fraud trickle throughout the entire economic and business system, whether auto, homes, stocks, bonds, and commercial paper, as well as intellectual property. At times, fraud activities seem insurmountable, but some are banding together to do something about it. The National Insurance Crime Bureau is one such entity. "[A] new agency—a merger of the National Automobile Theft Bureau and the Insurance Crime Prevention Institute—employs a national network of 165 investigators who help law enforcement prosecute insurance fraud perpetrators."[112] For information call 1-800-TEL-NICB.

Another resource center on fraud detection to contact is

> National Fraud Information Center/National Consumers League
> Fraud hotline—1-800-876-7060 or online complaint at: www.fraud.org
> 1701K Street, N.W., Suite 1200
> Washington, D.C. 20006
> phone: (202) 835-3323
> fax: (202) 835-0747
> www.nclnet.org/

In the case of insurance fraud contact:

> Coalition against Insurance Fraud
> 1012 14th Street, NW, Suite 200
> Washington, DC 20005
> phone: 202-393-7330
> fax: 202-393-7329
> info@InsuranceFraud.org
> www.insurancefraud.org

Fraudulent behavior, aside from its potential criminal behavior, may also trigger various sorts of civil liability.

5.4.2.13 Forgery

Property takings may be by simulation, forgery, or other deception. Individuals who create false documentation, false writings, or forged stamps, seals, trademarks, or other symbols of value, right, privilege, or identification may be subject to charges of forgery.[113] A common example of criminal forgery involves tampering with wills, deeds, contracts, commercial instruments, negotiable bonds, securities, or any other writing that influences, executes, authenticates, or issues something of monetary value. To constitute forgery, a fraudulent intent is always essential. There must not only be a false making of an instrument, but it must be with intent to defraud.[114]

715A.2 Forgery.

1. A person is guilty of forgery if, with intent to defraud or injure anyone, or with knowledge that the person is facilitating a fraud or injury to be perpetrated by anyone, the person does any of the following:

   a. Alters a writing of another without the other's permission.

   b. Makes, completes, executes, authenticates, issues, or transfers a writing so that it purports to be the act of another who did not authorize that act, or so that it purports to have been executed at a time or place or in a numbered sequence other than was in fact the case, or so that it purports to be a copy of an original when no such original existed.

   c. Utters a writing which the person knows to be forged in a manner specified in paragraph "a" or "b."

   d. Possesses a writing which the person knows to be forged in a manner specified in paragraph "a" or "b."[115]

5.4.2.14 Simulating Objects of Antiquity or Rarity

Security officials given the responsibility of protecting museum collections, art centers, or other nonprofit institutions dedicated to articles of antiquity or rarity should always be aware of possible reproduction or simulation of their employer's collections.

> Simulating objects of antiquity, rarity, etc.
>
> A person commits a misdemeanor of the first degree if, with intent to defraud anyone or with knowledge that he is facilitating a fraud to be perpetrated by anyone, he makes, alters or utters any object so that it appears to have value because of antiquity, rarity, source, or authorship which it does not possess.[116]

5.4.2.15 Fraudulent Destruction, Removal, or Concealment of Recordable Instruments or Their Tampering

Internal security, particularly in the area of personnel, payroll, and administrative matters, should give substantial thought to the preventative security measures that are presently in place or should be implemented.

> § 4103. Fraudulent destruction, removal or concealment of recordable instruments
> A person commits a felony of the third degree if, with intent to deceive or injure anyone, he destroys, removes or conceals any will, deed, mortgage, security instrument or other writing for which the law provides public recording.
> § 4104. Tampering with records or identification
> (a) Writings—A person commits a misdemeanor of the first degree if, knowing that he has no privilege to do so, he falsifies, destroys, removes or conceals any writing or record, or distinguishing mark or brand or other identification with intent to deceive or injure anyone or to conceal any wrongdoing.[117]

5.4.2.16 Bad Check and Credit Card Violations

Retail centers are regularly victimized by check and credit card fraud and related violations. Here too property is acquired without the proper payment of consideration. The seemingly endless stream of fraudulent and bounced checks received by commercial establishments is mind-boggling. The security industry must adopt an aggressive posture against these actors in order to protect pricing and value in the exchange of goods and services. Bad checks and credit card fraud drive up the prices. The language of bad check laws is fairly uniform.

§ 4105. Bad checks
a. OFFENSE DEFINED—

1. A person commits an offense if he issues or passes a check or similar sight order for the payment of money, knowing that it will not be honored by the drawee.

2. A person commits an offense if he, knowing that it will not be honored by the drawee, issues or passes a check or similar sight order for the payment of money when the drawee is located within this Commonwealth. A violation of this paragraph shall occur without regard to whether the location of the issuance or passing of the check or similar sight order is within or outside of this Commonwealth. It shall be no defense to a violation of this section that some or all of the acts constituting the offense occurred outside of this Commonwealth.

§ 4106. Access device fraud
a. OFFENSE DEFINED—A person commits an offense if he:

1. Uses an access device to obtain or in an attempt to obtain property or services with knowledge that:
    i. The access device is counterfeit, altered or incomplete;
    ii. The access device was issued to another person who has not authorized its use;
    iii. The access device has been revoked or canceled; or
    iv. For any other reason his use of the access device is unauthorized by the issuer or the device holder; or

2. Publishes, makes, sells, gives, or otherwise transfers to another, or offers or advertises, or aids and abets any other person to use an access device knowing that the access device is counterfeit, altered or incomplete, belongs to another person who has not authorized its use, has been revoked or canceled or for any reason is unauthorized by the issuer or the device holder; or

3. Possesses an access device knowing that it is counterfeit, altered, incomplete or belongs to another person who has not authorized its possession.[118]

Review the criminal penalties for bad checks at: http://www.ckfraud.org/penalties.html#criminal

5.4.3 Offenses against Public Order and Decency

Maintenance of public order is a public police function that has been increasingly transferred to the private sector.[119] Not surprisingly, security personnel have recently come up against troubled and volatile conditions experienced by the police in the mid-1960s, namely, riotous situations, disorderly persons, extreme disorderly conduct, harassment, public drunkenness, and other obstructive activities. As this transference of public control functions continues unabated, an understanding of the relevant statutes is imperative.

5.4.3.1 Riot

A person is guilty of riot, a felony of the third degree, if he participates with two or more others in a course of disorderly conduct:

1. With intent to commit or facilitate the commission of a felony or misdemeanor
2. With intent to prevent or coerce official action
3. When the actor or any other participant to the knowledge of the actor uses or plans to use a firearm or other deadly weapon[120]

Other provisions relating to public obstruction, trespass, and resisting arrest are close companions to crowd control. Pennsylvania and other jurisdictions have drafted aligned provisions dealing with similar situations such as

§ 5104. Resisting arrest or other law enforcement
A person commits a misdemeanor of the second degree if, with the intent of preventing a public servant from effecting a lawful arrest or discharging any other duty, the person creates a substantial risk of bodily injury to the public servant or anyone else, or employs means justifying or requiring substantial force to overcome the resistance.[121]
§ 5507. Obstructing highways and other public passages
(a) Obstructing—A person, who, having no legal privilege to do so, intentionally or recklessly obstructs any highway, railroad track or public utility right-of-way, sidewalk, navigable waters, other public passage, whether alone or with others, commits a summary offense, or, in case he persists after warning by a law officer, a misdemeanor of the third degree. No person shall be deemed guilty of an offense under this subsection solely because of a gathering of persons to hear him speak or otherwise communicate, or solely because of being a member of such a gathering.[122]
§ 7506. Violation of rules regarding conduct on Commonwealth property[123]
§ 5502. Failure of disorderly persons to disperse upon official order
Where three or more persons are participating in a course of disorderly conduct which causes or may reasonably be expected to cause substantial harm or serious inconvenience, annoyance or alarm, a peace officer or other public servant engaged in executing or enforcing the law may order the participants and others in the immediate vicinity to disperse. A person who refuses or knowingly fails to obey such an order commits a misdemeanor of the second degree.[124]

Handling the disruptive, the loud, and the fighters requires a charge of disorderly conduct.

§ 5503. Disorderly conduct
a. OFFENSE DEFINED—A person is guilty of disorderly conduct if, with intent to cause public inconvenience, annoyance or alarm, or recklessly creating a risk thereof, he:
   1. Engages in fighting or threatening, or in violent or tumultuous behavior;
   2. Makes unreasonable noise;
   3. Uses obscene language, or makes an obscene gesture; or
   4. Creates a hazardous or physically offensive condition by any act which serves no legitimate purpose of the actor.[125]

What is the likelihood of being arrested for using obscene language?

5.4.3.2 Public Drunkenness

A person is guilty of a summary offense if he appears in any public place manifestly under the influence of alcohol or a controlled substance, to the degree that he may endanger himself or other persons or property, or annoy persons in his vicinity.[126]

Ohio law defines voluntary intoxication in more specific terms stating that a violation of the disorderly conduct statute for public intoxication will only occur if the person is engaging in conduct "likely to be offensive or to cause inconvenience, annoyance, or alarm to persons of ordinary sensibilities."[127]

5.4.3.3 Other Public Order Provisions

Loitering,[128] obstruction of highways and other public places,[129] disrupting lawful meetings or processions,[130] desecration, theft, or sale of venerated objects[131] and vagrancy[132] are related public offenses of interest to the security professional. When one considers the homeless figures on the nation's streets, does vagrancy seem an enforceable statute? Ponder Wisconsin's vagrancy language:

> 947.02. Vagrancy.
> Any of the following are vagrants and are guilty of a Class C misdemeanor:
> (1) A person, with the physical ability to work, who is without lawful means of support and does not seek employment; or
> (2) A prostitute who loiters on the streets or in a place where intoxicating liquors are sold, or a person who, in public, solicits another to commit a crime against sexual morality; or
> (3) A person known to be a professional gambler or known as a frequenter of gambling places or who derives part of his or her support from begging or as a fortune teller or similar impostor.[133]

Critics of vagrancy statutes comment on the imprecision and vagaries of language employed. Civil libertarians bristle at language that seeks to measure whether a person looks employed or not, or whether one appears not to have a livelihood. Is it better that vagrants and other undesirables simply lay on the streets? Or does it make sense to round up the displaced for social service processing? Tension exists between those who urge decriminalization of the homeless or vagrancy statutes and those who see the loitering as a nuisance and trespass. As the public police system further transfers public order functions, private security will have to increasingly deal with these sorts of social pathology.

5.5 Criminal Culpability under the Federal Civil Rights Acts

While security operatives may directly act in a criminal manner, or either aid or abet others, or even neglect duties and responsibilities resulting in liability based upon omission, their particular actions, under diverse statutory and codified laws, may give rise to criminal culpability. In the area of the federal Civil Rights Act, the prosecutorial authority has the latitude to charge a criminal action. While the majority of litigation and actions under 42 U.S.C. § 1983 have been, and continue to be, civil in design and scope, Congress has enacted legislation that attaches criminal liability for persons or other legal entities acting under color of state law, ordinance, or regulation who are

a. Willfully depriving any inhabitant of a state of any right, privilege or immunity protected by the Constitution or the Laws of the United States, or

b. Willfully subjecting any inhabitant to a different punishment or penalty because such an inhabitant is an alien because of his race or color, then as prescribed for the punishment of citizen[134]

The body of case law and literature relative to section 1983 is now legion in size. Visit: http://corporate.findlaw.com/litigation-disputes/typical-section-1983-claims.html

---

While criminal liability can be grounded within the statutory framework, advocates of this liability must still pass the statutory and judicial threshold question, that is, whether or not the processes and functions of private justice can be arguably performed under "color of state law." As discussed previously, either the state action or the color of state law advocacy requires evidential proof of private action metamorphosing into a public duty or function or of governmental authorities depriving a citizen of certain constitutional rights. Criminal liability can also be imposed under the federal Civil Rights Act if, and when, a victim of illegal state action shows that the injurious action was the product of a conspiracy. The relevant provision as to conspiracy states:

1. A conspiracy by two or more persons;
2. For the purposes of injuring, oppressing, threatening or intimidating any citizen in the free exercise or enjoyment or past exercise of any right or privilege secured to him by the Constitution or laws of the United States.[135]

Various factual scenarios illustrate this statutory application:

■ Public police and private security personnel are engaged in a joint venture, cooperative effort, or alliance;

■ Public police solicit, request, entice, or encourage the activity of private law enforcement interests, knowing full well their activity is not legally sound; and

■ State officials, administrative heads, and agency policy makers hire, contract, or otherwise utilize the services of a private entity they know will make possible constitutional violations.

In sum, the pressing crossover question in the world of private security still remains whether or not private justice agents can be held to public scrutiny. The U.S. Supreme Court argued in *Evans v. Newton*[136] that:

Conduct that is formally "private" may become so entwined with governmental policies or so impregnated with governmental character as to become subject to the constitutional limitations placed upon state action ... when private individuals or groups are endowed by the State with powers or functions governmental in nature, they become agencies and instrumentalities of the State and subject to its Constitutional limitations.[137]

Contemporary judicial reasoning has yet to reach the point where private security practices are synonymous with public activities, though litigators are not shy about alleging this claim. Courts are less willing to entertain the argument as a basis for a case in chief or as argument for remedy. This judicial reticence has precipitated often scathing criticisms by practitioners and academics. The *Hofstra Law Review*, when assessing the constitutional ramifications of merchant detention statutes, concludes:

> By judicial decision and statute a "super police" has been created. The merchant detective has the same privileges as public law enforcement agents without the same restraints to neutralize the effect of a violation of constitutionally protected rights. The merchant detective is treated as a private citizen for purposes of defining his constitutional liabilities and yet he is granted tort immunity as though he were a public law enforcement agent.[138]

While this argument may have intellectual support, it generally disregards the practical realities of operating retail or other commercial establishments. Retail establishments and industrial units—whose chief justice function is asset protection—would find most public policing protections incompatible with their fundamental mission.

Various factual scenarios illustrate this statutory application:

- Public police and private security personnel are engaged in a joint venture, cooperative effort, or alliance;
- Public police solicit, request, entice, or encourage the activity of private law enforcement interests, knowing full well their activity is not legally sound;
- State officials, administrative heads, and agency policymakers hire, contract, or otherwise utilize the services of a private entity they know will make possible constitutional violations.

In sum, the pressing crossover question in the world of private security still remains whether or not private justice agents can be held to public scrutiny.

The detection and prevention of theft and shoplifting tends to be objective and performance based. However, there are overzealous methods and targeted groups that have borne the brunt of theft prevention at the retail and commercial level.[139] Hence, the Civil Rights Acts have been employed to bolster these arguments.

While criminal liability can be grounded within the statutory framework, advocates of this liability must still pass the statutory and judicial threshold question, that is, whether or not the processes and functions of private justice can be arguably performed under "color of state law." As discussed previously, either the state action or the color of state law advocacy requires evidential proof of private action metamorphosing into a public duty or function or of governmental authorities depriving a citizen of certain constitutional rights.

Criminal liability can also be imposed under the federal Civil Rights Act if, and when, a victim of illegal state action shows that the injurious action was the product of a conspiracy. The relevant provision as to conspiracy states:

1. A conspiracy by two or more persons;
2. For the purposes of injuring, oppressing, threatening or intimidating any citizen in the free exercise or enjoyment or past exercise of any right or privilege secured to him by the Constitution or laws of the United States.[140]

Various factual scenarios illustrate this statutory application:

- Public police and private security personnel are engaged in a joint venture, cooperative effort, or alliance;
- Public police solicit, request, entice, or encourage the activity of private law enforcement interests, knowing full well their activity is not legally sound; and
- State officials, administrative heads, and agency policy makers hire, contract, or otherwise utilize the services of a private entity they know will make possible constitutional violations.

In sum, the pressing crossover question in the world of private security still remains whether or not private justice agents can be held to public scrutiny.

5.6 Criminal Culpability and the Private Security Regulatory Process

Since the private security industry is subject to the regulatory oversight of governmental authorities, there is always a chance that criminal culpability will rest or reside in the failure to adhere to particular guidelines.

A repetitive theme originating with the RAND Study,[141] through the National Advisory Committee on Criminal Justice Standards and Goals, to the recent *Hallcrest Report II*, is the need for regulations, standards, education and training, and qualifications criteria for the security industry.[142] The National Advisory Committee on Criminal Justice Standards and Goals, citing the enormous power wielded by the private security industry, urges, through the adoption of a National Code of Ethics, professional guidelines (see Figure 5.13).

The National Advisory Committee further relates:

> Incidents of excessive force, false arrests and detainment, illegal search and seizure, impersonation of a public officer, trespass, invasion of privacy, and dishonest or unethical business practices not only undermine confidence and trust in the private security industry, but also infringe upon individual rights.[143]

In short, the commission recognizes that part of the security professional's measure has to be the avoidance of every criterion of crime and criminality. The regulatory and administrative processes involving licensure infer a police power to punish infractions of the promulgated standards.

A recent Arizona case, *Landi v. Arkules*,[144] delivers some eloquent thoughts on why licensing and regulation are crucial policy considerations. In declaring a New York security firm's contracts illegal due to a lack of compliance, the court related firmly:

> The statute imposes specific duties on licensees with respect to the confidentiality and accuracy of information and the disclosure of investigative reports to the client.[145] A license may be suspended or revoked for a wide range of misconduct, including acts of dishonesty or fraud, aiding the violation of court order, or soliciting business for an attorney.[146]

Ethical code for managers.

To recognize that our principal responsibilities are, in the service of our organizations and clients, to protect life and property as well as to prevent and reduce crime against our business, industry, or other organizations and institutions; and in the public interest, to uphold the law and to respect the constitutional rights of all persons.

To be guided by a sense of integrity, honor, justice, and morality in the conduct of business; in all personnel matters; in relationships with government agencies, clients, and employers; and in responsibilities to the general public.

To strive faithfully to render security services of the highest quality and to work continuously to improve our knowledge and skills and thereby improve the overall effectiveness of private security.

To uphold the trust of our employers, our clients, and the public by performing our functions within the law, not ordering or condoning violations of law; and ensuring that our security personnel conduct their assigned duties lawfully and with proper regard for the rights of others.

To respect the reputation and practice of others in private security, but to expose to the proper authorities any conduct that is unethical or unlawful.

To apply uniform and equitable standards of employment in recruiting and selecting personnel regardless of race, creed, color, sex, or age, and in providing salaries commensurate with job responsibilities and with training, education, and experience.

To cooperate with recognized and responsible law enforcement and other criminal justice agencies; to comply with security licensing and registration laws and other statutory requirements that pertain to our business.

To respect and protect the confidential and privileged information of employers and clients beyond the term of our employment, except where their interests are contrary to law or to this Code of Ethics.

To maintain a professional posture in all business relationships with employers and clients, with others in the private security field, and with members of other professions; and to insist that our personnel adhere to the highest standards of professional conduct.

To encourage the professional advancement of our personnel by assisting them to acquire appropriate security knowledge, education, and training.

Figure 5.13   Manager's code of ethics.

The Legislature's concern for the protection of the public from unscrupulous and unqualified investigators is woven into the legislative or regulatory intent of these controls. This concern for the public's protection precludes enforcement of an unlicensed investigator's fee contract.[147] The courts will not participate in a party's circumvention of the legislative goal by enforcing a fee contract to provide regulated services without a license.[148]

Hence, security professionals may incur criminal liability for failure to adhere to regulatory guidelines. States have not been shy about this sort of regulation. A California statute prohibiting the licensure of any investigator or armed guard who has a criminal conviction in the last 10 years was upheld.[149] A Connecticut statute for criminal conviction was deemed overly broad.[150]

As states and other governmental entities legislate standards of conduct and requirements criteria in the field of private security, the industry itself has not been averse to challenging the legitimacy of the regulations. Antagonists to the regulatory process urge a more privatized, free-market view and balk at efforts to impose criminal or civil liability for failure to meet or exceed statutory, administrative or regulatory rules and guidelines.[151] Some fascinating legal arguments have been forged by those challenging the right of government to regulate the security industry. The argument that state law preempts any local control of the security industry has failed on multiple grounds.[152] Other advocates attack regulation by alleged defects in due process.[153] Litigation has successfully challenged the regulatory process when ordinances, administrative rules, regulations, or other laws do not provide adequate notice, are discriminatory in design, or have other constitutional defects.[154] A legal action revoking an investigator's license was overturned despite a general investigator's criminal conviction since he merely pled nolo contendere rather than "guilty."[155] A plea in this manner is no admission, the court concluded, and thus failed the evidentiary burden of actual criminal commission. Other challenges to the validity and enforceability of the regulatory process in private security include the argument that such statutory oversight violates equal protection of law,[156] or that the regulatory process is an illegal and unfounded exercise of police power,[157] or an unlawful delegation of power.[158] As a general observation, these challenges are largely ineffective.[159]

Given the minimal intrusion inflicted upon the security industry by governmental entities, and the industry's own professional call for improvement of standards, litigation challenging the regulatory process should be used only in exceptional circumstances. The repercussions and ramifications for failure to adhere to the minimal regulatory standards are varied, ranging from fines, revocation, and suspension to actual imprisonment.[160]

Regulations, so says the State of Georgia, are in the "public interest." See: http://sos.ga.gov/index.php/licensing/plb/42

In *State v. Guardsmark*,[161] the court rejected the security defendant's contention that denial of licenses tended to be an arbitrary exercise. The court, accepting the statute's stringent licensure requirements and recognizing the need for rigorous investigation of applicants and testing, found no basis to challenge.[162] In *Guardsmark*, the crime cited under Illinois law was "engaging in business as a detective agency without a license."[163] Similarly, *State v. Bennett*[164] held the defendant liable in a prosecution for "acting as a detective without first having obtained a license."[165]

The fact that a security person, business, or industrial concern is initially licensed and granted a certificate of authority to operate does not ensure absolute tenure. Governmental control and administrative review of security personnel and agencies are ongoing processes. Revocation of a license or a certificate to operate has been regularly upheld in appellate reasoning. In *Taylor v. Bureau of Private Investigators and Adjustors*,[166] suspension of legal authority and license to operate as a private detective was upheld since the evidence clearly sustained a finding that the investigators perpetrated an unlawful entry into a domicile. The private detective's assertion that the regulation was constitutionally void because of its vagueness was rejected outright.[167]

License to operate or perform the duties indigenous to the security industry has also been revoked or suspended due to acts committed that involved moral turpitude. In *Otash v. Bureau of Private Investigators and Adjustors*,[168] the court tackled the definition of moral turpitude and explained that it could be best described as a conduct that was contrary to justice, honesty, and morality. Inclusive within the term would be fraudulent behavior with which the investigator was charged.[169] In *ABC Security Service, Inc. v. Miller*,[170] a plea of *nolo contendere* to a tax evasion charge was held as sufficient basis for revocation and suspension.[171] An opposite conclusion was reached in *Kelly v. Tulsa*,[172] in which an offense of public drunkenness was found generally not to be an act of moral turpitude that would result in a denial of application, loss, suspension, or revocation of licensing rights.

In summary, it behooves the security industry to stick to the letter of regulatory process. Failure to do so can result in actual criminal convictions or a temporary or permanent intrusion on the right to operate.

5.7 Criminal Culpability and Private Security Employers and Business Entities

Both corporations and individuals in the security industry may be convicted of actual criminal code violations, though in the former instance, this is an exceedingly rare event. This liability can attach either in an individual or vicarious sense. By *vicarious*, we mean that the employer is responsible for the conduct of their employees. Most jurisdictions, however, do impose a higher burden of proof in a case of vicarious liability since "the prosecution must prove that the employer knowingly and intentionally aided, advised or encouraged the employee's criminal conduct."[173]

Visit the *Yale Law Journal*'s recent treatment of corporate criminal liability in the Blackwater Security Firm case, see: http://www.yalelawjournal.org/comment/beating-blackwater-using-domestic-legislation-to-enforce-the-international-code-of-conduct-for-private-military-companies

---

Other legal issues make difficult a prosecution against corporations for criminal behavior. A broad critique corporate criminal intent can be summarized as follows:

> How can a corporation formulate specific or general intent, the mens rea necessary for a criminal conviction?
>
> More particularly, in violent acts of criminality such as rape, murder or robbery, to whom or on whose authority within the corporate structure would the responsibility lie?

Both queries pose difficult legal dilemmas.[174]

For a horrid example of security firm, corporate irresponsibility, visit: http://www.tampabay.com/news/publicsafety/crime/tampa-officials-reviewing-contract-with-security-firm-after-garage-shooting/2284967

While it is common to hear a sort of class warfare critique of the corporate heads of state, this type of "them versus us" will simply not do. To be culpable requires knowledge of the crime and its purpose. In the evolving analysis of corporate crime, a trend toward corporate responsibility has emerged.[175] Does a corporate officer and director who has actual knowledge of criminal behavior on the part of subordinates within the corporation bear some level of responsibility? Is a corporation responsible, as principal, for the acts of its agents both civilly and criminally? While "officers may be held criminally responsible on the presumption that it authorized the illegal acts"[176] that judgment will depend on the facts and circumstances of each case.[177]

There are other rationales for imposing criminal culpability on the corporate officers and directors. Criminal charges are regularly brought forth and eventual liability sometimes imposed for failure to uphold the rules and regulatory standards promulgated by government agencies, such as

- Occupational Health and Safety Act (OSHA)[178]
- The Food and Drug Administration (FDA)

- National Labor Relations Board (NLRB)
- Environmental Protection Act (EPA)
- Homeland Security Administration (HSA)
- National Transportation Safety Board (NTSB)

Government agencies are empowered to charge and assess criminal penalties and fines. OSHA is the classic federal agency with these sweeping powers.

Recent data demonstrates that OSHA is not shy about bringing for the criminal prosecutions. See: http://www.oshalawupdate.com/2012/12/18/osha-criminal-referrals-on-the-rise/

Other common corporate areas of criminality in business crime include securities fraud, antitrust activity, bank fraud, tax evasion, violations against the *Racketeer Influenced and Corrupt Organizations Act (RICO),* and acts involving bribery, international travel, and business practices.[179] Finding corporations criminally responsible for particular actions is not the insurmountable task it once was.

5.8 Criminal Culpability and Private Security Personnel

The nature and functions of security practice provides a ripe ground for violations of the criminal law. Hence, individual criminal cases, which tie factual behavior of the security operatives with specific elements in the wide array of federal, state and local crimes, are a matter of constant concern. There are repetitive forms of criminality witnessed in the private security industry. Review and evaluate the common scenarios below:

1. *Assault*[180]
   a. A security officer can easily create an apprehension of bodily harm in a detention case.[181]
   b. A security officer, in a crowd control situation, threatens, by a gesture, a private citizen.[182]
   c. Industrial security agent, protecting the physical perimeter, unjustly accosts a person with license and privilege to be on the premises.[183]
2. *Battery*[184]
   a. Security officer in a retail detention case offensively touches a suspected shoplifter.[185]
   b. Security officer uses excessive force in the restraint of an unruly participant in a demonstration.[186]
   c. Security officer utilizes excessive force to affect an arrest in an industrial location.[187]
3. *False arrest or imprisonment*[188]
   a. Security officer, in a jurisdiction with no merchant's privilege, arrests without probable cause, and motivated by malice toward a particular suspect who is eventually acquitted.
   b. Security officer restrains and detains a suspected shoplifter without probable cause.
   c. Security officer restrains and detains a suspected intruder on an industrial premises and does so in an abusive and physically harmful manner.

See how a security guard was held responsible under sexual assault statutes at: http://www.chicagotribune.com/news/local/breaking/ct-cps-guard-teen-sex-assault-charges-20160211-story.html

4. *Unlawful use of weapons*
    a. A security officer is not properly trained in the usage of weapons.
    b. A security officer does not possess a license.
    c. A security officer inappropriately utilizes weaponry best described as excessive force.
5. *Theft*[189]
    a. Security personnel steal, take by deception, fraud, or through simple unlawful acquisition property from their place of employment.
    b. Security personnel aid and abet outside individuals in conducting an inside theft.
6. *Manslaughter*[190]
    a. Security officer negligently drives an auto, which, in turn, kills either a pursued suspect or an innocent bystander.
    b. The security officer handles his or her weaponry in a grossly negligent way, thereby causing a fatality.
    c. The security officer reacts with excessive force in a property protection case causing the death of the suspect or an innocent bystander.
    d. Security officer in hot pursuit shoots a fleeing felon and injures an innocent bystander.[191]
7. *Murder*[192]
    a. A security officer kills another without proper investigation and with an extraordinary and wanton disregard of human life (see Figure 5.14).[193]
    b. Private military mercenaries kill without justification or right in a war zone.[194]
8. *Misprision*
    a. Security officer fails to report crimes or take actions necessary to prevent it.
    b. Security personnel purposely conceal a major capital offense.
9. *Compounding*
    a. Security officer makes a deal with a suspect in a theft or other criminal case for an agreement not to pursue the investigation.
    b. Security officer decides not to cooperate, for internal or economic reasons, with the prosecutorial staff assigned to the case.
10. *Solicitation*[195]
    a. Security officers or investigators entice, encourage, or solicit others to perform criminal acts.
    b. The security officer or private investigator encourages, solicits, or induces another to commit an illegal act for the purpose of acquiring a specific piece of evidence.
    c. Security investigator devises a plan that will ensnare a criminal; however, such tactics or plan may be construed as a case of entrapment.[196]
11. *Criminal conspiracy*[197]
    a. The security agent, investigator, or officer enters into an agreement with one or more individuals for the purposes of committing a criminal act such as internal theft.
    b. Security officer engages in conduct or in concert with other business entities which seek to illegally eavesdrop and investigate the personal backgrounds of prospective job applicants.
    c. The security company, in concert with other business interests, performs polygraph examination on prospective applicants in direct violation of state law.
    d. The security professional performs an overt act toward the commission of any crime which assists the principle perpetrator in effecting a successful criminal plan.[198] The range and extent of individual security crime is only limited by the roles, tasks, and duties undertaken by the industry's participants.

Department of Justice
U.S. Attorney's Office
Eastern District of Virginia

FOR IMMEDIATE RELEASE
Monday, December 5, 2016

Newport News Gangster Convicted of Racketeering and Murder Charges

NEWPORT NEWS, Va. – Michael Hopson, 39, of Newport News, was convicted today by a federal jury on charges of racketeering conspiracy, including acts of murder, attempted murder, robbery, obstruction of justice, murder in aid of racketeering, conspiracy and attempted murder in aid of racketeering, and other charges.

According to court records and evidence presented at trial, Hopson, (aka "Hop" aka "Big Homie") was the founding member and leader of the P-Stones, also referred to as the P-Stone Bloods and Cobra Stones, that operate primarily in the Denbigh area of Newport News. The P-Stones engage in violent crimes including murders, illegal drug trafficking, obstruction of justice and robberies that often target narcotics dealers and use stolen currency and inventory to purchase firearms and fund gang members' court dues.

According to evidence presented at trial, as the leader, Hopson planned, directed and participated in recruitment of members, including minors; collected monthly gang dues; carried out and ordered violations; ordered and presided over meetings; and organized other firearm and marijuana distribution. Hopson also served as a security officer at Denbigh High School, in which he used his security officer position to further the Black P-Stones gang by recruiting minors and selling narcotics to high school students.

According to evidence presented at trial, Hopson personally ordered multiple shootings and murders between October 2007 and June 2009, including:

- On Oct. 31, 2007, Hopson ordered P-Stone members to murder A.J., a member of the rival Thugs Relations street gang. At Hopson's direction, the P-Stones members attempted to lure A.J. from the home while armed. A.J. did not come out of the house and the P-Stone members left.
- On Nov. 6, 2007, a P-Stone, acting on Hopson's orders lured E.S., a 17-year-old P-Stone member, to a location in Newport News to kill him. Hopson had previously given him the "green light" for the killing of E.S. for his relations with Thug Relations. Once E.S. arrived he was shot and killed, and Hopson rewarded the P-Stone member with a promotion.
- On Dec. 10, 2008 Hopson authorized the murder of J.W., a Crip who was disrespectful to members of the P-Stones. Acting on those orders, two P-Stone members went to the home of J.W. and fired multiple rounds into the home. J.W.'s father, who was sitting in the living room when the assault occurred, was hit with debris from the bullet shrapnel and suffered injury to his eye.
- On March 9, 2009, Hopson ordered the murder of two members of 10-1 Mafia Crips, rivals of the P-Stones, for the beating of a P-Stone member. Acting on Hopson's orders, two P-Stone members shot multiple times into the home of the two 10-1 Mafia Crips.
- On April 17, 2009, Hopson ordered two P-Stones to fire multiple rounds into a home he knew to be occupied because the individuals inside the home were disrespectful to him.
- On June 12, 2009, Hopson ordered the murder of A.J., a Thug Relations member who was responsible for the murder of a P-Stone member. A P-Stone member acting on Hopson's orders shot and wounded A.J.

Hopson faces a mandatory penalty of life in prison when sentenced on March 3, 2017. The maximum statutory sentence of life is prescribed by Congress and is provided here for informational purposes, as the sentencing of the defendant will be determined by the court based on the statutory penalty, the advisory Sentencing Guidelines and other statutory factors.

Figure 5.14 A school security and safety officer was gangster, racketeer, and a murderer.
(Continued)

Dana J. Boente, U.S. Attorney for the Eastern District of Virginia; Assistant Attorney General Leslie R. Caldwell of the Justice Department's Criminal Division; and Special Agent in Charge Martin W. Culbreth of the Federal Bureau of Investigation's Norfolk, Virgina, Field Office made the announcement after the verdict was accepted by U.S. District Judge Arenda L. Wright Allen. Assistant U.S. Attorney Eric M. Hurt and Trial Attorney Marianne Shelvey of the Organized Crime and Gang Section in the Justice Department's Criminal Division prosecuted the case. FBI's Safe Streets Peninsula Task Force investigated the case, with the assistance of the Newport News Police Department and the James City County Police Department.

A copy of this press release may be found on the website of the U.S. Attorney's Office for the Eastern District of Virginia. Related court documents and information may be found on the website of the District Court for the Eastern District of Virginia or on PACER by searching for **Case No. 4:13-cr-96.**

USAO - Virginia, Eastern
Topic:
Violent Crime

Updated December 5, 2016

Figure 5.14 (Continued) A school security and safety officer was gangster, racketeer, and a murderer.

5.9 Classification of Criminal Offenses and Related Penalties

Common law and statutory guidelines also characterize criminal behavior into various classifications or types. Those classifications generally include

- Felony[199]
- Misdemeanor[200]
- Summary offense[201]
- Treason[202] and other infamous crimes

The security industry's concern will be the detection and apprehension of misdemeanants and felons whose crimes comprise the basic menu of criminal charges including assault, battery, theft and related property offenses, sexual offenses, intimidation and harassment, and white collar crime including forgery, credit card fraud, and the like. Treason and other infamous crimes emerge in cases of international terrorism and homeland security, and given the rising influence of private sector justice in the global war on terror, they should give rise to more involvement. The entire airspace industry is dependent upon personnel not only trained in security issues, but also the criminal law issues that surround breaches of security at airport facilities. Shoplifting and retail theft may be designated a "summary" offense. Summary offenses generally consist of public order violations, including failure to pay parking tickets, creating a temporary obstruction in a public place, public intoxication, or other offenses of a less serious nature that are rarely punishable by a term of imprisonment,[203] but are regularly witnessed by the security professional, like lower-level shoplifting. At common law, the designation of an act as a felony constituted an extremely serious offense. Penal and correctional response to felony behavior included the death penalty and forfeiture of all lands, goods, and other personal property. Generally, a felony was any capital offense, namely murder, manslaughter, rape, sodomy, robbery, larceny, arson, burglary, mayhem, and other violent conduct.[204] An alternative way of defining a felony was the severity of its corresponding punishment. Felony was defined "to mean offenses for which the offender, on conviction, may be punished by death or imprisonment in the state prison or penitentiary; but in the absence of such statute the word is used to designate such serious offenses as were formally punishable by death, or by forfeiture of the lands or goods of the offender."[205] In other words, a crime could be a felony or a misdemeanor not because of its severity or subsequent impact but due to the term of incarceration. Modern criminal analysis shows a confused and perplexing legislative decision making on the nature of a felony and a misdemeanor.

The President's Commission on Law Enforcement and Administration of Justice, in its *Task Force Report on the Courts*, relates:

> A study of the Oregon Penal Code revealed that 1,413 criminal statutes contained a total of 466 different types and lengths of sentences. The absence of legislative attention to the whole range of penalties may also be demonstrated by comparisons between certain offenses. A recent study of the Colorado Statutes disclosed that a person convicted of a first degree murder must serve ten (10) years before becoming eligible for parole, while a person convicted of a lesser degree of the same offense must serve at least fifteen (15) years; destruction of a house with fire is punishable by a maximum twenty (20) years imprisonment, but destruction of a house with explosives carries a ten (10) year maximum. In California, an offender who breaks into an automobile to steal the contents of the glove compartment is subject to a fifteen (15) year maximum sentence but if he stole the car itself, he would face a maximum ten (10) year term.
>
> Although each offense must be defined in a separate statutory provision, the number and variety of sentencing distinctions which result when legislatures prescribe a separate penalty for each offense are among the main causes of the anarchy in sentencing that is so widely deplored.[206]

In defining the term misdemeanor, legislatures and jurists use a process of elimination holding that an offense not deemed a felony is, deductively, a misdemeanor. Usually misdemeanors are offenses punishable by less than a year's incarceration. The popular perception that misdemeanors are not serious offenses may be a faulty impression. Criminal codes surprise even the most seasoned justice practitioner, who frequently finds little logic in an offense's definition, resulting classification, and corresponding punishment. For examples of this confusion, review selected state code provisions on "sexual offenses."[207]

5.10 Private Security and Defenses to Criminal Acts

An allegation of criminal activity can always be properly met with legitimate criminal defenses. Private security operatives are no different than any other citizen and entitled to personal integrity and safety by the use of self-defense and at the same time, permitted to protect their property interests with reasonable and proportionate force and if in an executive protection position, and allowed to protect and defend the third party as if self. A general overview of these principles is contained in the next few sections.

5.10.1 The Influence of Self-Help/Self-Protection

The idea of self-help and self-protection is as old as Western tradition itself. Since the time of the Romans and the Greeks, God's Chosen people, the Jews, and other early societies, there has always been a recognition that protection of self and property is a matter of right. Roman law, such as the *Code of Justinian* or the *Corpus Juris Civilis*, could not be more unequivocal about the right of individuals to rightfully defend oneself. The *Code* notes, in part:

> We grant to all persons the unrestricted power to defend themselves (*liberam resistendi cunctis tribuimus facultatem*), so that it is proper to subject anyone, whether a private person or a soldier, who trespasses upon fields at night in search of plunder, or lays by busy roads plotting to assault passers-by, to immediate punishment in accordance with the authority granted to all (*permissa cuicumque licentia dignus ilico supplicio subiugetur*). Let him suffer the death which he threatened and incur that which he intended.[208]

Most religious groups rely upon dogmatic teaching or texts, such as the Koran or the Bible, for instruction on the rights and limitations of self-help and self-defense. The Book of Exodus, by way of illustration, lays out a refined systematic defense of property rights when it notes:

> 1 If a man steals an ox or a sheep, and kills it or sells it, he shall repay five oxen for an ox, and four sheep for a sheep. 2 If a thief is found breaking in and is struck so that he dies, there shall be no bloodguilt for him, 3 but if the sun has risen on him, there shall be bloodguilt for him. He shall surely pay. If he has nothing, then he shall be sold for his theft. 4 If the stolen beast is found alive in his possession, whether it is an ox or a donkey or a sheep, he shall pay double. 5 If a man causes a field or vineyard to be grazed over, or lets his beast loose and it feeds in another man's field, he shall make restitution from the best in his own field and in his own vineyard. 6 If fire breaks out and catches in thorns so that the stacked grain or the standing grain or the field is consumed, he who started the fire shall make full restitution. 7 If a man gives to his neighbor money or goods to keep safe, and it is stolen from the man's house, then, if the thief is found, he shall pay double. 8 If the thief is not found, the owner of the house shall come near to God to show whether or not he has put his hand to his neighbor's property. 9 For every breach of trust, whether it is for an ox, for a donkey, for a sheep, for a cloak, or for any kind of lost thing, of which one says, "This is it," the case of both parties shall come before God. The one whom God condemns shall pay double to his neighbor. 10 If a man gives to his neighbor a donkey or an ox or a sheep or any beast to keep safe, and it dies or is injured or is driven away, without anyone seeing it, 11 an oath by the Lord shall be between them both to see whether or not he has put his hand to his neighbor's property. The owner shall accept the oath, and he shall not make restitution. 12 But if it is stolen from him, he shall make restitution to its owner. 13 If it is torn by beasts, let him bring it as evidence. He shall not make restitution for what has been torn. 14 If a man borrows anything of his neighbor, and it is injured or dies, the owner not being with it, he shall make full restitution. 15 If the owner was with it, he shall not make restitution; if it was hired, it came for its hiring fee.[209]

Thus, cultural and common law traditions, as well as religious and spiritual standards, provide a strong basis for the defense of person and things.

5.10.2 Personal Self-Defense

Much activity in the security industry is geared toward the protection of the person both as to self and third parties.[210] Indeed one of the fastest growing sectors in the industry regards celebrity and executive and industry leaders. As a result of this orientation, security professionals must understand defense tactics. If one unreasonably responds in a protection situation, allegations of criminal conduct may be in the offing. For the defender using excessive force, an assault or even a murder or manslaughter may be charged. In protection of person cases, "the obvious human instinct to meet physical aggression with counter force ... [must be balanced with] ... desirability in a civilized society ... of encouraging the resolution of disputes through peaceful means."[211] Since the preservation instinct is strong, conduct delineations regarding reasonable and justifiable force are critical policy questions. The Hallcrest Report I[212] fully delved into practitioner perception regarding the appropriate use of force as outlined in Table 5.2.[213]

5.10.2.1 Use of Force in Self-Protection

Imperative in security training is the topic of force in the application of self-defense principles, excessive force, and self-protection.[214] Professional bodies and groups, associations and the internal policies of agencies and organizations, all seek a clear and consistent policy on

Table 5.2 Use of Force Reported by Private Security Employees

	(N = 110) Proprietary	(N = 78) Contractual	
		Guard	Alarm
Incidence of Use			
In self-defense	54%	13%	53%
Evict a trespasser	39%	15%	12%
Deal with vandalism	18%	10%	44%
Prevent an assault	39%	8%	27%
Carry out a lawful search	37%	6%	31%
Detain someone	47%	12%	50%
Arrest someone	56%	4%	46%
		Guard and Alarm	
Expectations of Use			
Protect yourself	96%	92%	
Protect company property	43%	28%	
Detain someone	40%	18%	
Arrest someone	51%	9%	
Search someone		6%	

the defense of self. Think tanks such as the American Law Institute, by and through its *Model Penal Code* (MPC), propose a well-respected statutory design for the party acting in self-defense.[215]

1. Use of Force Justifiable for Protection of the Person. Subject to the provision of this Section and of Section 3.09 the use of force upon or toward another person is justifiable when the actor believes that such force is immediately necessary for the purpose of protecting himself against the use of unlawful force by such other person on the present occasion.
2. Limitations on Justifying Necessity for Use of Force.
   a. The use of force is not justifiable under this Section:
      i. To resist an arrest which the actor knows is being made by a peace officer, although the arrest is unlawful....
   b. The use of deadly force is not justifiable under this Section unless the actor believes that such force is necessary to protect himself against death, serious bodily harm, kidnapping or sexual intercourse compelled by force or threat, nor is it justifiable if:
      i. The actor, with the purpose of causing death or serious bodily harm, provoked the use of force against himself in the same encounter; or
      ii. The actor knows that he can avoid the necessity of using such force with complete safety by retreating or by surrendering possession of a thing to a person asserting a claim of right thereto, or by complying with a demand that he abstain from any action which he has no duty to take, except that:
         A. The actor is not obliged to retreat from his dwelling or his place of work unless he was the initial aggressor ...
         B. A public officer justified in using force in the performance of his duties, or a person justified in using force in his assistance or a person justified in using force in making an arrest or preventing an escape is not obliged to desist from efforts to perform such duty, effect such arrest or prevent such escape.[216]

Readily apparent from a first read of the MPC are the explicit restrictions on the use of force,[217] compelling the employer of force to think about its potential ramifications and limitations. First, force is not a permissible activity against law enforcement officers, though a few states accept extraordinary situations. Second, force is only tolerated in environments of heightened necessity or immediate need, when a victim of physical harm can objectively point to real and immediate bodily harm. Third, force is only to be employed in situations where a reasonably prudent person believes that he or she could suffer serious bodily harm, death, kidnapping, or sexual assault. "The requirement that the defendant be operating under the reasonable belief that he is in imminent danger of death, great bodily harm, or some felony, involve two elements: (1) the defendant in fact must have acted out of an honest, bona fide belief that he was in imminent danger and (2) the belief must be reasonable in light of the facts as they appeared to him."[218]

Security professionals, during the typical career, will likely confront the tension between the defense of self and the parameters for the use of force. Some cases will be easier than others. Violent aggression by suspects can be met by some level of proportionate response. Indeed, a slingshot should not be met with a rapid-fire weapon. The potential for abuse and disproportionate reaction is a natural risk in private policing for, as the Hallcrest Report I notes, "one inescapable fact is that firearms tend to be used when they are carried."[219] The report further explains that firearms' training, proper care, and usage thereof in the security industry are often abysmal and frighteningly inadequate exercises.

Evaluate the Self-Defense Implications:

- A security investigator catches a thief in the act. The thief reaches into his side pocket. Before he could remove the object, the security official fired a weapon, inflicting a fatal injury. Would this be a case of excessive force in the protection of self?
- Security officer comes upon a crime scene and sees a juvenile, with stolen goods in hand, riding his bike from the scene of a crime. As the juvenile accelerates his bicycle, he directs the path of the bike toward the security officer. The officer, in order to protect his life, even though he has an easy retreat and an opportunity to move in another direction, inflicts a fatal injury on the juvenile. Is this a case of excessive force?

Figure 5.15   Self-defense implications fact patterns.

For a curious ruling, covering a bevy of legal problems, including the sufficiency of probable cause determinations in private police action, see *Abraham v. Raso*[220] where the court remarks:

> This Court recognizes that N.J.S.A. 2C:3-7 provides in pertinent part that the use of deadly force is justifiable where the officer reasonably believes that the crime for which the arrest is being made was homicide, kidnapping, certain enumerated sex offenses, arson, robbery, burglary of a dwelling, or an attempt to commit one of these crimes, and where the officer believes that there is an imminent threat of deadly force to a third party or that the use of such force is necessary to prevent an escape. It is unclear to this Court, however, that this statutory provision defines the entire universe of situations in which an officer is privileged to use deadly force in the sense that the use of such force will not expose her to civil liability.[221]

See Figure 5.15.

Which of these two cases is contrary to the *Model Penal Code's* demand that the force exerted by a defender be proportionate to that being exhibited by the aggressor? Which case relies upon the objective reality the actor believes to be true when in fact it may or may not be?

While not all cases are easily resolved in self-defense analysis, courts generally construe case and fact based on what an ordinary, reasonable reaction might be. In conjunction, the analysis looks to other factors such as alternative means of defense, proportionality, and equivalency of force used between actors and potentiality for actual harm that is significant rather than minor trifles. Self-defense cases usually weigh circumstances in light of the security professional's reasonable and rational beliefs that corroborate the defense reaction.

5.10.3 *Protection of Other Persons*

Another typical task in the security industry is the protection of other persons. Persons of social importance such as entertainers, politicians, business executives, religious leaders, and other highly public and visible individual personalities rely heavily on the expertise of the security industry. Executive protection has become a multimillion dollar business.

To learn more about the protocol of Executive Protection, visit: http://www.cisworldservices.org/employment/executive_protection.html

What level of protective action is permissible in the protection of other persons?[222] The *Model Penal Code* again provides some general guidance:

1. Subject to the provisions of this Section and of Section 3.09, the use of force upon or toward the person of another is justifiable to protect a third person when:
   a. The actor would be justified under 3.04 in using such force to protect himself against the injury he believes to be threatened to the person whom he seeks to protect; and
   b. Under the circumstances as the actor believes them to be, the person whom he seeks to protect would be justified in using such protective force; and
   c. The actor believes that his intervention is necessary for the protection of the other person.[223]

At its heart, the MPC provides for a transferal of authority in the protection of self. In essence, one is permitted to defend another person entrusted to their care or oversight, as if defending oneself. In private sector justice, we witness this reality with great regularity. Indeed, the entire infrastructure of executive protection needs these parameters to know what defense can be exerted. In short, one may exert such force as is proportionate, reasonable, and necessary as the party entrusting this authority would be capable of. What the defender believes is also crucial. However, belief should not be governed by hypersensitivity and delusion, and it must be the product of a reasoned, well-defined justification. There should be "a threat, actual or apparent to the use of deadly force against the defender. The threat must have been unlawful and immediate. The defender must have believed that he was in imminent peril of death or serious bodily harm and that his response was necessary to save himself. These beliefs must not only have been honestly entertained, but also objectively reasonable in light of the surrounding circumstances."[224] "In addition, one acting in defense of another, when in the dwelling or workplace of the other, is no more obliged to retreat than he would be if he were in his own dwelling or workplace."[225]

The issue of self-defense for both the public and private justice system is a recurring policy consideration for management. The Case Western Reserve University School of Law, in its publication, *Private Police Training Manual,*[226] admonishes the public and private sector to prepare for a further influx of this type of activity since:

1. Confrontations between the police and the public are far more frequent.
2. Violence against officers has increased greatly.
3. Public clamor has been toward nonlethal weapons in the hands of police.
4. Police study groups are researching alternatives to violence.[227]

Certainly, as community pressure increases and civil and criminal litigation continues its influence on police and security planning, the role of self-defense of the person and the parameters, obligations, and standards of self-defense will become increasingly relevant.

The role of self-defense is further influenced by the evolution of defense technology and occupational hardware. Review the list below as only a partial example of defensive equipment available to public and private police systems.

1. Revolvers
2. Shotguns
3. Rifles
4. Machine guns

5. Flair guns
6. Armored vehicles
7. Helmets
8. Bullet proof vests
9. Combat shields
10. Tear gas
11. Grenade launchers
12. Batons
13. Water cannon
14. Military vehicles

Such an arsenal is bound to generate "defense" questions for industry planners and leaders.

For recent case and damage commentary on guns and potential liability in the security industry see: http://www.aele.org/law/Digests/civil143.html

5.10.4 Defense of Property

The value placed on personal property versus human life is markedly distinguishable. Most American jurisdictions, supported by common law tradition and well-entrenched case law precedent, have always placed a heavy burden on those seeking to employ force in the protection of personal property. The *Model Penal Code* confirms that tradition.

1. Use of Force Justifiable for the Protection of Property. Subject to the provisions of this Section and of Section 3.09, the use of force upon or toward the person of another is justifiable when the actor believes that such force is immediately necessary:

   a. To prevent or terminate an unlawful entry or other trespass upon land or a trespass against or the unlawful carrying away of tangible, movable property, provided that such land or movable property is, or is believed by the actor to be, in his possession or in the possession of another person for whose protection he acts; or

   b. To effect an entry or reentry upon land or to retake tangible movable property, provided that the actor believes that he or the person by whose authority he acts or a person from whom he or such other persons derives title was unlawfully dispossessed provided further, that:

      i. The force is used immediately or on fresh pursuit after such dispossession; or

      ii. The actor believed that the person against whom the force is used has no claim of right to the possession of the property and, in the case of land, the circumstances, as the actor believes them to be, are of such urgency that it would be an exceptional hardship to postpone the entry or reentry until a court order is obtained.[228]

Common sense and legal tradition dictate that the degree of force permissible is dependent on the totality of circumstances. Factual situations that include entry into one's domicile or residence, of course, heighten the right to exert force.[229] Simple thefts or property disputes of tangible property such as a television, a garden tool, or some other item do not justify the exertion of life-threatening force. On its face, the MPC insists that if a party desires to resolve a property dispute without the assistance of public law enforcement, he or she must do so immediately, hotly pursuing the item in question.

The use of deadly force in defense of property is justifiable if there has been an entry into the actor's dwelling which the actor neither believes nor has reason to believe is lawful, and the actor neither believes nor has reason to believe can be terminated by force less than deadly force. Otherwise, the use of deadly force in defense of property is not justifiable unless the actor believes either that the person against whom the deadly force is used is trying to dispossess him of his dwelling without a claim of right, or that deadly force is necessary to prevent a commission of a felony in the dwelling.[230]

The most confused cases occur when a dwelling place is involved. Numerous jurisdictions have grappled with the crosscurrents that occur in this area. Recent history indicates a movement toward favoring the owner of a domicile in the protection of his own property.[231] In *State v. Miller*[232], a North Carolina Court held:

When a trespasser enters upon a man's premises, makes an assault upon his dwelling, an attempt to force an entrance into a house in a manner such as would lead a reasonably prudent man to believe that the intruder intends to commit a felony or inflict some serious personal injury upon the inmates, a lawful occupant of the dwelling may legally prevent the entry, even by the taking of the life of the intruder.[233]

Applying these general standards, which of the following fact patterns signify an excessive use of force? (see Figure 5.16).

The initial fact pattern outlined is the best case for an excessive force charge and the reason is twofold: first, the utilization of excessive force did not have a basis in fact or a belief, which would lead the security officer to conclude that he or she was in imminent danger of harm; second, the force exerted was in the protection of assets or personal property, something the law does not favor. Alternatively, protection of the gold ingots was the responsibility of the security officer. His fault is not in his intention but his methodology.

The factual scenario outlined in the shoplifting case is a regular happenstance. The force exerted was reasonable in light of the weaponry employed by the shoplifter. While the weapons chosen were not strictly identical, their similar capacity to kill supports the officer's reasonable judgment.

Fact Pattern 1:

A security officer, responsible for the protection of a warehouse, is responding to an alarm. As he approaches the point of detection, he is confronted by a man, middle-aged, who is attempting to pilfer some gold ingots from the storage container. The security official professionally and respectfully requests that the thief halt and return the object of the theft. Thief disregards the request, and the security officer inflicts two fatal bullet wounds.

Fact Pattern 2:

A security officer in a retail establishment confronts a shoplifter. Shoplifter alights from the store; officer gives pursuit. After a scuffle in the parking lot the suspect pulls a switchblade and threatens to seriously harm the officer. The officer pulls his weapon and fires two projectiles into the suspect's leg which cause a serious, but not critical, injury.

Figure 5.16 Excessive force fact patterns.

5.11 Private Security Industry and the Relevance of Criminal Process and Procedure

Criminal process covers a good deal of territory including the materials relating to arrest, search, and seizure already dealt with in Chapter 3. Criminal process and procedure weighs and evaluates how a defendant is treated from initial arrest to post-trial motions after conviction and appeal. Criminal process and procedure covers not what the defendant does but rather how we move that defendant through the various stages of the justice system from booking to incarceration. And whether the private security industry need be concerned about process has long been a subject of discussion. To be sure, process is part and parcel of constitutional analysis whether a defendant was arrested based on sufficient facts and probable cause and whether a defendant is entitled to Miranda warnings, counsel, and confrontation rights, to name just a few.

As a general rule, the constitutional protections inherent in these basic criminal processes simply do not apply to private sector police. The industry unreservedly defends its explicit exemption from constitutional oversight based on express language in the Constitution. The Constitution, especially as to the Bill of Rights mention governmental authority, state action, or federal action but never its applicability to private citizens. That has been the general undertow guiding the security industry for most of its life. The *Burdeau*[234] decision could not be more explicit about its exemption.

> The Fourth Amendment gives protection against unlawful searches and seizures....
> Its protection applies to governmental actions. Its origin and history clearly shows
> that it was intended as a restraint upon the activity of sovereign authority and was not
> intended to be a limitation upon other than governmental agencies.[235]

However, the abject absence of an industry application, or even a suggested industry standard, is a source of constant concern for critics of the security industry. Antagonists of the private security industry, especially academics and law school professorial types, have vociferously argued that its secondary status or minor league position, when compared to public police, will remain a constant reality until the industry itself adopts well-defined procedural guidelines.[236]

The National Advisory Committee on Criminal Justice Standards and Goals calls for research and corresponding guidelines in these procedural areas:

1. General private security functions:
   a. Arrests
   b. Detentions
   c. Use of force (including firearms)
   d. Impersonation of and confusion of public law enforcement officers and
   e. Directing and controlling traffic
2. Specific investigatory functions:
   a. Search and seizure of private property
   b. Wiretapping, bugging, and other forms of surveillance
   c. Access of private security personnel to public law enforcement information and procedures for the safeguarding of the information
   d. Obtaining information from private citizens and the safeguarding of information and
   e. Interrogation[237]

The National Advisory Committee and other authoritative bodies see continued resistance to procedural standards somewhat similar to the public model as a negative for the industry. In addition, procedural regularity will bring a substantial reduction in the industry's rate of criminal and civil liability. In time, the argument is that a more enlightened, professional industry will make fewer mistakes, although this claim may be more ambition than a realistic conclusion. The *Hallcrest Report* observes:

> There are some overwhelming public safety issues which justify public concern for adequate controls on private security. The serious consequences of errors in judgment or incompetence demand controls which insure the client and the general public of adequate safeguards. If government is to allow private security a larger role in providing some traditional police services, then it needs to insure that sufficient training and appropriate performance standards exist for the participating security programs—both proprietary and contractual.[238]

Private police are increasingly carrying out once entrenched public functions. Russell Colling, in his work *Hospital Security*, concludes that the differences between the investigative protocol of the public officer from the private officer are really one of form and mission, and indeed the missions are very complimentary.

It is techniques and varying purposes that differentiate the security investigation from that of a law enforcement agency. This is not to say that the security investigation always has a different focus. A police investigation is conducted basically for the purpose of apprehending the perpetrator of a crime and locating evidence for the successful prosecution of a case. Security investigations, on the other hand, may involve, in addition to crimes, the gathering of information in regards to the violation of organizational rules and regulations; a job applicant's background, for conditions that may lead to criminal violations; the need for new security controls and procedures; liability claims or potential claims; unsafe conditions; or evidence needed to prove or disprove certain allegations.[239]

The process itself inherently serves the justice system—both the criminal and civil systems that depend upon hard facts and evidentiary quality to prove the case at hand.[240] While similarities abound between the public and private systems, the difference and distinction between these systems is undeniable. Public policing must, by nature, be more concerned about criminal felonies than any private security firm. Homicide is not as critical a concern for private security forces as it is for the investigator laboring in Chicago or New York City. Other felonies may be better suited to shared practice such as burglary, grand theft, and other forms of larceny, fraud and corrupt practice, assault and battery, all of which touch upon the day to day grind common to both systems.[241]

Public officers are clearly more concerned with arrest and prosecution than their private counterparts. This conclusion is further buttressed by the "general public" concerns within the same list of priorities. This prioritization, in and of itself, is a telling distinction, though it should not be viewed as justification for a sharp division. If anything, both public and private law enforcement share a generic goal—namely, the general enforcement of laws. As Bill Strudal points out in his article, *Giving the Police a Sense of Security*,

> Our goal, usually not shared by police and security is law enforcement … if we accept the premise that police and security have the same goals, then why don't we work together on a regular basis? There are differences; nobody can deny that … there

are many other gaps between the two forces, but none is insurmountable with good training and dialogue.[242]

If constitutional protections do not inure to defendants and litigants processed by private sector justice, then what protections do exist? Could it be argued that the line between private and public justice has become indistinguishable or at least so muddled that the roles blur? Are private citizens, subjected to arrest, search, and seizure actions by private police, entitled to some level of criminal due process that is fundamentally fair and not overly intrusive? Does the Fourth Amendment's strict adherence to the protection of rights solely in the public and governmental realm blindly disregard the reality of public policing? Is this an accurate assessment of what the general citizenry experiences? Or should the constitution be more generously applied to encompass the actions of private police and security operatives? All of these dilemmas are, at first glance, easy to answer, when assessing case law. Even despite the continuous resistance to said applications, the advocates for such arguments are perpetually persistent.

The unique and preferred legal status of private security has had much to do with its extraordinary growth and attractiveness for as the public system has been bogged down and manipulated by excessive judicial oversight, the private system conducts most of its affairs without similar legal oversight.[243]

To be sure, there is no completely safe harbor for the errant actions of private security operatives can trigger a host of legal responses, from the regulatory to the administrative, from the civil to the criminal. Indeed, the private sector officer need always be legally aware of his or her potential liability based on multiple theories and because of this, a serious series of protocols and safeguards must be adhered to when conducting investigations.[244] Private security is not immune to legal consequences although it possesses a constitutional edge when compared to the public police model.[245]

Harmed parties might allege that privacy laws were violated or that unlawful investigative practices may lead to a claim of trespass, assault, battery, or other civil or criminal action. Nothing the security operative does, in an unlawful investigative tactic, precludes legal actions for nuisance, defamation, intentional infliction of mental distress, or arguments concerning false light. Nothing the security operative carries out, in an unlawful investigative tactic, will shield him or her from consequences of damages or costs resulting from the illegal action. And this same conclusion can be reached as to criminal charges—for an investigation that seriously injures a targeted person, causes harm from a firearm or specialized restraint method may result in the initiation of a criminal complaint.

However, nothing, at least presently will provide a foundational basis for a traditional constitutional claim based on the Fourth Amendment of the United States Constitution.[246] The problem becomes particularly acute for these critics of the status quo when public and private parties share the results or fruits of the investigations.[247] While policymakers, theoreticians, and academics debate strenuously for a change in the status quo, judicial reasoning has yet to bridge the gap between the private and public security interest. On occasion, courts do, though with caution and trepidation, find an actionable state case by traditional and innovative procedural interpretations of the color of law standard.

When compared to the public system, private security personnel are not bogged down in a miasma of constitutional pin splitting involving arrest, search and seizure questions nor does it need to fret too much over cruel and unusual punishment standards or the many other constitutional challenges that are hurled at public police each and every day. The Constitution expressly, unambiguously, and clearly reserves these constitutional remedies to public policing along in that the language indicates the "No State shall…?" State action means governmental action and those employed by Securitas or Allied Barton are not state agents and no amount of wishful thinking can make it so. Of course, there is nothing to halt bad legal reasoning and the willful rejection of long standing and self-evident legal maxims—a common condition among contemporary judicial activists who act like social workers rather than jurists. Unfortunately, there are a few cases out there that challenge the status quo simply because that is what these judges want rather than this is what the law requires. This was clearly evident in the *Zelinski* and *Buswell* decisions.[248]

Of course, there are occasions when the entanglement between the public and private officers simply becomes too intimate not to find governmental, state action on the part of both parties, but these are the rare situations discoverable in fact and case law. Legal policy is never well founded when based on the aberration. For the foreseeable future, the constitutional advantages of the private security industry foretell an even more vibrant future than presently exists.

5.11.1 *Private Security and Miranda Warnings*

Noted thus far is the general premise that constitutional protections apply to governmental action rather than private action. In the matter of *Miranda v. Arizona*,[249] which extended warnings prior to custodial interrogation by public police officers, the reform effort has been to make applicable to private security officers.[250] This view is argued from many fronts including but not limited to the "public" nature of private security work; the linkages and connecting the industry has to governmental authorities in the matter of oversight, regulation, licensure, and the recurring belief that the private system is a side door to avoid constitutional protections. And the issue of Miranda rights may also inure to the benefit of security operatives accused of criminality—no case more prominent than the Blackwater incident in Iraq—where private security operatives killed terrorists. In *U.S. v. Slough*, 677[251], the DC District Court concluded that immunized statements to various government entities investigating the incident were improperly used by government prosecutors. Even more troubling, the court concluded that overzealous political reactions to these events causes prosecutors to disregard basic protections in these statements. The court concluded:

> From this extensive presentation of evidence and argument, the following conclusions ineluctably emerge. In their zeal to bring charges against the defendants in this case, the prosecutors and investigators aggressively sought out statements the defendants had been compelled to make to government investigators in the immediate aftermath of the shooting and in the subsequent investigation. In so doing, the government's trial team repeatedly disregarded the warnings of experienced, senior prosecutors, assigned to the case specifically to advise the trial team on Garrity and Kastigar issues, that this course of action threatened the viability of the prosecution. The government used the defendants' compelled statements to guide its charging decisions, to formulate its theory of the case, to develop investigatory leads and, ultimately, to obtain the indictment in this case. The government's key witnesses immersed themselves in the defendants' compelled statements, and the evidence adduced at the Kastigar hearing plainly demonstrated that these compelled statements shaped portions of the witnesses' testimony to the indicting grand jury. The explanations offered by the prosecutors and investigators in an attempt to justify their actions and persuade the court that they did not use the defendants' compelled testimony were all too often contradictory, unbelievable and lacking in credibility.[252]

The once invincible wall that immunized private security officers from this constitutional scrutiny is perpetually now under siege. One academic commentator recently opined:

> The inherent prevalence of corporate security personnel to detain, search, and arrest members of the public mandates that, in certain situations, they should be treated as state actors. One such situation occurs when a corporate store detective detains a customer or employee and questions him. There is too great a potential for coerced confessions and prolonged detentions without the protections of Miranda and probable cause.[253]

The inherent prevalence of corporate security personnel to detain, search, and arrest members of the public mandates that, in certain situations, they should be treated as state actors. One such situation occurs when a corporate store detective detains a customer or employee and questions him. There is too great a potential for coerced confessions and prolonged detentions without the protections of Miranda and probable cause.

There have been cracks in this solid wall of immunity. "In Moore v. Detroit Entertainment, L.L.C., the Michigan Court of Appeals utilized the nexus doctrine to hold the security personnel of Motor City Casino, a private entity, to be state actors and liable to plaintiffs under § 1983.9."[254]

A series of reports involving Cumberland Farm convenience stores, in Boston, allege an array of abuses by security guards who charged employees with theft. "Almost without exception, employees said they were subjected to the same procedure. Each was taken to a backroom, seated on an overturned milk crate, accused of theft and threatened with public humiliation or prosecution if they did not sign a confession of guilt. This process continued for years, but the accused individuals failed to take significant action because they did not know that other employees were similarly treated."[255] A host of Cumberland employees brought a class action against the employer.[256] So extensive were the alleged abuses that certain legal commentators, like Joan E. Marshall, made impassioned pleas in the *Dickinson Law Review* for extending Miranda protection to the private sector.

> Despite historical reasons for allowing merchants to practice so-called self-help in the protection of their property, the example of employee abuse by Cumberland Farms shows the need for new legislation to prevent the Fifth Amendment from becoming an anachronism. While some civil action may lie for harassment, the employee who is essentially robbed of his cash, his job, and his reputation is unlikely to feel vindicated even if victorious. Allowing evidence obtained in backroom interrogations to be turned over to the State for prosecution directly contradicts the Fifth Amendment guarantee that coerced confessions cannot and will not be used against an individual in a court of law.
>
> Clearly, courts will exclude confessions if they were not, "voluntarily" given following "reasonable" efforts by private security. Not all merchants, however, are interested in prosecuting their employees. Testimony from former Cumberland Farms' employees shows that there is a great deal of money to be gained by threatening employees. Private security guards in uniform carry visible authority. The courts and legislatures must recognize that this authority may be abused, particularly given the minimal restrictions placed in private security guards.[257]

The authority for this argument is more personal than precedential. In *Williams v. United States*,[258] the court found that a private detective who held a special police officer's card and badge granted, authorized, and licensed by the state and who was accompanied by a city police officer in obtaining evidence, was acting under color of state law.[259] The decision, though chronologically pre-Miranda, set some persuasive authority for *Tarnef v. State*.[260] In *Tarnef*, a private investigator, working under the direction of local police, was required to advise defendant of his constitutional rights before eliciting a statement.

Cases in which private security are acting in consort with, under the authority of, or at the encouragement or enticement of the public sector forge the nexus necessary for Miranda rights.[261] Cases involving moonlighting police officers and off-duty deputy sheriffs have held that Miranda rights are generally not required.[262] The California Supreme Court in a retail setting, held the Miranda rights inapplicable under the following reasoning:

1. Store detectives do not enjoy the psychological advantage of official authority when they confront a suspected shoplifter.
2. Store detectives believe that they must act with greater circumspection to avoid costly civil suits than do police officers. Thus, the compelling atmosphere inherent in custodial interrogation is diminished.
3. Store detectives may only detain those who shoplift in their presence, limiting any motivation they might otherwise have to vigorously seek confessions.
4. If a store detective engages in psychological or physical abuse or provides improper inducements, any resulting statements by a defendant would be involuntary and an exclusionary remedy would be available.[263]

VOLUNTARY STATEMENT

Date: _____ Time: _____

Location: _____

I, _____, am _____ years of age and my address is _____

_____. I have been advised and duly warned by _____ of my Right to the advice of counsel before making any statement, and that I do not have to make any statement at all, nor incriminate myself in any manner.

I hereby, expressly, waive my Right to the advice of counsel and voluntarily make the following statement to the aforesaid person, knowing that any statement I make may be used against me in the trial or trials for the offense or offenses concerning which the following statement is herein made.

I declare that the following statement is made of my own free will, without promise of hope or regard, without fear or threat of physical harm, without coercion, favor or offer of favor, without leniency of offer of leniency, by any person or persons whomsoever.

I have this statement consisting of _____ page(s), and I affirm to the trust and accuracy of the facts contained therein. This statement was completed at _____.m., on the _____ day of _____, 20 .

_____

Signature of Person giving Voluntary Statement

Witness: _____

Figure 5.17   Voluntary statement waiver of rights.

Consequently, the California court concluded that the traditional standards governing admissibility of voluntary statements were sufficient to protect the suspect's Fifth Amendment rights when confronted by a store detective, so it was not necessary to extend the greater protections established in Miranda.[264]

Some security companies and interrogator's employ Miranda-type documents to ensure future admissibility in the event of subsequent challenge. A Voluntary Statement is at Figure 5.17.

The form memorializes a knowing and volitional statement. A second suggestion is allow the person giving the statement to write out, in his or her hand, the substance of their statement. When public police are involved, either as investigators or participants, use Figure 5.18.

<u>WAIVER OF RIGHTS</u>

1. I, _____, have voluntarily requested to speak with of the _____ Security Department.

2. I am aware that criminal charges are currently pending against me in _____ County where I am charged with _____.

3. In addition, I am presently represented by _____, Esq., as to these pending charges. Nonetheless, I have specifically requested to speak to these Security Officers without the presence of my attorney. The _____ Security Officers have advised me of my absolute right to consult with my attorney prior to any conversation that I have with them. I also understand that prior to any conversation with the security officers I may consult with any counsel of my own choosing, or if I cannot afford or otherwise obtain a lawyer, a lawyer will be appointed for me.

4. Furthermore, the Security Officers have advised me of my Constitutional Rights against self-incrimination and I understand the following:

   a. I have the right to remain silent.

   b. Anything I say can and will be used against me in a Court of Law.

   c. I have the right to represented by an attorney.

   d. If I cannot afford an attorney, and want one, one will be appointed for me without charge.

   e. I have the right to discontinue my statement at any time in order to retain counsel, consult with counsel, or for any other reason.

5. Knowing my right to counsel and understanding that anything I say can and will be used against me, I hereby waive my right to counsel and I waive the right to remain silent, and I freely and voluntarily elect to speak with the _____ Security Officers.

6. I also acknowledge that no promises, threats or inducements of any kind whatsoever have been made to me by any law enforcement officer of any other person in order to encourage me to make this statement. And I have signed below in order to further verify my voluntary and knowing acceptance of this waiver of my rights.

_____   Signed: _____
Security Officer/Witness   Dated: _____ 20 _____
                                                           Time: _____ Hrs.
_____
Security Officer/Witness

Figure 5.18 Voluntary written waiver of rights.

5.12 Summary

This chapter advises the security professional and practitioner on potential criminal liabilities. While the majority of liability problems are civil in scope and design, criminal charges can be and are lodged against security personnel, agencies, businesses, and industrial concerns.

Individuals and corporations, either through their officers and directors or another entity, can be held criminally culpable for specific conduct. Also, the regulatory processes imposed at the state and local levels can, if not adhered to, result in criminal penalties such as fines and forfeiture of occupational rights. Loss of license, revocation and suspension, criminal conviction, and any other remedy legislated are acceptable means of enforcement. Arguments asserting due process violations or a failure of equal protection are not judicially favored. If the industry is ever to attain professional status or equal footing with its public counterparts, some have argued, it will have to stress higher standards and higher levels of procedural conduct.

This chapter also gave a schematic outline of the types of criminal behavior most frequently brought forth in a security setting and provided factual patterns for evaluation. Criminal defenses most often seen in the security sector were analyzed including self-defense and defense of others. Finally, some discussion was provided on the requirement of Miranda warnings, a procedural requirement firmly entrenched in the public sector, but as of yet, unless a sufficient nexus is shown between public and private functions, is not a requirement in private security custodial interrogation.

CASE EXAMPLES

Third-Party Crimes

Facts

A 40-year-old individual was shot during a robbery while waiting for an elevator in a city-owned building where he maintained residence. Injuries resulted in paralysis and substantial loss of earnings. Plaintiff alleged that the defendant's failure to maintain locks and lighting in the lobby and failure to provide adequate security personnel caused the injury.

Issue

Should a plaintiff be able to collect money damages from a municipality or other governmental entities for failure to provide protection against third-party criminal acts?

Miranda Rights—*Tarnef v. State*, 512 P. 2d. 923 (1973).

Facts

A private arson investigator working at the behest of local police and who had promised to turn all evidence acquired, both testimonial and tangible, over to public law enforcement, vigorously interrogated a defendant. Without any regard for constitutional guidelines, the investigator eventually acquired a great deal of information that was incriminating and subsequently turned it over to the local police.

Issue

Is a private security officer, working at the request and on behalf of public law enforcement, required to advise a defendant of his or her Miranda rights?

DISCUSSION QUESTIONS

1. What criminal penalties can result from failure to follow the regulatory and licensing processes?

2. What level of due process is required for the imposition of penalties or the termination of licensure by governmental authority?

3. Name four common circumstances in which a security officer might be criminally charged.

4. Discuss, in depth, the standards outlining the right to use force in self-protection.

5. In the protection of property, force is not a favored exercise. Explain.

6. Defendants in criminal cases initiated by the private security industry, have few procedural rights. Explain.

7. Are Miranda rights required in cases that involve private security?

NOTES

1. See Restatement of Torts §2.05 (1934); William L. Clark and William L. Marshall, *A Treatise on the Law of Crimes* 200 (1967); see also John E. Douglas and Mark Olshaker, *The Anatomy of Motive* (1999); Leo Katz, *Bad Acts and Guilty Minds: Conundrums of the Criminal Law* (1987).

2. See: *US v. Cejas*, 761 F. 3d 717 - Court of Appeals, 7th Circuit 2014.

3. See Charles P. Nemeth, *Criminal Law* (2012, 2nd edition); see also Stanton E. Samenow, *Inside the Criminal Mind* (2014); Lawrence Taylor, *Born to Crime: The Genetic Causes of Criminal Behavior* (1984).

4. Model Penal Code §2.01 (1–3) (1962).

5. See Nemeth, Criminal Law, at 77–83.

6. Edward T. Guy, John J. Merrigan, Jr., and John A. Wanat, *Forms for Safety and Security Management* 138 (1981).

7. George E. Dix and Michael M. Sharlot, *Basic Criminal Law, Cases and Materials* 151 (1980); see also Steven J. Rossen and Wilton S. Sogg, *Smith's Review of Criminal Law* (1985); Nemeth, *Criminal*, at 106; Katherine R. Tromble, Humpty Dumpty on mens rea standards: A proposed methodology for interpretation, *Vand. L. Rev.* 52 (1999); 521, 522. Note, Mens rea in federal criminal law, *Harv. L. Rev.* 111 (1998); 2402.

8. See: Brian W. Walsh and Tiffany M. Joslyn, *Without Intent: How Congress is eroding the Criminal Intent Requirement in Federal Law*, the Heritage Foundation and the National Association of Criminal Defense Lawyers, 2010, at 27.

9. See generally Tromble; Note, Mens rea; Douglas and Olshaker; Richard Rhodes, *Why They Kill: The Discoveries of a Maverick Criminologist* (1999); Katz; Frank Remington and Orrin L. Helstad, Mental element in crimes—A legislative problem, 1952 *Wisc. L. Rev.* 644 (1952); Rollin M. Perkins, A rationale of mens rea, *Harv. L. Rev.* 52 (1935); 905; Thomas A. Cowan, A critique of the moralistic conception of criminal law, *U. Pa. L. Rev.* 97 (1949); 502; *Dennis v. U.S.*, 341 U.S. 494 (1951).

10. See *State v. Jackson*, No. W2015-00134-CCA-R3-CD, 2016 Tenn. Crim. App. LEXIS 38 (Jan. 8, 2016).

11. See *State v. Perry*, 2016-Ohio-4852, available at http://www.supremecourt.ohio.gov/rod/docs/pdf/2/2016/2016-Ohio-1474.pdf.

12. See John S. Baker, Jr., Mens rea and state crimes: 50 years post-promulgation of the model penal code, *Crim Rep.* (BNA) 92 (November 28, 2012); 248.

13. Model Penal Code § 2.02 (1 and 2) (1962). See also Del. Code Ann. tit. 11, § 231 (2001); MO. Rev. Stat. § 562.016 (2001); remain the same changes to this provision Jonathan L. Marcus, Model penal code section 2.02(7) and willful blindness, *Yale L.J.* 102 (1993); 2231, 2232.

14. Clark and Marshall, at 270.

15. See Nemeth, Criminal, at 49–50; John E. Douglas, *Crime Classification Manual* (2013); *Dictionary of Criminal Justice Terms* (2005); 4 William Blackstone, *Commentaries* 5 (1941); Clark and Marshall, at §§2.01-2.04; Michael J. Pastor, Note: A tragedy and a crime?: Amadou Diallo, specific intent, and the federal prosecution of civil rights violations, *N.Y.U. J. Legis. & Pub. Pol'y* 6 (2002); 171; Adam Candeub, Consciousness and Culpability, *Ala. L. Rev.* 54 (2002); 113.

16 See Nemeth, *Criminal*, at 51–52.

17 Id. at 52–53.

18 See generally 2 Frederic Pollock, Sr. and Fredrick W. Maitland, *History of English Law* (1903); Blackstone; Clark and Marshall, at 108–115; Center for Criminal Justice, *Private Police Training Manual* 34 (1985); Nemeth, Criminal, at 50–53.

19 There are exceptions to this including Pennsylvania. See 18 Pa. Stat. Ann. §§1105 (2010).

20 See Blackstone, at 205.

21 *Bannon v. U.S.*, 156 U.S. 464 (1894).

22 Task Force on Administration on Justice, The President's Commission on Law Enforcement and Administration of Justice, Task Force Report: The Courts 15 (1967).

23 As an example, see New York's misdemeanor classification of sexual misconduct, at §§130.20. Critics claim it is nothing more than an actual aggravated sexual assault.

24 U.S. DOJ, Four former Blackwater employees found guilty of charges in fatal Nisur Square shooting in Iraq, https://www.justice.gov/opa/pr/four-former-blackwater-employees-found-guilty-charges-fatal-nisur-square-shooting-iraq, last visited February 20, 2017.

25 See generally Perkins; Herbert Wechsler and Jerome Michael, A rationale of the law of homicide, *Colum. L. Rev.* 37 (1937); 701; see Nemeth, Criminal, at 115.

26 Model Penal Code §210.1 (1962).

27 Id. at §210.2.

28 See Nemeth, Criminal, at 107–108; *People v. Erikson*, No. 25854 (Ca. Super. Ct. 1997); Edward Imwinkelried, Evidence pedagogy in the age of statutes, *J. Legal Educ.* 41 (1991); 227.

29 See Dan Barry et al, "Always agitated. Always mad": Omar Mateen, according to those who knew him, *New York Times* (June 18, 2016) at http://www.nytimes.com/2016/06/19/us/omar-mateen-gunman-orlando-shooting.html?_r=0.

30 *People v. Morris*, 187 N.W. 2d 434, 438-43 (Mich. App. 1971).

31 Id.

32 Westchester County District Attorney, Mount Vernon man sentenced in the murder of a security guard (October 1, 2015) at http://www.westchesterda.net/october-2015/2996-mount-vernon-man-sentenced-in-the-murder-of-a-security-guard.

33 See Nemeth, *Criminal*, at 168–171; Kenneth W. Simons, Does punishment for "culpable indifference" simply punish for "bad character"? Examining the requisite connection between mens rea and actus reus, *Buff. Crim. L.R.* 6 (2002); 219; Guyora Binder, The rhetoric of motive and intent, *Buff. Crim. L.R.* 6 (2002); 1.

34 See Nemeth, Criminal, at 113–114; Binder.

35 18 Pa. Cons. Stat. Ann. §2503 (a) (West 2010).

36 Id. at §2504 (a).

37 See Nemeth, *Criminal*, at 151–153; Simons; Binder.

38 Mo. Rev. Stat. §565.024 (2015); For an interesting case on intentionality, drug dealing and forfeiture punishments, see: *U.S. v. Solomon*, Criminal Nos. 13-40-ART-(5),(7),(8), 2016 U.S. Dist. LEXIS 150787 (E.D. Ky. 2016).

39 See Nemeth, *Criminal*, at 154; Dana K. Cole, Expanding felony-murder in Ohio: Felony-murder or murder-felony? *Ohio St. L.J.* 63 (2002); 15; Rudolph J. Gerber, The felony murder rule: Conundrum without principle, *Ariz. St. L.J.* 31 (1999); 763; Guyora Binder, The model penal code revisited: felony murder and mens rea default rules: A study in statutory interpretation, *Buff. Crim. L.R.* 4 (2000); 399.

40 Dix and Sharlot, at 470.

41 See Nemeth, *Criminal* at 154.

42 James J. Tomkovicz, The endurance of the felony-murder rule: A study of the forces that shape our criminal law, *Wash. & Lee L. Rev.* 51 (1994); 1429.

43 Model Penal Code §211.1 (1962).

44 See Nemeth, Criminal, at 218.

45 Model Penal Code §211.2 (1962).

46 18 Pa. Cons. Stat. § 302 (2010).

47 See 18 Pa. Cons. Stat. §§2705-710 (2010).

48 Guy et al., at 187.

49 Model Penal Code §212.1 (1962).

50 See *State v. Williams*, 526 P.2d 1244 (Ariz. 1974); *People v. Caudillo*, 580 P. 2d 274 (Cal. 1978); see also Richard Sanders, "Double offense" problems in kidnapping and false imprisonment cases, *Fla. B.J.*, Dec. 2003, at 10.

51 Model Penal Code §212.3 (1962).

52 Kelley V. Rea, The legal risks of conducting a security-initiated investigation, Sec. 28 (1991); 23; see also Richard A. Bales and Jeffrey A. McCormick, Workplace investigations in Ohio, *Cap. U. L. Rev.* 29 (2002); 30.

53 Robert L. Rabin, Pain and suffering and beyond: Some thoughts on recovery for intangible loss, *DePaul L. Rev.* 55 (2006); 359.

54 Brenda V. Smith, Checklist of state criminal laws prohibiting the sexual abuse of persons in custody of law enforcement, lock-up and jail authorities (2008) available at http://www.wcl.american.edu/nic/legal_responses_to_prison_rape/lock-up_fifty_state_checklist.pdf?rd=1.

55 John Ashby, Employment references: Should employers have an affirmative duty to report employee misconduct to inquiring prospective employers? *Ariz. L. Rev.* 46 (2004); 117; Mark Minuti, Employer liability under the doctrine of negligent hiring: Suggested methods for avoiding the hiring of dangerous employees, *Del. J. Corp. L.* 13 (1988); 501; *Henley v. Prince George's County*, 479 A.2d 1375, 1381 (Md. App. 1984), aff'd in part and rev'd in part, 503 A.2d 1333 (Md. 1986).

56 See Nemeth, Criminal, at 275–276; Henry L. Chambers, Jr., (Un)welcome conduct and the sexually hostile environment, *Ala. L. Rev.* 53 (2002); 733; Niloofar Nejat-Bina, Employers as vigilant chaperones armed with dating waivers: The intersection of unwelcomeness and employer liability in hostile work environment sexual harassment law, *Berkeley J. Emp. & Lab. L.* 20 (1999); 325.

57 Model Penal Code §213.1 (1962).

58 See Charles P. Nemeth, Judicial doubt or distrust: Court ordered psychiatric examination of rape victims, *Hum. Rights* 12 (1984); 1; David P. Bryden, Forum on the law of rape: Redefining rape, *Buff. Crim. L.R.* 3 (2000); 317. See also: Cameron Langford, Sexually assaulted by a security guard, *Courthouse News Service* November 21, 2013) at http://www.courthousenews.com/2013/11/21/63117.htm.

59 *State v. Norman*, 741 S.E.2d 683 (2013).

60 18 Pa. Cons. Stat. § 3126 (2010).

61 Id. at § 3127.

62 Kurt A. Decker, *A Manager's Guide to Employee Privacy* ((c) 1989 John Wiley & Sons, Inc. 1989).

63 33 Am. Jur. Trials, 286–289. Reprinted from Am Jur Trials with permission of Thomson Reuters.

64 See William C. Cunningham and Todd H. Taylor, The Hallcrest Report, Private Security and Private Police in America (1985).

65 See Nemeth, *Criminal*, at 379–382.

66 Robert A. Neale, Arson: The overlooked threat to homeland security, *Emergency Management Online Issue*, September 7, 2010, at http://www.emergencymgmt.com/safety/Arson-Homeland-Security.html.

67 Id.

68 Model Penal Code §220.1 (1962); see Nemeth, Criminal, at 387–390.

69 See Dix and Sharlot, at §410.

70 See 18 Pa. Cons. Stat. §§3301–3307 (2010).

71 NFPA, Inspection and testing form, http://www.nfpa.org/assets/files/AboutTheCodes/72/99InspecTestForm.pdf.

72 Clark and Marshall.

73 Id. at 984.

74 Id. at 986–987.

75 See Nemeth, Criminal, at 390.

76 See N.Y. Criminal Law §§140 (McKinney 1980); Nemeth, Criminal, at 390.

77 Nemeth, Private Security, at 245.

78 See Albert Coates, Criminal intent in burglary, *N.C. L. Rev.* 2 (1924); 110; see also *Champlin v. State*, 267 N.W.2d 295 (Wis. 1978); *State v. Ortiz*, 584 P.2d 1306 (N.M. 1978).

79 Clark and Marshall, at 1007.
80 See Nemeth, Criminal, at 377–379.
81 Model Penal Code §221.2 (1) (1962).
82 John Francis, *Security Officer Manual* (1992).
83 See Nemeth, Criminal, at 94–201.
84 Model Penal Code §222.1 (1) (1962).
85 Wayne R. Lafave and Austin W. Scott, Sr., *Criminal Law* 698–699 (1972); see also *People v. Woods*, 360 N.E.2d 1082 (N.Y. 1977); *Commonwealth v. Mays*, 375 A.2d 116 (Pa. Super. 1977).
86 Lafave and Scott, at 200.
87 See *People v. Beebe*, 245 N.W.2d 547 (Mich. App. 1976).
88 See Nemeth, Criminal, at 311–313.
89 James Cleary, *Prosecuting the Shoplifter, A Loss Prevention Strategy* (1986); Anne-Marie G. Harris, Shopping while black: Applying 42 U.S.C. § 1981 to cases of consumer racial profiling, *B.C. Third World L.J.* 23 (2003); 1; see also Center for Retail Research, *The Global Retail Theft Barometer* (10th ed., 2010); available at https://www.odesus.gr/images/nea/eidhseis/2011/GRTB-2010-11-Eng.pdf
90 See: Security guard charged in theft of Lakers title rings, *USA Today*, December 12, 2013, http://www.usatoday.com/story/sports/nba/lakers/2013/12/12/security-guard-charged-stealing-championship-rings/4006283.
91 Clark and Marshall, at 802.
92 Id. at 804–807.
93 Md. Code Ann. Criminal Law § 3-401 (West 2010).
94 Model Penal Code §223.2 (Proposed Official Draft 1962).
95 Guy et al., at 152.
96 Model Penal Code 56 (Tentative Draft 1953).
97 Model Penal Code §223.3 (1962).
98 See Nemeth, *Criminal*, at 318–322.
99 R.I. Gen. Laws § 11-41-4 (2009).
100 Model Penal Code §223.4 (1962).
101 See Nemeth, *Criminal*, at 331–335.
102 *Model Penal Code* §223.5 (1962).
103 Id. at §223.6; see Nemeth, *Criminal*, at 330–331.
104 Id. at §223.7; see Nemeth, *Criminal*, at 326–327.
105 See Nemeth, *Criminal*, at 328–329.
106 18 Pa. Cons. Stat. § 3929 (2010).
107 For a thorough analysis of retail theft and its legal and commercial applications, review James Cleary, *Prosecuting the Shoplifter, A Loss Prevention Strategy* (1986).
108 Id. at 19
109 Nemeth, *Private Security*, at 234–238 (2010).
110 Bill Zalud, Retail's 7 greatest security hits! *Sec.* 28 (1991); 34, 35.
111 See Nemeth, *Criminal*, at 336–339.
112 Note, Insurance firms toughen fraud fight, Sec. 29 (1992); 65.
113 See Nemeth, *Criminal*, at 339–346.
114 Clark and Marshall, at 954; See Me. Rev. Stat. Ann. tit. 17-A §702 (2009); Or. Rev. Stat. §165.013 (2009); *State v. Tarrence*, 985 P.2d 225 (Ore. App. 1999); *U.S. v. Sherman*, 52 M.J. 856 (U.S. Army Ct. Crim. App. 2000).
115 Iowa Code § 715A.2 (2008); *Iowa L. Rev.* 97 (May 2012); 1201–1258.
116 18 Pa. Cons. Stat. § 4102 (2010).
117 Id. at §§4103-4104.
118 Id. at §§4105-4106; see also Md. Code. Ann. Criminal Law §§8-103, 8-214 (West 2010).
119 See Cunningham and Taylor.
120 18 Pa. Cons. Stat. § 5501 (2010). (portions of this law are set to expire in 2017–2018).
121 Id. at § 5104.

122 Id. at § 5507.

123 Id. at § 7506.

124 Id. at § 5502.

125 Id. at § 5503; see Nemeth, *Criminal*, at 56, 102.

126 35 Pa. Cons. Stat. § 780-102; 18 Pa. Cons. Stat. § 5505 (2010).

127 Ohio Rev. Code Ann. §2917.11(B)(1) (West 2010).

128 18 Pa. Cons. Stat. § 5506 (2012).

129 Id. at § 5507.

130 Id. at § 5508; Ohio Rev. Code Ann. §2917.12(7) (West 2010).

131 Id. at § 5509.

132 Miss. Code Ann. §97-35-37 (2010).

133 Wis. Stat. § 947.02 (2010).

134 18 U.S.C. §242 (2010); see also Center for Criminal Justice, *Private Police Training Manual* (1985);
Rolando V. del Carmen and David L. Carter, An overview of civil and criminal liabilities of police
officers, *Pol. Chief,* Aug. 1985, at 46; see generally M. S. Vaughn and L. F. Coomers, Police civil
liability under Section 1983: When do police officers act under color of law? *J. Crim. Justice* 23 (1995);
395–415.

135 18 U.S.C. §241 (2010).

136 382 U.S. 296 (1966).

137 Id. at 299.

138 Note, Shoplifting law: Constitutional ramifications of merchant detention, *Hofstra L. Rev.* 1 (1973);
295, 310.

139 For an interesting discussion regarding racial profiling and retail theft/shoplifting see Anne-Marie
G. Harris, Shopping while black: Applying 42 U.S.C. § 1981 to cases of consumer racial profiling,
B.C. Third World L.J. 23 (2003); 1; see also Center for Retail Research, *The Global Retail Theft
Barometer* (10th ed. 2010) available at https://www.odesus.gr/images/nea/eidhseis/2011/GRTB-
2010-11-Eng.pdf; See: Greg B. Smith, Barneys agrees to pay $525G to settle racial profiling alle-
gations after civil rights review, *NY Daily News*, August 11, 2014, at http://www.nydailynews.
com/new-york/barneys-agrees-pay-525g-settle-racial-profiling-allegations-article-1.1899013;   NY
Attorney General's Office, A.G. Schneiderman announces agreement with barneys New York
to address discrimination against customers, August 11, 2014, https://ag.ny.gov/press-release/
ag-schneiderman-announces-agreement-barneys-new-york-address-discrimination-against.

140 18 U.S.C. §241 (2010).

141 James S. Kakalik and Sorrel Wildhorn, *Private Police in The United States: Findings and Recommendations*
(1971).

142 *Report of The Task Force on Private Security National Advisory Committee On Criminal Justice Standards
And Goals* (1976). See also William C. Cunningham, John J. Strauchs, and Clifford W. Vanmeter,
Private Security Trends 1970 To 2000: The Hallcrest Report 322 (1990).

143 Report of The Task Force, at 121; see also H. E. Barrineau, *Civil Liability in Criminal Justice* (2nd ed.
1994); Katheryn K. Russell, *The Color Of Crime* (1998).

144 835 P.2d 458 (Ariz. App. 1992).

145 A.R.S. § 32-2425 (2010).

146 A.R.S. § 32-2427 (2010).

147 *Shorten v. Milbank*, 11 N.Y.S.2d 387 (N.Y. Sup. 1939), aff'd 12 N.Y.S.2d 583 (1939).

148 Landi, 835 P.2d at 467.

149 *Schanuel v. Anderson*, 546 F. Supp. 519 (S.D. Ill. 1982), aff'd 708 F.2d 316 (C.A.7 Ill.).

150 *Smith v. Fussenich*, 440 F. Supp. 1077 (D.C. Conn. 1977).

151 See generally John C. Williams, Regulation of private detectives, private investigations and security
agencies, 86 A.L.R.3d 691(2010); Jeff Maahs and Craig Hemmens, Train in vain: A statutory analysis
of security guard training requirements, *Int'l J. Comp. & Applied Crim. Just.* 22 (1998); 91–101;
Courses and seminars, *Int'l Security Rev.*, Nov.–Dec. 1997, at 12.

152 See *Stewart v. County of San Mateo*, 54 Cal. Rptr. 599 (1966).

153 *State v. Zittel*, 462 P.2d 944 (Wash. 1969); *N.C. Assoc. of Licensed Detectives v. Morgan*, 195 S.E.2d 357 (N.C. Ct. App. 1973); *Norwood v. Ward*, 46 F.2d 312, aff'd. 283 U.S. 800, 75 L. Ed. 1422, 52 S. Ct. 494 (1930).

154 See generally *People v. Ro'Mar*, 559 P.2d 710 (Colo. 1977); *Martin v. Conlisk*, 347 F. Supp. 262, (D.C. Ill. 1972); *Wackenhut Corp. v. Calero*, 362 F. Supp. 715 (D.C. Puerto Rico 1973).

155 86 A.L.R. 829 (Supp. p.49); see also *People v. Corry*, 181 N.E. 603 (Ill. 1932).

156 See *ABC Security Service, Inc. v. Miller*, 514 S.W.2d 521 (Mo. 1974); Cf. *Schulman v. Kelly*, 255 A.2d 250 (N.J. 1969).

157 *State v. Guardsmark*, 190 N.W.2d 397 (Iowa 1971).

158 In Re Application of Hitchcock, 166 P. 849 (Cal. App. 1917); In Re Berardi, 129 A.2d 705 (N.J. 1957).

159 See Williams.

160 For an egregious example of fraud in regulatory process, see: How to score of bottle of McDonald's special sauce, at http://www.wesh.com/article/how-to-score-a-bottle-of-mcdonald-s-special-sauce/8635010 (fake licensure); Matthew Copeland, Toledo man arrested for working as unlicensed security guard, *WTOL* 11, July 12, 2016, at http://www.wtol.com/story/33998819/toledo-man-arrested-for-working-as-unlicensed-security-guard (working with no license).

161 Guardsmark, 190 N.W.2d.

162 See Williams.

163 Guardsmark, 190 N.W.2d, at 399.

164 14 S.W. 565 (Mo. 1890).

165 Id.

166 275 P.2d 579 (Cal. App. 1954).

167 Id.; See also *Donkin v. Director of Professional and Vocational Standards*, 49 Cal Rptr. 495 (1966).

168 41 Cal. Rptr. 263 (1964). See also *Agency for Investigation and Detection, Inc. v. Department of State*, 266 N.E.2d 310 (N.Y. 1965).

169 41 Cal. Rptr. 263 (1964).

170 514 S.W.2d 521 (Mo. 1974).

171 In Re Berardi, 129 A.2d 705 (N.J. 1957); see also *People v. King*, 194 N.E.2d 131 (N.Y. 1963).

172 569 P.2d 455 (Okl. 1977).

173 Schnabalk, The legal basis of liability, part II, *Sec. Mgmt.* 27 (1983); 29. See also Lawrence Friedman, In defense of corporate criminal liability, *Harv. J. L. & Pub. Pol'y* 23 (2000); 833; William A. Simpson, *Corporate Criminal Intent* (August 5, 2009), available at http://ssrn.com/abstract=1444543; *County of Santa Clara v Southern Pacific Railroad Company* 118 U.S. 394 (1886); *Arthur Andersen LLP v United States* 544 U.S. 696 (2005); *New York Cent. & H.R.R. Co. v. U.S.*, 212 U.S. 481 (1909); U.S. v. Bank of New England, N.A., 821 F.2d 844 (C.A.1 Mass. 1987).

174 For an excellent overview of corporate criminal liability, see: Charles Doyle, *Corporate Criminal Liability: An Overview of Federal Law*, Congressional Research Service (October 30, 2013), at https://fas.org/sgp/crs/misc/R43293.pdf.

175 See *W.T. Grant Co. v. Superior*, 23 Cap. App. 3d 284 (1972); *N.Y. Central & Hudson Railroad v. U.S.*, 212 U.S. 481 (1908); *People v. Canadian Fur Trappers Corp.*, 161 N.E. 455 (N.Y. 1928); see generally Shirley Baccus-Lobel, Criminal law, *S.M.U. L. Rev.* 52 (1999); 881, 910-911; Rolando V. del Carmen, *An Overview of Civil and Criminal Liabilities of Police Officers and Departments*, 9 *Am. J. Crim. L.* 33 (1981); Rolando V. del Carmen, *Civil and Criminal Liabilities of Police Officers*, in *Police Deviance* (T. Barker and D. L. Carter eds., 1994); Rolando V. del Carmen and Victor E. Kappeler, Municipal and police agencies as defendants: Liability for official policy and custom, *Am. J. Police* 10 (1991); 1–17.

176 Arthur J. Bilek, John C. Klotter, and R. Keegan Federal, *Legal Aspects of Private Security* 144 (1980).

177 See Norm Keith and Graham Walsh, *International Corporate Criminal Liability*, 8 World Focus, at http://www.asse.org/assets/1/7/NormKeith-GrahamWalsh-Article.pdf.

178 See Benjamin W. Mintz, Administrative separation of functions: OSHA and NLRB, *Cath. U. L. Rev.* 47 (1998); 917, at http://scholarship.law.edu/scholar/298/

179 Schnabalk.

180 See Nemeth, *Criminal*, 183–187; Roger T. Weitkamp, *Crimes and Offenses*, 16 Ga. St. U. L. Rev. 72, 73 (1999); Gloria F. Taft and Valeree R. Gordon, Criminal law (legislative survey—North Carolina), *Campbell L. Rev.* 21 (1999); 353, 353; Keith D. Harries, *Serious Violence: Patterns of Homicide and Assault In America* (1990).

181 For a representative statute see Ga. Code Ann. § 16-5-20(2) (West 2010).

182 See Model Penal Code § 211.1(c) (Proposed Official Draft 1962).

183 See Ga. Code Ann. § 16-5-20(1) (West 2010); MPC, at § 211.1(a).

184 Also called "assault and battery" or "aggravated assault" in some jurisdictions.

185 See *State v. Humphries*, 586 P.2d 130 (Wash. App. 1978).

186 See MPC, supra note 43, at §211.1(2).

187 See Id.

188 See Nemeth, at 178–179. See also Neb. Rev. Stat. § 38-314 (2010); MPC, at § 212.3; 18 Pa. Cons. Stat. Ann. § 2903 (West 2010); Colo. Rev. Stat § 18-3-303 (2010).

189 See Nemeth, at 254–263; Weitkamp, at 73; Taft and Valeree, at 353; James Gibson, How much should mind matter? Mens rea in theft and fraud sentencing, *Fed. Sentencing Rep.* 10 (1997); 136, 137.

190 See Nemeth, at 128–132; see also Pamela K. Lattimore and Cynthia A. Nahabedian, *The Nature of Homicide: Trends And Changes* (1997); Marvin E. Wolfgang, *Patterns in Criminal Homicide* (1975).

191 Jeremy Horder, *Provocation and Responsibility* (1992); Joshua Dressler, Provocation: Partial justification or partial excuse? *Mod. L. Rev.* 51 (1988); 467 ; Joshua Dressler, Rethinking heat of passion: A defense in search of a rationale, *J. Crim. L. Criminol.* 73 (1982); 421; Finbarr McAuley, Anticipating the past: The defense of provocation in Irish law, *Mod. L. Rev.* 50 (1987); 133; Andrew Von Hirsch and Nils Jareborg, *Provocation and Culpability in Responsibility, Character, and the Emotions* 241 (Ferdinand Schoeman ed., 1987).

192 See Nemeth, at 115–128; see also 2 Francis Wharton, *Wharton's Criminal Law* (Charles E. Torcia ed., 15th ed. 1993); Baccus-Lobel, at 910–911; John Rockwell Snowden, Second degree murder, malice, and manslaughter in Nebraska: New juice for an old cup, *Neb. L. Rev.* 76399, 410 (1997); 399, 410.

193 US DOJ, US Attorney's Office, *Newport News Gangster Convicted of Racketeering and Murder Charges* (May 12, 2016), at https://www.justice.gov/usao-edva/pr/newport-news-gangster-convicted-racketeering-and-murder-charges.

194 Jeffrey S. Thurnher, Drowning in Blackwater: How weak accountability over private security contractors significantly undermines counterinsurgency efforts, 2008 *Army Law.* 64 (2008); Craig S. Jordan, Who will guard the guards? The accountability of private military contractors in areas of armed conflict, 35 *N.E. J. Crim. Civ. Con.* 309 (2009); Oliver R. Jones, Implausible deniability: State responsibility for the actions of private military firms, *Conn. J. Int'l. L.* 24 (2009); 239; Gable F. Hackman, Lipping through the cracks: Can we hold private security contractors accountable for their actions abroad?, *Loy. J. Pub. Int. L.* 9 (2008); 251.

195 See Nemeth, Criminal, at 377, 378–379; see also William L. Clark and William L. Marshall, *A Treatise On The Law Of Crime* (6th ed., 1958); *People v. Burt*, 288 P.2d 503 (Cal. 1955).

196 Ex parte Moore, 356 U.S. 369 (1952).

197 See Nemeth, Criminal, at 377, 385–391; J. F. Mcsorley, *Portable Guide to Federal Conspiracy Law: Developing Strategies for Criminal and Civil Cases* (1996).

198 See Bilek et al., at 152; *Sears v. U.S.*, 343 F 2d 139 (5th Cir. 1965); *State v. St. Christopher*, 232 N.W.2d 798 (Minn. 1975). For an interesting case on security guards engaged in a trucking licensure DMV testing scandal with illegal aliens, see: *U.S. v. Harper*, 2015 U.S. Dist. LEXIS 140581 (E.D.N.Y. 2015).

199 See Nemeth, Criminal, at 49–50; John E. Douglas, *Crime Classification Manual* (2013); *Dictionary of Criminal Justice Terms* (2005); William Blackstone, *Commentaries* 4 (1941); 5; Clark and Marshall, at §§2.01-2.04; Michael J. Pastor, Note: A Tragedy and a crime?: Amadou Diallo, Specific intent, and the federal prosecution of civil rights violations, *N.Y.U. J. Legis. & Pub. Pol'y* 6 (2002); 171; Adam Candeub, Consciousness & culpability, *Ala. L. Rev.* 54 (2002); 113.

200 See Nemeth, Criminal, at 51–52.

201 See Nemeth, Criminal, at 52–53.

202 See generally 2 Frederic Pollock, Sr. and Fredrick W. Maitland, *History of English Law* (1903); Blackstone; Clark and Marshall, at 108–115; Center for Criminal Justice, *Private Police Training Manual* 34 (1985); Nemeth, *Criminal*, at 50–53.

203 There are exceptions to this including Pennsylvania. See 18 Pa. Stat. Ann. §§1105 (2010).

204 See Blackstone, *supra* note 10, at 205.

205 *Bannon v. U.S.*, 156 U.S. 464 (1894).

206 Task Force on Administration on Justice, *The President's Commission on Law Enforcement and Administration of Justice, Task Force Report: The Courts* 15 (1967).

207 As an example, see New York's misdemeanor classification of Sexual Misconduct, at §§130.20. Critics claim it is nothing more than an actual aggravated sexual assault.

208 Code Just. 3.27.1 (Valentinian, Theodosius and Arcadius 391). See also Will Tysse, The Roman legal treatment of self defense and the private possession of weapons in the code of Justinian, *J. Firearms and Pub. Pol'y*, 16.

209 22 Exodus 2:1.

210 National Institute of Justice, *Crime and Protection in America, A Study of Private Security and Law Enforcement Resources And Relationships* (1985). See Nemeth, at 389–407; Russell L. Christopher, Mistake of fact in the objective theory of justification: do two rights make two wrongs make two rights … ?, *J. Crim. L. Criminol.* 85 (1994); 295; Kent Greenawalt, The perplexing borders of justification and excuse, *Colum. L. Rev.* 84 (1984); 1897; George P. Fletcher, The right and the reasonable, *Harv. L. Rev.* 98 (1985); 949 2 Paul H. Robinson, *Criminal Law Defenses*, §3-3, Model Codifications, app. A (1984).

211 George E. Dix and Michael M. Sharlot, *Basic Criminal Law Cases and Materials* 527 (1980).

212 William C. Cunningham and Todd H. Taylor, *The Hallcrest Report, Private Security and Police in America* 92 (1985).

213 Site Surveys of Security Employees, Baltimore County, Maryland and Multnomah County (Portland), Oregon metropolitan areas. Hallcrest Systems, Inc., 1982. Stoneham, MA: Butterworth–Heinemann.

214 Shlomit Wallerstein, *Justifying the Right to Self-Defense: A Theory of Forced Consequences*, 91 VA. L. Rev. 999 (2005).

215 MPC, at §3.04.

216 MPC, at §3.04 (1 and 2).

217 For more information on the subject see Nemeth, *Criminal*, at 401–407; see also Christopher; Greenawalt; Fletcher; Robinson.

218 Summary of Pennsylvania Jurisprudence 2d, *Criminal Law* §7.19.

219 Cunningham and Taylor, at 94.

220 15 F. Supp. 2d 433 (N.J. 1998).

221 *Abraham v. Raso*, 15 F. Supp. 2d 433, 450 n.14 (N.J. 1998).

222 See Nemeth, Criminal, at 407–408; see Christopher; Greenawalt; Fletcher; Robinson.

223 MPC, at §3.05(1).

224 *U.S. v. Peterson*, 483 F. 2d 1222, 1223 (1973); see also *State v. Goodseal*, 183 N.W.2d 258 (Neb. 1971); *Commonwealth v. Martin*, 341 N.E. 885 (Mass. 1976); *Commonwealth v. Monico*, 366 N.E.2d 1241 (Mass. 1977).

225 Pennsylvania Jurisprudence, at §7:26.

226 Center for Criminal Justice, *Private Police Training Manual* 200 (1985).

227 Id.

228 MPC, at §3.06 (1).

229 See Nemeth, Criminal, at 408–409; see Christopher; Greenawalt; Fletcher; Robinson.

230 Pennsylvania Jurisprudence, § 7:36.

231 The State of New Jersey recently expanded the right of the homeowner to protect his or her interests with deadly force.

232 148 S.E. 2d 279, 281-282 (N.C. 1966).

233 Id.; see also *Law v. State*, 318 A.2d 859 (Md. App. 1974); *People v. Givens*, 186 N.E.2d 255 (Ill. 1962).

234 *Burdeau v. McDowell*, 256 U.S. 465 (1921).

235 Id. at 475.

236 See: Malcolm K. Sparrow, *Managing the Boundary Between Public and Private Policing*, September 2014, https://www.ncjrs.gov/pdffiles1/nij/247182.pdf; Certainly in the academic sectors, there is an ongoing demand for the extension of the constitution, yet the arguments lack precedent and legal logic. See M Rhead Enion, Constitutional limits on private policing and the state's allocation of force, *Duke L.J.* 59 (2009); 519, http://scholarship.law.duke.edu/cgi/viewcontent.cgi?article=1445&context=dlj.

237 Task Force on Private Security, at 127; see also Will Aitchison, *The Rights of Law Enforcement Officer* (4th ed. 2000); Rolando V. Del Carmen, *Criminal Procedure for Law Enforcement Personnel* (5th ed. 2001); del Carmen and Kappeler, at 1-17; S. M. Ryals, *Discovery and Proof in Police Misconduct Cases* (1995).

238 Cunningham and Taylor, at 264.

239 Russell Colling, *Hospital Security* 211 (Butterworth Publishers, 1982).

240 IACP, *National Policy Summit*, (2004) http://www.theiacp.org/Portals/0/pdfs/Publications/ACFAB5D.pdf.

241 See: COPS website, Private Security and Public Law Enforcement, http://www.cops.usdoj.gov/Default.asp?Item=2034.

242 Bill Strudel, *The Private Security Connection: Giving the Police a Sense of Security*, Police Chief, Feb. 1982, at 28–29; Law Commission of Canada, *In Search of Security: The Roles of Public Police and Private Agencies* (2002); George S. Rigakos, *The New Parapolice* (2002).

243 See: Malcolm K. Sparrow, *Managing the Boundary Between Public and Private Policing*, September 2014, https://www.ncjrs.gov/pdffiles1/nij/247182.pdf.

244 See Louis Klein, *Tips on Workplace Investigations*, at 34.

245 See: Ceil Goldberg, *A Training Triumph*, at 12.

246 Certainly in the academic sectors, there is an ongoing demand for the extension of the constitution, yet the arguments lack precedent and legal logic. See: M Rhead Enion, Constitutional limits on private policing and the state's allocation of force, *Duke L.J.* 59 (2009); 519, http://scholarship.law.duke.edu/cgi/viewcontent.cgi?article=1445&context=dlj.

247 See *US v. Cannon*, 703 F. 3d 407 (2013) where the search by a fire marshal led to the discovery of child pornography.

248 *State of Minnesota v. Buswell*, 449 N.W.2d 471, 474 (Minn. App. 1989); People v. Zelinski, 594 P. 2d 1000 (1979).

249 384 US 436 (1966).

250 *People v. Oxnell*, 166 N.W. 2d 279 (1968); see also Aitchison; Del Carmen, *Criminal Procedure*; del Carmen & Kappeler, at 1–17; Ryals. For an interesting case on how a fire inspection, not subject to constitutional scrutiny by its administrative nature, leading to eventual police probable cause, see: *State v. Dotson*, 450 S.W.3d 1 (Tenn. 2014).

251 F. Supp. 2d 112 (D.D.C. 2009).

252 *U.S. v. Slough*, F. Supp. 2d 112, 115 (D.D.C. 2009); See also: *U.S. v. Slatten*, 50 F. Supp. 3d 29, 2014 U.S. Dist. LEXIS 86636.

253 Sean James Beaton, Counterparts in modern policing: The influence of corporate investigators on the public police and a call for the broadening of the state action doctrine, *Touro Law Review* 26 (2012); 604, available at: http://digitalcommons.tourolaw.edu/lawreview/vol26/iss2/12; See Joan E. Marshall, The at-will employee and coerced confessions of theft: Extending fifth amendment protection to private security guard abuse, *Dick. L. Rev.* 96 (1991); 37, 3738, 40 (examining the potential abuses that present themselves when store detectives detain and interview employees suspected of theft). See also *Curley v. Cumberland Farms Dairy, Inc.*, 728 F. Supp. 1123, 1126 (D.N.J. 1990) (discussing former employees' claims under the Racketeer Influenced and Corrupt Organizations Act and state antiracketeering law arising out of the conduct of loss prevention specialists who allegedly extorted confessions and payments from employees suspected of theft).

254 Sean James Beaton, Counterparts in modern policing: The influence of corporate investigators on the public police and a call for the broadening of the state action doctrine, *Touro Law Review* 26 (2012); 604, available at: http://digitalcommons.tourolaw.edu/lawreview/vol26/iss2/12; *Moore v. Detroit*

Entm't, L.L.C., 755 N.W.2d 686, 699–700 (Mich. 2008) ("[D]efendants' joint engagement with the Detroit [P]olice in the arrest and detention of plaintiff also satisfies the symbiotic relationship or nexus test of action 'under color of state law.").

255 Joan E. Marshall, The at-will employee and coerced confessions of theft: Extending fifth amendment protection to private security guard abuse, *Dickinson L. Rev.* 96 (1991); 37, 40.

256 *Curly v. Cumberland Farms, Inc.*, 13 F.R.D. 77 (D. N.J. 1991).

257 Marshall, at 57; see also Aitchison; Del Carmen, *Criminal Procedure*; del Carmen and Kappeler, at 1–17; Ryals.

258 341 U.S. 97 (1951).

259 *Williams v. U.S.*, 341 U.S. 97 (1951); *City of Grand Rapids v. Impens*, 327 N.W.2d 278 (Mich. 1982).

260 512 P.2d 923 (Alaska 1973).

261 See *Griffin v. Maryland*, 378 U.S. 130 (1964); *People v. Jones*, 288 N.W.2d 385 (Mich. App. 1979).

262 See *People v. Faulkner*, 282 N.W.2d 377 (Mich. App. 1979).

263 R. Keegan Federal and Jennifer L. Fogleman, *Avoiding Liability in Retail Security: A Casebook* 168–169 (1986), quoting *Metigoruk v. Anchorage*, 655 P.2d 1317 (Alaska App. 1982).

264 Substantial authority concurs with the judgment of both the California and Alaska Supreme Courts regarding Miranda rights though given the Cumberland case, opinion may shift. See *Jelks v. State*, 411 So.2d 844 (Ala. Cr. App. 1982); *Bowman v. State of Indiana*, 468 N.E.2d 1064 (Ind. App. 4 Dist. 1984).

Chapter 6

Private Security Industry: The Collection, Preservation, and Interpretation of Evidence

6.1 Private Security's Role in the Integrity of Evidence and the Legal Process

By now it is quite evident that the private security industry plays a major, significant role in the delivery of justice services. The continuing evolution of the industry's role in once sacrosanct public functions only reaffirms the crucial role the industry assumes in the demands of justice in a free society. Even private security's harshest, most strident critics realize that without the services of private security, a gaping, colossal protection vacuum would exist in the distribution of justice and the protection of assets and facilities and related services. Public policing alone simply cannot fend off the escalating criminality or solely assure the integrity of community and governmental infrastructures. It is common knowledge that the security industry performs numerous functions, from crowd control to physical perimeter protection in public and private installations, and deterrent and preventative activities regarding shoplifting and other corporate crime and as the trend toward privatization continues, the integration of the private security industry into matters of criminal investigation, apprehension, and evidence gathering will undoubtedly grow. Hence understanding the law of private security must be coupled with a full understanding of the evidentiary principles that guide the protocols and practices of our justice model. That is the chief aim of this chapter—to introduce and analyze the more critical evidentiary and investigative practices that assure the fair and professional treatment of those who encounter the private sector operative. In previous chapters, the private security professional has been introduced to constitutional inquiry of private and state action, the definition of crimes and misdemeanors, and the wide array of legal actions based on intentional torts, negligence, and strict liability, as well as civil rights remedies, and other forms of liability including but not limited to vicarious versions where third parties are held accountable for actors under their supervision. Private security must have training and foundational knowledge in the law of civil action and crimes coupled with a recognition regarding

309

the demands that its proof requires. And if the industry is to make a meaningful contribution in the apprehension and subsequent prosecution of criminal behavior, its agents and officers need know and understand the evidentiary demands for a successful prosecution.

In the pages that follow, the reader is directed to the base elements that are essential to the law of evidence and its particular applications. In addition, the stress here will be on how evidentiary practices impact private sector officers trying to carry out their duties with due diligence and professionalism.

The legal integrity of any case will always depend on how an investigation is conducted; how evidence is collected, protected, and preserved and how an evidentiary chain of custody assures that the evidence offered can withstand legal and judicial scrutiny. Standard investigative practice calls for the security professional to attentively protect the crime scene and preserve the evidence. "Collection, preservation and the assurance of evidentiary integrity"[1] are central to any investigative regimen. This is true in any type of case consisting of criminal conduct or civil injuries; insurance investigations for arson, fraud, and vehicular accidents; terrorist acts; bomb threats; executive protection threats; intrusions into hotels, motels, colleges, and universities; violent labor disputes; workers' compensation, as well as suspected retail theft. This chapter presents a comprehensive analysis of methods and techniques employed by security investigators that insure the integrity of evidence and preserve the scene in a criminal or civil case.

6.2 Toolkit for Evidence Collection and Scene Preservation

Any successful protocol for evidence collection and scene preservation will require specific "tools" to get the job done. Security professionals use a mix of technology and old "gumshoe" processes. For example, the toolbox must minimally contain:

- Binoculars
- Blankets
- Brushes
- Bullhorns
- Cables
- Chains
- Chalk and chalkline
- Checklists
- Cutters
- First aid kits
- Flares or fuses
- Floodlamps
- Plaster of Paris
- Screwdriver
- Scribes
- Sketching supplies
- Spatula
- Sponges
- Sprays
- Stamps
- Steel measuring tape

- Swabs
- Syringes
- Tags
- Tape recorder
- Templates
- Thermometer
- Tinsnips
- Towels
- Transceivers
- Tubes
- Tweezers
- Vacuums
- Wax
- Wire
- Wrenches[2]

At the same time, the kit must be complemented with sophisticated technological innovations which assist the investigator. Some more common products that should be part of the investigative arsenal include

For evidence management (see Figure 6.1).[3]
Scene preservation (see Figure 6.2).[4]
Accident reconstruction (see Figure 6.3).[5]

Figure 6.1   EvidenceOnQ website.

Figure 6.2   FARO crime zone webpage.

Figure 6.3   FARO accident reconstruction software webpage.

6.2.1 Evidence at Scene: Preliminary Strategies and Responses

If the investigator is fortunate enough to have early access to the civil or criminal scene, securing the scene's physical integrity—the conditions surrounding the occurrence and the preservation of its evidence—whether evidence of personal injury, or damage to property or contraband, is a very critical responsibility. This initial scene search should be a planned, coordinated, and competent action that is legally permissible and does not interfere with or obstruct the function of public justice. Without exception, those laboring in the private sector in some investigative or evidentiary function must respect the priority of first responders—especially those entrusted with public official duties. In addition, the sanctity of a crime scene or reconstructive setting depends on the control of access, allowing only persons who have a legitimate investigative interest. As a rule, the larger the number of persons on the scene, the greater is the potential for scene contamination. Three fundamental priorities govern investigative and evidentiary policy upon initial visitation:

1. The acquisition and preservation of physical, real, documentary, and tangible evidence.
2. The notation of mental impressions regarding motive and modus operandi (MO).
3. Memorialize events and conditions at scene from the very outset whether by diagram, photographic or video-graphic means, or other permanent capturing of the setting.

Upon entry, the investigator must make every effort to preserve events and conditions for usage presently and over the long history of most litigation. The U.S. Department of Justice, through its National Institute of Justice, published a reference work for private and public law enforcement titled, *Crime Scene Search and Physical Evidence Handbook*,[6] which emphasizes the urgency of the preliminary review:

> Aside from any other consideration, the investigator should consider the crime scene as highly dynamic, that is, undergoing change; and fragile, in the sense that the evidence value of items it contains can be easily downgraded. Usually, there is only one opportunity to search the scene properly. Making a good preliminary survey of the layout helps to use that opportunity to best advantage.[7]

Preservation of the scene is a hallmark responsibility for the investigator since the scene will change by the mere passage of time and thus lose its primal innocence and integrity. "The investigator should first take into account all the information and opinions that have been accumulated by persons preceding him on the scene. The apparent physical focal point or points of the crime are of particular interest in this information exchange, as are the perceptions of other officers as to items or material having potential evidentiary value."[8] The maintenance of crime scene integrity begins with the observations of the first officer or investigative specialist on the scene. The protocol for the initial responder would be:

1. Note or log dispatch information (e.g., address/location, time, date, type of call, parties involved).
2. Be aware of any persons or vehicles leaving the crime scene.
3. Approach the scene cautiously, scan the entire area to thoroughly assess the scene, and note any possible secondary crime scenes. Be aware of any persons and vehicles in the vicinity that may be related to the crime.

4. Make initial observations (look, listen, smell) to assess the scene and ensure officer safety before proceeding.
5. Remain alert and attentive. Assume the crime is ongoing until determined to be otherwise.
6. Treat the location as a crime scene until assessed and determined to be otherwise.[9]

The Pennsylvania State Police, in its *Crime Laboratory Operations Manual*, corroborates the importance of this early evidentiary stage a wise series of initial actions. The security profession must;

- Form objectives of the search and deciding what to look for
- Take special note of evidence that may be easily destroyed such as shoeprints in dust, footprints, etc.
- Organize the search by making assignments for photographs, fingerprints, and evidence handling
- Decide on a search pattern and issuing instructions to assist personnel[10]

Review the recommended procedures for crime scene preservation at: http://www.ncjrs.gov/pdffiles1/nij/200160.pdf

The need to preserve physical evidence requires a resolute attempt to cordon off and secure the scene and its most current physical conditions to prevent—or at least minimize—any distortions or aberrations of the best possible reality. A few prototype forms for physical evidence collection are outlined in the forms that follow.[11] The checklist for physical evidence (see Figure 6.4[12]) is usable in both criminal and civil litigation.[13]

In Figure 6.5,[14] Physical Scene Investigation Checklist, the investigator is provided with step-by-step instructions on how to perform a preliminary review and examination. Note that the checklist includes reporting weather and lighting conditions; establishing a perimeter to secure the scene by keeping out foreign parties; observations regarding odors and the sensible policy of calling in additional help, if necessary.

Another important form is drawn from the Protection of the Scene Checklist at Figure 6.6.[15] By adhering to the standards and policies presented in this document, the private investigator insures the integrity of evidence collected and gathered. As noted above, many of the steps that protect the scene will require the "Toolkit" with specific needs for signs, lighting, flags, rope, chalk or crayon, barricades, and other security personnel needed to prevent intrusion.

While these suggestions are general in nature, as one zeroes in on specialized challenges, the techniques of collection and preservation will need further refinement. For example, when examining particular activities, such as bombs and explosives in executive protection situations, the focus on physical evidence becomes more targeted. Evidence gathering reflects the object of the investigative object and experienced investigators look for clues most relevant to the activity under investigation. So, in a case involving concealed explosive devices, an experienced professional may be looking for things that, on their natural face say less, but inferentially say far more such as

- Recently disturbed ground
- Sawdust
- Brickdust
- Wood chips

Checklist for Physical Evidence

	Yes	No	Does Not Apply
1. Were fingerprints located and photographed?			
2. Were latent fingerprints found, developed, and lifted?			
3. Did you call for a firearms examiner to help extract bullets from walls, ceilings, etc.?			
4. In homicide or woundings, did you obtain bullets removed by the medical examiner?			
5. Did you search for all possible types of physical evidence?			
6. Have you collected items of evidence that make jigsaw matches?			
7. In case of vehicular accident, did you recover paint, window glass, or headlight glass from victim's body or vehicle?			
8. Have you properly packed and marked evidence to go to the laboratory?			
9. Have you located footprints of shoes or bare feet in the out-of-doors scene and taken photographs and made casts?			
10. If there is an apprehended suspect, have you examined the inside of their shoes, the soles, and the welt for fine sand, clay or mud?			
11. Have you collected trace evidence by vacuum cleaning from suspect's clothing?			
12. Have you collected pieces of bed sheets, pillow slips, and other bedding involved in rape or homicide?			
13. Have you had someone in the family or close to the family look at the scene of indoor crimes to find out what has been disturbed?			
14. Has a list of missing objects been made?			
15. Have you checked for tools marks and broken glass that are signs of breaking and entering?			
16. Have you checked windows for broken glass or for bullet holes?			

Figure 6.4   Checklist for physical evidence.

- Electrical wire
- String
- Fishing line
- Dirty rope (fuses)
- Tin foil
- Partly opened drawers
- Fresh plaster or cement
- Loose floorboards
- Disturbed carpeting
- Loose electrical fittings
- Out-of-place objects
- Greasy paper wrapping, etc.[16]

Physical Scene Investigation Checklist

A. General:

1. If the investigator is weak in his knowledge of scene investigation he can do great harm to the investigation by inadvertently destroying the evidence.
2. An apparent suicide is always investigated as though it is a homicide.
3. A body should not be removed until all required investigation steps have been taken.
4. If the body must be moved (advancing fire, etc.), record in all ways possible the location and position of the body.

B. Approaching the Scene:

The investigation should begin as soon as the investigator becomes aware of the incident. All senses should be put to work—and most of all common sense must be used. BE ALERT! BE CURIOUS! Be complete in recording what you observe.

1. Observe vehicles (moving or parked)
2. Observe persons
3. Observe unusual conditions

C. Arrival at the Scene:

1. The first duty is always to the injured person. If the victim(s) shows any sign of life, he should be afforded all possible lifesaving measures.
2. Notation should be made regarding:
   a. Date
   b. Time of arrival
   c. Weather conditions
   d. Lighting conditions
3. The next duty is to establish a perimeter and secure the scene. Be observant for:
   a. Suspicious vehicles and persons at or around the immediate scene.
   b. Possible witnesses near or around the immediate scene (Be able to identify them for subsequent investigation—name, address, business and home phone numbers).
   c. Open doors, windows, unattached objects which could be associated with the offense.
   d. Points of entry and exit.
4. If the incident occurred within a closed area such as a house, be careful that your path of entry and exit does not destroy evidence. As examples, look for:
   a. Footprints in oil/tar/paint/snow/etc.
   b. Dusty prints on shiny floors
   c. Empty cartridges—projectiles
   d. Broken glass that could have latent fingerprints
   e. Cigarette/cigar butts, other smoking paraphernalia
5. Try to enter and exit by the same path, carefully keeping in mind all conditions as they existed upon your arrival.
6. Observe odors which may be lingering at the scene of the incident. The odor may be present upon arrival only, and may dissipate rapidly depending upon its chemical makeup. Examples include:
   a. Perfume—which could be a link between male and female suspects.
   b. Cooking gas—which could be an attempt to cover up a possible homicide.
   c. Gasoline—indicative of arson or possible cover-up of homicide.
   d. Any other unusual odors which would not otherwise be normally associated with the existing surroundings.

D. Calling for additional help:

Evaluate the condition at the scene and call for whatever additional help is indicated, such as:

1. Extra personnel (This would depend upon the nature of the incident, the layout of the buildings, or terrain to be protected.)
2. Ambulance
3. Fire Department (In some jurisdictions, fire departments handle rescue and ambulance services.)
4. Other Agencies (e.g., Medical Examiner/Coroner)

Figure 6.5 Crime scene investigation checklist.

Protection Of The Scene Checklist

A. Protection—Preservation—Control of the Scene:
  1. Protective measures are required:
     a. To record all persons at the scene.
     b. To prevent removal, destruction, rearrangement, or concealment of physical evidence.
     c. To preserve the scene in its natural state until such time as photographs have been taken and measurements, sketches, and notes are made.
     d. To keep out unauthorized persons who may unwittingly or purposely do some act which may interfere with the successful conclusion of the investigation and prevent the identification and apprehension of the perpetrator(s).
  2. Protection of areas adjoining or surrounding the exact spot where an incident occurred is vital.
     a. In buildings, evidence may be present that shows how the victim/perpetrator entered or left the premises.
     b. In an open area, evidence may be present that shows the route of travel.
     c. Physical evidence may have been dropped accidentally or hidden in adjacent areas.
     d. Fences, gates, bushes, or other shrubbery may contain fibers accidentally torn from clothing.
     e. Soft ground may contain foot, heel, or tire marks.
  3. The following is suggested scene protection equipment—to be carried as standard equipment in all investigative vehicles.
     a. 300 feet of rope or suitable material to rope off the scene.
     b. Emergency lighting (when practical).
     c. Flags easily visible at night to mark specific points of interest for overall pictures of out-of-door crime scene.
     d. 100-foot tape measure
     e. Chalk or crayon
     f. "Keep Out" signs
     g. Street closure barricade
B. Protection of the Scene:
  1. Open Scene—an area that is generally in open terrain and could be affected by the elements. Methods include:
     a. Roping off
     b. Barricading
     c. Use of existing barriers—fences, ditches, roads
     d. Use of natural barriers, such as hills, woods, and streams
  2. Closed Scene—an area that is generally not affected by the elements, e.g., buildings, houses. Methods include:
     a. Roping off
     b. Closing doors, windows
     c. Posting security measures (for lengthy crime scene operations)
     d. Security personnel

Figure 6.6   Crime scene protection checklist.

Crime scenes have come to depend upon a particular job—the Crime Scene Analyst. Read about the usual expectations for this position at: https://www.governmentjobs.com/careers/dallas/jobs/1277529/crime-scene-analyst

6.2.2 Scene Sketches and Other Graphic Portrayals

The investigator should make a representative sketch of the scene as a standard addition to the written report. Scene survey sketches are considered mandatory in most criminal and civil investigations. A scene sketch is a handmade or software-assisted secondary representation of conditions at a scene. Some typical uses of sketches are

- To refresh the memory of the investigator.
- To record the exact location of evidence found in relationship to pieces of furniture or fixed objects.
- To provide a permanent record.
- To assist all persons concerned in understanding facts.
- To supplement photographs and notes.

New and innovative approaches using cutting edge technology are now available to justice professionals when sketching the scene. See: http://www.crime-scene-vr.com/Product.html

While there is no absolute sketch method to follow, all sketches must be accurate, made to scale, and recorded uniformly.[17] If one aspect of a sketch is accurate, such as the dimensions of a field in which a body was found, and the position of an object within the field is only roughly estimated, the distortion thus introduced renders the sketch relatively useless. It is important that the coordinate distances of an item in the sketch be measured in the same manner.[18]

Sketching methods fall into these basic categorizations:

1. Triangulation (see Figure 6.7[19])
2. Baseline or coordinate (see Figure 6.8[20])
3. Cross projection (see Figure 6.9[21])
4. Rough and smooth (finished) sketches (see Figures 6.10[22] and 6.11[23])

6.2.2.1 Rules for Sketching

Regardless of the sketching method chosen,[24] the following rules apply:

- Decide what is to be sketched—the key features.
- Indicate North on the sketch. (Use a compass if necessary.)
- Control all measurements by using measuring tape or ruler.
- Have someone else verify all measurements. (Do not estimate distance by pacing.)
- Take two separate sets of measurements when noting the position of a body; one set from the head and another from the feet.
- Locate all objects accurately and identify all objects drawn in sketch either by numerals or letters. Draw "stick" figures to represent bodies.
- Include all essential items in the drawing.
- Make all sketch corrections at the scene.
- Record date, time, by whom drawn, case number, and names of persons who assisted with measurements.
- Use legend (drawing and charting symbols).

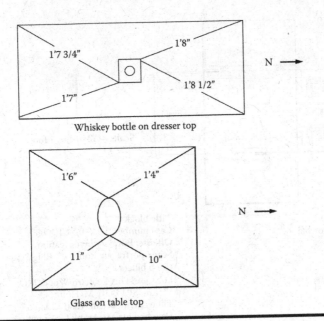

Whiskey bottle on dresser top

Glass on table top

Figure 6.7   Triangulation scene sketch.

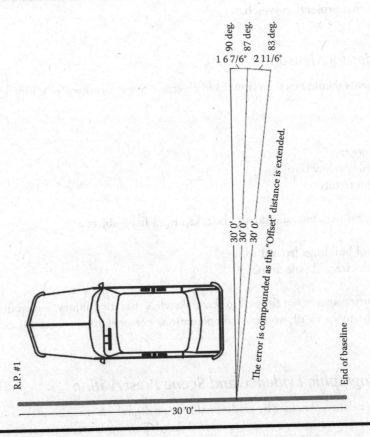

Figure 6.8   Baseline (coordinate) sketch.

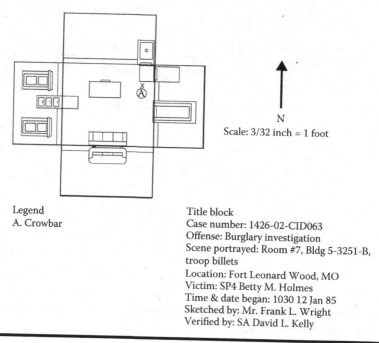

N

Scale: 3/32 inch = 1 foot

Legend
A. Crowbar

Title block
Case number: 1426-02-CID063
Offense: Burglary investigation
Scene portrayed: Room #7, Bldg 5-3251-B,
troop billets
Location: Fort Leonard Wood, MO
Victim: SP4 Betty M. Holmes
Time & date began: 1030 12 Jan 85
Sketched by: Mr. Frank L. Wright
Verified by: SA David L. Kelly

Figure 6.9   Cross projection sketch.

6.2.2.2 Rules for Measuring

All measurements should be taken from fixed objects.[25] Some locations for taking indoor measurements are

- Walls
- Room corners
- Door and window frames
- Bathroom fixtures

Outdoor measurements: should also be taken from fixed objects:

- Corners of buildings (record address)
- Light poles (record pole number)

Graphic portrayals are not limited to scene sketches. External injury and wound charts serve the investigator in cases of workers' compensation, personal injury, and disability cases (see Figure 6.12).

6.2.3 Photographic Evidence and Scene Preservation

Photographic evidence, whether by traditional film or digital means, also plays a key role in the development of an investigator's case. Traditional sketch portrayals are, at times, too subjective and individualized so to be fully reliable. Photographic evidence tends to formalize and memorialize

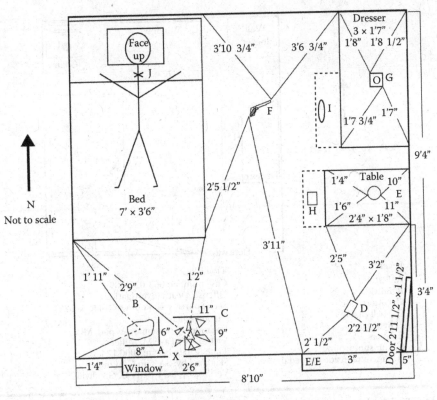

Legend

A. Hole
B. Red stain
C. Glass fragments
D. Shell casing
E. Glass
F. Pistol
G. Bottle
H. Canister
I. Cigarette
J. Neck injury

Title block

Case number: 0123-02-CID037
Offense: Undetermined death
Scene portrayed: Room #C-33, Bldg #3203,
    troop barracks
Location: Fort Leonard Wood, MO 65473
Victim: SGT Janet Williams
Time & date began: 1115 2 Jan 02
Sketched by: SA William Mac
Verified by: SA John Friend

Figure 6.10 Rough crime scene sketch.

the evidence in a fixed state. The scene shown in Figure 6.10 would be difficult to present accurately with a sketch or description alone. Evidence such as this must be depicted as accurately as possible in photographs since the scene—both in terms of the time and place but also the changeability of every scene or setting with the passage of time. As soon as objects such as vehicles and bodies are moved, the scene loses its original integrity (see Figure 6.13).

Private security investigators working in civil or criminal matters usually become adept photographers. However, since they frequently are not on the scene as early as public law enforcement investigators, cooperative arrangements, and relationships with public police are mandatory. "Probably more pictures for use in court are obtained from police photographers than any other source. Almost every police department is equipped with some photographic equipment, a camera or two at least, and in a city of any size, you will find a police photographic laboratory. Patrol

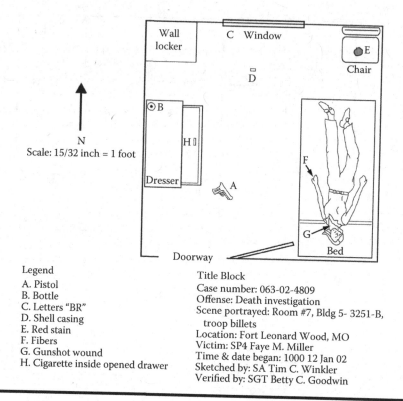

N

Scale: 15/32 inch = 1 foot

Legend
A. Pistol
B. Bottle
C. Letters "BR"
D. Shell casing
E. Red stain
F. Fibers
G. Gunshot wound
H. Cigarette inside opened drawer

Title Block
Case number: 063-02-4809
Offense: Death investigation
Scene portrayed: Room #7, Bldg 5- 3251-B,
 troop billets
Location: Fort Leonard Wood, MO
Victim: SP4 Faye M. Miller
Time & date began: 1000 12 Jan 02
Sketched by: SA Tim C. Winkler
Verified by: SGT Betty C. Goodwin

Figure 6.11   Finished crime scene sketch.

cars are often equipped with cameras. In special accident investigations, cars are more elaborately equipped as are the station wagons or trucks used as field crime investigation laboratories."[26]

Find out how digital photography is now the preferred method of photographic method at the crime scene, accident or other event at: https://www.fletc.gov/training-program/digital-photography-law-enforcement-level-2

Photography is also regularly employed by coroners, medical examiners, forensic experts, scientific experts, attorneys, claims adjusters, and government agencies. "Today law enforcement officials and attorneys everywhere realize the importance of photographing the scene of the crime. Good crime scene photographs are useful even though the case never reaches trial. They give police officials and attorneys the best possible pictorial record of the scene of the crime. Pictures also are useful when questioning witnesses and suspects. Often a guilty party will confess when confronted with indisputable photographic evidence... Throughout the world, the standard police practice is to make photographs of all scenes of serious crimes as soon as possible after discovery before anything is moved or even touched. This rule is so well known now that there is little excuse for anyone ignoring it."[27]

In order for photography to reach its primary evidentiary quality, it must precisely depict the scene, persons, or objects as found. It must also avoid being inflammatory or too gruesome for subsequent admission.[28] Thus, the investigator performing photographic functions is concerned about two fundamental queries:

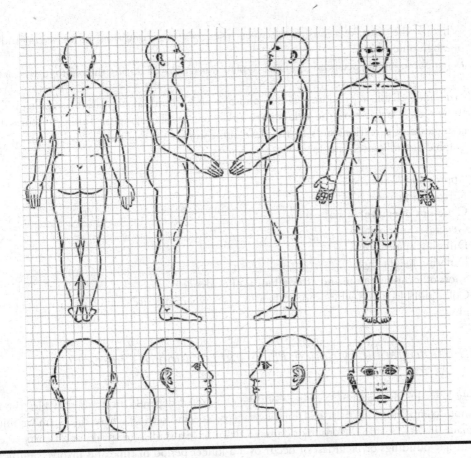

Figure 6.12   Blank wound chart.

Figure 6.13   Crime scene without vehicles to give perspective.

1. What is the time relationship between the event or condition in question and the photographic action?
2. What photographic perspective, angle, or plan was employed during the photographic action?

A true and reliable representation is a photographer's seminal obligation, since significant distortions reduce or destroy the evidentiary value of the photographs. Taking pictures from various angles and directions aids in the development of a reliable perspective. A professional photographic portfolio accounts for

- Approaches to the scene
- Surrounding areas
- Close-ups of entrances and exits
- General scenario shots
- Differing angle shots
- Differing height shots
- Shots of location before and after removal of evidence
- Color and black-and-white shots taken in cases where defense challenges gruesomeness of photos

6.2.3.1 Photographic Evidence: Place and Location of Crime or Civil Action Scene

Precisely how the photographic evidence will be conducted depends on many variables though none more compelling the than geographic place or specific setting where the harm or injury takes place. It may be that the crime or damage claim have a trail so to speak, or an entry or exit into multiple buildings or facilities, or occur over a longer period of time and involve significant movement or displacement. Hence, to collect properly, the photographic display will chronicle the events that unfolded in the place or locations where these events occurred.

In criminal cases, there is a general theorem that the scene be viewed both interiorly and exteriorly. The Federal Bureau of Investigation (FBI) gives specialized guidance for recording exterior and interior crime scene locations in its well-regarded *Crime Laboratory Operations Manual*:[29]

1. Exterior Locations:
   a. Establish the location of the scene by photographs from a distance to include a landmark.
   b. Take medium-distance photographs to show the relative position of closely related items of evidence.
   c. Take close-up photographs of individual items of evidence.
2. Interior Locations:
   a. Establish the location of the building by photograph.
   b. Photograph from eye level, rooms and other interior areas from typical observation points to show relative positions of all items within the area.
   c. Take medium-distance photographs to show the relative positions of closely related items of evidence.
   d. Take close-up photographs of individual items of evidence.

The "Photographer's Photo List" in Figure 6.14 aids in recording significant information.

Photographer's Photo List

Date of Complaint _____ Time _____

D# _____ Date Pictures Taken _____ Time _____

Victim's Name _____

Location _____

Type of Complaint _____

Investigating Officers _____

Photographer _____

_____

Camera _____ Focal Length _____

Lens Type – 1 _____ Diaphragm _____ Shutter _____

– 2 _____ Diaphragm _____ Shutter _____

Filter _____ Type of Lighting _____

Method of Printing _____ Enlarger Lens _____

Paper _____ Contrast _____

Exposure No.

_____   _____
_____   _____
_____   _____
_____   _____
_____   _____
_____   _____
_____   _____
_____   _____
_____   _____
_____   _____
_____   _____

Remarks:

Figure 6.14 Photo list.

A diversity of photographs gives a permanent, accurate perspective to a case that the limitations of memory do not permit. Pictures taken from various angles and directions assure a comprehensive and trustworthy record.

Look at the photos of an automobile accident (see Figures 6.15 through 6.18) from several different perspectives, including wide-angle, close-up, posterior, anterior, and aerial views. Can you make any conclusions or deductions regarding the condition of the vehicle? Consider why these pictures would be important in an investigation of an auto accident case.

6.2.3.2 Photographic Evidence and Special Applications

Just about every sort of criminal or civil case will come to depend on the use of photographic evidence to give it evidentiary permanency. No other technique of collection captures, in such a global and comprehensive fashion, the scope and sweep of the scene.

Figure 6.15   Wide-angle aerial view.

Figure 6.16   Close-up view.

Figure 6.17   Posterior view.

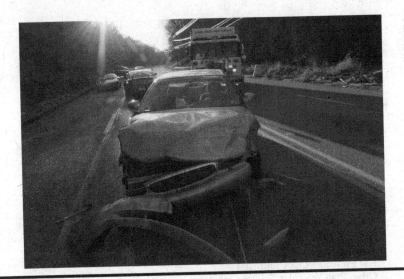

Figure 6.18 Anterior view.

6.2.3.2.1 Photographic Evidence: Vehicular Accidents and Related Auto Claims

Given the transiency of the automobile, capturing the essence of a collision has a present as well as a future urgency. It is obvious that vehicles involved in a crash or collision need be memorialized at that fixed point where the event occurred. Timeliness, always a pressing concern of the investigator, takes on added meaning in any case involving autos. On top of this, because of the need to get traffic moving again, officials must intrude at the scene and move evidence to prevent further accidents. The scene should be recorded promptly and accurately before removal of evidence. When photographing a vehicular accident scene, standard practice comprises pictures or notations of:

- The overall scene of the accident—from both approaches to the point of impact.
- The exact positions of the vehicles, injured persons, and objects directly connected to the accident.
- All points of impact, marks of impact, and damage to real property.
- All pavement obstructions and defects in the roadways.
- Close-ups of damage to vehicles. One photograph should show the front and one side, and another [photograph] should show the rear and other side of the vehicle.
- Skid marks. If possible, photographs should be taken before the vehicle has been removed and again after it has been moved.
- Tire tracks, glass, and other associated debris.[30]

A visual aid or checklist will assist the investigator who is required to photograph the scene. Pictures should reflect some of the issues included within Figure 6.19.[31]

An investigator whose practice is geared toward personal injury, insurance defense, or motor vehicle property damage claims must develop photographic skills. The photographer in this area of expertise should, at a minimum, consider these questions when photographing evidence:

1. What is the extent of damages to the vehicle?
2. What is the extent of personal or bodily injury to the victim, driver, pedestrian, or other interested parties?

Guideline Checklist—Auto Accident Scene

A. Scene:
1. Description/State of Repair of Road
2. Road/Weather/Lighting/Visibility, etc.
3. Description of Collision (abutment, other car(s), etc.)

B. Vehicles (Victim's And Others):
1. Make/Model, etc.
2. Speed (comparison with speed limit)
3. Direction Traveling
4. Safety Devices
   a. Lap Belts
   b. Shoulder Belts
   c. Other Restraints
   d. Locked Doors
   e. Cushioned Dash
   f. Pushout Windows
5. Vehicle Defects
6. Evidence of Alcohol/Drugs

C. Other Than Vehicular Collision (single vehicle, explosion, avalanche, etc.):
1. Description of Events
2. Evidence of Alcohol or Drugs

D. Victim:
1. Location at Moment of Accident
   a. Driver/Passenger (seat location)
   b. Body Location (post accident)
2. Clothing (description/condition)
3. Alcohol or Drugs Present (where, form)
4. Consistency of Injuries w/Accident

E. Other:
1. Possibility of Homicide
2. Possibility of Suicide

Figure 6.19   Auto accident scene checklist.

3. Have any parts or components of the vehicle been identified as or suspected of being defective and, if so, have they been properly photographed?
4. Has the automobile been photographed from various angles and directions?
5. Has the scene of the accident been photographed and fully identified?
6. Have injuries of victims, passengers, pedestrians, or other parties been photographed at various stages (e.g., at time of incident, during treatment, and at intervals thereafter)?

Various examples of photographic evidence pertaining to auto cases are assembled below. Answer the questions that accompany each photo (see Figures 6.20 through 6.22).

6.2.3.2.2 Photographic Evidence and Bodily Injuries

Depending on the time at which the pictures of bodily injuries are taken, conditions can either improve or worsen; however, injuries tend to worsen during the first two to three weeks in a bodily injury case. Fresh injuries tend to minimize the range and extent of damages. Take photographs at regular intervals in order to show bruised areas as they become more visible. In the majority of cases, a good investigator should photograph actual injuries and complement the photos with solid demonstrative evidence.

Figure 6.20 Overturned vehicle in high-speed collision: What evidence can be gleaned from this photographic evidence on the cause of the accident?

6.2.3.2.3 Photographic Evidence in Arson/Insurance Fraud Cases

Private investigators are often hired to investigate claims of insurance fraud involving the burning of the insured's vehicle. "When photographing the arson scene, complete coverage of the damage is important. But perhaps of even greater importance are objects or areas that are suspected to have been the point or points of initiation of fire. Close-up photographs should be made of all such objects or areas."[32]

Figure 6.21 Evidence of skid marks: Does a skid mark provide any evidence regarding the speed of the vehicle?

Figure 6.22 Vehicle from high-speed collision: Does this pictorial evidence provide any inferences or conclusions regarding the degree or angle of impact?

6.2.3.2.4 Photographic Evidence: Burglary/Criminal Trespass/Forcible Theft

In the protection of assets, the security investigator confronts cases of burglary and varied forms of larceny and theft. In cases of burglary, photographic proof of illegal breaking and entering assists the prosecution in meeting this elemental burden. See Figure 6.23 for a representation of photographic proof of forced entry.

When investigating property offenses, the photographer focuses on:

- The interior and exterior of the building.
- Damaged areas, particularly those around the points of entry and exit used by the criminal.

Figure 6.23 A case of burglary—Points of forced entry: Can you identify points or evidence of forced entry?

- Close-ups of damaged containers that were the target of the burglar—safes, jewelry boxes, strong boxes, etc.
- Tool marks, both up close and from a perspective that will allow the position of the mark with respect to the general scene to be noted.
- Fingerprints. Although fingerprints are of major interest to all types of investigations, they are of particular value in a burglary investigation. Fingerprints are photographed only when they are visible without development and when they cannot be lifted after they have been developed.[33]

6.2.3.3 *The Role of Comparative Micrography in Criminal and Civil Cases*

The comparative analysis of tool marks and fragments, the reconstruction of parts to a whole, ballistics comparisons, product reconstruction, and engineering failure analysis or other forms of microanalytical study are evidentiary forms heavily depended upon by investigative specialists. In cases where a product is alleged to be defective, comparative micrography plays an indispensable function—searching for stress points and fractures in materials often show defective design and manufacture. If it is alleged that alteration to product design, misuse, or a failure to follow instructions is an affirmative defense, comparative micrography can, at least in some cases, demonstrate the credibility of this type of argumentation. Investigators must scrutinize and evaluate the quality of this form of judgment, making sure that the comparison of a test plate and the actual sample is fair—that the test was performed under similar facts and circumstances (see Figure 6.24[34] for a helpful flow chart on how to insure the integrity of digital images).

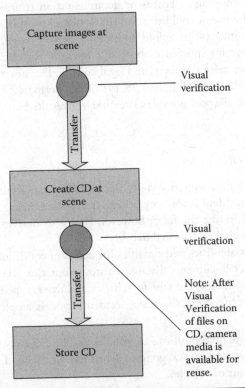

Figure 6.24 Digital image integrity flow chart.

6.3 Documentary Evidence in Criminal and Civil Cases

Proficient security investigators appreciate the crucial role that documentary evidence plays in the proof of most cases. Documentary evidence tends to trap a stated view of facts and conditions in a permanent rather than fluid form of evidence. The document, so it goes, speaks for its content and provides a window of understanding about a particular issue from a particular perspective. The range of scope of documentary evidence forms are simply too vast to fully catalog, but there are recurring forms that private sector specialists encounter. A summary review of the more common types follow.

6.3.1 Police Records

Police regularly complain that most the time expended in their job relates primarily to paperwork and secondarily to social work. Investigators will quickly discern the magnitude of documentation. Discovery of police documentation, from field notes to a final report, should be of professional interest to a security investigator working on a particular case. This is also true in the private sector systems too where investigators fill out many standardized forms and documents during the typical criminal or civil case.

6.3.1.1 Alcohol or Chemical Reports

There has been an increased emphasis on the defense and prosecution of driving while intoxicated or driving under the influence cases. Forms or documentation relative to states of intoxication are helpful. In addition, the rise of civil litigation that emerges from intoxicated behavior is on an upward incline. With the increase in opioid addictions, heroin usage, legalized marijuana, and an overall cultural tolerance for substance abuse, the lawsuits correlating to injury and damage claims are significant concerns for the social and legal culture. Documentary evidence, such as the Psycho-Physiological Test Results in Figure 6.25, provides a permanent measure of an intoxicated state. The Alcohol Influence Report provides Breathalyzer results by measuring alcohol vapor in the respiratory system.

6.3.1.2 Accident Reports

Police accident reports are relied upon heavily because they are fresh impressions of liability. Usually at the scene of an accident before any other party, police, emergency personnel, or private security operatives will transcribe the facts; however, they also may make judgments regarding conduct probative of either civil or criminal liability.

At first, the investigator identifies and classifies the accident conditions, persons, and property involved. Reports and other documents discussed throughout this text are filled out indicating time of day, location, environment, damage to vehicles and drivers, pedestrians, passengers, witnesses, and officials on the scene. Next, the initial accident report is supplemented by the following:

■ Measurements to locate final positions of vehicles and bodies of persons killed or injured.
■ Measurements to locate tire marks, gouges, debris left on the road.
■ Photos of final positions of vehicles.
■ Photos of tire marks, gouges, and debris left on the road.
■ Descriptions of damage to vehicles and measurements of collapse.

Psycho-Physiological Test Results

CD#   Subject

Date

1. Walking Heel-to-Toe
7 steps forward, turn to right/left, 4 steps back

_____ Staggering   _____ Performed correctly

_____ Unable to perform   _____ Falling off balance

_____ Other   _____ Did not follow instructions

                                                 _____ Off white line

2. Finger to nose
Right hand _____ times

                                                 _____ Missed nose _____ times

                                                 _____ Touched nose _____ times

                                                 _____ Did not follow instructions

                                                 _____ Performed correctly

Left hand _____ times

                                                 _____ Missed nose _____ times

                                                 _____ Touched nose _____ times

                                                 _____ Did not follow instructions

                                                 _____ Performed correctly

3. Bending forward
Eyes closed, feet together, tuck in chin, bend for 30 seconds

_____ falling   _____ Swaying side to side

_____ other   _____ Swaying front to back

                                                   _____ Little/no motion

                                                   _____ Did not follow instructions

4. Standing Erect
Eyes closed, feet together, arms alongside

_____ Falling   _____ Swaying side to side

_____ Other   _____ Swaying front to back

                                                   _____ Little/no motion

                                                   _____ Did not follow instructions

5. Alphabet
Ask subject to recite the alphabet

_____ Yes   _____ Recited correctly

_____ No   _____ Unable to recite correctly

6. Counting
Ask subject to count to ten

_____ Yes   _____ Forward 1-10

                                                   _____ Able to perform correctly

                                                   _____ Missed numbers

_____ no   _____ backwards 1-10

                                                   _____ Able to perform correctly

                                                   _____ Missed numbers

Other optional tests: Explain test and note observations

Officer's Signature   _____

Figure 6.25   **Psycho-physiological test results.**

- Photos of damage to vehicles.
- Blood samples for alcohol tests.
- Informal statements of people involved and other witnesses.
- Preliminary matching of contact damage between vehicles and between vehicles and road surface or fixed objects.
- Descriptions and photos of damage to such equipment as lamps, tires, batteries, safety belts, and obtaining these for test if possible.
- Samples of paint and glass for examination.
- Chemical tests for intoxication.
- Autopsies to determine cause of death.
- Medical descriptions of injuries.[35]

After this information is collected the investigator begins to map out or graphically portray the incident. It may involve activities such as

- Elementary ground photogrammetry
- Mapping from perspective template photos
- Matching vehicle damage areas and preparing maximum engagement, first contact, and disengagement diagrams
- Preparation of after-accident situation map
- Simple speed estimates from skid marks, yaw marks, and falls
- Determination of design speed and critical speed of curves and turns[36]

Yaw marks and other reference points can be photographically examined.

As discussed earlier, the investigator's comprehension of the accident site will be fostered by a scene sketch or other descriptive means. To construct an accident map, the investigator should follow the step-by-step instructions below.

1. Decide detail needed based on how map will be used:
   a. For *working* (reconstruction) *purposes*, minimum detail;
   b. For *display* (court) *purposes*, additional detail for realism.
2. Determine layout of roadways by inspection.
   a. Single roadway:
      i. Straight or curved;
      ii. Number of lanes.
   b. Junction of two or more roadways:
      i. Number of legs;
      ii. Number of lanes in each leg;
      iii. Which roadway edges align without offset or angle;
      iv. What angles between roadways are not right angles.
3. Draw on field sketch basic layout of roadways. Use light lines. Show approximate widths, angles, and curves (freehand).
4. Connect all edges which align by dashed line on field sketch.
5. If any leg is not square with the others, project one edge of it until it intercepts the edge of another leg to form an intercept.
6. Select RP (Reference Point or Points). Mark it on field sketch. Write description of RP on field sketch.

7. Mark accident RPs on field sketch if they are known.
8. Draw in edge returns (curves between edges of roadways), shoulders, sidewalks, etc., which may be needed.
9. Draw roadside objects which may be needed (fixed objects, etc.)
10. Draw in other things (buildings, fences, etc.) needed for display.
11. Indicate measurements to be made by dimension lines from coordinates or RPs to Items 3, 5, 7, 8, 9, and 10 above. Show measurements in series as much as possible (a series of measures from one point along a line).
12. Show additional measurements for curves and angles.
13. Add check measurements between important points.
14. Mark road surface (RP, etc.) if needed. Use yellow crayon.
15. Make measurements indicated. Record on field sketch.
16. Note grades, elevations, and character of surface. Record if needed.
17. Show north by arrow. (Add accident identifiers.)
18. Identify location by road name and, if needed, distance and direction to recognizable landmark. Give city or county and state.
19. Sign and date field sketch.[37]

Even a lifetime of field experience will not enable the investigator to claim perfection in auto accident analysis and reconstruction. As insurance companies seek ways of defending the onslaught of accident litigation, private security serves as the objective third party that provides information without bias or prejudice. Police reports are thoroughly examined in other portions of this text and come in paper documents as well as software packages to author and store in a documentary form.

Find out about a software program that investigators use in the field by laptop.
http://www.zeraware.com/portfolio/accident-investigation/

6.3.1.3 Domestic and Workplace Related Violence

Domestic violence is another recurring and escalating challenge for both public and private personnel entrusted with assuring safe environments. Spouses, children, and now increasingly victimized grandparents suffer from the tragedy of domestic violence in staggering numbers. Domestic violence encompasses "one person's use of emotional, physical, or sexual violence, or threat of violence to obtain control of another family member or intimate. Domestic violence may occur in the context of marriage, common-law relationships, or dating relationships and does not discriminate; it affects people from all walks of life, regardless of age, race, religious beliefs, educational background, income, or sexual preference."[38]

The fundamental dilemma for prosecution, under the historical offenses of assault, is the difficulty of proving a level of intentionality sufficient above and beyond the misdemeanor assault. Spousal abuse is far more complicated than a bar room brawl. On top of this, there is a general unwillingness on the part of the judicial system to invade the domestic province too aggressively. Courts do many things well but guarding the internal affairs of family is not its forte. Arguments and sometimes very heated exchanges between partners are natural over the life of any relationship. The fine and intricate lines between abuse and normal bickering are sometimes murky. Add to this the usual reticence witnessed in spouses that fight vigorously yet still hope to achieve a successful relationship, and the emotional crosscurrents can buffet the parties to positions that may not work in the world of common law assault. Any experienced law enforcement officer will tell amazing and befuddling stories of how complicated these affairs can be, of how today's diatribe and torrent of word and hand becomes forgiven before the first witness takes the stand. The complications of love and hate spoil the elemental logic of bodily injury, the intent to inflict and lack of privilege to do so.

More and more police departments are being expected to file and keep paperwork regarding these matters, and public outcry increases when police do not take an activist role in these matters. Domestic Violence Offense Report serves as the foundational document in the development of an evidentiary record sufficient to prove a case of violence. This type of document is quite effective in corroborating or supporting any claim for abuse as grounds for divorce or may serve as evidence in custody or visitation contests.

This same type of violence spills over into the workplace world. So significant are domestic violence issues to the American workplace that business and industry have coalesced to end or inhibit its presence and very negative influences in the workplace. Governmental responses regarding the scourge of domestic violence have been vigorous to say the least. With these types of cases reaching the public domain and its corresponding increases, the federal government has passed a host of laws to protect its employees from the impact of domestic violence.[39]

Legislatures have been frantically trying to halt the tide of domestic violence but the patterns are not being significantly altered, and if there are signs of improvement, it is because the raw data is impacted by less formal, intimate partner relationship other than traditional family structure. This skews data because the tendency is to categorize the data by marriage or partners rather than live in or changeable relationships. In essence, the one side sees assault while the other sees assault and spousal abuse. This is not a small matter statistically.

The Domestic Violence Resource Center paint a picture of extraordinary victimization to individuals that eventually impacts the workplace. In its recent report[40] they state:

- Nearly 33% of women killed in U.S. workplaces between 2003 and 2008 were killed by a current or former intimate partner.[41]
- Nearly one in four large private industry establishments reported at least one incidence of domestic violence, including threats and assaults, in 2005.[42]
- A survey of American employees found that 44% of full-time employed adults personally experienced domestic violence's effect in their workplaces, and 21% identified themselves as victims of intimate partner violence.[43]
- 64% of the respondents in a 2005 survey who identified themselves as victims of domestic violence indicated that their ability to work was affected by the violence. More than half of domestic violence victims (57%) said they were distracted, almost half (45%) feared getting discovered, and two in five were afraid of their intimate partner's unexpected visit (either by phone or in person).[44]
- Nearly two in three corporate executives (63%) say that domestic violence is a major problem in our society and more than half (55%) cite its harmful impact on productivity in their companies.[45]
- Nine in 10 employees (91%) say that domestic violence has a negative impact on their company's bottom line. Just 43% of corporate executives agree. Seven in ten corporate executives (71%) do not perceive domestic violence as a major issue at their company.[46]

- More than 70% of United States workplaces do not have a formal program or policy that addresses workplace violence.[47]
- Nearly 8 million days of paid work each year is lost due to domestic violence issues—the equivalent of more than 32,000 full-time jobs.[48]
- 96% of domestic violence victims who are employed experience problems at work due to abuse.[49]

Many aspects of domestic violence in the workplace can be mitigated by training and preparation of security staff in order that these professionals understand the offense's extraordinary complexity. To be sure, the problems of the home will never be completely separate from the workplace, but trained security professionals will be able to spot problems before harm has been caused; to mediate and remedy specific conflicts and to devise a plan or strategy that anticipates the employee laboring under severe emotional stress caused by domestic violence. The American Society for Industrial Security urges training in these distinct areas:

Background screening for job applicants to uncover information such as criminal records, frequent job changes or the falsification of data in the resume or job application. While there might be valid explanations for frequent job changes, it's recommended that organizations adopt a zero-tolerance policy toward falsified or unexplained data.

Uniform policies and procedures for reporting and disciplining employees who exhibit threatening behavior or engage in harassment, stalking, verbal abuse, theft, etc. To foster a fair and harmonious work environment, written policies and procedures must be universally applied and disseminated to all staff on the day they join the organization, so that no one can later claim he or she wasn't aware of the policies.

Conflict resolution training for both supervisors and employees. Staff should learn how to help defuse potential violence rather than exacerbate it.

Zero-tolerance policies and procedures regarding harassment and violence. These policies should be periodically reviewed to determine their effectiveness, and updated whenever necessary.

An employee grievance system. Employees who aren't given the chance to formally air complaints may silently stew in their resentments until a "trigger" unleashes suppressed anger. An effective grievance system involves transparency, communication and follow-up with those who come forward. If employees believe that nothing has been done to address their complaints, they might assume that management has swept the issues under the rug, which can fuel simmering resentment.

Job counseling for laid-off workers. Though job loss is a leading cause of workplace violence, few companies provide extended job counseling and outplacement services for terminated workers. Companies may reduce the risk of violence by demonstrating that they care enough about former employees to help them find new employment.

An effective crisis management plan. This plan should be communicated company-wide and periodically rehearsed—like a fire drill. Preparing for a crisis is an essential step, but if you fail to thoroughly educate, communicate and train the staff – and then follow-up with "after-action reports"—the plan's shortcomings may not be apparent until the worst possible moment.[50]

An unfortunate reality for commercial entities is the increase in violence in the workplace. The costs of violence are reason enough to adopt documentation policies. There are various reasons:

■ Businesses are beginning to realize the high costs of just one violent incident. These costs can include medical and psychiatric care as well as potential liability suits, lost business and productivity, repairs and clean-up, higher insurance rates, consultants' fees, increased security measures and—most important of all—the death or injury of valued employees and coworkers.
■ Threats and other violent, abusive behaviors are no longer tolerated in the workplace.
■ Executives, professionals, and administrative personnel are no longer immune to acts of violence in the workplace.
■ Layoffs, increased workload, having to do more with less, and other unpopular changes in the work environment have been associated with increased risk for violence.
■ Recent reports and surveys suggest that workplace violence impacts large numbers of employers and employees.
■ It's the right thing to do. Employers have both a moral and a legal obligation to provide a safe workplace for their employees, clients, and visitors.[51]

If violence occurs prepare a Threat Report like Figure 6.26.

6.3.1.4 Missing Person Reports

A "missing person" report is useful to investigators working on cases of insurance fraud, escape from prison, violation of probation and parole, change of identity, or other forms of subterfuge (see Figure 6.27[52] for a sample *Report of Person*).

6.3.1.5 Suspect Descriptions

Suspect descriptions provide a secondary view of identity and person shaped and framed by a party familiar with a suspect's features. While never a perfect match, the suspect description delivers a combination both visual and descriptive terminology. Two forms of suspect descriptions are outlined below. Abbreviated suspect descriptions can proved helpful during the initial investigation (see Figure 6.28). Figures 6.29 and 6.30 deliver a far more detailed series of variable that visualize the person under review.

6.3.2 Medical Records

Since medical records serve as the presumptive base or foundation for medical damage claims in civil litigation, their orchestration, control, and catalog always remain central to proper process in the investigative and evidentiary realm. The array of medical records and documentation defies listing, but suffice it to say, the private sector investigator, assigned to a negligence case, workers comp, disability claim, or other legal rationale for excuse from job performance cannot carry out his or her task without collecting and preserving these critical evidentiary records.

Standard medical records are indispensable in the investigation of any medical, personal injury, or related claim. Medical releases authorizing the transfer of information from a hospital, physician, consultant, emergency room, or employer should be signed. A general medical release, granted by the client, is given in Figure 6.31.[53]

Threat Report

Name of person(s) making threat _____

Relationship to company _____

Relationship to recipient of threat, if any _____

Name(s) of the recipients or victims _____

Date and location of incident _____

What happened immediately prior to the incident _____

_____

_____

The specific language of the threat _____

_____

Any physical conduct that would substantiate an intention to follow through with the threat _____

_____

How the threat-maker appeared, both physically and emotionally _____

_____

Names of others who were directly involved, and any actions they took _____

_____

_____

How the incident ended _____

_____

Names of witnesses _____

_____

What happened to the treat-maker after the incident _____

_____

What happened to other employees directly involved in the incident, if any ____

_____

Names of any supervisory staff involved and how they responded _____

_____

What event(s) triggered the incident _____

Any history leading up to the incident _____

The steps that have been taken to assure the threat will not be carried out _____

_____

Suggestions for preventing this type of incident from occurring again _____

_____

_____

Figure 6.26   Threat report.

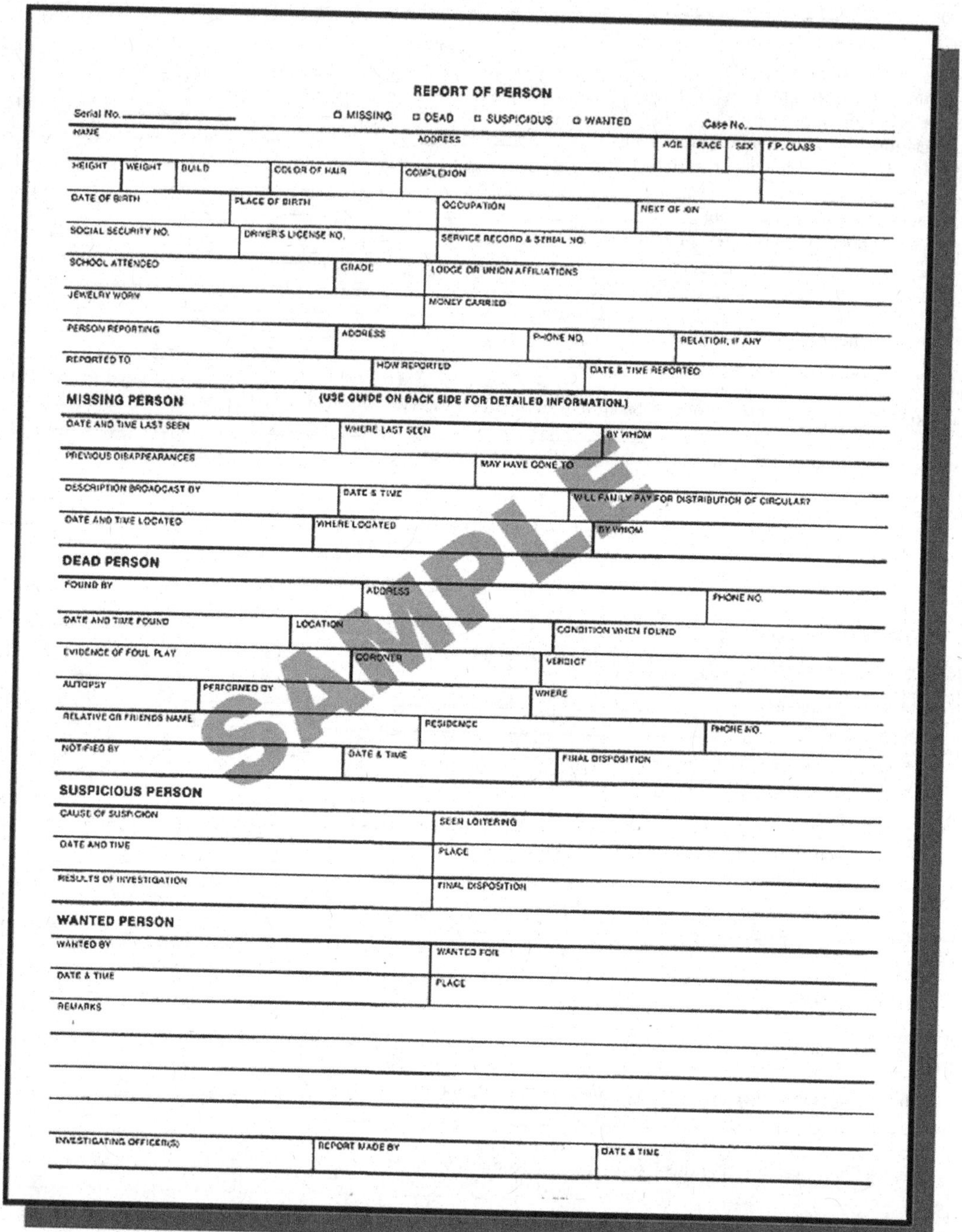

REPORT OF PERSON

Serial No. ______ ☐ MISSING ☐ DEAD ☐ SUSPICIOUS ☐ WANTED Case No. ______

NAME | ADDRESS | AGE | RACE | SEX | F.P. CLASS

HEIGHT | WEIGHT | BUILD | COLOR OF HAIR | COMPLEXION

DATE OF BIRTH | PLACE OF BIRTH | OCCUPATION | NEXT OF KIN

SOCIAL SECURITY NO. | DRIVER'S LICENSE NO. | SERVICE RECORD & SERIAL NO.

SCHOOL ATTENDED | GRADE | LODGE OR UNION AFFILIATIONS

JEWELRY WORN | MONEY CARRIED

PERSON REPORTING | ADDRESS | PHONE NO. | RELATION, IF ANY

REPORTED TO | HOW REPORTED | DATE & TIME REPORTED

MISSING PERSON (USE GUIDE ON BACK SIDE FOR DETAILED INFORMATION.)

DATE AND TIME LAST SEEN | WHERE LAST SEEN | BY WHOM

PREVIOUS DISAPPEARANCES | MAY HAVE GONE TO

DESCRIPTION BROADCAST BY | DATE & TIME | WILL FAMILY PAY FOR DISTRIBUTION OF CIRCULAR?

DATE AND TIME LOCATED | WHERE LOCATED | BY WHOM

DEAD PERSON

FOUND BY | ADDRESS | PHONE NO.

DATE AND TIME FOUND | LOCATION | CONDITION WHEN FOUND

EVIDENCE OF FOUL PLAY | CORONER | VERDICT

AUTOPSY | PERFORMED BY | WHERE

RELATIVE OR FRIENDS NAME | RESIDENCE | PHONE NO.

NOTIFIED BY | DATE & TIME | FINAL DISPOSITION

SUSPICIOUS PERSON

CAUSE OF SUSPICION | SEEN LOITERING

DATE AND TIME | PLACE

RESULTS OF INVESTIGATION | FINAL DISPOSITION

WANTED PERSON

WANTED BY | WANTED FOR

DATE & TIME | PLACE

REMARKS

INVESTIGATING OFFICER(S) | REPORT MADE BY | DATE & TIME

SAMPLE

Figure 6.27 Report of person.

Describe the Suspect.

The primary or most useful information to obtain when describing a suspect is:

Sex _____ Race _____ Age _____ Height _____ Weight _____

If a weapon is used it is very helpful to know if the weapon is a:

❑ Revolver

❑ Automatic

Other useful information is:

_____
Hair

_____
Color of eyes

_____
Glasses

_____
Moustache/Beard, Sideburns

_____
Complexion

_____
Tattoos, Amputations, Scars, or Marks

_____
Speech impediments or accents

_____
Distinguishable gait or limp

_____
Hat

_____
Shirt

_____
Coat

_____
Tie

_____
Pants and Shoes

Figure 6.28   Suspect description.

(Continued)

Vehicle Description.

The primary or most useful information to obtain when identifying a motor vehicle is the *license number*, **with state of issue or identifying colors.** _____
Other useful information is:

_____   _____   _____

What make?   Body Style? (2 dr., 4 dr., conv., etc.)   What year?

_____   _____

What color? Two color (two tone)?   Identifying dents, scratches?

The police can use answers to as many of these questions as possible. Please remember that wrong information is worse than no information at all. Answer only those questions that you're sure of.

1. How many suspects were there? _____
2. What did they do? _____
   _____
   _____
3. What did they say? _____
   _____
   _____
4. What did they take? _____
   _____
   _____

5. Which way did they go? _____
   _____
   _____

6. Were there any other witnesses? _____
   Names and addresses? _____
   _____
   _____

   Phone numbers? _____

7. Is there any other information you feel is important? _____
   _____
   _____
   _____
   _____

COMMUNITY
CRIME PREVENTION

MINNEAPOLIS
SAFE
POLICE

VISION
The City of Minneapolis is the safest place to live, work and visit.

For individuals with disabilities:
If you need this material in Braille, large print, computer disk, or cassette tape, call 612-673-2912. Sign language interpreters available — call 612-673-3220 or 612-673-2626 (TTY). Please allow two weeks for accommodation.

DESCSUSP.P65 6/03

Figure 6.28 (Continued)   **Suspect description.**

Details Description

1. SEX (Male, Female)
2. RACE (Caucasian, African American, Native American, Pacific Islander, Asian, etc.)
3. AGE _____
4. HEIGHT (Compare with person with whom you work) ____ ft. ____ in.
5. WEIGHT (Compare with person with whom you work) _____lbs.
6. PROBABLE NATIONALITY (American, English, Latin, Scandinavian, Japanese, etc.)
7. BUILD (slender, medium, heavy, stocky, athletic, very heavy, very thin, etc.)
8. POSTURE (erect, stooped, slumped, etc.)
9. COMPLEXION (fair, dark, red, tanned, pale, freckly, pimply, rough, smooth, etc.)
10. HEAD (large, medium, small, round, square, oblong, broad, inclined forward, backward, sideways)
11. HAIR (color _____; color at temples ____; baldness: frontal, top, receding at hairline, totally bald; texture: thick, thin, coarse, straight, wavy, kinky, curled, bushy; parted on right, left, middle, no part)
12. EYES (brown, blue, green, grey, hazel; clear, bloodshot; large, small, deep-set, protruding, straight, slanted, cross-eyed, narrow, squinting, close-set, wide apart; eyelashes: long, short; glass eye. If glasses worn: type, color of rims, etc.)
13. FOREHEAD (broad, narrow, high, low, receding, vertical, bulging)
14. EYEBROWS (thin, bushy, penciled, natural, arched, horizontal, slanting up or down, meeting)
15. NOSE (long, medium, short; thin, thick, straight, concave, convex, pointed, flat, turned up, turned down, pointed to right or left; nostrils: large, small, high, low, flared)
16. MUSTACHE OR BEARD (short, medium, long, pointed, ends turned up or down; thick, thin; type of beard or sideburns) Compare with color of hair
17. CHEEKS (full, fleshy, sunken, etc.)
18. CHEEKBONES (high, low, prominent, not prominent)
19. MOUTH (turned up or down at corners, held open or closed, distorted by speech or laughter)
20. LIPS (with reference to either upper or lower: thick, thin, puffy, overhanging, compressed, protruding, retracted over teeth; cracked, scarred; red, pale, blue)
21. TEETH (white, yellow, stained, loose, decayed, broken, filled, braced, capped, receding or projecting, false, prominent bridgework, etc.)
22. CHIN (small, large, normal, square, curved, pointed, flat, double, dimpled, protruding, receding, etc.)
23. JAW (long, short, wide, narrow, thin, fleshy, square, heavy, etc.)
24. EARS (small, medium, large, close to or projecting from head; oval, round, rectangular, triangular; pierced, cauliflowered, hairy; contour of the lobe, lower portion)
25. NECK (small, medium, long, straight, curved, thin, flat, goiterous, crooked; Adams' apple: flat, prominent, medium, absent)
26. SHOULDERS (small, heavy, narrow, broad, square, round, stooped, not equal, etc.)
27. HANDS (long, short, broad, narrow, thin, fleshy, rough, bony, soft, smooth, hairy, square, tapered, etc.)
28. FINGERS (short, long, slim, thick, tapered, square, stained, mutilated, etc.)
29. FINGERNAILS (length, description, foreign matter under nails; painted)
30. VOICE (pleasant, well-modulated, low, high, lisp or other impediment of speech, gruff, polite, regional or foreign accent)
    REMEMBER EXACT LANGUAGE USED _____

_____

_____

_____

Figure 6.29 Detailed suspect description.

(Continued)

31. WALK (long or short stride, energetic, slow, fast, springy step, limp)
32. APPEARANCE (loud, conservative, neat, sloppy)
33. CLOTHING: (list color, pattern, type, material, condition, how worn)

Hat or cap _____

Overcoat _____

Pants _____

Suit _____

Dress _____

Shirt _____

Tie _____

Shoes _____

Socks _____

Belt _____

Mask _____

34. JEWELRY (rings, watches, chains, earrings, tie pins, lapel pins, bracelets, cuff links, etc.)

Describe _____

35. PECULIARITIES (most important of all) (scars, marks, tattoos, moles, birthmarks)

Describe _____

36. TYPE OF WEAPON USED:

Name _____

Address _____

Date _____

Figure 6.29 (Continued)   Detailed suspect description.

Being attentive to privacy considerations and the emerging or existing legislation that guides the personal integrity of medical records is an ongoing security concern. Medical records prompt a host of ethical and practical dilemmas. The Electronic Privacy Information Center warns not only consumers but the investigators:

> Besides information about physical health, these records may include information about family relationships, sexual behavior, substance abuse, and even the private thoughts and feelings that come with psychotherapy. This information is often keyed to a social security number. Because of a lack of consistent privacy protection in the use of Social Security Numbers, the information may be easily accessible.
>
> Information from your medical records may influence your credit, admission to educational institutions, and employment. It may also affect your ability to get health insurance, or the rates you pay for coverage (OTA report). More importantly, having others know intimate details about your life may mean a loss of dignity and autonomy.[54]

THE STANFORD UNIVERSITY SAFETY & SECURITY REPORT

Describing a Suspect and Vehicle

Reporting a Crime | Suspect / Vehicle Description

Reporting Crime & Suspicious Activity

All students, faculty, staff and visitors at Stanford are encouraged to report all crimes and public safety related incidents to the Stanford Department of Public Safety in a timely manner.

Anytime you need **immediate** police, fire, or medical response, **dial 9-9-1-1** from University phones (all Stanford prefixes). From non-university phones, dial 9-1-1. Remember that 9-1-1 is a **free** call from pay phones and any cell phone. In addition, emergency phones with blue lights are located in many areas on campus. These phones are either blue emergency towers or pay phones with blue lights on top. For a **non-emergency** police response on campus, dial 723-9633.

Call 911 if you think a crime is in progress, which might be indicated by:

- A whistle, scream or call for help.
- A strange car repeatedly driving up and down the street.
- Seeing someone you don't know or recognize enter your neighbor's room or home, enter an office or lab with no apparent business or transaction, or loiter in a parking area or at a bike rack near your home, dorm, or work.

Remember that the police cannot be everywhere at once, and they depend on individuals in the community to assist them in crime prevention by reporting suspicious activities.

How to Describe a Suspect and Vehicle

INSTRUCTIONS: This form is to aid you describing a suspect or a suspect's vehicle. This does not take the place of phoning 9-911 or 911.
In an emergency, do not take the time to fill in this form.
Call 9-911 from a campus phone, or 911 from a non-campus phone or cell phone.

Date _____
Time _____
Location _____
Direction of Travel _____
Weapon _____

Figure 6.30 Stanford University Webpage regarding suspect and vehicle descriptions. (The City of New York owns all trademarks associated with the New York City Police Department. The copyright to the content of the NYPDShield.org website is owned by the City of New York and is used herein with permission. All rights reserved.) *(Continued)*

Suspect Information

Male _____   Female _____
Adult _____   Juvenile _____   Approximate Age _____
Race _____
Height _____   Weight _____
Hair Color _____
Eye Color _____
Mustache, bear, sideburns or other facial hair _____
Tattoos, scars or other identifying marks _____
Gait, limp or amputations _____

Suspect's Clothing

Hat _____
Glasses _____
Shirt type and color _____
Pants type and color _____
Shoes _____

Automobile Information

Make _____
Model _____
Color _____
Year _____
Body style (2-door, 4-door, convertible, truck, etc.) _____
License plate number _____
Distinguishing features (spoiler, racing stripes, tinting, damage, etc.) _____

Figure 6.30 (Continued)   Stanford University Webpage regarding suspect and vehicle descriptions. (The City of New York owns all trademarks associated with the New York City Police Department. The copyright to the content of the NYPDShield.org website is owned by the City of New York and is used herein with permission. All rights reserved.)

MEDICAL RELEASE

You are hereby authorized to release to the investigator any and all information, without limitation, that you possess. This release includes, but is not limited to, billing information, admission records, X-ray reports, lab reports, nurses' notes, progress reports, and discharge summaries.

This authorization shall not expire until expressly canceled. A copy of this release shall be as effective as an original.

Name: _____
NAME OF CLIENT

Dated: _____

Signature: _____

Figure 6.31   Medical release.

Efforts to federally control access to medical records are often seen legislative initiatives. In 104th U.S. Congress (1996), Congress poses the language of privacy, protection, and medical records, in the Medical Privacy in the Age of New Technologies Act of 1996.[55] Sanctions for privacy violations are also authorized:

> SEC. 311. WRONGFUL DISCLOSURE OF PROTECTED HEALTH INFORMATION.
> 1. *Offense*—Whoever knowingly—
>   a. Obtains protected health information relating to an individual in violation of this Act;
>   b. Discloses protected health information to another person in violation of this Act;
>   c. Coerces or attempts to coerce a health information trustee to disclose protected health information in violation of this title; or
>   d. Without authorization pursuant to this Act, identifies or attempt to identify an individual who is the subject of protected health information that a health information trustee has converted into coded health information, shall be punished as provided in subsection (b).
> 2. *Penalties*—A person referred to in subsection (a) shall be fined under title 18, United States Code, imprisoned not more than 1 year, or both, except that—
>   a. If the offense is committed under false pretenses, the person shall be fined under title 18, United States Code, imprisoned not more than 5 years, or excluded from participation in the program under title XVIII of the Social Security Act, the program under title XIX of such Act, or any other federally funded health care program, or any combination of such penalties.[56]

A policy statement or draft laying out the several parameters of information disclosure, release, and protection is an essential security function. Every office entrusted with the protection of records should implement a policy, similar to Figure 6.32.

Requesting hospital records from emergency rooms, consultants, or other medical professionals working for hospitals is standard investigative practice. See a client authorization request for hospital records in Figure 6.33.

Another example of a medical information request document that complements an investigative file is a request for a copy of an office record. In this case, the correspondence is usually directed to the treating physician's clerk or other paraprofessional who handles records. This should not be confused with a direct request for a medical evaluation or report, which is usually in the form of a standardized document such as a tabulated bill (see Figure 6.34).

Access request for every type of record whether, Admission and Discharge Records, Emergency Room Records, X-ray Reports, Medical Expense Records, Billing Statements, Payroll Information, Life Squad Reports, Death Certificates, etc., follow a similar format.

6.3.3 Documentary Evidence Involving Economic Damages

Customarily, investigators involved in cases of workers' compensation, disability, social security, or personal injury collect not only evidence of actual medical injuries, but also records concerning economic losses. Economic losses can take many forms, from losing the value of certain property to the loss of past, present, and future earnings capacity. Because of these factors, the investigator needs to gain access to employment and payroll records.

HIPAA Privacy Authorization Form

**Authorization for Use or Disclosure of Protected Health Information

(Required by the Health Insurance Portability and Accountability Act, 45 C.F.R. Parts 160 and 164)**

1. Authorization

I authorize _____ (healthcare provider) to use and disclose the protected health information described below to _____ (individual seeking the information).

2. Effective Period

This authorization for release of information covers the period of healthcare from:

a. ☐ _____ to _____.

OR

b. ☐ all past, present, and future periods.

3. Extent of Authorization

a. ☐ I authorize the release of my complete health record (including records relating to mental healthcare, communicable diseases, HIV or AIDS, and treatment of alcohol or drug abuse).

OR

b. ☐ I authorize the release of my complete health record with the exception of the following information:

☐ Mental health records

☐ Communicable diseases (including HIV and AIDS)

☐ Alcohol/drug abuse treatment

☐ Other (please specify): _____

Figure 6.32   HIPAA privacy authorization form.

(Continued)

4. This medical information may be used by the person I authorize to receive this information for medical treatment or consultation, billing or claims payment, or other purposes as I may direct.

5. This authorization shall be in force and effect until _____ (date or event), at which time this authorization expires.

6. I understand that I have the right to revoke this authorization, in writing, at any time. I understand that a revocation is not effective to the extent that any person or entity has already acted in reliance on my authorization or if my authorization was obtained as a condition of obtaining insurance coverage and the insurer has a legal right to contest a claim.

7. I understand that my treatment, payment, enrollment, or eligibility for benefits will not be conditioned on whether I sign this authorization.

8. I understand that information used or disclosed pursuant to this authorization may be disclosed by the recipient and may no longer be protected by federal or state law.

_____

Signature of patient or personal representative

_____

Printed name of patient or personal representative and his or her relationship to patient

_____

Date

Figure 6.32 (Continued)   HIPAA privacy authorization form.

An example of an authorization and request for employment records is given in Figure 6.35, along with inquiries about the client's payroll history, as well as the period of employment and the extent of weekly and overtime pay.

Often, employers compile and maintain records dealing with medical benefits because of a medical insurance, workers' compensation, or disability plan. A release or authorization for this information directed to the employer is given in Figure 6.36.

6.4 Preservation of Evidence

Collection and preservation of evidence and the assurance of its integrity during the investigative process are undeniable responsibilities of the public and private police system. Contamination of the evidence becomes problematic as to admissibility, constitutional regularity, and overall

Date:

To:

RE:

Our File No.:

Dear _____:

I have retained this firm to represent me in injuries sustained as a result of an accident that occurred on _____. Please send to this firm's address the medical records for this accident as well as a complete billing summary for services rendered to date. Please bill _____ for this report.

Sincerely,

_____

Patient Account #: _____

Figure 6.33 Client authorization to release hospital records.

credibility. Security professionals are continually concerned with whether or not the chain of custody of the evidence has been distorted, broken, contaminated, abused, reformulated, recast, or changed in any significant way. Every sort of evidence should be catalogued and packaged to track its life from collection to courtroom presentation and usage. Evidence such as tools, guns, glass fragments, hairs, fibers, body parts—any real, physical evidence—should be stored in an environment that maintains, as scientifically as possible, its original status.[57] "The investigator himself should bear in mind the possibility that he himself may destroy or contaminate evidence before it is noticed or recognized. Minute spurts of blood, particles of dust, dirt, and debris are not always obvious to the naked eye and can be destroyed or rendered worthless as evidence if the investigator is not sufficiently observant during his investigation. Defense counsel should recognize the possibility or probability of contamination having occurred and conduct his cross-examination accordingly."[58] In fact, chain of custody finding dictate a wide array of tactical decision regarding the use of evidence at trial or hearing. The legal "chain of custody" must be maintained at all times.[59] The Pennsylvania State Police, in their *Crime Laboratory Operations Manual*, offer timeless advice on the preservation of evidence.

> Each item of evidence should be placed in a suitable container, and this container should be properly identified and sealed. The laboratory can only aid in the investigation if

Date:

Name:
Address:

IN RE: Request for Copy of Office Record
          Name of Patient:
          Date of Injury:

Dear Dr. _____:

Please be advised that I am an investigator in the above-referenced case and have been given full power of attorney to seek information and records. Attached is a copy of the power of attorney. I am writing at this time to request a copy of the medical record that has been prepared by your office for this patient. Please send me a copy of this record as soon as possible.

I have enclosed a copy of a medical release which authorizes me to acquire this information. If there is any charge for copying or printing the requested material, please send a statement together with the requested information.

Sincerely,

Name of Investigator

Enclosure

Figure 6.34   Request for medical evaluation or report.

evidence has been preserved… As a general rule, to guarantee the value of the evidence collected, evidence should be packaged to:

1. *Prevent loss*—Package all evidence in such a manner that small items will not be lost from the container or in the seams or folds of a container. Envelopes are poor containers for small items such as paint chips, since they can leak out at the corners or become lodged in the folds and be difficult to remove without loss or damage. Pill boxes or plastic vials should be used for this type of evidence.
2. *Prevent contamination*—Separate items so that there is no mixing of items from various locations. NEVER place items from the scene and from the suspect in the same container. Each article of clothing from a victim or suspect of a crime should also be individually packaged and identified so that no trace evidence is transferred from one item to the next.
3. *Prevent alteration*—Handle and package the evidence in such a manner that it reaches the laboratory in the same condition as collected. Use common sense.[60]

The FBI, in its *Handbook for Forensic Science*,[61] has published guidelines on how evidence should be packaged, processed, and mailed for any analysis. See Figure 6.37[62] for a summary version of those packaging and safety standards.

Authorization and Request for Employment Records

To: _____   Re: _____

_____   Name of Employee

_____   _____

_____   Address

_____

S.S#: _____

You are hereby requested and authorized to furnish to my Attorney whose name and address is:

or my attorney's authorized representative, any information you may have regarding my past or present employment. Please provide copies of any records along with any other requested information. I would appreciate your full cooperation.

Dated: _____   _____

Employee

Additional Remarks: _____

_____

_____

_____

_____

_____

_____

Dated: _____   _____

Title

Figure 6.35   Authorization for employment records.

MEDICAL BENEFIT RELEASE FORM

This employee's records release authorizes you to furnish to the investigator named any record, information, or knowledge which is in your possession. This release includes, but is not limited to, information concerning my rates of pay, sick records, overtime records, vacation records, personnel records, injury and health records, tax and social security records, and insurance benefits records. The release shall remain valid until it is expressly canceled. A copy of this release shall be as effective as an original.

Name: NAME-OF-CLIENT

Social Security Number: ....

Date of Birth: ....

Name of Investigator: ....

Dated: _____   Signature _____

Figure 6.36   Medical benefit release form.

SUBMITTING EVIDENCE

Requesting Evidence Examinations

All requests for evidence examinations should be in writing, on agency letterhead, and addressed to the FBI Laboratory Evidence Management Program, unless otherwise indicated in the **Examinations** section.

Do not submit multiple cases under a single communication. Each case should be submitted with a separate communication and packaged separately.

All international law enforcement agency/police requests should be coordinated through the appropriate FBI legal attaché (LEGAT). LEGATs should fax the request to the Evidence Control Unit, 703-632-8334, prior to submitting any evidence to the Laboratory. Questions concerning international submissions should be directed to 703-632-8360.

Requests for evidence examinations must contain the following information:

- The submitting contact person's name, agency, address, and telephone number;
- Previous case-identification numbers, evidence submissions, and communications relating to the case;
- Description of the nature and the basic facts of the case as they pertain to evidence examinations;
- The name(s) of and descriptive data about the individual(s) involved (subject, suspect, victim, or a combination of those categories) and the agency-assigned, case-identification number;
- The violation;
- Reason for expedited examination, if requested;
- The name of the relevant prosecutor's office or prosecutor assigned, if available;
- A list of the evidence being submitted "herewith" (enclosed) or "under separate cover"

  - *Herewith* is limited to small items of evidence that are not endangered by transmitting in an envelope. Write on the envelope before placing evidence inside to avoid damaging or altering the evidence. The written communication should state: ***"Submitted herewith are the following items of evidence."***

  - Separate cover is used to ship numerous or bulky items of evidence. Include a copy of the communication requesting the examinations. The written communication should state: ***"Submitted under separate cover by [list the method of shipment] are the following items of evidence."***

- What type(s) of examination(s) is/are requested;
- Where the evidence should be returned and where the Laboratory report should be sent (a street address and phone number must be included); and
- A statement if there is local controversy or if other law enforcement agencies have an interest in the case.

Packaging and Shipping Evidence

Unless otherwise indicated in a specific Examination section, follow the below guidelines for packaging and shipping evidence. Please keep in mind the FBI case acceptance guidelines and limitations in the Introduction section.

Figure 6.37   FBI evidence submission guidelines.   *(Continued)*

- Prior to packaging and shipping evidence, call the pertinent unit for specific instructions.
- Take precautions to preserve the evidence.
- Wrap and seal each item of evidence separately to avoid contamination.
- Place the evidence in a clean, dry, and previously unused inner container.
- Seal the inner container with tamper-evident or filament tape.
- Affix EVIDENCE and BIOHAZARD labels, if appropriate, on the inner container. If any of the evidence needs to be examined for latent prints, affix a LATENT label on the inner container.
- Affix the evidence examination request and all case information between the inner and outer containers.
- Place the sealed inner container in a clean, dry, and previously unused outer container with clean packing materials. Do not use loose Styrofoam.
- Completely seal the outer container so that tampering with the container would be evident.
- All **shipments of suspected or confirmed hazardous materials** must comply with U.S. Department of Transportation and International Air Transport Association regulations. Title 49 of the Code of Federal Regulations (CFR) lists specific requirements that must be observed when preparing hazardous materials for shipment by air, land, or sea. In addition, the International Air Transport Association annually publishes Dangerous Goods Regulations detailing how to prepare and package shipments for air transportation.
- Title 49 CFR 172.101 provides a Hazardous Materials Table that identifies items considered hazardous for the purpose of transportation. Title 49 CFR 172.101 also addresses special provisions for certain materials, hazardous materials communications, emergency response information, and training requirements for shippers. A trained and qualified evidence technician must assist with the typing, labeling, packaging, and shipping of all hazardous materials.

Further information regarding shipping of Hazardous Materials or potential Chemical/Biological/ Radiological/Nuclear (CBRN) Material can be found in WMD/CBRN Evidence Examinations.

- U.S. Department of Transportation regulations and the following guidelines must be followed when shipping live ammunition:
- Package and ship ammunition separately from firearm(s).
- The outside of the container must be labeled **"ORM-D, CARTRIDGES, SMALL ARMS."**
- The Declaration of Dangerous Goods must include the number of packages and the gross weight in grams of the completed packages.

Unless otherwise indicated in the Examinations section, address the outer container as follows:

EVIDENCE MANAGEMENT PROGRAM
LABORATORY DIVISION
FEDERAL BUREAU OF INVESTIGATION
2501 INVESTIGATION PARKWAY
QUANTICO VA 22135

- Ship evidence by U.S. Postal Service Registered Mail, UPS, or FedEx.

Figure 6.37 (Continued) FBI evidence submission guidelines.

(Continued)

Adhesive, Caulk, and Sealant Examinations

Adhesives, caulks, and sealants can be compared by color and chemical composition with suspected sources. The source and manufacturer of adhesives, caulks, and sealants cannot be determined by compositional analysis.

Questions concerning adhesive, caulk, and sealant evidence should be directed to 703-632-8441.

Collection and packaging considerations:

- When possible, submit the item to which the adhesive, caulk, or sealant is adhered. If this is not possible, remove a sample of the material with a clean, sharp instrument and transfer it to a resealable plastic bag or leakproof container such as a screw top vial or plastic pill box.
- Submit a suspected source. Package separately.

Advanced Photography

Highly skilled Scientific & Technical Photographers can provide detailed and accurate on-site documentation using oblique and vertical aerial photography (also see GIS Mapping and Aerial Photography), 360-degree spherical photography, 360-degree spherical video, and high-resolution imagery for special operations, crime scenes, and special events. All photographs can be geo-referenced, allowing imagery to be used by Visual Information Specialists to prepare crime scene diagrams, digitally interactive scenes, and scenario reconstructions (also see Demonstrative Evidence and Special Event and Situational Awareness Support).

Questions concerning advanced photography can be directed to your Field Photographer or be directed to 703-632-8194.

Age of Document Examination

The earliest date a document could have been prepared may be determined by examining various physical characteristics, including watermarks, indented writing, printing, typewriting, and inks.

Questions concerning age of document examinations should be directed to 703-632-8444.

Collection and packaging considerations:

- Documentary evidence must be preserved in the condition in which it was found. It must not be unnecessarily folded, torn, marked, soiled, stamped, or written on or handled excessively. Protect the evidence from inadvertent indented writing.
- Mark documents unobtrusively by writing the collector's initials, date, and other information in pencil.
- Whenever possible, submit the original evidence. The lack of detail in photocopies makes examinations difficult and often will result in inconclusive opinions.

Altered or Obliterated Writing Examinations

Documents can be examined for the presence of altered or obliterated writing, and the original writing may be deciphered.

Questions concerning altered or obliterated writing should be directed to 703-632-8444.

Figure 6.37 (Continued) FBI evidence submission guidelines.   *(Continued)*

Collection and packaging considerations:

- Documentary evidence must be preserved in the condition in which it was found. It must not be unnecessarily folded, torn, marked, soiled, stamped, or written on or handled excessively. Protect the evidence from inadvertent indented writing.

- Mark documents unobtrusively by writing the collector's initials, date, and other information in pencil.

- Whenever possible, submit the original evidence. The lack of detail in photocopies makes examinations difficult and often will result in inconclusive opinions.

Anonymous Letter File

The Anonymous Letter File (ALF) contains images of anonymous and/or threatening communications submitted for examination. This file can be searched in an attempt to associate text from a communication in one case with text from communications in other cases.

Questions concerning the ALF should be directed to 703-632-8444.

Collection and packaging considerations:

- Documentary evidence must be preserved in the condition in which it was found. It must not be unnecessarily folded, torn, marked, soiled, stamped, or written on or handled excessively. Protect the evidence from inadvertent indented writing.

- Mark documents unobtrusively by writing the collector's initials, date, and other information in pencil.

- Whenever possible, submit the original evidence; however, photocopies are sufficient for reference file searches.

Anthropological Examinations

Anthropological examinations involve the analysis of skeletal remains (or potential skeletal remains). Examinations can result in the determination, interpretation, or estimation of:

- Whether material is skeletal (bone or tooth) versus some other material.
- Whether bones are human or nonhuman.
- Whether more than one individual is represented.
- Whether bones are modern or ancient.
- Biological information from certain bones (such as age, sex, ancestry, stature).
- Skeletal trauma type and timing (such as projectile, blunt, or sharp force trauma).
- Personal identification by comparison to known samples (such as medical records).
- Facial approximations, which are facilitated in conjunction with forensic imaging artists.

Forensic anthropologists are also available to assist in the detection and recovery of remains.

Questions concerning anthropological examinations should be directed to 703-632-8449. Case acceptance is based in part on the condition of the material; for cases with significant soft tissue remaining, please call 703-632-8449 for guidance prior to submission. In some cases, the determination of whether bones are human or nonhuman can be determined from submitted images (either by mail or by email). To submit images for analysis, please call 703-632-8449 for guidance.

Figure 6.37 (Continued) FBI evidence submission guidelines. *(Continued)*

Collection and packaging considerations:

- Collect bones (or small bone assemblages) individually in paper bags or other breathable material
- Tin foil may be formed around burned or very fragile bones.
- Sealed, plastic packaging may be acceptable for remains with fresh/wet tissue.
- As needed, include cold packs and/or 'BIOHAZARD' stickers.
- Minimize contact between bones and movement within the shipping container.
- If in doubt, please call for assistance.

Arson Examinations

Arson examinations can determine the presence of ignitable liquids introduced to a fire scene. Examinations of debris recovered from scenes can identify gasoline, fuel oils, and specialty solvents. Examinations generally cannot identify specific brands.

Questions concerning arson examinations should be directed to 703-632-7626.

Collection and packaging considerations:

- Search questioned arson scenes for candles, cigarettes, matchbooks, Molotov cocktails, fused chemical masses, or any electronic or mechanical devices an arsonist may have used.
- Search for burn trails on cloth or paper, burn trails on carpeted or hardwood floors, and the removal of personal property or commercial inventory.
- Ignitable liquids are volatile and easily lost through evaporation. Preserve evidence in airtight containers such as metal cans, glass jars, or heat-sealed plastic bags approved for fire debris. Do not fill containers to the top. Leave at least three inches of space between the evidence and top of the container. Pack to prevent breakage.

Bank Robbery Note File

The Bank Robbery Note File (BRNF) contains images of notes used in bank robberies. This file can be searched in an attempt to associate text from one bank robbery note with text from bank robbery notes in other cases. Digital submissions of demand notes for BRNF searches are accepted. FBI offices can attach the image(s) to their Electronic Communication/Lead Report via Sentinel. State and local law enforcement can submit the image(s) along with their request communication on agency letterhead to bankrobberysearch@ic.fbi.gov.

Questions concerning the BRNF should be directed to 703-632-8444.

Collection and packaging considerations:

- Documentary evidence must be preserved in the condition in which it was found. It must not be unnecessarily folded, torn, marked, soiled, stamped, or written on or handled excessively. Protect the evidence from inadvertent indented writing.
- Mark documents unobtrusively by writing the collector's initials, date, and other information in pencil
- Whenever possible, submit the original evidence; however, photocopies are sufficient for reference file searches.

Figure 6.37 (Continued) FBI evidence submission guidelines. *(Continued)*

Bank Security Dye Examinations

Bank dye packs contain dye to stain money and clothing and tear gas to disorient a robber. Items such as money and clothing can be analyzed for the presence of bank security dye and tear gas.

Questions concerning bank security dye evidence should be directed to 703-632-8441.

Collection and packaging considerations:

- Only evidence with visible red or pink stains will be examined.
- Do not submit large stained evidence (e.g., car seats). When possible, cut a small sample of the stained area and submit in a heat-sealed or resealable plastic bag.
- When cutting is not possible, transfer questioned stains by rubbing with a clean (dry or wet with alcohol) cotton swab. Use an unstained swab as a control. Air-dry the swab and pack in a heat-sealed or resealable plastic bag.
- Collect an unstained control sample, package separately, and submit it with the dye-stained evidence.

Biological Material Examination

The FBI Laboratory can provide expertise for conducting examinations on a variety of biological samples and related bioinformatic data. These examinations can assist in determination of such things as speciation, identification, relatedness, and designed genetic modifications. These examinations are conducted at FBI-designated partner laboratories. Examples of biological materials that can be examined include:

- Pathogenic microbes (including select agents).
- Non-pathogenic microbes.
- Animals.
- Plants.
- Insects.
- Biological toxins.
- Genetically modified organisms.
- Synthetically produced organisms or biological materials.

Questions regarding biological materials examinations should be directed to 703-632-7726. Call 703-632-7726 prior to submitting evidence.

Building Materials Examinations

Examinations can compare building materials such as brick, mortar, plaster, stucco, cement, and concrete.

Questions concerning building materials evidence should be directed to 703-632-8449.

Collection and packaging considerations:

- When building materials are penetrated or damaged, debris can adhere to people, clothing, tools, bags, and stolen items and can transfer to vehicles. If possible, submit the evidence to the Laboratory for examiners to remove the debris. Package each item in a separate leakproof container. Do not process tools for latent prints.

Figure 6.37 (Continued)   FBI evidence submission guidelines.

(Continued)

- Collect known samples from the penetrated or damaged areas.

- Ship known and questioned debris separately to avoid contamination. Submit known and questioned debris in leakproof containers such as film canisters or plastic pill bottles. Do not use paper or glass containers. Pack to keep lumps intact.

Bullet Examinations

A fired bullet can be examined to determine physical characteristics, including weight, caliber, bullet design, and general rifling characteristics (GRCs). GRCs are the number, width, and direction of twist of the rifling grooves imparted on a fired bullet by the barrel of a firearm. A microscopic examination of the bullet is conducted to determine if any marks of value are present.

If a suspect firearm is submitted, a direct microscopic comparison is done between test-fired bullets and the submitted questioned bullet.

If a suspect firearm is not submitted, the submitted fired bullets are intercompared to determine if they were fired from the same barrel. Using the GRC measurements, a search of the FBI Laboratory's GRC database will be conducted to produce a list of firearms that could have fired the bullet(s).

Questions concerning bullet examinations should be directed to 703-632-8442.

Collection and packaging considerations:

- Package bullets to prevent contact with other bullets.

- Bullets can be sent via Registered Mail through the U.S. Postal Service. Evidence must be packaged separately and identified by date, time, location, collector's name, case number, and evidence number.

- Do not mark bullets or other firearm-related evidence. The date, time, location, collector's name, case number, and evidence number must be on the container.

- Follow the U.S. Department of Transportation regulations if shipping live ammunition as listed in the Submitting Evidence section.

Bullet Jacket Alloy Examinations

Alloy classification can often differentiate among the bullet jacket alloys used by manufacturers to produce different varieties of bullets. As such, it can be used to exclude a bullet fragment as having originated from a particular type of ammunition. This analysis is most often helpful when attempting to determine which of a group of shooters may have fired a particular round at a crime scene when the fragment is too mutilated for direct comparison to a firearm.

Questions concerning bullet jacket alloy examinations should be directed to 703-632-8441.

Collection and packaging considerations:

- Ammunition components such as bullets and cartridge cases can be sent via Registered Mail through the U.S. Postal Service. Evidence must be packaged separately and identified by date, time, location, collector's name, case number, and evidence number.

- Do not mark bullets, cartridges, or cartridge cases. The date, time, location, collector's name, case number, and evidence number must be on the container.

- Follow the U.S. Department of Transportation regulations if shipping live ammunition as listed in the Submitting Evidence section.

Figure 6.37 (Continued)   FBI evidence submission guidelines.   *(Continued)*

7. Restored canine.

8. Restored front tooth.

- Place teeth and bone samples in clear paper or an envelope with sealed corners.
- Bone and teeth evidence can remain at room temperature before shipping to the Laboratory for analysis.

Preserving DNA Evidence - Long Term Storage

- Blood/saliva (known reference samples):
  - Refrigerate, do not freeze, liquid blood samples.
  - Store all samples (refrigerated, frozen (if dried), or room temperature), away from light and humidity.
- Blood/semen (evidence samples):
  - Store all samples (refrigerated, frozen (if dried), or room temperature), away from light and humidity
- DNA tubes/tissue samples:
  - Store refrigerated or frozen if possible.
  - It is recommended that these samples be stored in a refrigerator/freezer and isolated from evidence that has not been examined.

Drug Records Examinations

A drug records examination may identify the type of drug(s) distributed and/or manufactured; details of the operational hierarchy, including suppliers and/or customers; weights and quantities associated with the activity; price structures and gross sales; and other pertinent information.

Questions concerning drug records examinations should be directed to 703-632-7334, or 703-632-7356.

Collection and packaging considerations:

- Submission of original evidence is preferred; however, contributors may submit high-quality images or photocopies with prior authorization.

Embossing and Seals Examinations

An embossed or seal impression can be compared with a known source. Submit the impression and the device to the Laboratory.

Questions concerning embossing and seals should be directed to 703-632-8444.

Collection and packaging considerations:

- Documentary evidence must be preserved in the condition in which it was found. It must not be unnecessarily folded, torn, marked, soiled, stamped, or written on or handled excessively. Protect the evidence from inadvertent indented writing.
- Mark documents unobtrusively by writing the collector's initials, date, and other information in pencil.
- Whenever possible, submit the original evidence. The lack of detail in photocopies makes examinations difficult and often will result in inconclusive opinions.

Figure 6.37 (Continued)   FBI evidence submission guidelines.

(Continued)

Evidence Response Team

Evidence Response Teams (ERTs) can provide assistance in evidence collection and management from traditional search warrants to complex crime scenes. ERTs are especially valuable on large or complicated scenes and cases that are multijurisdictional.

When legal authority and resources permit, ERTs may be requested to assist other agencies by processing crime scenes, conducting searches, and providing training courses and consultations. ERTs can coordinate with the FBI Laboratory on advanced forensic examinations.

The ERT Program offers:

- Evidence identification, collection, and preservation.
- Multiple crime scene coordination.
- Photography: basic, advanced, and latent print.
- Crime scene diagramming and scene surveys.
- On scene latent print detection, development, and collection.
- Impression evidence documentation and collection: footwear, tire track, and toolmark.
- DNA evidence collection.
- Blood detection, collection, and documentation.
- Forensic light source for latent prints, trace, body fluids, and chemical residue.
- Trace evidence collection.
- Explosive residue collection.
- Postblast scene management.
- Arson evidence documentation and collection.
- Human remains recovery, processing, and mapping.
- Digital evidence collection.
- Humanitarian and mass disaster assistance.
- Training on crime scene management and various forensic disciplines.

Specialty Programs:

Forensic Canine Program

- Human Scent Evidence Team
- Victim Recovery Team

Underwater Evidence Program

- Underwater Search Evidence Response Team (USERT)
- Technical Dive Team (TDT), which conducts evidence collection operations in contaminated and deep water environments.

Questions concerning the Evidence Response Team should be directed to 540-368-8200 or the ERT Senior Team Leader in your local FBI office.

Figure 6.37 (Continued)   FBI evidence submission guidelines.

(Continued)

Explosives Examinations

Evidence resulting from an apparent explosion and/or recovery of an explosive device can be examined. Examinations are based on the premise that components and accessories used to construct the devices survive the explosion, although disfigured. The examinations can accomplish the following:

- Identify the components used to construct the device, such as switches, batteries, detonators, tapes, wires, and fusing systems.

- Identify the explosive main charge.

- Determine the construction characteristics.

- Determine the manner in which the device functioned or was designed or intended to function.

- Determine the specific assembly techniques employed by the builder(s) of the device.

- Preserve the trace evidence potentially present in the devices so that it is not destroyed or damaged during the examinations.

Questions concerning explosives evidence should be directed to 703-632-7626. Call the Laboratory at 703-632-7626 each time an explosive device or a related explosive item needs to be shipped. The communication accompanying the evidence must reference the telephone conversation accepting the evidence.

Collection and packaging considerations:

- **Explosives are hazardous materials and must be handled only by qualified public safety personnel, military explosives ordnance disposal personnel, or certified bomb technicians.**

- **Special packaging is required**, and the amount to be shipped is regulated. An FD-861 form (Mail/Package Alert) is required for shipping bomb components to the FBI Laboratory.

Explosives Residue Examinations

Instrumental analyses of explosives residue can determine whether substances are high-explosive, low-explosive, or incendiary mixtures; whether the composition of the substances is consistent with known explosives products; and the type of explosives. Explosives residue can be deposited on metal, plastic, wood, paper, glass, cloth, and other surfaces. Residue may be deposited after handling, storing, or initiating an explosive.

Questions concerning explosives residue evidence should be directed to 703-632-7626.

Collection and packaging considerations:

- Some explosives residue is water soluble and must be protected from moisture. Other residue evaporates quickly and must be collected as soon as possible in airtight containers such as metal cans, glass jars, or heat-sealed or resealable nylon or Mylar bags. Do not fill containers to the top. Leave a minimum of three inches between packaged evidence and the top of the container. Pack to prevent breakage. Ziplock storage bags are not suitable for shipping or storing explosives residue evidence.

- Collect and preserve control samples from the blast site.

- Extreme care must be taken to avoid contaminating explosives residue evidence.

Figure 6.37 (Continued) FBI evidence submission guidelines.

(Continued)

- Never store or ship explosives residue evidence with bulk explosive materials.
- Never store or ship explosives residue evidence from a crime scene with evidence from a search site.

Fabric Examinations

Fabric portions can be compared to determine if they physically match or exhibit the same construction and fiber composition. Fabric examinations can also determine whether a fabric has been damaged, the type of damage (e.g., cut, torn, punctured), and may determine the type of implement used. Impressions from fabric may be compared to known fabrics.

Questions concerning fabric evidence should be directed to 703-632-8449.

Collection and packaging considerations:

- When possible, submit the entire item of evidence.
- Examination-quality photographs, casts, and/or lifts of fabric impressions may be submitted when the substrate cannot be submitted.

FBI Disaster Squad

The FBI Disaster Squad consists of highly trained specialists from the FBI Laboratory Division. Upon official request, Disaster Squad assets are deployed to assist in the identification of casualties/victims through friction ridge analysis (fingerprints, palm prints, and footprints) at mass fatality incidents worldwide. Disaster Squad personnel use specialized postmortem fingerprint recovery techniques and equipment, including remote automated fingerprint search capabilities, to ensure precise and efficient forensic identification operations. The Disaster Squad also assists in printing the deceased at disaster scenes, collecting antemortem fingerprints of victims, and identifying friction ridge skin of the deceased.

Deployment of the FBI Disaster Squad requires consent from the disaster scene medical examiner or coroner, a ranking law enforcement or government official, a representative of the National Transportation Safety Board, or a representative of the U.S. Department of State. Requests for assistance must be made through the nearest FBI field office or the FBI's Strategic Information and Operations Center at **202-323-3300.**

Questions concerning the FBI Disaster Squad or postmortem fingerprint recovery techniques should be directed to 703-632-8443.

Feather Examinations

Feather examinations can determine bird species and can compare feathers found on clothing, vehicles, and other objects with feathers from the crime scene.

Questions concerning feather evidence should be directed to 703-632-8449.

Collection and packaging considerations:

- Submit feathers in heat-sealed or resealable plastic bags or paper bags.

Federal DNA Database (formerly Federal Convicted Offender) Examinations

The FBI Laboratory produces DNA profiles from buccal samples submitted by federal arresting and corrections agencies for comparison to DNA profiles from crime scene samples in the National DNA Index System (see also NDIS/CODIS).

DNA collection kits are provided at no charge to collection agencies, including Bureau of Prisons; federal probation districts; Court Services and Offender Supervision Agency, Washington, DC; and any federal agency that makes federal arrests or detains non-U.S. persons on immigration charges and is required by law to submit DNA samples.

Figure 6.37 (Continued) FBI evidence submission guidelines.

The integrity of evidence can also be protected by the use of tags, tapes, and various forms of labels.[63] Calling for a hands-off approach, evidence tamper tapes warn prospective individuals to keep out unless authorized. Property evidence tags are usually tied to the bag, box, or other packaging; they account for the exact chain of possession—from whom, to where, and what date and time is recorded (see Figures 6.38[64] and 6.39).[65]

In an age of communicable diseases, the security investigator must exercise caution in handling materials and in the storage of fluids and other perishable evidence. Using gloves, syringe needles, plastic vials, eyedroppers, and other devices assures not only the unchallengeable quality of the evidence, but also the safety of the person performing the investigative function.

For packaging and preservation requirements for the many of types of evidence, see the *FBI's Handbook of Forensic Services* at: https://www.fbi.gov/file-repository/handbook-of-forensic-services-pdf.pdf

Numerous commercial companies provide compact kits for the investigation of blood, collection of evidence in rape cases, ballistics analysis, gunshot residue tests, and other matter. Whatever the investigator chooses, if he or she is unsure of his or her skill or expertise in handling complicated evidence packages, he or she should defer to the expert. The American Society for Industrial Security affirms this position.

Collection and preservation of evidence are only a part of any professional investigation, but they frequently prove to be the most important part in solving a crime and prosecuting a suspect. An otherwise efficient investigation can be ruined by careless evidence handling or inadequate knowledge of this vital aspect of the work.[66]

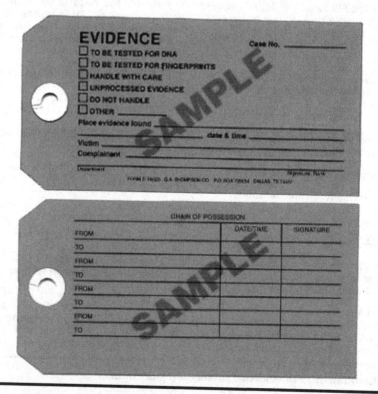

Figure 6.38 Evidence tag.

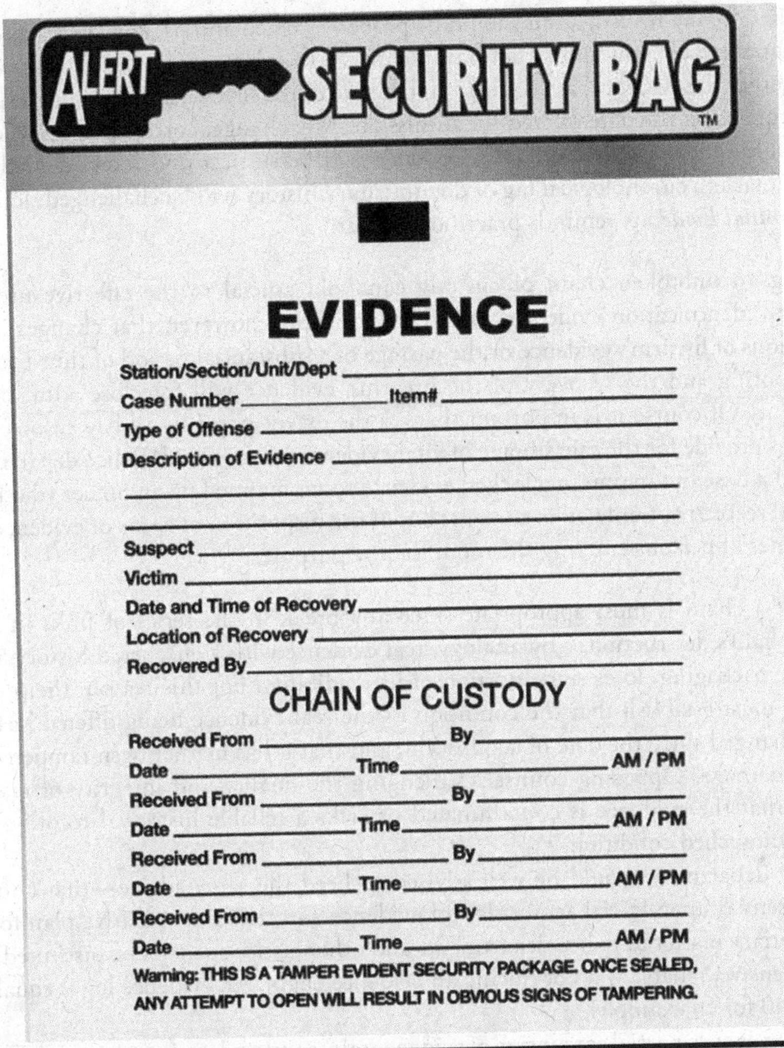

Figure 6.39 Evidence bag.

Just as the public police are concerned with, so too the private security investigator who must be wary of evidentiary flaws and contamination. To be certain, private security has always taken an active interest in the collection and preservation of evidence since it is so often on the front lines of first response. In that front line are laid the seedbeds for evidentiary integrity and utility at later litigation. As a result, when done the collection phase, the security industry need assure the long-term preservation of evidence.

6.4.1 Evidence: The "Chain of Custody"

Evidence acquired at the scene of a crime or place where harm is inflicted is forever subject to chain of custody challenges. Where has the evidence been? What is its history and geneology of usage? Has this evidence been altered, changed, or tampered with? Any evidence that has a history with unaccounted gaps in custodial control will always be suspect evidence.[67] As a result, evidence that is acquired in any investigation should be properly tagged and packaged with precautions to thoroughly preserve content and structural integrity.[68] In other words, the defense will raise the question whether the evidence, as acquired on the date of the investigation, compares in composition and nature as on the date offered for admission. Any change, corruption, or other alteration imputes a faulty and flawed chain. The evidence will be suspect and likely denied admission. Evidence that lacks a chronological tag or documentary history will be challenged. John Waltz, in his text, *Criminal Evidence*, reminds practitioners that:

> Tracing an unbroken chain of custody can hold crucial to the effective use of a firearm's identification evidence. This does not mean, however, that changes in the conditions of firearm's evidence or the passage of a substantial period of time between the shooting and the recovery of the firearm's evidence will foreclose admissibility at trial ... Of course it is important that, to the extent possible, all law enforcement agencies provide for the safe storage of vital evidence prior to trial. Police departments are well advised to maintain a locked evidence room manned by an officer who keeps detailed records not only of its contents but of the disposition of items of evidence and the names of persons entering the room for any purposes.[69]

The image of a chain is most appropriate since any break in the series of links in that chain imputes the chain's destruction.[70] By analogy, real evidence with a checkered history, whether as to location or packaging, loses some portion of its credibility. For this reason, the proponent of real evidence must establish that the condition of the real evidence being offered has remained basically unchanged since the date of acquisition, and that it has neither been tampered with nor suffered any damage. Opposing counsel challenging the quality and integrity of real evidence might argue that the evidence is contaminated or lacks a reliable historical record assuring its pristine and untouched condition.[71]

A security department would be well advised to heed the same advice—that chronological tracking is essential upon initial acquisition of evidence and that a cooperative plan for transference of evidentiary matter to police departments and other justice agencies be instituted. Evidence tags are inexpensive, reliable ways of tracing an evidence chain. An evidence log is equally helpful (see Figure 6.40 for an example).

Destruction or even partial corruption of evidence taints and undermines the proof. Documents, physical evidence, forensic materials, and other forms of evidence, used by both prosecution and defense, will only be able to withstand legal challenges if not subject to integrity challenges. While both parties may employ the evidence for its case in chief, the question of whether said evidence finds a willing tribunal will largely depend on the proof of how it has been handled and processed. The chain of custody requirements assure that the history of that evidence is one traceable and verifiable.[72] Destruction of evidence will also make discovery of said evidence, a compulsory grant by prosecution to defense, even more difficult for that evidence is untrustworthy. The exercise of procedural examination can be frustrated if relevant material is altered, concealed, or destroyed.[73] Destruction may also trigger constitutional violation when the agent who ruined the evidence did so with malice, fraud, or other intentional purpose and in collusion with public police entities. Whether by case law or statute, destroying evidence in all circumstances is a prohibited act.[74]

Visit an evidence company to review the many products to assure the integrity of evidence at: http://www.sirchie.com/

Prosecutor's Office					
Evidence Log					
Victim:			Page ____ of ____		
File/Investigation #:					
Crimes:					
Authority:					
Date:					

Item Number	Description of Items	Where Found	Found by Whom	Date & Time	Turned over to & Date (Lab #)

Figure 6.40   Evidence log.

6.5 Rules of Evidence for the Security Practitioner

While much of the evidence coverage thus far has been about applied principles of collection, information gathering and preservation strategies regarding evidence, from initial encounters at scene to eventual usage of trial, a look at fundamental definitions and concepts concerning evidence law is well worth a look for every security practitioner. To understand evidence surely demands real-world practical settings, but the practitioner must be forever mindful how evidence forms are argued and advocated in a more definitional and legalistic sense. A short summary follows.

6.5.1 The Nature and Classification and Evidence

Those first encountering the law of evidence are always stunned by its many form and varieties. In the most elemental sense, evidence—from the Latin verb *video*, meaning to see—and its preposition *ex*—meaning out of—gives a general sense of what all evidence really is—a source upon which a conclusion may or may not be reached. Evidence is what we deduce or conclude, derive, imply or intimate from what is before us. It can be as simple as a physical form such as blood and a bullet, by which we extract a finding, like this blood matches the murderer or this bullet causes this sort of marking. Or evidence may be noncorporeal such as reputation and character, motive and mental state, all of which can be proven or disproven with sufficient evidence. Private security, laboring on the front lines of so many protection systems, for both people and assets, better have a solid understanding of these forms of evidence for without that knowledge, the officer lacks the full understanding of the occupation he or she has undertaken. "Evidence" takes many forms, including testimony of a witness; real, tangible, physical and documentary evidence; chattels; microscopic fibers, biological material, and open forensic matter; character evidence; intellectual copyrights, trademarks, and patents; habits and customs; conviction records; public records; recordings, motion pictures, photographs, and videotapes; vital statistics; confessions; personal or professional reputation; mental state or condition; and judicially noticed findings.

6.5.1.1 Physical and Real Evidence

As the name implies, real or physical evidence is of a tangible form—felt, touched, sensed, and seen. Real evidence is the gun, the knife, the blood, and other actual composition.[75] Real evidence is the actual product, not a reproduction or a copy. It may be the actual weapon, forged check or deed, or other physical matter. In most litigation, there is a preference for the real over other evidentiary forms.

> As the trier of fact looks for the truth, what form of evidence is most convincing during its deliberations? Is the testimony of expert or lay witnesses regarding impressions and eyewitness accounts as persuasive as evidence in real format? Is the testimony of the plaintiff in a civil negligence case regarding experienced pain and suffering more probative than the actual exhibition of injuries inflicted in the plaintiff's body?[76]

While there may be some variety in responses based on the quality of the real and the illustrative and educational quality of secondary evidence forms, there is little doubt that the real evidence form can be compelling.

6.5.1.2 Direct Evidence

Direct evidence is the evidence that proves a fact or proposition directly rather than by secondary deduction or inference. Examples of direct evidence include eyewitness testimony, an oral confession of a defendant or the victim's first-hand account of a criminal assault. Direct evidence is the foundational support for many cases. The eyewitness testimony of an accident scene or a victim's testimony regarding their injuries has a primary quality that encompasses direct evidence. As a general rule, the more direct evidence amassed, the better the advocate's case.

6.5.1.3 Circumstantial Evidence

Indirect or circumstantial evidence, the bulk of evidentiary proof in most civil and criminal litigation, never speaks directly to innocence or guilt or liability or harm. A bullet in a murder case is only circumstantial evidence since it does not signify direct agency although its peripheral power of proof shows an agency connection. In essence, inferences are drawn from circumstances beyond the key action or parties.

6.5.1.4 Character Evidence

When is evidence of a person's character, either as a victim, defendant, party, or witness, relevant? In many ways, character is central to questions of integrity and credibility. Undermining character is a means of deflating the party that alleges something. A witness whose reputation is in doubt will be less persuasive than the man or woman with a sterling reputation in the community. Character, in this sense, has both individual and communal qualities. Put simply, what do others in the community think of the party? What is that person's reputation for honesty and fair dealing? Why should a person of ill-repute or one with a checkered history be believed at all? Character constitutes an effective method to either uplift or tear down a party.

FRE Rule 608 holds that opinion and reputation evidence of character is admissible under the following circumstances:

> The credibility of a witness may be attacked or supported by evidence in the form of opinion or reputation, but subject to these limitations: (1) the evidence may refer only to character for truthfulness or untruthfulness, and (2) evidence of truthful character is admissible only after the character of the witness for truthfulness has been attacked by opinion or reputation evidence or otherwise.[77]

At subsection (b) of the same rule, specific instances of conduct for the purpose of attacking or supporting the witness' credibility may be admitted if "probative of truthfulness or untruthfulness, be inquired into on cross-examination of the witness (1) concerning the witness' character for truthfulness or untruthfulness or (2) concerning the character for truthfulness or untruthfulness of another witness as to which character the witness being cross-examined has testified."[78]

Of corollary interest is FRE Rule 405 relaying that any opinion of character is permissible if not the result of individualized opinion but instead a community perception.[79] "Strictly speaking, a witness's personal opinion of someone's character is unacceptable. The character evidence adduced ought also be of the broad type impugned by the charges in the case. Negative character testimony of the type 'I have never heard anything ill of the defendant's character' will, however, be admitted."[80]

6.5.1.5 Documentary Evidence

Documentary evidence consists of memorialized writings or other inscriptions such as confessions, pleadings, contracts, memoranda, checks, or fraudulent bank notes. Documents are dealt with at every phase of the justice model from the investigatory to pretrial, from actual trial to appellate phases. A wide variety of examples for the documentary form, essential in the collection phase, are discussed in the first part of this chapter.

In documentary evidence, preference should always be for the original document rather than its copy, although the federal and state rules recognize how copies are now normative in many contexts. FRE Rule 1002, summarizes:

> To prove the content of a writing, recording, or photograph, the original writing, recording, or photograph is required, except as otherwise provided in these rules or by Act of Congress.[81]

Documentary matters involving public records, summaries, interrogatories, and depositions will also been covered.

6.5.1.6 Hearsay Evidence

Attorneys and legal scholars can spend a lifetime analyzing and deciphering the *hearsay doctrine*. Seasoned practitioners know the *hearsay rule* as an overrated evidentiary restriction. At its heart, hearsay evidence is an out of court declaration or statement, with the person who uttered it, being called the "declarant," unavailable to question or examine.[82] Additionally, it is hearsay because the statement of the declarant is offered to prove the truth of its content. This same statement is being testified to by a second or third party. As a result, the content of said statement cannot tested or evaluated under traditional cross examination. FRE Rule 801 (c) defines hearsay as follows:

> "Hearsay" is a statement, other than one made by the declarant while testifying at the trial or hearing, offered in evidence to prove the truth of the matter asserted.[83]

Therefore, that statement, being testified to at a trial or hearing, by a declarant witness other than the original declarant is hearsay.

The purpose of the statement is a key factor in whether the rule applies or not. It may or may not be hearsay. For what purpose is the out of court assertion being offered to the court? Is it being offered to prove the truth of the statement? Is it being offered to prove the truth of the writing or act? An out of court assertion that is offered for any purpose other than to prove its truth is not hearsay. An out of court assertion that has direct legal significance, regardless of its truth or falsity is not hearsay. For example, "an out of court assertion that constitutes, an offer or an acceptance, or a defamation, or a representation or a misrepresentation, or a guarantee or a notice, etc. is not hearsay."[84]

Why can't a witness testify to the statements of an out-of-court declarant when offered to prove the truth of the matter asserted? Foundationally, the exclusion rests on the opposing party's inability to cross-examine the content of the testimony being related. The out of court declarant is not available. James McCarthy in his work, *Making Trial Objections*, gives three principle reasons for the exclusion.

> First the declarant being quoted or relied on cannot be examined concerning his ability to perceive or retain the fact; thus, the right of cross-examination is denied. Second, no opportunity is given to the trier of fact to observe the demeanor of the defendant. Third, although the witness is under oath, the declarant is not.[85]

6.5.1.6.1 The Admission of Business Records

Business records are by nature inherently hearsay since the author of that record is not readily available to testify. Hearsay is inadmissible unless an exception has been fashioned. As is so often the case, especially in large corporate enterprises, record keeping is so voluminous and broad-based that it is difficult to tie authorship to any given document. The Federal Rules of Evidence fully recognize that business records themselves, while admittedly hearsay, are admissible. Federal Rule 803(6) provides:

> A memorandum, report, record, or data compilation, in any form, of acts, events, conditions, opinions, or diagnoses, made at or near the time by, or from information transmitted by, a person with knowledge, if kept in the course of a regularly conducted business activity, and if it was the regular practice of that business activity to make

the memorandum, report, record, or data compilation, all as shown by the testimony of the custodian or other qualified witness, unless the source of information or the method or circumstances of preparation indicate lack of trustworthiness. The term "business" as used in this paragraph includes business, institution, association, profession, occupation, and calling of every kind, whether or not conducted for profit.[86]

Records, in order to be regularly admissible, and outside the hearsay criterion, must be regularly kept. A presumption exists in the law that regularly kept records, automatically filled-in forms, and other autonomic exercises decrease the likelihood of deception and fraud in authorship.[87] For the most part, security record keeping, like surveillance reports, warehouse bills of lading, visitors' logs, shoplifting reports, and investigative task sheets, are robotic business records[88] that will be admitted despite their hearsay content.

Thus, business records will not be admitted in any subsequent litigation unless:

- The record was made at or near the time of the occurrence.
- It was the regular practice of the business to make such records.
- There are not indications of untrustworthiness in the record.
- The information in the record was made by, or with information from, a knowledgeable person.
- The record was made and kept in the normal course of a business.[89]

6.5.1.7 Judicially Noticed Evidence

Most jurisdictions automatically admit judicially noticed facts or conditions without advocacy of foundational requirements, formal identification, or authentication processes. The court notes the general acceptance of the fact or issue that it waives typical procedural requirements. The evidence is additionally deemed reliable enough not to need screening or scrutiny. In this case, such evidence is declared "judicially noticed." Judicially noticed evidence is that information "generally known by the community at large or which is so scientifically acceptable and reliable that it is given to be true and accurate."[90]

Generally, judicially noticed evidence is a straightforward fact, indisputable issue or a bit of common knowledge. That the sun rises and the sun sets is a fact that would be judicially noticed. A court can judicially notice that there are twenty-four hours in a day, or that a man is composed of certain chemical elements such as carbon and blood. However, the issue of whether or not blood plasma was infected with a virus is a matter not commonly known and therefore laden with actual or potential dispute. Facts or findings subject to multiple interpretations and diverse conclusions are not well suited to the realm of judicial notice.

The typical categories of judicially noticed evidence are

- Adjudicative findings of other courts
- Laws of science
- Natural principles widely accepted by the community
- Official records
- Government publications
- Legislative facts
- Judge's personal knowledge

- Public statutes
- Natural scientific forces
- Qualities and properties of matter

A court may judicially notice evidence under either a discretionary or mandatory scheme.[91] A party is entitled, upon timely request, to be heard regarding the propriety of taking judicial notice.[92] A request for evidence to be judicially noticed may be taken at any stage of the proceedings.[93] Jury instructions should contain a commentary about what evidence has been judicially noticed.[94]

Legal implications of the doctrine are obvious in that the proponent of the evidence need not prove relevance or other admissibility standards. In a sense, the doctrine of judicial notice promotes efficiency in the analysis of evidence. "The primary purpose of judicial notice is to achieve the maximum of convenience that is consistent with procedural fairness. In doing so, expert testimony with respect to statistics, scientific facts, and other natural phenomena may be avoided."[95]

6.5.1.8 Demonstrative Evidence

Comparatively, demonstrative evidence is an illustration of the real.[96] Its admissibility and utility depends upon these criteria:

1. Does it aid the trier of fact in discerning the truth?
2. Does it simplify complex problems? Does it educate the jury and tribunal? Is it persuasive? Does the demonstration appeal to multiple senses?[97]

Common forms of demonstrative evidence include the following:

- Maps
- Models
- Photographs
- Videotapes
  - Animation graphics
  - Experiments and simulations
- Movies
- Charts
- Graphs
- Reproductions
- Scale models
- Multiple views
- Cast models
- Sound recordings
- Artistic reproductions
- X-rays
- Thermographs
- Spectrograms
- Medical test results
- Chemical analysis[98]

Security personnel are increasingly relying upon animation and other graphics portrayals[99] to reconstruct a case during the investigative phase. Some of the more commonly used providers in the area are

The Association of Medical Illustrators
201 E. Main Street, Ste. 1405
Lexington, KY 40507
tel: 1-866-393-4AMI (or 1-866-393-4264)
e-mail: hq@ami.org
http://www.ami.org/
(information on medical illustrators in your area)

Wolf Technical Services, Inc.
9855 Crosspoint Blvd., Suite 126
Indianapolis, IN 46256-3336
Main: 317-842-6075
Toll Free: 800-783-9653
Fax: 317-842-6974
http://www.wolftechnical.com/
(Accident Reconstruction and Forensic Engineering)

ARCCA Incorporated
2288 Second Street Pike
Penns Park, PA 18943
Ph: 215-598-9750
Toll-Free: 1-800-700-4944
Fax: 215-598-9751
http://www.arcca.com
(illustrations and charts of crash simulations)

Visit one of the country's largest developer of medical and injury demonstrative exhibits at:
http://www.medicallegalexhibits.com

6.5.1.9 Testimonial Evidence: Lay Witnesses

As private security performs its investigatory functions, it must rely upon evidence provided by witnesses. The measure of witness competency will largely be determined by whether the witness is lay or expert. A wise practice is to evaluate lay witnesses in the field since these very individuals, who are providing crucial information, may be the best foundation upon which a case rests. If incompetent in the field, they will clearly be incompetent on the stand.[100] By competency, we merely hold that the witness capable of relating facts and conditions in a reliable and dependable way.

Lay competency is generally defined by Rule 602 of the Federal Rules of Evidence, as

1. The witness has the capacity to actually perceive, record and recollect impressions of fact (physical and mental capacity);
2. The witness in fact did perceive, record and recollect impressions having a tendency to establish a fact of consequence in the litigation (personal knowledge);

3. The witness be capable of understanding the obligation to tell the trust (oath or affirmation);
4. The witness possess the capacity to express himself understandably where necessary with the aid of an interpreter.[101]

Competency does not require genius but the capacity to perceive, record, and recollect impressions of fact as influenced by a wide assortment of social and biogenic factors.[102] Every lay witness, in order to be effective on the witness stand, need be evaluated in light of these criteria:

■ What is their present age level?
■ Do they have any personal habits that would indicate their powers of recollection and thought retention would be influenced by chemical or drug usage?
■ From an observational point of view, do these individuals appear intellectually ordered?
■ Would a street person, bag lady, or heroin abuser be a witness who could withstand the competency standard?
■ Did they have any personal knowledge of the events or is their viewpoint strictly the product of hearsay?[103]

Certain witnesses, such as children, a spouse, a coconspirator who has been granted immunity, or a person who has been adjudged insane, will have credibility concerns.[104] Lack of credibility, however, does not necessarily disallow a witness from taking the stand.[105]

Security practitioners should evaluate the levels of sincerity and credibility of any witness they interview during the investigative process. Employing simple human relations skills will often permit the security professional to judge the quality and credibility of any witness. When evaluating a witness, utilize the following checklist at Figure 6.41.[106]

The security officer needs to evaluate and weigh not only the physical and real evidence he collects, but also the testimony from interested as well as disinterested witnesses. Conduct the type of human observation that ferret out the unreliable in favor of the reliable lay witness. Make human judgments that work for the average person and avoid witnesses who are disgruntled individuals, abhorrent characters, and courtroom groupies whose sole purpose in life is to meddle in the affairs of others.[107]

6.5.1.10 Testimonial Evidence: Expert Witnesses

Experts are often defined as any witness that is not a lay witness. While it is a suitable definition, the complexities of expert testimony call for more.[108] It is now a given that experts populate our courtroom in both the criminal and civil realm. It is also commonly agreed upon that there has been a proliferation of experts, expert testimony and fields of acceptable expertise once envisioned.[109] These perceptions are the result of many factors such as media coverage of flamboyant expert witnesses to celebrated and often avant-garde litigation. However, the bulk of testimony given in any criminal or civil action is fundamentally "lay" in nature. An expert is entitled to give an opinion, but only in the context of his expertise, though a foundational test will have to be met before such testimony is proffered. In the case of a lay witness, foundational requirements must be laid as follows:

■ The witness's testimony is based upon his or her own unique perception.
■ The court is convinced that the testimony of the lay witness is helpful in arriving at the truth.

Witness Competency Checklist

Duty to tell truth: witness must understand the duty to tell the truth

_____ Is witness too young or to mentally incompetent to understand the difference between the truth and a lie?

_____ Does the witness have a prior conviction for perjury or criminal act based on dishonesty? (Federal Rules do not bar witness per se, but this factor can be used for impeachment.)

Ability to perceive: witness must have the ability to perceive the incident which is the subject matter of his testimony.

_____ Does witness have a handicap that would impair the ability to perceive, such as poor eyesight or lack of hearing?

_____ Did conditions such as darkness, fog, distance, noise level prevent the witness from perceiving?

_____ Was witness attentive or inattentive?

Ability to remember: witness must be able to remember what she perceived.

_____ Does witness have a medical or psychological handicap such as Alzheimer's disease, brain damage, schizophrenia, or other mental disorder that would prevent witness from remembering?

_____ Does witness remember other events accurately? Test with questions about physical setting, time frame, or historical information.

_____ Was witness distracted?

_____ Does witness have a problem remembering other information such as schoolwork, names, faces?

Ability to communicate: witness must be able to communicate to the jury.

Personal knowledge: witness cannot testify unless she has personal knowledge of the subject of her testimony. Rule 602.

_____ Was witness present during the event? Did witness actually see, hear, feel, smell or touch?

_____ Is witness relying on perceptions or relying on hearsay?

_____ An expert may testify on facts of which she has no personal knowledge but which has been disclosed to the expert at or before the hearing Rule 703.

Figure 6.41 Witness competency checklist.

- The witness does in actuality have an opinion.
- The witness is capable and competent to testify as to that opinion.
- Without the testimony, the trier of fact, namely the judge and jury would not have the best case presented.
- The witness is giving lay testimony rather than expert testimony.
- No opinion as to a rule or an interpretation of law will be permitted.[110]

Experts, on the other hand, must be qualified to testify in their areas of expertise. Rule 703 of the Federal Rules of Evidence[111] requires that an expert's opinion rest upon facts, data, or other information that he or she has actually seen or heard or has been communicated to the expert. Rule 704[112] permits the expert witness to attest to the ultimate issue of fact, though at one point in history the ultimate issue doctrine withheld that right. By ultimate issue, the expert is giving his or her assessment on the fundamental guilt or innocence of the defendant or the truth or falsity of a given issue at trial.[113]

Security companies must learn to develop collegial and long-standing relationships with experts in fields of mutual interest, such as engineering, hazardous materials, use of force and professional police practices, product liability, negligence, and intentional tortious conduct. The occasion may arise whereby the security company needs the assistance of an expert. Insist that the self-acclaimed expert prove his or her qualifications since the court will expect the scrutiny by reviewing these standardized qualifications:

■ The witness has specialized training in the field of his expertise.
■ The witness has acquired advanced degrees from educational institutions.
■ The witness has practiced in the field for a substantial period of time.
■ The witness taught courses in a particular field.
■ The witness has published books or articles in the particular field.
■ The witness belongs to professional societies or organizations in a particular field.
■ The witness has previously testified and been qualified as an expert before a court or administrative body on a particular subject to which he is being asked to render an opinion.[114]

6.5.1.11 Practical Exercise: Cross-Examination

Security operatives are frequently cross-examined on the witness stand.[115] How would you respond to the following queries?

1. "Your name and occupation, please?"
2. "So, you're a real live Pinkerton Detective. And who do you represent in this case?"
3. "In other words, you're being paid to testify for ABC Insurance Company against my client, isn't that correct?"
4. "Exactly how long did you conduct your spying in Mr. Smith's home and how long did you actually observe my client engaged in activity during this time?"
5. "So, for two (2) days you were paid to observe Mr. Smith for only a half hour. The insurance company must have been disappointed."
6. "You describe in your report the home of Mr. Smith and state that its approximate value is $65,000. Are you qualified to make such a statement?"
7. "Just how far away were you when you took these movies of Mr. Smith and don't you consider taking these movies without his permission a shameful invasion of Mr. Smith's right to privacy?"
8. "You state in your report that Mr. Smith exhibited no sign of discomfort or pain while moving about. Do you have a medical background that qualifies you to judge whether or not Mr. Smith was experiencing pain?"
9. "I understand that your presence in Mr. Smith's neighborhood created a great deal of anxiety among his neighbors, that they were concerned for the safety of their children with a stranger parked for two (2) days in their neighborhood with out of state license plates. Do you think you have a right to frighten innocent people while you are spying on my client for this big insurance company?"
10. "Do you get a percentage of any money the insurance company may save—Never mind. No further questions."[116]

There has been a proliferation of experts and consulting services in the security industry itself. Review a recent classified section of any industry magazine and you will find a plethora of ads for expert witness and consulting services (see Figure 6.42).[117]

Assuring the integrity of these or any other proposed expert is a problem, for the security industry and all other areas of expertise.[118] The International Association of Professional Security Consultants[119] is a member organization dedicated to assuring competency among its security experts.

Visit the IAPSC's website and explore the various events they promote. See: https://iapsc.org/

Use the following expert witness questionnaire when determining the qualifications of an expert (see Figure 6.43).[120]

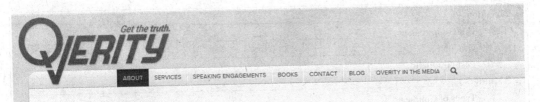

Phil Houston
Chief Executive Officer

Phil Houston is a nationally recognized authority on deception detection, critical interviewing, and elicitation. His 25-year career with the Central Intelligence Agency was highlighted by his service as a senior member of the Office of Security. In that capacity he conducted thousands of interviews and interrogations for the CIA and other federal agencies, both as an investigator and as a polygraph examiner. He is credited with developing a detection of deception methodology currently employed throughout the U.S. intelligence and federal law enforcement communities. The scope of Phil's work has covered criminal activity, personnel security, and key national security matters, including counter-intelligence and counter-terrorism. The fact that many of his interviews were conducted in foreign countries, coupled with six years of residence overseas, has given him unique insight and extensive experience in dealing with foreign cultures, particularly in the Far East.

Phil introduced the detection of deception methodology to the corporate world with the co-founding of Business Intelligence Advisors, where he served as Executive Vice President and worked with the company's largest clients in the U.S. and abroad. The story of his success in creating a commercial application and market for the detection of deception methodology is featured in the recently published book, *Broker, Trader, Lawyer, Spy* by Politico reporter Eamon Javers.

Phil holds a B.A. in Political Science from East Carolina University in Greenville, N.C.

Michael Floyd
Founding Partner

Mike Floyd provides training and consulting services for local, state, and federal law enforcement and intelligence agencies; high net-worth families; and large corporations and firms throughout North America, Europe, and Asia. He is widely recognized as a leading authority on interviewing, detection of deception, and elicitation in cases involving criminal activity, personnel screening, and national security issues.

Mike is the founder of Advanced Polygraph Services, where he spent 10 years conducting high-profile interviews and interrogations for law enforcement agencies, law firms, and private industry. During this period, he also worked with Wicklander & Zulawski as a lead instructor on detection of deception, interviewing, and interrogation, training hundreds of law enforcement officers throughout the United States. He has most recently been involved in providing training and consulting services in the areas of detection of deception and information collection to firms in the financial services and audit communities.

Mike began his career as a commissioned officer in the U.S. Army Military Police, serving in the U.S. and Asia. After spending six years on the staff of John E. Reid and Associates as a polygrapher and instructor on detection of deception, interviewing, and interrogation, he served in both the Central Intelligence Agency and the National Security Agency. Throughout a career that has spanned more than 35 years, he has conducted over 8,000 interviews and interrogations worldwide.

Figure 6.42 QVerity "About" webpage.

EXPERT WITNESS QUESTIONNAIRE

Name: _____

Address: _____

_____

Phone: _____

Business or Occupation: _____

Length of time in business/occupation: _____

Name of Organization: _____

Positions Held: _____

Prior Positions: _____

Education: _____

    Under Graduate: _____

    Graduate: _____

    Post Graduate: _____

Training: _____

    Types of Courses: _____

    Licenses/Certifications: _____

Professional Associations and Organizations: _____

Academic Background: _____

Expert Witness Experience: _____

Specializations: _____

Figure 6.43 Expert witness questionnaire.

A contract for the expert services of a security specialist lays out the professional expectations (see Figure 6.44).

6.6 A Potpourri of Evidentiary Principles

6.6.1 Burden of Proof

In criminal cases, the standard is beyond a reasonable doubt; in civil cases the standard is beyond a preponderance of the evidence, or by clear and convincing evidence.[121] While these rules are general, the burden challenges can be quite curious such as in crimes and civil actions, the advocate prove any sort of intentionality in a strict liability crime or tort. In addition, some misdemeanor level crimes mimic civil intentionality such as using "preponderance of the evidence" in tax and environmental cases.

(Date)

(Name)
(Address)

RE: Tammy Yeager v. Linda McConnell
                _____ County Common Pleas Court Case No. _____

Dear Mr. _____:

      This letter will confirm our conference of October 1, 1993, in connection with retaining your services as a security expert. As discussed, please evaluate this case to determine the following:

      (1) the pre-skid speed of the Yeager's vehicle.
      (2) to compare the time from Ms. Yeager's first reaction to the McConnell vehicle as a hazard to the interval of time that the McConnell vehicle was on Route 79 before impact; and
      (3) whether the presence of a guardrail on the south edge of Route 79 could have lessened the severity of the impact and resulting injuries.

      I am enclosing a check for $1,500.00 representing your retainer for work on this case. It is my understanding that, should the work be completed or stopped for any reason before using up the amount of the retainer, the balance will be refunded. It is my further understanding that your normal fee schedule for this type of work is as follows:

      Preparation Time..........................$.50.00/hour
      (Includes: background review, site visit, field work, engineering analysis, reports, meetings, depositions, travel time)

      Court Time.....$450.00/eight-hour day or part thereof
      All Expenses (Includes air fare, tolls, lodging, meals, mileage, film, prints, aerial photography, etc.)

      Under separate cover, I am forwarding a packet of background materials on this case for your review. You may feel free to contact my client, Ms. Tammy Yeager, at (412) 555-5387 if you need any information directly from her. I would ask that you not prepare a written report of your findings until I request it at a later date. Please note that the trial of this case has been scheduled for May 15, 1994.

      Mr. Todd Aloia is the paralegal in my office who will be assisting me on this case. Please feel free to contact either of us if you have questions. If the terms outlined above comport your understanding of your engagement on this case, please so indicate by signing the enclosed copy of this letter and return it to me in the envelope provided.

Very truly yours,
Attorney

Figure 6.44   Contract for expert services.

6.6.2 *Questions of Law versus Questions of Fact*

A trial judge saddled with the question of law must decide the applicability of a case decision, statute, or other regulation. A question of fact is an interpretation of events left best to the jury or a judge evaluating the case before it.

6.6.3 *The Nature of Relevancy*

Relevant evidence is evidence which tends to prove any matter provable in a civil or criminal action. FRE Rule 401 states:

      "Relevant evidence" means evidence having any tendency to make the existence of any fact that is of consequence to the determination of the action more probable or less probable than it would be without the evidence.[122]

To merit its qualification, relevant evidence must have a logical nexus or connection between its inherent value and a proposition it seeks to prove. "In other words, legal relevancy denotes, first of all, something more than a minimum of *probative value*. Each single piece of evidence must have a plus value."[123]

The textual content of FRE Rule 402 leads one to the conclusion that irrelevant evidence is not admissible and states "Evidence which is not relevant is not admissible."[124] But even irrelevant and minimally probative evidence has a place in the fact finder's menu according to some legal scholarship.[125]

6.6.4 *The Nature of Materiality*

Material evidence is that evidence that addresses a matter, the existence or nonexistence of which is provable in an action. FRE Rule 401 holds that evidence that has a "tendency to make the existence of any fact that is of consequence to the determination of the action more or less probable"[126] is material (if a fact or consequence). At common law, the terms *material* and *relevant* are often used interchangeably in conjunction with a party objecting to evidence as "irrelevant and immaterial." "Clarity in this area is, however, fostered by distinguishing between the propriety of the proof offered to establish it."[127]

6.7 Summary

This chapter provides a broad overview of legal principles, definitions, and standards relating to the laws of evidence. This chapter's coverage commenced with an overview of the essential relationship between investigative practice and the content and quality of evidence. Numerous forms, checklists, and other protocols are provided to assist the security practitioner as he or she seeks to collect and gather pertinent evidence. Rules and guidance on evidence integrity are also given, especially as to chain of custody requirements and keenly delineated requirements for proper scene sketching, graphic and demonstrative evidence forms, photographic technique, accident reconstruction, as well as specific crimes. The role of documentary evidence is also fully covered in both the investigative field and the courtroom. As private sector justice moves increasingly into public functions of law enforcement, it will have to master the art and science of crimes and their subsequent prosecutions. Equally essential to professional growth of the security industry is mastery of select evidentiary principles, which affect the investigative practice of the private security industry. Evaluating the quality of witnesses, their competency and credibility, and utilization of experts throughout all stages of criminal process are fully covered. Heeding the foundational rules and admission for evidence, whether real, testimonial, or expert in design, assures a worthwhile claim or case for the private sector entity. Assuring the quality of the evidence is just as critical. This chapter gives suggestions on packaging and preservation protocols. Finally, the reader is introduced to critical theoretical definition on the various evidence forms and how those "proofs" achieve successful advocacy of case or claim.

DISCUSSION QUESTIONS

1. Why are the rules of evidence and investigative practice so interdependent? How does a failure to adhere to proper investigative procedure cause potential harm to the integrity of legal evidence?

2. Research your jurisdiction's chain of custody definitions in your legal code—usually in criminal procedure provisions. What language is utilized to describe "chain of custody"?

3. How does one distinguish between real and demonstrative evidence?

4. It has been said that an expert witness may also qualify as a lay witness. How could this be so legally?

5. Discuss three types of evidence that are best described as not "physical" by design?

6. Why types of criminal laws are heavily dependent on the integrity of evidence to prove culpability?

7. Name three evidentiary principles or rules that private security officers must be as concerned about as public police officers.

NOTES

1 Charles P. Nemeth, *The Paralegal Resource Manual 3rd* 338 (2008).

2 W. Bennett and K. Hess, *Criminal Investigation* 42–43 (1981).

3 EvidenceOnQ website, at http://www.evidenceonq.com/products/evidence-management.html.

4 FARO website, at http://www.cadzone.com/the-crime-zone.

5 FARO website, at http://www.faro.com/measurement-solutions/applications/accident-reconstruction

6 U.S. Department of Justice, National Institute Of Justice, *Crime Scene Search And Physical Evidence HandBook* (U.S. Government Printing Office, 1973). See also FBI, *Crime Scene Investigation: A Guide for Law Enforcement* (1999), available at https://archives.fbi.gov/archives/about-us/lab/forensic-science-communications/fsc/april2000/twgcsi.pdf; BJA, Technical Working Group on Crime Scene Investigation, *Crime Scene Investigation: A Guide for Law Enforcement* (2013) available at https://www.nist.gov/sites/default/files/documents/forensics/Crime-Scene-Investigation.pdf.

7 Id. at 15.

8 Id.

9 United States Department of Justice, *Crime Scene Investigation: A Guide for Law Enforcement* 11 (2000).

10 Pennsylvania State Police, *Crime Laboratory* 2.1 (1985).

11 For a fascinating look at the new world of electronic crime scenes, such as computer hard drives, and the need for first responders to exercise the same caution on approach to a crime scene, see National Institute of Justice, *Electronic Crime Scene Investigation: A Guide for First Responders 2nd* (2008).

12 A. Joseph and H. Allison, *Handbook of Crime Scene Investigation* 29–31 (Allyn & Bacon, 1989); see also A. Moenssens and F. Inbau, *Scientific Evidence in Criminal Cases* (1987).

13 See also National Institute of Justice, *Crime Scene Investigation: A Reference for Law Enforcement Training* (2004).

14 The Forensic Sciences Foundation, Inc., *Death Investigation and Examination: Medicolegal Guidelines And Checklists* 9 (1986).

15 Id. at 11.

16 G. Knowles, *Bomb Security Guide* 69 (1976).

17 Al Lohner, *Crime Scene Diagramming Software Steadily Gains Converts*, NCJ 194850, Law Enforcement Technology, April 2002, at 58, 60–62, 63.

18 U.S. Department of Justice (2000), at 36.

19 Headquarters, Department of the Army, *Law Enforcement Investigations* 125 (2005), https://rdl.train.army.mil/soldierPortal/atia/adlsc/view/public/12038-1/FM/3-19.13/FM3_19X13.PDF.

20 Tacoma Police Department, *Forensic Services Policy and Procedure Manual* 4 (2004).

21 Department of the Army (2005), at 123.

22 Id. at 121.

23 Id. at 122.

24 Tim Dees, Crime scene drawing programs, *Law and Order*, Aug. 2001, at 12.

25 The Forensic Sciences Foundation, at 13.

26 C. Scott, 1 Photographic Evidence § 13 at 19 (1980).

27 Id. at 344–345.

28 David A. Bright and Jane Goodman-Delahunty, Gruesome evidence and emotion: anger, blame, and jury decision-making, *L. & Human Behav.*, 30 (2006); 183.

29 Pennsylvania State Police, at 2.2.

30 U.S. Department of Justice, (2005), at 44–45.

31 The Forensic Sciences Foundation, at 77.

32 U.S. Department of Justice, (2005), at 43.

33 Id. at 44.

34 Standards and guidelines best practices for maintaining the integrity of digital images and digital video, *For. Sci. Comm.*, April 2008, at Figure 2.

35 Traffic Institute, *Traffic Accident* at 4.

36 Ibid. at 5.

37 The Traffic Institute, *Measuring for Maps* 2 (SN 1097).

38 Roger T. Weitkamp, Crimes and offenses, *Ga. St. U. L. Rev.* 16 (1999); 72, 73.

39 US Department of Labor, Workplace Violence Resources, available at https://www.dol.gov/oasam/hrc/policies/dol-workplace-violence-program-appendices.htm#federallaws, last visited August 28, 2016.

40 Domestic Violence Resource Center, http://www.dvrc-or.org/dv-facts-stats, last visited August 28, 2016.

41 Hope M. Tiesman, et al., Workplace homicides among U.S. women: The role of intimate partner violence, *Annals of Epidemiology* 22 (2012); 277. http://www.annalsofepidemiology.org/article/S1047-2797(12)00024-5/abstract, last visited August 28, 2016.

42 US Dept. of Labor News, *Survey of Workplace Violence Prevention, 2005*, available at http://www.bls.gov/iif/oshwc/osnr0026.pdf, last visited August 28, 2016.

43 Corporate Alliance to End Partner Violence, Workplace violence, at http://www.caepv.org/getinfo/facts_stats.php?factsec=3, last visited August 28, 2016.

44 Ibid.

45 Corporate Alliance to End Partner Violence, *CEO & Employee Survey 2007*, http://www.caepv.org/about/program_detail.php?refID=34, last visited August 28, 2016.

46 Ibid.

47 Ibid.

48 CDC, Intimate Partner Violence: Consequences, http://www.cdc.gov/ViolencePrevention/intimatepartnerviolence/consequences.html, last visited August 28, 2016.

49 Click to Empower, Domestic Violence Facts, http://www.clicktoempower.org/domestic-violence-facts.aspx, last visited August 28, 2016.

50 Ken Carter, John Lawrence, and Ray Pohl, Workplace Violence: Prevention and Response 2–3 (Securitas, 2014), http://www.securitasinc.com/globalassets/us/files/knowledge-center/whitepapers/workplace-violence---prevention-and-response_whitepaper.pdf, last visited August 28, 2016.

51 The International Association of Chiefs of Police (IACP), Combating workplace violence, 1–2 (2002).

52 Report of Person, Form No. 114, G.A. Thompson Co., P.O. Box 64681, Dallas, TX 75206.

53 M. Houts, *Lawyer's Guide to Medical Proof* (1984).

54 Electronic Privacy Information Center, Medical Record Privacy, http://www.epic.org/privacy/medical.

55 H.R. 3482, 104th Cong. 2nd Sess. 1996.

56 H.R. 3482 Sec. 301.

57 The compelling nature of DNA evidence has surely heightened chain of custody concerns for both the public and private sector. See William P Kiley, The effects of DNA advances on police property rooms. *FBI Law Enforcement Bulletin*, Mar. 2009, at 20.

58 *Am. Jur. Trials* 555, 577 (1987).

59 Pennsylvania State Police, at 2.5.

60 Id. at 2.5.

61 FBI, *Handbook for Forensic Services* (U.S. Government Printing Office, 2007).

62 U.S. Department Of Justice, *Handbook of Forensic Science* 97–123 (1994).

63 FBI, (2007).

64 GA Thompson.

65 Packaging Horizons.

66 American Society for Industrial Security, at 28.

67 See Charles P. Nemeth, *Law and Evidence* 68–74 (2011).

68 See Arnold Markle, *Criminal Investigation and the Preservation of Evidence* (1977); Jill Witkowski, Can juries really believe what they see? New foundational requirements for the authentication of digital images, *Wash. U. J.L. & Pol'y* 10 (2002); 267.

69 John R. Waltz, *Criminal Evidence* 389–390 (1975); see also *Ignacio v. Territory of Guam*, 413 F.2d 513 (9th Cir. 1969), cert. denied, 397 U.S. 943 (1970).

70 See Nemeth, *Evidence*, at 66.

71 Charles P. Nemeth, *Evidence Handbook for Paralegals* 41 (1993).

72 See Robert Aronson and Jacqueline McMurtrie, Symposium: Ethics and evidence: III. The ethical limitations on prosecutors when preparing and presenting evidence: The use and misuse of high-tech evidence by prosecutors: Ethical and evidentiary issues, *Fordham L. Rev.* 76 (2007); 1453; James W. McElhaney, Proving Your Evidence Is Genuine, *A.B.A. J.*, May 1993, at 96; Joshua A. Perper et al., Suggested guidelines for the management of high-profile fatality cases, *Archives Pathology & Laboratory Med.* 132 (2008); 1630.

73 *Model Rules Of Prof'l Conduct* R. 3.4 cmt. (1989).

74 Jamie S. Gorelick, Stephen Marzen, and Lawrence Solum, *Destruction of Evidence* 200–202 (1989).

75 Nemeth, *Evidence*, at 49–79; see also Nicole J. De Sario, Merging technology with justice: How electronic courtrooms shape evidentiary concerns, *Clev. St. L. Rev.* 50 (2002–2003); 57. Richard Mahoney, *Evidence*, 2003 *N.Z. L. Rev.* 141 (2003).

76 Nemeth, *Paralegals*, at 32.

77 Fed. R. Evid. 608(a).

78 Fed. R. Evid. 608(b).

79 See Fed. R. Evid. 405.

80 Rowton L. & C. 520 (1865); Redgrave 74 Cr.App.R. 10 (1982).

81 Fed. R. Evid. 1002.

82 How the Sixth Amendment's confrontation clause entangles itself in hearsay problems is keenly critiqued in: Ellen Liang Yee, Confronting the "ongoing emergency": A pragmatic approach to hearsay evidence in the context of the Sixth Amendment, *Fla. St. U.L. Rev.* 35 (2008); 729.

83 Fed. R. Evid. 801(c).

84 Pennsylvania Bar Institute, *Evidence: A Statewide Institute*, 118 (1990).

85 James McCarthy, *Making Trial Objections*, 4–30 (1986).

86 Fed. R. Evid. §803 (6).

87 Nemeth, *Evidence*, at 150–151.

88 See *U.S. v. Reese*, 568 F.2d 1246 (6th Cir. 1977).

89 John A. Tarantino, *Trial Evidence Foundations* 6-24 (1986); see also *Cascade Lumber v. Cvitanovich*, 332 P.2d 1061 (Ore.1958); contra *Liner v. J.B. Tully and Co.*, 617 F.2d 327 (5th Cir. 1980); Jill Witkowski, Can juries really believe what they see? New foundational requirements for the authentication of digital images, *Wash. U. J.L. & Pol'y* 10 (2002); 267; Heather M. Bell, The year in review 2001: Cases from Alaska Supreme Court, Alaska Court of Appeals, U.S. Court of Appeals for the Ninth Circuit, and U.S. District Court for the District of Alaska, *Alaska L. Rev.* 19 (2002); 201; Lance Cole, The Fifth Amendment and compelled production of personal documents after *United States v. Hubbell*—New protection for private papers? *Am. J. Crim. L.* 29 (2002); 123.

90 Charles P. Nemeth, *Litigation, Pleadings and Arbitration*, 2nd ed. 402 (1990).

91 See Fed. R. Evid. 201 (c) & (d).

92 See Fed. R. Evid. 201(e).

93 See Fed. R. Evid. 201(f).

94 See Fed. R. Evid. 201(g).

95 Pennsylvania Bar Institute, *Evidence: A Statewide Institute*, 23 (1990).

96 Nemeth, *Evidence*, at 83–129; see also Katherine A. Godden, Cartoon criminals: The unclear future of computer animation in the Minnesota Criminal Courtroom—*State v. Stewart*, *Wm. Mitchell L. Rev.* 30 (2003); 355; De Sario; Mahoney.

97 Nemeth, *Paralegals*, at 55.

98 See *Moore v. Illinois*, 408 U.S. 786 (1972); *State v. Kazold*, 521 P.2d 990 (Ariz. 1974); In Re Air Crash Disaster, 635 F.2d 67 (2d Cir. 1980); *McCormick v. Smith*, 98 S.E.2d 448 (N.C. 1957); *U.S. v. Addeson*, 498 F.2d 741 (D.C. Cir. 1974); *State v. Mills*, 328 A.2d 410 (Vt. 1974); *Prouda v. McLaughlin*, 479 A.2d 447 (N.J. Super. Ct. Law Div. 1984).

99 See Stewart M. Casper, Looking fraudulent surveillance in the eye: How to refute distorted evidence, *Trial*, Jan. 1993, at 137; Greg Joseph, Demonstrative videotape evidence, *Trial*, June 1986, at 60, 63; Robert D. Peltz, Admissibility of "day in the life" films, *Fla. Bar J.*, Jan. 1989, at 55; Martha A. Churchill, Day in the life films subject to court challenge, *For Def.*, Dec. 1990, at 24; *Grimes v. Employer Mutual Liability Insurance Co.*, 73 F.R.D. 607 (D. Ala. 1977); *Bolstridge v. Central Maine Power Co.*, 621 F. Supp. 1202 (D. Me. 1985); Joyce Lynee Maderia, Lashing reason to the mast: Understanding judicial constraints on emotion in personal injury, *U.C. Davis L. Rev.* 40 (2006); 137; Philip K. Anthony and Donald E. Vinson, Demonstrative exhibits; A key to effective jury presentation, *For Def.*, Nov. 1986, at 13; David Tait, Rethinking the role of the image in justice: Visual evidence and science in the trial process, *Law, Probability & Risk* 6 (2007); 311.

100 Nemeth, *Evidence*, at 172–182; see also Jerome A. Hoffman, Special section on Alabama law: The Alabama Rules of Evidence: Their first half-dozen years, *Ala. L. Rev.* 54 (2002); 241; Ida-Gaye Warburton, The commandeering of free will: Brainwashing as a legitimate defense, *Cap. Def. J.* 16 (2003); 73; Lawrence M. Solan and Peter M. Tiersma, Hearing voices: Speaker identification in court, *Hastings L.J.* 54 (2003); 373.

101 See Fed. R. Evid. §§602; see also Michael Graham, *Handbook of Federal Evidence* (1981); Comment, Witness under Article VI of the proposed Federal Rules of Evidence, *Way. L. Rev.* 15 (1969); 1236; C.R. Kingston, Law of probabilities and the credibility of witnesses and evidence, *J. For. Sci.* 15 (1970); 18.

102 Frederick Overby, Preparing lay witnesses, *Trial*, Apr. 1990, at 88, 91; Judy Clarke, Trial preparation: The trial notebook, *Champion*, June 1995, at 4; Sandra Guerra Thompson, Beyond a reasonable doubt? Reconsidering uncorroborated eyewitness identification testimony, *U.C. Davis L. Rev.* 41 (2008); 1487.

103 See *U.S. v. Lyon*, 567 F.2d 777 (8th Cir. 1977) cert. denied, 435 U.S. 918; *U.S. v. Mandel*, 591 F. 2d 1347 (4th Cir. 1979).

104 Tarantino, supra note 136, at 3-11 to 3-22.

105 Marcus T. Boccaccini and Stanley L. Brodsky, Believability of expert and lay witnesses: Implications for trial consultation, *Prof. Psychol. Res. & Prac.* 33 (2002); 384–388.

106 Nancy Schleifer, *Litigation Forms and Checklists* 13–25 (1991).

107 *Mccormick on Evidence* §§43-108 (1972); Alan W. Mewitt, Psychiatric testimony as to credibility in criminal cases, *Crim. L.Q.* 13 (1970); 79.

108 William Pipkin, Expert opinion testimony: Experts, where did they come from and why are they here?, *Law & Psychol. Rev.* 13 (1989); 103; Anne Bowen Poulin, Credibility: A fair subject for expert testimony?, *Fla. L. Rev.* 59 (2007); 991; Jennifer L. Mnookin, Idealizing science and demonizing experts: An intellectual history of expert evidence, *Vill. L. Rev.* 52 (2007); 763; James S. Schutz, The expert witness and jury comprehension: An expert's perspective, *Cornell J.L. & Pub. Pol'y* 7 (1997); 107; Ric Simmons, Conquering the province of the jury: Expert testimony and the professionalization of fact-finding, *U. Cin. L. Rev.* 74 (2006); 1013; Harold A. Feder, The care and feeding of experts, *Trial*, June 1985, at 49; Stephen D. Easton, "Red rover, red rover, send that expert right over": Clearing the way for parties to introduce the testimony of their opponents' expert witnesses, *Smu L. Rev.* 55 (2002); 1427.

109 Nemeth, *Evidence*, at 202.

110 See Fed. R. Evid. §701; see also *U.S. v. Burnette*, 698 F.2d 1038 (9th Cir 1983), cert. denied, 103 S. Ct. 2106 (1983); *U.S. v. Jackson*, 569 F.2d 1003 (7th Cir. 1978), cert. denied, 437 U.S. 907.

111 Fed. R. Evid. §703.

112 Id. at §704.

113 Nemeth, *Evidence*, at 195–228.

114 Tarantino, at 4–5.

115 Nemeth, *Evidence*, at 186–189, 221–228; see also Fred Ferguson, Advocacy in the new millennium, *Alberta L. Rev.* 41 (2003); 527; Sanja Kutnjak Ivkovic et al., Jurors' evaluations of expert testimony: Judging the messenger and the message, *Law & Soc. Inquiry* 28 (2003); 441.
116 Pinkerton's Inc., *Investigations Department Training Manual* (1990).
117 Qverty Website, *About*, at http://www.qverity.com/team.
118 Note, Expert Witness: Corrupt or Inept?, Sec. 30 (1993); 98.
119 575 Market St. Suite 2125 San Francisco, CA 94105; Phone: (1) 415-536-0288; Fax: (1) 415-764-4915.
120 Nemeth, *Paralegals*, at 167–168.
121 Nemeth, *Evidence*, at 34–39; see also Kevin M. Clermont and Emily Sherwin, A comparative view of standards of proof, *Am. J. Comp. L.* 50 (2002); 243; Michele Taruffo, Rethinking the standards of proof, *Am. J. Comp. L.* 51 (2003); 659.
122 Fed. R. Evid. 401.
123 1 John H. Wigmore, *Evidence* 410 (1940).
124 Fed. R. Evid. 402.
125 Richard D Friedman, Anchors and flotsam: Is evidence law "Adrif,." *Yale L. J.* 107 (1998); 1921 (reviewing Mirjan R. Damaška, *Evidence Law Adrift* (1997)).
126 Fed. R. Evid. 401.
127 Michael Graham, *Evidence, Text, Rules, Illustrations and Problems* 13 (1983).

Chapter 7

Public and Private Law Enforcement: A Blueprint for Cooperation

7.1 Introduction: The Relationship between the Public and Private Sectors

How justice and protective services are delivered is a complex reality—a blending of both traditional, governmental structures, such as policing, corrections, and the judicial system with an emerging mentality of privatization—the view that these same services may be equally governed by private entities. Private security forces do, in fact, privately provide once sacrosanct public police services. Prisons, once solely the province of a civil service, governmental monopoly, now witness a host of private firms and companies erecting and overseeing prison operations. The same could be said about courts, code, and zoning enforcement, and literally every sector where law and justice have specified needs. This trend, known as privatization, is now entrenched in our landscape.

The interplay between public and private law enforcement and the modern delivery of public safety from privatized interest continues unabated. Everywhere across this rich country, public police entities engage the private sector, governments employ private sector companies for security of facilities and asset protection, communities turn to both arms of the justice model, and the military industrial complex appreciates the value of private sector involvement in military operations. Malcolm Sparrow's recent analysis for the National Institute of Justice captures this new reality of public–private cooperation.

> The boundary between public and private policing is messy and complex. Police executives deal with some aspect of it almost every day. Private investments in security continue to expand and public/private partnerships of myriad types proliferate, even as budgets for public policing stall or decline.[1]

It is the commonality of interests that spur on this unbridled growth in cooperation. Despite the differences in legal powers, employers, and mission, private security officers and public police have many similarities.[2]

The historical legacy that characterizes the relationship between the public and private justice systems is less than positive though continuously improving. In 1976, the Private Security Advisory Council, through the U.S. Department of Justice, delivered an insightful critique on the barriers to full and unbridled cooperation between the public and private law enforcement systems. Struggling with role definition and resource deployment, the relationship has been an uneasy but steady one. The council stressed the need to clarify role definitions and end the absurd and oft-practiced negative stereotyping.[3] The council cited various areas of conflict and ranked them in order of importance.

1. Lack of mutual respect
2. Lack of communication
3. Lack of cooperation
4. Lack of security enforcement knowledge of private security
5. Perceived competition
6. Lack of standards
7. Perceived corruption[4]

Put another way, each side operates from a series of perceptions, some accurate, others not. For the most part, the caricatures inhibit full cooperation. The Hallcrest Report I[5] decisively addressed this issue. In characterizing the police role as inclined toward crime detection, prevention, and control, security will always be to some extent the public police's antagonist. Private police give less attention to apprehension, crime detection, prevention, and technology than do their public counterparts. Comparatively, private security addresses similar subject matter but still dwells intently on the protection of assets, immediate deterrence, and commercial enforcement. Figure 7.1 provides a graphic illustration of the major distinctions between these two entities. Tables 7.1[6] and 7.2[7] further edify these occupational distinctions.

A cursory assessment of these figures shows fundamental agreement on the protection of lives and property. Departure occurs in the upper classifications of law enforcement since the thrust of any public police department must be for the eventual arrest and prosecution of suspects. In contrast, the private justice function is still concerned with preventive activities in the area of crime loss, fire prevention, and other order-maintenance functions. In the security manager

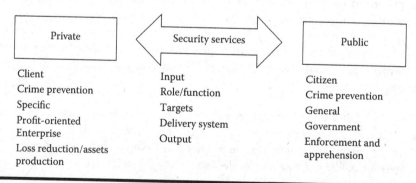

Figure 7.1 Comparison of public and private security services.

Table 7.1 Security Manager Rankings of Private Security Functions (Rank Ordered)

Proprietary Managers	*Contractual Managers*
1. Protection of lives and property	1. Protection of lives and property
2. Crime prevention	2. Crime prevention
3. Loss prevention	3. Loss prevention
4. Fire prevention	4. Fire prevention
5. Access control	5. Access control
6. Crime investigation	6. Order maintenance
7. Employee identification	7. Employee identification
8. Order maintenance	8. Crime reporting
9. Arrest/prosecution	9. Arrest/prosecution
10. Accident prevention	10. Information security
11. Crime reporting	11. Crime investigation
12. Information security	12. Accident prevention
13. Traffic control	13. Traffic control
N = 676	*N* = 545

rankings, criminal investigation and arrest and prosecution show up in the lower rankings. This prioritization, in and of itself, is a telling distinction, though it should not be viewed as justification for a sharp division. If anything, both public and private law enforcement share a generic goal—namely, the general enforcement of laws. As Bill Strudal points out in his article, "Giving the Police a Sense of Security,"

> Our goal, usually not shared by police and security is law enforcement ... if we accept the premise that police and security have the same goals, then why don't we work together on a regular basis? There are differences; nobody can deny that ... there are many other gaps between the two forces, but none is insurmountable with good training and dialogue.[8]

Table 7.2 Law Enforcement Executive Ratings of Law Enforcement Function (Rank Ordered)

1. Protection of lives and property
2. Arrest and prosecution of criminals
3. Investigation of criminal incidents
4. Maintaining public order
5. Crime prevention
6. Community relations
7. General assistance to the public
8. Traffic enforcement
9. Traffic control
N = 384

- Public Prosecutors and Law Enforcement Agencies
- Tort Investigation
- Publisher Actions
- Bank Investigations and Security
- Insurance Companies and Self-Insurer Investigations
- Railway, Bus, and Airlines Companies Security
- Motor Freight, Warehouse, and Freight Terminal Security
- Manufacturing, Wholesale Distributing, and Retail Security
- Hotel Security
- Character Investigations
- Surveillance
- Plant and Store Surveillance
- Undercover Investigations

Figure 7.2 Public and private sector employment opportunities.

The similarities between function, duty, and obligation are very apparent when the tasks of investigation are considered. The skills of the private sector are essentially identical to the public. Review Figure 7.2 to see the diverse opportunities shared and borne by both the private and public sectors.

Given the equal occupational capacity of both the private and public sectors to engage in these many activities, cooperation rather than division appears a wiser tactic. Surely, the concerns of private sector justice increasingly mirror that of the public model.[9]

Employee theft, property crime, and access controls are the top concerns of security professionals. Computer and information security concerns continue to increase as the most important security-related concerns.

Another recurring stumbling block, at least perceptually, is public law enforcement's attitude of superiority. Table 7.3[10] indicates that traditional law enforcement takes a dim view of the contribution of proprietary and contractual security when compared to its own role, though the merger of functions and roles will likely shrink this chasm in the near future. But there is a road to travel.[11]

In appraising the findings of this perceptual study, the Hallcrest II authors suggest:

> Here again, law enforcement executives gave markedly lower ratings than did the private security managers. They agreed, however, on the areas that deserved the highest and lowest ratings. Thus, both the law enforcement executives and the security managers felt that private security was relatively effective in reducing the dollar loss of crime, and relatively ineffective in apprehending larger numbers of criminals. This ranking is consistent with the preventive orientation of private security, which is more concerned with loss control than with arrest and prosecution for crimes. Consistent, too, is the finding that proprietary security managers gave themselves highest marks for maintaining order.[12]

Unfortunately, slight differences in approach and methodology have increased the divide between these camps. Critics of privatized police are often obsessively concerned with the procedural differences and distinctions between one system guided by constitutional dimensions, namely the public realm, while the private system "escapes" this oversight.[13]

Table 7.3 Private Security Contributions to Crime Prevention and Control

Ratings by Law Enforcement and Private Security Managers			
	Law Enforcement	Proprietary Security	Contractual Security
Overall contribution	2.2	1.5	1.2
Reduction in volume of crime	2.4	1.7	1.5
Reduction in direct dollar crime loss	2.2	1.6	1.5
Number of criminal suspects apprehended	2.6	1.9	2.0
Order maintenance	2.4	1.4	1.7
	N = 384	N = 676	N = 545

Scale: 1 = very effective, 2 = somewhat effective, 3 = not effective.

And with these attitudes in place, it becomes a much more difficult task to partner and cooperate. A 2004 Policy Summit cosponsored by public and private law enforcement associations list the main reasons why these alliances falter.

- Egos and turf battles
- Lack of resources (funds, staff)
- Lack of a product
- Overemphasis on structure or resource needs
- Insufficient commitment and support from higher levels of participating organizations
- Overemphasis on the social aspect and under emphasis on business
- Unwillingness of partners to share information, especially information that would
- Reflect poorly on the sharer
- Insufficient alignment of interests[14]

To the detriment of all, these petty differences continue to the present.[15] John Driscoll, in his article, "Public and Private Security Forces Unite in Dallas," asserts "this negative approach prevents the two similar entities from realizing their commonalities and capitalizing upon mutual cooperation."[16] Driscoll recounts the "Dallas experiment" that stresses interaction between the parties in sharing "criminal information bulletins, recruit[ing] class training blocks, field training officer and security officer meetings, and additional joint information seminars."[17] The elitist attitude taken by public law enforcement fosters a polarization between the public and private sectors.

Others conclude that while there may be a series of benefits emerging from the privatization movement, the detriments or the negatives outweigh the gains, especially in the realm of civil liberties and constitutional protections, specialized training and, as one commentator called it a "lack of stateness."[18] On the other hand, there are analysts who find these perceived negatives as purely positive results, which provide a more reasoned approach to dealing with crime and punishment.[19] The National Institute of Justice's New Perspectives in Policing charts the pros and cons of privatized services at Figure 7.3.[20]

Though role conflicts and perceptual views of the public and private sectors are compelling arguments, there are other forceful explanations for the natural tension between these competing interests. What is undeniable is the march forward into the public realm, with examples so numerous it is now difficult to catalog. Private sector operatives now watch over airports and parks, act as first responders and protectors of federal and state installations, deliver safety and security to the Olympics and sporting events, and conduct surveillance and assess critical infrastructure. In the final analysis, the playing field will be leveled a little more each day by the ever-growing numbers of private security forces.[21]

7.1.1 Public Interest versus Private Concerns

Public law enforcement is and has always been tasked with the needs of the public good. Few private security companies must be concerned with domestic disputes, the transportation of the deceased, stray animals, or protection of the homeless and other downtrodden individuals.[22] The Private Security Advisory Council characterized police work as a public interest function. Public police have "a wide range of responsibilities to protect essentially public concerns and their efforts are closely tied to statutorily mandated duties and the criminal justice system."[23]

The Advisory Council further relates that the police are burdened with constitutional limitations and must interpret and implement certain guidelines in the performance of their law enforcement duties. Additionally, public policing is further restrained by public budgeting and financing processes. Police management policies and an administrative hierarchy within most major police departments must evaluate and allocate their resources according to the needs and demands presently operating within their community structure.[24]

Norman Spain and Gary Elkin, in their article, "Private Security versus Law Enforcement," relate with precision:

> One of the traditional functions of the public police is to deter crime. In reality, their ability to do this is drastically limited. The primary reasons are that the police have little authority to change the conditions that foster crime and they have no authority to decide who will reside in their jurisdiction, whom they will police. Private security forces, on the other hand, may alter—at times drastically—the environment in which they operate. They can have walls and fences erected, doors sealed, windows screened, lights put up, and intrusion detectors installed. They can often play a decisive role in determining whom they have to monitor—who is to be an employee of the company—by conducting background investigations of potential employees.[25]

Such a supposition is difficult to dispute, since private security is primarily concerned with the concerns of private property assets and particular individuals. "Individuals and privately funded organizations and businesses undertake measures to provide protection for the perceived security needs which involve their private interests, not in the public domain. Private security is an option exercised to provide an additional or increased level of protection than that afforded by public law enforcement which must respond to the larger concerns of the public."[26]

Potential Benefits and Risks of Public/Private Police Partnerships

Grounds for Support and Engagement (the Benefits)

1. **Increased Effectiveness Through Public/Private Partnerships.** Collaboration between the public and private sectors enhances performance by sharing complementary skills, knowledge and resources. Partnerships facilitate information exchange and provide access to broader networks. All parties can benefit from properly functioning partnership arrangements.

2. **Alignment With the Ideals of Community Policing.** Community policing is essentially collaborative and involves sacrificing a purely "professional agenda" in favor of one negotiated with the community. The community, which includes businesses, should be able to participate in setting the crime-control agenda and should be encouraged to participate in carrying it out.

3. **Greater Equality in Protection.** The ability of the better off to protect themselves by purchasing private protection at their own expense allows the public police to concentrate their efforts on poorer and more vulnerable segments of the community. The overall effect, therefore, is to raise the floor in terms of levels of protection for the most vulnerable.

4. **Access to Specialized Skills and Technical Resources.** The private sector can provide the public police with highly skilled and technical specialists that the public sector could not routinely employ. Collaboration with the private sector thus makes highly skilled and specialist resources available for public purposes.

5. **Efficiencies Through Contracting Out.** Government operations should seek to exploit the efficiencies of private-sector competitive markets by contracting out any components of their operations that can be clearly specified and carved out, and for which competitive markets exist.

Grounds for Skepticism and Concern (the Risks)

1. **Lack of Accountability.** Private police are not subject to the same formal and legal systems of accountability that govern public police agencies. Nevertheless, they may carry weapons, use force, detain suspects and intrude on the privacy and rights of individuals. They may discover crimes and choose not to inform public authorities. The exercise of policing powers without commensurate accountability is inherently dangerous to society.

2. **Threats to Civil Liberties.** Many restrictions on the conduct of public police do not apply to private police (unless formally deputized by public agencies). For example, confessions extracted by private police without Miranda warnings and evidence obtained through unlawful searches conducted by private agents are not subject to exclusionary rules.

3. **Loss of "Stateness."** Policing services and security operations require judicious balancing of the multiple and often conflicting rights of different groups or individuals. Therefore, only state ("civic") institutions can be trusted to reflect the broad societal values required to carry out such functions. The particular interests of private clients and the for-profit motivations of commercial providers will inevitably distort the public agenda to some extent.*

4. **Threats to Public Safety.** Private police, who are not as well-trained as public police, may display poor judgment or overreact to situations, thus endangering public safety. Citizens may be confused about the status or rights of uniformed security personnel and may therefore act in ways that create danger for themselves or others.

5. **Greater Inequality in Protection.** The growth of private security exacerbates inequality regarding citizens' access to protection. Citizens will get the level of protection they can pay for. Those who are better off, and are able to purchase or enhance their own security, will reduce their commitment to public policing. Funding and support for public policing will suffer, which will ultimately result in lower levels of protection for the poorer and more vulnerable segments of society.

6. **Reputational Concerns.** Inadequate performance or improper conduct by private security personnel may produce reputational or litigation risk for public police if the public police have formally recognized, qualified, trained, contracted, or in some other way recognized or validated the operations of private operators. Such operators should therefore be kept at arm's length.

7. **Threats to Police Jobs.** Increased availability of lower skilled and lower paid security jobs, coupled with the contracting out of some police tasks to the private sector, may undermine job security and limit career prospects for public police. Competition from the private sector is inherently unfair because of their tolerance for lower training standards and access to cheaper labor.

*The term "stateness" has been used by other commentators as an umbrella term to cover a broader range of public-interest concerns. Several of these concerns, including loss of equity in public security and loss of public accountability, appear as separate items on this list. This paper will hereafter use the "stateness" term to focus more narrowly on the importance of judicious balancing of competing interests and values.

Figure 7.3 Benefits and risks of public/private partnerships.

7.1.2 Moral or Egalitarian Purpose

Entrance into the vocation of public law enforcement is considered by most a moral and social commitment—a vocation rather than a mere job. This career distinction is generally not applied to individuals who commit their lives to the service of private security. But is such a viewpoint fair and rational? Is not the protection of assets, governmental facilities, communities, business interests, or private proprietary holdings, or contributions in military and security initiatives a noble endeavor? If private security was not involved, what would be the state of American industry and its physical plants, the security of courthouses and judicial centers, transportation facilities, and neighborhood associations? How would the dynamic of the battlefield change in foreign wars? How would the allocation of military personnel be impacted? For that matter, how many more employees would the public sector have to hire, on the backs of already beleaguered taxpayers, to cover the diverse functions of private sector justice? By what standards are these judgments of moral superiority or social importance designed? Critics and theoreticians who scathingly condemn the nature of private justice often forget the historical contribution private security has provided. Long before the establishment of a formal, publicly funded police department in pre- and postcolonial America, private security interests were the only entities providing protection for individual persons, assets, and business interests. Remember that the nature of a system of town watches, the "hue and cry," calling for posse formation and community cooperation, constables, and part-time sheriffs could hardly be characterized as public in design.[27]

Judgments about private sector justice cannot be made in a vacuum but must be evaluated in light of the range of services the industry provides a troubled world. To be more particular, who would protect the majority of federal installations? Who would protect the majority of American museums? What force or body would ensure safety and protection in the college and university environment? What other bodies would provide adequate crowd control at entertainment events? What cost would society incur to ensure a public police officer in each bank? Should taxpayers' money be spent in the transportation of money and other negotiable instruments? What police department would provide adequate security for American corporations? How far could city budgets be stretched to provide a secured environment for its multiple retail establishments if security services were absent? When these queries are explored, public law enforcement's tendency to preach from a high moral pedestal is not as convincing. Richard Kobetz and H. H. Antony Cooper, in their article, "Two Armies: One Flag," cogently state:

> It is no exaggeration to aver that without the aid of those presently engaged in the various tasks of private security, the resources of public law enforcement would have to be expanded far beyond the limits that the taxpayer could afford and would pay. Even those who do not contribute directly to the cost of providing private security services benefit to some notable extent from their existence. Private security is not a public luxury. It represents a substantial contribution to the general security of the community. In their impact on the community public and private law enforcement are one and indivisible.[28]

7.1.3 A Caste System of Professionalism

Private security has long been an underclass when compared to public law enforcement. Differences in orientation, training, requirements, and social status accorded these positions have a great deal to do with the class or status differentiation. While much time and energy has been expended in the professionalization of public law enforcement,[29] negative stereotypes, justified or not, still exist concerning private security personnel. The most powerful trend is the continued growth of the private security industry, both in real terms and relative to law enforcement. In 1987, the director of the U.S. Justice Department's National Institute of Justice (NIJ) wrote that "cooperation becomes increasingly essential with the growth of the private security industry. [In policing] resources to meet the increasing demand have dwindled. In most major cities, police personnel have declined, and the number of police employees per 1000 population dropped 10% between 1975 and 1985. Shrinking tax revenues throughout the country and outright taxpayer revolts ... have curtailed growth in government. Police, like other public administrators, have become familiar with cutback management."[30] The Private Advisory Council expounds that these attitudes

> are based on incorrect assumptions that private security personnel perform the same job duties as patrol officers and investigators in law enforcement, and that a broad generalization can be made about the nature and personnel of all components of proprietary and contractual security—guards, private patrol services, private investigators, armored car guards and armed couriers, and alarm response runners and installers. Certainly, the security industry and private justice practitioners must concede there is a distinction between the level of training and qualifications for certification. The security industry has been its own worst enemy in this area by failing to promote high level, sophisticated standards of educational requirements.[31]

In response to the call for increased state and local regulation of the private security force, Richard Lukins, in his article "Security Training for the Guard Force," castigates the industry for its lack of action.

> This trend has not caught the affected components of the private security industry— the guard services and proprietary security managers—completely by surprise but it does not appear that they were totally prepared either. And certainly no one can say that our industry has established an imposing record of self-regulation.[32]

Lukins further relates that the present impression of a security guard as not more than "half a cop" will be deleterious to future professionalism in the security industry.[33] The quest for professionalism requires more than rhetoric. As outlined in Chapter 2 on regulation, licensing, and qualifications, the road to professionalism is filled with impediments. Those impediments—a lack of educational discipline or cogent body of knowledge, an accepted code of ethics, a prestige or status consensus on occupational roles, or a seal of social and governmental legitimacy—are all attainable goals.[34] To get beyond the characterization that a private security practitioner is nothing more than a play policeman, the industry must aggressively implement the standards of professionalism. On the other hand, much of that judgment is the result of prejudice and stereotype. "Private security is aware of this status differential imposed by many law enforcement personnel and deeply resent it since they feel that law enforcement neither understands nor empathizes with their crime prevention role. This in turn leads to a lower level of esteem by private security for law enforcement personnel."[35] Petty bickering and hate mongering further erodes the ambition of professionalism. Constructive suggestions regarding increased standards and performance objectives are more in order. Certification programs such as that offered by ASIS International and its

Certified Protection Professional programs make a real contribution to substantive professionalism. The CPP program's chief objectives are

1. To raise the professional standing of the field and to improve the practice of security management by giving special recognition to those security practitioners who, by passing examinations and fulfilling prescribed standards of performance, conduct, and education, have demonstrated a high level of competence and ethical fitness.
2. To identify sources of professional knowledge of the principles and practices of security and loss prevention, related disciplines, and laws governing and affecting the practice of security.
3. To encourage security professionals to carry out a continuing program of professional development.[36]

Attaining professionalism will require both dedication and perseverance. Howard C. Shook, former president of the International Association of Chiefs of Police (IACP), remarks that the private security sector has "proven its worth and can defend itself from detractors rather easily."[37] Harold Peterson, in his work *Private Security v. Public Law Enforcement*,[38] calls for a natural respect between the public and private sectors and highlights the unique and extremely sophisticated expertise exhibited by the private justice system. He warns the traditionalist in law enforcement that "[t]here are those in both the community and law enforcement who believe that the public police alone are responsible for crime reduction. If, as a chief, you think like this, I'm afraid that your agency will fail the public you serve."[39]

7.1.4 A Failure to Communicate and Cooperate

Predictably, a lack of respect between the public and private sector, leads to a lack of communication. The Private Security Advisory Council cogently concludes:

> Since many law enforcement personnel perceive themselves as having a higher degree of status than private security, and do not properly appreciate the role of private security in crime prevention, there will be a tendency to avoid communication with private security personnel. One might expect that private security would communicate freely with law enforcement as a perceived higher status group. But the intensity of feelings expressed by private security and the ambiguity of their relationship with law enforcement ... would seem to indicate an uncertainty as to the equality of status with law enforcement. Private security, then, would generally tend to avoid communication with law enforcement; without effective communication cooperation cannot be imposed.[40]

Like squabbling relatives, this state of interaction is counterproductive, but easily correctable. Many of the perceptions, viewpoints, and preconceived notions about the role of private security as it relates to public law enforcement that each party possesses are highly biased and unscientific. For example, it is ludicrous to argue that the training and educational requirements for all public law enforcement positions is markedly higher. Some major police departments, such as the city of Philadelphia, with a metropolitan area of more than six million people, historically required no more than an eighth-grade education for admission into the police department. While this may be an exception to the general requirement of a high-school diploma, it is folly for public police personnel to perceive their educational requirements as always being more rigorous. Of course, there has been a strong tendency toward higher educational requirements with a recent flurry of legislative activity concerning the regulation, licensing, and education mandated for private security.[41] The perception that only public policing has erudite training is fundamentally flawed.

Another rationale often espoused by the public sector, which justifies its lack of communication, is functional separation. Some see no benefits to communication because of distinct occupational roles. The perception that private security protects only those interests that are strictly private is incorrect. Consider Table 7.4,[42] charting the public functions performed by the private justice sector.

Those asserting a limited public role for private security inaccurately portray the industry. Private security personnel have willingly taken on, been legislatively granted, or freely pursued these traditionally public functions:

- Community protection and services
- Public housing protection
- Parking authority control and security
- Enforcement of motor vehicle laws
- Natural resource activities
- Waterways and port services
- Air and rail protection
- Animal control
- Court security
- Governmental office security
- Private prisons
- Code violation inspectors
- Special event security
- Governmental investigations

The call for cooperation and professional interchange is earnest and well-grounded. Professional associations and groups such as the American Society for Industrial Security have formulated liaison committees. Additionally, IACP has emphasized the unique capacities of the security industry, stating that it should be viewed as a complement to public law enforcement.[43] Even the current structure and bureaucratic makeup of the Department of Homeland Security (DHS) includes a Private Sector Commission, which is considered a significant contributor in the war on terror.[44]

There can be little dispute that privatization of public services or contracting out of government responsibility to private employers is a major trend. Not unexpectedly, much of this activity has been viewed with distrust and apprehension, particularly from those authorities that intend to ensure the vested interest of police. The Hallcrest Report I notes that this type of bickering and failure to communicate borders on the inane. The interest of the public will be better served through "constructive dialogue and creative planning by law enforcement and private security to facilitate contracting out of certain noncrime activities."[45] The report further notes that energy, time, and resources are being wasted in this debate and "could be better utilized in identifying areas for contracting out and developing tightly prescribed contract specifications of performance."[46] The momentum of privatization makes public reticence to

Table 7.4 Sites with Experience in Private Provision of Protection Services

State	Jurisdiction	Type of Service
Alaska	Anchorage	Parking meter enforcement Parking meter collection Parking lot security
Arizona	State Flagstaff Maricopa County Phoenix	Parking lot enforcement School crossing guards Building security Crowd control
California	Federal Hawthorns Los Angeles Los Angeles County Norwalk San Diego San Francisco Santa Barbara	US Department of Energy facility security Traffic control during peak hours Patrol streets surrounding private university Traffic and security for special events Building security Park security Park security Housing project security Park security Building security Airport security Prison transport
Colorado	Denver Fort Collins	Building security Building security
Connecticut	Hartford	Sport arena security
Florida	Dade County Fort Lauderdale Pensacola St. Petersburg	Courts, building security Airport, building security Airport security Park security
Hawaii	State	Parking lot enforcement
Idaho	State Idaho Falls	Regional medical center security School crossing guards
Kentucky	Lexington	Housing project security
Massachusetts	Boston	Hospital, courts, library security—city Library security—federal
Nevada	Federal	Nuclear test site security
New Jersey	Sport Authority	Sports arena security
New York	State Buffalo	Response to burglar alarms in state office County security—federal

(Continued)

Table 7.4 (*Continued*) Sites with Experience in Private Provision of Protection Services

State	Jurisdiction	Type of Service
	New York City	Security compounds for towed cars Shelter security Human Resources Administration security Building security Locate cars with outstanding tickets Arrests for retail store theft Management training; police Campus security
Pennsylvania	State Philadelphia Pittsburgh	Unemployment offices security Welfare offices security Parking enforcement Court security—federal Patrol city park High school stadium security School crossing guards Transfer of prisoners
Texas	Dallas/Fort Worth Houston	Airport security including baggage checking Building security
Utah	State	Building security Training for transit police
Washington	Seattle Tacoma	Building security Sports arena security
Washington, D.C.	District of Columbia Federal	Planning and management Building security

private sector justice even more unjustified. "But the trick to privatization is not only lowering costs, but also maintaining quality of service—particularly when the service in question is security."[47] The transference of public obligation to private interest is a trend likely to continue (see Table 7.5).[48]

The failure of public and private policing to communicate undermines and hinders the social order. Public law enforcement, in its own ignorance of the processes and functions of private law enforcement, simply chooses to disregard the reality of its professional counterpart. In the same vein, private security, particularly through its own internal decision making, management, and personnel practices, has done little to dissuade its reputation that it is a business first and foremost. As one commentator states,

Many problems are constant and intractable while the barriers remain; solutions become possible only as they fall away. Familiar roles are exchanged for others less accustomed. The experience is designed expressly to give practical insight into the domain and responsibility of others. It is a sobering feeling to have once in a while the

Table 7.5 Possibility of Transferring Responsibility to Private Security

Activity	Law Enforcement Executives (%)	Proprietary Security Managers (%)	Contract Security Managers (%)
Responding to burglar alarms	57	69	68
Preliminary investigations	40	88	68
Completing incident reports			
(a) Victim declines prosecution; for insurance purposes only	68	87	66
(b) Misdemeanors	45	81	63
Supplemental case reports	38	78	63
Transporting citizen arrests	35	32	38

privilege of walking a mile in someone else's moccasins. It is hoped that these shared experiences may be carried over into the day-to-day realities of professional life and provide a positive inspiration for cooperation and understanding.[49]

Failure of both the public and private justice systems to communicate and cooperate results in a staggering loss of human and professional resources. However, recent studies have shown steady and continuous improvement in the area of communication, both nationally and internationally—and that trend appears to be moving in a positive direction.[50]

In the earlier days of public–private cooperation, the results were not as encouraging. For examples, in the late 1970s the Private Security Advisory Council revealed an exceptionally low level of interaction between the public and private sectors. Its more salient findings included the following:

1. Less than one-half had conducted a survey to find out how many and what types of private security agencies operated in their areas
2. Only one-third of the agencies stated that they had an office or officer to provide liaison with private security
3. Only 25% of the agencies had policies or procedures for defining working roles of law enforcement in private security
4. Only 25% had policies covering interchange of information with private security
5. Less than 20% had procedures for cooperative actions with private security[51]

The lack of cooperation and communication negatively impacts both systems as evident in Table 7.6.[52]

There is a growing recognition of interdependency between law enforcement and the private security industry and have acknowledged a moral and legal obligation to open channels of communication and to professionally cooperation. To stagnate and not advance further the current relationship is debilitating to efforts to reduce criminality and assure a safer world. The continued

Table 7.6 Private Security Perceptions of Law Enforcement Cooperation on Criminal Incidents/Assistance Calls

	Security Managers	
	Proprietary (%)	Contract (%)
Degree of law enforcement cooperation		
Don't cooperate	2	7
Cooperative reluctantly	23	33
Cooperate fully	71	34
Interfere with private security investigation	2	4
Withhold needed information	9	15
	N = 676	N = 545
Law enforcement response to assistance requests		
Respond promptly	59	35
Respond slowly	3	10
Depends on situation	32	36
Have never called police	6	19
Law enforcement support for security employee decisions		
Support decisions	75	52
Do not support	1	4
Sometimes support	11	23
N/R	13	22
	N = 110	N = 78

practice of turf protection, stereotyping, and prejudicial analysis benefits no one. As Kobetz and Cooper relate:

> As soon as the essential unity of a mission is perceived and accepted, the special difficulties of responsibility and approach can be studied in detail. For too long, the other side—our common antisocial enemy—has seen matters in terms of "them versus us," is it not time that we, the public and the private providers of security, truly end this and in a practical and professional fashion begin to think of "us versus them"?[53]

7.2 Positive Programs on Interaction and Cooperation

The best remedy for the unfortunate divide between the public and private justice model is success by cooperation and integration.[54] Instead of diverse worlds, there need be the forging of a solid professional alliance. Public and private need see each system as distinct yet complimentary, unique yet dedicated to a similar mission. "While healthy competition and fraternal camaraderie are still in the distant future, the likelihood that more and more local police departments will recognize the hidden wealth that lies in police private security relations seems closer than ever."[55] In order to accomplish the objective of cooperation and communication, certain goals, objectives, and responsibilities must be met. Daniel E. McElory, in his article "A Professional Alliance," holds the following to be essential:

■ Recognize certain prescribed standards of performance, education, and high level of professional competence of individuals entering the field or presently employed in the industry.
■ Encourage the use of sound practices, principles of security, and loss prevention.
■ Promote mutual respect, cooperation, and communication between both sectors as well as increasing the knowledge of each other's functions.
■ Speak in a unified voice on issues that promote the industry at large.
■ Stress and promote programs designed for increasing professional development at all levels of employment.
■ Work to establish liaisons wherever possible that will serve to benefit the entire industry.
■ Pursue a program of true professionalism in thought, word, and deed.[56]

Factionalism is surely not a fixed state for either side of policing model. What appears more likely on the horizon is the recognition that these are two armies operating under one flag. The present landscape has many a story to tell about how these two theaters work in unity. Indeed, for some observers, the new partnering is not some fad or gimmick for the moment but a paradigm shift in how justice services shall be delivered in the century ahead.[57]

There is little question that the private sector brings skills and expertise to the table in areas where public law enforcement typically expends less effort and energy. For example, most technology has not been the province of government but more the invention of the private sector—especially the case in matters of surveillance, motion and sensor systems, alarms and related technology, as well as the demands and challenges of cyber threats and security.[58] For a sampling of these partnerships see Appendix 4. These are the true success stories in the life of private security—the ones where public and private work as comrades in arms.[59]

Review the current state of partnering between the public and private sector at: http://www.ilj.org/publications/docs/Operation_Partnership_Private_Security.pdf

7.2.1 College and Municipal Police Forces

The cooperation exhibited between city or municipal police and college or university security forces is a long-standing example of how these two worlds can effectively cooperate. William Bess, director of Campus Safety at Bowling Green State University, and Galen Ash, director at the Bowling Green Police Department, feel confident that they have mastered the art of interaction by identifying the essential elements in the recipe for successful cooperation:

1. Mutual assistance agreement
2. Support from the courts
3. Shared training programs
4. Efficient communications (technical)
5. Ongoing administrative working relations

6. Police/advisory committee participation
7. Shared crime prevention programs
8. Cooperative investigations and sharing of information
9. College educational programs
10. Informal daily contacts[60]

At Bowling Green, the private and public police model overcomes the preconceptions and caricatures so often applied to each model. Both parties indicate that rhetoric is easy, but activities that are planned and concerted are the elixirs that smooth over the distrustful state of affairs. At Northern Illinois University, the public and private police authorities are now so blended that it is difficult to see the distinction in its promotion for crime prevention and safety (see Figure 7.4).[61]

In its annual reporting to students, Northern Illinois officials praise the interactivity as almost second nature. See Figure 7.5[62] which lists all crucial contacts in the event of crime and emergency.

The interaction between public and private security, especially between college and university departments and the city or municipalities in which they are located, is an ongoing departmental obligation. In fact, college and university crime data reports, as required under the Clery Act, presuppose the cooperative, natural relationship that must exist between private forces working the campus and the local, federal, and state police agencies that have had significant interaction and have amassed crime data. The Clery Act requires private security forces and college officials to solicit crime date formally. Appendix 5[63] contains a recommended letter format between the private and public law enforcement entities.

The National Association of College and University Business Officers affirms the need for continuing interplay.

> The security department must be largely self-sufficient, but able to work harmoniously with other institutional departments. It should also maintain effective liaison with other law enforcement agencies, the courts, the prosecuting agencies and the press. It is also advisable that the local chief of police be informed of public functions to be held at the institution, so that he may be prepared to assist if necessary.[64]

Figure 7.4 University Police Officer communicating with security officer.

Crimes and emergencies can be reported by contacting any of the following authorities, 24 hours a day:	
Dial 911	Report emergencies or non-emergency criminal violations from a public, university building or residence hall phone or cell phone
Dial 815-753-1212	Report non-emergency requests for NIU Department of Police and Public Safety services or information
Emergency Assistance Call Boxes	Immediate connection to the NIU Department of Police and Public Safety Use any of the designated call boxes located throughout campus
Off-Campus Police Departments	815-748-8400 DeKalb Police Department 815-895-2155 DeKalb County Sheriff's Office 815-895-2123 Sycamore Police Department
In Person	Contact an NIU Department of Police and Public Safety officer on patrol, at any Community Safety Center in the residence halls, Northern View Community Center or the Department of Police and Public Safety at 395 Wirtz Drive in DeKalb
Online	Email: NIU Department of Police and Public Safety at niupd@niu.edu
Anonymous Tip Lines	Report information about a crime, illegal activities and/or violations of the Student Code of Conduct anonymously at 815-753-TIPS (8477) or Crimestoppers at 815-895-3272 or contact the DeKalb Police at cityofdekalb.com/612/iWatch with non-emergency information on any criminal activity

Figure 7.5 Northern Illinois University emergency contacts.

Find out about the International Association of Campus Law Enforcement Association at: http://www.iaclea.org/visitors/about/

Not all relationships are borne from good will. For example, at both the University of Pennsylvania and Temple University, the cost cutting of once public police forces erected a newer private sector model, which has resulted in efforts to unionize the private guard force. Allied Barton, the replacement company, has been met with severe labor organizing activities that reflect disgruntlement. On October 10, 2010, the private force voted to unionize.[65]

The influence of private sector policing on college campuses is multidimensional. With the implementation of new federal legislation on the reporting of the campus crime rate, *under* The Crime Awareness and Campus Security Act of 1990,[66] private sector justice computes the crime data. Campuses are required to collect and publish the following data:

1. A statement of current campus policies regarding procedures and facilities for students and others to report criminal actions or other emergencies occurring on campus and policies concerning the institution's response to such reports.
2. A statement of current policies concerning security and access to campus facilities, including campus residences, and security considerations used in the maintenance of campus facilities.

3. A statement of current policies concerning campus law enforcement, including—
   a. The law enforcement authority of campus security personnel;
   b. The working relationship of campus security personnel with state and local law enforcement agencies, including whether the institution has agreements with such agencies, such as written memoranda of understanding, for the investigation of alleged criminal offenses; and
   c. Policies that encourage accurate and prompt reporting of all crimes to the campus police and the appropriate law enforcement agencies.
4. A description of the type and frequency of programs designed to inform students and employees about campus security procedures and practices and to encourage students and employees to be responsible for their own security and the security of others.
5. A description of programs designed to inform students and employees about the prevention of crimes.
6. Statistics concerning the occurrence on campus, in or on noncampus buildings or property, and on public property during the most recent calendar year, and during the two preceding calendar years for which data are available:
   a. Of the following criminal offenses reported to campus security authorities or local police agencies:
      i. Murder;
      ii. Sex offenses, forcible or nonforcible;
      iii. Robbery;
      iv. Aggravated assault;
      v. Burglary;
      vi. Motor vehicle theft;
      vii. Manslaughter;
      viii. Arson; and
      ix. Arrests or persons referred for campus disciplinary action for liquor law violations, drug-related violations, and weapons possession; and
   b. Of the crimes described in sub clauses (I) through (VIII) of clause (i), of larceny-theft, simple assault, intimidation, and destruction, damage, or vandalism of property, and of other crimes involving bodily injury to any person, in which the victim is intentionally selected because of the actual or perceived race, gender, religion, sexual orientation, ethnicity, or disability of the victim that are reported to campus security authorities or local police agencies, which data shall be collected and reported according to category of prejudice.
7. A statement of policy concerning the monitoring and recording through local police agencies of criminal activity at off-campus student organizations that are recognized by the institution and that are engaged in by students attending the institution, including those student organizations with off-campus housing facilities.
8. A statement of policy regarding the possession, use, and sale of alcoholic beverages and enforcement of state underage drinking laws and a statement of policy regarding the possession, use, and sale of illegal drugs and enforcement of federal and state drug laws and a description of any drug or alcohol abuse education programs as required under section 1011i of this title.
9. A statement advising the campus community where law enforcement agency information provided by a state under section 14071(j) of Title 42, concerning registered sex offenders may be obtained, such as the law enforcement office of the institution, a local law enforcement agency with jurisdiction for the campus, or a computer network address.

10. A statement of current campus policies regarding immediate emergency response and evacuation procedures, including the use of electronic and cellular communication (if appropriate), which policies shall include procedures to:

    a. Immediately notify the campus community upon the confirmation of a significant emergency or dangerous situation involving an immediate threat to the health or safety of students or staff occurring on the campus, as defined in paragraph (6), unless issuing a notification will compromise efforts to contain the emergency;

    b. Publicize emergency response and evacuation procedures on an annual basis in a manner designed to reach students and staff; and

    c. Test emergency response and evacuation procedures on an annual basis.[67]

The International Association of Campus Law Enforcement Administration (IACLEA) has been a major implementer of the new policy. While the reporting requirements are administratively cumbersome, the "law has, however, delivered some good. Besides placating many victims' rights groups, it directs attention towards campus security with real and positive impact. As prospective students focus more on crime statistics as criteria for choosing a college, campuses will tend to beef up on-site security programs, by specifying integrated access control, communications and monitoring systems in dormitories, classrooms, parking lots and other facilities."[68] Local police departments, as well as state entities, increasingly rely on this information.

Crime is a growing reality on college campuses as is the paucity of funds to control and eradicate it. Universities and colleges are increasingly looking to the private sector to deliver safety and security on campus. Allied Barton, recently renamed the Penn Police Department, is the largest private police force in the Commonwealth of Pennsylvania. It operates on the campus of the University of Pennsylvania and works closely with the Philadelphia Police Department and delivers a wide array of services to the educational community including

- Campus fire safety
- Evacuation planning
- Drug and alcohol abuse
- Domestic abuse
- High risk/confrontational situation management
- Clery Act
- Access control
- Lock-outs and vehicle assists
- Campus escort services
- Residential life security
- Campus emergency preparedness[69]

Other companies are major players in the delivery of law enforcement services, and all of these entities work closely and cooperatively with public law enforcement.

7.2.2 Transit and Municipal Police Forces

In the areas of transit, transportation systems, and other public facilities from airports to bus stations, the role of private sector justice is clear. Transit systems are often large and complicated and present serious and significant security challenges for security professionals.

See how the Sacramento California Transit system utilizes both public and private police in the operation of its system at: http://www.sacrt.com/lightrail.stm#Security

Some transit systems, such as the City of Los Angeles and its five surrounding counties, employ a full-time transit police to oversee the safety of its operations.[70] Coupling a massive metropolitan area with a highly visible bus and transit service provides opportune laboratory conditions to test public–private cooperation. So sophisticated is the interaction between the private transit police and the surrounding City of Los Angeles and counties that in 1982 a grant of $375,000 was awarded from Los Angeles County for the purposes of "hiring off-duty local police officers to work on a part-time basis."[71] The benefits of the program over the years since its inception have been many and include a massive infusion of manpower, which has resulted in a decline of violent criminality in transit locations.[72] The intangible and indirect benefits of interaction and cooperation seem to be held in the highest regard. Harry Buzz, then assistant chief of the Transit Police Department, has written:

> The indirect benefits include development of working relationships between members of our local enforcement agencies. The part-time officers have gained respect for the professionalism of our department which they take back to their own agency. They have become more sensitized to transit crime and can, while working with their primary agency, handle unique transit related problems with confidence.
>
> Transit police officers have benefited from the exposure to highly trained and experienced officers of other agencies. Also, since transit police officers patrol most streets in Los Angeles County, especially the high crime areas, they are frequently called upon to provide backup to local jurisdictions. This is particularly true in the city of Los Angeles where LAPD is operating with extremely limited personnel resources. On many of these occasions, the officer being assisted has worked part time for our department and the other officers know each other.[73]

Aside from these remarkable benefits, the transit-LAPD experiment has dramatically increased the public's perception of safety. That, of course, is the greatest benefit of any policing process whether public or private.[74] Other transit programs that utilize private sector entities and officers include Seattle, Washington, Milwaukee, Wisconsin, and Phoenix, Arizona.

Review the U.S. Department of Transportation's Guide on security guidelines for mass transit at: https://www.transit.dot.gov/oversight-policy-areas/security-and-emergency-preparedness-action-items-transit-agencies

While in many cases interaction and cooperation between public and private law enforcement is impeded by an atmosphere of distrust and elitism, these examples indicate the capacity to change and to benefit from mutual dedication.

7.2.3 Private Security Industry and Law Enforcement Agencies

Public and private policing have a significant relational history. At the federal level, various agencies of government, from the DHS to the military branches, have come to heavily depend upon the services of private sector justice. As the Bureau of Justice Assistance notes in its Engaging Private Security to Promote Homeland Security, private sector justice can jump in with feet first. Private security can:

- Coordinate plans with the public sector regarding evacuation, transportation, and food services during emergencies.
- Gain information from law enforcement regarding threats and crime trends.
- Develop relationships so that private practitioners know whom to contact when they need help or want to report information.
- Build law enforcement understanding of corporate needs (e.g., confidentiality).
- Boost law enforcement's respect for the security field.[75]

The entire mission of homeland security presumes cooperation and alliances. Even the President's guiding mission statement on the defense of this nation notes:

> We will help ensure that the Federal Government works with states and local governments, and the private sector as close partners in a national approach to prevention, mitigation, and response.[76]

In homeland defense, the private sector justice model achieves extraordinary benefits for the collective. According to the Homeland Security Research Corporation, by 2011 the private sector "will trail only DHS in HLS industry procurement volume. This stems from the forecasted 50% private sector procurement growth from 2007 to 2011, totaling an accumulated $28.5B."[77] The face of private sector justice can be discovered across the DHS spectrum; from privatized forces seeking out terrorists in Iraq and Afghanistan to the protection of federal installations across the mainland, private sector justice makes extra ordinary contributions in the defense of the country.[78]

This same mentality extends to both states and localities. In Denver, Colorado, private security officers are now patrolling city locales in coordination with the Denver Police Department.[79] The City of Houston, Texas, is now training and enrolling nearly 300 security officers in specialized training from the local Academy to work side by side with the Houston Sheriff's department.[80]

Community policing inroads by private sector policing continues at a structural and institutional level as well. For example, entertainment and recreational communities like Seven Springs, Pennsylvania, have hired private security companies to deliver policing services. Near Orlando, at Metro West, full policing services are being delivered cooperatively between the City of Orlando and Critical Intervention Services[81] (see Figure 7.6).

No program has been as ambitious as the New York Police Department (NYPD) Shield endeavor, which seeks to integrate New York City's extraordinary resources of the private sector with its first-rate police department. As the center for all things security, New York City provides the perfect forum for the bulk of corporate security firms to be active players and partners in the prevention of terrorism and wide scale harm in the most populous region in the United States. NYPD has been an extraordinary success story in partnership (see Figure 7.7).[82]

Each of these entities seeks the promotion of safety and security by mutually agreed upon responsibilities and the appropriate delegation of power and authority to those properly entrusted.

Figure 7.6 Community oriented security officer. (Courtesy of CIS World Services.)

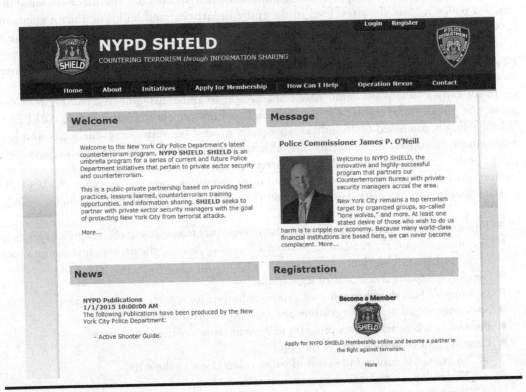

Figure 7.7 NYPD Shield website.

Public and private police must work together since the benefits are so measurable. Partnerships advance:

- Creative problem solving
- Increased training opportunities
- Information, data, and intelligence sharing
- Force multiplier opportunities
- Access to the community through private sector communications technology
- Reduced recovery time following disasters[83]

Another successful forging between public and private security forces is between the City of Amarillo, Texas, and a private security company Allstate Security Industries, Inc. The president of Allstate, as well as the chief of the Amarillo Police Department recognize that mutual cooperation benefits both departments. Commencing in August 1981, both entities devised a program whereby Allstate Security would begin responding to all alarm calls. In reviewing the findings of an internal study, the department revealed that "this procedure relieved the police department of the time-consuming responsibility of answering an average of eight alarms per day and saved the department approximately 3428 man hours, or the equivalent of adding 13 men per year to their police department. All of this was at no cost to the taxpayers."[84] The results of such cooperation are advantageous from an economic as well as a human point of view. As Allstate continues to pursue alarm calls, the policy frees up other public officers to perform more critical functions relating to investigative and apprehension processes. As it spreads out the many responsibilities, the policy reduces the stress level in the entire department and builds or affirms goodwill between the department, the security company, and the public at large. Given the success of this relationship, the program of mutual cooperation was expanded to include a neighborhood patrol program and a canine program. Current internal studies of these activities indicate a positive outcome.[85]

In the early 1980s, Washington state embarked on an ambitious joint endeavor between the public and private sector entitled the Washington Law Enforcement Executive Forum (WLEEF). "Membership is composed of 26 individuals equally divided between the private sector and law enforcement executives, including sheriffs, chiefs, the state patrol chief, and special agents in charge of the Seattle offices of the FBI and Secret Service, as well as representation from the state attorney general's office. Close relationship and open communication exist between the WLEEF and the Washington Association of Sheriffs and Police Chiefs."[86] WLEEF'S achievements include

- Funding a statewide loan executive program to enhance management of local police agencies;
- Providing support for the *Law Enforcement Executive Journal*, the nation's first law enforcement/business publication;
- Support computer crime control legislation;
- Funding and developing a state-wide toll-free hotline for reporting drunk drivers;
- Sponsoring legislation for regulation and training of private security personnel;
- Promoting a Business Watch program to prevent crimes against businesses;
- Creating an Economic Crime Task Force;
  - To assess the nature and extent of white-collar crime in the state,
  - To develop strategies to reduce such crime,
  - To promote appropriate legislative initiatives and revisions, and
  - To collect and disseminate information on economic crime.[87]

More recently, WLEEF has been an active participant in the state's 1991 legislation on the regulation and licensing of the private security industry. This joint endeavor produced a variety of positive results including

1. The philosophical and operational "gap" between public law enforcement and private security is not nearly as wide as often imagined.
2. Competitive security companies can work well together for legitimate common causes, such as training.
3. A high-quality training program can be put together in a short four-hour block.
4. Good communication between government and the security industry can go a long way toward making a licensing law workable and meaningful.
5. There are a lot of community resources available for training.[88]

Visit COPS USDOJ website at: https://cops.usdoj.gov/Default.asp?Item=2034

WLEEF, by and through its Operation Cooperation program, educates both ends of the justice spectrum on the benefits of cooperation. It designates particular structures and goals as well for the public–private consortium and delineates how intimate, how formal or informal these associations might be. Calling these partnerships, WLEEF finds plenty of room for distinctive relationship, examples being:

Degree of formality—Some programs are formal, incorporated ventures, such as 501(c)(3) nonprofits; others are merely "clubs" with bylaws and officers; while others are completely informal.

Specificity of mission—Some exist to solve specific problems, while others are general-purpose, networking organizations.

Leadership—Some collaborative programs are led by law enforcement, others by the private sector, and still others jointly by both fields.

Funding—Some programs have no budget, while others are well funded. There are many models for funding. For example, a partnership may receive money from participating organizations (including police agencies), from sponsors, or from police foundations or crime commissions.

Inclusiveness—A partnership may be a collaboration between law enforcement and private security or between law enforcement and the larger business sector, including more than security operations. On the law enforcement side, collaboration may include not only municipal police and sheriffs, but also state and federal law enforcement officers and school district and campus police. Cooperation also can be arranged between a single company and the local police department or between a federal agency and businesses throughout the country.[89]

WLEEF continues its aggressive promotion of cooperation between the public and private sector by laying out the essential ways in which these two worlds can cooperate.

In the final analysis, mutual cooperation, respect, and a passionate orientation toward professionalism all lead to safer communities. James A. Kirkley, then director of the Department of

Public Safety at the Claremont Colleges in Claremont, California, critiques the traditional separation of authority and power:

> It is now time for a total community effort. The high percentage of non-crime calls for service, the percentage of non-observable crimes, and the fiscal constraints placed upon you, make it ludicrous to expect the public police alone to be responsible for reducing crimes.
>
> Teamwork has long been recognized as an essential ingredient in winning. It is used in all sports, war, business, and even in police work … The time has come for the public sector and the private sector in law enforcement to work as a team.[90]

In many ways, the lines between the public and private police services continue to intermingle and blend—so much so that one entity naturally expects the other to come to its aid or that their stated powers of authority, training, and occupational function are hard to contrast. For example, the Vidant Medical Center, aligned with East Carolina University, describes its police department as almost a mirror image of the public counterpart for here private security officers do not see themselves as distinctive or different but rather part of the same operational mentality. On its Public Safety home page it notes:

> Officers of the Vidant Company Police Department have the same authority as municipal police officers to make arrests for both felonies and misdemeanors, charge for infractions, and to perform all the duties of a sworn law enforcement officer in the state of North Carolina. All of our police officers are certified by the state of North Carolina and commissioned through the North Carolina Attorney General's Office.[91]

The private security department further integrates its mission and activities across the entire neighborhood, the whole institutional setting and in roles and functions that have long been the exclusive province of the public police department. In its crime prevention tips and strategies, the department sets out suggestions and protocols that every public police department would be comfortable with (see Figure 7.8).[92]

The content here demonstrates not only a similarity in the knowledge base of these two entities but also an uncannily complimentary approach in how to protect people and assets. The consensus building for continual interaction and cooperation between the public and private sector has come of age.

7.3 Recommendations on the Future Public–Private Partnerships

The role of partnerships between public and private police entities has a far more dramatic impact than most practitioners realize. With each new venture, these diverse worlds tend to unify both in levels of competence and occupational functionality. With each new cooperative endeavor, information is shared, techniques are mutually assessed, adopted and critiqued. With each novel agreement, both sectors test the efficacy of techniques and protocols involving crime and communities. For nearly 50 years, the continuous call for cooperation and mutual partnership has not fallen upon deaf ears but an increasingly willing audience that sees the wisdom in working together.

Driving

- Avoid driving alone or at night.
- Know the area you are in. Beware of dead end streets.
- Make sure your car stays in good operating condition and be aware of the fuel level. Keep a flashlight, spare tire and jumper cables with you.
- Keep all car doors locked and windows closed while in or out of your car. Set your alarm or use an anti-theft device.
- Park in well-lit areas. Avoid parking next to vans, trucks with camper shells, or cars with tinted windows. Be especially alert in parking garages.
- Keep your keys in your hand when returning to your vehicle. If necessary, your keys can be used as a defensive weapon against an attacker.
- Park as close as you can to your destination and take notice of where you parked.
- Do not hide a key on or in your car.
- Inspect underneath car and in back seat before entering.
- Be cautious of anyone who gives you undue attention, asks for directions or in any other way tries to get too close. This includes someone offering help.
- Attract attention if approached (yell, make a scene, etc.)
- Never leave your car unoccupied with the motor running or with children inside.
- Do not leave packages or valuables on the seat of your car.
- When approaching your vehicle be aware of your surroundings.
- Do not approach your car alone if there are suspicious people in the area.
- Continue driving if someone tries to stop or follow you. Proceed to a well-lighted business or the police station before stopping. Police or security personnel may usually be found at the emergency department of a hospital. Do not lead someone to your home.
- Keep the car in gear at stop signs and traffic lights.
- If you see a stranded motorist, go to the nearest phone and call for help instead of stopping.

Automated Teller Machine (ATM)

- When using an Automated Teller Machine, try to use one in a well-lighted location. Withdraw only the cash you need.
- Protect your PIN by shielding the ATM keypad from anyone who is standing near you.
- Do not throw away your ATM receipt away at the ATM location.
- Be aware of your surroundings while using the machine.

At Home

- Lock all doors and windows when you leave the house, even for a few minutes.
- Make sure all doors to the outside are metal or solid; that they have good sturdy locks with deadbolts; that all windows have locks; and that you use all locks.
- Secure sliding glass doors with locks or bars.
- Make sure all entrances around your home are well-lit. Turn on these lights after dark.
- Trim or cut down bushes or trees that hide doors or windows or block your view or lighting.
- Never hide house keys on the outside.
- When leaving home for an extended time, have a neighbor or family member watch your house and pick up your newspapers and mail.
- Place indoor and outdoor lights on an automatic timer. Leave a radio or television on so the house looks and sounds occupied. Use security alarms and motion detectors if available.
- When children are home alone, make sure they know how to dial 911. Have an agreed upon contact for them to call.
- Train children not to let strangers inside the home and not to tell callers they are alone. Instruct them to keep all doors and windows locked.
- Warn children to look for signs of danger such as a broken, door ajar, or a strange car in the yard or street. Instruct them to go to a neighbor's house and call an adult or the Police Department.
- Teach children to walk and play with other children, not alone and to refuse rides or gifts from strangers in the neighborhood.

Figure 7.8 Crime prevention tips and strategies.

(Continued)

Stalking

A person who willfully and repeatedly contacts another person without permission can be charged with stalking. The following actions could be construed as stalking if they happen on more than one occasion:

- Following or appearing within the sight of another
- Approaching or confronting another individual in a public or private place
- Appearing at the work place or residence of another
- Entering or remaining on an individual's property
- Contacting by telephone
- Sending mail, email or instant messages

Stalking is a crime of power, control, obsession and intimidation. Do not ignore it. If you feel you are being watched or followed, you should:

- Notify police
- Notify work, family, and friends

Protect Yourself

- Do not walk alone. Always travel with friends.
- Tell the stalker to stop.
- Document everything. Keep a detailed record of any contact with the stalker, and save harassing phone calls or emails.
- Change your number to an unlisted number.
- Alert your neighbors, family, co-workers, etc., about your stalker.
- Vary the number of times and routes you take to work, etc.,
- Go to a police station if you think you are being followed.

Figure 7.8 (Continued)   Crime prevention tips and strategies.

The recommendations from various bodies, associations, think-tanks, and task forces has been consistent and such persistence is paying great dividends for both the private and public systems. A summary of those authorities is worth revisiting as our coverage of Private Security and the Law reaches its conclusions.

7.3.1 National Advisory Committee on Criminal Justice

The National Advisory Committee on Criminal Justice Standards and Goals, in its 1976 Report of The Task Force on Private Security, urged significant interaction and close cooperation. The report concludes:

> Over the past decade, the resources devoted to both public law enforcement and the private security industry have increased as the awareness of the need for greater crime prevention and control has grown. National leaders have called upon every private citizen, institution, and business to join their efforts with the criminal justice system to prevent crime. Although a closer cooperation between the private security and public law enforcement spheres offers a special opportunity for improved crime prevention, the relationship has often been ignored, overlooked or restrained. Recently, however, the potential of that meaningful working relationship between law enforcement and private security has been recognized.[93]

Theoretical concerns aside, practical, pragmatic considerations justify and even compel a policy of interaction. As this work has delved into the complex legal and policy questions involved in private security, one striking, recurring observation occurs—that for all the clamor about the differences of public and private security, there is really very little difference between the two entities. Therefore, the limitations and hesitations about a unified purpose are largely the result of hyperbole and exaggerated positions.

The National Advisory Committee enunciated specific standards, steadfastly encouraging cooperation, mutual respect, and regular interaction. Stated as specific goals, the report recommends:

Goal 6.1: Interaction Policies—Effective interaction between the private security industry and law enforcement agencies is imperative for successful crime prevention and depends to a large extent on published clear and understandable policies developed by their administrators. Policies should be developed to serve as guides for modification by appropriate agencies.[94]

Goal 6.2: Survey and Liaison with Private Security—Law enforcement agencies should conduct a survey and maintain a current roster of those security industry components operating in the agencies' jurisdictions, and designate at least one staff officer to serve as liaison with them.[95]

Goal 6.3: Policy and Procedures—For law enforcement agencies and the private security industry to most effectively work within the same jurisdiction, policies and procedures should be developed covering:

1. The delineation of working roles of law enforcement officers and private security personnel;
2. The continuous prompt and reasonable interchange of information; and
3. Cooperative actions between law enforcement agencies and the private security industry.[96]

Goal 6.4: Multi-Level Law Enforcement Training in Private Security—There should be a multi-level training program for public law enforcement officials, including but not limited to:

1. Role and mission of the private security industry;
2. Legal status and types of services provided by private service companies;
3. Interchange of information, crime reporting, and cooperative actions with the industry; and
4. Orientation in technical and operational procedures.[97]

Goal 6.5: Mistaken Identity of Private Security Personnel—Title, terms, verbal representations, and visual items that cause the public to mistake private security personnel for law enforcement officers should be eliminated; security employers should ensure that their personnel and equipment are easily distinguishable from public law enforcement personnel and equipment.[98]

Goal 6.6: State Regulation of Private Security, Uniforms, Equipment and Job Titles—Each state should develop regulations covering use and wear of private security uniforms, equipment, company names and personnel titles that do not conflict with those in use by law enforcement agencies within the state.[99]

Goal 6.7: Law Enforcement Personnel Secondary Employment—Law enforcement administrators should insure that secondary employment of public law enforcement personnel in the private security industry does not create a conflict of interest and that public resources are not used for private purposes.[100]

Goal 6.8: Law Enforcement Officer Employment as a Security Manager—No law enforcement officer should be a principal or a manager of a private security operation where such an association creates a conflict of interest.[101]

Goal 6.9: Private Investigatory Work—Law enforcement officers should be strictly forbidden from performing any investigatory work.[102]

The National Advisory Committee approaches the dilemma on multiple fronts. First, in order to ensure a cooperative environment between public and private sectors, it harkens for continuous and regular interaction and calls for the creation of a liaison officer and other committees to facilitate the interchange between public and private factions. The committee also urges the elimination of all conflict of interest situations, especially as relates to moonlighting and industrial involvement where either an actual or perceived conflict might exist. Finally, the committee, while insisting upon mutual respect and emulation of each other's tasks and duties, reminds the private sector that it cannot be copycat police officers and should not hold itself out, whether by uniform, badge, or other representation, as operating under the authority of the state or municipality where it is located. Such actions foster potential abuse and cause confusion in the public eye.

The Private Sector Office frequently lends its business expertise when evaluating particular security procedures such as air safety. See: http://tinet.ita.doc.gov/research/programs/ifs/DHS-OTTI_PilotStudyReport_v7-FINAL.pdf

---

7.3.2 The Hallcrest Report

The Hallcrest Report I accepts the fact that private security has "got its head together and found its purpose in life." Its recommendations now insist on a more proactive and participatory role in the elimination, prevention, and detection of criminality in society. Some of the following recommendations attest to this philosophical direction:

- Private security should be involved in community crime prevention.[103]
- Private security should be participants in the development of an Economic Crime Institute.[104]
- Private security should be required, through its associations, to develop crime loss reporting data and information.[105]
- Private industrial security firms should formulate employee awareness programs and specific corporate policies on business, business ethics, and crime.[106]
- Private security concerns should be involved in strategic planning, alternative policing arrangements, and in the transfer of selected police activities to the private sector.[107]
- Private security should provide the resources necessary to design a Private Security Resource Institute.[108]
- Private security should establish standard industrial classifications.[109]
- Private security should have total access to criminal histories.[110]
- Private security should be permitted to achieve an identity through uniforms and appropriate advertising.[111]
- Private security should develop the capacity to transfer its technology to the public sector.[112]
- Private security should support efforts to standardize qualifications, educational training, and certification.[113]

- Private security should provide educational opportunities for public law enforcement officials.[114]
- Private security should establish a task force of police and private security personnel for various purposes.[115]

As propounded above, these recommendations call for a more active involvement in crime prevention, deterrence, and apprehension than traditionally has been expected. Private security as an industry, can no longer expect to be insulated from either the government's regulatory process or public scrutiny. As the role of private security expands, both legally and socially, new responsibilities and obligations must be tackled. Given the high rate of public dissatisfaction over the performance of the public police systems, private police should view increased demands as a sign of confidence. The world's overall complexity makes it likely that security is here to stay and flourish. "The world has shrunk and most industries now face global competition. Businesses are not only concerned with the ethics and mores of a domestic environment, but must now deal with the values of a dynamic world market. Vast new technologies in communications have placed enormous pressures on businesses to protect their data and the assets that pass through these technologies."[116] Public policing, with its numerous restrictions and difficulties, can only envy the private police process.

7.3.3 The Private Sector Office of the Department of Homeland Security

Aside from professional associations, think-tanks, and other groups, the future for the private sector will be bound tightly to the activities of the DHS. From its earliest days, when it was referred to as the Office of Homeland Security, the National Strategy for Homeland Security,[117] the role of private security was to be a "close partnership."[118] Federal spending "on anti-terror since 9/11 has tripled.[119]... Estimates of private sector direct spending on increased security range from $10 billion to $127 billion."[120] Presidential Executive Orders since 9/11 repeatedly encourage cooperation between the two sectors in infrastructure, critical cybercrimes, incident response, and maritime and health policy.[121] How the private sector contributes to the fight against terrorism is a story worth telling. Since 9/11, governmental agencies have urged the participation of not only state and local governments, but also the active input and involvement of the general citizenry.[122] On top of this, there has been a continuous push for private business and commercial entities to be involved and an expectation that much of the American economy would need to be active players in the fight against terrorism. For example, America's chemical, water, utility, and nuclear sectors would have to be aggressively involved in the defense of their facilities, and thus the country itself.[123] Commercial interests could not simply wait for the government to do it all but instead had to jump into the mix of deterrence and prevention of terror. Infrastructure is largely owned by private enterprise and in need of a homeland defense plan. "Industries must plan to respond ... and undertake recovery under severe conditions where much of the infrastructure of the surrounding area is unavailable and site access is limited."[124] Preparedness is an industrial and commercial concern. And it is also the private citizen that encompasses the private sector as well. The question of how much more prepared private homes and families are has yet to be fully measured.[125]

Each facet of the private sector needs to understand:

- How communities are impacted by terrorism
- How to create a plan of response consistent with state and federal standards
- How to mitigate loss in the event of catastrophe and disaster

- How to be active partners in the development of homeland policy
- How to work closely with public agencies
- How to add new programs in traditional Neighborhood Watch programs that focus on terrorism[126]

The National Infrastructure Advisory Council, in its report on public–private sector intelligence coordination, identified 17 business and commercial sectors that need to be step up in the fight against terrorism:

- Communications
- Chemical and hazardous materials
- Commercial facilities
- Dams
- Defense industrial base
- Energy
- Emergency services
- Financial services
- Food and agriculture
- Government facilities
- Information technology
- National monuments and icons
- Nuclear power plants
- Postal and shipping
- Public health and health care
- Transportation
- Water[127]

On a second front, the role of private sector security firms and personnel can only be described as significant. The private sector portion of criminal justice operations grows at an almost immeasurable clip.[128] According to the Homeland Security Research Corporation, by 2011, the private sector "will trail only DHS in HLS industry procurement volume. This stems from the forecasted 50% private sector procurement growth from 2007 to 2011, totaling an accumulated $28.5B."[129] While there have been some slight pauses in that growth, the trend for private sector and DHS partnering is onward and upward according to the Homeland Security Research Council (see Figure 7.9).[130]

The face of private sector justice can be discovered across the DHS spectrum; from privatized forces seeking out terrorists in Iraq and Afghanistan to the protection of federal installations across the mainland, private sector justice makes extraordinary contributions in the defense of the country.[131] From Iraq to the local water facility, private sector justice operatives are engaged in a host of activities once exclusively reserved for the public sector. This trend, often labeled "privatization," assumes that the private sector, with its usual efficiencies and profit motivations, will carry out its task with greater effectiveness. Unions and entrenched government bureaucracies tend to be on the defensive with those promoting privatization. Those seeking greater accountability and freedom of operation tend to the privatized.[132] On paper, the concept is attractive, and in many cases, it is clear that the private sector can do a better job than the government in ensuring safety and security.[133] It will all depend on the subject matter of that security and the corresponding costs.

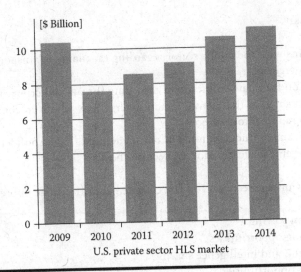

Figure 7.9   U.S. private sector HLS market.

To see how private security's premier professional association, the American Society for Industrial Security (ASIS), gets involved in the standards and practices of homeland security, see https://www.asisonline.org/Standards-Guidelines/Pages/default.aspx

In this sense, private sector justice is driven by bottom-line considerations more than its governmental counterpart. It is motivated by efficiencies never weighed or evaluated in the public sector. And given this general motivation to the profit mentality, there are those who critique it as being willing to cut corners so that the bottom line will be brighter. Quality allegedly suffers. Indeed, many are suspicious of the qualifications of those entrusted with security responsibilities from the private sector. Do recent attempts to increase qualification and conduct legitimate background investigations on security officer applicants calm frayed nerves?[134] Ian Patrick McGinley, when critiquing federal legislation to ensure suitable licensure and background requirements for security officers, found that the industry is in a state of market failure.

> Nevertheless, significant problems with leaving regulation to the market make this option unfeasible. For one, despite laudable attempts, the industry's self-regulation track record has been poor. Second, profit margins in the security industry are tight because many companies view security as a necessary evil. As a result, there is a race to the bottom—in terms of pricing and salaries—in order to gain a competitive advantage relative to other firms, resulting in less qualified officers.[135]

However, this argument does not pan out in so many governmentally operated entities. What of the public school system nationally? Are these systems not in crisis? What of public transportation systems? What of roads and bridges in near collapse? It is not difficult to discern where government fails to meet its mission. Privatization is evident everywhere—prisons, policing, and courts, to name just three, are examples of fields seeing these trends.[136] As the Bureau of Justice Assistance notes in its *Engaging Private Security to Promote Homeland Security*, private sector justice can jump in with feet first.

Private security can

- Coordinate plans with the public sector regarding evacuation, transportation, and food services during emergencies.
- Gain information from law enforcement regarding threats and crime trends.
- Develop relationships so that private practitioners know whom to contact when they need help or want to report information.
- Build law enforcement understanding of corporate needs (e.g., confidentiality).
- Boost law enforcement's respect for the security field.

Working together, private security and law enforcement can realize impressive benefits:

- Creative problem solving
- Increased training opportunities
- Information, data, and intelligence sharing
- Force multiplier opportunities
- Access to the community through private sector communications technology
- Reduced recovery time following disasters[137]

The National Defense Industrial Association (NDIA), another premier professional group for the private sector, argues as if the task of homeland is integral to any private security firm. Its mission unequivocally declares:

- To provide legal and ethical forums for the exchange of information, ideas, and recommendations between industry and government on homeland security issues.
- To promote a vigorous, robust, and collaborative government–industry homeland security team.
- To advocate for best-in-class, high-technology equipment, systems, training and support for America's first responder community.[138]

And not only is it capable of carrying out its own mission in the world of homeland security, but it should do so with collaboration and collegiality in regards to its public partners. The world of public–private is not distinct or radically different; rather, these are compatible and complementary domains where a shared mission is obvious. The Bureau of Justice Assistance in the Department of Justice urges the creation of partnerships between the public and private sector. To be a successful partnership, 12 essential components are needed.

- Common goals
- Common tasks
- Knowledge of participating agencies' capabilities and missions
- Well-defined projected outcomes
- A timetable
- Education for all involved
- A tangible purpose
- Clearly identified leaders
- Operational planning
- Agreement by all partners as to how the partnership will proceed

- Mutual commitment to providing necessary resources
- Assessment and reporting[139]

DHS formally encourages the interplay and cooperation between private sector justice entities and the public law enforcement function. Throughout DHS policymaking is the perpetual recognition that it cannot go alone and that it needs the daily cooperation of the private sector. Within its Office of Policy, DHS has erected a Private Sector Office, its chief aims being

- To engage individual businesses, trade associations, and other nongovernmental organizations to foster dialogue with the department
- To advise the secretary on prospective policies and regulations and in many cases on their economic impact
- To promote public–private partnerships and best practices to improve the nation's homeland security
- To promote department policies to the private sector

The Private Sector Office focuses on two major functions: The Business Outreach Group and Economics Group. In the first instance, DHS affirmatively connects with the business and commercial sector fully realizing that cooperation and joint endeavors fare better than isolation or turf protection. The Outreach Group seeks input and advice from the business sector before the institution or implementation of policy. The Outreach Group:

- Meets with private sector organizations and department components to promote public–private partnerships
- Promotes departmental policies
- Gathers private sector perspectives for use by the department

The Economics Group weighs policy in cost–benefit terms. Here DHS displays a deaf ear regarding the costs of policy implementation since each new regulation or requirement does have a corresponding price tag. As a result, the group looks at the impact of policy from various directions, including

- *Policy analysis*—Evaluates the economic impacts of departmental policies on the private sector.
- *Process analysis*—Evaluates departmental processes that will allow the private sector to operate efficiently while meeting national security needs.
- *Regulatory analysis*—Provides a resource to the department on regulatory/economic analyses.
- *Metrics*—Promotes the use of metrics to identify successes and areas needing improvement.
- *Benefits methodology*—Actively works on the development of methodologies to quantify the benefits of homeland security investments.

The Economics Group coordinates economic roundtables and publishes white papers and other studies that highlight cost–benefit.

Finally, DHS, not long after 9/11, instituted an advisory committee on private sector cooperation and collaboration. Members of the committee represent the full panoply of industry, corporate interests, and security firms with shared interests. From the outset of DHS, it was clear that policy-making would not occur without the input of industry and commerce. Outreach by both sectors is critical to partnering success though DHS appears to expect the first initiative from the public sector.

Visit the Private Sector Office of the DHS at: https://www.dhs.gov/about-private-sector-office

---

7.4 Summary

This chapter pragmatically examines the current cooperative programs between public and private law enforcement. While efforts to stress the commonality of interest between private and public justice are ongoing, there are still glaring differences regarding legal authority, rights, and obligations. There have been judicial, political, and social efforts to extend constitutional protections to private justice. While numerous attempts have been made to color the activities of private policing as a state action or a governmental exercise, which in turn affords more significant constitutional protections to the aggrieved suspect, no permanent bridge has yet been built. Private security, for all of its shortcomings, still has the upper hand procedurally when compared to the constraints and restraints of public policing.

Much of this chapter was concerned with the distinct, yet complementary functional approaches to crime prevention, deterrence, and policy interests of the public and private sectors, requirements in training and other qualifications, and a critical review of stereotypic and prejudicial perceptions of both law enforcement interests. In the final analysis, the preponderance of the evidence demonstrates that the public–private division is more an exercise in human prejudice than in logic or knowledge. Public–private cooperation generally manifests an intelligent exercise of combined resources to combat criminality in American society. Examples of the cooperation between college and municipal police departments, private transit police forces, and other private–public joint ventures were covered. While these examples are not scientifically probative, they are illustrative success stories.

Finally, recommendations from the National Committee on Criminal Justice Standards and Goals as well as the findings of The Hallcrest Reports I and II as well as the Private Sector Office of the Department of Homeland Security were covered in depth. The private security industry's involvement in public justice activities, tasks, and obligations signals increased responsibility for the industry and demands it to be a major contributor and policymaker in the elimination of crime and a safer world.

DISCUSSION QUESTIONS

1. Offer a few recommendations on how to improve the professional interaction of private police and public law enforcement.
2. Do police and private security have any professional interests that are largely antagonistic or are there surprising similarities of approach and occupational direction?
3. Does private sector justice have a moral or egalitarian purpose?
4. In your jurisdiction, are there any examples of mutual cooperation between public and private law enforcement?
5. What are some drawbacks of having a state or local police commission exercising regulatory oversight over the private security industry?

6. Pose three suggestions on how to equalize the status of public and private law enforcement.
7. Would it be feasible for state or other governmental regulators to require the security industry to donate time assisting public law enforcement in public order and/or public safety activities?

NOTES

1 Malcolm K. Sparrow, *Managing the Boundary between Public and Private Policing, New Perspectives in policing*, September 2014, https://www.ncjrs.gov/pdffiles1/nij/247182.pdf.
2 Arthur J. Bilek, James C. Klotter, and R. Keegan Federal, *Legal Aspects of Private Security* 180 (1980); See also: M. Rhead Enion, *Constitutional Limits on Private Policing and the State's Allocation of Force*, 59 Duke L.J.519 (2009–2010); James Pastor, *Security Law and Methods* (2006); The question of legal and constitutional advantage are forever on the minds of those thinking the industry lacks sufficient controls. Law reviews and academic journals are continuously critiquing the non-applicability of constitutional controls; Cooper J. Strickland, Regulation without agency: A practical response to private policing in *United States v. Day*, NC L. Rev. 89 (2010–2011); 1338; James F. Pastor, *Terrorism and Public Safety Policing: Implications for the Obama Presidency* (2009).
3 National Advisory Committee on Criminal Justice Standards and Goals, Private Security: Report of the Task Force on Private Security (1976); first one May 2016; Michael S. Klein and Craig Hemmens, Public regulation of private security: A statutory analysis of state regulation of security guards, *Criminal Justice Policy Review*, May 25, 2016; Stephen Rushin, The regulation of private police, *W. Va. L. Rev.* 115 (2012–2013); 159; see also *Operation Cooperation, Guidelines for Partnerships between Law Enforcement & Private Security Organizations* 11 (2000); Sean James Beaton, Counterparts in modern policing: The influence of corporate investigators on the public police and a call for the broadening of the state action doctrine, *Touro L. Rev.* 26 (2010–2011); 593.
4 National Advisory Committee, at 2; see also Operation Cooperation.
5 William C. Cunningham, John J. Strauchs, and Clifford W. VanMeter, *Private Security Trends 1970 to 2000: The Hallcrest Report II* 116 (1990); see also Operation Cooperation.
6 Cunningham et al., at 120; see also Operation Cooperation.
7 Cunningham et al., at 118.
8 Bill Strudel, The private security connection: Giving the police a sense of security, *Police Chief*, Feb. 1982, at 28–29; Law Commission of Canada, *In Search of Security: The Roles of Public Police and Private Agencies* (2002); George S. Rigakos, *The New Parapolice* (2002). See also: John Manzo, On the practices of private security officers: Canadian security officers' reflections on training and legitimacy, *Social Justice* 38 (2011); 107.
9 2001 Industry Forecast, *Security Mag.*, Chart 2 (2001). For an industry forecast until 2024, see the BLS data sheet at: http://www.bls.gov/ooh/protective-service/security-guards.htm#tab-6.
10 Cunningham et al., at 121; see also Operation Cooperation.
11 International Chiefs of Police, National Policy Summit: Building Private Security/Public Policing Partnerships to Prevent and Respond to Terrorism and Public Disorder (2004), available at https://ric-zai-inc.com/Publications/cops-w0704-pub.pdf; Rand Corp., Defense Institution Building: An Assessment (2016), http://www.rand.org/content/dam/rand/pubs/research_reports/RR1100/RR1176/RAND_RR1176.pdf.
12 Cunningham et al., at 121.
13 See: Elizabeth E. Job, Conceptualizing the private police, *Utah L. Rev.* 573, 582, 584 (2005).
14 International Chiefs of Police, at 18.
15 John E. Driscoll, Public and private security forces unite in Dallas, *Police Chief*, 1988, at 48; see also S. Ronald Hauri, Public–private security liaison: The synergy of cooperation, *Crime & Just. Int'l*, Oct. 1997, at 16; Operation Cooperation; Rob Chapman et al., The COPS Office announces a new online resource for private security and police partnerships, *Community Policing Dispatch* (Feb. 2011) 4.
16 Driscoll, at 48; see also Hauri.
17 Id.

18 Malcolm K. Sparrow, Managing the boundary between public and private policing, *New Perspectives in Policing*, September 2014, at 9, https://www.ncjrs.gov/pdffiles1/nij/247182.pdf.

19 See Nemeth, *Homeland Security: An Introduction to Principles and Practice*, 2nd edition, 164–171 (2010).

20 Sparrow, at 9.

21 Operation Cooperation; see also Pastor, Terrorism; James F. Pastor, *The Privatization of Police in America: An Analysis and Case Study* (2003). See also: Karena Rahall, The siren is calling: Economic and ideological trends towards privatization of public police forces, *U. Miami L. Rev.* 68 (2013–2014); 633.

22 Richard A. Lukins, Securing training for the guard force, *Security Mgmt.*, May 1976, at 32; For a comprehensive analysis of training and credentials for the private security industry, see: Kevin Strom et al., *The Private Security Industry: A Review of the Definitions, Available Data Sources, and Paths Moving Forward* 6.8 (December 2010), at https://www.ncjrs.gov/pdffiles1/bjs/grants/232781.pdf.

23 National Advisory Committee, at 5; see Mahesh K. Nalla & Don Hummer, Relations between police officers and security professionals: A study of perceptions, *Security J.* 12 (1999); 31.

24 National Advisory Committee, at 5; Hauri; Operation Cooperation, at 2–3.

25 Norman M. Spain and Gary L. Elkin, Private security versus law enforcement, *Security World* 16 (1979); 32; cite Elizabeth E. Joh, The paradox of private policing, *J. Crim. L. & Criminology* 95 (2004–2005); 49, http://scholarlycommons.law.northwestern.edu/cgi/viewcontent.cgi?article=7176&context=jclc; *see* Nalla and Hummer; Hauri.

26 National Advisory Committee, at 5.

27 E. J. Criscuoli, Jr., Building a professional complement to law enforcement, *Police Chief*, 1978, at 28; see also Robert R. Rockwell, Private guards: A viewpoint, *Security Mgmt.*, 1975, at 5; Nalla and Hummer; Hauri.

28 Richard W. Kobetz and H. H. A. Cooper, Two armies: One flag, *Police Chief*, 1978, at 28.

29 See generally Charles P. Nemeth, *Status Report on Contemporary Criminal Justice Education* (discussing education and its correlation to police professionalism) (1988).

30 Operation Cooperation.

31 National Advisory Committee, at 11.

32 Lukins, at 32.

33 Id.

34 Id. at 34; see also Pastor, Terrorism; Pastor, Privatization of Police; Malcolm K. Sparrow, Managing the Boundary between public and private policing, *New Perspectives in Policing*, September 2014, at 9, https://www.ncjrs.gov/pdffiles1/nij/247182.pdf.

35 See generally Private Security Advisory Council, *Codes of Ethics for Private Security Management and Private Security Employees* (1976); Private Security Advisory Council, *Model Security Guard Training Curricula* (1977); Private Security Advisory Council, *Report on the Meeting of April 21–23, 1976* (1976); Nemeth, *Status Report*, at 25.

36 Note, Certified protection security and law enforcement, *Security Mgmt.*, 1980, at 75. For a full survey of certifications and licensures provided by the American Society for Industrial Security see: https://www.asisonline.org/certification/Pages/default.aspx?utm_source=ASIS-Marketing&utm_medium=Banner-Stand&utm_content=Global-Conferences&utm_campaign=Certification-General.

37 Howard C. Shook, Certified protection professional progress report, *Security Mgmt.*, 1980, at 75. The age of private security is here to stay according to the US Department of Justice where partnerships between the public and private sectors are now normative. See: Kevin Strom et al., The Private Security Industry: A Review of the Definitions, Available Data Sources, and Paths Moving Forward 5.1-5.10 (Dec. 2010), at https://www.ncjrs.gov/pdffiles1/bjs/grants/232781.pdf.

38 Harold I. Peterson, Private security v. public law enforcement, *Police Chief*, 1983, at 26; See also Kimberly N. Brown, Outsourcing, data insourcing, and the irrelevant constitution, *Ga. L. Rev.* 49 (2014–2015); 607; see Nalla and Hummer; Hauri.

39 Peterson, at 27; see Nalla and Hummer; Hauri.

40 National Advisory Committee, at 12.

41 See Nemeth; see also Charles P. Nemeth, *Directory of Criminal Justice Education, Including Criminology, Law and Justice Related Education* (1991); Olson, A comparison of some characteristics of public and private security personnel, *J. Security Admin.* 1 (1978); 51 (for further breakdown of the stereotypes on age, income, and educational level).

42 Cunningham et al., at 275–276.

43 Kobetz and Cooper, at 33.

44 See Charles P. Nemeth, *Introduction to Homeland Security: Principles and Practice 3rd* (2017); see also K. C. Poulin and Charles P. Nemeth, *Private Security and Public Safety: A Community-Based Approach* (2004).

45 Cunningham and Taylor, at 185; see Nalla and Hummer; Hauri.

46 Cunningham and Taylor, at 186.

47 Stephen C. George, Privatization and integration, *Security* 29 (1992); 5.

48 Cunningham et al., at 272.

49 Cunningham and Taylor, at 187.

50 Mahesh K. Nalla and Joseph D. Johnson, Are police and security personnel warming up to each other? A comparison of officers' attitudes in developed, emerging, and transitional economies, *Policing* 32 (2009); 508.

51 National Advisory Committee, at 14.

52 Cunningham and Taylor, at 196.

53 Kobetz and Cooper, at 32.

54 The Law Enforcement-Private Security Consortium, Operation Partnership: Trends and Practices in Law Enforcement and Private Security Collaborations (2005), http://www.ilj.org/publications/docs/Operation_Partnership_Private_Security.pdf; see also Pastor, *Terrorism*; Pastor, *Privatization of Police*.

55 Harold W. Gray, Private security—Some comments, *Police Chief,* 1978, at 34; see also Bilek et al., at 206.

56 Daniel E. McElory, A professional alliance, *Security World,* 1979, at 34, 37–38.

57 Karena Rahall, The siren is calling: Economic and ideological trends toward privatization of public police forces, *U. Miami L. Rev.* 68 (2013–2014); 634.

58 See: Judith H. Germano, Cybersecurity Partnerships: A New Era of Public-Private Collaboration, NYU School of Law Center on Law & Security (2014) at http://www.lawandsecurity.org/wp-content/uploads/2016/08/Cybersecurity.Partnerships-1.pdf#page=1&zoom=auto.

59 Andrew Morabito and Sheldon Greenberg, Engaging the Private Sector to Promote Homeland Security: Law Enforcement-Private Security Partnerships (2005) at http://www.ncjrs.gov/pdffiles1/bja/210678.pdf.

60 William R. Bess and Galen L. Ash, City/university cooperation, *Police Chief,* 1982, at 42; See also Ronso, The U.S. Air Force security police: Is there a civilian counterpart? *Police Chief,* 1982, at 32; Bob Harkins, Building a university safety & security structure, *Campus Safety Magazine* (October 4, 2011) at http://www.campussafetymagazine.com/article/Building-a-College-and-University-Safety-and-Security-Structure#; BJA, Campus Security Guidelines, https://www.bja.gov/Publications/MCC_CampusSecurityGuidelines.pdf.

61 Northern Illinois University, 2016–2017 Annual Safety and Security Report 7 (2016) http://niu.edu/clery/annual_security_report.pdf. Copyright 2017. Board of Trustees of Northern Illinois University. All Rights Reserved.

62 Id. at 6. Copyright 2017. Board of Trustees of Northern Illinois University. All Rights Reserved.

63 *The Handbook for Campus Safety and Security Reporting* (2016), at https://www2.ed.gov/admins/lead/safety/handbook.pdf.

64 Bess and Ash.

65 Fabricio Rodriguea, Philadelphia Security Officer Union, *Social Policy* 4, 6 (Winter 2010).

66 20 U.S.C.A. § 1092 (West 2012). For a sample template that catalogs the required reporting requirements, see: Rio Salado College Annual Crime Statistics, 2010–2012, http://www.riosalado.edu/about/Documents/RSC-Crime-Statistics_2010-12.pdf.

67 20 U.S.C.A. § 1092(f) (West 2010). For a sample Clery Act Report, see: University of the West, Security and Fire Safety, Annual Report 2014 at http://www.uwest.edu/site/file/docs/pubs/UWest%20 Annual%20Security%20and%20Fire%20Safety%20Report%202014.pdf For the official *Clery Act Handbook*, published by the Department of Education, see: https://www2.ed.gov/admins/lead/safety/ handbook.pdf.

68 Note, Federal guidance lacking as colleges report crime statistics, *Security* 30 (1993); 12. Some colleges and universities publish more than what is required under the Clery Act. See Norwalk Community College, Annual Security Report 2016, at https://norwalk.edu/wp-content/uploads/2017/01/ annualsecurityreport.pdf.

69 Univ. of Penn, Div. of Public Safety, *Community Based Policing*, at https://www.publicsafety.upenn. edu/about/uppd/policing-at-penn.

70 John W. Powell, Security, *Coll. Univ. Bus. Admin.* 3 (1974); 5.

71 Harry Budds, Los Angeles transit police: A unique agency taking on unique challenges, *Police Chief*, 1982, at 30.

72 Id. at 31.

73 Id.

74 U.S. Dept. of Transportation, Federal Transit Administration, *Transit Security Handbook* (1998); 4 Transportation Research Board, *Public Transportation Security: Intrusion Detection for Public Transportation Facilities Handbook* (2004) at http://trb.org/publications/tcrp/tcrp_rpt_86v4.pdf.

75 Bureau of Justice Assistance, *Engaging the Private Sector to Promote Homeland Security: Law Enforcement–Private Security Partnerships* 11 (2003); Jon D. Michaels, Deputizing homeland security, *Tex. L. Rev.* 88 (2009–2010); 1435.

76 The White House Website, Homeland Security Page, at http://www.whitehouse.gov/issues/homeland-security.

77 Press Release, Homeland Security Research Corporation, Private Sector to Become 2nd Largest Homeland Security Industry Customer by 2011 (April 9, 2008); Sabrina Alimahomed, Homeland Security Inc.: public order, private profit, *Race & Class* 55 (2014); 82, http://troutinmilk.com/wp-content/uploads/2016/03/Homeland-Security-Inc.pdf.

78 For an examination of how these privatized practices prompt ethical concerns, *see* Kateri Carmola, *Private Security Contractors in the Age of New Wars: Risk, Law & Ethics* (2008). Huma T. Yasin, Playing catch-up: Proposing the creation of status-based regulations to bring private military contractor firms within the purview of international and domestic law, *Emory Int'l L. Rev.* 25 (2011); 411.

79 See: Noelle Phillips, Private security guards begin patrols on Denver's 16th Street Mall, *The Denver Post* (August 17, 2016) http://www.denverpost.com/2016/08/17/private-security-guards-denver-16th-street-mall.

80 See: James Pinkerton, Sheriff's Office training security guards to boost Harris force, *Houston Chronicle* (March 22, 2012), at http://www.chron.com/news/houston-texas/article/Sheriff-s-office-training-security-guards-3426972.php; See also: Office of the City Controller, Houston First Corporation *FY2012 Audit Follow-up Procedures*, (2012) http://www.houstontx.gov/controller/audit/ reports/2012-09.pdf.

81 MetroWest Website, Public Safety, at http://www.metrowestcommunity.com/public-safety; For a controversial reach, see how G4S took over certain public police function in Lincolnshire, England and ponder its rocky road at: G4S UK Website, Police, at http://www.g4s.uk.com/en-GB/What%20 we%20do/Sectors/Government/Police/.

82 NYPD Shield Website at http://www.nypdshield.org/public.

83 Bureau of Justice Assistance, at 11. See this same emphasis internationally at: Francois Bonnet et al., Plural policing of public places in France, *European J. Pol. Studies* 2 (2015); 285, at http://www. francoisbonnet.net/Articles/Bonnetetal2015PluralPolicing.pdf.

84 Dale Pancake, The New professionals: Cooperation between police departments and private security, *Police Chief*, 1983, at 34; James F. Pastor, Public–private policing arrangements & recommendations, *Homeland Sec. Rev.* 4 (2010); 71; see also James McGuire, Michael O'Mara, and Albert Ware, Training: The bridge that connects public and private police, *Police Chief*, 1983, at 38. See also: Ben Bradford et al., *The SAGE Handbook of Global Policing* (2016).

85 Pancake, at 35; David H. Bayley and Clifford D. Shearing, *The New Structure of Policing: Description, Conceptualization, and Research Agenda*—NCJ 187083 (2001); Elizabeth E. Joh, Conceptualizing the private police, *Utah L. Rev.* 2005 (2005); 574.

86 Cunningham et al., at 255.

87 Id. at 255–256.

88 Note, Private security and police join training forces in Washington, *Police Chief*, October 1992, at 170. Information regarding the program can be obtained from: Washington State Security Council, 6632 S. 191st Place, E-107, Kent, Washington 98032; (206) 872–2450; fax: (206) 872–1403.

89 Bureau of Justice Assistance, *Operation Cooperation: Guidelines for Partnerships between Law Enforcement and Private Security Organizations* 5 (2000), available at http://www.ilj.org/publications/docs/Operation_Cooperation.pdf. For a recent international and national study regarding communication between the two camps, see: Mahesh K. Nalla and Joseph D. Johnson, Are police and security personnel warming up to each other? A comparison of officers' attitudes in developed, emerging, and transitional economies, *Policing* 32 (2009); 508.

90 James A. Kirkley, The role of the police in private security, *Police Chief*, 1982 at, 35; see Nalla and Hummer; Hauri.

91 Vidant Medical Center, Vidant Company Police, at https://www.vidanthealth.com/medicalcenter/dynamic-detail.aspx?id=6680.

92 See: Vidant Medical Center, *Safety Tips from Vidant Company Police*, at https://www.vidanthealth.com/medicalcenter/dynamic-detail.aspx?id=6682.

93 National Advisory Committee.

94 Id.

95 Id., at 207.

96 Id., at 211.

97 Id., at 214.

98 Id., at 210.

99 Id., at 222.

100 Id., at 226.

101 Id., at 231.

102 Id., at 236.

103 Cunningham and Taylor, at 237; for a summary of the entire Report see, William C. Cunningham and Todd H. Taylor, *Crime and Protection in America: A Study of Private Security and Law Enforcement Resources and Relationships*, NCJ Number: 93660 (1984).

104 Cunningham and Taylor, at 241.

105 Id. at 242.

106 Id.

107 Id.

108 Id., at 247.

109 Id., at 249.

110 Id., at 250.

111 Id., at 254.

112 Id., at 259.

113 Id., at 262.

114 Id., at 265–266.

115 Id., at 271.

116 Ira S. Somerson, Preface to Security @ the Millennium, presentation at ASIS International Seminar and Exhibits, September 27–29, 1999. New Link R. Mccrie, Progress and problems of security in millennial society. An essay for the 25th volume of *Security Journal, Sec. J.* 25 (2012); 191.

117 Office of Homeland Security, Office of the President, National Strategy for Homeland Security 12 (2002). What the DHS intends and what the eventual result are often at odds. The general tendency of DHS is to meddle in every locale, so much so, that it makes things less safe. For example in its efforts to gauge the safety of critical infrastructure contractors, it may have created more opportunity for

the terrorist posing as a contractor to gain access to critical infrastructure. See: Sondra Bell Nensala, Homeland Security Presidential Directive 12: How HSPD-12 May Limit Competition Unnecessarily and Suggestions for Reform, *Publ Con. L.J.* 40 (2010–2011); 619.

118 Id.
119 Bart Hobijn, What will homeland security cost? *Fed. Res. Bank N.Y. Econ. Pol'y Rev.*, November 2002, at 23, available at http://www.ny.frb.org/research/epr/02v08n2/0211hobi.html; Bart Hobijn and Erick Sager, What has homeland security cost? An assessment: 2001–2005, *Current Issues in Economics and Finance* (2007); 13, https://papers.ssrn.com/sol3/papers2.cfm?abstract_id=971861. Charles P. Nemeth, *Introduction to Homeland Security: Principles and Practice 3rd* Chap. 3 (2017).
120 Id. at 28.
121 Diane Ritchey, Public and private security: Bridging the gap, *Security Mag. Online*, June 1, 2010, at 2, available at http://www.securitymagazine.com/articles/80710-public-and-private-security-bridging-the-gap-1.
122 This approach has been repeatedly advanced by those arguing for private policing systems working side by side with public policing systems. See J. F. Pastor, Public–private policing arrangements & recommendations, *The Homeland Security Review*, 4, 2010: 71; See also C. P. Nemeth and K. C Poulin, *The Prevention Agency*, 2006; C. P. Nemeth and K. C. Poulin, *Private Security and Public Safety: A Community Based Approach*, 2005; J. F. Pastor, *Terrorism and Public Safety Policing: Implications for the Obama Presidency*, 2010.
123 N. Santella and L. J. Steinberg, Accidental releases of hazardous materials and relevance, *Journal of Homeland Security & Emergency Management*, 8, 2011.
124 Santella and Steinberg, at 11.
125 M. Kano et al., Terrorism preparedness and exposure reduction since 9/11: The status of public readiness in the United States, *Journal of Homeland Security & Emergency Management*, 8, 2011.
126 J. Fleischman, Engaging the private sector in local homeland defense: The Orange County private sector terrorism response group, *Sheriff*, September/October, 2004: 33.
127 National Infrastructure Advisory Council, Public–private sector intelligence coordination: Final report and recommendations by the council, July 2006, 67.
128 C. P. Nemeth, *Private Security and the Law* (London: Elsevier, 2008), 12.
129 Homeland Security Research Corporation, Private Sector to Become 2nd Largest Homeland Security Industry Customer by 2011, news release, April 9, 2008.
130 Homeland Security Research, *U.S. Private Sector Homeland Security Market, 2010–2014* available at http://homelandsecurityresearch.com/2010/08/us-private-sector-homeland-security-market-2010-2014/.
131 For an examination of how these privatized practices prompt ethical concerns, see K. Carmola, *Private Security Contractors in the Age of New Wars: Risk, Law & Ethics* (New York: Routledge Press, 2008).
132 P. Starr, The meaning of privatization, *Yale L. & Pol'y Rev.* 6 (1988): 6. This article also appears in Alfred K. and S. Kamerman, eds., *Privatization and the Welfare State* (Princeton, NJ: Princeton University Press, 1989).
133 Fannie Chen, Structuring public–private partnerships: Implications from the "public–private investment program for legacy securities," *Columbia J. L. & Social Probl.* 46 (2013); 509.
134 Private Security Officer Employment Authorization Act of 2004, U.S. Code 28, 2004, § 534.
135 I. P. McGinley, Regulating 'Rent-A-Cops' Post 9/11: Why the private security officer employment act fails to address homeland security concerns, *Cardozo Pub. L., Pol'y & Ethics* 6 (2007); 145.
136 Charles P. Nemeth, *Private Security and the Investigative Process, 2nd ed.* (Boston: Butterworth Heinemann, 2000), 1–4.
137 Bureau of Justice Assistance, Engaging the private sector to promote homeland security: Law enforcement–private security partnerships, 11 (2003).
138 National Defense Industrial Association, www.ndia.org/Aboutus/pages/default.aspx.
139 Bureau of Justice Assistance, at 13.

Chapter 8

Selected Case Readings

Introduction

The following cases have been properly labeled "benchmark" precedent in the world of private security. Use them as reference points and as catalyst for further discussion. The cases emphasize the legal nuances of private sector justice, and even more compellingly tell the story of privatization and its apparent invincibility. Since *Burdeau v. McDowell*, the kingpin of private security cases, decided in 1921, the courts at both the state and federal levels have consistently ruled on this well-settled area of law. While activists on many fronts wish constitutional extension to private-sector operations, the reticence of jurists, even in the age of judicial activism, is quite remarkable. To be sure, the courts have been dependable and even more predictable. That sort of uniformity is rare and a reflection of how high the stakes are in the law of private security.

Aetna Casualty & Surety Company v. Pendleton Detectives of Mississippi, Inc. 182 F.3d 376, (5th Cir. 1999).

Before Garwood, Duhe, and Benavides, circuit judges.
Opinion: John M. Duhe, Jr., circuit judge

Aetna Casualty & Surety Company ("Aetna") sued Pendleton Detectives of Mississippi, Inc. ("Pendleton") for recovery of the amount of claims it paid for losses to its insured, The Merchants Company, Inc. ("Merchants"), resulting from Pendleton's negligence or breach of contract. The jury awarded Aetna $174,000 in damages. Subsequently, the district court granted Pendleton's Motion for Judgment as a Matter of Law and entered judgment for Pendleton. Aetna appeals arguing the district court erred, because Aetna presented sufficient evidence to sustain the jury's verdict. We agree, and reverse the district court's judgment and reinstate the jury's verdict.

Background

In August 1993, Pendleton contracted with Merchants to provide security for Merchants' Jackson, Mississippi, distribution warehouse facility. Merchants quickly determined that it was unsatisfied with Pendleton's service. Merchants complained that the gate was left open at times, guards arrived at work intoxicated, made personal phone calls, and entertained members of the opposite sex while on duty. In early 1995, Merchants determined through its inventories an unusually high amount of loss from its warehouse. Merchants suspected nightshift employee theft was responsible for the increased losses. Merchants fired its nightshift manager and notified Pendleton, but the problem only grew worse. After Merchants notified Pendleton again of the problem, it hired a private investigator posing as an employee to investigate the problem. The private investigator concluded employee theft was responsible for the losses. Additionally, several nightshift employees, while taking lie detector tests administered by a hired expert, admitted stealing large amounts of food from the warehouse. After receiving Merchants' complaints, Robert H. Pendleton, chairman of the board of Pendleton, sent Merchants a memo acknowledging that the guards' performance was below what was expected.

On January 31, 1996, Merchants submitted a claim of $430,266.68 for losses resulting from theft at its Jackson, Mississippi, warehouse. After settling the claim, Aetna sued to recover the amount as Merchants' legal subrogee and contractual assignee. Although the jury awarded $174,000 in damages to Aetna, the district court granted Pendleton's Motion for Judgment as a Matter of Law and entered a judgment for Pendleton on May 8, 1998. Merchants appeals.

Discussion

We review the district court's grant of a motion for judgment as a matter of law de novo, applying the same standard it used. See *Hill v. International Paper Co.*, 121 F.3d 168, 170 (5th Cir. 1997). A court may grant a judgment as a matter of law if after a party has been fully heard by the jury on an issue, "there is no legally sufficient evidentiary basis for a reasonable jury to have found for that party with respect to that issue." Fed. R. Civ. P. 50; *Conkling v. Turner*, 18 F.3d 1285, 1300 (5th Cir. 1994). A court should view the entire record in the light most favorable to the nonmovant, drawing all factual inferences in favor of the nonmoving party, and "leaving credibility determinations, the weighing of the evidence, and the drawing of legitimate inferences from the facts to the jury." *Conkling*, 18 F.3d at 1300 (citing *Anderson v. Liberty Lobby, Inc.*, 477 U.S. 242, 255, 91 L. Ed. 2d 202, 106 S. Ct. 2505 (1986)).

The district court based its ruling on Merchants' failure to introduce conclusive evidence that the thefts occurred while Pendleton guards were on duty. Although Pendleton's security expert, Robert Vause, testified that it was more likely than not that the theft occurred because of Pendleton's substandard service, the district court disregarded his testimony because his belief was based on the lax security environment created by Pendleton employees at Merchants' warehouse.

Merchants contends that it presented sufficient evidence to support the jury's verdict, while Pendleton asserts that Merchants did not prove its employees proximately caused Merchants' losses. Specifically, Pendleton argues Merchants failed to present direct evidence that Pendleton guards were on duty when the thefts occurred. While admitting that its security services were substandard, Pendleton contends that Merchants' restrictions on its security service caused the losses rather than Pendleton's substandard services.

To prove negligence, "a plaintiff must prove by a preponderance of the evidence each element of negligence: duty, breach of duty, proximate causation, and injury." *Lovett v. Bradford*, 676 So.

2d 893, 896 (Miss. 1996). Circumstantial evidence is sufficient to prove proximate cause under Mississippi law. See *K-Mart, Corp. v. Hardy*, 735 So. 2d 975, 1999 Miss. LEXIS 102, 1999 WL 145306, at *5 (Miss. 1999). "Negligence may be established by circumstantial evidence in the absence of testimony by eyewitnesses provided the circumstances are such as to take the case out of the realm of conjecture and place it within the field of legitimate inference." *Id*. (quoting *Downs v. Choo*, 656 So. 2d 84, 90 (Miss. 1995)); see *Davis v. Flippen*, 260 So. 2d 847, 848 (Miss. 1972). ("when the case turns on circumstantial evidence it should rarely be taken from the jury.")

Merchants presented the following evidence of Pendleton's negligent security practices: (1) guards slept on the job; (2) guards watched TV on the job; (3) guards drank on the job; (4) guards entertained guests of the opposite sex on the job; (5) guards left the gate to the warehouse open; (6) Pendleton's admission of failing to perform sufficient background checks on its guards; (7) the private investigator's conclusion that nightshift employees were responsible for the losses; (8) several of Merchants' nightshift employees' confessions to stealing large amounts of food; (9) Pendleton's contractual obligation to provide security from 4 p.m. to 8 a.m. and 24 hours a day on weekends; (10) Merchants' repeated reports of suspected employee theft to Pendleton; (11) the report of a person wearing a Pendleton baseball cap selling Merchants' products from the trunk of his car; and (12) Merchants' security expert's testimony that it was more probable than not that Pendleton's lax security practices caused the losses. Merchants argues the above evidence is sufficient to support the jury's verdict.

Pendleton argues that Merchants' restrictions on its security service caused the losses, and that, because of the limited nature of the security service Merchants requested, the loss would have occurred even had Pendleton performed its duties perfectly. Pendleton contends the following restrictions placed upon its service by Merchants prevented it from deterring the losses: (1) Pendleton was not allowed to go inside Merchants' warehouse; (2) Pendleton was not allowed to inspect the inside of trucks or employee vehicles leaving the facility; (3) Pendleton did not provide 24 hours a day protection 7 days a week; and (4) the Pendleton security officer's view of the employee parking lot was obstructed for a short period of time every hour while he conducted rounds of the premises.

At trial, Pendleton theorized that Merchant's former night shipping manager was involved in a large-scale scheme to steal food by colluding with truck drivers to falsify shipping documents and send sealed trucks full of food to nonexistent locations. Pendleton contended that because its guards lacked the authority to search sealed trucks as they left the gates of Merchants' facility, it was unable to prevent the losses Merchants suffered. However, Pendleton did not offer evidence that Merchants accused its truck drivers of stealing or that it ever suspected or investigated any occurrences of falsified shipping documents. Moreover, Merchants' evidence established that the substantial losses from theft continued long after Merchants fired the night shipping manager.

Merchants' evidence at trial sufficiently supports the jury's inference of causation between Pendleton's lax security practices and the losses Merchants suffered. The Security Instructions developed by Pendleton exclusively for Merchants expressly stated that the mission of Pendleton's post was "to maintain security of the property and prevent fires, theft, etc. during all hours." The Security Instructions required that Merchants' employees enter the facility only through a gate located next to the guard house and that Pendleton guards be stationed at the guard house during their entire shift except during the brief period of their rounds. These instructions also authorized Pendleton's guards to stop Merchants' employees and inspect any packages or bundles they were carrying, and mandated that Pendleton guards keep a "close check on the employee parking area to deter outsiders, or other employees, from tampering with or damaging employee vehicles." Additionally, while the guards' view of the employee parking lot was obstructed for a short period of time every hour during the rounds of the premises, the guards were to perform these rounds randomly rather than at a set time of day and were supposed to lock the gate while away, requiring employees to wait until the guard's return to exit the facility, thereby reducing the likelihood of employee theft during this brief absence.

The period of loss claimed by Merchants extended from October 1994 to December 1995. During this period, Merchants employed up to 90 nightshift employees, and Pendleton was required to conduct nearly 1000 shifts of security services. The jury's award of $174,000 to Aetna, an amount substantially smaller than the $430,266.68 Aetna demanded, evidences the jury's implicit conclusion that Pendleton caused at least some of Merchants' losses. The jury obviously concluded that while the night shipping manager Merchants fired in July 1995 caused some of the losses, Pendleton's substandard security practices also caused $174,000 of the losses Merchants suffered.

Based on the above evidence, a reasonable juror could not only have concluded that Pendleton's poor security practices allowed Merchants' nightshift employees to steal with impunity, but that in fact Pendleton's security officers were also involved in the theft from Merchants themselves. For the above reasons, we reverse the district court's decision and reinstate the jury's verdict.

REVERSED AND JURY VERDICT REINSTATED

Arthur Letourneau Et Al. V. The Department of Registration and Education et al., 212 Ill. App. 3d 717; 571 N.E.2d 783 (1991).

Justice White delivered the opinion of the court. Cerda, P. J., and Rizzi, J., concur.

Defendants appeal from a judgment entered by the circuit court of Cook County that reversed the revocation of plaintiffs' licenses to practice. We affirm the judgment of the circuit court.

Defendants are the Department of Registration and Education (the Department), now known as the Department of Professional Regulation; Gary L. Clayton (the Director), who was Director of Registration and Education at the pertinent times; the Illinois Private Detective, Private Alarm, and Private Security Board (the Board); and the Board's chairman, and five other members.

One plaintiff is Arthur Letourneau, to whom the record sometimes refers as Arthur LeTourneau. The other plaintiffs are the detective division, the security division, and the alarm division of Investigations International (the company). Of the four licenses and certificates revoked, two licenses (as a private detective and a private security contractor) were issued in Letourneau's name, and two certificates (as a private detective agency and as a private security contractor agency) were issued to Letourneau in the names of the company's detective division and security division, respectively. For convenience when referring collectively in this opinion to plaintiffs' licenses and certificates, the general term "licenses" is used.

A certificate as a private alarm contractor agency, issued in the name of the company's alarm division, and a license as a private alarm contractor, issued in Letourneau's name, were neither revoked nor involved in the disciplinary proceedings, but as licensees the holders thereof have joined as plaintiffs.

The central issue is whether revocation of plaintiffs' licenses was contrary to the manifest weight of the evidence, unsupported by substantial evidence, or arbitrary and unreasonable.

I. Statutory Background and Procedural History

Under the *Private Detective, Private Alarm, and Private Security Act of 1983* (Ill. Rev. Stat. 1985, ch. 111, par. 2651 et seq.) (the Act or the present Act), a licensee is subject to disciplinary sanctions for enumerated violations. (Ill. Rev. Stat. 1985, ch. 111, par. 2672(a).) A range of sanctions, including license revocation, is provided. Ill. Rev. Stat. 1985, ch. 111, par. 2675. In this cause, the department filed formal charges seeking disciplinary action against Letourneau and the company as respondents. The charges named Letourneau and the company's detective and security divisions as holders of the licenses in question. The charges alleged three substantive acts or omissions, said to constitute violations of the Act or of its precursor statute (the 1933 Act) (Ill. Rev. Stat. 1983, ch. 111, par. 2601 et seq.) (repealed eff. January 5, 1984)1 and therefore to constitute grounds for license revocation or suspension under Section 22 of the Act (Ill. Rev. Stat. 1985, ch. 111, par. 2672). The alleged violations were

a. Failure by the company since 1979 to register its employees with the department, in violation of Section 10b(4) of the 1933 Act and Section 15(c) of the present Act (Ill. Rev. Stat. 1983, ch. 111, par. 2622(4);Ill. Rev. Stat. 1985, ch. 111, par. 2665(c)).
b. Practice by the company as "a detective" while its "license" was nonrenewed from 1977 to October 1983, said to be in violation of Section 3 of the 1933 Act (Ill. Rev. Stat. 1983, ch. 111, par. 2603).
c. Practice by Ernest Rizzo since 1979 as a detective for the company despite a 1978 revocation of his detective license, in violation of Sections 16(b) and (f) of the 1933 Act and Sections 22(a)(3), (a)(14), (a)(15), and (a)(19) of the present Act (Ill. Rev. Stat. 1983, ch. 111, pars. 2628(b), (f); Ill. Rev. Stat. 1985, ch. 111, pars. 2672(a)(3), (a)(14), (a)(15), (a)(19)).

Under the version of the Act applicable to this cause, it was a continuing requirement for agency certification such as here that the agencies each have a full-time Illinois-licensed private detective or private security contractor in charge and that each such person reside in Illinois. (Ill. Rev. Stat. 1985, ch. 111, pars. 2664(d), (f).) "Residency" meant having established an actual domicile in Illinois for at least one year. (Ill. Rev. Stat. 1985, ch. 111, par. 2652(m).) The 1933 Act contained similar requirements for detective agencies. (Ill. Rev. Stat. 1983, ch. 111, pars. 2601, 2621.) The present Act has now been amended to repeal the requirement that a licensee in charge reside in Illinois. See Pub. Act 85-981, art. III, § 5, eff. January 1, 1988 (amending Ill. Rev. Stat. 1985, ch. 111, pars. 2664(d) through (f)).

During several sessions between January and July 1986, a hearing officer received testimony from 11 witnesses and admitted 75 exhibits into evidence. Attending from time to time and sometimes participating in the proceedings were several members of the board. On January 22, 1987, the board made and submitted its written findings of fact, conclusions of law, and recommendation that the licenses at issue be revoked. See Ill. Rev. Stat. 1985, ch. 111, par. 2674(d).

The board's factual findings were that:

Letourneau had been a Florida resident since at least 1980 and, while holding the licenses at issue, had falsely reported to the department since 1980 that he was an Illinois resident.
Letourneau and the company had practiced as a detective and detective agency from October 1977 to October 13, 1983, and from January 4, 1984, to January 7, 1985, without a license and without registering employees.
Letourneau and the company had since at least 1980 allowed Ernest Rizzo to practice as a detective without a license or supervision.
Letourneau and the company had practiced as a security contractor and security contractor agency from January 4, 1984, to January 7, 1985, without registering employees.
The board's legal conclusion was that Letourneau had violated the sections of the present Act and of the 1933 Act that he and the company were charged with violating.

Letourneau filed a motion for rehearing, but the director denied it. Adopting the board's findings of fact, conclusions of law, and recommendation, he then ordered that licenses at issue be revoked.

On April 28, 1987, Letourneau filed his complaint for administrative review in the circuit court of Cook County, seeking to have the director's revocation orders vacated. After briefing and argument, the court entered an order on August 10, 1988, reversing the department's revocation decision.

The trial judge stated that he was reversing the revocation orders because the findings of fact were without substantial foundation in the evidence. Specifically, the judge found that there was no evidence to support the director's finding that Letourneau had been a Florida resident since 1980 and that there was evidence that Letourneau had been an Illinois resident at the times in question. The judge also found that there was no evidence to support the director's finding that Letourneau had allowed Rizzo to practice as an unlicensed private detective and that the department's evidence in general was not strong enough to support the result of revocation. At a hearing on defendants' motion for reconsideration, the judge again stated that there was insufficient evidence to support the director's findings of fact and conclusions of law. Accordingly, he denied the motion for reconsideration, and this appeal followed. This opinion will refer to matters of evidence as required for discussion of the issues.

II. Analysis

A. Standard for Reviewing Findings of Fact

In reviewing the factual determinations made by the director, this court is limited to ascertaining whether his decision accorded with the manifest weight of the evidence and was supported by substantial evidence. *Massa v. Department of Registration & Education* (1987), 116 Ill. 2d 376, 385, 507 N.E.2d 814, 818; *Bruce v. Department of Registration & Education* (1963), 26 Ill. 2d 612, 622, 187 N.E.2d 711, 717; *Irving's Pharmacy v. Department of Registration & Education* (1979), 75 Ill. App. 3d 652, 658, 394 N.E.2d 627, 632.

The findings and conclusions of an administrative agency regarding questions of fact are to be considered prima facie true and correct. (Ill. Rev. Stat. 1989, ch. 110, par. 3–110; *Murdy v. Edgar* (1984), 103 Ill. 2d 384, 391, 469 N.E.2d 1085, 1088.) However, this does not mean that a court should automatically approve an agency decision merely because the agency heard witnesses and made findings. *Viera v. Illinois Racing Board* (1978), 65 Ill. App. 3d 94, 99, 382 N.E.2d 462, 466.

B. Letourneau's Residency

Defendants appear to regard Letourneau's residency as being relevant for two reasons, either of which might support disciplinary action.

First, as the sole individual to whom the company's agency licenses were issued, Letourneau (or some person employed by him) was required to be in charge of agency operations as a full-time, individually licensed Illinois resident, and failure to comply would violate the law. (See Ill. Rev. Stat. 1985, ch. 111, pars. 2664(d), (f); Ill. Rev. Stat. 1983, ch. 111, par. 2621.) Letourneau employed no such person; the question is whether Letourneau himself met the requirement. Second, Letourneau was required to avoid fraud or material deception in connection with licensure and to report his correct address and practice location to the department (Ill. Rev. Stat. 1985, ch. 111, pars. 2671(a), 2672(a)(1); Ill. Rev. Stat. 1983, ch. 111, pars. 2616, 2628(a)); according to defendants, failure to report a Florida residence would violate the law. However, though the department's briefs discuss such residency questions at length, its formal charges never clearly specified violation of either of these residency-related requirements. The only formal charge that even arguably might be read as pertaining to one or both of them was the charge that Rizzo had unlawfully practiced as a detective for the company.

Despite any deficiencies in the formal charges, one of the director's findings of fact was that Letourneau had been a Florida resident who falsely reported Illinois residency—thereby presumably violating the requirements that he report his correct address and avoid fraud or material deception (see Ill. Rev. Stat. 1985, ch. 111, pars. 2671(a), 2672(a)(1)). And one of the director's conclusions of law was that Letourneau had permitted his license to be used by an unlicensed person in order to operate without Letourneau's supervision or control (see Ill. Rev. Stat. 1985, ch. 111, par. 2672(a)(15))—which comes close to saying that Letourneau violated the requirement that he keep a full-time, Illinois-licensed individual who resides in Illinois in charge of his agencies (see Ill. Rev. Stat. 1985, ch. 111, pars. 2664(d), (f)).

The implication of defendants' treatment of the residency question is that Letourneau's non-residency, failure to report a correct address, failure to keep a full-time licensed resident in charge, and facilitation of Rizzo's unlicensed practice are actually all of a piece in common sense, and all unlawful under one statutory section or another. For the additional reason that plaintiffs make no issue of any incongruity in formal charges, findings of fact, and conclusions of law, Letourneau's alleged nonresidency is treated in this opinion as if it had been duly framed as a violation from the outset.

Defendants point to testimony by Letourneau's business partner and two alleged former employees (who testified under grants of immunity) that they never saw Letourneau in Illinois during the period in question. Defendants also point to evidence that departmental investigators were never able to find Letourneau at his Illinois addresses, that the company maintained a Florida office, and that Florida had issued detective licenses to an Arthur Letourneau. From this, defendants argue that they were entitled to use their expertise regarding normal conduct of a licensee in order to infer that Letourneau was not an Illinois resident.

Though Ernest Rizzo (whom, according to the formal charges, Letourneau had helped to engage in unlicensed practice) testified that he had known Letourneau for 20 years and that Letourneau was an Illinois resident, defendants argue that they were entitled to judge Rizzo's credibility adversely because of his failure to explain adequately a number of past actions and statements suggestive of unlicensed practice. In addition, defendants point to the testimony of one witness, a longtime Letourneau acquaintance, that he had dined with Letourneau in Florida in 1983 and that Letourneau, in the witness' words, had then "indicated" that he was a Florida resident.

Documentary evidence in the form of mail and utility bills shows Illinois addresses for Letourneau, but defendants argue that the addresses were actually Rizzo's. As a fact from which an adverse inference can be drawn, defendants point to Letourneau's refusal to answer questions at the administrative hearing on grounds of potential self-incrimination after the Department's counsel had referred to the possibility of criminal charges. Accordingly, defendants contend that the finding of Letourneau's nonresidency in Illinois was not against the manifest weight of the evidence.

In reply, besides referring to evidence already noted, plaintiffs point to other evidence that Letourneau was an Illinois resident. The department's investigator testified that he saw a license on the wall at an address previously stated by Letourneau to be his own. The department's investigators testified that mailboxes bearing Letourneau's name and containing mail addressed to him existed at addresses given by Letourneau. Responses in Letourneau's name were received by the department, after it had sent mail to Letourneau at his Illinois address, though defendants contend that the responses either did not bear Letourneau's personal signature at all or bore discrepant personal signatures. Letourneau also appeared before Illinois notaries public. In the circuit court, the trial judge referred to the need for "facts established by evidence,…evidence that is understood in law as being evidence." He continued:

> This is not a case which turns on the weight of the evidence or the credibility of the witnesses, quite frankly.

This is a case which must be reversed I believe because the findings are without substantial foundation in the evidence. A case by the state cannot be made from inferences, from presumptions, or from suspicions, or from indirect evidence. They have to be made by evidence that's credible, and sufficiently strong to warrant the result that is reached. There is no strong evidence here to support the result of revocation of Letourneau's license.

After referring to the department's grant of immunity to its witnesses, the trial judge remarked:

> The only basis for the conclusion that Mr. Letourneau resides in Florida is that one witness had dinner with Mr. Letourneau once in Florida in 1983 I believe, and yet the charge is that he lived there since 1980. That same witness said I hadn't seen him around, and I had dinner with him in '83. The fact that that witness had not seen Letourneau in Illinois does not mean that Letourneau resided in Florida during all of that hiatus.

The trial judge acknowledged the evidence of Florida detective licenses in the name of an Arthur Letourneau but stated:

> I am not sure that this Mr. Letourneau is the only Arthur Leto[ur]neau in the USA, and there was no attempt to demonstrate the Arthur Letourneau in Florida is the Arthur Letourneau that we are talking about here in Illinois.

So there clearly is no evidence to support the finding…that Letourneau has lived in Florida since 1980.

The judge then referred to evidence that Letourneau had received mail in his Illinois mailbox, was paying utility bills in Illinois, had registered his automobile in Illinois, and had responded to department notices mailed to Illinois. The judge also cited Rizzo's testimony that Letourneau lived in Illinois:

> Clearly the department is free to ignore Mr. Rizzo's testimony, but I find it incredible that they would ignore that testimony and accept testimony from someone who said he had dinner with Mr. Letourneau in Florida and give greater weight to the latter while giving no weight to the former.

Defendants were entitled to draw reasonable inferences from the evidence. (*Raymond Concrete Pile Co. v. Industrial Comm'n* (1967), 37 Ill. 2d 512, 517, 229 N.E.2d 673, 676.) In an administrative proceeding, defendants could also, in conjunction with other evidence, draw an inference adverse to Letourneau from his refusal to testify on grounds of potential self-incrimination. (*Giampa v. Illinois Civil Service Comm'n* (1980), 89 Ill. App. 3d 606, 613-14, 411 N.E.2d 1110,

1116.) If the issue is merely one of conflicting testimony and a witness' credibility, the administrative agency's determination should be sustained. (*Keen v. Police Board* (1979), 73 Ill. App. 3d 65, 70–71, 391 N.E.2d 190, 195.) An administrative agency may properly base its decision on circumstantial evidence. *Ritenour v. Police Board* (1977), 53 Ill. App. 3d 877, 882-83, 369 N.E.2d 135, 139.

In finding "no" evidence of Letourneau's nonresidency, the trial judge overlooked testimony that, in what may have been admissions against interest (see *Cox v. Daley* (1981), 93 Ill. App. 3d 593, 596-97, 417 N.E.2d 745, 748), Letourneau had said in about 1979 that he planned to move to Florida and had "indicated" in 1983 that he was now a Florida resident. In any event, the department presented what it contends was circumstantial evidence of Letourneau's Florida residency: the Florida licenses, inability to find him in Illinois, accumulation of several weeks' worth of mail in a mailbox, identity between Letourneau's claimed Illinois addresses and Rizzo's addresses, irregularities in Letourneau's purported signature on answers to mail sent to him at Illinois addresses, and the adverse inference from Letourneau's refusal to testify on the question of his residency.

Although the trial judge erred in concluding that there was no evidence that Letourneau had lived in Florida since 1980, the question remains whether the evidence offered by the department sufficiently supported the director's decision so that the decision can be said not to have been against the manifest weight of the evidence.

Defendants have not cited and we have not found any requirement that one must be a Florida resident in order to be licensed as a detective in that state, so the mere fact of Florida licensure would carry relatively little weight even if plaintiff were shown to have been the Florida licensee.

The Act did not expressly require the person in charge of a private detective agency always to remain within Illinois; all it required was that the person in charge be a resident of this state and be a "full-time Illinois licensed private detective." (See Ill. Rev. Stat. 1985, ch. 111, par. 2664(d).) Assuming that Letourneau did spend some time in Florida, such a fact is not substantial evidence that he thereby gave up Illinois residency, that while he was in Florida his Illinois agency operations actively continued without him, or that he was thereby prevented from being as much a "full-time Illinois licensed" individual as any other licensee who took vacations or went on trips out of state. The fact that departmental investigators failed to find Letourneau but found his mail in the mailbox is evidence that he was absent; it falls short of being substantial evidence that he was nonresident.

Assuming that any connection between Rizzo and Letourneau was lawful, a coincidence between Letourneau's Illinois addresses and Rizzo's is of little probative value. Any relationship between Letourneau and Rizzo in the nature of business association, friendship, or employment (unless of a type prohibited by the Act) is substantial evidence neither of Letourneau's nonresidency nor of his facilitation of unlicensed practice by Rizzo.

Letourneau would ordinarily have had a right to appoint someone his agent for signing documents; thus, purported irregularities in his signature are not substantial evidence of nonresidency. Because Letourneau's refusal to testify can lead to an adverse inference only in conjunction with other evidence (*Giampa*, 89 Ill. App. 3d 606, 411 N.E.2d 1110), the lack of other substantial evidence impairs the probative value of his refusal. And, given the other evidentiary shortcomings, a naked assertion of departmental expertise in judging licensees' conduct amounts to ipse dixit.

If the department had produced substantial evidence on the residency issue and it were simply a matter of weighing that evidence against Letourneau's or of judging the credibility of witnesses, the presumption of correctness in the director's findings would prevail over mere disagreements by plaintiffs or even by this court. However, as did the circuit court, we believe that no substantial evidence supported the director's finding of Letourneau's Florida residency and false statements of Illinois residency.

Still, the matter does not end here. The parties agree that the most serious charge against Letourneau was that he permitted the use of his agency certificates by Rizzo in order for Rizzo to engage in unlicensed practice. Thus, we must address the sufficiency of the director's findings on that issue.

C. Rizzo's Activities

Defendants point to considerable evidence as proving that Letourneau permitted Rizzo to use Letourneau's licenses and thus to operate without being licensed himself.

Repeated coincidences were demonstrated between Rizzo's address and those of Letourneau and the company. Letourneau, accompanied by Rizzo, had once attempted to obtain an agency certificate in the name of Ernest D. Rizzo, Ltd. In addition, Rizzo had contacted the department in behalf of Letourneau to discuss an agency name change and what kind of work Rizzo (whose license had been revoked) could now permissibly do for the company. Insurance procured by Letourneau was carried in Rizzo's name until corrected after departmental rejection. Checks payable to Rizzo had been deposited to the company's account. Rizzo signed purchase papers as owner of cars purchased by the company.

Raymond Rocke, testifying under a grant of immunity, said he had performed security work for the company under Rizzo as "boss." Though Rizzo testified that the witness was working without authority and was discharged by Letourneau, the testimony was impeached by Letourneau's certification to the department that the witness had been an employee after the "discharge." Rizzo also attempted to explain such matters as his deposition testimony that he was employed by the company, a magazine account of investigations he supposedly was conducting as a company subcontractor without being licensed, and a telephone directory advertisement for the company that carried Rizzo's name. Defendants argue that the credibility of Rizzo's explanations was simply judged adversely.

In addition, Letourneau refused to answer questions about Ed Rossi, whom he had listed as an employee and whose name the department contended was an alias for Rizzo. Rizzo matched the age and physical description of Rossi, and his social security number was a slightly transposed version of Rossi's. Rizzo acknowledged having used the name Ed Ross.

But plaintiffs respond that no witness, not even Rocke, testified to personal knowledge that since 1980 Rizzo had actually engaged in activities legally constituting practice as a private detective. One witness testified to Rizzo's having told him that Rizzo planned to be an employee but not a principal of a company to be formed by Letourneau. Rizzo himself denied having practiced as a detective in Illinois since 1978 or 1979.

Defendants contend that, despite Rizzo's denial of practicing as a detective, he admitted that he had investigated Rocke, ascertained the address and business of another person, conducted electronic sweeps to discover surveillance devices, and conducted "investigations for pay" on cases for Letourneau's attorney. However, these contentions by defendants lack force, because none of the described activity, unless it is part of a paid investigation, legally constituted practice as a private detective—except possibly, of course, for the very conduct of "investigations for pay." (See Ill. Rev. Stat. 1985, ch. 111, par. 2652(h).) As for the latter conduct, the most to which Rizzo's testimony admitted was serving a subpoena and checking for wiretaps at the attorney's request, apparently for pay in both cases. Neither serving a subpoena nor checking for a wiretap, even for pay, was itself necessarily practice as a private detective; it would only have been so if part of a paid investigation made to obtain information regarding several subjects specified by statute. (See Ill. Rev. Stat. 1985, ch. 111, par. 2652(h).) There was no testimony that Rizzo's admitted activity was part of any such statutorily specified investigation, much less that it was performed by use of Letourneau's licenses.

The director was entitled to judge the credibility of witnesses and to draw inferences from the evidence. However, the evidence offered to prove Rizzo's unlicensed practice did not constitute the substantial evidence required by law on what was admittedly the most serious charge against Letourneau. Thus, the circuit court correctly rejected the director's finding that Letourneau had permitted Rizzo to practice without a license by using Letourneau's licenses.

D. Other Disputed Factual Points

Defendants extensively discuss their contention that the director's findings regarding practice on inactive licenses and regarding nonregistration of employees should not have been reversed by the circuit court. Plaintiffs reply at length. Yet, the circuit court never "reversed" the director's findings on these issues.

The circuit court's order as drafted by plaintiffs' counsel did read that "the Court, having found no evidence to support the findings entered by the Department, orders that the Decision of the Department revoking the licenses of Arthur Letourneau be and is hereby reversed." However, the transcript reveals that the court focused entirely on the lack of substantial evidence for the findings on residency and on allowing Rizzo's unlicensed practice. Because of that lack, the court declared that "the decision by the department therefore is arbitrary and constitutes an abuse of the department's discretion. For all of these reasons the decision is reversed."

It is evident that the circuit court based reversal on the residency and Rizzo issues and on no other. We need not consider the director's findings and conclusions on other issues if his reversible findings on the residency and Rizzo issues were so central as to render his revocation decision an abuse of discretion.

E. License Revocation

An agency's exercise of discretion may be set aside if it was arbitrary or unreasonable or clearly violated the rule of law. (*Commonwealth Edison Co. v. Illinois Commerce Comm'n* (1988), 180 Ill. App. 3d 899, 907, 536 N.E.2d 724, 729.) The courts will not reweigh the evidence but will determine whether the final administrative decision just and reasonable in light of the evidence presented. *Davern v. Civil Service Comm'n* (1970), 47 Ill. 2d 469, 471, 269 N.E.2d 713, 714; *Sircher v. Police Board* (1978), 65 Ill. App. 3d 19, 20-21, 382 N.E.2d 325, 327.

The applicable rule, as phrased by many authorities, is that courts may not interfere with an administrative agency's discretionary authority unless it is exercised arbitrarily or capriciously or unless the administrative decision is against the manifest weight of the evidence. (E.g., *Massa v. Department of Registration & Education* (1987), 116 Ill. 2d 376, 388, 507 N.E.2d 814, 819; *Murdy v. Edgar* (1984), 103 Ill. 2d 384, 391, 469 N.E.2d 1085, 1088; *People ex rel. Stephens v. Collins* (1966), 35 Ill. 2d 499, 501, 221 N.E.2d 254, 255.) In terms of that formulation of the rule, it has been said that, when determining whether an administrative decision is contrary to the manifest weight of the evidence, a court should consider the severity of the sanction imposed. *Cartwright v. Illinois Civil Service Comm'n* (1980), 80 Ill. App. 3d 787, 793, 400 N.E.2d 581, 586; *Kelsey-Hayes Co. v. Howlett* (1978), 64 Ill. App. 3d 14, 17, 380 N.E.2d 999, 1002. *Contra Epstein v. Civil Service Comm'n* (1977), 47 Ill. App. 3d 81, 84, 361 N.E.2d 782, 785.

An alternative formulation of the rule is that, when judging whether an agency sanction is arbitrary or unreasonable, manifest weight of the evidence is not the applicable standard of review, because the reasonableness of the sanction, not the correctness of the agency's findings or reasoning, is the issue. E.g., *Brown v. Civil Service Comm'n* (1985), 133 Ill. App. 3d 35, 39, 478 N.E.2d 541, 544.

In any event, however, courts will not hesitate to grant relief from an adverse agency decision if that decision is not supported in the record by sufficient evidence. (*Basketfield v. Police Board* (1974), 56 Ill. 2d 351, 359, 307 N.E.2d 371, 375; *Feliciano v. Illinois Racing Board* (1982), 110 Ill. App. 3d 997, 1003, 443 N.E.2d 261, 266.) Thus, a court may reverse an order for imposing an unwarranted sanction. See *Feliciano*, 110 Ill. App. 3d at 1005, 443 N.E.2d at 267; *Cartwright*, 80 Ill. App. 3d at 793-94, 400 N.E.2d at 586.

On the questions of Letourneau's residency and Rizzo's activities, which clearly were the most important to the department and the director, the director's findings were unsupported by substantial evidence. We believe that the director's decision to revoke plaintiffs' licenses, based as it was primarily on such unsupported findings, represented an arbitrary and unwarranted sanction.

Accordingly, we affirm the judgment of the circuit court, which reversed the director's revocation of plaintiffs' licenses.

AFFIRMED.CERDA, P. J., AND RIZZI, J., CONCUR.

Stephanie P. Austin v. Paramount Parks, Inc., 195 F.3d 715 (4th Cir. 1999).

Before WIDENER and TRAXLER, Circuit Judges, and BUTZNER, Senior Circuit Judge. Judge Traxler wrote the opinion, in which Judge Widener and Senior Judge Butzner joined.

Paramount Parks, Inc. ("Paramount") operates an amusement park in Hanover County, Virginia known as "Paramount's Kings Dominion" ("Kings Dominion" or "the park"). While visiting Kings Dominion in May 1994, Stephanie P. Austin ("Austin") was positively identified by two of Kings Dominion's employees as a woman who had passed a bad check at the park less than one week earlier. After questioning Austin for several hours, a special police officer of the Kings Dominion Park Police Department caused a warrant to be issued for Austin's arrest on a charge of grand larceny. The same officer thereafter caused a second warrant to be issued, this time for Austin's arrest on charges of forgery and uttering a forged writing. The Commonwealth's Attorney's Office, with the assistance of the arresting officer, actively prepared the case against Austin over the next nine months. The charges were dismissed before trial, however, once the Commonwealth's Attorney's Office realized that one of the employees who had identified Austin as having passed the bad check in question had later identified another park guest in connection with the same offense.

Austin subsequently brought this civil action against Paramount, asserting a variety of claims arising from her arrests and prosecution on the preceding charges. At trial, the jury returned general verdicts for Austin on her claim under 42 U.S.C.A. § 1983 (West Supp. 1998) and on several claims under Virginia law, and awarded her compensatory and punitive damages. The district court ultimately entered judgment in favor of Austin, denied Paramount's motion for judgment as a matter of law, and awarded Austin attorney's fees and expenses under 42 U.S.C.A. § 1988 (West Supp. 1998) upon finding her to be a prevailing party on the § 1983 claim. This appeal followed.

We conclude that Paramount was entitled to judgment as a matter of law on Austin's § 1983 claim because Austin failed to establish that any deprivation of her federal rights was caused by an official policy or custom of Paramount. We further conclude that Virginia law compels judgment as a matter of law in favor of Paramount on Austin's state-law claims because Virginia law shields a private employer from liability when a special police officer takes an action in compliance with a public duty to enforce the law. Accordingly, we reverse the denial of Paramount's motion for judgment as a matter of law, vacate the judgment in favor of Austin, vacate the award of attorney's fees and expenses, and remand with instructions that judgment as a matter of law be entered in favor of Paramount.

I.

The Loss Prevention Department at Kings Dominion ("Loss Prevention") is responsible for providing safety to park guests and employees, preserving park assets, and enforcing Virginia law and park rules and regulations. The security operations group of Loss Prevention consists of special police officers associated with the Kings Dominion Park Police Department, and seasonal uniformed security officers. Unlike the uniformed security officers, the special police officers are sworn conservators of the peace who are authorized to carry firearms, make arrests, and perform the same functions that law enforcement officers in the Commonwealth of Virginia perform. The special police officers derive this authority from an appointment order issued annually, on Paramount's application, by the judges of the Circuit Court of Hanover County under Va. Code Ann. § 19.2-13 (Michie Supp. 1999).

The Sheriff of Hanover County had supervisory authority over the special police officers of the Park Police Department that was expressly acknowledged in both the Circuit Court's appointment order and the Park Police Department's Policy and Procedure Manual ("Manual") in force at the time of the events in question. Specifically, the appointment order provided that the special police officers "work only under the control and direction of the Sheriff of Hanover County." This directive was reiterated in the Manual, which provided that the Park Police Department "has direct affiliation with the Hanover County Sheriff's Department and is under the direction of the Sheriff of Hanover County." The Manual further provided: The Chain of Command and authority for all Kings Dominion Park Police shall be as follows involving official law enforcement:

1. Sheriff of Hanover County
2. Lieutenant of Kings Dominion Park Police
3. Kings Dominion Park Police Sergeant
4. Kings Dominion Park Police Corporal
5. Kings Dominion Park Police Officer

Although the Park Police Department fell under Loss Prevention in the organizational structure at Kings Dominion, the testimony at trial established that the special police officers performed their law enforcement duties without interference from park management. Chancellor L. Hester ("Hester"), who served as Manager of Loss Prevention at the time of the events in question, provided uncontradicted testimony that his role in matters of law enforcement was limited to ensuring that guests suspected of committing crimes at the park were treated courteously and professionally. As to decisions pertaining to law enforcement, however, Hester testified that he "let the police officers do the work," knowing that those officers received assistance and direction from the Hanover County Sheriff's Department and the Commonwealth's Attorney's Office. The annual training that the special police officers received reflected this division. Hester provided instruction on interpersonal skills, while the Sheriff's Department and the Commonwealth's Attorney's Office taught law enforcement classes on such topics as the laws of arrest, the conducting of interviews, self-defense, and searches and seizures.

The principal events giving rise to the present litigation occurred at Kings Dominion on May 15, 1994, when a guest arrived at the park's Season Pass office and submitted a check for $360 under the name of "Donita Morgan." Japata Taylor ("Taylor"), a park cashier, accepted the check and proceeded to retrieve $360 worth of Kings Dominion currency, known as "Scooby dollars," which guests use to purchase merchandise for sale within the park. Meanwhile, a guest at the next window submitted a check under the name of "Catherine May" to Joshua Stone ("Stone"), another park cashier. Because the Season Pass office did not have enough Scooby dollars to cash the two checks, Taylor and Stone contacted their supervisor, Deborah Samuel ("Samuel"). Samuel then had a chance to observe "Donita Morgan" and "Catherine May" after obtaining a sufficient amount of Scooby dollars from the park's Cash Control office.

Several days later, Loss Prevention learned that both the "Donita Morgan" check accepted by Taylor and the "Catherine May" check accepted by Stone were fraudulent. In fact, numerous fraudulent checks under these and other names had been passed at Kings Dominion during the May 14–15 weekend. Loss Prevention suspected that a group of individuals were operating an illegal check-cashing scheme at the park using fraudulent identification cards and fraudulent checks,4 and provided the park's cashiers with a memorandum listing various names under which bad checks had already been passed, including "Catherine May." The cashiers were directed to immediately inform Loss Prevention should a guest submit a check under a listed name.

Sergeant Cindy Gatewood ("Gatewood") of the Park Police Department supervised the investigation into the apparent check-cashing scheme. On the morning of Saturday, May 21, 1994, six days after Taylor and Stone had accepted the "Donita Morgan" check and the "Catherine May" check, respectively, Gatewood obtained verbal descriptions of the suspects from Samuel, Taylor, and Stone. According to Gatewood's testimony at trial, Samuel described "Donita Morgan" as a "middle-aged black woman with twisted hair." Taylor described the suspect as "a black female, five foot five, five foot six, average build, twisted hair braids, sunglasses." After obtaining verbal statements, Gatewood asked each of the three employees to prepare written statements. In her written statement, Taylor described "Donita Morgan" as a woman who had braided hair and wore Chanel sunglasses. Samuel, in her written statement, described her as "a middle-aged black woman with glasses, long twisted braids, and a lot of children."

Austin, an African American woman who at the time was a twenty-three-year-old student at the University of Maryland, was among the more than 20,000 guests of Kings Dominion on Saturday, May 21. That evening, Taylor saw Austin in the park and identified her as the "Donita Morgan" suspect from the previous weekend. Taylor alerted Loss Prevention accordingly. Officer Michael Drummer ("Drummer") of the Park Police Department subsequently approached Austin and escorted her to the Loss Prevention office. After being contacted at home and apprised of the situation, Gatewood arranged for Investigator Robert Schwartz ("Schwartz") of the Hanover County Sheriff's Department to meet her at the Loss Prevention office. In the interim, Samuel went to the Loss Prevention office and, like Taylor, identified Austin as the "Donita Morgan" suspect from the previous weekend.

After arriving at the Loss Prevention office, Schwartz advised Austin of her Miranda rights. He and Gatewood then informed Austin that two employees had positively identified her as having passed a fraudulent "Donita Morgan" check at the Season Pass office on May 15, 1994, and questioned Austin for several hours as to her whereabouts on that date. According to Gatewood's testimony at trial, Austin stated that she was at a banquet at the University of Maryland on May 15, 1994, but Austin refused to provide any information which would allow that statement to be verified. Consistent with his role as Manager of Loss Prevention, Hester occasionally appeared for several minutes to observe the questioning. Hester testified at trial that his purpose in doing so "was to make sure that our folks were handling their duties properly, that the police were in the process of moving this situation forward, and that the people involved in it were being handled professionally and properly."

Based primarily upon the accounts of Taylor and Samuel, whom Gatewood described at trial as "more than a hundred percent sure that Miss Austin was the one who had written a check to them," Gatewood decided to arrest Austin. Before doing so, however, Gatewood contacted Seward M. McGhee ("McGhee") of the Commonwealth's Attorney's Office, who advised Gatewood that Austin could be charged only with grand larceny until the bank had processed and returned the bad "Donita Morgan" check at issue. Schwartz thereafter transported Austin to the Hanover County Magistrate's office, where Gatewood caused a warrant to be issued for Austin's arrest on a charge of grand larceny in violation of Va. Code Ann. § 18.2-95 (Michie Supp. 1999).

On the following day, Sunday, May 22, 1994, a significant development occurred with respect to the investigation into the check-cashing scheme at Kings Dominion. Specifically, a guest named Annette Williams arrived at the Season Pass office and submitted a check under the name of "Catherine May." The park cashier who accepted the check recognized "Catherine May" from the memorandum distributed in connection with the scheme and immediately contacted Loss Prevention. Simultaneously, a guest named Tonya Williams submitted a check at the Season Pass office under the name of "Demetry Gordon."

Gatewood subsequently arrived at the Season Pass office in response to the cashier's call. When Gatewood asked Annette Williams to come to the Loss Prevention office, Tonya Williams became visibly agitated. Gatewood described the situation at trial in the following manner: "a friend of [Annette Williams] got very verbal and upset and said she didn't understand why I was taking her friend away, so I invited her to come to the office with me." During this encounter, Samuel saw Tonya Williams, an African American woman who had braided hair, and identified her as the woman who had submitted the "Donita Morgan" check to Taylor one week earlier.

Gatewood subsequently brought Annette Williams and Tonya Williams to the Loss Prevention office for questioning. During the questioning, the women maintained their respective false identities as Catherine May and Demetry Gordon. Later that day, after Annette Williams and Tonya Williams had left the park, Gatewood discovered their actual identities when a guest named Gladys Ann Williams was brought to the Loss Prevention office after submitting a fraudulent check at the Season Pass office under the name of "Michelle Lockhart." In a detailed confession, Gladys Ann Williams confirmed the existence of a check-cashing scheme, provided the names and aliases of the other participants in the scheme, and provided information concerning the source from whom they had obtained fraudulent identification cards and fraudulent checks.

That evening, Samuel alerted Hester at Loss Prevention that she had recognized Tonya Williams as the woman who had submitted the "Donita Morgan" check to Taylor on May 15, 1994. Hester's unrefuted testimony indicates that he personally informed Gatewood of this development later that evening. Samuel's observation, along with written statements filed by other park employees, led Gatewood and Hester to conclude that Tonya Williams was one of several women who had passed bad checks at the park under the name of "Donita Morgan." When asked at trial whether she specifically informed McGhee that Samuel had identified Tonya Williams as "Donita

Morgan," Gatewood responded that "I'm not sure if I told him those exact words, but he was advised that there was more than one Donita Morgan." Ultimately, Gatewood testified, McGhee advised her that "there's more than one person, you have your witnesses, and we're going to go forward with the case, if there's a scheme, and bust the scheme."

Gatewood thereafter caused a warrant to be issued for Austin's arrest on charges of forgery and uttering a forged writing in violation of Va. Code Ann. § 18.2-172 (Michie 1996). According to Gatewood's uncontradicted testimony at trial, she did so only after consulting McGhee once the "Donita Morgan" checks from May 15, 1994, had been processed by the bank and returned to Kings Dominion. Specifically, Gatewood testified that McGhee "told me when the checks came in, I was to give him a call. I did, and he advised me to go get the warrants." Gatewood subsequently informed Hester that she spoke to McGhee and that she intended to bring additional charges against Austin. In this regard, Hester testified at trial that Gatewood "indicated to me somewhere in that period of time, I don't remember the exact date or anything, that [McGhee] and she had had a conversation, and the charges were being amended, yes, sir, I was aware of that." Gatewood did not serve Austin with the second arrest warrant until July 14, 1994, when Austin returned to the Hanover County Magistrate's Office for a preliminary hearing on the charge of grand larceny. Austin was not further detained and was allowed to remain out on her original bond.

In January 1995, a Hanover County general district court conducted a preliminary hearing on the charges pending against Austin. Based primarily upon Gatewood's testimony, the court found probable cause to certify the charges for trial. In so doing, the court indicated that it would have dismissed the charges had Austin presented any evidence supporting her alibi: "if I would have had any evidence at all that there was a banquet on May the 15th and if, in fact, [Austin] could have come in here and presented that [she] attended a banquet on May the 15th, then there would be no question in my mind." Although a Hanover County grand jury subsequently indicted Austin on the charges, the matter did not proceed to trial. Rather, in April 1995, McGhee had the charges dismissed. McGhee did so apparently upon learning that Samuel, only one day after identifying Austin as having passed the "Donita Morgan" check to Taylor on May 15, 1994, identified Tonya Williams in connection with the same offense.

II.

Austin initiated the present litigation by filing a civil action in Maryland state court, naming Paramount as the only defendant. Following Paramount's removal of the action to the district court, Austin filed an eight-count second amended complaint, counts one through five of which contained claims arising under Virginia law for false arrest, false imprisonment, malicious prosecution, assault and battery, and negligence, respectively. Counts six through eight, on the other hand, contained claims arising under federal law. With respect to her § 1983 claim asserted in count six, Austin alleged primarily that she suffered a deprivation of her federal constitutional rights as a result of Paramount's policy of causing individuals suspected of passing bad checks at Kings Dominion to be detained, arrested, and prosecuted, even without probable cause, to deter other park guests from engaging in such conduct. Austin also alleged that Paramount failed to exercise due care in the hiring, retention, training, and supervision of employees who participated in the investigation, detention, and arrest of individuals suspected of passing bad checks at Kings Dominion, and that such failure manifested a conscious disregard for Austin's rights. These latter allegations essentially reiterated the allegations supporting Austin's state-law negligence claim asserted in count five.

B.

Paramount next maintains that it was entitled to judgment as a matter of law on Austin's § 1983 claim either because Paramount was not a state actor or because Austin failed to establish that an official policy or custom of Paramount caused a deprivation of her federal rights. We review de novo a district court's denial of a Rule 50(b) motion for judgment as a matter of law, viewing the evidence in the light most favorable to the prevailing party and drawing all reasonable inferences in her favor. See *Konkel v. Bob Evans Farms Inc.*, 165 F.3d 275, 279 (4th Cir.), cert. denied,145 L. Ed. 2d 155, 1999 U.S. LEXIS 5882, 120 S. Ct. 184 (U.S. 1999).

Section 1983 provides in relevant part as follows:

> Every person who, under color of any statute, ordinance, regulation, custom, or usage, of any State ... subjects, or causes to be subjected, any citizen of the United States or other person within the jurisdiction thereof to the deprivation of any rights, privileges, or immunities secured by the Constitution and laws, shall be liable to the party injured in an action at law, suit in equity, or other proper proceeding for redress.

42 U.S.C.A. § 1983. To prevail against Paramount on her § 1983 claim, Austin had the burden to establish that she was "deprived of a right secured by the Constitution or laws of the United States, and that the alleged deprivation was committed under color of state law." *American Mfrs. Mut. Ins. Co. v. Sullivan*, 526 U.S. 40, 119 S. Ct. 977, 985, 143 L. Ed. 2d 130 (1999). Paramount does not dispute that Austin's rights under the Fourth and Fourteenth Amendments were violated when Gatewood effected the July 14, 1994 arrest without probable cause. However, Paramount does dispute that it was a state actor for purposes of § 1983 merely because it employed Gatewood as a special police officer.

The question of whether Paramount was a state actor is a thorny one, but one which we need not decide here because Austin's clear failure to show that an official policy or custom of Paramount was the moving force behind Austin's July 14, 1994 arrest negates the necessity of addressing the issue. For purposes of our review we will assume, without holding, that Paramount was a state actor and proceed to consider Paramount's challenge to Austin's assertion that Paramount had an official policy or custom justifying the imposition of liability under § 1983.

Our analysis begins with general principles of municipal liability. In *Monell v. Department of Soc. Servs.*, 436 U.S. 658, 56 L. Ed. 2d 611, 98 S. Ct. 2018 (1978), the Supreme Court held that municipalities and other local governmental bodies constitute "persons" within the meaning of § 1983, see id. at 688–89. The Court, however, has consistently refused to impose § 1983 liability upon a municipality under a theory of respondeat superior. See *Board of the County Comm'rs v. Brown*, 520 U.S. 397, 403, 137 L. Ed. 2d 626, 117 S. Ct. 1382 (1997). Rather, under *Monell* and its progeny, a municipality is subject to § 1983 liability only when "it causes such a deprivation through an official policy or custom." *Carter v. Morris*, 164 F.3d 215, 218 (4th Cir. 1999). We have determined that "municipal policy may be found in written ordinances and regulations, in certain affirmative decisions of individual policy-making officials, or in certain omissions on the part of policy-making officials that manifest deliberate indifference to the rights of citizens." Id. (internal citations omitted). Municipal custom, on the other hand, may arise when a particular practice "is so persistent and widespread and so permanent and well settled as to constitute a custom or usage with the force of law." *Id.* (internal quotation marks omitted).

We have recognized, as has the Second Circuit, that the principles of § 1983 municipal liability articulated in *Monell* and its progeny apply equally to a private corporation that employs special police officers. Specifically, a private corporation is not liable under § 1983 for torts committed by special police officers when such liability is predicated solely upon a theory of respondeat superior. See *Powell v. Shopco Laurel Co.*,678 F.2d 504 (4th Cir. 1982); *Rojas v. Alexander's Dep't Store, Inc.*, 924 F.2d 406 (2d Cir. 1990); see also *Sanders v. Sears, Roebuck & Co.*, 984 F.2d 972, 975-76 (8th Cir. 1993) (concluding that private corporation is not subject to § 1983 liability under theory of respondeat superior regarding acts of private security guard employed by corporation); *Iskander v. Village of Forest Park*, 690 F.2d 126, 128 (7th Cir. 1982) (same). Rather, a private corporation is liable under § 1983 only when an official policy or custom of the corporation causes the alleged deprivation of federal rights. See *Rojas*, 924 F.2d at 408; *Sanders*, 984 F.2d at 976; *Iskander*, 690 F.2d at 128.

In her second amended complaint, Austin primarily alleged in support of her § 1983 claim that she suffered a deprivation of her federal constitutional rights as a result of Paramount's policy of causing individuals suspected of passing bad checks at Kings Dominion to be detained, arrested, and prosecuted, even without probable cause, to deter other park guests from engaging in such conduct. At trial, however, Austin was unable to present any evidence to substantiate those allegations. Rather, Austin's evidence focused on her alternative theory of § 1983 liability, also alleged in the second amended complaint, that Paramount failed to exercise due care in training employees who participated in the investigation, detention, and arrest of individuals suspected of passing bad checks at Kings Dominion, and that such failure manifested a conscious disregard for Austin's rights. Indeed, the district court, in denying Paramount's motion for judgment as a matter of law on the § 1983 claim at the close of Austin's evidence, relied solely upon this theory:

> I think there's evidence from which [Austin] can argue in this case that really it was a pretty patchy situation at [Kings Dominion], that they really didn't have any clear-cut training program to educate their personnel on dealing with customers who are suspected of passing bad checks. They did something, but arguably it was pretty patchy, and it seems to me it could be argued that it was deliberately indifferent.

On appeal, however, Austin has abandoned the preceding theory of § 1983 liability, obviously because the general verdict in favor of Paramount on the negligence claim contained in count five and the adverse interrogatory answers on the § 1983 claim showed that the jury rejected Austin's claim of inadequate training. Now, Austin presents a theory of § 1983 liability that resembles the reasoning offered by the district court in disposing of Paramount's Rule 49(b) motion and is purportedly reconcilable with the jury's verdict. Specifically, Austin argues that Hester was a policymaker who acquiesced in Gatewood's intention to effect the July 14, 1994 arrest of Austin on charges of forgery and uttering a forged writing, and who thereby subjected Paramount to liability. We find this claim untenable.

1.

The Supreme Court has recognized that, under appropriate circumstances, a municipality may incur § 1983 liability for a single decision of a policymaking official. See *Pembaur v. City of Cincinnati*, 475 U.S. 469, 480, 89 L. Ed. 2d 452, 106 S. Ct. 1292 (1986) (plurality opinion) (holding county liable under § 1983 when county prosecutor instructed sheriff's deputies to forcibly enter plaintiff's place of business to serve capiases upon third parties); *Carter*, 164 F.3d at 218 ("Municipal policy may be found…in certain affirmative decisions of individual policy making officials, or in certain omissions on the part of policy-making officials that manifest deliberate indifference to the rights of citizens.") (internal citations omitted). In determining whether an individual constitutes a "policy-making official" in this sense, courts inquire whether the individual speaks "with final policy-making authority for the local governmental actor concerning the action alleged to have caused the particular constitutional or statutory violation at issue." *Jett v. Dallas Indep. Sch. Dist.*, 491 U.S. 701, 737, 105 L. Ed. 2d 598, 109 S. Ct. 2702 (1989); see *Pembaur*, 475 U.S. at 481 ("Municipal liability attaches only where the decision maker possesses final authority to establish municipal policy with respect to the action ordered."). Whether the individual in question exercises such authority "is not a question of fact in the usual sense." *City of St. Louis v. Praprotnik*, 485 U.S. 112, 124, 99 L. Ed. 2d 107, 108 S. Ct. 915 (1988). Rather, the inquiry "is dependent upon an analysis of state law," *McMillian v. Monroe County, Alabama*, 520 U.S. 781, 786, 138 L. Ed. 2d 1, 117 S. Ct. 1734 (1997), requiring review of "the relevant legal materials, including state and local positive law, as well as custom or usage having the force of law." *Jett*, 491 U.S. at 737 (internal quotation marks omitted). A district court's determination of whether an individual exercises final policymaking authority in a particular area is reviewed de novo. See *Scala v. City of Winter Park*, 116 F.3d 1396, 1399 (11th Cir. 1997); *Gillette v. Delmore*, 979 F.2d 1342, 1349 (9th Cir. 1992).

The foregoing principles of § 1983 "policy-maker" liability were articulated in the context of suits brought against municipalities and other local government defendants. Nevertheless, these principles are equally applicable to a private corporation acting under color of state law when an employee exercises final policymaking authority concerning an action that allegedly causes a deprivation of federal rights. See *Howell v. Evans*, 922 F.2d 712, 724-25, vacated after settlement, 931 F.2d 711 (11th Cir. 1991) (assessing whether prison medical director employed by private corporation exercised final policy-making authority for employer concerning equipment and staff procurement). In the present appeal, Austin asserts that Paramount's liability under § 1983 derives from Hester's single decision to acquiesce in Gatewood's intention to effect Austin's July 14, 1994 arrest on charges of forgery and uttering a forged writing. Accordingly, the relevant "policy-maker" inquiry is whether Hester, as a matter of state and local positive law, or custom or usage having the force of law, see *Jett*, 491 U.S. at 737, exercised final policymaking authority concerning arrests effected by the special police officers of the Park Police Department. We are satisfied that he did not.

First, nothing in the positive law of the Commonwealth of Virginia or of Hanover County granted Hester any policymaking authority concerning arrests effected by the special police officers. In particular, nothing in the Virginia statute authorizing the appointment of special police officers granted a private corporation or any of its employees authority over the law enforcement functions performed by those officers. See Va. Code Ann. § 19.2-13(A). Moreover, nothing in the appointment order issued by the Circuit Court of Hanover County granted any authority over the special police officers' law enforcement functions to any of Paramount's employees, including the Manager of Loss Prevention. Indeed, the appointment order explicitly mandated that those officers "work only under the control and direction of the Sheriff of Hanover County."

Second, nothing in the written policies of Paramount or of Kings Dominion granted Hester any policymaking authority over arrests effected by the special police officers. *The Park Police Department's Policy and Procedure Manual* provided that the Park Police Department "has direct affiliation with the Hanover County Sheriff's Department and is under the direction of the Sheriff of Hanover County." The manual further provided: The Chain of Command and authority for all Kings Dominion Park Police shall be as follows involving official law enforcement:

1. Sheriff of Hanover County
2. Lieutenant of Kings Dominion Park Police
3. Kings Dominion Park Police Sergeant
4. Kings Dominion Park Police Corporal
5. Kings Dominion Park Police Officer

Aside from effectively illustrating the final authority of the Sheriff of Hanover County over the special police officers, the preceding list conspicuously omitted any reference to the Manager of Loss Prevention.

Third, even viewing the evidence at trial in the light most favorable to Austin and drawing all reasonable inferences in her favor, we cannot conclude that Hester had any policymaking authority concerning arrests effected by the special police officers as a matter of custom or usage having the force of law. See *Jett*, 491 U.S. at 737. At trial, Austin presented no evidence that Hester had ever directed a special police officer to effect an arrest or that he had ever prevented the same. Moreover, there was no evidence that the special police officers routinely consulted Hester or obtained his approval concerning impending arrests. Nor was there any evidence that Gatewood consulted Hester or obtained his approval concerning the two arrests in the present litigation. Rather, Gatewood's testimony regarding the events preceding those arrests demonstrates that she consulted only McGhee of the Commonwealth's Attorney's Office. Furthermore, when asked whether he knew that Gatewood planned to bring additional charges against Austin, Hester testified that "[Gatewood] indicated to me somewhere in that period of time…that [McGhee] and she had had a conversation, and the charges were being amended, yes, sir, I was aware of that." Although certainly suggesting that Gatewood kept Hester informed as to the status of Austin's case, this testimony in no way indicates that Gatewood attempted either to consult with Hester or to obtain his approval regarding her decision to bring additional charges against Austin. Put simply, there was no evidence that Hester, despite his title of Manager of Loss Prevention, in practice exercised any control over the decisions of the special police officers regarding detention and/ or arrests of park guests suspected of criminal offenses in this case or any other case. Indeed, the uncontradicted testimony was to the contrary. In fact, we find no support in the record for any specific policymaking authority given to or exercised by Hester regarding matters of law enforcement. The questions simply were not asked, nor was evidence ever produced in this regard.

In light of the foregoing analysis, we have no basis upon which to conclude that Hester exercised final policymaking authority concerning arrests effected by the special police officers of the Park Police Department. Because Austin's position on Paramount's liability under § 1983 rests entirely upon her theory that Hester was a "policy maker," we are satisfied that she failed to establish that any deprivation of her federal rights was caused by an official policy or custom of Paramount. Accordingly, we conclude that Paramount was entitled to judgment as a matter of law on Austin's § 1983 claim.

2.

Because Paramount was entitled to judgment as a matter of law on Austin's § 1983 claim, Austin cannot be considered a prevailing party on that claim for purposes of § 1988. We therefore vacate the district court's award of attorney's fees and expenses. Accordingly, we need not address the issue presented in Austin's cross-appeal, which pertains solely to the district court's calculation of that award.

C.

Lastly, we turn to the issue of whether Paramount is entitled to judgment as a matter of law on Austin's state-law claims for false arrest (July 14, 1994) and malicious prosecution. Again, we review de novo the district court's denial of Paramount's Rule 50(b) motion for judgment as a matter of law, viewing the evidence in the light most favorable to Austin and drawing all reasonable inferences in her favor. See *Konkel*, 165 F.3dat 279.

The Virginia Supreme Court has established that a private employer may not be held liable under a theory of respondeat superior for torts committed by a special police officer when he or she acts as a public officer, as opposed to an agent, servant, or employee of the employer. See *Norfolk & W. Ry. Co. v. Haun*, 167 Va. 157, 187 S.E. 481, 482 (Va. 1936); *Glenmar Cinestate, Inc. v. Farrell*, 223 Va. 728, 292 S.E.2d 366, 369-70 (Va. 1982). The court elaborated upon this key distinction in *Glenmar*: Moreover, we held in *N. & W. Ry. Co. v. Haun*, 167 Va. 157, 187 S.E. 481 (1936), that a special police officer appointed by public authority, but employed and paid by a private party, does not subject his employer to liability for his torts when the acts complained of are performed in carrying out his duty as a public officer. The test is: in what capacity was the officer acting at the time he committed the acts for which the complaint is made? If he is engaged in the performance of a public duty such as the enforcement of the general laws, his employer incurs no vicarious liability for his acts, even though the employer directed him to perform the duty. On the other hand, if he was engaged in the protection of the employer's property, ejecting trespassers or enforcing rules and regulations promulgated by the employer, it becomes a jury question as to whether he was acting as a public officer or as an agent, servant, or employee.

292 S.E.2d at 369-70.

In the present litigation, the only viable factual predicate for Austin's claims for false arrest (July 14, 1994) and malicious prosecution is that Gatewood lacked probable cause to effect the July 14, 1994 arrest and further lacked probable cause to assist with the prosecution of the pertinent charges. It is without question, however, that Gatewood effected Austin's arrest and assisted with the prosecution in the course of performing her public duty to enforce the Commonwealth of Virginia's law against forgery and uttering a forged writing. See Va. Code Ann. § 18.2-172. Accordingly, under Glenmar, the issue of whether Gatewood acted in her capacity as a public officer was not one for the jury's resolution.

Because Austin presented no evidence that Gatewood acted other than in her capacity as a public officer in effecting Austin's July 14, 1994 arrest and assisting with the prosecution, Paramount cannot be held vicariously liable with respect to Austin's claims for false arrest (July 14, 1994) and malicious prosecution. See *Glenmar*, 292 S.E.2d at 369 ("If [the officer was] engaged in the performance of a public duty such as the enforcement of the general laws, his employer incurs no vicarious liability for his acts...."). We conclude, therefore, that Paramount was entitled to judgment as a matter of law on both claims.

IV.

In summary, we conclude that Paramount was entitled to judgment as a matter of law on Austin's § 1983 claim because Austin failed to establish that any deprivation of her federal rights was caused by an official policy or custom of Paramount. We further conclude that, because Gatewood was engaged in the performance of her public duty to enforce Virginia law when she effected Austin's July 14, 1994 arrest and assisted with the prosecution, Paramount was entitled to judgment as a matter of law on Austin's claims for false arrest (July 14, 1994) and malicious prosecution. Accordingly, we reverse the denial of Paramount's Rule 50(b) motion for judgment as a matter of law, vacate the judgment in favor of Austin, vacate the award of attorney's fees and expenses, and remand with instructions that judgment as a matter of law be entered in favor of Paramount.

VACATED AND REMANDED

Beverly Jean Whitehead, et al. v. USA-One, Inc., 595 SO. 2D 867 (ALA. SUP. 1992).

Maddox, Almon, Shores, Houston, and Steagall, JJ., concur.
Opinion: per curiam.

Beverly Jean Whitehead, Carla Prewett, and Blair Marques were all tenants at Sharpsburg Manor apartments in Birmingham in 1988. In April and May of that year, a man broke into each of their apartments and sexually assaulted them. On June 11, 1988, the same man who had previously assaulted Whitehead broke into Whitehead's apartment again and raped her. Alfred Zene was apprehended that evening, and he later pleaded guilty to second degree burglary for the June 11 break-in; he was sentenced to 25 years in prison.

Whitehead, Prewett, and Marques all sued USA-One, Inc., the company hired to provide gate attendants at Sharpsburg Manor; Rime, Inc., the owner of Sharpsburg Manor; and Regal Development Company, the manager of the apartment complex, alleging negligence, wantonness, and breach of contract. They also sued Zene, alleging assault. Whitehead, Prewett, and Marques reached a pro tanto settlement with Rime and Regal Development Company, and the trial court entered a summary judgment for USA-One and made that judgment final pursuant to Rule 54(b), A.R.Civ.P.

Whitehead, Prewett, and Marques appeal from that judgment, arguing that USA-One voluntarily assumed a duty to protect them from the criminal acts of a third party. They rely on *Gardner v. Vinson Guard Service, Inc.*, 538 So.2d 13 (Ala. 1988), in support of that argument.

In *Gardner*, Vinson Guard Service had an oral contract with Van's Photo, Inc., to provide security guards at one of its facilities. Specifically, Vinson Guard Service was to "provide protection for vehicles in the parking lot of Van's Photo and to protect employees traveling to and from their vehicles" and to "patrol the perimeter around the facility and to make their presence evident." 538 So.2d at 14. A Van's Photo employee arrived for work one morning after a burglary had occurred and was told by the security guard on duty that it was safe to go in the building because the burglar had fled. Approximately 15 minutes after the employee went inside, she was attacked by a second burglar. In reversing the summary judgment for Vinson Guard Service on the plaintiff's negligence claim, this Court held that there was a jury question as to whether Vinson Guard Service had assumed a duty to protect the Van's Photo employees while they were inside the building. We also held that, although a breach of contract cause of action might exist for a third-party beneficiary, no such cause of action existed in that case.

We find no evidence here that USA-One had a contractual duty to protect Whitehead, Prewett, and Marques or that it assumed a duty to protect them. The contract between Rime and Shelby Securities, Inc., USA-One's predecessor in interest, states at paragraph nine: "It is expressly understood and agreed that this contract is entered into solely for the mutual benefit of the parties herein and that no benefits, rights, duties, or obligations are intended or created by this contract as to third parties not a signatory hereto."

Although USA-One's duties were not expressly stated in the contract, Dorothy Holland, the manager of Sharpsburg Manor, and Barrell Lamar Walker, a former employee of USA-One, described in their depositions the extent of USA-One's responsibilities. Walker said that the gate attendants primarily checked cars entering and exiting the complex, that they kept daily logs, and that they made periodic "rounds" of the premises. Holland said that the attendants served as an after-hours answering service, that is, that they had the telephone numbers of the maintenance person and the manager on duty in case a resident called the gate with a problem the attendant could not handle. Holland stated more specifically regarding the attendants' duties:

"Q: All right. Other than answering—filling an answering service, did [USA-One]—did you have an understanding that they were supposed to provide anything else?

"A: Yes.

"Q: What was that?

"A: They make rounds of all the public areas. This means they check the swimming pools to make sure at the proper time that people are out of the pools. Some of them are 9:00, some are 10:00, the pools. And they check the maintenance shop doors. They check the pump house doors. They walk through breezeways. They walk around buildings, they do all sorts of things.

"Q: How many—you call them guards, don't you?

"A: No, we call them gate attendants.

"Q: All right. How many gate attendants were on duty each night?

"A: Until—well, they fluctuated. They had different hours at different times. Depending upon the nights we had the heaviest traffic, they would—there would be one, two persons up to say, midnight. And then after midnight, to 5:00 in the morning, there would be one who rode. They wouldn't stay in the gate house at all, he rode around and made checks more frequently.

"Q: Midnight to—

"A: 5:00. Daylight, whatever time it is.

"Q: And what would happen at 5:00?

"A: He would leave.

"Q: Would you have any gate attendants whatsoever after 5:00 in the morning?

"A: After 5:00, no.

"Q: And the first gate attendant to show up would be at 2:00, or what time?

"A: Gate attendant?

"Q: Yes.

"A: When the office closed.

"Q: At 5:00.

"A: Yes. And we closed at 5:30. They would come a little before that time to get information and pick up the keys and this sort of thing.

"Q: Did you make inquiries about their whereabouts after the first Whitehead incident?

"A: Did I make—

"Q: Did you ask these gate attendants where they were during the night of the first Whitehead incident?

"A: Yes.

"Q: What did they tell you?

"A: They were there. They were making—or a person was.

"Q: One person was making rounds?

"A: Yes.

"Q: And the other person—

"A: They report back to the attendant.

"Q: Pardon me?

"A: They report back to their station, and are there periodically.

"Q: So, both were making rounds, reporting back to their station periodically, right? Is that what they told you?

"A: This is what their duties were each night until a certain hour of night, and it depends on the—we have to look at the guard reports to see.

"...

"Q: And now, what did you do after this Marques incident with regard to security force? Did you talk to the gate attendants? Did you talk to them, personally, at all?

"A: Uh-huh (positive response).

"Q: All right. Were any changes made?

"A: They were—just what they're permitted to do. You know, they cannot make an arrest.

"Q: Right.

"A: And they just made rounds more frequently, rode around more frequently, rode on the street areas and inside the complex itself. And the police did, too, at all times. They were there day and night.

"Q: In what way did the gate attendants follow your suggestions about more frequent patrolling?

"A: Yes, they did [sic]. In fact, I would check on it at times to make sure they were doing that. I called the gate house to see if they were there, and asked if they made rounds.

"Q: Did they—did they continue to use two people during the hours that you've earlier testified about, 12:00 to 5:00?

"A: It seems that we made some changes in some of the hours, but I can't remember exactly what they were. But they still went off duty at 5:00 or 5:30 in the morning, because it was daylight at that time.

"Q: I just want to get a bearing on like, more frequently is—they began patrolling more frequently. How long did they do that? They just spent more time in the car and less time in the gate?

"A: No. We asked them to walk. Drive to an area, get out and walk around, and—they used to do a lot of that, anyway. We just asked them to do it more frequently.

"Q: Did you ever have any complaints prior to any of these incidents about the gate attendants?

"A: Complaints, like?

"Q: Like they weren't doing their job?

"A: Spasmodically. Not as a usual thing.

"Q: All right.

"A: They're only there for limited times, and they're only there for limited services to perform.

"Q: After the first Whitehead incident, when you understood that the fellow—the assailant had said 'they're waiting for me in the car outside,' did you check with the guards to determine whether they had identified the license tag numbers or cars entering and exiting that evening?

"A: Well, now, we don't offer security-type security. They can—people like this watch and wait until there is no one around to appear. He could be at one end of the complex, and far away from that. You can't be everywhere at the same time, no way."

As opposed to the duties of the security company in *Gardner v. Vinson Guard Service*, supra, it is clear both from the contract here as well as from the deposition testimony of Walker and Holland that the employees of USA-One were at Sharpsburg Manor for the benefit of Rime. We are unpersuaded by the plaintiffs' reliance on *Nail v. Jefferson County Truck Growers Ass'n, Inc.*, 542 So.2d 1208 (Ala. 1988), to show that USA-One voluntarily assumed a duty to protect them.

Nail involved a shootout between competing produce retailers at the Jefferson County Farmers' Market over leased space at the market. The retailers sued the owner and manager of the market, alleging a negligent failure to prevent injuries caused by the intentional tort of a third person. The trial court entered a judgment notwithstanding the verdict, for the owner and manager of the market, and the retailers appealed, arguing that the market had voluntarily assumed a duty to protect them because, three days before the shootout, the market had hired a third security guard to patrol the area where the violence occurred. On the day of the shooting, however, only two guards were present, because one guard was sick. The retailers produced evidence that a replacement guard was usually called in when a guard was absent and that, on the day in question, the market did not provide a replacement guard even though it had knowledge of the "growing rancor" between the retailers. In reversing the J.N.O.V. with regard to one of the retailers, this Court stated, "The hostility in this case fermented over a period of several weeks before the shootout, and Market was apprised of the growing animosity. We hold that evidence was sufficient for the jury reasonably to conclude violence in Shed One was foreseeable." 542 So.2d at 1212.

Here, the fact that the gate attendants patrolled the grounds of Sharpsburg Manor "more frequently" after the second assault is insufficient to establish that USA-One undertook to protect the residents of the apartment complex. We hold, therefore, that the summary judgment for USA-One was correct, and it is due to be affirmed.

AFFIRMED. MADDOX, ALMON, SHORES, HOUSTON, AND STEAGALL, JJ., CONCUR.

Burdeau v. McDowell, 256 U.S. 465; 41 S. Ct. 574; 65 L. Ed. 1048 (1921).

Appeal from an order of the District Court requiring that certain books and papers be impounded with the clerk and ultimately returned to the appellee, and enjoining officers of the Department of Justice from using them, or evidence derived through them, in criminal proceedings against him. The facts are stated in the opinion, post, 470.

COUNSEL: The Solicitor General for appellant:

It was not shown that any book, paper, or other document which was the private property of appellee was delivered to or was ever in the possession of appellant.

It is difficult to see how it can be said, with any show of reason, that there was any stealing of books and papers in this case. Certainly there was no invasion of appellee's right of privacy. Everything that was taken into possession was found in the office of the company itself, with the exception of a few papers which were in the private office of appellee, but which it is admitted related to the business of the company, and were, therefore, such papers as the company was entitled to have delivered to it. They were, in fact, delivered to its auditor by appellee's representative.

If the employee has left papers of his own commingled with those of the company, he certainly cannot be said to be the sole judge of whether a particular paper is his or belongs to the company. He has brought about a condition under which the company has the right to inspect everything in the office before allowing anything to be removed. The inspection, therefore, is entirely lawful, and any information of crime or other matters which may be thus acquired is lawfully acquired and may properly be used. In the present case, appellee's representative was allowed to be present and make a list or take copies of all papers examined. A paper furnishing evidence of crookedness in the conduct of the company's affairs certainly relates to a matter in which the company is interested; and if the unfaithful employee has left it in the company's files, or in the company's office, there is no principle of law under which he can lawfully claim the right to have it returned to him. He has parted with the private possession of it, and his surrender of possession has not been brought about by any invasion of his constitutional rights.

Even if it could be said that the company or its representatives stole these papers from the appellee, this would not preclude their use in evidence if they should thereafter come to the hands of the federal authorities. The court found, as the evidence clearly required, that no department of the Federal Government had anything whatever to do with the taking of these papers and that no federal official had any knowledge that an investigation of any kind was being made, nor did such knowledge come to any federal official until several months later. It would scarcely be insisted by anyone that, if the Government should discover that someone has stolen from another a paper which shows that the latter has committed a crime, the thief could not be called as a witness to testify to what he has discovered. If the paper were still in his possession, he could be subpoenaed to attend and produce the paper. The same thing is accomplished when the Government, instead of issuing a subpoena duces tecum, takes the paper and holds it as evidence. The rightful owner, while it is being so held, is no more entitled to its return than one who has been arrested for carrying a pistol is entitled to have the pistol returned to him pending a trial.

It must always be remembered that "a party is privileged from producing the evidence but not from its production." *Johnson v. United States*, 228 U.S. 457, 458.

Moreover, the Fourth Amendment protects only against searches and seizures which are made under governmental authority, real or assumed, or under color of such authority. If papers have been seized, even though wrongfully, by one not acting under color of authority, and they afterwards come to the possession of the Government, they may be properly used in evidence. *Weeks v. United States*, 232 U.S. 383; *Gouled v. United States*, 255 U.S. 298; *Boyd v. United States*, 116 U.S. 616; *Adams v. New York*, 192 U.S. 585; *Johnson v. United States*, supra; *Perlman v. United States*, 247 U.S. 7.

Mr. E. Lowry Humes, with whom Mr. A. M. Imbrie and Mr. Rody P. Marshall were on the brief, for appellee:

> The issue in this proceeding was the title and right of possession of certain private papers alleged to have been stolen. The right to private property can be as effectually asserted against the Government as it can against an individual, and the Government has no greater right to stolen property than the private citizen. The receiver of stolen goods has no right superior to the right of the thief and the officer or agent of the Government who receives stolen goods is in no better position to retain the fruits and advantages of the crime than the humble private citizen. *Boyd v. United States*, 116 U.S. 616, 624; *Weeks v. United States*, 232 U.S. 383, 398. The right which the appellee asserted was a right which the court had jurisdiction to recognize and preserve.

The courts of the United States are open to the citizen for the enforcement of his legal and constitutional rights, and the right to private property may be asserted as a mere legal right or it may be asserted under the guarantees of the Constitution.

Abuses of individuals involving the deprivation of the right to the possession, use and enjoyment of private property are adequately redressed by the assertion of the legal rights of the individual in either courts of law or equity. The resort to the limitations of the Constitution may be necessary to curb the excesses of the Government.

In the case at bar there can be no question but that replevin would lie against both the thief and the receiver of the stolen goods to recover the private property of the appellee. But the legal remedy by replevin would have been inadequate as the injury could not be measured in damages. It was necessary to resort to the equitable powers of the court. The fact that the appellant happened to be an officer or employee of the Government provided no immunity to him that could prevent the owner of private property from asserting his legal rights in either a court of law or of equity. Quite to the contrary, the very fact that he was an officer of the court, enlarged rather than diminished the authority of the court to exercise control over and deal with the stolen papers which had come into his possession as such officer of the court.

In this case the proceeding is properly a much more summary proceeding than in a case against a stranger to the court where the formality and difficulty of securing jurisdiction over both the person and the property might be involved.

The right of a court of equity to order and decree the return of private property and papers is well recognized, as is illustrated by the following cases. *McGowin v. Remington*, 12 Pa. St. 56; *Dock v. Dock*, 180 Pa. St. 14; *Pressed Steel Car Co. v. Standard Steel Car Co.*, 210 Pa. St. 464.

This is an independent proceeding having for its purpose the recovery of property in equity. The law side of the court provided no adequate remedy. The court in adjudicating the case properly found that the papers had been stolen; that they were private and personal papers of the appellee, and that they were in the hands of an officer of the court, and that the owner was entitled to their return. Up to this point no constitutional question is involved. It is, however, respectfully submitted that had the court below refused under the evidence and the facts in this case to order the return of the books and papers, and dismissed the proceeding, and if subsequently a criminal proceeding had been instituted against the appellee and the stolen books and papers been admitted in evidence over objection, then appellee would have been denied the constitutional right guaranteed him under the Fifth Amendment to the Constitution in that he would have been "compelled in" a "criminal case to be a witness against himself." If this conclusion is not correct then a means has been found by which private prosecutors and complainants and those personally interested in the prosecution and persecution of alleged offenders can, by the mere acquiescence of the Government, deprive citizens of the United States of the constitutional rights guaranteed to them by both the Fourth and Fifth Amendments.

Judges: McKenna, Holmes, Day, Van Devanter, Pitney, McReynolds, Brandeis, Clarke

Opinion by: DAY

Opinion: MR. JUSTICE DAY delivered the opinion of the court.

J. C. McDowell, hereinafter called the petitioner, filed a petition in the United States District Court for the Western District of Pennsylvania asking for an order for the return to him of certain books, papers, memoranda, correspondence and other data in the possession of Joseph A. Burdeau, appellant herein, Special Assistant to the Attorney General of the United States.

In the petition it is stated that Burdeau and his associates intended to present to the grand jury in and for the Western District of Pennsylvania a charge against petitioner of an alleged violation of § 215 of the Criminal Code of the United States in the fraudulent use of the mails; that it was the intention of Burdeau and his associates, including certain post-office inspectors cooperating with him, to present to the grand jury certain private books, papers, memoranda, etc., which were the private property of the petitioner; that the papers had been in the possession and exclusive control of the petitioner in the Farmers Bank Building in Pittsburgh. It is alleged that during the spring and summer of 1920 these papers were unlawfully seized and stolen from petitioner by certain persons participating in and furthering the proposed investigation so to be made by the grand jury, under the direction and control of Burdeau as special assistant to the Attorney General, and that such books, papers, memoranda, etc., were being held in the possession and control of Burdeau and his assistants; that in the taking of the personal private books and papers the person who purloined and stole the same drilled the petitioner's private safes, broke the locks upon his private desk, and broke into and abstracted from the files in his offices his private papers; that the possession of the books, papers, etc., by Burdeau and his assistants was unlawful and in violation of the legal and constitutional rights of the petitioner. It is charged that the presentation to the grand jury of the same, or any secondary or other evidence secured through or by them, would work a deprivation of petitioner's constitutional rights secured to him by the Fourth and Fifth Amendments to the Constitution of the United States.

An answer was filed claiming the right to hold and use the papers. A hearing was had before the District Judge, who made an order requiring the delivery of the papers to the clerk of the court, together with all copies memoranda and data taken therefrom, which the court found had been stolen from the offices of the petitioner at rooms numbered 1320 and 1321 in the Farmers Bank Building in the City of Pittsburgh. The order further provided that upon delivery of the books, papers, etc., to the clerk of the court the same should be sealed and impounded for the period of ten days, at the end of which period they should be delivered to the petitioner or his attorney unless an appeal were taken from the order of the court, in which event, the books, papers, etc., should be impounded until the determination of the appeal. An order was made restraining Burdeau, Special Assistant Attorney General, the Department of Justice, its officers and agents, and the United States Attorney from presenting to the United States Commissioner, the grand jury or any judicial tribunal, any of the books, papers, memoranda, letters, copies of letters, correspondence, etc., or any evidence of any nature whatsoever secured by or coming into their possession as a result of the knowledge obtained from the inspection of such books, papers, memoranda, etc.

In his opinion the District Judge stated that it was the intention of the Department of Justice, through Burdeau and his assistants, to present the books, papers, etc., to the grand jury with a view to having the petitioner indicted for the alleged violation of § 215 of the Criminal Code of the United States, and the court held that the evidence offered by the petitioner showed that the papers had been stolen from him, and that he was entitled to the return of the same. In this connection the District Judge stated that it did not appear that Burdeau, or any official or agent of the United States, or any of the Departments, had anything to do with the search of the petitioner's safe, files, and desk, or the abstraction therefrom of any of the writings referred to in the petition, and added that "the order made in this case is not made because of any unlawful act on the part of anybody representing the United States or any of its Departments but solely upon the ground that the Government should not use stolen property for any purpose after demand made for its return." Expressing his views, at the close of the testimony, the judge said that there had been a gross violation of the Fourth and Fifth Amendments to the Federal Constitution; that the Government had not been a party to any illegal seizure; that those Amendments, in the understanding of the court, were passed for the benefit of the States against action by the United States, forbidden by those Amendments, and that the court was satisfied that the papers were illegally and wrongfully taken from the possession of the petitioner, and were then in the hands of the Government.

So far as is necessary for our consideration certain facts from the record may be stated. Henry L. Doherty & Company of New York were operating managers of the Cities Service Company, which company is a holding company, having control of various oil and gas companies. Petitioner was a director in the Cities Service Company and a director in the Quapaw Gas Company, a subsidiary company, and occupied an office room in the building owned by the Farmers Bank of Pittsburgh. The rooms were leased by the Quapaw Gas Company. McDowell occupied one room for his private office. He was employed by Doherty & Company as the head of the natural gas division of the Cities Service Company. Doherty & Company discharged McDowell for alleged unlawful and fraudulent conduct in the course of the business. An officer of Doherty & Company and the Cities Service Company went to Pittsburgh in March, 1920, with authority of the president of the Quapaw Gas Company to take possession of the company's office. He took possession of room 1320; that room and the adjoining room had McDowell's name on the door. At various times papers were taken from the safe and desk in the rooms, and the rooms were placed in charge of detectives. A large quantity of papers were taken and shipped to the auditor of the Cities Service Company at 60 Wall Street, New York, which was the office of that company, Doherty & Company and the Quapaw Gas Company. The secretary of McDowell testified that room 1320 was his private office; that practically all the furniture in both rooms belonged to him; that there was a large safe belonging to the Farmers Bank and a small safe belonging to McDowell; that on March 23, 1920, a representative of the company and a detective came to the offices; that the detective was placed in charge of room 1320; that the large safe was opened with a view to selecting papers belonging to the company, and that the representative of the company took private papers of McDowell's also. While the rooms were in charge of detectives both safes were blown open. In the small safe nothing of consequence was found, but in the large safe papers belonging to McDowell were found. The desk was forced open, and all the papers taken from it. The papers were placed in cases, and shipped to Doherty & Company, 60 Wall Street, New York.

In June, 1920, following, Doherty & Company, after communication with the Department of Justice, turned over a letter, found in McDowell's desk to the Department's representative. Burdeau admitted at the hearing that as the representative of the United States in the Department of Justice he had papers which he assumed were taken from the office of McDowell. The communication to the Attorney General stated that McDowell had violated the laws of the United States in the use of the mail in the transmission of various letters to parties who owned the properties which were sold by or offered to the Cities Service Company; that some of such letters, or copies of them taken from McDowell's file, were in the possession of the Cities Service Company, that the Company also had in its possession portions of a diary of McDowell in which he had jotted down the commissions which he had received from a number of the transactions, and other data which, it is stated, would be useful in the investigation of the matter before the grand jury and subsequent prosecution should an indictment be returned.

We do not question the authority of the court to control the disposition of the papers, and come directly to the contention that the constitutional rights of the petitioner were violated by their seizure, and that having subsequently come into the possession of the prosecuting officers of the Government, he was entitled to their return. The Amendments involved are the Fourth and Fifth, protecting a citizen against unreasonable searches and seizures, and compulsory testimony against himself. An extended consideration of the origin and purposes of these Amendments would be superfluous in view of the fact that this court has had occasion to deal with those subjects in a series of cases. *Boyd v. United States,* 116 U.S. 616; *Adams v. New York,* 192 U.S. 585; *Weeks v. United States,* 232 U.S. 383; *Johnson v. United States,* 228 U.S. 457; *Perlman v. United States,* 247 U.S. 7; *Silverthorne Lumber Co. v. United States,* 251 U.S. 385; and *Gouled v. United States,* 255 U.S. 298.

The Fourth Amendment gives protection against unlawful searches and seizures, and as shown in the previous cases, its protection applies to governmental action. Its origin and history clearly show that it was intended as a restraint upon the activities of sovereign authority, and was not intended to be a limitation upon other than governmental agencies; as against such authority it was the purpose of the Fourth Amendment to secure the citizen in the right of unmolested occupation of his dwelling and the possession of his property, subject to the right of seizure by process duly issued.

In the present case the record clearly shows that no official of the Federal Government had anything to do with the wrongful seizure of the petitioner's property, or any knowledge thereof until several months after the property had been taken from him and was in the possession of the Cities Service Company. It is manifest that there was no invasion of the security afforded by the Fourth Amendment against unreasonable search and seizure, as whatever wrong was done was the act of individuals in taking the property of another. A portion of the property so taken and held was turned over to the prosecuting officers of the Federal Government. We assume that petitioner has an unquestionable right of redress against those who illegally and wrongfully took his private property under the circumstances herein disclosed, but with such remedies we are not now concerned.

The Fifth Amendment, as its terms import is intended to secure the citizen from compulsory testimony against himself. It protects from extorted confessions, or examinations in court proceedings by compulsory methods.

The exact question to be decided here is: May the Government retain incriminating papers, coming to it in the manner described, with a view to their use in a subsequent investigation by a grand jury where such papers will be part of the evidence against the accused, and may be used against him upon trial should an indictment be returned?

We know of no constitutional principle which requires the Government to surrender the papers under such circumstances. Had it learned that such incriminatory papers, tending to show a violation of federal law, were in the hands of a person other than the accused, it having had no part in wrongfully obtaining them, we know of no reason why a subpoena might not issue for the production of the papers as evidence. Such production would require no unreasonable search or seizure, nor would it amount to compelling the accused to testify against himself.

The papers having come into the possession of the Government without a violation of petitioner's rights by governmental authority, we see no reason why the fact that individuals, unconnected with the Government, may have wrongfully taken them, should prevent them from being held for use in prosecuting an offense where the documents are of an incriminatory character.

It follows that the District Court erred in making the order appealed from, and the same is Reversed.

Dissent by: BRANDEIS

Dissent: MR. JUSTICE BRANDEIS dissenting, with whom MR. JUSTICE HOLMES concurs.

Plaintiff's private papers were stolen. The thief, to further his own ends, delivered them to the law officer of the United States. He, knowing them to have been stolen, retains them for use against the plaintiff. Should the court permit him to do so?

That the court would restore the papers to plaintiff if they were still in the thief's possession is not questioned. That it has power to control the disposition of these stolen papers, although they have passed into the possession of the law officer, is also not questioned. But it is said that no provision of the constitution requires their surrender and that the papers could have been subpoenaed. This may be true. Still I cannot believe that action of a public official is necessarily lawful, because it does not violate constitutional prohibitions and because the same result might have been attained by other and proper means. At the foundation of our civil liberty lies the principle which denies to government officials an exceptional position before the law and which subjects them to the same rules of conduct that are commands to the citizen. And in the development of our liberty insistence upon procedural regularity has been a large factor. Respect for law will not be advanced by resort, in its enforcement, to means which shock the common man's sense of decency and fair play.

State of Minnesota v. Jeffrey Scott Buswell, 449 N.W.2d 471 (Minn. App. 1989).

Parker, Presiding Judge, Crippen, Judge, and Bowen, *Judge. Bowen, Judge, dissenting.
Opinion by: Crippen

Appellants contend their Fourth Amendment rights were violated by security agent searches at the gateway to Brainerd International Raceway. The trial court concluded the policing activity was private. We reverse and remand.

Facts

Each appellant was charged with possession of controlled substances. After a consolidated omnibus hearing, the trial court determined that the evidence seized was the product of a private search and denied appellants' motions to suppress the evidence. Appellants waived their rights to a jury trial and were found guilty as charged by the trial court.

Appellant Dale Jay Schmidt was stopped in his borrowed pickup camper by Bruce Gately, a private security agency employee outside the entrance to Brainerd International Raceway on August 18, 1988. Gately asked Schmidt to unlock the back door of the camper portion of his vehicle so Gately could see if any persons were attempting to enter the race without paying the admission fee. After Schmidt unlocked the back door, Gately looked into the rear of the camper, entered it, opened a closet and discovered a small, green tackle box which contained cocaine. Gately then handcuffed Schmidt and his passenger to a fence pending the arrival of law enforcement officials.

Appellants Jeffrey Scott Buswell and Gary Lee Schwartzman were also stopped by Gately upon their arrival at the racetrack on August 18. While searching their converted bus, Gately discovered contraband inside a closet and a closet drawer. Subsequently, Buswell and Schwartzman were handcuffed to a fence and law enforcement officials were summoned. More contraband was found after the bus was seized and searched, and cocaine was discovered on appellants after they were taken into custody.

In each instance, the searches were conducted by a private security guard employed by North Country Security. North Country Security is owned by Keith Emerson, a Brainerd police officer and a special deputy for the Crow Wing County Sheriff's office.

Emerson contracted with the Brainerd raceway to provide security at the track, which is located on private property about six miles outside Brainerd, in Crow Wing County. He was responsible for hiring security guards and managing the security arrangements. For the weekend at issue, Emerson employed 127 guards, seven of whom were police officers.

In May of 1988, prior to the racing season, Emerson conferred with the Crow Wing County Sheriff and a local Bureau of Criminal Apprehension agent to determine the procedures that would be employed when his security guards seized contraband or uncovered other illegal activity. It was agreed that if any circumstances encountered by Brainerd security guards seemed to warrant an arrest, Emerson would be called first. After reviewing the situation, he would then decide whether to call in law enforcement officers. Arrangements were made for Emerson to contact Dave Bjerja, a Crow Wing County deputy sheriff and a special BCA agent, when someone was held for further police action.

At approximately 6 a.m. on the day of the searches, Emerson convened a meeting with his employees to discuss security arrangements for the weekend's races. At this meeting, Emerson told his employees that vehicles were to be searched for nonpaying persons. Emerson testified, however, that there was also a standing rule that vehicles are checked on a random basis for contraband.

ISSUE

Did the searches conducted by private security personnel at the entrance to Brainerd International Raceway constitute public police action, governed by Fourth Amendment limitations?

Analysis

Appellants contend the random searches at issue were not private activity and should have been subject to the constraints set forth by the Fourth and Fourteenth Amendments. They argue that there was sufficient evidence of public action to implicate the constitutional prohibitions against unreasonable and warrantless searches and that evidence obtained was illegally seized and should have been suppressed.

It is well-settled that the Fourth Amendment applies only to governmental action. *Burdeau v. McDowell*, 256 U.S. 465, 475, 65 L. Ed. 1048, 41 S. Ct. 574 (1921). This rule of law has been followed in Minnesota. See *State v. Kumpula*, 355 N.W.2d 697, 701 (Minn. 1984); *State v. Hodges*, 287 N.W.2d 413, 416 (Minn. 1979). The difficulty often arises, however, as it does here, in determining when governmental action occurs. There is no single authority directly bearing on this issue.

The public–private classification is made with awareness that constitutional rights of the citizen must be protected. We are to liberally construe those constitutional provisions which provide for the security of person and property. See *Coolidge v. New Hampshire*, 403 U.S. 443, 453-54, 29 L. Ed. 2d 564, 91 S. Ct. 2022 (1971). Courts have recognized the dangers in creating a simplistic division between private and public sectors when interpreting the Fourth Amendment.

To err on the side of a restrictive interpretation of the Fourth Amendment would be to sanction the possibility of widespread abuse of the privacy rights of individuals by private security guards.
* * * *

Ill-trained in the subtleties of the law of search and seizure, private security guards are more likely than public law-enforcement officials to conduct illegal searches and seizures. In addition, private security guards have accoutrements of office that tend to radiate an air of authority not possessed by other private individuals. Of particular importance are the uniform and badge, both regulated by the state.

People v. Holloway, 82 Mich. App. 629, 267 N.W.2d 454, 459 (1978) (Kaufman, Judge, concurring).

The Supreme Court formulated the following standard in Coolidge:

> The test…is whether [the private citizen], in light of all the circumstances of the case, must be regarded as having acted as an "instrument" or agent of the state.

Coolidge, 403 U.S. at 487. The Court recently reiterated this position and stated that the Fourth Amendment does not apply to a private search or seizure unless the private party acted as an instrument or agent of the government. *Skinner v. Railway Labor Executives Ass'n*, 489 U.S. 602, 109 S. Ct. 1402, 1411, 103 L. Ed. 2d 639 (1989).

Case law identifies several determinants of public involvement. Our consideration of these factors leads us to the conclusion that the searches in the present case were public. As these factors are examined here, we review the record with respect for the additional rule of law that appellants have the burden to show by a preponderance of evidence that the security searches here were not private in nature. *United States v. Feffer*, 831 F.2d 734, 739 (7th Cir. 1987).

1. Official Police Involvement.

Whether a private party should be considered an agent or instrument of the government for purposes of the Fourth Amendment turns initially on the degree of the government's participation in the private party's activities. *Skinner*, U.S. at, 109 S. Ct. at 1411. "The fact that the government has not compelled a private party to perform a search does not, by itself, establish that the search is a private one." Id. Governmental participation may be found where the government does something more than adopt a passive position toward underlying private conduct. *Id.*

Before a private party's actions can be attributed to the government, some degree of government instigation must be shown. *United States v. Luciow*, 518 F.2d 298, 300 (8th Cir. 1975). This may be in the form of governmental direction, authorization, or knowledge of the illegality. Id. The Fourth Amendment may apply if the government participates in a search or encourages a private party to conduct a search. *Gundlach v. Janing*, 536 F.2d 754, 755 (8th Cir. 1976).

A search is not private in nature if it has been ordered or requested by a government official. 1 W. LaFave, Search and Seizure § 1.8(b), at178 (2d ed. 1987). Similarly, governmental involvement has been found to exist when private security guards act pursuant to customary procedures agreed to in advance by the police. See *Murray v. Wal-Mart, Inc.*, 874 F.2d 555, 559 (8th Cir. 1989); *El Fundi v. Deroche*, 625 F.2d 195, 196 (8th Cir. 1980).

In the instant case, a meeting occurred where public officials and private security personnel reached an understanding regarding arrest procedures to be utilized upon the discovery of contraband by the private guards. Although this meeting dealt with the aftermath of searches, and not the manner of searching, the meeting produced a standing arrangement for contacts by the supervising security agent with police during the hours of operation, and a police officer was designated on call to assist with arrests. Emerson testified he was to be the intermediary between the security person conducting the search and the police; as he explained: "They wanted a law enforcement officer making the phone calls which would be for two reasons. One, I am in charge of security and I am a licensed officer."

2. Service of Public Policing Function.

Regardless of direct police involvement, systematic use of random contraband searches serves the general public interest and may reflect pursuit of criminal convictions as well as protection of private interests. *Marsh v. Alabama*, 326 U.S. 501, 90 L. Ed. 265, 66 S. Ct. 276 (1946), supplies the basis for concluding that private investigators and police may be subject to the Fourth Amendment where they are with some regularity engaged in the "public function" of law enforcement. *Id.* at 506. See 1 W. LaFave, § 1.8(d) at 200. See also *Feffer*, 831 F.2d at 739 (private purpose to assist police considered along with government acquiescence in conduct).

Private security guards may share with police an interest in public prosecutions premised on the results of a private search. Here, as already pointed out, the interest of the police was demonstrated in the prior meetings between Emerson and law enforcement officials regarding the procedures to be used. Where some presearch contact between the private party conducting the search and a potentially interested government official is shown, influence may be inferred. 1 W. LaFave, § 1.8(e) at 211 n. 151. The security guards were clearly aiming at discovery of contraband and public prosecution of offenses thus discovered. This was so notwithstanding any private interest in controlling drug-induced misconduct. Emerson testified that vehicles were to be checked on a random basis for contraband.

In addition, private security personnel were utilized here to police a major public activity. Private security guards have been increasingly used as supplements for police protection and perform functions similar to licensed police officers. Here, Emerson employed approximately 127 guards, seven of whom were police officers, for the weekend races at the Brainerd raceway overseeing approximately 78,000 spectators.

Finally, the police-like clothing, equipment, and procedures gave North Country Security personnel the appearance of public authorities. See *Holloway*, 82 Mich. App. at, 267 N.W.2d at 459-60. They wore grey uniforms with badges. Gately carried handcuffs and a gun. Emerson acknowledged that the security guards might look like police officers to the average person. Combined with the use of the police arrest process (handcuffing appellants to fences, conducting body searches), the role of these private security agents extended to a police function, not merely affording private protection.

3. Boundaries of Reasonable Private Policing.

When intrusion goes beyond a reasonable and legitimate means for protecting private property, the practice suggests a need for constitutional protection of individual liberty. *Commonwealth v. Leone*, 386 Mass. 329, 435 N.E.2d 1036, 1041 (1982). The public does not reasonably anticipate, we conclude, a private prerogative for random searches, a regular part of admission to a public event, which are more intrusive than permitted for police authorities. We have examined, in this regard, the nature of the intrusion in the circumstances of this case.

Gately's searches of appellants' vehicles were evidently conducted without consent. Appellants were not given the option of being searched or leaving the raceway. Moreover, Gately exceeded the announced scope of the searches. Although appellants were told that he was only looking for persons trying to enter the race without paying, Gately searched areas of appellants' vehicles which could not possibly have hidden a person. He also testified that the purpose of the searches was to look for contraband as well as trespassers.

4. Police Personnel.

Finally, the identity of private security employees as off-duty policemen is an additional factor to be weighed. See *Williams v. United States*, 341 U.S. 97, 99, 95 L. Ed. 774, 71 S. Ct. 576 (1951) (special police officer who operated a detective agency acted under color of law, and not as a private person, when he used brutal methods to obtain confessions from alleged thieves after being hired by a privately-owned company). Such officers are formally affiliated with the government and usually given authority beyond that of an ordinary citizen. Thus, they may be treated as state agents and subject to the constraints of the Fourth Amendment. *Leone*, 386 Mass. at…435 N.E.2d at 1040 (1982) (comparing public and "purely private" searches).

Emerson, a long-time licensed police officer and special deputy, directed and authorized the searches and instructed security personnel. As a result, private actions became entwined with governmental policies. See *Evans v. Newton*, 382 U.S. 296, 299, 15 L. Ed. 2d 373, 86 S. Ct. 486 (1966). Emerson cannot escape Fourth Amendment limitations by directing a third party to perform a search he could not otherwise conduct himself. See *United States v. West*, 453 F.2d 1351, 1356 (3rd Cir. 1972).

In sum, we observe a combination of factors requiring the conclusion that the activity of private security personnel in this case took on a public character. There was significant official police involvement as indicated by the presearch meetings between Emerson and law enforcement officials. North Country Security agents were engaged in the "public function" of law enforcement. Emerson, as well as a number of the security agents, were licensed police officers. Finally, the searches involved a significant degree of intrusion.

Decision

Because the trial court concluded the search was private, it did not address evidence and argument on the Fourth Amendment issue. On remand, the trial court must weigh the issues for unreasonableness in the search activity, including consent for the scope of the search and the question of whether any contraband was found in the agent's plain view.

Reversed and remanded.

Dissent by: BOWEN

Dissent: BOWEN, Judge (dissenting).

I respectfully dissent. The record before us and before the trial court does not support the majority's conclusion, even applying the majority's criteria, that the searches here were public rather than private.

I agree with the majority that the test, enunciated in *Coolidge v. New Hampshire*, 403 U.S. 443, 487, 29 L. Ed. 2d 564, 91 S. Ct. 2022 (1971), and most recently reiterated by the Supreme Court in *Skinner v. Railway Labor Executives Association*, 489 U.S. 602, 109 S. Ct. 1402, 1411, 103 L. Ed. 2d 639 (1989), is whether the private citizen who conducted the search and seizure acted as an instrument or agent of the government. I part company with the majority, however, on the issue of whether the application of their criteria, or any other criteria recognized by case law, establishes that either Gately or his boss, Emerson, acted here as an instrument or agent of Crow Wing County or the State of Minnesota.

The meeting between Emerson and law enforcement personnel, discussing procedures to be followed upon discovery of contraband, was not initiated by the BCA or by the county sheriff;

rather, it was held to inform Emerson how to contact a law enforcement officer to take over after Emerson or one of his employees discovered contraband and made a citizen's arrest on the BIR property. The law enforcement personnel attending the meeting gave no instructions as to how searches or arrests were to be made. They did, however, insist that one individual, Emerson, call them in, rather than be subjected to the prospect of being called by any of 60 security guards. On the law enforcement side, one deputy sheriff, Dave Bjerga, was assigned as the individual to be called by Emerson. Bjerga, however, was not standing by awaiting calls, but went on performing his regular duties. (In fact, when he was called by Emerson about the searches and arrests here, he was on his way to Long Prairie on another case.) The meeting was the result of Emerson's legitimate concern, on behalf of his private employer, about the logistics of promptly turning over citizen's arrestees to a peace officer, both to comply with statutory requirements and to avoid liability for false arrest. The meeting did not constitute the government instigation or participation required to make these "public" searches. See 1 W. LaFave, Search and Seizure § 1.8(b), at 178 (2d ed. 1987).

BIR had an obvious legitimate interest in avoiding open drug use or drug-induced behavior on its property, something which could jeopardize its continuation in business. BIR initiated entrance-gate vehicle searches to insure that no one entered without having paid for admission, as well as to keep order. The record is devoid of any evidence that BIR's primary purpose was the assistance of public authorities in the prosecution of persons for drug violations.

Admittedly, Gately's searches would not have passed Fourth Amendment muster had they been public searches. However, I can find no authority for assuming a nexus between the unreasonableness of a search and its public or private nature. The fact that Gately engaged in conduct forbidden to a police officer does not make his searches public.

Finally, the fact that seven of Emerson's 127 employees were moonlighting policemen from other jurisdictions does not bring this case within *Williams v. United States*, 341 U.S. 97, 95 L. Ed. 774, 71 S. Ct. 576 (1951). These security guards are not formally affiliated with the government and have no authority beyond that of an ordinary citizen. We cannot treat them as state agents on the record before us. In referring to Emerson as "along-time licensed police officer and special deputy," the majority fails to note that Emerson was a Brainerd police officer, that the BIR is not located in the City of Brainerd, and that Emerson had no authority as a special deputy to make arrests. Neither Emerson nor Gately could lawfully conduct a search or make an arrest except as a private citizen. Nor did either of them hold himself out as a police officer in making the searches and arrests in question.

I find nothing in the majority's reasoning, or in this record, to convince me that Emerson's and Gately's conduct was government-instigated, or that the state or county participated therein. I believe the searches were private searches, not covered by the fourth amendment; I would affirm the judgments of conviction.

Kelley et al. v. Baker Protective Services, Inc., 198 Ga. App. 378; 401 S.E.2d 585 (1991).

Sognier, Chief Judge. McMurray, P. J., and Carley, J., concur.
Opinion by: Sognier

Forrest Kelley and Janet Kelley brought a wrongful death suit against Baker Protective Services, Inc. and its predecessor, Burns International Investigation Services, Inc., for the negligent hiring and retention of an employee, David Scott Goza, an unarmed security guard involved in the

Selected Case Readings   ■   465

murder of Mark Stephen Kelley, the plaintiffs' son. The trial court granted the defendants' motion for summary judgment, and the Kelleys appeal.

We affirm. The record establishes that Goza, who began working for appellee Burns International Investigation Services, Inc. (hereinafter "appellee") in November 1986, was the sole security guard at the Hormel Plant in Tucker, Georgia on January 19, 1987. Goza allowed appellants' decedent and three other men (none of them Hormel employees) to enter the plant premises, apparently to conduct a drug deal. Two of the men then murdered appellants' decedent and the fourth man. Goza did not participate in the murders but did assist in the disposal of the bodies. It is uncontroverted that a background investigation performed on Goza by appellee and various State agencies revealed that Goza had no convictions for any crimes or any record of criminal activity or dangerous propensities, or that any accusations of criminal activities or violent behavior had been made against Goza. Appellants' own investigation into Goza's background uncovered only a traffic warning ticket. Although appellants place great emphasis on evidence in the record indicating that Goza's training as an unarmed security guard did not comport with O.C.G.A. § 43-38-7.1 (a) (training of unarmed private security guards) and the rules and regulations promulgated by the Georgia Board of Private Detective and Security Agencies pursuant to O.C.G.A. § 43-38-4 (d) (3), in his deposition Goza acknowledged that he knew, without being so instructed by anyone at appellee, that he was not supposed to participate in illegal drug transactions or in murdering anyone while on his job.

"'For [appellee] to be negligent in hiring and retaining any employee with violent and criminal propensities, it would be necessary that [appellee] knew or should have known of those dangerous propensities alleged to have resulted in [appellants' decedent's death.] (Cits.) The record contains absolutely no evidence which would authorize a finding that appellee knew or should have known that [Goza] was violently or criminally prone. [Cit.]" *Southern Bell Tel. &c. Co. v. Sharara*, 167 Ga. App. 665, 666 (307 S.E.2d 129) (1983). See also *Big Brother/Big Sister &c. v. Terrell*, 183 Ga. App. 496, 497 (1) (359 S.E.2d 241) (1987); *Edwards v. Robinson-Humphrey Co.*, 164 Ga. App. 876, 880 (298 S.E.2d 600) (1982). The submission of evidence by appellee that it did not know of Goza's criminal propensities after investigating his criminal and employment record and the absence of any evidence controverting appellee's evidence or indicating that appellee should have known of Goza's criminal propensities entitled appellee to summary judgment. *Southern Bell*, supra at 667 (1).

We are not persuaded by appellants' arguments that the trial court's judgment was erroneous. First, we do not agree with appellants that the training Goza was required by statute and agency regulations to receive was designed to uncover the trainee's latent character defects for purposes of placing the employer on notice that the trainee possessed violent or criminal propensities. Thus, appellee's failure to provide that training does not avail appellants. Next, in view of Goza's testimony that he was totally aware that illegal drug transactions and murder were not part of his employment with appellee, we cannot agree with appellants that appellee, in its training, was negligent in failing to state these prohibitions to Goza explicitly. Finally, we cannot agree that a question for jury resolution was created by appellants' supposition, unsupported by any evidence in the record, that Goza would not have allowed the men onto the Hormel plant premises where the murder of their son occurred had appellee informed Goza during his training that participating in drug deals and murder was not appropriate while he was on the job. Appellants having failed to counter appellee's evidence by setting forth specific facts showing that there is a genuine issue for trial, the trial court did not err by granting summary judgment in favor of appellee. O.C.G.A. § 9-11-56 (e).

JUDGMENT AFFIRMED.

Leroy Ross v. Texas One, 796 S.W.2d 206 (Tx. App. 1990).

Justices Whitham, Gordon Rowe, and Baker. Opinion By Justice Gordon Rowe.
Opinion by: Rowe

ROWE, Justice. Leroy Ross appeals from rendition of a summary judgment in favor of Texas One Partnership, doing business as Ewing Estates Apartments. Ross suffered injuries incurred when a security guard patrolling the Ewing Estates Apartments shot Ross with a shotgun. Ross sued James Neal, individually and doing business as Neal Security Company; Johnny Thompson, the security guard; and Texas One Partnership, the owner of the apartments. Texas One moved for summary judgment, contending that it could not be held liable as a matter of law because the security company was an independent contractor. The trial court granted summary judgment in favor of Texas One and severed that action from the rest of the case. In eight points of error, Ross asserts that the trial court erred in granting the summary judgment. We affirm the trial court's judgment.

Summary judgment is proper if the summary judgment record shows that there is no genuine issue as to any material fact and that the movant is entitled to judgment as a matter of law. See Tex. R. Civ. P. 166a(c). The purpose of summary judgment is the elimination of patently unmeritorious claims or untenable defenses; it is not intended to deprive litigants of their right to a full hearing on the merits of any real issue of fact. *Gulbenkian v. Penn*, 151 Tex. 412, 416, 252 S.W.2d 929, 931 (1952). In reviewing the propriety of a summary judgment, we are bound by these standards: (1) the movant has the burden of showing that there is no genuine issue of material fact and that it is entitled to judgment as a matter of law; (2) in deciding whether there is a disputed material fact issue, evidence favorable to the nonmovant will be taken as true; and (3) every reasonable inference must be indulged in favor of the nonmovant and any doubts must be resolved in its favor. *Nixon v. Mr. Property Management Co.*, 690 S.W.2d 546, 548-49 (Tex. 1985).

In the seventh point of error, Ross contends that the summary judgment was erroneously granted because a material fact issue existed as to whether the security company acted as an agent of Texas One. In its motion for summary judgment, Texas One asserted, among other things, that the security company was an independent contractor. The general rule is that an owner of premises is not liable for harm arising out of activity conducted by, and under the control of, an independent contractor. See *Exxon Corp. v. Quinn*, 726 S.W.2d 17, 19 (Tex. 1987); *Abalos v. Oil Dev. Co. of Texas*, 544 S.W.2d 627, 631 (Tex. 1976). The doctrine of respondeat superior is not applicable in such a situation. *Phillips Pipe Line Co. v. McKown*, 580 S.W.2d 435, 438 (Tex. Civ. App.—Tyler 1979, writ ref'd n.r.e.).

An agency relationship cannot be presumed to exist. *Johnson v. Owens*, 629 S.W.2d 873, 875 (Tex. App.—Fort Worth 1982, writ ref'd n.r.e.). Although the question of agency is generally one of fact, *Horne v. Charter Nat'l Ins. Co.*, 614 S.W.2d 182, 184 (Tex. Civ. App.—Fort Worth 1981, writ ref'd n.r.e.), the question of whether a principal–agent relationship exists under established facts is a question of law for the court. *Norton v. Martin*, 703 S.W.2d 267, 272 (Tex. App.—San Antonio 1985, writ ref'd n.r.e.). Thus, the existence of an agency relationship can be a question of law to be determined by the agreement between, and the words and conduct of, the parties. See *Mercedes-Benz of North America, Inc. v. Dickenson*, 720 S.W.2d 844, 858 (Tex. App.—Fort Worth 1986, no writ). In other words, if the facts are uncontroverted or otherwise established, the existence of an agency relationship is a pure question of law. See *American Int'l Trading Corp. v. Petroleos Mexicanos*, 835 F.2d 536, 539 (5th Cir. 1987) (applying Texas law). Proof of agency requires a showing that the alleged principal has the right to assign the agent's task and the right to control the means and details of the process to be used to accomplish the task. *Johnson v. Owens*, 629 S.W.2d at 875.

On the other hand, an independent contractor is one who, in the pursuit of an independent business, undertakes a specific job for another person, using his own means and methods, without submitting himself to the other's control regarding details of the job. *Pitchfork Land and Cattle Co. v. King*, 162 Tex. 331, 338, 346 S.W.2d 598, 602-03 (1961). Thus, the primary test used to decide whether a party is an independent contractor involves determination as to which of the parties to the relationship possesses the "right of control" over the details of the work. See *Newspapers, Inc. v. Love*, 380 S.W.2d 582, 590 (Tex. 1964). Factors used to determine whether one is an independent contractor include: (1) the independent nature of the contractor's business; (2) his obligation to supply necessary tools, supplies, and materials; (3) his right to control the progress of the work except as to final results; (4) the time for which he is employed; and (5) the method by which he is paid, whether by the time or by the job. *Pitchfork*, 346 S.W.2d at 603. When the controlling facts are undisputed and only one reasonable conclusion can be inferred from those facts, the question of whether a party is an independent contractor is a question of law. *Id.*

A contract between the parties which establishes an independent contractor relationship is determinative of the parties' relationship in the absence of extrinsic evidence indicating that the contract was a subterfuge or that the hiring party exercised control in a manner inconsistent with the contractual provisions. See *Newspapers, Inc.*, 380 S.W.2d at 590, 592. The contract between Texas One and the security company specified certain tasks to be undertaken by the security company, but it did not grant to Texas One the right to control the methods and details involved in accomplishing those tasks. The contract provided that the security company would be self-employed and responsible for all insurance.

Ross emphasizes the fact that the contract specified several tasks to be accomplished, as opposed to the one "specific piece of work" referred to in the Pitchfork case. See *Pitchfork*, 346 S.W.2d at 602. This distinction has little or no bearing on the question of whether the security company was an independent contractor. We find no authority suggesting that an independent contractor relationship is confined only to cases in which the contractor undertakes only one task. Ross notes that the contract contemplated that the security company would provide services for an indefinite period of time. Although the period of employment is a factor to be considered, *Pitchfork*, 346 S.W.2d at 603, it is certainly not determinative, since the primary test involves the right of control. We note that the contract granted to both Texas One and the security company the right to terminate the contract upon thirty days' written notice. Ross relies on the fact that the security company was to be paid at regular intervals rather than for any discrete job. The method of payment may be considered, id., but it is not a controlling factor in relation to the ultimate "right of control" test.

We conclude that the contract, viewed alone, established an independent contractor relationship between Texas One and the security company. The contract did not provide that Texas One would possess the right to control the manner and means to be used in accomplishing the tasks assigned to the security company. The contract merely specified some of the tasks to be undertaken. It expressly provided that the security company would be self-employed.

The question remains as to whether the contract was a sham designed to conceal the true relationship between the parties. Establishing that the contract was such a subterfuge requires evidence that Texas One actually exercised control over the details of the work performed by the security company. See *Newspapers, Inc.*, 380 S.W.2d at 590, 592. The summary judgment proof included excerpts from the deposition of James Neal, the owner of the security company. Neal testified that he and another man that he hired as a supervisor were responsible for supervising the security guards employed by the security company. He stated that he had established certain rules and regulations governing the conduct of his security guards. Neal said that he was not an employee of the Ewing Estates Apartments (Texas One), and he stated that his security company provided services to Texas One as an independent contractor. He testified that his company was hired to provide security services using his expertise as he saw fit. Neal said that he used his own means and methods in performing the security services for the Ewing Estates Apartments. This deposition testimony was uncontroverted.

Ross suggests that this testimony was not competent summary judgment evidence because it came from an interested witness. According to the applicable rule, uncontroverted testimonial evidence of an interested witness can provide a basis for summary judgment if the evidence is clear, positive, and direct, otherwise credible and free from contradictions and inconsistencies, and it could have been readily controverted. See Tex. R. Civ. P. 166a(c). We note that, although Neal was an interested witness, we do not see that it was necessarily in his interest to testify to facts that would support the elimination of a fellow defendant. In any event, Ross does not explain how the requirements of rule 166a(c) were not satisfied. In our view, Neal's testimony was clear, positive, direct, otherwise credible, and free from contradictions and inconsistencies. His testimony was consistent with the provisions of the contract between Texas One and the security company. Neal was not the only person who could have testified about the right of control and the nature of the relationship between Texas One and the security company. Under these circumstances, we conclude that Neal's testimony was subject to being readily controverted. See *Kimble v. Aetna Cas. & Sur. Co.*, 767 S.W.2d 846, 848-49 (Tex. App.—Amarillo 1989, writ denied); *Fitzgerald v. Caterpillar Tractor Co.*, 683 S.W.2d 162, 164 (Tex. App.—Fort Worth 1985, writ ref'd n.r.e.). Neal's deposition testimony was competent summary judgment evidence as authorized by rule 166a(c).

Applying the primary "right of control" test, Neal's uncontradicted testimony indicates that the security company was an independent contractor. Other factors that can be considered support this determination. Neal stated that his company performed security work for a number of other customers besides Texas One. This certainly indicates that the security company was a business independent of Texas One. Neal testified that his company supplied the necessary tools and materials used by the security guards (badges, flashlights, guns, ammunition, handcuffs, etc.).

Ross argues that some of the tasks delineated in the contract between Texas One and the security company raise reasonable inferences that the security company personnel received directions from Texas One. Ross notes that the contract provided that the security personnel would show apartments and pass out notices. However, we view the contractual provisions as merely designating some of the tasks to be accomplished. The fact that additional information would have to be conveyed to the security company personnel before the tasks could be carried out does not imply that Texas One would exercise control over the details of the assigned jobs. Specifying the apartments to be shown or the types of notices to be distributed would involve description of the tasks to be accomplished, as opposed to direction as to the manner and means of accomplishment. There was no evidence indicating, for example, that the security personnel were required to follow a script or checklist when showing apartments. Neal testified that the security guards received training arranged by the security company. There was no evidence that Texas One provided any training to the security company personnel.

Based on the evidence and reasonable inferences, we determine that the security company was an independent contractor as a matter of law. We overrule the seventh point of error.

In his first point of error, Ross contends that the trial court erred in granting summary judgment because his petition gave fair notice of an alleged intentional tort, an issue which was not addressed by Texas One's motion for summary judgment. Of course, when allegations in a plaintiff's petition are not controverted by a defendant's summary judgment motion or proof, the granting of summary judgment in favor of the defendant is improper. See *Pollard v. Missouri Pac. R.R.*, 759 S.W.2d 670, 671 (Tex. 1988).

Assuming for the moment that Texas One would be liable for an intentional tort committed by the security company, we nevertheless conclude that Ross's first point of error lacks merit. His petition simply did not allege an intentional tort. The petition describes the alleged shooting incident and then alleges numerous specific acts and omissions, including the shooting itself, which were described as constituting negligence or gross negligence. One of the listed acts of negligence or gross negligence was "willfully discharging a firearm at the Plaintiff with the malicious intent to cause bodily harm and/or death." In a paragraph requesting exemplary damages, Ross alleged "acts and/or omissions of wanton, willful and malicious misconduct." Read in context, the allegations now asserted to be allegations of intentional conduct were in fact allegations of gross negligence. Ross suggests that shooting someone with a gun may be presumed to be intentional. We reject this contention because of the obvious possibility that any given shooting may well have been negligent as opposed to intentional.

Ross relies on the rule that a petition will be construed liberally in favor of the pleader when there are no special exceptions. See *Roark v. Allen*, 633 S.W.2d 804, 809 (Tex. 1982). That rule does not help Ross because his petition contained no fair indication that an intentional tort was being alleged. To be sufficient, a petition must provide fair and adequate notice of the facts upon which the pleader's claim is based, and the opposing party must be supplied with information sufficient to enable him to prepare a defense. *Id.* at 810. Ross's petition specifically alleged both negligence and gross negligence, whereas allegations of intentional conduct were conspicuously absent. Allegations of wantonness, willfulness, and malice were raised in the context of charges of gross negligence and a request for exemplary damages. Ross suggests that Texas One could have specially excepted to the petition to seek clarification. This argument is without merit. We are aware of no authority indicating that a defendant must specially except because a plaintiff has wholly failed to plead an alternative cause of action. Our judicial system rests upon the foundation of adversary presentation, *Fikes v. Ports*, 373 S.W.2d 806, 808 (Tex. Civ. App.—Fort Worth 1963, writ ref'd n.r.e.), and one party is under no obligation to help his adversary plead an unpleaded cause of action. We overrule the first point of error.

We now address the question of whether the summary judgment was warranted in view of the exceptions to the general rule that an owner of premises is not liable for harm caused by the activity of an independent contractor. Ross argues in his second point of error that the summary judgment was erroneously granted because a material fact issue existed as to the personal character of the premises owner's duties owed to the public when taking measures to protect its property. In support of this point of error, Ross relies on *Dupree v. Piggly Wiggly Shop Rite Foods, Inc.*, 542 S.W.2d 882 (Tex. Civ. App.—Corpus Christi 1976, writ ref'd n.r.e.). In that case, the court of appeals held that a grocery chain was liable for an incident of false imprisonment perpetrated by employees of an independent contractor. *Id.* at 890.

There is a crucial distinction between that case and the case before us: the fact that the court was dealing with a case involving an intentional tort, false imprisonment. The court considered an exception to the general rule that an owner of premises is not liable for the conduct of an independent contractor. The court described the exception in this manner:

> [B]ecause of the "personal character" of duties owed to the public by one adopting measures to protect his property, owners and operators of enterprises cannot, by

securing special personnel through an independent contractor for the purposes of protecting property, obtain immunity from liability for at least the intentional torts of the protecting agency or its employees.

Id. at 888; see Annotation, Liability of One Contracting for Private Police or Security Service for Acts of Personnel Supplied, 38 A.L.R.3d 1332, 1339 (1971). The court then analyzed what it described as the leading case adopting this exception, a case involving the intentional tort of false arrest. See *Adams v. F. W. Woolworth Co.*, 144 Misc. 27, 257 N.Y.S. 776 (N.Y. Sup. Ct. 1932). The court quoted extensively from the New York case, including the following:

> This is not the case of a contractor doing his work negligently. Where negligence is the sole basis of the liability, the doctrine of respondeat superior has been held inapplicable to independent contracts. Negligence does not enter into the tort of false arrest. The act itself, if not justified under statute…is tortious, irrespective of negligence.

Dupree, 542 S.W.2d at 889. The court cited a number of other cases from other jurisdictions and stated:

> The weight of the above authorities seems to be that one may not employ or contract with a special agency or detective firm to ferret out the irregularities of its customers or employees and then escape liability for the malicious prosecution or false arrest on the ground that the agency and or its employees are independent contractors…. Such cases adopting this policy have been founded on the principle that he who expects to derive advantage from an act which is done by another for him, must answer for any intentional injury which a third party may sustain from it.

Id. (emphasis added). The *Dupree* court adopted the exception as stated above, and the language used by the court demonstrates that it viewed the exception as applying to intentional torts. The court stated its holding in this way:

> We hold that *Piggly Wiggly* by securing through the guise of an independent contractor, security guards to protect its property by various means, cannot obtain immunity from liability for false imprisonment which such store owner would not be equally entitled to if such owner itself directly selected and paid the agents expressly retaining the power of control and removal, When a store owner undertakes these functions its duties are personal and nonassignable and where the company arranges for and accepts the service, it will not be permitted to say that the relationship of master and servant as far as responsibility is concerned, does not exist. Negligence does not enter into the tort of false imprisonment. The act itself is tortious irrespective of negligence.

Id. at 890 (emphasis in original). Although the court made some abstract statements about nondelegable duty cases involving only negligence, see *id.*, it is clear that the court's holding was based on the fact that the tortious act was intentional. Because the case before us does not involve an intentional tort, Dupree is inapplicable. We therefore overrule Ross's second point of error.

In the third point of error, Ross maintains that the trial court erred in granting summary judgment because a material fact issue existed as to the inherently dangerous activity performed by the security company. There is an exception to the general rule of a hiring party's nonliability for harm caused by an independent contractor. One who hires an independent contractor is liable for injuries caused by the contractor's failure to exercise due care in performing work which is inherently dangerous. *Loyd v. Herrington*, 143 Tex. 135, 138, 182 S.W.2d 1003, 1004 (1944); *Gragg v. Allen*, 481 S.W.2d 452, 454 (Tex. Civ. App.—Waco 1972, writ dism'd w.o.j.). The theory underlying this kind of liability is that one who engages a contractor to do inherently dangerous work remains subject to an absolute, nondelegable duty to see that the work is performed with that degree of care which is appropriate to the circumstances. *Loyd*, 182 S.W.2d at 1004.

The Texas case most closely analogous to this case is *Gessell v. Traweek*, 628 S.W.2d 479 (Tex. App.—Texarkana 1982, writ ref'd n.r.e.). In *Gessell*, a house owned by Elmer Gessell was occupied by his daughter and son-in-law, Betsy and T. W. Larkin. One evening, T. W. Larkin went outside the house to investigate a noise. When he saw a pickup truck speeding away, he shot at the truck, and one of the occupants of the truck was injured. The injured plaintiff argued that T. W. Larkin was an independent contractor hired by Gessell to protect the house and the premises and that the work to be performed was inherently dangerous. *Id.* at 481. The court of appeals quoted two relevant sections of the Restatement (Second) of Torts. Those provisions state:

> One who employs an independent contractor to do work which the employer should recognize as likely to create during its progress a peculiar risk of physical harm to others unless special precautions are taken, is subject to liability for physical harm caused to them by the failure of the contractor to exercise reasonable care to take such precautions, even though the employer has provided for such precautions in the contract or otherwise.

RESTATEMENT (SECOND) OF TORTs § 416 (1965).

One who employs an independent contractor to do work involving a special danger to others which the employer knows or has reason to know to be inherent in or normal to the work, or which he contemplates or has reason to contemplate when making the contract, is subject to liability for physical harm caused to such others by the contractor's failure to take reasonable precautions against such danger.

Id. § 427. The court of appeals then stated that "these sections have no application where the negligence of the contractor creates a new risk not inherent in the work itself." *Gessell*, 628 S.W.2d at 482. The court held as a matter of law that the work of caring for and protecting the property was not inherently dangerous. See *id.* at 482.

Ross argues that the present case is significantly different from the Gessell case. He notes that there was summary judgment evidence that Texas One discussed the use of firearms with the security company. The contract between Texas One and the security company listed the duties of the security company, and those duties included stopping vandalism and drug traffic. Texas One knew that security company personnel were carrying weapons and provided an office on the premises for storage of those weapons. Based on these facts and "reasonable inferences" associated therewith, Ross argues that there was a factual issue as to whether the work undertaken by the security company was inherently dangerous. Specifically, Ross contends that a fact finder could reasonably infer that confrontations would take place between the armed guards and third parties.

At least one Texas court has noted, however, that it has been held that the protection of one's property with firearms does not, in and of itself, constitute an inherently dangerous activity. See *Dupree*, 542 S.W.2d at 888 (citing *Brien v. 18925 Collins Avenue Corp.*, 233 So. 2d 847 (Fla. Dist. Ct. App. 1970), and 38 A.L.R.3d 1332, 1340). In the cited Florida case, the plaintiff appealed from a summary judgment granted in favor of the premises owner. *Brien*, 233 So. 2d at 847-48.

The appellate court held as a matter of law that an owner of real property who hires an independent contractor security company to protect his property is not liable for harm allegedly caused by the negligent discharge of a firearm by an employee of the security company. *Id.* at 849. The court reasoned that lawful activity involving the use of firearms is not inherently dangerous activity. *Id.* The court's holding is consistent with the previously discussed Gessell case.

We conclude that owners of premises should be able to hire independent contractors for purposes of providing armed security and protection of their property without being exposed to automatic liability for the negligent discharge of firearms by employees of the independent contractor. We do not consider it particularly uncommon that protection of property may involve stopping vandalism or drug trafficking. In any event, the summary judgment record contains no indication that the incident involved in this case was related to vandalism or drug trafficking. We follow Brien and hold as a matter of law that the work undertaken by the security company in this case was not inherently dangerous work. The alleged negligent act of discharging the shotgun was not a risk inherent in the work contracted for. See *Gessell*, 628 S.W.2d at 482. We overrule the third point of error.

In his fourth point of error, Ross contends that the summary judgment was erroneous because a material fact issue existed as to whether the activities complained of were contemplated by the contract or in furtherance of the premises owner's business. This point of error is without merit because the "exceptions" to the general rule of nonliability allegedly relied on by Ross simply do not exist, and Ross's reliance on certain cases is misplaced. He states that a party who hires an independent contractor may be found liable for the contractor's activities that are reasonably contemplated by the contract. He cites *Texas Compensation Insurance Co. v. Matthews*, 504 S.W.2d 545, 549 (Tex. Civ. App.—Dallas 1973), rev'd, 519 S.W.2d 630 (Tex. 1974), for this proposition. We note initially that Ross failed to inform this Court that the cited case was reversed. Secondly, the case does not state the proposition asserted by Ross. This Court in Matthews held that the acts of an independent contractor are the acts of the hiring party to the extent that they are required by the contract. 504 S.W.2d at 549. The Court also based its decision on the rule that when work required by a contract is necessarily dangerous, the premises owner and the contractor have a duty to take precautions against the danger. Id. The other case cited by Ross in support of his nonexistent "exception" states that an employer may be held liable for injuries which might reasonably have been contemplated by the parties and which result directly from inherently dangerous work. See *Loyd*, 182 S.W.2d at 1004.

Ross states the other "exception" to the rule of nonliability in this manner: a party who hires an independent contractor may be found liable for the contractor's activities that are in furtherance of the hiring party's business and/or part of the contractor's duties as agent of the hiring party. Of course, if a contractor is in fact an agent of the hiring party, there is no need to resort to an exception to the general rule of nonliability for the acts of independent contractors. In any event, we have already determined that the security company was not an agent of Texas One. We conclude that Ross is apparently attempting to suggest that the security company was in fact Texas One's agent, since the cases he cites in support of his second "exception" involve questions as to whether there was an agency relationship. See *Moore's, Inc. v. Garcia*, 604 S.W.2d 261, 264 (Tex. Civ. App.—Corpus Christi 1980, writ refd n.r.e.); *Patrick v. Miss New Mexico-USA Universe Pageant*, 490 F. Supp. 833, 839 (W.D. Tex. 1980). We find no merit in the fourth point and overrule it.

In the fifth point of error, Ross contends that the trial court erred in granting summary judgment because a material fact issue existed as to whether Texas One used reasonable care in keeping the premises under its control in a safe condition. In arguing this point of error, Ross relies on a number of premises defect cases. However, the present case is not such a case; it is a case involving injury caused by activity conducted on the premises. See *Redinger v. Living, Inc.*, 689 S.W.2d 415, 417 (Tex. 1985). Ross also invokes cases holding that a premises owner may be liable for the acts of an independent contractor if the owner has the right to control, or exercises actual control over, the contractor's acts. See *Pollard*, 759 S.W.2d at 671; *Redinger*, 689 S.W.2d at 418. *Redinger* states that a premises owner may be liable for harm caused by an independent contractor even if the owner retains only some control over the contractor, albeit not the degree of control which would subject him to liability as a master. The owner's role must involve more than a general right to order work to start or stop, to inspect progress, or to receive reports. *Redinger*, 689 S.W.2d at 418.

We have previously discussed the questions of right of control and exercise of control in connection with the seventh point of error. The summary judgment record simply does not indicate that any material fact issues existed regarding control. Both *Pollard* and *Redinger* are readily distinguishable from this case. Ross's reliance on *Nixon v. Mr. Property Management Co.*, 690 S.W.2d 546 (Tex. 1985), is also misplaced because *Nixon* was a premises defect case, and the asserted negligence per se was committed by the premises owner. As noted, the present case is not a premises defect case, and it involves the acts of an independent contractor. We overrule the fifth point of error.

Ross maintains in his sixth point of error that the summary judgment was erroneous because a material fact issue existed as to whether Texas One was negligent in hiring the security company. An employer has a duty to use ordinary care in employing an independent contractor. *Smith v. Baptist Memorial Hosp. Sys.*, 720 S.W.2d 618, 627 (Tex. App.—San Antonio 1986, writ ref'd n.r.e.). One who hires an independent contractor may be held responsible for the contractor's acts if the employer knew or should have known that the contractor was incompetent and a third party is injured because of that incompetency. *Texas American Bank v. Boggess*, 673 S.W.2d 398, 400 (Tex. App.—Fort Worth 1984, writ dism'd by agr.). Thus, one who hires an independent contractor has a duty of ordinary care and reasonable inquiry.

The summary judgment record shows that while the contract between Texas One and the security company was being negotiated, Neal provided to Texas One documentation showing that the security company was licensed by the State of Texas. The record also contains affidavits indicating that Texas One contacted two references regarding the security company. Both references provided favorable reports about the security company. This evidence is uncontroverted. In the absence of controverting evidence or other evidence concerning the duty of reasonable inquiry, we find no basis for Ross's assertion that a material fact issue existed as to whether Texas One knew or should have known that the security company was incompetent when hired. We overrule the sixth point of error.

In the eighth point of error, Ross argues that the trial court erred in granting summary judgment because Texas One's operative pleading did not provide a basis for the summary judgment. Although the record before us does not indicate that Texas One's first amended answer (raising the issues dealt with in the motion for summary judgment) had been separately filed, the answer was attached to Texas One's motion for summary judgment. Moreover, we find no indication that Ross raised this alleged error at the trial court level. Had Ross objected to the alleged defect in pleadings, the defect could have been easily cured. See *Jones v. McSpedden*, 560 S.W.2d 177, 179-80 (Tex. Civ. App.—Dallas 1977, no writ). Because the error now raised on appeal was not brought to the attention of the trial court, any error was waived. See Tex. R. App. P. 52(a); Tex. R. Civ. P. 90, 166a(c). We overrule the eighth point of error.

WE AFFIRM THE JUDGMENT OF THE TRIAL COURT.

Marta Rivas & Alberto Rivas v. Nationwide Personal Security Corporation, 559 So. 2d 668, 15 Fla. L. Weekly D 871 (Fl. App. 1990).

Judges: Hubbart and Cope and Goderich, JJ.
Opinion by: Per Curiam

This is an appeal by the plaintiffs Marta and Alberto Rivas from a final judgment entered in an action for personal injuries arising out of an assault and battery committed by the defendant Arthur Hinton while he was employed at a supermarket for the defendant Nationwide Personal Security Corporation. The jury returned a verdict of $25,000 in compensatory damages and zero dollars in punitive damages against both defendants on the plaintiff Marta Rivas' claim—as well as a verdict of zero dollars against both defendants on the plaintiff Alberto Rivas' claim. The trial court thereafter granted the defendant Nationwide Personal Security Corporation's renewed motion for directed verdict on the plaintiff Marta Rivas' claim. We affirm in part and reverse in part.

First, the plaintiffs are not entitled, as urged, to a new trial based on (1) the trial court's unobjected-to comments during voir dire of the jury and (2) the trial court's refusal to allow two of the plaintiffs' witnesses to testify through an interpreter. The trial court's comments were in no way improper and fall far short of constituting a fundamental error. See *Lusk v. State*, 446 So.2d 1038, 1042 (Fla.), cert. denied, 469 U.S. 873, 105 S. Ct. 229, 83 L. Ed. 2d 158 (1984); *Little v. Bankers Nat'l Life Ins. Co.*, 369 So.2d 637, 638 (Fla. 3d DCA 1979); cf. *Whitenight v. International Patrol & Detective Agency, Inc.*, 483 So.2d 473 (Fla. 3d DCA), rev. denied, 492 So.2d 1333 (Fla. 1986). Moreover, there is no showing that the trial court abused its discretion in refusing an interpreter, as requested, inasmuch as the two witnesses in question testified satisfactorily in English; indeed, there is no indication in this record that their testimony was in any way garbled or incomplete. *Bolender v. State*, 422 So.2d 833, 836-37 (Fla. 1982), cert. denied, 461 U.S. 939, 103 S. Ct. 2111, 77 L. Ed. 2d 315 (1983). This being so, (1) the final judgment entered upon the jury verdict as to the defendant Arthur Hinton on both plaintiffs' claims is affirmed and (2) the final judgment entered in favor of the defendant Nationwide Security Corporation on the plaintiff Alberto Rivas' claim is affirmed.

Second, the trial court, however, committed reversible error in directing a verdict in favor of the defendant Nationwide Personal Security Corporation on the plaintiff Marta Rivas' claim. Contrary to the trial court's determination, we conclude that on this record a jury question was presented as to whether the assault and battery sued upon was committed by the defendant Arthur Hinton within the scope of his employment with the defendant Nationwide Personal Security Corporation. The defendant Hinton was on the job in the supermarket when he became embroiled in a job dispute with the supermarket manager; the plaintiff Marta Rivas, a supermarket cashier, screamed for help when Hinton began choking the manager; Hinton then struck Marta Rivas to silence her and thus diffuse a disruptive situation in the store. In our view, the jury was entitled to conclude, as it did by special interrogatory verdict, that the assault and battery sued upon arose out of a job dispute and was therefore within the scope of Hinton's employment with Nationwide Personal Security Corporation. *Gonpere Corp. v. Rebull*, 440 So.2d 1307 (Fla. 3d DCA 1983); *Parsons v. Weinstein Enter., Inc.*, 387 So.2d 1044 (Fla. 3d DCA 1980); *Lay v. Roux Laboratories, Inc.*, 379 So.2d 451 (Fla. 1st DCA 1980); *Williams v. Florida Realty & Management Co.*, 272 So.2d 176 (Fla. 3d DCA 1973); *Forster v. Red Top Sedan Serv., Inc.*, 257 So.2d 95 (Fla. 3d DCA 1972); *Sixty-Six, Inc. v. Finley*, 224 So.2d 381 (Fla. 3d DCA 1969); *Columbia by the Sea, Inc. v. Petty*, 157 So.2d 190 (Fla. 2d DCA 1963). This being so, the final judgment entered upon the directed verdict in favor of the defendant Nationwide Personal Security Corporation on the plaintiff Marta

Rivas' claim is reversed, and the cause is remanded to the trial court with directions to enter judgment in favor of the plaintiff Marta Rivas based on the jury verdict previously returned.

AFFIRMED IN PART; REVERSED IN PART AND REMANDED.

N.C. Private Protective Services Board v. Gray, Inc., D/B/A Superior Security, 87 N.C. App. 143; 360 S.E.2d 135 (1987).

Judges: Jack Cozort, Judge. Judges Charles L. Becton and John C. Martin concur.
Opinion by: Cozort

Gray, Inc., formerly d/b/a Superior Security, is a guard and patrol company that was, at all times relevant to this appeal, licensed by the North Carolina Private Protective Services Board (the Board). On August 26, 1985 Gray was notified by letter from the Board that a hearing was scheduled for October 4, 1985 to look into allegations that Gray had failed to register unarmed guards and armed guards in accordance with Chapter 74C of the North Carolina General Statutes and regulations adopted pursuant to those statutes. The hearing was rescheduled for December 18, 1985. On December 18, 1985 the Board and Gray entered into a stipulation agreement which stated, among other things, that, in 1983, Gray employed six armed guards and twenty-two unarmed guards which were not registered with the Board; and, in 1984, Gray employed twenty-seven armed guards and twenty unarmed guards which were not registered with the Board. Gray and the Board had agreed to all terms of a settlement except for a $2000.00 "reimbursement" to which Gray objected. On March 21, 1986 the Board issued its final agency decision which, among other things, assessed a civil penalty of $2000.00 and an order for Gray to submit $1071.36 in back registration fees and interest for the unregistered guards.

On April 28, 1986 Gray petitioned for judicial review asking that the $2000.00 assessment be reversed and the matter remanded to the Board for entry of a modified decision. On November 17, 1986, Superior Court Judge Donald L. Smith granted the relief requested by Gray and remanded the case to the Board, ordering that the $2000.00 civil penalty be stricken, and that the Board reconsider "its final agency decision in light of State, *ex rel. Lanier v. Vines*, 274 N.C. 486, 164 S.E. 2d 161 (1968)." The Board appeals. We reverse.

The trial court did not state its reasons for modifying the decision of the agency, as is required under the last sentence of N.C. Gen. Stat. §150A-51 (1983), which provides: "If the court reverses or modifies the decision of the agency, the judge shall set out in writing, which writing shall become a part of the record, the reasons for such reversal or modification." By the trial court's reference to Lanier, id., and by the briefs submitted by the Board and Gray, it is evident that the trial court based its decision on a legal conclusion that the authority of the Board to assess a civil penalty, under N.C. Gen. Stat. § 74C-17(c), violated Art. IV. § 3 of the North Carolina Constitution.

That section provides:

> The General Assembly may vest in administrative agencies established pursuant to law such judicial powers as may be reasonably necessary as an incident to the accomplishment of the purposes for which the agencies were created. Appeals from administrative agencies shall be to the General Court of Justice.

In *Lanier*, our Supreme Court was called upon to consider the constitutionality of statutes which empowered the Commissioner of Insurance to assess a civil penalty of up to $25,000.00, in addition to, or in lieu of, license revocation, against those found in violation of certain insurance laws. In an opinion by Justice Lake, the court found the statute to be in violation of Art. IV, § 3:

The power to revoke a license granted to an insurance agent by the Commissioner, pursuant to chapter 58 of the General Statutes, is "reasonably necessary" to the effective policing of the activities of such agents so as to protect the public from fraud and imposition, one of the purposes for which the Department of Insurance was established. The power to hold hearings and determine facts relating to the conduct of such agent is "reasonably necessary" to the effective and just exercise of the power to grant and revoke such license. The grant of such judicial power to the Commissioner for that purpose is clearly within the authority conferred upon the Legislature by Art. IV, § 3, of the Constitution.

We find, however, no reasonable necessity for conferring upon the Commissioner the judicial power to impose upon an agent a monetary penalty, varying, in the Commissioner's discretion, from a nominal sum to $25,000 for each violation.

Whether a judicial power is "reasonably necessary as an incident to the accomplishment of a purpose for which" an administrative office or agency was created must be determined in each instance in the light of the purpose for which the agency was established and in the light of the nature and extent of the judicial power undertaken to be conferred. We have before us only the attempted grant to the Commissioner of Insurance of the judicial power to impose upon an insurance agent, for one or more of the violations of law specified in G.S. 58-44.6, a penalty, varying in the Commissioner's discretion from a nominal sum to $25,000. We hold such power cannot be granted to him under Art. IV, § 3, of the Constitution of North Carolina.

Lanier, Comr. of Insurance v. Vines, 274 N.C. at 497, 164 S.E. 2d at 167-68. Our review of Lanier leads us to the conclusion that the trial court below erred in its apparent conclusion that N.C. Gen. Stat. § 74C-17(c) violated Art. IV, § 3 of the N.C. Constitution. We note initially that the trial court's action in striking the penalty in its entirety and remanding the cause to the Board to "reconsider its final agency decision in light of... Lanier...and proceed as otherwise is provided or required by Chapter 74C of the General Statutes of North Carolina" (emphasis supplied) is subject to being interpreted as a conclusion by the trial court that Lanier stands for the proposition that administrative agencies are constitutionally barred from assessing civil penalties. We do not find Lanier to mean that all administrative civil penalties are per se in violation of the State Constitution, and we so hold. Rather, the granting of the judicial power to assess a civil penalty must be "reasonably necessary" to the purposes for which the agency was created and with appropriate guidelines for the exercise of the discretion.

Viewing the case at bar in light of Justice Lake's guidelines from *Lanier,* we hold that the authority of the Board under N.C. Gen. Stat. § 74C-17(c) to assess a civil penalty of up to $2000.00 in lieu of revocation or suspension of a license is not an unconstitutional attempt to confer a judicial power on a state agency. This case is readily distinguishable from the situation in *Lanier.* In *Lanier,* the Commissioner could assess a fine from a nominal amount up to $25,000.00 for each violation, in his discretion, and in addition to license revocation or suspension. Under N.C. Gen. Stat. § 74C-17(c), the civil penalty is limited to $2000.00, must be in lieu of license revocation or suspension, and the Board has been given statutory guidance in determining the amount of the penalty: "In determining the amount of any penalty, the Board shall consider the degree and extent of the harm caused by the violation." N.C. Gen. Stat. § 74C-17(c) (1985). We find the provision authorizing civil penalties to be reasonably necessary to the Board in fulfilling its duties to require that those who hold themselves out as providing private protective services to citizens must meet high standards of training and professionalism. The Board's decision was not in violation of any constitutional provisions, and the trial court erred in concluding to the contrary.

We have reviewed the Board's decision under the other five standards set out in N.C. Gen. Stat. § 150A-51 (1983),13 and we find the decision of the agency should be affirmed. The decision of the Superior Court modifying the Board's decision is reversed, and the matter is remanded to the Superior Court for entry of an order affirming the decision of the Board.

REVERSED AND REMANDED.

Andrew J. Neuens v. City of Columbus, 169 F. Supp. 2d 780 (S.D. Ohio, 2001).

Judges: Alegnon L. Marbley, United States District Court.
Opinion by: Alegnon L. Marbley

I. Introduction

This matter is before the Court on all of the Defendants' Motions for Summary Judgment. Defendant City of Columbus, which also filed a Motion for Summary Judgment, has been dismissed as a party by stipulation. Jurisdiction lies under 42 U.S.C. § 1983. A hearing on the Motions for Summary Judgment was held on October 12, 2001.

For the following reasons, the Court hereby GRANTS summary judgment as to the state claim for intentional infliction of emotional distress, and DENIES summary judgment as to the federal claim under 42 U.S.C. § 1983 and the state claim for negligence.

II. FACTS

Because this case comes before the Court on the Defendants' Motions for Summary Judgment, the Court views the facts in the light most favorable to the Plaintiff.

On the evening of December 25, 1998, the Plaintiff, Andrew Neuens, went out with two friends, Nate Faught and Chad Spinosi. The men went first to a neighborhood establishment, then to a dance club. Subsequently, they decided to go to the Waffle House restaurant to eat. They arrived at the Waffle House at 3385 E. Dublin-Granville Road at approximately 2:00 a.m., the morning of December 26, 1998.

According to the Plaintiff, the Waffle House restaurant is fairly small. The outer door leads into a small foyer or hallway, and an inner door opens from that foyer into the restaurant. Inside, the cash registers are directly across from the doorway. To the right of the registers is a jukebox, behind which are three of the restaurant's booths.

When the Plaintiff and his companions entered the Waffle House, they seated themselves in the first booth nearest the door, behind the jukebox. The Plaintiff sat alone on the side of the booth that allowed him to face the door and cash registers. Mr. Faught and Mr. Spinosi sat across from him, facing the other booths. Upon entering the restaurant, the men noticed a security guard, Defendant John Padgett, by the door.

Soon after the Plaintiff and his friends began to eat the food they had ordered, a group of people consisting of Defendants Bridges, Parker, and Kincaid, along with another man and two women ("Defendant group"), entered the restaurant. Prior to entering the Waffle House, the Defendant group had been at a bowling alley. While there, some members of the group, including Defendant Parker, engaged in a fight, which Defendant Bridges, who is a police officer, took no action to prevent, stop, or report. According to the Plaintiff, the Defendant group began creating problems as soon as they entered the Waffle House by acting "loud, drunk, and obnoxious." Defendant Bridges acknowledged that at least two members of his group were visibly inebriated, and that he himself had probably consumed alcohol that night, as well. When they came in, the Defendant group seated itself at the third booth behind the jukebox.

According to the Plaintiff, the Defendant group continued to harass the Plaintiff and his companions even after they sat down at their booth. Specifically, Defendant Kincaid yelled expletives toward them. Although neither the Plaintiff nor his friends had ever met anyone in the Defendant group prior to that encounter, apparently some members of the Defendant group mistook the Plaintiff and his friends for the people with whom they had fought at the bowling alley earlier that evening.

As the Plaintiff, Mr. Faught, and Mr. Spinosi finished their meals, the tension between the two groups grew. Margaret Tracy, the waitress for both tables, believed that the tension was escalating to the point that it would ultimately lead to violence. According to Waffle House policy as printed in the Waffle House employee handbook, if an employee sees a situation in the restaurant that she believes will imminently turn to violence, she has a duty to report that situation to a manager. Despite this Waffle House rule, Ms. Tracy did not report the situation that she observed between the Plaintiff and the Defendants to her manager. According to her deposition testimony, however, Ms. Tracy did inform the security guard, Defendant Padgett, that she was concerned that a fight would soon erupt.

When the Plaintiff and his companions finished eating their meal, Defendant Padgett approached their table and advised them to leave the restaurant. Subsequently, Mr. Spinosi got out of the booth, and turned to walk out of the restaurant. According to the Plaintiff, as soon as Mr. Spinosi got up, the Defendant group also got up, passed the Plaintiff's table, and moved toward the exit. Before Mr. Spinosi reached the outer door, but after he had gone through the inner door, Defendant Parker pushed him from behind. As Mr. Spinosi turned around, he was then punched twice in the face, first by Defendant Parker, and then by Defendant Kincaid.

The Plaintiff stood up from his table after the Defendant group had already passed by. As he approached the cash register, he heard a commotion behind him, and turned to see what was happening. The next thing the Plaintiff remembers is waking up in the hospital hours later. The Plaintiff subsequently learned that Defendant Parker, after punching Mr. Spinosi, walked toward the register and punched the Plaintiff from behind, knocking him to the floor, unconscious. Apparently, Defendant Parker then kicked the Plaintiff in the head. Defendant Officer Bridges admits seeing Defendant Parker standing near the Plaintiff, but denies seeing Defendant Parker punch or kick him. Nonetheless, at that point, Defendant Bridges grabbed Defendant Parker and pulled him out of the restaurant. The Defendant group then departed the Waffle House in two separate vehicles.

It is unclear whether Defendant Padgett tried physically to restrain Defendants Kincaid and Parker during this incident. Mr. Faught testified during his deposition that the security guard did nothing other than caution the other members of the Defendant group not to get involved. After the Defendant group left, however, Defendant Padgett radioed his employer, Defendant Smith Detective & Security, Inc. ("SDSI" or "Smith Security") for backup. After contacting his employer, a Smith Security supervisor and a uniformed Columbus police officer arrived at the Waffle House within four minutes.

As a result of this incident, the Plaintiff was taken to a hospital, where he was treated for injuries to his eye, severe lacerations to his eyebrows and lips, and a concussion, along with other minor injuries. On December 23, 1999, the Plaintiff filed a Complaint against Defendants City of Columbus, Ohio, Officer Bridges, Ernest Parker, Josh Kincaid, John Padgett, Smith Detective & Security, Inc., and J. Thomas & Co., Inc. (d/b/a Waffle House). The Complaint raised federal claims against the City of Columbus and Officer Bridges for violations of 42 U.S.C. § 1983 and 42 U.S.C. § 1985. The Complaint additionally raised state claims against the Defendants for assault and battery, intentional infliction of emotional distress, negligent infliction of emotional distress, and negligence.

III. Standard of Review

Summary judgment is appropriate "if the pleadings, depositions, answers to interrogatories, and admissions on file, together with the affidavits, if any, show there is no genuine issue as to any material fact and the moving party is entitled to judgment as a matter of law." FED. R. CIV. P. 56(c). The movant has the burden of establishing that there are no genuine issues of material fact, which may be accomplished by demonstrating that the nonmoving party lacks evidence to support an essential element of its case. *Celotex Corp. v. Catrett*, 477 U.S. 317, 322-23, 91 L. Ed. 2d 265, 106 S.Ct. 2548 (1986); *Barnhart v. Pickrel, Schaeffer & Ebeling Co.*, 12 F.3d1382, 1388-89 (6th Cir. 1993). The nonmoving party must then present "significant probative evidence" to show that "there is [more than] some metaphysical doubt as to the material facts." *Moore v. Philip Morris Cos.*, 8 F.3d 335, 340 (6th Cir. 1993) (citation omitted). "Summary judgment will not lie if the dispute is about a material fact that is 'genuine,' that is, if the evidence is such that a reasonable jury could return a verdict for the non-moving party." *Anderson v. Liberty Lobby, Inc.*, 477 U.S. 242, 248, 91 L. Ed. 2d 202, 106 S. Ct. 2505 (1986); see also *Matsushita Elec. Indus. Co. v. Zenith Radio Corp.*, 475 U.S. 574, 587, 89 L. Ed. 2d 538, 106 S. Ct. 1348 (1986) (finding summary judgment appropriate when the evidence could not lead a trier of fact to find for the nonmoving party).

In evaluating a motion for summary judgment, the evidence must be viewed in the light most favorable to the nonmoving party. *Adickes v. S.H. Kress & Co.*, 398 U.S. 144, 157, 26 L. Ed. 2d 142, 90 S. Ct. 1598 (1970). In responding to a motion for summary judgment, however, the nonmoving party "may not rest upon its mere allegations...but...must set forth specific facts showing that there is a genuine issue for trial." FED. R. CIV. P. 56(e); see Celotex, 477 U.S. at 324; *Searcy v. City of Dayton*, 38 F.3d 282, 286 (6th Cir. 1994). Furthermore, the existence of a mere scintilla of evidence in support of the nonmoving party's position will not be sufficient; there must be evidence on which the jury could reasonably find for the nonmoving party. *Anderson*, 477 U.S. at 251; *Copeland v. Machulis*, 57 F.3d 476, 479 (6th Cir. 1995).

IV. Discussion

A. Federal Claims

The Plaintiff's First Amended Complaint asserted federal claims under 42 U.S.C. §§ 1983 and 1985 against the City of Columbus and Defendant Officer Bridges. On June 25, 2001, a Stipulation was entered dismissing the City of Columbus as a party. At the hearing on the Motions for Summary Judgment, the Plaintiff acknowledged that he is no longer pursuing his claim under § 1985. Therefore, the only remaining federal claim is the § 1983 claim brought against Defendant Bridges. Specifically, the Plaintiff asserts that Defendant Bridges violated his right to substantive due process, protected by the Fourteenth Amendment to the United States Constitution. Defendant Officer Bridges has asserted the affirmative defense of qualified immunity against this claim.

1.42 U.S.C. § 1983

The Plaintiff has alleged that Defendant Bridges infringed the Plaintiff's constitutional rights in violation of 42 U.S.C. § 1983.15 To succeed on a§ 1983 claim, the plaintiff must show that (1) a person acting under color of law (2) deprived him of his rights secured by the United State Constitution or its laws. *O'Brien v. City of Grand Rapids*, 23 F.3d 990, 995 (6th Cir. 1994). At oral argument on the Motions for Summary Judgment, Defendant Bridges conceded that he was acting under color of law at the time of this incident. Therefore, the Court addresses only the issue of whether Defendant Bridges deprived the Plaintiff of his substantive due process rights under the Fourteenth Amendment.

The Due Process Clause of the Fourteenth Amendment does not impose upon the state an affirmative duty to protect its citizens against private acts of violence; rather, the amendment only limits the state's ability to take affirmative action that denies an individual of life, liberty, or property without due process. *DeShaney v. Winnebago County Dep't of Social Servs.*, 489 U.S. 189, 195, 103 L. Ed. 2d 249, 109 S. Ct. 998 (1989). Nonetheless, the state may be liable for private acts when the state acts in some way to increase the danger to individuals from those private acts. Id. at 201. ("While the State may have been aware of the dangers that [the plaintiff] faced in the free world, it played no part in their creation, nor did it do anything to render him any more vulnerable to them.") The Sixth Circuit has relied on *DeShaney* to establish a state-created danger theory of substantive due process liability. *Kallstrom v. City of Columbus*, 136 F.3d 1055, 1066 (6th Cir. 1998); *Gazette v. City of Pontiac*, 41 F.3d 1061, 1065 (6th Cir. 1994). ("In DeShaney, the Supreme Court...stated that a duty to protect can arise in a noncustodial setting if the state does anything to render an individual more vulnerable to danger.")

Specifically, a plaintiff must show three elements to succeed on a state-created danger claim. First, the Plaintiff must demonstrate that the state actor took affirmative actions that "either create or increase the risk that an individual will be exposed to private acts of violence." *Kallstrom*, 136 F.3d at 1066 (citing *Sargi v. Kent City Bd. of Educ.*, 70 F.3d 907, 913 (6th Cir. 1995)). Second, the Plaintiff must show that the state actor created a "special danger," which can be done through a showing that the state's actions placed the specific victim at risk, as opposed to placing the general public at risk. Id. (explaining that this element is necessary to distinguish actions giving rise to liability from actions that the state takes every day that can potentially increase any person's risk of harm, such as releasing someone from police custody). Third, the state actor must have known, or clearly should have known, that his actions "specifically endangered an individual." *Id.* (citations omitted).

The affirmative action requirement of the state-created danger claim arises out of *DeShaney's* holding that the state generally is under no obligation to protect citizens from the private acts of others. Although it is true that the state cannot be liable when it has done nothing to increase the risk of harm to an individual, the converse is also true. Thus, "if the state puts a man in a position of danger from private persons and then fails to protect him, it will not be heard to say that its role was merely passive; it is as much an active tortfeasor as if it had thrown him into a snake pit." *Kallstrom*, 136 F.3d at 1066 (quoting *Bowers v. DeVito*, 686 F.2d 616, 618 (7th Cir. 1982)). Accordingly, state actors have been found liable for violating an individual's right to substantive due process when they have affirmatively placed that individual in a position of increased risk of harm. See *Kallstrom*, 136 F.3d at 1066 (finding that the city's affirmative act of giving personal information regarding officers and their families to defense counsel for a violent gang that the officers helped to prosecute placed the officers in serious risk of harm); *Davis v. Brady*, 143 F.3d 1021, 1023-25 (6th Cir. 1998) (concluding that officers placed the plaintiff in greater harm than he would have been if they had not acted at all when they abandoned the plaintiff, while he was inebriated, on an unfamiliar highway, and was subsequently hit by a car); *Stemler v. City of Florence*, 126 F.3d 856, 868-69 (6th Cir. 1997) (stating that officers did not merely fail to protect the victim, but increased her risk of harm when they took her out of her friend's car and physically placed her in the truck of her intoxicated boyfriend, who subsequently crashed into a guardrail, killing the victim). Furthermore, state actors have been found liable when they have deliberately decided not to act in a certain way, such that their inaction increased the risk of harm to a particular individual. See *Culberson v. Doan*, 125 F. Supp. 2d 252 (S.D. 2000); *Sheets v. Mullins*,109 F. Supp. 2d 879 (S.D. Ohio 2000); *Smith v. City of Elyria*, 857 F. Supp. 1203 (N.D. Ohio 1994).

In Culberson, the police chief was alerted to the fact that the body of the decedent whose murder was being investigated was probably located in a certain pond. *Culberson*, 125 F. Supp. 2d at 268. Although the police chief was alerted to this fact in the presence of the suspected killer, a man who was a good friend of the police chief, he nonetheless determined not to secure the decedent's body, and to postpone searching the pond until the next day, despite the risk that the evidence could be tampered with or the body removed. *Id*. The next day, when the pond was drained, no body was found, but there were footprints on the bottom of the pond and muddy prints coming out of the water, indicating that someone could have recently removed something from the pond. *Id*. at 269. The court determined that these facts presented a genuine issue of material fact as to whether the police chief made the plaintiffs more vulnerable to the danger that their daughter's body would be removed from the pond. *Id*. Thus, the court determined that the plaintiffs raised a genuine issue of material fact when the defendant's alleged affirmative action was a "deliberate choice" not to act in such a way as to prevent the ultimate harm.

In *Sheets*, the plaintiff called the police, seeking help to retrieve her daughter from the father, Roger Montgomery, who had custody of the daughter and who had assaulted and threatened the plaintiff with a gun and a knife, and threatened to kill their daughter. *Sheets*, 109 F. Supp. 2d at 882. The officer, however, (1) told the plaintiff that she would have to go to court to try to get custody of the child, rather than try to get her daughter back herself; (2) stopped looking for Montgomery after not finding him at his home, even though the plaintiff had already said he was elsewhere; and (3) failed to indicate to officers who took over his shift that Montgomery had threatened to kill the child over whom he had physical custody. *Id*. Furthermore, when Montgomery called the officer, with whom he was close friends, a couple days later, the officer failed to try to ascertain his location. *Id*. at 883. Four days after the plaintiff made her initial complaints, Montgomery killed the child and himself. *Id*. Based on these facts, the court found that the plaintiff had raised a genuine issue of material fact as to whether the officer increased the danger to the baby who was killed. *Id*. at 890. Thus, the court in Sheets, like the court in Culberson, looked to the officer's decisions not to act in such a way that could have prevented the crime to conclude that the plaintiff posed a genuine issue as to whether the officer's actions increased the risk of harm to the minor child.

In *Smith*, the plaintiffs alleged that officers who were called out to a woman's home when she sought to have her ex-husband removed there from refused to remove him and merely told

482 ■ *Private Security and the Law*

the woman to initiate eviction proceedings if she wanted him out. *Smith*, 857 F. Supp. at 1206. Furthermore, the officers told the ex-husband that if his ex-wife continued to throw his belongings out of the house, he could bring them back in. *Id.* Subsequently, the ex-husband stabbed and killed the woman. *Id.* at 1207. The court found that "the facts here support a claim that the police officers' affirmative acts created or increased the danger to [the decedent]. The police officers did not merely fail to perform their duties; they told [the ex-husband] that he did not have to leave, and advised him to go back if [his ex-wife] tried to throw him out." *Id.* at 1210. Thus, the court found that the plaintiffs had presented sufficient evidence to prevent summary judgment on their substantive due process claim, on the ground that the private actor may have used the "apparent authority" given to him by the officers to remain in his ex-wife's home, where he later killed her. *Id.* (finding that the plaintiffs raised a genuine issue of material fact as to whether the police officers "affirmatively increased the danger to [the decedent] while limiting her ability to help herself and [making] her more vulnerable to attack").

Here, as in the above cited cases, the Plaintiff has presented sufficient evidence to raise a genuine issue of material fact as to whether Defendant Officer Bridges' actions on the night of the altercation increased the Plaintiff's vulnerability to harm, giving rise to liability under the state-created danger theory. Specifically, a reasonable trier of fact could conclude that, although Defendant Bridges took no part in either the planning or commission of this assault, he made a deliberate decision not to prevent his friends from acting as they did, either at the Waffle House or earlier at the bowling alley. A reasonable trier of fact could conclude that this purposeful decision by Defendant Bridges, evidenced by his failure to prevent, intervene in, or report the altercations, caused Defendants Parker and Kincaid to feel more bold in their assault on the Plaintiff. A trier of fact might conclude that, were it not for the presence and tacit approval of their friend, the police officer, Defendants Parker and Kincaid would not have acted toward the Plaintiff as they did. Like the ex-husband in Smith, Defendants Parker and Kincaid may have used the apparent authority given to them by Defendant Bridges to attack, assault and batter the Plaintiff. Thus, Defendant Bridges' affirmative decision could be found to be the affirmative act that formed the basis of a substantive due process violation because that decision created an atmosphere of increased danger to the Plaintiff.

In addition to the affirmative act requirement, the Plaintiff must show that the Defendant's actions created a "special danger" that placed the Plaintiff specifically at risk. *Sheets*, 109 F. Supp. 2d at 889. This Court finds that the Plaintiff has presented sufficient evidence for a reasonable trier of fact to conclude that Defendant Bridges's failure to act under the circumstances created a danger specifically to the Plaintiff and his companions. As alleged herein, the evidence gives no indication that anyone else in the restaurant, let alone in the general public, would have been endangered by Defendant Bridges' actions.

Finally, the Plaintiff must show that the Defendant knew or should have known that his actions would result in harm to the Plaintiff, the specific individual who was ultimately harmed. See *Duvall v. Ford*, 1999 U.S. App. LEXIS 15161, No. 98-5777, 1999 WL 486531, at *3 (6th Cir. July 1, 1999) (determining that the defendants' conduct of releasing a prisoner into a work release program with minimal supervision without first checking his criminal background was too attenuated from the ultimate harm resulted after the prisoner escaped from that program for the defendants to have known that their actions would cause harm to the victim); *Gazette*, 41 F.3d at 1066-67 (concluding that there could be no substantive due process violation because the defendant police officers' failure to aggressively investigate a missing person's report was too remote from the ultimate harm of the victim's death for them to have known that such harm could result from their actions). A reasonable trier of fact could conclude that, under the circumstances,

Defendant Bridges knew or should have known that his failure to prevent his friends from acting as they did would result in harm specifically to the Plaintiff.

Based on the foregoing, the Court finds that the Plaintiff has presented sufficient evidence to raise genuine issues of material fact as to whether Defendant Bridges infringed the Plaintiff's right to substantive due process under a state-created danger theory of liability. The Court, therefore, DENIES the Defendant's Motion for Summary Judgment on the Plaintiff's § 1983 claim.

2. Qualified Immunity

Government officials sued in their individual capacities are entitled to seek qualified immunity. *Harlow v. Fitzgerald*, 457 U.S. 800, 818, 73 L. Ed. 2d 396, 102 S. Ct. 2727 (1982). Qualified immunity extends to individuals performing discretionary functions unless their actions violate "clearly established statutory or constitutional rights of which a reasonable person would have known." *Id.* A right is "clearly established" if "[a] reasonable official would understand that what he is doing violates that right." *Anderson v. Creighton*, 483 U.S. 635, 640, 97 L. Ed. 2d 523, 107 S. Ct. 3034 (1987). This means only that the unlawfulness of the act must have been apparent in light of preexisting law, even if the precise action at issue was not previously held to be unlawful. *Id.* at 640.

At the time of this incident, it was clearly established within the Sixth Circuit that an individual has a right to be free from state-created danger. *Kallstrom*, 136 F.3d at 1066; Gazette, 41 F.3d at 1065 (citing *DeShaney* for the proposition that there may be a duty to protect when the state leaves an individual more vulnerable to danger than he would have been had the state actor not intervened at all). The Sixth Circuit and district courts within the circuit had clearly recognized that a state actor can be liable if he acts so as to significantly increase the risk of danger to an individual from a third party. See discussion supra Part IV.A.1. Based on the state of the case law in December 1998, the Court finds that a reasonable person in Defendant Bridges's position would have known that a state actor could be liable under § 1983 for taking actions that increase an individual's vulnerability to harm from third parties. Therefore, Defendant Bridges is not entitled to the affirmative defense of qualified immunity.

B. State Law Claims

The Plaintiff has raised numerous state law claims against each of the Defendants. First, the Plaintiff asserted claims of assault and battery against Defendants Parker, Kincaid, and Bridges. He subsequently voluntarily dismissed that claim as against Defendant Bridges, and Defendants Parker and Kincaid have not filed motions for summary judgment. Second, the Plaintiff asserted a claim of intentional infliction of emotional distress against Defendants Parker, Kincaid, and Bridges. Only Defendant Bridges has filed a Motion for Summary Judgment on that claim. Third, the Plaintiff asserted claims of negligence against Defendants J. Thomas & Co. ("Waffle House"), SDSI, and John Padgett. Each of those Defendants has filed a Motion for Summary Judgment. Therefore, for the purpose of ruling on the Defendants' Motions for Summary Judgment, the Court will discuss only the Plaintiff's claims of intentional infliction of emotional distress and negligence.

1. Intentional Infliction of Emotional Distress

The Plaintiff's First Amended Complaint alleged a cause of action for intentional infliction of emotional distress against Defendants Bridges, Kincaid, and Parker. Only Defendant Bridges has moved for summary judgment with respect to this claim.

In order to prove a claim of intentional infliction of emotional distress, the plaintiff must show that the defendant intentionally or recklessly caused him serious emotional distress by extreme and outrageous conduct. *McNeil v. Case W. Reserve Univ.*, 105 Ohio App. 3d 588, 664 N.E.2d 973, 975 (Ohio 1995) (citing *Yeager v. Local Union 20*, 6 Ohio St. 3d 369, 453 N.E.2d 666 (Ohio 1983)). The behavior complained of must go beyond the intentionally tortious or even the criminal. *Yeager*, 453 N.E.2d at 671. Rather, the conduct must be so extreme and outrageous as "'to be regarded as atrocious, and utterly intolerable in a civilized community.'" 453 N.E.2d at 671 (quoting Rest. 2d of Torts § 46, cmt. d (1965)). Furthermore, the emotional distress allegedly suffered must be serious. *Id.* In order to defeat a Motion for Summary Judgment on a claim of intentional infliction of emotional distress, the plaintiff must present evidence sufficient to create a genuine issue of material fact as to the defendant's behavior and the severity of the injury suffered. *McNeil*, 664 N.E.2d at 975-76; see *Uebelacker v. Cincom Systems, Inc.*, 48 Ohio App. 3d 268, 549 N.E.2d 1210, 1220 (Ohio Ct. App. 1988) (finding that the plaintiff raised a genuine issue of material fact as to his emotional distress when he submitted along with his pleadings an affidavit from his wife detailing the various symptoms of his distress).

The Court finds that the Plaintiff has not presented sufficient evidence to create a genuine issue of material fact on his claim of intentional infliction of emotional distress. First, even when viewed in the light most favorable to the Plaintiff, Defendant Bridges' actions, while possibly negligent or even reckless, do not rise to the level of extreme or outrageous conduct, as that standard has been interpreted by the case law. See *Retterer v. Whirlpool Corp.*, 111 Ohio App. 3d 847, 677 N.E.2d 417, 421-23 (Ohio Ct. App. 1996) (upholding the lower court's grant of summary judgment for the defendants on a claim of intentional infliction of emotional distress where, among other things, the defendants, the plaintiff's supervisors at work, repeatedly called him into their office under threat of termination and then restrained him by his wrists as they "poked" and "tickled" him on his chest and stomach so that he would "jump and flop"); *McNeil*, 664 N.E.2d at 976 (finding no extreme or outrageous conduct by the employer when an employee continuously harassed and threatened to assault a fellow employee).

Even if a trier of fact finds that the Defendant did make a conscious decision to allow his friends to commit assault and battery upon the Plaintiff and then help them flee, those actions without more are not extreme and outrageous. Second, although the Plaintiff has alleged that he has suffered emotional distress to the point of not being able to perform normal daily functions or work for some period of time, this bare allegation without any evidentiary support is insufficient to defeat the Defendant's Motion for Summary Judgment. See *Hockenberry v. Village of Carrollton*, 110 F. Supp. 2d 597, 605 (N.D. Ohio 2000) (granting summary judgment for the defendant where the plaintiff failed to provide any specific evidence that would support his allegation that he and his family suffered serious emotional distress).

Therefore, the Court hereby GRANTS summary judgment in favor of Defendant Bridges on the Plaintiff's claim of intentional infliction of emotional distress.

2. Negligence

The Plaintiff has asserted claims of negligence against the Waffle House, SDSI, John Padgett, and Officer Bridges.

In order to assert a successful claim of negligence under Ohio law, a plaintiff must show that (1) the defendant owed a duty to the plaintiff; (2) the defendant breached that duty; and (3) as a result of that breach, the defendant proximately caused actual loss or damage to the plaintiff. *Mussivand v. David*, 45 Ohio St. 3d 314, 544 N.E.2d 265, 270 (Ohio 1989); *Deeds v. Am. Sec.*, 39 Ohio App. 3d 31, 528 N.E.2d 1308, 1311 (Ohio Ct. App. 1987).

a. Officer Bridges

The Plaintiff states in his Memorandum Contra Defendant Bridges' Motion for Summary Judgment that he asserted a state law claim of negligence against Defendant Bridges. In the First Amended Complaint, however, the Plaintiff raised allegations of negligence only as to Defendants Waffle House, SDSI, and Padgett. The Plaintiff has not subsequently amended his Complaint to add a claim of negligence against Defendant Bridges.

Under the Federal Rules of Civil Procedure, "[a] pleading which sets forth a claim for relief... shall contain...a short and plain statement of the claim showing that the pleader is entitled to relief." FED. R. CIV. P. 8 (a). Furthermore, a plaintiff may not use a summary judgment motion to raise a claim that he failed to state in his complaint. *Lombard v. MCI Telecomm. Corp.*, 13 F. Supp. 2d 621, 626 (N.D. Ohio 1998) (citations omitted). Although usually this rule applies to prevent a plaintiff from asserting additional claims in his own motion for summary judgment, it applies equally here, where the Plaintiff is attempting to use the Defendant's Motion for Summary Judgment to state a claim that he omitted from his Complaint.

Based on the above rules, the Court finds that the Plaintiff has not adequately set forth a claim of negligence against Defendant Bridges in his Complaint, and he cannot now use the Defendant's Motion for Summary Judgment to do so. Defendant Bridges' Motion for Summary Judgment on the Plaintiff's alleged negligence claim is GRANTED.

b. Waffle House

The Plaintiff alleges that the Waffle House is negligent because it had a duty to provide a safe, secure, and reasonable environment to Waffle House patrons, and breached that duty when it allowed the Defendants to strike him.

As the owner of the premises on which this incident occurred, the Waffle House owed the Plaintiff, an invitee, a duty of ordinary care. *Newton v. Penn. Iron & Coal, Inc.*, 85 Ohio App. 3d 353, 619 N.E.2d 1081, 1083 (Ohio Ct. App. 1993) (recognizing the common law rule that landowners owe a duty of ordinary care to invitees, people whom the landowner invites onto his land for his own benefit). Where the premises owner does not, and in the exercise of ordinary care could not, know of a danger that causes injury to the invitee, the owner is not liable for the injury. *Howard v. Rogers*, 19 Ohio St. 2d 42, 249 N.E.2d 804, 807 (Ohio 1969). Such knowledge of a danger depends on the foreseeability of the harm. *Daily v. K-Mart Corp.*, 9 Ohio Misc. 2d 1, 458 N.E.2d 471, 474 (Ohio Com. Pl. 1981). Foreseeability of the harm may arise from prior incidents of a similar nature on the premises. *Townsley v. Cincinnati Gardens, Inc.*, 39 Ohio App. 2d 5, 314 N.E.2d 409, 411 (Ohio Ct. App. 1974). Ohio courts, however, have ruled that a totality of the circumstances approach is the preferable method for determining whether the ultimate harm was foreseeable. *Reitz v. May Co. Dept. Stores*, 66 Ohio App. 3d 188, 583 N.E.2d 1071, 1074 (Ohio Ct. App. 1990). Under either approach, the ultimate harm may be generally foreseeable, based on the type of activity that could be expected to occur on the premises at any time, specifically foreseeable due to the particular circumstances leading up to the harm. See 583 N.E.2d at 1075 (discussing Rest. 2d of Torts § 344, which provides that if the premises owner, based on his past experience or knowledge of his business, "should reasonably anticipate careless or criminal conduct on the part of third persons, either generally or at some particular time, he may be under a duty to take precautions against it").

The Court believes that the Plaintiff has presented sufficient evidence to raise a genuine issue of material fact as to whether the harm that the Plaintiff incurred was foreseeable to the Waffle House. The Plaintiff has presented evidence that, under the totality of the circumstances approach, this particular incident was foreseeable based on the behavior of the Defendants and their interactions with the Plaintiff and his companions throughout their time at the Waffle House on this particular night. Additionally, the Plaintiff has presented some evidentiary support for his claim that, not only was the incident foreseeable, but it was actually foreseen by at least one Waffle House employee.

The Court finds, based on the above, that a reasonable trier of fact could find that the harm to the Plaintiff was foreseeable to the Waffle House. Furthermore, a trier of fact drawing such a conclusion could also find that the Waffle House breached its duty of ordinary care when it failed to prevent this foreseeable harm. Therefore, the Court DENIES Defendant Waffle House's Motion for Summary Judgment as to the Plaintiff's claim of negligence.

c. SDSI and John Padgett

SDSI has a contract with the Waffle House to provide security for the restaurant. Under the contract, SDSI assigns one of its employee security guards to work in the restaurant. On the night in question, SDSI employee John Padgett was the security guard at the Waffle House.

The Plaintiff alleges that SDSI and Security Officer John Padgett were negligent because they breached their duty to provide a safe, secure, and reasonable environment to Waffle House patrons. The claim against SDSI is premised on a respondeat superior theory of liability for the Security Officer's negligence, as well as claims of negligent hiring, retention, and supervision of Defendant Padgett. As to the respondeat superior theory, the Plaintiff alleges that because the security officer acted negligently while acting as an employee of SDSI, within the scope of his employment, SDSI can be liable for his negligence. See *Cooper v. Grace Baptist Church of Columbus, Ohio, Inc.*, 81 Ohio App. 3d 728, 612 N.E.2d 357, 362 (Ohio Ct. App. 1992) (asserting that for respondeat superior to apply, the employee must be liable for a tort committed in the scope of his employment).The Plaintiff bases his allegation of Defendant Padgett's negligence on his failure to prevent the harm to the Plaintiff, particularly in light of the fact that, according to the Plaintiff, a Waffle House waitress had notified him that a fight was probably going to ensue.

Ohio law imposes no heightened duty to prevent a third party from harming another absent a special relationship between the would-be rescuer and the victim. *Gelbman v. Second Nat'l Bank of Warren*, 9 Ohio St. 3d 77, 458 N.E.2d 1262, 1263 (Ohio 1984) (citing Rest. 2d of Torts §§ 314, 315). In the case of private security guards, an increased duty to protect individuals from harm by third parties will be imposed only when such a duty is specified in the guard's contract. *Eagle v. Mathews-Click-Bauman, Inc.*, 104 Ohio App. 3d 792, 663 N.E.2d 399, 402 (Ohio Ct. App. 1995). In the absence of such a contractual duty, private security officers may be held liable in negligence only for failure to exercise ordinary care. *Id.*

The Court believes that the Plaintiff has presented sufficient evidence to raise a genuine issue of material fact as to whether Defendant Padgett breached a duty to exercise ordinary care. Although Defendants SDSI and Padgett have asserted that the contract between SDSI and Waffle House specifies that guards are hired only to protect the Company's property, and therefore have no heightened duty under Ohio law to protect customers from harm by third parties, the Plaintiff has presented evidence that, in practice, the guards had additional duties that were not specifically written into the terms of the contract. Both the Waffle House and SDSI have acknowledged that the manager at the Waffle House would tell Defendant Padgett what he was supposed to do each night he reported for work. On the night in question, the manager told Padgett, among other things, to prevent any "rowdiness," and help provide "crowd control." Although Defendant Padgett has claimed that his instructions from the Waffle House manager pertained only to his duty to protect the Company's property, a question of fact remains as to whether such instructions really go beyond the protection of property, and extend to the protection of customers.

The Court finds that a reasonable trier of fact could conclude that the manager's instructions to Defendant Padgett did, in fact, relate to persons and not just property. As such, under *Eagle v. Mathews-Click-Bauman*, Defendant Padgett would be subject to a heightened standard of care, which the trier of fact may find he breached by failing to prevent the harm to the Plaintiff. The Court also finds, however, that a reasonable trier of fact could conclude that the manager's instructions really did not extend Defendant Padgett's duties beyond the protection of property. Were the trier of fact to so find, it could nonetheless conclude that Defendant Padgett breached his duty of ordinary care under the circumstances. Under either standard, the Court believes that if a breach by Defendant Padgett were found, the trier of fact could further conclude that SDSI is liable for Defendant Padgett's breach under a respondeat superior theory of liability. Therefore, the Court DENIES summary judgment to Defendants SDSI and Padgett on the Plaintiff's claim of negligence.

V. Conclusion

Based on the foregoing, the Court DENIES summary judgment as to the 42 U.S.C. § 1983 claim and the negligence claims, and GRANTS summary judgment as to the claim of intentional infliction of emotional distress.

IT IS SO ORDERED.
ALGENON L. MARBLEY

Barry Walker v. May Department Stores Co., 83 F. Supp. 2d 525 (E.D. Pa. 2000).

Judges: J. Curtis Joyner, J.

MEMORANDUM AND ORDER

Joyner, J.
January 24, 2000

This case has been brought before the Court on motion of the defendants for summary judgment. For the reasons which follow, the motion shall be granted in part and denied in part.

Statement of Facts

On January 3, 1997, the plaintiff, Barry Walker, was observed via closed circuit television in the Strawbridge's department store in Center City Philadelphia by defendant Kim Stone, a store detective. In Ms. Stone's opinion, Mr. Walker, whom she had apprehended less than a week before for shoplifting, was acting suspiciously and she believed he may have again taken store merchandise without paying for it. Using the store security department's radio system, Ms. Stone directed uniformed guard Robert Bryant, who was in the vicinity of Mr. Walker, to follow him and try to "spook him" into dropping the shopping bag that he was carrying.

By the time that Mr. Bryant could locate the plaintiff, he was already out of the Strawbridge's store and in the Gallery mall, walking toward the Food Court area. Mr. Bryant began to follow

Mr. Walker, but was soon passed by Anthony Battle, a plainclothes store detective, who caught up to the plaintiff and stopped him outside of the McDonald's Restaurant. According to the plaintiff, Mr. Battle pushed him toward the wall of the McDonald's, grabbed him by the arm and asked him what he had in the bag. According to Mr. Battle and Mr. Bryant, however, Mr. Battle put his arm around the plaintiff's shoulders and asked him what was in the bag. The plaintiff produced a receipt for three of the items that he was carrying from the nearby Ross store and since Mr. Bryant's search of the remaining contents of the bag revealed no tags or other marks identifying them as Strawbridge's merchandise, the items were returned to the plaintiff and he was released, with apologies from Mr. Bryant.

Mr. Walker followed Messrs. Bryant and Battle back into the Strawbridge's store to complain of the treatment that he had received and to get their names. Neither man would identify themselves but Mr. Battle introduced the plaintiff to Anthony Robinson, one of the security managers on duty, who in turn, listened to his complaint and gave him the phone number and name of his supervisor, Philip Bonafiglia. Mr. Walker contends that he tried to reach Mr. Bonafiglia on several occasions, but was unsuccessful. Plaintiff thereafter filed this lawsuit against Strawbridges and its employees, alleging negligence, "intentional actions," and "discrimination." Discovery in this matter having now been completed, Defendants move for summary judgment in their favor as a matter of law.

Standards Governing Summary Judgment Motions

The standards for determining whether summary judgment is properly entered in cases pending before the district courts are governed by Fed.R.Civ.P. 56. Subsection (c) of that rule states, in pertinent part,

> The judgment sought shall be rendered forthwith if the pleadings, depositions, answers to interrogatories, and admissions on file, together with the affidavits, if any, show that there is no genuine issue as to any material fact and that the moving party is entitled to a judgment as a matter of law. A summary judgment, interlocutory in character, may be rendered on the issue of liability alone although there is a genuine issue as to the amount of damages.

In this way, a Motion for Summary Judgment requires the court to look beyond the bare allegations of the pleadings to determine if they have sufficient factual support to warrant their consideration at trial. *Liberty Lobby, Inc. v. Dow Jones & Co.*, 267 U.S. App. D.C. 337, 838 F.2d 1287 (D.C. Cir. 1988), cert. denied, 488 U.S. 825, 109 S. Ct. 75, 102 L. Ed. 2d 51 (1988). See Also: *Aries Realty, Inc. v. AGS Columbia Associates*, 751 F. Supp. 444 (S.D. N.Y. 1990).

As a general rule, the party seeking summary judgment always bears the initial responsibility of informing the district court of the basis for its motion and identifying those portions of the pleadings, depositions, answers to interrogatories and admissions on file, together with the affidavits, if any, which it believes demonstrate the absence of a genuine issue of material fact. *Celotex Corp. v. Catrett*, 477 U.S. 317, 106 S. Ct. 2548, 91 L. Ed. 2d 265 (1986). In considering a summary judgment motion, the court must view the facts in the light most favorable to the party opposing the motion and all reasonable inferences from the facts must be drawn in favor of that party as well. *U.S. v. Kensington Hospital*, 760 F. Supp. 1120 (E.D. Pa. 1991); *Schillachi v. Flying Dutchman Motorcycle Club*, 751 F. Supp. 1169 (E.D. Pa. 1990).

When, however, "a Motion for Summary Judgment is made and supported [by affidavits or otherwise], an adverse party may not rest upon the mere allegations or denials of the adverse party's pleading, but the adverse party's response...must set forth specific facts showing that there is a genuine issue for trial. If the adverse party does not so respond, summary judgment, if appropriate may be entered against [it]." Fed.R.Civ.P. 56(e).

A material fact has been defined as one which might affect the outcome of the suit under relevant substantive law. *Boykin v. Bloomsburg University of Pennsylvania*, 893 F. Supp. 378, 393 (M.D.Pa. 1995) citing *Anderson v. Liberty Lobby, Inc.*, 477 U.S. 242, 106 S. Ct. 2505, 91 L. Ed. 2d 202 (1986). A dispute about a material fact is "genuine" if "the evidence is such that a reasonable jury could return a verdict for the nonmoving party." *Id.*, citing *Anderson*, 477 U.S. at 248, 106 S. Ct. at 2510.

Discussion

A. Immunity from Civil Liability under Pennsylvania's Retail Theft Statute, 18 Pa.C.S. § 3929.

Defendants first argue that they are entitled to summary judgment in their favor on all counts of the complaint because they are effectively immune under the Pennsylvania Retail Theft Statute, 18 Pa.C.S. § 3929. Specifically, that statute provides in relevant part:

> (c) Presumptions—Any person intentionally concealing unpurchased property of any store or other mercantile establishment, either on the premises or outside the premises of such store, shall be prima facie presumed to have so concealed such property with the intention of depriving the merchant of the possession, use or benefit of such merchandise without paying the full retail value thereof within the meaning of subsection (a), and the finding of such unpurchased property concealed, upon the person or among the belongings of such person, shall be prima facie evidence of intentional concealment, and, if such person conceals, or causes to be concealed, such unpurchased property, upon the person or among the belongings of another, such fact shall also be prima facie evidence of intentional concealment on the part of the person so concealing such property.
>
> (d) Detention—A peace officer, merchant or merchant's employee or an agent under contract with a merchant, who has probable cause to believe that retail theft has occurred or is occurring on or about a store or other retail mercantile establishment and who has probable cause to believe that a specific person has committed or is committing the retail theft may detain the suspect in a reasonable manner for a reasonable time on or off the premises for all or any of the following purposes: to require the suspect to identify himself, to verify such identification, to determine whether such suspect has in his possession unpurchased merchandise taken from the mercantile establishment and, if so, to recover such merchandise, to inform a peace officer, or to institute criminal proceedings against the suspect. Such detention shall not impose civil or criminal liability upon the peace officer, merchant, employee or agent so detaining.

It should be noted that store employees who stop, detain and search individuals who they reasonably suspect of retail theft do not act under color of state authority and hence it is not necessary to first apply for or obtain a search warrant. *Commonwealth v. Lacy*, 324 Pa. Super. 379, 471 A.2d 888, 890 (1984); *Commonwealth v. Martin*, 300 Pa. Super. 497, 446 A.2d 965, 968 (1982). However, since the Retail Theft Statute does require that probable cause have existed to justify a stop and to trigger a shopkeeper's immunity, the threshold issue with which we are now faced is whether or not Mr. Bryant and Mr. Battle had the requisite probable cause to stop and detain Mr. Walker.

Probable cause has been said to be a fluid concept turning on the assessment of probabilities in particular factual contexts not readily or even usefully reduced to a neat set of legal rules. *Illinois v. Gates*, 462 U.S. 213, 232, 103 S. Ct. 2317, 2329, 76 L. Ed. 2d 527 (1983). Probable cause is determined by the totality of the circumstances based upon a practical, common-sense decision whether, given all the facts presented, including the veracity and basis of knowledge of any persons supplying hearsay information, there is a fair probability that a crime has been or is being committed by the suspect or that contraband or evidence of a crime will be found in a particular place. See: *Illinois v. Gates*, 462 U.S. at 238, 103 S. Ct. at 2332; *Sharrar v. Felsing*, 128 F.3d 810, 817-818 (3rd Cir. 1997); *Commonwealth v. Banks*, 540 Pa. 453, 454, 658 A.2d 752, 753 (1995). Probable cause thus means more than mere suspicion but does not require the police to have evidence sufficient to prove guilt beyond a reasonable doubt. *Cronin v. West Whiteland Township*, 994 F. Supp. 595 (E.D.Pa. 1998). It should further be noted that the appropriate inquiry for application of the "shopkeeper privilege" focuses only on whether the merchant or his agent had probable cause at the moment he decided to detain the plaintiff. *Doe v. Dendrinos*, 1997 U.S. Dist. LEXIS 2052 (E.D.Pa. 1997). In this case, the totality of the circumstances reflect that the plaintiff was stopped because (1) Kim Stone observed him as a previously known shoplifter in the store one week after he had previously been detained and questioned for shoplifting; (2) Ms. Stone believed he may have been carrying a shopping bag full of Strawbridge's merchandise and she directed store guard Robert Bryant to follow him and try to scare him into dropping the bag; and (3) Store Detective Anthony Battle also heard the radio transmission from Stone to Bryant and decided to assist Bryant. When Battle saw the plaintiff turn around and look over his shoulder, he recognized him from his earlier shoplifting incident one week previously and made the decision to stop the plaintiff when he caught up to him outside the McDonald's Restaurant. Given that it appears that the plaintiff may have been stopped solely because he had been caught shoplifting one week before and was carrying a shopping bag, we cannot find that there is no material issue of fact as to whether these circumstances, without more, constituted sufficient probable cause to believe that the plaintiff was again shoplifting on the day at issue so as to trigger the "shopkeeper's immunity" under the Retail Theft Statute. Defendant's Motion for Summary Judgment on this basis must therefore be denied.

B. Entitlement to Summary Judgment on Punitive Damages

Defendants next assert that since there is no evidence in this case to support a claim for punitive damages, they are likewise entitled to judgment in their favor as a matter of law on plaintiff's punitive damages claims. We agree.

In order to impose punitive damages, the wrongful conduct must be outrageous and conduct is said to be outrageous when it is "malicious, wanton, reckless, willful or oppressive." *Rizzo v. Haines*, 520 Pa. 484, 506, 555 A.2d 58, 69 (1989); *Trotman v. Mecchella*, 421 Pa. Super. 620, 618 A.2d 982, 985 (1992). Such conduct must show the actor's evil motive or reckless indifference to the rights of others. *Trotman v. Mecchella*, 618 A.2d at 985, citing *Feld v. Merriam*, 506 Pa. 383, 485 A.2d 742 (1984) and *Hess v. Hess*, 397 Pa. Super. 395, 399, 580 A.2d 357, 359 (1990). In assessing punitives, the trier of fact can properly consider the character of the defendant's act, the nature and extent of the harm to the plaintiff that the defendant caused or intended to cause and the wealth of the defendant. *Feld v. Merriam*, 485 A.2d at 748. See Also: *Polselli v. Nationwide Mutual Fire Insurance Co.*, 23 F.3d 747, 751 (3rd Cir. 1994).

In applying these principles to the case at hand, we first observe that despite having captioned two counts of his complaint as seeking damages for "Intentional Acts," virtually plaintiff's entire complaint alleges nothing more than negligence on the part of the defendants. This, coupled with the complete lack of any evidence that any of the defendants acted other than negligently, let alone recklessly, maliciously, willfully or oppressively or with an evil motive, warrants the entry of judgment in defendants' favor as a matter of law. Summary judgment shall therefore be entered in favor of all of the defendants with respect to plaintiff's claims for punitive damages.

C. Summary Judgment as to Defendant Anthony Robinson

Finally, Defendants assert that summary judgment is properly entered with regard to defendant Robinson, as there is no evidence that he played any role in the plaintiff's stop and detention. Again, we agree.

A careful review of the entire record in this case reflects that Mr. Robinson in no way participated in the stop or the decision to stop and detain Mr. Walker for suspected shoplifting on January 3, 1997. To the contrary, Mr. Robinson's only contact with the plaintiff occurred after he followed Messrs. Bryant and Battle back into the store after he had been detained and searched. At that time, Mr. Battle introduced Mr. Robinson to the plaintiff as a supervisor who would hear his complaints about how Mr. Bryant and Mr. Battle had treated him. Mr. Robinson did nothing more than listen to the plaintiff's complaints and give him the name and telephone number of his supervisor. We thus find that there is no basis upon which Mr. Robinson could be held liable to Mr. Walker and we therefore shall enter judgment in favor of this defendant as a matter of law as to all of the plaintiff's claims against him.

An order follows.

Order

AND NOW, this 24th day of January, 2000, upon consideration of Defendants' Motions for Summary Judgment and Plaintiff's Response thereto, it is hereby ORDERED that the Motions are GRANTED in PART and DENIED in PART and Judgment is entered in favor of all Defendants on Plaintiff's claims for punitive damages and in favor of Defendant Anthony Robinson on all Counts of the Plaintiff's Complaint.

BY THE COURT:

J. CURTIS JOYNER, J.

Kyong Wood & Sheila Copeland v. The City of Topeka, Case No. 01-4016-SAC (Kansas 2003).

Judges: Sam A. Crow, U.S. District Senior Judge.

Opinion by: Sam A. Crow

This case comes before the court on the motion of the Kroger Co., d.b.a. Dillon Stores Division ("Dillons"), and American Sentry Security System, Inc., ("Sentry") to dismiss the case. Defendant City of Topeka has previously been dismissed as a party. See Dk. 56. Plaintiffs represent that after the City's dismissal, plaintiff Sheila Copeland is no longer a plaintiff in the case, as "she has no claims against defendants Dillons or Sentry." (Dk. 53, p. 2).

Plaintiff brings 42 U.S.C. § 1983 and supplemental state law claims against Dillons and Sentry based upon an incident in which she was detained at a Dillons store due to suspicion of shoplifting and/or destruction of property. Defendants move to dismiss the case, alleging that it fails to state a claim for relief, pursuant to Fed. R.Civ.P. 12(b)(6). Specifically, defendants allege that plaintiff has failed to properly plead state action, or action under color of law, as is required for all § 1983 cases.

Before examining the merits of the motions, the court addresses plaintiff's objection that defendants failed to follow the local rules regarding the manner in which motions and supporting memoranda are to be filed. D.Kan. R. 7.1 states, in pertinent part, that motions in civil cases "shall be accompanied by a brief or memorandum...." This rule contemplates that a motion and its supporting memorandum shall be filed as two separate pleadings, not as one, as both defendants have done.

The court believes that the violation apparently flows from defense counsels' lack of familiarity with the rules, rather than from blatant disregard for their requirements. Accordingly, the court shall permit the pleadings to remain as they are, but advises counsel for defendants that they shall not be excused from any future lack of compliance with the court's rules. The court thus examines the merits of the motions to dismiss.

12(b)(6) Standards

A court may dismiss a complaint for "failure to state a claim upon which relief can be granted." Fed. R. Civ. P. 12(b)(6). Dismissal should not be granted "unless it appears beyond doubt that the plaintiff can prove no set of facts in support of his claim which would entitle him to relief," *GFF Corp. v. Associated Wholesale Grocers, Inc.*, 130 F.3d 1381, 1384 (10th Cir. 1997) (quoting *Conley v. Gibson*, 355 U.S. 41, 45-46, 2 L. Ed. 2d 80, 78 S. Ct. 99 (1957)), or unless an issue of law is dispositive, *Neitzke v. Williams*, 490 U.S. 319, 326, 104 L. Ed. 2d 338, 109 S. Ct. 1827 (1989). "The purpose of Rule 12(b)(6) is to allow a defendant to test whether, as a matter of law, the plaintiff is entitled to legal relief even if everything alleged in the complaint is true." *Mayer v. Mylod*, 988 F.2d 635, 638 (6th Cir. 1993); see *Hospice of Metro Denver, Inc. v. Group Health Ins. of Oklahoma*, 944 F.2d 752, 753 (10th Cir. 1991).

The Tenth Circuit has observed that the federal rules "erect a powerful presumption against rejecting pleadings for failure to state a claim." *Maez v. Mountain States Tel. and Tel., Inc.*, 54 F.3d 1488, 1496 (10th Cir. 1995) (quoting *Morgan v. City of Rawlins*, 792 F.2d 975, 978 (10th Cir. 1986)). A court judges the sufficiency of the complaint accepting as true all well-pleaded facts, as distinguished from conclusory allegations, *Maher v. Durango Metals, Inc.*, 144 F.3d 1302, 1304 (10th Cir. 1998), 1219, and drawing all reasonable inferences from those facts in favor of the plaintiff. *Witt v. Roadway Express*, 136 F.3d 1424, 1428 (10th Cir.), cert. denied, 525 U.S. 881, 142 L. Ed. 2d 154, 119 S. Ct. 188 (1998); see *Southern Disposal, Inc. v. Texas Waste Management*, 161 F.3d 1259, 1262 (10th Cir. 1998). It is not the court's function "to weigh potential evidence that the parties might present at trial." *Miller v. Glanz*, 948 F.2d 1562, 1565 (10th Cir. 1991). The court construes the allegations in the light most favorable to the plaintiff. *Scheuer v. Rhodes*, 416 U.S. 232, 236, 40 L. Ed. 2d 90, 94 S. Ct. 1683 (1974); *Hall v. Bellmon*, 935 F.2d 1106, 1109 (10th Cir. 1991).

These deferential rules, however, do not allow the court to assume that a plaintiff "can prove facts that it has not alleged or that the defendants have violated the...laws in ways that have not been alleged." *Associated General Contractors v. California State Council of Carpenters*, 459 U.S. 519,

526, 74 L. Ed. 2d 723, 103 S. Ct. 897 (1983) (footnote omitted). Dismissal is a harsh remedy to be used cautiously so as to promote the liberal rules of pleading while protecting the interests of justice. *Cayman Exploration Corp. v. United Gas Pipe Line Co.*, 873 F.2d 1357, 1359 (10th Cir. 1989).

§ 1983 Requirements

Defendants claim that plaintiff has failed to allege that they, as private security guards and/or store employees, acted under color of law, as is required for all § 1983 claims.

It is well established that private actors are not usually subject to liability under § 1983.

Plaintiffs alleging a violation of § 1983 must demonstrate they have been deprived of a right "secured by the Constitution and the laws of the United States," and that the defendants deprived them of this right acting under color of law. *Lugar v. Edmondson Oil Co.*, 457 U.S. 922, 930, 102 S. Ct. 2744, 73 L. Ed. 2d 482 (1982) (citations omitted). "Thus, the only proper defendants in a Section 1983 claim are those who represent [the state] in some capacity, whether they act in accordance with their authority or misuse it." See *Gallagher v. Neil Young Freedom Concert*, 49 F.3d 1442, 1447 (10th Cir. 1995) (citations and quotations omitted). However, a defendant need not be an officer of the state in order to act under color of state law for purposes of § 1983. (citation omitted). Rather, courts have applied four separate tests to determine whether a private party acted under color of law in causing an alleged deprivation of federal rights: (1) the nexus test; (2) the symbiotic relation test; (3) the joint action test; and (4) the traditional public powers test or public functions test. See *Gallagher*, 49 F.3d at 1447.

Sigmon v. Community Care HMO, Inc., *234 F.3d 1121, 1125(10th Cir. 2000)*

Plaintiff states that the gravamen of her argument is not that the defendants conspired with the City of Topeka officers to violate her civil rights, but that they engaged in other acts sufficient to meet the requirements of the joint action test. Compare *Anaya v. Crossroads Managed Care Systems*, 195 F.3d 584, 596 (10th Cir. 1999) ("a requirement of the joint action charge… is that both public and private actors share a common, unconstitutional goal."); *Hunt v. Bennett*, 17 F.3d 1263, 1268 (10th Cir. 1994) (§ 1983 pleadings must specifically present facts tending to show agreement and concerted action).

Defendants allege that none of the acts they engaged in are sufficient, under any of the four tests noted above, to meet plaintiff's burden to plead state action. Defendants rely primarily upon the general rule that "an individual does not act under color of law merely by reporting an alleged crime to police officers who take action thereon." *Benavidez v. Gunnell*, 722 F.2d 615, 618 (10th Cir. 1983). Nor does the making of a citizen's arrest constitute acting under color of law for § 1983 purposes. See *Carey v. Continental Airlines*, 823 F.2d 1402, 1404 (10th Cir. 1987); *Lee v. Town of Estes Park*, 820 F.2d 1112, 1114-15 (10th Cir. 1987); see also, *Cruz v. Donnelly*, 727 F.2d 79 (3d Cir. 1984) (finding no acts under color of law where a shopkeeper called the police to search a suspected shoplifter, but the police found nothing); see generally *Sarner v. Luce*, 129 F.3d 131, [published in full-text format at 1997 U.S. App. LEXIS 29814], 1997 WL 687449, *1 (10th Cir. 1997) (finding plaintiff failed to plead overt or significant action by the other defendants such that defendant was a state actor).

These same principles apply to merchants, as the Tenth Circuit has stated:

> Generally, merchants are not considered to be acting under color of law for purposes of 1983 when they detain a person suspected of shoplifting or other crimes, call the police, or make a citizen's arrest. See *Gramenos v. Jewel Cos.*, 797 F.2d 432, 435-36

(7th Cir. 1986), cert. denied, 481 U.S. 1028, 95 L. Ed. 2d 525, 107 S. Ct. 1952 (1987); *Cruz v. Donnelly*, 727 F.2d 79, 81 (3d Cir. 1984); *White v. Scrivner Corp.*, 594 F.2d 140, 142-43 (5th Cir. 1979); *Hurt v. G.C. Murphy Co.*, 624 F. Supp. 512, 514 (S.D. W. Va.), aff'd, 800 F.2d 260 (4th Cir. 1986); cf. *Flagg Bros. v. Brooks*, 436 U.S. 149, 165-66, 56 L. Ed. 2d 185, 98 S. Ct. 1729 (1978) (holding that state enacted provisions which permit self-help do not automatically convert private action into state action); *Carey*, 823 F.2d at 1404 (holding that complaint to police and citizen's arrest by Continental Airlines employee does not constitute state action).

Jones v. Wal-Mart Stores, Inc., 33 F.3d 62, 1994 WL 387887, *3 (10th Cir. 1994) (Table).

Analysis

The court has reviewed plaintiff's complaint to determine whether it sufficiently alleges facts showing the defendants acted under the color of law as required by 42 U.S.C. § 1983. Two paragraphs of plaintiff's § 1983 claim refer generally to state action. Paragraph 2 states:

> Defendants used their powers under color of state law to direct and control the City police department for purposes that were adverse to plaintiffs...and were detrimental to the public welfare and safety.

Paragraph 8 states:

> Defendants the Kroger Co., d.b.a. Dillons, and Sentry wrongfully invoked the police power of the City of Topeka. The City of Topeka, by and through its police officers, wrongfully acceded to the request and participated in the unlawful actions of the other defendants.

These conclusory allegations fall far short of meeting the pleading requirements in § 1983 cases. See *Fries v. Helsper*, 146 F.3d 452, 458 (7th Cir.), cert. denied, 525 U.S. 930, 142 L. Ed. 2d 278, 119 S. Ct. 337 (1998) ("Mere allegations of joint action or a conspiracy do not demonstrate that the defendants acted under color of state law and are not sufficient to survive a motion to dismiss").

The factual allegations of plaintiff's complaint, incorporated by reference, include the following allegations of acts by defendants, prior to the arrival of the City of Topeka police officers: "A Dillons security guard supplied by Sentry came up behind [plaintiff] in the parking lot and without notice or warning grabbed her hand, removing her car keys"; "one or more employees of Dillons wrongfully detained and falsely imprisoned plaintiff"; "the guard then directed [plaintiff] to go back into the store where the security guard was joined by another guard"; the "security guards refused to allow [plaintiff] to call her husband or get a glass of water that she had requested"; the security guards did not respond to her when she asked if she was being charged; and "Dillons security guards together pulled her arms behind her in a forceful and painful manner, and placed handcuffs on her forcibly pushed (sic) her backward causing her to strike a railing in the room, [injuring her]." Dk 1, p. 3.

City of Topeka police officers then arrived, having been called by one or more Dillons employees. The following allegations relate to acts thereafter: "The police officers declined to take plaintiff's complaint" that she had been "physically injured by the treatment of Dillons security guards";

one of the officers called her residence and stated that plaintiff had been arrested for shoplifting; and when plaintiff asked one or more of the City officers to loosen her handcuffs, "at first the officer declined, telling her that if she didn't move her hands, the cuffs would not be so tight." Dk. 1, p. 4. Plaintiff's daughter then arrived, demanded that plaintiff's handcuffs be removed, and was removed from the detention room by one of the police officers who told her that her mother was going to be charged with criminal damage to property. The remaining relevant allegation is that "together the security guards and Topeka police watched a video on multiple occasions that purported to record the action of [plaintiff]. Thereafter, the officers removed the cuffs from [plaintiff] and allowed her and Sheila Copeland to leave." Dk. 1, p. 4. No charges were filed against plaintiff or her daughter.

Nothing in plaintiff's complaint sufficiently alleges that defendants, or either of them, engaged in acts under color of state law. Instead, the seizure and subsequent treatment of plaintiff at Dillons cannot be fairly attributed to the City of Topeka under any of the tests for state action. For a merchant or its security officers to call the police when they suspect shoplifting or destruction of property is insufficient to constitute state action. No acts allegedly taken by officers of the City of Topeka at the scene reveal prior collusion with defendants, or compliance with any requests by the defendants, or either of them, let alone the requisite joint action. Plaintiff's assertion that defendants "directed and controlled" the City police department is conclusory and unsupported by the facts alleged in the complaint. No allegations in the complaint support a conclusion that plaintiff's treatment resulted from any concerted action, prearranged plan, customary procedure, or policy that substituted the judgment of a private party for that of the police, or allowed a private party to exercise state power. See *Carey*, 823 F.2d at 1404. Thus even if everything alleged in the complaint is true, plaintiff fails to state a claim under § 1983.

State Law Claims

Plaintiff's complaint includes state law claims of false arrest and imprisonment, assault and battery, and outrage and/or negligent infliction of emotional distress. Over these claims, this court has no original jurisdiction.

Having dismissed the federal claims over which this court has original jurisdiction, the court in the exercise of its statutory discretion declines to assume supplemental jurisdiction over the plaintiff's state law claims against the defendants. 28 U.S.C. § 1367 (c)(3); see *Tonkovich v. Kansas Bd. of Regents*, 254 F.3d 941, 945 (10th Cir. 2001). The plaintiff advances no substantial reasons for exercising such jurisdiction. "Given the relative lack of pretrial proceedings—including a total absence of discovery—considerations of 'judicial economy, convenience, fairness' do not favor 'retaining jurisdiction.'" *Tonkovich*, 254 F.3d at 945 (quoting in part *Anglemyer v. Hamilton County Hosp.*, 58 F.3d 533, 541 (10th Cir. 1995)). At this juncture, the most common response is to dismiss the state law claims without prejudice. *Roe v. Cheyenne Mountain Conference Resort, Inc.*, 124 F.3d 1221, 1237 (10th Cir. 1997).

Plaintiff requests that the state law claims "should be remanded to state court for trial" so that she will not lose her remedies for defendant's behavior. Given the state's savings statute, see K.S.A. § 60-518, plaintiff's fear of losing her state law remedies is unfounded. The court finds no unique circumstances justifying its exercise of supplemental jurisdiction.

IT IS THEREFORE ORDERED that Dillons' motion to dismiss (Dk. 42), and Sentry's motion to dismiss (Dk. 37) are granted.

IT IS FURTHER ORDERED that the court declines to exercise supplemental jurisdiction over the remaining state law claims and dismisses the same without prejudice.

Dated this 23rd day of May, 2003, Topeka, Kansas.
Sam A. Crow, U.S. District Senior Judge

The People v. Virginia Alvinia Zelinski, 24 Cal. 3d 357; 594 P.2d 1000 (1979).

Opinion by Manuel, J., with Tobriner, Mosk, Richardson, and Newman, JJ., concurring. Bird, C. J., concurred in the result. Separate dissenting opinion by Clark, J.

Virginia Zelinski was charged with unlawful possession of a controlled substance, heroin (Health & Saf. Code, § 11350). A motion to suppress evidence pursuant to Penal Code Section 1538.5 was denied. She entered a plea of guilty and appeals. (Pen. Code, § 1538.5, subd. (m).) We reverse.

On March 21, 1976, Bruce Moore, a store detective employed by Zody's Department Store, observed defendant place a blouse into her purse. Moore alerted Ann O'Connor, another Zody detective, and the two thereafter observed defendant select a pair of sandals, which she put on her feet, and a hat, which she put on her head. Defendant also took a straw bag into which she placed her purse. Defendant then selected and paid for a pair of blue shoes and left the store.

Detectives Moore and O'Connor stopped defendant outside the store. Moore placed defendant under arrest for violation of Penal Code Section 484 (theft) and asked her to accompany him and detective O'Connor into the store. Defendant was taken by O'Connor to the security office where Pat Forrest, another female store detective, conducted a routine "cursory search in case of weapons" on the person of defendant.

Moore testified that he reentered the security office when the search of defendant's person was completed, opened defendant's purse to retrieve the blouse taken from Zody's, and removed the blouse and a pill vial that lay on top of the blouse. Moore examined the vial, removed a balloon from the bottle, examined the fine powdery substance contained in the balloon, and set the vial and balloon on the security office desk to await the police who had been called.

Detective O'Connor, who testified to the search of defendant's person by Forrest, was initially confused as to whether the pill vial containing the balloon had been taken from the defendant's purse or from her brassiere. On cross-examination, O'Connor was certain that she saw Forrest taking it from defendant's brassiere. According to O'Connor, the pill bottle was placed on the security office desk where detective Moore shortly thereafter opened it and examined the powdery substance in the balloon. Later the police took custody of the vial and defendant was thereafter charged with unlawful possession of heroin.

(1a) (2a) Defendant's appeal involves two questions—(1) whether store detectives Moore, O'Connor, and Forrest exceeded the permissible scope of search incident to the arrest and (2) if they did, whether the evidence thus obtained should be excluded as violative of defendant's rights under federal or state Constitutions. We have concluded that the narcotics evidence was obtained by unlawful search and that the constitutional prohibition against unreasonable search and seizure affords protection against the unlawful intrusive conduct of these private security personnel.

(3) Store detectives and security guards are retained primarily to protect their employer's interest in property. They have no more powers to enforce the law than other private persons. (See *Private Police in California: A Legislative Proposal* (1975) 5 Golden Gate L. Rev. 115,129-134; cf. *Stapleton v. Superior Court* (1968) 70 Cal.2d 97, 100-101, fn.3 [73 Cal. Rptr. 575, 447 P.2d 967].) Like all private persons, security employees can arrest or detain an offender (Pen. Code, § 837) and search for weapons (Pen. Code, § 846) before taking the offender to a magistrate or delivering

him to a peace officer (Pen. Code, §§ 847, 849). Store personnel Moore and O'Connor were acting under this statutory authority when they arrested defendant and took her into custody for leaving the store with stolen merchandise.

(4) Merchants have traditionally had the right to restrain and detain shoplifters. At the time of the incident at Zody's, merchants were protected from civil liability for false arrest or false imprisonment in their reasonable efforts to detain shoplifters by a common law privilege that permitted detention for a reasonable time for investigation in a reasonable manner of any person whom the merchant had probable cause to believe had unlawfully taken or attempted to take merchandise from the premises. (*Collyer v. S.H. Kress & Co.* (1936) 5 Cal.2d 175 [54 P.2d 20].) That privilege has since been enacted into statute as subdivision (e) of Penal Code Section 490.5.

Thus, pursuant to the Penal Code or the civil common law privilege, store personnel Moore and O'Connor had authority to arrest or detain defendant. The question remains, however, whether they exceeded their authority in their subsequent search for and seizure of evidence.

(5) The permissible scope of search incident to a citizen's arrest is set out in *People v. Sandoval* (1966) 65 Cal.2d 303, 311, footnote 5 [54 Cal. Rptr. 123, 419 P.2d 187]: "A citizen effecting such an arrest is authorized only to 'take from the person arrested all offensive weapons which he may have about his person' (Pen. Code, § 846), not to conduct a search for contraband 'incidental' to the arrest, or to seize such contraband upon recovering it. [Citation.] We reject the suggestion of *People v. Alvarado* (1962) 208 Cal. App. 2d 629, 631 [25 Cal. Rptr. 437], that the search of one private individual or his premises by another is lawful simply because 'incidental' to a lawful citizen's arrest." (See also *People v. Cheatham* (1968) 263 Cal. App. 2d 458, 462, fn. 2 [69 Cal. Rptr. 679]; *People v. Sjosten* (1968) 262 Cal. App. 2d 539 [68 Cal. Rptr. 832]; *People v. Martin* (1964) 225 Cal. App. 2d 91, 94 [36 Cal. Rptr. 924].) The rationale behind the rule is that, absent statutory authorization, private citizens are not and should not be permitted to take property from other private citizens.

(6) The limits of the merchant's authority to search is now expressly stated in Penal Code Section 490.5. Paragraph of subdivision (e) provides that "During the period of detention any items which a merchant has reasonable cause to believe are unlawfully taken from his premises and which are in plain view may be examined by the merchant for the purposes of ascertaining the ownership thereof." (Italics added.) Neither the statute nor the privilege which it codified purport to give to the merchant or his employees the authority to search.

(1b) In the present case, instead of holding defendant and her handbag until the arrival of a peace officer who may have been authorized to search, the employees instituted a search to recover goods that were not in plain view. Such intrusion into defendant's person and effects was not authorized as incident to a citizen's arrest pursuant to Section 837 of the Penal Code (Sandoval, supra, 65 Cal.2d at p. 311, fn. 5), or pursuant to the merchant's privilege subsequently codified in subdivision (e) of Section 490.5. It was unnecessary to achieve the employees' reasonable concerns of assuring that defendant carried no weapons30 and of preventing loss of store property. As a matter of law, therefore, the fruits of that search were illegally obtained.

(2b) The People contend that the evidence is nevertheless admissible because the search and seizure were made by private persons. They urge that *Burdeau v. McDowell* (1921) 256 U.S. 465 [65 L. Ed. 1048, 41 S. Ct. 574, 13 A.L.R. 1159], holding that Fourth Amendment proscriptions against unreasonable searches and seizures do not apply to private conduct, is still good law and controlling. (See *People v. Randazzo* (1963) 220 Cal. App. 2d 768, 770-775 [34 Cal. Rptr. 65]; *People v. Superior Court* (Smith) (1969) 70 Cal.2d 123, 128-129 [74 Cal. Rptr. 294, 449 P.2d 230],["...acquisition of property by a private citizen from another person cannot be deemed reasonable or unreasonable..."]; cf. *Stapleton v. Superior Court*, supra, 70 Cal.2d at p. 00, fn. 2.)

Defendant contends, on the other hand, that only by applying the exclusionary rule to all searches conducted by store detectives and other private security personnel can freedoms embodied in the Fourth Amendment of the federal Constitution and article I, Section 13 of the state Constitution be protected from the abuses and dangers inherent in the growth of private security activities.

More than a decade ago we expressed concern that searches by private security forces can involve a "particularly serious threat to privacy" (*Stapleton*, supra, 70 Cal.2d at pp. 100-101, fn. 3); in *Stapleton* and later in *Dyas v. Superior Court* (1974) 11 Cal. 3d 628, 633 [114 Cal. Rptr. 114, 522 P.2d 674], we left open the question whether searches by such private individuals should be held subject to the constitutional proscriptions. We now address the problem.

Article I, Section 13 of the California Constitution provides in part that: "The right of the people to be secure in their persons, houses, papers and effects against unreasonable seizures and searches may not be violated...." Although the constitutional provision contains no language indicating that the "security" protected by the provision is limited to security from governmental searches or seizures, California cases have generally interpreted this provision as primarily intended as a protection of the people against such governmentally initiated or governmentally directed intrusions. The exclusionary rule, fashioned to implement the rights secured by the constitutional provision, has therefore been applied to exclude evidence illegally obtained by private citizens only where it served the purpose of the exclusionary rule in restraining abuses by the police of their statutory powers. (*Stapleton v. Superior Court*, supra, 70 Cal.2d 97; *People v. Cahan* (1955) 44 Cal.2d 434 [282 P.2d 905, 50 A.L.R.2d 513]; *Mapp v. Ohio* (1961) 367 U.S. 643 [6 L. Ed. 2d 1081, 81 S. Ct. 1684, 84 A.L.R.2d 933]; cf. *People v. Payne* (1969) 1 Cal. App. 3d 361 [81 Cal. Rptr. 635]; *People v. Randazzo*, supra, 220 Cal. App. 2d 768; *People v. Cheatham*, supra, 263 Cal. App. 2d 458, 461-462; cf. *People v. Millard* (1971) 15 Cal. App. 3d 759, 761-762 [93 Cal. Rptr. 402]; *People v. Superior Court* (Smith), supra, 70 Cal.2d 123; *People v. Mangiefico* (1972) 25 Cal. App. 3d 1041, 1947-1048 [102 Cal. Rptr. 449].

We have recognized that private security personnel, like police, have the authority to detain suspects, conduct investigations, and make arrests. They are not police, however, and we have refused to accord them the special privileges and protections enjoyed by official police officers. (See *People v. Corey* (1978) 21 Cal. 3d 738 [147 Cal. Rptr. 639, 581 P.2d 644].) We have excluded the fruits of their illegal investigations only when they were acting in concert with the police or when the police were standing silently by. (*Stapleton*, supra, 70 Cal.2d at p. 103.) We are mindful, however, of the increasing reliance placed upon private security personnel by local law enforcement authorities for the prevention of crime and enforcement of the criminal law and the increasing threat to privacy rights posed thereby. Since Stapleton was decided, the private security industry has grown tremendously, and, from all indications, the number of private security personnel continues to increase today. A recent report prepared by the Private Security Advisory Council to the United States Department of Justice describes this phenomenon in the following terms:

> A vast army of workers are employed in local, state and federal government to prevent crime and to deal with criminal activity. Generally thought of as the country's major crime prevention force are the more than 40,000 public law enforcement agencies with their 475,000 employees. While they constitute the...most visible component of the criminal justice system, another group has been fast rising in both numbers and responsibility in the area of crime prevention. With a rate of increase exceeding even that of the public police, the private security sector has become the largest single group in the country engaged in the prevention of crime. (Private Security Adv. Coun. to U.S. Dept. of Justice, LEAA, Report on the Regulation of Private Security Services (1976) p. 1.)

Realistically, therefore, we recognize that in our state today illegal conduct of privately employed security personnel poses a threat to privacy rights of Californians that is comparable to that which may be posed by the unlawful conduct of police officers. (See generally, *Private Police in California—A Legislative Proposal*, supra, 5 Golden Gate L. Rev. 115; Bassiouni, Citizen's Arrest: The Law of Arrest, Search and Seizure for Private Citizens and Private Police (1977) p. 72.) Moreover, the application of the exclusionary rule can be expected to have a deterrent effect on such unlawful search and seizure practices since private security personnel, unlike ordinary private citizens, may regularly perform such quasi-law enforcement activities in the course of their employment. (See "Seizures by Private Parties: Exclusion in Criminal Cases" (1967) 19 Stan. L. Rev. 608, 614-615.)

In the instant case, however, we need not, and do not, decide whether the constitutional constraints of article I, Section 13, apply to all of the varied activities of private security personnel, for here the store security forces did not act in a purely private capacity but rather were fulfilling a public function in bringing violators of the law to public justice. For reasons hereinafter expressed, we conclude that under such circumstances, that is, when private security personnel conduct an illegal search or seizure while engaged in a statutorily authorized citizen's arrest and detention of a person in aid of law enforcement authorities, the constitutional proscriptions of article I, Section 13 are applicable.

Although past cases have not applied the constitutional restrictions to purely private searches, we have recognized that some minimal official participation or encouragement may bring private action within the constitutional constraints on state action. (*Stapleton v. Superior Court*, supra, 70 Cal.2d 97, 101.) (7) As noted by the United States Supreme Court in *United States v. Price* (1965) 383 U.S. 787 [16 L. Ed. 2d 267, 86 S. Ct. 1152], a person does not need to be an officer of the state to act under color of law and therefore be responsible, along with such officers, for actions prohibited to state officials when such actions are engaged in under color of law. (*Id.*, p. 794, and fn. 7 thereunder [16 L. Ed. 2d at p. 272]; cf. *Burton v. Wilminton Pkg. Auth.* (1961) 365 U.S. 715, 725 [6 L. Ed. 2d 45, 52, 81 S. Ct. 856]; *Weeks v. U.S.* (1914) 232 U.S. 383, 398 [58 L. Ed. 652, 657, 34 S. Ct. 341]; *Marsh v. Alabama* (1946) 326 U.S. 501 [90 L. Ed. 265, 66 S. Ct. 276].)

(2c) In the instant case, the store employees arrested defendant pursuant to the authorization contained in Penal Code Section 837, and the search which yielded the narcotics was conducted incident to that arrest. Their acts, engaged in pursuant to the statute, were not those of a private citizen acting in a purely private capacity. Although the search exceeded lawful authority, it was nevertheless an integral part of the exercise of sovereignty allowed by the state to private citizens. In arresting the offender, the store employees were utilizing the coercive power of the state to further a state interest. Had the security guards sought only the vindication of the merchant's private interests they would have simply exercised self-help and demanded the return of the stolen merchandise. Upon satisfaction of the merchant's interests, the offender would have been released. By holding defendant for criminal process and searching her, they went beyond their employer's private interests.

(8) (See fn. 10.) Persons so acting should be subject to the constitutional proscriptions that secure an individual's right to privacy, for their actions are taken pursuant to statutory authority to promote a state interest in bringing offenders to public accounting. Unrestrained, such action would subvert state authority in defiance of its established limits. It would destroy the protection those carefully defined limits were intended to afford to everyone, the guilty and innocent alike. It would afford de facto authorizations for searches and seizures incident to arrests or detentions made by private individuals that even peace officers are not authorized to make. Accordingly, we hold that in any case where private security personnel assert the power of the state to make an

arrest or to detain another person for transfer to custody of the state, the state involvement is sufficient for the court to enforce the proper exercise of that power (cf. *People v. Haydel* (1974) 12 Cal. 3d 190, 194 [115 Cal. Rptr. 394, 524 P.2d 866]) by excluding the fruits of illegal abuse thereof. We hold that exclusion of the illegally seized evidence is required by article I, Section 13 of the California Constitution.

The judgment (order granting probation) is reversed.

Dissent by: Clark

Dissent: Clark, J. I dissent for the reasons expressed in my dissenting opinion in *Dyas v. Superior Court* (1974) 11 Cal. 3d 628, 637-638 [114 Cal. Rptr. 114, 522 P.2d 674]. The judgment should be affirmed.

1. Plaintiffs received their licenses under the present Act by derivation from previous licensure under the 1933 Act. (See Ill. Rev. Stat. 1985, ch. 111, par. 2656.) Plaintiffs have made no issue of whether derivative licenses may be revoked on account of any breached present obligation of derivative licensees not to have violated the 1933 Act, even though nonderivative licensees arguably have no such present obligation. Thus, we may deem any such issue waived. Supreme Court Rules 341(e)(7), (f) (113 Ill. 2d Rules 341(e)(7), (f)). But compare Ill. Rev. Stat. 1985, ch.\1, pars. 1001, 1101, 1103 (unless contradicted by terms of particular statute, general rule is that identical new statutory provisions continue old ones and that new law is not construed as repealing old law for purposes of offenses or claims under old) with Ill. Rev. Stat. 1985, ch. 111, par. 2656 (derivative licensees have "same rights and obligations" as nonderivative licensees).

2. If the company was operating without a certificate of authority as a detective agency, the operation violated Section 3a of the 1933 Act (Ill. Rev. Stat. 1983, ch. 111, par. 2604) rather than Section 3. However, the director's eventual finding of fact was that both Letourneau and the company had practiced without licensure as a private detective and a detective agency, respectively—which in Letourneau's case did violate Section 3. The director's conclusion of law was merely that Letourneau violated Section 3, the company going unmentioned.

    Because plaintiffs have made no issue of variances between the formal charges and the findings of fact and conclusions of law, the question may be deemed waived. But see *Bruce v. Department of Registration & Education* (1963), 26 Ill. 2d 612, 620, 187 N.E.2d 711, 715-16 (respondent entitled to notice of charges that must be met); *Jim M'Lady Olds, Inc. v. Secretary of State* (1987), 162 Ill. App. 3d 959, 961-62, 516 N.E.2d 346, 347-48 (same).

3. Va. Code Ann. § 19.2-13(A) provides in relevant part: Upon the application of any corporation authorized to do business in the Commonwealth or the owner, proprietor or authorized custodian of any place within the Commonwealth and the showing of a necessity for the security of property or the peace, the circuit court of any county or city, in its discretion, may appoint one or more special conservators of the peace who shall serve as such for such length of time as the court may designate, but not exceeding four years under any one appointment. The order of appointment may provide that a special conservator of the peace shall have all the powers, functions, duties, responsibilities and authority of any other conservator of the peace within such geographical limitations as the court may deem appropriate, whenever such special conservator of the peace is engaged in the performance of his duties as such.

4. The fraudulent checks were used to obtain Scooby dollars, which in turn were used to purchase park merchandise. The merchandise would then be returned for a refund in cash.

5. While Schwartz transported Austin, Gatewood proceeded to the Hanover County Magistrate's Office with Octavia Marie Eaton ("Eaton"), whom Stone and Taylor had identified as the "Catherine May" suspect from the previous weekend. Eaton was ultimately brought to trial on charges of grand larceny, forgery, and uttering forged checks, but the trial court dismissed the charges on the basis that Eaton's guilt could not be established beyond a reasonable doubt. Eaton subsequently brought a civil action against Paramount, asserting various claims under Virginia law. The United States District Court for the Eastern District of Virginia entered summary judgment in favor of Paramount, however, holding that no genuine issue of fact existed as to whether Gatewood had probable cause to believe that Eaton had committed the offenses in question. On appeal, this court agreed and affirmed. See *Eaton v. Paramount Parks, Inc.*, 141 F.3d 1158, 1998 WL 163833 (4th Cir. 1998) (per curiam) (unpublished).

6. Before trial, Paramount moved for summary judgment on each count asserted in Austin's second amended complaint. The district court granted the motion solely with respect to counts seven and eight. Austin does not challenge that ruling on appeal.

7. At trial, the district court instructed the jury that Hester was "a policy maker of defendant Paramount Parks, Inc.," but failed to specify the area in which Hester purportedly exercised final policy making authority for Paramount.

8. It is worth remembering that the jury found Austin's July 14, 1994 arrest was not effected pursuant to a policy, custom, or practice of Paramount, notwithstanding the district court's instruction that Hester was a "policy maker" of Paramount. The net result in this case is that there was neither a legal nor a factual basis to find Paramount liable under § 1983 based upon a policy.

9. In light of our analysis in part III.B., we are satisfied that there is no basis for the jury's finding that Austin's July 14, 1994 arrest was based upon Hester's actions. Indeed, the record is devoid of any evidence that Hester participated in or approved the decision to effect that arrest or that he could have prevented that arrest upon learning of Gatewood's intention to bring additional charges.

10. Although certain individuals may have been liable for their acts in regard to Austin's arrest and prosecution, Austin did not join them as defendants in the present litigation. Rather, Austin chose to bring suit only against Paramount.

    *Acting as judge of the Court of Appeals by appointment pursuant to Minn. Const. art. VI, § 2.

11. Although some of the court's language suggests that the independent contractor relationship was a subterfuge, the court did not specifically consider the propriety of the jury finding that the security company was an independent contractor.

12. The 1985 rewrite of the Administrative Procedure Act (APA) contains no such requirement. See N.C. Gen. Stat. § 150B-51 (1985). The new APA applies to contested cases commenced on or after January 1, 1986.

13. The court may affirm the decision of the agency or remand the case for further proceedings; or it may reverse or modify the decision if the substantial rights of the petitioners may have been prejudiced because the agency findings, inferences, conclusions, or decisions are
    a. In violation of constitutional provisions; or
    b. In excess of the statutory authority or jurisdiction of the agency; or
    c. Made upon unlawful procedure; or
    d. Affected by other error of law; or
    e. Unsupported by substantial evidence admissible under G.S. 150A-29(a) or G.S.150A-30 in view of the entire record as submitted; or
    f. Arbitrary or capricious.

If the court reverses or modifies the decision of the agency, the judge shall set out in writing, which writing shall become a part of the record, the reasons for such reversal or modification. N.C. Gen. Stat. § 150A-51 (1983).

14. Defendant Padgett claims that although Ms. Tracy did speak to him, their conversation concerned clearing a table for customers, not the impending violence. He claims that he was never made aware of the situation, and had no knowledge of the potential for violence. For the present purposes, however, the Court must assume that Ms. Tracy did, in fact, warn Defendant Padgett about the situation.

15. The relevant portion of that statute reads:

> Every person who, under color of any statute, regulation, custom, or usage of any State or Territory or the District of Columbia, subjects, or causes to be subjected, any citizen of the United States or other person within the jurisdiction thereof to the deprivation of any rights, privileges, or immunities secured by the Constitution and laws, shall be liable to the party injured in an action at law, suit in equity, or other proper proceeding for redress....42 U.S.C. § 1983.

16. Arguably, the *Culberson* decision is distinguishable because the court in that case relied on the fact that the decedent's body had been taken into the "functional custody" of the police chief once he started to search around the pond to find a state-created danger. *Culberson*, 125 F. Supp. 2d at 269. Here, however, Defendant Bridges had neither physical nor functional custody over the Plaintiff. Nonetheless, the Court finds *Culberson* instructive to the extent that the court in that case found the police chief's decision not to act may have increased the Plaintiff's vulnerability to the harm of losing the decedent's body.

17. The Plaintiff has, in fact, presented his theory that Defendant Bridges helped plan the actions of Defendants Parker and Kincaid and was intending to act as their "back-up." The Plaintiff, however, has not presented sufficient evidence to support this theory as a basis for defeating the Defendant's Motion for Summary Judgment.

18. On July 2, 2001, a Stipulation of Voluntary Dismissal was entered as to the Plaintiff's claims under state law for negligent infliction of emotional distress as to all Defendants and as to the claim for assault and battery against Defendant Bridges. Those claims were dismissed with prejudice.

19. The Plaintiff has alleged a separate count of "respondeat superior" against SDSI. This should really be included in the negligence claim, as it merely supplies one theory upon which Defendant SDSI can be found negligent.

20. Plaintiff argues that Mr. Robinson should be held responsible for Strawbridge's alleged failure to properly train its employees with regard to stopping and detaining individuals for suspected shoplifting. We note, however, that this is not a § 1983 action whereby liability may be imposed upon a policy-making official for the failure to train its police-employees and even if it were there has been no showing of deliberate indifference to the need for more or better training or supervision or that plaintiff's purported injuries resulted from a custom, policy or practice on the part of the defendants. See, for example, *City of Canton v. Harris*, 489 U.S. 378, 109 S. Ct. 1197, 103 L. Ed. 2d 412 (1989); *Monell v. Department of Social Services*, 436 U.S. 658, 98 S. Ct. 2018, 56 L. Ed. 2d 611 (1978). Likewise, there is no evidence that Mr. Robinson is a "policy maker."

21. The court need not decide the status of plaintiff Sheila Copeland, Kyong Wood's daughter, given the court's decision herein on the motions to dismiss the case. For convenience, the court will refer herein to Kyong Wood as "plaintiff."

22. Sentry's motion/memorandum neither incorporates Dillons' motion, which expressly relies upon the stated rule, nor cites to Rule 12(b)(6). Nonetheless, the court finds that Sentry's motion is appropriately brought pursuant to that rule.

23. There is some evidence that Moore commenced search of the purse prior to the search of defendant's person by Forrest.

24. Moore, who had worked in undercover narcotics operations with the police and private agencies, suspected the substance was heroin.

25. Forrest did not testify.

26. Insofar as applicable to private persons, the statutes provide: Section 837: "A private person may arrest another: 1. For a public offense committed or attempted in his presence. 2. When the person arrested has committed a felony, although not in his presence. 3. When a felony has been in fact committed and he has reasonable cause for believing the person arrested to have committed it."

    Section 846: "Any person making an arrest may take from the person arrested all offensive weapons which he may have about his person, and must deliver them to the magistrate before whom he is taken."

    Section 847: "A private person who has arrested another for the commission of a public offense must, without unnecessary delay, take the person arrested before a magistrate, or deliver him to a peace officer...."

    Section 849: "(a) When an arrest is made without a warrant by a peace officer or private person, the person arrested, if not otherwise released, shall, without unnecessary delay, be taken before the nearest or most accessible magistrate in the county in which the offense is triable, and a complaint stating the charge against the arrested person shall be laid before such magistrate."

27. Subdivision (e) became effective on January 1, 1977. The Legislature made clear that the provisions of subdivision (e) of Section 490.5 "do not constitute a change in, but are declaratory of, the existing law, and such provisions shall not be interpreted to amend or modify Sections 837, 847, and 849 of the Penal Code." (Stats. 1976, ch. 1131, § 3, p. 5049.)

28. In *People v. Bush* (1974) 37 Cal. App. 3d 952 [112 Cal. Rptr. 770], seizure of a baggie of marijuana by an off duty policeman who effected an arrest was upheld as a seizure of contraband in plain view. Because the officer in Bush was acting outside of his jurisdiction, the court was compelled to treat the arrest as a citizen's arrest. Insofar as Bush suggests that the permissible scope of search incident to a citizen's arrest goes beyond the right to disarm the offender, as provided in Penal Code section 846, it is disapproved.

29. Contrast the extensive decisional law which has expanded the scope of permissible search by a police officer as an incident to arrest despite lack of statutory authorization. (See *Chimel v. California* (1969) 395 U.S. 752 [23 L. Ed. 2d 685, 89 S. Ct. 2034]; *Preston v. U.S.* (1964) 376 U.S. 364, 367 [11 L. Ed. 2d 777, 780, 84 S. Ct. 881]; *People v. Superior Court* (Kiefer) (1970) 3 Cal. 3d 807, 813 [91 Cal. Rptr. 729, 478 P.2d 449, 45 A.L.R.3d 559]; *People v. Norman* (1975) 14 Cal. 3d 929 [123 Cal. Rptr. 109, 538 P.2d 237].)

30. The record discloses no specific facts or circumstances which warranted a search for weapons. According to detective Moore, a "cursory" and routine search for weapons was made because weapons had been found on other occasions. We express no opinion as to the validity of a routine search for weapons after a petty theft (see *People v. Brisendine* (1975) 13 Cal. 3d 528, 536-538 [119 Cal. Rptr. 315, 531 P.2d 1099]), and the People do not rely upon the weapons search as justification for seizure of the narcotics. But, even if we concede the right to search for weapons, the detectives were not justified in seizing and examining the contents

of an opaque bottle in the course of such a limited search. (*Brisendine*, supra, 13 Cal. 3d at p. 543.) A container of pills carried on an individual's person or in his immediate effects does not ordinarily feel like a weapon (*People v. Mosher* (1969) 1 Cal. 3d 379, 394 [82 Cal. Rptr. 379, 461 P.2d 659]), and the person conducting the search is not entitled to engage in "fanciful speculation" as to what the item might be (*People v. Collins* (1970) 1 Cal. 3d 658, 663 [83 Cal. Rptr. 179, 463 P.2d 403]).

31. See Kelsen, General Theory of Law and State (Harvard University Press, 1949) pages 18–20, 50–51.

32. We distinguish action taken pursuant to statutory authority which promotes a state interest (here, enforcement of the penal laws) from action taken pursuant to statute which merely establishes the procedure for regulation of private interests. (See, for example, *Garfinkle v. Superior Court* (1978) 21 Cal. 3d 268 [146 Cal. Rptr. 208, 578 P.2d 925].) Thus, when a merchant exercises his common law privilege (now embodied in Pen. Code, § 490.5), to detain a person suspected of taking merchandise, the merchant is exercising a purely private and self-interested right to protect his property. His conduct does not assume the color of law until he formally arrests the suspected thief, as any citizen is empowered to do (Pen. Code, § 837), or, alternatively, continues the detention for delivery of the suspect to a peace officer who may arrest. Detention and search of a shoplifter, followed by release by the merchant, brings into play no state interest that concerns us here.

Douglas Moore v. Detroit Entertainment, L.L.C., 279 Mich. App. 195; 755 N.W.2d 686 (Mich. App. 2008)

Opinion by: Elizabeth L. Gleicher

Plaintiff commenced this action alleging multiple state-law intentional torts and a violation of 42 USC 1983 after Detroit Entertainment, L.L.C., doing business as Motor City Casino, through several casino employees, denied plaintiff entry into the casino, thereafter detained him inside the casino, and ultimately banned him permanently from the casino. Defendant appeals as of right, challenging various aspects of a final judgment entered by the trial court after a jury trial, at the conclusion of which the jury returned a special verdict in plaintiff's favor. Plaintiff cross-appeals, contesting the trial court's pretrial order granting summary disposition of his abuse-of-process and malicious-prosecution claims. We affirm.

I. Underlying Facts and Proceedings

Plaintiff and five companions traveled to the Motor City Casino on the evening of September 14, 2002, to take advantage of a complimentary meal and to gamble. When the group's Metro car arrived at the casino's valet entrance, some members of the group, including plaintiff, held cups containing alcoholic beverages, but disposed of the cups when advised that they could not enter the casino with them. Much trial testimony disputed whether (1) plaintiff stumbled while alighting from the group's Metro car and approaching the valet lobby, (2) plaintiff's speech was slurred, (3) plaintiff's eyes appeared glassy, or (4) plaintiff's breath smelled of alcohol.

There is no dispute, however, that in the valet lobby, defendant Jose Oscar Martinez, a casino security manager who had obtained "PA 330 certification" under MCL 338.1079, barred plaintiff's entry on the basis that he appeared inebriated and thus constituted a potential liability to the casino. Plaintiff and some of his companions expressed disbelief, denied that plaintiff was intoxicated, and asked to speak with a manager. But the evidence diverged concerning the extent of plaintiff's physical reaction to Martinez's announcement: some testimony described that while protesting his exclusion and demanding a manager, plaintiff may have made "nonchalant" gestures with his arm or hand, although this testimony varied regarding plaintiff's proximity to Martinez at the time of the gestures, while other testimony recounted that plaintiff seemed to have intentionally pointed a finger or directed an open hand that made contact with Martinez's chest. Many witnesses recalled seeing Martinez step backward.

Other nearby casino security personnel announced that an assault had occurred, which prompted plaintiff and his companions to depart from the valet lobby and walk across the street. A group consisting of several casino security officers, at some point accompanied by two Detroit police officers, eventually confronted plaintiff and his companions. Another PA 330-certified casino security manager, John Grzadzinski, offered plaintiff the choice to either return to the casino to discuss the alleged assault, or to place himself in the custody of the Detroit Police Department. At trial, Grzadzinski replied affirmatively to plaintiff's counsel's inquiry whether the Detroit police officers present likewise "suggested to [plaintiff] that he go back with [Grzadzinski] into the casino, is that right?" Richard Novak, one of plaintiff's companions and his longtime business attorney, recounted at trial that after Grzadzinski announced the two choices "loud enough for everybody to hear," Novak spoke with the Detroit police officers present in the group, and "asked the DPD" whether they agreed with Grzadzinski's two alternative proposals. According to Novak, the officers "said we don't care, it's your call." Plaintiff, who initially declined to return to the casino, ultimately elected, on Novak's advice, to allow himself to be escorted back to the casino's security office.

In a detention room, pursuant to casino policies and applicable administrative rules, plaintiff underwent a pat-down search and the removal and inventory of his personal property, before being left alone in the locked detention room. At plaintiff's request, someone later escorted him to a bathroom. On returning to the detention room, against plaintiff's expressed wishes, security personnel locked him back inside the detention room. Ultimately, Grzadzinski obtained plaintiff's signature on an "86 form" permanently banning him from the casino, although Grzadzinski denied plaintiff's requests that Novak review the form or that plaintiff receive a copy of the form.

The trial evidence established that plaintiff's detention period was about 2-1/2 hours. Plaintiff then left the Motor City Casino with his companions, and everyone went to the Greektown Casino.

In May 2003, a Wayne County Sheriff's deputy arrested plaintiff at Detroit Metropolitan Airport when he learned plaintiff had outstanding assault and battery warrants arising from the September 14, 2002, incident at the Motor City Casino. The criminal proceedings against plaintiff were temporarily terminated in September 2003, when the 36th District Court dismissed the charge without prejudice because no prosecution witnesses appeared. Sometime in 2005, plaintiff discovered the existence of resurrected arrest warrants relating to September 14, 2002. After a December 2005 trial in the 36th District Court, a jury acquitted plaintiff.

II. Challenges to 42 USC § 1983 Special Verdict

Defendant first contends that the trial court erred by denying its motion for a directed verdict regarding plaintiff's § 1983 claim. Defendant specifically challenges the trial court's ruling as a matter of law that the casino, through the conduct of its PA 330-certified security officers, acted under color of state law during the September 14, 2002, detention of plaintiff.

A

This Court reviews de novo a trial court's ruling on a litigant's motion for a directed verdict. *Candelaria v. B C Gen Contractors, Inc,* 236 Mich App 67, 71; 600 NW2d 348 (1999). In reviewing the trial court's ruling, this Court examines the evidence presented and all legitimate inferences arising therefrom in the light most favorable to the nonmoving party. *Farm Credit Serv's of Michigan's Heartland, PCA v. Weldon,* 232 Mich App 662, 668; 591 NW2d 438 (1998). "A directed verdict is appropriate only when no material factual question exists upon which reasonable minds could differ." *Candelaria, supra* at 71-72. "If reasonable jurors could honestly have reached different conclusions, neither the trial court nor this Court may substitute its judgment for that of the jury." *Hunt v. Freeman,* 217 Mich App 92, 99; 550 NW2d 817 (1996). The "appellate court recognizes the jury's and the judge's unique opportunity to observe the witnesses, as well as the factfinder's responsibility to determine the credibility and weight of trial testimony." *Zeeland Farm Serv's, Inc v. JBL Enterprises, Inc,* 219 Mich App 190, 195; 555 NW2d 733 (1996).

B

According to 42 USC 1983, any person who experiences "the deprivation of any rights, privileges, or immunities secured by the Constitution and laws" because of the actions of another person acting "*under color of any statute, ordinance, regulation, custom, or usage, of any State*" may file an action seeking relief against the party that caused the deprivation. (Emphasis added.) The dispute in this appeal focuses on the "under color of" state law element of a § 1983 claim.

The United States Court of Appeals for the Sixth Circuit recently examined, in relevant part as follows, the contours of the requisite state-action element:

> The issue in this appeal is whether Plaintiffs can demonstrate that Defendant acted "under color of state law" by showing that Defendant's conduct constituted state action. See *Lugar v. Edmondson Oil Co, Inc,* 457 U.S. 922, 942; 102 SCt 2744; 73 L Ed 2d 482 (1982) .... Section 1983 does not, as a general rule, prohibit the conduct of private parties acting in their individual capacities. ... However, "[a] private actor acts under color of state law when its conduct is "'fairly attributable to the state.'" *Romanski v. Detroit Entertainment, LLC,* 428 F3d 629, 636 (CA 6, 2005)] (quoting *Lugar [supra* at 937]).
>
> "What [conduct] is fairly attributable [to the state] is a matter of normative judgment, and the criteria lack rigid simplicity." *Brentwood [Academy v. Tennessee Secondary School Athletic Ass'n,* 531 U.S. 288, 295; 121 S Ct 924; 148 L Ed 2d 807 (2001). The Supreme Court and this Court, however, have provided several significant milestones to guide our inquiry as to whether Defendant's conduct constitutes state action. As we recognized in *Chapman v. Higbee Co,* 319 F3d 825, 833 (CA 6, 2003),] "[t]he Supreme Court has developed three tests for determining the existence of state action in a particular case: (1) the public function test, (2) the state compulsion test, and (3) the symbiotic relationship or nexus test." Of these three tests, the only one relevant to the instant case is the public function test. Under the public function test, courts have found "state action present in the exercise by a private entity of powers traditionally exclusively reserved to the State." *Jackson v. Metro Edison Co,* 419 U.S. 345, 352; 95 S Ct 449; 42 L Ed 2d 477 (1974). The Supreme Court has found this requirement satisfied where the state permitted a private entity to hold elections, allowed a private company

to own a town, or established private ownership of a municipal park. However, the Supreme Court has explicitly declined to decide the question of "whether and under what circumstances private police officers may be said to perform a public function for purposes of § 1983." *Romanski*, 428 F3d at 636. [*Lindsey v. Detroit Entertainment, LLC,* 484 F3d 824, 827-828 (CA 6, 2007) (some citations omitted).]

C

The trial court in this case invoked *Romanski, supra,* when finding that Martinez, Grzadzinski, and other casino security personnel acted under color of state law in detaining plaintiff. Because the parties argue at length concerning the propriety of the trial court's application of *Romanski,* we now turn to a careful examination of *Romanski.*

Romanski involved a casino patron's claim against the instant defendant. In *Romanski,* the plaintiff, age 72, "took a walk around the gaming floor," during which she "noticed a five cent token lying in a slot machine's tray. Seeing no chair at the machine, she picked up the token and returned to the machine at which she had earlier played, intending to use the token there." *Romanski, supra* at 632. Several casino security officers descended on the plaintiff and advised her that the casino had a "policy not to permit patrons to pick up tokens, which appeared to be abandoned, found at other slot machines, a practice known as 'slot-walking,'" despite the fact that the casino had not posted notice of such a policy. *Id.* at 633. One defendant security officer, Marlene Brown, recalled that because Romanski "became loud and belligerent," several security personnel escorted her to the casino's "small and windowless" security office "located off the casino's floor." *Id.* at 633.

According to Romanski, once they had taken their seats, Brown accused Romanski of stealing the token, whereupon Brown counted Romanski's money and removed one nickel from Romanski's winnings. [Brown's supervisor JoEtta] Stevenson asked Romanski to turn over her social security card and driver's license; Romanski complied and these items were photocopied. Romanski was then photographed. Romanski testified that she acquiesced to these requests because Brown said she was a police officer, had a badge, and appeared to have handcuffs. ... [A] uniformed casino security officer stood just outside the room for the duration of the questioning. Romanski was ejected from the casino for a period of 6 months; Stevenson made the final decision to eject, or "86," Romanski. ... Although unknown to Romanski at the time, it is now undisputed that Brown and some of her colleagues on the casino's security staff were licensed under state law as "private security police officer[s]." MCL 338.1079. By virtue of being so licensed, a private security police officer has "the authority to arrest a person without a warrant as set forth for public peace officers ... when that private security police officer is on the employer's premises." MCL 338.1080. The statute additionally requires that private security police officers make arrests only when they are on duty and in "the full uniform of their employer." *Id.* It is undisputed that Brown was on duty during the events of this case. It is also undisputed that Brown was not wearing the uniform worn by some of the other security guards, but Defendants have never contended that this rendered Brown out of uniform for purposes of MCL 338.1080; indeed, *Defendants have conceded from the beginning that the statute applies in this case. Their argument is simply that the power admittedly conferred on Brown by the statute did not make her actions under color of state law. See 42 USC 1983.* [*Romanski, supra* at 633 (emphasis added).]

The plaintiff filed an amended complaint that contained several state-law tort claims and "a claim under 42 USC § 1983 that Defendants had violated Romanski's Fourth Amendment rights," specifically "that Defendants, acting under color of state law, had arrested her without probable cause because the token she picked up was abandoned, that is, not the casino's property." *Romanski, supra* at 634.

When the defendants sought summary judgment of Romanski's § 1983 claim on the basis that they had not acted under color of state law, the district court denied the motion, holding "as a matter of law that Defendants had acted under color of state law ... because Brown, the defendant who initiated Romanski's detention, did so while on duty in her capacity as a licensed private security police officer empowered with the same arrest authority as a public police officer." *Romanski, supra* at 635. A jury found in the plaintiff's favor regarding her § 1983 claim that the defendants violated her Fourth Amendment rights, and consequently awarded "$500 in punitive damages against Brown, and $875,000 in punitive damages against the casino." *Id.* The district court denied a motion for a judgment notwithstanding the verdict, and the defendants appealed. *Id.* at 635–636.

The Sixth Circuit affirmed in *Romanski*, rejecting the defendants' contention that they did not qualify as state actors. The Sixth Circuit commenced its analysis by surveying federal caselaw that had considered whether private security officers acted under color of state law, including *Payton v. Rush-Presbyterian-St Luke's Med Ctr*, 184 F3d 623, 627-630 (CA 7, 1999), in which "the Seventh Circuit held that private police officers licensed to make arrests could be state actors under the public function test." *Romanski, supra* at 637. In discussion highly relevant to the instant case, the Sixth Circuit ascertained and applied the following guiding principles:

> [T]he crucial fact in [*Payton*]—assumed to be true there but indisputable here—was that by virtue of their status as on-duty special police officers, licensed by the city of Chicago, the defendants enjoyed "virtually the same power as public police officers." *Id.* at 629. Indeed, the defendants in *Payton* operated under an ordinance which provided that special police officers licensed under it "shall possess the powers of the regular police patrol at the places for which they are respectively appointed or in the line of duty for which they are engaged." *Id.* at 625.
> * * *
> Payton illustrates a line that has been drawn in the case law. The line divides cases in which a private actor exercises a power traditionally reserved to the state, but not exclusively reserved to it, for example, the common law shopkeeper's privilege, from cases in which a private actor exercises a power exclusively reserved to the state, for example, the police power. Where private security guards are endowed by law with plenary police powers such that they are de facto police officers, they may qualify as state actors under the public function test. ... The rationale of these cases is that when the state delegates a power traditionally reserved to it alone-the police power-to private actors in order that they may provide police services to institutions that need it, a "plaintiff's ability to claim relief under § 1983 [for abuses of that power] should be unaffected." Payton, supra at 629.
> On the other side of the line illustrated by *Payton* are cases in which the private defendants have some police-like powers but not plenary police authority. ... A subset of these cases are cases in which a private institution's security employees have been dispatched to protect the institution's interests or enforce its policies. The canonical example here is when a store avails itself of the common law shopkeeper's privilege ... .

Like the district court, we think this case falls on the *Payton* side of the line. It is undisputed that Brown (and some of her colleagues) were private security police officers licensed under [MCL 338.1079]. This means that Brown's qualifications for being so licensed were vetted by Michigan's department of state police, *id.* § (1), and that Brown was subject to certain statutes administered by that department. *Id.* § (2); *see* MCL 338.1067, MCL 338.1069. More critical for present purposes are the undisputed facts that Brown was on duty and on the casino's premises at all times relevant to this case. *These undisputed facts lead to an inescapable conclusion of law—namely, that at all times relevant to this case, Brown "had the authority to arrest a person without a warrant as set forth for public peace officers ... ." [MCL 338.1080]. One consequence of Brown's possession of this authority, the authority to make arrests at one's discretion and for any offenses, is clear: at all times relevant to this case, Brown was a state actor as a matter of law.*

Unlike the common law privileges at issue in *Wade v. Byles*, 83 F3d 902 (CA 7, 1996)] (the use of deadly force in self-defense, the right to detain for trespass, and the right to carry a weapon) and *Chapman[, supra*, 319 F3d 825] (the shopkeeper's privilege), which may be invoked by any citizen under appropriate circumstances, the plenary arrest power enjoyed by private security police officers licensed pursuant to MCL 338.1079 is a power traditionally reserved to the state alone. ...

Defendants contend that *Wade* ought to control here because, as in that case, private security police officers' power to make arrests is subject to spatial or geographic limits. *See* [MCL 338.1080]. But the spatial or geographic limitation in *Wade* was profound—it prohibited housing authority security guards from exercising their (already minimal) powers anywhere except in the lobbies of buildings operated by the housing authority. *See Wade,* [*supra* at 906]. By contrast, [MCL 338.1080] invests private security police officers with full arrest authority on the entirety of their employer's premises, which makes this case distinguishable from *Wade* and similar to *Payton* and *Henderson* [*v. Fisher*, 631 F2d 1115 (CA 3, 1980)], each of which involved a statute or ordinance that imposed or contemplated some spatial or geographic limits on the private defendants' police powers. *See Payton,* [*supra* at 625](special police officers "shall possess the powers of the regular police patrol *at the places for which they are respectively appointed*) (emphasis added) ...; *Henderson, supra* at 1117–1119 (authority of the university police was limited to the university campus in question). *Furthermore, as we have discussed, private security police officers in Michigan are endowed with plenary arrest authority, see* [MCL 338.1080], while the defendant in *Wade* was permitted to exercise only what were in effect citizens' arrests. [*Romanski, supra* at 637–639 (emphasis added; some citations omitted).]

D

The Sixth Circuit subsequently addressed § 1983 claims filed by several plaintiffs who underwent similar detentions by Motor City Casino security personnel in *Lindsey, supra* at 826. The *Lindsey* court did not question or criticize the legal principles espoused or the conclusion reached by the court in *Romanski*, which it reviewed in detail. *Lindsey, supra* at 828–831. The Sixth Circuit held, however, that the defendants in *Lindsey* had not acted under color of state law, citing the following factual distinction:

Plaintiffs argue that *Romanski* supports a finding that Defendant's security personnel were likewise state actors in this case. We disagree. Unlike *Romanski*, where it was undisputed that Defendant's security personnel were licensed under [MCL 338.1079], *here, exactly the opposite appears to be the case.* Plaintiffs' complaint alleges that: "At the time of the seizure[s] and detention[s] ..., none of [Defendant's] security guards were authorized to make misdemeanor arrests. ..."

If Defendant's security personnel had in fact been licensed pursuant to [MCL 338.1079], they would have had misdemeanor arrest authority at the time that they seized and detained Plaintiffs. Hence, Plaintiffs' allegation that Defendant's security personnel lacked such authority is by implication an assertion that Defendant's security personnel were not licensed under [MCL 338.1079]. Moreover, at oral argument, Plaintiffs were asked to point the Court to any information in the record that suggested that Defendant's security personnel were licensed pursuant to [MCL 338.1079] at the time of Plaintiffs' arrests, and Plaintiffs could point to no such information. *Plaintiffs have therefore not carried their burden of demonstrating that any of Defendant's security guards were licensed under [MCL 338.1079], and we must proceed under the assumption that all of Defendant's security personnel who interfaced with Plaintiffs were not so licensed.*

The fact that Defendant's security personnel were *not* licensed in this case means that, under the facts of this case, Defendant's conduct in detaining Plaintiffs was not "fairly attributable to the state." ...

* * *

This analysis [in *Romanski*] demonstrates that the fact that Michigan delegated a part of the police power to licensed private security guards, which it had traditionally and exclusively reserved for itself, was the key fact that justified finding state action in *Romanski*. Although the police power that Michigan bestowed upon licensed security guards pursuant to [MCL 338.1080] was limited in certain respects, the plaintiff in *Romanski* could point to an identifiable police power—the power of arrest—which was not possessed by the citizens of Michigan at large, but instead resided only in the state, its agents, and those persons who the state empowered and regulated by statute. By contrast, Plaintiffs here cannot point to any powers above and beyond those possessed by ordinary citizens that the state of Michigan had delegated to Defendant's unlicensed security personnel at the time of Plaintiffs' arrests. The instant case is thus squarely within the rule of *Chapman*, where this Court held that a merchant exercising the "shopkeeper's privilege" was not a state actor under the public function test. [*Chapman, supra* at 834]. Because Plaintiffs cannot demonstrate that Defendant's security personnel were licensed under [MCL 338.1079], they cannot show that Defendant engaged in action attributable to the state. Plaintiffs therefore cannot demonstrate that Defendant deprived them of their rights secured by the Constitution by acting under color of state law, and their § 1983 claim must fail. [*Lindsey, supra* at 829–831 (emphasis added; some citations omitted).]

E

After reviewing the record in this case, we find that it falls squarely within the facts and legal analysis presented in *Romanski*, which properly concluded as a matter of law that the state-licensed private security officers involved in the casino detention acted under color of state law. Here, the parties do not dispute that at the time of plaintiff's detention on September 14, 2002, Martinez, security manager Chenine McDowell, and Grzadzinski had obtained certification pursuant to MCL 338.1079. During trial, Martinez, McDowell, and Grzadzinski elaborated on the training they had received, under the tutelage of a Detroit police officer and through the Michigan State Police, to obtain their statutory certifications, which they understood to invest them with the authority to make certain arrests inside the casino. Because the record indisputably establishes that Martinez and others involved in plaintiff's detention on September 14, 2002, primarily Grzadzinski and McDowell, had obtained state licensure pursuant to MCL 338.1079, and, consequently, pursuant to MCL 338.1080, Martinez, Grzadzinski, and McDowell all possessed the power to arrest plaintiff on casino premises for his alleged assault ("a part of the police power" that the state "had traditionally and exclusively reserved for itself," *Lindsey, supra* at 831, citing *Romanski, supra* at 637), and Martinez, Grzadzinski, and McDowell arranged for plaintiff to be held within the casino's security detention room on the basis of this statutory authority, we conclude that the trial court correctly ruled as a matter of law that defendant, through Martinez, Grzadzinski, and McDowell, acted under color of state law for purposes of § 1983.

We stress that ours is decidedly a fact-specific holding, in accordance with the United States Supreme Court's observations in *Lugar, supra* at 939, that the state-action inquiry is "necessarily fact-bound," and that a court's approach to the inquiry must be closely tailored to the evidence before it. We further emphasize that our holding is entirely inconsistent with the notions that licensed, private security guards are always state-actors, or that the mere performance of a task specifically authorized by a state statute confers state actor status. Contrary to the dissent's hyperbolic and dire prophesy, Michigan's day-care providers, plumbers, barbers, beauticians, electricians, and cab drivers need not fear an onslaught of litigation triggered by our ruling today. Those licensed professionals obviously do not qualify as state actors because they do not exercise powers "traditionally exclusively reserved to the State." *Jackson, supra* at 352. No portion of our opinion conflicts with the oft-repeated principle, first articulated in *Jackson*, that "[t]he mere fact that a business is subject to state regulation does not by itself convert its action into that of the State for purposes of the Fourteenth Amendment." *Id.* at 350.

In the instant case, the casino's employees arrested and detained a casino customer because they suspected that he had committed an assault and battery. Those employees' ability to arrest plaintiff derived solely from their special state licensure. Officers of the Detroit Police Department expressly approved the casino employees' actions. These facts conclusively demonstrate that the casino's employees exercised powers "traditionally exclusively reserved to the state," and did so with the encouragement and approbation of the state itself.

Indeed, the record of state action here far exceeds the state action involved in *Romanski*. Here, licensed security guards effectuated an arrest to investigate a violent crime, while Mrs. Romanski's detention arose from a suspected larceny. The power to arrest and detain a larcenous customer does not rest exclusively with the state of Michigan, but resides in all Michigan security guards by virtue of MCL 338.1079(2). Furthermore, the city police officers here watched and helped direct the security personnel's decision to take plaintiff into custody, while the security personnel in *Romanski* acted in the absence of any police presence. We therefore reject as completely unfounded the dissent's suggestion that our decision unreasonably expands state-action concepts.

Although defendant urges that we reject *Romanski* as a nonbinding intermediate federal appellate court decision, this Court plainly may adopt as persuasive a "lower federal court decision" involving federal law. *Abela v. General Motors Corp*, 469 Mich 603, 607; 677 NW2d 325 (2004). Furthermore, as noted, we view the similar relevant facts and applicable legal analysis in *Romanski* as persuasive in this case, and defendant has not identified, and we have not located, any

United States Supreme Court decision casting doubt on the state-actor conclusion in *Romanski*. The Supreme Court declined to consider the holding in *Romanski*, denying certiorari at 549 U.S. 946; 127 S Ct 209; 166 L Ed 2d 257 (2006).

F

We additionally note that the United States Supreme Court has provided a succinct principle to aid in the analysis of the state-action requirement in § 1983 cases, which we view as instructive to our state-action conclusion in this case. "[I]n the usual case we ask whether the State provided a mantle of authority that enhanced the power of the harm-causing individual actor." *Nat'l Collegiate Athletic Ass'n v. Tarkanian*, 488 U.S. 179, 192; 109 S Ct 454; 102 L Ed 2d 469 (1988). The instant record establishes indisputably that plaintiff's detention within the locked casino security room commenced immediately after a combined force of Detroit police officers and casino security personnel confronted plaintiff, his attorney, and his other companions as they attempted to leave the casino grounds. Both Grzadzinski and Richard Novak testified that the Detroit police officers authorized, and indeed encouraged, defendant's security personnel to seize plaintiff and escort him back to the casino. This evidence strongly supports our conclusion that the state "provided a mantle of authority" that constrained plaintiff to subject himself to detention by defendant.

> [T]o act "under color of" state law for § 1983 purposes does not require that the defendant be an officer of the State. It is enough that he is a willful participant in joint action with the State or its agents. Private persons, jointly engaged with state officials in the challenged action, are acting "under color" of law for purposes of § 1983 actions. [*Dennis v. Sparks*, 449 U.S. 24, 27-28; 101 S Ct 183; 66 L Ed 2d 185 (1980).]

In *Chapman, supra*, at 835, the Sixth Circuit, sitting en banc, concluded that a customer's detention by a store security guard could qualify as an act "that may fairly be attributed to the state." The security guard, an off-duty, armed, uniformed sheriff's deputy, initiated a strip search of the customer, and store policy mandated "police intervention in strip search situations … ." *Id.* at 835. Utilizing the "symbiotic or nexus test," the Sixth Circuit held that a genuine issue of material fact existed "as to whether the security officer acted under "color of state law" when he initiated the search. *Id.* at 834–835. The Sixth Circuit explained that a § 1983 claimant could satisfy the symbiotic or nexus test by demonstrating "that there is a sufficiently close nexus between the government and the private party's conduct so that the conduct may be fairly attributed to the state itself." *Chapman, supra* at 834.

The testimony in the instant case established not only a close working relationship between defendant's security personnel and the Detroit police officers posted near the casino, but a joint and cooperative effort to detain plaintiff either in a city jail cell or its casino equivalent. We therefore hold, in conformity with the *Chapman* majority, that defendants' joint engagement with the Detroit police in the arrest and detention of plaintiff also satisfies the symbiotic relationship or nexus test of action "under color of state law."

> In response to defendant's protestation on appeal that in the trial court plaintiff never proposed the symbiotic relationship or nexus test as a potential basis for finding state action, we observe that we have the authority to consider this question of law for the first time on appeal because all facts necessary for its resolution appear in the existing

record. *Royce v. Chatwell Club Apartments*, 276 Mich App 389, 399; 740 NW2d 547 (2007), application for leave to appeal held in abeyance 743 NW2d 213 (2008).

G

We do not find persuasive defendant's suggestion that the "private detention" of plaintiff could not constitute state action. According to this argument, defendant's employees' "conduct in detaining, processing and eventually 86'ing Plaintiff, constituted, at most, an "arrest' for purposes of state civil liability," and the jury's rejection of plaintiff's false arrest claim eliminated defendant's "state action" liability. In our view, this distinction lacks a meaningful difference, particularly under the circumstances presented here. Defendant's security personnel restrained plaintiff's freedom of movement because they believed he assaulted and battered Martinez. Defendant's employees' entitlement to detain plaintiff—either momentarily or for two hours and 15 minutes—derived directly from their state licensure. Their conduct, therefore, qualified as state action, and deprived plaintiff of a right "secured by the Constitution." See *Davis v. Mississippi*, 394 U.S. 721, 726-727; 89 S Ct 1394; 22 L Ed 2d 676 (1969), in which the United States Supreme Court observed that "the Fourth Amendment was meant to prevent wholesale intrusions upon the personal security of our citizenry, whether these intrusions be termed 'arrests' or 'investigatory detentions,'" and *Dunaway v. New York*, 442 U.S. 200, 216; 99 S Ct 2248; 60 L Ed 2d 824 (1979) (observing that "detention for custodial interrogation-regardless of its label-intrudes so severely on interests protected by the Fourth Amendment as necessarily to trigger the traditional safeguards against illegal arrest").

The trial testimony here shows that when plaintiff and his companions were surrounded by casino security personnel and Detroit police officers, Grzadzinski offered plaintiff two choices, go with the police or return to the casino security office to discuss the matter; at no time was plaintiff advised he could simply continue his departure from casino property. Although plaintiff's testimony suggested that he returned to the casino voluntarily, other trial testimony shows that after Grzadzinski escorted plaintiff to the casino detention room, plaintiff remained there against his will for more than two hours. Under these circumstances, the jury reasonably could have found a violation of § 1983.

The dissent also asserts that "[t]he security guards never exercised any power to arrest," *ante* at , and points to the jury's verdict that "no false arrest occurred in this case." [Citation omitted] Although defendants did not *falsely* arrest plaintiff, the evidence demonstrates that he was detained, placed into custody, and thereafter subjected to the will of defendant's security personnel. In *People v. Gonzales*, 356 Mich 247, 253; 97 NW2d 16 (1959), our Supreme Court adopted the following definition of "arrest":

> An arrest is the taking, seizing, or detaining of the person of another, either by touching or putting hands on him, or by any act which indicates an intention to take him into custody and subjects the person arrested to the actual control and will of the person making the arrest. The act relied upon as constituting an arrest must have been performed with the intent to effect an arrest and must have been so understood by the party arrest. [Internal quotation marks and citation omitted.]

The jury's rejection of plaintiff's false-arrest claim does not alter the fact that defendant's security officers restricted plaintiff's freedom of movement during the two hours and 15 minutes of his detention, and did so on the basis of the authority provided by MCL 338.1080 to the security officers. The dissent has identified no basis other than MCL 338.1080 that would have permitted plaintiff's arrest and detention, and we are unaware of any. The licensing statute provided the mantel of authority for defendant's security personnel, and imbued them with virtually the same powers as the Detroit police officers who explicitly approved defendants' decision to escort plaintiff back to the casino.

H

We also find unpersuasive defendant's related suggestion that no state action existed here because, although several of its officers had certification under MCL 338.1079 and the authority to arrest pursuant to MCL 338.1080, they routinely did not employ their authority to arrest casino patrons. We agree with the following portion of *Romanski*, in which the Sixth Circuit rejected this precise contention:

> Finally, we address Defendants' repeated representation that, although empowered to make arrests under [MCL 338.1080], Brown and the other casino employees licensed under the statute are, as a matter of casino policy, not permitted to exercise this statutory authority to effectuate arrests. For this argument Defendants again rely on *Wade*, in which the very document that was the source of the defendant's police-type powers, his contract with the public housing authority, at the same time imposed profound limits on those powers. *See Wade*, [*supra* at 905-906]. Here the source of Brown's power to make arrests is a statute that includes no qualitative limits on that power, so *Wade* is inapplicable. Defendants do not cite a case in which a private security officer licensed to make arrests as under [MCL 338.1080] was held not to be a state actor on the ground that the officer's employer substantially circumscribed the arrest power conferred on the officer by having been licensed. [*Romanski, supra* at 639–640.]

I

We additionally reject that *Grand Rapids v. Impens,* 414 Mich 667; 327 NW2d 278 (1982), on which defendant and the dissent rely heavily, controls the state-actor analysis in this case. In *Impens*, the Michigan Supreme Court considered "whether a signed statement procured by private security guards, one of whom was an off-duty deputy sheriff, may be admitted into evidence against a defendant even though no *Miranda* warnings were given." *Id*. at 670 (citation omitted). The Supreme Court surveyed several decisions holding "that private security guards who receive direct assistance from public police officers or who work in close connection with the police may be acting under color of state law, subject to constitutional restrictions." *Id*. at 674. The Supreme Court concluded, in relevant part, as follows:

> We do not believe that the activities of the store security guards and the city police in this case demonstrated the coordinated effort necessary to constitute state action. The Meijer security personnel were working with the view of furthering their employer's interest only; they were not acting as police agents. Their role may be viewed as an extension of the common-law shopkeepers' privilege to detain for a reasonable period of time a person suspected of theft or failure to pay. There was no complicity with the police department or any indication that their acts were instigated or motivated by the police.
> * * *

Defendant also contends that Meijer security personnel qualified as law enforcement officers because state action has granted them greater authority than that possessed by private citizens. ... [D]efendant believes that the licensing statutes which regulate private security guards demonstrate the requisite degree of state action to bring their activities under color of state law, subject to constitutional restraints. See MCL 338.1051 *et seq.* ... ..We disagree. We do not believe that the mere licensing of security guards constitutes sufficient government involvement to require the giving of *Miranda* warnings. ...

      * * *

Our statute specifically states that "private security police employed for the purpose for guarding the property and employees of their employer and generally maintaining plant security for their employer" need not be licensed. MCL 338.1079. ... This language speaks to the exact function performed by Meijer's security personnel. We do not believe that qualification for such licensing exclusion equates the actions of private security guards with those of law enforcement officers. [*Impens, supra* at 675–677 (citation omitted).]

The Supreme Court did not elaborate regarding whether the defendant security officers had obtained state licensing, thus investing them with the authority to make arrests pursuant to MCL 338.1080. The Supreme Court made no reference whatsoever to MCL 338.1080.

As reflected in the following portion of *Romanski*, which we also find persuasive, the Sixth Circuit likewise considered the effect of the Michigan Supreme Court's decision in *Impens* on the question of state action in the context of a § 1983 action:

The dissent's repeated reliance on *City of Grand Rapids v. Impens* ... is misplaced. There, private security officers suspected the defendant and two others of shoplifting. *Id.* at 279. The officers *asked* the three individuals to come to the security office. *Id.* The officers searched the three and found merchandise on one of the other individuals. *Id.* The officers then elicited information from the defendant to complete a "Loss Prevention Department Voluntary Statement." *Id.* The officers read the statement to the defendant and asked the defendant to sign it, which he did. *Id.* "There was no indication that defendant would not be released if the statement were not signed." *Id.* Prior to his trial, the defendant moved to suppress the signed statement, arguing that it was obtained in violation of *Miranda. Id.* The Michigan Court held that the private security officers were not required to give *Miranda* warnings. *Id.* at 282.

One obvious distinction between the instant case and *Impens* is that *Impens* did not involve an arrest in any form. There, the defendant was not held against his will. He was asked to go to the security office; he was asked to sign a form. There was no indication of arrest.

The key distinction, however, is that the security officers did not exercise power exclusively reserved to the states. The contested conduct was the security officers' elicitation of the defendant's statements. Simply put, asking questions in a noncustodial setting is a power not within the exclusive province of the state. [*Romanski, supra* at 638 n 2 (some emphasis added).]

The dissent asserts that *Impens* should control the outcome of this case because it held that "the simple fact of licensure would not transform a private security guard into a state actor."

As we have emphasized, however, "the simple fact of licensure" did not "transform" defendant's security guards into state actors. Rather, their licensure triggered the security guards' exercise of a power traditionally and exclusively reserved to the state. And unlike the security guards in *Impens,* defendant's security personnel here employed a "coordinated effort" with police officers, thus unquestionably acting as "police agents." These distinctions are not "immaterial," as the dissent claims, but central to the *Impens* decision, at least according to the justices who wrote and joined that opinion.

We conclude that, irrespective of whether the trial court may have employed incorrect logic, the court correctly distinguished *Impens* from the instant case. *Coates v. Bastian Bros, Inc,* 276 Mich App 498, 508-509; 741 NW2d 539 (2007) (observing that this Court "will not reverse if the right result is reached, albeit for the wrong reason").

J

Defendant alternatively maintains that the trial court should have ordered a new trial, in light of the defective jury instructions concerning plaintiff's § 1983 claim. This Court reviews for an abuse of discretion a trial court's ultimate decision whether to grant a new trial, but considers "de novo any questions of law that arise." *Kelly v. Builders Square, Inc,* 465 Mich 29, 34; 632 NW2d 912 (2001).

> This Court reviews claims of instructional error de novo. MCR 2.516(D)(2) states that the trial court must give a jury instruction if a party requests such instruction and it is applicable to the case. We review for abuse of discretion the trial court's determination whether a standard jury instruction is applicable and accurate. The trial court's jury instructions must include all the elements of the plaintiffs' claims and should not omit any material issues, defenses, or theories of the parties that the evidence supports. ... If, on balance, the theories of the parties and the applicable law are adequately and fairly presented to the jury, no error requiring reversal occurs. Reversal based on instructional error is only required where the failure to reverse would be inconsistent with substantial justice. MCR 2.613(A) ... . [*Lewis v. LeGrow,* 258 Mich App 175, 211-212; 670 NW2d 675 (2003).]

1

Defendant first complains that the trial court erred by failing to explain to the jury that the casino could only face vicarious liability for any constitutional violation by its employees "pursuant to a custom, policy or practice of th[e] employer." (Defendant's brief, p 33.) Before instructing the jury, the trial court agreed, over plaintiff's objection, to instruct the jury regarding the concept of respondeat superior. But when instructing the jury, the trial court failed to incorporate any reference to vicarious liability. After the jury retired to deliberate, defense counsel apprised the trial court that it had "omitted instructing on private security officer, MCL 338 [.1079]." Plaintiff's counsel replied that he had no objection to the private-security-officer instruction, and the following exchange then occurred:

> *The Court:* Alright, I'll give it. Anything else?
> *Defense Counsel:* No, we've been through it all.

The jury returned and received instruction with respect to the authority of private security officers, after which the parties again discussed the propriety of the instructions:

> *The Court*: Gentlemen, are the, is the Plaintiff satisfied with the instructions and form of the verdict?
> *Plaintiff's Counsel*: Your Honor, other than the previously positions [sic], yes your Honor.
> *The Court*: And the Defendant.
> *Defense Counsel*: Ditto.

The above-quoted exchanges reflect defendant's forfeiture ("No, we've been through it all") and waiver of a vicarious-liability-instruction objection, because defense counsel ultimately and affirmatively expressed satisfaction with the instructions to the jury. Defendant's expression of satisfaction with the instructions, which omitted the vicarious-liability instruction, constitutes a waiver that extinguishes any error concerning vicarious liability. *Grant v. AAA Michigan/Wisconsin, Inc (On Remand)*, 272 Mich App 142, 148; 724 NW2d 498 (2006).

2

Defendant next maintains that the trial court insufficiently defined for the jury the parameters of a Fourth Amendment violation, but we once again conclude that defendant waived any claim of error. After the jury began deliberating, it requested clarification regarding the Fourth Amendment, prompting the following exchange:

> *The Court*: And then they say re-read Fourth Amendment, Fourteenth Amendment parameters. Well technically it's not in evidence. What I propose to do is just tell them what the Fourth Amendment is, that citizens of the United States shall be protected against unlawful searches and seizures. And the Fourteenth Amendment applies that to Michigan. Any objections?
> *Plaintiff's Counsel*: No your Honor.
> *Defense Counsel*: I do your Honor. I think you've read the illegal search and seizure instruction. And I think to instruct them in something different at this point may even cause greater confusion.
> *The Court*: Well shall I simply—
> *Plaintiff's Counsel*: Reread that instruction.
> *The Court*: Reread that instruction[?]
> *Defense Counsel*: Yes, I think that's the way it should be done.

The trial court proceeded to reiterate to the jury the two constitutional elements of § 1983, but did not include the detailed paragraph regarding probable cause that initially had followed the § 1983 elements. Nonetheless, when the trial court inquired whether "[d]efendant [was] satisfied," his counsel affirmatively replied, "Yes your Honor." To the extent that the trial court's reinstruction-at defense counsel's request-qualified as erroneous, defense counsel's affirmative expression of satisfaction with the trial court's charge extinguished any error. *Grant, supra* at 148.

> Ladies and gentlemen, I'm now going to begin a series of instructions on .... unlawful search. Under the Constitution of the United States, that is the Fourth Amendment,

every person has the right not to be subjected to unreasonable searches and seizures. In order to prove this claim, Plaintiff must prove by a preponderance of evidence each of the following elements. First, the Defendant intentionally violated Plaintiff's constitutional right by conducting an unreasonable search and seizure. Second, that the Defendant's acts were the proximate cause of damages sustained by the Plaintiff.

Additional instructions. ...

It is also a statement of our law that any person who assaults or assaults and batters an individual shall be guilty of a misdemeanor. This is the definition of probable cause. If an arrest is lawful when made, there has not been a false arrest or false imprisonment. Instead, claims of false arrest and false imprisonment require Plaintiff prove that the arrest or detention lacked probable cause. Probable cause that a particular person has committed a crime is established by a reasonable ground of suspicion supported by circumstances sufficiently strong in themselves to warrant the cautious person in the belief that the accused is guilty of the offense. If you find the Defendants had probable cause to believe that Plaintiff committed an assault on the Motor City Casino security officer, then you decide, you must decide that Motor City Casino personnel were entitled to detain Plaintiff.

After reviewing these instructions in their entirety, we conclude that they adequately describe the legal principles governing a determination whether defendants unlawfully searched or seized plaintiff, in violation of the Fourth Amendment. *Lewis, supra* at 211-212.

III. Challenges to Punitive-Damages Award

Defendant next contends that the trial court should have granted a new trial on the issue of § 1983 punitive damages because the jury's award was inconsistent with its rejection of plaintiff's counts alleging false arrest, assault and battery, and intentional infliction of emotional distress, and with plaintiff's request for exemplary damages.

Our review of the record leads us to conclude, however, that the entirety of the jury's special verdict comports with the trial evidence and the trial court's careful and extended delineation of the distinctions between, and components of, compensatory damages, exemplary damages, and punitive damages. As this Court has observed, "The Michigan Supreme Court has repeatedly held that the jury's verdict must be upheld, even [if] it is arguably inconsistent, if there is an interpretation of the evidence that provides a logical explanation for the findings of the jury." *Allard v. State Farm Ins Co*, 271 Mich App 394, 407; 722 NW2d 268 (2006) (internal quotation marks omitted). Furthermore, a reviewing court must make "every attempt ... to harmonize a jury's verdicts. Only where verdicts are so logically and legally inconsistent that they cannot be reconciled will they be set aside." *Id.* (internal quotation marks omitted).

The jury's finding that defendants unlawfully detained plaintiff (special verdict question 1), its somewhat similar finding that defendants falsely imprisoned plaintiff (special verdict question 3), coupled with its rejections of plaintiff's other proffered tort claims, namely false arrest, assault and battery, and intentional infliction of emotional distress (special verdict questions 2, 4, and 5), suggest that the jury viewed defendants' initial arrest or seizure of plaintiff and the placement of plaintiff in the casino's security office as premised on probable cause that plaintiff may have unlawfully touched Martinez, but concluded that defendants eventually detained plaintiff against his will, or extended the seizure's duration for too long. The jury's special verdicts 1 through 5 find support in the evidence and appear to be at a minimum reasonably consistent.

Regarding defendant's specific challenge to the jury's awards of damages, in special verdict question 6 the jury found that defendant had caused plaintiff $125,000 in "non-economic loss compensatory damages," which the trial court explained should "fairly and adequately compensate[] him" "for mental anguish, fright and shock and embarrassment." The jury then rejected the claim that plaintiff would sustain future compensatory damages. (Special verdict question 7.) In special verdict question 8, the jury considered and rejected the claim that plaintiff had endured exemplary damages, which the trial court defined as "injury to Plaintiff's feelings," in this case "humiliation, outrage or indignity." Lastly, the jury found that defendants had violated "plaintiff's right to be free from unreasonable searches and seizures under the [f]ourth and [f]ourteenth [a] mendments to the U.S. Constitution" (special verdict question 9), and awarded plaintiff $400,000 in punitive damages (special verdict question 10), which the trial court described as an amount "appropriate to punish the Defendants or to deter the Defendants and others from like conduct in the future."

In summary, we fail to detect any manner by which the jury rendered an inconsistent verdict regarding defendant's liability or plaintiff's entitlement to the three distinct types of damages he sought. *Allard, supra* at 407.

IV. Challenges to False-Imprisonment Special Verdict

Defendant additionally asserts that the trial court erred by denying its motion for a directed verdict with respect to plaintiff's false-imprisonment count because Grzadzinski indisputably had probable cause to detain plaintiff. The trial testimony plainly reflects that plaintiff and the several members of his group offered recollections of the September 14, 2002, confrontation that differed markedly from the testimony of Martinez, Grzadzinski, McDowell, and Jeanne Snyder, plaintiff's former fiancee, regarding the important issues whether (1) plaintiff made nonchalant arm gestures, (2) plaintiff might have been close to or distant from Martinez at the time plaintiff gestured, and (3) plaintiff intentionally poked, punched, struck, or otherwise touched Martinez's chest. Given the widely contradictory testimony offered in these areas, which were central to a determination whether defendant possessed probable cause through its security personnel to arrest or detain plaintiff, it was the jury's prerogative to resolve this issue of fact, including the inherent credibility questions. *Zeeland Farm Serv's, supra* at 195; *Hunt, supra* at 99. Consequently, the trial court properly denied a directed verdict on plaintiff's false-imprisonment count.

Alternatively, defendant suggests that the trial court should have granted a new trial because it inadequately explained to the jury the elements of false imprisonment, and that the instructions given did not support the jury's rejection of the false-arrest claim while finding liability for false imprisonment. The trial court read to the jury four paragraphs of instructions differentiating the elements of false arrest from false imprisonment. As defendant acknowledges, these instructions very closely tracked Michigan Model Civil Jury Instructions 116.01 ("False Arrest-Definition"), 116.02 ("False Imprisonment-Definition"), 116.20 ("False Arrest-Burden of Proof"), and 116.21 ("False Imprisonment-Burden of Proof"). Defendant also concedes that within the next two to four paragraphs, the trial court fleshed out, in the context of plaintiff's § 1983 claim, the concept of probable cause necessary to render a search or seizure reasonable and lawful.

We conclude that, taken as a whole, the trial court's extended and indisputably accurate recitation of the relevant legal principles regarding false arrest, false imprisonment, and probable cause fully and fairly set forth for the jury the elements of false arrest and false imprisonment. *Lewis, supra* at 211–212. And as discussed in part III of this opinion, applying the false-arrest and false-imprisonment instructions to the facts of this case demonstrates that the jury likely, and reasonably, viewed the casino's initial detention of plaintiff in its security area as supported by probable cause that he assaulted Martinez, but deemed plaintiff's more than two-hour detention locked in the casino's security office as unsupported by any legal basis, and therefore amounting to false imprisonment.

V. Remittitur Request Concerning Noneconomic-Damages Award

Defendant lastly complains that the trial court should have remitted the jury's award of $125,000 in compensatory damages, which lacked support in the trial evidence, especially given that the jury rejected that defendants had intentionally inflicted emotional distress.

> In determining whether remittitur is appropriate, a trial court must decide whether the jury award was supported by the evidence. This determination must be based on objective criteria relating to the actual conduct of the trial or the evidence presented. The power of remittitur should be exercised with restraint. If the award for economic damages falls reasonably within the range of the evidence and within the limits of what reasonable minds would deem just compensation, the jury award should not be disturbed. A trial court's decision regarding remittitur is reviewed for an abuse of discretion. We review all of the evidence in the light most favorable to the nonmoving party. [*Silberstein v. Pro-Golf of America, Inc,* 278 Mich. App. 446, 462; 750 N.W.2d 615 (2008) (citations omitted).]

Plaintiff testified that he endured extreme embarrassment on multiple occasions because of defendants' detention of him for more than two hours on September 14, 2002, their decision to eject and ban him from the casino, and Martinez's pursuit of criminal assault and battery charges against him. Specifically, plaintiff averred that on a daily basis he experienced extreme feelings of upset and embarrassment because of (1) the casino's treatment of him on September 14, 2002; (2) his May 2003 Metro Airport arrest on an outstanding assault and battery warrant while attempting to pick up his girlfriend; (3) his September 2003 appearance in the 36th District Court for a scheduled criminal trial; (4) his 2005 discovery of the existence of more arrest warrants stemming from September 14, 2002; (5) the 2005 jury trial for assault and battery that ultimately ended in his acquittal; and (6) his testimony in the instant civil case. Although plaintiff did not substantiate that he experienced any significant change in the course of his daily activities, his testimony that defendants' conduct caused him extreme upset and embarrassment on multiple occasions, especially when viewed in the light most favorable to plaintiff, amply supports the jury's award of $125,000 in noneconomic compensatory damages.

Affirmed.
Borrello, J., concurred.
/s/ Elizabeth L. Gleicher
/s/ Stephen L. Borrello

Dissent by: Peter D. O'Connell

Dissent:

O'Connell, P.J. (*dissenting*).

I respectfully dissent. In my opinion, the trial court erred when it failed to grant defendant's motion for directed verdict regarding plaintiff's 42 USCS § 1983 claim because private security guards are not state actors. The trial court also erred by adopting federal precedent as persuasive and rejecting the Michigan Supreme Court's reasoning in *Grand Rapids v. Impens*, 414 Mich 667, 670; 327 NW2d 278 (1982). I would reverse the decision of the trial court.

In order to maintain an action under § 1983, a plaintiff is required to establish that he or she was "deprived of a right secured by the Constitution or laws of the United States" and that the defendant was a "state actor," that is, acting under color of state law at the relevant time. *Am Mfrs Mut Ins Co v. Sullivan*, 526 U.S. 40, 49; 119 S Ct 977; 143 L Ed 2d 130 (1999). "[M]erely private conduct, no matter how discriminatory or wrongful" will not support a § 1983 claim. *Id.* at 50 (internal quotation marks and citations omitted). The plaintiff bears the burden to show state action because it is an element of the claim. *Brentwood Academy v. Tenn Secondary School Athletic Ass'n*, 531 U.S. 288, 308-309; 121 S Ct 924; 148 L Ed 2d 807 (2001). Accordingly, in order for plaintiff to maintain his § 1983 claim, he was required to establish that the casino's private security officers were state actors.

The trial court held as a matter of law that the casino's private security guards were acting under color of state law by virtue of the fact that they were certified under MCL 338.1079, relying on *Romanski v. Detroit Entertainment, LLC*, 428 F3d 629, 636 (CA 6, 2005). "Although state courts are bound by the decisions of the United States Supreme Court construing federal law, there is no similar obligation with respect to decisions of the lower federal courts." *Abela v. Gen Motors Corp*, 469 Mich 603, 606; 677 NW2d 325 (2004) (citations omitted). On the other hand, Michigan Supreme Court cases on point are binding on lower courts, regardless of whether the lower courts agree with the decision. *Detroit v. Vavro*, 177 Mich App 682, 685; 442 NW2d 730 (1989). In my opinion, it is clear that the trial court erred by not following the Michigan Supreme Court decision in *Impens*, because the logic behind the decision is controlling and dispositive of the issue.

In *Impens*, our Supreme Court impliedly determined that private security guards are not state actors simply because they are certified under MCL 338.1079. Indeed, at least one federal district court recognized this fact:

> Plaintiff here has not identified any state or local legislation that confers broad police powers upon security personnel. In fact, Michigan's security guard licensing statute limits the powers of security guards. Pursuant to the statute, upon obtaining a license, a private security officer is granted "the authority to arrest a person without a warrant" to the same extent possessed by public police officers, but only when this officer "is on the employer's premises." Mich. Comp. Laws § 338.1080. This authority is further limited to the security guard's "hours of employment as a private security police officer and does not extend beyond the boundaries of the property of the employer." Mich. Comp. Laws § 338.1080.
>
> The limited powers conferred under this statute do not convert private security guards into state actors. This has been confirmed by the definitive arbiter of the proper meaning of this statute, the Michigan Supreme Court. ...
>
> [In *Impens*, t]he Michigan Supreme Court held that the defendant had not identified any state action that would trigger the requirement of *Miranda* warnings. In so ruling, the Court specifically rejected the defendant's contention that "the licensing statutes which regulate private security guards demonstrate the requisite degree of state action to bring their activities under color of state law, subject to constitutional restraints." 327 N.W.2d at 281. Instead, the Court concluded that "we do not believe that the mere licensing of security guards constitutes sufficient government

involvement to require the giving of *Miranda* warnings." 327 N.W.2d at 281. This Court, of course, is bound by the views of Michigan's highest court as to the extent of authority conferred under the Michigan security guard licensing statute. [*Smith v. Detroit Entertainment, LLC,* 338 F Supp 2d 775,780-781 (ED Mich, 2004) (emphasis added).]

In my opinion, this is the better analysis, because it recognizes the implications of the logic behind *Impens* and gives the ruling of our state's highest court the deference the law requires. It is this case, and not *Romanski*, on which the trial court should have relied.

The majority attempts to avoid the application of *Impens* with immaterial distinctions. Specifically, the majority notes that our Supreme Court did not determine whether the security officers in the *Impens* case had been licensed and that the opinion made no reference MCL 338.1080. A review of the opinion indicates that it was unnecessary for the *Impens* Court to determine whether the security officers were licensed. The Court "[did] not believe that the mere licensing of security guards constitutes sufficient government involvement to require the giving of *Miranda* warnings." *Id.* at 676. Accordingly, it was unnecessary for the Court to determine, or even mention, whether the security guards were licensed because the simple fact of licensure would not transform a private security guard into a state actor.

Similarly, the Court's failure to reference MCL 338.1080 does not render *Impens* inapposite. MCL 338.1080 provides for a limited power of arrest to those security guards licensed under MCL 338.1079. Because the power to arrest under MCL 338.1080 is conferred solely by licensure under MCL 338.1079, if licensure alone does not constitute state action, then acknowledgment that licensure confers an arrest power is similarly insufficient. Importantly, in the instant case, plaintiff was not arrested, but voluntarily went with the security officers back to the casino's security office. The security guards never exercised any power to arrest. Accordingly, it must be simply the existence of this limited power of arrest pursuant to MCL 338.1080 that gave the security officers in the present case a police power traditionally and exclusively reserved to the state. Such a conclusion broadly confers "state actor" status to all security guards who are licensed under MCL 338.1080 and is at odds with *Impens*.

One of the men who aided in the apprehension in *Impens* was an off-duty deputy sheriff. The Court held that his presence did not constitute "color of law," in part because he was off-duty and identified himself as a store employee. *Impens, supra* at 677. If the mere existence of arrest authority under MCL 338.1080 were sufficient to confer "state actor" status, there would be no logical basis for our Supreme Court's holding that the off-duty deputy sheriff in *Impens* was not acting under color of law, because even off-duty, he still had the power to arrest. The holding of the United States Court of Appeals for the Sixth Circuit, sitting en banc, in *Chapman v. The Higbee Co,* 319 F3d 825 (CA 6, 2003), is similarly irreconcilable with the majority's broad conclusion. The security guard in *Chapman* was "an off-duty sheriff's deputy, wearing his official sheriff's department uniform, badge, and sidearm." *Id.* at 834. As a police officer, the security guard possessed plenary police power. Yet the *Chapman* court did not conclude that mere possession of that authority resulted in state action. Instead, it examined the specific actions taken by the security officer, which included a strip search, and noted that store policy mandated police involvement for such an action. *Id.* at 834–835. If the security guards in *Impens* and *Chapman* were not state actors, despite having been licensed by the state as police officers with full arrest powers, it is clear that licensure under MCL 338.1079 alone cannot transform the casino's private security guards into state actors in the present case.

The majority argues that because the security guards were licensed under MCL 338.1079, they had the power to arrest plaintiff pursuant to MCL 338.1080, and that because plaintiff was held in a room on the basis of this authority, the security guards acted under color of state law. Application of such reasoning to other Michigan statutes would result in absurd and unintended outcomes that would destroy the "state actor" requirement of § 1983 altogether. Under MCL 764.16, private persons are given the authority to make arrests under certain situations. Every security guard who is unlicensed and, therefore, without authority under MCL 338.1080, still has the limited power given to all private persons under MCL 764.16. Having received authority from the state to arrest, any security guard who locked someone in an office pursuant to that authority becomes a state actor, notwithstanding all the prior case law that finds such actions to be that of private individuals. See, for example, *Lindsey v. Detroit Entertainment, LLC*, 484 F3d 824, 827-828 (CA 6, 2007). The fact that a private person has the power to arrest does not transform the person into a state actor. Rather, it would be the exercise of that power that would create state action. That is why the presence of state action is "fact-specific, and ... determined on a case-by-case basis." *Id.* at 834.

It takes very little imagination to envision the havoc that would result from the application of the majority's holding. Whether it is the licensed day-care provider who places a four-year-old child in "time-out" for hitting another child, or the licensed cab driver who refuses to let a passenger leave the cab until the fare is paid, the majority would conclude that because MCL 764.16 gives these private persons the power to arrest, they are state actors. Thousands of everyday private actions would be distorted into state action for which plaintiffs will seek monetary remedies from taxpayer funds and overwhelm our already burdened courts.

Because I find *Impens* controlling, *Romanski* is inapplicable, and the trial court erred in relying on it to deny defendant's motion for directed verdict. The simple fact of licensure under MCL 338.1079 cannot, does not, and should not transform private security guards into state actors. To hold otherwise expands state action to a point that strains credulity.

I would reverse the decision of the trial court.

/s/ Peter D. O'Connell

Ramirez v. Fifth Club, Inc., 114 S.W. 3d 574 (Tex. App. 2004)

Before Justices Kidd, Puryear and Pemberton.
Opinion by: Mack Kidd

This case stems from an altercation at an Austin nightclub. Luis a/k/a Louis Medrano and David A. West were employed to work as security personnel for the club. Roberto, Adolfo, and Laura Ramirez were all allegedly assaulted by West or Medrano. Following a ten-day jury trial, a jury found Fifth Club and West liable for injuries to Roberto but determined that West and Medrano were not liable to Adolfo and Laura because they were functioning as peace officers and entitled to official immunity.

Adolfo and Laura appeal, arguing West and Medrano were not entitled to official immunity and that the district court erred in submitting a jury question on official immunity. Fifth Club and West appeal, contesting the legal and factual sufficiency of seven jury findings favoring Roberto. We will affirm the judgment of the district court.

Background

Factual Background

The facts of this case were hotly contested at trial. What is undisputed is that on September 16, 2000, Roberto Ramirez and his brother, Adolfo Ramirez, attended a party to celebrate the baptism of their cousin. After the party, around 12:30 or 1:00 a.m. on September 17, Roberto and Adolfo arrived at Club Rodeo with some friends. Roberto and Adolfo were, at some point, denied admission into Club Rodeo. West and Medrano, both of whom were working security in the Club Rodeo parking lot, were signaled by the Club Rodeo doorman and proceeded to the doorway of the club. An altercation between Roberto and West ensued, during which Roberto's head struck a wall, fracturing a bone in his skull. Apparently, Adolfo intervened in the altercation between Roberto and West, causing Medrano to restrain Adolfo.

Eventually, West and Medrano took Roberto, who was unconscious, and Adolfo into the parking lot and handcuffed them. Laura Ramirez, who was dropping off another brother at Club Rodeo, soon arrived to find her brothers Roberto, who had regained consciousness, and Adolfo lying handcuffed on the parking-lot pavement. She and West became embroiled in a verbal altercation, and West eventually handcuffed Laura and placed her under arrest as well. Both Medrano and an eyewitness called 911; Austin Police Department (APD) officers soon arrived and transported Roberto, Adolfo, and Laura Ramirez to the city jail.

Trial Proceedings

Roberto sued West for assault, false imprisonment, malicious prosecution, intentional infliction of emotional distress, negligence, and malice, and he sued Fifth Club for negligence and respondeat superior.

Adolfo sued Medrano for assault, false imprisonment, malicious prosecution, intentional infliction of emotional distress, negligence, and malice. He sued West for negligence and malice, and he sued Fifth Club for negligence and respondeat superior.

Laura sued West for assault, false imprisonment, malicious prosecution, intentional infliction of emotional distress, negligence, and malice. Laura sued Fifth Club for negligence and respondeat superior.

West and Medrano asserted the affirmative defense of official immunity. At the time of this incident, peace officers outside of their jurisdiction could make a warrantless arrest of a person who commits a felony, a breach of the peace, or public intoxication within the officer's presence or view. *See* Act of May 29, 1993, 73d Leg., R.S., ch. 900, § 3.02, 1993 Tex. Gen. Laws 3586, 3715 (amended 2003) (current version at Tex. Code Crim. Proc. Ann. art. 14.03(d) (West Supp. 2004)) (hereinafter cited as Former Tex. Code Crim. Proc. Ann. art. 14.03(d)). West and Medrano argued that they observed Roberto, Adolfo, and Laura commit felonies, breaches of the peace, public intoxication, or some combination thereof. Because West and Medrano were commissioned by Huston-Tillotson College to function as peace officers, they assert they were entitled to function as peace officers and were therefore entitled to official immunity. *See id.*; *see also* Tex. Educ. Code Ann. § 51.212 (West 1996) (permitting private institutions of higher education to commission campus security personnel); Tex. Code Crim. Proc. Ann. art. 2.12(8) (West Supp. 2004) (defining officers commissioned under chapter 51, education code, as "peace officers").

At the conclusion of a 10-day jury trial, the district court submitted questions to the jury regarding official immunity. The jury granted official immunity to West for his actions toward Laura and to Medrano for his actions toward Adolfo, but refused to grant official immunity to West for his actions toward Roberto.

Based on its official-immunity findings, the jury did not reach any liability questions stemming from Laura's and Adolfo's complaints. The jury did, however, find both West and Fifth Club liable to Roberto and awarded him $80,000 for physical pain and mental anguish sustained in the past, $20,000 for mental anguish that he will reasonably sustain in the future, $2100 for loss of earning capacity in the past, $7000 for physical impairment sustained in the past, $1198 for medical care in the past, and $35,000 as exemplary damages against Fifth Club.

Issues on Appeal

Adolfo and Laura appeal, arguing that the submission of the immunity question to the jury was in error because the education code only authorized West and Medrano to function as peace officers while working for Huston-Tillotson. *See* Tex. Educ. Code Ann. § 51.212. They therefore request that the cause be remanded so a jury can determine whether Fifth Club, West, or Medrano are liable to Adolfo and Laura for the injuries they allegedly sustained.

Fifth Club and West also appeal and argue that the evidence is legally and factually insufficient to support the jury's finding that (1) Fifth Club is responsible for the acts of West; (2) Fifth Club was negligent and that its proportionate responsibility for the damages to Roberto was 55 percent; (3) Roberto was entitled to an award of $80,000 for past physical pain and mental anguish and $20,000 for future physical pain and mental anguish; (4) Roberto was entitled to an award of $7000 for physical impairment in the past; (5) Fifth Club or West acted with malice; (6) Fifth Club should pay Roberto $ 35,000 in exemplary damages; and (7) West was not entitled to official immunity.

Discussion

Laura's and Adolfo's Issue: Authority to Act as "Peace Officers"

Laura and Adolfo argue in one issue that they are entitled to a remand because the district court improperly submitted to the jury a question regarding official immunity for West and Medrano. West and Medrano were both employed by Huston-Tillotson College, a private institution of higher education, as campus security personnel. In empowering private institutions to hire security personnel, the legislature provided:

> The governing boards of private institutions of higher education, including private junior colleges, are authorized to employ and commission campus security personnel for the purpose of enforcing the law of this state on the campuses of private institutions of higher education. Any officer commissioned under the provisions of this section is vested with all the powers, privileges, and immunities of peace officers *while on the property* under the control and jurisdiction of the respective private institution of higher education *or otherwise in the performance of his assigned duties.*

Tex. Educ. Code Ann. § 51.212 (emphasis added). Because this section states that a campus officer has the powers, privileges, and immunities of peace officers "while on the property ... or otherwise in the performance of his assigned duties," Laura and Adolfo argue that West and Medrano could not function as peace officers while working at Club Rodeo.

However, article 2.12 of the code of criminal procedure unambiguously defines "officers commissioned under ... Subchapter E, Chapter 51, Education Code" as "peace officers," Tex. Code Crim. Proc. Ann. art. 2.12(8), and former article 14.03(d) provides:

> A peace officer *who is outside his jurisdiction* may arrest, without warrant, a person who commits an offense within the officer's presence or view, if the offense is a felony, a violation of Title 9, Chapter 42, Penal Code [disorderly conduct and related offenses], a breach of the peace, or an offense under Section 49.02, Penal Code [public intoxication]. A peace officer making an arrest

under this subsection shall, as soon as practicable after making the arrest, notify a law enforcement agency having jurisdiction where the arrest was made. The law enforcement agency shall then take custody of the person committing the offense and take the person before a magistrate in compliance with Article 14.06 of this code.

Former Tex. Code Crim. Proc. Ann. art. 14.03(d). We believe the interaction between these statutes is clear. Section 51.212 of the education code establishes the jurisdiction for campus security personnel. Within this jurisdiction, campus security personnel are "vested with *all* the powers, privileges, and immunities of peace officers." Tex. Educ. Code Ann. § 51.212 (emphasis added). But former article 14.03(d) acts as an exception to the general rule that a peace officer's authority to act is limited to his own geographic jurisdiction. *Brother v. State*, 85 S.W.3d 377, 383 & n.3 (Tex. App.—Fort Worth 2002, no pet.); *see also Angel v. State*, 740 S.W.2d 727, 734 (Tex. Crim. App. 1987) (plurality opinion) (legislature likely used term "jurisdiction" to restrict geographic scope of peace officer's power, rights, and authority). Outside of their primary jurisdiction, officers are vested with the *limited* authority to arrest for certain enumerated offenses committed within the officer's presence or view. Former Tex. Code Crim. Proc. Ann. art. 14.03(d).

After thoroughly analyzing the education code, the code of criminal procedure, and Texas case law, Laura and Adolfo argue that interpreting former article 14.03(d) to include campus security personnel commissioned under section 51.212 of the education code would lead to absurd results. First, they argue that article 2.123 of the code of criminal procedure expressly addresses the limited circumstances under which officers commissioned by private institutions may act as peace officers outside their ordinary jurisdiction. This section provides in part:

a. Within counties under 200,000 population, the chief of police of a municipality or the sheriff of the county, if the institution is outside the corporate limits of a municipality, that has jurisdiction over the geographical area of a private institution of higher education, provided the governing board of such institution consents, may appoint up to 50 peace officers who are commissioned under Section 51.212, Education Code, and who are employed by a private institution of higher education located in the municipality or county, to serve as adjunct police officers of the municipality or county. Officers appointed under this article shall aid law enforcement agencies in the protection of the municipality or county in a geographical area that is designated by agreement on an annual basis between the appointing chief of police or sheriff and the private institution.
b. The geographical area that is subject to designation under Subsection (a) of this article may include only the private institution's campus area and an area that:
   1. Is adjacent to the campus of the private institution;
   2. Does not extend further than a distance of one mile from the perimeter of the campus of the private institution; and
   3. Is inhabited primarily by students or employees of the private institution.
c. A peace officer serving as an adjunct police officer may make arrests and exercise all authority given peace officers under this code only within the geographical area designated by agreement between the appointing chief of police or sheriff and the private institution.
d. A peace officer serving as an adjunct police officer has all the rights, privileges, and immunities of a peace officer but is not entitled to state compensation and retirement benefits normally provided by the state to a peace officer.

Tex. Code Crim. Proc. Ann. art. 2.123(a)–(d) (West Supp. 2004). Laura and Adolfo argue that this specific section, which explains the circumstances under which a campus security officer at a private educational institution may function outside of his jurisdiction, should control over the more general former article 14.03(d). See, for example, *Horizon/CMS Healthcare Corp. v. Auld*, 34 S.W.3d 887, 901, 43 Tex. Sup. Ct. J. 1151 (Tex. 2000) ("more specific statute controls over the more general"). However, this rule of statutory construction only applies when different code provisions are "irreconcilable." *See id.*; *see also* Tex. Gov't Code Ann. § 311.026(a) (West 1998). ("If a general provision conflicts with a special or local provision, the provisions shall be construed, if possible, so that effect is given to both.")

Here, we do not find that article 2.123 and former article 14.03(d) conflict. The fundamental difference between these two articles is that article 2.123 provides the specific circumstances, including geographic restrictions, for when a campus security officer may exercise *all* the rights, privileges, and immunities of a peace officer, while former article 14.03(d) provides an additional situation where a peace officer, including a campus security officer, can exercise the *limited* function of arresting an individual for specific offenses committed within the officer's presence or view. *Compare* Tex. Code Crim. Proc. Ann. art. 2.123(d) ("peace officer serving as an adjunct police officer has all the rights, privileges, and immunities of a peace officer"), *with* Former Tex. Code Crim. Proc. Ann. art. 14.03(d) (peace officer must follow procedure for making warrantless arrest outside his jurisdiction for *limited* range of offenses). Article 2.123 allows a campus security officer functioning as an adjunct officer to make *all* arrests, but only within a specified geographic area. Tex. Code Crim. Proc. Ann. art. 2.123(c). Former article 14.03(d), on the other hand, allows a campus security officer to make a warrantless arrest without regard to geographic boundaries within the state *only if* the offense is committed "within the officer's presence or view" and *only if* the offense observed is specifically listed. *See* Former Tex. Code Crim. Proc. Ann. art. 14.03(d). We conclude that the plain language of these two articles does not conflict, and we overrule Laura's and Adolfo's issue insofar as it is based on article 2.123 of the code of criminal procedure.

Next, Laura and Adolfo point to section 51.203 of the education code to support their argument that West and Medrano were not entitled to official immunity. Section 51.203 provides in part:

a. The governing boards of each state institution of higher education and public technical institute may employ and commission peace officers for the purpose of carrying out the provisions of this subchapter. The primary jurisdiction of a peace officer commissioned under this section includes all counties in which property is owned, leased, rented, or otherwise under the control of the institution of higher education or public technical institute that employs the peace officer.
b. Within a peace officer's primary jurisdiction, a peace officer commissioned under this section:
   1. Is vested with all the powers, privileges, and immunities of peace officers;
   2. May, in accordance with Chapter 14, Code of Criminal Procedure, arrest without a warrant any person who violates a law of the state; and
   3. May enforce all traffic laws on streets and highways.
c. Outside a peace officer's primary jurisdiction a peace officer commissioned under this section is vested with all the powers, privileges, and immunities of peace officers and may arrest any person who violates any law of the state if the peace officer:
   1. Is summoned by another law enforcement agency to provide assistance;
   2. Is assisting another law enforcement agency; or
   3. Is otherwise performing his duties as a peace officer for the institution of higher education or public technical institute that employs the peace officer.

Tex. Educ. Code Ann. § 51.203(a)–(c) (West Supp. 2004).

Laura and Adolfo argue that construing former article 14.03(d) to include campus security personnel commissioned by *private* institutions under section 51.212 of the education code would empower such officers with *more* power than similar officers commissioned by *public* institutions of higher education under section 51.203 of the education code. This argument stems from the fact that section 51.203(c) limits the instances when an officer commissioned by a *public* institution may act outside of his primary jurisdiction, yet section 51.212 contains no such restrictions. *See id.* §§ 51.203(c),.212. Therefore, according to Laura and Adolfo, construing former article 14.03(d) to include campus security personnel at private institutions would grant them *more* power than similar officers at public institutions, who can only act outside of their jurisdiction when the limited circumstances described in section 51.203(c) apply.

We disagree with Laura's and Adolfo's reading of the statutes in question. Section 51.203(c) of the education code describes three instances when a campus officer at a public institution who is outside of his primary jurisdiction is "vested with *all* the powers, privileges, and immunities of peace officers and may arrest any person who violates *any* law of the state." *Id.* § 51.203(c) (emphasis added). Section 51.203(c) is narrowly tailored to describe the circumstances under which a campus police officer maintains *full* peace-officer status, even if outside the officer's jurisdiction. This does not conflict with former article 14.03(d), which empowers campus police officers—those employed by public and private institutions alike—to make warrantless arrests for a small number of offenses committed within the officer's presence or view. *See* Former Tex. Code Crim. Proc. Ann. art. 14.03(d). Because section 14.03(d) applies equally to campus officers employed by public institutions and campus officers employed by private institutions and is not in conflict with section 51.203 of the education code, we overrule Laura's and Adolfo's issue insofar as it is based on section 51.203 of the education code.

Finally, Laura and Adolfo cite numerous cases in support of their argument that former article 14.03(d) cannot apply to West and Medrano, but these cases are easily distinguishable from the situation now before us. See, for example, *Perkins v. State*, 812 S.W.2d 326 (Tex. Crim. App. 1991) (article 14.03(d) not at issue); *Brother v. State*, 85 S.W.3d 377 (Tex. App.—Fort Worth 2002, no pet.) (same); *State v. Backus*, 881 S.W.2d 591 (Tex. App.—Austin 1994, pet. ref'd) (pertinent facts occurred before legislature amended former article 14.03(d) to include additional alcoholic-beverage offenses); *State v. Carroll*, 855 S.W.2d 128 (Tex. App.—Austin 1993, no pet.) (same); *Garza v. State*, 822 S.W.2d 174 (Tex. App.—San Antonio 1991, no pet.) (article 14.03(d) not at issue). In citing these cases, Laura and Adolfo focus on where West and Medrano were empowered to function with *full* peace-officer authority, yet they fail to address that the legislature specifically provided for *limited* situations in which peace officers, *outside of their jurisdiction*, may make warrantless arrests for a limited number of offenses committed within their presence or view. *See* Former Tex. Code Crim. Proc. Ann. art. 14.03(d).

We conclude that article 2.12(8) and former article 14.03(d) of the code of criminal procedure are clear and unambiguous and do not conflict with sections 51.203 or 51.212 of the education code, or with article 2.123 of the code of criminal procedure. *See* Tex. Code Crim. Proc. Ann. arts. 2.12(8), 2.123; Former Tex. Code Crim. Proc. Ann. art. 14.03(d); Tex. Educ. Code Ann. §§ 51.203,.212. We therefore hold that the district court properly submitted the question of official immunity to the jury. We overrule Laura's and Adolfo's sole issue.

Fifth Club's and West's Issues: Legal and Factual Sufficiency

In seven issues, Fifth Club and West challenge the legal and factual sufficiency of the jury's findings. When reviewing a no-evidence challenge, we consider all the evidence in the light most favorable to the judgment, making every reasonable inference in its favor. *Associated Indem. Corp. v. CAT Contracting, Inc.*, 964 S.W.2d 276, 285-86, 41 Tex. Sup. Ct. J. 389 (Tex. 1998). We will uphold the jury's finding if more than a scintilla of evidence supports it. *Burroughs Wellcome Co. v. Crye*, 907 S.W.2d 497, 499, 38 Tex. Sup. Ct. J. 848 (Tex. 1995). The evidence supporting a finding is more than a scintilla if reasonable minds could arrive at the finding given the facts proved in the particular case. *Id.* When reviewing a factual-sufficiency challenge, we consider all the evidence and uphold the jury's verdict unless we find that (1) the evidence is too weak to support the finding or (2) the finding is so against the overwhelming weight of the evidence as to be manifestly unjust. *Cain v. Bain*, 709 S.W.2d 175, 176, 29 Tex. Sup. Ct. J. 214 (Tex. 1986).

Because all seven issues turn on an examination of the evidence presented at trial, a recounting of the evidence before the jury is necessary. The parties hotly contested what actually happened at Club Rodeo, and we will address their different accounts of the incident in turn.

The Plaintiffs' Account

Roberto and Adolfo both testified that when they were waiting in line in a front hallway to enter Club Rodeo, the club doorman allowed two men to cut in front of Roberto and Adolfo. Adolfo complained to the doorman, who then said Adolfo was not getting in. Adolfo apologized and showed his identification to the doorman, who said, "Get the [expletive] out of here." Roberto told the doorman not to speak to Adolfo that way, and the doorman then said Roberto was not getting into Club Rodeo either.

At this point, Roberto was under the impression that his friends, who were at the cash register, had already paid for his and Adolfo's admission. He told the doorman that if their money was returned, he and Adolfo would leave. Upon learning that their friends had not, in fact, already paid for their admission, Roberto and Adolfo turned around to leave. As Roberto was walking toward the exit, West approached from behind and grabbed his hands. When Roberto resisted West's effort to restrain Roberto's hands, West allegedly "got very mad" and pushed Roberto's face against a limestone or concrete wall, fracturing a bone in Roberto's skull and rendering him unconscious. When Roberto regained consciousness, he was lying handcuffed in the parking lot.

Adolfo testified that after West pushed Roberto into the wall, West "was beating [Roberto] several times," prompting Medrano to tell West "that was enough." When Adolfo tried to push West away from Roberto, Medrano grabbed Adolfo by the neck and threw him to the floor. Medrano dragged Adolfo outside, where Medrano and West allegedly kicked both Adolfo and Roberto after they had been handcuffed.

Laura Ramirez, who was dropping off another brother at Club Rodeo, soon arrived to find her brothers Roberto and Adolfo lying handcuffed on the parking-lot pavement. She exited her vehicle and attempted to ascertain what had happened from West, who was initially nonresponsive. West told Laura to move her car, but Laura attempted to move closer to Roberto, whose face was swollen and bleeding. West again told Laura to move her car, allegedly telling her "it wasn't [her] [expletive] business what was happening there."

Laura inquired about Roberto's injuries, which West admitted to causing. Laura stated she was going to call an attorney and returned to her truck to get her cellular phone. When Laura obtained her phone, West grabbed her from behind, threw her against a car, handcuffed her, told her she was under arrest, and pushed her to the ground. While Laura was handcuffed on the ground, Thomas Romero, Club Rodeo's manager at that time, purportedly laughed at and mocked Laura's predicament. Laura testified that at no point did West ever identify himself as a police officer, and at no point did she touch West or Medrano.

APD officers arrived after being called by both a witness to the incident and Medrano. APD officers transported Adolfo, Roberto, and Laura to jail. Roberto and Adolfo spent two days in jail, and were subsequently no-billed by the grand jury for assault on a police officer, the only crime with which they were charged. Laura spent three days in jail, purportedly for assault on a police officer, but was never charged with any crime.

The Defendants' Account

Fifth Club, West, and Medrano present a much different account of the events of September 17. Fifth Club's doorman testified that when he asked for Roberto's identification to get into the club, Roberto seemed intoxicated and shoved his ID against the doorman's chest. The doorman asked Roberto to leave, and Roberto refused. The doorman threatened to call the police if Roberto did not leave, and Roberto again refused. The doorman then signaled with a flashlight to West and Medrano that they were needed inside the club.

West was sitting in his car in the parking lot when the doorman signaled that he and Medrano, who was near the entrance, were needed inside the club. West and Medrano proceeded inside the club, where the doorman informed them that Roberto was intoxicated and should not enter the club. Roberto and Adolfo refused to leave, at which point Medrano grabbed Roberto by the wrist or hand to escort him out. Roberto pulled away and was then grabbed by West. As West was escorting Roberto to the door, Roberto kneed West in the groin, and West lost his grip on Roberto. West then pushed Roberto against a wall. Roberto attempted to strike West, at which point West began to throw a forearm at Roberto. Adolfo then punched West in the head, causing West and Roberto to fall either against the wall or onto the floor. Roberto was not moving, and West surmised he may have passed out. West handcuffed Roberto and moved him outside.

After Adolfo punched West, Medrano pushed Adolfo out the door of the club, and Adolfo tried to kick and punch Medrano. Both Medrano and Adolfo fell to the ground outside the door to the club. Adolfo repeatedly kicked Medrano while Adolfo was on the ground, causing Medrano to strike Adolfo with a flashlight several times while saying, "Police, stop kicking me." Medrano eventually subdued and handcuffed Adolfo.

Laura soon arrived, parking her car where it would block APD efforts to arrest and transport Roberto and Adolfo. She immediately threatened to sue West, who repeatedly asked her to move her car. West escorted Laura by the elbow to her car, and Laura snatched her elbow away from West and elbowed him. West then informed Laura she was under arrest and handcuffed her. Romero, Club Rodeo's manager, testified via deposition that he simply told Laura, "If you calm down, they'll probably let you go." APD officers then transported Roberto, Adolfo, and Laura to jail.

Issue 7: Whether West was Entitled to Official Immunity

Fifth Club and West argue that West was entitled to official immunity as a matter of law because he was functioning as a peace officer during the early morning hours of September 17. This argument, however, presupposes that Roberto committed one of the enumerated offenses in former article 14.03(d) within West's presence or view, thereby entitling West to function as a peace officer. *See* Former Tex. Code Crim. Proc. Ann. art. 14.03(d). To be entitled to immunity, West was required to show that he was acting at all relevant times pursuant to his authority as a peace officer and that his actions were discretionary and in good faith. *City of Lancaster v. Chambers*, 883 S.W.2d 650, 653, 37 Tex. Sup. Ct. J. 980 (Tex. 1994).

Here, the district court presented to the jury the following question and instructions regarding official immunity:

> Could a reasonably prudent officer, under the same or similar circumstances, have believed that the disputed conduct of David West was justified based on the information David West possessed when the conduct occurred?
>
> You are instructed that David West may arrest someone if he reasonably believed the person committed an offense within his presence or view if the offense is a felony, a breach of the peace, public intoxication, disorderly conduct, criminal trespass, interference with an arrest, assault, assault on a police officer, or failure to obey a lawful order.
>
> The term "breach of the peace" includes all violations of the public peace or order, or decorum; in other words, it signifies the offense of disturbing the public peace or tranquility enjoyed by the citizens of a community; a disturbance of the public tranquility by any act or conduct inciting to violence or tending to provoke or excite others to break the peace; a disturbance of public order by an act of violence, or by any act likely to produce violence, or which, by causing consternation and alarm disturbs the peace and quiet of the community.
>
> A person commits an offense if the person appears in a public place while intoxicated to the degree that the person may endanger the person or another.

The jury was essentially asked to determine two questions. First, whether West was entitled to "switch hats" and transform from his role as private security for the club into a separate role as a peace officer. Next, if West was acting within his authority as a peace officer, the jury was asked to determine whether his actions were in good faith. Fifth Club and West argue that the evidence conclusively shows that West acted as a "reasonably prudent officer" and was entitled to immunity, but they ignore that the jury, from the evidence presented, could have concluded that Roberto never committed a crime within West's presence or view that entitled him to function as a peace officer under former article 14.03(d) and arrest Roberto. There is, at best, conflicting evidence of whether Roberto committed any crimes at all, and the jury is the sole judge of the credibility of witnesses and the weight to be given to their testimony. *Golden Eagle Archery, Inc. v. Jackson*, 116 S.W.3d 757, 761, 46 Tex. Sup. Ct. J. 1133 (Tex. 2003).

Additionally, Fifth Club and West assert that because West and another one of their witnesses testified that West's actions were reasonable, the jury's refusal to grant official immunity to West was based on factually insufficient evidence. We disagree. Even Officer Payne, an expert witness for Fifth Club and West, testified that he had never seen an officer slam someone's head into a wall, and had never seen an officer hit a suspect who was already handcuffed, as West was alleged to have done. Officer Tidwell, an expert witness for Roberto, testified that the crimes allegedly committed by Roberto would not justify an officer slamming a suspect's head against a wall. Officer Tidwell also testified it would not have been reasonable for West to grab Roberto's arms from behind without announcing his presence as a police officer. We hold the evidence was both legally and factually sufficient to support the jury's finding that West was not entitled to official immunity for his actions toward Roberto, and we overrule Fifth Club's and West's seventh issue.

Issue 1: Whether Fifth Club is Responsible for West's Actions

The district court submitted to the jury the following question: "On the occasion in question was David West acting in the furtherance of a mission for the benefit of Fifth Club, Inc. and subject to control by Fifth Club, Inc. as to the details of the mission?" The jury answered, "Yes." Fifth Club now asserts that it is not responsible for West's actions because he was acting as a peace officer.

This Court has previously explained the process for determining when a security guard ceases functioning as an employee and functions instead as a peace officer:

> In determining the status of a police officer, we ask "in what capacity was the officer acting at the time he committed the acts for which the complaint is made?" If the officer is performing a public duty, such as the enforcement of general laws, the officer's private employer incurs no vicarious responsibility for that officer's acts, even though the employer may have directed the activities. If the officer was engaged in *protecting the employer's property, ejecting trespassers, or enforcing rules and regulations promulgated by the employer*, however, the trier of fact decides whether the officer was acting as a public officer or as a servant of the employer.

Mansfield v. C.F. Bent Tree Apartment Ltd. P'ship, 37 S.W.3d 145, 149 (Tex. App.—Austin 2001, no pet.) (emphasis added). As explained above, there is both legally and factually sufficient evidence to support a conclusion that West was not acting as a peace officer under former article 14.03(d) when Roberto's injuries were inflicted. We therefore reject Fifth Club's contention that it is not responsible for West's actions because he was functioning as a peace officer.

Fifth Club also asserts it is not responsible for West's actions because he was an independent contractor. In the employment context, it is the right of control that commonly justifies imposing liability on the employer for the actions of the employee, and an employer may be vicariously liable for his independent contractor's acts if he retains the "right to control the means, methods, or details of the independent contractor's work." *St. Joseph Hosp. v. Wolff*, 94 S.W.3d 513, 542, 46 Tex. Sup. Ct. J. 142 & n.91 (Tex. 2003) (quoting *Baptist Mem'l Hosp. Sys. v. Sampson*, 969 S.W.2d 945, 947, 41 Tex. Sup. Ct. J. 833 (Tex. 1998)).

An employer can also be liable for the acts of an independent contractor if the "personal character exception" applies. *See Ross v. Texas One P'ship*, 796 S.W.2d 206, 213 (Tex. App.—Dallas 1990), *writ denied*, 806 S.W.2d 222, 34 Tex. Sup. Ct. J. 293 (Tex. 1991) (per curiam); *Duran v. Furr's Supermarkets, Inc.*, 921 S.W.2d 778, 787 (Tex. App.—El Paso 1996, writ denied). If the duties being carried out by an independent contractor are of a personal character owed to the public by one adopting measures to protect his property, owners and operators of enterprises cannot, by securing independent contractors for the purpose of protecting property, obtain immunity from liability for at least the intentional torts of those hired. *See Ross*, 796 S.W.2d at 213; *Duran*, 921 S.W.2d at 787–88.

Here, the uncontroverted evidence established that the doorman signaled West and Medrano to enter the club and remove Roberto and Adolfo. The doorman then directed West and Medrano to eject Adolfo and Roberto, which they did. Salim Salem, one of Fifth Club's owners, testified that it was the club's responsibility to ensure the safety of patrons and that one of the reasons for hiring outside security like West was to deter crime, both inside and outside the club. This is evidence that West was carrying out the exact functions he was hired to perform, and was performing those functions at the direction of Club Rodeo employees. We hold that the record contains both legally and factually sufficient evidence that West was acting in the furtherance of a mission for the benefit of Fifth Club and subject to control by Fifth Club as to the details of the mission. We overrule Fifth Club's and West's first issue.

Issue 2: Fifth's Club's Negligence and Apportionment of Responsibility

Fifth Club and West next argue there is insufficient evidence to support the jury's finding that Fifth Club was negligent and that its proportionate responsibility was 55%. Roberto claims that Fifth Club was negligent in both its hiring and retention of West and Medrano. Salim Salem testified that he did not personally hire the off-duty peace officers who worked as outside security, but instead entrusted another officer to make these arrangements. Fifth Club gave this officer no instructions, did not require applicants to fill out applications, and was not even aware of which officers were working. Although Fifth Club had policy manuals for inside security, including directives not to use profanity with customers because profanity can "escalate[] an incident," the manuals were not provided to security personnel working outside. Finally, Fifth Club failed to perform background checks on any of the security personnel working outside. Roberto presented expert testimony that Fifth Club's conduct in hiring and retaining West constituted gross negligence and proximately caused the injuries to Roberto. We conclude there was legally and factually sufficient evidence to support the jury's finding that Fifth Club was negligent.

Regarding the jury's apportionment of 55% of the responsibility to Fifth Club, the jury is given wide latitude in performing its sworn duty to serve as fact finder in allocating responsibility. Tex. Civ. Prac. & Rem. Code Ann. § 33.003 (West Supp. 2004); *Rosell v. Central West Motor Stages, Inc.*, 89 S.W.3d 643, 659 (Tex. App.—Dallas 2002, no pet.). Even if the evidence could support a different percentage allocation of responsibility, an appellate court may not substitute its judgment for that of the jury. *Rosell*, 89 S.W.3d at 659. We conclude the evidence is legally and factually sufficient to support the jury's finding, and we overrule Fifth Club's and West's second issue.

Issues 5 and 6: Malice Finding and Exemplary Damages

Fifth Club challenges the jury's award of exemplary damages against Fifth Club and the jury's finding that both Fifth Club and West acted with malice. Here, Roberto's expert testified that Fifth Club acted with gross negligence in hiring and retaining West. An employer can also be liable for exemplary damages due to the malicious acts of an employee if the employee was unfit and the corporation was grossly negligent in employing him. *Mobil Oil Corp. v. Ellender*, 968 S.W.2d 917, 921, 41 Tex. Sup. Ct. J. 763 (Tex. 1998). We conclude the evidence was legally and factually sufficient to support an award of exemplary damages.

Fifth Club also argues that the amount of $35,000 in exemplary damages is excessive. Exemplary damages must be reasonably proportioned to actual damages. *Alamo Nat'l Bank v. Kraus*, 616 S.W.2d 908, 910, 24 Tex. Sup. Ct. J. 343 (Tex. 1981). There is no set rule of ratio between the amount of actual and exemplary damages that will be considered reasonable. *Ethicon, Inc. v. Martinez*, 835 S.W.2d 826, 835 (Tex. App.—Austin 1992, writ denied). An award of exemplary damages rests largely in the discretion of the fact finder and will not be set aside as excessive unless the amount is so large as to indicate that it is the result of passion, prejudice, or corruption, or that the evidence has been disregarded. *Id.* Factors to consider when determining whether an exemplary-damages award is reasonable include: (1) the nature of the wrong, (2) the character of the conduct involved, (3) the degree of culpability of the wrongdoer, (4) the situation and sensibilities of the parties concerned, and (5) the extent to which such conduct offends a public sense of justice and propriety. *Id.*

Here, the jury awarded over $110,000 in actual damages and $35,000 in exemplary damages. Examining the *Kraus* factors to determine whether this proportion is reasonable, we note first that the nature of the wrong consists of serious bodily injury inflicted by Fifth Club personnel to Roberto, who subsequently spent two days in jail for crimes for which he was later no-billed. We concluded above that the evidence is legally and factually sufficient to support the jury's findings that Fifth Club is responsible for West's actions and that Fifth Club was itself grossly negligent. Second, Fifth Club delegated the hiring of security officers to a third party, failed to perform background checks, did not require applications to be completed, did not provide policy manuals or instructions to outside security personnel, and was not even aware of the identities of the security personnel it was employing. Moreover, there is evidence in the record that Club Rodeo's manager laughed at and mocked Laura while she was handcuffed. It is undisputed that West and Medrano were paid in full at the end of their shift and that Fifth Club took no action as a result of this incident. Third, regarding Fifth Club's culpability, the jury heard expert testimony that Fifth Club's conduct constituted gross negligence and proximately caused Roberto's injuries. Fourth, considering the situation and sensibilities of the parties concerned, we concluded that the evidence is legally and factually sufficient to support the conclusion that Roberto suffered, and continues to suffer from, injuries proximately caused by Fifth Club's gross negligence. Finally, Fifth Club's conduct offends a public sense of justice and propriety. Fifth Club representatives testified that personnel such as West were hired, in part, to protect its patrons. However, Fifth Club did nothing to ensure that the security personnel hired were qualified for employment. Furthermore, Fifth Club failed to inform its outside security personnel of club policies, as it did with other club employees. This is the type of conduct exemplary damages is meant to punish and deter. In light of the *Kraus* factors, the jury's award of exemplary damages equal to approximately one third the amount of actual damages is not clearly wrong and unjust. *See Kraus*, 616 S.W.2d at 910; *Martinez*, 835 S.W.2d at 835. We therefore overrule Fifth Club's exemplary-damages issue.

Issues 3 and 4: Award for Physical Pain, Mental Anguish, and Physical Impairment

Fifth Club and West argue that the evidence is insufficient to support three awards: $80,000 for physical pain and mental anguish Roberto sustained in the past, $20,000 for mental anguish that he will reasonably sustain in the future, and $7000 for physical impairment he suffered in the past. Matters of past and future physical pain, mental anguish, and physical impairment are particularly within the jury's province. *Marvelli v. Alston*, 100 S.W.3d 460, 482 (Tex. App.—Fort Worth 2003, pet. denied). As long as sufficient probative evidence exists to support the jury's verdict, neither the reviewing court nor the trial court is entitled to substitute its judgment for that of the jury. *Id.* (citing *Larson v. Cactus Util. Co.*, 730 S.W.2d 640, 641, 30 Tex. Sup. Ct. J. 331 (Tex. 1987)); see also *Rehabilitation Facility at Austin, Inc. v. Cooper*, 962 S.W.2d 151, 155 (Tex. App.—Austin 1998, no pet.).

Roberto presented evidence at trial that he suffered a fracture of his left zygomatic arch, a bone in his skull. His face was swollen and bloody. When he arrived at the jail after the incident, it was determined he needed to be taken to the hospital for treatment. While in the hospital, he asked that his daughter not be allowed to see him in his condition. He could not sleep or eat when in jail, was in pain, and had problems communicating following this incident. Roberto had recurring headaches, required additional visits to the doctor, and missed a week of work. We conclude the evidence is legally and factually sufficient to support an award for physical pain and mental anguish Roberto sustained in the past.

Roberto's wife testified that at the time of trial, over a year after the incident, Roberto continued to have trouble talking to people, was "always tossing and turning," and was having nightmares. She testified he was eating less, suffering from depression, and pushing her away. We conclude the evidence is legally and factually sufficient to support an award for physical pain and mental anguish that Roberto will reasonably sustain in the future.

Physical impairment, sometimes called loss of enjoyment of life, encompasses the loss of the injured party's former lifestyle. *Dawson v. Briggs*, 107 S.W.3d 739, 752 (Tex. App.—Fort Worth 2003, no pet.). To recover damages for past impairment, the plaintiff must prove that the effect of his physical impairment extends beyond any impediment to his earning capacity and beyond any pain and suffering and mental anguish to the extent that it produces a separate and distinct loss that is substantial and for which he should be compensated. See *Golden Eagle Archery, Inc. v. Jackson*, 116 S.W.3d 757, 772, 46 Tex. Sup. Ct. J. 1133 (Tex. 2003); *Blankenship v. Mirick*, 984 S.W.2d 771, 777 (Tex. App.—Waco 1999, pet. denied); *Lawson-Avila Constr., Inc. v. Stoutamire*, 791 S.W.2d 584, 599 (Tex. App.—San Antonio 1990, writ denied).

Here, Roberto suffered a fracture to a bone in his skull. He spent a week recovering from this injury, had difficulty eating and communicating with others, and sought to avoid his daughter so that she would not observe his condition. His wife testified that before the incident he used to exercise and eat frequently; after the incident he would not eat, had difficulty communicating, and would spend time in his room by himself. This represents more than a scintilla of evidence of physical impairment in the past, and we cannot say the jury's decision to award damages for physical impairment suffered in the past is "so contrary to the overwhelming weight of the evidence as to be clearly wrong and unjust." See *Crye*, 907 S.W.2d at 499; *Cain*, 709 S.W.2d at 176. Accordingly, the evidence is legally and factually sufficient to support the jury's award for physical impairment in the past. Our review of the record also leads us to conclude that there is legally and factually sufficient evidence to support the amount of all damages the jury awarded. We therefore overrule Fifth Club's and West's third and fourth issues.

Conclusion

We have overruled Laura's and Adolfo's one issue on appeal, and Fifth Club's and West's seven issues. The final judgment of the district court is therefore affirmed.

Mack Kidd, Justice

State of Louisiana v. Steven Michael Presson, 986 So. 2d 843(La. Ct. App. 2008)

Before Caraway, Peatross and Moore, JJ.
Opinion by: Caraway

The defendant was convicted of operating a motor vehicle while intoxicated, fourth offense. He was ultimately sentenced to twelve years at hard labor, to run consecutively with another sentence being served for a prior conviction. For the following reasons, defendant's conviction is affirmed, and the sentence is amended.

Facts

At approximately 5:00 p.m. on November 13, 2006, Clay Morgan, a security officer at Willis-Knighton Hospital ("WK"), received a report of possible automobile theft in the hospital parking lot. Morgan and his acting supervisor, Jerry Johnson, arrived at the parking lot at the same time and approached the defendant, Steven Michael Presson ("Presson"). Presson explained that he locked his keys in the car. Johnson smelled alcohol on Presson's breath and inquired about how much alcohol he had consumed. Although the details of their conversation are not known, Johnson advised Presson not to drive due to his suspected intoxication. Once the security officers unlocked the defendant's vehicle, they had the car driven to the north hospital parking lot by a third party, and left the scene.

Presson admitted at trial that Johnson informed him that he smelled alcohol on his breath and told him not to drive his car. Nevertheless, by 5:20 p.m. and in spite of the explicit warning against driving, Morgan observed Presson drive away in the vehicle. Morgan immediately notified Johnson, who stated he would contact the local police and begin following Presson.

Shreveport Police Department Officer Scott Deen was on patrol when he received a dispatch concerning a possible DWI. Officer Deen was told that the WK security officer (Johnson) was following the suspect (Presson) and Johnson was giving directions while driving behind the defendant. These directions were relayed to the responding officers, including Officer Deen. The police were ultimately directed to the Circle K convenience store at the corner of Fairfield Avenue and Jordan Street.

When Officer Deen arrived at Circle K at 5:30 p.m., Presson, Johnson, and other police officers were already there. Presson was outside of his car, which was parked in the Circle K lot. Officer Deen, a police force veteran experienced in DWI field sobriety testing, approached Presson. He also detected the odor of alcohol on defendant's breath. After he was *Mirandized*, Presson submitted to the standard field sobriety tests.

Presson was asked to recite the alphabet. Officer Deen noted his speech was slurred and "thick tongued," indicators of intoxication. Next, he was asked to hold one foot up six inches above the ground for thirty seconds. Presson did not mention any condition he suffered from that could cause poor performance on this particular test. Within a few seconds, defendant placed his foot back down on the ground three times and also had to use his arms for balance, further indicating he was intoxicated. Officer Deen performed the HGN (horizontal gaze nystagmus) test, but no testimony was elicited at trial as to Presson's actual performance on this test.

Officer Deen believed Presson was intoxicated and transported him to the Traffic Unit for additional chemical testing. After defendant was advised of his rights relating to chemical testing, he consented to take the breath test. At 6:12 p.m., the Intoxilyzer 5000 revealed Presson's blood alcohol concentration level was 0.085%.

Presson was charged by bill of information with operating a motor vehicle while intoxicated, fourth offense. During trial, the defendant admitted drinking some alcohol earlier on the day of his arrest, admitted his encounter with the security officers in the WK parking lot, and admitted being told not to drive because of his suspected intoxication. However, he denied that he was intoxicated when he left WK in his car.

Presson testified that he was upset because his mother was ill, and his car had overheated (causing him to pull into Circle K). He drank some Jagermeister and another "quarter of a pint," but only after he had already parked his car at Circle K. He blamed his poor performance on the field sobriety tests on a purported brain injury. Defendant admitted at least three prior DWI convictions during the ten years preceding the instant offense.

The unanimous jury found the defendant guilty as charged. The trial court originally sentenced defendant to fifteen years at hard labor to run concurrently with any other sentence he was then serving. Both parties filed timely motions for reconsideration, and as a result, Presson's sentence was reduced to twelve years at hard labor, to run consecutively to any other sentence Presson was serving, as required by La. R.S. 14:98(E)(4)(b) (Presson had previously received the benefits of suspension of sentence and probation as a DWI fourth offender for his conviction in Suit No. 225,931). This appeal ensued.

Discussion

Presson contends in his first assignment of error that the evidence was insufficient to prove he was guilty beyond a reasonable doubt of driving while intoxicated. He argues that even though his blood alcohol concentration was 0.085% after his arrest, no evidence showed that he operated his car while he was intoxicated. Rather, he argues, the evidence only proved he became legally intoxicated after parking his car at Circle K.

When issues are raised on appeal both as to the sufficiency of the evidence and as to one or more trial errors, the reviewing court should first determine the sufficiency of the evidence. The reason for reviewing sufficiency first is that the accused may be entitled to an acquittal under *Hudson v. Louisiana*, 450 U.S. 40, 101 S. Ct. 970, 67 L. Ed. 2d 30 (1981), if a rational trier of fact, viewing the evidence in accord with *Jackson v. Virginia*, 443 U.S. 307, 99 S. Ct. 2781, 61 L. Ed. 2d 560 (1979), in the light most favorable to the prosecution, could not reasonably conclude that all of the elements of the offense have been proved beyond a reasonable doubt. *State v. Hearold*, 603 So. 2d 731 (La. 1992); *State v. Bosley*, 29,253 (La. App. 2d Cir. 4/2/97), 691 So. 2d 347, *writ denied*, 97-1203 (La. 10/17/97), 701 So. 2d 1333.

This standard, now legislatively embodied in La. C. Cr. P. art. 821, does not provide the appellate court with a vehicle to substitute its own appreciation of the evidence for that of the fact finder. *State v. Robertson*, 96-1048 (La. 10/4/96), 680 So. 2d 1165. The appellate court does not assess the credibility of witnesses or reweigh evidence. *State v. Smith*, 94-3116 (La. 10/16/95), 661 So. 2d 442.

The *Jackson* standard is applicable in cases involving both direct and circumstantial evidence. An appellate court reviewing the sufficiency of evidence in such cases must resolve any conflict in the direct evidence by viewing that evidence in the light most favorable to the prosecution. When the direct evidence is thus viewed, the facts established by the direct evidence and inferred from the circumstances established by that evidence must be sufficient for a rational trier of fact to conclude beyond a reasonable doubt that defendant was guilty of every essential element of the crime. *State v. Sutton*, 436 So. 2d 471 (La. 1983); *State v. Owens*, 30,903 (La. App. 2d Cir. 9/25/98), 719 So. 2d 610, *writ denied*, 98-2723 (La. 2/5/99), 737 So. 2d 747.

When circumstantial evidence forms the basis of the conviction, such evidence must exclude every reasonable hypothesis of innocence. La. R.S. 15:438. The court does not determine whether another possible hypothesis suggested by the defendant could afford an exculpatory explanation of the events; rather, when evaluating the evidence in the light most favorable to the prosecution, the court determines whether the possible alternative hypothesis is sufficiently reasonable that a rational juror could not have found proof of guilt beyond a reasonable doubt under *Jackson v. Virginia, supra. State v. Davis*, 92-1623 (La. 5/23/94), 637 So. 2d 1012, *cert. denied*, 513 U.S. 975, 115 S. Ct. 450, 130 L. Ed. 2d 359 (1994); *State v. Owens*, 30,903 (La. App. 2d Cir. 9/25/98), 719 So. 2d 610, *writ denied*, 98-2723 (La. 2/5/99), 737 So. 2d 747.

Where there is conflicting testimony about factual matters, the resolution of which depends upon a determination of the credibility of the witnesses, the matter is one of the weight of the evidence, not its sufficiency. *State v. Allen*, 36,180 (La. App. 2d Cir. 9/18/02), 828 So. 2d 622, *writs denied*, 02-2595 (La. 3/28/03), 840 So. 2d 566, *and* 02-2997 (La. 6/27/03), 847 So. 2d 1255, *cert. denied*, 540 U.S. 1185, 124 S. Ct. 1404, 158 L. Ed. 2d 90 (2004).

In the absence of internal contradiction or irreconcilable conflict with physical evidence, one witness's testimony, if believed by the trier of fact, is sufficient support for a requisite factual conclusion. *State v. White*, 28,095 (La. App. 2d Cir. 5/8/96), 674 So. 2d 1018, *writs denied*, 96-1459 (La. 11/15/96), 682 So. 2d 760, and 98-0282 (La. 6/26/98), 719 So. 2d 1048.

La. R.S. 14:98 provides in pertinent part:

> A. (1) The crime of operating a vehicle while intoxicated is the operating of any motor vehicle, aircraft, watercraft, vessel, or other means of conveyance when:
> (a) The operator is under the influence of alcoholic beverages; or
> (b) The operator's blood alcohol concentration is 0.08 percent or more by weight based on grams of alcohol per one hundred cubic centimeters of blood; or
> * * * *

Thus, the state need only prove to the jury that the defendant was operating a vehicle and that the defendant was under the influence of alcohol. La. R.S. 14:98(A)(1)(a); *State v. Minnifield*, 31,527 (La. App. 2d Cir. 1/20/99), 727 So. 2d 1207, *writ denied*, 99-0516 (La. 6/18/99), 745 So. 2d 19. To convict a defendant of driving while intoxicated, fourth offense, the state must also prove that the defendant has had three prior valid convictions, as defined in La. R.S. 14:98(F)(1). *State v. Inzina*, 31,439 (La. App. 2d Cir. 12/9/98), 728 So. 2d 458.

This court has noted that the term "operating" is broader than the term "driving." The jurisprudence generally holds that in order to operate a motor vehicle, the defendant must have exercised some control or manipulation over the vehicle, such as steering, backing, or any physical handling of the controls for the purpose of putting the car in motion. *State v. Johnson*, 580 So. 2d 998, 1001 (La. App. 3d Cir. 1991); *City of Bastrop v. Paxton*, 457 So. 2d 168 (La. App. 2d Cir. 1984). It is not necessary that these actions have any effect on the engine, nor is it essential that the car move in order for the state to prove the element of operation. *Id.*

An officer must conduct a general observation of the defendant for a period of 15 minutes prior to testing, whereby the defendant shall not have ingested alcohol, alcoholic beverages, regurgitated, vomited or taken anything by mouth. *State v. Meredith*, 36,483 (La. App. 2d Cir. 12/11/02), 833 So. 2d 1125.

Some behavioral manifestations, independent of any scientific test, are sufficient to support a charge of driving while intoxicated. *State v. McDonald*, 33,013 (La. App. 2d Cir. 3/1/00), 754 So. 2d 382, 386; *State v. Pitre*, 532 So. 2d 424 (La. App. 1st Cir. 1988), *writ denied*, 538 So. 2d 590 (La. 1989). It is not necessary that a conviction for DWI be based upon a blood or breath alcohol test, and the observations of an arresting officer may be sufficient to establish a defendant's guilt. Intoxication is an observable condition about which a witness may testify. *State v. Allen*, 440 So. 2d 1330 (La. 1983); *State v. Blackburn*, 37,918 (La. App. 2d Cir. 1/28/04), 865 So. 2d 912; *State v. McDonald, supra.*

The evidence conclusively established that Presson was intoxicated by the time police arrived at the scene, after defendant was out of his vehicle. There is an irrebuttable presumption of intoxication when a person's blood alcohol concentration level is 0.08% or more. La. R.S. 14:98(A)(2); *State v. Downer*, 460 So. 2d 1184 (La. App. 2d Cir. 1984), *superseded by statute*, as recognized by *State v. McGuire*, 493 So. 2d 559 (La. 1986). The central issue presented in this appeal is whether defendant was intoxicated while he "operated" his car after leaving the WK parking lot.

The uncontroverted evidence shows that when Presson was initially confronted in the hospital parking lot shortly after 5:00 p.m., there was a strong smell of alcohol on his breath. It is clear that the WK security officers suspected that defendant was already intoxicated at that time, and they specifically instructed him not to drive his car. Nonetheless, Presson disobeyed their instructions and drove away at 5:20 p.m.

Although there is an evidentiary gap due to Johnson's unavailability to testify at trial, other testimony reveals that Johnson was able to follow Presson and remained in contact with police, reporting Presson's trip between WK and Circle K. Once police arrived at Circle K, Presson and Johnson were already parked. The evidence shows that Officer Deen immediately detected alcohol on defendant's breath, defendant's speech was slurred and "thick-tongued," and defendant failed at least two of three standardized field sobriety tests. The police records show that the police officers first came into contact with defendant at 5:30 p.m. Although Presson disputes the exact timing, he nevertheless admitted at trial that the police arrived no more than eight minutes after he first drove into the Circle K parking lot. There was no evidence that defendant consumed any alcohol once police arrived on the scene.

Defendant's version of the events is that he consumed some Jagermeister earlier in the day, prior to his encounter with WK security officers in the hospital parking lot, then drank another "quarter of a pint" after he parked at Circle K, but before the police arrived. The only possible hypothesis of innocence which can be advanced under these facts is that the defendant parked and *exited* his car at Circle K, and then consumed enough alcoholic beverages to become intoxicated prior to the arrival of police shortly thereafter. Any consumption of alcoholic beverages while parked, but still in the car, would be sufficient to constitute "operation" because he still had control of the vehicle. As explained above, movement of the vehicle is not the determinative factor. *See, State v. Johnson, supra.* Given the facts of this case, however, this hypothesis is not reasonable. Moreover, the physical evidence and circumstantial evidence demonstrate that Presson's self-serving version of the events could be rejected by the jury.

There was no evidence that any alcoholic beverage containers were found in Presson's car or in the vicinity thereof. There were no eyewitnesses or direct proof that Presson actually drank any alcoholic beverages outside of his vehicle during the brief interval at Circle K. The sequence of events does not support this hypothesis. The evidence suggests that everything happened within a span of ten minutes (i.e., between the time defendant left the WK parking lot until the time he was stopped by police). During this time, according to defendant, he drove from WK to Circle K, at the intersection of Jordan and Fairfield, parked his car, used a pay phone to find a motel room, and then drank enough Jagermeister to affect his speech and impair his performance on the field sobriety tests minutes later. Defendant's version of the events finds little support when the overall timeline of his actions is considered, and on credibility grounds, the jury clearly rejected his testimony.

The only reasonable hypothesis is that defendant was already intoxicated when he drove out of the WK parking lot. Viewing the evidence in a light most favorable to the prosecution, a rational trier of fact could have concluded beyond a reasonable doubt that every reasonable hypothesis of innocence had been excluded. The evidence was sufficient to support defendant's conviction. This assignment is therefore without merit.

The defendant's second assignment of error argues that his sentence is excessive in that it does take his emotional state at the time of the commission of the offense, or his personal or work history, into consideration. Further, the trial court did not consider his longstanding substance abuse problem.

Because defendant's motion for reconsideration of the July 18, 2007 resentencing was untimely, and merely urges that his sentence is excessive, the defendant is relegated only to a claim of constitutional excessiveness. A sentence violates La. Const. art. 1, § 20 if it is grossly out of proportion to the seriousness of the offense or nothing more than a purposeless and needless infliction of pain and suffering. *State v. Smith*, 2001-2574 (La. 1/14/03), 839 So. 2d 1; *State v. Dorthey*, 623 So. 2d 1276 (La. 1993); *State v. Bonanno*, 384 So. 2d 355 (La. 1980). A sentence is considered grossly disproportionate if, when the crime and punishment are viewed in light of the harm done to society, it shocks the sense of justice. *State v. Weaver*, 2001-0467 (La. 1/15/02), 805 So. 2d 166; *State v. Lobato*, 603 So. 2d 739 (La. 1992); *State v. Hogan*, 480 So. 2d 288 (La. 1985); *State v. Bradford*, 29,519 (La. App. 2d Cir. 4/2/97), 691 So. 2d 864.

A trial court has broad discretion to sentence. Absent a showing of manifest abuse of that discretion, this court may not set aside a sentence as excessive. *State v. Guzman*, 99-1528 and 99-1753 (La. 5/16/00), 769 So. 2d 1158; *State v. June*, 38,440 (La. App. 2d Cir. 5/12/04), 873 So. 2d 939.

At the time of the instant offense, La. R.S. 14:98(E)(1)(a) provided:

> Except as otherwise provided in Subparagraph (4)(b) of this Subsection, on a conviction of a fourth or subsequent offense, notwithstanding any other provision of law to the contrary and regardless of whether the fourth offense occurred before or after an earlier conviction, the offender shall be imprisoned with or without hard labor for not less than ten years nor more than thirty years and shall be fined five thousand dollars. Sixty days of the sentence of imprisonment shall be imposed without the benefit of probation, parole, or suspension of sentence. The court, in its discretion, may suspend all or any part of the remainder of the sentence of imprisonment. If any portion of the sentence is suspended, the offender shall be placed on supervised probation with the Department of Public Safety and Corrections, division of probation and parole, for a period of time not to exceed five years, which probation shall commence on the day after the offender's release from custody.

La. R.S. 14:98(E)(4)(b) provided:

> If the offender has previously received the benefit of suspension, probation, or parole as a fourth offender, no part of the sentence may be imposed with benefit of suspension of sentence, probation, or parole, and no portion of the sentence shall be imposed concurrently with the remaining balance of any sentence to be served for a prior conviction for any offense.

Prior to imposing sentence, the trial court reviewed the facts of the instant offense and defendant's extensive criminal history, including more than ten prior arrests and/or convictions for DWI. See also, *State v. Presson*, 39,688 (La. App. 2d Cir. 4/6/05), 900 So. 2d 240 (in affirming this defendant's prior DWI fourth offense conviction, this court noted that "defendant had a predisposition to commit the offense of driving while intoxicated" based on his prior criminal record). Indeed, he was on probation for DWI, fourth offense, when the instant offense was committed. The record shows that defendant previously underwent evaluation and treatment for substance abuse in Suit No. 225,931 (*see, State v. Presson, supra*), contrary to his contention here, but that did nothing to preclude his commission of this offense. The trial judge noted that defendant had received a "series of breaks" over the past twenty years, but he has continued to drink and drive. Considering these factors, and notwithstanding defendant's request to consider his emotional state as a mitigating factor, the trial court concluded he was in need of incarceration, that a lesser sentence would deprecate the seriousness of the offense, and that these circumstances were likely to recur based upon his habitual intemperate conduct.

The trial court originally sentenced defendant to fifteen years at hard labor concurrent with any other sentence he was then serving. After reconsideration at the behest of both parties, defendant's sentence was reduced to twelve years at hard labor but made to run consecutively to any other sentence he was serving, as required by La. R.S. 14:98(E)(4)(b) (the record confirms that defendant previously received the benefits of suspension of sentence and probation as a DWI fourth offender.)

Considering this defendant's prior DWI fourth offense conviction (to say nothing of his other DWI multiple offense convictions), and the fact that the defendant was on probation when he committed this offense, the sentence imposed in this case is not constitutionally excessive. *See, State v. Masters*, 37,967 (La. App. 2d Cir. 12/17/03), 862 So. 2d 1121. In terms of prison time, the defendant's sentence barely exceeds the statutory minimum mandated in this case. On this record, nothing about this sentence shocks the sense of justice. This assignment is therefore without merit.

Error Patent

A review of the record reveals two errors patent.

The trial court did not impose the twelve year sentence without benefit of probation, parole, or suspension of sentence, as mandated by La. R.S. 14:98(E)(4)(b). The trial court explicitly found that La. R.S. 14:98(E)(4)(b) applied when it ordered the consecutive sentence. La. R.S. 15:301.1 is self-activating, however, and makes the denial of benefits self-operative. *See, State v. Williams*, 00-1725 (La. 11/28/01), 800 So. 2d 790; *State v. Batts*, 43,142 (La. App. 2d Cir. 4/2/08), 979 So. 2d 684, 2008 WL 867290.

La. R.S. 14:98(E)(1)(a) provides that upon conviction of DWI, fourth offense, in addition to the prison sentence, the offender "shall be fined five thousand dollars." Here, the trial court did not impose the mandatory fine, resulting in an illegally lenient sentence.

A court of appeal has the authority on its own motion to correct the sentence imposed under La. R.S. 14:98(E)(1)(a) by directing the trial court to add the mandatory fine of $ 5000 as required by the statute. *State v. Decrevel*, 03-0259 (La. 5/16/03), 847 So. 2d 1197; *State v. Williams, supra.* Further, an appellate court may amend a defendant's sentence without the necessity of remanding the matter to the trial court. *State v. Sermons*, 41,746 (La. App. 2d Cir. 2/28/07), 953 So. 2d 958, *writ denied*, 07-0789 (La. 11/2/07), 966 So. 2d 601. The defendant's sentence is therefore amended to impose the statutorily mandated fine of $ 5000.

Decree

For the foregoing reasons, the defendant's conviction is affirmed, the sentence is amended to impose the mandatory $5000 fine and to recognize the denial of benefits in accordance with La. R.S. 14:98(E)(4)(b), and the sentence, as amended, is affirmed.

CONVICTION AFFIRMED; SENTENCE AFFIRMED AS AMENDED.

Wesley Locke v. Ozark City Board of Education, 910 So. 2d 1247 (Ala. 2005)

Judges: SEE, Justice. Nabers, C.J., and Harwood, Stuart, and Bolin, JJ., concur.
Opinion by: SEE

Wesley Locke appeals from a summary judgment in favor of the defendant, the Ozark City Board of Education. We reverse and remand.

I.

Wesley Locke is a physical education teacher employed by the Dale County Department of Education. For a number of years, Locke also served as an umpire for high school baseball games. Locke was a member of the Southeast Alabama Umpires Association ("SAUA"), which provides officials to athletic events sponsored by the Alabama High School Athletic Association ("AHSAA").

On March 30, 1999, Locke was serving as the head umpire in a baseball game between Carroll High School and George W. Long High School. The game was being played at Carroll High School, and the principal and the athletic director of Carroll High School were in attendance; however, Carroll High School did not provide police protection or other security personnel for the game. After the baseball game, Mixon Cook, the parent of one of the baseball players for Carroll High School, attacked Locke, punching him three times in the face—in his right eye, on the right side of his face, and on the left side of his neck. As a result, Locke sustained physical injuries to his neck and face that caused him pain, discomfort, scarring, and blurred vision. Locke sued the Ozark City Board of Education ("the Board") alleging breach of contract.

Locke specifically alleged that because Carroll High School, through the Board, is a member of the AHSAA, it is therefore required to follow the rules and regulations of the AHSAA. According to Locke, the AHSAA Directory provides that all school principals have the duty to "insure good game administration and supervision by providing for the following: ... adequate police protection" at athletic events. Locke alleged that, by not fulfilling its duty under the Directory, the Board breached its contract with the AHSAA by failing to provide police protection at the baseball game, that he was an intended third-party beneficiary of the contract, and that he was injured as a result of the Board's breach of the contract.

The Board moved for a summary judgment, arguing that it did not have a duty to protect Locke, that Locke was not an intended third-party beneficiary of the contract between it and AHSAA, that Locke's claims were tort claims and not contract claims, that the Board is not responsible for the criminal actions of a third party, and that the Board did not breach "any alleged contract" with AHSAA. The trial court entered a summary judgment in favor of the Board. Locke appeals.

II.

The standard for review of a summary judgment is well established:

> "The standard of review applicable to a summary judgment is the same as the standard for granting the motion, that is, we must determine whether there was a genuine issue of material fact and, if not, whether the movant was entitled to a judgment as a matter of law. Our review is further subject to the caveat that this Court must review the record in a light most favorable to the nonmovant and resolve all reasonable doubts against the movant. *Wilson v. Brown*, 496 So. 2d 756, 758 (Ala. 1986); *Harrell v. Reynolds Metals Co.*, 495 So. 2d 1381 (Ala. 1986). See also *Hanners v. Balfour Guthrie, Inc.*, 564 So. 2d 412 (Ala. 1990)."
>
> "... Ala. Code 1975 § 12-21-12, mandates that the [nonmovants] meet their burden by 'substantial evidence.' *Bass v. SouthTrust Bank of Baldwin County*, 538 So. 2d 794, 797-98 (Ala. 1989). Under the substantial evidence test the nonmovant must present 'evidence of such weight and quality that fair-minded persons in the exercise of

impartial judgment can reasonably infer the existence of the fact sought to be proved.'
West v. Founders Life Assurance Co. of Florida, 547 So. 2d 870, 871 (Ala. 1989)."

Brewer v. Woodall, 608 So. 2d 370, 372 (Ala. 1992).

III.

For the purposes of this appeal, we assume that the AHSAA Directory constitutes [*1250] a valid contract between the Board and AHSAA.

> (The Board's brief, p. 11.) Because there apparently is a genuine issue of material fact as to whether the AHSAA Directory is a contract between the AHSAA and the Board, we do not review that question. This Court "will address on appeal only those issues presented and for which supporting authorities have been cited to the court." *Messer v. Messer*, 621 So. 2d 1343, 1344 (Ala. Civ. App. 1993).

On appeal, Locke first argues that he is an intended third-party beneficiary of a contract between the Board and the AHSAA. "If one person makes a promise for the benefit of a third party, such beneficiary may maintain an action thereon, though the consideration does not move from the latter." *Franklin Fire Ins. Co. v. Howard*, 230 Ala. 666, 667-68, 162 So. 683, 684 (1935).

> To recover under a third-party beneficiary theory, the complainant must show: (1) that the contracting parties intended, at the time the contract was created, to bestow a direct benefit upon a third party; (2) that the complainant was the intended beneficiary of the contract; and (3) that the contract was breached.

H.R.H. Metals, Inc. v. Miller, 833 So. 2d 18, 24 (Ala. 2002) (quoting *Sheetz, Aiken & Aiken, Inc. v. Spann, Hall, Ritchie, Inc.*, 512 So. 2d 99, 101-02 (Ala. 1987)). Further, "it has long been the rule in Alabama that one who seeks recovery as a third-party beneficiary of a contract must establish that the contract was intended for his direct, as opposed to incidental, benefit." *Morris Concrete, Inc. v. Warrick*, 868 So. 2d 429, 434 (Ala. Civ. App. 2003) (quoting *McGowan v. Chrysler Corp.*, 631 So. 2d 842, 848 (Ala. 1993) (quoting in turn *Mills v. Welk*, 470 So. 2d 1226, 1228 (Ala. 1985))). "We look[] to the complaints and the surrounding circumstances of the parties to ascertain the existence of that direct benefit." *Holley v. St. Paul Fire & Marine Ins. Co.*, 396 So. 2d 75, 80 (Ala. 1981)(citing *Zeigler v. Blount Bros. Constr. Co.*, 364 So. 2d 1163 (Ala. 1978)); see also *Anderson v. Howard Hall Co.*, 278 Ala. 491, 179 So. 2d 71 (1965).

In *Zeigler*, this Court addressed what is necessary to establish status as a third-party beneficiary of a contract. 364 So. 2d at 1163. In that case, a dam commissioned by a power company and built by a contractor collapsed. 364 So. 2d at 1165. Zeigler, a customer of the electrical power company, sued the contractor that had built the dam, arguing that his status as a consumer of electrical power made him a third-party beneficiary of the contract between the electrical power company and the contractor. *Id.* Specifically, Zeigler argued that because the contractor failed to construct the dam properly and the dam subsequently collapsed, he was being forced to pay higher bills for electricity than he would have had to pay had the dam been properly constructed. *Id.*

In determining whether Zeigler was a third-party beneficiary of the contract under the "surrounding circumstances" test, this Court looked to whether the power company itself was directly benefited by the contract, or whether the benefit manifested itself mainly to third parties.

Zeigler, 364 So. 2d at 1166. This Court noted that the contract itself did not mention third parties or any benefits third parties would reap from the construction of the dam. *Id*. This Court found that "performance of the contracts would, and did, result in an enhancement of [the power company's] real and riparian property holdings, to the direct benefit of the [power company] itself." 364 So. 2d at 1166. This Court further noted that there was no evidence indicating that the power company had considered the fees their customers would have to pay if the dam was built, and that there was no evidence indicating that a properly constructed dam would have necessarily resulted in lower electrical bills for the consumer. *Zeigler*, 364 So. 2d at 1166. Therefore, this Court held that because the contract directly benefited the power company and would not necessarily benefit the customer, Zeigler was an incidental, rather than an intended direct, beneficiary of the contract between the power company and the contractor. *Id*.

On the other hand, in *H.R.H. Metals, Inc.*, Vulcan Materials Company contracted with H.R.H Metals, Inc., to purchase and remove three buildings located on property belonging to Vulcan. 833 So. 2d at 21. H.R.H. signed a contract with Vulcan that provided, in pertinent part:

> [H.R.H] covenants to follow Vulcan's safety rules and to maintain its own safety and health program for its employees, subcontractors, and agents sufficient to prevent injury or illness to such persons resulting from their presence on the Vulcan premises....

H.R.H. Metals, Inc., 833 So. 2d at 21. H.R.H. hired a subcontractor, Carl Miller, to demolish and remove one of the buildings. *Id*. at 22. While in the process of demolishing the building, Miller walked across a skylight and fell 20 feet, seriously injuring himself. *Id*. Miller sued H.R.H., alleging, among other things, that H.R.H. had breached its contract with Vulcan to provide safety equipment to subcontractors, that he was a third-party beneficiary of the contract between Vulcan and H.R.H, that H.R.H. had breached that contract, and that he had been injured by H.R.H.'s breach of the contract.

On appeal, this Court noted that in order for a person to be a third-party beneficiary of a contract, the contracting parties must have intended to bestow benefits on third parties. *H.R.H. Metals, Inc.*, 833 So. 2d at 24. This Court held that to ascertain the intent of the parties "we must first look to the contract itself, because while 'the intention of the parties controls in construing a written contract,' 'the intention of the parties is to be derived from the contract itself where the language is plain and unambiguous.'" *H.R.H. Metals, Inc.*, 833 So. 2d at 24 (quoting *Loerch v. National Bank of Commerce of Birmingham*, 624 So. 2d 552, 553 (Ala. 1993)). We then noted that the contract between H.R.H. and Vulcan specifically provided that H.R.H. was to "maintain its own safety and health program for its employees, subcontractors, and agents *sufficient to prevent injury or illness to such persons resulting from their presence on the Vulcan premises*." 833 So. 2d at 25. This Court held that "the emphasized language reflects an intention on the part of the contracting parties to bestow a direct benefit on [the plaintiff] ...." 833 So. 2d at 25.

In this case, the Board argues that "Locke was not an intended beneficiary of the AHSAA contract." The Board relies on *Gardner v. Vinson Guard Service, Inc.*, 538 So. 2d 13 (Ala. 1988), in which a corporation hired a security company to provide protection in the corporation's parking lot to its employees as they were arriving at and leaving work. 518 So. 2d at 13. The instructions to the security guards specified certain times and places female employees would be arriving at work, and provided that the security guards were to escort them into the building. *Id*. at 14. The security guards were also to perform security checks around the perimeter of the company's property at certain intervals. *Id*. However, the contract also provided that, "Guards will use bathroom facilities in [the company's] building, but will not visit or linger in the building for any extended period of time." *Gardner*, 538 So. 2d at 14.

One morning, when a group of female employees, including the plaintiff, arrived for work, a security guard met them at the door and told them that "he had interrupted someone trying to break into the cigarette machine and that there was no need to call the police because the man had left and he (the security guard) had recovered all of the merchandise." 538 So. 2d at 14. The security guard further informed the female employees that he had apprehended the man and that they could safely enter the building to start work. *Id.* A short time later, a female employee, Hazel Gardner, entered a bathroom in the building where she was attacked by a second man who had apparently broken into the building. *Id.* Gardner and her husband sued the security company, alleging, among other things, breach of contract. Gardner argued that she was a third-party beneficiary of the contract between the security company and her employer. *Gardner*, 538 So. 2d at 14. The company moved for a summary judgment, and the trial court granted that motion.

On appeal, this Court upheld the summary judgment for the security company. However, it was not, as the Board contends, because this Court found that Gardner was not an intended third-party beneficiary. This Court stated that "in their brief, the Gardners argue that a cause of action may exist for a third-party beneficiary for a breach of contract. We do not dispute that a cause of action may exist, but we can find no contractual duty imposed upon [the security company]." *Gardner*, 538 So. 2d at 15. Thus, in *Gardner* this Court held that the security guards did not have a contractual duty to protect Gardner inside the building; it did not hold that Gardner was not a third-party beneficiary.

The Board also cites *DuPont v. Yellow Cab Co. of Birmingham*, 565 So. 2d 190 (Ala. 1990), in support of its argument that Locke is not an intended third-party beneficiary of the contract between the Board and AHSAA. In *DuPont*, a school board contracted with a cab company to provide drivers and maintenance for school buses. 565 So. 2d at 192. The cab company subcontracted with another company to provide drivers for the buses. *Id.* One of the buses was not maintained properly, and the driver was injured when the brakes failed, causing the bus to collide with a tree. *Id.* at 191. The driver sued the cab company, alleging that he was a third-party beneficiary of the contract between the school board and the cab company. *Id.* The trial court found that the driver was not a third-party beneficiary of the contract and entered a summary judgment for the cab company.

This Court stated that the cab company "was under an obligation, independent of the contract, to maintain its fleet of vehicles for the safety of its drivers." *DuPont*, 565 So. 2d at 192 (citing § 25-1-1, Ala. Code 1975). The contract at issue in *DuPont* provided solely for the transportation of students to and from school; therefore, the only group that could benefit from the contract was the students. 565 So. 2d at 192. We held, therefore, that the only "reasonable inference" that could be drawn from the contract was that the children riding the school buses, not the drivers, were the intended direct beneficiaries of the contract, and we affirmed. *Dupont*, 565 So. 2d at 192.

In this case, the contract between the Board and the AHSAA specifically provides that principals are to "provide good game administration and supervision by providing ... adequate police protection." Therefore, we must determine from the surrounding circumstances whether Locke is an intended direct beneficiary.

The contract before us between the Board and the AHSAA, like the one in *H.R.H.* and unlike the one in *Zeigler*, anticipates the existence of a third party. SAUA, which provided umpires, specifically Locke, for the game, provides officials only to athletic events that are sponsored by the AHSAA. The contract states that the purpose of "adequate police protection" is to "provide good game administration and supervision." Game administration and supervision necessarily involve umpires. The fact that the AHSAA and the Board intended for the police protection to directly benefit the umpires, who are involved in game administration and supervision, is evidenced by the letter from the AHSAA sanctioning Carroll High School for the incident involving Locke. The AHSAA stated:

> According to information received ... there were administrators present at the baseball game from both schools but there was no police protection provided. ... At the conclusion of the game, Mr. Mixon Cook made his way to the area where the umpires were exiting the field. Mr. Wesley Locke, Jr., the umpire in chief was struck three times in the face and neck area by Mr. Mixon Cook, a parent of a Carroll High School athlete. Mr. Cook used his fist with striking blows to Mr. Locke's right eye, left neck area and right side of his face. Because of this physical attack by Mr. Mixon Cook on the game official, Mr. Wesley Locke, Jr., Carroll High School is assessed a monetary fine of $1,000.00 and placed on probation for a period of one year.

Because this matter is before us on the appeal of a summary judgment, we need determine only whether Locke, as the nonmovant, has presented substantial evidence creating a genuine issue of material fact as to whether he was an intended direct beneficiary of the contract. We hold, based on the plain language of the contract and on the surrounding circumstances, that the contract anticipates third-party umpires, that the contract was intended to directly benefit umpires like Locke, and that Locke has presented substantial evidence creating a genuine issue of fact as to whether he was an intended direct beneficiary of the contract between the Board and the AHSAA.

IV.

The Board next argues that Locke's allegations sound in tort rather than in contract. Locke argues that his claim sounds in contract because, he says, the Board had a contractual duty to provide police protection at the baseball game Locke was umpiring, the Board failed to do so, and as a result Locke was assaulted by a spectator. Locke relies on *Sims v. Etowah County Board of Education*, 337 So. 2d 1310, 1313 (Ala. 1976), in which this Court stated: "'It will be observed that a negligent *failure* to perform a contract express or implied ... is but a breach of the contract.'" (quoting *Berry v. Druid City Hosp. Bd.*, 333 So. 2d 796, 799 (Ala. 1976)(quoting in turn *Vines v. Crescent Transit Co.*, 264 Ala. 114, 119, 85 So. 2d 436, 440 (1955))). On the other hand, it is true that

> if in performing [the contract], it is alleged that the defendant negligently caused personal injury or property damage to plaintiff, the remedy is in tort, for it is not the breach of a contract express or implied, but the breach of an implied duty to exercise due care not to injure plaintiff or her property which is the gravamen of the action.

Vines, 264 Ala. at 119, 85 So. 2d at 440.

Cook testified that if police protection had been provided, he would not have attacked Locke. Therefore, viewing the record in a light most favorable to Locke, the nonmovant, we conclude that he has presented substantial evidence showing that the Board failed to perform its contractual duties and that as a result of the Board's breach of the contract Locke was harmed. Locke's complaint sounds in contract, not in tort.

V.

The Board argues that "absent special relationships or circumstances, a person has no duty to protect another from criminal acts of a third person." *Steiger v. Huntsville City Bd. of Educ.*, 653 So. 2d 975 (Ala. 1995) (quoting *Young v. Huntsville Hosp.*, 595 So. 2d 1386, 1387 (Ala. 1992)). While this is a correct statement of law, the principle applies to claims sounding in tort, not to those in contract. *See Steiger*, 653 So. 2d at 978 ("We have noted, 'It is difficult to impose liability on one person for an intentional criminal act committed by a third person.' In this case, the Board has no tort liability. The only liability it could have to plaintiff Steiger is through a contract theory.") (citations omitted). Locke has presented evidence indicating that one of the purposes of the contract was providing "good game administration and supervision ...." Viewed in a light most favorable to Locke, this evidence creates a question of material fact as to whether the Board had a contractual duty to protect Locke from the criminal acts of third parties at sporting events by providing adequate police protection.

VI.

Finally, the Board argues that it did not breach the contract with the AHSAA. The Board concedes that the AHSAA Directory "provides that the school principal is required to insure good game administration and supervision by providing for adequate police protection." The Board, however, also offers testimony from Dan Washburn, the executive director of the AHSAA, to the effect that the AHSAA has recommended that "security at non-revenue games ... be in the form of administrators ...." Nevertheless, "it is elementary that it is the terms of the written contract, not the mental operations of one of the parties, that control its interpretation." *Harbison v. Strickland*, 900 So. 2d 385, 391, 2004 Ala. LEXIS 275, *13 (Ala. 2004) (quoting *Kinmon v. J.P. King Auction Co.*, 290 Ala. 323, 325, 276 So. 2d 569, 570 (1973)). The AHSAA Directory specifically provides that "adequate police protection" is to be provided at all athletic events sponsored by the AHSAA. Locke has offered undisputed evidence that there was no police protection at the baseball game at which he was injured and that the Board provided police protection at other athletic events. Further, a letter sent by the AHSAA to the Board, fining the Board for the incident involving Locke, specifically cites the fact that no police protection was provided at the baseball game. There is a genuine issue of material fact as to whether the Board provided "adequate" police protection at the baseball game at which Locke was injured under its contract with the AHSAA; therefore, a summary judgment is not appropriate as to this issue.

VII.

Locke has presented substantial evidence indicating that the Board and the AHSAA intended to provide a direct benefit to umpires, that he was an intended direct beneficiary of the contract, and that the Board breached the contract. Locke's complaint sounds in contract, and the evidence, viewed in a light most favorable to Locke, presents a question of material fact as to whether the Board had a contractual duty to protect Locke from the criminal acts of third parties and whether the Board did in fact provide adequate police protection at the game. For these reasons, a summary judgment was not appropriate. Therefore, the summary judgment in favor of the Board is reversed, and this case is remanded for proceedings consistent with this opinion.

REVERSED AND REMANDED

Nabers, C.J., and Harwood, Stuart, and Bolin, JJ., concur.

Michael Wells v. Securitas Security Services USA, Inc. and The University of Michigan, Case No. 07-15500 (E.D. Mich. 2009)

Judges: Present: The Honorable Lawrence P. Zatkoff, United States District Judge.
Opinion by: Lawrence P. Zatkoff

I. Introduction

This matter comes before the Court on Defendants' respective motions for summary judgment [dkt 27 & 28]. The parties have fully briefed the motions. The Court finds that the facts and legal arguments are adequately presented in the parties' papers such that the decision process would not be significantly aided by oral argument. Therefore, pursuant to E.D. Mich. L.R. 7.1(e) (2), it is hereby ORDERED that the motions be resolved on the briefs submitted. For the reasons set forth below, Defendant Securitas Security Services' motion for summary judgment is GRANTED, and Defendant The University of Michigan's motion for summary judgment is GRANTED.

Also before the Court is Plaintiff's motion for leave to file a sur-reply brief [dkt 39]. In this motion, Plaintiff contends that Securitas's reply brief to its motion for summary judgment "contains multiple misstatements of fact and law." Defendants respond that the Federal and Local Rules do not contemplate sur-reply briefs, that Plaintiff's proposed sur-reply is redundant of his initial responses, and that Plaintiff's proposed sur-reply brief exceeds the page limitation imposed on reply briefs by E.D. Mich. L.R. 7.1. Because this matter is before the Court on summary-judgment motions filed by Defendants, the Court must construe all facts in favor of Plaintiff as the nonmoving party. Therefore, Plaintiff's concerns of factual misstatements are immaterial, and the Court finds no other compelling reason to consider Plaintiff's sur-reply brief. Accordingly, Plaintiff's motion for leave to file sur-reply brief is HEREBY DENIED.

II. Background

Securitas provides private security officers to clients throughout the United States. Securitas's predecessor hired Plaintiff as a security officer in 2000. Generally, prior to assigning its employees to a client, Securitas sends its employees to interview with the client. If the client finds the employee to be satisfactory, the employee is assigned to that client. Pursuant to that process, Plaintiff was assigned to the central power plant of the University of Michigan in the fall of 2002. In December 2002, Plaintiff was promoted to the position of site supervisor for the central power plant.

In January 2006, an employee of the University named Gerald Avery sexually assaulted another employee of the University, Katherine McCarty. McCarty reported the assault in March of that same year. The University of Michigan investigated the incident and ultimately suspended Avery for one month without pay, demoted his position, transferred him to another plant, and entered into a "Last Chance Settlement Agreement" with Avery whereby the latter was "not to make any effort to contact, talk to or otherwise seek out [McCarty]." At that time, Avery was the chief steward for his union, Local 547, International Union of Operating Engineers—a position that apparently required him to visit the central power plant periodically.

On April 4, 2007, Plaintiff encountered McCarty in an agitated state. McCarty informed Plaintiff of Avery's 2006 assault against her. She further informed Plaintiff that she had seen Avery on the premises of the power plant earlier that morning. McCarty, however, misrepresented the terms of the Last Chance Settlement Agreement to Plaintiff, indicating that Avery was not permitted at the central power plant while McCarty was on the premises. McCarty indicated to Plaintiff that she had seen Avery at the power plant on several other occasions and that his presence upset her.

Plaintiff contacted the University's Department of Public Safety ("DPS") on behalf of McCarty. At that time, he had not independently verified the actual terms of the Last Chance Settlement Agreement. It is not entirely clear what Plaintiff conveyed to DPS during his initial phone call but approximately one week later, DPS Officer Kevin Rice came to the power plant to speak with McCarty about the incident. Plaintiff was present during the meeting between Rice and McCarty but did not contribute to it. DPS had not previously known about the 2006 assault and, after an investigation, Avery was convicted of a charge of aggravated assault.

On April 13, 2007, DPS Detective Mike Mathews issued Avery a "No Contact Order" pursuant to which he was forbidden from entering the central power plant or otherwise being in McCarty's presence for the duration of the DPS investigation. McCarty told Plaintiff about the No Contact Order on April 16, 2007. Plaintiff, in turn, attempted to contact individuals through the chain of command. Finding no one available, Plaintiff ultimately contacted the University's Associate Director of Utilities, William Verge, so that the power plant's post orders would reflect that Avery was not to be permitted on site. Verge was apparently upset that he had not been informed of this fact by the power plant's manager, Richard Wickboldt, such that Verge "got in [Wickboldt's] face about it" and "read Wickboldt the riot act."

At some point after Plaintiff's discussion with Verge, Securitas's branch manager, Diane Logan, informed Plaintiff that Wickboldt was upset with him because he got him into trouble with Verge. Another security guard at the power plant, Leonard Pagel, observed Wickboldt casting ominous looks at Plaintiff. On approximately April 27, 2007, Wickboldt emailed Logan to inform her of new chain-of-command procedures regarding whom security officers should approach in Wickboldt's absence. Wickboldt also met with Logan and requested that Plaintiff be removed from the power plant. On that same day, Logan informed Plaintiff that he would be removed from the power plant.

Karen Triplett, Securitas's scheduler, offered Plaintiff four other assignments, including a demotion at the power plant. None of the alternatives involved supervisory positions, and three of the alternatives required Plaintiff to take a pay reduction. The sole alternative that would have compensated Plaintiff at the same rate was a temporary position that might not have exceeded 30 days. Plaintiff declined these positions and worked his last day at the power plant on September 20, 2007.

On September 25, 2007, Plaintiff embarked on an out-of-state vacation. While he was out of town, his mother checked his mail and discovered a letter from Belinda Hamilton, Securitas's human resources manager, assigning Plaintiff to a new position effective October 1, 2007. Plaintiff called Triplett and informed her that he would not be able to begin work on October 1. He left a voice message to the same effect with Hamilton on the morning of October 1. On October 3, Securitas terminated Plaintiff's employment for consecutive unexcused work absences. Plaintiff had not interviewed or interacted with representatives at his prospective new site at any time.

Plaintiff now brings suit alleging that Defendants, as joint employers, retaliated against him in violation of Title VII of the Civil Rights Act of 1964. Specifically, Plaintiff contends that he opposed a violation of the Act and suffered an adverse employment action as a result.

III. Legal Standard

Summary judgment is proper where "the pleadings, depositions, answers to interrogatories, and admissions on file, together with the affidavits, if any, show that there is no genuine issue as to any material fact and the moving party is entitled to judgment as a matter of law." Fed. R. Civ. P. 56(c); *Thompson v. Ashe*, 250 F.3d 399, 405 (6th Cir. 2001). The moving party bears the initial burden of demonstrating the absence of any genuine issue of material fact, and all inferences should be made in favor of the nonmoving party. *Celotex Corp. v. Catrett*, 477 U.S. 317, 323, 106 S. Ct. 2548, 91 L. Ed. 2d 265 (1986).

To support its motion, the moving party may show "that there is an absence of evidence to support the nonmoving party's case." *Id.* at 325. Although all inferences must be drawn in favor of the nonmoving party, this Court bears no obligation to imagine favorable facts where the non-moving party has alleged none. The moving party must also set forth facts sufficient to establish its case: "[T]he mere existence of a scintilla of evidence in support of the plaintiff's position will be insufficient [to defeat a motion for summary judgment]; there must be evidence on which the jury could reasonably find for the plaintiff." *Anderson v. Liberty Lobby, Inc.*, 477 U.S. 242, 252, 106 S. Ct. 2505, 91 L. Ed. 2d 202 (1986).

IV. Analysis

Securitas argues that Plaintiff is unable to establish a prima facie case of a retaliation claim because he did not engage in an activity protected by Title VII. Even if Plaintiff's involvement amounted to a protected activity, Securitas argues that Plaintiff did not "oppose" any Title VII violation. Securitas further contends that Plaintiff reported the assault to the University, not to Securitas. As such, Securitas maintains that it was not aware of Plaintiff's alleged "opposition" to a Title VII violation. Securitas points to the alternative positions offered to Plaintiff as evidence that he suffered no adverse employment action. Finally, Securitas takes the position that, even if Plaintiff establishes a prima facie case, the University was entitled to request officer reassignment and that alone provides a sufficient nondiscriminatory reason for Plaintiff's transference.

Plaintiff responds that he did engage in a protected activity by assisting McCarty and that he only needed to have a good faith belief that he was opposing sexual harassment. Plaintiff argues that Securitas knew of his protected activity but nevertheless subjected him to an adverse employment action by removing him from the power plant and offering unacceptable alternatives. Finally, Plaintiff maintains that Securitas's proffered nondiscriminatory reasons for his termination are pretextual.

To survive Defendants' motions for summary judgment, Plaintiff must establish a prima facie case of discrimination. If Plaintiff succeeds in establishing a prima facie case of retaliation, the burden of production shifts to the employer to articulate a legitimate, nondiscriminatory reason to justify its action and to rebut Plaintiff's prima facie case. *McDonnell Douglas Corp. v. Green*, 411 U.S. 792, 93 S. Ct. 1817, 36 L. Ed. 2d 668 (1973). After the employer offers such evidence, the burden returns to Plaintiff to prove by a preponderance of the evidence that the legitimate reason set forth by the employer was mere pretext for discrimination. *Ang v. Procter & Gamble Co.*, 932 F.2d 540, 548 (6th Cir. 1998).

A prima facie case of retaliation under Title VII requires Plaintiff to establish that: "(1) [he] engaged in activity protected by Title VII; (2) this exercise of protected rights was known to defendant; (3) defendant thereafter took adverse employment action against the plaintiff, ... and (4) there was a causal connection between the protected activity and the adverse employment action." *Morris v. Oldham County Fiscal Court*, 201 F.3d 784, 792 (6th Cir. 2000). Establishing a prima facie case is "the first prong of analysis which defeats a motion for dismissal prior to trial." *EEOC v. Avery Dennison Corp.*, 104 F.3d 858, 861 (6th Cir. 1997). Plaintiff's burden at the prima-facie stage of proceedings "is minimal, requiring [him] to put forth some evidence to deduce a causal connection between the retaliatory action and the protected activity and requiring the court to draw reasonable inferences from that evidence, providing it is credible." *Id.* Still, Plaintiff, in this Title VII action, "has the burden of proving by the preponderance of the evidence a prima facie case of discrimination." *Tex. Dep't of Cmty. Affairs v. Burdine*, 450 U.S. 248, 252-53, 101 S. Ct. 1089, 67 L. Ed. 2d 207 (1981).

Under Title VII, an individual engages in a protected activity when he "has opposed any practice made an unlawful employment practice by this subchapter, or because he has made a charge, testified, assisted, or participated in any manner in an investigation, proceeding, or hearing under this subchapter." 42 U.S.C. § 2000e-3(a). The federal courts "have generally granted less protection for opposition than for participation in enforcement proceedings." *Booker v. Brown & Williamson Tobacco Co.*, 879 F.2d 1304, 1312 (6th Cir. 1989). For Plaintiff to engage in a protected opposition activity under Title VII, he "must make an overt stand against suspected illegal discriminatory action." *Comiskey v. Auto. Indus. Action Group*, 40 F. Supp. 2d 877, 898 (E.D. Mich. 1999). Therefore, "a vague charge of discrimination … is insufficient to constitute opposition to an unlawful employment practice." *Booker*, 879 F.2d at 1313. At the same time, opposition "need not rise to the level of a formal complaint in order to receive statutory protection." *Allen v. Advanced Digital Info. Corp.*, 500 F. Supp. 2d 93, 109 (N.D.N.Y. 2007). There is no exhaustive list of opposition activities, but they include "making complaints to management, writing critical letters to customers, protesting against discrimination by industry or by society in general, and expressing support of coworkers who have filed formal charges." *Sumner v. United States Postal Serv.*, 899 F.2d 203, 209 (2d Cir. 1990).

Here, Plaintiff alleges that he "opposed" sexual harassment in a number of ways, thereby entitling him to the protections of Title VII. Although it is not entirely clear what Plaintiff conveyed to DPS during his phone call, the Court construes the facts of the matter in his favor for the purpose of Defendants' summary-judgment motions. Therefore, the Court accepts as true that Plaintiff was reporting in good-faith what he believed was an incident of sexual harassment. Plaintiff also prepared a brief incident report in which he wrote that Avery "was in the building … in violation of an agreement that was made with the Human Resources dept., which states that Gerald Avery isn't supposed to be in the building when Katherine McCarty is." Also in the report, which Plaintiff submitted to both a University contact and his superior within Securitas, Plaintiff wrote that he left a message for DPS "in accordance with the Securitas Security Officer Handbook section on Reporting Unsafe Conditions and Security Risks." Plaintiff did not mention harassment in the incident report. Finally, at the request of McCarty, Plaintiff was present when Officer Rice interviewed her but he did not contribute to the interview. Plaintiff also submits that his phone call informing Verge that Avery was banned from the power plant was an act of opposition. These actions, however, do not constitute opposition to an unlawful employment practice.

In *Sawicki v. American Plastic Toys, Inc.*, 180 F. Supp. 2d 910 (E.D. Mich. 2001), the plaintiff brought suit for retaliation, alleging that her employment was terminated for "protesting the alleged sexual harassment of coworkers and subordinates by another employee." *Id.* at 912. In that case, the plaintiff learned that four female employees had been subjected to harassment by a coworker. Having access to a typewriter, "the plaintiff typed up the complaint, the subordinates signed the complaint, and the plaintiff delivered the complaint to the defendant … . The plaintiff also mailed a copy of the complaint to … the human resources manager." *Id.* at 913. The company commenced an investigation as a result of the complaint and interviewed the plaintiff, who indicated that she had witnessed one incident of potential harassment but "could offer no further first-hand knowledge of Taylor's misconduct." *Id.* In *Sawicki*, the plaintiff failed to "offer some evidence that she actually opposed the misconduct." *Id.* at 916. Therefore, the court held that the plaintiff's conduct did not amount to "opposition":

> [I]t could not have been clear to management that the plaintiff intended to file suit on behalf of her subordinates, or that she personally opposed the misconduct. It was plaintiff's duty as a supervisor who was approached by her subordinates with a complaint to take action, investigate or send the complaint up the line of authority. That conduct, however, cannot constitute "opposition" on this record.

Id. at 919. In this case, Plaintiff merely called DPS to facilitate McCarty's complaint, an action explicitly required of him in his capacity as security guard. Like the actions of the plaintiff in *Sawicki*, Plaintiff's actions did not indicate personal opposition to perceived sexual harassment. See *Moore v. City of Philadelphia*, 461 F.3d 331, 350 (3d Cir. 2006) ("If litigants claim to be retaliated against for having opposed discrimination, they must have stood in opposition to it-not just objectively reported its existence or attempted to serve as an intermediary."). Therefore, the Court finds that Plaintiff's actions in this matter do not amount to opposition under Title VII and therefore, his prima facie case of retaliation necessarily fails.

Even if Plaintiff's actions could be considered "opposition," he would not be able to establish the causation element of the prima facie case. Construing the facts of the case in the light most favorable to Plaintiff, the Court finds that Wickboldt wanted Plaintiff removed from the power plant because Plaintiff got Wickboldt into trouble by contacting Verge directly. There is no indication that Wickboldt's displeasure had anything to do with the fact that Plaintiff allegedly reported an instance of potential sexual harassment.

The record reveals that both Defendants treated Plaintiff unfairly. The facts of the case establish that Plaintiff was dutiful and vigilant in carrying out the responsibilities of his position as security guard. In attempting to follow the chain of command regarding what Plaintiff in good faith believed to be a serious security concern, Plaintiff inadvertently got Wickboldt in trouble with a supervisor and immediately thereafter, Wickboldt asked that Plaintiff be reassigned. That the University of Michigan removed Plaintiff from his position for his attentiveness to McCarty's wellbeing is appalling. That Securitas did not present Plaintiff with a suitable replacement opportunity is equally appalling. Finally, that Securitas terminated Plaintiff's employment despite the fact that he informed Securitas of his vacation and despite the fact that Securitas did not follow its typical interviewing process is a gross disservice to an employee who did nothing wrong. Plaintiff very well may have legal recourse on an alternate theory of recovery. Unfortunately for Plaintiff, however, he is unable to establish a prima facie case for retaliation under Title VII. Specifically, Plaintiff's actions with respect to McCarty do not amount to "opposition" of an unlawful employment practice. Because Plaintiff cannot establish a prima facie case against either Defendant, both motions for summary judgment must be granted.

V. Conclusion

For the above reasons, Plaintiff's motion for leave to file sur-reply brief is HEREBY DENIED.

IT IS FURTHER ORDERED that Defendants' motions for summary judgment [dkt 27 & 28] are both GRANTED.

IT IS SO ORDERED.

/s/ Lawrence P. Zatkoff

Nick White v. Martel Moylan, Melissa Bilodeau, Carolyn Hill, and Macys's Department Store, 554 F. Supp. 2d 263(D. Conn. 2008)

Judges: Alvin W. Thompson, United States District Judge.
Opinion by: Alvin W. Thompson

Ruling On Motion To Dismiss

Pro se plaintiff Nick White ("White") brought this action against defendants Martel Moylan ("Moylan"), Melissa Bilodeau ("Bilodeau"), Carolyn Hill ("Hill") and Macy's Department Store ("Macy's"), alleging, *inter alia*, a violation of 42 U.S.C. § 1983. Pursuant to Fed. R. Civ. P. 12(b)(2) and 12(b)(1), Macy's has moved to dismiss this action for lack of personal jurisdiction and lack of subject matter jurisdiction. However, although Macy's moves to dismiss the plaintiff's complaint, its memorandum addresses only the plaintiff's § 1983 claim. For the reasons set forth below, Macy's motion is being granted, but the plaintiff is being granted leave to replead.

I. Factual Allegations

For purposes of this motion, the court takes the following factual allegations set forth in the Complaint as true.

On November 17, 2006, Bilodeau and Hill, who worked as security directors at Macy's, accused White of shoplifting items from Macy's. Officer Moylan from the Enfield Police Department was dispatched to the store. The security directors and the officer reviewed the store's surveillance footage, which showed White entering the store with two bags. These two bags contained expensive merchandise along with the receipts for those items. The security directors and the officer switched White's property with other merchandise from Macy's and accused White of shoplifting. White was charged with larceny in the fourth degree. On August 22, 2007, the charge was dismissed.

II. Legal Standard

A. Fed. R. Civ. P. 12(b)(2)

On a Rule 12(b)(2) motion to dismiss for lack of personal jurisdiction, the plaintiff bears the burden of showing that the court has jurisdiction over the defendant. *Metropolitan Life Insurance Co. v. Robertson-Ceco Corp.*, 84 F.3d 560, 566 (2d Cir.1996). "Prior to trial, however, when a motion to dismiss for lack of jurisdiction is decided on the basis of affidavits and other written materials, the plaintiff need only make a prima facie showing. The allegations in the complaint must be taken as true to the extent they are uncontroverted by the defendant's affidavits. If the parties present conflicting affidavits, all factual disputes are resolved in the plaintiff's favor, and the plaintiff's prima facie showing is sufficient notwithstanding the contrary presentation by the moving party." *Seetransport Wiking Trader Schiffarhtsgesellschaft MBH & Co., Kommanditgesellschaft v. Navimpex Centrala Navala*, 989 F.2d 572, 580 (2d Cir. 1993).

B. Fed. R. Civ. P. 12(b)(1)

A claim is properly dismissed for lack of subject matter jurisdiction under Fed. R. Civ. P. 12(b)(1) when the court lacks the statutory or constitutional power to adjudicate the claim. *Nowak v.*

Ironworkers Local 6 Pension Fund, 81 F.3d 1182, 1187 (2d Cir. 1996). On a Rule 12(b)(1) motion to dismiss, the party asserting subject matter jurisdiction "bears the burden of proving subject matter jurisdiction by a preponderance of the evidence." *Aurecchione v. Schoolman Transp. Sys., Inc.*, 426 F.3d 635, 638 (2d Cir. 2005). When reviewing a motion to dismiss for lack of subject matter jurisdiction, the court may consider evidence outside the pleadings. *See Makarova v. United States*, 201 F.3d 110, 113 (2d Cir. 2000).

The standards for dismissal under Fed R. Civ. P. 12(b)(1) and 12(b)(6) are identical. *See Lerner v. Fleet Bank, N.A.*, 318 F.3d 113, 128 (2d Cir. 2003). [HN5] When deciding a motion to dismiss under Rule 12(b)(6), the court must accept as true all factual allegations in the complaint and must draw inferences in a light most favorable to the plaintiff. *Scheuer v. Rhodes*, 416 U.S. 232, 236, 94 S. Ct. 1683, 40 L. Ed. 2d 90 (1974). Although a complaint "does not need detailed factual allegations, a plaintiff's obligation to provide the 'grounds' of his 'entitle[ment] to relief' requires more than labels and conclusions, and a formulaic recitation of the elements of a cause of action will not do." *Bell Atlantic Corporation v. Twombly*, 127 S. Ct. 1955, 1965, 167 L. Ed. 2d 929 (2007). "Factual allegations must be enough to raise a right to relief above the speculative level, on the assumption that all allegations in the complaint are true (even if doubtful in fact)." *Id.* (citations omitted). The plaintiff must plead "only enough facts to state a claim to relief that is plausible on its face." *Id.* at 1974. "The function of a motion to dismiss is 'merely to assess the legal feasibility of the complaint, not to assay the weight of the evidence which might be offered in support thereof.'" *Mytych v. May Dept. Store Co.*, 34 F. Supp. 2d 130, 131 (D. Conn. 1999), quoting *Ryder Energy Distribution v. Merrill Lynch Commodities, Inc.*, 748 F.2d 774, 779 (2d Cir. 1984). "The issue on a motion to dismiss is not whether the plaintiff will prevail, but whether the plaintiff is entitled to offer evidence to support his claims." *United States v. Yale New Haven Hosp.*, 727 F. Supp. 784, 786 (D. Conn. 1990) (citing *Scheuer*, 416 U.S. at 232). In its review of a motion to dismiss for failure to state a claim, the court may consider "only the facts alleged in the pleadings, documents attached as exhibits or incorporated by reference in the pleadings and matters of which judicial notice may be taken." *Samuels v. Air Transport Local 504*, 992 F.2d 12, 15 (2d Cir. 1993).

When considering the sufficiency of the allegations in a *pro se* complaint, the court applies "less stringent standards than [those applied to] formal pleadings drafted by lawyers. ..." *Haines v. Kerner*, 404 U.S. 519, 92 S. Ct. 594, 30 L. Ed. 2d 652 (1972). *See also Branham v. Meachum*, 77 F.3d 626, 628-29 (2d Cir. 1996). The court should interpret the plaintiff's complaint to raise the strongest arguments that it suggests. *See Burgos v. Hopkins*, 14 F.3d 787, 790 (2d Cir. 1994).

III. Discussion

A. Motion to Dismiss for Lack of Personal Jurisdiction

Macy's moves to dismiss this action for lack of personal jurisdiction because there is no legal entity known as "Macy's Department Store," the named defendant in this action. Macy's has submitted an affidavit from Louise Kusnierz ("Kusnierz"), the operations manager for the Macy's store in Enfield. Kusnierz avers that "[a]lthough Macy's East, an Unincorporated Division of Macy's Retail Holdings, Inc. owns and operates retail stores in Connecticut, there is no legal entity known as 'Macy's Department Store.'" (Def.'s Mot., (Doc. No. 30), Ex. A. at P 3). She also avers that "'Macy's Department Store' does not own or control a store at Enfield Mall in Enfield, Connecticut. On November 17, 2006, the store was owned and controlled by an entity known as

Macy's East, an Unincorporated Division of Federated Retail Holdings, Inc." (*Id.* at P 4). Because the court lacks personal jurisdiction over an entity that does not exist, the defendant's motion to dismiss on this basis is being granted with leave to file an amended complaint correctly stating the defendant's legal name.

B. Motion to Dismiss for Lack of Subject Matter Jurisdiction

The plaintiff brings claims against Macy's pursuant to § 1983, alleging violations of his constitutional rights under the Fourth and Fourteenth Amendments. Under § 1983, an individual may bring an action against any person, who under color of state law, deprives him or her of any rights, privileges, or immunities protected by the Constitution or laws of the United States. *See* 42 U.S.C. § 1983. "A plaintiff pressing a claim of violation of his constitutional rights under § 1983 is thus required to show state action." *Tancredi v. Metropolitan Life Insurance Co.*, 316 F.3d 308, 312 (2d Cir.2003).

The Second Circuit has stated:

> In order to satisfy the state action requirement where the defendant is a private entity, the allegedly unconstitutional conduct must be fairly attributable to the state. Conduct that is ostensibly private can be fairly attributed to the state only if there is such a close nexus between the State and the challenged action that seemingly private behavior may be fairly treated as that of the State itself. State action may properly be found where the state exercises coercive power over, is entwined in [the] management or control of, or provides significant encouragement, either overt or covert to, a private actor, or where the private actor operates as a willful participant in joint activity with the State or its agents, is controlled by an agency of the State, has been delegated a public function by the state, or is entwined with governmental policies.

Tancredi, 316 F.3d at 312-313 (internal citations and quotation marks omitted). Here, Macy's argues that the court lacks subject matter jurisdiction over the plaintiff's § 1983 claim because the plaintiff has not alleged that Macy's acted under color of state law or that it exercised power possessed by virtue of state law.

Although "[g]enerally, the acts of private security guards, hired by a store, do not constitute state action under § 1983," there are two circumstances in which courts have held that the actions of private security guards do constitute state action. *Josey v. Filene's, Inc.*, 187 F. Supp. 2d 9, 16 (D.Conn. 2002). "First, private guards may be sued when they are given the authority of state law. Second, security guards are considered to be acting under state law if they are willful participants in the joint activity of the State or its agents." *Id.* (internal citations and quotation marks omitted). However, "courts within the Second Circuit have repeatedly held that store security personnel are not state actors when they detain or call for the arrest of suspected shoplifters." *Jones v. J.C. Penney's Dept. Stores, Inc.*, 2005 U.S. Dist. LEXIS 17468, 2007 WL 1577758 at *7 (W.D.N.Y. 2007) (collecting cases).

Although White does not allege that the security directors at Macy's were given authority of state law, he does set forth allegations from which a reasonable inference can be drawn that they operated as willful participants in a joint activity with a state agent. Specifically, White alleges that "Melissa Bilodeau and Carolyn Hill security directors along with Officer Martel learned that the [plaintiff's] two bags had (high priced) merchandise and switched the [plaintiff's] merchandise with the stores merchandise only to say that the [plaintiff] was shoplifting in the Macy's department store." (Compl. at 9). Thus, the plaintiff alleges that the security directors did more than simply detain the plaintiff and call for his arrest and also that the officer did more than simply apprehend White upon his arrival. The plaintiff alleges that the security directors wilfully participated with a state agent in fabricating a reason to arrest White for shoplifting. Although "[a] mere conclusory allegation that a private entity acted in concert with a state actor does not suffice to state a § 1983 claim against the private entity," *Ciambriello v. County of Nassau*, 292 F.3d 307, 324 (2d Cir. 2002), the plaintiff's allegations are not merely conclusory. White has set forth specific facts that, if true, would support a finding that the private security directors employed by Macy's were willful participants in joint activity with a state actor. Construing the *pro se* plaintiff's complaint liberally and accepting all of the allegations set forth therein as true, as the court must do when deciding a motion to dismiss, the court concludes that the plaintiff has sufficiently alleged that the security directors employed by Macy's acted under the color of state law.

However, Macy's cannot be held vicariously liable under § 1983 for the constitutional torts of its employees based on a theory of respondeat superior. *See Rojas v. Alexander's Department Store, Inc.*, 924 F.2d 406, 408 (2d Cir. 1990) (citations omitted) ("Private employers are not liable under § 1983 for the constitutional torts of their employees, unless the plaintiff proves that 'action pursuant to official … policy of some nature caused a constitutional tort.'); *Mejia v. City of New York*, 228 F. Supp. 2d 234, 243 (E.D.N.Y. 2002) ("[N]either a municipality nor a private corporation can be held vicariously liable under § 1983 for the actions of its employees."). Therefore, assuming *arguendo* that the security directors employed by Macy's acted under color of state law, Macy's cannot be held liable for constitutional torts committed by them unless the plaintiff can establish that Macy's deprived him of his constitutional rights by virtue of an official policy or custom of the corporation. *See Monell v. New York Dep't of Soc. Servs.*, 436 U.S. 658, 694, 98 S. Ct. 2018, 56 L. Ed. 2d 611 (1978) (It is only "when the execution of the government's policy or custom, whether made by its lawmakers or by those whose edicts or acts may fairly be said to represent official policy, inflicts the injury that the government as an entity is responsible under § 1983."); *Rojas*, 924 F.2d at 408-09 (applying *Monell's* rationale to private employers). Because the plaintiff fails to set forth any facts alleging that Macy's caused the alleged constitutional violation by its security directors, the court is granting Macy's motion to dismiss the plaintiff's § 1983 claim against it, with leave to replead.

In an order dated May 7, 2008, the court dismissed without prejudice this case as to Hill and Bilodeau because the plaintiff failed to provide the court with the addresses for service for either defendant as directed by the court. (*See* Order (Doc. No. 29)). Therefore, the security director defendants are no longer parties in this case. At this time, the plaintiff has federal and state law claims against Moylan and state law claims against Macy's remaining in the case.

IV. Conclusion

For the reasons set forth above, Defendant Macy's Department Store's Motion to Dismiss (Doc. No. 30) is hereby GRANTED, with leave to replead within 30 days being granted to the plaintiff.

It is so ordered.

Dated this 20th day of May 2008 at Hartford, Connecticut.

/s/ AWT

Alvin W. Thompson

United States District Judge

Washington County v. Washington County Deputy Sheriff's Association, 2009 WI App 116; 320 Wis. 2d 570; 772 N.W.2d 697 (Wis. Ct. App. 2009)

Judges: Before Fine, Kessler and Brennan, JJ.
Opinion by: Brennan

BRENNAN, J. The Washington County Deputy Sheriff's Association (WCDSA) appeals the trial court's order prohibiting arbitration of its grievance against the Sheriff. The trial court declared that the Sheriff's decision to staff the security screening station at the Washington County Justice Center with special deputies was part of the Sheriff's constitutionally protected powers and could not be limited by a collective bargaining agreement. We reverse because we conclude that staffing the x-ray and metal detector security screening station is not one of those "certain immemorial, principal, and important duties of the sheriff at common law that are peculiar to the office of sheriff and that characterize and distinguish the office." *Kocken v. Wisconsin Council 4 0*, 2007 WI 72, P39, 301 Wis. 2d 266, 732 N.W.2d 828.

Background

Washington County started the planning for a new justice center in 2005. The design included a new secure entrance, which did not exist previously. The purpose for the building was to bring the courts and other offices all into one wing of Washington County's court complex. During the 2006 county budget process, Sheriff Brian Rahn proposed to the County Board Committee that the security screening station be staffed with two full-time deputy sheriffs for the additional security needs of the newly constructed justice center. He made the request partly due to some security concerns expressed by judges. The County Board Committee, without reaching a conclusion, then discussed with Sheriff Rahn the possibility of privatizing the staffing of the security screening station. Sheriff Rahn reworked his proposal and came back to the County Board Committee with an alternative proposal of staffing the security screening station with two part-time special deputies. The County Board Committee approved the alternate proposal. Sheriff Rahn testified at his deposition that he would have preferred the full-time deputy sheriffs and only made the alternate proposal because the County was considering privatizing the staff for the security screening station. He testified that the final decision on hiring the special deputies was his own.

In May 2006, the WCDSA filed a grievance claiming that the hiring of the part-time special deputies, who were nonunion, was a violation of the collective bargaining agreement. The WCDSA petitioned the Wisconsin Employment Review Commission ("WERC") for arbitration. The County filed a declaratory judgment lawsuit and a petition for an injunction to prevent the arbitration. The parties submitted briefs and affidavits, and the trial court held a hearing on the County's motions. The trial court made a factual finding, which is undisputed by the parties, describing the nature of the job involved in the grievance:

> The nature of the job to which Sheriff Rahn assigned the Special Deputies was performing courthouse entrance security screening duties, *including manning a walk-through metal detector and an x-ray machine to look for weapons and other things that were not permitted in the Justice Center.*
> (Emphasis added.)

The trial court granted the County's motion declaring that the grievance was not substantively arbitrable because the decision to staff the security screening station with special deputies was part of the Sheriff's constitutionally protected duties. The trial court granted the County's injunction request and ordered the WCDSA to withdraw the grievance. WCDSA appeals.

The facts in this case are undisputed, with one exception. WCDSA contends that the County Board Committee made the decision that special deputies would be hired. The County contends that the Sheriff made that decision. The trial court's order of February 28, 2008, included the specific factual finding that the Sheriff made the decision to staff the security screening station with special deputies.

Standards of Review

We review the trial court's decision granting the County's motion for declaratory judgment without deference to the decision of the trial court. *See Ball v. District No. 4, Area Bd.*, 117 Wis. 2d 529, 537, 345 N.W.2d 389 (1984).

We review the disputed issue of fact in this case, whether the County or the Sheriff made the decision to staff the security screening station with part-time special deputies, under the "clearly erroneous" standard. *See Noll v. Dimiceli's, Inc.*, 115 Wis. 2d 641, 643, 340 N.W.2d 575 (Ct. App. 1983). The finding is not "clearly erroneous" when there is credible evidence in the record to support it. *See Insurance Co. of N. Am. v. DEC Int'l, Inc.*, 220 Wis. 2d 840, 845, 586 N.W.2d 691 (Ct. App. 1998).

I. The Trial Court's Disputed Factual Finding Is Not "Clearly Erroneous"

WCDSA argues that the decision to staff the security screening station with special deputies was really made by the County Board Committee and, therefore, the staffing decision was not part of the Sheriff's exercise of his constitutionally protected powers. The County argues that the Sheriff made the staffing decision. The trial court found that the Sheriff made the staffing decision. That finding was not clearly erroneous.

There is evidence in the record supporting the trial court's finding that the Sheriff was the one who made the decision. In his deposition testimony, Sheriff Rahn stated that he was the first to propose two full-time deputy sheriffs to staff the new security screening station. He agreed that if the County Board Committee had approved his initial proposal to hire two new full-time deputies, he would have staffed the security screening station with the new deputies. He acknowledged that he only revised the proposal because the County officials required him to do so. But on redirect by the County's attorney, Sheriff Rahn testified that he revised the proposal because the County officials advised him to come back with additional options after they had discussed privatization of the staff at the security screening station. When directly asked who made the decision to staff the secure entrance with the special deputies, he said he did.

WCDSA argues that by discussing privatization of the positions, the County, in effect, was making the decision to staff the security screening station with special deputies. But this argument ignores two obvious facts. First, the County only discussed, and did not order, privatization. And second, the topic being discussed was hiring private-sector security officers, not part-time special deputies of the Washington County Sheriff's Department. WCDSA does not offer any evidence from the record demonstrating that it was the County that initiated or ordered the special deputies. Accordingly, the record supports the trial court's finding that it was the Sheriff who decided to staff with special deputies; and we cannot say that finding was clearly erroneous.

II. The Sheriff's Constitutionally Protected Duties

The main issue on appeal is whether the Sheriff's decision to staff x-ray and metal detector machines with part-time special deputies is one of the Sheriff's constitutionally protected duties. A sheriff cannot be constrained by a collective bargaining agreement if he acts on his constitutional powers. *See Wisconsin Prof'l Police Ass'n v. Dane County*, 106 Wis. 2d 303, 305, 316 N.W.2d 656 (1982) (WPPA I); *Dunn County v. WERC*, 2006 WI App 120, P15, 293 Wis. 2d 637, 718 N.W.2d 138. If the Sheriff's decision to staff the security screening station with special deputies was not part of his constitutionally protected duties, then it is substantively arbitrable under the collective bargaining agreement.

The Wisconsin Constitution does not define the duties of a sheriff, but case law has described examples and a method of analysis. Initially, the definition of whether duties were part of the sheriff's constitutionally protected powers focused on a historical analysis of whether they were long-standing established duties of the sheriff at common law such as housing the county's prisoners in the jail. *See State ex rel. Kennedy v. Brunst*, 26 Wis. 412, 414 (1870). But, in *State ex rel. Milwaukee County v. Buech*, 171 Wis. 474, 177 N.W. 781 (1920), the Wisconsin Supreme Court shifted the focus of the analysis to those duties that characterized and distinguished the office of sheriff, rather than whether they existed at common law. *See Buech*, 171 Wis. at 481-82. "If the duty is one of those immemorial principal and important duties that characterized and distinguished the office of sheriff at common law, the sheriff 'chooses his own ways and means of performing it.'" *See Wisconsin Prof'l Police Ass'n v. Dane County*, 149 Wis. 2d 699, 710, 439 N.W.2d 625 (Ct. App. 1989) *(WPPA II)* (quoting WPPA I, 106 Wis. 2d at 314).

To properly determine whether the assigned job is within constitutional protection, we first examine the nature of the job or duty. *See WPPA I*, 106 Wis. 2d at 312. The trial court made a finding here on the nature of the security screening station job:

> The nature of the job to which Sheriff Rahn assigned the Special Deputies was performing courthouse entrance security screening duties, including manning a walk-through metal detector and an x-ray machine to look for weapons and other things that were not permitted in the Justice Center.

Neither party has disputed this finding on appeal. Accordingly, we must determine whether manning the walk-through metal detector and x-ray machine to look for weapons and other things that are not permitted in the Justice Center are duties that are "one of these immemorial principal and important duties that characterized and distinguished the office of sheriff at common law." *See WPPA II*, 149 Wis. 2d at 710.

No Wisconsin case has yet addressed whether the staffing of security screening stations is part of the sheriff's constitutionally protected duties. Part of the reason for this is that such stations have not existed until recent times. Now, however, it is common to see metal detector screening stations at airports, schools, sporting events and both private and public building entrances. The record states clearly that the Washington County Justice Center secure entrance is new with the 2006 opening of the building. Certainly, it cannot be said that staffing the security screening station at the Washington County Justice Center is a time immemorial duty of the sheriff.

Nonetheless, the County argues that staffing the screening station machines is part of the Sheriff's inherent constitutional powers because it is similar to: (1) "attendance upon the courts," which the Wisconsin Supreme Court has determined to be part of the Sheriff's constitutional powers, *see WPPA I*, 106 Wis. 2d at 313 (court security officer is part of sheriff's constitutionally protected duties) (citing *Brunst*, 26 Wis. at 415; *see also* WIS. STAT. § 59.27(3) (2007-08); and (2) the sheriff's general law enforcement powers, which our supreme court has also found to be constitutionally protected, *Washington County v. Deputy Sheriff's Ass'n*, 192 Wis. 2d 728, 741, 531 N.W.2d 468 (Ct. App. 1995) (assigning municipal officers to patrol Harleyfest is part of the sheriff's constitutionally protected duties).

We first address the County's argument that manning the security screening station machines is similar to "attendance upon the courts." In *Dunn County*, we held that the assignment of bailiffs to attend upon the court and supervision over their schedules is one of the sheriff's constitutionally protected duties. *See id.*, 293 Wis. 2d 637, P15 (citing *WPPA I*, 106 Wis. 2d at 312).

More recently, in a series of three decisions, we have held that execution of orders issued by the county's judges is part of the sheriff's constitutionally protected duty of attendance upon the court. In *WPPA II*, we held that "when the sheriff executes an arrest warrant issued by the court to bring a prisoner before the court the sheriff attends upon the court." *Id.*, 149 Wis. 2d at 707. In *Brown County Sheriff's Department Non-Supervisory Labor Ass'n v. Brown County*, 2009 WI App 75, 318 Wis. 2d 774, 767 N.W.2d 600, 2009 Wisc. App. LEXIS 289, we held that transportation of the county's prisoners was part of the sheriff's constitutionally protected duties. *See id.*, P8. And, in *Milwaukee County Deputy Sheriff's Ass'n v. Clarke*, No. 2008AP2290, 2009 WI App 123, 320 Wis. 2d 486, 772 N.W.2d 216, 2009 Wisc. App. LEXIS 390, slip op. (WI App June 2, 2009, recommended for publication), we held that transporting prisoners and effectuating other orders of the county's judges is part of the sheriff's constitutional duty to attend upon the courts. *See id.*, P29. The exception to this line of cases is where the sheriff is transporting prisoners from other jurisdictions as a revenue-generating operation. *Ozaukee County v. Labor Ass'n of Wis.*, 2008 WI App 174, P31, 315 Wis. 2d 102, 763 N.W.2d 140. When the sheriff is executing orders from jurisdictions other than his own, he is not acting within his constitutional powers. *Id.*

The nature of the job of security screening is not similar to these other examples of attendance upon the courts. Operating the metal detector and x-ray machine at an entrance to the Washington County Justice Center, which houses offices, as well as courts, is not at all comparable to being the court's security officer within the courtroom. The visitors of the Justice Center include visitors and employees of the housed offices, as well as the courts. The deputies at the security screening station are not stationed *in* the courts nor do they patrol or monitor the courtrooms in any way. The security screening station deputies have no function that relates to executing judges' orders. And, screening for things *other than weapons* "and other things not permitted in the Justice Center" is too far a stretch to meet the description of attending upon the courts. None of the security screening station deputies' duties compares in any way to those duties of the sheriff that we have held are constitutionally protected as part of the Sheriff's recognized duty to attend upon the courts.

The County next argues that manning the screening station machines here is part of the Sheriff's constitutional duties because they are similar to other duties that have been found to be constitutionally protected, such as providing law enforcement. The Wisconsin courts have determined that maintaining law and order and preserving the peace are parts of the sheriff's constitutionally protected duties. *See Manitowoc County v. Local 986B*, 168 Wis. 2d 819, 830, 484 N.W.2d 534 (1992) (per curiam) (reassignment of deputy from patrol to undercover drug investigations); *Washington County*, 192 Wis. 2d at 741 (sheriff's assignment of municipal officers to augment his county-wide law enforcement duty for Harleyfest).

Here, waiving the metal-detecting wand or listening for the buzzer to ring at the county's combined-use office building is a far cry from the sheriff's county-wide law enforcement responsibilities noted above. It is a function frequently performed by private security guards at airports, schools, movie theaters, retail stores, and public buildings.

The nature of the job of security screening is really administrative. Duties of the sheriff that are excluded from constitutional protection have been described as "internal management and administrative duties" or "mundane and common administrative duties." *Heitkemper v. Wirsing,* 194 Wis. 2d 182, 193, 533 N.W.2d 770 (1995). Examples of "internal management and administrative duties" are: (1) preparation of food for inmates in the jail, *Kocken,* 2007 WI 72, 301 Wis. 2d 266, P75, 732 N.W.2d 828; (2) hiring and firing procedures of deputy sheriffs, *see Buech,* 171 Wis. at 482; *Heitkemper,* 194 Wis. 2d at 193; (3) day-to-day scheduling of overtime and emergency coverage and limited-term employee coverage other than court officers, *Dunn County,* 2006 WI App 120, 293 Wis. 2d 637, P23, 718 N.W.2d 138; and (4) money-generating transport of federal prisoners in the county's jail under a rental contract with the federal government, *Ozaukee County,* 2008 WI App 174, 315 Wis. 2d 102, 763 N.W.2d 140, PP32–33.

All of the above determined administrative duties have some connection to the sheriff's constitutionally protected duties, but cannot be said to be tasks that lend character and distinction to the office of sheriff. Operating the machines involved in screening is a mundane task that is done in many places by private security officers. These have not traditionally been the sheriff's tasks to perform. They are too far removed from the courtroom itself, the orders of the judges and the function of law enforcement. Because staffing metal detector and x-ray machines is similar to the duties that the courts have considered "mundane and commonplace," " internal management and administrative," *Heitkemper,* 194 Wis. 2d at 193, we reverse the order of the trial court.

By the Court.—Order reversed and cause remanded.

United States of America v. Jeffrey Craig, No. 2:04-CR-156 (D. Vt. 2009)

Judges: William K. Sessions III, U.S. District Court Chief Judge.
Opinion by: William K. Sessions III

Defendant Jeffrey Craig is charged with four counts of possessing a firearm in or affecting commerce as an unlawful user of a controlled substance, in violation of 18 U.S.C. § 922(g)(3); one count of receiving a firearm that has been shipped or transported in interstate commerce while under indictment for a crime punishable by imprisonment for a term exceeding one year, in violation of 18 U.S.C. §§ 922(n) and 924(a)(1)(D); and one count of possessing a firearm in or affecting commerce as a fugitive from justice, in violation of 18 U.S.C. § 922(g)(2). Craig filed a Motion to Suppress Evidence and to Dismiss (Docs. 15, 27) based on three separate encounters with law enforcement officials between September 2002 and January 2008. The Court held hearings on this motion on October 2 and 10, 2008, and the parties filed supplemental post-hearing briefs on November 10, 2008. Based on the evidence submitted by the parties and the arguments of counsel, the Court issues the following opinion.

Discussion

This case stems from three separate events: (1) Craig's detention at a concert site in Wilmington, Vermont on September 1, 2002; (2) interviews of Craig by Alcohol, Tobacco, & Firearms ("ATF") agents conducted in Burlington, Vermont on September 20 and 23, 2002; and (3) Craig's detention by Burlington police officers at the City Market in Burlington on January 25, 2008. Since these are factually distinct situations, the Court addresses each separately.

A. The September 2002 Concert

Factual Background

The Strangefolk-Garden of Eden Music Festival (the "Concert") took place at Haystack Mountain in Wilmington, Vermont from August 31 to September 2, 2002. This was an outdoor concert venue with a stage and areas set aside for camping and parking. The Concert promoter hired Green Mountain Concert Security ("GMC Security") and the Rutland County Sheriff's Department ("Rutland Sheriffs") to provide security during the Concert. GMC Security patrolled the area in front of the stage and the vendor areas, and searched cars as they entered the venue. The Rutland Sheriffs patrolled the area in back of the stage, the parking and camping areas, the main gate and ticketing area, and the areas along the access roads. Rutland Sheriffs were present at the entrance area but did not participate in the vehicle searches. The Rutland Sheriffs and GMC Security had separate command posts, but they were in radio communication. They also had an agreement that if a person troubled GMC Security, GMC Security would bring that person to the Rutland Sheriffs, who would eject or arrest the person, or take other steps as necessary.

At approximately 8 p.m. on August 31, 2002 Craig entered the Concert venue in a white jeep. At the main entrance security checkpoint, GMC Security officers searched Craig's jeep and found what appeared to be illegal mushrooms in the jeep. When the officers removed the mushrooms and disposed of them, Craig became agitated and gave the security officers a hard time. Ryan Wheeler, a GMC Security officer, approached Craig and asked him to leave the Concert. Later that evening, Wheeler obtained approval from the production staff to remove Craig, but GMC Security could not locate Craig that evening. The next morning, September 1, 2002, at approximately 10 a.m., Wheeler and Kevin Cheney, the owner of GMC Security, saw Craig's jeep in an area where it was not allowed to be parked. Wheeler and Cheney then encountered Craig and advised him that he was going to be removed from the Concert grounds. Wheeler and Cheney did not physically restrain Craig, but called the Rutland Sheriffs to escort Craig off the property. The Rutland Sheriffs did not ask Wheeler and Cheney to detain Craig until they arrived.

In response to Wheeler's call at approximately 10:30 a.m. on September 1, 2002, Sergeant William Skeens and Deputy Kim Hunter were dispatched to the area where Craig's jeep was parked. When Skeens and Hunter arrived, GMC Security officers were speaking with Craig near the jeep, and Hunter observed a portable lamppost behind the jeep, blocking Craig in. Craig told the two GMC Security officers, Wheeler and Cheney, and the two Rutland Sheriffs, Skeens and Hunter, that he wanted the lamppost removed so he could leave, but there is no evidence that Craig said this to the GMC Security officers before Skeens and Hunter arrived. The GMC Security officers told Skeens and Hunter that they wanted Craig removed from the Concert grounds because he had been out of control the previous night. Skeens approached Craig while Hunter talked to the GMC Security officers. After Skeens introduced himself to Craig and they shook hands, Craig identified himself and told Skeens that he had been a real jerk the previous night, but was OK now.

As Skeens talked to Craig, he noticed a slight odor of marijuana coming from Craig. Skeens observed Craig patting his bulging pants pockets in a manner that made Skeens suspect that he was hiding something; Hunter also noticed Craig's bulky pants. Skeens told Craig that with his years of experience, he believed that Craig possessed an illegal substance, and he requested that Craig turn it over to him if he did. Craig removed from his pants pockets 21 baggies containing what appeared to be marijuana. Skeens estimated that approximately five minutes elapsed between the time he arrived and Craig emptied his pants pockets.

Skeens asked Craig to go to the command post with him. Craig agreed, and rode with Skeens and Hunter in their police cruiser to the command post. Skeens entered the command post while Craig stood outside. At least one other deputy was outside keeping an eye on Craig and would have stopped him from leaving. Skeens began the paperwork to charge Craig with possession of marijuana, but Captain Steve Benard, who was in the command post, suggested obtaining consent to search Craig's jeep. Skeens showed Craig the consent card and explained that Craig did not have to sign it. Craig asked what would happen if he didn't sign it, and Skeens replied that he would get a search warrant and search the car. Craig signed the consent card, and Hunter, along with two other officers, went to Craig's jeep and searched the interior. The officers did not find anything in the interior of the car. Lifting the interior door coverings, the officers found empty plastic bags and a scale. The officers asked Craig if they could continue the search in the area of the command post. Craig agreed, gave them the keys, and the jeep was moved to the command post. Craig told the officers that the jeep contained approximately two pounds of marijuana and a pistol. After searching, the officers found four sealed plastic bags containing approximately two and a half pounds of marijuana, a loaded Glock .45 caliber automatic pistol, and $ 2548.00 in cash. Craig also had $ 1393.00 in cash in his wallet.

Throughout this encounter, Skeens noted that Craig was polite and cooperative, spoke freely about the marijuana, and told Skeens that he sells marijuana at concerts.

Analysis

Craig contends that GMC Security officers acted as agents of the Rutland Sheriffs and illegally detained him on September 1, 2002. As a result, Craig seeks to suppress the items seized from him and the statements he made that day.

The government is prohibited from conducting "unreasonable searches and seizures." U.S. Const. amend. IV. "[A] wrongful search or seizure conducted by a private party does not violate the Fourth Amendment and [] such private wrongdoing does not deprive the government of the right to use evidence that it has acquired lawfully." *United States v. Walter*, 447 U.S. 649, 656, 100 S. Ct. 2395, 65 L. Ed. 2d 410 (1980) (citing *Coolidge v. New Hampshire*, 403 U.S. 443, 487–490, 91 S. Ct. 2022, 29 L. Ed. 2d 564 (1971)). "However, where a private party acts as an 'instrument or agent' of the state in effecting a search or seizure, fourth amendment interests are implicated." *Walther v. United States*, 652 F.2d 788, 791 (9th Cir. 1981) (citing *Coolidge*, 403 U.S. at 487); accord *United States v. Bennett*, 709 F.2d 803, 805 (2d Cir. 1983); *United States v. Shahid*, 117 F.3d 322, 325 (7th Cir. 1997).

> [D]e minimis or incidental contacts between the citizen and law enforcement agents prior to or during the course of a search or seizure will not subject the search to fourth amendment scrutiny. The government must be involved either directly as a participant or indirectly as an encourager of the private citizen's actions before we deem the citizen to be an instrument of the state. The requisite degree of governmental participation involves some degree of knowledge and acquiescence in the search.

Walther, 652 F.2d at 791–92 (citations omitted).

Two critical factors to determine whether a private party acts as an 'instrument or agent' of the government are (1) the government's knowledge and acquiescence in the search or seizure and (2) the intent of the party performing the search or seizure. *Walther,* 652 F.2d at 792; *see also Bennett,* 709 F.2d at 805 ("[a] private person cannot act unilaterally as an agent or instrument of the state; there must be some degree of governmental knowledge and acquiescence.") (citations omitted). "Other useful criteria are whether the private actor acted at the request of the government and whether the government offered the private actor a reward." *Shahid,* 117 F.3d at 325 (citations omitted).

To determine whether GMC Security acted as an instrument or agent of the government, the Court first considers whether the Rutland Sheriffs knew of or acquiesced in GMC Security's detention of Craig. As part of coordinating security for the Concert, there was an understanding or agreement that any person troubling GMC Security would be brought to the Rutland Sheriffs for further action, such as removal from the Concert or arrest. Arguably, the Rutland Sheriffs were on notice and aware that GMC Security might be detaining and bringing people to the Rutland Sheriffs. And that is exactly what occurred in this case. GMC Security officers advised Craig that he was going to be removed by the Rutland Sheriffs and blocked his jeep with a portable lamppost, making it impossible for him to leave. Skeens and Hunter were summoned to remove Craig from the Concert grounds, and although they did not ask GMC Security to handcuff or physically restrain Craig, Craig was prevented from leaving until they arrived. When Skeens and Hunter arrived, Craig asked the GMC Security officers, Wheeler and Cheney, and the Rutland Sheriffs, Skeens and Hunter, to remove the lamppost so he could leave, but there is no evidence that Craig asked the GMC Security officers whether he could leave before the Rutland Sheriffs arrived. Based on these facts, the Court finds that the Rutland Sheriffs knew of and acquiesced in GMC Security's detention of Craig.

This is not the end of the inquiry, however. The Court must also consider GMC Security's intent in detaining Craig. At the time of the incident, Wheeler stated that he "held [Craig] until he could be escorted off property by the Rutland County Sheriffs." Def.'s Ex. D, Wheeler Statement, September 1, 2002. In an interview conducted on September 26, 2008, Wheeler reiterated that he "advised Craig he was going to remove him from the property" and he "contacted the Rutland County Sheriff's Officers and requested they assist Craig from the property." Govt.'s Ex. 16, Report of Investigation, September 26, 2008. Cheney stated that after seeing Craig's jeep parked in an improper area, he "requested assistance from Rutland County Sheriff Officers who were patrolling in the area in removing Craig from the venue property." Govt.'s Ex. 17, Report of Investigation, October 1, 2002. Skeens also reported that GMC Security called the Rutland Sheriffs to request "that [Craig] be removed today because of his behavior last nite [sic] and in not wanting to have anymore problems today resulting in the same type [of] behavior." Def.'s Ex. K, Skeens Affidavit, September 1, 2002.

This makes clear that GMC Security's intent in holding Craig was to have him removed from the Concert grounds. There is no evidence that GMC Security intended to detain Craig on suspicion of criminal behavior. There is also no evidence that GMC Security acted at the request of the Rutland Sheriffs. In fact, the evidence shows exactly the opposite—GMC Security requested the Rutland Sheriffs' assistance.

Similarly, there is no evidence that the Rutland Sheriffs offered or gave GMC Security any kind of reward for detaining Craig. These facts resemble those in *United States v. Abney,* where an off-duty police officer working as a private security guard questioned a person suspected of using counterfeit money and asked him to empty his pockets. The private security guard was not wearing a police uniform, identified himself as a security guard, and did not arrest, pat down, or physically restrain the suspect. The private security guard also testified that he acted to further the security interests of the private store in not receiving counterfeit notes. In those circumstances, the court determined that the private security guard was not acting as an agent or instrument of the government. *United States v. Abney,* No. 03 CR 60(JGK), 2003 U.S. Dist. LEXIS 15055, 2003 WL 22047842 at *5-*6 (S.D.N.Y. August 29, 2003).

Like the security guard in Abney, GMC Security officers testified that they were acting to protect the interests of their employer, the Concert promoter, by avoiding any problems or confrontations at the Concert. The evidence here falls short of establishing that GMC Security acted as an instrument or agent of the government. Since the Fourth Amendment does not apply to private party action, there is no constitutional violation.

Craig also contends that the Rutland Sheriffs' continued detention of him violated his constitutional rights. This contention is not supported by the evidence. When Skeens and Hunter arrived at the place where Craig's jeep was parked and Craig was speaking to GMC Security officers, Skeens approached Craig and began speaking with him. Craig admitted that he had been a real jerk the night before. Skeens noticed the odor of marijuana coming from Craig and that Craig was patting his bulky pants pockets, as if he were hiding something. Based on his years of experience, Skeens told Craig that he believed that Craig possessed an illegal substance, and Skeens requested that Craig turn it over to him if he did. Craig removed 21 bags of marijuana from his pants pockets. According to Skeens, approximately five minutes passed between the time he began speaking with Craig and when Craig emptied his pockets. Based on Skeen's observations, there was reasonable suspicion that Craig had been or was going to be engaging in criminal activity and his brief detention was permissible to further the investigation.

Craig's motion to suppress evidence and statements obtained from him as a result of his detention and search at the Concert is denied.

...

ORDER

For the foregoing reasons, the Court denies Craig's Motion to Suppress Evidence and to Dismiss (Docs. 15, 27) in its entirety.

Dated at Burlington, Vermont this 4th day of February, 2009.

/s/ William K. Sessions III

Travis A. Roddey, as the Personal Representative of the Estate of Alice Monique Beckham Hancock, deceased, Petitioner, v. Wal-Mart Stores East, LP, U.S. Security Associates, Inc., and Derrick L. Jones, Respondents.

Opinion No. 27615.
Supreme Court of South Carolina.
Heard October 8, 2015.
Filed March 30, 2016.

John S. Nichols and Blake Alexander Hewitt, both of Bluestein Nichols Thompson & Delgado, LLC, of Columbia; S. Randall Hood and William Angus McKinnon, both of McGowan Hood & Felder, LLC, of Rock Hill; and Brent Paul Stewart, of Stewart Law Offices, LLC, of Rock Hill, for Petitioner.

W. Howard Boyd, Jr., and Stephanie G. Flynn, both of Gallivan, White & Boyd, PA, of Greenville, for Respondents.

TOAL, Acting Justice.

Petitioner appeals the court of appeals' decision affirming the trial court's grant of Wal-Mart's motion for a directed verdict on Petitioner's negligence claim. We reverse and remand for a new trial.

Factual/Procedural Background

The following facts are undisputed. On June 20, 2006, Alice Hancock waited in her vehicle in the parking lot of Wal-Mart while her sister, Donna Beckham, attempted to shoplift several articles of clothing.[1] Hope Rollings, a Wal-Mart customer service manager, noticed Beckham attempting to shoplift and alerted several other employees, including fellow manager Shawn Cox and the on-duty security guard Derrick Jones of U.S. Security Associates, Inc. (USSA), which provided security in the Wal-Mart parking lot pursuant to a contract with Wal-Mart.

Ultimately, Beckham exited Wal-Mart without the clothing. However, Jones approached her in the parking lot. Beckham ran towards Hancock's vehicle, and Jones followed her in his truck and blocked Hancock's vehicle with his truck. After Beckham entered Hancock's vehicle, Hancock turned the vehicle around and drove towards the parking lot's exit, with Jones following. Hancock exited the parking lot onto a highway, and Jones followed. Approximately two miles from Wal-Mart, Hancock's vehicle left the highway and crashed. Hancock died at the scene of the accident.

Travis Roddey, the personal representative of Hancock's estate (Petitioner), brought an action alleging negligence on the part of Wal-Mart, USSA, and Jones. At trial, there was varying witness testimony, especially with regard to the course of events that occurred between Jones and the two Wal-Mart customer service managers—Rollings and Cox—and between Jones and Beckham.

Beckham testified that when she exited Wal-Mart, she heard Jones yelling from his vehicle, "Hey, I need to talk to you." According to Beckham, Jones "zoomed in on [them]" and blocked Hancock's vehicle as she entered Hancock's backseat. Beckham testified that she remained crouched in the backseat as they drove, but looked up periodically to see Jones following behind them at a close distance with his emergency lights on and frequently flashing his high beam headlights. Beckham testified that about two miles from Wal-Mart, Hancock remarked that "he's still on our ass," Beckham observed Jones "on [their] bumper," and then Hancock's vehicle "shot off to the left" and crashed.

Rollings testified that when she saw Beckham attempting to shoplift, she radioed Cox,[2] and instructed the door greeters to stop Beckham and ask for a receipt if she exited the store. Rollings explained that she then walked to the parking lot and notified Jones of the suspected shoplifting. Rollings testified that she did not have authority or responsibility over Jones, and that she did not intend for Jones to approach, delay, or stop Beckham. Rollings acknowledged that Wal-Mart policy prohibited employees from pursuing shoplifters beyond the parking lot,[3] but testified that she could not radio Jones to tell him to stop pursuing Hancock's vehicle because only one person could speak into the radio at a time, and other employees were using the radio during the incident. Further, she remembered Cox telling Jones to "[j]ust get the tag number [from Hancock's vehicle,]" but was unsure whether Cox knew that Jones was pursuing Hancock's vehicle when Cox gave the instruction to Jones.

Cox testified that the night of the incident, Rollings notified her of Beckham's shoplifting. After Beckham abandoned the clothing and exited Wal-Mart, Cox walked outside and saw Jones driving down the aisle of the parking lot where Hancock's vehicle was parked. Cox testified that Hancock's vehicle struck a median in the parking lot and headed toward the exit, at which point Cox instructed: "Get her tag number." Cox testified that she did not intend for Jones to follow Hancock out of the parking lot and acknowledged that it was Wal-Mart policy not to pursue shoplifters, but stated that Jones was not a Wal-Mart employee. According to Cox, she observed Jones's truck two car lengths behind Hancock's vehicle as they exited the parking lot, but that Jones was less than two car lengths behind as she saw them driving away.

Jones testified that the night of the incident, he received a call on his radio informing him that Beckham shoplifted and that she was exiting Wal-Mart. According to Jones, he asked: "[W] hat do you want me to do because I'm a security officer; I'm not a police officer. I cannot detain, so what do you want me to do?" Jones testified that he was instructed to delay Beckham by talking to her. When he saw her exit the store, he attempted to engage her in conversation, at which point she ran to Hancock's vehicle. Jones testified that he then blocked Hancock's vehicle with his truck "because the whole time all [he was] hearing from [Wal-Mart] was, 'You've got to get that license plate tag. We need that license plate tag number.'" Jones testified that at the time, he was under the impression that if he did not get the license plate tag number, he could be fired for not doing his job. According to Jones, both Rollings and Cox repeatedly instructed him to get the license plate tag number. After telling them that he could not see the tag number and that Hancock's vehicle was "about to leave the parking lot," Jones testified that through the radio, someone said, "Man, well, you got to do what you got to do. You need to get that license plate tag number."

Jones knew that he was not supposed to leave the parking lot, but stated that he felt pressure due to the instruction to "do what you got to do," which Jones interpreted to mean pursuing Hancock's vehicle beyond the parking lot. Jones testified that even after he told Wal-Mart employees over the radio that Hancock's vehicle was leaving the parking lot, Wal-Mart employees continued to instruct him to obtain the license plate tag number. Jones stated that he was in radio communication with Wal-Mart employees until a highway on-ramp, where he witnessed Hancock's vehicle almost cause an accident. He then lost sight of Hancock's vehicle until he later saw lights flashing on the side of the road, where he found Beckham screaming for help and Hancock severely injured.

Jeff Gross, Petitioner's expert witness in parking lot security, guard force, and loss prevention, testified that several of Wal-Mart's policies were violated "through tacit approval of [Wal-Mart]." Gross further testified that Wal-Mart "didn't do anything to stop [Jones]. ... [T]hey told him to go out and get [the] license plate number, with that they didn't give any other instruction or guidance." Gross stated that "the very headwaters of this problem starts with [Wal-Mart employees] not following their own policies [and] asking [Jones] to do something that [Wal-Mart] specifically says they won't do themselves and they don't want their contractors to do." Finally, Gross testified that Cox witnessed the pursuit and had enough time to process the information, yet chose not to use the radio to instruct Jones to end the pursuit. Based on the testimony of the parties involved in the incident, Gross opined that there was sufficient range on the radios to communicate beyond the Wal-Mart parking lot.

Chip Tipton, a representative for Wal-Mart, testified that he saw no evidence that any Wal-Mart employee violated Wal-Mart policies, and found no fault in the employees' failure to instruct Jones to end the pursuit. Regardless, Tipton stated that he did not believe the radio's range would have enabled Wal-Mart employees to call Jones back because there were often issues with radio transmission inside Wal-Mart itself.

At the conclusion of Petitioner's case, Wal-Mart moved for a directed verdict on three grounds: (1) Petitioner presented no evidence that Wal-Mart breached its duty of care; (2) Wal-Mart's actions were not the proximate cause of Hancock's death as a matter of law; and (3) Hancock's fault in causing her own death was more than fifty percent as a matter of law. The trial court granted the motion on Wal-Mart's first two grounds, finding insufficient evidence that Wal-Mart was negligent, and that even if Wal-Mart was negligent, there was a lack of proximate cause because the events were not foreseeable. The trial court stated that at that point, it could not find Hancock more than fifty percent negligent as a matter of law. Upon the conclusion of trial, the jury found that Hancock was sixty-five percent at fault, and that USSA and Jones were collectively thirty-five percent at fault.

The court of appeals affirmed the trial court's decision to grant Wal-Mart's motion for a directed verdict in a split opinion. See *Roddey v. Wal-Mart Stores E.*, LP, 400 S.C. 59, 732 S.E.2d 635 (Ct. App. 2012). Chief Judge Few found that the trial court should not have directed a verdict on the basis that there was insufficient evidence of Wal-Mart's negligence because evidence existed that Wal-Mart employees violated Wal-Mart policies. Chief Judge Few further found that the actions of Jones and Hancock were foreseeable. Nevertheless, Chief Judge Few determined that the trial court should have granted Wal-Mart's directed verdict motion on the following grounds: (1) the jury's factual determination of fault apportionment between Hancock, Jones, and USSA was binding on Petitioner even though Wal-Mart's actions were not included in the jury's analysis and (2) Hancock was more than fifty percent at fault as a matter of law. Judge Short concurred in a separate opinion, finding that Wal-Mart was entitled to a directed verdict because it was not foreseeable that Jones would leave the parking lot and continue to aggressively pursue Hancock for several miles.

Judge Huff dissented, agreeing with Chief Judge Few that evidence existed from which a jury could find that Wal-Mart was negligent, and that negligence proximately caused the injuries that occurred. Judge Huff also stated that while a jury still could have found Hancock sixty-five percent negligent even after considering Wal-Mart's liability, it could also have conceivably found—after factoring in Wal-Mart's negligence—that Hancock was less than fifty percent at fault. Accordingly, Judge Huff opined that the trial court should have submitted the issues of negligence and proximate cause to the jury.

We granted Petitioner's petition for a writ of certiorari to review the court of appeals' decision pursuant to Rule 242, SCACR.

Standard of Review

When ruling on a motion for a directed verdict, the trial court must view all evidence and all reasonable inferences in the light most favorable to the nonmoving party, and if the evidence is susceptible of more than one reasonable inference, the trial court should submit the case to the jury. *Unlimited Servs., Inc., v. Macklen Enters., Inc.*, 303 S.C. 384, 386, 401 S.E.2d 153, 154 (1991). In a comparative negligence case, the trial court should grant a directed verdict motion if the sole reasonable inference from the evidence is the nonmoving party's negligence exceeded fifty percent. *Bloom v. Ravoira*, 339 S.C. 417, 422, 529 S.E.2d 710, 712 (2000). Comparing the negligence of two parties is ordinarily a question of fact for the jury. Creech v. S.C. Wildlife & Marine Res. Dep't, 328 S.C. 24, 32, 491 S.E.2d 571, 575 (1997). This Court is "reticent to endorse directed verdicts in cases involving comparative negligence." *Thomasko v. Poole*, 349 S.C. 7, 11, 561 S.E.2d 597, 599 (2002).

Analysis

Viewing the evidence in the light most favorable to the nonmoving party—Petitioner—we find that there is evidence from which a jury could determine that Wal-Mart was negligent, and that its negligence proximately caused the injuries in this case. Accordingly, we hold that the trial court should have submitted to the jury the issues of Wal-Mart's negligence and proximate cause, and we remand for a new trial as to all of the defendants.

I. Evidence of Wal-Mart's Breach of its Duty of Care

To prove a cause of action for negligence, a plaintiff must show: (1) the defendant owes a duty of care to the plaintiff; (2) the defendant breached that duty by a negligent act or omission; (3) the defendant's breach was the actual and proximate cause of the plaintiff's injury; and (4) the plaintiff suffered an injury or damages. *Madison ex rel. Bryant v. Babcock Ctr., Inc.*, 371 S.C. 123, 135, 638 S.E.2d 650, 656 (2006). In a given case, a court may establish and define the standard of care by looking to the common law, statutes, administrative regulations, industry standards, or a defendant's own policies and guidelines. Id. at 140, 638 S.E.2d at 659. Evidence of a company's deviation from its own internal policies is relevant to show the company deviated from the standard of care, and is properly admitted to show the element of breach. *Peterson v. Nat'l R.R. Passenger Corp.*, 365 S.C. 391, 397, 618 S.E.2d 903, 906 (2005); see also *Caldwell v. K-Mart Corp.*, 306 S.C. 27, 31, 410 S.E.2d 21, 24 (Ct. App. 1991) (holding that K-Mart's loss prevention manual was relevant on the material issue of the reasonableness of K-Mart's actions, and noting that in negligence cases, internal policies or self-imposed rules are often admissible as relevant on the issue of failure to exercise due care (citations omitted)).

There is evidence that Wal-Mart breached its duty of care, and therefore, the trial court erred in finding that the directed verdict was proper on that ground. While a jury could conclude from the evidence that Wal-Mart employees merely requested Jones to delay Beckham or obtain the license plate tag number of Hancock's vehicle in a manner that did not violate Wal-Mart's policies, there is also evidence that Wal-Mart employees violated Wal-Mart's policies by instructing Jones to engage in the pursuit that occurred. Specifically, there is evidence indicating that Wal-Mart employees directed Jones to obtain Hancock's license plate tag number while observing Jones following Hancock's vehicle in the parking lot and even after Jones stated that Hancock's vehicle was leaving the parking lot. Accordingly, there is evidence from which a jury could find that Wal-Mart employees either instructed Jones to act in violation of Wal-Mart's policies, or acquiesced in Jones's improper pursuit of Hancock and Beckham.

II. Proximate Cause

To show proximate cause, a plaintiff must show both causation in fact and legal cause. Madison, 371 S.C. at 146, 638 S.E.2d at 662 (citing Oliver v. S.C. Dep't of Highways & Pub. Transp., 309 S.C. 313, 316, 422 S.E.2d 128, 130 (1992)). A plaintiff proves causation in fact by establishing that the injury would not have occurred "but for" the defendant's negligence, and legal cause by establishing foreseeability. Id. (citing Oliver, 309 S.C. at 316, 422 S.E.2d at 130). "Foreseeability is determined by looking at the natural and probable consequences of the complained of act, although it is not necessary to prove that a particular event or injury was foreseeable." Id. (citations omitted). The defendant's negligence does not have to be the sole proximate cause of the plaintiff's injury; instead, the plaintiff must prove the defendant's negligence was at least one of the proximate causes of the injury. Id.

An intervening force may be a superseding cause that relieves an actor from liability, but for there to be relief from liability, the intervening cause must be one that could not have been reasonably foreseen or anticipated. *Rife v. Hitachi Const. Mach. Co.*, 363 S.C. 209, 217, 609 S.E.2d 565, 569 (Ct. App. 2005). In other words, the intervening negligence of a third party will not excuse the first wrongdoer if such intervention ought to have been foreseen in the exercise of due care. *Bishop v. S.C. Dep't of Mental Health*, 331 S.C. 79, 89, 502 S.E.2d 78, 83 (1998). "In such case, the original negligence still remains active, and a contributing cause of the injury." Id. Accordingly, if the intervening acts are set into motion by the original wrongful act and are the foreseeable result of the original act, the "final result, as well as every intermediate cause, is considered in law to be the proximate result of the first wrongful cause." *Wallace v. Owens-Ill., Inc.*, 300 S.C. 518, 521, 389 S.E.2d 155, 157 (Ct. App. 1989).

As an initial matter, there is evidence that "but for" Wal-Mart employees instructing Jones to obtain Hancock's license plate tag number, the accident would not have occurred. Moreover, viewing the evidence in the light most favorable to Petitioner, the trial court erred in finding the directed verdict was proper as to foreseeability, because there is more than one reasonable inference as to whether the consequences of the Wal-Mart employees' actions were foreseeable. It is a natural and probable consequence that a contracted security guard would follow instructions from Wal-Mart employees telling him to "do what you got to do," including pursuing a suspect off-premises. Furthermore, Wal-Mart's own policies demonstrate that Wal-Mart recognized the danger of pursuing a shoplifting suspect, and it was reasonably foreseeable that instructing a contracted security guard to engage in such pursuit would be dangerous.

We find that there is sufficient testimony indicating that upon the Wal-Mart employees' instruction to obtain Hancock's license plate tag number, Jones's actions were not independent unforeseeable intervening acts. There was evidence presented that: Wal-Mart employees' instructions led Jones to drive through Wal-Mart's parking lot in pursuit of Beckham; Wal-Mart employees directed Jones to obtain Hancock's license plate tag number while observing Jones pursue Beckham and Hancock in his patrol vehicle, with both vehicles being operated recklessly; and Wal-Mart continued to instruct Jones to obtain the tag number even after Jones informed them that Hancock's vehicle was leaving the parking lot.

Accordingly, there is evidence that Jones's acts—which were the foreseeable results of Wal-Mart employees' actions—were set into motion by the original wrongful acts of Wal-Mart. We therefore reverse the court of appeals' decision to uphold trial court's grant of a directed verdict on the issue of proximate cause.

III. Apportionment of Fault

Unlike Chief Judge Few, we do not view Wal-Mart's liability as strictly derivative of Jones's or USSA's liability. In addition to Petitioner's claim that Jones was Wal-Mart's agent and thus, Wal-Mart is vicariously liable for his conduct, Petitioner also alleged that Wal-Mart was liable based on its failure to properly supervise Jones and Wal-Mart's improper advice or instruction to Jones to follow Hancock to obtain her license plate tag number. Considering Wal-Mart's potential liability, it is conceivable that a jury could find that the collective fault of the defendants was over fifty percent and that Hancock was less than fifty percent at fault. [4] In light of the reversal of the directed verdict as to Wal-Mart's liability, the only appropriate remedy in this situation is a new trial.

Conclusion

Based on the foregoing, we reverse the court of appeals' decision and remand for a new trial as to all defendants.

REVERSED AND REMANDED.

BEATTY and HEARN, JJ., concur. PLEICONES, C.J., dissenting in a separate opinion in which KITTREDGE, J., concurs.

CHIEF JUSTICE PLEICONES.

I respectfully dissent and would affirm the decision of the Court of Appeals. I agree with Chief Judge Few:

Even under [Petitioner's] theory of the case, Wal-Mart's conduct merely provides some explanation of what motivated Jones' actions. Wal-Mart's negligence could affect how much of the remaining 35% of fault is attributable to Jones, for if Jones was motivated by Wal-Mart's improper actions, arguably he would bear less of the fault for Hancock's death. However, Wal-Mart's actions can have no effect on Hancock's fault. Wal-Mart obviously did not advise or instruct Hancock to flee, nor did it enable her actions by failing to adequately supervise her. There is no evidence in the record that Hancock knew anything about what Wal-Mart told Jones. Therefore, Wal-Mart's alleged conduct could not have reduced Hancock's proportion of fault in the way it could have reduced that of Jones. Even if the jury had been permitted to consider Wal-Mart in its apportionment of fault, Wal-Mart's conduct could not have affected the jury's determination that Hancock was 65% at fault.

Because Wal-Mart's conduct could not have reduced Hancock's fault, [Petitioner] is bound by the jury's finding that she was 65% at fault, and the trial court's decision to grant Wal-Mart a directed verdict could not have prejudiced [Petitioner]. Therefore, I believe we must affirm. See *O'Neal v. Carolina Farm Supply of Johnston, Inc.*, 279 S.C. 490, 497, 309 S.E.2d 776, 780 (Ct.App. 1983) (affirming directed verdict without deciding whether trial court erred because jury's verdict made error harmless).

Roddey v. Wal-Mart Stores E., LP, 400 S.C. 59, 68, 732 S.E.2d 635, 639-40 (Ct. App. 2012).

Moreover, I am not convinced that even if Petitioner were entitled to a new trial against Wal-Mart, it would be proper to require USSA and Jones to face the possibility of liability in a second trial having been absolved in the first. In arguing for a joint retrial, Petitioner relies on *Williams v. Slade*, 431 F.2d 605 (5th Cir. 1970). In Williams, the "innocent" passenger sued both the driver of the automobile in which she was riding and the driver of the other car involved in the accident. The trial court directed a verdict in favor of one of the drivers, and the jury returned a verdict in favor of the other. In Williams, either of the defendants, or both, might have been liable to the plaintiff. Here, however, Wal-Mart could not be liable unless USSA and Jones were also responsible, and unlike the Williams' innocent plaintiff, a jury could (and did) find Hancock to be most at fault. I am unable to determine why the majority concludes, without discussion, that both USSA and Jones should again face a jury trial and the possibility of liability.

KITTREDGE, J., concurs.

1. Beckham testified that Hancock was unaware of her intention to shoplift from Wal-Mart.
2. Cox testified that the night of the incident, the following employees had radios: Cox, Rollings, Jones, and assistant manager Chuck Campbell.
3. Specifically, Wal-Mart's policy for investigating and detaining suspected shoplifters provides:

NEVER pursue a fleeing Suspect more than approximately 10 feet beyond the point you are located when the Suspect begins to run to avoid detention. Ten feet is about three long steps. This limitation applies both inside and outside the facility.

NEVER pursue a Suspect who is in a moving vehicle.
NEVER pursue a Suspect off the Facility's property.
NEVER use a moving vehicle to pursue a Suspect.
TERMINATE the pursuit of a Suspect, if the Suspect begins to enter a vehicle.

LET THE SUSPECT GO, rather than continue a pursuit that is likely to injure or cause harm to someone. Further, the Guidelines for Private Security Contractors provide that security contractors are prohibited from using their vehicles in an attempt to apprehend any suspects, and only allow their vehicles to leave Wal-Mart property for gas or maintenance of the vehicle. These guidelines also note that it is the responsibility of Wal-Mart management to enforce Wal-Mart policies and procedures.

4. The dissent, by adopting Chief Judge Few's rationale, merely assumes the outcome of the jury's deliberations when it is impossible to know what would influence the jury's comparison if the jury was permitted to consider Wal-Mart's liability. Here, we cannot say that the sole reasonable inference to be drawn from the evidence was that Hancock was more than fifty percent negligent in light of the testimony that Wal-Mart employees instructed Jones to follow Hancock. Bloom, 339 S.C. at 422, 529 S.E.2d at 713 ("In a comparative negligence case, the trial court should only determine judgment as a matter of law if the sole reasonable inference which may be drawn from the evidence is that the plaintiff's negligence exceeded fifty percent." (citation omitted)). Therefore, it would be inappropriate for this Court to speculate. See *Thomasko*, 349 S.C. at 11, 561 S.E.2d at 599 ("Because the term is relative and dependant on the facts of a particular case, comparing the negligence of two parties is ordinarily a question of fact for the jury. For these reasons, this Court is reticent to endorse directed verdicts in cases involving comparative negligence." (internal citations omitted)).

Gordon Pellegrini and Keith Cervone, Plaintiffs, v. Duane Reade Inc., Sottile Security Co. And John Does 1-5, Defendants.

Docket No. 156317/2012. 2015 NY Slip Op 31352(U)
July 22, 2015.
Supreme Court, New York County.
DECISION/ORDER
CYNTHIA S. KERN, J.S.C.

Plaintiffs bring this action to recover for assault; battery; false arrest and imprisonment; malicious prosecution; abuse of process; negligent training; negligence; and intentional and negligent infliction of emotional distress. Defendant Duane Reade Inc. ("Duane Reade") now moves for partial summary judgment dismissing plaintiffs' causes of action for false arrest and imprisonment; malicious prosecution; abuse of process; intentional infliction of emotional distress; negligent infliction of emotional distress and negligent training and striking plaintiffs' demand for punitive damages. Defendant Sottile Security Co. ("Sottile") cross-moves for partial summary judgment dismissing plaintiffs' causes of action for intentional infliction of emotional distress; negligent infliction of emotional distress and negligent training and to strike plaintiffs' demand for punitive damages. As set further below, Duane Reade's motion is granted only in part and Sottile's motion is granted in its entirety.

The relevant facts are as follows. Plaintiffs' claims revolve around an incident at a Duane Reade store ("the store") located at 194 East 2nd Street, New York, New York on the night of October 29, 2011. On that night, plaintiffs Gordon Pellegrini ("Pellegrini") and Keith Cervone ("Cervone") planned to attend a Halloween party in Brooklyn. Before heading to the party in Brooklyn, Cervone testified that they decided to go to a corner deli and buy beers. Cervone testified that at the deli he purchased two 22 ounce cold Miller Genuine Draft bottles of beer and put them in his jacket's front pocket. The plaintiffs then decided to go to the Duane Reade store directly across the street to get snacks. At the time the plaintiffs entered the store, plaintiffs were carrying tennis rackets, which they claim were part of their Halloween costumes.

Cervone testified that he walked around the store looking for snacks and at one point he picked up a "Jason" Halloween mask that Duane Reade had for sale, put it on and walked around the store wearing the mask. Cervone testified that he was in the store for about 15 minutes. As Cervone attempted to leave the store with the beers and Halloween mask, security guard Jyotish Chakraborty ("Chakraborty"), who worked for defendant Sottile, stopped Cervone. Cervone testified that Chakraborty yelled at him, accused him of shoplifting the beers and grabbed his right arm and pushed him up against the wall. Cervone further attests that at this time he told Chakraborty the he did not steal anything and that he had purchased the beers across the street. According to Chakraborty, Cervone never told him that he purchased the bottles before he came to the store. Rather, Chakraborty testified that he saw Cervone take the bottles from the Duane Reade cooler. The surveillance footage of the incident shows that after Chakraborty stopped Cervone, Cervone began dancing around and playing "air guitar." Cervone eventually took off the mask and tried to leave again with the bottles in his pocket. At this point, Chakraborty removed the bottles from Cervone's pocket and placed them on the register counter. Chakraborty then told the cashier to call the manager and Cervone exited the store where co-plaintiff Pelligrini was waiting outside.

Plaintiffs allege they were standing outside the store discussing what had happened and what they should do when Chakraborty and Duane Reade employee Richard Arnold ("Arnold") came outside. A Duane Reade customer wearing a plaid shirt also exited the store at this time (the "customer"). The parties dispute what occurred next. According to Pelligrini, Arnold, without provocation, punched him in the face. Cervone also testified that Arnold punched Pelligrini in the face. Cervone further testified that the other "guard," believed to be Chakraborty, along with the customer grabbed Cervone and pulled him back into the vestibule of the store. He testified that the customer was trying to pull his jacket over his head and the security guard was hitting him from behind. He further testified that he fell down at this point and both Chakraborty and Arnold kicked him until he lost consciousness. He then woke up on the curb with no pants on and no jacket. Surveillance footage from the store shows that at one point Cervone and the customer were fighting within the store. Chakraborty testified that he was not outside at this time and he watched as Arnold, one of the plaintiffs and the customer entered the vestibule. According to Chakraborty, they were all punching each other when they came into contact with him and he got punched in the face.

After this altercation, the police were called and plaintiffs left the area of the store. However, when plaintiffs were about a block from the store, they were stopped by squad cars and arrested. According to the criminal complaint, an employee of Duane Reade told the police that he had observed two men enter the Duane Reade store; at the time of their entry, neither of them was carrying any beer; a short while later the two men attempted to leave the store without paying while one of them was carrying several beers; he attempted to prevent the men from exiting the store's property, whereupon one of them men punched him about the face and body and the other man struck him about the head with a tennis racket. Plaintiffs were charged with (a) one count of first-degree robbery; (b) two counts of second-degree assault; and (c) one count of fourth-degree criminal possession of a weapon. All charges were eventually dismissed.

Plaintiffs now bring the instant action asserting nine causes of action: (1) assault; (2) battery; (3) false arrest and imprisonment; (4) malicious prosecution; (5) abuse of process; (6) intentional infliction of emotional distress; (7) negligent infliction of emotional distress; (8) negligent training; and (9) negligence. The first, second, fifth, sixth, seventh, eighth, and ninth causes of action are asserted against both defendants, while the second, third, and fourth causes of action are asserted against Duane Reade only. Both defendants now move for partial summary judgment dismissing plaintiffs' sixth, seventh and eighth causes of action and striking plaintiffs' demand for punitive damages. Duane Reade also seeks summary judgment dismissing the third, fourth and fifth causes of action asserted against it.

On a motion for summary judgment, the movant bears the burden of presenting sufficient evidence to demonstrate the absence of any material issues of fact. See *Alvarez v. Prospect Hosp.*, 68 N.Y.2d 320, 324 (1986). Summary judgment should not be granted where there is any doubt as to the existence of a material issue of fact. See *Zuckerman v. City of New York*, 49 N.Y.2d 557, 562 (1980). Once the movant establishes a prima facie right to judgment as a matter of law, the burden shifts to the party opposing the motion to "produce evidentiary proof in admissible form sufficient to require a trial of material questions of fact on which he rests his claim." Id.

In the present case, as an initial matter, Duane Reade's motion for summary judgment dismissing plaintiffs' third cause of action for false arrest and imprisonment is granted as Duane Reade has established that there is no issue of fact as to its liability under this claim. To establish a claim for false arrest or false imprisonment, plaintiff must establish that: "(1) the defendant intended to confine him, (2) the plaintiff was conscious of the confinement, (3) the plaintiff did not consent to the confinement, and (4) the confinement was not otherwise privileged." *Broughton v. State of New York*, 37 N.Y.2d 451, 456 (1975). "It is well settled in this State's jurisprudence that a civilian complainant, by merely seeking police assistance or furnishing information to law enforcement authorities who are then free to exercise their own judgment as to whether an arrest should be made and criminal charges filed, will not be held liable for false arrest or malicious prosecution." *Du Chateau v. Metro-North Commuter R. R. Co.*, 253 A.D.2d 128, 131 (1st Dept 1999). "Nor does identifying plaintiff as the perpetrator of a crime, signing the summons or testifying at trial give rise to tort liability." Id. Rather, there must be evidence that defendant "encouraged the police to arrest plaintiff or intended to confine him." *Berrios v. Our Lady of Mercy Med. Ctr.*, 20 A.D.3d 361, 362 (1st Dept 2005).

Here, the court finds that no issues of fact exist as to Duane Reade's involvement in plaintiffs' arrest as the undisputed evidence demonstrates that Duane Reade did not encourage the police to arrest plaintiffs or intend to confine them. As an initial matter, the record indicates that Duane Reade employees neither confined plaintiffs in the store against their will, nor took part in the physical arrest of plaintiffs by the NYPD. Further, according to the criminal complaint, it is clear that plaintiffs' arrest was based upon NYPD's conversations with Chakraborty and the customer who was also involved in the altercation. Although the criminal complaint does not identify Chakraborty by name, it is clear from the record as a whole that the Duane Reade employee identified in the complaint must be Chakraborty as it is undisputed that he was the only individual who stopped plaintiff Cervone from exiting the store. As Chakraborty is not actually a Duane Reade employee but employed by Sottile, his actions cannot be attributed to Duane Reade to hold it liable. Thus, there is no evidence that Duane Reade encouraged the police to arrest plaintiffs and plaintiffs cannot maintain a claim for false arrest and imprisonment against Duane Reade.

Similarly, Duane Reade's motion for summary judgment dismissing plaintiffs' fifth cause of action for abuse of process is granted as Duane Reade has demonstrated that plaintiffs cannot maintain this claim as a matter of law. "Abuse of process has three elements: (1) regularly issued process, either civil or criminal, (2) an intent to do harm without excuse or justification, and (3) use of the process in a perverted manner to obtain a collateral objective." Id. As the Court of

Appeals has recognized, this tort "is frequently confused with malicious prosecution." *Board of Educ. of Farmingdale Union Free School Dist. v. Farmingdale Classroom Teachers Assn., Local 1889. AFT FL-CIO*, 38 N.Y.2d 397, 400 (1975). Thus, the Court clarified the distinction between abuse of process and malicious prosecution claims by explaining that abuse of process is when process is issued lawfully but to accomplish some unjustified purpose, while malicious prosecution is when one maliciously causes process to issue without justification. Id.

Here, plaintiffs fail to identify any lawful process used by Duane Reade to accomplish some unjustified purpose to sustain a claim for abuse of process. Plaintiffs claim that Duane Reade committed an abuse of process by (1) making intentionally false and misleading statements to the police; (2) providing incomplete and misleading video to the District Attorney's Office; and (3) failing to produce any evidence of the beer other than what appears on the video. However, none of these assertions, even accepting them as true, is a lawful process used to accomplish an unjustified purpose. Rather, these assertions, if supported by adequate evidence, would support a malicious prosecution claim. Thus, plaintiffs' claim for abuse of process must be dismissed.

However, Duane Reade's motion for summary judgment dismissing plaintiffs' fourth cause of action for malicious prosecution is denied as there remain issues of fact as to whether Duane Reade failed to provide a complete and unaltered copy of the store's surveillance footage to the District Attorney. "In order to recover for malicious prosecution, a plaintiff must establish four elements: that a criminal proceeding was commenced; that it was terminated in favor of the accused; that it lacked probable cause; and that the proceeding was brought out of actual malice." *Cantalino v. Danner*, 96 N.Y.2d 391, 394 (2001). "New York law has long equated the civil defendant's failure to make a full and complete statement of the facts to the District Attorney or the court, or holding back information that might have affected the results, with that defendant's initiation of a malicious prosecution." *Ramos v. City of New York*, 285 A.D.2d 284, 299 (1st Dept 2001).

Here, the record sufficiently supports plaintiffs' claim, for purposes of denying Duane Reade's motion for summary judgment, that Duane Reade did not turn over complete and unaltered surveillance footage to the District Attorney. The footage provided to the District Attorney included several clips from the night in question. Indeed, there was footage from at least three different camera angles, including from camera "1" that was pointed directly on the entrance of the store. However, mysteriously absent from what was provided was the footage of plaintiffs entering the store. While Duane Reade provided footage from camera "1" starting at 1:16, there is no footage from this camera prior to that time, which is when plaintiffs entered the store allegedly with the beers they were being charged with stealing. Footage from this time period was provided for other cameras within the store, but not for camera "1." Duane Reade offers no real explanation for this missing footage. Rather, Duane Reade argues that plaintiffs' argument as to the missing video is disingenuous as plaintiffs never moved for spoliation. However, the absence of a motion for spoliation does not, contrary to Duane Reade's contention, negate the reality that no such footage has been produced and no explanation has been given to account for the missing video that could have showed Cervone entering the store with the beer. Thus, on its face, the video footage presented to the District Attorney raises an issue of fact as to whether Duane Reade provided a full and complete copy of its surveillance footage to the District Attorney precluding summary judgment as to plaintiffs' claim for malicious prosecution.

Both Duane Reade and Sottile's motions for summary judgment dismissing plaintiffs' sixth and seventh causes of action for intentional and negligent infliction of emotional distress are granted as defendants have demonstrated that plaintiffs cannot recover under these claims as a matter of law. Both intentional and negligent infliction of emotional distress require allegations that the defendant's conduct is "so outrageous in character, and so extreme in degree, as to go beyond all possible bounds of decency and to be regarded as atrocious, and utterly intolerable in a civilized community." *Berrios v. Our Lady of Mercy Med. Ctr.*, 20 A.D.3d 361, 362 (1st Dept 2005). In the present case, upon review of the record, the court finds that neither defendant's conduct rises to level of conduct that is so shocking and outrageous that it exceeds all reasonably bounds of decency.

Additionally, both Duane Reade and Sottile's motions for summary judgment dismissing plaintiffs' eighth cause of action for negligent training is granted as plaintiffs do not seek punitive damages for defendants' alleged negligent training of their respective employees. "Generally, where an employee is acting within the scope of his or her employment, the employer is liable for the employee's negligence under a theory of respondeat superior and no claim may proceed against the employer for negligent hiring, retention, supervision or training." *Talavera v. Arbit*, 18 A.D.3d 738 (2nd Dept 2005). "This is because if the employee was not negligent, there is no basis for imposing liability on the employer, and if the employee was negligent, the employer must pay the judgment regardless of the reasonableness of the hiring or retention or the adequacy of the training." *Karron v. New York City Tr. Auth.*, 241 A.D.2d 323, 324 (1st Dept 1997). "An exception exists where the injured plaintiff is seeking punitive damages from the employer based on alleged gross negligence in the hiring or retention of the employee." Id. (internal citations omitted).

Here, plaintiffs cannot maintain a claim for negligent hiring against either defendant as plaintiffs do not seek punitive damages based on defendants' alleged negligent training of their respective employees. In their complaint, plaintiffs do not seek an award of punitive damages based on defendants' alleged negligent training of their employees. Indeed, although plaintiffs seek punitive damages in regard to their other seven causes of action, they seek only compensatory damages for their negligent training claim. Thus, defendants' motions for summary judgment dismissing plaintiffs' claim for negligent training must be granted.

Finally, the remainder of defendants' motion seeking summary judgment striking plaintiffs' demand for punitive damages is granted as defendants' employees conduct was not aimed at the public generally. "Punitive damages are permitted when the defendant's wrongdoing is not simply intentional but evinces a high degree of moral turpitude and demonstrate such wanton dishonesty as to imply a criminal indifference to civil obligations." *Ross v. Louise Wise Servs.*, Inc., 8 N.Y.3d 478, 489 (2007) (internal quotations omitted). "[A] private party seeking to recover punitive damages must not only demonstrate egregious tortious conduct by which he or she was aggrieved, but also that such conduct was part of a pattern of similar conduct directed at the public generally." *Rocanova v. Equitable Life Assurance Society*, 83 N.Y.2d 603, 613 (1994); see also *1 Mott St., Inc. v. Con Edison*, 33 A.D.3d 531, 532 (1st Dept 2006). Here, defendants' employees conduct cannot, as a matter of law, support an award of punitive damages as the record contains no evidence that the conduct of either employee was aimed at the public generally. Rather, the evidence in the record demonstrates that the complained about conduct in this proceeding was directed only at plaintiffs.

Accordingly, it is hereby

ORDERED that Duane Reade's motion for partial summary judgment dismissing plaintiffs' third, fifth, sixth, seventh and eighth causes of action and to strike plaintiffs' demand for punitive damages is granted but is otherwise denied; and it is further

ORDERED that Sottile's motion for partial summary judgment dismissing plaintiffs' sixth, seventh, and eighth causes of action and to strike plaintiffs' demand for punitive damages is granted. This constitutes the decision and order of the court.

Luís M. Martínez, Plaintiff, v. Christopher Linden Espey, et al., Defendant.

Case No. 2:14-cv-02318-MHH.
United States District Court, N.D. Alabama, Southern Division.
February 24, 2016.
MEMORANDUM OPINION AND ORDER
MADELINE HUGHES HAIKALA, District Judge.

Plaintiff Luís Martínez is a citizen of El Salvador residing in Alabama under temporary protected status. On May 10, 2014, Mr. Martínez went to Courtyard Oyster Bar's restaurant to play pool. Defendant Christopher Espey, a former marine, also happened to be at the restaurant. Mr. Martínez alleges that while he was playing pool, Mr. Espey threatened him, commented on his race, and struck him in the face with a pool stick, rendering him unconscious.

Mr. Martínez filed suit in this Court, asserting a state law assault and battery claim against Mr. Espey and various state and federal claims against Courtyard. This case is before the Court on Courtyard's motion to dismiss. (Doc. 16). For the reasons discussed below, the Court grants in part and denies in part Courtyard's motion to dismiss.

I. Standard of Review

Rule 12(b)(6) enables a defendant to move to dismiss a complaint for "failure to state a claim upon which relief can be granted." Fed. R. Civ. P. 12(b)(6). Pursuant to Rule 8(a)(2), a complaint must contain, "a short and plain statement of the claim showing that the pleader is entitled to relief." Fed. R. Civ. P. 8(a)(2). "Generally, to survive a [Rule 12(b)(6)] motion to dismiss and meet the requirement of Fed. R. Civ. P. 8(a)(2), a complaint need not contain 'detailed factual allegations,' but rather 'only enough facts to state a claim to relief that is plausible on its face.'" *Maledy v. City of Enterprise*, 2012 WL 1028176, at *1 (M.D. Ala. March 26, 2012) (quoting *Bell Atl. Corp. v. Twombly*, 550 U.S. 544, 555, 570 (2007)). "Specific facts are not necessary; the statement need only 'give the defendant fair notice of what the … claim is and the grounds upon which it rests.'" *Erickson v. Pardus*, 551 U.S. 89, 93 (2007) (quoting Twombly, 550 U.S. at 555). In deciding a Rule 12(b)(6) motion to dismiss, a court must view the allegations in a complaint in the light most favorable to the nonmoving party. *Watts v. Fla. Int'l Univ.*, 495 F.3d 1289, 1295 (11th Cir. 2007). A court must accept well-pled facts as true. *Grossman v. Nationsbank*, N.A., 225 F.3d 1228, 1231 (11th Cir. 2000).

II. Factual and Procedural History

On May 10, 2014, Mr. Martínez went to Courtyard to play pool. (Doc. 14, ¶¶ 11, 13). When Mr. Martínez entered Courtyard, he paid a fee at the door. (Doc. 14, ¶ 17). While Mr. Martínez played pool, another patron, Mr. Espey, made a negative remark about Mr. Martínez's race. (Doc. 14, ¶ 13). Next, Mr. Espey signaled with his hands that he would cut Mr. Martínez's throat. (Doc. 14, ¶ 13). When Mr. Martínez started to leave the bar, Mr. Espey struck him in the face with a pool stick. (Doc. 14, ¶ 13). Mr. Martínez fell to the ground unconscious. (Doc. 14, ¶ 14). [1] The police later arrested Mr. Espey as a result of his assault on Mr. Martínez. (Doc. 14, ¶ 12).

An off-duty police officer working at Courtyard as a security officer witnessed the altercation between Mr. Martínez and Mr. Espey. (Doc. 14, ¶ 17). This officer saw the encounter between

Mr. Martínez and Mr. Espey escalate, but the officer did not intervene. (Doc. 14, ¶¶ 17, 18). Mr. Martínez alleges that on other occasions, the security officer intervened in similar confrontations between white males. (Doc. 14, ¶ 19).

Seeking a remedy for the injuries that he allegedly sustained because of his encounter with Mr. Espey, Mr. Martínez filed this lawsuit. Mr. Martínez asserts a state law claim against Mr. Espey for assault and battery. (Doc. 14, p. 7). Mr. Martínez also asserts claims against Courtyard under the following theories: (1) assault and battery; (2) equal protection under the Fourteenth Amendment to the U.S. Constitution; (3) equal protection under the Alabama Constitution; (4) selective enforcement under the Fourteenth Amendment to the U.S. Constitution; (5) failure to obtain liability insurance for a security officer pursuant to Alabama Code § 6-5-338(c); (6) negligent/reckless training and supervision; and (7) breach of contract and/or breach of warranty. (Doc. 14, pp. 8-14). [2] Courtyard filed a motion to dismiss, to which Courtyard attached several documents. (*See* Doc. 16-1). In opposition to the motion, Mr. Martínez asked the Court to convert Courtyard's motion to dismiss into a motion for summary judgment pursuant to Federal Rule of Civil Procedure 12(d). (Doc. 17, p. 6). Mr. Martínez's response included an affidavit concerning discovery that he argues he needs to address Courtyard's arguments. (Doc. 17, p. 7). Courtyard filed a motion to strike the affidavit concerning discovery. (Doc. 18). On this record, the Court considers Courtyard's motion to strike and motion to dismiss.

III. Analysis

A. Courtyard's Motion to Strike

Courtyard's motion to strike Mr. Martínez's request for discovery is moot because the Court has not considered the attachments to Courtyard's motion to dismiss that gave rise to Mr. Martínez's request for discovery. (Doc. 16-1; Doc. 17, pp. 6–7).

"A judge need not convert a motion to dismiss into a motion for summary judgment" pursuant to Rule 12(d) if the judge "does not consider matters outside the pleadings." *Harper v. Lawrence Cnty., Ala.*, 592 F.3d 1227, 1232 (11th Cir. 2010) (internal quotations omitted). "According to case law, not considering such matters is the functional equivalent of excluding them—there is no more formal step required." *Id.* Because the Court has not considered the exhibits attached to Courtyard's motion to dismiss, the Court does not have to reach Mr. Martínez's request for discovery or Courtyard's motion to strike Mr. Martínez's request.

B. Mr. Martínez's Respondeat Superior Claims

Mr. Martínez brings his assault and battery, equal protection, and selective enforcement claims against Courtyard under the theory of respondeat superior. Mr. Martínez contends that Courtyard is vicariously liable for its security officer's failure to intervene and stop Mr. Espey from striking Mr. Martínez. (Doc. 14, ¶¶ 27, 34, 37, 40). "For [Courtyard] to be liable under the doctrine of respondeat superior, [the officer] would have to be acting in the line and scope of his employment with [Courtyard] when the events complained of occurred." *Whitely v. Food Giant, Inc.*, 721 So. 2d 207, 209 (Ala. Civ. App. 1998) (citing *Hudson v. Muller*, 653 So. 2d 942 (Ala. 1995)). "The Alabama Supreme Court has held that when an off-duty police officer witnesses an offense for which the perpetrator is arrested, the officer's status changes, and he is then acting in his capacity as a police officer and not his capacity as a security guard." *Whitely*, 721 So. 2d at 209 (citing

Dinmark v. Farrier, 510 So. 2d 819 (Ala. 1987) and *Perry v. Greyhound Bus Lines,* 491 So. 2d 926 (Ala. 1986)); see also *Dinmark,* 510 So. 2d at 821 (noting that the status of an off-duty police officer working as a security guard changes to that of an on-duty police officer when the officer witnesses criminal acts committed in his presence).

Mr. Martínez alleges that the security officer witnessed Mr. Espey utter ethnic slurs, make threatening gestures, and strike Mr. Martínez in the face with a pool stick. (Doc. 14, ¶¶ 18, 19). Mr. Espey was arrested as a result of this altercation. (Doc. 14, ¶¶ 12, 15). When the officer witnessed the ethnic slurs and threatening gestures, his status changed from security guard to police officer. See *Whitley,* 721 So. 2d at 209 (holding that grocery store was not liable under respondeat superior for actions of offduty police officer because at the moment the officer witnessed a man approaching a woman while making a fist, the officer's status changed to that of a police officer). Therefore, Courtyard is not vicariously liable for the officer's failure to intervene in the altercation. The Court dismisses with prejudice Mr. Martínez's claims under respondeat superior for assault and battery, equal protection, and selective enforcement.

Mr. Martínez's complaint also states that Courtyard is "vicariously responsible for the wrongful acts and omissions of defendant Espey." (Doc. 14, ¶ 2). "In vicarious liability analysis, there are three types of relationships: master/servant; principal/agent; and independent contractor." *S. Trust Bank v. Jones, Morrison, Womack & Dearing, P.C.,* 939 So. 2d 885, 903 (Ala. Civ. App. 2005) (citing *Restatement (Second) of Agency* § 2 (1958)). Mr. Martínez has not alleged a relationship between Mr. Espey and Courtyard that would give rise to vicarious liability. Moreover, under Alabama law, a master or principal typically is not subject to vicarious liability for the criminal acts of an alleged servant or agent. *See E. Ala. Behavioral Med., P.C. v. Chancey,* 883 So. 2d 162, 168 (Ala. 2003). Therefore, the Court dismisses with prejudice Mr. Martínez's assault and battery claim against Courtyard.

C. Failure to Obtain Liability Insurance

In Count V of the complaint, Mr. Martínez asserts that Courtyard failed to obtain liability insurance for its off-duty police officer. (Doc. 14, pp. 12-13). Under Alabama law, private employers who hire off-duty police officers as security guards must obtain liability insurance. Ala. Code § 6-5-338(c). The Alabama Code states:

> Every private, nongovernmental person or entity who employs a peace officer during that officer's "off-duty" hours to perform any type of security work or to work while in the uniform of a peace officer shall have in force at least $100,000 of liability insurance, which insurance must indemnify for acts the "off-duty" peace officer takes within the line and scope of the private employment. The failure to have in force the insurance herein required shall make every individual employer, every general partner of a partnership employer, every member of an unincorporated association employer, and every officer of a corporate employer individually liable for all acts taken by an "off-duty" peace officer within the line and scope of the private employment.

Ala. Code § 6-5-338(c). Private employers who fail to obtain the necessary insurance are individually liable for the officer's acts that are "within the line and scope of the private employment." *Id.*

As explained above, when an off-duty police officer witnesses an offense for which the perpetrator is arrested, the officer's status changes from security guard to police officer. *See Whitely,*

721 So. 2d at 209. "In other words, once [the officer] witnessed a crime, he would be outside the 'line and scope' of his employment" with Courtyard and thus outside the scope of § 6-5-338(c) so that Courtyard would not be liable for the officer's acts. *Media General Operations, Inc. v. Stovall*, 2007 WL 3379753, at *7 (M.D. Ala. 2007). Mr. Martínez alleges that the off-duty police officer witnessed the altercation that led to Mr. Espey's arrest. (Doc. 14, ¶ 18). Because the off-duty officer's status changed when he witnessed the altercation between Mr. Martínez and Mr. Espey, § 6-5-338 does not apply in this case. The Court dismisses with prejudice Mr. Martínez's claim for failure to obtain liability insurance to the extent that it relates to the officer's failure to intervene.

D. Negligent/Reckless Training and Supervision

In Count VI of the complaint, Mr. Martínez alleges that Courtyard was negligent or reckless in training and supervising the off duty police officer. (Doc. 14, p. 13). Under Alabama law, "[i]n the master and servant relationship, the master is held responsible for his servant's incompetency when notice or knowledge, either actual or presumed, of such unfitness has been brought to him." *Lane v. Central Bank of Ala., N.A.*, 425 So. 2d 1098, 1100 (Ala. 1983) (citing *Thompson v. Havard*, 235 So. 2d 853, 858 (1970)). Mr. Martínez contends that Courtyard employed the off-duty police officer as a security guard. (Doc. 14, ¶ 5, 34). Plaintiff also alleges that Courtyard "failed to furnish sufficient guidelines." (Doc. 14, ¶ 44). Although these factual allegations are sparse, they are sufficient to give Courtyard fair notice of the grounds for Mr. Martínez's negligence/wantonness claim. Therefore, the Court denies Courtyard's motion to dismiss Mr. Martínez's negligent/reckless training and supervision claim.

E. Breach of Contract and/or Warranty

Mr. Martínez's final count alleges that "[t]here exists an implied contract between Defendant Oyster Bar and Plaintiff for the protection of a paying patron invitee in the establishment." (Doc. 14, p. 14). In Alabama, "a duty may be imposed on a store owner to take reasonable precautions to protect invitees from criminal attack in the exceptional case where the store owner possessed actual or constructive knowledge that criminal activity which could endanger an invitee was a probability." *Broadus v. Chevron USA, Inc.*, 677 So. 2d 199, 203 (Ala. 1996) (citing *Ortell v. Spencer Companies*, 477 So. 2d 299 (Ala. 1985)). The Court will construe Mr. Martínez's "breach of contract" claim as a premises liability claim. [3]

Mr. Martínez alleges that he was an invitee at Courtyard and that Mr. Espey criminally attacked him. (Doc. 14, ¶¶ 12, 47). Mr. Martínez also alleges that the altercation between himself and Mr. Espey was "foreseeable." (Doc. 14, ¶ 2). Again, although Mr. Martínez's allegations are sparse, they are sufficient to put Courtyard on notice of the nature of Mr. Martínez's premises liability claim. The Court therefore denies Courtyard's motion to dismiss this claim.

IV. Conclusion

For the reasons explained above, the Court GRANTS Courtyard's motion to dismiss in part. The Court DISMISSES WITH PREJUDICE Mr. Martínez's claims against Courtyard for assault and battery, equal protection, selective enforcement, and failure to obtain liability

insurance (Counts I, II, III, IV, and V). Mr. Martínez's claims against Courtyard for negligent/ reckless training and supervision (Count VI) and premises liability (Count VII) will go forward.
[4] Courtyard's motion to strike is MOOT. (Doc. 18).

The Court directs the Clerk to please TERM Docs. 16 and 18.

DONE and ORDERED.

1. Because Mr. Martínez was unconscious, he does not know how many times Mr. Espey struck him with the pool stick. (Doc. 14, ¶ 14). Based on his injuries, Mr. Martínez believes that Mr. Espey struck him multiple times. (Doc. 14, ¶ 14).
2. Document 14 is Mr. Martínez's first amended complaint.
3. When a complaint satisfies Rule 8's notice and plausibility requirements, "the form of the complaint is not significant if it alleges facts upon which relief can be granted, even if it fails to categorize correctly the legal theory giving rise to the claim." *Keene v. Prine*, 477 Fed. Appx. 575, 583 (11th Cir. 2012) (finding that plaintiff stated a claim because her complaint, though "not a model of clarity," should have put the defendant on notice of the claim leveled against it).
4. Because the Court is dismissing Mr. Martínez's federal claims, leaving only Mr. Martínez's state negligent/reckless training and supervision and premises liability claims against Courtyard, the Court must assess whether it is left with an independent basis for subject matter jurisdiction. *See RES-GA Cobblestone, LLC v. Blake Const. & Dev., LLC*, 718 F.3d 1308, 1313 (11th Cir. 2013) ("Federal courts operate under a continuing obligation to inquire into the existence of subject matter jurisdiction whenever it may be lacking.") (citing *Baltin v. Alaron Trading Corp.*, 128 F.3d 1466, 1468 (11th Cir. 1997)). The Court finds that under 28 U.S.C. § 1332, it has a basis for invoking federal subject matter jurisdiction over Mr. Martínez's two remaining claims. Federal diversity jurisdiction requires diversity of citizenship and an amount in controversy that exceeds $75,000. 28 U.S.C. § 1332. As to diversity of citizenship, Mr. Martínez is a citizen of a foreign country and is diverse from both defendants, who are citizens of Alabama. As to the amount in controversy, Mr. Martínez plausibly alleges that his cause of action meets the jurisdictional amount in controversy requirement. In his amended complaint, Mr. Martínez seeks both compensatory and punitive damages for each of his claims. (Doc. 14). Under Alabama law, Mr. Martínez potentially may recover punitive damages under his wantonness theory. *See Galaxy Cable, Inc. v. Davis*, 58 So. 3d 93, 100 (Ala. 2010) (citing Ala. Code § 6-11-20). Therefore, Mr. Martínez potentially may recover a judgment in excess of $75,000, given both the nature of Mr. Martínez's alleged injuries and his punitive damages claims. *See Federated Mut. Ins. Co. v. McKinnon Motors, LLC*, 329 F.3d 805, 807 (11th Cir. 2003) ("Generally, '[i]t must appear to a legal certainty that the claim is really for less than the jurisdictional amount to justify dismissal.'"); *see also Roe v. Michelin N. Am., Inc.*, 613 F.3d 1058, 1061-62 (11th Cir. 2010) (a federal district court may "make 'reasonable deductions, reasonable inferences, or other reasonable extrapolations' from the pleadings to determine whether it is facially apparent" that the court has subject matter jurisdiction over a cause of action); *id.* at 1162 ("Put simply, a district court need not 'suspend reality or shelve common sense in determining whether the face of a complaint … establishes the jurisdictional amount…. Instead, courts may use their judicial experience and common sense in determining whether the case stated in a complaint meets federal jurisdictional requirements.'").

Yavon Martin and Elizabeth Martinez, Plaintiffs, v. J.C. Penney Corporation, Inc., Yesennia Bolanos, Kenneth Fingerman, John Pena, and David Rodriguez, Defendants.

No. 13-CV-1985.

United States District Court, E.D. New York.

28 F.Supp.3d 153 (2014)

Signed June 9, 2014.

Filed June 10, 2014.

Anthony Patrick Malecki, Ayanna Tamara Blake, Daniela Elizabeth Nanau, Michael J. Borrelli, Alexander T. Coleman, Law Offices of Borrelli & Associates, Great Neck, NY, for Plaintiffs. Steven F. Goldstein, Gina M. Arnedos, Steven F. Goldstein, LLP, Carle Place, NY, for Defendant.

MEMORANDUM AND ORDER

JACK B. WEINSTEIN, Senior District Judge:

I. Introduction

Plaintiffs Yavon Martin and Elizabeth Martinez assert claims against defendants J.C. Penney Corporation, Inc. ("J.C. Penney"), Yesennia Bolanos, Kenneth Fingerman, John Pena, and David Rodriguez for violations of 42 U.S.C. § 1981, New York State Human Rights Law, the New York City Administrative Code, and state tort law resulting from the detention and questioning of plaintiffs on suspicion of shoplifting.

Defendants have moved for summary judgment with respect to plaintiffs' state and federal discrimination claims on the following grounds: (1) plaintiffs were not treated differently than other J.C. Penney shoppers, (2) plaintiffs were not prevented from purchasing merchandise, (3) the court lacks jurisdiction over the NYHRL and NYCHRL claims, and (4) there is no proof of discrimination. The motion does not address plaintiffs' state law tort claims.

Because there are questions of material fact, defendants' motion for summary judgment on plaintiffs' discrimination claims is denied. Trial will commence on November 3, 2014. *See* Scheduling Order, June 9, 2014.

II. Facts

Plaintiffs' discrimination claims stem from an incident at a J.C. Penney store in Queens, New York on October 22, 2012.

Plaintiffs are "dark-skinned females who dress in stereotypically male attire." Pl.'s Rule 56.1(b) Counter Statement ("Pl.'s Rule 56.1(b)") ¶ 110, ECF No. 40. At the time of the incident in question, Martin held herself out as a male and is currently investigating the surgical process of transitioning from female to male. *Id.* ¶¶ 9, 11; *see also* Def.'s Rule 56.1(b) Statement ("Def.'s Rule 56.1(b)"). It is undisputed that both plaintiffs were in defendants' J.C. Penney store on October 22, 2012, dressed in masculine attire. Compl. ¶ 15; Def.'s Mem. in Supp. of Def.'s Mot. for Summ. J. ("Def.'s Mem.") I, ECF No. 34.

Plaintiffs arrived at the J.C. Penney store around 3:00 or 3:30 p.m. *See* Pl.'s Rule 56.1(b) ¶ 14; Def.'s Rule 56.1(b) ¶ 14. They spent fifteen to twenty minutes shopping in the men's department, before taking selected items into the fitting room in the men's department. *See* Pl.'s Rule 56.1(b) ¶ 16, 46, 49; Def.'s Rule 56.1(b) ¶ 16–20.

Shortly after plaintiffs entered the store, individual defendants Pena and Bolanos, J.C. Penney loss prevention specialists, began watching them as they shopped for merchandise. Pl.'s Rule 56.1(b) ¶ 8.1; Pena assumed plaintiffs were male and Bolanos admitted some confusion as to their genders. *Id.* ¶¶ 62, 105. Both Pena and Bolanos testified that they made the determination that plaintiffs were not white, but were unable to identify their races. *Id.* ¶¶ 68, 69, 104.

Plaintiffs were observed picking up between four and six items of merchandise prior to entering the fitting rooms. *Id.* ¶ 111. Pena and Bolanos testified that they created a list of the merchandise plaintiffs brought into the fitting room with them. *Id.* ¶ 113. Pena contacted the third loss prevention specialist, defendant Rodriguez, requesting assistance with two "males" who entered the fitting room. *Id.* ¶ 115. Pena followed plaintiffs into the fitting room area, while Bolanos watched from the camera room. *Id.* ¶ 114.

Plaintiffs exited the fitting rooms, leaving some merchandise with the attendant, including at least one shirt. *Id.* ¶ 116. Pena searched the fitting rooms and testified to finding price tags left behind. *Id.* ¶ 117. None of the defendants could recall what merchandise the price tags matched or whether they created a record of the tags that were recovered. *Id.* While Pena searched the fitting rooms, Bolanos watched plaintiffs exit the fitting rooms with approximately three items on a surveillance camera. *Id.* ¶ 118.

Plaintiffs testified that they discarded several items on shelves and racks prior to exiting the store. Pena recovered some of these items. *Id.* ¶¶ 119-122. Defendants Pena and Bolanos determined that more than one item of merchandise was missing and, despite being unable to identify the specific missing item or items, made a determination to detain plaintiffs. *Id.* ¶ 123.

Pena and Rodriguez stopped plaintiffs just outside the entrance to J.C. Penney and demanded that they return to the store. *Id.* ¶¶ 26, 52, 126. Plaintiffs allege Pena and Rodriguez proceeded to grab Martinez by the arm and grab Martin by the shoulder and force them back into the store. *Id.* ¶ 130.

Plaintiffs were led past customers and employees to the security office in the back of the store. *Id.* ¶ 132. Defendant Bolanos was in the security office when plaintiffs arrived. *Id.* ¶ 132.

They allege that defendants patted them down, emptied the contents of their bags, and required them to strip off layers of their clothing to search for the missing merchandise. *Id.* ¶ 133–34. Plaintiffs contend that they attempted to tell defendants where they had left the merchandise in the store but were detained by defendants for almost an hour. *Id.* ¶ 135.

Eventually the manager, defendant Fingerman, entered the security office and told the plaintiffs that they were free to leave. *Id.* ¶¶ 35, 82, 136.

J.C. Penney's requires a five-step process be followed prior to its loss prevention specialists detaining a suspected shoplifter: (1) shoplifter must enter an area where merchandise is located; (2) suspect must select merchandise from store; (3) suspect must conceal merchandise in some manner; (4) specialist must maintain observation of the suspect and merchandise; (5) suspect must pass all points of sale and exit the store. *Id.* ¶ 124. Plaintiffs allege defendants "grossly deviated from their own policies and failed to follow the five-step process" with respect to plaintiffs by failing to determine what items were missing or concealed prior to detaining them. *Id.* ¶ 125.

III. Burden of Proof

Summary judgment is appropriate if "there is no genuine issue as to any material fact and if the moving party is entitled to judgment as a matter of law." Anderson v. Liberty Lobby, Inc., 477 U.S.

242, 250, 106 S.Ct. 2505, 91 L.Ed.2d 202 (1986); see for example, *Mitchell v. Washingtonville Cent. Sch. Dist.*, 190 F.3d 1, 5 (2d Cir.1999). If, after construing the evidence in the light most favorable to the nonmoving party and drawing all reasonable inferences in its favor, there is no genuine issue as to any material fact and the movant is entitled to a judgment as a matter of law, summary judgment is warranted. Fed.R.Civ.P. 56(a); see Anderson, 477 U.S. at 247-50, 255, 106 S.Ct. 2505.

Evidence offered to demonstrate a genuine dispute regarding a material fact must consist of more than "conclusory allegations, speculation or conjecture." *Cifarelli v. Vill. of Babylon*, 93 F.3d 47, 51 (2d Cir.1996); see *Del. & Hudson Ry. v. Consol. Rail Corp.*, 902 F.2d 174, 178 (2d Cir.1990) ("Conclusory allegations will not suffice to create a genuine issue"). "If the non-movant fails to come forth with evidence sufficient to permit a reasonable juror to return a verdict in his or her favor on an essential element of the claim, summary judgment is granted." *Guisto v. Stryker Corp.*, 293 F.R.D. 132 (E.D.N.Y. 2013) (*quoting Burke v. Jacoby*, 981 F.2d 1372, 1379 (2d Cir.1992)); *see for example, Anderson*, 477 U.S. at 248-49, 106 S.Ct. 2505.

IV. Federal Law Section 1981 Claim

A. Law

To establish an equal benefits claim under 42 U.S.C. § 1981, a plaintiff must allege facts supporting the following elements: "(1) the plaintiff is a member of a racial minority; (2) an intent to discriminate on the basis of race by the defendant; and (3) the discrimination concerned one or more of the activities enumerated in the statute (i.e., make and enforce contracts, sue and be sued, give evidence, etc.)." *Mian v. Donaldson, Lufkin & Jenrette Sec. Corp.*, 7 F.3d 1085, 1087 (2d Cir.1993); *Brown v. City of Oneonta*, 221 F.3d 329, 339 (2d Cir.2000).

Section 1981(a) provides in relevant part that:

> All persons within the jurisdiction of the United States shall have the same right in every State and Territory to make and enforce contracts, to sue, be parties, give evidence, and *to the full and equal benefit of all laws and proceedings for the* **security** *of persons and property as is enjoyed by white citizens,* and shall be subject to like punishment, pains, penalties, taxes, licenses, and exactions of every kind, and to no other.

42 U.S.C.A. § 1981 (West) (emphasis added). The Second Circuit has broadly construed section 1981's equal benefit clause as applying to "racially motivated torts that deprive a plaintiff of the equal protection of laws or proceedings for the **security** of persons and property." *Phillip, supra*, 316 F.3d 291, 297-98 (2d Cir.2003); *see Jones v. J.C. Penney's Dep't Stores, Inc.*, 03-CV920A, 2007 WL 1577758 (W.D.N.Y. May 31, 2007) *aff'd sub nom. Jones v. J.C. Penny's Dep't Stores Inc.*, 317 Fed.Appx. 71 (2d Cir.2009).

B. Application of Law to Facts

Plaintiffs contend defendants violated section 1981's "equal benefit" clause by subjecting them to false imprisonment, assault and battery because of their race. J.C. Penney argues that the equal benefit claim must be dismissed because plaintiffs cannot demonstrate that they were targeted by J.C. Penney employees because of race.

Plaintiffs' allegations that defendants assaulted, battered, and falsely imprisoned them on suspicion of shoplifting because of the color of their skin fall within the ambit of "laws or proceedings for the security of persons and property" protected by 1981's equal benefit clause. Phillip, 316 F.3d at 297-98; see *Jones v. J.C. Penney's Dept. Stores, Inc.*, 2007 WL 1577758, at *18 (W.D.N.Y. May 31, 2007) (holding allegations that store defendants racially discriminated against plaintiff by arresting and prosecuting for shoplifting because of race supported a claim for violation of full and equal benefit of the laws under § 1981 so long as defendants' challenged actions constitute a tort); *Chapman v. Higbee Co.*, 319 F.3d 825, 833 (6th Cir.2003) (holding store security officer's decision to stop and search African American customer for shoplifting was racially motivated and supported customer's claim under § 1981 equal benefit clause); *See Pierre v. J.C. Penney Co. Inc.*, 340 F. Supp.2d 308 (E.D.N.Y 2004) (holding black customer's allegations that retail store security guards accused her of shoplifting, detained her, and attempted to force her to sign a false confession because of her race stated claim under § 1981 equal benefit clause based on alleged violations of state laws against assault and battery and false imprisonment).

Disputed issues of material fact exist with respect to defendants' discriminatory intent in detaining plaintiffs as suspected shoplifters. "A finding of discriminatory intent is a finding of fact, as are findings of discrimination, and causation." *Tolbert v. Queens Coll.*, 242 F.3d 58, 70 (2d Cir.2001) (internal citations omitted). "An invidious discriminatory purpose may often be inferred from the totality of the relevant facts." *Id.* A reasonable jury could conclude based on defendants' surveillance of plaintiffs and *1 5 8 their alleged failure to conform with store policy that plaintiffs were intentionally discriminated against based on the color of their skin.158

V. State and City Law Claims

A. Law

1. Election of Remedies

NYSHRL and NYCHRL each contain an election of remedies provision. When a plaintiff pursues a complaint with the State Division on Human Rights regarding an alleged discriminatory practice, they are barred from maintaining a separate action under state law. See N.Y. Exec. Law § 297(9); N.Y. Admin. Code § 8-502; *McPherson v. Plaza Athenee, NYC*, 2012 WL 3865154, 2012 U.S. Dist. LEXIS 127822 (S.D.N.Y. September 4, 2012) (*citing N.Y.C.* Admin. Code § 8-502(a)).

2. Race Discrimination

Claims of race discrimination pursuant to the accommodation provisions of NYSHRL and NYCHRL are subject to the same analysis as a claim of race discrimination under Section 1981, although those brought under the NYCHRL may be construed more liberally. *See Drayton v. Toys "R" Us Inc.*, 645 F.Supp.2d 149, 163-64 (S.D.N.Y.2009); N.Y.C. Admin. Code § 8-130; *Williams v. New York City Housing Authority*, 61 A.D.3d 62, 67-68, 872 N.Y.S.2d 27 (1st Dep't 2009) ("The provisions of this title shall be construed liberally for the accomplishment of the uniquely broad and remedial purposes thereof....").

3. Sex and Gender Discrimination

Unlike Section 1981, the accommodation provisions of NYSHRL and NYCHRL protect against discrimination on the basis of sex and gender, respectively.

The public accommodation provision of the NYSHRL protects against discrimination "because of age, race, creed, color, national origin, sexual orientation, military status, sex, marital status, or disability." N.Y. Exec. Law § 291(2).

The NSCHRL public accommodation provision protects against discrimination on the basis of "actual or perceived race, creed, color, national origin, age, gender, disability, marital status, sexual orientation or alienage or citizenship status." N.Y.C. Admin. Code § 107(4)(a). "The term 'gender' shall include actual or perceived sex and shall also include a person's gender identity, self-image, appearance, behavior or expression, whether or not that gender identity, self-image, appearance, behavior or *Martin v. JC Penney Corp., Inc.*, 28 F. Supp. 3d 153—Dist. Court, ED expression is different from that traditionally associated with the legal sex assigned to that person at birth." N.Y.C. Admin. Code § 8-102.

B. Application of Law to Facts

Plaintiffs bring claims under the accommodation provisions of NYSHRL and NYCHRL for discrimination based on sex/gender and on race.

They filed a complaint with the State Division on Human Rights for the same alleged acts of discriminatory conduct by defendants as brought in the instant action seeking money damages. *See* DHR Compl., April 15, 2013, ECF No. 33, Ex. F. The instant action, however, was filed before any complaint with the division was filed. *See* Compl., April 8, 2013, ECF No. 1. The election of remedies provisions in NYSHRL and NYCHRL do not apply to plaintiffs who initiate their suit prior to asserting a claim with the division. Plaintiffs have not violated the election of remedies provisions and are not foreclosed from bringing this suit.

With respect to their sex and gender claims, plaintiffs are in the unusual position of being females alleging that they were discriminated against for being male. Their claims are premised on allegations that they were discriminated against because of their perceived male sex, rather than their actual female sex.

Plaintiffs state cognizable gender discrimination claims under NYCHRL's broad protections against discrimination based on "actual or perceived" gender, where gender is defined as "actual or perceived sex." N.Y. Exec. Law § 291(2).

Plaintiffs also state valid claims for sex discrimination under NYSHRL. Unlike the NYCHRL, the language of the accommodation provision in the NYSHRL does not explicitly provide protection for "actual or perceived" sex. It simply prohibits discrimination "because of sex." Since the statute is to be "construed liberally" to accomplish its purpose, defendants should not be permitted to avoid responsibility for some discriminatory acts motivated by sex and not others. N.Y. Exec. Law § 290. Discrimination based on an individual's perceived sex is discrimination "because of sex" in the same way that discrimination based on an individual's actual sex is.

For the reasons stated above, *see supra* Part IV., material issues of fact exist as to plaintiffs' discriminatory intent in detaining plaintiffs. A reasonable jury could conclude that plaintiffs were intentionally discriminated against based on the color of their skin and their perceived male sex.

VI. Conclusion

Defendants' motion for summary judgment is denied.

SO ORDERED.

State v. Buswell

460 N.W.2d 614 (1990)

STATE of Minnesota, Petitioner, Appellant, v. Jeffrey Scott BUSWELL, Gary Leek Schwartzman, and Dale Jay Schmidt, Respondents.

Nos. C5-89-555, CX-89-1166 and C5-89-1169.

Supreme Court of Minnesota.

August 31, 1990.

Rehearing Denied October 8, 1990.

Hubert H. Humphrey, III, Atty. Gen., William F. Klumpp, Jr., Asst. Atty. Gen., St. Paul, and Stephen C. Rathke, Crow Wing County Atty., Brainerd, for appellant.

Robert W. Owens, Jr., Heuer & Associates, Minneapolis, for Jeffrey Buswell.

Steven J. Meshbesher, John J. Leunig, Meshbesher, Birrell & Dunlap, Minneapolis, for Gary Schwartzmann.

Richard D. Genty, Winsted, for Dale Schmidt.

Heard, considered and decided by the court en banc.

KELLEY, Justice.

Resolution of this case requires that we examine the extent to which searches of motor vehicles that turn up contraband seized by private security guards, who later turn the contraband over to government authorities for use in criminal prosecutions, constitute governmental actions subject to the limitations on unreasonable search and seizure of the Fourth Amendment to the United States Constitution. In denying the respondents' motions to suppress the contraband seized by private security guards, the trial court ruled that, on the facts of these cases, the search and seizure of the contraband was the product of a private search and, therefore, not subject to Fourth Amendment constraints against unreasonable searches and seizures. The court of appeals disagreed. It held that there was sufficient governmental involvement in the search to transform it into government action, and remanded the case to the trial court for determination of whether the searches were reasonable. State v. Buswell, 449 N.W.2d 471 (Minn. App.1989).

Because the determination of whether sufficient governmental involvement exists to transform a private search into governmental action is a question of fact to be determined by the trial court, *United States v. Koenig*, 856 F.2d 843, 847 (7th Cir.1988); *United States v. Walther*, 652 F.2d 788, 791 (9th Cir.1981), and because we are unable to conclude that the trial court's holding that each of the searches here was private was clearly erroneous, we reverse the court of appeals, reinstate the trial court's orders refusing to suppress the evidence, and affirm the convictions of these respondents.

The Brainerd International Raceway (BIR) operates an automobile racetrack on private property approximately six miles outside the City of Brainerd in Crow Wing County, Minnesota. The BIR was not within the jurisdiction of the City of Brainerd. In 1988 BIR contracted for security services at the track during the summer racing season with a company called North Country Security. Keith Emerson, whose primary employment was as a member of the City of Brainerd police force, owned and operated North Country Security. At the time, all City of Brainerd police officers, including Emerson, held appointments as special deputies for Crow Wing County. However, none of the Brainerd police officers, including Emerson, had independent powers of arrest outside the city limits of Brainerd except as directed by the Crow Wing County Sheriff or by a regularly deputized sheriff.

*616 In 1988 North Country Security's contract with BIR called for North Country Security to be paid a set figure for security on a given race weekend. In return, it was North Country

Security's responsibility to hire guards and manage all security arrangements at the track during a race meet. The weekend commencing August 18, 1988, was the largest weekend of that year's racing season; approximately 78,000 persons attended the raceway between Thursday and Sunday. North Country Security employed 127 guards, only six or seven of whom were licensed police officers employed in any governmental jurisdiction, to provide security during this meet. None of the off-duty police officers employed that weekend were from law enforcement agencies having any jurisdiction covering the Brainerd International Raceway.

In May 1988, before the commencement of BIR's 1988 racing season, Emerson had conferred in general terms with the Crow Wing County Sheriff and the local Minnesota Bureau of Criminal Apprehension agent relative to procedures to be employed for making arrests should security guards of North Country Security uncover illegal activity during a race meet. This conference resulted in agreement that if any incident encountered by North Country Security guards seemed to warrant an arrest for a crime, Emerson would first be notified, and, he, in turn, would decide whether to call in official law enforcement agencies. The arrangement was strictly procedural. No agreement was made relating to the type or number of searches by security personnel, nor were any official law enforcement personnel assigned to be present at the BIR during a race meet. However, if Emerson decided to report discovered criminal activity, a specific deputy or agent was "on call" to respond to the report.

Part of the responsibility of North Country Security on a race weekend was to see that only ticket holders entered the raceway grounds. North Country Security attempted to discharge that duty generally, and specifically on the weekend of August 18, 1988, by randomly stopping and searching vehicles seeking entry to the raceway to look for "stowaways."

After the gates were opened on August 18, 1988, a number of vehicles, including those operated by these respondents, were searched by security guards before being permitted to enter the grounds. The primary motivation for the searches was to insure that persons without admission tickets not enter the track; a secondary reason was to prevent illegal drugs from entering the premises, and to keep other contraband such as mopeds and fireworks out of the race track grounds.[1] No written warning was given to entrants that their vehicles might be searched for "stowaways" or illegal drugs, firecrackers or other prohibited items. However, Emerson had established a policy for North Country Security employees that before a search took place, occupants of vehicles were to be provided an option to refuse to consent to a search and not enter the track premises.

Security guard Bruce Gateley, who was not an off-duty public police officer licensed or employed as a law enforcement officer in any jurisdiction, actually conducted the searches of the vehicles occupied by the respondents. At the time of the search of each vehicle he was wearing North Country Security standard uniform and was carrying a sidearm and handcuffs. Before making each search, however, contrary to the policy established by Emerson, Gateley failed to secure consent to the search or inform the occupants of the option to refuse.

*617 On August 18, 1988, his procedure was to inform the occupants of each vehicle that the purpose of a search was to spot "stowaways," after which he proceeded to search the inside of the vehicle. This procedure was followed when he searched Respondent Schmidt's pick-up camper. After entering the camper, Gateley found no "stowaways," but did open a small closet in which a fishing tackle box which contained what appeared to be cocaine was located. Thereupon Gateley handcuffed Schmidt to a fence, and contacted Emerson, who himself notified law enforcement officers pursuant to the protocol previously established in May of 1988.

Using the same procedure, Gateley later stopped and searched a converted Greyhound bus occupied by Respondents Buswell and Schwartzman. While searching the bus for nonpaying persons, Gateley found cocaine, marijuana, and other drug paraphernalia in one of the closets.

Both Schwartzman and Buswell were likewise handcuffed to the fence, and Emerson was again contacted so he could inform law enforcement officials of the situation.

The law enforcement official notified by Emerson was Crow Wing County Deputy Sheriff Bjerga, who, with other officers, responded by going to the race track. After further investigation they arrested all three respondents and charged them with possession of controlled substances.

After the trial court had denied the respondents' motions to suppress the drugs seized in the search, the parties by agreement submitted the cases to the trial court on stipulated facts. The respondents were adjudged to be guilty and subsequently sentenced. This appeal followed.

The limited issue presented by this appeal is whether the trial court's ruling that the searches were not governmental actions subject to the constraints of the Fourth Amendment to the United States Constitution was clearly erroneous.

Before addressing that issue, however, we deem it appropriate to note and briefly discuss a related but nondeterminative issue; to wit, whether the conduct of Gateley, had he been a governmental law enforcement official at the time, would have violated the "unreasonable searches and seizures" clause of the Fourth Amendment, thereby rendering the contraband seized subject to suppression. We have not the slightest doubt that these searches, which can charitably be characterized as being "outrageous," would violate the Fourth Amendment and result in suppression had they been made by one exercising governmental action. See, *Mapp v. Ohio*, 367 U.S. 643, 655, 81 S. Ct. 1684, 1691, 6 L. Ed. 2d 1081 (1961); see also *State v. Mitchell*, 285 Minn. 153, 172 N.W.2d 66, 73 (1969) (marijuana seized by police subsequent to a warrantless, unconstitutional search of an entire house was suppressed). Indeed, the state concedes that if the searches by Gateley constituted state action, the Fourth Amendment rights of these respondents were violated.[2]

However, no matter how egregious the conduct of Gateley in making these searches, the contraband was properly admitted into evidence if, at the time, he enjoyed the status of a private citizen. The Fourth Amendment was intended as a restraint upon the activities of the government. It was never intended to be a limitation upon other than governmental agencies. *Burdeau v. McDowell*, 256 U.S. 465, 475, 41 S. Ct. 574, 576, 65 L. Ed. 1048 (1921). Thus, a private search, even if unreasonable, *618 will not result in evidence seized being suppressed because there is no constitutional violation. *United States v. Jacobsen*, 466 U.S. 109, 113, 104 S. Ct. 1652, 1656, 80 L. Ed. 2d 85 (1984); *United States v. Pryba*, 502 F.2d 391, 397-398, n. 39, 40, 42 (D.C.Cir.1974).[3]

However, the mere fact that a private individual made the search and seized the contraband does not always isolate his or her conduct from Fourth Amendment scrutiny. If, "in the light of all the circumstances of the case" the private individual "must be regarded as having acted as an instrument or agent of the state" when conducting the search, the search is subject to Fourth Amendment constraints. *Skinner v. Railway Executives Ass'n*, 489 U.S. 602, 109 S. Ct. 1402, 1411, 103 L. Ed. 2d 639 (1989); *Coolidge v. New Hampshire*, 403 U.S. 443, 487, 91 S. Ct. 2022, 2048, 29 L. Ed. 2d 564 (1971). The determination of whether the private person acted as an agent of the state is one of fact to be decided on a case-by-case basis after consideration of all the facts and circumstances relative to the search. *Skinner v. United States*, 489 U.S. at ____, 109 S. Ct. at 1411; *United States v. Koenig*, 856 F.2d 843 (7th Cir.1988); *United States v. Walther*, 652 F.2d 788, 791 (9th Cir.1981). "Whether a private party should be deemed an agent or instrument of the government for Fourth Amendment purposes necessarily turns on the degree of the government's participation in the private party's activities." *Skinner*, 489 U.S. at ____, 109 S. Ct. at 1411.

Federal courts have considered a variety of factors to determine whether government participation recasts the private individual as an instrument or agent of the state. In *United States v. Walther*, 652 F.2d 788 (9th Cir.1981), the Ninth Circuit stressed two "critical factors": (1) whether the government knew of and acquiesced in the search and (2) whether the search was conducted to assist law enforcement efforts or to further the private party's own ends. Walther, 652 F.2d at 792. Other circuits have adopted the Walther critical factor analysis either in whole or in part. See, for example, *United States v. Pierce*, 893 F.2d 669, 673 (5th Cir.1990); *Pleasant v. Lovell*, 876 F.2d 787, 797 (10th Cir.1989); *United States v. Feffer*, 831 F.2d 734, 739 (7th Cir.1987).[4]

These Walther criteria, as well as criteria suggested by other cases, are helpful in that they direct the trial court to focus on the significance and impact of the government's involvement in the search. The concern is whether the conduct of the government was such as to make the actions of a private individual the government's actions for the purpose of a Fourth Amendment analysis. Although the criteria set forth in Walther are helpful, the diversity in factual settings involving private searches mandates an individual case-by-case analysis in which precedent plays but a small part. As previously noted, final determination of whether the government's involvement was such as to transform a private search into a governmental search subject to the constraints of the Fourth Amendment is a question of fact to be resolved by the trial court. Moreover, such factual determinations will be reversed only if clearly erroneous. *United States v. Walther*, 652 F.2d *619 788 (1981) (dictum); *United States v. Botero*, 589 F.2d 430, 433 (9th Cir.1978), cert. denied 441 U.S. 944, 99 S. Ct. 2162, 60 L. Ed. 2d 1045 (1979); *United States v. Koenig*, 856 F.2d 843, 849 (7th Cir.1988); *United States v. Feffer*, 831 F.2d 734 (7th Cir. 1987).

Respondents advance several arguments in support of their contention that Gateley and North Country Security were acting as instruments or agents of the state when the searches and seizures were made. We examine these arguments keeping in mind the two factor Walther test and watching for clear indices of significant government involvement which would convert the conduct of the BIR security force into government action. First, respondents contend that the May meeting between Emerson and Crow Wing County law enforcement officials at which arrest procedures were formulated indicates that the state knew of, ordered, encouraged, and acquiesced in the vehicle searches by North County Security guards, and, therefore, the guards were instruments or agents of the government. In advancing this argument, respondents rely, in part, upon Walther, 652 F.2d 788, where the court concluded that an airline employee who had seized an overnight case, found drugs upon opening it, and then contacted narcotic agents from the Drug Enforcement Agency, who then arrested the owner, was an instrument of the government. There, unlike the cases before us today, the airline employee had been a paid Drug Enforcement Agency informant for at least five years before the search and expected compensation for the search there at issue.

Contrasted to Walther, the facts surrounding the searches here differ dramatically. The records in these cases contain nothing to indicate that law enforcement officials did anything to persuade North Country Security employees to conduct searches in any particular manner, or to search for any particular items.[5] Law enforcement personnel did know that searches for stowaways would occur at entry gates. But, nothing in the record indicates that law enforcement officials knew the searches would violate BIR policy and be conducted without first obtaining the consent of the vehicle occupants. Furthermore, not only is the record devoid of evidence that law enforcement officials were aware of or encouraged the specific searches in question, but apparently, similar searches resulting in an arrest had not occurred during the 1988 racing season. The record contains not one reference to any search which occurred between the May meeting and the August 18, 1988 race at which Gateley, or any other officer searched for, found, or turned over contraband to law enforcement officials, or any evidence that he received, or even expected, compensation for so doing. In short, unlike Walther, there is no indication that Gateley or North County Security conducted the searches with the government's objectives in mind. The government in no way "knew of" or "acquiesced in" the search. Walther, 652 F.2d at 792.

Mere antecedent contact between law enforcement and a private party is inadequate to trigger the application of the exclusionary remedy under the Fourth Amendment. *United States v. Coleman*, 628 F.2d 961, 965 (6th Cir.1980). It is only when the government takes some type of initiative or steps to promote the search, that a private citizen is deemed to be an agent or instrument of the government. *Pleasant v. Lovell*, 876 F.2d 787, 796-97 (10th Cir.1989). But when the extent of governmental involvement amounts to no more than responding to requests for arrests and discussions concerning arrest procedure, the Fourth Amendment exclusionary sanctions are not triggered. See, for example, *United States v. Koenig*, 856 F.2d 843 (7th Cir.1988); *United States v. Ramirez*, *620 810 F.2d 1338 (5th Cir.) cert. denied, 484 U.S. 844, 108 S. Ct. 136, 98 L. Ed. 2d 93 (1987); *State v. Sanders*, 185 N.J.Super. 258, 448 A.2d 481 (App.Div.1982); *United States v. Capra*, 372 F. Supp. 609 (S.D.N.Y. 1974).

Respondents next focus upon the status of Emerson, whose primary employment was as a City of Brainerd police officer. They suggest that the government cannot avoid the constraints of the Fourth Amendment by directing a third party to perform an illegal search. See, for example, *United States v. West*, 453 F.2d 1351, 1356 (3rd Cir.1972). This argument fails for two reasons. First, Emerson was not acting as a government agent; his duties at the BIR were not those of a government law enforcement agent. At the BIR he had only the power to make a citizen's arrest because he was outside the jurisdiction in which he had any authority as a licensed public officer. The two jobs were distinctly separated. See, for example, *United States v. McGreevy*, 652 F.2d 849 (9th Cir.1981); *Commonwealth v. Leone*, 386 Mass. 329, 334-36, 435 N.E.2d 1036, 1048-41 (1982).

Furthermore, nothing in the records of these cases suggests that Emerson directed a third party, the security guards, to conduct searches without first asking consent of the vehicle occupants, or to exceed the scope of that consent given, or to look for contraband outside the area in plain view. To the contrary, the evidence indicates Emerson's policy was to ask vehicle occupants if guards could conduct a search, inform the occupants of the scope of the search, and inform the occupants that if the search was refused, the search would not be conducted and the vehicle occupants would be prevented from entering the raceway. In other words, no evidence points to Emerson as the original instigator of the searches. The evidence seems clear that it was the race track management who requested vehicle searches for nonpaying attenders, and for other items that might be used to disrupt the raceway weekend program. These facts support the trial court's implicit findings that there was no significant government involvement in these searches.

That being so, we could end our analysis at this point. However, we proceed to examine the trial court's findings that the searches were conducted by private persons and were for private rather than governmental purposes. This leads us to consider the second Walther factor an analysis of the purpose of the search to see if the trial court's conclusion that it was private has support in the evidence, keeping in mind that searches conducted for private purposes which turn up evidence of crime do not turn into state action merely because that evidence is later turned over to law enforcement officials. *United States v. Bulgier*, 618 F.2d 472 (7th Cir.1980). The trial court found legitimate private purposes for the search. Without doubt there exists evidence to support that conclusion. The BIR primarily sought to prevent people for entering the raceway without first paying admission. Additionally, the BIR had legitimate private reasons to prevent illegal drugs, mopeds, and fireworks from entering the raceway in order to minimize disruptive behavior of patrons, to prevent injury to or discomfort of other patrons, and to reduce the possibility of destruction to property.

Accordingly, we are unable to conclude that the trial court arrived at a clearly erroneous finding when it found that the searches and seizures in this case were private and, thus, not subject to

Fourth Amendment constraints.[6] Clearly, evidence *621 existed to support that result. Therefore, we reverse the decision of the court of appeals, and the judgment of the trial court is reinstated.

YETKA, J., files dissenting opinion in which WAHL and KEITH, JJ., join.

YETKA, Justice (dissenting).

Because the security agents here worked as instruments or agents of the state and thus were governed by the fourth amendment's prohibition against unreasonable searches and seizures, I dissent.

The fourth amendment applies to searches and seizures effected by a private party acting "as an instrument or agent of the Government." *Skinner v. Railway Labor Executives Ass'n*, 489 U.S. 602, 109 S. Ct. 1402, 1411, 103 L. Ed. 2d 639 (1989). The degree of government participation in the private party's activities sufficient to make the private party its instrument or agent is a question to be resolved "in light of all the circumstances." *Coolidge v. New Hampshire*, 403 U.S. 443, 487, 91 S. Ct. 2022, 2048, 29 L. Ed. 2d 564 (1971). According to the Supreme Court, the fact that the government did not compel a private party to perform a search does not, by itself, establish that the search is a private one. *Skinner*, 109 S. Ct. at 1411. Rather, fourth amendment protection can apply where the government has done "more than adopt a passive position toward the underlying private conduct." Id.

In *Skinner*, federal regulations authorized, but did not compel, a private railroad to test employees to detect drug and alcohol use. The court found that, by removing legal barriers to testing, pre-empting collective bargaining agreements prohibiting testing, and indicating a strong preference for testing and a desire to share in the fruits of these intrusions, the government encouraged, endorsed and participated in the testing so as to implicate the fourth amendment. Id. at 1412.

Although there is no evidence that the county law enforcement officials compelled North Country Security to search vehicles, as in *Skinner*, they clearly adopted more than a passive position towards this conduct. At their meeting before the race season opened, Emerson, the owner and operator of North Country Security, and county law enforcement officials discussed the search and seizure of controlled substances at the gate of BIR. Emerson testified that the security guards agreed to contact him if they found contraband while searching vehicles for stowaways. Emerson would then call the county officials. They also agreed that the guards would hold persons possessing contraband until county officials arrived. An official was on call to make arrests if Emerson called. In short, the law enforcement officials here, like the government in Skinner, knew that private parties would be conducting searches and raised no legal barriers to these searches or to the prospect of private security guards forcibly holding people at the race track. Indeed, the county officials planned to use the fruits of those searches.

In *Skinner*, the Court discussed as a threshold matter whether the government endorsed searches and, after concluding that the fourth amendment applied, analyzed the validity of those searches. *Skinner*, 109 S. Ct. at 1411-22. The Court did not require the defendants to establish, as the majority suggests the defendants should here, that the government encouraged a particular manner of or objectives for searching people, nor does the Supreme Court require the government to provide incentives to private actors in order to implicate the fourth amendment. Establishing that the county officials knew that there would be security personnel at BIR searching vehicles and detaining people until they arrived is evidence that county officials acquiesced in the searches. This is official state action. Accordingly, I would *622 hold that the security company here acted as an agent of the state and that defendants are entitled to the protection of the fourth amendment.

This same result follows from applying the test set out in *United States v. Walther*, 652 F.2d 788 (9th Cir.1981), and adopted by the majority. Majority Op. at 618. Under this test, courts determine if a private party acts as an agent of the government by considering (1) whether the government knew of and acquiesced in the search and (2) whether the search was conducted to assist law enforcement efforts or to further the private party's own ends. Id. at 792. As discussed above, the government knew of and acquiesced in the searches here. The searches benefited the government as well as BIR. BIR could have fulfilled its security needs simply by denying admittance to the race track. Certainly assisting law enforcement is a commendable practice, but, in this case, it should be exercised within the restraints of the Constitution.

Emerson's status as an experienced police officer and special deputy for the Crow Wing County Sheriff's Department is not essential to finding state action. This fact does, however, lend additional weight to finding state involvement here. Emerson instructed Gately, a North Country security guard, to search every vehicle entering BIR during a 2-hour period the morning of the race. He was close enough to see Gately search defendants' vehicles and handcuff the defendants to a fence. Emerson's close contact with law enforcement officials as an employee raises the concern that his security agents, under his direction, conducted police work and circumvented the Constitution under the guise of private security work. Even though, as the majority notes, Emerson only had the power to make a citizen's arrest at the BIR, searches effected pursuant to that authority are not immune to fourth amendment scrutiny. See *State v. Schinzing*, 342 N.W.2d 105, 108-11 (Minn.1983); *State v. Filipi*, 297 N.W.2d 275, 277-79 (Minn. 1980).

Significant policy considerations underlie this issue. I agree with the Supreme Court of California that "searches by private security forces can involve a particularly serious threat to privacy." *People v. Zelinski*, 24 Cal. 3d 357, 365, 155 Cal. Rptr. 575, 579, 594 P.2d 1000, 1004 (1979). First, it seems to me incongruous to give private individuals who do not receive the equivalent training of official police forces broader authority to make searches and seizures than police officials themselves. Second, here, the security guards were clad in a police-like uniform, including a hat, badge, shoulder patches and belt with a flashlight. Gately also carried handcuffs and a sidearm. The security guards looked like and were acting like law enforcement officials. Private investigators and security guards who regularly engage in the "public function" of law enforcement should be subject to fourth amendment constraints. See *Marsh v. Alabama*, 326 U.S. 501, 66 S. Ct. 276, 90 L. Ed. 265 (1946) (company-owned town acting in a public function subject to first amendment constraints); 1 W. LaFave, Search and Seizure § 1.8(d) at 200 (2d ed. 1987).

In general, it is important to note that the Constitution itself would not have been ratified if the original drafters had not promised to write the Bill of Rights. The colonists took the language in our Bill of Rights from a 700-year history of English law and were determined to put in writing fundamental rights upon which the government cannot infringe. They did not intend to leave these fundamental rights to chance, interpretation or an unwritten constitution such as the British still have. I am concerned that the majority opinion, in effect, waters down the Bill of Rights. The Bill of Rights should be changed by amending the Constitution itself, not by judicial interpretation.

As the majority acknowledges, the action taken by the security agents in searching the vehicles would undoubtedly violate the fourth amendment to the United States Constitution if performed by law enforcement *623 officials. Majority Op. at 617-618. Because I would find that North Country Security acted as an agent of Crow County law enforcement officials, I would affirm the court of appeals.

WAHL, Justice (dissenting).

I join the dissent of Justice Yetka.

KEITH, Justice (dissenting).

I join the dissent of Justice Yetka.

NOTES

1. Crowd and patron conduct is difficult to control during a race of this magnitude, involving tens of thousands of patrons and extending over several days. In authorizing searches for illegal drugs, mopeds and fireworks, BIR hoped to minimize incidents that might result in damage to patrons or property. Although not specifically involving illegal drugs, fireworks, or small motorized vehicles, the "flavor" of the type of conduct some patrons engage in after overuse of mood altering substances (there alcohol), thereby endangering not only themselves, but, as well, other patrons, is presented in *Rieger v. Zackoski*, 321 N.W.2d 16 (Minn.1982). See also *State v. Borden*, 455 N.W.2d 482 (Minn.App. 1990). ⋅

2. Originally the state took the position (1) that each respondent had consented to the search made and (2) that Gateley found the illegal contraband in plain view during each search. Both arguments were patently meritless and the latter was absolutely opprobrious. The evidence revealed that under the guise of looking for "stowaways," Gateley opened a small closet of Schmidt's camper and saw a closed fishing tackle box which, when opened, contained the drugs found. Similarly, during a search of a small closet in the bus, Gateley found drugs and drug paraphernalia. It would have been obvious to anyone that neither closet (or the tackle box) could hide a "stowaway," moped, or any other sizable items that the BIR had an interest in excluding from the track premises. Later, at oral argument the state altered its position, and conceded that if the searches constituted state action, suppression of the contraband would have been proper under the exclusionary rules.

3. Our analysis today is limited to the public-private search dichotomy which, as indicated in the cases cited in the body of the opinion, arises from the Fourth Amendment to the United States Constitution. We do not reach the issue of whether this search violated Art. I, § 10 of the Minnesota Constitution. That issue has neither been raised nor discussed on appeal, and at the trial court level, at least one respondent failed to move that the evidence be suppressed under the Minnesota Constitution. We note, however, that Art. I, § 10 of the Minnesota Constitution like its federal counterpart, the Fourth Amendment, purports to constrain only unreasonable searches by governmental authority.

4. In *United States v. Luciow*, 518 F.2d 298 (8th Cir.1975), the Eighth Circuit seemingly stressed a different factor, to wit, that before a private individual's action can be attributed to the government, some degree of government instigation of the search must be shown. Id. at 300 (citing *United States v. Valen*, 479 F.2d 467 (3rd Cir.1973), cert. denied 419 U.S. 901, 95 S. Ct. 185, 42 L. Ed. 2d 147 (1974)). See also *United States v. Coleman*, 628 F.2d 961, 965 (6th Cir.1980) (police did not instigate, encourage, or participate in search).

5. The dissent suggests that at the May meeting Emerson and law enforcement officials "discussed the search and seizure of controlled substances at the gate of BIR." Dissent at D-2. This is somewhat misleading as nothing in the record indicates that searches and seizures of controlled substances at the main gate were specifically discussed. Rather, the group determined that for any incident, not only those dealing with controlled substances, Emerson would be the sole contact with both the Crow Wing County Sheriff's Office and the BCA.

6. As did the court of appeals, we express our concern that egregious searches by private security guards escape the penalty of suppression, whereas similar conduct by licensed law enforcement officers would not. We take notice that private security guards often possess professional police knowledge and skill, and may conduct searches with the goal of obtaining evidence of crime. See, for example, *State v. Keyser*, 117 N.H. 45, 47, 369 A.2d 224, 225 (1977). The court of appeals in its opinion addressed this concern by determining that private security

guards may be subject to Fourth Amendment constraints when they regularly engage in the "public function" of law enforcement. State v. Buswell, 449 N.W.2d at 475. See also *People v. Holloway*, 82 Mich.App. 629, 635, 267 N.W.2d 454, 459-60 (Kaufman, J. concurring). It offends our sense of rationality and proportionality that a person who performs acts similar to a law enforcement official is able to circumvent the constraints of the fourth amendment merely because the private sector pays the bill. But, we cannot ignore the clear line of precedents starting with *Burdeau v. McDowell* which hold that the fourth amendment only gives protection against unlawful government actions.

U.S. v. Charles E. Brooks

Memorandum

Defendant Charles E. Brooks has filed a Motion to Suppress (Docket No. 40), to which the United States filed a Response in opposition (Docket No. 46). On January 22, 2014, the court held an evidentiary hearing concerning the motion. (Docket No. 63.) For the reasons stated herein, the motion will be denied.

Background

Based on the record before the court, including testimony and evidence presented at the January 22, 2014 suppression hearing, the court makes the following findings of fact:

The events relevant to this case took place at the "Fallbrook Apartments" in Nashville, Tennessee ("Fallbrook"). Fallbrook is privately owned by Alco Dellway Partners LP ("Alco"). Although Fallbrook is privately owned, many of its residents receive so-called "Section 8" housing benefits under 42 U.S.C. § 1437f.

As a condition of their lease agreements at Fallbrook, residents of Fallbrook must adhere to a set of "Community Rules," which include the following terms concerning conduct:

5. Conduct

a. The resident(s) on the Lease is responsible not only for their [sic] own actions but the conduct of his/her household members, guest(s), and visitor(s), while in the apartment or on the property. Any violation of these policies, and/or Lease terms is considered noncompliance with the Lease.

....

c. Residents and his/her guest(s) will not engage in, or participate in, such conduct which interferes with the quiet and peaceful enjoyment of the other residents living in the apartment property. No act of a resident and/or guest which threatens, intimidates, is deemed as harassing others, is physically violent with or without injury to another person and/or property, or has unacceptable social conduct, will be tolerated. Residents are responsible for the conduct of their guests. If a guest creates a nuisance or otherwise disturbs other residents at the community, he or she will be required to leave the community immediately. Any such incident(s) will be considered a violation of the Community Rules and the Lease Agreement. Additionally, where applicable, such incidents will be reported to local law enforcement.

d. Acts of intimidation, harassment, including sexual harassment, verbal abuse, physical threat or violence, or social misconduct of, or to, any employee of this apartment property by any person will not be tolerated. Any such incident(s) will be considered a violation of the Community Rules and the Lease Agreement. Additionally, where applicable, such incidents will be reported to local law enforcement.

...

g. Management has the right to ban any person(s) from the premises that is involved in any criminal activity, including but not limited to drug and firearm activity .... Persons evicted for any reason, or who are placed on the criminal trespass list, are not permitted back on the property. If Resident allows such a person to visit, it is grounds for immediate eviction.

(Docket No. 46, Ex. 5 (at pp. 3-4).) The Community Rules also contain a preamble stating that Fallbrook "was developed for the purpose of providing decent, safe, sanitary, and affordable housing," that "each resident is entitled to the exclusive use and enjoyment of their apartment in a peaceful, quiet, and private environment," and that the rules "are not meant to infringe on the rights of any one resident but, rather, to protect the right of all the residents, the owners, managing agents, and the property as a whole." (Id. at p. 1.) The Community Rules state that "[a]ll City, County, State, and Federal Laws apply to each resident, their household members and all guest(s)." (Id.)

To enforce the Community Rules, Alco contracted with a private security firm, Tennessee Protection Agency ("TPA"), which provided security officers for Fallbrook during the relevant time frame. Fallbrook also maintained a "Criminal Trespass List," which listed individuals who would not be allowed on the property because they had engaged in criminal activity or had otherwise engaged in disruptive activity that violated the Community Rules. (See Docket No. 46, Ex. 6 ("Criminal Trespass List").) The TPA security officers possessed a copy of the Criminal Trespass List, which was apparently updated on a rolling basis as necessary.

During the relevant time frame, TPA officers maintained a security checkpoint at the only roadway entrance to Fallbrook during the evening hours. As a general matter, TPA officers would stop cars at the checkpoint, ask for identification of the individuals in the car, and cross-reference those names against the Criminal Trespass List. If an individual in a car was on the Criminal Trespass List, TPA officers would have the individual step out of the car, at which point TPA officers would detain the attempted trespasser until a Metro Nashville Police Department ("MNPD") police officer arrived. Both sides of the gate at the checkpoint contained posted signs stating in large letters that "ALL PERSONS AND VEHICLES ENTERING THIS PROPERTY MAY BE SUBJECT TO SEARCH AT ANY TIME" and that "NO FIREARMS ALLOWED ON THIS PROPERTY." (See Trial Exhibits, Government's Exhibit 2.) The right side of the gate (from the perspective of an entrant) also contained posted signs stating "NO TRESPASSING" and "NOTICE TO VISITORS: ALL PERSONS ENTERING THIS PROPERTY SHOULD PROCEED DIRECTLY TO RESIDENT'S UNIT: NO LOITERING, TRESPASSING, GAMBLING OR ILLEGAL ACTIVITY IS PERMITTED IN THE COMMON AREAS. VIOLATORS WILL BE SUBJECT TO ARREST." (Id.)

The TPA did not, as a matter of course, share the Criminal Trespass List with the MNPD, nor did MNPD attempt to add names to that list. According to MNPD Officer Terry Denton, who was responsible for the East Precinct geographic area encompassing Fallbrook, his interactions with the Fallbrook facility were limited to situations in which the facility alerted him that someone was trespassing on its property. MNPD Lieutenant Doug Vinson, who supervises MNPD officers in the East Precinct, testified that the MNPD does not post officers at Fallbrook, although officers under his command do respond to calls for service related to it. Lieutenant Vinson testified that it is common knowledge that Fallbrook utilizes private security and that the property at Fallbrook is a high crime area. According to police records provided to the court, the MNPD received 4667 emergency calls related to incidents at Fallbrook between September 18, 1998 and September 17, 2013. (See Trial Exhibits, Government's Exhibit 3, CAD Reports (reflecting dispatch calls).)

The record contains no evidence that TPA officers (either generally or specifically in this case) falsely identified themselves as public police officers, nor does the record contain evidence that TPA officers' uniforms or conduct in any way violated applicable provisions of the Tennessee Private Protective Services Licensing and Regulatory Act ("PPSLRA"), which is discussed in the Analysis section herein. The record also indicates that, in compliance with the PPSLRA, TPA security personnel received training classes in concealed weapons and other security matters and that this training included instruction on how to make a "citizen's arrest," when an individual broke the law in the TPA officer's presence.

The incident at issue in this case occurred on November 1, 2012. That night, TPA Officers Charles Black and Smith were running the checkpoint, checking the IDs of the individuals attempting to enter the complex. At approximately 7 p.m., T.S. Springer (the driver), Tashika Davis (a passenger in the front seat), and defendant Brooks (a passenger behind the driver in the back seat) arrived at the checkpoint in a Chrysler Sebring. Davis was a resident of Fallbrook. TPA Officers Black and Smith, who were standing together near a speed bump in front of the gate, stopped the car and approached it, holding their flashlights. The car's driver's side window was down, and the back seat window (closest to Brooks) was partially open. Apparently before he or TPA Officer Smith had a chance to ask for IDs, TPA Officer Black (1) saw Brooks unsuccessfully attempt to dispose of a "blunt" (a marijuana cigarette) by throwing it out of the car window and (2) smelled a marijuana odor coming from the car. Black heard Brooks tell the driver of the car to "go, go, go," at which point Smith moved to place himself in front of the car. Black then saw Brooks shuffling quickly from side-to-side within the back passenger seat, attempting to disguise something in his hand by cupping it out of the officers' line of sight. Black alerted Smith that Brooks had something in his hand, and Brooks therefore drew his weapon as a precautionary measure. Black placed his hand on his own weapon but did not draw it. According to Black, the car stopped. At this point, Black intended to detain the car's occupants until a Metro Nashville police officer could arrive to formally arrest Brooks.

At the same time that this incident was unfolding, MNPD Officer Denton was present at Fallbrook, where he was issuing an unrelated citation in the vicinity of the checkpoint. While he was issuing the citation, MNPD Officer Denton heard Black and Smith and the associated "commotion," at which point Denton moved to assist. Officer Denton arrived within a few seconds and shined his flashlight into the car. Denton shouted at the car's driver to place the car in park. While Denton was shining his flashlight into the car, Officer Smith observed a bag of marijuana and pointed it out to Officer Denton. Officer Denton, Black, and Smith removed the passengers from the car and handcuffed them. Officer Denton formally arrested Brooks.

Another MNPD Officer, Michael Boguskie, arrived and conducted a probable cause search of the car. Upon searching the vehicle, he found the following items: (1) a sandwich bag containing approximately 53 grams of marijuana, (2) a small baggie containing approximately 0.5 grams of marijuana, and (3) a pistol visible in the car's rear floorboard on the driver's side, where Brooks had been seated. Brooks was charged with possession with intent to distribute marijuana and with being a felon in possession of a firearm.

Motion to suppress standard

The Fourth Amendment provides that "[t]he right of the people to be secure in their houses against unreasonable searches and seizures, shall not be violated." U.S. Const. amend. IV. The Fourth Amendment therefore bars the government from conducting unreasonable searches and seizures. *United States v. Moon*, 513 F.3d 527, 537 (6th Cir. 2008). Where the Fourth Amendment applies, "searches 'conducted without a warrant issued upon probable cause [are] per se unreasonable ... subject only to a few specifically established and well-delineated exceptions." *Moon*, 513 F.3d at 537 (quoting *Schneckloth v. Bustamonte*, 412 U.S. 218, 219 (1973)). To redress and deter violations of the Fourth Amendment, courts apply the exclusionary rule and will suppress the fruits of an unconstitutional search or seizure. *Wong Sun v. United States*, 371 U.S. 471, 485 (1963).

The Fourth Amendment, however, does not provide protection against searches by private individuals acting in a private capacity. *United States v. Lambert*, 771 F.2d 83, 89 (6th Cir. 1985) ("[T]he Fourth Amendment proscribes only governmental action and does not apply to a search or seizure, even an unreasonable one, conducted by a private individual not acting as an agent of the government or with the participation or knowledge of any government official."); *United States v. Coleman*, 628 F.2d 961, 965 (6th Cir. 1980) ("[T]he Fourth Amendment proscribes only governmental action, and does not apply to a search or seizure, even an unreasonable one, effected by a private individual not acting as an agent of the government or with the participation or knowledge of any governmental official"); see also *United States v. Smythe*, 84 F.3d 1240, 1243 (10th Cir. 1996) ("Fourth Amendment protection against unreasonable searches and seizures 'is wholly inapplicable to a search or seizure, even an unreasonable one, effected by a private individual.'") (citing *United States v. Jacobsen*, 466 U.S. 109, 113 (1984)); *United States v. Day*, 591 F.3d 679, 683 (4th Cir. 2010). Although the Fourth Amendment typically applies only to governmental actors, courts have recognized that, under certain limited circumstances, searches and seizures by private entities may be imputed to the government. Thus, "if the government coerces, dominates or directs the actions of a private person" conducting the search or seizure, the private person's search or seizure may be "transformed into a governmental search." *Smythe*, 84 F.3d at 1242; see also Day, 591 F.3d at 683 (stating that a defendant must show that "an agency relationship exists" between the government and the private individual). The inquiry is, essentially, "whether there is a sufficiently close nexus between the State and the challenged action of the [private actor] so that the action of the latter may be fairly treated as that of the State itself." *Jackson v. Metro. Edison Co.*, 419 U.S. 345, 351 (1974). Ultimately, "whether a private individual's conduct is imputed to the government 'turns on the degree of the Government's participation in the private party's activities, a question that can only be resolved in light of all the circumstances'." *United States v. Booker*, 728 F.3d 535, 541 (6th Cir. 2013) (quoting *Skinner v. Ry. Labor Execs. Ass'n*, 489 U.S. 602, 614-15 (1989)) (internal quotation marks within quotation omitted).

Analysis

I. The Parties' Positions

In their written submissions and at oral argument, the parties have presented a grab bag of arguments.

As the court construes Brooks' position(s), Brooks argues that (1) TPA Officers Smith and Black (a) were performing a "public function" at Fallbrook, which function is subject to Fourth Amendment requirements under the "public function" test set forth by the Sixth Circuit in *Romanski v. Detroit Entm't, L.L.C.*, 428 F.3d 629, 636-640 (6th Cir. 2006); and (b) seized Brooks without probable cause; and/or (2) that the TPA checkpoint was per se unconstitutional.

The government argues that the court should only apply the "agency" standard set forth by the Sixth Circuit in Lambert. The government argues that Brooks cannot meet this test or, if the court chooses to address it, the public function test. The government also argues that no "seizure" occurred until Officer Denton approached the car, because the car continued to move and, therefore, did not surrender. Finally, the government argues that (1) even if the Fourth Amendment applies, the security checkpoint was not per se unconstitutional and/or (2) even if the TPA Officers violated Brooks' Fourth Amendment rights, suppression of the evidence is not an appropriate remedy.

In sum Brooks' arguments—and the government's response thereto—focus on the TPA officers' conduct and authority at the Fallbrook security checkpoint, where the car was initially stopped. Brooks does not challenge the subsequent search of the car by the MNPD. Therefore, the court will similarly focus its analysis on whether, in stopping the car in which Brooks was riding, TPA Officers Black and Smith engaged in actions sufficiently attributable to the government to justify application of the Fourth Amendment.

II. Seizure

"Stopping and detaining a motorist constitutes a seizure within the meaning of the Fourth Amendment," and "[p]assengers ... are also considered seized during a traffic stop." *United States v. Stepp*, 680 F.3d 651, 661 (6th Cir. 2012); *City of Indianapolis v. Edmond*, 531 U.S. 32, 40 (2000); *Mich. Dep't of State Police v. Sitz*, 496 U.S. 444, 450 (1990) (vehicle stop at police sobriety checkpoint constitutes a "seizure" within the meaning of the Fourth Amendment); *Delaware v. Prouse*, 440 U.S. 648, 654 (1979) ("[S]topping an automobile and detaining its occupants constitute a 'seizure' within the meaning of [the Fourth and Fourteenth] Amendments, even though the purpose of the stop is limited and the resulting detention quite brief.").

The court finds as a matter of fact that the car stopped at the checkpoint and that the car was stopped when MNPD Officer Denton approached it. Therefore, the court rejects the government's position that, if the Fourth Amendment applies, no seizure actually occurred because the car never "surrendered" to the TPA officers at the checkpoint. The evidence shows that TPA Officer Smith blocked the car's path, and the court credits TPA Officer Black's recollection that the car did not move after Smith stood in its path upon learning that its occupants were engaged in potentially criminal activity and may have been attempting to speed away. Thus, if the Fourth Amendment applied to their conduct, Smith and Black "seized" Brooks and the other passengers in the car by stopping them at the security checkpoint. Cf. *United States v. Seymour*,—F. 3d—, 2014 WL 128120, at *4 (6th Cir. January 14, 2014) (finding that passenger was not seized during traffic stop, where passenger leaped out of vehicle before it came to a complete stop). Indeed, Brooks himself has argued that he was seized and "arrested" by the TPA Officers. Of course, the fact of a seizure merely begs the questions that the court must resolve: can Smith and Black's actions in stopping the vehicle be imputed to the government for Fourth Amendment purposes and/or was the security checkpoint unconstitutional ab initio?

III. The Public Function Test and the Lambert Agency Test

The parties have introduced multiple proposed "tests" to determine whether the Fourth Amendment applied to the actions of the TPA Officers, but they have provided little guidance to the court as to why the court should apply one test over another. The parties' confusion in this regard is understandable, because federal caselaw reflects a polyglot of approaches to the state action inquiry, many of which gloss over, or explicitly decline to address, some confounding issues left unresolved by the Supreme Court in this area of the law. See, for example, Romanski, 428 F.3d at 632 (stating that Supreme Court developed three tests for determining the existence of "state action" for purposes of § 1983 - the "public function" test, the "state compulsion" test, and the "symbiotic relationship test"); Lambert, 752 F.2d at 227 (articulating an "agency" test in context of motion to suppress in criminal case); Day, 591 F.3d 683 (in a criminal case involving a motion to suppress, applying both Lambert-like "agency test" from criminal cases and Romanski § 1983 "public function" test, and acknowledging but declining to address whether it was appropriate to apply a "a 'free-standing' public function test or to utilize such a test as part of analyzing the first factor of the agency test"); see also *State of New Mexico v. Santiago*, 217 P.3d 89, 83 (N.M. 2009) (construing Fourth Amendment) (in addressing motion to suppress, applying both Lambert-like agency test and Romanski "public function" test, but noting that "[o]ur courts have not previously applied the public-function doctrine in the context of the Fourth Amendment, and we have found only limited authority from other jurisdictions that have done so."). Here, the parties essentially argue past each other as to which of these tests should apply, without fully addressing these difficult doctrinal issues.

As the best the court can discern, courts apply the state action test or tests that best fit the factual circumstances presented. For example, in Romanski, the Sixth Circuit addressed whether a private casino could be held liable under § 1983 when its security guards allegedly arrested the plaintiff without probable cause. 428 F.3d at 632. The plaintiff had picked up a five-cent token left at a slot machine, at which point a plain-clothes private casino security officer detained her for violating an un-posted casino policy against picking up tokens. Id. 632-33. When the plaintiff protested, the officers escorted her to a windowless "security office," where they copied the plaintiff's license and social security card, photographed her, and removed a nickel from her winnings. Id. at 633. The officers chose to eject the plaintiff from the casino, but refused the plaintiff's request to collect her friends at a lunch buffet (where they were eating), and refused to permit the plaintiff to use the bathroom without being accompanied by a security officer. Id. at 633–34. The casino notified the Michigan State Police about the incident, but otherwise the police had no role in it. Id. at 634. Under these circumstances, the Sixth Circuit applied the "public function" test, which seeks to determine whether a private entity (here, the casino security team) performs a public function by "exercising powers traditionally reserved to the state." Id. at 637. The Sixth Circuit determined that Michigan's plenary delegation of its police power to the casino security guards satisfied the "public function" test, meaning that those guards constituted "state actors" for purposes of § 1983. Id. at 636-640. Following Romanski, some courts, including the Fourth Circuit, have applied the Romanski public function test in criminal cases in which the actions of private security officers are challenged as per se attributable to the government. See, for example, Day, 591 F.3d at 687–89 (private security officers at a private housing complex); Santiago, 217 P.2d at 86–87 (private mall security officers).

By contrast, in Lambert, the Sixth Circuit addressed whether a housekeeper's retrieval of inculpatory evidence from the defendant's home and provision of that evidence to the Federal Bureau of Investigation was subject to the Fourth Amendment. Id. at 89. Briefly, a housekeeper claimed that the homeowner and his friends had openly used illegal drugs in front of her; concerned about the negative effects of drug use, she approached the FBI 25 times concerning the homeowner's activities. Id. at 86. Despite the FBI's explicit instructions not to remove objects from the house, the housekeeper removed a thermos containing a white powder that she (correctly) believed was cocaine, which she furnished to the FBI. Id. at 87. The defendant argued that this evidence should be suppressed because the housekeeper had violated his Fourth Amendment rights. Id. at 89. Under the circumstances, the Sixth Circuit applied an "agency" test to determine whether (1) "the police instigated, encouraged or participated in the search," and (2) the housekeeper "engaged in the search with the intent of assisting the police in their investigative efforts." Id. (citing *United*

States v. Howard, 752 F.2d 220, 227 (6th Cir. 1985)). Concluding that the FBI had not instigated, encouraged, or participated in the search, the court held that the housekeeper's search was a "private search" not subject to the purview of the Fourth Amendment. Id.; see also *United States v. Hardin*, 559 F.3d 404 (6th Cir. 2007) (where agents ordered apartment manager to determine if suspect was located at a particular residence, without which agents would have lacked probable cause, apartment manager's search in compliance with agent's demands constituted state action); *Howard*, 752 F.2d at 227–28 (insurance company investigator did not act as an "agent of the government," where the investigator entered property in the interest of determining liability of the insurance company with respect to suspected arson).

As Romanski and Lambert indicate, it does not appear that one test is meant to be exclusive of the other; rather, the facts of each case influence the proper test to apply. Having canvassed the cases cited by the parties here, it may be that the Lambert agency test applies where a private actor who otherwise would not be subject to the Fourth Amendment engages in specific activity functionally attributable to the government, whereas the Romanski public function test applies more appropriately to situations in which a party claims that a class of people—such as casino security guards—constitute state actors by virtue of the function they perform.

Furthermore, the government has not presented a meaningful basis for its position that the court should decline to apply the "public function" test because Romanski was a § 1983 case. As the Fourth Circuit noted in Day, the Supreme Court has held that the § 1983 "under color of law" inquiry mirrors the "state action" requirement of the Fourteenth Amendment. Day, 591 F.3d at 691 (citing *Lugar v. Edmonson Oil Co., Inc.*, 457 U.S. 922 (1982)). The Due Process Clause of the Fourteenth Amendment made the Fourth Amendment applicable to the states. *United States v. Booker*, 728 F.3d 535, 545 (6th Cir. 2013). Here, the government, citing to a Ninth Circuit case, simply points out that the Fourth Amendment is not triggered simply because of the existence of "state action." *Arpin v. Santa Clara Valley Transp. Agency*, 261 F.3d 912, 924 (9th Cir. 2001). That is not a controversial proposition: in Arpin, the Ninth Circuit was merely pointing out that, notwithstanding a finding of "state action" for purposes of § 1983, the Fourth Amendment would not apply unless the underlying "state action" at issue involved a "search" and/or "seizure" -that is, the types of government conduct to which the Fourth Amendment protection against unreasonable searches and seizures applies. Id. Here, there was a "seizure" of Brooks, which would trigger Fourth Amendment protections (via the Fourteenth Amendment) if the security officers who seized Brooks were performing a public function and/or otherwise acting as agents of the MNPD or the State of Tennessee. In sum, if there is any meaningful reason why the court should not consider the § 1983 state action standard articulated by the Sixth Circuit in Romanski under the circumstances presented here, the government has not adequately articulated it.

Here, the public function test seems to best fit the factual circumstances at issue. Be that as it may, the court need not resolve whether one test or the other (or both) is the "right" one, because the facts satisfy neither test for the reasons stated in the next section. Therefore, as other courts have done under similar circumstances, the court will assume arguendo that it is appropriate to analyze the actions of private security guards in a criminal case under both the public function and the agency tests. See, for example, Day, 591 F.3d 679; Santiago, 147 N.M. at 82–88.

IV. Burden of Proof

The government has identified multiple Sixth Circuit decisions indicating that, when a defendant argues that a private party's actions should nevertheless be treated as government action for purposes of the Fourth Amendment, the burden of proving state action for Fourth Amendment purposes rests on the defendant. See, for example, *United States v. Freeland*, 562 F.2d 383, 385 (6th Cir. 1977) ("Where a motion to suppress evidence has been made, the burden of establishing that the evidence was secured by an unlawful search is on the moving party. It was thus incumbent upon Freeland to demonstrate that sufficient governmental involvement existed to invoke the proscriptions of the Fourth Amendment."); *United States v. Coleman*, 6528 F.2d 961, 965 (6th Cir. 1980) ("To establish an unlawful search here, [the defendant] must demonstrate that the search was not a private search even though [a private person] alone actively searched the truck."); see also Day, 591 F.3d at 683 (where defendant contends that a private party acted as a state actor for Fourth Amendment purposes, defendant bears the burden to prove the requisite agency relationship between the individual and the government). Brooks has not identified any contrary legal authority. Therefore, the court finds that the burden is on Brooks to demonstrate that the TPA security officers' conduct, and/or that the checkpoint itself, fell within the scope of the Fourth Amendment.

III. Whether the Seizure by TPA Officers Smith and Black Constituted State Action

A. Lambert/Agency Test

Under the Lambert test, Brooks must show that (1) the MNPD instigated, encouraged or participated in the seizure by TPA Officers Smith and Black and (2) that TPA Officers Smith and Black "engaged in the [seizure] with the intent of assisting the police in their investigative efforts." 771 F.2d at 89. Here, Brooks has not made either showing.

First, in stopping the car on the night in question, Smith and Black effectuated a stop that, subject to the state action requirement, would otherwise constitute a "seizure" under the Fourth Amendment. Officers Smith and Black did not conduct the stop at the instigation or encouragement of law enforcement; instead, they did so in the normal course of their duties as TPA security personnel, who were charged with enforcing the Criminal Trespass List on behalf of Alco at Fallbrook. Although the MNPD may generally have been aware of TPA's work as a security firm at Fallbrook, the fact that MNPD responded when TPA alerted them to criminal violations occurring at Fallbrook does not establish "encouragement" - it merely establishes that the MNPD was fulfilling its obligation to respond to complaints from private citizens and property owners about criminal activity. Although Officer Denton happened to be in the area when Smith and Black stopped the car, it was Smith and Black who seized the car in the first instance, without any involvement or encouragement from Officer Denton. Indeed, after Black ascertained that a crime had been committed in his presence (marijuana possession) and witnessed Brooks making furtive moves in the car's back seat, Black had Smith step in the path of the car to prevent its escape and to detain it until law enforcement could arrive to effectuate a formal arrest. Neither Denton nor the MNPD "instructed or encouraged" the TPA officers to seize cars attempting to enter Fallbrook, nor did they instruct, encourage, or participate in the TPA officers' initial decision to stop the car at the checkpoint and their subsequent decision to detain it upon realizing that illegal and perhaps dangerous activity was taking place in their presence. See Lambert, 771 F.2d at 89.

Second, the evidence shows that Officers Smith and Black were not seeking to assist the police in crime prevention and investigation efforts when (1) they stopped the car at the checkpoint as a matter of course and (2) after seeing evidence of plain sight illegal activity committed by Brooks and/or others in the car (as well as suspicious movements by Brooks in the back seat thereafter), seizing the car by blocking its path until a formal arrest could be made. The evidence shows that, in stopping the car at the checkpoint and in detaining the car thereafter, Officers Smith and Black were enforcing their employer's interest in enforcing the Criminal Trespass List and in keeping Fallbrook free from trespassers and criminal activity on the premises, in compliance with the Community Rules. Again, the fact that the MNPD may have been aware that TPA utilized a checkpoint for these purposes and often alerted the MNPD to criminal activity does not establish that the TPA (and, by extension, Alco) primarily intended to assist the MNPD's general interest in investigating crimes… "[W]here … the intent of the private party conducting the search is entirely independent of the government's intent to collect evidence for use in a criminal prosecution, … the private party is not an agent of the government." Howard, 752 F.2d at 227.

B. Public Function Test

1. Romanski and the "Line" Between Payton and Wade. Under the public function test, a private entity is said to be performing a public function if it is exercising powers traditionally reserved to the state, such as holding elections, taking private property under the eminent domain power, or operating a company-owned town. Romanski, 428 F.3d at 636. As the Sixth Circuit has observed, the Supreme Court has expressly left open the question of whether and under what circumstances private security officers may be said to perform a public function for purposes of § 1983. Id. (citing *Flagg Bros., Inc. v. Brooks*, 436 U.S. 149, 155 (1978)). Nevertheless, the Sixth Circuit and other circuit courts have found that, under appropriate circumstances, private security guards can perform a "public function" subject to the Fourth Amendment. See Romanski, 428 F.3d at 640; see also *Payton v. Rush-Presbytarian*, 184 F.3d 623, 627-30 (7th Cir. 1999) (special police officers with plenary police powers); *Henderson v. Fisher*, 631 F.2d 1115 (3d Cir. 1980) (university policeman with plenary police authority throughout campus); cf. Day, 591 F.3d at 687–689 (private security guards at apartment complex did not perform a public function, where Virginia granted security guards arrest authority that was "circumscribed" and "essentially the same as that of any private citizen").

In Romanski, the Sixth Circuit considered the application of the public function test to private security guards at a casino in Michigan. The Sixth Circuit looked to the Seventh Circuit decisions in *Payton v. Rush-Presbytarian–St. Luke's Med. Ctr.*, 184 F.3d 623, 628 (7th Cir. 1999) and *Wade v. Byles*, 83 F.3d 902, 905–906 (7th Cir. 1996), as providing persuasive guidance as to the "line" beyond which private security guards may be considered state actors. In *Payton*, the Seventh Circuit had considered whether private individuals designated as "special police officers" under Chicago city ordinances could be held liable as state actors while performing security functions at a Chicago-area hospital. 183 F.3d at 625-630. The ordinances at issue vested the special police officers with "the powers of the regular police patrol for which they are respectively appointed or in the line of duty for which they are engaged," and required those officers to "conform to and be subject to all rules and regulations governing police officers of the city." Id. at 625 (emphases added). Under the circumstances, the court found that the special police officers at issue were "de facto police on [the defendant's] premises" and that "no legal difference exists between a privately employed special officer with full police powers and a regular Chicago police officer," thereby qualifying them as state actors subject to constitutional constraints. Id. at 630.

By contrast, in Wade, the Seventh Circuit had held that private security guards under contract with the Chicago Housing Authority (the "CHA," a governmental entity) did not engage in state action. 83 F.3d 903-04. There, the CHA provided security for residents of its housing projects (i.e., government-affiliated housing projects), through (1) a CHA-maintained police force whose jurisdiction was limited to CHA property, but who were "statutorily vested with all the powers of city and state police"; (2) CHA's own in-house armed security guards; and (3) private security guards with whom the CHA contracted to provide security for the lobbies of CHA buildings. Id. The primary responsibility of the private security guards was to control access to the CHA buildings by monitoring the identification of people entering and leaving the buildings. Id. at 904. If a guest did not show proper identification or refused to sign in, the private security guards could ask the person to leave and, if the person refused, they would call the police and either wait for police to arrive or arrest the individual for criminal trespass pending police arrival. Id. The private security guards were permitted to carry firearms, permitted to use deadly force in self-defense, had limited arrest authority, and could exercise their limited powers only in the building lobbies. Id. The Seventh Circuit observed that the security guards "possessed powers no greater than those of armed security guards who are commonly employed by private companies to protect private property." Id. at 906. The court also observed that private citizens generally possessed power to carry a gun, the power to arrest someone for criminal trespass pending arrival of the police, and the power to use deadly force in self-defense, meaning that those were not powers exclusively reserved to the police. Id. Accordingly, the court found that the CHA officers were not state actors for purposes of § 1983. Id. at 906–07.

Examining Payton and Wade, the Sixth Circuit in Romanski characterized Payton as exemplifying the proposition that, "[w]here security guards are endowed by law with plenary police powers such that they are de facto police officers, they may qualify as state actors under the public function test." Romanski, 428 F.3d at 637. The Sixth Circuit characterized Wade as exemplifying the "other side of the line," in which the private defendants have some police-like powers but not plenary police authority. Id.

The casino security officers at issue in Romanski operated pursuant to a Michigan statute granting them "the authority to arrest a person without a warrant as set forth for public peace officers." Id. at 638 (quoting Mich. Comp. Laws § 338.1080). The Sixth Circuit construed the Michigan statute as delegating "plenary police power" to private security guards at the casino, because (subject to geographic limits) the security guards had been vested with essentially the same arrest powers as the police, without any qualitative limits. See 428 F.3d at 639 n.3 (stating that, in Michigan, "a licensed private security officer's arrest power is plenary in the sense that while on her employer's property during working hours, a private security officer can make warrantless arrests to the same extent as a public police officer"). Accordingly, the Sixth Circuit concluded that the circumstances presented in Romanski "fall[] on the Payton side of the line," meaning that the casino security guards performed a public function subject to constitutional constraints. Id.

2. Application. Here, the dividing line identified by the Sixth Circuit in Romanski compels a finding that the TPA security officers at Fallbrook were not state actors.

Security guards in Tennessee, including the TPA officers here, operate under the PPSLRA, which sets forth licensing requirements and restrictions for certain forms of private security. See generally Tenn. Code Ann. § 62-35-101 et seq. The PPSLRA applies to, inter alia, "security and patrol guard service," defined as "protection of persons or property, or both, from criminal activities, including, but not limited to: (A) Prevention or detection, or both, of intrusion, unauthorized entry, larceny, vandalism, abuse, fire or trespass on private property; (B) Prevention, observation or detection of any unauthorized activity of private property; (C) Enforcement of rules, regulations or local or state laws on private property; [and] (D) Control, regulation or direction of the flow or movements of the public, whether by vehicle or otherwise[,] on private property." Id. § 62-35-102(16)(A)-(D). Security firms and security officers subject to the PPSLRA must register with and be approved by the state, subject to training and examination requirements, including special additional training for armed security guards. The PPSLRA contains multiple provisions specifically barring security guards from engaging in activities that could give the false impression that the guards are public peace officers. For example, § 62-35-127 proscribes the following conduct:

While performing any function of a security guard and patrol service, no person shall:

1. Wear or display any badge, insignia, shield, patch, or pattern that:
   a. Indicates or tends to indicate that the person is a sworn peace officer;
   b. Contains or includes the word "police" or the equivalent of the word "police"; or
   c. Is similar in wording to any law enforcement agency in this state.
2. Have or utilize any vehicle or equipment that:
   a. Displays the word "police," "law enforcement officer," or the equivalent of those words or
   b. Has any sign, shield, accessory or insignia that may indicate that the vehicle or equipment belongs to a public law enforcement agency.

Similarly, under Tenn. Code Ann. § 62-35-128:

No security guard shall wear any military or police-style uniform, except for rainwear or other foul-weather clothing, unless the uniform has

1. Affixed over the left breast pocket on the outermost garment and on any cap a badge or insignia distinct in design from that utilized by any law enforcement agency in this state, unless the licensed security officer is in plain clothes and
2. Affixed over the right breast pocket on the outermost garment a name plate or tape with the name of the security guard/officer on it, unless the licensed security officer is in plain clothes.

Moreover, the PPSLRA makes it unlawful "for any contract security company to publish any advertisement, letterhead, circular, statement or phrase of any sort that suggests that the company is a government agent or instrumentality" or to "[m]ake any statement that would reasonably cause another person to believe that the security guard/officer functions as a sworn peace officer or other government official." Id. § 62-35-134(b). Here, there is no indication in the evidentiary record that Smith, Black, or the TPA generally violated any provision of the PPSLRA.

Although Brooks attempts to analogize the PPSLRA to the Michigan statute at issue in Romanski, the comparison is fundamentally flawed. Unlike the Michigan statutory scheme, the PPSLRA does not purport to grant "plenary arrest power" to private security guards. Indeed, Tennessee has a broad "citizen's arrest" statute, which permits private citizens to make arrests under the following circumstances:

A private person may arrest another: (1) For a public offense committed in the arresting person's presence; (2) When the person arrested has committed a felony, although not in the arresting person's presence; or (3) When a felony has been committed, and the arresting person has reasonable cause to believe that the person arrested committed the felony.

Tenn. Code Ann. § 40-7-109. Thus, under Tennessee law, private citizens possess some arrest powers, including the authority to arrest another person who commits "a public offense" in that person's presence, without regard to whether the offense constitutes a felony or misdemeanor. Accordingly, construing the PPSLRA and the Tennessee citizen's arrest statute in harmony, private security guards possess the same power to arrest as private citizens in Tennessee. See Tenn. Op. Atty. Gen. No. 03-018, 2003 WL 912608, at *4 (February 19, 2003) ("Arrest powers for security officers exist only as they do for private citizens"). In sum, under Tennessee law, certain arrest powers, including the authority to arrest another person for committing a crime in that person's presence, are not exclusively reserved to public peace officers—and it is those nonexclusive police powers that private security guards may exercise. Furthermore, subject to restrictions specifically preventing them from identifying or otherwise giving the impression that they are public officers, the PPSLRA authorizes private security officers to prevent and detect "unauthorized entry," "trespass," and "unauthorized activity" on private property, as well as the enforcement of "rules" and the "flow or movements of the public, whether by vehicle or otherwise" on private property.

Coming back to the Romanski analysis, it is clear that TPA officers (and private security guards within Tennessee more generally) do not possess "plenary arrest power." Moreover, the circumstances here are even less indicative of state action than Wade (the Seventh Circuit decision that the Sixth Circuit construed as appropriately finding a lack of state action), where the security guards at issue conducted necessary security functions at a public housing facility owned and operated by a city government entity, the CHA. Here, the TPA officers manned a checkpoint at a private facility owned and operated by a private entity, not a public one. Furthermore, the TPA officers were tasked with enforcing the Community Rules, which included preventing "trespassers" from entering the (private) property after those individuals had broken the Community Rules and the associated lease terms—perhaps, but not necessarily, by committing a crime on the Fallbrook grounds. The record contains no indication that the TPA officers violated the requirements of the PPSLRA. Moreover, the gates openly disclosed that anyone entering the property was subject to search, that the property owner reserved the right to exclude trespassers, and that illegal activity of any kind was forbidden on the property.

In sum, the TPA officers exercised essentially the same nonexclusive police powers as private citizens in Tennessee, and the record does not show that the TPA officers somehow held themselves out as public peace officers at the checkpoint, or that Alco in any way sought to encourage that impression. Under the circumstances, the mere fact that Tennessee law required the TPA officers to register with the state and receive specialized training (among other prerequisites) is insufficient to establish that the TPA officers were performing "public functions" exclusively reserved to the state of Tennessee.

Accordingly, the court finds that TPA Officers Black and Smith, in operating the security checkpoint, were not acting as governmental actors subject to the Fourth Amendment.

C. Whether the Fallbrook Security Checkpoint Was Per Se Unconstitutional

In reliance on the Tennessee Supreme Court decision in *State v. Hayes*, 188 S.W.3d 505 (Tenn. 2006), Brooks argues that the security checkpoint at Fallbrook was per se unconstitutional.

In *Hayes*, the federally subsidized Chattanooga Housing Authority ("CHA"), a governmental entity, operated a public housing facility called Poss Homes. Id. at 508. According to the Tennessee Supreme Court, "[t]he CHA operates its own police department, which has full concurrent jurisdiction with the Chattanooga Police Department inside Poss Homes." Id. at 508. The CHA issued special identification badges to Poss Home residents. Id. CHA officers maintained a security checkpoint at a "thoroughfare that had been 'ceded' to the CHA by the City of Chattanooga." Id. at 509. The CHA officers claimed that the checkpoint was established simply for checking IDs to see whether individuals lived at Poss Homes. Id. at 508–509. The evidence indicated that CHA officers may have selectively enforced this policy, because it operated the checkpoint "about two to three times a week ... at random ...usually late afternoon," and officers "'usually' stopped both motorists and pedestrians." Id. at 509. The evidence also showed that CHA officers did more than simply check for CHA-issued ID badges; instead, the defendant's arresting officer testified that, even after checking those IDs, he would typically ask for a driver's license, and "sometimes for registration and insurance, and after that I would make a decision on what I was going to do." Id. at 509.

Analyzing these facts, the Hayes court concluded that the checkpoint was unconstitutional under both the Fourth Amendment (to the United States Constitution) and under the Tennessee Constitution. The court looked to the line of cases dealing with the narrow categories of circumstances under which the government may establish targeted security checkpoints and/or roadblocks on the roadways at which cars may be "seized" without probable cause. See, for example, *United States v. Martinez-Fuerte*, 428 U.S. 543, 545 (1976) (brief, suspicionless seizures of motorists at Border Patrol checkpoints permissible); Sitz, 496 U.S. at 455 (upholding sobriety checkpoints aimed at removing drunk drivers from the road); *Delaware v. Prouse*, 440 U.S. 648, 663 (1979) (suggesting that a roadblock aimed at verifying drivers' licenses and vehicle registrations would be permissible in pursuit of highway safety). The Hayes court also cited *City of Indianapolis v. Edmond*, 531 U.S. 31, 48 (2000), for the proposition that "roadblocks aimed at general crime control contravene the Fourth Amendment." Hayes, 188 S.W.3d at 512 (citing Edmond [no pinpoint citation]); see Edmond, 531 U.S. at 48 (declining to approve state police roadblocks "whose primary purpose is ultimately indistinguishable from the general interest in crime control"). Essentially, the Hayes court concluded that the CHA's security checkpoint constituted an effort by the government to engage in general crime prevention by stopping people without probable cause, a practice which the court therefore found to be unconstitutional under Edmond. See Hayes, 188 S.W.3d at 512–513.

Crucially, whether the CHA officers were governmental actors for Fourth Amendment purposes was not at issue in Hayes; that is, the parties and the court in that case appear to have agreed that the Fourth Amendment applied to the CHA officers. That assumption is understandable and entirely consistent with the Romanski "public function" analysis, because the CHA officers in Hayes (1) worked for a public entity at a public facility and (2) exercised police power concurrent with the powers of the local Chattanooga police force—that is, the type of "plenary police power" that, under Romanski, compels application of the Fourth Amendment to any searches conducted by those officers.

Thus, although Hayes addresses the constitutionality of public police checkpoints focused on general crime deterrence at public housing facilities, Hayes does not address the threshold issue presented here, which is whether private security guards operating a security checkpoint on private residential property were government actors for purposes of the Fourth Amendment. Therefore, as to that threshold issue, Hayes is entirely inapposite.

Because the court has found that the TPA officers at Fallbrook are not state actors, the court need not address (as the Hayes court did) whether the Fallbrook checkpoint constituted a constitutionally impermissible attempt by the police to engage in general crime deterrence by seizing and/or searching people without probable cause. Accordingly, the court expresses no opinion about the persuasiveness of the Hayes court's analysis with respect to government-affiliated checkpoints at public housing facilities in Tennessee.

D. Summary

In sum, the court finds that the initial seizure of the car by TPA Security Guards Black and Smith at the checkpoint did not implicate the Fourth Amendment. Accordingly, Black and Smith were permitted to stop the car in which Brooks was riding (as they did with all cars attempting to enter Fallbrook that night) to check the identification of its occupants against the Criminal Trespass List.

Finally, although the parties have devoted short shrift to the constitutionality of the evidence uncovered following the routine stop by TPA Officers Black and Smith, the court observes that the remaining evidence was lawfully gathered. Once Black observed Brooks' attempt to throw a marijuana cigarette out of the back window and smelled marijuana, Black had sufficient cause to support a "citizen's arrest" of Brooks and the other passengers under Tennessee law—a point that Brooks does not appear to dispute. At the time, Brooks, likely realizing his predicament, shouted at the driver to "go, go, go" in an effort to evade the TPA officers, but Brooks and Smith prevented the car from moving. By happenstance, MNPD Officer Denton was in the area and approached the car just a few seconds after this series of events. By that time, Black had already determined that Brooks had committed a crime in his presence (marijuana possession, at least). Black then saw a bag of marijuana in plain sight and pointed it out to Officer Denton, after which Black and Smith assisted Denton in formally arresting Brooks. Testimony at the hearing indicated that the evidence discovered during the subsequent search of the car was in plain sight and, therefore, not subject to the warrant requirement. See *Texas v. Brown*, 460 U.S. 730, 740 (1983) (no legitimate expectation of privacy in objects that would be entirely visible to officer as a private citizen); *United States v. Witherspoon*, 82 F.3d 697, 699 (6th Cir. 1996). Regardless, given that TPA Officer Black had witnessed Brooks attempt to dispose of a marijuana cigarette and saw him shifting around in the backseat attempting to hide something else from the TPA Officers—perhaps additional evidence of drug possession—it was reasonable to believe that a search of the vehicle following Brooks' arrest would yield evidence relevant to Brooks' arrest for drug possession. See *Arizona v. Gant*, 556 U.S. 332, 347 (2009) ("If there is probable cause to believe a vehicle contains evidence of criminal activity [related to the arrest], *United States v. Ross*, 456 U.S. 798, 820-821 [] (1982), authorizes a search of any area of the vehicle in which the evidence might be found.")

Because the court will deny the Motion to Suppress for the reasons stated herein, the court need not reach the government's alternative argument that, even if a Fourth Amendment violation occurred, suppression is not warranted.

Conclusion

For the reasons stated herein, Brooks' Motion to Suppress will be denied.

An appropriate order will enter.

ALETA A. TRAUGER

United States District Judge

U.S. v. Slough

641 F3d 544 (D.C. Cir. 2011).

WILLIAMS, Senior Circuit Judge:

The district court dismissed an indictment against the five defendants on the ground that the evidence presented to the grand jury, and indeed the decision to prosecute two of the defendants, were tainted by statements of the defendants that for purposes of this appeal are conceded to have been compelled within the meaning of *Garrity v. New Jersey*, 385 U.S. 493, 87 S.Ct. 616, 17 L.Ed.2d 562 (1967). We reverse and remand as to four of the defendants; the government itself moved to dismiss the indictment against Nicholas Slatten, without prejudice to possible later re-indictment, and the district court's grant of the motion has taken Slatten out of the case for now. *United States v. Slough*, 677 F.Supp.2d 112, 115-116 n. 2 (D.D.C. 2009).

On September 16, 2007 a car bomb exploded near the Izdihar Compound in Baghdad, where a U.S. diplomat was conferring with Iraqi officials. American security officials ordered a team from Black-water Worldwide to evacuate the diplomat to the Green Zone. See U.S. Department of State, U.S. Embassy Baghdad, (Draft) Use of Deadly Force Incident at Nisur Square—Baghdad: Preliminary Report and Findings, September 23, 2007, at 2. Another Blackwater team, Raven 23, headed out of the Green Zone to block traffic at the Nisur Square traffic circle and thus assure the diplomat's safe passage back. (In fact, because a checkpoint had fortuitously been closed, the escort convoy never passed through Nisur Square.) Id. Raven 23 positioned its four vehicles on the south side of the Square and its members started gesturing to stop traffic. Shots were fired; the dispute over who fired at whom and when is the substantive crux of the criminal case underlying this appeal. When the shooting stopped, 14 Iraqi civilians were dead and 20 wounded. Slough, 677 F.Supp.2d at 116.

Within hours of the incident, the Department of State's Diplomatic Security Service ("DSS") conducted brief interviews with each of the 19 members of Raven 23. Id. at 117. Among the 19 were the five defendants in this case, Paul Slough, Nicholas Slatten, Evan Liberty, Dustin Heard and Donald Ball. [Redacted.]

We have redacted material that on the parties' view might spread "taint" from statements of defendants that are deemed compelled for purposes of this case, or the release of which would disclose witnesses' grand jury testimony, except to the extent hitherto disclosed elsewhere. The interests protected by the redaction should in due course become moot, and we direct the parties to notify the court when that occurs.

On September 18, 2007, two days after the incident, all Raven 23 members submitted sworn written statements to the State Department, using a form that included a guarantee that the statement and the information or evidence derived therefrom would not be used in a criminal proceeding against the signer. Slough, 677 F.Supp.2d at 118–19. The government conceded before the district court that under Garrity the September 18 statements must be treated as having been compelled; as to the September 16 statements, the district court so found and the government does not appeal that finding.

The defendants were re-interviewed later. Slough, 677 F.Supp.2d at 117–20. But because the defendants invoked only the statements of September 16 and September 18 as sources of potential taint of the evidence presented to the grand jury, id. at 120–21, only those statements are relevant to this appeal.

The incident almost immediately became the focus of media attention in both the United States and Iraq. Some of the early articles, published within a few days of the incident, reported that the Blackwater team was attacked, and purported to quote from and otherwise rely on a State Department "incident report," presumably prepared at least in part on the basis of the interviews and statements. See, for example, Adam Zagorin Brian Bennett, Iraq Limits Blackwater's Operations, Time, September 17, 2007, http://www.time.com/time/world/article/ 0,8599,1662586,00.html; Sabrina Tavernise, U.S. Contractor Banned by Iraq Over Shootings, N.Y. Times, September 18, 2007, at Al. These very same articles, however, also cite Blackwater representatives as making the same assertion ([Redacted.]). See Tavernise. The articles also cite Iraqi officials' statements that Blackwater guards used excessive force. Joshua Partlow Walter Pincus, Iraq Bans Security Contractor, Wash. Post, September 18, 2007, at Al; Sinan Salaheddin, Iraq Plans Review of Foreign Security Firm Status, Assoc. Press, September 18, 2007.

The September 18 written statements were also leaked to the media. On September 28, 2007, ABC News reported that it had obtained all 19 of the September 18 sworn statements and quoted from some of them. See The Blotter, First Images of Controversial Blackwater Incident, ABC

News, September 28, 2007, http://blogs.abcnews. conVtheblotter/2007/09/exclusivefirst.html. Defendant Slough's statement was later posted online in its entirety, [Redacted.], and news reports by ABC News and the *New York Times*, among others, reproduced parts of defendants' and other team members' September 18 statements. [Redacted.]

The witnesses that the government relied on most heavily before the grand jury—Raven 23 members Adam Frost, Matthew Murphy and Mark Mealy—admitted to having read these news reports, and it soon became apparent that parts of their testimony may have been tainted by their exposure. In an effort to safeguard its case, the government decided to present a redacted case to a second grand jury, which returned an indictment against the defendants, finding that there was probable cause to believe that defendants committed (and attempted to commit) voluntary man-slaughter and weapons violations. Slough, 677 F.Supp.2d at 127-28.

The defendants moved to dismiss the indictment as tainted. As required by *Kastigar v. United States*, 406 U.S. 441, 92 S.Ct. 1653, 32 L.Ed.2d 212 (1972), the district court held a hearing to determine the existence and extent of any taint. It found that exposure to defendants' statements had tainted much of the evidence presented to the second grand jury—the testimony of security guards Frost and Murphy and Iraqi witnesses and victims, Frost's written journal, the factual proffer and debriefing of Jeremy Ridgeway (a Raven 23 member who had been indicted and had pleaded guilty), and physical evidence recovered by DSS from the scene of the crime—and had also tainted the prosecutors' decision to indict defendants Heard and Ball. The district court thus dismissed the indictment as to all five defendants. The government now appeals. We review the district court's findings that the government used a defendant's immunized statement for clear error, *United States v. North*, 910 F.2d 843, 855 (D.C. Cir. 1990) (" North I"), a standard that is met for any finding that was "induced by an erroneous view of the law," *United States v. Kilroy*, 27 F.3d 679, 687 (D.C. Cir. 1994) (internal quotations omitted).

The Fifth Amendment bars the government from compelling self-incriminating testimony from individuals. If the government nevertheless decides to require an individual to testify, it must offer him immunity that puts him in "substantially the same position as if [he] had claimed his privilege." See *Kastigar*, 406 U.S. at 458–59, 92 S.Ct. 1653. In a later prosecution of the individual, the government cannot use his immunized testimony itself or any evidence that was tainted—substantively derived, "shaped, altered, or affected," North I, 910 F.2d at 863—by exposure to the immunized testimony. Nor can the government use it to develop investigatory leads, to focus an investigation on a witness, *Kastigar*, 406 U.S. at 460, 92 S.Ct. 1653, or to motivate another wit-ness to give incriminating testimony. *United States v. Rinaldi*, 808 F.2d 1579, 1584 n. 7 (D.C. Cir. 1987). In North itself, for example, after North gave his immunized testimony former National Security Advisor Robert C. McFarlane had requested a second hearing before special investigat-ing committees "in order to respond" thereto, and we found error in the district court's having admitted McFarlane's trial testimony without having determined "what use—if any" he had made of North's. North I, 910 F.2d at 864. More generally, evidentiary content (potentially including a witness's whole testimony, as where his very availability was derived from or caused by immunized statements) will share the constitutional ban on use of the immunized statements. Kilroy, 27 F.3d at 687. Below we deal explicitly with situations where evidence's content or availability is derived from both immunized statements and independent factors.

In building a case against a defendant who received use immunity for his statements, the gov-ernment must prove, by a preponderance of the evidence, that "all of the evidence it proposes to use was derived from legitimate independent sources." North I, 910 F.2d at 854 (quoting *Kastigar*, 406 U.S. at 461–62, 92 S.Ct. 1653, internal quotations omitted). As the district court observed, proof that a witness was "never exposed to immunized testimony" or that the investigators memorialized (or "canned") a witness's testimony before exposure, Slough, 677 F.Supp.2d at 132 (citing North I, 910 F.2d at 872), would obviously satisfy the requirement. But a failure by the government to make either showing does not end the district court's inquiry. North I requires the court to parse the evidence "witness-by-witness" and "if necessary, ... line-by-line and item-by-item," 910 F.2d at 872, and to "separate the wheat of the witnesses' un-spoiled memory from the chaff of [the] immunized testimony," id. at 862. This sifting is particularly important in cases where, as here, a witness was exposed to a defendant's immunized statement but testifies to facts not included in that statement.

In sifting the record as to taint of the evidence before the indicting grand jury, the district court made a number of systemic errors based on an erroneous legal analysis.

First, the district court erred by treating evidence, including the testimony of Frost, Murphy, Ridgeway and the Iraqi witnesses, and the Frost journal, as single lumps and excluding them in their entirety when at the most only some portion of the content was tainted—it made no effort to decide what parts of the testimony or the journal were free of taint. Prima facie, this error applies (for example) to all elements of testimony that do not overlap with the content of the immunized statements. North I requires the court to segregate tainted parts of the evidence from those parts that either could not have been tainted (because there is no overlap) or were shown to be untainted by a preponderance of the evidence. 910 F.2d at 872. Even in instances where there could be no possible claim that the immunized statements caused the witness to speak up (as in some variant of the McFarlane instance), the district court found that the government had failed to fulfill its burden; yet the court never identified what the government could have done besides pointing to the complete absence of overlap, or why it should have been required to show more.

The district court excluded, for example, all of the testimony of Frost and Murphy, finding that the two guards "had been thoroughly immersed" in defendants' immunized statements by virtue of having read news reports about the Nisur Square incident. Slough, 677 F.Supp.2d at 144. But Frost's and Murphy's grand jury testimony included specific recollections with no referent either in defendants' immunized statements or news reports derived therefrom. [Redacted.] As these elements of Frost's testimony have no antecedent in the immunized statements, they cannot be tainted (unless somehow the statements caused Frost's testimony in some subtler way). Similarly, [Redacted.]. The list goes on, as the government points out in its briefs. Appellant Br. at 62–64; Appellant Reply. Br. at 13 (describing parts of Frost's and Murphy's testimony not overlapping with the statements); Appellant Br. at 89–93 (describing parts of Jeremy Ridgeway's statements that could not have been tainted); Appellant Reply Br. at 26–27 (describing parts of Iraqi witness testimony that did not overlap with any immunized statements that appeared in news reports). We will not catalog every instance of nonoverlap here, but North's mandate that the district court parse the record "line-by-line" clearly requires such review, not only for the rest of Frost's and Murphy's testimony, but also for the Iraqi witnesses' testimony and Ridgeway's proffer and statement.

In *United States v. North*, 920 F.2d 940 (D.C. Cir. 1990) (" North II"), we noted that the defendant bears the burden of laying "a firm 'foundation' resting on more than 'suspicion'" that proffered evidence was tainted by exposure to immunized testimony. Id., at 949 n. 9 (quoting from *Lawn v. United States*, 355 U.S. 339, 348-49, 78 S.Ct. 311, 2 L.Ed.2d 321 (1958)). A witness's prior exposure to immunized statements can hardly be said to meet that burden as to completely nonoverlapping points—defense counsel conceded as much at oral argument. See Oral Arg. Transcript 54, 56, 58. Of course, defendants may fill that gap by submitting additional evidence; again, the McFarlane episode in the North case may be a model, though it is worth noting that our disposition there left unresolved whether McFarlane's responding to North's testimony in fact constituted a forbidden "use" within the meaning of *Kastigar*. North I, 910 F.2d at 864.

Second (and closely related), the district court erred by failing to conduct a proper independent-source analysis as required by *Kastigar*, 406 U.S. at 460, 92 S.Ct. 1653, and Rinaldi 808 F.2d at 1582. In particular, the district court erred by finding that any evidence responding to allegations that Raven 23 was attacked was tainted, even where no information specific to a particular defendant was included, and the supposedly tainting sources in fact encompassed multiple, equivalent assertions by nondefendants. Many of the news reports were based on the State Department spot and incident reports, which, in turn, were in part based on statements by all 19 guards ([Redacted.]), not simply the five defendants' immunized statements. See, for example, Zagorin Bennett (citing from the incident report that "the motorcade was engaged with small arms fire from several locations" and "returned fire").

Moreover, the State Department reports were not the only sources offered in the news stories to support the claim of [Redacted.]—the very same articles also cite Blackwater representatives as making the claim. There is no suggestion in the district court's opinion that Blackwater management learned the specifics of [Redacted.] from the State Department reports; [Redacted.] Where two independent sources of evidence, one tainted and one not, are possible antecedents of particular testimony, the tainted source's presence doesn't ipso facto establish taint. (Moreover, a witness's testimony need not have any exterior antecedent, that is, any precursor other than the witness's perceptions of what happened.) Speaking of a government decision to pursue a line of investigation, for instance, the Second Circuit said, "[I]f it appears that that pursuit could have been motivated by both tainted and independent factors, the court must determine whether the government would have taken the same steps 'entirely apart from the motivating effect of the immunized testimony.'" *United States v. Nanni*, 59 F.3d 1425, 1432 (2d Cir. 1995) (citing *United States v. Biaggi*, 909 F.2d 662, 689 (2d Cir. 1990); Biaggi in turn drew on broader legal sources, such as those governing claims of dismissal for exercise of First Amendment rights, *Mt. Healthy City School District Board of Education v. Doyle*, 429 U.S. 274, 97 S.Ct. 568, 50 L.Ed.2d 471 (1977)). The same principle—a goal of removing any net effect on either side—must apply to any circumstance (e.g., a segment of testimony, a witness's decision to speak up) claimed to be an effect of immunized testimony. Immunity, properly construed, "leaves the witness and the Federal Government in substantially the same position as if the witness had claimed his privilege." *Kastigar*, 406 U.S. at 458–59, 92 S.Ct. 1653 (emphasis added, internal quotations omitted) (quoting *Murphy v. Waterfront Comm'n*, 378 U.S. 52, 79, 84 S.Ct. 1594, 12 L.Ed.2d 678 (1964)). To preserve that symmetry, obviously courts cannot bar the government from use of evidence that it would have obtained in the absence of the immunized statement.

The district court also found that these early news reports tainted Frost's journal and his testimony when he addressed the claim of [Redacted.] (Indeed, when armed guards shoot a number of people in a crowd, it doesn't take Hercule Poirot to start wondering what the crowd was doing.) The district court erred by failing to consider whether Frost's testimony and journal, as well as other evidence challenging the story that [Redacted.], were more probably than not derived from sources other than defendants' immunized statements.

Third, the district court applied the wrong legal standard when it excluded Frost's journal and his testimony simply because the news reports based on some of the immunized statements were "a cause" for his writing it. Slough, 677 F.Supp.2d at 151. Defendants cite our language in Hylton to the effect that if Hylton's immunized statements "were a cause of [a key witness's] decision to plead and testify against Hylton, [the witness's] testimony was impermissible even if the government had prior knowledge of [the witness's] role." 294 F.3d at 134. But Hylton did not decide that any causal role was necessarily fatal. To do so would have been to reverse North Ts (and Rasagar's) references to independent sources, as well as Kastigar's own explicit view that immunity, properly applied, "leaves the witness and the Federal Government in substantially the same position as if the witness had claimed his privilege." Kastigar, 406 U.S. at 458–59, 92 S.Ct. 1653 (internal quotations omitted). Finally, Hylton's entire focus was on explaining why a defendant was correctly asserting ineffective assistance of counsel, because of the latter's failure to make a Kastigar objection, not on resolving the nuances of multiple sources or causes.

Thus, only if the government on remand fails to establish by a preponderance that Frost would have written the journal or testified in the absence of exposure to defendants' immunized statements would use of the journal and testimony be barred under Kastigar. Of course, the defendants' communications transmitted to Frost via the media are relevant against the government in this analysis only to the extent that they actually added to the information flowing through from nondefendant sources.

This takes us to a fourth systemic error. To the extent that evidence tainted by the impact of one defendant's immunized statements may be found to have accounted for the indictment of that defendant, it does not follow that the indictment of any other defendant was tainted. The district court assumed the contrary. Slough, 677 F.Supp.2d at 166 n. 66. Although the prosecution presented a single indictment against all five defendants, each defendant was charged individually and therefore the presence, extent and possible harmfulness of the taint must be assessed individually.

Defendants argue that the government proceeded on a joint liability theory that would render defendant-by-defendant taint assessment unsuitable. They point to a prosecutor's statement to the grand jury that it was "charging [the defendants] jointly, with each of these shootings because they're working together." Grand Jury Tr., December 2, 2008, p.m., at 10–11. But in context the reference does not suggest government adoption of the broad theory espied by defendants. The prosecutor had explained to the grand jury that for aider and abettor liability a defendant need not have fired a fatal or wounding shot. Even shots that hit no one could aid and abet directly harmful shots by making it "difficult for victims to run that direction to safety." Grand Jury Tr., November 20, 2008, a.m., at 16. But guilt was individual: a vote to indict required jurors to be satisfied "that there's probable cause that each of the people we've identified … did, in fact, shoot their weapons that day … [a]nd joined in this, in what happened." Id. In context it is plain that the snippet identified by defendants is no more than a reference back to the government's aider and abettor theory.

The exact language might suggest that the government led the grand jury to believe that shooting, without regard to incoming fire, was itself an adequate basis for a manslaughter indictment. But the passage quoted was simply the government's explanation of the workings of aider and abettor liability; else-where the government made clear that firing in self-defense would not qualify. See Grand Jury Tr., December 4, 2007, a.m., at 11–12 (explaining to the grand jury that if it is "objectively reasonable for you to believe that you need to use [deadly] force to defend yourself, somebody's shooting from this car, and you apply force to that car, that's obviously justified conduct").

As we noted, the district court found the indictments of Heard and Ball independently and fatally tainted on the theory that their immunized statements motivated the prosecutor's decision to seek their indictment. Neither Kastigar nor North states that nonevidentiary uses of immunized statements are barred. Kastigar prohibits the use of immunized evidence as an "investigatory lead" to other derivative evidence that would then be used against the defendant. 406 U.S. at 460, 92 S.Ct. 1653. In North I, after a substantial review of the various circuits' decisions on the matter, we concluded: "Thus, even assuming without deciding that a prosecutor cannot make nonevidentiary use of immunized testimony, in the case before us the [Independent Counsel] did not do so." 910 F.2d at 860. We then went on (though under the heading "'Non-evidentiary' Use," id. at 856) to rule out the use of immunized testimony to refresh the memories of witnesses, id. at 860-63. That is, of course, an indirect evidentiary use.

Here, as the government does not challenge the factual finding on the decision to indict, we must assume its correctness and are thus forced to resolve the issue left unsettled in North I. In the absence of clear Supreme Court or D.C. Circuit precedent, North I turned to relevant decisions in other circuits for guidance and noted a circuit split: the Third and Eight Circuits suggested that Kastigar banned all nonevidentiary uses; the First, Second, Ninth, and Eleventh Circuits found otherwise. North I, 910 F.2d at 857. Since North was decided, the Seventh Circuit has joined the latter group, holding that Kastigar is not concerned with "the exercise of prosecutorial discretion." *United States v. Cozzi*, 613 F.3d 725, 729 (7th Cir. 2010) (citing a number of post-North I decisions; internal quotations omitted). In the end, at least as to decisions to indict, we join those circuits refusing to find such decisions vulnerable on the ground of links to immunized statements. The Eleventh Circuit observed in *United States v. Byrd*, 765 F.2d 1524, 1531 (11th Cir. 1985), that such a rule would turn use immunity into transactional immunity. That is a bit of an over-statement; after all, prosecutors could, by construction of firewalls (along with the associated incremental personnel costs), assure that such decisions were made without risk of taint. But defendants' proposed rule clearly would entangle the court in what has hitherto normally been internal prosecutorial decision-making. And it would open a new field for courts' having to make complex causal judgments of the sort already required to assure clean evidence.

Continuing its discussion of nonevidentiary uses, Slough, 677 F.Supp.2d at 158–65, the district court also asserted that defendants' September 16 statements must have been useful to the prosecution and must have guided the government's investigation, id. at 163, but it never detailed what statements, independent of innocent sources, played exactly what role. We cannot uphold the judgment of dismissal to the extent that it rests on such vague propositions.

We further note that the district court lumped physical evidence collected by the DSS under the nonevidentiary-use rubric and found it to be tainted. Slough, 677 F.Supp.2d at 164–65. Insofar as physical evidence was presented to the grand jury, that classification is surely wrong—if the immunized statements led to discovery of physical evidence that was before the grand jury, it should be analyzed as an evidentiary use. As with uses purportedly leading to testimony or to the Frost journal, the district court's judgment was subject to the same errors reviewed above as to nonphysical evidence. (We note that especially as to physical evidence, but in principle as to all evidence alleged to be tainted, the independent sources that might undercut any taint would include actual facts on the ground, such as the locations of vehicles that were shot and bullet strikes, which would lead investigators to look for shell casings from any incoming fire, not to mention make inquiries of potential witnesses.)

If the excluded physical evidence was not presented to the grand jury, as the government's briefs suggest, Appellant Br. at 117 n. 43; Appellant Reply Br. at 38, then the district court's consideration and exclusion of that evidence appears premature. The district court acknowledged as much, noting that the "search [for physical evidence that it excluded] may have been highly relevant to the criminal case eventually brought against the defendants." Slough, 677 F.Supp.2d at 165. To the extent that the court ordered the Kastigar hearing simply to determine the status of the indictment, it would not properly reach the issue of possible use at trial. North II, 910 F.2d at 947–48.

Finally, although the district court disapproved of the prosecutor Kohl's explanation to the grand jury that some of defendants' statements were immunized, it did not find that mentioning the existence of immunized statements constituted a prohibited use under Kastigar. See Slough, 677 F.Supp.2d at 128. As the district court appears not to have relied on Kohl's explanation, we will not rule on the matter.

We find that the district court's findings depend on "an erroneous view of the law." Kilroy, 27 F.3d at 687. We thus vacate and remand the case for the court to determine, as to each defendant, what evidence—if any—the government presented against him that was tainted as to him, and, in the case of any such presentation, whether in light of the entire record the government had shown it to have been harmless beyond a reasonable doubt. North I, 910 F.2d at 873.

So ordered.

Appendix 1: Florida Statutes (2010)

TITLE 32. REGULATION OF PROFESSIONS AND OCCUPATIONS (CHS. 454–493)
CHAPTER 493. PRIVATE INVESTIGATIVE, PRIVATE SECURITY, AND REPOSSESSION SERVICES
PART I. GENERAL PROVISIONS

§ 493.6100. Legislative intent

The Legislature recognizes that the private security, investigative, and recovery industries are rapidly expanding fields that require regulation to ensure that the interests of the public will be adequately served and protected. The Legislature recognizes that untrained persons, unlicensed persons or businesses, or persons who are not of good moral character engaged in the private security, investigative, and recovery industries are a threat to the welfare of the public if placed in positions of trust. Regulation of licensed and unlicensed persons and businesses engaged in these fields is therefore deemed necessary.

History: SS. 2, 11, ch. 90–364; s. 4, ch. 91–429; s. 1, ch. 94–172.

§ 493.6101. Definitions

1. "Department" means the Department of Agriculture and Consumer Services.
2. "Person" means any individual, firm, company, agency, organization, partnership, or corporation.
3. "Licensee" means any person licensed under this chapter.
4. The personal pronoun "he" or the personal pronoun "she" implies the impersonal pronoun "it."
5. "Principal officer" means an individual who holds the office of president, vice president, secretary, or treasurer in a corporation.

6. "Advertising" means the submission of bids, contracting, or making known by any public notice or solicitation of business, directly or indirectly, that services regulated under this chapter are available for consideration.

7. "Good moral character" means a personal history of honesty, fairness, and respect for the rights and property of others and for the laws of this state and nation.

8. "Conviction" means an adjudication of guilt by a federal or state court resulting from plea or trial, regardless of whether imposition of sentence was suspended.

9. "Unarmed" means that no firearm shall be carried by the licensee while providing services regulated by this chapter.

10. "Branch office" means each additional location of an agency where business is actively conducted which advertises as performing or is engaged in the business authorized by the license.

11. "Sponsor" means any Class "C," Class "MA," or Class "M" licensee who supervises and maintains under his or her direction and control a Class "CC" intern; or any Class "E" or Class "MR" licensee who supervises and maintains under his or her direction and control a Class "EE" intern.

12. "Intern" means an individual who studies as a trainee or apprentice under the direction and control of a designated sponsoring licensee.

13. "Manager" means any licensee who directs the activities of licensees at any agency or branch office. The manager shall be assigned to and shall primarily operate from the agency or branch office location for which he or she has been designated as manager.

14. "Firearm instructor" means any Class "K" licensee who provides classroom or range instruction to applicants for a Class "G" license.

15. "Private investigative agency" means any person who, for consideration, advertises as providing or is engaged in the business of furnishing private investigations.

16. "Private investigator" means any individual who, for consideration, advertises as providing or performs private investigation. This does not include an informant who, on a one-time or limited basis, as a result of a unique expertise, ability, vocation, or special access and who, under the direction and control of a Class "C" licensee or a Class "MA" licensee, provides information or services that would otherwise be included in the definition of private investigation.

17. "Private investigation" means the investigation by a person or persons for the purpose of obtaining information with reference to any of the following matters:

   a. Crime or wrongs done or threatened against the United States or any state or territory of the United States, when operating under express written authority of the governmental official responsible for authorizing such investigation.

   b. The identity, habits, conduct, movements, whereabouts, affiliations, associations, transactions, reputation, or character of any society, person, or group of persons.

   c. The credibility of witnesses or other persons.

   d. The whereabouts of missing persons, owners of unclaimed property or escheated property, or heirs to estates.

   e. The location or recovery of lost or stolen property.

   f. The causes and origin of, or responsibility for, fires, libels, slanders, losses, accidents, damage, or injuries to real or personal property.

   g. The business of securing evidence to be used before investigating committees or boards of award or arbitration or in the trial of civil or criminal cases and the preparation therefor.

18. "Security agency" means any person who, for consideration, advertises as providing or is engaged in the business of furnishing security services, armored car services, or transporting prisoners. This includes any person who utilizes dogs and individuals to provide security services.
19. "Security officer" means any individual who, for consideration, advertises as providing or performs bodyguard services or otherwise guards persons or property; attempts to prevent theft or unlawful taking of goods, wares, and merchandise; or attempts to prevent the misappropriation or concealment of goods, wares or merchandise, money, bonds, stocks, choses in action, notes, or other documents, papers, and articles of value or procurement of the return thereof. The term also includes armored car personnel and those personnel engaged in the transportation of prisoners.
20. "Recovery agency" means any person who, for consideration, advertises as providing or is engaged in the business of performing repossessions.
21. "Recovery agent" means any individual who, for consideration, advertises as providing or performs repossessions.
22. "Repossession" means the recovery of a motor vehicle as defined under s. 320.01(1), a mobile home as defined in s. 320.01(2), a motorboat as defined under s. 327.02, an aircraft as defined in s. 330.27(1), a personal watercraft as defined in s. 327.02, an all-terrain vehicle as defined in s. 316.2074, farm equipment as defined under s. 686.402, or industrial equipment, by an individual who is authorized by the legal owner, lienholder, or lessor to recover, or to collect money payment in lieu of recovery of, that which has been sold or leased under a security agreement that contains a repossession clause. As used in this subsection, the term "industrial equipment" includes, but is not limited to, tractors, road rollers, cranes, forklifts, backhoes, and bulldozers. The term "industrial equipment" also includes other vehicles that are propelled by power other than muscular power and that are used in the manufacture of goods or used in the provision of services. A repossession is complete when a licensed recovery agent is in control, custody, and possession of such repossessed property. Property that is being repossessed shall be considered to be in the control, custody, and possession of a recovery agent if the property being repossessed is secured in preparation for transport from the site of the recovery by means of being attached to or placed on the towing or other transport vehicle or if the property being repossessed is being operated or about to be operated by an employee of the recovery agency.
23. "Felony" means a criminal offense that is punishable under the laws of this state, or that would be punishable if committed in this state, by death or imprisonment in the state penitentiary; a crime in any other state or a crime against the United States which is designated as a felony; or an offense in any other state, territory, or country punishable by imprisonment for a term exceeding 1 year.

History: SS. 2, 11, ch. 90–364; s. 4, ch. 91–429; s. 10, ch. 94–241; s. 5, ch. 96–407; s. 1137, ch. 97–103; s. 1, ch. 97–248; s. 34, ch. 2001–36; s. 4, ch. 2002–295; s. 1, ch. 2005–143.

§ 493.6102. Inapplicability of this chapter

This chapter shall not apply to:

1. Any individual who is an "officer" as defined in s. 943.10(14) or is a law enforcement officer of the United States Government, while such local, state, or federal officer is engaged in her or his official duties or when performing off-duty security activities approved by her or his superiors.

2. Any insurance investigator or adjuster licensed by a state or federal licensing authority when such person is providing services or expert advice within the scope of her or his license.

3. Any individual solely, exclusively, and regularly employed as an unarmed investigator in connection with the business of her or his employer, when there exists an employer–employee relationship.

4. Any unarmed individual engaged in security services who is employed exclusively to work on the premises of her or his employer, or in connection with the business of her or his employer, when there exists an employer–employee relationship.

5. Any person or bureau whose business is exclusively the furnishing of information concerning the business and financial standing and credit responsibility of persons or the financial habits and financial responsibility of applicants for insurance, indemnity bonds, or commercial credit.

6. Any attorney in the regular practice of her or his profession.

7. Any bank or bank holding company, credit union, or small loan company operating pursuant to chapters 516 and 520; any consumer credit reporting agency regulated under 15 U.S.C. ss. 1681 et seq.; or any collection agency not engaged in repossessions or to any permanent employee thereof.

8. Any person who holds a professional license under the laws of this state when such person is providing services or expert advice in the profession or occupation in which that person is so licensed.

9. Any security agency or private investigative agency, and employees thereof, performing contractual security or investigative services solely and exclusively for any agency of the United States.

10. Any person duly authorized by the laws of this state to operate a central burglar or fire alarm business. However, such persons are not exempt to the extent they perform services requiring licensure or registration under this chapter.

11. Any person or company retained by a food service establishment to independently evaluate the food service establishment including quality of food, service, and facility. However, such persons are not exempt to the extent they investigate or are retained to investigate criminal or suspected criminal behavior on the part of the food service establishment employees.

12. Any person who is a school crossing guard employed by a third party hired by a city or county and trained in accordance with s. 316.75.

13. Any individual employed as a security officer by a church or ecclesiastical or denominational organization having an established physical place of worship in this state at which nonprofit religious services and activities are regularly conducted or by a church cemetery to provide security on the property of the organization or cemetery, and who does not carry a firearm in the course of her or his duties.

14. Any person or firm that solely and exclusively conducts genealogical research, or otherwise traces lineage or ancestry, by primarily utilizing public records and historical information and databases.

15. Any licensed Florida-certified public accountant who is acting within the scope of the practice of public accounting as defined in chapter 473.

History: SS. 2, 11, ch. 90–364; s. 16, ch. 91–248; s. 4, ch. 91–429; s. 2, ch. 94–172; s. 6, ch. 96–407; s. 1138, ch. 97–103; s. 69, ch. 97–190; s. 2, ch. 97–248; s. 35, ch. 2001–36; s. 2, ch. 2005–143; s. 23, ch. 2006–312, eff. January 1, 2007.

§ 493.6103. Authority to make rules

The department shall adopt rules necessary to administer this chapter. However, no rule shall be adopted that unreasonably restricts competition or the availability of services requiring licensure pursuant to this chapter or that unnecessarily increases the cost of such services without a corresponding or equivalent public benefit.

History: SS. 2, 11, ch. 90–364; s. 4, ch. 91–429.

§ 493.6104. Advisory council

1. The department shall designate an advisory council, known as the Private Investigation, Recovery, and Security Advisory Council, to be composed of 11 members. One member must be an active law enforcement officer, certified under the Florida Criminal Justice Standards and Training Commission, representing a statewide law enforcement agency or statewide association of law enforcement agencies. One member must be the owner or operator of a business that regularly contracts with Class "A," Class "B," or Class "R" agencies. Nine members must be geographically distributed, insofar as possible, and must be licensed pursuant to this chapter. Two members must be from the security profession, one of whom represents an agency that employs 20 security guards or fewer; two members must be from the private investigative profession, one of whom represents an agency that employs five investigators or fewer; one member shall be from the repossession profession; and the remaining four members may be drawn from any of the professions regulated under this chapter.

2. Council members shall be appointed by the Commissioner of Agriculture for a 4-year term. In the event of an appointment to fill an unexpired term, the appointment shall be for no longer than the remainder of the unexpired term. No member may serve more than two full consecutive terms. Members may be removed by the Commissioner of Agriculture for cause. Cause shall include, but is not limited to, absences from two consecutive meetings.

3. Members shall elect a chairperson annually. No member may serve as chairperson more than twice.

4. The council shall meet at least 4 times yearly upon the call of the chairperson, at the request of a majority of the membership, or at the request of the department. Notice of council meetings and the agenda shall be published in the Florida Administrative Weekly at least 14 days prior to such meeting.

5. The council shall advise the department and make recommendations relative to the regulation of the security, investigative, and recovery industries.

6. Council members shall serve without pay; however, state per diem and travel allowances may be claimed for attendance at officially called meetings as provided by s. 112.061.

7. A quorum of six members shall be necessary for a meeting to convene or continue. All official action taken by the council shall be by simple majority of those members present. Members may not participate or vote by proxy. Meetings shall be recorded, and minutes of the meetings shall be maintained by the department.

8. The director of the Division of Licensing or the director's designee shall serve, in a nonvoting capacity, as secretary to the council. The Division of Licensing shall provide all administrative and legal support required by the council in the conduct of its official business.

History: SS. 2, 11, ch. 90–364; s. 4, ch. 91–429; s. 3, ch. 94–172; s. 526, ch. 97–103; s. 5, ch. 2002–295.

§ 493.6105. Initial application for license

1. Each individual, partner, or principal officer in a corporation, shall file with the department a complete application accompanied by an application fee not to exceed $ 60, except that the applicant for a Class "D" or Class "G" license shall not be required to submit an application fee. The application fee shall not be refundable.

   a. The application submitted by any individual, partner, or corporate officer shall be approved by the department prior to that individual, partner, or corporate officer assuming his or her duties.

   b. Individuals who invest in the ownership of a licensed agency, but do not participate in, direct, or control the operations of the agency shall not be required to file an application.

2. Each application shall be signed by the individual under oath and shall be notarized.

3. The application shall contain the following information concerning the individual signing same:

   a. Name and any aliases.

   b. Age and date of birth.

   c. Place of birth.

   d. Social security number or alien registration number, whichever is applicable.

   e. Present residence address and his or her residence addresses within the 5 years immediately preceding the submission of the application.

   f. Occupations held presently and within the 5 years immediately preceding the submission of the application.

   g. A statement of all convictions.

   h. One passport-type color photograph taken within the 6 months immediately preceding submission of the application.

   i. A statement whether he or she has ever been adjudicated incompetent under chapter 744.

   j. A statement whether he or she has ever been committed to a mental institution under chapter 394.

   k. A full set of fingerprints on a card provided by the department and a fingerprint fee to be established by rule of the department based upon costs determined by state and federal agency charges and department processing costs. An applicant who has, within the immediately preceding 6 months, submitted a fingerprint card and fee for licensing purposes under this chapter shall not be required to submit another fingerprint card or fee.

   l. A personal inquiry waiver which allows the department to conduct necessary investigations to satisfy the requirements of this chapter.

   m. Such further facts as may be required by the department to show that the individual signing the application is of good moral character and qualified by experience and training to satisfy the requirements of this chapter.

4. In addition to the application requirements outlined in subsection (3), the applicant for a Class "C," Class "CC," Class "E," Class "EE," or Class "G" license shall submit two color photographs taken within the 6 months immediately preceding the submission of the application, which meet specifications prescribed by rule of the department. All other applicants shall submit one photograph taken within the 6 months immediately preceding the submission of the application.

5. In addition to the application requirements outlined under subsection (3), the applicant for a Class "C," Class "E," Class "M," Class "MA," Class "MB," or Class "MR" license shall include a statement on a form provided by the department of the experience which he or she believes will qualify him or her for such license.

6. In addition to the requirements outlined in subsection (3), an applicant for a Class "G" license shall satisfy minimum training criteria for firearms established by rule of the department, which training criteria shall include, but is not limited to, 28 hours of range and classroom training taught and administered by a Class "K" licensee; however, no more than 8 hours of such training shall consist of range training. If the applicant can show proof that he or she is an active law enforcement officer currently certified under the Criminal Justice Standards and Training Commission or has completed the training required for that certification within the last 12 months, or if the applicant submits one of the certificates specified in paragraph (7)(a), the department may waive the foregoing firearms training requirement.

7. In addition to the requirements under subsection (3), an applicant for a Class "K" license shall:
   a. Submit one of the following certificates:
      i. The Florida Criminal Justice Standards and Training Commission Firearms Instructor's Certificate.
      ii. The National Rifle Association Police Firearms Instructor's Certificate.
      iii. The National Rifle Association Security Firearms Instructor's Certificate.
      iv. A Firearms Instructor's Certificate from a federal, state, county, or municipal police academy in this state recognized as such by the Criminal Justice Standards and Training Commission or by the Department of Education.
   b. Pay the fee for and pass an examination administered by the department which shall be based upon, but is not necessarily limited to, a firearms instruction manual provided by the department.

8. In addition to the application requirements for individuals, partners, or officers outlined under subsection (3), the application for an agency license shall contain the following information:
   a. The proposed name under which the agency intends to operate.
   b. The street address, mailing address, and telephone numbers of the principal location at which business is to be conducted in this state.
   c. The street address, mailing address, and telephone numbers of all branch offices within this state.
   d. The names and titles of all partners or, in the case of a corporation, the names and titles of its principal officers.

9. Upon submission of a complete application, a Class "CC," Class "C," Class "D," Class "EE," Class "E," Class "M," Class "MA," Class "MB," or Class "MR" applicant may commence employment or appropriate duties for a licensed agency or branch office. However, the Class "C" or Class "E" applicant must work under the direction and control of a sponsoring licensee while his or her application is being processed. If the department denies application for licensure, the employment of the applicant must be terminated immediately, unless he or she performs only unregulated duties.

History: SS. 2, 11, ch. 90–364; s. 1, ch. 91–248; s. 4, ch. 91–429; s. 1, ch. 93–49; s. 527, ch. 97–103; s. 3, ch. 97–248.

§ 493.6106. License requirements; posting

1. Each individual licensed by the department must:
   a. Be at least 18 years of age.
   b. Be of good moral character.
   c. Not have been adjudicated incapacitated under s. 744.331 or a similar statute in another state, unless her or his capacity has been judicially restored; not have been involuntarily placed in a treatment facility for the mentally ill under chapter 394 or a similar statute in any other state, unless her or his competency has been judicially restored; and not have been diagnosed as having an incapacitating mental illness, unless a psychologist or psychiatrist licensed in this state certifies that she or he does not currently suffer from the mental illness.
   d. Not be a chronic and habitual user of alcoholic beverages to the extent that her or his normal faculties are impaired; not have been committed under chapter 397, former chapter 396, or a similar law in any other state; not have been found to be a habitual offender under s. 856.011(3) or a similar law in any other state; and not have had two or more convictions under s. 316.193 or a similar law in any other state within the 3-year period immediately preceding the date the application was filed, unless the individual establishes that she or he is not currently impaired and has successfully completed a rehabilitation course.
   e. Not have been committed for controlled substance abuse or have been found guilty of a crime under chapter 893 or a similar law relating to controlled substances in any other state within a 3-year period immediately preceding the date the application was filed, unless the individual establishes that she or he is not currently abusing any controlled substance and has successfully completed a rehabilitation course.
   f. Be a citizen or legal resident alien of the United States or have been granted authorization to seek employment in this country by the United States Bureau of Citizenship and Immigration Services.
      i. An applicant for a Class "C," Class "CC," Class "D," Class "DI," Class "E," Class "EE," Class "M," Class "MA," Class "MB," Class "MR," or Class "RI" license who is not a United States citizen must submit proof of current employment authorization issued by the United States Citizenship and Immigration Services or proof that she or he is deemed a permanent legal resident alien by the United States Citizenship and Immigration Services.
      ii. An applicant for a Class "G" or Class "K" license who is not a United States citizen must submit proof that she or he is deemed a permanent legal resident alien by the United States Citizenship and Immigration Services, together with additional documentation establishing that she or he has resided in the state of residence shown on the application for at least 90 consecutive days before the date that the application is submitted.
      iii. An applicant for an agency or school license who is not a United States citizen or permanent legal resident alien must submit documentation issued by the United States Citizenship and Immigration Services stating that she or he is lawfully in the United States and is authorized to own and operate the type of agency or school for which she or he is applying. An employment authorization card issued by the United States Citizenship and Immigration Services is not sufficient documentation.
   g. Not be prohibited from purchasing or possessing a firearm by state or federal law if the individual is applying for a Class "G" license or a Class "K" license.

2. Each agency shall have a minimum of one physical location within this state from which the normal business of the agency is conducted, and this location shall be considered the primary office for that agency in this state.
    a. If an agency desires to change the physical location of the business, as it appears on the agency license, the department must be notified within 10 days of the change, and, except upon renewal, the fee prescribed in s. 493.6107 must be submitted for each license requiring revision. Each license requiring revision must be returned with such notification.
    b. The Class "A," Class "B," or Class "R" license and any branch office or school license shall at all times be posted in a conspicuous place at the licensed physical location in this state where the business is conducted.
    c. Each Class "A," Class "B," Class "R," branch office, or school licensee shall display, in a place that is in clear and unobstructed public view, a notice on a form prescribed by the department stating that the business operating at this location is licensed and regulated by the Department of Agriculture and Consumer Services and that any questions or complaints should be directed to the department.
    d. A minimum of one properly licensed manager shall be designated for each agency and branch office location.
3. Each Class "C," Class "CC," Class "D," Class "DI," Class "E," Class "EE," Class "G," Class "K," Class "M," Class "MA," Class "MB," Class "MR," or Class "RI" licensee shall notify the division in writing within 10 days of a change in her or his residence or mailing address.

History: SS. 2, 11, ch. 90–364; s. 2, ch. 91–248; s. 4, ch. 91–429; s. 2, ch. 93–49; s. 4, ch. 94–172; s. 528, ch. 97–103; s. 83, ch. 2004–5; s. 1, ch. 2006–165, eff. July 1, 2006.

§ 493.6107. Fees

1. The department shall establish by rule examination and biennial license fees which shall not exceed the following:
    a. Class "M" license—manager Class "AB" agency: $75.
    b. Class "G" license—statewide firearm license: $150.
    c. Class "K" license—firearms instructor: $100.
    d. Fee for the examination for firearms instructor: $75.
2. The department may establish by rule a fee for the replacement or revision of a license which fee shall not exceed $30.
3. The fees set forth in this section must be paid by certified check or money order or, at the discretion of the department, by agency check at the time the application is approved, except that the applicant for a Class "G" or Class "M" license must pay the license fee at the time the application is made. If a license is revoked or denied or if the application is withdrawn, the license fee shall not be refunded.
4. The department may prorate license fees.
5. Payment of any license fee provided for under this chapter authorizes the licensee to practice his or her profession anywhere in this state without obtaining any additional license, permit, registration, or identification card, any municipal or county ordinance or resolution to the contrary notwithstanding. However, an agency may be required to obtain a city and county occupational license in each city and county where the agency maintains a physical office.

History: SS. 2, 11, ch. 90–364; s. 3, ch. 91–248; s. 4, ch. 91–429; s. 5, ch. 94–172; s. 529, ch. 97–103.

§ 493.6108. Investigation of applicants by Department of Agriculture and Consumer Services

1. Except as otherwise provided, prior to the issuance of a license under this chapter, the department shall make an investigation of the applicant for a license. The investigation shall include:
    a.
        i. An examination of fingerprint records and police records. When a criminal history analysis of any applicant under this chapter is performed by means of fingerprint card identification, the time limitations prescribed by s. 120.60(1) shall be tolled during the time the applicant's fingerprint card is under review by the Department of Law Enforcement or the United States Department of Justice, Federal Bureau of Investigation.
        ii. If a legible set of fingerprints, as determined by the Department of Law Enforcement or the Federal Bureau of Investigation, cannot be obtained after two attempts, the Department of Agriculture and Consumer Services may determine the applicant's eligibility based upon a criminal history record check under the applicant's name conducted by the Department of Law Enforcement and the Federal Bureau of Investigation. A set of fingerprints taken by a law enforcement agency and a written statement signed by the fingerprint technician or a licensed physician stating that there is a physical condition that precludes obtaining a legible set of fingerprints or that the fingerprints taken are the best that can be obtained is sufficient to meet this requirement.
    b. An inquiry to determine if the applicant has been adjudicated incompetent under chapter 744 or has been committed to a mental institution under chapter 394.
    c. Such other investigation of the individual as the department may deem necessary.
2. In addition to subsection (1), the department shall make an investigation of the general physical fitness of the Class "G" applicant to bear a weapon or firearm. Determination of physical fitness shall be certified by a physician or physician assistant currently licensed pursuant to chapter 458, chapter 459, or any similar law of another state or authorized to act as a licensed physician by a federal agency or department or by an advanced registered nurse practitioner currently licensed pursuant to chapter 464. Such certification shall be submitted on a form provided by the department.
3. The department shall also investigate the mental history and current mental and emotional fitness of any Class "G" applicant, and may deny a Class "G" license to anyone who has a history of mental illness or drug or alcohol abuse.

History: SS. 2, 11, ch. 90–364; s. 4, ch. 91–429; s. 3, ch. 93–49; s. 6, ch. 94–172; s. 230, ch. 96–410; s. 4, ch. 97–248; s. 6, ch. 2002–295; s. 1, ch. 2005–76.

§ 493.6109. Reciprocity

1. The department may adopt rules for
    a. Entering into reciprocal agreements with other states or territories of the United States for the purpose of licensing persons to perform activities regulated under this chapter who are currently licensed to perform similar services in the other states or territories; or

b. Allowing a person who is licensed in another state or territory to perform similar services in this state, on a temporary and limited basis, without the need for licensure in state.

2. The rules authorized in subsection (1) may be promulgated only if:

   a. The other state or territory has requirements which are substantially similar to or greater than those established in this chapter.

   b. The applicant has engaged in licensed activities for at least 1 year in the other state or territory with no disciplinary action against him or her.

   c. The Commissioner of Agriculture or other appropriate authority of the other state or territory agrees to accept service of process for those licensees who are operating in this state on a temporary basis.

History: SS. 2, 11, ch. 90–364; s. 4, ch. 91–429; s. 530, ch. 97–103; s. 7, ch. 2002–295.

§ 493.6110. Licensee's insurance

A Class "B" agency license may not be issued unless the applicant first files with the department a certification of insurance evidencing commercial general liability coverage. The coverage shall provide the department as an additional insured for the purpose of receiving all notices of modification or cancellation of such insurance. Coverage shall be written by an insurance company which is lawfully engaged to provide insurance coverage in Florida. Coverage shall provide for a combined single-limit policy in the amount of at least $300,000 for death, bodily injury, property damage, and personal injury. Coverage shall insure for the liability of all employees licensed by the department while acting in the course of their employment.

1. The licensed agency shall notify the department of any claim against such insurance.

2. The licensed agency shall notify the department immediately upon cancellation of the insurance policy, whether such cancellation was initiated by the insurance company or the insured agency.

3. The agency license shall be automatically suspended upon the date of cancellation unless evidence of insurance is provided to the department prior to the effective date of cancellation.

History: SS. 2, 11, ch. 90–364; s. 4, ch. 91–248; s. 4, ch. 91–429; s. 3, ch. 2005–143.

§ 493.6111. License; contents; identification card

1. All licenses issued pursuant to this chapter shall be on a form prescribed by the department and shall include the licensee's name, license number, expiration date of the license, and any other information the department deems necessary. Class "C," Class "CC," Class "D," Class "E," Class "EE," Class "M," Class "MA," Class "MB," Class "MR," and Class "G" licenses shall be in the possession of individual licensees while on duty.

2. Licenses shall be valid for a period of 2 years, except for Class "A," Class "B," Class "AB," Class "R," and branch agency licenses, which shall be valid for a period of 3 years.

3. The department shall, upon complete application and payment of the appropriate fees, issue a separate license to each branch office for which application is made.

4. Notwithstanding the existence of a valid Florida corporate registration, no agency licensee may conduct activities regulated under this chapter under any fictitious name without prior

written authorization from the department to use that name in the conduct of activities regulated under this chapter. The department may not authorize the use of a name which is so similar to that of a public officer or agency, or of that used by another licensee, that the public may be confused or misled thereby. The authorization for the use of a fictitious name shall require, as a condition precedent to the use of such name, the filing of a certificate of engaging in business under a fictitious name under s. 865.09. No licensee shall be permitted to conduct business under more than one name except as separately licensed nor shall the license be valid to protect any licensee who is engaged in the business under any name other than that specified in the license. An agency desiring to change its licensed name shall notify the department and, except upon renewal, pay a fee not to exceed $30 for each license requiring revision including those of all licensed employees except Class "D" or Class "G" licensees. Upon the return of such licenses to the department, revised licenses shall be provided.

5. It shall be the duty of every agency to furnish all of its partners, principal corporate officers, and all licensed employees an identification card. The card shall specify at least the name and license number, if appropriate, of the holder of the card and the name and license number of the agency and shall be signed by a representative of the agency and by the holder of the card.

 a. Each individual to whom a license and identification card have been issued shall be responsible for the safekeeping thereof and shall not loan, or let or allow any other individual to use or display, the license or card.

 b. The identification card shall be in the possession of each partner, principal corporate officer, or licensed employee while on duty.

 c. Upon denial, suspension, or revocation of a license, or upon termination of a business association with the licensed agency, it shall be the duty of each partner, principal corporate officer, manager, or licensed employee to return the identification card to the issuing agency.

6. A licensed agency must include its agency license number in any advertisement in any print medium or directory, and must include its agency license number in any written bid or offer to provide services.

History: SS. 2, 11, ch. 90–364; s. 5, ch. 91–248; s. 4, ch. 91–429; s. 4, ch. 93–49; s. 1, ch. 98–335.

§ 493.6112. Notification to Department of Agriculture and Consumer Services of changes of partner or officer or employees

1. After filing the application, unless the department declines to issue the license or revokes it after issuance, an agency or school shall, within 5 working days of the withdrawal, removal, replacement, or addition of any or all partners or officers, notify and file with the department complete applications for such individuals. The agency's or school's good standing under this chapter shall be contingent upon the department's approval of any new partner or officer.

2. Each agency or school shall, upon the employment or termination of employment of a licensee, report such employment or termination immediately to the department and, in the case of a termination, report the reason or reasons therefor. The report shall be on a form prescribed by the department.

History: SS. 2, 11, ch. 90–364; s. 4, ch. 91–429; s. 8, ch. 2002–295.

§ 493.6113. Renewal application for licensure

1. A license granted under the provisions of this chapter shall be renewed biennially by the department, except for Class "A," Class "B," Class "AB," Class "R," and branch agency licenses, which shall be renewed every 3 years.
2. No less than 90 days prior to the expiration date of the license, the department shall mail a written notice to the last known residence address for individual licensees and to the last known agency address for agencies.
3. Each licensee shall be responsible for renewing his or her license on or before its expiration by filing with the department an application for renewal accompanied by payment of the prescribed license fee.
   a. Each Class "A," Class "B," or Class "R" licensee shall additionally submit on a form prescribed by the department a certification of insurance which evidences that the licensee maintains coverage as required under s. 493.6110.
   b. Each Class "G" licensee shall additionally submit proof that he or she has received during each year of the license period a minimum of 4 hours of firearms recertification training taught by a Class "K" licensee and has complied with such other health and training requirements which the department may adopt by rule. If proof of a minimum of 4 hours of annual firearms recertification training cannot be provided, the renewal applicant shall complete the minimum number of hours of range and classroom training required at the time of initial licensure. If the licensee fails to complete the required 4 hours of annual training during the first year of the 2-year term of the license, the license shall be automatically suspended. The licensee must complete the minimum number of hours of range and classroom training required at the time of initial licensure and submit proof of completion of such training to the department before the license may be reinstated. If the licensee fails to complete the required 4 hours of annual training during the second year of the 2-year term of the license, the licensee must complete the minimum number of hours of range and classroom training required at the time of initial licensure and submit proof of completion of such training to the department before the license may be renewed. The department may waive the firearms training requirement if:
      i. The applicant provides proof that he or she is currently certified as a law enforcement officer or correctional officer under the Criminal Justice Standards and Training Commission and has completed law enforcement firearms requalification training annually during the previous 2 years of the licensure period;
      ii. The applicant provides proof that he or she is currently certified as a federal law enforcement officer and has received law enforcement firearms training administered by a federal law enforcement agency annually during the previous 2 years of the licensure period; or
      iii. The applicant submits a valid firearm certificate among those specified in s. 493.6105(6)(a) and provides proof of having completed requalification training during the previous 2 years of the licensure period.
   c. Each Class "DS" or Class "RS" licensee shall additionally submit the current curriculum, examination, and list of instructors.

    d. Each Class "K" licensee shall additionally submit one of the certificates specified under s. 493.6105(6) as proof that he or she remains certified to provide firearms instruction.

4. A licensee who fails to file a renewal application on or before its expiration must renew his or her license by fulfilling the applicable requirements of subsection (3) and by paying a late fee equal to the amount of the license fee.

5. No license shall be renewed 3 months or more after its expiration date. The applicant shall submit a new, complete application and the respective fees.

6. A renewal applicant shall not perform any activity regulated by this chapter between the date of expiration and the date of renewal of his or her license.

History: SS. 2, 11, ch. 90–364; s. 6, ch. 91–248; s. 4, ch. 91–429; s. 43, ch. 95–144; s. 531, ch. 97–103; s. 2, ch. 98–335.

§ 493.6114. Cancellation or inactivation of license

1. In the event the licensee desires to cancel her or his license, she or he shall notify the department in writing and return the license to the department within 10 days of the date of cancellation.

2. The department, at the written request of the licensee, may place her or his license in inactive status. A license may remain inactive for a period of 3 years, at the end of which time, if the license has not been renewed, it shall be automatically canceled. If the license expires during the inactive period, the licensee shall be required to pay license fees and, if applicable, show proof of insurance or proof of firearms training before the license can be made active. No late fees shall apply when a license is in inactive status.

History: SS. 2, 11, ch. 90–364; s. 4, ch. 91–429; s. 532, ch. 97–103.

§ 493.6115. Weapons and firearms

1. The provisions of this section shall apply to all licensees in addition to the other provisions of this chapter.

2. Only Class "C," Class "CC," Class "D," Class "M," Class "MA," or Class "MB" licensees are permitted to bear a firearm and any such licensee who bears a firearm shall also have a Class "G" license.

3. No employee shall carry or be furnished a weapon or firearm unless the carrying of a weapon or firearm is required by her or his duties, nor shall an employee carry a weapon or firearm except in connection with those duties. When carried pursuant to this subsection, the weapon or firearm shall be encased in view at all times except as provided in subsection (4).

4. A Class "C" or Class "CC" licensee 21 years of age or older who has also been issued a Class "G" license may carry, in the performance of her or his duties, a concealed firearm. A Class "D" licensee 21 years of age or older who has also been issued a Class "G" license may carry a concealed firearm in the performance of her or his duties under the conditions specified in s. 493.6305(2). The Class "G" license shall clearly indicate such authority. The authority of any such licensee to carry a concealed firearm shall be valid throughout the state, in any location, while performing services within the scope of the license.

5. The Class "G" license shall remain in effect only during the period the applicant is employed as a Class "C," Class "CC," Class "D," Class "MA," Class "MB," or Class "M" licensee.

6. In addition to any other firearm approved by the department, a licensee who has been issued a Class "G" license may carry a.38 caliber revolver; or a.380 caliber or 9 millimeter semiautomatic pistol; or a.357 caliber revolver with.38 caliber ammunition only while performing duties authorized under this chapter. No licensee may carry more than two firearms upon her or his person when performing her or his duties. A licensee may only carry a firearm of the specific type and caliber with which she or he is qualified pursuant to the firearms training referenced in subsection (8) or s. 493.6113(3)(b).

7. Any person who provides classroom and range instruction to applicants for Class "G" licensure shall have a Class "K" license.

8. A Class "G" applicant must satisfy the minimum training criteria as set forth in s. 493.6105(6) and as established by rule of the department.

9. Whenever a Class "G" licensee discharges her or his firearm in the course of her or his duties, the Class "G" licensee and the agency by which she or he is employed shall, within 5 working days, submit to the department an explanation describing the nature of the incident, the necessity for using the firearm, and a copy of any report prepared by a law enforcement agency. The department may revoke or suspend the Class "G" licensee's license and the licensed agency's agency license if this requirement is not met.

10. The department may promulgate rules to establish minimum standards to issue licenses for weapons other than firearms.

11. The department may establish rules to require periodic classroom training for firearms instructors to provide updated information relative to curriculum or other training requirements provided by statute or rule.

12. The department may issue a temporary Class "G" license, on a case-by-case basis, if:
    a. The agency or employer has certified that the applicant has been determined to be mentally and emotionally stable by either:
        i. A validated written psychological test taken within the previous 12-month period.
        ii. An evaluation by a psychiatrist or psychologist licensed in this state or by the Federal Government made within the previous 12-month period.
        iii. Presentation of a DD form 214, issued within the previous 12-month period, which establishes the absence of emotional or mental instability at the time of discharge from military service.
    b. The applicant has submitted a complete application for a Class "G" license, with a notation that she or he is seeking a temporary Class "G" license.
    c. The applicant has completed all Class "G" minimum training requirements as specified in this section.
    d. The applicant has received approval from the department subsequent to its conduct of a criminal history record check as authorized in s. 493.6121(6). s. 493.6108(1).

13. In addition to other fees, the department may charge a fee, not to exceed $ 25, for processing a Class "G" license application as a temporary Class "G" license request.

14. Upon issuance of the temporary Class "G" license, the licensee is subject to all of the requirements imposed upon Class "G" licensees.

15. The temporary Class "G" license is valid until the Class "G" license is issued or denied. If the department denies the Class "G" license, any temporary Class "G" license issued to that individual is void, and the individual shall be removed from armed duties immediately.

16. If the criminal history record check program referenced in s. 493.6121(6) s. 493.6108(1). is inoperable, the department may issue a temporary "G" license on a case-by-case basis, provided that the applicant has met all statutory requirements for the issuance of a temporary "G" license as specified in subsection (12), excepting the criminal history record check stipulated there; provided, that the department requires that the licensed employer of the applicant conduct a criminal history record check of the applicant pursuant to standards set forth in rule by the department, and provide to the department an affidavit containing such information and statements as required by the department, including a statement that the criminal history record check did not indicate the existence of any criminal history that would prohibit licensure. Failure to properly conduct such a check, or knowingly providing incorrect or misleading information or statements in the affidavit shall constitute grounds for disciplinary action against the licensed agency, including revocation of license.

17. No person is exempt from the requirements of this section by virtue of holding a concealed weapon or concealed firearm license issued pursuant to s. 790.06.

History: SS. 2, 11, ch. 90–364; s. 7, ch. 91–248; s. 4, ch. 91–429; s. 7, ch. 94–172; s. 533, ch. 97–103; s. 5, ch. 97–248; s. 1, ch. 2005–69.

§ 493.6116. Sponsorship of interns

1. Only licensees may sponsor interns. A Class "C," Class "M," or Class "MA" licensee may sponsor a Class "CC" private investigator intern; a Class "E" or Class "MR" licensee may sponsor a Class "EE" recovery agent intern.
2. An internship may not commence until the sponsor has submitted to the department the notice of intent to sponsor. Such notice shall be on a form provided by the department.
3. Internship is intended to serve as a learning process. Sponsors shall assume a training status by providing direction and control of interns. Sponsors shall only sponsor interns whose place of business is within a 50-mile distance of the sponsor's place of business and shall not allow interns to operate independently of such direction and control, or require interns to perform activities which do not enhance the intern's qualification for licensure.
4. No sponsor may sponsor more than six interns at the same time.
5. A sponsor shall certify a biannual progress report on each intern and shall certify completion or termination of an internship to the department within 15 days after such completion or termination. The report must be made on a form provided by the department and must include at a minimum:
   a. The inclusive dates of the internship.
   b. A narrative part explaining the primary duties, types of experiences gained, and the scope of training received.
   c. An evaluation of the performance of the intern and a recommendation regarding future licensure.

History: SS. 2, 11, ch. 90–364; s. 4, ch. 91–429; s. 8, ch. 94–172; s. 68, ch. 95–144.

§ 493.6117. Division of Licensing Trust Fund

There is created within the Division of Licensing of the department a Division of Licensing Trust Fund. All moneys required to be paid under this chapter shall be collected by the department and deposited in the trust fund. The Division of Licensing Trust Fund shall be subject to the service charge imposed pursuant to chapter 215. The Legislature shall appropriate from the fund such amounts as it deems necessary for the purpose of administering the provisions of this chapter. The unencumbered balance in the trust fund at the beginning of the year shall not exceed $100,000, and any excess shall be transferred to the General Revenue Fund unallocated.

History: SS. 2, 11, ch. 90–364; s. 4, ch. 91–429.

§ 493.6118. Grounds for disciplinary action

1. The following constitute grounds for which disciplinary action specified in subsection (2) may be taken by the department against any licensee, agency, or applicant regulated by this chapter, or any unlicensed person engaged in activities regulated under this chapter.
   a. Fraud or willful misrepresentation in applying for or obtaining a license.
   b. Use of any fictitious or assumed name by an agency unless the agency has department approval and qualifies under s. 865.09.
   c. Being found guilty of or entering a plea of guilty or nolo contendere to, regardless of adjudication, or being convicted of a crime that directly relates to the business for which the license is held or sought. A plea of nolo contendere shall create a rebuttable presumption of guilt to the underlying criminal charges, and the department shall allow the individual being disciplined or denied an application for a license to present any mitigating circumstances surrounding his or her plea.
   d. A false statement by the licensee that any individual is or has been in his or her employ.
   e. A finding that the licensee or any employee is guilty of willful betrayal of a professional secret or any unauthorized release of information acquired as a result of activities regulated under this chapter.
   f. Proof that the applicant or licensee is guilty of fraud or deceit, or of negligence, incompetency, or misconduct, in the practice of the activities regulated under this chapter.
   g. Conducting activities regulated under this chapter without a license or with a revoked or suspended license.
   h. Failure of the licensee to maintain in full force and effect the commercial general liability insurance coverage required by s. 493.6110.
   i. Impersonating, or permitting or aiding and abetting an employee to impersonate, a law enforcement officer or an employee of the state, the United States, or any political subdivision thereof by identifying himself or herself as a federal, state, county, or municipal law enforcement officer or official representative, by wearing a uniform or presenting or displaying a badge or credentials that would cause a reasonable person to believe that he or she is a law enforcement officer or that he or she has official authority, by displaying any flashing or warning vehicular lights other than amber colored, or by committing any act that is intended to falsely convey official status.

j. Commission of an act of violence or the use of force on any person except in the lawful protection of one's self or another from physical harm.

k. Knowingly violating, advising, encouraging, or assisting the violation of any statute, court order, capias, warrant, injunction, or cease and desist order, in the course of business regulated under this chapter.

l. Soliciting business for an attorney in return for compensation.

m. Transferring or attempting to transfer a license issued pursuant to this chapter.

n. Employing or contracting with any unlicensed or improperly licensed person or agency to conduct activities regulated under this chapter, or performing any act that assists, aids, or abets a person or business entity in engaging in unlicensed activity, when the licensure status was known or could have been ascertained by reasonable inquiry.

o. Failure or refusal to cooperate with or refusal of access to an authorized representative of the department engaged in an official investigation pursuant to this chapter.

p. Failure of any partner, principal corporate officer, or licensee to have his or her identification card in his or her possession while on duty.

q. Failure of any licensee to have his or her license in his or her possession while on duty, as specified in s. 493.6111(1).

r. Failure or refusal by a sponsor to certify a biannual written report on an intern or to certify completion or termination of an internship to the department within 15 working days.

s. Failure to report to the department any person whom the licensee knows to be in violation of this chapter or the rules of the department.

t. Violating any provision of this chapter.

u. For a Class "G" licensee, failing to timely complete recertification training as required in s. 493.6113(3)(b).

v. For a Class "K" licensee, failing to maintain active certification specified under s. 493.6105(6).

w. For a Class "G" or a Class "K" applicant or licensee, being prohibited from purchasing or possessing a firearm by state or federal law.

x. In addition to the grounds for disciplinary action prescribed in paragraphs (a)–(t), Class "R" recovery agencies, Class "E" recovery agents, and Class "EE" recovery agent interns are prohibited from committing the following acts:

   i. Recovering a motor vehicle, mobile home, motorboat, aircraft, personal watercraft, all-terrain vehicle, farm equipment, or industrial equipment that has been sold under a conditional sales agreement or under the terms of a chattel mortgage before authorization has been received from the legal owner or mortgagee.

   ii. Charging for expenses not actually incurred in connection with the recovery, transportation, storage, or disposal of repossessed property or personal property obtained in a repossession.

   iii. Using any repossessed property or personal property obtained in a repossession for the personal benefit of a licensee or an officer, director, partner, manager, or employee of a licensee.

   iv. Selling property recovered under the provisions of this chapter, except with written authorization from the legal owner or the mortgagee thereof.

   v. Failing to notify the police or sheriff's department of the jurisdiction in which the repossessed property is recovered within 2 hours after recovery.

vi. Failing to remit moneys collected in lieu of recovery of a motor vehicle, mobile home, motorboat, aircraft, personal watercraft, all-terrain vehicle, farm equipment, or industrial equipment to the client within 10 working days.

vii. Failing to deliver to the client a negotiable instrument that is payable to the client, within 10 working days after receipt of such instrument.

viii. Falsifying, altering, or failing to maintain any required inventory or records regarding disposal of personal property contained in or on repossessed property pursuant to s. 493.6404(1).

ix. Carrying any weapon or firearm when he or she is on private property and performing duties under his or her license whether or not he or she is licensed pursuant to s. 790.06.

x. Soliciting from the legal owner the recovery of property subject to repossession after such property has been seen or located on public or private property if the amount charged or requested for such recovery is more than the amount normally charged for such a recovery.

xi. Wearing, presenting, or displaying a badge in the course of performing a repossession regulated by this chapter.

y. Installation of a tracking device or tracking application in violation of s. 934.425.

2. When the department finds any violation of subsection (1), it may do one or more of the following:
   a. Deny an application for the issuance or renewal of a license.
   b. Issue a reprimand.
   c. Impose an administrative fine not to exceed $1000 for every count or separate offense.
   d. Place the licensee on probation for a period of time and subject to such conditions as the department may specify.
   e. Suspend or revoke a license.

3. The department may deny an application for licensure citing lack of good moral character only if the finding by the department of lack of good moral character is supported by clear and convincing evidence. In such cases, the department shall furnish the applicant a statement containing the findings of the department, a complete record of the evidence upon which the determination was based, and a notice of the rights of the applicant to an administrative hearing and subsequent appeal.

4. Notwithstanding the provisions of paragraph (1)(c) and subsection (2):
   a. If the applicant or licensee has been convicted of a felony, the department shall deny the application or revoke the license unless and until civil rights have been restored by the State of Florida or by a state acceptable to Florida and a period of 10 years has expired since final release from supervision.
   b. A Class "G" applicant who has been convicted of a felony shall also have had the specific right to possess, carry, or use a firearm restored by the State of Florida.
   c. If the applicant or licensee has been found guilty of, entered a plea of guilty to, or entered a plea of nolo contendere to a felony and adjudication of guilt is withheld, the department shall deny the application or revoke the license until a period of 3 years has expired since final release from supervision.
   d. A plea of nolo contendere shall create a rebuttable presumption of guilt to the underlying criminal charges, and the department shall allow the person being disciplined or denied an application for a license to present any mitigating circumstances surrounding his or her plea.

e. The grounds for discipline or denial cited in this subsection shall be applied to any disqualifying criminal history regardless of the date of commission of the underlying criminal charge. Such provisions shall be applied retroactively and prospectively.

5. Upon revocation or suspension of a license, the licensee shall forthwith return the license which was suspended or revoked.

6. The agency license and the approval or license of each officer, partner, or owner of the agency are automatically suspended upon entry of a final order imposing an administrative fine against the agency, until the fine is paid, if 30 calendar days have elapsed since the entry of the final order. All owners and corporate or agency officers or partners are jointly and severally liable for agency fines. Neither the agency license or the approval or license of any officer, partner, or owner of the agency may be renewed, nor may an application be approved if the owner, licensee, or applicant is liable for an outstanding administrative fine imposed under this chapter. An individual's approval or license becomes automatically suspended if a fine imposed against the individual or his or her agency is not paid within 30 days after the date of the final order, and remains suspended until the fine is paid. Notwithstanding the provisions of this subsection, an individual's approval or license may not be suspended nor may an application be denied when the licensee or the applicant has an appeal from a final order pending in any appellate court.

7. An applicant or licensee shall be ineligible to reapply for the same class of license for a period of 1 year following final agency action resulting in the denial or revocation of a license applied for or issued under this chapter. This time restriction shall not apply to administrative denials wherein the basis for denial was:

a. An inadvertent error or omission on the application;

b. The experience documented by the department was insufficient at the time of application;

c. The department was unable to complete the criminal background investigation due to insufficient information from the Department of Law Enforcement, the Federal Bureau of Investigation, or any other applicable law enforcement agency; or

d. Failure to submit required fees.

History: SS. 2, 11, ch. 90–364; s. 8, ch. 91–248; s. 4, ch. 91–429; s. 5, ch. 93–49; s. 9, ch. 94–172; s. 534, ch. 97–103; s. 6, ch. 97–248; s. 4, ch. 2005–143.

§ 493.6119. Divulging investigative information; false reports prohibited

1. Except as otherwise provided by this chapter or other law, no licensee, or any employee of a licensee or licensed agency shall divulge or release to anyone other than her or his client or employer the contents of an investigative file acquired in the course of licensed investigative activity. However, the prohibition of this section shall not apply when the client for whom the information was acquired, or the client's lawful representative, has alleged a violation of this chapter by the licensee, licensed agency, or any employee, or when the prior written consent of the client to divulge or release such information has been obtained.

2. Nothing in this section shall be construed to deny access to any business or operational records, except as specified in subsection (1), by an authorized representative of the department engaged in an official investigation, inspection, or inquiry pursuant to the regulatory duty and investigative authority of this chapter.

3. Any licensee or employee of a licensee or licensed agency who, in reliance on subsection (1), denies access to an investigative file to an authorized representative of the department shall state such denial in writing within 2 working days of the request for access. Such statement of denial shall include the following:
   a. That the information requested was obtained by a licensed private investigator on behalf of a client; and
   b. That the client has been advised of the request and has denied permission to grant access; or
   c. That the present whereabouts of the client is unknown or attempts to contact the client have been unsuccessful but, in the opinion of the person denying access, review of the investigative file under conditions specified by the department would be contrary to the interests of the client; or
   d. That the requested investigative file will be provided pursuant to a subpoena issued by the department.
4. No licensee or any employer or employee of a licensee or licensed agency shall willfully make a false statement or report to her or his client or employer or an authorized representative of the department concerning information acquired in the course of activities regulated by this chapter.

History: SS. 2, 11, ch. 90–364; s. 4, ch. 91–429; s. 535, ch. 97–103.

§ 493.6120. Violations; penalty

1. Any person who violates any provision of this chapter except s. 493.6405 commits a misdemeanor of the first degree, punishable as provided in s. 775.082 or s. 775.083.
2. Any person who is convicted of any violation of this chapter shall not be eligible for licensure for a period of 5 years.
3. Any person who violates or disregards any cease and desist order issued by the department commits a misdemeanor of the first degree, punishable as provided in s. 775.082 or s. 775.083. In addition, the department may seek the imposition of a civil penalty not to exceed $ 5,000.
4. For a second or subsequent violation, a felony of the third degree, punishable as provided in s. 775.082, s. 775.083, or s. 775.084, and the department may seek the imposition of a civil penalty not to exceed $10,000.
5. Any person who was an owner, officer, partner, or manager of a licensed agency at the time of any activity that is the basis for revocation of the agency or branch office license and who knew or should have known of the activity, shall have his or her personal licenses or approval suspended for 3 years and may not have any financial interest in or be employed in any capacity by a licensed agency during the period of suspension.

History: SS. 2, 11, ch. 90–364; s. 4, ch. 91–429; s. 6, ch. 93–49; s. 536, ch. 97–103.

§ 493.6121. Enforcement; investigation

1. The department shall have the power to enforce the provisions of this chapter, irrespective of the place or location in which the violation occurred, and, upon the complaint of any person or on its own initiative, to cause to be investigated any suspected violation

thereof or to cause to be investigated the business and business methods of any licensed or unlicensed person, agency or employee thereof, or applicant for licensure under this chapter.

2. In any investigation undertaken by the department, each licensed or unlicensed person, applicant, agency, or employee shall, upon request of the department provide records and shall truthfully respond to questions concerning activities regulated under this chapter. Such records shall be maintained in this state for a period of 2 years at the principal place of business of the licensee, or at any other location within the state for a person whose license has been terminated, canceled, or revoked. Upon request by the department the records must be made available immediately to the department unless the department determines that an extension may be granted.

3. The department shall have the authority to investigate any licensed or unlicensed person, firm, company, partnership, or corporation when such person, firm, company, partnership, or corporation is advertising as providing or is engaged in performing services which require licensure under this chapter or when a licensee is engaged in activities which do not comply with or are prohibited by this chapter; and the department shall have the authority to issue an order to cease and desist the further conduct of such activities, or seek an injunction, or take other appropriate action pursuant to s. 493.6118(2)(a) or (c).

4. In the exercise of its enforcement responsibility and in the conduct of any investigation authorized by this chapter, the department shall have the power to subpoena and bring before it any person in the state, require the production of any papers it deems necessary, administer oaths, and take depositions of any persons so subpoenaed. If any person fails or refuses to comply with a proper subpoena to be examined or fails or refuses to answer any question about her or his qualifications or the business methods or business practices under investigation or refuses access to agency records in accordance with s. 493.6119, the circuit court of Leon County or of the county wherein such person resides may issue an order on the application of the department requiring such person to comply with the subpoena and to testify. Such failure or refusal shall also be grounds for revocation, suspension, or other disciplinary action. The testimony of witnesses in any such proceeding shall be under oath before the department or its agents.

5. In order to carry out the duties of the department prescribed in this chapter, designated employees of the Division of Licensing of the Department of Agriculture and Consumer Services may obtain access to the information in criminal justice information systems and to criminal justice information as defined in s. 943.045, on such terms and conditions as are reasonably calculated to provide necessary information and protect the confidentiality of the information. Such criminal justice information submitted to the division is confidential and exempt from the provisions of s. 119.07(1).

6. The department shall be provided access to the program that is operated by the Department of Law Enforcement, pursuant to s. 790.065, for providing criminal history record information to licensed gun dealers, manufacturers, and exporters. The department may make inquiries, and shall receive responses in the same fashion as provided under s. 790.065. The department shall be responsible for payment to the Department of Law Enforcement of the same fees as charged to others afforded access to the program.

7. The department may institute judicial proceedings in the appropriate circuit court seeking enforcement of this chapter or any rule or order of the department.

8. Any investigation conducted by the department pursuant to this chapter is exempt from s. 119.07(1) until:

a. The investigation of the complaint has been concluded and determination has been made by the department as to whether probable cause exists;

b. The case is closed prior to a determination by the department as to whether probable cause exists; or

c. The subject of the investigation waives her or his privilege of confidentiality.

History: SS. 2, 11, ch. 90–364; s. 17, ch. 91–248; s. 4, ch. 91–429; s. 5, ch. 92–183; s. 2, ch. 93–197; s. 10, ch. 94–172; s. 69, ch. 95–144; s. 326, ch. 96–406; s. 1139, ch. 97–103; s. 7, ch. 97–248; s. 9, ch. 2002–295; s. 2, ch. 2006–165, eff. July 1, 2006.

§ 493.6122. Information about licensees; confidentiality

The residence telephone number and residence address of any Class "C," Class "CC," Class "E," or Class "EE" licensee maintained by the department is confidential and exempt from the provisions of s. 119.07(1), except that the department may provide this information to local, state, or federal law enforcement agencies. When the residence telephone number or residence address of such licensee is, or appears to be, the business telephone number or business address, this information shall be public record.

History: SS. 2, 11, ch. 90–364; s. 18, ch. 91–248; s. 4, ch. 91–429; s. 327, ch. 96–406.

§ 493.6123. Publication to industry

1. The department shall have the authority to periodically, through the publication of a newsletter, advise its licensees of information that the department or the advisory council determines is of interest to the industry. Additionally, this newsletter shall contain the name and locality of any licensed or unlicensed person or agency against which the department has filed a final order relative to an administrative complaint and shall contain the final disposition. This newsletter shall be published not less than two or more than four times annually.

2. The department shall develop and make available to each Class "C," Class "D," and Class "E" licensee and all interns a pamphlet detailing in plain language the legal authority, rights, and obligations of his or her class of licensure. Within the pamphlet, the department should endeavor to present situations that the licensee may be expected to commonly encounter in the course of doing business pursuant to his or her specific license, and provide to the licensee information on his or her legal options, authority, limits to authority, and obligations. The department shall supplement this with citations to statutes and legal decisions, as well as a selected bibliography that would direct the licensee to materials the study of which would enhance his or her professionalism. The department shall provide a single copy of the appropriate pamphlet without charge to each individual to whom a license is issued, but may charge for additional copies to recover its publication costs. The pamphlet shall be updated every 2 years as necessary to reflect rule or statutory changes, or court decisions. Intervening changes to the regulatory situation shall be noticed in the industry newsletter issued pursuant to subsection (1).

History: SS. 2, 11, ch. 90–364; s. 4, ch. 91–429; s. 537, ch. 97–103.

§ 493.6124. Use of state seal; prohibited

No person or licensee shall use any facsimile reproduction or pictorial portion of the Great Seal of the State of Florida on any badge, credentials, identification card, or other means of identification used in connection with any activities regulated under this chapter.

History: SS. 2, 11, ch. 90–364; s. 4, ch. 91–429.

§ 493.6125. Maintenance of information concerning administrative complaints and disciplinary actions

The department shall maintain statistics and relevant information, by profession, for private investigators, recovery agents, and private security officers which details:

1. The number of complaints received and investigated.
2. The number of complaints initiated and investigated by the department.
3. The disposition of each complaint.
4. The number of administrative complaints filed by the department.
5. The disposition of all administrative complaints.
6. A description of all disciplinary actions taken by profession.

History: SS. 2, 11, ch. 90–364; s. 4, ch. 91–429; s. 19, ch. 94–172; s. 49, ch. 95–196.

§ 493.6126. Saving clauses

1. No judicial or administrative proceeding pending on October 1, 1990, shall be abated as a result of the repeal and reenactment of this chapter.
2. All licenses valid on October 1, 1990, shall remain in full force and effect until expiration or revocation by the department. Henceforth, all licenses shall be applied for and renewed in accordance with this chapter.

History: SS. 2, 11, ch. 90–364; s. 4, ch. 91–429.

§ 493.6201. Classes of licenses

1. Any person, firm, company, partnership, or corporation which engages in business as a private investigative agency shall have a Class "A" license. A Class "A" license is valid for only one location.
2. Each branch office of a Class "A" agency shall have a Class "AA" license. Where a person, firm, company, partnership, or corporation holds both a Class "A" and Class "B" license, each additional or branch office shall have a Class "AB" license.
3. Any individual who performs the services of a manager for a:
   a. Class "A" private investigative agency or Class "AA" branch office shall have a Class "MA" license. A Class "C" or Class "M" licensee may be designated as the manager, in which case the Class "MA" license is not required.

b. Class "A" and "B" agency or a Class "AB" branch office shall have a Class "M" license.

4. Class "C" or Class "CC" licensees shall own or be an employee of a Class "A" agency, a Class "A" and Class "B" agency, or a branch office. This does not include those who are exempt under s. 493.6102, but who possess a Class "C" license solely for the purpose of holding a Class "G" license.

5. Any individual who performs the services of a private investigator shall have a Class "C" license.

6. Any individual who performs private investigative work as an intern under the direction and control of a designated, sponsoring Class "C" licensee or a designated, sponsoring Class "MA" or Class "M" licensee must have a Class "CC" license.

7. Only Class "M," Class "MA," Class "C," or Class "CC" licensees are permitted to bear a firearm, and any such licensee who bears a firearm shall also have a Class "G" license.

8. A Class "C" or Class "CC" licensee may perform bodyguard services without obtaining a Class "D" license.

History: SS. 3, 11, ch. 90–364; s. 4, ch. 91–429; s. 11, ch. 94–172; s. 70, ch. 95–144; s. 8, ch. 97–248.

§ 493.6202. Fees

1. The department shall establish by rule examination and biennial license fees, which shall not exceed the following:
   a. Class "A" license—private investigative agency: $450.
   b. Class "AA" or "AB" license—branch office: $125.
   c. Class "MA" license—private investigative agency manager: $75.
   d. Class "C" license—private investigator: $75.
   e. Class "CC" license—private investigator intern: $60.

2. The department may establish by rule a fee for the replacement or revision of a license, which fee shall not exceed $30.

3. The fees set forth in this section must be paid by certified check or money order or, at the discretion of the department, by agency check at the time the application is approved, except that the applicant for a Class "G," Class "C," Class "CC," Class "M," or Class "MA" license must pay the license fee at the time the application is made. If a license is revoked or denied or if the application is withdrawn, the license fee shall not be refunded.

History: SS. 3, 11, ch. 90–364; s. 4, ch. 91–429; s. 12, ch. 94–172.

§ 493.6203. License requirements

In addition to the license requirements set forth elsewhere in this chapter, each individual or agency shall comply with the following additional requirements:

1. Each agency or branch office shall designate a minimum of one appropriately licensed individual to act as manager, directing the activities of the Class "C" or Class "CC" employees.

2. An applicant for a Class "MA" license shall have 2 years of lawfully gained, verifiable, full-time experience, or training in:

   a. Private investigative work or related fields of work that provided equivalent experience or training;

   b. Work as a Class "CC" licensed intern;

   c. Any combination of paragraphs (a) and (b);

   d. Experience described in paragraph (a) for 1 year and experience described in paragraph (e) for 1 year;

   e. No more than 1 year using:

      i. College coursework related to criminal justice, criminology, or law enforcement administration; or

      ii. Successfully completed law enforcement-related training received from any federal, state, county, or municipal agency; or

   f. Experience described in paragraph (a) for 1 year and work in a managerial or supervisory capacity for 1 year.

3. An applicant for a Class "M" license shall qualify for licensure as a Class "MA" manager as outlined under subsection (2) and as a Class "MB" manager as outlined under s. 493.6303(2).

4. An applicant for a Class "C" license shall have 2 years of lawfully gained, verifiable, full-time experience, or training in one, or a combination of more than one, of the following:

   a. Private investigative work or related fields of work that provided equivalent experience or training.

   b. College coursework related to criminal justice, criminology, or law enforcement administration, or successful completion of any law enforcement-related training received from any federal, state, county, or municipal agency, except that no more than 1 year may be used from this category.

   c. Work as a Class "CC" licensed intern.

5. Effective January 1, 2008, an applicant for a Class "MA," Class "M," or Class "C" license must pass an examination that covers the provisions of this chapter and is administered by the department or by a provider approved by the department. The applicant must pass the examination before applying for licensure and must submit proof with the license application on a form approved by rule of the department that he or she has passed the examination. The administrator of the examination shall verify the identity of each applicant taking the examination.

   a. The examination requirement in this subsection does not apply to an individual who holds a valid Class "CC," Class "C," Class "MA," or Class "M" license.

   b. Notwithstanding the exemption provided in paragraph (a), if the license of an applicant for relicensure has been invalid for more than 1 year, the applicant must take and pass the examination.

   c. The department shall establish by rule the content of the examination, the manner and procedure of its administration, and an examination fee that may not exceed $100.

6.

   a. A Class "CC" licensee shall serve an internship under the direction and control of a designated sponsor, who is a Class "C," Class "MA," or Class "M" licensee.

   b. Effective September 1, 2008, an applicant for a Class "CC" license must have completed at least 24 hours of a 40-hour course pertaining to general investigative techniques and this chapter, which course is offered by a state university or by a school, community college, college, or university under the purview of the Department of Education, and the applicant must pass an examination. The certificate evidencing satisfactory completion of at least 24 hours of a 40-hour course must be submitted with the application for a Class "CC" license. The remaining 16 hours must be completed and an examination passed within 180 days. If documentation of completion of the required training is not submitted within the specified timeframe, the individual's license is automatically suspended or his or her authority to work as a Class "CC" pursuant to s. 493.6105(9) is rescinded until such time as proof of certificate of completion is provided to the department. The training course specified in this paragraph may be provided by face-to-face presentation, online technology, or a home study course in accordance with rules and procedures of the Department of Education. The administrator of the examination must verify the identity of each applicant taking the examination.

c. Effective January 1, 2012, before submission of an application to the department, the applicant for a Class "CC" license must have completed a minimum of 40 hours of professional training pertaining to general investigative techniques and this chapter, which course is offered by a state university or by a school, community college, college, or university under the purview of the Department of Education, and the applicant must pass an examination. The training must be provided in two parts, one 24-hour course and one 16-hour course. The certificate evidencing satisfactory completion of the 40 hours of professional training must be submitted with the application for a Class "CC" license. The training specified in this paragraph may be provided by face-to-face presentation, online technology, or a home study course in accordance with rules and procedures of the Department of Education. The administrator of the examination must verify the identity of each applicant taking the examination.

  i. Upon an applicant's successful completion of each part of the approved course and passage of any required examination, the school, community college, college, or university shall issue a certificate of completion to the applicant. The certificates must be on a form established by rule of the department.

  ii. The department shall establish by rule the general content of the training course and the examination criteria.

  iii. If the license of an applicant for relicensure has been invalid for more than 1 year, the applicant must complete the required training and pass any required examination.

d. An individual who submits an application for a Class "CC" license on or after September 1, 2008, through December 31, 2011, who has not completed the 16-hour course must submit proof of successful completion of the course within 180 days after the date the application is submitted. If documentation of completion of the required training is not submitted by that date, the individual's license shall be automatically suspended until proof of the required training is submitted to the department. An individual licensed on or before August 31, 2008, is not required to complete additional training hours in order to renew an active license beyond the total required hours, and the timeframe for completion in effect at the time he or she was licensed applies.

7. In addition to any other requirement, an applicant for a Class "G" license shall satisfy the firearms training set forth in s. 493.6115.

History: SS. 3, 11, ch. 90–364; s. 9, ch. 91–248; s. 4, ch. 91–429; s. 1, ch. 2007–232, eff. July 1, 2007.

§ 493.6301. Classes of licenses

1. Any person, firm, company, partnership, or corporation which engages in business as a security agency shall have a Class "B" license. A Class "B" license is valid for only one location.
2. Each branch office of a Class "B" agency shall have a Class "BB" license. Where a person, firm, company, partnership, or corporation holds both a Class "A" and Class "B" license, each branch office shall have a Class "AB" license.
3. Any individual who performs the services of a manager for a:
   a. Class "B" security agency or Class "BB" branch office shall have a Class "MB" license. A Class "M" licensee, or a Class "D" licensee who has been so licensed for a minimum of 2 years, may be designated as the manager, in which case the Class "MB" license is not required.
   b. Class "A" and Class "B" agency or a Class "AB" branch office shall have a Class "M" license.
4. A Class "D" licensee shall own or be an employee of a Class "B" security agency or branch office. This does not include those individuals who are exempt under s. 493.6102(4) but who possess a Class "D" license solely for the purpose of holding a Class "G" license.
5. Any individual who performs the services of a security officer shall have a Class "D" license. However, a Class "C" licensee or a Class "CC" licensee may perform bodyguard services without a Class "D" license.
6. Only Class "M," Class "MB," or Class "D" licensees are permitted to bear a firearm, and any such licensee who bears a firearm shall also have a Class "G" license.
7. Any person who operates a security officer school or training facility must have a Class "DS" license.
8. Any individual who teaches or instructs at a Class "DS" security officer school or training facility must have a Class "DI" license.

History: SS. 4, 11, ch. 90–364; s. 10, ch. 91–248; s. 4, ch. 91–429; s. 13, ch. 94–172; s. 71, ch. 95–144; s. 7, ch. 96–407; s. 9, ch. 97–248.

§ 493.6302. Fees

1. The department shall establish by rule biennial license fees, which shall not exceed the following:
   a. Class "B" license—security agency: $450.
   b. Class "BB" or Class "AB" license—branch office: $125.
   c. Class "MB" license—security agency manager: $75.
   d. Class "D" license—security officer: $45.
   e. Class "DS" license—security officer school or training facility: $60.
   f. Class "DI" license—security officer school or training facility instructor: $60.
2. The department may establish by rule a fee for the replacement or revision of a license, which fee shall not exceed $30.
3. The fees set forth in this section must be paid by certified check or money order or, at the discretion of the department, by agency check at the time the application is approved, except

that the applicant for a Class "D," Class "G," Class "M," or Class "MB" license must pay the license fee at the time the application is made. If a license is revoked or denied or if the application is withdrawn, the license fee shall not be refunded.

History: SS. 4, 11, ch. 90–364; s. 4, ch. 91–429; s. 14, ch. 94–172.

§ 493.6303. License requirements

In addition to the license requirements set forth elsewhere in this chapter, each individual or agency shall comply with the following additional requirements:

1. Each agency or branch office shall designate a minimum of one appropriately licensed individual to act as manager, directing the activities of the Class "D" employees.
2. An applicant for a Class "MB" license shall have 2 years of lawfully gained, verifiable, full-time experience, or training in:
    a. Security work or related fields of work that provided equivalent experience or training;
    b. Experience described in paragraph (a) for 1 year and experience described in paragraph (c) for 1 year;
    c. No more than 1 year using:
        i. Either college coursework related to criminal justice, criminology, or law enforcement administration; or
        ii. Successfully completed law enforcement-related training received from any federal, state, county, or municipal agency; or
    d. Experience described in paragraph (a) for 1 year and work in a managerial or supervisory capacity for 1 year.
3. An applicant for a Class "M" license shall qualify for licensure as a Class "MA" manager as outlined under s. 493.6203(2) and as a Class "MB" manager as outlined under subsection (2).
4.
    a. An applicant for a Class "D" license must complete a minimum of 40 hours of professional training at a school or training facility licensed by the department. The department shall by rule establish the general content and number of hours of each subject area to be taught.
    b. An applicant may fulfill the training requirement prescribed in paragraph (a) by submitting proof of:
        i. Successful completion of the total number of required hours of training before initial application for a Class "D" license; or
        ii. Successful completion of 24 hours of training before initial application for a Class "D" license and successful completion of the remaining 16 hours of training within 180 days after the date that the application is submitted. If documentation of completion of the required training is not submitted within the specified timeframe, the individual's license is automatically suspended until such time as proof of the required training is provided to the department. However, any person whose license has been revoked, suspended pursuant to subparagraph 2., or expired for 1 year or longer is considered, upon reapplication for a license, an

initial applicant and must submit proof of successful completion of 40 hours of professional training at a school or training facility licensed by the department as prescribed in paragraph (a) before a license will be issued. Any person whose license was issued before January 1, 2007, and whose license has been expired for less than 1 year must, upon reapplication for a license, submit documentation of completion of the total number of hours of training prescribed by law at the time her or his initial license was issued before another license will be issued. This subsection does not require an individual licensed before January 1, 2007, to complete additional training hours in order to renew an active license, beyond the required total amount of training within the timeframe prescribed by law at the time she or he was licensed.

5. An applicant for a Class "G" license shall satisfy the firearms training outlined in s. 493.6115.

History: SS. 4, 11, ch. 90–364; s. 11, ch. 91–248; s. 4, ch. 91–429; s. 15, ch. 94–172; s. 3, ch. 2006–165, eff. January 1, 2007.

§ 493.6304. Security officer school or training facility

1. Any school, training facility, or instructor who offers the training outlined in s. 493.6303(4) for Class "D" applicants shall, before licensure of such school, training facility, or instructor, file with the department an application accompanied by an application fee in an amount to be determined by rule, not to exceed $60. The fee shall not be refundable.
2. The application shall be signed and notarized and shall contain, at a minimum, the following information:
   a. The name and address of the school or training facility and, if the applicant is an individual, her or his name, address, and social security or alien registration number.
   b. The street address of the place at which the training is to be conducted.
   c. A copy of the training curriculum and final examination to be administered.
3. The department shall adopt rules establishing the criteria for approval of schools, training facilities, and instructors.

History: SS. 4, 11, ch. 90–364; s. 4, ch. 91–429; s. 538, ch. 97–103.

§ 493.6305. Uniforms, required wear; exceptions

1. Class "D" licensees shall perform duties regulated under this chapter in a uniform which bears at least one patch or emblem visible at all times clearly identifying the employing agency. Upon resignation or termination of employment, a Class "D" licensee shall immediately return to the employer any uniform and any other equipment issued to her or him by the employer.
2. Class "D" licensees may perform duties regulated under this chapter in nonuniform status on a limited special assignment basis, and only when duty circumstances or special requirements of the client necessitate such dress.
3. Class "D" licensees who are also Class "G" licensees and who are performing limited, special assignment duties may carry their authorized firearm concealed in the conduct of such duties.

4. Class "D" licensees who are also Class "G" licensees and who are performing bodyguard or executive protection services may carry their authorized firearm concealed while in nonuniform as needed in the conduct of such services.

History: SS. 4, 11, ch. 90–364; s. 12, ch. 91–248; s. 4, ch. 91–429; s. 10, ch. 97–248; s. 30, ch. 99–7.

§ 493.6401. Classes of licenses

1. Any person, firm, company, partnership, or corporation which engages in business as a recovery agency shall have a Class "R" license. A Class "R" license is valid for only one location.
2. Each branch office of a Class "R" agency shall have a Class "RR" license.
3. Any individual who performs the services of a manager for a Class "R" recovery agency or a Class "RR" branch office must have a Class "MR" license. A Class "E" licensee may be designated as the manager, in which case the Class "MR" license is not required.
4. Any individual who performs the services of a recovery agent must have a Class "E" license.
5. Any individual who performs repossession as an intern under the direction and control of a designated, sponsoring Class "E" licensee or a designated, sponsoring Class "MR" licensee shall have a Class "EE" license.
6. Class "E" or Class "EE" licensees shall own or be an employee of a Class "R" agency or branch office.
7. Any person who operates a repossessor school or training facility or who conducts an Internet-based training course or a correspondence training course must have a Class "RS" license.
8. Any individual who teaches or instructs at a Class "RS" repossessor school or training facility shall have a Class "RI" license.

History: SS. 5, 11, ch. 90–364; s. 14, ch. 91–248; s. 4, ch. 91–429; s. 7, ch. 93–49; s. 2, ch. 2007–232, eff. July 1, 2007.

§ 493.6402. Fees

1. The department shall establish by rule biennial license fees which shall not exceed the following:
   a. Class "R" license—recovery agency: $450.
   b. Class "RR" license—branch office: $125.
   c. Class "MR" license—recovery agency manager: $75.
   d. Class "E" license—recovery agent: $75.
   e. Class "EE" license—recovery agent intern: $60.
   f. Class "RS" license—repossessor school or training facility: $60.
   g. Class "RI" license—repossessor school or training facility instructor: $60.
2. The department may establish by rule a fee for the replacement or revision of a license, which fee shall not exceed $30.
3. The fees set forth in this section must be paid by certified check or money order, or, at the discretion of the department, by agency check at the time the application is approved, except

that the applicant for a Class "E," Class "EE," or Class "MR" license must pay the license fee at the time the application is made. If a license is revoked or denied, or if an application is withdrawn, the license fee shall not be refunded.

History: SS. 5, 11, ch. 90–364; s. 4, ch. 91–429; s. 17, ch. 94–172.

§ 493.6403. License requirements

1. In addition to the license requirements set forth in this chapter, each individual or agency shall comply with the following additional requirements:
   a. Each agency or branch office must designate a minimum of one appropriately licensed individual to act as manager, directing the activities of the Class "E" or Class "EE" employees. A Class "E" licensee may be designated to act as manager of a Class "R" agency or branch office in which case the Class "MR" license is not required.
   b. An applicant for Class "MR" license shall have at least 1 year of lawfully gained, verifiable, full-time experience as a Class "E" licensee performing repossessions of motor vehicles, mobile homes, motorboats, aircraft, personal watercraft, all-terrain vehicles, farm equipment, or industrial equipment.
   c. An applicant for a Class "E" license shall have at least 1 year of lawfully gained, verifiable, full-time experience in one, or a combination of more than one, of the following:
      i. Repossession of motor vehicles as defined in s. 320.01(1), mobile homes as defined in s. 320.01(2), motorboats as defined in s. 327.02, aircraft as defined in s. 330.27(1), personal watercraft as defined in s. 327.02, all-terrain vehicles as defined in s. 316.2074, farm equipment as defined under s. 686.402, or industrial equipment as defined in s. 493.6101(22).
      ii. Work as a Class "EE" licensed intern.
2. Beginning October 1, 1994, an applicant for a Class "E" or a Class "EE" license must have completed a minimum of 40 hours of professional training at a school or training facility licensed by the department. The department shall by rule establish the general content for the training.

History: SS. 5, 11, ch. 90–364; s. 15, ch. 91–248; s. 4, ch. 91–429; s. 8, ch. 93–49; s. 18, ch. 94–172; s. 11, ch. 94–241; s. 5, ch. 2005–143.

§ 493.6404. Property inventory; vehicle license identification numbers

1. If personal effects or other property not covered by a security agreement are contained in or on a recovered vehicle, mobile home, motorboat, aircraft, personal watercraft, all-terrain vehicle, farm equipment, or industrial equipment at the time it is recovered, a complete and accurate inventory shall be made of such personal effects or property. The date and time the inventory is made shall be indicated, and it shall be signed by the Class "E" or Class "EE" licensee who obtained the personal property. The inventory of the personal property and the records regarding any disposal of personal property shall be maintained for a period of 2 years in the permanent records of the licensed agency and shall be made available, upon demand, to an authorized representative of the department engaged in an official investigation.

2. Within 5 working days after the date of a repossession, the Class "E" or Class "EE" licensee shall give written notification to the debtor of the whereabouts of personal effects or other property inventoried pursuant to this section. At least 45 days prior to disposing of such personal effects or other property, the Class "E" or Class "EE" licensee shall, by United States Postal Service proof of mailing or certified mail, notify the debtor of the intent to dispose of said property. Should the debtor, or her or his lawful designee, appear to retrieve the personal property, prior to the date on which the Class "E" or Class "EE" licensee is allowed to dispose of the property, the licensee shall surrender the personal property to that individual upon payment of any reasonably incurred expenses for inventory and storage. If personal property is not claimed within 45 days of the notice of intent to dispose, the licensee may dispose of the personal property at her or his discretion, except that illegal items or contraband shall be surrendered to a law enforcement agency, and the licensee shall retain a receipt or other proof of surrender as part of the inventory and disposal records she or he maintains.
3. Vehicles used for the purpose of repossession by a Class "E" or Class "EE" licensee must be identified during repossession by the license number of the Class "R" agency only, local ordinances to the contrary notwithstanding. These vehicles are not "wreckers" as defined in s. 713.78. The license number must be displayed on both sides of the vehicle and must appear in lettering no less than 4 inches tall and in a color contrasting from that of the background.

History: SS. 5, 11, ch. 90"364; s. 4, ch. 91–429; s. 9, ch. 93–49; s. 539, ch. 97–103; s. 11, ch. 97–248; s. 6, ch. 2005–143.

§ 493.6405. Sale of motor vehicle, mobile home, motorboat, aircraft, personal watercraft, all-terrain vehicles, farm equipment, or industrial equipment by a licensee; penalty

1. A Class "E" or Class "EE" licensee shall obtain, prior to sale, written authorization and a negotiable title from the owner or lienholder to sell any repossessed motor vehicle, mobile home, motorboat, aircraft, personal watercraft, all-terrain vehicles, farm equipment, or industrial equipment.
2. A Class "E" or Class "EE" licensee shall send the net proceeds from the sale of such repossessed motor vehicle, mobile home, motorboat, aircraft, personal watercraft, all-terrain vehicles, farm equipment, or industrial equipment to the owner or lienholder, within 20 working days after the licensee executes the documents which permit the transfer of legal ownership to the purchaser.
3. A person who violates a provision of this section commits a felony of the third degree, punishable as provided in s. 775.082, s. 775.083, or s. 775.084.

History: SS. 5, 11, ch. 90–364; s. 4, ch. 91–429; s. 7, ch. 2005–143.

§ 493.6406. Repossession services school or training facility

1. Any school, training facility, or instructor who offers the training outlined in s. 493.6403(2) for Class "EE" applicants shall, before licensure of such school, training facility, or instructor, file with the department an application accompanied by an application fee in an amount

to be determined by rule, not to exceed $60. The fee shall not be refundable. This training may be offered as face-to-face training, Internet-based training, or correspondence training.

2. The application shall be signed and notarized and shall contain, at a minimum, the following information:

   a. The name and address of the school or training facility and, if the applicant is an individual, his or her name, address, and social security or alien registration number.

   b. The street address of the place at which the training is to be conducted or the street address of the Class "RS" school offering Internet-based or correspondence training.

   c. A copy of the training curriculum and final examination to be administered.

3. The department shall adopt rules establishing the criteria for approval of schools, training facilities, and instructors.

History: SS. 5, 11, ch. 90–364; s. 4, ch. 91–429; s. 540, ch. 97–103; s. 3, ch. 2007–232, eff. July 1, 2007.

Appendix 2: List of Associations and Groups

Academy of Security Educators and Trainers (A.S.E.T.)
16 Penn Plaza Suite 1570
New York, NY 10001
Toll free: 800-947-5827
Phone: 212-268-4555
Fax: 212-563-4783
www.academyofsecurity.org

The Association of Medical Illustrators
201 E. Main Street, Ste. 1405
Lexington, KY 40507
Toll free: 866-393-4AMI (or 866-393-4264)
www.ami.org

American Bankers Association
1120 Connecticut Avenue, N.W.
Washington, DC 20036
Toll free: 1-800-BANKERS
www.aba.com

American Polygraph Association
P.O. Box 8037
Chattanooga, TN 37414-0037
Toll free: 800-APA-8037
Phone: 423-892-3992
Fax: 423-894-5435
www.polygraph.org

American Risk and Insurance Association
716 Providence Road
Malvern, PA 19355-3402
Phone: 610-640-1997
Fax: 610-725-1007
www.aria.org

AOPA Air Safety Foundation
Aircraft Owners and Pilots Association
421 Aviation Way
Frederick, MD 21701
Toll free: 800-872-2672
Fax: 301-695-2375
www.aopa.org/asf

Academy of Security Educators & Training—A.S.E.T.
16 Penn Plaza Suite 1570
New York, NY 10001
Toll free: 800-947-5827
Phone: 212-268-4555
Fax: 212-563-4783
www.personalprotection.com
www.academyofsecurity.org

Association of Contingency Planners
www.acp-international.com

Association of Management Consulting Firms
370 Lexington Avenue, Suite 2209
New York, NY 10017
Phone: 212-262 3055
Fax: 212-262 3054
www.amcf.org

The American Safe Deposit Association (ASDA)
P.O. Box 519
Franklin, IN 46131, USA
Phone: 317-738-4432
Fax: 317-738-5267

The Associated Locksmiths of America, Inc.
3500 Easy St.
Dallas, TX 75247
Toll free: 800-532-2562
Phone: 214-819-9733
www.aloa.org

The Association of Medical Illustrators
201 E. Main Street, Ste. 1405
Lexington, KY 40507
Toll free: 1-866-393-4AMI
Fax: 1-866-393-4264
www.ami.org

Automatic Fire Alarm Association
National Headquarters
P.O. Box 1659

Jasper, GA 30143
Phone: 678-454 -FIRE (3473)
www.afaa.org
National Headquarters

National Headquarters
81 Mill Street
Suite 300
Gahanna, OH 43230
844-GET-AFAA (844-438-2322)
614-416-8076
614-453-8744 Fax

Aviation Crime Prevention Institute, Inc.

226 N. Nova Road
Ormond Beach, FL 32174, USA
Toll free: 800-969-5473
Phone: 386-341-7270
Fax: 386-615-3378
www.acpi.org
P.O. Box 730118 Ormond Beach, FL 32173
Office: 1 386-843-ACPI (2274)
Toll Free: 1800-969-5473

Bank Administration Institute (BAI)

115 S. LaSalle Street
Suite 3300
Chicago, IL 60603-3801
Toll free: 800-224-9889
Phone: 312-683-2464
Fax: 800-375-5543 or 312-683-2373
www.bai.org

Board of Certified Safety Professionals

208 Burwash Avenue Savoy
Illinois 61874-9510
Phone: 217-359-9263
Fax: 217-359-0055
www.bcsp.org

2301 W. Bradley Avenue
Champaign, IL 61821
Phone: +1 217-359-9263
Fax: +1 217-359-0055

Computer Crime Research Center

Box 8010
Zaporozhye 95
Ukraine, 69095
www.crime-research.org

Information Systems Security Association (ISSA)

9220 SW Barbur Blvd #119-333
Portland, OR 97219
Toll free: 866-349-5818
Phone: 206-388-4584
Fax: 206-299-3366
www.issa.org

12100 Sunset Hills Road, Suite 130
Reston, VA 20190
+1 866 349 5818 (USA toll-free)
Virginia: +1 703 234 4077 (local/international)
Fax: +1 703 435 4390 (local/international)

The Institute of Internal Auditors

247 Maitland Avenue
Altamonte Springs, FL 32701-4201
Phone: 407-937-1100
Fax: 407-937-1101
www.theiia.org

International Association of Bomb Technicians & Investigators (IABTI)

P.O. Box 160
Goldvein, VA 22720-0160
Phone: 540-752-4533
Fax: 540-752-2796
www.iabti.org

1120 International Parkway, Suite 105
Fredericksburg, VA 22406

International Association of Campus Law Enforcement Administrators (IACLEA)

342 North Main Street
West Hartford, CT 06117
Phone: 860-586-7517
www.iaclea.org

International Association of Computer Investigative Specialists (IACIS)

P.O. Box 2411
Leesburg, VA. 20177
Toll free: 888-884-2247
www.iacis.com

International Association of Financial Crimes Investigators

1020 Suncast Lane, Suite 102
El Dorado Hills, CA 95762
Phone: 916-939-5000
Fax: 916-939-0395
www.iafci.org

International Association of Health Care Security and Safety
P.O. Box 5038
Glendale Heights, IL 60139
Phone: 630-529-3913
Fax: 630-529-4139
www.iahss.org

International Association of Professional Security Consultants
525 SW 5th Street, Suite A
Des Moines, IA 50309-4501
Phone: 515-282-8192
Fax: 515-282-9117
www.iapsc.org

575 Market St. Suite 2125
San Francisco, CA 94105
Phone: (1) 415-536-0288
Fax: (1) 415-764-4915

International Association of Security and Investigative Regulators
PO Box 93
Waterloo, IA 50704
Toll free: 888- 35-IASIR - (888-354-2747)
Fax: 319-232-1488
www.iasir.org

International Bodyguard Association (IBA)
International Headquarters
Castle Cosey
Castlebellingham
Co. Louth
Ireland
Phone: +353 42 9382849
www.ibabodyguards.com

IBA HQ
Suite 206
33 Parkway
London
NW1 7PN
UK
Telephone: + 353 87 1940 787 or +44 7720 823 855
Fax: + 353 53 9130822

International Council of Shopping Centers
1221 Avenue of the Americas, 41st fl.
New York, NY 10020-1099
Phone: 646-728-3800
Fax: 732-694-1755
www.icsc.org
Fax: +1 732 694 1690

International Foundation for Protection Officers
PO Box 771329
Naples, FL 34107-1329
Phone: 239-430-0534
Fax: 239-430-0533
www.ifpo.org

1250 Tamiami Tr. N Ste. 206
Naples, FL. 34102

International Guards Union of America
420 Hardwicke Dr.
Knoxville, TN 37923
Toll free: 866-776-4662
Fax: 865-531-4703
www.theigua.org

P.O. Box 4098
Oak Ridge, TN 37831
Phone: 865-456-9110

International Organization for Black Security Executives
P.O. Box 4436
Upper Marlboro, MD 20775
Toll free: 888-884-6273
Fax: 301-352-7807
www.iobse.com

2340 Powell St., #327
Emeryville, CA 94608
1-510-648-4292

International Professional Security Association
Northumberland House, 11
The Pavement
Popes Lane, Ealing, London England W5 4NG
Phone: +44 (0)20 8832 7417
Fax: +44 (0)20 8832 7418
www.ipsa.org.uk

IPSA, Railway House, Railway Road, Chorley, Lancashire, PR6 0HW – United Kingdom
Phone: 0845 873 8114 (International +44 1257 249945)
Fax: 0845 873 8115 (International +44 1257 241146)

Jewelers Security Alliance
6 East 45th Street
New York, NY 10017, USA
Toll free: 800-537-0067
Fax: 212-808-9168
www.jewelerssecurity.org

National Association of Investigative Specialists
P.O. Box 82148
Austin, TX 78708
Phone: 512-719-3595
Fax: 512-719-3594
www.pimall.com/nais/nais.j.html

National Association of Legal Investigators
235 N. Pine Street
Lansing, MI. 48933
Toll Free: 866-520-NALI (6254)
Phone: 517-702-9835
Fax: 517-372-1501
www.nalionline.org

National Burglar& Fire Alarm Association
2300 Valley View Lane Suite 230
Irving, TX 75062
Toll Free: 888-447-1689
Phone: 214-260-5970
Fax: 214-260-5979
www.alarm.org

National Center for Computer Crime Data
1222 17th Avenue
Santa Cruz, CA 95062
Phone: 831-475-4457
Fax: 831-475-5336

National Council of Investigation & Security Services
7501 Sparrows Point Blvd.
Baltimore, Maryland 21219-1927
Toll free: 800-445-8408
Fax: 410-388-9746
www.nciss.org

National Crime Prevention Institute Justice Administration
206 McCandless Hall
University of Louisville
Louisville, KY 40292
Phone: 502-852-8577
Fax: 502-852-6990

National Criminal Justice Reference Service
P.O. Box 6000
Rockville, MD 20849-6000
Toll free: 800-851-3420
Phone: 301-519-5500
Fax: 301-519-5212

301-240-5830 (fax)
www.ncjrs.gov

National Fire Protection Association
1 Batterymarch Park
Quincy, MA 02169-7471
Phone: 617-770-3000
Fax: 617-770-0700
www.nfpa.org

National Fire Sprinkler Association
40 Jon Barrett Road
Patterson, NY 12563
Phone: 845-878-4200
Fax: 845-878-4215
www.nfsa.org

National Property Management Association
28100 US Highway 19 North, Suite 400
Clearwater, FL 33761
Phone: 727-736-3788
Fax: 727-736-6707
www.npma.org

3525 Piedmont Road
Building 5, Suite 300
Atlanta, GA 30305
P: 404-477-5811
F: 404-240-0998

National Safety Council
1121 Spring Lake Dr.
Itasca, IL 60143-3201
Toll free: 800-621-7615
Phone: 630-285-1121
Fax: 630-285-1315
www.nsc.org

The Professional Investigators and Security Association
P.O. Box 220012
Chantilly, VA 20153
http://vapisa.com/contact/

Security Industry Association
635 Slaters Lane, Suite 110
Alexandria, VA 22314
Toll free: 866-817-8888
Fax: 703-683-2469
www.siaonline.org

8405 Colesville Road, Ste. 500
Silver Spring, MD 20910
Main: 301-804-4700
Fax: 301-804-4701

Security Industry Authority
P.O. Box 1293
Liverpool
L69 1AX
England
Phone: 0844 892 1025
Fax: 0844 892 0975
www.sia.homeoffice.gov.uk

Security Sales & Integration, Bobit Publishing, Inc.
3520 Challenger Street
Torrance, CA 90503
Phone: 310-533-2400
Fax: 310-533-2502
www.securitysales.com

EH Publishing, Inc.
111 Speen Street
Framingham, MA 01701
Phone: 508.663.1500
Fax: 508.663.1598

Appendix 3: Sample Forms

Exhibit 3A.1—Issuer's Bond

Exhibit 3A.2—Application for Private Detective Employee or Private Security Guard Employee
https://www.nh.gov/safety/divisions/nhsp/ssb/permitslicensing/documents/dssp247.pdf

Exhibit 3A.3—Affidavit of Experience
http://forms.freshfromflorida.com/16023.pdf

Exhibit 3A.4—Application for Private Detective or Security Service License
http://www.ct.gov/despp/lib/despp/slfu/private_detectives/dps-366_pi_security_serv_app_03-15.pdf

Exhibit 3A.5—Private Security Guard Company / Qualifying Principal License Application
http://www.dol.wa.gov/forms/690001.pdf

Exhibit 3A.6—Private Security Instructor Application
http://www.dcjs.virginia.gov/forms/privateSecurity/pss_ia.pdf

Exhibit 3A.7—Renewal of Registration Application
https://www.dcjs.virginia.gov/forms/privatesecurity/pss_rr.pdf

Exhibit 3A.8—Training Session Notification Form
http://www.dcjs.virginia.gov/forms/privatesecurity/pss_tsn.pdf

Exhibit 3A.9—Application for Company License
http://sos.ga.gov/PLB/acrobat/Forms/31%20Application%20-%20Company%20License.pdf

Exhibit 3A.10—Application for Employee Registration
http://sos.ga.gov/PLB/acrobat/Forms/31%20Application%20-%20Employee%20Registration.pdf

Exhibit 3A.11—Private Security Guard License Application
http://www.dol.wa.gov/forms/690008.pdf

GEORGIA BOARD OF PRIVATE DETECTIVE & SECURITY AGENCIES

STATE OF GEORGIA

BOND

BOND NUMBER: _____   _____ **COUNTY**

KNOW ALL MEN BY THESE PRESENTS

That we, _____
Principal/Licensee, and _____ , as

_____ as Surety/Company, are held and firmly bound unto **HIS EXCELLENCY**, Governor of Georgia, and his successors in office in the just sum of **TWENTY-FIVE THOUSAND AND NO/100 ($25,000) DOLLARS,** for the payment of which, well and truly to be made, we bind ourselves, our heirs, executors and administrators, each and every one of them, jointly and severally, by these presents.

It is further understood and agreed that this bond is for a period beginning on the _____ day of _____ , and ending on the _____ day of _____ , _____ .

Whereas, the above bound Principal/Licensee has made application to the Georgia Board of Private Detective & Security Agencies for a license as Private Detective/Security Agency in accordance with the laws governing the Private Detective and Security Agencies in the State of Georgia;

It is a condition of this bond that the said Principal/Licensee is to comply with all of the laws governing the acts of Private Detective and Security Agencies in Georgia.

A further condition of this bond is that the Principal/Licensee and Surety/Company to this bond shall be subject to suit by action thereon for the purpose of indemnifying any persons aggrieved by any act of the Principal/Licensee, which act is in violation of Code Section 43-38 and would be grounds for denial, suspension, or revocation of a license under Code Section 43-38-11. Any and all damages paid shall not exceed the amount of this bond.

Now, should the said Principal/Licensee, faithfully perform all his duties under Code Section 43-38 as a Private Detective/Security Agency during the term for which he has been licensed, then the above bond is to be void upon expiration of his license, else to be in full force and effect.

IN WITNESS WHEREOF, the Principal/Licensee and Surety/Company have caused these presents to be duly signed and executed under seal, this _____ day of _____ , _____ .

_____
Signature of Principal/Licensee

_____
Surety/Company – Name of Company

Countersigned:

_____
Address

_____   _____
Resident Agency   By Attorney-in-Fact

IMPORTANT: BOND MUST BE SIGNED – POWER OF ATTORNEY MUST BE ATTACHED

CANCELLATION CLAUSE – No licensee shall cancel or cause to be canceled a bond … issued pursuant to this Code section unless the board is so informed in writing by certified mail or statutory overnight delivery at least 30 days prior to the proposed cancellation. O.C.G.A. Section 43-38-6(d)(1).

Rev. 04/04

Exhibit 3A.1   Issuer's bond.

State of New Hampshire
DEPARTMENT OF SAFETY
DIVISION OF STATE POLICE

APPLICATION FOR: (check appropriate box)

☐ **Private Investigator Employee** ☐ **Security Guard Employee** ☐ **Bail Bondsman Employee**

PART 1: FOR ALL LICENSE APPLICANTS

A) **Answer all required questions. Failure to do so will delay the processing of your application.**
B) **False answers will result in a denial of a license.**
C) Type or print all information.
D) Fee of $5.00 plus a $25.00 criminal record check fee pursuant to RSA 106-F:8III and Saf-C 2205.02 and a $10.00 background investigative fee pursuant to RSA 106-F:8III and Saf – C 2205.03.
E) Armed Status: Add $26.50 for fingerprinting. Fingerprinting scheduled by appointment only at (603) 223-3873.

1) Name of Agency you are going to be employed by:

2) Address of Agency:

3) Name of Applicant:	First	Middle Initial	Last	4) Maiden Name:	

5) Present Address: Street		City	State	Zip Code
Mailing Address: (if different)		City	State	Zip Code

6) Date of Birth	7) Age	8) Place of Birth		9) Soc. Sec. No.	10) Sex	11) Height

12) Weight	13) Hair	14) Eyes	15) List and describe all scars, marks, tattoos and their location or state "NONE"

16) Driver's License Number : _____   State: _____

17) United States Citizen?   YES ☐   NO ☐   **If "NO" you must provide the following:**

   AR#: _____   **Country of Citizenship:** _____

18) Previous Employment (company name and address)

19) List three (3) persons, unrelated to you, of whom an inquiry can be made as to your character, integrity, and reputation. Give the full name and mailing address as these persons will be sent questionnaires. Failure to respond to the questionnaire will delay this application for a license.

1. Full Name	Mailing Address (street, city , state, zip code)
2. Full Name	Mailing Address (street, city, state, zip code)
3. Full Name	Mailing Address (street, city, state, zip code)

20) List any special schools or courses taken to qualify you for the type of license sought. (optional)

DSSP247 (Rev 09/12)

Exhibit 3A.2   Application for private detective employee or private security guard employee.
(Continued)

21) Have you had any experience for the type of license sought? YES ☐ NO ☐ If YES, explain fully in block 30.

22) Have you ever applied for a Private Investigator, Security Guard or Bail Bondsman license in N.H. before? If yes, give date of application. YES ☐ NO ☐ If YES, explain fully in block 30.

23) Have you ever been convicted of a felony or misdemeanor that has not been pardoned or annulled by a court in this state or nation? YES ☐ NO ☐ If YES, explain fully in block 30.

24) Have you ever been convicted of a crime associated with theft, honesty, fraud, use or sale of controlled substances or misdemeanor crimes of violence, domestic violence or abuse of any type that has not been pardoned or annulled by a court in this state or nation? YES ☐ NO ☐ If YES, explain fully in block 30.

25) Have you ever been treated for mental illness or an emotional disorder or confined to an institution? YES ☐ NO ☐ If YES, explain fully in block 30.

26) Are you or have you ever been a user of drugs or narcotics? (Except under the direction of a doctor) YES ☐ NO ☐ If YES, explain fully in block 30.

27) Has any license (Private Investigator, Security Guard or Bail Bondsman) applied for or issued to you, a partnership or corporation which you were a member ever been denied, revoked or suspended in this or any other state or territory? YES ☐ NO ☐ If YES, explain fully in block 30.

28) Are you currently the subject of an active domestic violence Protective Order in New Hampshire or any other jurisdiction in the United States, its possessions or territories? YES ☐ NO ☐ If YES, explain fully in block 30.

29) Military service: YES ☐ NO ☐
If YES, branch and type of discharge: _____

30) If "YES" on questions 23 – 28, please explain here: (attach separate sheet if necessary)
_____

PART 2 – FOR ARMED LICENSE APPLICANTS ONLY:

If you intend to carry a firearm while employed, complete the following; **(NOTE – a pistol permit does not allow the carrying of a firearm while employed as a security guard, investigator or bondsman).** In addition, an ARMED license must be obtained by completing an approved firearms course given by a certified firearms instructor).

31) Date, location of firearms qualification and name of certified firearms instructor: (An armed license will not be issued until a complete qualification form had been received and approved).

Date: _____ Location: _____ Instructor: _____

PART 3 – FOR ALL LICENSE APPLICANTS:

Applicant's Name (please print) _____

I certify that I have read the following application and affirm that every statement contained herein is true and correctly set forth and I also certify that I am familiar with all state laws, regulations and local ordinances relating to the license for which I am applying, for the locations in which I intend to conduct operations.

Signature of Applicant: _____ Date: _____
(False statements punishable under N.H. RSA 641:3)

EMAIL ADDRESS: _____

By providing an email address, you are acknowledging that the Permits and Licensing Unit may handle your application in whole or part via electronic mail.

MAKE CHECKS PAYABLE TO: STATE OF N.H. - TREASURER

Exhibit 3A.2 (Continued)   Application for private detective employee or private security guard employee.

ADAM H. PUTNAM
COMMISSIONER

Florida Department of Agriculture and Consumer Services
Division of Licensing
AFFIDAVIT OF EXPERIENCE
Chapter 493, Florida Statutes
Post Office Box 5767♦Tallahassee, FL 32314-5767♦(850) 245-5691
www.mylicensesite.com

Section 493.6105, F.S. requires the applicant for a Class "C" Private Investigator license, a Class "E" Recovery Agent license, or a Class "M", "MA", "MB", and "MR" Manager license to "include a statement on a form provided by the department of the experience he or she believes will qualify him or her for such license."

INSTRUCTIONS: Fill out this form completely, providing complete and comprehensive details about the duties you performed. Do not sign the form until you are in the presence of a Notary Public. If you have been honorably discharged from military service and would like to use related military experience toward satisfaction of the experience requirement, attach a copy of your DD214 to this completed form. Mail your completed form with your application to the P.O. Box referenced above.

EXPERIENCE WHICH CANNOT BE VERIFIED BY THE DIVISION OF LICENSING OR EXPERIENCE WHICH WAS ACQUIRED UNLAWFULLY WILL NOT BE COUNTED TOWARD THE EXPERIENCE REQUIREMENT OUTLINED UNDER CHAPTER 493, FLORIDA STATUTES.

LAST NAME

FIRST NAME

MI

SOCIAL SECURITY NUMBER   SEE REVERSE.

ALIEN REGISTRATION NUMBER
A

If you are an alien, you must also provide your 8- or 9-digit Alien Registration Number.

TYPE OF LICENSE for which you are applying

COMPLETE ONE. If you are applying for more than one class of agency license, a separate Affidavit of Experience form is required for each.

◯ CLASS "C" PRIVATE INVESTIGATOR LICENSE

◯ CLASS "MA" PRIVATE INVESTIGATIVE AGENCY MANAGER

◯ CLASS "E" RECOVERY AGENT LICENSE

◯ CLASS "MB" SECURITY AGENCY MANAGER

◯ CLASS "M" PRIVATE INVESTIGATIVE AND SECURITY BRANCH MANAGER

◯ CLASS "MR" RECOVERY AGENCY MANAGER

APPLICANT INFORMATION (RELATED EXPERIENCE)

NAME OF EMPLOYER: _____   Phone #: _____
                                              (INCLUDE AREA CODE)

ADDRESS: _____

CITY, STATE ZIP CODE: _____

JOB TITLE: _____   DATES OF EMPLOYMENT: _____
                                       FROM (MM/YY)   TO (MM/YY)

EXACT DUTIES WHICH RELATE TO THE LICENSE SOUGHT AND PERCENTAGE OF TIME DEVOTED TO THESE DUTIES. **BE SPECIFIC:**

_____

_____

_____

_____

_____

NAME AND TITLE OF INDIVIDUAL WHO CAN VERIFY EMPLOYMENT: _____

PHONE NUMBER: _____
              (INCLUDE AREA CODE)

FDACS-16023 Rev. 03/14
Page 1 of 2

Exhibit 3A.3   Affidavit of experience.

(Continued)

NAME OF EMPLOYER: _____ Phone #: _____
                                                              (INCLUDE AREA CODE)
ADDRESS: _____

CITY, STATE ZIP CODE: _____

JOB TITLE: _____ DATES OF EMPLOYMENT: _____
                                                          FROM (MM/YY)   TO (MM/YY)
EXACT DUTIES WHICH RELATE TO THE LICENSE SOUGHT AND PERCENTAGE OF TIME DEVOTED TO THESE DUTIES. BE SPECIFIC:

_____

_____

_____

NAME AND TITLE OF INDIVIDUAL WHO CAN VERIFY EMPLOYMENT: _____
PHONE NUMBER: _____
                (INCLUDE AREA CODE)

NAME OF EMPLOYER: _____ Phone #: _____
                                                              (INCLUDE AREA CODE)
ADDRESS: _____

CITY, STATE ZIP CODE: _____

JOB TITLE: _____ DATES OF EMPLOYMENT: _____
                                                          FROM (MM/YY)   TO (MM/YY)
EXACT DUTIES WHICH RELATE TO THE LICENSE SOUGHT AND PERCENTAGE OF TIME DEVOTED TO THESE DUTIES. BE SPECIFIC:

_____

_____

_____

NAME AND TITLE OF INDIVIDUAL WHO CAN VERIFY EMPLOYMENT: _____
PHONE NUMBER: _____
                (INCLUDE AREA CODE)

I,_____, do hereby swear or affirm
that the work experience listed herein accurately reflects my employment history and the job duties I have performed, and
that this work experience is related to the license for which I have applied.

_____   _____
SIGNATURE OF APPLICANT   DATE SIGNED

STATE OF FLORIDA
        COUNTY OF_____
The foregoing application was sworn to (or affirmed) and subscribed before me this _____ day of _____, 20____ by:

_____   _____
PRINT NAME OF APPLICANT   NOTARY SIGNATURE

☐ PERSONALLY KNOWN   ☐ PRODUCED IDENTIFICATION
                                          _____
TYPE OF IDENTIFICATION PRODUCED _____   PRINT, TYPE, OR STAMP NAME OF NOTARY

USE OF SOCIAL SECURITY NUMBERS: Sections 493.6105, 493.6304, and 493.6406, Florida Statutes (F. S.), in conjunction with section 119.071(5) (a) 2, F. S., mandates that the Department of Agriculture and Consumer Services, Division of Licensing, obtain social security numbers from applicants. Applicant social security numbers are maintained and used by the Division of Licensing for identification purposes, to prevent misidentification, and to facilitate the approval process by the Division. The Department of Agriculture and Consumer Services, Division of Licensing, will not disclose an applicant's social security number without consent of the applicant to anyone outside of the Department of Agriculture and Consumer Services, Division of Licensing, or as required by law. [See Chapter 119, F. S., 15 U.S.C. ss. 1681 et seq., 15 U.S.C. ss. 6801 et seq., 18 U.S.C. ss. 2721 et seq., Pub. L. No. 107-56 (USA Patriot Act of 2001), and Presidential Executive Order 13224.]

Exhibit 3A.3 (Continued)   Affidavit of experience.

DEPARTMENT OF EMERGENCY SERVICES AND PUBLIC PROTECTION
DIVISION OF STATE POLICE
1111 Country Club Road Middletown, CT 06457-9294

Application for Private Detective or Security Service License

Check Type of License Desired:

Individual (including DBA)	Corporate (including LLC & Inc.)
☐ Private Detective	☐ Private Detective, Inc.
☐ Private Detective Fire Investigator	☐ Private Detective Fire Investigator, Inc.
☐ Security Service	☐ Security Service, Inc.

Applicant is: ☐ Licensee   ☐ Corporate Official   ☐ Proprietary Licensee

Personal Information:

Name of Applicant		Social Security #:		
Date of Birth	Place of Birth	Height	Weight	Sex
Hair Color	Eye Color	Scars/Marks/Tattoos	Race	
Firearms Permit No./State		Driver's License No./State		
Home phone		Business phone		
Address				

Prior home addresses for past five years: *(use additional paper if needed)*

From	To	Street/City/Town/State/Zip

Employment history – Begin with present or most current and work backwards, Include dates of employment, duties/responsibilities, reason for leaving employment. *(Use additional paper if needed or attach resume)*

Statement of Citizenship: (attach proof of citizenship)

Are you a citizen of the United States? ☐ Yes ☐ No	If naturalized, detail when and where:

Have you ever used any other name(s)? If so, list name(s) used: *(Use additional paper if needed)*

Are you currently vested with police powers? ☐ Yes ☐ No

1.

Exhibit 3A.4   Application for private detective or security service license.   *(Continued)*

Education: (Indicate highest degree received (Attach copy of high school diploma/GED certificate or college transcript)

Degree/Diploma	Year Degree Awarded:	Name of College/University
☐ High School ☐ Associate Degree ☐ Baccalaureate Degree ☐ Masters/Doctorate Degree ☐ Other _____		

List any schools or courses, which you believe qualifies you for the type of license applied for:
(The Commissioner of Emergency Servicse and Public Protection may, at his discretion, substitute up to one year of experience upon proof of satisfactory participation in a course of instruction pertinent to the license applied for. **Include copies of training certificates. (Attach additional sheets of paper as required).**

Private Investigator Applicants: Does the applicant meet the minimum five years of <u>full time</u> investigative experience or ten years of experience as a police officer with a state or organized municipal police department? ☐ Yes ☐ No If "No " Explain: (*Submit qualifying documentation*)
(Please reference CGS 29-154a)

Security Applicants: Does the applicant meet the minimum five years supervisory experience under a licensed security agency or ten years as a police officer with a state or organized municipal police department? ☐ Yes ☐ No If "No " Explain: (*Submit qualifying documentation*)
(Please reference CGS 29-161h)

Criminal and Motor Vehicle Record:
Have you ever been arrested for a criminal offense? ☐ Yes ☐ No   If Yes, explain:

Date/Place	Jurisdiction/Court	Charge

Have you ever been arrested on a motor vehicle charge? ☐ Yes ☐ No   If Yes, explain:

Date/Place	Jurisdiction/Court	Charge

DPS-366-C (Revised 3/12)

An Affirmative Action/Equal Opportunity Employer

Page 2

Exhibit 3A.4 (Continued)   Application for private detective or security service license.

(Continued)

Military Service: ☐ Yes ☐ No *(If "Yes" DD-214 or NGB-22 must be attached)*

Military branch or component	Highest Rank Attained	Type of Discharge

Business Information:

Proposed Trade Name*	Address of Home Office

Type Organization ☐ Individual ☐ Corporate	Date & Place of Incorporation *(attach Certificate of Incorporation or Trade Certificate)*

Connecticut Addresses	Telephone Numbers
Branch Manager's Name:& D.O.B.	

* Subject to approval by the Commissioner of Emergency Services and Public Protection.

Names, addresses, dates of birth, and proposed titles of all corporate officials:
(use additional paper if necessary)

Are you currently licensed as a private investigator/security service in any other state?
☐ Yes ☐ No   If "Yes," Explain:

State	Lic. Number	Type of License	Date License Expires

DPS-366-C (Revised 3/12)

An *Affirmative Action/Equal Opportunity Employer*

Page 3

Exhibit 3A.4 (Continued)   Application for private detective or security service license.
(Continued)

You must submit the following items with this application. *(Use check boxes to indicate items are attached. Incomplete packages will be returned)*

☐ Two photographs (2" x 2" passport style)

☐ Verification from State Agency

☐ Documentation of employment

☐ Copy of Motor Vehicle Driver's License

☐ DD-214 or NGB-22, military discharge documentation which includes type of discharge and reenlistment codes

☐ High school diploma/ GED cert., college transcript or other proof of training

☐ Full credit bureau report; summary not accepted

☐ Trade name, LLC or Incorporation papers.

☐ Two fingerprint cards - 1 green (state card) with $50.00 payable to Treasurer, State of Connecticut, and 1 blue (FBI card) with $14.75 payable to the Treasurer, State of Connecticut. Submit prints with bank or postal money order only. **NO CASH.**

☐ Motor vehicle abstract for LICENSEE only, for the past three years. Obtain the abstract from the motor vehicle licensing agency in the state of the licensee's residence for the past three years.

☐ Also required are four letters of personal reference, LICENSEE ONLY. These letters of reference must be original letters and must be sent directly from the author to the Special Licensing & Firearms Unit. FORM LETTERS ARE NOT ACCEPTABLE AND WILL BE RETURNED.

Corporate Applicants: Submit this application(DPS-366-C) along with:

☐ Two fingerprint cards - 1 green (state card) with $50.00 payable to Treasurer, State of Connecticut and 1 blue (FBI card) with $14.75 payable to the Treasurer, State of Connecticut. Submit prints with bank or postal money order only. NO CASH.

☐ Two photographs (approximately 2" x 2" passport style)

Proprietary Applicants:

☐ Submit only the DPS-366-C – **NO FEES OR ADDITIONAL DOCUMENTATION REQUIRED.**

Applications must be complete.
Authorization for Release of Personal Information

All of the information on this application must be verifiable or it will not be considered for licensing. False, misleading or omitted information may be the basis for denial of a license. "Any person who violates any provision shall be fined not more than $5,000.00 or imprisoned for not more than one year or both."

STATE OF

_____
(Signature of Applicant)

SS

_____
Date of Oath

COUNTY OF: _____

PERSONALLY APPEARED: _____

ADDRESS: _____

Signer of the foregoing application and made oath of truth of matters contained before me.

My Commission Expires: _____

_____
Notary Public, Justice of Peace or Commissioner of Superior Court

DPS-366-C (Revised 3/12)

An Affirmative Action/Equal Opportunity Employer

Page 4

Exhibit 3A.4 (Continued) Application for private detective or security service license.

WASHINGTON STATE DEPARTMENT OF
dol LICENSING

Private Security Guard Company/
Qualifying Principal
License Application

For validation only   001-070-299-0009

Send this completed form with a check or money order, payable to the
Department of Licensing, to: **Private Security Guard Program,**
Department of Licensing, PO Box 35001, Seattle WA 98124-3401

29989-APPLICATIONS

This is an application for:
☐ Company with principal – **$330**   ☐ Armed endorsement – additional **$10**
☐ Change of principal – **$80**   ☐ Armed endorsement – additional **$10**

Company information

TYPE OR PRINT UBI number	Company name	
		Number of partners *(if partnership)*

Type of business *(check one)*
☐ Sole proprietor ☐ Partnership ☐ Corporation ☐ Foreign corporation

Company address *(street address in Washington state)*

City		State **WA**	ZIP code

(Area code) Telephone number	(Area code) Fax number	Company email

Company mailing address *(if different)*

City		State	ZIP code

Branch office address *(Street, city, state, ZIP code)*

Branch office address *(Street, city, state, ZIP code)*

To show additional branches, attach pages.

Principal information

TYPE OR PRINT   Name *(Last, First, Middle initial)*

Social Security number required*	Date of birth *(mm/dd/yyyy)*	Citizenship ☐ U.S. citizen ☐ Resident alien

Home address

City		State	ZIP code

(Area code) Home telephone number	Email	Gender ☐ Male ☐ Female

Requirement under which you will be qualifying for license: *(check one)*
☐ Three years experience as a manager, supervisor, or administrator in the security business or a related field
☐ Examination *(see next page)*

*All applicants are required by federal and state law to provide their Social Security number (SSN) for use in child support enforcement programs (42 U.S.C. 666(a)(13) and RCW 74.20A.320). It may also be used for education loan repayment programs and identification of records with similar names. Submission of your SSN is mandatory; failure to submit it will result in denial of your application.

Criminal history

Answer the questions below. If you answer "Yes," attach a detailed explanation.

In this state or any other jurisdiction are you or have you:

1. Within the last 10 years, had any action (fine, suspension, revocation, censure, surrender, etc.) taken against any professional or occupational license, certification, or permit held by you? . . . . . ☐ Yes ☐ No

2. Currently under indictment, or is there a criminal complaint, charge, or information pending against you? . . . . ☐ Yes ☐ No

PSG-690-001 (R/4/16)WA Page 1 of 3

Exhibit 3A.5   Private security guard company/qualifying principal license application.
(Continued)

Criminal history (continued)

3. Within the last 10 years, defaulted or been convicted of or entered a plea of no contest to a gross misdemeanor or felony crime? (Don't include traffic offenses.) . . . . □ Yes □ No

What were you convicted of?	Date	Name of court	City and state	Misdemeanor, gross misdemeanor, or felony?
1.				
2.				

To show additional convictions, attach pages.

Fingerprinting

All security guards must have fingerprint-based background checks. For information about the fingerprinting and background check process, go to www.dol.wa.gov/business/fingerprinting.html.

Experience (You must provide proof of your past employment)

Document your experience **beginning with your most recent or current position.** Acceptable forms of proof include: copies of payroll check stubs showing company name and pay period, copies of your federal tax return for the periods listed, certification from the employer verifying your status, duties, and time employed. Verification of license/registration from another state/jurisdiction is acceptable **only** if that state/jurisdiction has requirements that meet or exceed those of Washington State. Use the enclosed verification form for out-of-state work history.

Type of experience *(Manager, supervisor, administrator)*	From *(Month-day-year)*	To *(Month-day-year)*
Company name		
Company address *(Number and street, city, state, ZIP code)*		

Type of experience *(Manager, supervisor, administrator)*	From *(Month-day-year)*	To *(Month-day-year)*
Company name		
Company address *(Number and street, city, state, ZIP code)*		

Exam scheduling

Exams are given at driver licensing offices across the state. Select the location where you would like to take your exam, putting a "1" for your first choice and a "2" for your second choice. A licensing representative will contact you for scheduling.

	Bellingham		Kent		Puyallup		Union Gap
	Bel-Red		Lynnwood		Renton		Vancouver (136th Ave)
	Bremerton		Olympia		Seattle (25th Ave)		Walla Walla
	Clarkston		Omak		Smokey Point		Wenatchee
	Everett		Parkland		Spokane (Sprague Ave)		
	Federal Way		Port Angeles		Sunnyside		
	Kennewick		Port Townsend		Tacoma (Yakima Ave)		

Applicant authorization and certification

Do you authorize all organizations and government agencies (local, state, federal, or foreign) to release any information, files, or records requested to this Department to process your application? . . . . □ Yes □ No

I certify under penalty of perjury under the laws of the state of Washington that the foregoing is true and correct.

	X
Date and place signed	Applicant signature

Providing false information in this application may be cause for the denial, suspension, or revocation of your private security guard license in the state of Washington.

PSG-690-001 (R/4/16)WA Page 2 of 3

Exhibit 3A.5 (Continued)   Private security guard company/qualifying principal license application.

(Continued)

Application requirements
- Appropriate fee
- Applicant must be at least 21 years old
- Prior to licensing, the armed principal applicant must attend an eight-hour Firearms Certification course through the Criminal Justice Training Commission. The Department will be notified directly when the certificate is issued.
- If principal is applying for a license under the exam requirement, a licensing representative will contact you to schedule an exam
- Be prepared to provide a Certificate of Insurance prior to issuance of your license. The company must have comprehensive general liability coverage of at least $25,000 for bodily or personal injury and $25,000 for property damage. This certificate does not have to be submitted with the application packet and may be faxed to us when the license is ready to be issued (fax (360) 570-7888).
  The certificate holder on the insurance must read:
  Department of Licensing
  Private Security Guard Licensing Program
  PO Box 9649
  Olympia, WA 98507-9649
- Provide an address list of any branch offices maintained by the company
- US corporations must submit a:
  - copy of the Articles of Incorporation filed with the Washington Secretary of State
  - list of all officers and directors with an address for each
  - letter from the governing body of the corporation designating the applicant as "principal"
- Partnerships or limited partnerships must also submit:
  - a fee for each partner other than the principal
  - one completed application for each partner
    Each partner must apply for licensure in order to be eligible to own or operate the company. Each must meet the same eligibility requirements as the principal of the company.
- In addition, foreign corporations must submit a certified copy of the Certificate of Authority to conduct business in the state of Washington

Frequently asked questions
Q. What is a company principal?
A. The individual who, in order to own or operate a private security guard company, must meet the minimum qualifications of three years experience or pass the state exam.

Q. How often are the exams given for principals and certified trainers?
A. They are scheduled within two to three weeks after we receive your application.

Q. Where will I take the exam?
A. The exams are scheduled at driver licensing offices around the state. When the exam is completed, it will be returned to this office to be scored. A letter with your score will be mailed to you approximately 10 days after you've taken your exam.

Q. How often can I take the exam?
A. There's no limit on the number of times you may take the exam as long as there's at least seven working days between them.

Q. How do I get rescheduled if I don't pass?
A. A reexam application will be mailed to you with your results. Complete and return the application with the $25 fee to be rescheduled.

Q. If I'm just working for myself and do not want to hire employees, do I still have to get a company license?
A. Yes, anyone who works as a private security guard must either be licensed as a company principal or as a security guard under another company.

Q. How do my employees get licensed?
A. Once your company is licensed, you can submit applications for your employees. They are required to complete eight hours of pre-assignment training from a licensed certified trainer. The certified trainer must sign the certification box on the front of the Security Guard Application.

Q. How do I become a certified trainer?
A. Once you are licensed, submit a certified trainer exam application and $25.

Q. May I have a certified trainer from another company give my employees the training?
A. Yes, provided the trainer is currently employed and holds a valid certified trainer's license.

PSG-690-001 (R/4/16)WA Page 3 of 3

Exhibit 3A.5 (Continued) Private security guard company/qualifying principal license application.

COMMONWEALTH OF VIRGINIA
Department of Criminal Justice Services
P.O. Box 1300 • Richmond, VA 23218
Phone: (804) 786-4700 • Fax: (804) 786-6344 www.dcjs.virginia.gov/pss

Status Hotline
(804) 786-1132
1-877-9STATUS

INITIAL INSTRUCTOR CERTIFICATION APPLICATION – $50.00 plus $10.00 per category

IMPORTANT INFORMATION

➤ A Fingerprint Application, Fingerprint Card, and $50.00 non-refundable fee is required for registration pursuant to § 9.1-145.A of the *Code of Virginia*. Please ensure that an Instructor Application is submitted within 120 days of submitting the fingerprint application. Note: a criminal history records check may take up to 45 days to process.

➤ A DCJS instructor development course training must be completed within the 3 years prior to your application for certification, or submit a partial training exemption application for an instructor development course that meets or exceeds standards established by the DCJS. For additional information, please go online at www.dcjs.virginia/pss.

➤ Third Party Documentation verifying the types and dates or experience must be attached to this application. To be eligible the experience must be either:

> Three (3) years managerial/supervisory experience in a private security services business, a federal, military police, state, or local law enforcement agency or in related field
> **OR**
> Five (5) years general experience in private security or a related field
> **OR**
> One (1) year experience as an instructor or teacher at an accredited educational institution or agency in the subject matter for which certification is requested or in a related field
> **AND**
> Have a minimum of 2 years previous work experience for those subjects in which certification is requested.

➤ If requesting to become a certified firearms instructor, a range qualification completed with a **Virginia** Criminal Justice Agency, Academy, Correctional Department or Certified Private Security School is required. The qualification must be with a semi-automatic handgun, revolver, AND shotgun at 85% or better.

> If requesting to provide patrol rifle training, a range qualification completed with a **Virginia** Criminal Justice Agency, Academy, Correctional Department or Certified Private Security School is required. The qualification must be at 85% or better.

➤ The initial instructor certification fee **includes one** category of training. A separate fee of **$10.00** will be charged for each additional category of training as identified in 6VAC20-171-100. B. 4. of the Regulations Relating to Private Security Services.

Applicant Information		
SSN or DCJS ID Number:	Last Name:	First Name: / MI:
Mailing Address (Street/Apt.#):		City, State, Zip:
Email Address:		Fax: ( )
Home Phone: ( )	Business Phone: ( )	Cell: ( )
Employment Information		
School Name:		DCJS School ID Number:

Exhibit 3A.6 Private security instructor application.

(Continued)

Training Information

Has a Partial Training Exemption Application been submitted? ☐ Yes ☐ No

Has a General Instructor Entry-Level Training Enrollment application been submitted? ☐ Yes ☐ No

Instruction Category(s) Requested *(check each that apply)*

☐ Security Officers/Couriers/Alarm respondent (armed and unarmed) to include Arrest Authority. (01, 05)

☐ Private Investigators. (02)

☐ Locksmiths, Electronic Security Personnel to include Central Station Dispatchers. (25, 30, 35, 38, 39)

☐ Armored car Personnel. (03)

☐ Personal Protection Specialist. (32)

☐ Detector Canine Handlers (4ED), Security Canine Handlers. (4ES)

☐ Special Conservators of the Peace pursuant to § 9.1-150 of the *Code of Virginia*. (06)

☐ Bail Bondsmen pursuant to § 9.1-185 of the *Code of Virginia*. Bail Enforcement Agents pursuant to § 9.1-186 of the *Code of Virginia*. (40, 44)

☐ Firearms. (Check all that apply)
    ☐ Entry Level Handgun (07)
    ☐ Security Officer Handgun (75)
    ☐ Shotgun (08)
    ☐ Advanced Handgun (09)
    ☐ Patrol Rifle (10)

Affirmation

I, the undersigned, certify that all information contained on this application is true and correct to the best of my knowledge and I have not omitted any pertinent information. I understand that any misrepresentation, falsification or omission of pertinent information may be cause for denial and may result in criminal charges. I understand that I am responsible for maintaining full compliance with *Virginia Code* Sections 9.1-138 through 9.1-150 and the Regulations Relating to Private Security Services 6 VAC 20-171.

Signature Required: _____ Date: _____
                                                                                mm/dd/yy

Applications are valid for 12 months from the date of submittal.

All fees are non-refundable. Applications received without payment will be returned.

Submit a check or money order payable to the TREASURER OF VIRGINIA,
or pay by credit card using the Credit Card form available at www.dcis.virginia.gov/forms/privatesecurity/pss_cc.pdf
— this form must be included with your application package when paying by credit card.

Exhibit 3A.6 (Continued) Private security instructor application.

COMMONWEALTH OF VIRGINIA
Department of Criminal Justice Services
P.O. Box 1300 • Richmond, VA 23218
Phone: (804) 786-4700 • Fax: (804) 786-6344 www.dcjs.virginia.gov/pss

Status Hotline
(804) 786-1132
1-877-9STATUS

Private Security Services –
RENEWAL REGISTRATION APPLICATION 2-YEAR REGISTRATION – FEE $20.00
IMPORTANT INFORMATION

➢ Application and In-service Training must be completed prior to expiration date for issuance of registration. If you are going to carry or have access to a firearm, you must also maintain a Firearms Endorsement and complete all required firearms training.

➢ You may add or remove categories without additional fees at renewal. If adding the Armored Car category, a Fingerprint Application, Fingerprint Card, and a $50.00 non-refundable fee are required for registration if you have **not** submitted fingerprints within 120 days a criminal history records check may take up to 45 days to process.

➢ If your current registration is expired, you have **60 days** from the date your registration expired to submit a non-refundable reinstatement fee of **$10.00** and meet all of the renewal requirements. If 60 day reinstatement period has passed; you cannot use this form as you **must** complete the initial registration process.

Applicant Information

SSN or DCJS ID Number:	Last Name:	First Name:	MI:

Mailing Address (Street/Apt.#): ☐ *Check if New Address*   City, State, Zip:

Physical Address (if different that mailing address):   City, State, Zip:

Email Address:

Home Phone: ( )	Business Phone: ( )	Fax: ( )

Registration Category(s) Requested (check all that apply) * Armored Car Personnel, Armed Personal Protection Specialist and Armed Security Officers are required to maintain a firearm endorsement.

☐ *Armored Car Personnel
☐ * Armed Security Officer/Courier
☐ *Armed Personal Protection Specialist
☐ Private Investigator

☐ Security Canine Handler
☐ Detector Canine Handler
☐ Alarm Respondent
☐ Unarmed Security Officer/Courier
☐ Unarmed Personal Protection Specialist

☐ Electronic Security Technician
☐ Electronic Security Technician Assistant
☐ Electronic Security Sales Representative
☐ Locksmith
☐ Central Station Dispatcher

Criminal History

Have you **been convicted** or **found guilty of a felony or misdemeanor** (not including minor traffic violations) in Virginia or any other jurisdiction to include military court martial or currently under protective orders within the **past two years?**
☐ Yes *   ☐ No   * If Yes, **please attach a** Private Security Criminal History Supplement Form **and all requested criminal history documentation.**

Affirmation

I, the undersigned, certify that all information contained on this application is true and correct to the best of my knowledge and have not omitted any pertinent information. I understand that any misrepresentation, falsification or omission of pertinent information may be cause for denial and may result in criminal charges. I understand that I am responsible for maintaining full compliance with *Virginia Code* Sections 9.1-138 through 9.1-150 and the Regulations Relating to Private Security Services 6 VAC 20-171.

Signature Required: _____   Date: _____
                                                                                                                          mm/dd/yy

All fees are non-refundable. Applications received without payment will be returned.

Submit a check or money order payable to the TREASURER OF VIRGINIA,
or pay by credit card using the Credit Card form available at www.dcjs.virginia.gov/forms/privatesecurity/pss_cc.pdf
— this form must be included with your application package when paying by credit card.

01/2015

Page 1 of 1

Exhibit 3A.7   Renewal of registration application.

COMMONWEALTH OF VIRGINIA
Department of Criminal Justice Services
P.O. Box 1300 • Richmond, VA 23218
Phone: (804) 786-4700 • Fax: (804) 786-6344 www.dcjs.virginia.gov/pss

Status Hotline
(804) 786-1132
1-877-9STATUS

TRAINING SESSION NOTIFICATION FORM

IMPORTANT INFORMATION

➤ Must be postmarked or received **no less than seven (7) calendar days** prior to the beginning or the training session.

➤ You may only provide one category of training per session notification.

Applicant Information	Submittal ☐	Cancelation ☐	
DCJS School ID Number: 88-	School Name:		Trading As:
Primary Instructor:			DCJS ID Number: 99-
Location of Training (if different than School):			City, State, Zip:
Range Name:			Code:
Start Date:	Start Time: (Military Format)	End Date:	End Time: (Military Format)

Entry level Subjects

- ☐ 01E Security Officer Core Subjects
- ☐ 02E Private Investigator
- ☐ 03E Armored Car Personnel
- ☐ 4ES Security Canine Handler
- ☐ 4ED Detector Canine Handler
- ☐ 05E Armed Security Officer Arrest Authority
- ☐ 06E Special Conservator of the Peace Core Subjects
- ☐ 25E Locksmith

- ☐ 30E Electronic Security Subjects
- ☐ 32E Personal Protection Specialist
- ☐ 35E Electronic Security Technician
- ☐ 38E Central Dispatcher
- ☐ 39E Electronic Security Sales Representative
- ☐ 40E Bail Bondsman
- ☐ 44E Bail Enforcement Agent

In-Service Subjects

- ☐ 01I Security Officer Core Subjects
- ☐ 02I Private Investigator
- ☐ 03I Armored Car Personnel
- ☐ 4IS Security Canine Handler
- ☐ 4ID Detector Canine Handler
- ☐ 06I Special Conservator of the Peace Core Subjects

- ☐ 25 I Locksmith
- ☐ 30I Electronic Security Subjects
- ☐ 32I Personal Protection Specialist
- ☐ 40I Bail Bondsman
- ☐ 44I Bail Enforcement Agent

Firearms Training

- ☐ 07E Entry- Level Handgun
- ☐ 075E Security Officer Handgun
- ☐ 07R Handgun Re-Training

- ☐ 08E Shotgun Training
- ☐ 08R Shotgun Re-Training
- ☐ 10E Patrol Rifle Training

- ☐ 09E Advanced Handgun Training
- ☐ 09R Advanced Handgun Re-Training
- ☐ 10R Patrol Rifle Re-Training

Additional Instructors During Session

Name:	DCJS ID Number: 99-
Name:	DCJS ID Number: 99-
Training School Director:	
Signature Required: _____ *Training School Director*	Phone: ( ) Ext.:
Date: *mm/dd/yy*	

04/2015

Page 1 of 1

Exhibit 3A.8   Training session notification form.

GEORGIA STATE BOARD OF PRIVATE DETECTIVE & SECURITY AGENCIES
237 COLISEUM DRIVE
MACON, GA 31217
TELEPHONE: 478.207.2440

INFORMATION SHEET FOR COMPANY LICENSURE

IMPORTANT: Review the Qualifications for Examination listed below **BEFORE MAKING APPLICATION. Ensure that you can qualify for the examination before you make application; otherwise, you risk the loss of the application fee. Application fees are NON-REFUNDABLE.**
All company licenses are valid for up to two years, and expire on June 30 of odd years. Renewal fees will be due at that time to maintain the license. If your application for licensure is approved, your initial license may be valid for a shorter time period, due to the relation between the date your initial license is issued and the expiration date of all company licenses.

QUALIFICATIONS FOR PRIVATE DETECTIVE EXAMINATION *(FROM O.C.G.A.§ 43-38-6)*:

1. An applicant must be at least eighteen (18) years of age;
2. An applicant is a citizen of the United States, or a registered resident alien;
3. An applicant is of good moral character;
4. An applicant has not been convicted of a felony or any crime involving the illegal use, carrying, or possession of a dangerous weapon or any crime involving moral turpitude(see O.C.G.A. § 43-38-6(4) for board discretion in granting licensure);
5. An applicant has not committed an act constituting dishonesty or fraud;
6. An applicant must have at least one of the following qualifications:
   A. Two (2) years of full-time experience as a registered private detective employee with a licensed detective company;
   B. Two (2) years of full-time experience in law enforcement with a federal, state, county, or municipal police department as defined in OCGA § 35-8-2 (8);
   C. A four (4)-year degree in criminal justice or a related field from an accredited college or university.

QUALIFICATIONS FOR PRIVATE SECURITY EXAMINATION *(FROM O.C.G.A.§ 43-38-6)*:

1. An applicant must be at least eighteen (18) years of age;
2. An applicant is a citizen of the United States, or a registered resident alien;
3. An applicant is of good moral character;
4. An applicant has not been convicted of a felony or any crime involving the illegal use, carrying, or possession of a dangerous weapon or any crime involving moral turpitude(see O.C.G.A. § 43-38-6(4) for board discretion in granting licensure);
5. An applicant has not committed an act constituting dishonesty or fraud;
6. An applicant must have at least one of the following qualifications:
   A. Two (2) years of full-time experience as a supervisor or administrator in in-house security operations, or with a licensed security agency;
   B. Two (2) years of full-time experience in law enforcement with a federal, state, county, or municipal police department as defined in OCGA § 35-8-2 (8);
   C. A four (4)-year degree in criminal justice or a related field from an accredited college or university.

Exhibit 3A.9 Application for company license.

THE APPLICATION PROCESS

Submit a completed application. NOTE: Applicants for company license who intend to provide both private detective and private security services must submit a separate application (an application for Private Detective Company, and an application for Private Security Company.) A completed application consists of the following information:

1. A company application with each question on the application answered to the best of the applicant's ability. The employee registration application is a necessary part of the company application package.
2. Applicants approved by the Board to take the appropriate exam must schedule the examination with PSI. The approval notification from PSI will direct approved applicants to the PSI website to schedule an examination.
3. A completed LiveScan fingerprinting from an approved GAPS service site. Register for fingerprinting at www.ga.cogentid.com. If you prefer, you can register by phone at 1.888.439.2512.

**When registering, the ORI number to use is GA920240Z.
The Verification Code is 920240Z.
The reason for registration is Private Detective/Security Business**

   **NOTE: If the applying company is a partnership or corporate entity, the fingerprints submitted must be for the designee of the company.
4. A 2"X2" frontal view photograph of the applicant attached in the designated area on the Employee Registration Application included in this package.
   **NOTE: If the applying company is a partnership or corporate entity, the applicant will be the designee of the company.
5. An original NOTARIZED letter of experience from the applicant's employer where the two years of experience was obtained. The letter must include the exact dates of full-time employment, and positions and duties held by the applicant. If the experience used to qualify the applicant is from law enforcement, the letter must include P.O.S.T. certification qualifications. The letter must be signed by the personnel department of the company/organization, or by a responsible officer/supervisor of the company/organization, on company letterhead.
   **NOTE: Certificates, Letters of Commendation, copies of licenses, resumes, self-written letters of experience, and like documents ARE NOT ACCEPTABLE as proof of two years of experience.
6. If the applying company is an out-of-state company, submit an original NOTARIZED letter of certification from the state(s) in which the company holds or has held a license. Additionally, the individual making application as the license holder for the company must submit an original NOTARIZED letter of certification from the state(s) in which the individual holds or has held a license or registration.
7. If the applying company is a Georgia corporate entity, submit CERTIFIED documentation that the applicant for the company is a corporate officer. If the applying company is an LLC, partnership, or any other entity, submit CERTIFIED documentation that the applicant for the company is an officer of the entity.
8. If applying with a four-year degree in criminal justice or a related field from an accredited college or university, the applicant must submit an original CERTIFIED transcript or letter in a sealed envelope from the institution. The sealed transcript or letter must be submitted with the application.
   **NOTE: A copy of the transcript or letter will not suffice. If the degree is not in criminal justice, the Board will review the transcript to determine if the courses completed for the degree are sufficient to grant licensure based on the degree.
9. The applicant must also submit an Application for Employee Registration to obtain a personal registration.

Rev. 06/29/12

2

Exhibit 3A.9 (Continued) Application for company license.   (Continued)

**NOTE*: An application for a weapon permit is not required to be submitted if the license holder will not carry a weapon.

10.   Original Surety Bond ($25,000) OR

Original Certificate of Liability Insurance ($1 million) OR
Certified Audited Financial Statement (in excess of $50,000).

**NOTE*: Bond/Insurance/Financial Statement is not required until successful completion of exam.

Disapproved applicants will be notified by the Board office

EXAMINATIONS

The Board does not provide study material. The very broad nature of the scope of practice makes it difficult to provide study material.

**The Board office staff does not have information on where study material may be obtained.

The Private Detective examination will consist of questions in the following areas:
- Legal observation/surveillance
- Gun safety and handling
- Obtaining and preserving evidence
- Interview/interrogation
- Client relation/administration

The Security Company examination will consist of questions in the following areas:
- Search and seizure
- Use of force
- Rights of privacy
- Carrying arms
- Transfer of detainee/offender
- Scope of services
- Developing service plans/contracts
- Liability

**If you have a disability and may require an accommodation, complete the "Request for Disability Accommodation Guidelines" form and return with your application and acceptable documentation of your disability.

Successful applicants must submit to the Board office the remaining items necessary to complete the application:
1.   Appropriate License Fee.
2.   Original $25,000 Surety Bond with the company name exactly as it appears on the application, OR
3. $1 million ($1,000,000) General Liability Certificate of Insurance, indicating the policy number AND the certificate holder as: Georgia State Board of Private Detective & Security Agencies, 237 Coliseum Drive, Macon, GA 31217, OR
4.   A certified audited financial statement showing a net worth in excess of $50,000.00.
5.   Any other information requested by the Board.

Once all the required information and fee has been submitted, processed, reviewed, and determined complete, the license will be issued.

Rev. 06/29/12

3

Exhibit 3A.9 (Continued)   Application for company license.   *(Continued)*

HELPFUL HINTS

- Review the qualifications before you apply. Ensuring that you qualify for the license you seek to obtain before submitting an application and fee will help prevent the loss of the non-refundable application fee, should you discover later that you are not qualified.
- Ensure that the training instructor utilized by the company is certified by the Board. To verify that a prospective instructor is certified by the Board, you can verify licensure on our website by clicking the link entitled "License Verification" and following the instructions.
- Review your application thoroughly before you submit it to the Board office. Every question must be answered to the best of your ability. Failure to do so will result in delays in Board review. Ensure that the Application for Employee Registration is included in your submission.
- You may have your fingerprints processed at an approved GAPS service site prior to submitting your application. When registering, the ORI number to use is GA920240Z. The Verification Code is 920240Z. The reason for registering is Private Detective/Security Business. Your application will not be reviewed by the Board until we receive the results of your fingerprint-based background check.
- Ensure that the proof of experience is original and notarized by the employer with whom you received the experience. Remember that certificates and letters of commendation will not suffice for proof of experience. Failure to do so will result in delay in Board review.
- Ensure that the appropriate fee is paid for the application you are submitting.
- Ensure that the bond or certificate of insurance indicates your company name exactly as it appears on your application. Also ensure that the certificate of insurance indicates the holder as the Georgia State Board of Private Detective & Security Agencies, 237 Coliseum Drive, Macon, GA 31217. Failure to ensure that this information is accurate will result in delay in issuing your license. Also ensure that the bond is signed by the applicant. Do not write the business name in the signature line.
- If applying as a corporate entity, ensure that the proper corporate documents are submitted that indicate that the designee for the company license is an officer of the corporation.

All information should be mailed to the Board office by addressing correspondence to:

Georgia State Board of Private Detective & Security Agencies
237 Coliseum Drive, Macon, GA 31217

Exhibit 3A.9 (Continued)   Application for company license.   *(Continued)*

GEORGIA BOARD OF PRIVATE DETECTIVE & SECURITY AGENCIES

FEE SCHEDULE

ALL APPLICATION FEES ARE NON-REFUNDABLE

COMPANY LICENSURE FEES

INITIAL LICENSURE	APPLICATION FEE	LICENSE FEE	TOTAL FEE
Detective Company	$100.00	$300.00	$400.00
Security Company	$100.00	$500.00	$600.00

ADDITIONAL COMPANY FEES

Replacement Fee for Lost or Destroyed License	$ 25.00
Application Fee for Change of Company Name	$ 25.00
Application Fee for Change of Address	$ 25.00
Renewal Fee - Detective Company	$ 300.00
Late Renewal Fee – Detective Company	$400.00
Reinstatement Fee – Detective Company	$450.00
Renewal Fee - Security Company	$500.00
Late Renewal Fee – Security Company	$600.00
Reinstatement Fee – Security Company	$750.00
Renewal Fee - Detective & Security Company	$700.00
Late Renewal Fee – Detective & Security Company	$800.00

EMPLOYEE REGISTRATION FEES

Unarmed Detective Employees	$ 45.00
Armed Detective Employees	$ 70.00
Armed Security Guard Employees	$ 70.00
Renewal Fee – All Employee Registrations	$ 65.00
Late Renewal Fee – All Employee Registrations	$ 80.00
Fee for Additional Weapon, or Change of Weapon Type	$ 25.00
Replacement Fee for Lost or Destroyed License	$ 25.00

TRAINING INSTRUCTOR FEES

Certification of Training Instructor Fee	$100.00
Renewal Fee	$100.00
Late Renewal Fee	$150.00
Replacement Fee for Lost or Destroyed License	$ 25.00

Rev. 06/29/12

5

Exhibit 3A.9 (Continued) Application for company license.

(Continued)

GEORGIA BOARD OF PRIVATE DETECTIVES
& SECURITY AGENCIES
237 COLISEUM DRIVE
MACON, GA 31217
TELEPHONE 478.207.2440
www.sos.ga.gov/plb/detective

DO NOT WRITE IN THIS SECTION
RECEIPT # _____
AMOUNT _____
APPLICANT # _____
INITIAL _____ DATE _____

APPLICATION FOR COMPANY LICENSE

APPLICATION IS BEING MADE FOR (CHECK APPROPRIATE BOX):

☐ PRIVATE DETECTIVE AGENCY

☐ PRIVATE SECURITY AGENCY   ☐ IN-HOUSE SECURITY COMPANY

☐ REINSTATEMENT OF LICENSE NO. _____   *REINSTATEMENT IS AT THE BOARD'S DISCRETION

TRADE NAME OF BUSINESS: _____

_____

FEDERAL EMPLOYER'S ID: _____

EMAIL ADDRESS (FOR CORRESPONDENCE FROM BOARD): _____

PERSON AUTHORIZED TO HOLD LICENSE FOR THE COMPANY(DESIGNEE):

_____

_____

RESIDENCE ADDRESS   CITY   STATE   ZIP CODE   TELEPHONE

GENDER: _____ MALE _____ FEMALE   DATE OF BIRTH : _____/_____/_____

PLACE OF BIRTH: _____

SOCIAL SECURITY NO.*: _____-____-_____

*THIS INFORMATION IS AUTHORIZED TO BE OBTAINED &
DISCLOSED TO STATE & FEDERAL AGENCIES PURSUANT TO
O.C.G.A. § 19-11-1 & O.C.G.A. § 20-3-295, 42 U.S.C.A. § 551 & 20
U.S.C.A. § 1001.

MAILING ADDRESS OF BUSINESS (ADDRESS USED TO MAIL LICENSE & RENEWAL NOTICES):

_____

_____

STREET ADDRESS OR P.O. BOX

CITY   STATE   ZIP CODE   COUNTY   TELEPHONE

PHYSICAL LOCATION ADDRESS OF BUSINESS (ADDRESS WILL APPEAR ON LICENSE & ONLINE):

_____

_____

ADDRESS (P.O. BOX NOT ACCEPTABLE

CITY   STATE   ZIP CODE   COUNTY   TELEPHONE

Rev. 06/29/12   6

Exhibit 3A.9 (Continued)   Application for company license.   *(Continued)*

As part of a background investigation to determine suitability for the issuance of a license by the Georgia Board of Private Detective & Security Agencies, please answer the following questions. If you answer "Yes" to any questions, give a brief explanation of your answer. Attach additional pages, if necessary.

1. Has the company ever been the subject of an investigation or litigation that was conducted by a federal, state, or local agency?_____ ☐ YES ☐ NO

2. Has the company ever had a professional license or certification revoked, suspended, or modified for any reason? _____ ☐ YES ☐ NO

3. Has the company or any principal ever been reprimanded, placed on probation, or otherwise disciplined by a professional licensing or certification body? _____ ☐ YES ☐ NO

4. Has any principal ever been disciplined or cited for a breach of ethics or unprofessional conduct? _____ ☐ YES ☐ NO

5. Has any principal ever resigned or been discharged from any position with pending criminal or administrative charges? _____ ☐ YES ☐ NO

6. Has the company ever been prohibited from doing business with the State of Georgia, the United States Government, or any local or state government? _____ ☐ YES ☐ NO

7. Is the agency now, or has the agency previously been licensed as a private detective &/or private security agency in Georgia, or in any other state? If so, list the state(s) and the expiration date(s) of the license(s). _____ ☐ YES ☐ NO

8. Has the agency ever had a license revoked, suspended, or otherwise sanctioned by any board or agency, or have you ever been denied issuance of, or, pursuant to disciplinary proceedings, refused renewal of a license by any board or agency in Georgia or any other state? **If so, you must attach a detailed explanation.** ☐ YES ☐ NO

Exhibit 3A.9 (Continued) Application for company license.

(Continued)

QUALIFYING EXPERIENCE OF THE LICENSE HOLDER LISTED ON PAGE 1

Have you ever held a position of supervisor or administrator with a licensed private security agency or with in-house security operations? If so, provide the following information: ☐ YES ☐ NO

Agency or In-House Operations Name: _____

No. of Security Personnel
Title Held: _____ No. of Years: _____ Under Your Supervision: _____

You must provide an <u>original notarized</u> letter from the employer, verifying your experience.

Have you been employed full-time with a licensed private detective agency? If so, list your registration number _____ and agency name _____ ☐ YES ☐ NO

You must also provide verification of experience as detailed in the instructions.

Have you ever held a license for a private investigative agency, private security agency, or licensed in-house security operations? If so, provide the following information: ☐ YES ☐ NO

Agency or In-House Operations Name: _____

Other Business Name(s) Used : _____

Agency License Number: _____

Are you now, or have you ever been certified through P.O.S.T.? ☐ YES ☐ NO
If yes, you must provide a copy of your certification.
If yes , provide the type of certification: _____ .

Have you ever had a disciplinary action taken against your certification? **If yes, you must provide documentation of the case, including the final outcome.** ☐ YES ☐ NO

Have you served in the armed forces? **Attach a copy of your Form DD-214.** ☐ YES ☐ NO

If so, please list the highest rank achieved: _____

List any duties assigned or experience gained that you feel qualify you to hold a license for private detective or security agency:

_____

_____

Have you obtained a four-year degree from a college, university, or institution of higher learning with a major in Criminal Justice or a related field? If yes, complete the following: ☐ YES ☐ NO

Name of Institution: _____ Degree(s) Earned: _____

In what field(s)?: _____

** You must provide an <u>original</u> <u>certified</u> copy of the transcript or an <u>original</u> letter from the institution verifying this information. **

Rev. 06/29/12   8

Exhibit 3A.9 (Continued)   Application for company license.   *(Continued)*

OWNERSHIP/RELATIONSHIP INFORMATION

SOLE PROPRIETORSHIP

OWNER NAME: _____

RESIDENCE: _____

STREET(NOT A P.O. BOX)   CITY   STATE ZIP CODE   TELEPHONE

CORPORATIONS & LIMITED LIABILITY COMPANIES

DATE REGISTERED WITH GA SECRETARY OF STATE: _____

LIST PRINCIPAL OFFICERS/MEMBERS
(ATTACH ADDITIONAL PAGES, IF NECESSARY)

NAME: _____   TITLE: _____

RESIDENCE: _____

STREET(NOT A P.O. BOX)   CITY   STATE ZIP CODE   TELEPHONE

NAME: _____   TITLE: _____

RESIDENCE: _____

STREET(NOT A P.O. BOX)   CITY   STATE ZIP CODE   TELEPHONE

NAME: _____   TITLE: _____

RESIDENCE: _____

STREET(NOT A P.O. BOX)   CITY   STATE ZIP CODE   TELEPHONE

PARTNERSHIPS

LIST PARTNERS
(ATTACH ADDITIONAL PAGES, IF NECESSARY)

NAME: _____   TITLE: _____

RESIDENCE: _____

STREET(NOT A P.O. BOX)   CITY   STATE ZIP CODE   TELEPHONE

NAME: _____   TITLE: _____

RESIDENCE: _____

STREET(NOT A P.O. BOX)   CITY   STATE ZIP CODE   TELEPHONE

NAME: _____   TITLE: _____

RESIDENCE: _____

STREET(NOT A P.O. BOX)   CITY   STATE ZIP CODE   TELEPHONE

Rev. 06/29/12

Exhibit 3A.9 (Continued)   Application for company license.   *(Continued)*

AFFIDAVIT OF AUTHORIZATION OF THE DESIGNEE

DESIGNEE FOR A CORPORATION OR LLC

PLEASE PRINT NAMES

I, _____, HEREBY NAME
PRESIDENT, SECRETARY, OR MANAGING MEMBER OF CORPORATION OR LLC

_____
              DESIGNEE

AS THE DESIGNATED AGENT FOR THE CORPORATION OR LLC THAT APPEARS ON THIS
APPLICATION FOR LICENSURE. THIS AFFIDAVIT GIVES THE DESIGNEE ALL RIGHTS AND
RESPONSIBILITIES OF A LICENSE HOLDER ON BEHALF OF THE CORPORATION OR LLC AND
SHALL PROVIDE THAT ACTIONS OR OMISSIONS OF THE CORPORATION OR LLC, ITS OFFICERS,
MEMBERS, EMPLOYEES, AGENTS, ASSIGNS, OR DESIGNEES IN VIOLATION OF THE GEORGIA
PRIVATE DETECTIVE & SECURITY AGENCIES ACT OR IN VIOLATION OF THE GEORGIA BOARD
OF PRIVATE DETECTIVE & SECURITY AGENCIES RULES SHALL SUBJECT THE LICENSE
HOLDER AND THE CORPORATION OR LLC TO ANY SANCTIONS WHICH MAY BE IMPOSED
UNDER THE GEORGIA PRIVATE DETECTIVE & SECURITY AGENCIES ACT OR UNDER THE
GEORGIA BOARD OF PRIVATE DETECTIVE & SECURITY AGENCIES RULES.

WE UNDERSTAND THAT THE LICENSE IS NOT TRANSFERRABLE, AND SHOULD THE
DESIGNATED AGENT TERMINATE EMPLOYMENT OR OTHERWISE BECOMES UNAUTHORIZED
TO HOLD THE LICENSE, A NEW APPLICATION WILL BE REQUIRED.

SIGNATURES

_____   _____
PRESIDENT, SECRETARY, OR MANAGING MEMBER OF CORPORATION OR LLC   DATE

_____   _____
      DESIGNATED LICENSE HOLDER   DATE

STATE OF GEORGIA
COUNTY OF _____

SUBSCRIBED AND SWORN TO BEFORE ME THIS

_____ DAY OF _____, _____

_____
           NOTARY PUBLIC
MY COMMISSION EXPIRES: _____   SEAL

Rev. 06/29/12   10

Exhibit 3A.9 (Continued)   **Application for company license.**   *(Continued)*

AFFIDAVIT OF AUTHORIZATION OF THE DESIGNEE

DESIGNEE FOR A PARTNERSHIP

PLEASE PRINT NAME

WE, THE BELOW NAMED PARTNERS, HEREBY NAME _____

DESIGNEE

AS THE DESIGNATED AGENT FOR LICENSURE OF THE BUSINESS THAT APPEARS ON THIS APPLICATION FOR LICENSURE. THIS AFFIDAVIT GIVES THE DESIGNEE ALL RIGHTS AND RESPONSIBILITIES OF A LICENSE HOLDER ON BEHALF OF THE PARTNERSHIP AND SHALL PROVIDE THAT ACTIONS OR OMISSIONS OF THE PARTNERSHIP, ITS OFFICERS, EMPLOYEES, AGENTS, ASSIGNS, OR DESIGNEES IN VIOLATION OF GEORGIA PRIVATE DETECTIVE & SECURITY AGENCIES ACT OR IN VIOLATION OF THE GEORGIA BOARD OF PRIVATE DETECTIVE & SECURITY AGENCIES RULES SHALL SUBJECT THE LICENSE HOLDER AND THE PARTNERSHIP TO ANY SANCTIONS WHICH MAY BE IMPOSED UNDER THE GEORGIA PRIVATE DETECTIVE & SECURITY AGENCIES ACT OR UNDER THE GEORGIA BOARD OF PRIVATE DETECTIVE & SECURITY AGENCIES BOARD RULES.

WE UNDERSTAND THAT THE LICENSE IS NOT TRANSFERRABLE, AND SHOULD THE DESIGNATED AGENT TERMINATE EMPLOYMENT OR OTHERWISE BECOMES UNAUTHORIZED TO HOLD THE LICENSE, A NEW APPLICATION WILL BE REQUIRED.

SIGNATURES

_____   _____   _____   _____
PARTNER   DATE   DESIGNEE   DATE

_____   _____
PARTNER   DATE

STATE OF GEORGIA
COUNTY OF _____

SUBSCRIBED AND SWORN TO BEFORE ME THIS

_____ DAY OF _____, _____

_____
NOTARY PUBLIC
MY COMMISSION EXPIRES: _____

SEAL

Exhibit 3A.9 (Continued)   **Application for company license.**

(Continued)

Provide information on the types of services your agency will offer:

_____

_____

_____

AFFIDAVIT

I hereby swear and affirm that all information provided in this application is true and correct to the best of my knowledge and belief. I further swear and affirm that I have read and understand the current state laws and rules and regulations of the Georgia Board of Private Detective & Security Agencies, and I agree to abide by these laws and rules, as amended from time to time.

I also understand that if I have made a false statement on the application, or if I am found to have been convicted of a felony and have not had all of my civil rights restored pursuant to the law, **the Board may suspend my registration without a prior hearing.** I shall be entitled to a hearing after the suspension of my registration.

By signing this application, electronically or otherwise, I hereby swear and affirm one of the following to be true and accurate pursuant to O.C.G.A. § 50-36-1:

1) _____ I am a United States citizen 18 years of age or older. **Please submit a copy of your current Secure and Verifiable Document(s) such as driver's license, passport, or other document as indicated on pages 13 and 14 of the application.**

2) _____ I am not a United States citizen, but I am a legal permanent resident of the United States 18 years of age or older, or I am a qualified alien or non-immigrant under the Federal Immigration and Nationality Act 18 years of age or older with an alien number issued by the Department of Homeland Security or other federal immigration agency. **Please submit a copy of your current immigration document(s) which includes either your Alien number or your I-94 number and, if needed, SEVIS number.**

STATE OF GEORGIA
COUNTY OF _____

_____
SIGNATURE OF THE APPLICANT

SUBSCRIBED AND SWORN TO BEFORE ME THIS

_____ DAY OF _____, _____

_____
DATE

_____
NOTARY PUBLIC
MY COMMISSION EXPIRES: _____

Exhibit 3A.9 (Continued)   Application for company license.   *(Continued)*

GEORGIA BOARD OF PRIVATE DETECTIVE & SECURITY AGENCIES

STATE OF GEORGIA

BOND

BOND NUMBER: _____

_____
COUNTY

KNOW ALL MEN BY THESE PRESENTS

That we,_____
Principal/Licensee, and _____, as

_____ as Surety/Company, are held and firmly bound
unto **HIS EXCELLENCY**, Governor of Georgia, and his successors in office in the just sum of **TWENTY-FIVE THOUSAND
AND NO/100 ($25,000) DOLLARS,** for the payment of which, well and truly to be made, we bind ourselves, our heirs, executors
and administrators, each and every one of them, jointly and severally, by these presents.

It is further understood and agreed that this bond is for a period beginning on the _____ day of
_____, _____, and ending on the _____ day of _____,
_____.

Whereas, the above bound Principal/Licensee has made application to the Georgia Board of Private Detective & Security
Agencies for a license as Private Detective/Security Agency in accordance with the laws governing the Private Detective and
Security Agencies in the State of Georgia;

It is a condition of this bond that the said Principal/Licensee is to comply with all of the laws governing the acts of Private
Detective and Security Agencies in Georgia.

A further condition of this bond is that the Principal/Licensee and Surety/Company to this bond shall be subject to suit by
action thereon for the purpose of indemnifying any persons aggrieved by any act of the Principal/Licensee, which act is in violation
of Code Section 43-38 and would be grounds for denial, suspension, or revocation of a license under Code Section 43-38-11. Any
and all damages paid shall not exceed the amount of this bond.

Now, should the said Principal/Licensee, faithfully perform all his duties under Code Section 43-38 as a Private
Detective/Security Agency during the term for which he has been licensed, then the above bond is to be void upon expiration of his
license, else to be in full force and effect.

IN WITNESS WHEREOF, the Principal/Licensee and Surety/Company have caused these presents to be duly signed
and executed under seal, this _____ day of _____, _____.

_____
Signature of Principal/Licensee

_____
Surety/Company – Name of Company

Countersigned: _____
Address

_____   _____
Resident Agency   By Attorney-in-Fact

IMPORTANT: BOND MUST BE SIGNED – POWER OF ATTORNEY MUST BE ATTACHED

CANCELLATION CLAUSE – No licensee shall cancel or cause to be canceled a bond … issued pursuant to
this Code section unless the board is so informed in writing by certified mail or statutory overnight delivery at
least 30 days prior to the proposed cancellation. O.C.G.A. Section 43-38-6(d)(1).

13

Exhibit 3A.9 (Continued) Application for company license.

(Continued)

GEORGIA BOARD OF PRIVATE DETECTIVES
& SECURITY AGENCIES
237 COLISEUM DRIVE
MACON, GA 31217
TELEPHONE 478.207.2440
www.sos.ga.gov/plb/detective

```
DO NOT WRITE IN THIS SECTION
RECEIPT # _____
AMOUNT _____
APPLICANT # _____
INITIAL _____ DATE _____
```

APPLICATION FOR EMPLOYEE REGISTRATION

TYPE OF WEAPON APPLIED FOR (CHECK ALL THAT APPLY):
☐ NO WEAPON**THIS DESIGNATION ONLY APPLIES TO PRIVATE DETECTIVE EMPLOYEES

☐ EXPOSED   ☐ SHOTGUN ** ☐ CONCEALED **
** REQUIRES WRITTEN REQUEST FROM EMPLOYER, DETAILING DUTIES

TYPE OF REGISTRATION APPLIED FOR (CHECK ONLY ONE TYPE):
☐ PRIVATE DETECTIVE EMPLOYEE   ☐ PRIVATE SECURITY GUARD EMPLOYEE

☐ IN-HOUSE DETECTIVE EMPLOYEE   ☐ IN-HOUSE SECURITY GUARD EMPLOYEE   ☐ REINSTATEMENT OF REGISTRATION # _____

EMPLOYEE NAME:

_____
FIRST   MIDDLE   LAST   SUFFIX (JR, SR, ETC)

SOCIAL SECURITY NO.*: _____-___-_____   PLACE OF BIRTH:
*THIS INFORMATION IS AUTHORIZED TO BE OBTAINED &
DISCLOSED TO STATE & FEDERAL AGENCIES PURSUANT TO
O.C.G.A. § 19-11-1 & O.C.G.A. § 20-3-295, 42 U.S.C.A. § 551 & 20   CITY   STATE OR COUNTRY
U.S.C.A. § 1001.

GENDER   : _____ MALE   _____ FEMALE   DATE OF BIRTH : _____/_____/_____

RESIDENCE ADDRESS (P.O. BOX NOT ACCEPTABLE)

_____
STREET   CITY   COUNTY   STATE   ZIP CODE   TELEPHONE

EMAIL ADDRESS (TO BE USED FOR NOTIFICATIONS FROM THE BOARD)

COMPANY: _____ **LICENSE NO.** _____

MAILING ADDRESS OF COMPANY (FOR MAILING LICENSE & RENEWAL NOTICE. WILL APPEAR ON LICENSE & ONLINE)

_____
STREET OR P.O. BOX   CITY   COUNTY   STATE   ZIP CODE   TELEPHONE

COMPANY EMAIL ADDRESS (TO BE USED FOR NOTIFICATIONS FROM THE BOARD)

14

Exhibit 3A.9 (Continued)   Application for company license.   *(Continued)*

BACKGROUND INVESTIGATION QUESTIONNAIRE

As part of a background investigation to determine your suitability for the issuance of a registration by the Georgia Board of Private Detective & Security Agencies, you are required to answer the following questions. If you answer "Yes" to any questions, give a brief explanation of your answer, including dates and places of arrest(s) &/or conviction(s) **with documentation**. Attach additional pages, if necessary. **Convictions will require certified copies of final court dispositions to be included with this application. Failure to provide final dispositions will delay consideration of your application.**

1. Are there currently any charges pending against you for a criminal offense? ☐ YES ☐ NO

2. Are you under indictment or information in any court for a felony, or any other crime, for which a judge could imprison you for more than one year? ☐ YES ☐ NO

3. Have you been convicted in any court of a felony, or any other crime, for which the judge could have imprisoned you for more than one year, even if you received a shorter sentence including probation? ☐ YES ☐ NO

4. Have you ever entered a plea pursuant to the provisions of the "Georgia First Offender Act", or any other first offender act? **You must respond "Yes", if you pled and completed probation as a First Offender.** ☐ YES ☐ NO

5. Are you a fugitive from justice? ☐ YES ☐ NO

6. Are you an unlawful user of, or addicted to, marijuana, or any depressant, stimulant, or narcotic drug, or any other controlled substance? ☐ YES ☐ NO

7. Have you ever been adjudicated mentally defective (which includes having been adjudicated incompetent to manage your own affairs), or have you ever been committed to a mental institution? ☐ YES ☐ NO

8. Have you been discharged from the Armed Forces under dishonorable conditions? ☐ YES ☐ NO

9. Are you subject to a court order restraining you from harassing, stalking, or threatening your child or an intimate partner or child of such partner? ☐ YES ☐ NO

10. Have you been convicted in any court of a misdemeanor crime of domestic violence? ☐ YES ☐ NO

11. Have you ever renounced your United States citizenship? ☐ YES ☐ NO

12. Are you an alien illegally in the United States? ☐ YES ☐ NO

13. Have you, or any company in which you are or were a principal, ever been the subject of an investigation or litigation that was conducted by a federal, state, or local agency? ☐ YES ☐ NO

15

Exhibit 3A.9 (Continued)   Application for company license.

(Continued)

14. Have you ever had a professional license or certification revoked, suspended, or modified for any reason? _____ ☐ YES ☐ NO
_____

15. Have you ever been reprimanded, placed on probation, or otherwise disciplined by a professional licensing or certification body? _____ ☐ YES ☐ NO

16. Have you ever been disciplined or cited for a breach of ethics or unprofessional conduct? ☐ YES ☐ NO
_____

17. Have you ever resigned or been discharged from any position with criminal or administrative charges pending against you? _____ ☐ YES ☐ NO
_____

18. Have you ever been prohibited from doing business with the State of Georgia, the United States Government, or any local or state government? _____ ☐ YES ☐ NO
_____

19. Have you ever been registered with a licensed company as a private detective or security guard employee in this state? If so, list registration number, company, and approximate date of registration: _____ ☐ YES ☐ NO

20. Have you completed the required basic training for this registration? Submit a copy of the completion certificate. **If you cannot provide a copy, submit a letter to the Board detailing when you completed the training; otherwise, you will be required to complete the training.** ☐ YES ☐ NO

AFFIDAVIT OF EMPLOYER

I certify and declare that the employee for whom this application is made has been given the minimum training required under the rules and regulations of the Board, or will complete the minimum training required under the rules and regulations of the Board within 6 (six) months of hire, and that the training certificate will be maintained in the employee's file with the company. I further certify and declare that a name character background check has been made by my company on the employee, which indicates that the employee has had no felony convictions and has not displayed a disregard for the law.

STATE OF GEORGIA
COUNTY OF _____   _____
                                        SIGNATURE OF THE EMPLOYER

SUBSCRIBED AND SWORN TO BEFORE ME THIS   _____
                                                        DATE
_____ DAY OF _____, _____

_____
              NOTARY PUBLIC
MY COMMISSION EXPIRES: _____

16

Exhibit 3A.9 (Continued)   Application for company license.   *(Continued)*

ADDRESS HISTORY

STARTING WITH YOUR CURRENT ADDRESS, LIST YOUR PREVIOUS ADDRESSES FOR THE PAST **FIVE(5)** YEARS. DATES MUST BE PROVIDED, **WITHOUT GAPS**. IF NECESSARY, USE ADDITIONAL PAGES.

DATES						
FROM	TO	STREET ADDRESS	CITY	STATE	ZIP CODE

EMPLOYMENT HISTORY

STARTING WITH YOUR CURRENT EMPLOYER, LIST YOUR EMPLOYMENT FOR THE PAST **FIVE (5)** YEARS. ALL TIME MUST BE ACCOUNTED FOR, INCLUDING PERIODS OF UNEMPLOYMENT. ALL BLOCKS MUST BE COMPLETED. IF NECESSARY, USE ADDITIONAL PAGES.

DATES				
FROM	TO	EMPLOYER	POSITION HELD	SUPERVISOR

17

Exhibit 3A.9 (Continued)   Application for company license.   (*Continued*)

ADDITIONAL EXPERIENCE

List any additional experience you have which has not been addressed and which you feel qualifies you for registration under the Private Detective and Security Agencies Act. Attach any documentation necessary as proof of training and/or experience.

_____

_____

_____

_____

_____

AFFIDAVIT OF EMPLOYEE

I hereby swear and affirm that all information provided in this application is true and correct to the best of my knowledge and belief. I further swear and affirm that I have read and understand the current state laws and rules and regulations of the Georgia Board of Private Detective & Security Agencies, and I agree to abide by these laws and rules, as amended from time to time.

I also understand that if I have made a false statement on the application, or if I am found to have been convicted of a felony and have not had all of my civil rights restored pursuant to the law, **the Board may suspend my registration without a prior hearing.** I shall be entitled to a hearing after the suspension of my registration.

By signing this application, electronically or otherwise, I hereby swear and affirm one of the following to be true and accurate pursuant to O.C.G.A. § 50-36-1:

1) _____ I am a United States citizen 18 years of age or older. **Please submit a copy of your current Secure and Verifiable Document(s) such as driver's license, passport, or other document as indicated on pages 8 and 9 of the application.**

2) _____ I am not a United States citizen, but I am a legal permanent resident of the United States 18 years of age or older, or I am a qualified alien or non-immigrant under the Federal Immigration and Nationality Act 18 years of age or older with an alien number issued by the Department of Homeland Security or other federal immigration agency. **Please submit a copy of your current immigration document(s) which includes either your Alien number or your I-94 number and, if needed, SEVIS number.**

STATE OF GEORGIA
COUNTY OF _____

SUBSCRIBED AND SWORN TO BEFORE ME THIS

_____ DAY OF _____, _____

_____
NOTARY PUBLIC
MY COMMISSION EXPIRES: _____

_____
SIGNATURE OF THE APPLICANT

_____
DATE

Exhibit 3A.9 (Continued) Application for company license. *(Continued)*

INFORMATION FOR OBTAINING A WEAPON PERMIT WITH YOUR REGISTRATION

DO NOT SUBMIT THIS INFORMATION IF YOU ARE NOT REQUESTING A WEAPON

TRAINING INFORMATION

PROVIDE THE FOLLOWING INFORMATION RELATED TO YOUR TRAINING

PLACE WHERE THE REQUIRED BASIC TRAINING WAS HELD:

_____
NAME OF COMPANY/FACILITY & LOCATION

DATE OF COMPLETION OF REQUIRED BASIC TRAINING:

_____
DATE

LIST THE NAME & LICENSE NUMBER OF YOUR INSTRUCTOR:

_____   _____
INSTRUCTOR NAME   LICENSE NO.

PLACE WHERE THE REQUIRED WEAPON TRAINING WAS HELD:

_____

DATE OF COMPLETION OF REQUIRED BASIC TRAINING:

_____
DATE

LIST THE NAME & LICENSE NUMBER OF YOUR INSTRUCTOR:

_____   _____
INSTRUCTOR NAME   LICENSE NO.

19

Exhibit 3A.9 (Continued)   Application for company license.   (*Continued*)

BOARD RULE 509-4-.01(1) & (2) WEAPONS. AMENDED.

(1) No person licensed by the board to carry a firearm shall carry any firearm which is not in operable condition and capable of firing live ammunition, and when carrying such a weapon, the licensee shall have on his person live ammunition capable of being fired in the weapon which he carries.

(2) No person licensed or registered by the board to provide security services shall carry a firearm while performing services for a private security agency or in-house security agency except while providing actual security services or while going directly to and from work (no stopovers allowed en route to or from work). Under no condition will a licensee, registrant or any other employee or agent of a licensee carry any sort of firearm or have anyone accompanying them who is carrying a firearm while soliciting new or prospective clients.

TRAINING AFFIDAVITS

I have read Board Rule 509-4-.01(1) & (2) and understand my responsibility to abide by the mandates of the rule. If granted a permit, I shall wear the firearm in the manner prescribed by law.

_____   _____
                DATE   SIGNATURE OF THE APPLICANT

STATE OF GEORGIA
COUNTY OF _____

SUBSCRIBED AND SWORN TO BEFORE ME THIS

_____ DAY OF _____, _____

_____
                NOTARY PUBLIC
MY COMMISSION EXPIRES: _____

I declare that the above employee is qualified to carry a firearm by reason of having received classroom instruction in the use of firearms by a board-approved instructor, having received firearm range instruction, and having passed the Firearm Training Curriculum for Handguns as required in Rule 509-3-.10.

_____   _____
                DATE   SIGNATURE AND TITLE OF THE EMPLOYER

STATE OF GEORGIA
COUNTY OF _____

SUBSCRIBED AND SWORN TO BEFORE ME THIS

_____ DAY OF _____, _____

_____
                NOTARY PUBLIC
MY COMMISSION EXPIRES: _____

20

Exhibit 3A.9 (Continued)   Application for company license.   *(Continued)*

EMPLOYER REQUEST FOR CONCEALED WEAPON PERMIT

This form must be completed by the employer and accompanied by an application for a concealed weapon permit for the referenced employee. A detailed description of the duties of the employee and the need for the employee to carry a concealed weapon must be made, with complete justification in support of the request.

I hereby make request for a concealed weapon permit to be issued to _____.

Print Name of Employee

I have detailed below the specific duties that the employee will be assigned, along with complete justification of the necessity of carrying of a weapon in a concealed manner:

_____

_____

_____

_____

_____

_____

_____

_____

_____

I certify and declare that the information presented in this request for a concealed weapon permit is a true description of the actual job duties that are or will be assigned to the above-named employee and a true representation of the facts in support of the necessity for carrying a concealed weapon in the performance of these duties. I understand that any intentional misrepresentation of the facts in support of this application for concealed weapon permit will be grounds for disciplinary action by the Board up to and including revocation of my license.

STATE OF GEORGIA
COUNTY OF _____

SUBSCRIBED AND SWORN TO BEFORE ME THIS

_____ DAY OF _____, _____

_____
            NOTARY PUBLIC
MY COMMISSION EXPIRES: _____

_____
SIGNATURE OF THE LICENSE HOLDER

_____
            DATE

21

Exhibit 3A.9 (Continued)   Application for company license.   *(Continued)*

EMPLOYER REQUEST FOR SHOTGUN PERMIT

This form must be completed by the employer and accompanied by an application for a shotgun permit for the referenced employee. A detailed description of the duties of the employee and the need for the employee to carry a shotgun must be made, with complete justification in support of the request.

I hereby make request for a shotgun permit to be issued to _____.

Print Name of Employee

I have detailed below the specific duties that the employee will be assigned, along with complete justification of the necessity of carrying of a shotgun:

_____

_____

_____

_____

_____

_____

_____

I certify and declare that the information presented in this request for a shotgun permit is a true description of the actual job duties that are or will be assigned to the above-named employee and a true representation of the facts in support of the necessity for carrying a shotgun in the performance of these duties. I understand that any intentional misrepresentation of the facts in support of this application for shotgun permit will be grounds for disciplinary action by the Board up to and including revocation of my license.

STATE OF GEORGIA
COUNTY OF _____

SUBSCRIBED AND SWORN TO BEFORE ME THIS

_____ DAY OF _____, _____

SIGNATURE OF THE LICENSE HOLDER

_____
DATE

_____
NOTARY PUBLIC
MY COMMISSION EXPIRES: _____

Rev. 05/09/11

22

Exhibit 3A.9 (Continued) Application for company license.

(Continued)

EMPLOYEE REGISTRATION INFORMATION

This application must be filed by the **licensee (employer)** for every employee who will be employed by the licensee (employer) as a private investigator or armed security guard. Company owners or designated license holders for corporations, LLC's, or partnerships must have an employee registration. The fee for the registration for the owner/designee is the same as for all other employees. **EMPLOYEES APPLYING FOR BOTH PRIVATE DETECTIVE AND SECURITY GUARD REGISTRATION MUST SUBMIT SEPARATE APPLICATIONS.**

NOTE: Unarmed security guards are not required to be registered with the Georgia Board of Private Detective & Security Agencies; however, unarmed security guards must be trained according to the Board standards and are governed by the Board as mandated in OCGA 43-38-7.1.

This application must be submitted by the **licensee (employer)** on behalf of any employee hired to work as a private investigator or armed security guard, even if the employee has an active registration with another employer. **No employee may use an existing registration to work for a company, other than the company that is indicated on the registration.** A registration is only valid when the employee is performing investigative or armed security duties for the employer listed on the registration. The category for Reinstatement of Registration Number on the application is only to be used if the employee is reinstating a registration that has lapsed for the same employer. The employee must also physically carry the registration at all times while on duty, at the place of employment, or any time that the employee is in uniform. Armed registrations must be carried by the employee while a weapon is carried on duty, in uniform, or in route directly to and from the post or place of employment **(Board Rule 509-4-.01).**

APPLICATION PROCESSING

The application must be complete in order to process the application. Incomplete applications will be returned to the **licensee (employer)** for completion. The **licensee (employer)** is responsible for ensuring that the application is complete and correctly prepared. Failure to submit a complete application will result in unnecessary delays in processing and may be grounds for disapproval of the application by the Board. **Please list a valid email address so the Board office staff may correspond quickly with you in the event that more information is needed to complete the application.**

Fingerprinting for all applications is required through Cogent Services. The ORI number to use when registering is **GA920240Z**. The Verification Code is **920240Z**. The Reason for registering is **Private Detective/Security Business**. The website to register is http://www.ga.cogentid.com/index.htm.

Please allow 25 business days for processing the application. The timeframe allows our staff time to receive the application, perform data entry of basic information for tracking purposes, receive fingerprint results from Cogent Services, and review the details provided in the application.

Applicants who must answer **Yes** to questions concerning criminal history or disciplinary actions taken against them by any professional licensing or certification agency must submit **certified** documentation of court dispositions, agency orders, or any other documentation to provide a complete answer to such questions. Failure to provide this information will result in additional delays in processing, and may be grounds for disapproval of the application by the Board.

1

Exhibit 3A.10   Application for employee registration.

(Continued)

GEORGIA BOARD OF PRIVATE DETECTIVE & SECURITY AGENCIES

FEE SCHEDULE

ALL APPLICATION FEES ARE NON-REFUNDABLE

COMPANY LICENSURE FEES

INITIAL LICENSURE	APPLICATION FEE	LICENSE FEE	TOTAL FEE
Detective Company	$100.00	$300.00	$400.00
Security Company	$100.00	$500.00	$600.00

ADDITIONAL COMPANY FEES

Replacement Fee for Lost or Destroyed License	$ 25.00
Application Fee for Change of Company Name	$ 25.00
Application Fee for Change of Address	$ 25.00
Renewal Fee - Detective Company	$ 300.00
Late Renewal Fee – Detective Company	$400.00
Reinstatement Fee – Detective Company	$450.00
Renewal Fee - Security Company	$500.00
Late Renewal Fee – Security Company	$600.00
Reinstatement Fee – Security Company	$750.00
Renewal Fee - Detective & Security Company	$700.00
Late Renewal Fee – Detective & Security Company	$800.00

EMPLOYEE REGISTRATION FEES

Unarmed Detective Employees	$ 45.00
Armed Detective Employees	$ 70.00
Armed Security Guard Employees	$ 70.00
Renewal Fee – All Employee Registrations	$ 65.00
Late Renewal Fee – All Employee Registrations	$ 80.00
Fee for Additional Weapon, or Change of Weapon Type	$ 25.00
Replacement Fee for Lost or Destroyed License	$ 25.00

TRAINING INSTRUCTOR FEES

Certification of Training Instructor Fee	$100.00
Renewal Fee	$100.00
Late Renewal Fee	$150.00
Replacement Fee for Lost or Destroyed License	$ 25.00

2

Exhibit 3A.10 (Continued)   Application for employee registration.   *(Continued)*

GEORGIA BOARD OF PRIVATE DETECTIVES
& SECURITY AGENCIES
237 COLISEUM DRIVE
MACON, GA 31217
TELEPHONE 478.207.2440
www.sos.ga.gov/plb/detective

DO NOT WRITE IN THIS SECTION
RECEIPT # _____
AMOUNT _____
APPLICANT # _____
INITIAL _____ DATE _____

APPLICATION FOR EMPLOYEE REGISTRATION

TYPE OF WEAPON APPLIED FOR (CHECK ALL THAT APPLY):
☐ **NO WEAPON**THIS DESIGNATION ONLY APPLIES TO PRIVATE DETECTIVE EMPLOYEES**

☐ **EXPOSED**   ☐ **SHOTGUN ** **   ☐ **CONCEALED ** **
** REQUIRES WRITTEN REQUEST FROM EMPLOYER, DETAILING DUTIES

TYPE OF REGISTRATION APPLIED FOR (CHECK ON LY ONE TYPE):
☐ PRIVATE DETECTIVE EMPLOYEE   ☐ PRIVATE SECURITY GUARD EMPLOYEE

☐ IN-HOUSE DETECTIVE EMPLOYEE   ☐ IN-HOUSE SECURITY GUARD EMPLOYEE   ☐ REINSTATEMENT OF REGISTRATION # _____

EMPLOYEE NAME:

_____

FIRST	MIDDLE	LAST	SUFFIX (JR, SR, ETC)

SOCIAL SECURITY NO.*: _____ - _____ - _____   PLACE OF BIRTH:
*THIS INFORMATION IS AUTHORIZED TO BE OBTAINED &
DISCLOSED TO STATE & FEDERAL AGENCIES PURSUANT TO
O.C.G.A. § 19-11-1 & O.C.G.A. § 20-3-295, 42 U.S.C.A. § 551 & 20
U.S.C.A. § 1001.   CITY _____ STATE OR COUNTRY

GENDER   : _____ MALE _____ FEMALE   DATE OF BIRTH : _____ / _____ / _____

RESIDENCE ADDRESS (P.O. BOX NOT ACCEPTABLE)

_____

STREET	CITY	COUNTY	STATE	ZIP CODE	TELEPHONE

EMAIL ADDRESS (TO BE USED FOR NOTIFICATIONS FROM THE BOARD)

COMPANY: _____ **LICENSE NO.** _____

MAILING ADDRESS OF COMPANY (FOR MAILING LICENSE & RENEWAL NOTICE. WILL APPEAR ON LICENSE & ONLINE)

_____

STREET OR P.O. BOX	CITY	COUNTY	STATE	ZIP CODE	TELEPHONE

COMPANY EMAIL ADDRESS (TO BE USED FOR NOTIFICATIONS FROM THE BOARD)

3

Exhibit 3A.10 (Continued)   Application for employee registration.   *(Continued)*

BACKGROUND INVESTIGATION QUESTIONNAIRE

As part of a background investigation to determine your suitability for the issuance of a registration by the Georgia Board of Private Detective & Security Agencies, you are required to answer the following questions. If you answer "Yes" to any questions, give a brief explanation of your answer, including dates and places of arrest(s) &/or conviction(s) **with documentation**. Attach additional pages, if necessary. **Convictions will require certified copies of final court dispositions to be included with this application. Failure to provide final dispositions will delay consideration of your application.**

1. Are there currently any charges pending against you for a criminal offense? ☐ YES ☐ NO

2. Are you under indictment or information in any court for a felony, or any other crime, for which a judge could imprison you for more than one year? ☐ YES ☐ NO

3. Have you been convicted in any court of a felony, or any other crime, for which the judge could have imprisoned you for more than one year, even if you received a shorter sentence including probation? ☐ YES ☐ NO

4. Have you ever entered a plea pursuant to the provisions of the "Georgia First Offender Act", or any other first offender act? **You must respond "Yes", if you pled and completed probation as a First Offender.** ☐ YES ☐ NO

5. Are you a fugitive from justice? ☐ YES ☐ NO

6. Are you an unlawful user of, or addicted to, marijuana, or any depressant, stimulant, or narcotic drug, or any other controlled substance? ☐ YES ☐ NO

7. Have you ever been adjudicated mentally defective (which includes having been adjudicated incompetent to manage your own affairs), or have you ever been committed to a mental institution? ☐ YES ☐ NO

8. Have you been discharged from the Armed Forces under dishonorable conditions? ☐ YES ☐ NO

9. Are you subject to a court order restraining you from harassing, stalking, or threatening your child or an intimate partner or child of such partner? ☐ YES ☐ NO

10. Have you been convicted in any court of a misdemeanor crime of domestic violence? ☐ YES ☐ NO

11. Have you ever renounced your United States citizenship? ☐ YES ☐ NO

12. Are you an alien illegally in the United States? ☐ YES ☐ NO

13. Have you, or any company in which you are or were a principal, ever been the subject of an investigation or litigation that was conducted by a federal, state, or local agency? ☐ YES ☐ NO

4

Exhibit 3A.10 (Continued) Application for employee registration. *(Continued)*

14. Have you ever had a professional license or certification revoked, suspended, or modified for any reason? _____   ☐ YES ☐ NO
_____

15. Have you ever been reprimanded, placed on probation, or otherwise disciplined by a professional licensing or certification body? _____   ☐ YES ☐ NO
_____

16. Have you ever been disciplined or cited for a breach of ethics or unprofessional conduct? _____   ☐ YES ☐ NO
_____

17. Have you ever resigned or been discharged from any position with criminal or administrative charges pending against you? _____   ☐ YES ☐ NO
_____

18. Have you ever been prohibited from doing business with the State of Georgia, the United States Government, or any local or state government? _____   ☐ YES ☐ NO
_____

19. Have you ever been registered with a licensed company as a private detective or security guard employee in this state? If so, list registration number, company, and approximate date of registration: _____   ☐ YES ☐ NO
_____

20. Have you completed the required basic training for this registration? Submit a copy of the completion certificate. **If you cannot provide a copy, submit a letter to the Board detailing when you completed the training; otherwise, you will be required to complete the training.**   ☐ YES ☐ NO

AFFIDAVIT OF EMPLOYER

I certify and declare that the employee for whom this application is made has been given the minimum training required under the rules and regulations of the Board, and that the training certificate will be maintained in the employee's file with the company. I further certify and declare that a name character background check has been made by my company on the employee, which indicates that the employee has had no felony convictions and has not displayed a disregard for the law.

STATE OF GEORGIA
COUNTY OF _____

SUBSCRIBED AND SWORN TO BEFORE ME THIS

_____ DAY OF _____, _____

_____
NOTARY PUBLIC
MY COMMISSION EXPIRES: _____

_____
SIGNATURE OF THE EMPLOYER

_____
DATE

5

Exhibit 3A.10 (Continued)   Application for employee registration.

(Continued)

EMPLOYMENT HISTORY

ADDRESS HISTORY

STARTING WITH YOUR CURRENT ADDRESS, LIST YOUR PREVIOUS ADDRESSES FOR THE PAST **FIVE(5)** YEARS. DATES MUST BE PROVIDED, **WITHOUT GAPS**. IF NECESSARY, USE ADDITIONAL PAGES.

DATES		STREET ADDRESS	CITY	STATE	ZIP CODE
FROM	TO				

STARTING WITH YOUR CURRENT EMPLOYER, LIST YOUR EMPLOYMENT FOR THE PAST **FIVE (5)** YEARS. ALL TIME MUST BE ACCOUNTED FOR, INCLUDING PERIODS OF UNEMPLOYMENT. ALL BLOCKS MUST BE COMPLETED. IF NECESSARY, USE ADDITIONAL PAGES.

DATES		EMPLOYER	POSITION HELD	SUPERVISOR
FROM	TO			

ADDITIONAL EXPERIENCE

6

Exhibit 3A.10 (Continued) **Application for employee registration.** *(Continued)*

List any additional experience you have which has not been addressed and which you feel qualifies you for registration under the Private Detective and Security Agencies Act. Attach any documentation necessary as proof of training and/or experience.

_____

_____

_____

_____

_____

AFFIDAVIT OF EMPLOYEE

I hereby swear and affirm that all information provided in this application is true and correct to the best of my knowledge and belief. I further swear and affirm that I have read and understand the current state laws and rules and regulations of the Georgia Board of Private Detective & Security Agencies, and I agree to abide by these laws and rules, as amended from time to time.

I also understand that if I have made a false statement on the application, or if I am found to have been convicted of a felony and have not had all of my civil rights restored pursuant to the law, **the Board may suspend my registration without a prior hearing.** I shall be entitled to a hearing after the suspension of my registration.

By signing this application, electronically or otherwise, I hereby swear and affirm one of the following to be true and accurate pursuant to O.C.G.A. § 50-36-1:

1) _____   I am a United States citizen 18 years of age or older. **Please submit a copy of your current Secure and Verifiable Document(s) such as driver's license, passport, or other document as indicated on pages 8 and 9 of the application.**

2) _____   I am not a United States citizen, but I am a legal permanent resident of the United States 18 years of age or older, or I am a qualified alien or non-immigrant under the Federal Immigration and Nationality Act 18 years of age or older with an alien number issued by the Department of Homeland Security or other federal immigration agency. **Please submit a copy of your current immigration document(s) which includes either your Alien number or your I-94 number and, if needed, SEVIS number.**

STATE OF GEORGIA
COUNTY OF _____

SUBSCRIBED AND SWORN TO BEFORE ME THIS

_____ DAY OF _____, _____

_____
NOTARY PUBLIC
MY COMMISSION EXPIRES: _____

_____
SIGNATURE OF THE APPLICANT

_____
DATE

Exhibit 3A.10 (Continued)   Application for employee registration.   *(Continued)*

INFORMATION FOR OBTAINING A WEAPON PERMIT WITH YOUR REGISTRATION

DO NOT SUBMIT THIS INFORMATION IF YOU ARE NOT REQUESTING A WEAPON

TRAINING INFORMATION

PROVIDE THE FOLLOWING INFORMATION RELATED TO YOUR TRAINING

PLACE WHERE THE REQUIRED BASIC TRAINING WAS HELD:

_____
NAME OF COMPANY/FACILITY & LOCATION

DATE OF COMPLETION OF REQUIRED BASIC TRAINING:

_____
DATE

LIST THE NAME & LICENSE NUMBER OF YOUR INSTRUCTOR:

_____   _____
                                        LICENSE NO.
INSTRUCTOR NAME

PLACE WHERE THE REQUIRED WEAPON TRAINING WAS HELD:

_____

DATE OF COMPLETION OF REQUIRED BASIC TRAINING:

_____
DATE

LIST THE NAME & LICENSE NUMBER OF YOUR INSTRUCTOR:

_____   _____
                                        LICENSE NO.
INSTRUCTOR NAME

8

Exhibit 3A.10 (Continued)   **Application for employee registration.**   *(Continued)*

BOARD RULE 509-4-.01(1) & (2) WEAPONS. AMENDED.

(1) No person licensed by the board to carry a firearm shall carry any firearm which is not in operable condition and capable of firing live ammunition, and when carrying such a weapon, the licensee shall have on his person live ammunition capable of being fired in the weapon which he carries.

(2) No person licensed or registered by the board to provide security services shall carry a firearm while performing services for a private security agency or in-house security agency except while providing actual security services or while going directly to and from work (no stopovers allowed en route to or from work). Under no condition will a licensee, registrant or any other employee or agent of a licensee carry any sort of firearm or have anyone accompanying them who is carrying a firearm while soliciting new or prospective clients.

TRAINING AFFIDAVITS

I have read Board Rule 509-4-.01(1) & (2) and understand my responsibility to abide by the mandates of the rule. If granted a permit, I shall wear the firearm in the manner prescribed by law.

_____	_____
DATE	SIGNATURE OF THE APPLICANT

STATE OF GEORGIA
COUNTY OF _____

SUBSCRIBED AND SWORN TO BEFORE ME THIS

_____ DAY OF _____, _____

_____
NOTARY PUBLIC
MY COMMISSION EXPIRES: _____

I declare that the above employee is qualified to carry a firearm by reason of having received classroom instruction in the use of firearms by a board-approved instructor, having received firearm range instruction, and having passed the Firearm Training Curriculum for Handguns as required in Rule 509-3-.10.

_____	_____
DATE	SIGNATURE AND TITLE OF THE EMPLOYER

STATE OF GEORGIA
COUNTY OF _____

SUBSCRIBED AND SWORN TO BEFORE ME THIS

_____ DAY OF _____, _____

_____
NOTARY PUBLIC
MY COMMISSION EXPIRES: _____

9

Exhibit 3A.10 (Continued)   Application for employee registration.   *(Continued)*

This form must be completed by the employer and accompanied by an application for a concealed weapon permit for the referenced employee. A detailed description of the duties of the employee and the need for the employee to carry a concealed weapon must be made, with complete justification in support of the request.

EMPLOYER REQUEST FOR CONCEALED WEAPON PERMIT

I hereby make request for a concealed weapon permit to be issued to _____.
                                                                     Print Name of Employee

I have detailed below the specific duties that the employee will be assigned, along with complete justification of the necessity of carrying of a weapon in a concealed manner:

_____

_____

_____

_____

_____

_____

_____

_____

I certify and declare that the information presented in this request for a concealed weapon permit is a true description of the actual job duties that are or will be assigned to the above-named employee and a true representation of the facts in support of the necessity for carrying a concealed weapon in the performance of these duties. I understand that any intentional misrepresentation of the facts in support of this application for concealed weapon permit will be grounds for disciplinary action by the Board up to and including revocation of my license.

STATE OF GEORGIA
COUNTY OF _____

SUBSCRIBED AND SWORN TO BEFORE ME THIS

_____ DAY OF _____, _____

_____
          NOTARY PUBLIC
MY COMMISSION EXPIRES: _____

_____
SIGNATURE OF THE LICENSE HOLDER

_____
                DATE

10

Exhibit 3A.10 (Continued) Application for employee registration.   *(Continued)*

EMPLOYER REQUEST FOR SHOTGUN PERMIT

> This form must be completed by the employer and accompanied by an application for a shotgun permit for the referenced employee. A detailed description of the duties of the employee and the need for the employee to carry a shotgun must be made, with complete justification in support of the request.

I hereby make request for a shotgun permit to be issued to _____.

Print Name of Employee

I have detailed below the specific duties that the employee will be assigned, along with complete justification of the necessity of carrying of a shotgun:

_____

_____

_____

_____

_____

_____

_____

I certify and declare that the information presented in this request for a shotgun permit is a true description of the actual job duties that are or will be assigned to the above-named employee and a true representation of the facts in support of the necessity for carrying a shotgun in the performance of these duties. I understand that any intentional misrepresentation of the facts in support of this application for shotgun permit will be grounds for disciplinary action by the Board up to and including revocation of my license.

STATE OF GEORGIA
COUNTY OF _____

SUBSCRIBED AND SWORN TO BEFORE ME THIS

_____ DAY OF _____, _____

_____
NOTARY PUBLIC
MY COMMISSION EXPIRES: _____

_____
SIGNATURE OF THE LICENSE HOLDER

_____
DATE

11

Exhibit 3A.10 (Continued)   Application for employee registration.

WASHINGTON STATE DEPARTMENT OF
LICENSING

Private Security Guard License Application

Send this completed form with a check or money order payable to the Department of Licensing, to: **Public Protection Services, Department of Licensing, PO Box 35001, Seattle WA 98124-3401**

Telephone: (360) 664-6611

For validation only   001-070-299-0010

‖‖‖‖‖‖‖‖‖‖‖‖‖‖‖‖‖‖‖‖‖‖‖‖‖‖‖
29910-APPLICATIONS

This is an application for:
- ☐ New security guard applicant – **$91**
- ☐ Verification of firearm eligibility – **$10**
- ☐ Transfer/Rehire – **$25**
- ☐ Dual licensure – **$25**, must recertify with Washington State Criminal Justice Training Center
- ☐ Renewal – **$85**, armed security guards must recertify with Washington State Criminal Justice Training Center
- ☐ Late renewal – **$90** (not required when renewing with a transfer/rehire application)
- ☐ Certified trainer endorsement renewal – **$15** (in addition to the renewal fee)
- ☐ Duplicate license – **$10**

Applicant information

Previous license
Have you been a licensed security guard in the state of Washington within the last two years? . . . . ☐ Yes ☐ No
If yes: License number _____ Expiration date _____

TYPE OR PRINT Name *(Last, First, Middle)*

Social Security number required*	Date of birth *(mm/dd/yyyy)*	Citizenship ☐ U.S. citizen ☐ Resident alien

Residence address

City		State	ZIP code

(Area code) Home telephone number	Email	Gender ☐ Male ☐ Female

*All applicants are required by federal and state law to provide their Social Security number (SSN) for use in child support enforcement programs (42 U.S.C. 666(a)(13) and RCW 74.20A.320). It may also be used for education loan repayment programs and identification of records with similar names. Submission of your SSN is mandatory; failure to submit it will result in denial of your application.

Company information

Company name	Security guard company license number (not UBI)

Company address *(street address as it appears on the license)*

City		State	ZIP code

(Area code) Company telephone number	(Area code) Company fax number	Company email

Certification of preassignment testing/training (New applicants only)

Temporary card number	Date issued	Expiration date *(60 days)*
Name of certified trainer	License number of certified trainer	Expiration date

Certification
I hereby certify under penalty of perjury under the laws of the state of Washington, that the above named applicant has successfully completed the preassignment training and testing requirements as outlined in WAC 308-18-300. Incorrect answers were reviewed with the applicant and the test results have been verified and signed by me.

_____   **X** _____
Date and place   Signature of certified trainer

PSG-690-008 (R/4/16)WA Page 1 of 2

Exhibit 3A.11   Private security guard license application.   *(Continued)*

Criminal history

Answer the questions below. If you answer "Yes," attach a detailed explanation.

In this state or any other jurisdiction are you or have you:

1. Within the last 10 years, had any action (fine, suspension, revocation, censure, surrender, etc.) taken against any professional or occupational license, certification, or permit held by you? . . . . . ☐ Yes ☐ No

2. Currently under indictment, or is there a criminal complaint, charge, or information pending against you? . . . . ☐ Yes ☐ No

3. Within the last 10 years, defaulted or been convicted of or entered a plea of no contest to a gross misdemeanor or felony crime? (Don't include traffic offenses.) . . . . ☐ Yes ☐ No

What were you convicted of?	Date	Name of court	City and state	Misdemeanor, gross misdemeanor, or felony?
1.				
2.				

To show additional convictions, attach pages.

Fingerprinting

All security guards must have fingerprint-based background checks. For information about the fingerprinting and background check process, go to www.dol.wa.gov/business/fingerprinting.html.

Armed applicants

- Be at least 21 years old and be licensed as an unarmed security guard.
- Submit a completed security guard license application and pay the $10 armed endorsement fee.
- Have a current firearms certificate. To be an armed security guard you must attend an eight-hour firearms certification course certified by the Criminal Justice Training Commission, telephone (206) 835-7300. When you complete the firearms training, they will issue a certificate. We cannot issue you an armed license until we receive your firearms certificate. RCW 18.170.040(c)
- Alien residents need to submit proof of an alien firearm license. Visit dol.wa.gov for information on how to get your alien firearms license.

Armed renewal

By renewing the armed private security guard license with the Department, the principal partner or principal owner for the private security guard company is declaring that the armed security guard has met the requirements for annual proficiency with the firearms for which he/she is certified.

Applicant authorization and certification

Do you authorize all organizations and government agencies (local, state, federal, or foreign) to release any information, files, or records requested to this Department to process your application? . . . ☐ Yes ☐ No

I certify under penalty of perjury under the laws of the state of Washington that the foregoing is true and correct.

_____   **X**
Date and place   _____
                                                                     Applicant signature

Providing false information in this application may be cause for the denial, suspension, or revocation of your private security guard license in the state of Washington.

Exhibit 3A.11 (Continued) Private security guard license application.

Appendix 4: Operation Partnership: Trends and Practices in Law Enforcement and Private Security Collaborations

Appendix C: Selected Partnerships

The following are some of the more formally organized law enforcement-private security (LE-PS) partnerships that were reviewed during the Operation Partnership study. Many have been in operation for 20 years or more. The web sites listed for contact information were current as of July 2009.

Anaheim Crime Alert Network (C.A.N.). In the early 1980s, Anaheim (California) Police Department (APD) burglary detectives launched C.A.N. to address crimes in hotels. Collaborators now include the APD's Tourist Oriented Policing Team and private security members representing all segments of the hospitality industry, with about 50 members participating in monthly meetings and 400 persons attending the C.A.N. annual training conference. anaheimoc.org/Articles/Archive/Webpage101091.asp

Boise Organized Retail Theft/Fraud Prevention and Interdiction Network. During the past 19 years, the Network has contributed to early identification and arrest of hundreds of suspects involved in merchandise refund fraud, credit card fraud, drug trafficking, vehicle theft, armed robbery, and other crimes. Hundreds of thousands of dollars' worth of merchandise have been recovered and large-scale organized theft rings disbanded. www.cityofboise.org/Departments/Police/CommunityOutreachDivision/CrimePrevention/page5794.aspx

Boston Consortium for Higher Education. Public Safety Group. The Boston Consortium, composed of 14 Boston area colleges and universities, encourages collaboration for cost saving and quality improvement across numerous communities of practice, including public safety. Public Safety Group projects have included participation in statewide disaster planning for higher education, training on handling campus protests, and development of a campus police information network. www.boston-consortium.org/about/what_is_tbc.asp

Chicago Building Owners and Managers Association (BOMA). Formed more than 20 years ago by proprietary security directors of large buildings in the Chicago Police Department's

First Precinct, the Committee expanded its membership after September 11, 2001, to include employees of contract security firms. Activities include daily fax alerts from the police, an emergency radio alert system, e-mail alerts, and use of closed circuit television (CCTV) to share photos of suspects. www.boma-chicago.org/about/staff.asp for BOMA staff contact information

Dallas Law Enforcement and Private Security (LEAPS) Program. Formed in the 1980s to foster better communication among police and private security, the Dallas Police Department's LEAPS partnership has sponsored numerous training workshops for private security and a fax information distribution network. www.leaps.us/contact.php

Energy Security Council. Created in 1982 and based in Houston, Texas, the Energy Security Council (ESC) is a nonprofit corporation funded by private-sector members. The ESC Law Enforcement Liaison Committee, composed of ESC members who conduct investigations, works with law enforcement on oil field theft cases, trains law enforcement on the oil and gas industry, and shares information and intelligence on trends, crime patterns, and suspects. www.energysecuritycouncil.org/index.cfm/MenuItemID/149.htm

Frontline Defense Initiative (FDI) of the Institute for Public Safety Partnerships (IPSP) is housed at the University of Illinois, Chicago, and is one of about 15 educational programs offered by the IPSP. FDI training is designed specifically for private security, hospitality, and other industries that are in a position to notice potential terrorist activity. www.ipsp.us/trainings.cfm#frontline

Grand Central Partnership (GCP), a business improvement district incorporated in 1988, covers 68 blocks in Midtown Manhattan and employs about 45 uniformed public safety officers, trained by the New York City Police Department (NYPD), who patrol neighborhood streets and may assist the NYPD with investigations. In addition, approximately 15 NYPD officers, with department approval, work with the GCP on their days off. www.grandcentralpartnership.org/what_we_do/protect.asp

Greater Chicago Hotel Loss Prevention Association (GCHLPA). The GCHLPA partnership began in the early 1980s when a few security professionals joined together to address pickpocketing in a tourist area and is now concerned with virtually any crime committed in or near hotels. Its members represent 46 hotels, three local police departments, and the Federal Bureau of Investigation, U.S. Secret Service, U.S. Department of Homeland Security, and Office of Emergency Management. www.ilssa.org/gchlpa/GCHLPA_Info.htm

Hillsborough County (Florida) Public Safety and Security Partnership. This partnership has addressed auto thefts, graffiti, gang activities, disturbances at nightclubs, and other problems. The sheriff's department has a long history of involvement in community policing and regularly involves community resource deputies at partnership meetings; and a founding partner, Critical Intervention Services, has devoted a portion of its web site to partnership concerns. www.safetampabay.org

Illinois Association of Chiefs of Police, Public and Private Police Liaison Committee (PPPLC). Founded in 1975 with goals related to education, liaison, and legislation, the committee is led by two chairpersons—an active police chief and a private security representative selected by private-sector members of the committee. Activities include homeland security training for private security personnel. www.ilchiefs.org. For current PPPLC chairs, www.ilchiefs.org/subpage.asp?pagenumber=46358.

InfraGard. Founded in 1996, InfraGard is a partnership among the Federal Bureau of Investigation and businesses, academic institutions, state and local law enforcement, and others. InfraGard has more than 70 chapters nationwide whose purpose is to share and analyze information and intelligence to prevent hostile acts against the United States. www.infragard.net (Select "Find Your Chapter" for contact information).

Michigan Intelligence Operations Center for Homeland Security. The state fusion center's initial activities included developing a business plan for privatesector collaboration. All 13 critical infrastructure sectors (utilities, medical, education, automotive industry, etc.) are represented on the advisory board. www.michigan.gov/mioc

Michigan State University (MSU) Critical Incident Protocol–Community Facilitation Program. Developed by the MSU School of Criminal Justice and funded by the U.S. Department of Homeland Security, the program's goal is to build public-private partnerships across the nation for critical incident management. The program is active in 39 communities in 23 states. Activities include joint planning and tabletop and full-scale exercises. cip.insu.edu

Minneapolis SafeZone Collaborative for Downtown. SafeZone accomplishments include installing CCTV cameras downtown; establishing a common police-private security radio channel; creating a web site that allows its 900 members to share police incident reports, videos and photos, and other information; and delivering training events. Officially launched in 2005, the Minneapolis SafeZone partnership won a community policing award from the International Association of Chiefs of Police. www.minneapolissafezone.org

Nassau County SPIN (Security/Police Information Network), started by the Nassau County (New York) Police Department in 2004, has a membership of some 1,600 businesses, trade associations, civic associations, government agencies, hospitals, utilities, and others. Information is shared within SPIN primarily by e-mail, as well as through text messaging and meetings. www.police.co.nassau.ny.us/SPIN/spininfo.htm

Overseas Security Advisory Council (OSAC). OSAC, a Federal Advisory Committee, is a highly structured partnership involving the U.S. Department of State, federal law enforcement, numerous corporations doing business overseas, and academia. OSAC has a 34-member core council, an executive office, and more than 100 country councils. www.osac.gov/About/index.cfm

Philadelphia Center City District (CCD). The CCD, a business improvement district with a long history of public/private cooperation, has private security officers (called community service representatives) who work closely with Philadelphia Police Department officers on a daily basis. In addition, the Philadelphia Crime Prevention Council, created by the CCD in 1997, has expanded over the years and now devotes about half of its efforts to homeland security and disaster preparedness issues. www.centercityphila.org/about/Safe.php

Southeast Wisconsin Homeland Security Partnership, Inc. This nonprofit organization was formed in 2004, serves seven southeast Wisconsin counties, and has more than 200 members. The partnership tests and validates responses to homeland security threats and major disasters; works to develop cost-effective policy and technology solutions; and has facilitated resource sharing (e.g., equipment, expertise). www.swhsp.org

Southeast Transportation Security Council. This corporate security-law enforcement partnership was formed in 2002 to facilitate prevention and recovery of stolen cargo in the transportation industry. In addition to operating several task forces, the Council operates a blast fax system reaching about 200 law enforcement agencies, provides member access to the Georgia Cargo Theft Alert System, and offers POST-certified training. www.setsc.org

Target and BLUE. This program of the Target Corporation includes many efforts to collaborate with and support law enforcement agencies across the country by providing grants, materials, expertise, information, forensic services, and investigative support. In 2007, Target received the FBI Director's Community Leadership Award for extraordinary contributions to communities and law enforcement. For more information, contact the Outreach Programs Manager at AP. Community@Target.com

U.S. Secret Service Electronic Crimes Task Forces and Working Groups. This is a nation-wide network of 24 task forces involves federal, state, and local law enforcement, private industry, and academia in preventing and investigating attacks on the nation's financial and other critical infrastructures. Although the task forces differ somewhat in areas of emphasis and other characteristics, priorities include crimes involving significant economic impact, organized criminal groups, and schemes using new technologies. www.secretservice.gov/ectf.shtml

Washington Law Enforcement Executive Forum (WLEEF). Founded in 1980 by the Washington Association of Sheriffs and Police Chiefs, WLEEF is one of the longest lived LE-PS partnerships in the nation. Over the years, WLEEF has sponsored numerous legislative, training, information sharing, and other initiatives. www.waspc.org/index.php?c=Law%20 Enforcement%20Executive%20Forum

Wilmington Downtown Visions. Downtown Visions, a business improvement district, sponsors public safety initiatives that include deployment of private security personnel (community resource officers); use of CCTV cameras at strategic locations; and in cooperation with the Wilmington Police Department, a new "bridge program" to help prepare individuals for law enforcement careers. www.downtownvisions.org/safety-division/bridge-program

Appendix 5: Sample Letter to a Local Law Enforcement Agency to Request Crime Statistics

January 21, 2016

(Name)
Research Analyst
Metropolitan Police Department
300 Indiana Ave. NW, Suite 5126
Washington, DC 20001

Dear (Name),

Under the federal *Jeanne Clery Disclosure of Campus Security Policy and Campus Crime Statistics Act (Clery Act)*, postsecondary schools are required to disclose statistics for certain crimes that occurred on campus and on public property within and immediately adjacent to school-owned buildings and property. In the statistics we are required to include crimes that were reported to our department as well as crimes reported to local and state law enforcement agencies.

I am requesting that your department provide me with **crime statistics for 2015** for the following offenses that occurred on our campus or on public property within and immediately adjacent to our property:

- Murder/Non-negligent Manslaughter
- Manslaughter by Negligence
- Rape
- Fondling
- Incest
- Statutory Rape
- Robbery
- Burglary
- Aggravated Assault

- Motor Vehicle Theft
- Arson

Please specify if any of the above-listed offenses were categorized as Hate Crimes. In addition, please include statistics for any incidents of Larceny-Theft, Simple Assault, Intimidation, or Destruction/Damage/Vandalism of Property that were classified as Hate Crimes. I also need the category of bias for each Hate Crime according to the eight categories for which we are required to report: Race, Religion, Sexual Orientation, Gender, Gender Identity, Disability, Ethnicity, and National Origin.

Please include statistics for **arrests** only for the following Uniform Crime Reporting (UCR) categories:

- Liquor Law Violations
- Drug Abuse Violations
- Weapons: Carrying, Possessing, etc.

Please include **separate** statistics for all incidents of Domestic Violence, Dating Violence, and Stalking. For *Clery Act* reporting, we are required to use the following definitions for these terms:

Domestic Violence: The term "domestic violence" includes felony or misdemeanor crimes of violence committed by a current or former spouse or intimate partner of the victim, by a person with whom the victim shares a child in common, by a person who is cohabitating with or has cohabitated with the victim as a spouse or intimate partner, by a person similarly situated to a spouse of the victim under the domestic or family violence laws of the jurisdiction receiving grant monies, or by any other person against an adult or youth victim who is protected from that person's acts under the domestic or family violence laws of the jurisdiction.

Dating Violence: The term "dating violence" means violence committed by a person—(A) who is or has been in a social relationship of a romantic or intimate nature with the victim; and (B) where the existence of such a relationship shall be determined based on a consideration of the following factors:

1. The length of the relationship.
2. The type of relationship.
3. The frequency of interaction between the persons involved in the relationship.

Stalking: The term "stalking" means engaging in a course of conduct directed at a specific person that would cause a reasonable person to—(A) fear for his or her safety or the safety of others; or (B) suffer substantial emotional distress.

I am requesting the required statistics for the following areas that are considered to be "on campus":

1900-2200 blocks of Pennsylvania Ave.
2300 block of K St.
2000-2300 blocks of I St.
2000-2300 blocks of H St.

2000-2300 blocks of G St.
1900-2200 blocks of F St.

I also need crime statistics for the following specific addresses:

1129 New Hampshire Ave.
2400 Virginia Ave.
2601 Virginia Ave.
1776 G St.
2011 I St.
2020 K St.
2021 K St.

I would appreciate it if you would forward this information to me as soon as you get an opportunity. We are in the process of publishing our annual report, and we will need to include these statistics in the final draft.

In addition, if a serious crime that may cause an ongoing threat to our campus community is reported to your department, we would appreciate it if you would notify our University Police Department immediately. The institution has a legal responsibility to notify the campus community in a timely manner about any crimes on and immediately around the campus that pose an ongoing threat to the community.

Thank you for your attention to this matter.

Sincerely,

(Name)
Chief of University Police
(Phone Number)

Index